The Fielding Bible

Volume II

John Dewan

Baseball Info Solutions

www.baseballinfosolutions.com

Published by ACTA Sports

A Division of ACTA Publications

www.actasports.com

Cover by Tom A. Wright

Cover Photo by Scott Jordan Levy

First Edition: February 2009

Published by:
ACTA Sports, a division of ACTA Publications
5559 W. Howard Street, Skokie, IL 60077
(800) 397-2282
www.actasports.com
www.actapublications.com

ISBN: 978-0-87946-371-7
ISSN: 1946-7524

Printed in the United States of America

Table of Contents

This book is dedicated to Bill James, Steve Moyer, and Pat Quinn.
Because of them, my lifelong passion for baseball has gone beyond anything I could imagine.

Acknowledgements

We did it again. Volume II. After all the work involved in Volume I, it surprises me that this one was even more work. The phrase "labor of love" can be overused, but there is no better expression. Again, it would not have happened without a large, strong supporting cast. The book only names one author, but that is the opposite of the collaborative effort required.

My friend and partner, Bill James inspired and supported this book every step of the way. He always found time despite all his other projects (during his free time from his job with the Red Sox, he works on BillJamesOnline.com, The Bill James Handbook 2009, The Bill James Gold Mine 2009, and a soon to be published book on crime).

Another partner, Steve Moyer, runs Baseball Info Solutions (BaseballInfoSolutions.com). This book depends on his expertise and BIS' comprehensive, thorough, highly-detailed data collection. No other data source comes close to meeting this book's requirements.

Pat Quinn of BIS was with me on the first *Fielding Bible*. He continued his excellent work on this one. He literally moved in with me and my family (and away from his family) for 12 days to finish the book. Among other things, he helped me format the book and present all the numbers in charts so that they pop off the page and make sense to the reader.

Still another business partner, Greg Pierce (ACTAsports.com), did editing and everything else a publishing company provides to make a successful book.

While I am covering partners, my partner for life, my wife, Sue Dewan, never ceases to go the extra mile to support my other love, analyzing baseball. Her patience and her willingness to do still one more favor is impossible to measure.

Of course, Steve Moyer doesn't work alone at BIS. Damon Lichtenwalner, company vice president, designed, programmed, managed, and worked non-stop to make sure every Information Technology aspect of this book sings. His contributions are immeasurable.

We expanded our Research and Development in the past few months. The three new guys, along with Pat Quinn, are an extension of my brain. Analyzing, programming, writing—they can do it all. They are practically co-authors. Thank you Rob Burckhard, Steve Goodfriend, and Ben Jedlovec.

BIS staff also includes Dan Casey, Austin Diamond, Matt Lorenzo, Tony Pellegrino, Todd Radcliffe, Jeff Spoljaric, Annemarie Stella, Jim Swavely, and Jon Vrecsics.

Several places I mention the folks who watch the games and enter every little detail accurately into the computer. They wrote our Defensive Scouting Reports. Thanks to our 2008 Video Scout crew Jake Argue, Steve Gleason, Jeremy Gordon, Brian Johnston, Matt Kelliher-Gibson, Steve Landefeld, Brian Powalish, Kurt Wimpe, Mike Wolverton, and J.D. Wyborny.

Likewise, Greg Pierce isn't a one-man band. ACTA Sports staff includes Andrew Yankech, Charles Fiore, Donna Ryding, Mary Eggert, and Brendan Gaughan.

All those people belong to one related entity or another. Yet, wait, there are still more people who helped. Eric Ferguson and Steve Moyer edited the Defensive Scouting Reports. Dave Studenmund from The Hardball Times (HardballTimes.com) and Cindy Quinn helped out as well.

A huge thank you to all of you readers. This book was impossible without you.

And finally, my kids, Jason and Erica. They are the best teenagers in the world. (For those of you who have teenage kids, you'll understand when I say that in some ways that sentence is an oxymoron.) I put more time into this book than into my kids over the last few months, but nothing is more important in my life than they are. Now with the book done, the time shift has begun.

Introduction

Welcome back. And hi to those of you who are new to *The Fielding Bible*. We've been busy since the first volume of The Fielding Bible came out three years ago and we've got a ton of new stuff for you.

Our mission remains to try to discover the best ways to evaluate defense in baseball. Bill James wrote the introduction to the first volume and he shared with us how there has been a great evolution in creating and capturing information about batting and pitching in baseball, but fielding was far behind the curve. Up until recently, fielding stats pretty much remained unchanged for over a century.

Now we're trying to correct that situation. The first book, and now this second volume, are steps in the direction of greater understanding about defense in baseball. They are not the only steps. People like Chris Dial, Mitchel Lichtman, Dave Pinto, Dave Studenmund, Tom Tango, John Walsh, the guys over at Baseball Prospectus are all doing fantastic research in this area. (My apologies to anyone I've left out!).

Here's a summary of some of the things we're doing in this book.

- Defensive Runs Saved. Baseball is about scoring and preventing runs. We use the Plus/Minus System, Double Play abilities, Outfielder Arms, Bunt Defense by corner infielders, Pitcher Stolen Base defense, Catcher Stolen Base defense and the catcher's ability to Handle Pitchers and convert it all into Defensive Runs Saved. This is probably the biggest theme of the book.

- Total Runs for every player. We combine Runs Created, Baserunning Runs, and Defensive Runs Saved to determine an overall value of every player in baseball in 2008.

- Bill James' Misplays/Good Plays. This has been an exclusive team product and is now making its world

premiere to the public. It's a revolutionary, ground-breaking concept in measuring defensive abilities. Bill has a huge essay in the book, and we present extensive leaderboards for 2008.

- Defensive Scouting Reports. As in the first volume, we share our scouting reports on the defensive abilities of every regular and semi-regular position player in baseball. We added catchers in this volume.

- Measuring Catcher Defense. We've taken Catcher ERA to the next level as we begin to unravel a catcher's ability to handle pitchers. We're also restating traditional stolen base and caught stealing data to runs saved for catchers.

- Measuring Pitcher Defense. We're introducing pitcher plus/minus values and runs saved to measure their abilities to field their position, but we're also evaluating pitchers for their ability to control the running game.

- Analysis of Defensive Positioning. We've looked at this from two standpoints. First, we are sharing Baseball Info Solution's Defensive Positioning software to show hitter tendencies. Only teams have ever seen this before. It answers the question, "How should we position the defense for this hitter?" It's a huge advance beyond typical hitter spray charts. Second, we're analyzing how positioning can help specific players and defense in baseball overall.

- Nate McLouth vs. Carlos Gomez. McLouth won a Gold Glove, Gomez didn't. What's the deal with that?

- Shallow, Medium, and Deep. Looking at McLouth-Gomez, we found that breaking down our outfield data by depth of batted ball is really helpful. We've now added this information to our registers for every outfielder in baseball.

- Plus/Minus System enhancements. In the last three years, we've been working steadily, and will continue to work steadily, to improve the Plus/Minus System. One of the newer additions is the Manny Adjustment. It factors into the system a way of handling stadiums with high walls.
- Complete Registers of defensive information for every player. The One-Year Register is back for 2008, and the Volume I Three-Year Register is now a Six-Year Register.
- Plus a ton more. We have special features on Manny vs. Alfonso Soriano vs. Carl Crawford, and Troy Tulowitzki vs. Juan Uribe. Bill James' Universal Fielding Percentage. Revised Zone Ratings and Defensive Replacements. Team plus/minus totals. Bunts, GDPs, Pivots, Outfielder Arm sections—back from the first volume, but now with Runs Saved based on updated data.

We hope you enjoy it.

John Dewan
Chicago, Illinois

Defensive Runs

Baseball is all about runs. Runs determine the score. Runs are all over the statistics. How many runs did he drive in? What's his earned run average? In the first volume of *The Fielding Bible* we developed metrics that help us better understand defense in baseball. We speculated that we would try to translate the new defensive metrics into runs. That's what we've done here in *Volume II*. We've taken all the metrics we had and converted them to runs.

24 States Analysis (or The Run Matrix)

Take your pick. What do you want to call it? On Bill James Online (BillJamesOnline.com), it's called "24 States Analysis". I'm a big fan of The Matrix movie series so I'll go with "The Run Matrix". It sounds like a complicated concept, but in reality it's not that difficult. It's simply a chart that tells you how many runs score in an inning following each of the possible 24 situations in an inning (or as we call them "states"). The 24 states are determined by how many men are out (zero, one or two) and how many men are on which bases. There are eight combinations of men on base: none out, man on first, man on second, man on third, men on first and second, men on first and third, men on second and third, and bases loaded. Eight base-situations times three out-situations gives you 24 states. Here's the Run Matrix for 2008:

Run Matrix - 2008

Runners	Outs		
	0	1	2
None on	.521	.279	.108
Man on first	.900	.528	.227
Man on second	1.150	.695	.335
Man on third	1.499	.969	.346
Men on first and second	1.530	.919	.464
Men on first and third	1.769	1.159	.481
Men on second and third	2.006	1.422	.589
Bases loaded	2.306	1.586	.799

It looks more complicated than it is. The figure in the chart for none on and no outs is .521. That simply means that anytime this situation occurred in an inning

during 2008, an average of .521 runs were scored after that point. Or, take the bases loaded with one out, the run expectancy is 1.586. Adding up every situation that occurred like that in 2008, we find that 1.586 runs scored on average after a team had the bases loaded and one out.

The key way that we use this chart is to look at it before and after a play. Let's say there's a man on first with one out. The expected runs at that point are .528. The next play is a groundball to the shortstop. He boots it for an error and we now have men on first and second with one out. The expected runs went from .528 to .919. That's an increase of .391 (.919 minus .528) runs. The play itself, the error, cost the team .391 runs. We don't have to follow it through and count the rest of the inning. We know what the value of the ending state is and can use it. The term that we are using in this book for this is Defensive Runs (or Defensive Runs Saved or simply Runs Saved). Since the error cost the team runs, it becomes a negative when stated as Defensive Runs. The value of the error is -.391 defensive runs.

Plus/Minus Runs Saved

The Plus/Minus System is the most important method (or metric) that we use to evaluate defense. By going through each play in our database and using the run matrix table, we have converted plus/minus into plus/minus runs saved. We'll skip the rest of the math, but if you want to know more about it, head over to the last section of this article. When we were all done, we came up with a value of runs saved per plus/minus point by position. Here are the values we use throughout this book:

Plus/Minus Runs per Plus/Minus Point

Pitcher	.75
First Base	.73
Second Base	.76
Third Base	.76
Shortstop	.76
Left Field	.56
Center Field	.56
Right Field	.58

For example, if a pitcher has a +4 plus/minus rating, it translates into three runs saved (.75 x 4). It works similarly for every position. For the corner infielders and the outfielders, we use enhanced plus/minus. These plus/minus run factors are remarkably consistent among the infield positions and separately among the outfield positions.

Runs Saved for Every Metric

Similar to Plus/Minus Runs Saved, we have developed different ways to come up with defensive runs saved for each metric. These are explained throughout the book. For first basemen, for example, we use plus/minus runs saved and bunt runs saved. Bunt runs saved are explained on page 363. Here's a summary by position:

Position	Runs Saved Metric Used
First Basemen	Plus/minus runs saved
	Bunt runs saved
Second Basemen	Plus/minus runs saved
	GDP runs saved
Third Basemen	Plus/minus runs saved
	Bunt runs saved
Shortstops	Plus/minus runs saved
	GDP runs saved
Outfielders	Plus/minus runs saved
	Outfielder arm runs saved
	HR saving runs saved
Catchers	Adjusted earned runs saved
	Stolen base runs saved
Pitchers	Plus/minus runs saved
	Stolen base runs saved

Robbing Home Runs

The grand slam of all defensive plays is robbing a home run. You can't make a better play than a reach over the fence to bring back a homer in terms of run value. On average, it saves 1.6 runs. That's the average number of runs that score on home runs after counting up all the runs on solo shots, two-run home runs, three-run dingers and grand slams. Here's the list of the best fence-climbing outfielders over the last three years, based on the database at Baseball Info Solutions:

HR Saving Plays

Torii Hunter	7
Gary Mathews Jr.	5
Corey Patterson	4
Carlos Beltran	3
Andruw Jones	3
Corey Hart	3
Nick Markakis	3
Jermaine Dye	3
Raul Ibanez	3
Jason Bay	3

Defensive Runs Saved by Position

On the next pages, we have defensive runs saved for every regular player over the last three years: for each year and for the three years combined. For position players we show the 35 guys with the most innings in each year, and separately for the three years combined. For pitchers, we use the 175 pitchers with the most innings.

When we finally came up with all the methods to do runs saved and figured them out for every player, the key question was "Do the results make sense?" You can judge for yourself as you look through these ranked lists, but we were very pleased how they came out. We think they provide excellent information to identify the best defensive players in baseball.

Let's go through each position together.

First Base—Albert Pujols has the most runs saved at first base over the last three years. He won The Fielding Bible Award in each of those years, but if I were to vote all over again for 2008, I'd still pick Mark Teixeira. Not only did Teixeira save a couple more runs, he had the most Good Plays (see page 40) in all of baseball. Lyle Overbay and Adrian Gonzalez are a contrast on the three-year chart. Overbay has a ton of trouble with bunts (-7 runs saved) while Gonzalez is the best there is handling bunts (8 runs saved).

Second Base—Chase Utley's incredible 33 runs saved in 2008 launches him to the top of the three-year list. Mark Ellis is second and is tied with Mark Gruzielanek for the most runs saved on double plays over three years with 11. Surprisingly, 2008 Fielding Bible Award winner Brandon Phillips has a low total on double plays (-5).

Third Base—Pedro Feliz is the surprise winner over the last three years, finishing two runs ahead of two-time Fielding Bible Award winner, Adrian Beltre. Feliz won the award in 2007, splitting up Beltre's two awards. Handling bunts is where Feliz passes Beltre. The best players handling bunts are generally National Leaguers—there may be a bias in the data that we should look at in the future.

Shortstop—After being so dominant on defense, Adam Everett is no surprise at the top of the list. Except that he missed huge chunks of playing time over the last two seasons. His one-year total of 34 runs saved in 2006 is higher than the 33 runs saved over three years by second-place finisher, Jimmy Rollins. The best double-play man over the three years is Orlando Cabrera.

Left Field—This one is a complete surprise. Alfonso Soriano has saved an incredible 33 runs for his teams in the last three years with his throwing arm alone. When you have 42 baserunner kills and the next best has less than half (19), that explains it. Take a look at the article about Soriano on page 255. This may be one case where Defensive Runs is indicating the player that saved the most runs but is not indicating the best defensive player at the position. During his first two years in the outfield, opposing runners didn't know better than to try to run on Soriano. He had 34 total kills in 2006 and 2007. But in 2008 they learned something (well, a little), so his still MLB-leading kill total in left field dropped to eight. With two Fielding Bible Awards, Carl Crawford is clearly the best left fielder in baseball.

Center Field—Carlos Beltran also has two Fielding Bible Awards and several Gold Gloves. And he has the most defensive runs saved in center field over the last three years. Andruw Jones remains right up there with Beltran despite his lost season of 2008. The best outfield arm from center field over the three years was Aaron Rowand with 17 runs saved. And the best player at any position pulling back home run balls to his side of the fence was Torii Hunter with 11 runs saved.

Right Field—Alex Rios leads right field by a wide margin with 49 runs saved over three years. He is very consistent with totals of 19 ('06), 16 ('07) and 14 ('08) runs saved in those three years. The best throwing arm is Jeff Fancoeur with 25 runs saved, followed closely by Nick Markakis with 21.

Catcher—Jason Kendall has 27 runs saved. Yadier Molina is the runner-up with 19. They did it two different ways. Kendall got most of his runs by calling for the right pitches, helping his battery mates keep down their earned run averages (23 adjusted earned runs saved over the

three years). Molina stopped the running game cold with 14 runs saved.

Pitcher—The Gambler, Kenny Rogers, doesn't gamble with grounders. He gobbles 'em up better than anyone out there. Well, Greg Maddux might take exception. Rogers had the best total with 27 runs saved. Maddux beat out Kenny with plus/minus runs (25 to 20) but Mad Dog's ineffectiveness with the running game cost him overall. Rogers gained 7 runs with his ability to hold runners while Maddux lost 11. The best pitcher at holding runners in baseball is Mark Buehrle with 12 runs saved.

Wins

To translate runs to wins, there's a great, easy rule of thumb. Each 10 runs is worth a win. Chase Utley has 64 runs saved over the last three years, while Jeff Kent has -41. That's a difference of 105 runs, about 10 wins.

Math for Plus/Minus Runs Saved

Beware! The math is off leash in this section. Here's how we developed the plus/minus runs per plus/minus point chart shown earlier in this article.

Let's start with this example: nobody on and no outs, and the batter hits a hard groundball to Stephen Drew at shortstop, specifically to Vector 197 (slightly to a normal shortstop's right). Before the groundball, the run expectancy was .521 (from the run matrix chart). If Drew gets the out, there is now one out and still nobody on base, a run expectancy of .279, a drop of .242. If he doesn't make the play, the runner reaches first with nobody out, which has a run expectancy of .900, a .379 run increase.

The Plus/Minus System gives us the percentage of the time that a hard groundball to Vector 197 was successfully converted to an out by the shortstop last year: 85.6%. The shortstop will make the play most of the time, but not always. We determine that the average shortstop will contribute $(.856) \times (.242) + (1 - .856) \times (-.379) = .153$ runs on the play. If Drew converts the out, his play was worth $.242 - .153 = .091$ runs above the average shortstop.

Obviously, this can get complicated. For outfielders, for instance, a fliner or flyball that falls in safely could easily become a single, double, or triple depending on a number of things, including the runner. Also, baserunners don't always behave predictably. Some take extra bases, some don't. (We take the outfielder's arm into account in the OF Arms section on page 375.) As a result, we average all of these outcomes together based on the frequency of each.

After repeating this procedure for every play, we found that there was still plenty of "noise" in the run values that had nothing to do with the fielder's defensive ability. For example, converting a difficult play with two outs and the bases loaded could be worth two full runs, but the same play with two outs and nobody on was worth a tenth of that, at no fault of the fielder. This is a situational bias that the fielder has little control over. (Unless you want to start arguing about "clutch fielding". We'll save that argument for another time!)

To adjust for this bias, we took a look at how many runs each plus/minus point was worth. How many runs was Chase Utley's +46 plays worth? At second base, it turned out that the average plus/minus point was worth .76 runs. That's 35 plus/minus runs saved for Utley in 2008.

First Basemen - 3-Year Runs Saved

Player	Plus/Minus	Bunts	Total
Albert Pujols	60	1	61
Casey Kotchman	32	-1	31
Kevin Youkilis	18	1	19
Doug Mientkiewicz	19	-2	17
Mark Teixeira	15	1	16
Lance Berkman	16	0	16
Lyle Overbay	22	-7	15
Joey Votto	13	2	15
Carlos Pena	14	0	14
Todd Helton	6	2	8
James Loney	4	4	8
Nick Johnson	2	6	8
Daric Barton	9	-1	8
Derrek Lee	3	1	4
Dan Johnson	4	-2	2
Scott Hatteberg	-1	2	1
Adrian Gonzalez	-9	8	-1
Justin Morneau	0	-2	-2
Ross Gload	-5	1	-4
Miguel Cabrera	-4	-1	-5
Nomar Garciaparra	-8	1	-7
Nick Swisher	-6	-1	-7
Ryan Howard	-11	3	-8
Carlos Delgado	-13	4	-9
Adam LaRoche	-14	1	-13
Paul Konerko	-7	-6	-13
Ryan Garko	-9	-4	-13
Sean Casey	-14	0	-14
Richie Sexson	-15	-1	-16
Conor Jackson	-16	0	-16
Kevin Millar	-14	-3	-17
Dmitri Young	-20	-1	-21
Jason Giambi	-22	0	-22
Prince Fielder	-33	0	-33
Mike Jacobs	-36	1	-35

First Basemen - 2007 Runs Saved

Player	Team	Plus/Minus	Bunts	Total
Albert Pujols	StL	27	2	29
Casey Kotchman	LAA	18	0	18
Todd Helton	Col	7	2	9
Lyle Overbay	Tor	9	0	9
Ryan Klesko	SF	6	3	9
Kevin Youkilis	Bos	7	1	8
Ross Gload	KC	4	1	5
Doug Mientkiewicz	NYY	5	0	5
Adam LaRoche	Pit	2	1	3
James Loney	LAD	1	2	3
Andy Phillips	NYY	4	-1	3
Carlos Pena	TB	3	-1	2
Carlos Delgado	NYM	1	1	2
Scott Thorman	Atl	1	0	1
Ryan Howard	Phi	-4	4	0
Justin Morneau	Min	0	-1	-1
Mark Teixeira	2 tms	-3	2	-1
Lance Berkman	Hou	-2	1	-1
Dan Johnson	Oak	-1	-1	-2
Brad Wilkerson	Tex	-2	0	-2
Adrian Gonzalez	SD	-5	2	-3
Paul Konerko	CWS	-2	-1	-3
Tony Clark	Ari	-3	0	-3
Derrek Lee	ChC	-3	-1	-4
Sean Casey	Det	-2	-2	-4
Conor Jackson	Ari	-4	0	-4
Kevin Millar	Bal	-5	0	-5
Jeff Conine	2 tms	-5	0	-5
Mike Jacobs	Fla	-7	1	-6
Scott Hatteberg	Cin	-7	1	-6
Ryan Garko	Cle	-7	-1	-8
Prince Fielder	Mil	-11	0	-11
Richie Sexson	Sea	-11	-1	-12
Nomar Garciaparra	LAD	-13	0	-13
Dmitri Young	Was	-16	-1	-17

First Basemen - 2008 Runs Saved

Player	Team	Plus/Minus	Bunts	Total
Mark Teixeira	2 tms	17	0	17
Joey Votto	Cin	13	3	16
Albert Pujols	StL	15	0	15
Lance Berkman	Hou	13	0	13
Carlos Pena	TB	10	1	11
Casey Kotchman	2 tms	10	-1	9
Lyle Overbay	Tor	8	-2	6
Derrek Lee	ChC	4	1	5
Daric Barton	Oak	5	-1	4
Kevin Youkilis	Bos	4	0	4
Todd Helton	Col	4	0	4
Miguel Cairo	Sea	0	2	2
James Loney	LAD	-1	2	1
Adrian Gonzalez	SD	-4	4	0
Ryan Howard	Phi	0	0	0
Rich Aurilia	SF	-1	1	0
Chad Tracy	Ari	-1	0	-1
Chris Davis	Tex	-2	1	-1
Justin Morneau	Min	-1	-2	-3
John Bowker	SF	-3	0	-3
Sean Casey	Bos	-3	0	-3
Kevin Millar	Bal	-2	-2	-4
Paul Konerko	CWS	-1	-3	-4
Conor Jackson	Ari	-4	0	-4
Nick Swisher	CWS	-4	0	-4
Miguel Cabrera	Det	-4	-1	-5
Ryan Garko	Cle	-2	-3	-5
Ross Gload	KC	-5	0	-5
Adam LaRoche	Pit	-6	0	-6
Garrett Atkins	Col	-7	0	-7
Richie Sexson	2 tms	-8	0	-8
Carlos Delgado	NYM	-11	2	-9
Prince Fielder	Mil	-9	-1	-10
Jason Giambi	NYY	-13	0	-13
Mike Jacobs	Fla	-20	-3	-23

First Basemen - 2006 Runs Saved

Player	Team	Plus/Minus	Bunts	Total
Albert Pujols	StL	18	-1	17
Doug Mientkiewicz	KC	11	-1	10
Kendry Morales	LAA	8	0	8
Scott Hatteberg	Cin	6	1	7
Kevin Youkilis	Bos	7	0	7
Nick Johnson	Was	0	6	6
Nomar Garciaparra	LAD	5	1	6
Travis Lee	TB	5	1	6
Chris Shelton	Det	5	0	5
Richie Sexson	Sea	4	0	4
Lance Berkman	Hou	5	-1	4
Ryan Shealy	2 tms	5	-1	4
Dan Johnson	Oak	4	-1	3
Justin Morneau	Min	1	1	2
Adrian Gonzalez	SD	0	2	2
Shea Hillenbrand	2 tms	4	-2	2
Mark Teixeira	Tex	1	-1	0
Lyle Overbay	Tor	5	-5	0
Mike Lamb	Hou	-1	0	-1
Carlos Delgado	NYM	-3	1	-2
Nick Swisher	Oak	-1	-1	-2
Andy Phillips	NYY	-1	-1	-2
Jeff Conine	Bal	-2	0	-2
Todd Helton	Col	-5	0	-5
Ben Broussard	2 tms	-4	-1	-5
Craig Wilson	2 tms	-5	0	-5
Paul Konerko	CWS	-4	-2	-6
Mike Jacobs	Fla	-9	3	-6
Sean Casey	2 tms	-9	2	-7
Ryan Howard	Phi	-7	-1	-8
Conor Jackson	Ari	-8	0	-8
Kevin Millar	Bal	-7	-1	-8
Adam LaRoche	Atl	-10	0	-10
Prince Fielder	Mil	-13	1	-12
Jason Giambi	NYY	-12	0	-12

Second Basemen - 3-Year Runs Saved

Player	Plus/Minus	GDP	Total
Chase Utley	64	-1	63
Mark Ellis	43	11	54
Aaron Hill	34	10	44
Placido Polanco	23	7	30
Orlando Hudson	22	3	25
Mark Grudzielanek	7	11	18
Jose Lopez	11	6	17
Adam Kennedy	14	3	17
Jose Valentin	20	-3	17
Jamey Carroll	6	8	14
Brandon Phillips	18	-5	13
Howie Kendrick	4	6	10
Dustin Pedroia	6	3	9
Robinson Cano	-3	9	6
Josh Barfield	8	-3	5
Kaz Matsui	0	5	5
Brian Roberts	2	2	4
Akinori Iwamura	-2	5	3
Aaron Miles	0	2	2
Ian Kinsler	-9	9	0
Freddy Sanchez	-4	3	-1
Kelly Johnson	-1	-1	-2
Alexi Casilla	-5	2	-3
Tadahito Iguchi	-12	6	-6
Ronnie Belliard	-12	4	-8
Mark Loretta	-14	6	-8
Dan Uggla	-11	1	-10
Mark DeRosa	-6	-6	-12
Jose Castillo	-13	0	-13
Marcus Giles	-15	0	-15
Craig Biggio	-15	-5	-20
Luis Castillo	-15	-8	-23
Ray Durham	-21	-2	-23
Rickie Weeks	-21	-3	-24
Jeff Kent	-32	-9	-41

Second Basemen - 2007 Runs Saved

Player	Team	Plus/Minus	GDP	Total
Robinson Cano	NYY	13	9	22
Aaron Hill	Tor	17	4	21
Orlando Hudson	Ari	15	2	17
Mark Ellis	Oak	14	2	16
Chase Utley	Phi	17	-2	15
Kaz Matsui	Col	9	4	13
Placido Polanco	Det	8	3	11
Brandon Phillips	Cin	8	1	9
Jose Lopez	Sea	4	3	7
Ian Kinsler	Tex	5	2	7
Mark Grudzielanek	KC	5	2	7
Howie Kendrick	LAA	5	1	6
Josh Barfield	Cle	4	-2	2
Geoff Blum	SD	2	0	2
Kelly Johnson	Atl	0	1	1
Brian Roberts	Bal	0	0	0
Mike Fontenot	ChC	0	0	0
Freddy Sanchez	Pit	-4	3	-1
Ronnie Belliard	Was	-1	0	-1
Aaron Miles	StL	-1	0	-1
Jamey Carroll	Col	-1	0	-1
Dustin Pedroia	Bos	-4	2	-2
Alexi Casilla	Min	-3	1	-2
Mark DeRosa	ChC	0	-3	-3
Adam Kennedy	StL	-1	-2	-3
Tadahito Iguchi	2 tms	-7	3	-4
Marcus Giles	SD	-5	0	-5
B.J. Upton	TB	-4	-1	-5
Luis Castillo	2 tms	-2	-4	-6
Ray Durham	SF	-8	0	-8
Danny Richar	CWS	-8	0	-8
Rickie Weeks	Mil	-13	1	-12
Dan Uggla	Fla	-14	1	-13
Jeff Kent	LAD	-10	-3	-13
Craig Biggio	Hou	-13	-5	-18

Second Basemen - 2008 Runs Saved

Player	Team	Plus/Minus	GDP	Total
Chase Utley	Phi	35	-2	33
Mark Ellis	Oak	19	5	24
Adam Kennedy	StL	14	3	17
Dustin Pedroia	Bos	11	1	12
Placido Polanco	Det	11	0	11
Brandon Phillips	Cin	13	-3	10
Asdrubal Cabrera	Cle	3	7	10
Mike Fontenot	ChC	8	0	8
Clint Barmes	Col	7	1	8
Joe Inglett	Tor	5	0	5
Akinori Iwamura	TB	-2	5	3
Aaron Miles	StL	1	2	3
Dan Uggla	Fla	3	-1	2
Freddy Sanchez	Pit	2	0	2
Tadahito Iguchi	2 tms	0	2	2
Jose Lopez	Sea	0	1	1
Rickie Weeks	Mil	2	-2	0
Howie Kendrick	LAA	-3	3	0
Jamey Carroll	Cle	-3	2	-1
Edgar Gonzalez	SD	1	-2	-1
Alexi Casilla	Min	-3	1	-2
Mark Grudzielanek	KC	-5	3	-2
Brian Roberts	Bal	-3	0	-3
Kelly Johnson	Atl	-1	-2	-3
Orlando Hudson	Ari	-3	0	-3
Alexei Ramirez	CWS	-6	0	-6
Ian Kinsler	Tex	-11	4	-7
Kaz Matsui	Hou	-8	0	-8
Damion Easley	NYM	-5	-3	-8
Ray Durham	2 tms	-8	-1	-9
Mark DeRosa	ChC	-6	-3	-9
Jeff Kent	LAD	-8	-3	-11
Robinson Cano	NYY	-13	0	-13
Felipe Lopez	2 tms	-11	-2	-13
Luis Castillo	NYM	-11	-2	-13

Second Basemen - 2006 Runs Saved

Player	Team	Plus/Minus	GDP	Total
Aaron Hill	Tor	19	6	25
Jamey Carroll	Col	10	6	16
Jose Valentin	NYM	18	-2	16
Chase Utley	Phi	12	3	15
Mark Ellis	Oak	10	4	14
Mark Grudzielanek	KC	7	6	13
Orlando Hudson	Ari	10	1	11
Neifi Perez	2 tms	8	2	10
Jose Lopez	Sea	7	2	9
Tony Graffanino	2 tms	12	-3	9
Placido Polanco	Det	4	4	8
Brian Roberts	Bal	5	2	7
Josh Barfield	SD	6	-1	5
Joe Inglett	Cle	2	2	4
Adam Kennedy	LAA	1	2	3
Dan Uggla	Fla	0	1	1
Ian Kinsler	Tex	-3	3	0
Aaron Miles	StL	0	0	0
Kaz Matsui	2 tms	-1	1	0
Ronnie Belliard	2 tms	-5	4	-1
Craig Biggio	Hou	-2	0	-2
Robinson Cano	NYY	-3	0	-3
Todd Walker	2 tms	-2	-1	-3
Luis Castillo	Min	-2	-2	-4
Tadahito Iguchi	CWS	-5	1	-4
Brandon Phillips	Cin	-3	-3	-6
Ray Durham	SF	-5	-1	-6
Hector Luna	2 tms	-6	0	-6
Mark Loretta	Bos	-11	4	-7
Marcus Giles	Atl	-10	0	-10
Jose Castillo	Pit	-11	0	-11
Rickie Weeks	Mil	-10	-2	-12
Jorge Cantu	TB	-16	-1	-17
Jeff Kent	LAD	-14	-3	-17
Jose Vidro	Was	-16	-6	-22

Third Basemen - 3-Year Runs Saved

Player	Plus/Minus	Bunts	Total
Pedro Feliz	42	8	50
Adrian Beltre	47	1	48
Joe Crede	42	-1	41
Scott Rolen	35	4	39
Brandon Inge	39	0	39
Ryan Zimmerman	26	6	32
Nick Punto	20	4	24
Troy Glaus	18	0	18
Jack Hannahan	16	1	17
Mike Lowell	15	-1	14
David Wright	4	8	12
Andy Marte	13	-2	11
Eric Chavez	10	-1	9
David Bell	4	-2	2
Chipper Jones	-5	6	1
Chone Figgins	-1	1	0
Abraham Nunez	-1	1	0
Aramis Ramirez	-3	1	-2
Morgan Ensberg	-3	1	-2
Maicer Izturis	-2	0	-2
Hank Blalock	-5	2	-3
Kevin Kouzmanoff	-5	1	-4
Alex Gordon	-2	-2	-4
Chad Tracy	-5	-2	-7
Casey Blake	-7	-1	-8
Mike Lamb	-8	-1	-9
Melvin Mora	-7	-5	-12
Alex Rodriguez	-6	-7	-13
Ramon Vazquez	-14	1	-13
Mark Reynolds	-14	0	-14
Ty Wigginton	-20	-3	-23
Jose Bautista	-27	0	-27
Miguel Cabrera	-30	2	-28
Garrett Atkins	-32	0	-32
Edwin Encarnacion	-38	-5	-43

Third Basemen - 2007 Runs Saved

Player	Team	Plus/Minus	Bunts	Total
Pedro Feliz	SF	21	3	24
Ryan Zimmerman	Was	16	4	20
Brandon Inge	Det	17	0	17
David Wright	NYM	10	3	13
Scott Rolen	StL	11	2	13
Aramis Ramirez	ChC	11	0	11
Nick Punto	Min	8	1	9
Melvin Mora	Bal	5	1	6
Eric Chavez	Oak	8	-2	6
Mike Lowell	Bos	5	0	5
Adrian Beltre	Sea	5	0	5
Alex Gordon	KC	5	0	5
Troy Glaus	Tor	7	-2	5
Chipper Jones	Atl	2	2	4
Abraham Nunez	Phi	4	0	4
Maicer Izturis	LAA	3	0	3
Wes Helms	Phi	2	0	2
Alex Rodriguez	NYY	2	-1	1
Mike Lamb	Hou	0	-1	-1
Chone Figgins	LAA	-2	0	-2
Greg Dobbs	Phi	-3	1	-2
Kevin Kouzmanoff	SD	-3	0	-3
Ramon Vazquez	Tex	-2	-1	-3
Travis Metcalf	Tex	-3	0	-3
Casey Blake	Cle	-4	-1	-5
Mark Reynolds	Ari	-6	1	-5
Akinori Iwamura	TB	-6	-1	-7
Morgan Ensberg	2 tms	-6	-1	-7
Ty Wigginton	2 tms	-8	0	-8
Edwin Encarnacion	Cin	-11	-2	-13
Josh Fields	CWS	-14	0	-14
Miguel Cabrera	Fla	-18	2	-16
Jose Bautista	Pit	-17	1	-16
Garrett Atkins	Col	-22	-1	-23
Ryan Braun	Mil	-31	-1	-32

Third Basemen - 2008 Runs Saved

Player	Team	Plus/Minus	Bunts	Total
Adrian Beltre	Sea	24	0	24
Jack Hannahan	Oak	16	0	16
Ryan Zimmerman	Was	8	3	11
Blake DeWitt	LAD	8	3	11
Scott Rolen	Tor	10	0	10
Chipper Jones	Atl	8	2	10
Evan Longoria	TB	8	1	9
Chone Figgins	LAA	8	1	9
Joe Crede	CWS	10	-1	9
Troy Glaus	StL	5	2	7
David Wright	NYM	2	3	5
Pedro Feliz	Phi	5	0	5
Mike Lowell	Bos	5	0	5
Geoff Blum	Hou	5	0	5
Ian Stewart	Col	3	1	4
Andy Marte	Cle	5	-3	2
Andy LaRoche	2 tms	1	-1	0
Kevin Kouzmanoff	SD	-2	1	-1
Bill Hall	Mil	1	-2	-1
Alex Rodriguez	NYY	1	-3	-2
Jose Castillo	2 tms	-4	2	-2
Brian Buscher	Min	-2	0	-2
Casey Blake	2 tms	-3	0	-3
Jose Bautista	2 tms	-2	-1	-3
Ty Wigginton	Hou	-4	-2	-6
Ramon Vazquez	Tex	-8	1	-7
Mike Lamb	2 tms	-7	0	-7
Jorge Cantu	Fla	-8	0	-8
Garrett Atkins	Col	-8	0	-8
Mark Reynolds	Ari	-8	-1	-9
Aramis Ramirez	ChC	-9	0	-9
Alex Gordon	KC	-7	-2	-9
Carlos Guillen	Det	-7	-2	-9
Melvin Mora	Bal	-10	-1	-11
Edwin Encarnacion	Cin	-16	-1	-17

Third Basemen - 2006 Runs Saved

Player	Team	Plus/Minus	Bunts	Total
Joe Crede	CWS	24	-1	23
Brandon Inge	Det	21	0	21
Pedro Feliz	SF	16	5	21
Adrian Beltre	Sea	18	1	19
Scott Rolen	StL	14	2	16
Nick Punto	Min	12	2	14
Freddy Sanchez	Pit	8	3	11
Morgan Ensberg	Hou	7	2	9
Andy Marte	Cle	8	1	9
Troy Glaus	Tor	6	0	6
Mike Lowell	Bos	5	-1	4
Eric Chavez	Oak	2	1	3
David Bell	2 tms	4	-2	2
Ryan Zimmerman	Was	2	-1	1
Corey Koskie	Mil	-2	2	0
Vinny Castilla	2 tms	-2	2	0
Willy Aybar	2 tms	-1	1	0
Garrett Atkins	Col	-2	1	-1
Hank Blalock	Tex	-3	2	-1
Mark Teahen	KC	0	-2	-2
Aramis Ramirez	ChC	-5	1	-4
Abraham Nunez	Phi	-5	1	-4
B.J. Upton	TB	-4	0	-4
Chad Tracy	Ari	-3	-2	-5
Maicer Izturis	LAA	-5	0	-5
Wilson Betemit	2 tms	-6	1	-5
David Wright	NYM	-8	2	-6
Aubrey Huff	2 tms	-7	1	-6
Melvin Mora	Bal	-2	-5	-7
Tony Batista	Min	-8	0	-8
Miguel Cabrera	Fla	-9	0	-9
Aaron Boone	Cle	-12	2	-10
Alex Rodriguez	NYY	-9	-3	-12
Edwin Encarnacion	Cin	-11	-2	-13
Chipper Jones	Atl	-15	2	-13

Shortstops - 3-Year Runs Saved

Player	Plus/Minus	GDP	Total
Adam Everett	44	4	48
Jimmy Rollins	31	2	33
Omar Vizquel	27	2	29
Troy Tulowitzki	26	3	29
Jack Wilson	20	5	25
J.J. Hardy	24	0	24
John McDonald	20	1	21
Jose Reyes	20	0	20
Jason Bartlett	23	-3	20
Tony F Pena	14	2	16
Khalil Greene	12	1	13
Yunel Escobar	15	-2	13
Cesar Izturis	11	0	11
Rafael Furcal	8	1	9
Ryan Theriot	7	2	9
Alex Gonzalez	6	2	8
Cristian Guzman	5	3	8
Ronny Cedeno	3	0	3
Orlando Cabrera	-6	6	0
Stephen Drew	-3	2	-1
Juan Uribe	-3	1	-2
Angel Berroa	-5	3	-2
Edgar Renteria	-3	0	-3
Miguel Tejada	-9	1	-8
Bobby Crosby	-14	5	-9
Carlos Guillen	-11	1	-10
Royce Clayton	-6	-4	-10
Jhonny Peralta	-17	3	-14
Julio Lugo	-9	-5	-14
Yuniesky Betancourt	-24	4	-20
David Eckstein	-19	-1	-20
Michael Young	-25	1	-24
Hanley Ramirez	-31	2	-29
Felipe Lopez	-26	-3	-29
Derek Jeter	-51	1	-50

Shortstops - 2007 Runs Saved

Player	Team	Plus/Minus	GDP	Total
Troy Tulowitzki	Col	27	3	30
John McDonald	Tor	20	0	20
Tony F Pena	KC	14	2	16
Omar Vizquel	SF	15	1	16
Jason Bartlett	Min	14	1	15
Adam Everett	Hou	14	1	15
Jack Wilson	Pit	8	4	12
Jose Reyes	NYM	10	1	11
Rafael Furcal	LAD	5	2	7
Jimmy Rollins	Phi	5	1	6
Khalil Greene	SD	5	1	6
J.J. Hardy	Mil	5	1	6
Ryan Theriot	ChC	4	2	6
Orlando Cabrera	LAA	2	3	5
Alex Gonzalez	Cin	3	2	5
Bobby Crosby	Oak	2	1	3
Cesar Izturis	2 tms	-1	2	1
Royce Clayton	2 tms	2	-1	1
Stephen Drew	Ari	-1	1	0
Edgar Renteria	Atl	-1	1	0
Julio Lugo	Bos	1	-2	-1
Jhonny Peralta	Cle	-2	0	-2
Juan Uribe	CWS	-5	1	-4
Miguel Tejada	Bal	-3	-2	-5
Jeff Keppinger	Cin	-5	0	-5
Yuniesky Betancourt	Sea	-8	1	-7
Mark Loretta	Hou	-5	-2	-7
Carlos Guillen	Det	-9	-1	-10
Felipe Lopez	Was	-10	0	-10
Josh Wilson	2 tms	-11	0	-11
Michael Young	Tex	-11	-1	-12
David Eckstein	StL	-11	-1	-12
Brendan Harris	TB	-14	-1	-15
Derek Jeter	NYY	-26	3	-23
Hanley Ramirez	Fla	-28	1	-27

Shortstops - 2008 Runs Saved

Player	Team	Plus/Minus	GDP	Total
Jimmy Rollins	Phi	17	-2	15
Cesar Izturis	StL	15	-1	14
Mike Aviles	KC	11	2	13
J.J. Hardy	Mil	14	-2	12
Cristian Guzman	Was	10	2	12
Yunel Escobar	Atl	15	-3	12
Jack Wilson	Pit	12	0	12
Omar Vizquel	SF	7	1	8
Marco Scutaro	Tor	9	-1	8
Miguel Tejada	Hou	5	2	7
Erick Aybar	LAA	6	0	6
Nick Punto	Min	3	3	6
Ryan Theriot	ChC	5	0	5
Orlando Cabrera	CWS	1	2	3
Maicer Izturis	LAA	2	1	3
Troy Tulowitzki	Col	3	-1	2
Hanley Ramirez	Fla	2	-1	1
Angel Berroa	LAD	0	0	0
Jose Reyes	NYM	-2	0	-2
Jason Bartlett	TB	-1	-1	-2
Khalil Greene	SD	-3	1	-2
Tony F Pena	KC	-2	0	-2
John McDonald	Tor	-1	-1	-2
Stephen Drew	Ari	-4	1	-3
Michael Young	Tex	-6	1	-5
Julio Lugo	Bos	-2	-3	-5
Juan Castro	2 tms	-3	-2	-5
Jhonny Peralta	Cle	-8	2	-6
Bobby Crosby	Oak	-10	4	-6
Brendan Harris	Min	-7	1	-6
Edgar Renteria	Det	-7	0	-7
Derek Jeter	NYY	-8	-1	-9
David Eckstein	Tor	-10	0	-10
Jeff Keppinger	Cin	-11	0	-11
Yuniesky Betancourt	Sea	-14	1	-13

Shortstops - 2006 Runs Saved

Player	Team	Plus/Minus	GDP	Total
Adam Everett	Hou	31	3	34
Clint Barmes	Col	21	3	24
Craig Counsell	Ari	14	5	19
Bill Hall	Mil	15	-2	13
Jimmy Rollins	Phi	9	3	12
Jose Reyes	NYM	12	-1	11
Khalil Greene	SD	10	-1	9
Jason Bartlett	Min	10	-3	7
Omar Vizquel	SF	5	0	5
Juan Castro	2 tms	4	1	5
Alex Cora	Bos	3	2	5
Edgar Renteria	Atl	5	-1	4
Ronny Cedeno	ChC	4	0	4
Alex Gonzalez	Bos	3	0	3
John McDonald	Tor	1	2	3
Rafael Furcal	LAD	3	-1	2
Juan Uribe	CWS	2	0	2
David Eckstein	StL	2	0	2
Stephen Drew	Ari	2	0	2
Jack Wilson	Pit	0	1	1
Yuniesky Betancourt	Sea	-2	2	0
Carlos Guillen	Det	-2	2	0
Hanley Ramirez	Fla	-5	2	-3
Angel Berroa	KC	-6	2	-4
Ben Zobrist	TB	-4	0	-4
Jhonny Peralta	Cle	-7	1	-6
Bobby Crosby	Oak	-6	0	-6
Michael Young	Tex	-8	1	-7
Orlando Cabrera	LAA	-9	1	-8
Julio Lugo	2 tms	-8	0	-8
Miguel Tejada	Bal	-11	1	-10
Royce Clayton	2 tms	-8	-3	-11
Derek Jeter	NYY	-17	-1	-18
Felipe Lopez	2 tms	-16	-3	-19
Marco Scutaro	Oak	-20	0	-20

Left Fielders - 3-Year Runs Saved

Player	Plus/Minus	OF Arm	HR Save	Total
Alfonso Soriano	9	33	0	42
Carl Crawford	19	3	0	22
Willie Harris	18	3	0	21
Reed Johnson	8	12	0	20
Eric Byrnes	13	0	0	13
Emil Brown	6	4	2	12
Matt Diaz	10	1	0	11
Jason Michaels	7	1	2	10
Scott Podsednik	7	1	2	10
Matt Murton	8	2	0	10
Luke Scott	11	-1	0	10
Josh Willingham	-9	16	0	7
Andre Ethier	4	3	0	7
Ryan Braun	4	3	0	7
Dave Roberts	7	-2	0	5
Jay Payton	-7	8	3	4
Craig Monroe	-7	9	2	4
Shannon Stewart	6	-3	0	3
Matt Holliday	0	-2	3	1
Carlos Quentin	-4	4	0	0
Chris Duncan	-3	2	0	-1
Adam Lind	0	-2	0	-2
Barry Bonds	-3	-3	3	-3
Hideki Matsui	-7	4	0	-3
Frank Catalanotto	-2	-2	0	-4
Carlos Lee	-3	-4	2	-5
Garret Anderson	-1	-4	0	-5
Marcus Thames	-8	1	0	-7
Raul Ibanez	-24	12	4	-8
Delmon Young	-14	3	0	-11
Jason Bay	-11	-7	4	-14
Luis Gonzalez	-13	-6	2	-17
Manny Ramirez	-35	7	0	-28
Pat Burrell	-41	11	0	-30
Adam Dunn	-35	-4	0	-39

Left Fielders - 2007 Runs Saved

Player	Team	Plus/Minus	OF Arm	HR Save	Total
Alfonso Soriano	ChC	-1	17	0	16
Eric Byrnes	Ari	14	1	0	15
Geoff Jenkins	Mil	10	0	0	10
Ryan Church	Was	6	4	0	10
Willie Harris	Atl	10	0	0	10
Scott Hairston	2 tms	7	1	0	8
Matt Diaz	Atl	6	1	0	7
Jason Michaels	Cle	1	3	2	6
Scott Podsednik	CWS	4	2	0	6
Emil Brown	KC	3	2	0	5
Joey Gathright	KC	3	-1	3	5
Craig Monroe	2 tms	-1	3	2	4
Moises Alou	NYM	1	1	2	4
Adam Lind	Tor	5	-1	0	4
Rob Mackowiak	2 tms	5	-1	0	4
Matt Holliday	Col	2	1	0	3
Reggie Willits	LAA	2	1	0	3
Reed Johnson	Tor	1	2	0	3
Carlos Lee	Hou	1	0	0	1
Carl Crawford	TB	0	1	0	1
Hideki Matsui	NYY	-5	6	0	1
Chris Duncan	StL	-2	2	0	0
Garret Anderson	LAA	-2	2	0	0
Shannon Stewart	Oak	3	-5	0	-2
Frank Catalanotto	Tex	-1	-1	0	-2
Josh Willingham	Fla	-10	7	0	-3
Jay Payton	Bal	-6	1	0	-5
Jason Kubel	Min	-4	-3	2	-5
Barry Bonds	SF	-6	-1	0	-7
Jason Bay	Pit	-11	1	2	-8
Luis Gonzalez	LAD	-7	-5	2	-10
Raul Ibanez	Sea	-14	0	2	-12
Pat Burrell	Phi	-15	2	0	-13
Manny Ramirez	Bos	-13	-1	0	-14
Adam Dunn	Cin	-16	-2	0	-18

Left Fielders - 2008 Runs Saved

Player	Team	Plus/Minus	OF Arm	HR Save	Total
Carl Crawford	TB	13	0	0	13
Willie Harris	Was	11	2	0	13
Josh Willingham	Fla	4	5	0	9
Conor Jackson	Ari	6	3	0	9
Ryan Braun	Mil	4	3	0	7
Johnny Damon	NYY	4	1	2	7
Brandon Boggs	Tex	3	4	0	7
Jay Payton	Bal	2	2	3	7
Ben Francisco	Cle	2	4	0	6
Matt Holliday	Col	5	0	0	5
Alfonso Soriano	ChC	-1	6	0	5
Fred Lewis	SF	2	3	0	5
Luke Scott	Bal	6	-1	0	5
Matt Joyce	Det	2	2	0	4
David DeJesus	KC	4	-1	0	3
Wily Mo Pena	Was	4	-1	0	3
Juan Pierre	LAD	3	-3	2	2
Carlos Quentin	CWS	-4	4	0	0
Chase Headley	SD	2	-2	0	0
David Murphy	Tex	-3	3	0	0
Garret Anderson	LAA	1	-2	0	-1
Gregor Blanco	Atl	2	-3	0	-1
Carlos Lee	Hou	0	-2	0	-2
Eric Byrnes	Ari	-1	-1	0	-2
Emil Brown	Oak	1	-3	0	-2
Manny Ramirez	2 tms	-5	2	0	-3
Pat Burrell	Phi	-11	6	0	-5
Marcus Thames	Det	-6	1	0	-5
Raul Ibanez	Sea	-11	5	0	-6
Adam Lind	Tor	-5	-1	0	-6
Luis Gonzalez	Fla	-7	0	0	-7
Jason Bay	2 tms	-7	-3	2	-8
Jack Cust	Oak	-8	0	0	-8
Adam Dunn	2 tms	-9	-1	0	-10
Delmon Young	Min	-14	3	0	-11

Left Fielders - 2006 Runs Saved

Player	Team	Plus/Minus	OF Arm	HR Save	Total
Alfonso Soriano	Was	11	10	0	21
Melky Cabrera	NYY	7	5	2	14
Reed Johnson	Tor	6	8	0	14
Raul Ibanez	Sea	1	7	2	10
Emil Brown	KC	2	5	2	9
Carl Crawford	TB	6	2	0	8
Andre Ethier	LAD	2	5	0	7
Ryan Langerhans	Atl	8	-1	0	7
Matt Diaz	Atl	6	1	0	7
Matt Murton	ChC	4	2	0	6
Scott Podsednik	CWS	4	-1	2	5
Dave Roberts	SD	9	-4	0	5
Barry Bonds	SF	3	-2	3	4
Luke Scott	Hou	4	0	0	4
Jason Michaels	Cle	6	-3	0	3
David DeJesus	KC	-1	2	2	3
Juan Rivera	LAA	-3	6	0	3
Jason Bay	Pit	7	-5	0	2
Brad Wilkerson	Tex	1	1	0	2
Jay Payton	Oak	-3	5	0	2
Josh Willingham	Fla	-3	4	0	1
Nick Swisher	Oak	1	0	0	1
Jeff Conine	2 tms	-2	3	0	1
Luis Gonzalez	Ari	1	-1	0	0
Craig Monroe	Det	-6	6	0	0
Frank Catalanotto	Tor	1	-1	0	0
Kevin Mench	2 tms	1	-2	0	-1
Carlos Lee	2 tms	-4	-2	2	-4
Garret Anderson	LAA	0	-4	0	-4
Cliff Floyd	NYM	-3	-1	0	-4
Preston Wilson	2 tms	-5	-1	0	-6
Matt Holliday	Col	-7	-3	3	-7
Adam Dunn	Cin	-10	-1	0	-11
Manny Ramirez	Bos	-17	6	0	-11
Pat Burrell	Phi	-15	3	0	-12

Center Fielders - 3-Year Runs Saved

Player	Plus/Minus	OF Arm	HR Save	Total
Carlos Beltran	33	6	5	44
Andruw Jones	24	6	5	35
Corey Patterson	22	4	6	32
Alfredo Amezaga	18	11	0	29
Shane Victorino	10	10	0	20
Willy Taveras	4	13	2	19
Carlos Gomez	18	1	0	19
Adam Jones	6	10	0	16
Mike Cameron	13	-1	3	15
Curtis Granderson	12	0	2	14
Marlon Byrd	3	6	3	12
Chris Young	13	-4	2	11
Cody Ross	8	3	0	11
Coco Crisp	10	-2	2	10
Juan Pierre	13	-7	2	8
Vernon Wells	2	5	0	7
Ichiro Suzuki	-2	9	0	7
B.J. Upton	-5	12	0	7
Eric Byrnes	4	1	2	7
Gary Matthews Jr.	-6	4	8	6
Aaron Rowand	-12	17	0	5
Grady Sizemore	3	-2	3	4
Brian Anderson	3	1	0	4
Torii Hunter	-5	-4	11	2
Melky Cabrera	-12	12	0	0
Chris Duffy	-4	1	2	-1
David DeJesus	-6	0	2	-4
Josh Hamilton	-8	2	2	-4
Lastings Milledge	-5	1	0	-4
Joey Gathright	-2	-3	0	-5
Mark Kotsay	-18	10	0	-8
Johnny Damon	-4	-6	2	-8
Jim Edmonds	-19	4	0	-15
Kenny Lofton	-13	-7	2	-18
Nate McLouth	-26	1	0	-25

Center Fielders - 2007 Runs Saved

Player	Team	Plus/Minus	OF Arm	HR Save	Total
Andruw Jones	Atl	12	7	3	22
Curtis Granderson	Det	11	3	2	16
Coco Crisp	Bos	15	1	0	16
Alfredo Amezaga	Fla	8	7	0	15
Carlos Beltran	NYM	13	-1	0	12
Aaron Rowand	Phi	-2	11	0	9
Jacque Jones	ChC	7	2	0	9
Nook Logan	Was	11	-3	0	8
Ichiro Suzuki	Sea	2	3	0	5
Mike Cameron	SD	1	1	3	5
Vernon Wells	Tor	4	1	0	5
Corey Patterson	Bal	1	1	3	5
Jerry Owens	CWS	6	-1	0	5
B.J. Upton	TB	1	4	0	5
Bill Hall	Mil	-1	5	0	4
Torii Hunter	Min	0	0	3	3
Nick Swisher	Oak	2	1	0	3
Felix Pie	ChC	3	0	0	3
David DeJesus	KC	-1	1	2	2
Hunter Pence	Hou	-1	3	0	2
Chris Duffy	Pit	-2	2	2	2
Juan Pierre	LAD	5	-4	0	1
Willy Taveras	Col	-5	4	2	1
Josh Hamilton	Cin	-1	2	0	1
Chris Young	Ari	-2	0	2	0
Marlon Byrd	Tex	-2	2	0	0
Mark Kotsay	Oak	-4	4	0	0
Ryan Freel	Cin	-4	4	0	0
Grady Sizemore	Cle	0	-1	0	-1
Jim Edmonds	StL	-6	5	0	-1
Melky Cabrera	NYY	-12	9	0	-3
Kenny Lofton	2 tms	-7	-1	2	-6
Nate McLouth	Pit	-5	-1	0	-6
Gary Matthews Jr.	LAA	-13	0	2	-11
Dave Roberts	SF	-11	-1	0	-12

Center Fielders - 2008 Runs Saved

Player	Team	Plus/Minus	OF Arm	HR Save	Total
Carlos Beltran	NYM	14	4	3	21
Carlos Gomez	Min	16	1	0	17
Shane Victorino	Phi	8	7	0	15
Adam Jones	Bal	4	7	0	11
Corey Patterson	Cin	6	2	3	11
Cody Ross	Fla	7	3	0	10
Alex Rios	Tor	4	6	0	10
Chris Young	Ari	12	-3	0	9
Mike Cameron	Mil	7	0	0	7
Jody Gerut	SD	7	0	0	7
Carlos Gonzalez	Oak	3	4	0	7
Melky Cabrera	NYY	2	3	0	5
Matt Kemp	LAD	-1	6	0	5
Michael Bourn	Hou	2	0	2	4
Jacoby Ellsbury	Bos	4	-1	0	3
Grady Sizemore	Cle	1	1	0	2
B.J. Upton	TB	-6	8	0	2
Aaron Rowand	SF	-4	5	0	1
Willy Taveras	Col	-2	2	0	0
Mark Kotsay	Atl	-8	7	0	-1
Ichiro Suzuki	Sea	-7	6	0	-1
Torii Hunter	LAA	-4	-1	3	-2
Rick Ankiel	StL	-11	7	2	-2
Coco Crisp	Bos	-1	-2	0	-3
Skip Schumaker	StL	-2	-2	0	-4
Josh Hamilton	Tex	-7	0	2	-5
Lastings Milledge	Was	-6	0	0	-6
Joey Gathright	KC	-6	0	0	-6
Reed Johnson	ChC	-6	0	0	-6
Curtis Granderson	Det	-6	-1	0	-7
Nick Swisher	CWS	-6	-1	0	-7
David DeJesus	KC	-6	-3	0	-9
Vernon Wells	Tor	-10	-2	0	-12
Jim Edmonds	2 tms	-14	1	0	-13
Nate McLouth	Pit	-21	2	0	-19

Center Fielders - 2006 Runs Saved

Player	Team	Plus/Minus	OF Arm	HR Save	Total
Willy Taveras	Hou	11	7	0	18
Andruw Jones	Atl	15	-1	2	16
Corey Patterson	Bal	15	1	0	16
Vernon Wells	Tor	8	6	0	14
Gary Matthews Jr.	Tex	4	2	6	12
Carlos Beltran	NYM	6	3	2	11
Randy Winn	SF	8	-2	2	8
Shane Victorino	Phi	3	3	0	6
Juan Pierre	ChC	7	-4	2	5
Curtis Granderson	Det	7	-2	0	5
Eric Byrnes	Ari	2	0	2	4
Grady Sizemore	Cle	2	-2	3	3
Mike Cameron	SD	5	-2	0	3
Cory Sullivan	Col	-1	4	0	3
Alfredo Amezaga	Fla	3	0	0	3
David DeJesus	KC	1	2	0	3
Joey Gathright	2 tms	5	-3	0	2
Brian Anderson	CWS	2	0	0	2
Brady Clark	Mil	4	-2	0	2
Rocco Baldelli	TB	2	0	0	2
Jeremy Reed	Sea	1	1	0	2
Torii Hunter	Min	-1	-3	5	1
Steve Finley	SF	3	-2	0	1
Chone Figgins	LAA	-2	2	0	0
Reggie Abercrombie	Fla	-2	2	0	0
Jim Edmonds	StL	1	-2	0	-1
Coco Crisp	Bos	-4	-1	2	-3
Chris Duffy	Pit	-2	-1	0	-3
Johnny Damon	NYY	-1	-5	2	-4
Aaron Rowand	Phi	-6	1	0	-5
Rob Mackowiak	CWS	-6	0	0	-6
Mark Kotsay	Oak	-6	-1	0	-7
Jose Bautista	Pit	-11	2	0	-9
Kenny Lofton	LAD	-6	-6	0	-12
Ken Griffey Jr.	Cin	-16	1	2	-13

Right Fielders - 3-Year Runs Saved

Player	Plus/Minus	OF Arm	HR Save	Total
Alex Rios	25	24	0	49
Franklin Gutierrez	32	2	0	34
Randy Winn	24	7	0	31
Nick Markakis	5	21	4	30
Ichiro Suzuki	16	9	2	27
Jeff Francoeur	1	25	0	26
Brian Giles	23	-5	2	20
Austin Kearns	17	2	0	19
Shane Victorino	3	15	0	18
Jayson Werth	4	11	0	15
Ryan Ludwick	2	12	0	14
Hunter Pence	0	12	0	12
Delmon Young	-3	14	0	11
Nelson Cruz	8	3	0	11
Corey Hart	7	-4	5	8
Geoff Jenkins	2	6	0	8
Justin Upton	4	3	0	7
J.D. Drew	6	0	0	6
Matt Kemp	0	6	0	6
Juan Encarnacion	8	-3	0	5
Jeremy Hermida	3	-2	2	3
Magglio Ordonez	-10	12	0	2
Mark Teahen	-2	2	2	2
Jacque Jones	-1	0	2	1
Xavier Nady	-4	3	0	-1
Vladimir Guerrero	-11	7	2	-2
Andre Ethier	-2	-2	2	-2
Jose Guillen	-11	8	0	-3
Trot Nixon	-3	-5	0	-8
Michael Cuddyer	-34	25	0	-9
Ken Griffey Jr.	-14	0	0	-14
Shawn Green	-10	-7	0	-17
Bobby Abreu	-28	9	0	-19
Brad Hawpe	-37	10	0	-27
Jermaine Dye	-39	-4	4	-39

Right Fielders - 2007 Runs Saved

Player	Team	Plus/Minus	OF Arm	HR Save	Total
Jeff Francoeur	Atl	6	13	0	19
Shane Victorino	Phi	5	13	0	18
Alex Rios	Tor	7	9	0	16
Franklin Gutierrez	Cle	12	-2	0	10
Jayson Werth	Phi	4	6	0	10
Austin Kearns	Was	10	-1	0	9
Randy Winn	SF	7	2	0	9
Andre Ethier	LAD	9	-2	2	9
Mark Teahen	KC	3	5	0	8
Delmon Young	TB	-4	11	0	7
Jeremy Hermida	Fla	4	1	2	7
Corey Hart	Mil	6	-2	3	7
Magglio Ordonez	Det	2	3	0	5
Nick Markakis	Bal	-3	5	2	4
Nelson Cruz	Tex	4	0	0	4
Nick Swisher	Oak	3	1	0	4
Jose Guillen	Sea	-4	7	0	3
J.D. Drew	Bos	3	0	0	3
Carlos Quentin	Ari	2	1	0	3
Xavier Nady	Pit	1	1	0	2
Michael Cuddyer	Min	-13	13	0	0
Vladimir Guerrero	LAA	-3	3	0	0
Luke Scott	Hou	-1	1	0	0
Travis Buck	Oak	2	-2	0	0
Brian Giles	SD	1	-3	0	-2
Matt Kemp	LAD	-1	-1	0	-2
Juan Encarnacion	StL	-2	0	0	-2
Jack Cust	Oak	-2	-1	0	-3
Trot Nixon	Cle	-5	-1	0	-6
Cliff Floyd	ChC	-5	-1	0	-6
Bobby Abreu	NYY	-8	1	0	-7
Shawn Green	NYM	-5	-2	0	-7
Ken Griffey Jr.	Cin	-5	-3	0	-8
Brad Hawpe	Col	-10	-1	0	-11
Jermaine Dye	CWS	-24	-2	2	-24

Right Fielders - 2008 Runs Saved

Player	Team	Plus/Minus	OF Arm	HR Save	Total
Franklin Gutierrez	Cle	17	5	0	22
Nick Markakis	Bal	6	14	0	20
Ichiro Suzuki	Sea	8	5	2	15
Denard Span	Min	7	6	2	15
Alex Rios	Tor	9	5	0	14
Randy Winn	SF	9	3	0	12
Ryan Ludwick	StL	1	11	0	12
Hunter Pence	Hou	-1	12	0	11
Ryan Sweeney	Oak	3	6	0	9
Brian Giles	SD	13	-5	0	8
Brad Wilkerson	2 tms	5	2	0	7
Elijah Dukes	Was	6	0	0	6
Justin Upton	Ari	2	3	0	5
Ryan Church	NYM	5	0	0	5
Jayson Werth	Phi	0	5	0	5
Geoff Jenkins	Phi	-1	6	0	5
Gabe Gross	2 tms	0	4	0	4
Kosuke Fukudome	ChC	1	2	0	3
Corey Hart	Mil	0	0	2	2
Xavier Nady	2 tms	-2	3	0	1
Jay Bruce	Cin	-2	3	0	1
Michael Cuddyer	Min	-5	5	0	0
Jeff Francoeur	Atl	-7	5	0	-2
Magglio Ordonez	Det	-3	1	0	-2
Jeremy Hermida	Fla	1	-3	0	-2
Vladimir Guerrero	LAA	-2	-2	2	-2
Austin Kearns	Was	1	-3	0	-2
Jose Guillen	KC	-6	2	0	-4
Bobby Abreu	NYY	-12	7	0	-5
J.D. Drew	Bos	-4	-1	0	-5
Ken Griffey Jr.	2 tms	-9	3	0	-6
Mark Teahen	KC	-5	-3	2	-6
Jermaine Dye	CWS	-7	-2	0	-9
Andre Ethier	LAD	-11	0	0	-11
Brad Hawpe	Col	-21	-1	0	-22

Right Fielders - 2006 Runs Saved

Player	Team	Plus/Minus	OF Arm	HR Save	Total
Alex Rios	Tor	9	10	0	19
Brian Giles	SD	9	3	2	14
Austin Kearns	2 tms	6	6	0	12
Ichiro Suzuki	Sea	8	4	0	12
Randy Winn	SF	8	2	0	10
Jeff Francoeur	Atl	2	7	0	9
J.D. Drew	LAD	7	1	0	8
Mark DeRosa	Tex	6	2	0	8
Juan Encarnacion	StL	10	-3	0	7
Brad Hawpe	Col	-6	12	0	6
Nick Markakis	Bal	2	2	2	6
Reggie Sanders	KC	7	-1	0	6
Jay Payton	Oak	3	0	2	5
Damon Hollins	TB	5	-1	0	4
Geoff Jenkins	Mil	3	0	0	3
Casey Blake	Cle	1	2	0	3
Jacque Jones	ChC	-1	2	0	1
Carlos Quentin	Ari	-2	1	2	1
Vladimir Guerrero	LAA	-6	6	0	0
Magglio Ordonez	Det	-9	8	0	-1
Milton Bradley	Oak	-4	1	2	-1
Jason Lane	Hou	-3	2	0	-1
Trot Nixon	Bos	1	-3	0	-2
Jeremy Hermida	Fla	-2	0	0	-2
Moises Alou	SF	0	-2	0	-2
Jose Guillen	Was	-1	-1	0	-2
Xavier Nady	2 tms	-3	-1	0	-4
Jeromy Burnitz	Pit	-9	5	0	-4
Kevin Mench	Tex	-5	1	0	-4
Emil Brown	KC	-1	-3	0	-4
Jermaine Dye	CWS	-8	0	2	-6
Bobby Abreu	2 tms	-8	1	0	-7
Bernie Williams	NYY	-6	-1	0	-7
Michael Cuddyer	Min	-16	7	0	-9
Shawn Green	2 tms	-5	-5	0	-10

Catchers - 3-Year Runs Saved

Player	Earned Runs	Stolen Bases	Total
Jason Kendall	23	4	27
Yadier Molina	5	14	19
Jose Molina	6	10	16
Ivan Rodriguez	9	6	15
Gerald Laird	5	10	15
Ronny Paulino	11	1	12
Chris Snyder	5	4	9
David Ross	3	6	9
Russell Martin	4	4	8
Yorvit Torrealba	2	5	7
Rod Barajas	3	4	7
Brian McCann	10	-4	6
Bengie Molina	4	2	6
Joe Mauer	5	1	6
Kelly Shoppach	1	2	3
A.J. Pierzynski	7	-5	2
Ramon Hernandez	0	2	2
Carlos Ruiz	3	-2	1
Miguel Olivo	-6	6	0
Kurt Suzuki	-4	2	-2
Paul Bako	0	-3	-3
Brad Ausmus	9	-13	-4
Gregg Zaun	2	-6	-4
Dioner Navarro	-5	0	-5
Jason Varitek	1	-7	-6
Mike Napoli	-3	-4	-7
Paul Lo Duca	-5	-5	-10
Johnny Estrada	1	-12	-11
Jorge Posada	-5	-7	-12
Brian Schneider	-16	2	-14
Victor Martinez	-8	-6	-14
Josh Bard	-2	-12	-14
John Buck	-4	-11	-15
Michael Barrett	-4	-13	-17
Kenji Johjima	-19	1	-18

Catchers - 2007 Runs Saved

Player	Team	Earned Runs	Stolen Bases	Total
Yadier Molina	StL	6	7	13
Russell Martin	LAD	4	5	9
Joe Mauer	Min	5	3	8
A.J. Pierzynski	CWS	7	0	7
Ivan Rodriguez	Det	5	2	7
Jason Kendall	2 tms	14	-8	6
Gerald Laird	Tex	0	6	6
Yorvit Torrealba	Col	6	0	6
David Ross	Cin	2	4	6
Chris Snyder	Ari	3	2	5
Carlos Ruiz	Phi	3	1	4
Gregg Zaun	Tor	7	-3	4
Bengie Molina	SF	4	-1	3
Ronny Paulino	Pit	2	-1	1
Victor Martinez	Cle	-2	2	0
Jose Molina	2 tms	0	0	0
Brian McCann	Atl	1	-2	-1
Mike Redmond	Min	-1	0	-1
Paul Lo Duca	NYM	0	-2	-2
Brad Ausmus	Hou	4	-6	-2
Dioner Navarro	TB	0	-3	-3
Ramon Hernandez	Bal	0	-3	-3
Mike Napoli	LAA	-1	-2	-3
Chris Iannetta	Col	-2	-1	-3
Jason Varitek	Bos	-2	-2	-4
Miguel Olivo	Fla	-5	1	-4
Brian Schneider	Was	-7	1	-6
Jorge Posada	NYY	-1	-6	-7
Kenji Johjima	Sea	-10	3	-7
Josh Bard	SD	2	-9	-7
Kurt Suzuki	Oak	-7	0	-7
Miguel Montero	Ari	-3	-4	-7
John Buck	KC	-4	-4	-8
Michael Barrett	2 tms	-5	-3	-8
Johnny Estrada	Mil	0	-9	-9

Catchers - 2008 Runs Saved

Player	Team	Earned Runs	Stolen Bases	Total
Jason Kendall	Mil	4	8	12
Jose Molina	NYY	5	7	12
Bengie Molina	SF	1	6	7
Brian McCann	Atl	7	-1	6
Gerald Laird	Tex	5	1	6
Kurt Suzuki	Oak	3	2	5
Rod Barajas	Tor	4	1	5
Ivan Rodriguez	2 tms	3	0	3
Chris Snyder	Ari	2	1	3
Miguel Olivo	KC	0	3	3
Jason Varitek	Bos	3	-2	1
Ramon Hernandez	Bal	3	-2	1
Yadier Molina	StL	-2	3	1
Jesus Flores	Was	2	-1	1
Joe Mauer	Min	1	-1	0
Chris Iannetta	Col	2	-2	0
Kenji Johjima	Sea	2	-2	0
Jeff Mathis	LAA	3	-3	0
Brad Ausmus	Hou	2	-2	0
Matt Treanor	Fla	1	-1	0
Geovany Soto	ChC	3	-4	-1
Dioner Navarro	TB	-5	4	-1
Yorvit Torrealba	Col	-2	1	-1
Ryan Doumit	Pit	0	-2	-2
Brian Schneider	NYM	-2	0	-2
Carlos Ruiz	Phi	0	-2	-2
Paul Bako	Cin	0	-2	-2
Chris Coste	Phi	1	-3	-2
Russell Martin	LAD	-2	-1	-3
Kelly Shoppach	Cle	-2	-2	-4
John Baker	Fla	-1	-3	-4
Gregg Zaun	Tor	-4	-1	-5
Mike Napoli	LAA	-3	-3	-6
A.J. Pierzynski	CWS	-5	-3	-8
John Buck	KC	-1	-7	-8

Catchers - 2006 Runs Saved

Player	Team	Earned Runs	Stolen Bases	Total
Ronny Paulino	Pit	9	1	10
Jason Kendall	Oak	5	4	9
Damian Miller	Mil	5	2	7
Ivan Rodriguez	Det	1	4	5
Yadier Molina	StL	1	4	5
Ramon Hernandez	Bal	-3	7	4
Jose Molina	LAA	1	3	4
A.J. Pierzynski	CWS	5	-2	3
David Ross	Cin	2	1	3
Gerald Laird	Tex	0	3	3
Russell Martin	LAD	2	0	2
Mike Napoli	LAA	1	1	2
Yorvit Torrealba	Col	-2	4	2
Brian McCann	Atl	2	-1	1
Miguel Olivo	Fla	-1	2	1
John Buck	KC	1	0	1
Rod Barajas	Tex	-1	2	1
Mike Piazza	SD	7	-6	1
Henry Blanco	ChC	-2	3	1
Jorge Posada	NYY	-3	3	0
Eliezer Alfonzo	SF	-1	0	-1
Dioner Navarro	2 tms	0	-1	-1
Brad Ausmus	Hou	3	-5	-2
Joe Mauer	Min	-1	-1	-2
Johnny Estrada	Ari	1	-3	-2
Jason Varitek	Bos	0	-3	-3
Gregg Zaun	Tor	-1	-2	-3
Bengie Molina	Tor	-1	-3	-4
Michael Barrett	ChC	2	-7	-5
Paul Lo Duca	NYM	-5	-1	-6
Brian Schneider	Was	-7	1	-6
Toby Hall	2 tms	-3	-3	-6
Josh Bard	2 tms	-4	-2	-6
Kenji Johjima	Sea	-11	0	-11
Victor Martinez	Cle	-6	-9	-15

Pitchers - 3-Year Runs Saved

Player	Plus/Minus	Stolen Bases	Total
Kenny Rogers	20	7	27
Mark Buehrle	6	12	18
Aaron Cook	10	6	16
Zach Duke	10	6	16
Johan Santana	9	5	14
Greg Maddux	25	-11	14
Jon Garland	6	7	13
Tom Glavine	6	6	12
Justin Verlander	2	9	11
Jeff Suppan	8	2	10
Jeff Francis	8	2	10
Jesse Litsch	8	2	10
Jarrod Washburn	4	5	9
Chris Capuano	4	5	9
Bronson Arroyo	3	5	8
Javier Vazquez	6	2	8
Paul Maholm	3	5	8
Chien-Ming Wang	6	2	8
Erik Bedard	6	2	8
Dontrelle Willis	5	3	8
Joel Pineiro	7	1	8
Brandon Webb	11	-4	7
Jamie Moyer	2	5	7
Felix Hernandez	7	0	7
Jake Westbrook	6	1	7
Brett Tomko	7	0	7
Casey Fossum	7	0	7
Roy Oswalt	2	4	6
Wandy Rodriguez	1	5	6
Jeremy Guthrie	5	1	6
Zack Greinke	3	3	6
Livan Hernandez	4	1	5
Tim Hudson	6	-1	5
James Shields	1	4	5
Doug Davis	0	5	5
Adam Wainwright	1	4	5
Adam Eaton	1	4	5
Noah Lowry	3	2	5
Kyle Kendrick	6	-1	5
Gil Meche	1	3	4
Chad Billingsley	0	4	4
Josh Fogg	4	0	4
Shaun Marcum	3	1	4
Brian Bannister	2	2	4
Steve Trachsel	4	0	4
John Danks	4	0	4
Woody Williams	5	-1	4
Kameron Loe	3	1	4
Chris Carpenter	2	2	4
Barry Zito	-3	6	3
Scott Olsen	-2	5	3
John Smoltz	3	0	3
Fausto Carmona	4	-1	3
Randy Wolf	1	2	3
Todd Wellemeyer	1	2	3
Ryan Dempster	4	-1	3
Chris Sampson	1	2	3
Rodrigo Lopez	1	2	3
Micah Owings	1	2	3
Brad Thompson	0	3	3
Aaron Heilman	5	-2	3
Brandon Backe	0	3	3
Andy Pettitte	-2	4	2
Carlos Zambrano	-4	6	2
Mike Mussina	6	-4	2
Kyle Lohse	-1	3	2
Vicente Padilla	-1	3	2
Andy Sonnanstine	-2	4	2
Sean Marshall	2	0	2
Shawn Chacon	2	0	2
Tim Redding	2	0	2
Josh Johnson	1	1	2
Cha Seung Baek	0	2	2
Kip Wells	2	0	2
Saul Rivera	3	-1	2
Derek Lowe	4	-3	1
Ted Lilly	0	1	1
Cole Hamels	4	-3	1
Odalis Perez	0	1	1
John Maine	0	1	1
Joe Saunders	-1	2	1
Claudio Vargas	1	0	1
Carlos Villanueva	1	0	1
Clay Hensley	2	-1	1
Ryan Madson	1	0	1
Jeremy Affeldt	3	-2	1
Matt Guerrier	0	1	1
Jason Marquis	3	-3	0
Oliver Perez	0	0	0
Matt Morris	1	-1	0
Kelvim Escobar	2	-2	0
Daisuke Matsuzaka	2	-2	0
Tom Gorzelanny	0	0	0
Jamey Wright	-3	3	0
Jeremy Sowers	1	-1	0
Zach Miner	-1	1	0
Mark Redman	-2	2	0
Chan Ho Park	1	-1	0
Carlos Marmol	1	-1	0
Scott Feldman	4	-4	0
Jake Peavy	5	-6	-1
David Bush	2	-3	-1
Miguel Batista	1	-2	-1
Brett Myers	2	-3	-1
Ramon Ortiz	-2	1	-1
Mike Pelfrey	-3	2	-1
Julian Tavarez	-2	1	-1
Brian Burres	0	-1	-1
Sidney Ponson	-5	4	-1
CC Sabathia	-3	1	-2
John Lackey	-1	-1	-2
Ian Snell	1	-3	-2
Scott Baker	-2	0	-2
Curt Schilling	-4	2	-2
Jon Lester	-5	3	-2
Chad Gaudin	-2	0	-2
Jorge de la Rosa	-2	0	-2
Brian Moehler	-3	1	-2
Jeff Weaver	-4	2	-2
Kyle Davies	0	-2	-2
Orlando Hernandez	0	-2	-2
Chuck James	0	-2	-2
Ubaldo Jimenez	2	-4	-2
Taylor Buchholz	0	-2	-2
Edinson Volquez	-1	-1	-2
Jon Rauch	-2	0	-2
Matt Belisle	-2	0	-2
Jason Schmidt	-3	1	-2
Ryan Franklin	-4	2	-2
Joe Blanton	-3	0	-3
Nate Robertson	-6	3	-3
Paul Byrd	-5	2	-3
Braden Looper	-4	1	-3
Ricky Nolasco	-5	2	-3
Kevin Correia	-5	2	-3
Anthony Reyes	-4	1	-3
David Wells	-3	0	-3
Roy Halladay	0	-4	-4
Carlos Silva	-5	1	-4
Boof Bonser	-5	1	-4
Jason Jennings	-2	-2	-4
Rich Hill	-2	-2	-4
Dustin McGowan	2	-6	-4
Tony Armas Jr.	-2	-2	-4
Jorge Sosa	-5	1	-4
Jonathan Sanchez	-2	-2	-4
Dan Haren	-4	-1	-5
Matt Cain	-6	1	-5
Cliff Lee	-7	2	-5
Tim Wakefield	5	-10	-5
Scott Kazmir	-9	4	-5
Ben Sheets	-3	-2	-5
Jon Lieber	-5	0	-5
Pedro Martinez	-2	-3	-5
Chad Qualls	-6	1	-5
Josh Beckett	-5	-1	-6
Ervin Santana	-7	1	-6
Mark Hendrickson	-5	-1	-6
Jason Bergmann	-5	-1	-6
Matt Garza	-7	1	-6
Freddy Garcia	0	-6	-6
Byung-Hyun Kim	-2	-4	-6
Brad Penny	-6	-1	-7
Jeremy Bonderman	-5	-2	-7
Edwin Jackson	-7	0	-7
Tim Lincecum	-4	-3	-7
Aaron Harang	-6	-2	-8
Kevin Millwood	-4	-4	-8
Jose Contreras	-2	-6	-8
Jered Weaver	-4	-4	-8
Randy Johnson	-6	-2	-8
Gavin Floyd	-1	-8	-9
A.J. Burnett	-5	-7	-12
Daniel Cabrera	-12	-6	-18
Chris Young	-3	-15	-18

23

Pitchers - 2008 Runs Saved

Player	Team	Plus/Minus	Stolen Bases	Total
Kenny Rogers	Det	12	3	15
Jesse Litsch	Tor	6	2	8
Aaron Cook	Col	3	4	7
Greg Maddux	2 tms	10	-3	7
Zack Greinke	KC	3	3	6
Zach Duke	Pit	4	2	6
Ryan Dempster	ChC	5	0	5
Justin Verlander	Det	3	2	5
Jeff Suppan	Mil	3	2	5
Mark Buehrle	CWS	0	4	4
Javier Vazquez	CWS	4	0	4
Paul Maholm	Pit	2	2	4
Scott Olsen	Fla	2	2	4
Jon Garland	LAA	2	2	4
Greg Smith	Oak	-2	6	4
Hiroki Kuroda	LAD	3	1	4
Livan Hernandez	2 tms	2	2	4
Kyle Kendrick	Phi	5	-1	4
Glen Perkins	Min	2	2	4
Doug Davis	Ari	3	1	4
Adam Wainwright	StL	2	2	4
R.A. Dickey	Sea	2	2	4
Brandon Webb	Ari	4	-1	3
Roy Oswalt	Hou	2	1	3
Bronson Arroyo	Cin	2	1	3
Vicente Padilla	Tex	2	1	3
Tim Hudson	Atl	3	0	3
Sean Gallagher	2 tms	3	0	3
Micah Owings	Ari	2	1	3
Phil Dumatrait	Pit	2	1	3
Chad Billingsley	LAD	1	1	2
Mike Pelfrey	NYM	-1	3	2
Felix Hernandez	Sea	3	-1	2
Mike Mussina	NYY	2	0	2
Joe Saunders	LAA	2	0	2
Joe Blanton	2 tms	1	1	2
John Danks	CWS	2	0	2
Andy Sonnanstine	TB	0	2	2
Brian Bannister	KC	1	1	2
Paul Byrd	2 tms	-1	3	2
Jason Marquis	ChC	3	-1	2
Kevin Slowey	Min	1	1	2
Joel Pineiro	StL	1	1	2
Rich Harden	2 tms	1	1	2
Jeff Francis	Col	2	0	2
Justin Duchscherer	Oak	1	1	2
Jeremy Sowers	Cle	2	0	2
Fausto Carmona	Cle	2	0	2
Darrell Rasner	NYY	1	1	2
Adam Eaton	Phi	1	1	2
Chad Gaudin	2 tms	0	2	2
Josh Rupe	Tex	1	1	2
Brian Bass	2 tms	1	1	2
Erik Bedard	Sea	2	0	2
Cole Hamels	Phi	2	-1	1
James Shields	TB	-1	2	1
Gil Meche	KC	2	-1	1
Ted Lilly	ChC	-1	2	1
Oliver Perez	NYM	1	0	1
Jeremy Guthrie	Bal	2	-1	1
Carlos Zambrano	ChC	-1	2	1
Tim Redding	Was	1	0	1
Barry Zito	SF	-1	2	1
Armando Galarraga	Det	1	0	1
Daisuke Matsuzaka	Bos	2	-1	1
Jarrod Washburn	Sea	0	1	1
Shaun Marcum	Tor	1	0	1
John Maine	NYM	0	1	1
Wandy Rodriguez	Hou	0	1	1
Zach Miner	Det	1	0	1
Pedro Martinez	NYM	2	-1	1
Carlos Villanueva	Mil	1	0	1
Clayton Kershaw	LAD	0	1	1
Seth McClung	Mil	0	1	1
Chan Ho Park	LAD	1	0	1
Aaron Laffey	Cle	0	1	1
Justin Masterson	Bos	2	-1	1
Jamey Wright	Tex	1	0	1
Glendon Rusch	2 tms	1	0	1
Matt Harrison	Tex	0	1	1
Johan Santana	NYM	-2	2	0
Ben Sheets	Mil	-1	1	0
Nick Blackburn	Min	-1	1	0
Todd Wellemeyer	StL	-2	2	0
John Lannan	Was	0	0	0
Josh Beckett	Bos	-1	1	0
Johnny Cueto	Cin	-1	1	0

Player	Team	Plus/Minus	Stolen Bases	Total
Scott Baker	Min	-1	1	0
Nate Robertson	Det	-1	1	0
Brandon Backe	Hou	-2	2	0
Jorge Campillo	Atl	0	0	0
Scott Kazmir	TB	-2	2	0
Sidney Ponson	2 tms	-2	2	0
Ryan Rowland-Smith	Sea	0	0	0
Jo-Jo Reyes	Atl	0	0	0
Kevin Correia	SF	-2	2	0
Chien-Ming Wang	NYY	0	0	0
Chad Durbin	Phi	-1	1	0
Josh Johnson	Fla	0	0	0
Carlos Marmol	ChC	0	0	0
Shawn Chacon	Hou	-1	1	0
Hong-Chih Kuo	LAD	0	0	0
Manny Corpas	Col	0	0	0
Derek Lowe	LAD	1	-1	0
Ubaldo Jimenez	Col	1	-1	0
Edinson Volquez	Cin	1	-1	0
Brett Myers	Phi	2	-2	0
Tim Wakefield	Bos	2	-2	0
Brian Burres	Bal	1	-1	0
Tom Gorzelanny	Pit	1	-1	0
Josh Banks	SD	2	-2	0
Saul Rivera	Was	2	-2	0
Matt Cain	SF	-2	1	-1
Ricky Nolasco	Fla	-2	1	-1
Jon Lester	Bos	-2	1	-1
Braden Looper	StL	-2	1	-1
Jamie Moyer	Phi	-2	1	-1
Randy Wolf	2 tms	-2	1	-1
David Bush	Mil	0	-1	-1
Edwin Jackson	TB	-2	1	-1
Jake Peavy	SD	0	-1	-1
Dana Eveland	Oak	-1	0	-1
Manny Parra	Mil	-2	1	-1
Odalis Perez	Was	-2	1	-1
Scott Feldman	Tex	2	-3	-1
Cha Seung Baek	2 tms	-2	1	-1
Mark Hendrickson	Fla	0	-1	-1
Jorge de la Rosa	Col	-1	0	-1
Chris Sampson	Hou	-2	1	-1
Joba Chamberlain	NYY	-1	0	-1
Salomon Torres	Mil	-2	1	-1
Collin Balester	Was	-2	1	-1
CC Sabathia	2 tms	-2	0	-2
Roy Halladay	Tor	-1	-1	-2
Cliff Lee	Cle	-3	1	-2
A.J. Burnett	Tor	-2	0	-2
Dan Haren	Ari	-2	0	-2
Kyle Lohse	StL	-2	0	-2
Ian Snell	Pit	0	-2	-2
Jonathan Sanchez	SF	0	-2	-2
Carlos Silva	Sea	-2	0	-2
Jose Contreras	CWS	0	-2	-2
Dustin McGowan	Tor	-1	-1	-2
Chris Young	SD	0	-2	-2
Brad Penny	LAD	-2	0	-2
Ryan Madson	Phi	-1	-1	-2
Dennis Sarfate	Bal	-2	0	-2
Ryan Franklin	StL	-2	0	-2
Aquilino Lopez	Det	-2	0	-2
Andy Pettitte	NYY	-5	2	-3
Matt Garza	TB	-3	0	-3
Jered Weaver	LAA	-2	-1	-3
John Lackey	LAA	-3	0	-3
Brian Moehler	Hou	-2	-1	-3
Jason Bergmann	Was	-2	-1	-3
Garrett Olson	Bal	-1	-2	-3
Luke Hochevar	KC	-2	-1	-3
Boof Bonser	Min	-2	-1	-3
Miguel Batista	Sea	0	-3	-3
Kyle Davies	KC	-2	-1	-3
Andrew Miller	Fla	-2	-1	-3
Jeff Bennett	Atl	-3	0	-3
J.P. Howell	TB	-2	-1	-3
Radhames Liz	Bal	-2	-1	-3
Chris Volstad	Fla	-2	-1	-3
Joel Hanrahan	Was	-1	-2	-3
Tim Lincecum	SF	-2	-2	-4
Kevin Millwood	Tex	-1	-3	-4
Sean Green	Sea	-4	0	-4
Ervin Santana	LAA	-4	-1	-5
Gavin Floyd	CWS	0	-5	-5
Jair Jurrjens	Atl	-1	-4	-5
Aaron Harang	Cin	-3	-2	-5
Randy Johnson	Ari	-5	-2	-7
Daniel Cabrera	Bal	-5	-3	-8

Pitchers - 2007 Runs Saved

Player	Team	Plus/Minus	Stolen Bases	Total
Johan Santana	Min	4	2	6
Jeff Francis	Col	4	2	6
Jon Garland	CWS	3	3	6
Tim Hudson	Atl	4	1	5
Mark Buehrle	CWS	2	3	5
Chien-Ming Wang	NYY	5	0	5
Jarrod Washburn	Sea	3	2	5
Aaron Cook	Col	5	0	5
Joel Pineiro	2 tms	5	0	5
Bronson Arroyo	Cin	1	3	4
Tom Glavine	NYM	2	2	4
Jamie Moyer	Phi	2	2	4
Woody Williams	Hou	4	0	4
Wandy Rodriguez	Hou	2	2	4
Brett Tomko	2 tms	4	0	4
Chris Sampson	Hou	3	1	4
Mike Maroth	2 tms	1	3	4
CC Sabathia	Cle	1	2	3
Javier Vazquez	CWS	2	1	3
Andy Pettitte	NYY	2	1	3
James Shields	TB	2	1	3
Dontrelle Willis	Fla	2	1	3
Derek Lowe	LAD	2	1	3
Greg Maddux	SD	8	-5	3
Doug Davis	Ari	-1	4	3
Erik Bedard	Bal	2	1	3
Jeremy Guthrie	Bal	1	2	3
Brian Bannister	KC	1	2	3
Shaun Marcum	Tor	2	1	3
Chris Capuano	Mil	2	1	3
Kameron Loe	Tex	3	0	3
Joe Kennedy	3 tms	2	1	3
Yovani Gallardo	Mil	2	1	3
Horacio Ramirez	Sea	2	1	3
Saul Rivera	Was	2	1	3
Jake Peavy	SD	4	-2	2
Roy Oswalt	Hou	1	1	2
Jeff Suppan	Mil	2	0	2
John Smoltz	Atl	2	0	2
Barry Zito	SF	1	1	2
Kyle Lohse	2 tms	1	1	2
Adam Eaton	Phi	0	2	2
Steve Trachsel	2 tms	2	0	2
Noah Lowry	SF	1	1	2
Jake Westbrook	Cle	2	0	2
Sergio Mitre	Fla	2	0	2
Chad Billingsley	LAD	0	2	2
John Danks	CWS	2	0	2
Odalis Perez	KC	2	0	2
Chad Durbin	Det	2	0	2
Jason Hirsh	Col	2	0	2
Jesse Litsch	Tor	2	0	2
Zach Duke	Pit	1	1	2
Randy Wolf	LAD	1	1	2
Heath Bell	SD	2	0	2
Kason Gabbard	2 tms	2	0	2
Carlos Zambrano	ChC	-1	2	1
Gil Meche	KC	-1	2	1
Ted Lilly	ChC	1	0	1
Livan Hernandez	Ari	2	-1	1
Adam Wainwright	StL	-1	2	1
Matt Morris	2 tms	2	-1	1
Josh Fogg	Col	2	-1	1
Kip Wells	StL	2	-1	1
Chuck James	Atl	1	0	1
Orlando Hernandez	NYM	2	-1	1
Kyle Davies	2 tms	2	-1	1
Brad Thompson	StL	-1	2	1
Kyle Kendrick	Phi	1	0	1
Ramon Ortiz	2 tms	1	0	1
Edgar Gonzalez	Ari	0	1	1
Shawn Hill	Was	1	0	1
Shawn Chacon	Pit	1	0	1
Robinson Tejeda	Tex	2	-1	1
Peter Moylan	Atl	2	-1	1
Matt Guerrier	Min	1	0	1
Aaron Heilman	NYM	2	-1	1
Tim Redding	Was	1	0	1
Kevin Gregg	Fla	1	0	1
Joaquin Benoit	Tex	0	1	1
Ryan Franklin	StL	0	1	1
Aaron Harang	Cin	0	0	0
Fausto Carmona	Cle	0	0	0
Carlos Silva	Min	-1	1	0
Justin Verlander	Det	-2	2	0
Miguel Batista	Sea	-1	1	0
Felix Hernandez	Sea	-1	1	0
Nate Robertson	Det	-1	1	0
Paul Maholm	Pit	0	0	0
Oliver Perez	NYM	0	0	0
Matt Chico	Was	-1	1	0
David Wells	2 tms	-1	1	0
Micah Owings	Ari	-1	1	0
Lenny DiNardo	Oak	-1	1	0
Andy Sonnanstine	TB	-2	2	0
Jorge de la Rosa	KC	-1	1	0
Zack Greinke	KC	0	0	0
Anthony Reyes	StL	-1	1	0
Joe Saunders	LAA	-1	1	0
Brandon Webb	Ari	2	-2	0
Kelvim Escobar	LAA	2	-2	0
Jason Marquis	ChC	2	-2	0
David Bush	Mil	1	-1	0
Justin Germano	SD	2	-2	0
Ian Snell	Pit	-1	0	-1
Daisuke Matsuzaka	Bos	0	-1	-1
Tom Gorzelanny	Pit	-1	0	-1
Matt Cain	SF	-2	1	-1
John Maine	NYM	-1	0	-1
Dustin McGowan	Tor	4	-5	-1
Ervin Santana	LAA	-1	0	-1
Jeff Weaver	Sea	-1	0	-1
Scott Baker	Min	0	-1	-1
Julian Tavarez	Bos	-2	1	-1
Brian Burres	Bal	-1	0	-1
Vicente Padilla	Tex	-2	1	-1
Mike Bacsik	Was	-2	1	-1
Matt Albers	Hou	0	-1	-1
Buddy Carlyle	Atl	-1	0	-1
Sean Marshall	ChC	-1	0	-1
Jason Jennings	Hou	0	-1	-1
Roger Clemens	NYY	1	-2	-1
Taylor Buchholz	Col	0	-1	-1
Dustin Moseley	LAA	-1	0	-1
Scott Proctor	2 tms	0	-1	-1
Tony Pena	Ari	-2	1	-1
Matt Garza	Min	-2	1	-1
Rick VandenHurk	Fla	-1	0	-1
Roy Halladay	Tor	-1	-1	-2
Brad Penny	LAD	-2	0	-2
Josh Beckett	Bos	-2	0	-2
Chad Gaudin	Oak	-1	-1	-2
Paul Byrd	Cle	-2	0	-2
Cole Hamels	Phi	-1	-1	-2
Matt Belisle	Cin	-2	0	-2
Braden Looper	StL	-2	0	-2
Boof Bonser	Min	-3	1	-2
Mike Mussina	NYY	1	-3	-2
Curt Schilling	Bos	-2	0	-2
Claudio Vargas	Mil	-2	0	-2
Mark Hendrickson	LAD	-2	0	-2
Jason Bergmann	Was	-2	0	-2
Carlos Villanueva	Mil	-2	0	-2
Jorge Sosa	NYM	-2	0	-2
Josh Towers	Tor	0	-2	-2
Bartolo Colon	LAA	-3	1	-2
Cliff Lee	Cle	-2	0	-2
Joel Peralta	KC	-1	-1	-2
Jon Rauch	Was	-2	0	-2
Ubaldo Jimenez	Col	1	-3	-2
Jonathan Broxton	LAD	-2	0	-2
Bob Howry	ChC	-2	0	-2
Joe Blanton	Oak	-2	-1	-3
John Lackey	LAA	-2	-1	-3
Scott Kazmir	TB	-5	2	-3
Rich Hill	ChC	-2	-1	-3
Tim Lincecum	SF	-2	-1	-3
Ben Sheets	Mil	0	-3	-3
Brandon McCarthy	Tex	-1	-2	-3
Kevin Correia	SF	-2	-1	-3
Tony Armas Jr.	Pit	-2	-1	-3
Jason Hammel	TB	-1	-2	-3
Chad Qualls	Hou	-3	0	-3
Scott Olsen	Fla	-5	1	-4
Jeremy Bonderman	Det	-2	-2	-4
Jered Weaver	LAA	-2	-2	-4
Byung-Hyun Kim	3 tms	-2	-2	-4
Tim Wakefield	Bos	1	-6	-5
Kevin Millwood	Tex	-4	-1	-5
Dan Haren	Oak	-4	-2	-6
Jose Contreras	CWS	-4	-2	-6
A.J. Burnett	Tor	-1	-5	-6
Edwin Jackson	TB	-5	-1	-6
Chris Young	SD	-1	-7	-8
Daniel Cabrera	Bal	-7	-3	-10

Pitchers - 2006 Runs Saved

Player	Team	Plus/Minus	Stolen Bases	Total
Kenny Rogers	Det	7	3	10
Mark Buehrle	CWS	4	5	9
Johan Santana	Min	7	1	8
Zach Duke	Pit	5	3	8
Chris Capuano	Mil	2	4	6
Tom Glavine	NYM	4	2	6
Justin Verlander	Det	1	5	6
Dontrelle Willis	Fla	3	2	5
Felix Hernandez	Sea	5	0	5
Brandon Webb	Ari	5	-1	4
Chris Carpenter	StL	2	2	4
John Lackey	LAA	4	0	4
Aaron Cook	Col	2	2	4
Jamie Moyer	2 tms	2	2	4
Greg Maddux	2 tms	7	-3	4
Paul Maholm	Pit	1	3	4
Cory Lidle	2 tms	4	0	4
Kirk Saarloos	Oak	4	0	4
Ron Villone	NYY	2	2	4
Dan Haren	Oak	2	1	3
Chien-Ming Wang	NYY	1	2	3
Jon Garland	CWS	1	2	3
Erik Bedard	Bal	2	1	3
Jeff Suppan	StL	3	0	3
Jarrod Washburn	Sea	1	2	3
Scott Olsen	Fla	1	2	3
Josh Fogg	Col	2	1	3
Steve Trachsel	NYM	3	0	3
Noah Lowry	SF	2	1	3
Josh Johnson	Fla	2	1	3
Casey Fossum	TB	3	0	3
Brian Moehler	Fla	1	2	3
Scott Elarton	KC	2	1	3
Hector Carrasco	LAA	3	0	3
Ruddy Lugo	TB	2	1	3
Andy Pettitte	Hou	1	1	2
Jake Westbrook	Cle	2	0	2
Miguel Batista	Ari	2	0	2
Jeff Francis	Col	2	0	2
Mike Mussina	NYY	3	-1	2
Gil Meche	Sea	0	2	2
Claudio Vargas	Ari	2	0	2
Mark Redman	KC	0	2	2
Jae Seo	2 tms	1	1	2
Jaret Wright	NYY	1	1	2
Cole Hamels	Phi	3	-1	2
Kyle Lohse	2 tms	0	2	2
Sean Marshall	ChC	2	0	2
Anibal Sanchez	Fla	2	0	2
Runelvys Hernandez	KC	1	1	2
Elizardo Ramirez	Cin	1	1	2
Luke Hudson	KC	1	1	2
Brad Hennessey	SF	2	0	2
Salomon Torres	Pit	1	1	2
Mark Mulder	StL	2	0	2
Bronson Arroyo	Cin	0	1	1
John Smoltz	Atl	1	0	1
Roy Oswalt	Hou	-1	2	1
Kevin Millwood	Tex	1	0	1
Javier Vazquez	CWS	0	1	1
Rodrigo Lopez	Bal	-1	2	1
Clay Hensley	SD	1	0	1
Ian Snell	Pit	2	-1	1
Kris Benson	Bal	1	0	1
Joel Pineiro	Sea	1	0	1
Eric Milton	Cin	0	1	1
Wandy Rodriguez	Hou	-1	2	1
James Shields	TB	0	1	1
Shawn Chacon	2 tms	2	-1	1
Enrique Gonzalez	Ari	0	1	1
Boof Bonser	Min	0	1	1
Bruce Chen	Bal	0	1	1
Casey Janssen	Tor	-1	2	1
Mike Thompson	SD	2	-1	1
Pedro Astacio	Was	1	0	1
John Maine	NYM	1	0	1
Aaron Heilman	NYM	2	-1	1
Jon Lester	Bos	-1	2	1
Matt Capps	Pit	0	1	1
John Thomson	Atl	2	-1	1
Barry Zito	Oak	-3	3	0
Livan Hernandez	2 tms	0	0	0
Carlos Zambrano	ChC	-2	2	0
Ervin Santana	LAA	-2	2	0
Curt Schilling	Bos	-2	2	0
Vicente Padilla	Tex	-1	1	0
Brett Myers	Phi	0	0	0

Player	Team	Plus/Minus	Stolen Bases	Total
Kelvim Escobar	LAA	0	0	0
Daniel Cabrera	Bal	0	0	0
Ricky Nolasco	Fla	-1	1	0
Ryan Madson	Phi	0	0	0
Odalis Perez	2 tms	0	0	0
Brett Tomko	LAD	0	0	0
Adam Loewen	Bal	-1	1	0
Julian Tavarez	Bos	0	0	0
Fernando Nieve	Hou	0	0	0
Juan Cruz	Ari	0	0	0
Jon Rauch	Was	0	0	0
Tim Corcoran	TB	0	0	0
Chad Billingsley	LAD	-1	1	0
Darren Oliver	NYM	0	0	0
Roy Halladay	Tor	2	-2	0
David Bush	Mil	1	-1	0
Jose Contreras	CWS	2	-2	0
Woody Williams	SD	1	-1	0
Tim Wakefield	Bos	2	-2	0
Scot Shields	LAA	1	-1	0
Jason Schmidt	SF	-2	1	-1
Matt Morris	SF	-1	0	-1
Randy Johnson	NYY	0	-1	-1
Cliff Lee	Cle	-2	1	-1
Ted Lilly	Tor	0	-1	-1
Jeff Weaver	2 tms	-3	2	-1
Tony Armas Jr.	Was	0	-1	-1
Chan Ho Park	SD	0	-1	-1
Jered Weaver	LAA	0	-1	-1
Jorge Sosa	2 tms	-2	1	-1
Victor Santos	Pit	-2	1	-1
Roger Clemens	Hou	1	-2	-1
Taylor Buchholz	Hou	0	-1	-1
Oliver Perez	2 tms	-1	0	-1
Aaron Sele	LAD	-1	0	-1
Scott Proctor	NYY	-1	0	-1
Rich Hill	ChC	0	-1	-1
Tomo Ohka	Mil	-2	1	-1
Jeremy Affeldt	2 tms	-1	0	-1
Brad Halsey	Oak	-1	0	-1
Zach Miner	Det	-1	0	-1
Oscar Villarreal	Atl	-1	0	-1
Geoff Geary	Phi	-1	0	-1
Chad Qualls	Hou	-2	1	-1
Jeremy Sowers	Cle	-1	0	-1
Gustavo Chacin	Tor	-1	0	-1
Scott Baker	Min	-1	0	-1
Joel Zumaya	Det	-1	0	-1
Derek Lowe	LAD	1	-3	-2
Doug Davis	Mil	-2	0	-2
Jake Peavy	SD	1	-3	-2
Joe Blanton	Oak	-2	0	-2
Jason Marquis	StL	-2	0	-2
Ramon Ortiz	Was	-3	1	-2
Carlos Silva	Min	-2	0	-2
Jon Lieber	Phi	-2	0	-2
Brad Radke	Min	-3	1	-2
Byung-Hyun Kim	Col	0	-2	-2
Esteban Loaiza	Oak	-2	0	-2
Scott Kazmir	TB	-2	0	-2
John Koronka	Tex	-2	0	-2
Chuck James	Atl	-1	-1	-2
Ben Sheets	Mil	-2	0	-2
Mike O'Connor	Was	0	-2	-2
Jake Woods	Sea	-2	0	-2
Seth McClung	TB	-1	-1	-2
Anthony Reyes	StL	-2	0	-2
Sidney Ponson	2 tms	-3	1	-2
Brandon McCarthy	CWS	-1	-1	-2
Aaron Harang	Cin	-3	0	-3
Tim Hudson	Atl	-1	-2	-3
Jason Jennings	Col	-2	-1	-3
Nate Robertson	Det	-4	1	-3
CC Sabathia	Cle	-2	-1	-3
Matt Cain	SF	-2	-1	-3
Brad Penny	LAD	-2	-1	-3
Paul Byrd	Cle	-2	-1	-3
Mark Hendrickson	2 tms	-3	0	-3
Orlando Hernandez	2 tms	-2	-1	-3
Jamey Wright	SF	-5	2	-3
Francisco Liriano	Min	-2	-1	-3
Jimmy Gobble	KC	-3	0	-3
Jeremy Bonderman	Det	-3	-1	-4
Josh Beckett	Bos	-2	-2	-4
A.J. Burnett	Tor	-2	-2	-4
Pedro Martinez	NYM	-2	-2	-4
Freddy Garcia	CWS	-1	-6	-7
Chris Young	SD	-2	-6	-8
Jason Johnson	3 tms	-7	-3	-10

Defensive Misplays

Bill James

The concept of an error *is* an error. Back when I was young and knew everything, I used to fulminate about fielding errors. It would have been much better, I argued, if the statistical founding fathers (the Seminal Statisticians? The Founding Figure Filberts?) had never come up with this concept. A batter hits two ground balls toward third, and winds up on first base both times. One of them the third baseman reaches but drops; that's an error. The other one the third baseman never gets to; that's a hit. What's the difference? Why distinguish between them at all?

Now that I am older and not as radical, I accept the distinction without regular complaint. The concept of an error, engrained as it is in the sport, involves three mistakes. The first is trying to take the concept of "per opportunity" success, which works for batters and works for pitchers, and applying it to fielders. It doesn't work—in fact, it doesn't work in any sport. Defensive players, in all sports, are not presented with "opportunities"; defensive players have to make their own plays. It's a flawed premise.

The other two mistakes are:

1) That the concept of an error is too general. It puts together events which are essentially unalike. All singles take a batter out of the batter's box, and move him to first base. All doubles put the batter on second base. All walks are fundamentally alike, and all strikeouts. Different things may happen after the play and different things may happen during the play, but there are common elements in them all that make for easy definition.

Errors, on the other hand, have all kinds of different outcomes. Some simply extend an at bat, allowing it to reach some other conclusion. Some put the batter on first base; some on second base. Some advance a runner who is already on base, from first to second or from second to third or from third to home or from first to home; we're all over the map here.

An error can be a wild throw or a dropped pop up. Falling down can be an error, or kicking the ball while trying to pick it up. The category is so general that it fails to describe the event.

2) That it involves an unnecessary value judgment on the part of the scorer.

The unifying concept of the error is that the fielder has done something wrong. This is a lousy way to measure anything—even misbehavior. The "error" requires a person who is not a part of the action to enter his judgment about what ought to have happened in the place where there should be a description of what did happen. What are we talking about here, a counterfactual universe?

I have ranted about all of this before, albeit not recently. The point here is that *a Defensive Misplay is not a type of error.* A defensive misplay is a very specific observation of a very narrowly defined event, created in such a way as to keep the scorer's use of judgment to an absolute minimum.

What we are doing here is kind of halfway between sabermetrics and scouting. Scouting is organized observation. Defensive Misplays are very limited but extremely highly organized observations. We watch the games, carefully, repeatedly, and we make "notes" about what happens. Those notes are sorted into very narrow categories: Second baseman juggles the ball and loses the opportunity for a Double Play. Two outfielders converge on a pop up and let it drop between them.

Fielder pulls his foot off the bag unnecessarily, losing the out. Fielder neglects to cover his base.

Employing a staff of researchers, we watch every major league game carefully for all of these plays—and 50 others. And anything else a fielder might do that is clearly substandard, in case something were to happen that we have never seen before.

There are 54 separate Defensive Misplays that our system recognizes; the goal, remember, is to describe the event, such that a person reading a scoring summary can understand what happened. DM 38, for example, is:

Failing to anticipate the wall – Outfielder goes to the outfield wall, allowing a ball to bounce over his head back toward the infield, allowing a runner or runners to take bases which they might not have been able to take had the fielder turned and played the ball off the wall.

The scorer has to ask himself only two questions:

1) Did the outfielder go to the wall in an effort to catch the ball, and
2) Did the ball bounce over his head back toward the infield?

Perfectly straightforward questions, involving no element of judgment on the part of the scorer. Did this happen or did it not?

If those two things happened, then, *unless it is perfectly and absolutely clear that it made no difference,* it is a defensive misplay—DM 38. The scorer does not ask himself "Did the fielder have a real chance to catch the ball?" or "Should the fielder have chased the ball to the wall in that situation?" or "Should an ordinary fielder have known that he could not catch the ball at the wall?" or anything like that. It's two simple questions: Did he chase the ball to the wall, and did the ball bounce over his head back toward the infield?

The one element of discretion is that there has to be some possible consequence to the misplay. There would be no consequence here (thus no misplay) if, for example, another fielder was in position to play the ricochet off the wall. If the left fielder chases the ball to the wall but the center fielder plays the carom, that's not a misplay, that's teamwork. If the batter who hit the ball off the wall winds up on first base and no other runners were on base, then obviously the failed effort to catch the ball at the wall didn't cost the team, so there's no misplay. If the ball is hit 360 feet off the wall and Jose Reyes is running, obviously you're not stopping him at first base, so if he gets a double, that's not a misplay, either.

Otherwise, our scorer is NOT supposed to make any judgment about "I don't think he could have stopped him from going to second even if he had played the ball off the wall" or "I don't think he could have thrown out the runner at home from there anyway." It's just a misplay.

Think about it: If the fielder chases the ball to the wall and doesn't catch it, what was the value in going to the wall? None. If you chase the ball to the wall and it comes off the wall over your head, what is the possibility that this delays your getting the ball back to the infield? 100%. Therefore, if you do these two things and the runners are moving, it's a misplay. If you're slow getting the ball back to the infield and there are runners moving, that's a misplay. Whether you *could* have saved a base if you hadn't gone to the wall, whether you should have known you couldn't catch the ball. . .we're not getting into that. You were slow getting the ball back to the infield with the runners moving; that's a misplay. Period.

Another Defensive Misplay for an outfielder is breaking back on a ball that lands in front of you. Again, two simple observations are required of the scorer:

1) Did the fielder break back?
2) Did the ball land in front of him?

That's all—no judgment about "would the fielder have caught the ball if he had broken in immediately" or anything like that. Just the facts.

In reality, when an outfielder breaks back and the ball lands in front of him, that was essentially *always* a catchable ball. If the ball is so far in front of you that you couldn't get to it even if you broke right, then it's obvious that the ball is in front of you. The outfielder only breaks back if it's not obvious. If you break back even half a step, you've lost four-five steps coming in, at a minimum.

That's DM-29, breaking back on a ball that lands in front of you.

There were 224 instances in the majors in 2008 when an outfielder chased the ball to the wall, didn't catch it, and let it bounce back toward the infield. Bobby Abreu and Nate McLouth tied for the lead, doing this six times each.

That is the ninth most common misplay. The most common defensive misplay is a wild pitch/catcher's misplay (DM 54). It's a wild pitch, yes, but the catcher COULD have caught it. If the catcher gets his glove on the ball but doesn't stop it, or blocks the ball but can't locate it, it's a wild pitch, yes, but the catcher could have made the play.

The second most-common Defensive Misplay is a ground ball that just goes right through an infielder, under his glove or through his legs. By our count there were 1,693 ground balls in 2008 that evaded the glove of an infielder who was in position to field the ball. 570 of those were scored as errors—a third of them—while the other 1,123 were scored as Defensive Misplays (DM-1). The major league leader in letting the ball get by him was Orlando Cabrera, with 22 (18 Defensive Misplays, plus 4 Errors on similar plays.) Arizona third baseman Mark Reynolds actually messed up that play 24 times (13 Defensive Misplays, 11 Errors.)

Reynolds overall led major league third baseman both in Errors (34) and Defensive Misplays (33); his total of 67 Errors + Defensive Misplays was the highest in the major leagues. The major league leaders in Defensive Misplays by position were:

P—Scott Olsen
C—Ramon Hernandez
1B—Ryan Howard
2B—Rickie Weeks
3B—Mark Reynolds
SS—Orlando Cabrera
LF—Delmon Young
CF—Aaron Rowand, Lastings Milledge,
    and B. J. Upton (tie, 34 each)
RF—Brad Hawpe

What WERE those plays, exactly? Every position has its own mix of Defensive Misplays, and every fielder has a unique set. Different players make different mistakes. But the mistakes that THESE players made were:

Scott Olsen, Florida pitcher, had 7 Defensive Misplays. He bobbled the ball and lost the play at first twice, missed first base on a 3-1 play one time, failed to cover first once, threw wide to a base once (losing an out), missed a tag once, allowing a runner to get back to the base safely, and let a ball go through his legs or under his glove once.

The four most common misplays for a pitcher are
1) Letting a ball go through his legs or under his glove,
2) Failing to cover first,
3) Failing to catch a ball that bounces off his glove, and

4) Falling asleep on a baserunner.

That isn't what it's called, "falling asleep" on a baserunner. What it is technically called is "Slow reaction allowing baserunner to steal". (Catcher, pitcher, or infielder fails to react to stolen base attempt, allowing runner to steal easily due to inattention.) Those four plays account for about half of Defensive Misplays by pitchers.

Ramon Hernandez, Baltimore catcher, had 49 Defensive Misplays, of which 34 were failing to stop Wild Pitches that weren't really all that wild. His other Misplays were exceptionally poor throws on stolen base attempts (seven times), backing away from a foul pop up (twice; that's the Alfonse/Gaston play where two fielders converge on a ball and let it drop between them), missing the tag after a throw from the infielder (twice), failing to catch the ball or tag the runner after a throw from the outfield (once), failing to locate a pop up that landed near him (once), hesitating before throwing to a base on a tap in front of the plate (once), and throwing off-target to a base (once. . .that's not on a stolen base play; that's on a force play, where he might have had a play with a good throw).

The "error" gives the fielder the benefit of the doubt on that play, saying that there's no error because we don't know whether he would have gotten the out anyway, so let's give the batter a hit. The Defensive Misplay says "that was a bad throw; we don't know whether there was a play there or not and we're not going to get into that, but that was definitely a bad throw."

The overwhelming majority of Defensive Misplays by catchers are wild pitches that could have been stopped.

Ryan Howard, Philadelphia first baseman, had 37 Misplays, of which 9 were balls that rolled under his glove or between his legs. For the sake of clarity, he actually had 16 of those plays—7 of which were ruled errors, the other 9 of which were not. He also had 9 catchable throws from other infielders that he did not come up with, three potential double-play balls that he didn't handle smoothly, letting the lead runner get away, two plays on which he passed up the out at first in an effort to get another runner, then didn't get the other runner, two ground balls that he bobbled or juggled for a minute, losing the out at first, two plays on which he threw wide to another base, losing the out, two plays on which he took the out at first when he clearly could have had an out at another base, one play on which he juggled the relay from the outfield, one bad throw on a double play (losing the second out), one time when he pulled his foot off the bag before he recorded the out, one play on which he abandoned the base in an effort to make the play, didn't make the play and lost the opportunity to take the throw at first, one time when he cut in front of another infielder in an unsuccessful effort to make a play (interfering with the other fielder), one time when he misread a pop up, took a long route to it and didn't get there, one time when he hesitated or double-pumped before making a throw, losing the out, and one fly ball or line drive that bounced off his glove.

OK, there's a lot of ways that a first baseman can mess up a play, right? Which is a point worth making: people think playing first base is nothing, but there's an awful lot of ways to mess up a play over there. And we're not saying that Howard is a bad first baseman; he also had 64 especially *good* plays. We'll get to those in a moment. But. . .he did make a lot of mistakes.

The two plays that Howard made 9 times each—letting a ball roll past him and failing to corral a throw from another infielder—are by far the most common Defensive Misplays by first basemen, and account for over one-half of first basemen's DM totals.

Rickie Weeks, Milwaukee's ersatz second baseman, had 44 diverse Defensive Misplays. These were:

Letting a ball roll under his glove or between his legs—9 times

Juggling or dropping a ball on which a smooth play might have gotten an out—7 times

Making a poor throw on a double-play try—6 times

Making a poor throw—4 times

Mishandling the pivot on a double-play try (juggling or dropping the ball)—3 times

Having a ball hit in the air bounce off his glove—2 times

Mishandling the start of a double play attempt, losing one out—2 times

Cutting off a better-positioned fielder and failing to make the play—2 times

Letting a pop up drop for a hit because of confusion with another fielder—once

Failing to catch the ball and apply a tag on a throw from another infielder—once

Failing to catch the ball and apply a tag after a throw from an outfielder—once

Colliding with another fielder—once

Losing a fly ball in the sun—once

Hesitating or double-clutching before making a throw, losing the play—once

Ball stuck in glove—once

Letting a runner who had been picked off get back to the base—once

Giving away the lead runner to take the play at first (when he clearly could have gotten the other runner)—once

I really like Rickie Weeks, and I feel strongly that he has major league ability that just hasn't come out yet. One of the reasons it hasn't come out yet—one of several—is that they keep playing him at second base, and he really is not much of a second baseman. I would compare him to Don Buford, a player of three or four generations ago who came up as a highly-touted second baseman for the White Sox, but never really could put it together as a second baseman. But Earl Weaver moved him to left field, and he was a very valuable player as a left fielder/leadoff man.

An average major league second baseman makes about one Defensive Misplay for every six games, or 28 a year, and there is a wide diversity in what those plays are. But the most common is letting a ball roll under your glove or between your legs.

At third base, as I said before, the major league leader in Defensive Misplays was Arizona's Mark Reynolds, who had 33, of which 13 were balls that rolled under his glove or between his legs. The other 20 were:

Off target throws to first (not scored as error) (4)

Line drives that whizzed right by him (3)

Balls that he juggled a second before throwing (3)

Double-play balls that he didn't come up with cleanly, missing the lead runner (2)

Failed to locate a foul pop up that landed near him (2)

A poor throw to second on a double-play ball, losing one out (1)

A Bad Fielder's Choice—passed up the play at first in a failed effort to make a different play (1)

Failed to catch a throw from the outfield and apply a tag (1)

Cut off a better positioned fielder (1)

Passed up a lead runner to take the out at first (when he clearly could have gotten the lead runner) (1)

Line drive bounced off his glove (1)

The most common Defensive Misplays for third basemen are (1) Ground balls that go through the fielder,

(2) Ground balls that the fielder picks up but juggles or drops before he throws, and (3) Wide throws to first.

Most of the leaders in Defensive Misplays are younger players with relatively little experience, like Reynolds and Weeks, Milledge and Upton. At shortstop, however, we have a veteran player who has long been a highly-regarded fielder, Orlando Cabrera. Cabrera had 18 plays that just went under his glove or right past him in 2008. No other major league shortstop had more than 10. And if we didn't count those plays, Cabrera would still have been second in the majors in Defensive Misplays at short, with 22 (behind the other Chicago shortstop, Ryan Theriot. Theriot had only 5 singles that went right past him, but 25 assorted other boo-boos.)

I'm going to skip the full accounting of Cabrera's other mistakes, because the point of doing that was to help you understand the system, and we've covered most of the types of Misplays that infielders make by now. But Cabrera also led major league shortstops in off-target throws to first/not scored as error, with eight. And obviously, we don't count those if the out is recorded.

In left field, the major league leader in Defensive Misplays was the walking mistake machine, Delmon Young. Young, who must surely be the worst percentage player in baseball, made fifteen different types of misplays, an average of two times apiece, actually a total of 29 Misplays. Which were:

Mishandled a ball after a safe hit, allowing runners to advance (5)

Dived for the ball and didn't catch it, let it get behind him (4)

Chased a ball to the wall, allowing it to bounce off the wall over his head (3)

Fly ball hit his glove and bounced off (not scored as error) (2)

Took a bad route to the ball (2)

Broke in the wrong direction (2)

Slow recovery of the ball, allowing runner to advance (2)

Shied away from the wall on a catchable ball (2)

Failed to locate a pop up near him, dropped for a hit (1)

Turned the wrong way on a ball (1)

Fell down chasing the ball (1)

Broke back on a ball that landed in front of him (1)

Poor throw after a hit, allowing runner to advance (1)

Wasted throw after a hit, allowing other runner to advance (1)

Missing the cutoff man, allowing runner to advance (1)

"Taking a bad route to the ball". . .again, you might think that's a judgment call, but when you watch the games, particularly on video where you can watch it again and again, it really isn't. Basically, if an outfielder has a hook in his path toward the ball—that is, if he is running one direction and then has to turn and go another direction—that's what the scouts call a bad route. Most of the time it's a fielder who thinks he can get to the ball by running laterally, runs several steps laterally, then realizes he is not going to get to the ball and has to retreat. Delmon only did that twice; some outfielders do it a lot more. Rick Ankiel led the majors, with six. But we only count it as a bad route if he doesn't make the play; if he catches the ball anyway it's no harm, no foul. I'd guess that some outfielders take a bad route 25 times a year, but we only count the times that they get burned by it.

A bad route is different from breaking in the wrong direction. Occasionally a left fielder will break left, but the ball hooks and goes to the right of him. And both of these are different from turning the wrong way on a ball. Turning the wrong way on a ball has to do with actually catching it, the position your body is in when you're actually trying to catch the ball. A bad route or breaking in the wrong direction has to do with getting in position to catch the ball, as opposed to actually catching it.

In center field there was a three-way tie for the lead, so I'm going to cut those guys a break, and talk instead about the most frequent Misplays for outfielders. Major league outfielders were charged by our scorers with 2,326 Misplays in 2008, or between 75 and 80 per team. Center fielders make significantly more than left or right fielders, because they have more challenging plays. The 25 most common Misplays for outfielders, and the number of times that each occurred in 2008, are:

1) Ball bounces off the glove, no error (304). Sometimes an outfielder makes a nice run toward a ball, but the ball bounces off his glove. The Official Scorer's judgment may be that the play could not have been made with an ordinary effort on the part of the fielder, so there's no error. Our take on it is "OK, it's not an error, but when a major league outfielder gets his glove on a ball, you would like him to catch it." Most of the time they do, but sometimes they don't.

2) Wasted throw after a hit or error (279). Often described as missing the cutoff man; see note below on wasted throw after a catch. If we added together all of the "Missed the cutoff man" categories, they would be easily the most common misplays by outfielders.

3) Failed dive for the ball (247). Again, if another fielder is backing you up so that there is no consequence to the dive, that's no harm/no foul. But if you dive for the ball and let it get behind you with no backup, that's not good.

4) Failing to anticipate the wall (224). The play that I described at the start of the article. . .outfielder chases the ball to the wall and lets it ricochet back toward the infield.

5) Mishandling the ball after a safe hit (215). Fielder picks up the ball, juggles it or drops it, runner keeps running and they give him a double or a triple, when it might have been a single or double if the fielder had picked up the ball cleanly.

6) Bad Route (170).

7) Wall Difficulties (131). Pulling up short of the wall because you don't know quite where it is, ball drops on the warning track.

8) Breaking in the Wrong Direction (121).

9) Wasted throw after a catch (60). This is a bit of a controversial one, because many times the fielder hasn't actually done anything that he shouldn't have done. Runners on first and third, runner on third tags up, throw home, runner safe at home, runner from first moves to second.

The fielder didn't do anything **wrong**. He's not supposed to concede the run in that situation; he's supposed to try to throw the guy out if he can. But at the same time, the fact is that if the fielder had simply thrown the ball to second, keeping the other runner at first, the outcome would have been better for the defense. We're not making value judgments here; we're making a record of what happens. The clear fact is that the fielder made a choice that didn't work out for his team, a choice that made the situation worse, not better. That's a Defensive Misplay, like it or not.

Many times this is described by the announcers as overthrowing the cutoff man. But MOST outfielders' arms simply are not strong enough to allow them to throw on a flat line 200 or more feet. Only a few players can really do that. Most players have to make a choice: do I throw home, or do I throw to the cutoff man? If you choose wrong, that's what we enter as a wasted throw after a catch.

10) Losing the ball in the sun, the lights, or the roof (52).

11) Letting a pop up drop for a hit (46). This is a two-man Defensive Misplay. If one player calls the other one off and then lets the ball drop, it's a Defensive Misplay against the guy who called for the ball. If neither fielder calls for the ball and they both watch it drop, it's a Defensive Misplay against BOTH fielders.

12) Overrunning the ball (45). Base hit in front of you, outfielder charges in to pick up the ball but runs past it and has to stop and get it.

13) Slow recovery (41). Outfielder takes his own sweet time getting to the ball and getting it back to the infield, allowing the baserunner to pick up an extra base. Perhaps the most irritating Defensive Misplay. B. J. Upton was the only major league outfielder to do it three times last year, while Manny, Delmon Young, Lastings Milledge, Aaron Rowand and Corey Patterson did it twice each.

14) Bad throw to the plate, allowing runner to score (34). This is only a Misplay if it's really a BAD throw, off-line so the catcher has to chase it, and then only in a situation where just an ordinary throw would have nailed the runner.

15) Bad throw back to the infield, allowing a runner to advance (33). Actually, I've never understood why this *isn't* an error, but very often it isn't. In our system we have several instructions covering bad throws in specific situations, and then there is this "collection" category that catches bad throws not in any of those specific situations. We don't want a category of just "bad throws", because we'd prefer for the note to describe, as specifically as possible, what it was that the fielder did, and what the consequence was.

15) Slipping (33). Fielder falls down while chasing the ball. Lonnie Smith would do this more than 33 times a year all by himself.

17) Breaking back on a ball that lands in front of you (32).

17) Missing the cutoff man (32). The backup category when "Wasted Throw after a Hit" or "Wasted Throw after a Catch" somehow don't quite apply. It's a play on which the outfielder TRIES to include the cutoff man among the people he is shooting at, but throws off-target and allows runners to move up. Again, I don't quite understand why this is not scored as an error, but it almost never is.

19) Colliding with another fielder (31).

20) Giving up on a play (30). Fielder abandons the effort to make a play in the mistaken belief that somebody else will catch it.

21) Failing to locate a foul pop up (28).

22) Throw to the wrong base (27). Fielder throws to third, trying to prevent runner moving first-to-third, but just allows the batter to move up to second. Again, there are several similar descriptions, like "Wasted throw after a hit" and "Missing the cut-off man." You kind of have to be into our system to understand exactly what the distinctions are.

23) Failing to locate/failing to reach a pop up in fair territory (23).

24) Off-line throw after a hit, allowing runner to advance (22).

25) Hesitating before throwing (17).

In right field, the leader in Defensive Misplays was Brad Hawpe, with 33. But special recognition should be given to Justin Upton, who had not only 27 Misplays but also 11 errors in just 860 innings in right field—about 95 games. But he's just a kid; you put a 20-year-old in the majors, you've got to expect some mistakes.

All of Brad Hawpe's misplays, without exception, were on the list above. There were six balls that he got his glove on but didn't catch, which was the most in the majors except for Aaron Rowand with seven, and there were five times that he chased the ball to the wall and let it bounce back toward the infield, which was the most in the majors except for Abreu and McLouth.

The Other Side of the Ledger

OK, so far we've talked a lot about players who made mistakes, and about how many mistakes they made, and I think in all candor that I've been very disciplined about not making fun of them for this. Now let's look on the sunny side for a moment.

On the sunny side we have two types of excellence:
1) Not making mistakes, and
2) Making outstanding plays.

We could figure "not making mistake rates" either per inning or per touch. My preference would be per inning, but it's John Dewan's book and his preference is per touch, so we'll do both. They're usually the same.

What is a "touch"? A touch is any time the fielder records:

    a) a Putout,

    b) an Assist,

    c) an Error,

    d) a Passed Ball,

    e) a Defensive Misplay, or

    f) any time he is the first fielder to handle a ball after a safe hit.

For the sake of clarity, fielders *do* sometimes touch the ball without being credited with a touch. Catchers touch the ball after almost every pitch, but this is usually uneventful, and we have enough things to keep track of, thank you very much. But suppose that the ball is grounded to right with a runner on first, second baseman is the cutoff man, play goes 9-4-5 but the runner is safe at third. There's no play; it's a 1B9, so as we score the game, the second baseman and third baseman never touched the ball, even though they really did.

The concept of a "touch" was invented, I think, because some whiners and losers and traditionalists and other scoundrels always wanted to know how many "opportunities" each player had for a defensive misplay. Maybe there is no such thing as a stupid question, but that's a nice try. A fielder can mess up any play that he's involved in—and, in fact, fielders not infrequently mess up plays that they shouldn't rightfully have had anything to do with. Any time a fielder near you catches the ball, you have the opportunity to run into him at top speed if you're into that kind of thing, the old Elio Chacon play.

Anyway, if it was up to me, I'd have told the people who wanted to know how many "opportunities" each player had for a misplay to mind their own business, but John wanted to try to get along, so we started counting these "touches". We could figure that the least mistake-prone fielders are either those who have the fewest Misplays per inning—my way—or the fewest Misplays per touch—John's way. The leaders in fewest Misplays per inning, among regular and near-regular players were:

P—Big Game James Shields (Zero in 215 innings)
C—Kurt Suzuki (21 in 1,215 innings)
1B—Derek Lee (12 in 1,339 innings)
2B—Orlando Hudson (9 in 905 innings)
3B—Mike Lowell (6 in 935 innings)
SS—Derek Jeter (17 in 1,259 innings)
LF—Jason Bay (9 in 1,345 innings)
CF—Curtis Granderson (14 in 1,188 innings)
RF—Nick Markakis (12 in 1,367 innings)

Switching to Defensive Misplays per touch, we have the same leaders except at pitcher. Ubaldo Jimenez replaces Big Game James Shields at pitcher. They both had no Defensive Misplays, as did other pitchers including Jake Peavy, Nick Blackburn, Josh Beckett, Jeff Francis, Ian Snell, R. A. Dickey, and Scott Baker. But among the pitchers who had no defensive misplays, Shields had the most innings, while Jimenez had the most touches by far, with 54.

Jimenez, however, was charged with 4 errors, which is rather a lot. So that gives us yet a third leader (or is this a fourth?): Fewest Defensive Misplays + Errors per touch. Nick Blackburn. Blackburn pitched 193 innings, 36 touches, with no errors and no misplays.

Otherwise the leaders are the same, but you can get another set of positional leaders by looking at Defensive Misplays + Errors, per touch. I'm leery of this, because I don't want people to start thinking that Defensive Misplays are like errors. They're like errors in some ways; in other ways they're not like errors at all. But anyway, we can figure who the least mistake-prone fielders are, as well, by adding together Errors and Misplays. Then you get some different guys:

P—Nick Blackburn
C—Bengie Molina
1B—Casey Kotchman
2B—Placido Polanco
3B—Mike Lowell
SS—Derek Jeter
LF—Jason Bay
CF—Torii Hunter
RF—Nick Markakis

We have to draw an arbitrary line to decide who is a "regular", so let's note some of the players arbitrarily excluded:

Humberto Quintero, Houston catcher, caught only 447 innings (50 games), but was charged with only one error and six Defensive Misplays—both figures quite outstanding, and both better by any standard than Suzuki, although Suzuki worked many more innings.

Nick Swisher and Todd Helton at first base, although they didn't qualify as regulars, both had quite exceptional error and misplay rates, as did Tadahito Iguchi and Adam Kennedy at second. Omar Vizquel at short, although he doesn't get around much any more, had only eight misplays and two errors in 658 innings, a lower rate even than Jeter. Mark Kotsay in center field had 378 touches with only six misplays and no errors—a mistake rate less than half Torii Hunter's, and he played 696 innings there, so he didn't miss being a regular (900

innings) by a huge margin. And Franklin Gutierrez in right, although he didn't quite qualify as a regular, had a better mistake rate than Nick Markakis.

The *most* remarkable "non-mistake maker" in baseball in 2008, however, actually doesn't appear on any of these lists. It's Jacoby Ellsbury. The Red Sox rookie played 346 innings in left field with only two misplays and no errors—by far the best mistake rate of any left fielder playing 125 or more innings. In center field he played 547 innings with no errors and a misplay rate, per touch or per inning, just a hair behind Curtis Granderson (although also behind several other players who didn't quite qualify as regulars, like Kotsay, Cody Ross, Skip Schumacher and Vernon Wells.)

And in right field, Ellsbury played 281 innings and handled 123 touches with no errors and no misplays—by far the most innings and the most touches by any major league player with a clean record at any one position in 2009.

You know, I saw probably 50 Red Sox games live last year and the rest on TV, and Jacoby played well, but I honestly wouldn't have guessed that he was playing *that* well in the field. He is extraordinarily fast, of course, but when he came up in 2007, he had a lot of trouble with walls. . .I mean a lot of trouble. It seemed like any time he had to play a ball at the wall or off the wall, something went wrong.

Last year he was better, but I really had no idea that he had come so far. Adding it together, he played 1,174 innings in the outfield (130 games), being involved in 622 plays with zero errors and only 11 misplays. Rookie or no rookie, that's a remarkable record.

Good Fielding Plays

That's one way to look at fielding excellence: not making mistakes. But Jason Bay, who made fewer mistakes in 2008 than any other left fielder, is really not a Gold Glove candidate. He's a big guy who takes a while to get his legs lined out, but he catches what he gets to. Perhaps a better way to look at fielding excellence is to look for players who make outstanding plays.

OK, let me tell you the real reason that we score Good Fielding Plays, or GFP. The real reason is: common decency. Suppose that you were a major league player. How would you feel if somebody studied every moment of every game on video, and made notes of every little mistake that you made, but paid no attention when you did something well? You'd think that was unfair, right?

That's really the main reason that we study GFP; yes, we learn something from doing it, yes it has some place in the evaluation of fielders, but in the main, we do it because it's not right NOT to do it.

I wish I could tell you that the scoring of Good Fielding was—like the scoring of Defensive Misplays is—almost entirely objective. It isn't. For some reason, it is simply not a parallel problem. We *can* define Defensive Misplays in such a way that it is extremely clear what is and what is not a Defensive Misplay. We would like to be able to do the same for Good Fielding Plays. We would also like peace in the Middle East and a date with Gwyneth Paltrow, but so far we're 0-for-3.

The essential definition of a Good Fielding Play is *a play that is made when it appears most likely that it cannot be made.* The problem arises in this way. A Defensive Misplay always has a consequence. A Defensive Misplay occurs only when something a defensive player does results in the loss of a base, an out, or the *opportunity* for an out. In other words, it may not be clear whether he could have thrown out the runner on that play, but he had a shot at it; there was an opportunity to make a play. He juggled the ball and lost the opportunity; that's a Misplay. It may be a base hit, but it's also a Misplay.

The problem is that *when a fielder makes an exceptional fielding play, the consequence is exactly the same as if he had made a routine play.* When the second baseman fields the ball behind second and throws out the runner, the consequence is the same as if he had fielded the ball in his normal position and thrown out the runner. How do you draw a line between them?

We try. We have 27 Good Fielding Plays (GFP) that we score. . .let me run here an abbreviated scoring manual:

1) Ground ball out – Fielder turns a ground ball that seemed likely to be a hit into an out.

2) Infielder line drive out – Infielder catches a line drive that seemed likely to be a hit.

(There are several more like this. . .catching fly balls, catching pop outs, etc., after they seemed destined to hit the ground.)

3) Handling difficult throw – Fielder (normally first baseman) handles difficult throw from another player and records out. This applies to throws in the dirt or throws wide of the bag.

4) Keeping the ball in the infield – Fielder stops a ground ball that seemed likely to be heading into the outfield, preventing the possibility of a runner or runners from advancing.

5) Quick double-play pivot - Fielder makes exceptionally quick pivot to complete a double play on a ball that seemed more likely to be a forceout.

6) Double play despite aggressive slide - Fielder is able to complete difficult double play despite aggressive slide by runner from first.

7) Infielder assist – Infielder takes relay throw from outfielder and makes throw to a base to record an out.

8) Outfielder throws batter out at first – Outfielder (in almost every instance a right fielder) fields a ground ball or line drive and throws the **batter** out at first.

9) Holds to single – Fielder holds runner to a single on a ball that seemed more likely to be an extra base hit.

10) Reaches into stands – Fielder reaches into the stands, dugout or camera well to catch a pop up or fly ball.

11) Robs home run – Outfielder catches ball that would have been a Home Run had he not caught the ball.

12) Catcher pick off – Catcher picks runner off base. (Note: A catcher picking a runner off base is one of the few plays which are almost always a Good Fielding Play. If the runner sort of wanders off base and gets himself out, and all the catcher does is stay awake, then that might not be a GFP. But, since there is never an expectation that the catcher is going to nail a runner off base, it is almost always a GFP when it does occur.)

OK, some of those are pretty objective. A fielder either reaches into the stands to make a play, or he does not. A fielder either goes over the fence to catch a home run, or he does not. But how do you decide whether a second baseman was or was not "exceptionally quick" on the pivot, or whether the double play would have been completed had he not been?

We just have to decide, because we think we should. We've watched a lot of baseball games; we kind of know whether that looks like a double-play ball or whether it doesn't.

Of the 27 GFP that we recognize, all happened at least 25 times in 2008, except GFP 19 ("Outfielder throws batter out at first"), which never happened at all. Let's look at the major league leaders in some of these types of plays:

Ground ball out. The ground ball out—snagging a ground ball hit before it can reach the outfield and throwing the guy out—is by far the most common GFP, accounting for 32% of all GFP. The major league leader at this, by a wide margin, was David Wright, with 51. Adrian Beltre was second in the majors with 41.

Infielder catching a line drive out. Major league leader was Teixeira, with 8. Plus two or three in the playoffs.

Catching a fly ball that seemed likely to drop in for a hit. Major league leader was Nate McLouth, with 27. Which I suppose explains the Gold Glove.

Catching a pop up that seemed likely to drop for a hit. Major league leader was Ryan Theriot, with 6.

Catching a foul pop up that didn't look like anybody would reach it. Major league leader was Ryan Howard, with 6.

Saving a bad throw. Major league leader was Justin Morneau, with 44. However, Todd Helton had almost as many (42), while playing barely over half as many innings at first base. Helton is really incredible on that play.

Catching a wild throw. Catching a wild throw is different from saving a bad throw. A bad throw is a throw that is wide enough that it seems likely to pull the first baseman off the base, allowing the batter to reach safely. If you get the out at first, that's saving a bad throw.

A wild throw, on the other hand, is a ball thrown so badly that you're not getting the out at first; you're just trying to keep the runner at first base, or keep him wherever he is. The leader at saving a wild throw was Casey Kotchman, with 12.

Keeping the ball in the infield. Major league leader was Longoria, with 7.

Good force play. Basically, a force play on a ball on which it appeared you'd have to take the out at first. Major league leader was Jimmy Rollins with 8.

Quick start on the DP. Major league leader was Tejada, with 8. Miguel.

Quick pivot on DP. Major league leaders were Iwamura and Ugly Dan Uggla, with 8 each. Obviously we use a pretty high standard.

Completing the DP despite aggressive slide. Major league leader was Michael Young, with 9.

Throwing out a runner after a hit or an error. Major league leader was Nick Markakis, with 10. Technically, it is an outfield assist, but I hate the term "outfield assist", since it sounds wimpy and manifestly fails to describe that which it is supposed to describe.

Holds batter to a single on what looked like a double. Major league leader was the much-maligned Pat Burrell, with 8.

Going into the stands to make a play. Denard Span and Kevin Youkilis did it three times each, only players to make 3.

Robbing the batter of a home run. I think John wants to cover these. . .I'll leave it for him. See page 12.

Stopping a ball that looked like a wild pitch. Major league leader was Kurt Suzuki, with 9.

We could also run down the leaders in GFP position by position, but we've got a whole book to talk about fielders, and that wasn't really the point of this exercise. The point here was to get you to understand the practical workings of these concepts, *Defensive Misplay* and *Good Fielding Play.*

I'm as proud of these as of anything I've ever invented, I guess, but I can take no credit for them. All of the work of counting these was done by the video scouts of Baseball Info Solutions, guys who watch every pitch of every game and make notes about everything that happens. And, yes, it's a dream job, but that lasts about two days and then it's work.

I've wanted to have this data for about ten years now, been talking about it and arguing for it, and finally, here it is. Steve Moyer, President for Life of Baseball Info Solutions, has brought together and trained and equipped and organized and supervised a team of people to make this a reality. I certainly could never have done it, and I just can't tell you how pleased I am to have the data.

Misplay/Good Play Leaders and Touches

I hope you enjoyed the previous article by Bill James about Defensive Misplays and Good Fielding Plays. It's a revolutionary, ground-breaking addition to our techniques for measuring defense in baseball. When Bill first proposed the idea to Baseball Info Solutions to track this data, I thought it might be overkill. The level of detail was nearly overwhelming. But based on Bill's track record, we were determined to give it a chance. From past experience working with Bill, his ideas nearly always pan out. This one did too. In a big way.

Now I will say I disagree with something Bill wrote in the previous article. He wasn't totally on board with my concept of Touches. Here's my definition of Touches:

A Touch is an estimate of the number of plays on which a fielder touches the ball. We use this as a technique to determine opportunities for defensive misplays and good plays. It won't include every possible touch of the baseball on a play, but it will include 99% of the significant touches. For example, a batter hits a single to left. We will count that as a Touch for the left fielder who fielded the ball. Theoretically, the left-fielder could misplay the ball both fielding it and throwing it, but we will only count the play as one Touch, or good play/ misplay opportunity. The left fielder will throw the ball back to the infield, usually to the shortstop or second baseman. In theory, that could be an opportunity for the infielder. However, this is such a routine play, we will only count it as a Touch if the infielder actually makes an error, defensive misplay, or good play on the play.

The concept of Touches is needed for this new metric that Bill invented. In measuring defense, it's clear that some players have more opportunities than others. As an example, when comparing two left fielders on two different teams, one of the left fielders might be on a team with a predominantly right-handed groundball pitching staff, while the other isn't. The first left fielder will get far less opportunities to be involved in a play than the second. Here's an example:

Eric Byrnes played in 420 innings for the Diamondbacks and Jay Payton played 407 for the Baltimore Orioles. Despite the fact that he played a few more innings than Payton, Byrnes had a lot fewer touches. Byrnes had 166 touches and Payton had 237. The way we calculate touches is to count every ball that the outfielder caught, every ball he fielded as a hit, every ball that he dropped, and every ball that he made any other kind of error. The only thing I can think of that's not counted 100% of the time is a foul flyball. If it's caught it counts, but if it drops in foul territory without an error being made we're not counting it (yet—maybe we'll add it in the future). The only other thing I can think of is some bizarre situation where the outfielder is picking up a ball that first was touched by another outfielder or where he is running in to participate in an infield rundown play. We're pretty much counting 99% of the possible situations where the outfielder could get a misplay or a good play.

Byrnes had 3.6 chances (touches) per nine innings, Payton had 5.2. That's a big difference. Byrnes had 7 good plays and Payton had 12. Looking at Good Plays per Inning we get 1.7% for Byrnes and 2.9% for Payton. Using Good Plays per Touch we get 4.2% for Byrnes and 5.0% for Payton. I am much more comfortable using the rate based on Touches than the one based on Innings.

Good Play and Misplay Leaderboards

The following pages contain the leaderboards for good fielding plays and defensive misplays for 2008. I'm going to walk you through each page, sharing some of my observations:

2008 Good Fielding Plays – Mark Teixeira's 93 good fielding plays were the most in baseball by a wide margin. His defensive prowess is well known, as is that of most of the other guys on the boards: David Wright, Jimmy Rollins, Carlos Gomez, Nick Markakis, Kenny Rogers and Yadier Molina. The two surprises are Robinson Cano and Pat Burrell.

2008 Defensive Misplays and Errors – A lot of the leaders in misplays plus errors are no surprise either: Ryan Howard, Rickie Weeks, Mark Reynolds. But Orlando Cabrera was a Gold Glove shortstop in 2007, yet led all 2007 shortstops in defensive misplays by a wide margin. Robinson Cano and Pat Burrell bring themselves back to more of what we expected by also appearing among the leaders in misplays and errors.

2008 Net (GFP minus DME) – To get a more complete picture of each player, we take his Good Fielding Plays and subtract his Defensive Misplays plus Errors to get a Net number. This net figure gives us another real good indicator of the best defensive players in baseball by position. If you gave a Gold Glove or Fielding Bible Award to any of these guys, no one should complain.

1B	Mark Teixera	+71
2B	Dustin Pedroia	+35
3B	David Wright	+38
SS	Jimmy Rollins	+32
LF	Jacoby Ellsbury	+13
CF	Jacoby Ellsbury	+10
RF	Nick Markakis	+26
P	Kenny Rogers	+7
C	Rod Barajas	+7

Well, maybe some would complain about Jacoby Ellsbury receiving two awards, one for left field and one for center field. Bill James commented on the remarkable numbers posted by Ellsbury. The guy simply didn't make any mistakes last year. Not only did he lead left fielders and center fielders in limited playing time, he was also on the leaderboard for right fielders (tied for seventh with +6).

2008 GFP per Touch – Now we get a flavor of who some of the best players were, based on the number of opportunities they had. Erick Aybar's skill at shortstop comes through as he leads the shortstop position by a wide margin. Alexi Castilla nabbed the top spot at second base over Orlando Hudson and Brandon Phillips. Interesting.

2008 DME per Touch – We see a couple of new names that we didn't see on the list of overall DME leaders. Mike Jacobs at first base for Florida and Tony Pena at shortstop for Kansas City give their respective teams some nightmares. Pitchers cringe at the rate of misplays and errors made by outfielders Alfonso Soriano, Rick Ankiel and Justin Upton.

2008 Net per Touch – Some of the names of fielders who show up here that are not on the overall Net list are Todd Helton at first base, Orlando Hudson at second, and Eric Byrnes in left field. These guys are outfielders who are known for their defense. The guy that surprised me at the top of the shortstop position was Maicer Izturis. Omar Vizquel and Jimmy Rollins were expected. They finished second and third to Maicer. His brother Cesar received a Gold Glove Award a few years ago, but I have newfound respect for this Izturis.

The remaining leaderboards break good plays and misplays into groupings. The groupings give us a way of seeing some of the specific areas of strength and weakness on the part of individual players. The groupings are:

- Grounders
- Flies and Liners
- Throwing
- Catching Throws
- Double Plays
- Preventing Extra Bases
- Fences and Walls
- Covering Bases
- Catcher Specific Plays

Some notes from these pages:
- The best players fielding grounders were Mark Teixeira, Dustin Pedroia, David Wright and Jimmy Rollins. The worst were Prince Fielder, Rickie Weeks, Mark Reynolds and Orlando Cabrera.
- The best infielders handling line drives and pop-ups were Lance Berkman, Orlando Hudson, Joe Crede, and Ryan Theriot.
- The best outfielders on flies and liners were Jacoby Ellsbury, Nate McLouth, and Brian Giles.
- Good throwing performances were put in by Mark Teixeira, Alex Rios, and Nick Markakis.
- The best at catching throws was Casey Kotchman. Jhonny Peralta stood out among shortstops.

- The best double play men were Brian Roberts by a wide margin at second base, Michael Young, and Joe Crede.
- Jermaine Dye was excellent at preventing runners from taking an extra base when balls were hit to him in right field.
- Nate McLouth, Bobby Abreu. and Brad Hawpe had trouble with fences and walls.
- Miguel Cabrera had some problems covering the base in his first year as a first baseman. Not good when that's your main job.
- Jason Kendall had more pitch blocks (balls in the dirt) by a wide margin.
- Yadier Molina had the most good plays involving baserunners, but his brother Bengie had difficulty preventing wild pitches.

2008 Good Fielding Plays

1B - GFP			2B - GFP			3B - GFP			SS - GFP	
Teixeira,Mark	93		Cano,Robinson	69		Wright,David	78		Rollins,Jimmy	65
Kotchman,Casey	76		Phillips,Brandon	66		Beltre,Adrian	62		Aybar,Erick	55
Morneau,Justin	70		Pedroia,Dustin	66		Hannahan,Jack	53		Cabrera,Orlando	55
Loney,James	69		Uggla,Dan	62		Crede,Joe	52		Hardy,J.J.	52
Pena,Carlos	64		Utley,Chase	57		Kouzmanoff,Kevin	49		Young,Michael	51
Berkman,Lance	64		Roberts,Brian	57		Longoria,Evan	49		Reyes,Jose	51
Howard,Ryan	64		Hudson,Orlando	48		Zimmerman,Ryan	48		Betancourt,Yuniesky	49
Millar,Kevin	64		Casilla,Alexi	47		Reynolds,Mark	46		Tejada,Miguel	49
Pujols,Albert	62		Polanco,Placido	42		Blake,Casey	45		Ramirez,Hanley	48
Helton,Todd	60		Lopez,Jose	41		Hall,Bill	40		Theriot,Ryan	48

LF - GFP			CF - GFP			RF - GFP	
Burrell,Pat	32		Gomez,Carlos	34		Markakis,Nick	41
Ibanez,Raul	30		Upton,B.J.	32		Dye,Jermaine	30
Young,Delmon	27		McLouth,Nate	31		Pence,Hunter	27
Holliday,Matt	24		Sizemore,Grady	28		Fukudome,Kosuke	25
Braun,Ryan	24		Cameron,Mike	26		Suzuki,Ichiro	24
Bay,Jason	23		Beltran,Carlos	25		Giles,Brian	23
Lewis,Fred	21		Bourn,Michael	24		Ludwick,Ryan	22
Crawford,Carl	20		4 tied with	22		Hart,Corey	22
Quentin,Carlos	18					Gutierrez,Franklin	22
Willingham,Josh	18					2 tied with	20

P - GFP			C - GFP	
Rogers,Kenny	12		Molina,Yadier	20
Hernandez,Felix	10		Barajas,Rod	16
Litsch,Jesse	9		Kendall,Jason	16
Maddux,Greg	7		Molina,Bengie	11
Santana,Johan	6		Schneider,Brian	11
Peavy,Jake	6		Martin,Russell	11
13 tied with	5		Hernandez,Ramon	11
			McCann,Brian	10
			Mathis,Jeff	10
			3 tied with	9

2008 Defensive Misplays and Errors

1B - DME

Howard,Ryan	56
Fielder,Prince	47
Votto,Joey	44
Jacobs,Mike	36
Barton,Daric	33
Cabrera,Miguel	33
Loney,James	30
Morneau,Justin	29
Delgado,Carlos	29
Giambi,Jason	28

2B - DME

Weeks,Rickie	59
Utley,Chase	48
Johnson,Kelly	45
Cano,Robinson	42
Lopez,Jose	41
Uggla,Dan	40
Roberts,Brian	37
Phillips,Brandon	34
Iwamura,Akinori	34
Kinsler,Ian	33

3B - DME

Reynolds,Mark	67
Encarnacion,Edwin	47
Gordon,Alex	46
Wright,David	40
Ramirez,Aramis	39
Cantu,Jorge	38
Kouzmanoff,Kevin	37
Hall,Bill	36
Mora,Melvin	34
2 tied with	33

SS - DME

Cabrera,Orlando	56
Ramirez,Hanley	47
Betancourt,Yuniesky	46
Theriot,Ryan	44
Escobar,Yunel	43
Bartlett,Jason	42
Young,Michael	41
Renteria,Edgar	41
Tejada,Miguel	41
Reyes,Jose	40

LF - DME

Young,Delmon	37
Ibanez,Raul	33
Soriano,Alfonso	29
Lewis,Fred	26
Braun,Ryan	25
Quentin,Carlos	24
Burrell,Pat	23
Boggs,Brandon	22
Dunn,Adam	21
Lee,Carlos	21

CF - DME

Upton,B.J.	41
Gomez,Carlos	40
Milledge,Lastings	39
Rowand,Aaron	38
Young,Chris	34
Victorino,Shane	29
Taveras,Willy	27
Ankiel,Rick	26
McLouth,Nate	25
3 tied with	24

RF - DME

Hawpe,Brad	42
Upton,Justin	38
Abreu,Bobby	34
Hart,Corey	32
Pence,Hunter	28
Guerrero,Vladimir	23
Ordonez,Magglio	23
Giles,Brian	22
Francoeur,Jeff	22
2 tied with	21

P - DME

Burnett,A.J.	9
Olsen,Scott	9
Gaudin,Chad	8
Kuroda,Hiroki	8
Meche,Gil	8
Floyd,Gavin	8
6 tied with	7

C - DME

Hernandez,Ramon	24
McCann,Brian	21
Molina,Yadier	19
Martin,Russell	17
Johjima,Kenji	15
Kendall,Jason	15
Saltalamacchia,J	14
Doumit,Ryan	14
4 tied with	13

2008 Net (GFP minus DME)

1B - Net		2B - Net		3B - Net)		SS - Net	
Teixeira,Mark	+71	Pedroia,Dustin	+35	Wright,David	+38	Rollins,Jimmy	+32
Kotchman,Casey	+58	Phillips,Brandon	+32	Beltre,Adrian	+33	Aybar,Erick	+20
Helton,Todd	+50	Hudson,Orlando	+30	Longoria,Evan	+22	Wilson,Jack	+19
Gload,Ross	+43	Cano,Robinson	+27	Crede,Joe	+21	Hardy,J.J.	+18
Berkman,Lance	+42	Uggla,Dan	+22	Hannahan,Jack	+20	Vizquel,Omar	+15
Millar,Kevin	+42	Casilla,Alexi	+20	Rodriguez,Alex	+16	Rodriguez,Luis	+14
Morneau,Justin	+41	Roberts,Brian	+20	Zimmerman,Ryan	+16	Izturis,Maicer	+13
Pena,Carlos	+40	Cabrera,Asdrubal	+19	Blake,Casey	+15	Tulowitzki,Troy	+13
Pujols,Albert	+40	Polanco,Placido	+18	Kouzmanoff,Kevin	+12	Izturis,Cesar	+12
Loney,James	+39	2 tied with	+17	2 tied with	+11	3 tied with	+11

LF - Net		CF - Net		RF - Net	
Ellsbury,Jacoby	+13	Ellsbury,Jacoby	+10	Markakis,Nick	+26
Bay,Jason	+10	Gardner,Brett	+9	Gutierrez,Franklin	+14
Burrell,Pat	+9	Kemp,Matt	+8	Dye,Jermaine	+12
Chavez,Endy	+6	Ross,Cody	+8	Fukudome,Kosuke	+8
Holliday,Matt	+5	Wells,Vernon	+7	Winn,Randy	+7
Dellucci,David	+5	Matthews Jr.,Gary	+7	Chavez,Endy	+7
Crawford,Carl	+5	Reed,Jeremy	+6	Ellsbury,Jacoby	+6
Schumaker,Skip	+5	Gerut,Jody	+6	Suzuki,Ichiro	+6
7 tied with	+4	McLouth,Nate	+6	Griffey Jr.,Ken	+5
		Cabrera,Melky	+5	6 tied with	+4

P - Net		C - Net	
Rogers,Kenny	+7	Barajas,Rod	+7
Hernandez,Felix	+6	Holm,Steve	+3
Litsch,Jesse	+5	Burke,Jamie	+3
Peavy,Jake	+4	Molina,Bengie	+3
12 tied with	+3	Chavez,Raul	+3
		Cancel,Robinson	+2
		Hoover,Paul	+2
		Casanova,Raul	+2
		Ramirez,Max	+2
		10 tied with	+1

2008 GFP per Touch

1B GFP per Touch

Helton,Todd	6.7 %
Swisher,Nick	6.5 %
Gload,Ross	6.2 %
Teixeira,Mark	6.1 %
Kotchman,Casey	5.7 %
Pena,Carlos	5.7 %
Giambi,Jason	5.5 %
Davis,Chris	5.4 %
Millar,Kevin	5.2 %
Morneau,Justin	4.9 %

2B GFP per Touch

Casilla,Alexi	10.7 %
Hudson,Orlando	10.0 %
Phillips,Brandon	9.5 %
Pedroia,Dustin	9.2 %
Uggla,Dan	8.9 %
Cano,Robinson	8.9 %
Barmes,Clint	8.4 %
Roberts,Brian	7.9 %
Carroll,Jamey	7.8 %
Kennedy,Adam	7.8 %

3B GFP per Touch

Wright,David	16.9 %
Crede,Joe	16.8 %
Hannahan,Jack	16.3 %
Beltre,Adrian	14.9 %
Zimmerman,Ryan	14.4 %
Stewart,Ian	14.2 %
Longoria,Evan	13.3 %
Blake,Casey	12.8 %
Hall,Bill	12.7 %
Bautista,Jose	12.5 %

SS GFP per Touch

Aybar,Erick	12.5 %
Rollins,Jimmy	10.6 %
Wilson,Jack	10.1 %
Aviles,Mike	10.0 %
Izturis,Maicer	9.8 %
McDonald,John	9.7 %
Castro,Juan	8.9 %
Vizquel,Omar	8.9 %
Pena,Tony F	8.6 %
Scutaro,Marco	8.3 %

LF GFP per Touch

Burrell,Pat	5.8 %
Harris,Willie	5.3 %
Payton,Jay	5.1 %
Lewis,Fred	5.0 %
Crawford,Carl	4.9 %
Cust,Jack	4.7 %
Anderson,Garret	4.6 %
Willingham,Josh	4.6 %
Boggs,Brandon	4.4 %
Ibanez,Raul	4.3 %

CF GFP per Touch

Ellsbury,Jacoby	5.9 %
Gathright,Joey	5.4 %
Kemp,Matt	5.1 %
Cameron,Mike	4.7 %
Ankiel,Rick	4.7 %
Upton,B.J.	4.3 %
Cabrera,Melky	4.2 %
Gerut,Jody	4.2 %
Bourn,Michael	4.2 %
Gomez,Carlos	4.1 %

RF GFP per Touch

Cuddyer,Michael	7.1 %
Suzuki,Ichiro	6.5 %
Jenkins,Geoff	5.9 %
Markakis,Nick	5.9 %
Griffey Jr.,Ken	5.6 %
Bruce,Jay	5.2 %
Gutierrez,Franklin	5.2 %
Dye,Jermaine	5.2 %
Span,Denard	5.1 %
Church,Ryan	5.1 %

P GFP per Touch

Kershaw,Clayton	21.7 %
Hernandez,Felix	21.3 %
McGowan,Dustin	20.0 %
Redding,Tim	17.9 %
Lopez,Aquilino	16.7 %
Chamberlain,Joba	16.7 %
Torres,Salomon	15.4 %
Rogers,Kenny	14.8 %
Peavy,Jake	14.6 %
2 tied with	14.3 %

C GFP per Touch

Molina,Yadier	13.1 %
Barajas,Rod	12.1 %
Schneider,Brian	9.0 %
Shoppach,Kelly	8.3 %
Kendall,Jason	7.7 %
Flores,Jesus	7.0 %
Treanor,Matt	6.9 %
Mathis,Jeff	6.9 %
Martin,Russell	6.1 %
Molina,Bengie	5.9 %

2008 DME per Touch

1B DME per Touch

Jacobs,Mike	3.9 %
Bowker,John	3.8 %
Howard,Ryan	3.6 %
Votto,Joey	3.6 %
Aurilia,Rich	3.6 %
Jackson,Conor	3.5 %
Fielder,Prince	3.1 %
Giambi,Jason	3.0 %
Barton,Daric	2.9 %
Davis,Chris	2.7 %

2B DME per Touch

Weeks,Rickie	9.8 %
Matsui,Kaz	6.7 %
Lopez,Felipe	6.6 %
Johnson,Kelly	6.6 %
Miles,Aaron	6.5 %
Gonzalez,Edgar	6.5 %
DeRosa,Mark	6.3 %
Barmes,Clint	6.2 %
Casilla,Alexi	6.2 %
Utley,Chase	6.1 %

3B DME per Touch

Reynolds,Mark	16.6 %
Encarnacion,Edwin	12.5 %
Buscher,Brian	12.2 %
Castillo,Jose	11.9 %
Gordon,Alex	11.6 %
DeWitt,Blake	11.5 %
Hall,Bill	11.4 %
Cantu,Jorge	11.1 %
Ramirez,Aramis	10.7 %
Figgins,Chone	10.7 %

SS DME per Touch

Pena,Tony F	9.0 %
Lugo,Julio	8.2 %
Aybar,Erick	8.0 %
Bartlett,Jason	7.8 %
Theriot,Ryan	7.5 %
Cabrera,Orlando	7.4 %
McDonald,John	7.4 %
Eckstein,David	7.3 %
Betancourt,Yuniesky	7.2 %
Ramirez,Hanley	7.2 %

LF DME per Touch

Soriano,Alfonso	7.2 %
Boggs,Brandon	7.0 %
Lewis,Fred	6.2 %
Young,Delmon	5.4 %
Blanco,Gregor	5.3 %
Cust,Jack	5.0 %
Thames,Marcus	5.0 %
Headley,Chase	4.8 %
Ibanez,Raul	4.7 %
Payton,Jay	4.6 %

CF DME per Touch

Ankiel,Rick	6.1 %
Milledge,Lastings	5.8 %
Upton,B.J.	5.5 %
Swisher,Nick	5.1 %
Taveras,Willy	5.0 %
Gomez,Carlos	4.9 %
Rowand,Aaron	4.8 %
Victorino,Shane	4.6 %
Edmonds,Jim	4.5 %
Gonzalez,Carlos	4.4 %

RF DME per Touch

Upton,Justin	9.9 %
Hawpe,Brad	7.7 %
Jenkins,Geoff	7.3 %
Bruce,Jay	7.3 %
Guerrero,Vladimir	6.4 %
Cuddyer,Michael	5.9 %
Abreu,Bobby	5.3 %
Hart,Corey	5.1 %
Dukes,Elijah	5.1 %
Kearns,Austin	4.9 %

P DME per Touch

Kuo,Hong-Chih	35.7 %
Gaudin,Chad	32.0 %
Lackey,John	29.2 %
Johnson,Randy	29.2 %
Green,Sean	28.6 %
Miller,Andrew	26.3 %
Bennett,Jeff	23.8 %
McClung,Seth	23.8 %
3 tied with	23.1 %

C DME per Touch

Hernandez,Ramon	12.4 %
Molina,Yadier	12.4 %
Baker,John	12.3 %
Olivo,Miguel	11.8 %
Johjima,Kenji	11.5 %
Treanor,Matt	9.9 %
Schneider,Brian	9.8 %
McCann,Brian	9.8 %
Martin,Russell	9.5 %
Napoli,Mike	9.4 %

2008 Net (GFP minus DME) per Touch

1B Net per Touch	
Helton,Todd	5.6 %
Swisher,Nick	5.5 %
Gload,Ross	4.8 %
Teixeira,Mark	4.7 %
Kotchman,Casey	4.3 %
Pena,Carlos	3.6 %
Millar,Kevin	3.4 %
Cairo,Miguel	3.4 %
Berkman,Lance	3.0 %
Garko,Ryan	2.9 %

2B Net per Touch	
Hudson,Orlando	6.2 %
Kennedy,Adam	4.9 %
Pedroia,Dustin	4.9 %
Phillips,Brandon	4.6 %
Casilla,Alexi	4.6 %
Cabrera,Asdrubal	4.2 %
Kendrick,Howie	3.9 %
Cano,Robinson	3.5 %
Uggla,Dan	3.2 %
Roberts,Brian	2.8 %

3B Net per Touch	
Wright,David	8.2 %
Beltre,Adrian	7.9 %
Crede,Joe	6.8 %
Hannahan,Jack	6.2 %
Longoria,Evan	6.0 %
Zimmerman,Ryan	4.8 %
Stewart,Ian	4.7 %
Rodriguez,Alex	4.3 %
Blake,Casey	4.3 %
Lowell,Mike	3.3 %

SS Net per Touch	
Izturis,Maicer	6.4 %
Vizquel,Omar	5.3 %
Rollins,Jimmy	5.2 %
Wilson,Jack	4.7 %
Aybar,Erick	4.5 %
Aviles,Mike	2.9 %
Hardy,J.J.	2.8 %
Punto,Nick	2.7 %
Tulowitzki,Troy	2.7 %
Scutaro,Marco	2.5 %

LF Net per Touch	
Byrnes,Eric	2.4 %
DeJesus,David	1.6 %
Burrell,Pat	1.6 %
Bay,Jason	1.5 %
Harris,Willie	1.3 %
Crawford,Carl	1.2 %
Anderson,Garret	0.9 %
Holliday,Matt	0.8 %
Payton,Jay	0.4 %
Willingham,Josh	0.3 %

CF Net per Touch	
Ellsbury,Jacoby	3.1 %
Kemp,Matt	1.9 %
Ross,Cody	1.7 %
Gerut,Jody	1.7 %
Wells,Vernon	1.5 %
Schumaker,Skip	1.0 %
Gathright,Joey	1.0 %
Cabrera,Melky	1.0 %
McLouth,Nate	0.8 %
Cameron,Mike	0.7 %

RF Net per Touch	
Markakis,Nick	3.8 %
Gutierrez,Franklin	3.3 %
Dye,Jermaine	2.1 %
Suzuki,Ichiro	1.6 %
Fukudome,Kosuke	1.6 %
Griffey Jr.,Ken	1.4 %
Winn,Randy	1.2 %
Cuddyer,Michael	1.2 %
Span,Denard	1.1 %
Church,Ryan	1.1 %

P Net per Touch	
Lopez,Aquilino	16.7 %
Rupe,Josh	13.3 %
Hernandez,Felix	12.8 %
Torres,Salomon	11.5 %
Durbin,Chad	11.1 %
Bedard,Erik	10.0 %
Haren,Dan	10.0 %
Peavy,Jake	9.8 %
Baker,Scott	9.1 %
2 tied with	8.7 %

C Net per Touch	
Barajas,Rod	5.3 %
Molina,Bengie	1.6 %
Molina,Yadier	0.7 %
Kendall,Jason	0.5 %
Navarro,Dioner	-0.6 %
Iannetta,Chris	-0.8 %
Schneider,Brian	-0.8 %
Shoppach,Kelly	-0.9 %
Suzuki,Kurt	-1.3 %
Zaun,Gregg	-1.8 %

2008 GFP and DME on Grounders

1B - GFP on Grounders

Teixeira,Mark	30
Loney,James	22
Kotchman,Casey	19
Votto,Joey	18
Berkman,Lance	18
Gonzalez,Adrian	18
Gload,Ross	17
Pujols,Albert	16
Millar,Kevin	16
Lee,Derrek	15

2B - GFP on Grounders

Cano,Robinson	42
Pedroia,Dustin	39
Phillips,Brandon	35
Utley,Chase	32
Uggla,Dan	29
Casilla,Alexi	28
Hudson,Orlando	23
Roberts,Brian	22
Kinsler,Ian	22
Weeks,Rickie	21

3B - GFP on Grounders

Wright,David	56
Beltre,Adrian	42
Hannahan,Jack	36
Zimmerman,Ryan	36
Blake,Casey	34
Crede,Joe	32
Kouzmanoff,Kevin	31
Longoria,Evan	31
Ramirez,Aramis	30
2 tied with	28

SS - GFP on Grounders

Rollins,Jimmy	41
Cabrera,Orlando	32
Reyes,Jose	31
Escobar,Yunel	31
Ramirez,Hanley	29
Izturis,Cesar	28
Crosby,Bobby	27
Aybar,Erick	27
Young,Michael	27
Hardy,J.J.	27

P - GFP on Grounders

Hernandez,Felix	8
Rogers,Kenny	7
Litsch,Jesse	7
Dempster,Ryan	5
Maddux,Greg	5
Kuroda,Hiroki	5
Ponson,Sidney	4
Marquis,Jason	4
Kershaw,Clayton	4
Webb,Brandon	4

C - GFP on Grounders

Mathis,Jeff	5
Kendall,Jason	5
Ruiz,Carlos	4
Molina,Bengie	3
Molina,Jose	3
McCann,Brian	3
12 tied with	2

1B - DME on Grounders

Fielder,Prince	21
Howard,Ryan	19
Pena,Carlos	15
Jacobs,Mike	13
Berkman,Lance	12
Giambi,Jason	11
Votto,Joey	11
Konerko,Paul	10
Garko,Ryan	10
Delgado,Carlos	10

2B - DME on Grounders

Weeks,Rickie	24
Johnson,Kelly	19
Cano,Robinson	19
Lopez,Jose	18
Roberts,Brian	18
Utley,Chase	18
Kinsler,Ian	16
Phillips,Brandon	16
Pedroia,Dustin	14
Casilla,Alexi	13

3B - DME on Grounders

Reynolds,Mark	31
Gordon,Alex	25
Ramirez,Aramis	24
Wright,David	23
Bautista,Jose	21
Hall,Bill	19
Blake,Casey	18
Encarnacion,Edwin	18
Crede,Joe	17
DeWitt,Blake	17

SS - DME on Grounders

Cabrera,Orlando	26
Drew,Stephen	21
Renteria,Edgar	19
Guzman,Cristian	19
Ramirez,Hanley	18
Bartlett,Jason	18
Hardy,J.J.	18
Betancourt,Yuniesky	17
Peralta,Jhonny	17
4 tied with	16

P - DME on Grounders

Johnson,Randy	4
18 tied with	3

C - DME on Grounders

Doumit,Ryan	2
Paulino,Ronny	1
Montero,Miguel	1
Flores,Jesus	1
Schneider,Brian	1
Johjima,Kenji	1
Martin,Russell	1
McCann,Brian	1

2008 Net (GFP minus DME) Grounders

1B - Net Grounders

Teixeira,Mark	+21
Loney,James	+13
Helton,Todd	+13
Kotchman,Casey	+13
Gonzalez,Adrian	+12
Gload,Ross	+11
Millar,Kevin	+9
Pujols,Albert	+9
3 tied with	+7

2B - Net Grounders

Pedroia,Dustin	+25
Cano,Robinson	+23
Phillips,Brandon	+19
Cabrera,Asdrubal	+17
Uggla,Dan	+17
Casilla,Alexi	+15
Utley,Chase	+14
Kennedy,Adam	+13
Hudson,Orlando	+13
3 tied with	+9

3B - Net Grounders

Wright,David	+33
Beltre,Adrian	+26
Zimmerman,Ryan	+25
Hannahan,Jack	+23
Longoria,Evan	+17
Blake,Casey	+16
Kouzmanoff,Kevin	+15
Crede,Joe	+15
Rodriguez,Alex	+15
Rolen,Scott	+13

SS - Net Grounders

Rollins,Jimmy	+25
Izturis,Cesar	+20
Aviles,Mike	+19
Escobar,Yunel	+18
Crosby,Bobby	+17
Reyes,Jose	+15
Aybar,Erick	+15
Berroa,Angel	+12
Rodriguez,Luis	+12
Jeter,Derek	+12

P - Net Grounders

Hernandez,Felix	+8
Litsch,Jesse	+5
Rogers,Kenny	+4
Marquis,Jason	+4
Maddux,Greg	+4
Kershaw,Clayton	+4
Dempster,Ryan	+4
11 tied with	+3

C - Net Grounders

Kendall,Jason	+5
Mathis,Jeff	+5
Ruiz,Carlos	+4
Molina,Jose	+3
Molina,Bengie	+3
10 tied with	+2

2008 Good Fielding Plays on Flies and Liners

1B - GFP on Flies and Liners

Howard,Ryan	12
Berkman,Lance	12
Teixeira,Mark	10
Lee,Derrek	10
Kotchman,Casey	9
Loney,James	7
Morneau,Justin	7
Pena,Carlos	7
5 tied with	6

2B - GFP on Flies and Liners

Ramirez,Alexei	11
Hudson,Orlando	11
Roberts,Brian	11
Ellis,Mark	10
Pedroia,Dustin	9
Utley,Chase	9
Polanco,Placido	8
Uggla,Dan	8
Phillips,Brandon	8
2 tied with	7

3B - GFP on Flies and Liners

Reynolds,Mark	10
Wright,David	9
Crede,Joe	8
Mora,Melvin	8
Cantu,Jorge	8
Hannahan,Jack	8
Beltre,Adrian	7
Hall,Bill	7
3 tied with	6

SS - GFP on Flies and Liners

Theriot,Ryan	15
Bartlett,Jason	9
Jeter,Derek	8
Ramirez,Hanley	8
Betancourt,Yuniesky	8
Escobar,Yunel	7
Cabrera,Orlando	7
4 tied with	6

LF - GFP on Flies and Liners

Ibanez,Raul	17
Crawford,Carl	16
Braun,Ryan	14
Quentin,Carlos	14
Lewis,Fred	13
Ellsbury,Jacoby	12
Young,Delmon	12
Burrell,Pat	12
Thames,Marcus	11
Harris,Willie	11

CF - GFP on Flies and Liners

McLouth,Nate	27
Gomez,Carlos	26
Sizemore,Grady	26
Upton,B.J.	20
Cameron,Mike	20
Granderson,Curtis	19
Beltran,Carlos	18
Bourn,Michael	16
Hamilton,Josh	16
Taveras,Willy	16

RF - GFP on Flies and Liners

Giles,Brian	22
Dye,Jermaine	19
Markakis,Nick	19
Suzuki,Ichiro	15
Winn,Randy	14
Hart,Corey	14
Fukudome,Kosuke	13
Pence,Hunter	13
Jenkins,Geoff	13
2 tied with	12

P - GFP on Flies and Liners

Lohse,Kyle	3
Hamels,Cole	3
17 tied with	2

C - GFP on Flies and Liners

Barajas,Rod	4
McCann,Brian	3
Suzuki,Kurt	3
Varitek,Jason	2
Schneider,Brian	2
Bard,Josh	2
Iannetta,Chris	2
13 tied with	1

2008 Defensive Misplays and Errors on Flies and Liners

1B - DME on Flies and Liners

Jacobs,Mike	8
Barton,Daric	8
Morneau,Justin	7
Overbay,Lyle	6
Howard,Ryan	6
Kotchman,Casey	6
Fielder,Prince	6
Loney,James	5
Delgado,Carlos	5
Pujols,Albert	5

2B - DME on Flies and Liners

Ramirez,Alexei	9
Uggla,Dan	8
Grudzielanek,Mark	7
Weeks,Rickie	7
Cano,Robinson	6
Iwamura,Akinori	6
Phillips,Brandon	6
Durham,Ray	6
3 tied with	5

3B - DME on Flies and Liners

Reynolds,Mark	7
Kouzmanoff,Kevin	7
Hannahan,Jack	7
Ramirez,Aramis	6
Blake,Casey	6
8 tied with	5

SS - DME on Flies and Liners

Pena,Tony F	8
Tejada,Miguel	7
Reyes,Jose	7
Aviles,Mike	6
Bynum,Freddie	6
Renteria,Edgar	5
Aybar,Erick	5
Cabrera,Orlando	5
Jeter,Derek	5
Crosby,Bobby	5

LF - DME on Flies and Liners

Soriano,Alfonso	18
Braun,Ryan	18
Young,Delmon	15
Quentin,Carlos	13
Lewis,Fred	12
Ibanez,Raul	12
Ramirez,Manny	12
Burrell,Pat	10
Dunn,Adam	9
Willingham,Josh	9

CF - DME on Flies and Liners

Milledge,Lastings	19
Gomez,Carlos	19
Rowand,Aaron	17
Ankiel,Rick	16
Upton,B.J.	14
Young,Chris	14
Edmonds,Jim	13
Sizemore,Grady	13
Hunter,Torii	12
Granderson,Curtis	12

RF - DME on Flies and Liners

Hawpe,Brad	21
Hart,Corey	17
Upton,Justin	17
Pence,Hunter	16
Abreu,Bobby	11
Dye,Jermaine	11
Ludwick,Ryan	11
Span,Denard	10
Ordonez,Magglio	9
6 tied with	8

P - DME on Flies and Liners

Batista,Miguel	2
Davis,Doug	2
Broxton,Jonathan	2
Bannister,Brian	2
Washburn,Jarrod	2
Perez,Rafael	2
Coffey,Todd	2
Padilla,Vicente	2
74 tied with	1

C - DME on Flies and Liners

Hernandez,Ramon	4
15 tied with	2

2008 Net (GFP minus DME) Flies and Liners

1B - Net Flies and Liners

Berkman,Lance	+10
Teixeira,Mark	+9
Lee,Derrek	+8
Howard,Ryan	+6
Konerko,Paul	+6
Youkilis,Kevin	+5
Garko,Ryan	+4
Votto,Joey	+4
Pena,Carlos	+4
3 tied with	+3

2B - Net Flies and Liners

Hudson,Orlando	+11
Roberts,Brian	+7
Ellis,Mark	+7
Polanco,Placido	+6
Casilla,Alexi	+6
Utley,Chase	+5
Pedroia,Dustin	+4
Kennedy,Adam	+4
7 tied with	+3

3B - Net Flies and Liners

Crede,Joe	+6
Wright,David	+5
Guillen,Carlos	+5
Cantu,Jorge	+5
Stewart,Ian	+4
Helms,Wes	+4
Mora,Melvin	+4
6 tied with	+3

SS - Net Flies and Liners

Theriot,Ryan	+12
Betancourt,Yuniesky	+8
Bartlett,Jason	+6
Hardy,J.J.	+5
Escobar,Yunel	+5
Ramirez,Hanley	+4
Vizquel,Omar	+4
7 tied with	+3

LF - Net Flies and Liners

Ellsbury,Jacoby	+12
Crawford,Carl	+10
DeJesus,David	+8
Chavez,Endy	+6
Schumaker,Skip	+5
Ibanez,Raul	+5
Byrnes,Eric	+5
Dellucci,David	+5
6 tied with	+4

CF - Net Flies and Liners

McLouth,Nate	+17
Sizemore,Grady	+13
Cabrera,Melky	+10
Jones,Adam	+10
Gerut,Jody	+10
Cameron,Mike	+10
Ellsbury,Jacoby	+10
Beltran,Carlos	+9
Wells,Vernon	+8
Reed,Jeremy	+8

RF - Net Flies and Liners

Giles,Brian	+15
Markakis,Nick	+13
Suzuki,Ichiro	+10
Dye,Jermaine	+8
Winn,Randy	+8
6 tied with	+6

P - Net Flies and Liners

14 tied with	+2

C - Net Flies and Liners

Barajas,Rod	+4
Bard,Josh	+2
Suzuki,Kurt	+2
Zaun,Gregg	+1
Schneider,Brian	+1
Holm,Steve	+1
Iannetta,Chris	+1
McCann,Brian	+1
Thigpen,Curtis	+1
Casanova,Raul	+1

2008 Good Fielding Plays on Throwing

1B - GFP on Throws	
Teixeira,Mark	7
Overbay,Lyle	5
Fielder,Prince	5
Votto,Joey	3
Swisher,Nick	3
Aurilia,Rich	3
Pujols,Albert	3
Konerko,Paul	3
Loney,James	3
4 tied with	2

2B - GFP on Throws	
Pedroia,Dustin	6
Phillips,Brandon	5
Uggla,Dan	4
Easley,Damion	3
Barmes,Clint	3
Hernandez,And	3
Lopez,Felipe	3
Sanchez,Freddy	3
Johnson,Kelly	3
Utley,Chase	3

3B - GFP on Throws	
Kouzmanoff,Kevin	4
Aybar,Willy	3
Bautista,Jose	3
11 tied with	2

SS - GFP on Throws	
Rollins,Jimmy	5
Wilson,Jack	5
Betancourt,Yuniesky	4
Aybar,Erick	4
Escobar,Yunel	4
8 tied with	3

LF - GFP on Throws	
Burrell,Pat	10
Young,Delmon	8
Soriano,Alfonso	7
Bay,Jason	7
Ibanez,Raul	7
Willingham,Josh	6
Braun,Ryan	6
Lewis,Fred	6
6 tied with	5

CF - GFP on Throws	
Upton,B.J.	9
Rios,Alex	8
Kemp,Matt	7
Bourn,Michael	5
Ross,Cody	5
Victorino,Shane	5
5 tied with	4

RF - GFP on Throws	
Markakis,Nick	13
Ludwick,Ryan	9
Pence,Hunter	8
Nady,Xavier	7
Church,Ryan	7
Abreu,Bobby	7
Guillen,Jose	7
5 tied with	6

P - GFP on Throws	
14 tied with	1

C - GFP on Throws	
Molina,Bengie	6
Molina,Yadier	6
Kendall,Jason	5
Quintero,Humberto	3
Ross,David	3
Hundley,Nick	3
Nieves,Wil	3
Hernandez,Ramon	3
Barajas,Rod	3
8 tied with	2

2008 Defensive Misplays and Errors on Throwing

1B - DME on Throws	
Votto,Joey	11
Howard,Ryan	10
Gonzalez,Adrian	7
Giambi,Jason	7
Delgado,Carlos	6
Loney,James	6
Cabrera,Miguel	6
Barton,Daric	6
3 tied with	5

2B - DME on Throws	
Weeks,Rickie	13
Sanchez,Freddy	11
Uggla,Dan	10
Utley,Chase	10
Matsui,Kaz	10
Roberts,Brian	9
Lopez,Jose	8
Polanco,Placido	8
Cano,Robinson	8
3 tied with	7

3B - DME on Throws	
Reynolds,Mark	24
Encarnacion,Edwin	17
Zimmerman,Ryan	15
Cantu,Jorge	14
Gordon,Alex	14
Mora,Melvin	12
Hannahan,Jack	11
Kouzmanoff,Kevin	11
Hall,Bill	10
Rodriguez,Alex	10

SS - DME on Throws	
Crosby,Bobby	20
Betancourt,Yuniesky	17
Escobar,Yunel	17
Bartlett,Jason	17
Aviles,Mike	16
Cabrera,Orlando	15
Ramirez,Hanley	15
Young,Michael	15
Peralta,Jhonny	14
Theriot,Ryan	14

LF - DME on Throws	
Ibanez,Raul	11
Quentin,Carlos	8
Burrell,Pat	8
Crawford,Carl	7
Lee,Carlos	6
Boggs,Brandon	6
8 tied with	5

CF - DME on Throws	
Upton,B.J.	10
Victorino,Shane	10
Jones,Adam	10
Taveras,Willy	9
Rowand,Aaron	8
Byrd,Marlon	7
Cabrera,Melky	7
Gomez,Carlos	7
McLouth,Nate	7
2 tied with	6

RF - DME on Throws	
Abreu,Bobby	10
Guillen,Jose	8
Kearns,Austin	8
Guerrero,Vladimir	8
Giles,Brian	8
Francoeur,Jeff	8
Suzuki,Ichiro	7
Wilkerson,Brad	7
Nady,Xavier	7
Upton,Justin	7

P - DME on Throws	
Gaudin,Chad	5
Lackey,John	5
Olson,Garrett	4
Meche,Gil	4
Zambrano,Carlos	4
Campillo,Jorge	4
Lowe,Mark	4
Richard,Clayton	4
Cueto,Johnny	4
19 tied with	3

C - DME on Throws	
Mathis,Jeff	12
Hernandez,Ramon	9
Molina,Yadier	9
Treanor,Matt	9
McCann,Brian	9
Saltalamacchia,J	9
Martin,Russell	9
6 tied with	7

2008 Net (GFP minus DME) Throwing

1B - Net Throws

Teixeira,Mark	+5
Overbay,Lyle	+3
Fielder,Prince	+2
12 tied with	+1

2B - Net Throws

Pedroia,Dustin	+4
Hernandez,And	+3
15 tied with	+1

3B - Net Throws

Lowrie,Jed	+1
McDonald,John	+1
Youkilis,Kevin	0
Aybar,Willy	0
Harris,Brendan	0
Branyan,Russell	0
31 tied with	-1

SS - Net Throws

Santiago,Ramon	+2
Barmes,Clint	+1
Janish,Paul	+1
Izturis,Maicer	+1
Bocock,Brian	+1
Burke,Chris	+1
Bloomquist,Willie	+1
Ochoa,Ivan	+1
3 tied with	0

LF - Net Throws

Lewis,Fred	+4
Braun,Ryan	+4
Bay,Jason	+4
Soriano,Alfonso	+4
Anderson,Garret	+4
Young,Delmon	+3
10 tied with	+2

CF - Net Throws

Rios,Alex	+6
Gardner,Brett	+4
Ross,Cody	+3
Kemp,Matt	+3
Matthews Jr.,Gary	+2
Gross,Gabe	+2
Schumaker,Skip	+2
Payton,Jay	+2
11 tied with	+1

RF - Net Throws

Markakis,Nick	+9
Ludwick,Ryan	+7
Church,Ryan	+6
Pence,Hunter	+5
Werth,Jayson	+5
Balentien,Wladimir	+3
Griffey Jr.,Ken	+3
Sweeney,Ryan	+3
9 tied with	+2

P - Net Throws

Santana,Ervin	+1
Gonzalez,Gio	+1
Dickey,R.A.	+1
Shell,Steven	+1
Hensley,Clay	+1
Snell,Ian	+1
6 tied with	0

C - Net Throws

Ross,David	+2
Molina,Bengie	+2
Snyder,Chris	+2
Quintero,Humberto	+2
Inge,Brandon	+1
Ellis,A.J.	+1
Redmond,Mike	+1
Iannetta,Chris	+1
Burke,Jamie	+1
Holm,Steve	+1

2008 GFP and DME on Catching Throws

1B- GFP on Catching Throws

Morneau,Justin	47
Kotchman,Casey	45
Helton,Todd	42
Teixeira,Mark	39
Pena,Carlos	38
Millar,Kevin	38
Giambi,Jason	37
Delgado,Carlos	36
Howard,Ryan	36
Pujols,Albert	35

2B- GFP on Catching Throws

Uggla,Dan	9
Cano,Robinson	6
Sanchez,Freddy	5
Hudson,Orlando	4
Inglett,Joe	4
8 tied with	3

3B- GFP on Catching Throws

Rodriguez,Alex	2
Wright,David	2
Hall,Bill	2
Beltre,Adrian	2
Inge,Brandon	2
Cantu,Jorge	2
19 tied with	1

SS-GFP on Catching Throws

Peralta,Jhonny	7
Guzman,Cristian	5
Janish,Paul	4
Bruntlett,Eric	4
Reyes,Jose	4
Eckstein,David	3
Rollins,Jimmy	3
Theriot,Ryan	3
Young,Michael	3
14 tied with	2

P - GFP on Catching Throws

22 tied with	1

C - GFP on Catching Throws

Shoppach,Kelly	3
Martin,Russell	3
Kendall,Jason	2
Barajas,Rod	2
Navarro,Dioner	2
Schneider,Brian	2
17 tied with	1

1B-DME on Catching Throws

Votto,Joey	16
Morneau,Justin	15
Howard,Ryan	15
Fielder,Prince	12
Cabrera,Miguel	10
Barton,Daric	9
Jacobs,Mike	9
Loney,James	8
Overbay,Lyle	8
Teixeira,Mark	8

2B-DME on Catching Throws

Lopez,Jose	6
Casilla,Alexi	5
Lopez,Felipe	5
Johnson,Kelly	5
Pedroia,Dustin	5
Ramirez,Alexei	5
Ellis,Mark	4
9 tied with	3

3B-DME on Catching Throws

Feliz,Pedro	4
Figgins,Chone	3
10 tied with	2

SS-DME on Catching Throws

Betancourt,Yuniesky	8
Escobar,Yunel	6
Young,Michael	6
Reyes,Jose	5
Cabrera,Orlando	5
Guzman,Cristian	4
Aybar,Erick	4
Theriot,Ryan	4
8 tied with	3

P- DME on Catching Throws

Padilla,Vicente	2
Carmona,Fausto	2
Lindstrom,Matt	2
Perez,Rafael	2
Santana,Johan	2
47 tied with	1

C-DME on Catching Throws

Molina,Yadier	5
Hernandez,Ramon	4
Suzuki,Kurt	4
Olivo,Miguel	4
7 tied with	3

2008 Net (GFP minus DME) Catching Throws

1B - Net Catching Throws

Kotchman,Casey	+42
Helton,Todd	+37
Pena,Carlos	+36
Giambi,Jason	+32
Morneau,Justin	+32
Millar,Kevin	+31
Gload,Ross	+31
Delgado,Carlos	+31
Teixeira,Mark	+31
Pujols,Albert	+30

2B - Net Catching Throws

Uggla,Dan	+6
Sanchez,Freddy	+5
Inglett,Joe	+3
Cano,Robinson	+3
Hudson,Orlando	+3
Polanco,Placido	+3
5 tied with	+2

3B - Net Catching Throws

Inge,Brandon	+2
14 tied with	+1

SS - Net Catching Throws

Peralta,Jhonny	+7
Janish,Paul	+4
Bruntlett,Eric	+3
Counsell,Craig	+2
Punto,Nick	+2
Rodriguez,Luis	+2
Harris,Brendan	+2
17 tied with	+1

P - Net Catching Throws

21 tied with	+1

C - Net Catching Throws

Shoppach,Kelly	+2
Martin,Russell	+2
9 tied with	+1

2008 GFP and DME on Double Plays

1B - GFP on Double Plays

Barton,Daric	4
10 tied with	2

2B - GFP on Double Plays

Roberts,Brian	18
Iwamura,Akinori	13
Pedroia,Dustin	12
Phillips,Brandon	12
Uggla,Dan	10
Sanchez,Freddy	10
Lopez,Jose	10
Cano,Robinson	10
5 tied with	9

3B - GFP on Double Plays

Crede,Joe	6
Hannahan,Jack	5
Beltre,Adrian	4
Longoria,Evan	4
Feliz,Pedro	3
Inge,Brandon	3
Rodriguez,Alex	3
11 tied with	2

SS - GFP on Double Plays

Hardy,J.J.	15
Tejada,Miguel	14
Aybar,Erick	14
Young,Michael	14
Aviles,Mike	11
Cabrera,Orlando	10
Wilson,Jack	10
Tulowitzki,Troy	9
Reyes,Jose	9
Betancourt,Yuniesky	8

P - GFP on Double Plays

Floyd,Gavin	2
33 tied with	1

C - GFP on Double Plays

Martin,Russell	2
Kendall,Jason	2
Rodriguez,Ivan	2
Hundley,Nick	1
Molina,Yadier	1
Doumit,Ryan	1

1B - DME on Double Plays

Howard,Ryan	4
Loney,James	2
Berkman,Lance	2
Aurilia,Rich	2
Pujols,Albert	2
Delgado,Carlos	2
Fielder,Prince	2
Jackson,Conor	2
Pena,Carlos	2
Young,Dmitri	2

2B - DME on Double Plays

Weeks,Rickie	12
Utley,Chase	9
Gonzalez,Edgar	6
Iwamura,Akinori	6
Miles,Aaron	5
Phillips,Brandon	5
Uggla,Dan	5
6 tied with	4

3B - DME on Double Plays

Cantu,Jorge	4
Lamb,Mike	3
Reynolds,Mark	3
Encarnacion,Edwin	3
13 tied with	2

SS - DME on Double Plays

Ramirez,Hanley	6
Hardy,J.J.	5
Renteria,Edgar	4
Tulowitzki,Troy	4
Betancourt,Yuniesky	4
Guzman,Cristian	4
Izturis,Cesar	4
8 tied with	3

P - DME on Double Plays

Cook,Aaron	2
27 tied with	1

C - DME on Double Plays

2008 Net (GFP minus DME) Double Plays

1B - Net Double Plays

Barton,Daric	+3
Gonzalez,Adrian	+2
Garko,Ryan	+2
Cabrera,Miguel	+2
Sandoval,Pablo	+2
Overbay,Lyle	+2
Cantu,Jorge	+2
10 tied with	+1

2B - Net Double Plays

Roberts,Brian	+15
Kendrick,Howie	+8
Pedroia,Dustin	+8
Ramirez,Alexei	+7
Iwamura,Akinori	+7
Sanchez,Freddy	+7
Phillips,Brandon	+7
Lopez,Jose	+7
Hudson,Orlando	+7
5 tied with	+6

3B - Net Double Plays

Crede,Joe	+6
Beltre,Adrian	+4
Hannahan,Jack	+4
Inge,Brandon	+3
Rodriguez,Alex	+3
Blake,Casey	+2
Longoria,Evan	+2
Marte,Andy	+2
17 tied with	+1

SS - Net Double Plays

Young,Michael	+14
Aybar,Erick	+13
Tejada,Miguel	+11
Aviles,Mike	+11
Hardy,J.J.	+10
Wilson,Jack	+8
5 tied with	+7

P - Net Double Plays

Floyd,Gavin	+2
29 tied with	+1

C - Net Double Plays

Martin,Russell	+2
Rodriguez,Ivan	+2
Kendall,Jason	+2
Doumit,Ryan	+1
Molina,Yadier	+1
Hundley,Nick	+1

2008 GFP and DME on Preventing Extra Bases

1B - GFP on Extra Bases

Sexson,Richie	3
Teixeira,Mark	3
Votto,Joey	2
Tatis,Fernando	2
Pena,Carlos	2
Kotchman,Casey	2
16 tied with	1

2B - GFP on Extra Bases

Phillips,Brandon	5
Lopez,Jose	5
Weeks,Rickie	3
8 tied with	2

3B - GFP on Extra Bases

Longoria,Evan	7
Wright,David	6
Rodriguez,Alex	6
Kouzmanoff,Kevin	5
LaRoche,Andy	5
Encarnacion,Edwin	4
Dobbs,Greg	4
Bautista,Jose	4
Lamb,Mike	4
Beltre,Adrian	4

SS - GFP on Extra Bases

Rollins,Jimmy	5
Crosby,Bobby	5
Greene,Khalil	5
Theriot,Ryan	5
Reyes,Jose	4
6 tied with	3

LF - GFP on Extra Bases

Burrell,Pat	10
Holliday,Matt	9
Young,Delmon	7
Willingham,Josh	6
Ibanez,Raul	6
Bay,Jason	5
Braun,Ryan	4
Anderson,Garret	4
Crawford,Carl	4
Gonzalez,Luis	4

CF - GFP on Extra Bases

Gomez,Carlos	5
Jones,Adam	4
Rowand,Aaron	4
Cabrera,Melky	4
Blanco,Gregor	3
Cameron,Mike	3
Wells,Vernon	3
Hamilton,Josh	3
16 tied with	2

RF - GFP on Extra Bases

Fukudome,Kosuke	8
Dye,Jermaine	8
Markakis,Nick	8
Gutierrez,Franklin	7
Griffey Jr.,Ken	7
Rios,Alex	5
Hamilton,Josh	5
Pence,Hunter	5
Francoeur,Jeff	5
5 tied with	4

1B - DME on Extra Bases

Aurilia,Rich	1
Broussard,Ben	1
Lo Duca,Paul	1

2B - DME on Extra Bases

Lopez,Jose	2
Johnson,Kelly	2
Pedroia,Dustin	1
Durham,Ray	1
DeWitt,Blake	1
Eckstein,David	1
Castillo,Luis	1
Hudson,Orlando	1
Grudzielanek,Mark	1
Cano,Robinson	1

3B - DME on Extra Bases

Freel,Ryan	1
Zimmerman,Ryan	1
Helms,Wes	1

SS - DME on Extra Bases

Bynum,Freddie	1
Punto,Nick	1
Berroa,Angel	1
Ochoa,Ivan	1
Gonzalez,Edgar	1
Young,Michael	1
Burriss,Emmanuel	1

LF - DME on Extra Bases

Young,Delmon	11
Lewis,Fred	8
Ibanez,Raul	6
Thames,Marcus	6
Holliday,Matt	6
Headley,Chase	5
Boggs,Brandon	5
Dunn,Adam	5
11 tied with	3

CF - DME on Extra Bases

Milledge,Lastings	11
Upton,B.J.	11
Gomez,Carlos	10
Young,Chris	9
Beltran,Carlos	6
Jones,Adam	5
7 tied with	4

RF - DME on Extra Bases

Hawpe,Brad	9
Upton,Justin	8
Bruce,Jay	6
Francoeur,Jeff	5
Jenkins,Geoff	5
Giles,Brian	5
Abreu,Bobby	5
Choo,Shin-Soo	5
7 tied with	4

2008 Net (GFP minus DME) Preventing Extra Bases

1B - Net Extra Bases

Sexson,Richie	+3
Teixeira,Mark	+3
Pena,Carlos	+2
Kotchman,Casey	+2
Tatis,Fernando	+2
Votto,Joey	+2
15 tied with	+1

2B - Net Extra Bases

Phillips,Brandon	+5
Weeks,Rickie	+3
Lopez,Jose	+3
Ellis,Mark	+2
Velez,Eugenio	+2
Polanco,Placido	+2
Scutaro,Marco	+2
Roberts,Brian	+2
24 tied with	+1

3B - Net Extra Bases

Longoria,Evan	+7
Rodriguez,Alex	+6
Wright,David	+6
Kouzmanoff,Kevin	+5
LaRoche,Andy	+5
Encarnacion,Edwin	+4
Lamb,Mike	+4
Bautista,Jose	+4
Beltre,Adrian	+4
Dobbs,Greg	+4

SS - Net Extra Bases

Crosby,Bobby	+5
Rollins,Jimmy	+5
Theriot,Ryan	+5
Greene,Khalil	+5
Reyes,Jose	+4
6 tied with	+3

LF - Net Extra Bases

Burrell,Pat	+7
Willingham,Josh	+6
Anderson,Garret	+4
Holliday,Matt	+3
Gonzalez,Luis	+3
9 tied with	+2

CF - Net Extra Bases

Blanco,Gregor	+3
Cabrera,Melky	+2
Anderson,Brian	+2
Ellsbury,Jacoby	+2
16 tied with	+1

RF - Net Extra Bases

Dye,Jermaine	+7
Markakis,Nick	+5
Hamilton,Josh	+5
Fukudome,Kosuke	+5
Griffey Jr.,Ken	+4
Gutierrez,Franklin	+4
Span,Denard	+3
Rios,Alex	+3
Chavez,Endy	+3
3 tied with	+2

2008 GFP, DME, and Net on Fences and Walls

LF - GFP on Fences and Walls	
Payton,Jay	2
10 tied with	1

CF - GFP on Fences and Walls	
Beltran,Carlos	2
Patterson,Corey	2
Hunter,Torii	2
10 tied with	1

RF - GFP on Fences and Walls	
Span,Denard	4
Ellsbury,Jacoby	2
Gutierrez,Franklin	2
Guerrero,Vladimir	2
Snider,Travis	1
Bruce,Jay	1
Sweeney,Ryan	1
Hart,Corey	1
Suzuki,Ichiro	1

LF - DME on Fences and Walls	
Lee,Carlos	5
Young,Delmon	5
Scott,Luke	4
Murphy,Daniel	4
Soriano,Alfonso	4
Ibanez,Raul	4
Lewis,Fred	4
6 tied with	3

CF - DME on Fences and Walls	
McLouth,Nate	7
Upton,B.J.	6
Rowand,Aaron	6
Young,Chris	6
Jones,Adam	5
Hunter,Torii	5
Hamilton,Josh	5
Taveras,Willy	5
Sizemore,Grady	5
3 tied with	4

RF - DME on Fences and Walls	
Abreu,Bobby	8
Hawpe,Brad	8
Pence,Hunter	6
Teahen,Mark	6
Upton,Justin	6
Ordonez,Magglio	5
Hart,Corey	5
Dukes,Elijah	4
Guerrero,Vladimir	4
10 tied with	3

LF - Net Fences and Walls	
Langerhans,Ryan	+1
Werth,Jayson	+1
Gload,Ross	+1
Guillen,Jose	+1
Pierre,Juan	+1
Payton,Jay	0
Infante,Omar	0
Kapler,Gabe	0
Bay,Jason	0
39 tied with	-1

CF - Net Fences and Walls	
Patterson,Corey	+1
Willits,Reggie	+1
Maier,Mitch	+1
Gardner,Brett	+1
Pie,Felix	+1
Beltran,Carlos	0
Gutierrez,Franklin	0
22 tied with	-1

RF - Net Fences and Walls	
Span,Denard	+2
Gutierrez,Franklin	+2
Ellsbury,Jacoby	+2
Snider,Travis	+1
Sweeney,Ryan	+1
20 tied with	-1

2008 Defensive Misplays on Covering Bases

1B - DME on Covering Bases

Cabrera,Miguel	5
Gonzalez,Adrian	3
Bowker,John	3
Fielder,Prince	3
Tracy,Chad	3
LaRoche,Adam	3
7 tied with	2

2B - DME on Covering Bases

Johnson,Kelly	4
Utley,Chase	3
Grudzielanek,Mark	2
Fontenot,Mike	2
Hudson,Orlando	2
Uggla,Dan	2
Ellis,Mark	2
DeRosa,Mark	2
16 tied with	1

3B - DME on Covering Bases

Figgins,Chone	2
13 tied with	1

SS - DME on Covering Bases

Reyes,Jose	2
Theriot,Ryan	2
Infante,Omar	2
Cabrera,Orlando	2
Hu,Chin-lung	2
16 tied with	1

P - DME on Covering Bases

Olsen,Scott	3
Sabathia,CC	3
Cabrera,Daniel	3
Lincecum,Tim	3
Perez,Odalis	3
10 tied with	2

C - DME on Covering Bases

Suzuki,Kurt	1
Barrett,Michael	1

2008 Catcher Specific Plays

Catcher Stolen Bases and Pickoffs GFP	
Molina,Yadier	7
Chavez,Raul	3
Mathis,Jeff	3
Barajas,Rod	2
Ruiz,Carlos	2
McCann,Brian	2
20 tied with	1

Catcher Wild Pitches GFP	
Suzuki,Kurt	9
Johjima,Kenji	8
Molina,Bengie	8
Soto,Geovany	5
Martin,Russell	4
Schneider,Brian	4
Inge,Brandon	4
Hundley,Nick	3
Doumit,Ryan	3
Iannetta,Chris	3

Catcher Plate Blocks GFP	
Suzuki,Kurt	4
Molina,Yadier	4
Johjima,Kenji	4
Martin,Russell	4
Flores,Jesus	4
Shoppach,Kelly	4
Barajas,Rod	4
Martinez,Victor	4
3 tied with	3

Catcher Pitch Blocks GFP	
Kendall,Jason	497
Suzuki,Kurt	425
Martin,Russell	418
Mathis,Jeff	395
Molina,Yadier	377
Soto,Geovany	370
Varitek,Jason	356
Molina,Bengie	350
Doumit,Ryan	346
Hernandez,Ramon	345

Catcher Stolen Bases and Pickoffs DME	
Hernandez,Ramon	7
Rodriguez,Ivan	6
Ross,David	6
Cash,Kevin	6
McCann,Brian	6
Baker,John	6
Snyder,Chris	5
Kendall,Jason	5
Napoli,Mike	5
3 tied with	4

Catcher Wild Pitches DME	
Molina,Bengie	41
Mauer,Joe	36
Hernandez,Ramon	34
Kendall,Jason	33
Doumit,Ryan	32
Martin,Russell	31
Molina,Yadier	31
Pierzynski,A.J.	31
3 tied with	29

Pitcher Defense

Each year, pitcher defense gets about five minutes of attention when the Gold Gloves are announced. Then the topic is shelved for another year. We decided to dust this topic off and take a closer look. Let me once again share with you what I wrote as a Stat of the Week and later published in *The Bill James Handbook 2009*.

Who are the best fielding pitchers?

September 18, 2008

Greg Maddux has won the National League Gold Glove Award for pitchers in 17 of the last 18 years. The American League Award has gone to Kenny Rogers in five of the last eight years. But are they truly the best fielding pitchers in baseball? Were they really the best in each and every year that they won? Aren't these two guys getting pretty old? Aren't there some younger studs out there to take their places?

Surely there must be other pitchers who are good fielders that should have won a few of those awards. No other award has a string of winners like this. Think of the MVP Award, the Cy Young Award, the Silver Slugger Award, Relief Man of the Year Award, etc. The key difference between these awards and the Gold Glove awards is that statistics are much more strongly considered. Gold Glove voters historically have not relied much on fielding statistics. With good reason: There haven't been many new reliable statistics in fielding for 100 years.

Until now (I hope). There are several new systems out there, and the Plus/Minus System from my book, The Fielding Bible, *seems to be working pretty well. Video Scouts at Baseball Info Solutions chart each and every batted ball, including batted ball speed, type and direction. Using that information, the Plus/Minus System determines how well each fielder handles batted balls within each category compared to other fielders. A plus five (+5) in the system, for example, says this particular* fielder successfully handled five more balls than the average fielder at his position.

When we published the first volume of The Fielding Bible *three years ago, we hadn't yet developed a Plus/Minus System for pitchers. But we have since then. Complete plus/minus results for pitchers will be available in* The Fielding Bible—Volume II, *available in February of 2009. So let's see how Maddux and Rogers come out when measured by that system.*

Here's the surprise: Greg Maddux and Kenny Rogers are far and away the two best fielding pitchers in the Plus/Minus System since we started it in 2003. Here are the Plus/Minus leaders for pitchers since 2003:

Greg Maddux	+56
Kenny Rogers	+53
Livan Hernandez	+30

It is incredible that Maddux and Rogers are number one and number two while the number three guy, Livan Hernandez, is a very distant third. This says two things to me: 1) The Gold Glove voters know what they're doing when it comes to pitchers. Relying primarily on visual evidence, they've seen the excellent glove work by Maddux and Rogers. 2) The Plus/Minus System works. It comes up with the same answers as the Gold Glove voters.

Of course, there are some huge exceptions to this correlation. For example, Derek Jeter has won three Gold Gloves but never fares well in the Plus/Minus System, and Adam Everett has worn four "Plus/Minus Crowns" as the highest-rated shortstop in baseball but has never won a Gold Glove.

Lest you think that despite having the highest 6-year plus/minus numbers doesn't necessarily mean that Maddux and Rogers should win nearly every year, here are their yearly numbers, along with their rank in all of

Major League Baseball and their Gold Gloves (GG) and Fielding Bible Awards (FBA).

	Maddux			Rogers		
	+/-	Rank	Award	+/-	Rank	Award
2003	+7	3		+6	6	
2004	+10	2	GG	+10	4	GG
2005	+6	6	GG	+12	1	GG
2006	+10	1	GG, FBA	+8	3	GG
2007	+10	1	GG	+1	---	
2008	+13	2	tba	+16	1	tba

* Data through 9/15/08, courtesy Baseball Info Solutions.

Rogers or Maddux has had the highest plus/minus figure among pitchers in each of the last four years. They're not just getting older, they're getting better. Despite his injuries, age, and less-effective pitching, Kenny Rogers has the highest figure again this year, with Maddux right behind him.

Giving the Gold Gloves to Maddux in the National League and Rogers in the American is a no-brainer once again. But who should win The Fielding Bible Award, which only recognizes one winner in all of Major League Baseball? That's easy too. It's Kenny Rogers, but not simply because his plus/minus figure is slightly better. It's because of his control of the running game. Rogers is exceptionally good at it, while Maddux is notoriously bad. Here are the figures:

Rogers—only three attempted stolen bases all season, two of them caught, plus three runners picked off. Maddux—26 attempted steals, only three caught, no runners picked off.

In early November, we'll see what both the Gold Glove and Fielding Bible Award voters have to say.

Here's what the voters decided. The Fielding Bible Award went to Kenny Rogers. The Gold Glove voters chose Greg Maddux in the National League and Mike Mussina in the American. (The Fielding Bible Award goes to one player per position throughout baseball, while one player per position from each league wins a Gold Glove.) Before commenting on the merits of these winners, first the research. We've studied pitcher defense extensively since my comments were written.

Pitcher Plus/Minus and Runs Saved

As we've done throughout this book, we've converted plus/minus values to runs saved. For pitchers, it works out almost exactly the same as it does for the other two middle infielders. (Yes, I'm calling a pitcher a middle infielder—what would you call him?) After looking at detailed play-by-play information and combining it with the expected runs in the run matrix chart, we found that each plus/minus point is worth .75 runs. Shortstops and second basemen came out almost exactly the same, .76 runs per plus/minus point.

Greg Maddux wound up with a plus/minus value of +14 for the 2008 season. To translate to runs, we multiply by .75 to get 11 (rounded up from 10.5). That means that Greg Maddux saved 11 runs defensively for the two teams he played for in 2008. That's in comparison to what an "average" pitcher would do with the same types of batted balls hit to him. The 11 plus/minus runs saved for Maddux in 2008 was second only to Kenny Rogers. Rogers had a plus/minus figure of +16 which translates to 12 runs saved.

Controlling the Running Game

Who has greater control of the running game in baseball, the pitcher or the catcher? Obviously the strength of the catcher's arm is a key, as is the quickness of his release and the accuracy of his throws. But the pitcher comes into play as well. How well does he hold the runner? How often does he make throws to first? How quick is his release to the plate? How good is his pickoff move and how often does he nab runners with that move? Do more or fewer runners run against him than other pitchers? Are more (or less) caught?

Looking at the data from the last six years, the best and worst catchers in baseball had these caught stealing rates:

Best Catcher Caught Stealing Rates

Yadier Molina	43%
Jose Molina	40%
Henry Blanco	38%
Gerald Laird	37%
Brian Schneider	35%
David Ross	35%

Worst Catcher Caught Stealing Rates

Josh Bard	15%
Michael Barrett	18%
A.J. Pierzynski	18%
Chad Moeller	19%
Johnny Estrada	19%
Gregg Zaun	19%

Now let's look at the best and worst pitchers in controlling the running game:

Best Pitcher Caught Stealing Rates

Brandon Backe	66%
Kenny Rogers	58%
Mark Buehrle	56%
Carlos Zambrano	55%
Justin Verlander	52%
Adam Wainwright	52%

Worst Pitcher Caught Stealing Rates

Chris Young	10%
Tim Lincecum	14%
Kevin Millwood	14%
Ted Lilly	18%
Pedro Martinez	18%
Jake Peavy	18%

What you can clearly see here is that the spread between the best and worst pitchers is bigger than the spread between the best and worst catchers. When I look at this, it confirms to me what most people can see by watching baseball closely: the pitcher has greater control of the running game than the catcher.

If you look at stolen base frequency, you see an even stronger control of the running game by pitchers. Fewer runners run on Pudge Rodriguez than other catchers. But the magnitude of the difference compared to pitchers is far smaller. Let's compare Pudge to Mike Piazza, who was known for his lack of arm strength. In their most extreme seasons Pudge allowed about half of the number of stolen base attempts as Piazza. The difference between the most extreme pitchers is much larger. In 2008, for example, in about the same number of innings, Cliff Lee only allowed three stolen base attempts while Gavin Floyd allowed 42.

There's a big irony here when it comes to Gold Glove voting. When the voters vote for catcher Gold Gloves, they put a strong emphasis on the catcher's throwing ability. I would say an over-emphasis. But when voting for pitcher Gold Gloves, they put almost zero emphasis on the pitcher's ability to control the running game. Yet we see here that pitchers have a bigger influence on the running game.

For me, this stops here and now. When I've been considering my Fielding Bible Award ballots I certainly have been factoring in the pitcher's ability to control the running game, but I've only been doing it indirectly. Even in the Stat of the Week article I wrote, I said Greg Maddux was a no-brainer to win the 2008 award. Well, I was the no-brainer to write that. Greg Maddux is legendary for his inability to control basestealers.

How do we make this stop? We do what we've been doing in this book all along. We measure runs saved.

Stolen Base Runs Saved for Pitchers

The mission is to convert pitcher stolen base data into runs saved. To do this, we need to break it into two components, caught stealing rate and stolen base frequency, just as we looked at them when we were comparing catchers and pitchers.

Before getting into the tedious details, I'm going to give you the results for the six most extreme pitchers in baseball. There were four pitchers who saved four or more runs for their teams by controlling the running game (Greg Smith, Dallas Braden, Aaron Cook and Mark Buehrle). There were two pitchers who cost their team at least four runs (Gavin Floyd and Jair Jurrjens). Here's a complete chart of their stolen base numbers and the runs associated with those numbers:

Pitcher	SB Opps	SB	CCS	PCS	PPO	Runs Saved		
						CS/PO	Freq	Tot
Greg Smith, Oak	213	11	1	11	5	6	0	6
Dallas Braden, Oak	88	1	2	0	7	4	0	4
Aaron Cook, Col	204	5	8	0	4	4	0	4
Mark Buehrle, CWS	232	5	2	5	2	3	1	4
Jair Jurrjens, Atl	201	28	3	0	0	-3	-1	-4
Gavin Floyd, CWS	188	38	3	1	0	-3	-2	-5

Let's go through the chart. Stolen Base Opportunities (SB Opps) are defined as the number of times a runner was on first base with second base open when that pitcher was on the mound. We are ignoring possible opportunities to steal second or home. For simplicity, we didn't use them because steals of third and home are so infrequent compared to second base steals. Stolen Bases (SB) include all bases stolen while that pitcher was on the mound. Runners caught stealing are broken between those where the catcher made the throw

(CCS), and those where the pitcher made the throw and the catcher was not involved (PCS). Pitcher pickoffs are abbreviated as PPO. PCS and PPO are pretty much the same thing. The pitcher throws over to the base and runner is out. But technically, it's called a caught stealing if the runner makes any movement to the next base. Otherwise it's a pickoff.

The first component of Pitcher Stolen Base Runs Saved is calculated based on how often runners were caught by way of a catcher caught stealing, pitcher caught stealing, or pitcher pickoff (CS/PO). The second component is based on how often runners attempt to steal on the pitcher (Freq).

Considering the first component, look at Greg Smith. Eleven runners caught stealing on his throws to the base, and another five picked off. Very impressive. No wonder he comes out on top of the CS/PO Rate component (and overall as well).

Interesting side note: Mark Buehrle and Gavin Floyd, two extremes in controlling the running game, both pitch for the same team, the Chicago White Sox. Their catcher, A.J. Pierzynski, benefits when Buehrle is on the mound and suffers with Floyd pitching. In the catcher defense section we talk about how we adjust for this when evaluating catcher stolen base defense. (Oh, and look at the next table. Another Sox pitcher, John Danks, isn't exactly helping A.J. out either.)

The Frequency component is intriguing as well. Here are the pitchers who have the most and least stolen base attempts per opportunity (100 or more opportunities).

Most and Fewest Stolen Base Attempts per Opportunity - 2008

	SB Opps	Attempts	Att/Opp
Tim Wakefield, Bos	160	37	23.1%
Gavin Floyd, CWS	188	42	22.3
Scott Feldman, Tex	148	27	18.2
Greg Maddux, SD-LAD	165	29	17.6
John Danks, CWS	177	31	17.5
Nick Blackburn, Min	202	4	2.0%
Kenny Rogers, Det	176	3	1.7
Cliff Lee, Cle	206	3	1.5
Roy Oswalt, Hou	199	2	1.0
Braden Looper, StL	168	1	0.6

Only one stolen base attempt against Braden Looper all year. And it's amazing that three of the best five pitchers at holding runners are right-handed (Blackburn,

Oswalt, Looper).

Let me take you through how we get from these stolen base numbers to Stolen Base Defensive Runs Saved. Looking at the expected number of runs scored before and after each stolen base related event, we found the following values:

Increase in Run Expectancy

Stolen Base	0.19 runs
Caught Stealing/Pickoff	-0.43 runs

We then assigned 65% of the responsibility for stolen bases and catcher caught stealing to the pitcher and 35% to the catcher. Pitcher caught stealing and pickoffs were assigned as 100% for the pitcher. Stolen bases are counted as -0.19 x .65 x SB (restated as negative because we're calling it runs saved). Catcher caught stealing are 0.43 x .65 x CCS. Pitcher caught stealing and pickoffs are done as .43 x PCS and .43 x PPO. Add these all up and you get the first component of runs saved for pitchers.

For the frequency component, we look at their frequency rate compared to league average. If their frequency is above league average, they lose the other 35% of the runs we were attributing to the catcher for attempts above league average. If they are below league average in frequency, they get credit for the league run value of a stolen base attempt for each attempt they are below average. I won't bore you to death going through a detailed calculation.

Total Defensive Runs Saved for Pitchers

Now we put plus/minus runs saved together with stolen base runs saved to get Defensive Runs Saved for pitchers. Let's look at the last six years of Greg Maddux's career:

Greg Maddux

	Plus/Minus Runs Saved	Stolen Base Runs Saved	Total Runs Saved
2003	5	-2	3
2004	7	-2	5
2005	4	-4	0
2006	8	-4	4
2007	8	-5	3
2008	10	-3	7
Total	42	-20	22

Greg Maddux had the most plus/minus runs saved in baseball over the six years. His actual plus/minus of +54 translated into the 42 runs saved. But his inability to control the running game gave back nearly half those runs. Nevertheless, his net total of 22 runs saved is still the fifth highest total out of the 175 pitchers with the most innings in those six years (who were active in 2008). That's how good he was on comebackers hit anywhere near him.

Here's the complete top ten list:

Defensive Runs Saved Last Six Years

1	Kenny Rogers	50
2	Mark Buehrle	34
3	Tom Glavine	30
4	Livan Hernandez	27
5	Greg Maddux	22
	Jake Westbrook	22
7	Dontrelle Willis	21
8	Johan Santana	20
9	Jon Garland	19
10	Zach Duke	18
	Mark Mulder	18

This list shows the best defensive pitchers in baseball over the last six years.

In 2008 Rogers led the league in most defensive runs saved (15) for the year, just as he did in 2006 and 2004. Fielding Bible Award voters got it right. But the Gold Glove voters gave their American League award to Mike Mussina instead. Moose only had two defensive runs saved in 2008, ranking number 31 among 175 pitchers. Not a Gold Glove performance. But he pitched better than Rogers. That's why I think he got the Gold Glove award over the Gambler. It's funny, because Rogers won a Gold Glove in five of the previous eight years, and the voters sure like to give the pitching Gold Glove consistently to the same person. Yet, Rogers didn't get the award. The only explanation is his pitching. He had his worst year in a long time, while Mussina went 20 and 9. Mussina gets his seventh Gold Glove, but his first since 2003. Just as there is a minimum hitting standard to win a Gold Glove, there appears to be one for pitching as well. That's my opinion; I could be wrong.

In the National League Maddux had seven defensive runs saved, and despite his stolen base woes, his performance was good for third place in baseball overall. Plus, it was the best figure in the National League. He should have and did win the NL Gold Glove.

When I said Maddux should win the Gold Glove in my Stat of the Week, I didn't know all this. Even a blind dog finds a bone once in a while.

Rogers was ranked first in baseball by a wide margin with 15 defensive runs saved in 2008. Maddux was third with seven. Eight defensive runs saved by Jesse Litsch of Toronto allowed him to sneak between Rogers and Maddux for second place.

For the complete picture of runs saved by pitchers, take a look at the one-year and six-year registers. Because of the number of pitchers, we don't show separate figures for plus/minus runs saved and stolen base runs saved. But it's not hard to figure from each chart. To get plus/minus runs saved, multiply plus/minus by .75. To get stolen base runs saved, take total runs saved (RS) and subtract plus/minus runs saved.

McCarver and Carlton

Bill James

For some reason I got interested in the issue of Tim McCarver and Steve Carlton. I am always trying to figure out some way to get a better handle on catcher's defense. What I am trying to get to here is the question of whether there is real and substantial reason to credit some of Steve Carlton's success on the mound to Tim McCarver being behind the mask. Of course I am old and I remember all of this stuff, so let me recount the history very briefly for those of you who are younger or weren't paying attention.

Tim McCarver

Tim McCarver I think was a bonus baby, back in the days before the amateur draft started in the mid-sixties. He was signed by the Cardinals as a 17-year-old in 1959, got major league roster time immediately because the rules required it, and reached the majors for real in 1963, still only 21 years old.

The Cardinals weren't desperate for catching. Their catchers in 1962 (Gene Oliver and Carl Sawatski) hit .259 with 25 homers, 81 RBI and 78 walks, not counting what they contributed as pinch hitters. They were both big, powerful guys who could put a hurt on a baseball, and they were not totally inept in the field. The Cardinals in '62 allowed only 73 stolen bases with 39 runners caught stealing—very decent numbers.

McCarver was a lot quicker behind the plate and threw better at that time and hit for a better average, so he won the job—plus, even as a very young player, McCarver always got great reviews for his ability to work with pitchers. The Cardinals in those years had a good farm system, producing a lot of talent. They won the National League in 1964, 1967 and 1968, and won the World Series in '64 and '67.

One of the young players they produced was Steve Carlton, who came up in '65. He was a factor on the powerhouse Cardinals of the sixties, but he wasn't a star at that time. He wasn't on the '64 team at all, and was a third starter type on the '67 and '68 teams, although everybody knew he had good stuff.

The Cardinals didn't win in '69, and after the '69 season their ownership, in a display of dazzling obtuseness, decided to blow up the team. The Cardinals produced more talent in the 1970s than they had in the 1960s, but they spent the entire decade fighting with their team over money, rules and haircuts. McCarver by '69 had had some shoulder issues and didn't throw well anymore, plus of course the quickness of his youth had gotten away from him, so by 1969 he was a smart veteran catcher who didn't throw too well anymore and had had back-to-back disappointing seasons with the bat. The Cardinals decided to move Joe Torre, an ex-catcher who was playing first base for them, back behind the plate.

McCarver bounced around, going to Philadelphia, where he was briefly re-united with Steve Carlton, then to Montreal, back to St. Louis (to try to tutor the young Ted Simmons and to heal the wounds left by his departure four years earlier), and then to Boston. Released by the Red Sox in June, 1975, McCarver signed with the Phillies on July 1.

Steve Carlton

Steve Carlton is one of the compelling personalities of baseball history. Similar in build to Sandy Koufax, he was the Miss America of scouting: a big lefty with a natural motion and a big-time fastball. He got to the majors quickly and with unreliable location, but in 1969 he was 17-11 with the second-best ERA in the majors, 2.17.

McCarver was traded that winter, and Carlton, for no apparent reason, took a huge step backward in 1970, losing 19 games. Joe Torre, a great hitter and a great manager, was never intended by God to be a catcher. Torre and Carlton just didn't work. In 1971 Torre moved to third base and won the NL MVP Award, while Carlton, working with Ted Simmons, won 20 games.

In February, 1972, baseball was in the middle of its first serious labor confrontation in sixty years, and Carlton was refusing to sign with the Cardinals. The Cardinals, featuring the same genius that they would show throughout the decade, traded Carlton to the Phillies for Rick Wise, and told the press loudly and repeatedly that Carlton was nothing special, that he had been lucky to win 20 games and that Rick Wise was just as good a pitcher and a much better hitter.

Carlton had a historic year. Pitching 346 innings—in a strike-shortened season—Carlton won 27 games for a terrible, terrible, terrible team. He struck out 310 batters and had a 1.97 ERA. He lost five straight games in May, dropping him to 5-6 at the end of May, then got onto a fantastic roll, going 4-0 in June, 6-0 in July, 6-2 in August, 5-2 in September, and winning his only start in October.

Carlton had gotten into Eastern philosophy, and, when he was on a roll, he talked about that quite a bit with the press and through the media, how this had helped him to overcome the negativity that sometimes in the past had weighed him down. But in '73, Negativity had a great year. Carlton, though still an above-average pitcher, lost 20 games. He was booed sometimes in Veteran's Stadium, and he was ridiculed in a few newspaper articles for the philosophical insights that had been widely applauded the year before.

Carlton stopped talking to the press, a practice about which he would become increasingly insistent over the next ten years. Sealed off from the press, he came to be perceived, perhaps unfairly, as arrogant and hostile. At the same time, Carlton had developed some *serious* workout habits. He worked harder at staying in shape than anyone in baseball. He would climb into a vat of dry rice, up to his neck, and exercise inside the rice. He ate carefully. He emerged gradually, over the years, as the strongest man in baseball. Gus Hoefling, his trainer during his glory years, insisted that Carlton was as strong as an NFL linebacker, with the focus on building up his muscles on his back and shoulders.

The Phillies, winners of only 59 games in 1972, moved gradually toward contention: 71 wins in '73, 80 in '74, 86 in '75. But Carlton, despite his overpowering stuff, despite his superb conditioning and despite his history of success, was not dominating. After going 13-20 in 1973 he was 16-13 in '74, and was 6-6 through June of 1975.

Also, Phillies catcher Bob Boone was breaking down. The Phillies had been catching him every day—145 games in 1973, 146 in '74. He opened the '75 season hitting over .300 through May, still playing almost every day, and then just hit the wall in June. I'm sure injuries played some role in it, don't know what they were, but in any case he just *entirely* stopped hitting. It began to occur to the Phillies that letting the young catcher play every game might not be the smartest thing they could do.

McCarver and Carlton

It occurred to somebody, then, that
a) Bob Boone needed some regular days off, and
b) One way to get him regular rest would be to sign McCarver to work with Steve Carlton.

This may have been Carlton's idea. Carlton had had a fine year working with McCarver in '69, and had gone south badly when McCarver left the Cardinals in '70. Anyway, they tried McCarver as Carlton's personal catcher in '75, with fairly good results, but McCarver didn't hit and couldn't throw anymore, so then for a time Johnny Oates was Carlton's catcher. Oates was traded, and at the start of '76 Bob Boone was back to catching Carlton and everybody else. Carlton in April of '76 was winless with an ERA of 12.00. They decided to try McCarver again.

For three years following that, the pairing of McCarver and Carlton clicked like Fred Astaire and Ginger Rogers. Carlton re-emerged as one of baseball's best pitchers. McCarver hit .299 in '76-'77 (97 for 324), with lots of walks giving him on-base percentages over .400 and almost as many RBI as walks; in the 324 at bats he had 24 doubles and 9 homers. The Phillies won the division both years. McCarver wasn't as good in '78, but the Phillies still won, and then he wasn't as good again in '79, and the Phillies didn't win. McCarver was released after the '79 season, although he was invited back for the stretch run in 1980.

Research

So I got interested in the question of whether or not we could really conclude, based on the data, that part of what made Carlton great was McCarver. I put Carlton's career record in a spreadsheet, and looked up the catcher for each appearance—the starting catcher, or the catcher who was in the game at the time Carlton entered, for the games that Carlton pitched in relief early and late in his career. (There were a handful of games in Carlton's career in which he worked with two different catchers, but I didn't get into that.)

Steve Carlton's Record With and Without Tim McCarver

Player	G	GS	IP	H	R	ER	BB	SO	W	L	Pct	ERA
McCarver	234	226	1676.0	1439	606	528	518	1287	119	67	.640	2.84
Others	507	483	3541.2	3233	1524	1336	1315	2849	210	177	.543	3.40

Carlton in his career was substantially better with McCarver as his catcher than with other catchers—a winning percentage almost a hundred points better and an ERA 56 points better.

Early in the '72 season, with Carlton pitching well but not winning consistently, the Phillies traded McCarver to Montreal for John Bateman, another veteran catcher. Bateman was Carlton's catcher—and the Phillies' catcher—when Carlton made his historic run in '72. With that exception (Bateman), Carlton had a better winning percentage and a better ERA with McCarver than with any other catcher.

OK, so Carlton was much better with McCarver than with other catchers. So what? What does that prove?

Actually, it doesn't prove anything. I was hoping that the data would shake out so that it could be analyzed to reach a definitive conclusion as to whether Carlton was better with McCarver or not. In fact, though, it doesn't. There are two possibilities:

   a) that Carlton was better because McCarver caught him, and

   b) that McCarver happened to catch Carlton when Carlton was having good years.

But which is it?

I think, in all honesty, that the better argument is for (a)—that McCarver made Carlton better.

McCarver met up with Carlton at three points in his career—

1) When Carlton first came to the majors,

2) In 1972, but only for 12 games in 1972, and

3) In 1975, at a time when Carlton was having trouble getting the momentum of his career re-established.

McCarver, being a little older than Carlton, was out of baseball before Carlton began his exit struggles, so McCarver did dodge those. But McCarver did not catch Carlton in 1980, when Carlton was the best pitcher in baseball, and he did not catch him while he was on his historic roll in 1972. He didn't catch him in '81 and '82, when Carlton was a combined 36-15.

McCarver caught Carlton in '69, when Carlton was 17-11 with a 2.17 ERA, but didn't catch him in 1970, when Carlton was 10-19 with a 3.73 ERA. Is that proof

that McCarver helped Carlton to succeed? No. But it seems to me that it's a point in favor of the argument.

There's actually more to it than just McCarver and Carlton. The '69 Cardinals, McCarver's last team there, had three young pitchers who would win 734 games among them—Carlton, Jerry Reuss and Mike Torrez. In '69, mostly with McCarver, they were a combined 28-15. In '70, without McCarver, they were 25-37, and the Cardinals gave them all away in the year after that. Maybe, if they had kept McCarver, it might have made a difference.

Maybe some of it is luck, but McCarver played for eight teams that won their league or division—the Cardinals in '64, '67 and '68, the Red Sox in '75, and the Phillies in '76, '77, '78 and '80.

In 1976 Bob Boone caught Carlton in four starts, during which Carlton was 0-1 with an ERA of 10.06, and McCarver caught him in 31 starts, during which Carlton was 20-6 with a 2.64 ERA. If there was more data like that, we would have no trouble concluding that McCarver was central to Carlton's success. But there isn't.

If we could aggregate 1969 and 1970 as one unit, and compare Carlton with McCarver and Carlton without McCarver within that unit, we would have no trouble concluding that McCarver was central to Carlton's success. But we can't.

If McCarver had caught Carlton when Carlton was winning every start in '72, perhaps we could conclude that McCarver was central to Carlton's success. But he wasn't.

All we can really say for sure is that it is reasonable, based on the record, to think that McCarver may have made Carlton better, but that there's no clear proof of it.

Carlton worked with 32 catchers in his major league career, of whom six were named "John"—John Bateman, Johnny Oates, Johnny Edwards, John Romano, John Wockenfuss, and John Russell. The other 26 were McCarver, Bob Boone, Bo Diaz, Ted Simmons, Ozzie Virgil, Joe Torre, Rick Dempsey, Darren Daulton, Mike Ryan, Keith Moreland, Dave Ricketts, Tim Laudner, Bob Melvin, Larry Cox, Chris Bando, Ron Karkovice, Jerry McNertney, Ron Hassey, Jim Essian, Tom Nieto, Andy Allanson, Sal Butera, Carlton Fisk, Pat Corrales, Bob

Uecker, and Bob Stinson. This chart summarizes the data catcher by catcher:

Player	G	IP	BB	SO	W	L	Pct	ERA
McCarver	234	1676.0	518	1287	119	67	.640	2.84
Boone	146	1080.0	404	904	69	46	.600	3.25
Diaz	79	603.0	181	555	38	27	.585	3.09
Simmons	47	357.2	130	223	22	14	.611	3.25
Virgil	40	260.2	110	187	14	13	.519	3.42
Bateman	27	235.0	58	188	20	4	.833	1.57
Torre	24	165.2	76	137	8	14	.364	4.07
Oates	15	107.2	47	93	6	7	.462	3.52
Dempsey	14	68.1	41	48	3	6	.333	5.16
Daulton	12	66.0	26	46	3	6	.333	5.54
Ryan	9	61.2	27	53	2	5	.286	4.99
Edwards	9	60.1	13	45	3	5	.375	2.55
Moreland	7	54.0	17	62	3	1	.750	1.33
Ricketts	9	46.1	10	48	2	3	.400	2.89
Laudner	7	28.1	12	12	1	3	.250	9.85
Melvin	6	30.0	16	18	1	3	.250	5.10
Cox	4	32.2	14	29	2	2	.500	2.48
Romano	5	31.1	6	23	3	1	.750	1.44
Wockenfuss	4	28.2	9	22	0	2	.000	4.08
Russell	5	24.1	21	24	1	2	.333	8.14
Bando	7	27.1	17	17	2	2	.500	6.26
Karkovice	4	27.1	11	14	3	1	.750	2.30
McNertney	3	23.2	19	25	2	1	.667	5.70
Hassey	4	24.0	9	18	1	1	.500	4.13
Essian	2	19.1	9	15	1	1	.500	1.40
Nieto	3	14.1	9	9	0	1	.000	3.14
Allanson	2	13.2	5	6	0	1	.000	4.61
Butera	3	10.0	7	4	0	2	.000	12.60
Fisk	2	12.0	5	8	0	1	.000	6.00
Corrales	2	11.2	5	4	0	1	.000	4.63
Uecker	5	10.0	0	10	0	0	.000	2.70
Stinson	1	7.0	1	2	0	1	.000	5.14

We have to note Carlton's remarkably poor records with most of the catchers with whom he worked only briefly. A little more than three-fourths of Carlton's career games were with one of six catchers—McCarver, Boone, Bo Diaz, Ted Simmons, Ozzie Virgil and John Bateman. He had winning records and ERAs no higher than 3.42 with each of those six, a total of 282-171, 2.98 ERA.

But that leaves 168 career games with 26 other catchers, and in those games Carlton's record was a remarkably bad 47-73, 4.21 ERA. Yes, some of those games—about 40% of them—did occur while Carlton's career was flaming out, but Carlton's "flameout" period, dating it to the beginning of 1985, is only 84 games, with a record of 16-37. And almost all of the games in '85 were with Ozzie Virgil and Bo Diaz, who were two of Carlton's "major" catchers. That leaves a lot of bad games there that aren't explained by the fact that he was pitching his way out of the league.

This chart gives Carlton's year-by-year record with McCarver catching and with other catchers.

Catcher	Year	G	IP	W	L	ERA
McCarver	1965	8	14	0	0	2.57
Uecker	1965	5	10	0	0	2.70
Ricketts	1965	2	1	0	0	0.00
Catcher	Year	G	IP	W	L	ERA
McCarver	1966	7	40	3	2	2.68
Corrales	1966	2	11	0	1	4.63
Catcher	Year	G	IP	W	L	ERA
McCarver	1967	20	126	9	5	3.44
Ricketts	1967	5	36	2	3	2.75
Romano	1967	5	31	3	1	1.44
Catcher	Year	G	IP	W	L	ERA
McCarver	1968	24	170	10	6	2.96
Edwards	1968	9	60	3	5	2.55
Ricketts	1968	1	2	0	0	21.60
Catcher	Year	G	IP	W	L	ERA
McCarver	1969	26	201	15	9	2.10
Torre	1969	4	27	2	2	3.33
Ricketts	1969	1	8	0	0	0.00
Catcher	Year	G	IP	W	L	ERA
Torre	1970	20	139	6	12	4.22
Simmons	1970	14	115	4	7	3.13
Catcher	Year	G	IP	W	L	ERA
Simmons	1971	33	243	18	7	3.30
McNertney	1971	3	24	2	1	5.70
Stinson	1971	1	7	0	1	5.14
Catcher	Year	G	IP	W	L	ERA
Bateman	1972	27	235	20	4	1.57
McCarver	1972	12	100	6	5	2.52
Ryan	1972	2	11	1	1	5.56

Catcher	Year	G	IP	W	L	ERA
Boone	1973	33	243	12	16	3.70
Ryan	1973	7	50	1	4	4.86

Catcher	Year	G	IP	W	L	ERA
Boone	1974	33	239	13	10	3.46
Cox	1974	4	33	2	2	2.48
Essian	1974	2	19	1	1	1.40

Catcher	Year	G	IP	W	L	ERA
Oates	1975	15	107	6	7	3.52
Boone	1975	13	86	5	5	3.66
McCarver	**1975**	**9**	**62**	**4**	**2**	**3.48**

Catcher	Year	G	IP	W	L	ERA
McCarver	**1976**	**31**	**236**	**20**	**6**	**2.64**
Boone	1976	4	17	0	1	10.06

Catcher	Year	G	IP	W	L	ERA
McCarver	**1977**	**36**	**283**	**23**	**10**	**2.64**

Catcher	Year	G	IP	W	L	ERA
McCarver	**1978**	**34**	**247**	**16**	**13**	**2.84**

Catcher	Year	G	IP	W	L	ERA
McCarver	**1979**	**27**	**196**	**13**	**9**	**3.62**
Boone	1979	8	55	5	2	3.62

Catcher	Year	G	IP	W	L	ERA
Boone	1980	38	304	24	9	2.34

Catcher	Year	G	IP	W	L	ERA
Boone	1981	17	136	10	3	2.85
Moreland	1981	7	54	3	1	1.33

Catcher	Year	G	IP	W	L	ERA
Diaz	1982	36	280	22	10	3.15
Virgil	1982	2	16	1	1	2.25

Catcher	Year	G	IP	W	L	ERA
Diaz	1983	35	271	14	15	3.08
Virgil	1983	2	12	1	1	3.65

Catcher	Year	G	IP	W	L	ERA
Virgil	1984	24	164	11	5	3.85
Diaz	1984	5	36	2	0	1.96
Wockenfuss	1984	4	28	0	2	4.08

Catcher	Year	G	IP	W	L	ERA
Virgil	1985	11	65	1	5	2.37
Diaz	1985	3	15	0	2	4.70
Daulton	1985	2	12	0	1	6.75

Catcher	Year	G	IP	W	L	ERA
Daulton	1986	10	55	3	5	5.27
Melvin	1986	6	30	1	3	5.10
Karkovice	1986	4	27	3	1	2.30
Hassey	1986	4	24	1	1	4.13
Russell	1986	5	24	1	2	8.14
Fisk	1986	2	12	0	1	6.00
Virgil	1986	1	4	0	1	6.75

Catcher	Year	G	IP	W	L	ERA
Dempsey	1987	14	68	3	6	5.16
Bando	1987	7	27	2	2	6.26
Laudner	1987	3	19	1	2	6.27
Nieto	1987	3	14	0	1	3.14
Allanson	1987	2	14	0	1	4.61
Butera	1987	3	10	0	2	12.60

Catcher	Year	G	IP	W	L	ERA
Laudner	1988	4	10	0	1	16.76

Molina is to Pudge as Pudge is to Inge

Mike Mussina finished a brilliant pitching career with his first 20-win season in 2008 at the age of 39. On the Yankees roster with Mussina were two of the best catchers over the last 10+ years, Jorge Posada and Ivan (Pudge) Rodriguez. But it was a third catcher, who in eight previous seasons had never appeared in even half his team's games, that caught 32 of Mussina's 34 starts. Jose Molina was Mike Mussina's personal caddy during the 2008 season. Molina also became the personal caddy for another superb veteran pitcher during the last two months of the year–Andy Pettitte.

Why do two of the best pitchers for over a decade prefer to pitch to Jose Molina behind the plate than two of baseball's best catchers? The *New York Daily News* ran a story by John Harper about Mussina and Molina in early August after the Yankees trade for Pudge Rodriguez. Here's Harper's take on the trade:

"It's nothing against Ivan Rodriguez. The Yankees could have traded for Johnny Bench in his prime and Mike Mussina would have said, 'That's nice, but I'll keep Molina.'"

Earlier, in July, Mussina shared this about Molina with Tylor Kepner of the *New York Times*:

"Calling a game, catching the game, throwing the ball, blocking balls, being a leader on the field—he's a No. 1 catcher," Mussina said. "He knows how I think now. He's important. He's real important."

On July 31st, Andy Pettitte had a horrible outing with Ivan Rodriguez behind the plate, giving up 11 hits and 9 earned runs in 5 1/3 innings. According to the *New York Journal News*, Pettitte asked to no longer throw to Pudge and asked for Molina to become his personal catcher.

Molina caught all ten of Pettitte's final ten starts.

Catcher ERA and Earned Runs Saved

So Mussina and Pettitte both like Molina better, better than one of the best defensive catchers of all time, Pudge Rodriguez, and better than one of the best overall catchers of the last decade, Jorge Posada. But do the numbers back them up?

Now, before we look at the numbers, I want to throw out a caveat. Whether the numbers do or do not back Mussina/Pettitte up, we have to take them with a grain of salt. Over the course of a season a full-time starting pitcher in this era won't get more than 30 to 35 starts, and 35 is rare. That's a small sample size. And when you start breaking down the data into smaller groupings (i.e. so many starts with catcher A, this many with catcher B, and a couple more with catcher C) the sample size becomes an even greater problem. Sample size is always something to consider. If a hitter gets eight hits in 20 at-bats, no one truly believes he is a .400 hitter. But if he goes 80 for 200, people start to believe that there is something special about the guy. Having said this, it's worth looking at the data and interpreting it with this in mind.

OK, enough with the stat lesson. Here's the data for Mussina and Pettitte by catcher in 2008.

Mike Mussina

Catcher	G	GS	Catcher Innings	ER	ERA
Jose Molina	32	32	190.1	68	3.22
All Others	2	2	10.0	7	6.30
The Others:					
Jorge Posada	1	1	7.0	2	2.57
Chad Moeller	1	1	3.0	5	15.00
Ivan Rodriguez	0	0	0	0	---
Total	**34**	**34**	**200.1**	**75**	**3.37**

Andy Pettitte

Catcher	G	GS	Catcher Innings	ER	ERA
Jose Molina	18	18	112.2	52	4.15
All Others	15	15	91.1	51	5.03
The Others:					
Jorge Posada	8	8	46.1	28	5.44
Chad Moeller	6	6	39.2	14	3.18
Ivan Rodriguez	1	1	5.1	9	15.19
Total	**33**	**33**	**204.0**	**103**	**4.54**

Some observations:

- Pettitte's bad outing with Pudge was the only outing with Pudge.
- Pettitte has his best ERA with Moeller catching, but only six outings.
- Both Mussina and Pettitte had better overall ERAs with Molina catching, although Molina only missed two starts with Mussina.

The data does back up Mussina and Pettitte. They both wanted Molina and they both pitched better with him. In Mussina's case, the better indicator is not the ERA in the two starts without Molina, but the fact that he had a tremendous season at age 39 with Molina catching nearly all his games.

But again, the sample size is small. Let's add in the other key Yankee pitchers with Molina catching.

Molina catching Yankee pitchers

Pitcher	G	GS	Catcher Innings	ER	ERA	Pitcher Overall ERA
Mike Mussina	32	32	190.1	68	3.22	3.37
Andy Pettitte	18	18	112.2	52	4.15	4.54
Chien-Ming Wang	8	8	55.1	23	3.74	4.07
Joba Chamberlain	23	5	47.1	12	2.28	2.60
Mariano Rivera	35	0	39.1	5	1.14	1.40
Jose Veras	35	0	35.0	9	2.31	3.59
Kyle Farnsworth	31	0	30.2	10	2.93	4.48

Every pitcher who threw 30 or more innings to Jose Molina for the Yankees in 2008 had a better ERA with Molina than they did overall. If you sum these amounts for all Yankee pitchers, you find that the pitchers had a collective 3.69 ERA with Molina catching. That's Molina's Catcher ERA; we've been keeping this stat for many years now. The Yankee pitching staff overall ERA was 4.28. Molina looks like he made a real difference.

We're still working with a small sample size, but this is starting to build.

One reason Molina's catcher ERA looks good is because he caught almost every game of the Yankees best pitcher, Mike Mussina. This artificially lowers Molina's catcher ERA. But wait. We just said Molina made Mussina's ERA better and now we're saying Mussina made Molina's ERA better. We could keep going round and round like this but there is a solution. It's Earned Runs Saved.

Earned Runs Saved is a number that tells you how many earned runs the catcher saved for his pitcher. I'll do Molina and Mussina as an example. If Molina caught every one of Mussina's games, his earned runs saved would be zero because there's no basis for comparison. But he didn't and here's how it works.

Mussina's overall ERA was 3.37. If Mussina had a 3.37 ERA with Molina catching in the 190.1 innings he caught, Mussina would have allowed 71.3 runs. Instead, the Mussina-Molina combination only allowed 68 runs. That's 3.3 runs saved. We round this off and simply count this as 3 runs saved.

This technique works better than comparing catcher ERA to staff ERA, or even comparing one catcher's catcher ERA to another, even on the same team.

Here's the summary of Earned Runs Saved for Yankee catchers in 2008:

New York Yankees 2008
Earned Runs Saved by Catcher

Catcher	Innings Caught	Earned Runs Saved
Jose Molina	737.0	31
Jorge Posada	234.1	-18
Chad Moeller	225.0	9
Ivan Rodriguez	223.1	-32
Francisco Cervelli	14.0	-4
Chris Stewart	8.0	0
Total	**1441.2**	**-14**

Detroit Tigers 2008
Earned Runs Saved by Catcher

Catcher	Innings Caught	Earned Runs Saved
Ivan Rodriguez	706.1	53
Brandon Inge	493.2	-37
Dane Sardinha	122.2	3
Dusty Ryan	122.1	-19
Total	**1445.0**	**-1**

Why doesn't the Earned Runs Saved add up to zero for the Yankees? If every pitcher only pitched on the Yankees, it would. But because several of them pitched for more than one team, it doesn't add up. Basically, we're factoring in how other catchers on other teams caught the same pitchers. The negative number for Yankee catchers as a whole suggests that other teams' catchers did a better job with Yankee pitchers in 2008 than Yankee catchers did. LaTroy Hawkins is an example. He had a 5.71 ERA with the Yankees and 0.43 ERA with Houston. That accounted for -9 of the -14.

For the league as a whole, Earned Runs Saved does add up to zero.

What's up with Pudge's -32? The one outing with Pettitte cost him six earned runs. Remember, nine were allowed in the outing. Three were "expected." Here are the other pitchers who had a worse ERA with Pudge catching: Sidney Ponson, -6 ER saved in 48 innings. Edwar Ramirez, -6 in only 12.1 innings. Jose Veras, -6 in 8.2 innings. Darrell Rasner, -4 in 26.1 innings. Joba Chamberlain, -4 in 8.1 innings. All the other pitchers came out even. That's a lot of lost runs in not very many innings.

If these numbers are to be believed, Ivan Rodriguez didn't do a very good job of handling pitchers in his brief stint with the Yankees last year. He also played for the Tigers. Let's see how the Tigers catchers did overall:

Wow. Pudge was a ton better. Going by these numbers, Inge and Ryan cost the Tiger pitching staff 56 runs. And Pudge helped by 53.

Let's compare Pudge and Inge by pitcher:

Pitcher	Ivan Rodriguez		Brandon Inge	
	Innings	ERA	Innings	ERA
Kenny Rogers	111.1	4.04	51.2	8.71
Justin Verlander	95.2	3.95	76.0	5.57
Armando Galarraga	87.1	3.81	55.0	3.93
Nate Robertson	85.2	5.57	53.2	9.06
Jeremy Bonderman	60.2	4.45	10.2	4.50
Zach Miner	45.0	2.60	51.1	5.08
Aquilino Lopez	38.1	2.58	30.2	4.11
Todd Jones	30.2	5.28	8.0	4.50

With the exception of Todd Jones (only 8 innings with Inge), every pitcher with the Tigers for whom Rodriguez caught 30 or more innings had a better ERA with Pudge catching than with Inge catching.

Here's what we seem to have then:

- Molina was better than Pudge for the Yankees—every pitcher with 30 or more innings had a better ERA.
- Pudge was better than Inge for the Tigers—every pitcher with 38 or more innings had a better ERA.

Despite the sample size, it looks like a very good case for the simple conclusion that among the three of them, Jose Molina handled pitchers better than Pudge Rodriguez last year. And Pudge Rodriguez handled pitchers better than Brandon Inge. Their earned runs saved totals for 2008:

Jose Molina   31   earned runs saved
Ivan Rodriguez   21   earned runs saved
Brandon Inge   -37   earned runs saved (or 37 earned runs lost)

Adjusted Earned Runs Saved

But I don't believe it. I made a convincing case, but I don't believe it. Or, to be more specific, I don't believe it entirely. I think it's a good technique, about as good as I can come up with given the data. But there just isn't that much data. Remember that sample size caveat? That's a problem here. Six earned runs lost in one outing? That can't be entirely the catcher's fault, can it? A simple explanation could be that Pettitte simply didn't have it that day. Another problem is that, even with pitcher and catcher movement in the league, of all the catchers in baseball you still don't have very many catchers catching each pitcher. What we're mostly doing is comparing catchers on a team. That's why it worked so nicely with Pudge, as he caught significantly for two different teams in 2008.

On the other hand, I do believe that Molina was more effective than Pudge in 2008. I do believe that Molina was more effective than Posada. I do believe that Pudge was more effective than Inge. I do believe that Pudge was more effective than Dusty Ryan. I do, I do, I do.

How do we handle this dilemma? Here's how I handled it. A credibility factor. We're calling it Earned Runs Saved. But I'm not going to count every run. I've decided to believe the data 33%. How did I arrive at that number? It is pretty much out of the air. But I shared my dilemma about this technique with Bill James. Recognizing that there was "noise" in the data, he put together a what-if scenario that says, what if the catchers do have underlying skill differences, but because of the noise in the data, the data only reflects the differences some of the time. Is the data still useful? Bill's simulation said yes, which helped verify my gut reaction to use a credibility factor. In fact, Bill said that, based on his simulation, the best credibility factor is, in fact, based on how well the data reflects the underlying skill level. If the data reflects 20% of the underlying skill, the best credibility factor is 20%.

I chose 33%. Sort of. In effect, I actually chose a much smaller number. I weighted the data by the number of innings caught by the catcher relative to a full-season of team innings (I used 1,440 innings). For example, in Brandon Inge's case, where he only caught 493.2 innings, the credibility factor comes out to 11%. The fewer the innings caught, the less I believe the Earned Runs Saved numbers.

One other adjustment we do is park effects. If a pitcher pitches at Coors, then goes to the Dodgers, we have to adjust. That's built in as well.

Brandon Inge's -37 Earned Runs Saved number becomes -4 Adjusted Earned Runs Saved. The three adjustments are:

- 33% credibility drops the -37 down to -12.21.
- 34.5% loss in credibility for innings caught drops it down further to -4.21.
- Detroit was a hitter's park in 2008, but this only affects multi-team pitchers. -4.21 goes up slightly.
- Round to -4 Adjusted Earned Runs Saved.

If you're still with me, congratulations. You got through the boring stuff. Now on to the good stuff: actually comparing players.

Multi-Year Data

After studying the data using this technique, the merits start to really come through when looking at multiple years. Here are the leaders and trailers in Adjusted Earned Runs Saved over the last six years (among catchers who are still active):

Leaders and Trailers – Last Six Years
Adjusted Earned Runs Saved

1	Jason Kendall	23
2	Paul Lo Duca	18
3	Ivan Rodriguez	17
4	Chris Snyder	12
	Gregg Zaun	12
31	Michael Barrett	-9
32	Jorge Posada	-15
33	Jason Varitek	-17
34	Victor Martinez	-18
35	Kenji Johjima	-19

The Molina brothers?

8	Yadier Molina	9
10	Jose Molina	8
15	Bengie Molina	4

All are well above average. Looking at just the last three years we have:

**Leaders and Trailers – Last Three Years
Adjusted Earned Runs Saved**

1	Jason Kendall	23
2	Ronny Paulino	11
3	Brian McCann	10
4	Ivan Rodriguez	9
	Brad Ausmus	9
29	Dioner Navarro	-5
	Paul Lo Duca	-5
	Jorge Posada	-5
32	Miguel Olivo	-6
33	Victor Martinez	-8
34	Brian Schneider	-16
35	Kenji Johjima	-19

Again, the Molina brothers are above average:

7	Jose Molina	6
8	Yadier Molina	5
12	Bengie Molina	4

Unresolved Techniques

After reading the Bill James' Carlton-McCarver article (prior to this one), I had the idea to use multi-year data to come up with earned runs saved. I worked at this many, many hours. It seems reasonable that you might be able to compare pitchers and catchers working with each other over multiple years. The short answer: it don't work. Or, more likely: I'm not smart enough to make it work yet. The noise in the data got so loud, I couldn't think any more. Some of the key problems were park factors (which I think I handled), pitcher effectiveness from one year to the next having nothing to do with the catcher (very noisy—I tried breaking into smaller chunks), and differing run environments from year to year (real noisy—I got my ear muffs to work a bit, but not very well).

I tried to break the data into two-year chunks, three-year chunks, five years and career based. I could see some patterns, but it jumped all over the place and I wasn't comfortable using it. The career method, which was inspired by Carlton-McCarver, has promise, but it ain't ready for prime time yet. The credibility based one-year method, which is what the Adjusted Earned Runs Saved technique is, worked the best.

Just a quick note here. In *The Hardball Times Baseball Annual 2009*, Craig Wright comes up with some data and his own method that shows Mike Piazza was an above-average handler of pitchers. The one-year technique that I came up with is showing the same thing. Piazza has 105 Earned Runs Saved for his career, adjusted for park factors. Using the credibility adjustment, this would come out to 20 to 30 career Adjusted Earned Runs Saved for Piazza. The career technique is showing even more dramatic results, maybe 50 to 70 runs or more, but the technique is still under construction.

In the next chapter, I did use the career technique to come up with Catcher Stolen Base Runs Saved and it worked well. I think.

Catcher Stolen Bases Saved

A.J. Pierzynski only threw out 10% of the baserunners who attempted to steal against him for the White Sox in 2008. That's the lowest rate of his career, going all the way back to 1998. He's never been known for having a great arm, but has he actually gotten worse?

Short answer: No, not by much. It's Gavin Floyd.

Last year Gavin Floyd was the worst pitcher in baseball at controlling the running game. There were more stolen base attempts (42) with Floyd on the mound than with any other pitcher in baseball. And only five were caught. In the Pitcher Defense article (page 63), we estimated that Floyd's inability to control runners cost the White Sox an MLB-high five runs.

Floyd pitched 206 innings for the Sox in 2008 after having only tossed 70 in 2007. Those extra 136 innings with the worst holding pitcher in baseball on the mound make a difference in how his catchers' stolen base numbers look.

A.J. Pierzynski (and his backup, Toby Hall) had the dubious pleasure of being behind the plate with three of the worst pitchers in baseball at controlling the running game:

Pitcher	Stolen Base Attempts	Caught	Pct
Gavin Floyd	42	5	12%
Octavio Dotel	17	1	6%
Jose Contreras	17	1	6%

But they also enjoyed one of the best:

Mark Buehrle (plus two pickoffs)	12	7	58%

The other White Sox pitchers were all pretty average with the running game.

How do we sort this out? How much of A.J.'s ineffectiveness is attributable to the three pitchers who can't hold runners, and how much is attributable to his own problems? Is any of Mark Buehrle's effectiveness attributable to Pierzynski, or is Buehrle simply helping A.J.'s numbers because of what he does?

Before we proceed, let me point something out. When we measure catcher caught stealing percentage, we do something different than you might see elsewhere. When A.J. was catching last year, there were 117 attempts and 21 runners caught stealing. Some folks count that as an 18% caught stealing rate for Pierzynski. We don't. We take out the 10 runners caught stealing by the pitcher (pitcher originates the throw to nail the runner) from both the attempts and the runners caught to get 107 attempts against A.J. with 11 runners caught. That rounds to 10%.

Stolen Bases Saved

In the previous article, we developed a method to come up with Earned Runs Saved for catchers, and we are using the same method for Stolen Bases Saved. Because of the wide variety of pitchers that a catcher handles, and because the pitcher has even more control of the running game than the catcher does, we need to try to develop a level playing field to evaluate each catcher's ability to prevent stolen bases.

This time I am going to give you the results first, and then walk you through the technique. Here are the catchers who were the best and worst at saving stolen bases in 2008:

Catcher	Stolen Base Attempts	Caught Stealing Percentage	Stolen Bases Saved
Jason Kendall, Mil	96	40%	11
Jose Molina, NYY	75	43%	11
Bengie Molina, SF	104	32%	8
Dioner Navarro, TB	73	36%	6
Yadier Molina, StL	52	32%	4
Miguel Olivo, KC	33	39%	4
Jorge Posada, NYY	41	8%	-6
Geovany Soto, ChC	94	21%	-6
Jarrod Saltshaker, Tex	49	15%	-6
John Buck, KC	71	11%	-10

The three Molina brothers are in the top five. Wow, what did they feed those boys when they were growing up?

Geovany Soto's 21% caught stealing rate looks a little high in the company of the other three trailers on the list. Why does he show up? Partly it's because he played a lot. But it's also because he had two pitchers who are excellent at controlling runners on the staff, Carlos Zambrano and Ted Lilly. Because those guys are so good, Soto's adjusted numbers don't look as good.

Here are the best and worst over the last six years:

Catcher	Stolen Base Attempts	Caught Stealing Percentage	Stolen Bases Saved
Yadier Molina	224	43%	30
Jose Molina	275	40%	26
Brian Schneider	426	35%	21
Ivan Rodriguez	383	34%	18
Henry Blanco	219	38%	18
Jason Varitek	484	21%	-20
Gary Bennett	197	16%	-23
Brad Ausmus	433	23%	-23
Johnny Estrada	372	19%	-26
Michael Barrett	458	18%	-28

The two Molina brothers are numbers one and two. Third brother Bengie had six runs saved and ranked twelfth among the 35 catchers we rank.

To come up with stolen bases saved, we did the same thing we did for earned runs saved. But in this case, instead of looking at an individual pitcher's ERA for a season and relating each catcher's performance with that pitcher, we looked at lifetime data for the pitcher in controlling the running game. This was the career technique that I talked about in the last chapter. When doing Catcher Earned Runs Saved, we had trouble using the career technique because a pitcher's pitching performance is so volatile over his career. Not so for controlling the running game. As a rule, pitchers are very consistent over their careers in how they hold runners. To be sure, there are some variations, but if you were to compare consistency for pitchers between effectiveness, measured in ERA, and controlling the running game, there's no comparison. The career technique works.

In the last chapter I mentioned how Mike Piazza's numbers looked good for handling pitchers. As everyone would expect, it's not so with the running game. Over his career, Mike Piazza had -98 Stolen Bases Saved (98 stolen bases lost) while his contemporary, Pudge Rodriguez, has 136 Stolen Bases Saved so far in his career.

Here are some of the other key catchers and their career Stolen Bases Saved we calculated based on data back to 1974 (thank you, Retrosheet!).

Catcher	Stolen Bases Saved
Gary Carter	25
Jim Sundberg	51
Todd Hundley	-38
Ivan Rodriguez	136
Mike Piazza	-98
Lance Parrish	61
Tony Pena	47
Benito Santiago	16
Mike Scioscia	-25
Darrin Fletcher	-70

Stolen Bases Runs Saved for Catchers

Converting to runs saved was easy. Each stolen base saved is worth .62 runs. So, for example, Rodriguez has saved his teams about 84 runs over his career (136 x .62).

Overview of the Plus/Minus System

The Plus/Minus System is the key technique that we use to study defense in baseball. We developed the system for the first volume of *The Fielding Bible*. In order to evaluate the system we did a historical comparison against Gold Glove winners. The comparison showed a strong correlation to the award winners, but just as important, it recognized some of the players that the voters were slow to recognize. Like Orlando Hudson and Albert Pujols. Hudson and Pujols both eventually received Gold Glove Awards but the Plus/Minus System was pointing to each of these players two years earlier.

We are continually working to improve the system. Since the introduction of the system in 2006 we have introduced a number of enhancements. My favorite is the "Manny Adjustment" where we factor in stadiums that have high walls like the Green Monster in Boston and the Baggie in Minnesota. A summary of enhancements are at the end of this article.

Here's the question that we try to answer with the Plus/Minus System:

How many plays did this player make above or below those an average player at his position would make?

That's what you should think to yourself when you're looking at all those plus and minus numbers. The average is zero. If a player makes one play more than the average, that's +1.

Baseball Info Solutions reviews videotape of every game in Major League Baseball. Every play is entered into the computer where we record the exact direction, distance, speed, and type of every batted ball. Direction and distance is done on a computer screen by simply clicking the exact location of the ball on a replica of the field shown on the screen. Speed is recorded as soft, medium, and hard, while types of batted balls are groundball, liner, fly, fliner, and bunt. We introduced the fliner in the 2006 season. A fliner is a ball that is hard to categorize because it's somewhere between a fly and a liner, so it becomes a fliner.

The computer totals all softly hit groundballs on Vector 206, for example, and determines that these types of batted balls are converted into outs by the shortstop only 26% of the time. Therefore, if, on this occasion, the shortstop converts a slowly hit ball on Vector 206 into an out, that's a heck of a play, and it scores at +.74. The credit for the play made, 1.00, minus the expectation that it should be made, which is 0.26. If the play isn't made—by anybody—it's -.26 for the shortstop.

The key is if a player makes a play on a specific type of batted ball, hit to a specific location on the field, and hit at a specific speed, he gets credit if at least one other player in MLB that season missed that exact ball sometime during the season. A player who misses a play on a specific type of batted ball, hit to a specific location on the field, and hit at a specific speed, loses credit if at least one other player made the same play some other time.

Add up all the credits the player gets and loses based on each and every play when he's on the field and you get his plus/minus number (rounded to the nearest integer). Let's continue with the Vector 206 example. Vector 206 is a line extending from home plate towards the hole between the normal shortstop and third base positions, but not the exact hole. It's closer to the normal shortstop position. Shortstops fielded a softly hit groundball there 26% of the time in 2008. Medium hit balls on that vector were fielded 47% of the time, while hard hit balls were only fielded at a 25% rate. Overall, there are 90 vectors we use for fair territory on the field. One more factor we add for outfielders is the distance of every batted ball.

Each and every position has at least one special adjustment to improve accuracy. Let's go through each position:

First Base – There is a big difference between how a first baseman positions himself, depending on whether he's holding the runner or not. To approximate this, we break down all plays involving first basemen into two categories, Holding Required and Holding Not Required. Holding Required is any situation where there's a man on first with second base open. We may refine this in the future, but we found that since the outcomes are very different with runners being held this adjustment made an important difference in improving the accuracy of the first base plus/minus numbers.

A second adjustment for first basemen is Enhanced Plus/Minus. Basic Plus/Minus counts the number of plays above or below what could be expected by an average first baseman. Enhanced Plus/Minus takes the "value" of those made plays and hits into account. Here's the question that we try to answer with Enhanced Plus/

Minus: *How many bases does the player save for his team above those saved by the average first baseman?*

Second Base and **Shortstop** – The key adjustment for these two positions is made on hit-and-run plays. We consider any play where the runner on first is breaking towards second a hit-and-run play. It may have been intended as a straight steal, but if the batter hits the ball, it becomes a hit-and-run in practice, at least from the standpoint of the defense. On these plays, either the second baseman or the shortstop is breaking towards second to cover a possible throw and the dynamics of the defense change completely. For the Plus/Minus System, we use Hit-and-Run as another variable.

We don't use the Enhanced Plus/Minus adjustment for middle infielders, since almost all of the plays they don't make become singles, rather than extra-base hits.

Third Base – At third base we make the same Enhanced Plus/Minus adjustment as first base, but not the Holding Required adjustment.

Outfield – A key addition that we made to the system in 2005 was to move from three types of balls hit into the air to six different kinds. Prior to doing the Plus/Minus System for the 2004 season, we had three types of balls hit to the outfield: soft, medium and hard. Initially, we didn't think that a distinction between line drives and flyballs was necessary. If it's hard hit, it's hard hit. However, after doing extensive video analysis for Johnny Damon to see why his plus/minus number was so low in 2004, we discovered that the distinction was necessary. It's pretty obvious, now that we know it. A hard hit flyball simply stays in the air longer than a hard hit liner, giving the fielder more time to make the play. That gave us six types of balls hit to the outfield, with soft, medium, and hard hit flyballs and soft, medium, and hard hit liners.

In 2006, we moved to nine categories as we added in soft, medium, and hard "fliners."

In 2007, we introduced the "Manny Adjustment." In this adjustment we eliminate any ball that hits an outfield wall that is out of reach of the outfielder (i.e. too high on the wall). Basically, we're treating a ball hitting a wall out of reach in the same way we treat a home run. They can't be caught so they are left out of the universe of plays to consider.

For outfielders, we also use the Enhanced version of the system, since balls not fielded by outfielders frequently wind up as extra-base hits.

Summary of Enhancements

Here is a complete summary of enhancements made to the Plus/Minus System since the publication the first volume of *The Fielding Bible* in February, 2006.

The system for outfielders was modified to count all batted balls hit within about five feet as the same location. This generally resulted in more extreme (higher and lower) plus/minus figures for outfielders. All years were restated.

Also for outfielders: We added a new category called a "fliner." Previously we categorized balls hit in the air as a fly or a liner. But there are a lot of balls hit in the air that are in between. We call them fliners, and using this new category we are able to get better precision. This was implemented for 2006.

Also for outfielders: The Manny Adjustment was added beginning in 2007. In this adjustment we eliminate from consideration all balls that hit an outfield wall that are too high on the wall and out of reach in the same way that we remove home runs.

For balls hit in the air in the infield (pop-ups and line drives), all batted balls within about three feet count as the same location. Again, all years were restated for the "air" component of infielders' plus/minus.

For all positions: the vector system was changed to polar coordinates. Previously we used about 260 vectors in the field of play. Starting in 2006, we have a system using 90 vectors in the field of play. This allows us to use the standard 360 degree circle to measure all batted balls including foul balls hit anywhere on the field.

Over the years we have reviewed several other possible enhancements, such as using multi-year data as a basis to calculate an individual year. Other than those mentioned above, however, none of them provided any improvement in the system and were discarded.

Plus/Minus Leaders and Trailers

The next few pages summarize the leaders in plus/minus by position for the last six years, three years, and for 2008 by itself. Trailers are also included. For outfielders and corner infielders, enhanced plus/minus scores are listed to account for the impact of extra-base hits.

Some observations on the leader boards:

- Occasionally an average defensive player will post a particularly good season. However, the three-year leader boards clearly identify the best defensive players in baseball. Take a look at the top five at each position on the 2006-2008 Plus/Minus Leaders page and there's no doubt about it. The six-year leader boards separate the players who have been among the best and most consistent defenders at each position over time.
- Similarly, the three-year (and six-year) trailers make it pretty clear who baseball's worst defenders are.
- Six winners of a 2008 "Plus/Minus Crown" (the highest Plus/Minus score for the year) at their respective positions also won Fielding Bible Awards in 2008. Of those six, two (Adrian Beltre and Jimmy Rollins) also won a Gold Glove. Plus/Minus Crown, Fielding Bible Award, and Gold Glove: the triple crown of defense.
- Last year we put "The Manny Adjustment" into the Plus/Minus System. This adjustment came about because of parks with high outfield walls like the Green Monster in Fenway and the Baggie in the Metrodome. This is a specific adjustment to the calculation of plus/minus numbers for outfielders. We eliminate from consideration all balls that hit an outfield wall that are too high on the wall and out of reach of the defender in the same way that we remove home runs hit over the wall. The effect was to improve plus/minus numbers for Manny Ramirez and for other outfielders who play in parks with high outfield fences. In 2007, Manny had a -38 before the adjustment and a -24 afterwards. It's still a very poor performance, reflecting Manny's ineptitude as a defender, but not incredibly atrocious as represented by -38. As a result, Manny is no longer the 3-year trailer in left field. His three-year plus/minus figure of -64 "improves" to second worst, as Pat Burrell takes over the dubious distinction of having the worst plus/minus figure over the last three years in left field at -72.
- Adam Everett and Adrian Beltre have each posted +134 plus/minus figures over six seasons, tied for the best in baseball. Manny Ramirez, even after the adjustment that bears his name, finishes dead last at -150. To be fair, the Manny Adjustment has only been around for the last two years.
- In the six-year leader boards, Craig Counsell finished seventh among second basemen (+36) and tenth among shortstops (+23).
- The Yankees have had some of the worst defensive players over the past six years. In the six-year leader boards, Jason Giambi ranks third from the bottom at first base (-45), Robinson Cano comes in sixth worst at second (-31), Derek Jeter ranks dead last at short (-131), Hideki Matsui is fourth-worst in left (-39), Melky Cabrera has compiled a -29 in center since reaching the majors (sixth-worst), and Bobby Abreu ranks third from last (-60). Even two former Yankee pitchers ranked in the bottom six: Randy Johnson at -17 and Sidney Ponson at -15. Former Yankee Alfonso Soriano managed to rank tied for worst at second base despite having played the outfield the past three seasons.

2003-2008 Plus/Minus Leaders

First Basemen
Leaders

Pujols, Albert	+107
Teixeira, Mark	+74
Mientkiewicz, Doug	+58
Kotchman, Casey	+36
Overbay, Lyle	+30
Youkilis, Kevin	+25
Erstad, Darin	+23
Votto, Joey	+18
Shealy, Ryan	+16
Berkman, Lance	+15

Second Basemen
Leaders

Utley, Chase	+116
Hudson, Orlando	+106
Ellis, Mark	+91
Polanco, Placido	+56
Kennedy, Adam	+56
Hill, Aaron	+46
Counsell, Craig	+36
Roberts, Brian	+35
Phillips, Brandon	+30
Grudzielanek, Mark	+24

Third Basemen
Leaders

Beltre, Adrian	+134
Rolen, Scott	+93
Feliz, Pedro	+91
Crede, Joe	+62
Inge, Brandon	+54
Chavez, Eric	+49
Zimmerman, Ryan	+34
Punto, Nick	+28
Blum, Geoff	+27
Counsell, Craig	+23

Shortstops
Leaders

Everett, Adam	+134
Rollins, Jimmy	+82
Wilson, Jack	+76
Vizquel, Omar	+56
Furcal, Rafael	+48
Izturis, Cesar	+48
Bartlett, Jason	+45
Hardy, J.J.	+43
Barmes, Clint	+41
Tulowitzki, Troy	+34

First Basemen
Trailers

Jacobs, Mike	-53
Sexson, Richie	-49
Giambi, Jason	-45
Fielder, Prince	-45
Delgado, Carlos	-40
LaRoche, Adam	-35

Second Basemen
Trailers

Soriano, Alfonso	-40
Kent, Jeff	-40
Weeks, Rickie	-39
Rivas, Luis	-35
Castillo, Jose	-31
Cano, Robinson	-31

Third Basemen
Trailers

Wigginton, Ty	-75
Encarnacion, Edwin	-46
Cabrera, Miguel	-43
Bautista, Jose	-37
Atkins, Garrett	-35
Teahen, Mark	-32

Shortstops
Trailers

Jeter, Derek	-131
Young, Michael	-106
Berroa, Angel	-66
Lopez, Felipe	-49
Ramirez, Hanley	-40
Peralta, Jhonny	-37

Left Fielders
Leaders

Crawford, Carl	+88
Johnson, Reed	+45
Harris, Willie	+32
Byrnes, Eric	+31
Podsednik, Scott	+31
Werth, Jayson	+27
Murton, Matt	+24
Langerhans, Ryan	+23
Scott, Luke	+21
Wilkerson, Brad	+19

Center Fielders
Leaders

Jones, Andruw	+79
Beltran, Carlos	+71
Patterson, Corey	+50
Hunter, Torii	+47
Cameron, Mike	+39
Pierre, Juan	+35
Reed, Jeremy	+34
Amezaga, Alfredo	+33
Gomez, Carlos	+32
Granderson, Curtis	+31

Right Fielders
Leaders

Suzuki, Ichiro	+84
Rios, Alex	+57
Gutierrez, Franklin	+55
Kearns, Austin	+43
Giles, Brian	+40
Winn, Randy	+40
Drew, J.D.	+39
Clark, Brady	+35
Nixon, Trot	+23
Kapler, Gabe	+22

Pitchers
Leaders

Maddux, Greg	+54
Rogers, Kenny	+47
Hernandez, Livan	+28
Westbrook, Jake	+27
Glavine, Tom	+23
Mussina, Mike	+21
Webb, Brandon	+20
Willis, Dontrelle	+16
Trachsel, Steve	+16
Ramirez, Horacio	+15

Left Fielders
Trailers

Ramirez, Manny	-150
Dunn, Adam	-98
Burrell, Pat	-72
Matsui, Hideki	-39
Ibanez, Raul	-28
Young, Delmon	-25

Center Fielders
Trailers

Griffey Jr., Ken	-82
Edmonds, Jim	-58
McLouth, Nate	-48
Cruz, Jose	-31
Kotsay, Mark	-31
Cabrera, Melky	-29

Right Fielders
Trailers

Hawpe, Brad	-73
Dye, Jermaine	-70
Abreu, Bobby	-60
Cuddyer, Michael	-54
Guerrero, Vladimir	-32
Stairs, Matt	-29

Pitchers
Trailers

Cabrera, Daniel	-27
Bonderman, Jeremy	-21
Johnson, Randy	-17
Lee, Cliff	-15
Ponson, Sidney	-15
Franklin, Ryan	-13

2006-2008 Plus/Minus Leaders

First Basemen
Leaders

Pujols,Albert	+82
Kotchman,Casey	+43
Overbay,Lyle	+31
Mientkiewicz,Doug	+26
Youkilis,Kevin	+25
Berkman,Lance	+22
Teixeira,Mark	+21
Pena,Carlos	+19
Votto,Joey	+18
Shealy,Ryan	+14

Second Basemen
Leaders

Utley,Chase	+84
Ellis,Mark	+57
Hill,Aaron	+45
Hudson,Orlando	+29
Polanco,Placido	+29
Phillips,Brandon	+24
Kennedy,Adam	+18
Lopez,Jose	+14
Barfield,Josh	+11
Fontenot,Mike	+11

Third Basemen
Leaders

Beltre,Adrian	+63
Feliz,Pedro	+55
Crede,Joe	+55
Inge,Brandon	+50
Rolen,Scott	+47
Zimmerman,Ryan	+33
Punto,Nick	+26
Glaus,Troy	+23
Hannahan,Jack	+21
Lowell,Mike	+20

Shortstops
Leaders

Everett,Adam	+58
Rollins,Jimmy	+42
Vizquel,Omar	+36
Tulowitzki,Troy	+34
Hardy,J.J.	+33
Bartlett,Jason	+30
Reyes,Jose	+27
Wilson,Jack	+26
McDonald,John	+26
Barmes,Clint	+26

First Basemen
Trailers

Jacobs,Mike	-50
Fielder,Prince	-45
Giambi,Jason	-30
Young,Dmitri	-28
Jackson,Conor	-22
Sexson,Richie	-21

Second Basemen
Trailers

Kent,Jeff	-42
Weeks,Rickie	-28
Durham,Ray	-27
Lopez,Felipe	-21
Castillo,Luis	-20
Loretta,Mark	-19

Third Basemen
Trailers

Encarnacion,Edwin	-51
Atkins,Garrett	-42
Cabrera,Miguel	-40
Bautista,Jose	-37
Wigginton,Ty	-27
Boone,Aaron	-20

Shortstops
Trailers

Jeter,Derek	-67
Ramirez,Hanley	-40
Lopez,Felipe	-34
Young,Michael	-33
Betancourt,Yuniesky	-32
Harris,Brendan	-28

Left Fielders
Leaders

Crawford,Carl	+33
Harris,Willie	+33
Byrnes,Eric	+23
Scott,Luke	+19
Cabrera,Melky	+19
Diaz,Matt	+17
Soriano,Alfonso	+16
Murton,Matt	+15
Johnson,Reed	+15
Hairston,Scott	+15

Center Fielders
Leaders

Beltran,Carlos	+60
Jones,Andruw	+44
Patterson,Corey	+39
Amezaga,Alfredo	+33
Gomez,Carlos	+32
Cameron,Mike	+23
Young,Chris	+23
Pierre,Juan	+22
Granderson,Curtis	+21
Victorino,Shane	+18

Right Fielders
Leaders

Gutierrez,Franklin	+55
Rios,Alex	+44
Winn,Randy	+42
Giles,Brian	+40
Kearns,Austin	+29
Suzuki,Ichiro	+27
Schierholtz,Nate	+17
Cruz,Nelson	+15
Hart,Corey	+12
Chavez,Endy	+12

Pitchers
Leaders

Maddux,Greg	+34
Rogers,Kenny	+26
Webb,Brandon	+15
Duke,Zach	+13
Cook,Aaron	+12
Suppan,Jeff	+11
Santana,Johan	+11
Litsch,Jesse	+11
Francis,Jeff	+10
Ramirez,Horacio	+10

Left Fielders
Trailers

Burrell,Pat	-72
Ramirez,Manny	-64
Dunn,Adam	-61
Ibanez,Raul	-42
Young,Delmon	-25
Gonzalez,Luis	-24

Center Fielders
Trailers

McLouth,Nate	-46
Edmonds,Jim	-34
Kotsay,Mark	-33
Griffey Jr.,Ken	-24
Rowand,Aaron	-23
Cabrera,Melky	-22

Right Fielders
Trailers

Dye,Jermaine	-67
Hawpe,Brad	-66
Cuddyer,Michael	-58
Abreu,Bobby	-48
Griffey Jr.,Ken	-24
Guerrero,Vladimir	-20

Pitchers
Trailers

Cabrera,Daniel	-15
Kazmir,Scott	-10
Broxton,Jonathan	-9
Lee,Cliff	-9
Johnson,Jason	-8
Garza,Matt	-8

2008 Plus/Minus Leaders

First Basemen
Leaders

Teixeira, Mark	+23
Pujols, Albert	+20
Berkman, Lance	+18
Votto, Joey	+18
Kotchman, Casey	+14
Pena, Carlos	+14
Overbay, Lyle	+11
Barton, Daric	+7
Lee, Derrek	+6
Youkilis, Kevin	+6

Second Basemen
Leaders

Utley, Chase	+46
Ellis, Mark	+25
Kennedy, Adam	+18
Phillips, Brandon	+17
Pedroia, Dustin	+15
Polanco, Placido	+14
Fontenot, Mike	+11
Barmes, Clint	+9
Inglett, Joe	+7
Ojeda, Augie	+6

Third Basemen
Leaders

Beltre, Adrian	+32
Hannahan, Jack	+21
Scutaro, Marco	+17
Rolen, Scott	+13
Crede, Joe	+13
Longoria, Evan	+11
Figgins, Chone	+11
DeWitt, Blake	+11
Jones, Chipper	+10
Zimmerman, Ryan	+10

Shortstops
Leaders

Rollins, Jimmy	+23
Escobar, Yunel	+20
Izturis, Cesar	+20
Hardy, J.J.	+19
Wilson, Jack	+16
Aviles, Mike	+15
Guzman, Cristian	+13
Scutaro, Marco	+12
Vizquel, Omar	+9
Aybar, Erick	+8

First Basemen
Trailers

Jacobs, Mike	-28
Giambi, Jason	-18
Delgado, Carlos	-15
Fielder, Prince	-12
Sexson, Richie	-11
Atkins, Garrett	-9

Second Basemen
Trailers

Cano, Robinson	-17
Lopez, Felipe	-15
Kinsler, Ian	-15
Castillo, Luis	-14
Durham, Ray	-11
Matsui, Kaz	-11

Third Basemen
Trailers

Encarnacion, Edwin	-21
Mora, Melvin	-13
Ramirez, Aramis	-12
Atkins, Garrett	-11
Cantu, Jorge	-11
Reynolds, Mark	-11

Shortstops
Trailers

Betancourt, Yuniesky	-19
Keppinger, Jeff	-14
Eckstein, David	-13
Crosby, Bobby	-13
Cintron, Alex	-12
Jeter, Derek	-11

Left Fielders
Leaders

Crawford, Carl	+23
Harris, Willie	+20
Jackson, Conor	+11
Scott, Luke	+10
Chavez, Endy	+10
Holliday, Matt	+9
Willingham, Josh	+8
DeJesus, David	+8
Schumaker, Skip	+8
Braun, Ryan	+7

Center Fielders
Leaders

Gomez, Carlos	+29
Beltran, Carlos	+25
Young, Chris	+21
Victorino, Shane	+14
Ross, Cody	+13
Gerut, Jody	+13
Cameron, Mike	+12
Amezaga, Alfredo	+12
Patterson, Corey	+10
Anderson, Josh	+10

Right Fielders
Leaders

Gutierrez, Franklin	+29
Giles, Brian	+22
Winn, Randy	+16
Rios, Alex	+16
Suzuki, Ichiro	+13
Span, Denard	+12
Markakis, Nick	+11
Dukes, Elijah	+11
Chavez, Endy	+11
Murphy, David	+11

Pitchers
Leaders

Rogers, Kenny	+16
Maddux, Greg	+14
Litsch, Jesse	+8
Kendrick, Kyle	+7
Dempster, Ryan	+6
Webb, Brandon	+5
Duke, Zach	+5
Vazquez, Javier	+5
Hill, Shawn	+5
Acosta, Manny	+5

Left Fielders
Trailers

Young, Delmon	-25
Burrell, Pat	-19
Ibanez, Raul	-19
Cust, Jack	-15
Dunn, Adam	-15
Matthews Jr., Gary	-12

Center Fielder
Trailers

McLouth, Nate	-37
Edmonds, Jim	-25
Ankiel, Rick	-19
Wells, Vernon	-17
Kotsay, Mark	-15
Suzuki, Ichiro	-13

Right Fielders
Trailers

Hawpe, Brad	-37
Abreu, Bobby	-20
Ethier, Andre	-19
Griffey Jr., Ken	-16
Dye, Jermaine	-12
Francoeur, Jeff	-12

Pitchers
Trailers

Johnson, Randy	-7
Cabrera, Daniel	-6
Pettitte, Andy	-6
Papelbon, Jonathan	-5
Green, Sean	-5
Santana, Ervin	-5

The Fielding Bible Awards

After the publication of the first volume of *The Fielding Bible*, Bill James sent me one of his occasional patented long letters with an idea. Every time I get one of these long letters from Bill it details some great new idea. (One of these letters became the Misplays/Good Plays system that Bill invented and was implemented by Baseball Info Solutions.) On this occasion Bill's idea was The Fielding Bible Awards.

The intent of the Fielding Bible Awards is to provide an alternative to the Gold Glove Awards. Instead of giving an award to one player in each league at each position, we want to recognize the best of the best and only award one player for all of Major League Baseball at each position. At the same time we want to correct several of the problems inherent in the Gold Glove process. Things like a voting process that can easily award a Gold Glove to the wrong player. Or the lack of distinction among outfield positions. Or lack of information about the actual voters and vote totals.

We've been giving the awards for three years now. Each year we announce the winners (and complete ballot information) on November 1st in the *Bill James Handbook*. Just by coincidence (OK, maybe not entirely), that's about a week before the Gold Glove awards are announced. As you can see by some of the things in this book, different award winners between the two processes gives us a lot of material to discuss.

At the back of this article we have more information about the process. Here is a run-down of the winners by position over the last three years.

First Base

2006   Albert Pujols
2007   Albert Pujols
2008   Albert Pujols

How does it feel, Albert, to belong to a club that has only you as a member? This is our third year of The Fielding Bible Awards, and Albert Pujols won his third straight award at first base. Along the way, he has picked up fifteen first place votes among Fielding Bible Award voters, out of a possible thirty. The well-traveled Mark Teixeira has finished runner-up twice, including finishing two points behind in last year's voting. He will try to unseat Pujols in 2009 and become the first Yankee to bring home a Fielding Bible Award.

Second Base

2006   Orlando Hudson
2007   Aaron Hill
2008   Brandon Phillips

While Brandon Phillips improved on his third place finish in 2007 to lead the pack last year, Mark Ellis, Chase Utley, and Orlando Hudson have each finished in the top five all three years of Fielding Bible Award voting. Ellis finished runner-up for the second time in three years, and plus/minus leader Utley finished third but garnered the most first place votes (4). For a more detailed breakdown of Phillips and Utley, refer to the Chase Utley article on page 151. Aaron Hill played only 55 games in 2008 and fell off the ballot after first and fourth place finishes the previous seasons.

Third Base

2006   Adrian Beltre
2007   Pedro Feliz
2008   Adrian Beltre

Beltre ran away with his second Fielding Bible Award in 2008, topping a strong rookie performance from second-place finisher Evan Longoria by 36 points. Beltre left nothing to chance this time, capturing 8 of 10 first place votes after squeaking into first place on a tiebreaker in 2006. Scott Rolen finished third this season after placing a close second the previous two seasons. Pedro Feliz dropped to eighth last year after an award in 2007.

Shortstop

2006	Adam Everett
2007	Troy Tulowitzki
2008	Jimmy Rollins

Jimmy Rollins won his first Gold Glove in 2007, and last year he easily won with his first Fielding Bible Award. The year started slow for Rollins, but he got it going and overtook Yunel Escobar in the last week of the season to win the Plus/Minus Crown with +23. Rollins also led all shortstops with the most Good Fielding Plays (65) by a good margin over Orlando Cabrera (55) and Erick Aybar (55). Injuries helped drop Troy Tulowitzki to eighth last year after he comfortably took the crown as a rookie. Adam Everett claimed 98 points in the first Fielding Bible Awards and finished second in 2007 despite playing only 66 games due to injury.

Left Field

2006	Carl Crawford
2007	Eric Byrnes
2008	Carl Crawford

Carl Crawford missed most of the month of September but still won the 2008 Fielding Bible Award with 87 points. Crawford also took home the trophy in 2006 and finished a mere three points behind Eric Byrnes in 2007. The Rays left fielder has collected 19 of 30 first place votes since the inception of the Fielding Bible Awards. In the "former infielders now playing left field" category, Willie Harris improved from fifth to second in 2008 and Alfonso Soriano dropped to 11th after third and sixth place finishes in 2007 and 2006.

Center Field

2006	Carlos Beltran
2007	Andruw Jones
2008	Carlos Beltran

Like Carl Crawford in left, Carlos Beltran won the award for center fielders in 2006 but finished second in 2007 to Andruw Jones in a close battle. In 2008 Minnesota's rookie speedster Carlos Gomez (74 points) finished second and is profiled in detail in the McLouth vs. Gomez chapter of this book. Jones fell off the ballot in 2008 after first and second place finishes previously. Despite aging just as quickly as the rest of us, Torii Hunter continues to rise in the voting, from seventh to sixth to fourth.

Right Field

2006	Ichiro Suzuki
2007	Alex Rios
2008	Franklin Gutierrez

Franklin Gutierrez led all right fielders in plus/minus in 2007 with +20, although he did not win the Fielding Bible Award. To show that 2007 was no fluke, however, Gutierrez led them again this year with +29. Here's the amazing part: he did it while playing only 88 games in right field in 2007 and only 97 games this year. Nick Markakis improved from seventh to fifth to second in the balloting over the three years, while Alex Rios dropped to fifth after finishing first and second in the first two Fielding Bible Award votes. Ichiro (!) placed fourth in 2008, first in 2006, and managed to finish third as a center fielder in 2007.

Catcher

2006	Ivan Rodriguez
2007	Yadier Molina
2008	Yadier Molina

Maybe his brothers are getting jealous; they're creeping up on him. But it's a repeat Fielding Bible Award for Yadier Molina in 2008 (88 points). Jose Molina finished tied for second with Jason Kendall of the Brewers this year at 63 points. With Bengie Molina placing eighth in the voting, it's the first time any set of two brothers, much less three, have cracked the top ten in our Fielding Bible Award voting. That record may stand for quite some time. Pudge edged out Yadier in 2006, and Joe Mauer has made strong showings, finishing in the top five each season.

Pitcher

2006	Greg Maddux
2007	Johan Santana
2008	Kenny Rogers

Greg Maddux and Kenny Rogers have dominated pitchers' fielding for years. Maddux has won the National League Gold Glove Award for pitchers in 18 of the last 19 years, while the American League Award has gone to Rogers in five of the last nine years. Maddux finished runner-up to Rogers in Fielding Bible Award voting in 2008 and to Johan Santana in 2007, but took home the first pitcher Fielding Bible Award in 2006. For more discussion of pitcher fielding and control of the running game, see the pitcher fielding section on page 63.

The Fielding Bible Award Process

While *The Fielding Bible* puts a lot of emphasis on the numbers, especially my Plus/Minus System, I feel that visual observation and subjective judgment are still very important parts of determining the best defensive players. Also, I think people have a right to know who is voting and all the players they are voting for. Therefore, in setting up the Fielding Bible Awards, we took the following Bill James inspired steps:

1. *We appointed a panel of experts to vote.* We have a panel of ten experts plus three "tie-breaker" ballots.

2. *We rate everybody in one group*. The Gold Glove vote is divided into National League and American League. We make ours different by putting everybody together. Besides, is playing shortstop in the American League one thing and playing shortstop in the National League a different thing, or are they really very much the same thing? We want to say who the best fielder was at each position last year in Major League Baseball, period. So we have a single ballot.

3. *We use a ten-man ballot*. We use a ten-man ballot (I'm referring to the players listed, not the panel of experts). Ten points for first place, nine points for second place, etc, down to one point for tenth place. We feel strongly that a ten-man ballot with weighted positions leads to more accurate outcomes.

4. *We define the list of candidates.* Only players who actually were regulars at the position are candidates. This eliminates the possibility of a vote going to somebody who wasn't really playing the position.

5. *We publish the balloting results.* We summarize the voting at each position, clearly identifying whom everybody voted for. Publishing the actual vote totals encourages the voters to take their votes more seriously. Also, we feel the public will have more respect for the voting if they have more insight into the process.

There is something cool about having 10 experts and a 10-man ballot, because that gives each position 100 possible points. If all 10 voters place one player first on their ballot, he scores 100. That hasn't happened yet.

Here are the tie-breaker rules (we needed the first two tie-breakers our very first year):
1. Most first-place votes wins.
2. Count the tie-breaker ballots.
3. Award goes to player with the higher plus/minus rating.

Ballots are due on the Tuesday after the end of the regular season and published, as we said, in *The Bill James Handbook* on November 1 of each year.

One-Year Register

We've made three key additions to the One-Year Register since the publication of the first *Fielding Bible*. We've added pitcher registers. We've add catcher registers. We've added runs saved for every position.

Pitchers

Pitchers make their debut in Volume II of *The Fielding Bible*. Pitcher defense is often taken for granted but there are clear cut and consistent differences in the defensive skills of pitchers. The data is broken into three sections for each pitcher: Basic, Holding Runners (Holding), and Plus/Minus (+/-).

The first four columns under the Basic heading are the player's basic fielding statistics: innings, total chances (putouts plus assists plus errors), errors, and fielding percentage. After the basic columns is a section for holding runners, which displays stolen base attempts, catcher caught stealing, pitcher caught stealing, pitcher pickoffs, and caught stealing percentage. There is a subtle but official distinction between pitcher caught stealing and pitcher pickoffs. When the pitcher throws to first and the runner dives back to the bag and is called out, that's a pickoff. If the runner makes any movement towards the next base, that's officially a caught stealing.

While not necessarily done with a glove, holding runners is an integral way for pitchers to prevent runs. As such, we are officially declaring holding runners to be part of pitcher defense. In his 174 innings in 2008, Kenny Rogers allowed only three stolen base attempts, with two getting thrown out by the catcher. The southpaw also picked off three runners (in case prospective thieves needed another disincentive to run on Rogers). To fully grasp the impact of holding runners, compare Rogers to Angel starter Jered Weaver, who pitched in 177 innings and had 25 stolen base attempts by runners, with catchers throwing out only five of them and Weaver picking off two. Rogers, who is also an excellent fielder, saved 15 runs, while Weaver didn't save any, and in fact cost his team three runs with a subpar score of -3. For more on this, take a look at the Pitcher Defense chapter on page 63.

The next four columns are the pitcher's plus/minus score on balls to his right, balls hit right at him, balls to his left, and his total plus/minus score. The final two columns are the pitcher's runs saved (RS) and rank. The pitcher register is the only section where runs saved and rank are based on total runs saved for the player. For pitchers, total runs saved is determined by adding together stolen base runs saved and plus/minus runs saved. Ranks for all pitchers are based on the 175 pitchers with the most innings in baseball. This allows for about six pitchers per team to be considered.

Catchers

Catchers are new to *Volume II* as well. Catcher data is also broken into three sections, including Basic, Pitcher Handling, and Stolen Bases. The basic data includes games at catcher, games started at catcher, total innings caught, putouts, assists, errors, wild pitches while catching, passed balls, double plays, and fielding percentage.

Pitcher Handling is in the middle of the catcher chart. This section seeks to quantify the catcher's impact on the pitcher, and the runs the duo surrender. The first three columns are the catcher's wins, losses, and winning percentage. Catchers earn the game's decision when they start the game. One interesting note about the catcher's record in 2008 is that several backups had relatively high winning percentages, albeit in relatively few decisions. Take A.J. Pierzynski's backup in Chicago, Toby Hall. In

36 decisions, Hall posted a winning percentage of .611. New York Met backup Ramon Castro was an even .600 in 40 decisions. Even Florida's Mike Rabelo posted a .621 winning percentage, but in 29 decisions. After the catcher's basic record there is a tally of the number of earned runs scored while he was behind the plate, along with the earned run average while he was catching (Catcher ERA—CERA). The next three columns are focused on runs saved, with earned runs saved, adjusted earned runs saved, and rank. The rank is based on the adjusted earned runs saved column. The 35 catchers with the most innings caught in 2008 are ranked. For more on Catcher Defense, check out the chapter beginning on page 75. Atlanta's Brian McCann led catchers with seven runs saved, while 2008 first-time All-Star Dioner Navarro, with the upstart Tampa Bay Rays, brought up the rear with a score of -5, tied with A.J. Pierzynski.

Catchers also differ from the other fielders in the content of the last section of the One-Year Register. Where other fielders have the familiar plus/minus columns, catchers have a section dedicated to stolen bases, which begins with stolen base attempts, catcher caught stealing, pitcher caught stealing, catcher pickoffs, and caught stealing percentage. Cardinal backstop Yadier Molina led catchers with seven pickoffs in 2008, four more than anyone else, while a total of only 19 catchers recorded even one pickoff. Stolen bases saved, runs saved based on stolen bases, and rank based on stolen base runs saved are in the last three columns.

Other Positions

For the other seven positions on the field, the first eight columns, under the heading "Basic", are simply the player's basic fielding statistics at the position—games, games started, innings, putouts, assists, errors, double plays, and fielding percentage.

After fielding percentage, there is one additional column for second basemen, third basemen, shortstops, and outfielders entitled Rng. This is range factor per nine

innings, the number of plays that the fielder made per nine innings.

New for this volume are runs saved for every position. The plus/minus section for every position now has plus/minus runs saved and corresponding rank. To make room for it, we grouped all outs recorded by a player into the Outs Made column. In this version of the Bible, no distinction is made between outs made on groundballs or balls in the air.

For outfielders, we've expanded the data and have given them a plus/minus score for balls hit to three different outfield depths: shallow, medium, and deep. These columns are creatively called shallow, medium, and deep and are located after the player's basic plus/minus score. Luckily, the findings in these columns are more enlightening than the column names. The speedy Carl Crawford seems to get to every ball hit his way and is +10 on balls hit shallow, +7 on medium, and +6 on deep. Pat Burrell, on the other hand, is a whopping -22 on deep balls, but a +7 on shallow. Positioning problem for Burrell? Maybe. After the positioning columns, are the enhanced plus/minus scores, the runs saved, and the player's rank. We rank the 35 players with the most innings in the field at each position.

The middle section of each chart is position specific, as it was in the original Fielding Bible. Corner infielders have a section dedicated to bunts, middle infielders have a double-play section, and the outfielders have a section for throwing. To each of these we've added, once again, runs saved. This gives an excellent way to evaluate and compare player effectiveness in those situations. For instance, San Diego first baseman Adrian Gonzalez led all first basemen with four bunt runs saved, while David Wright of the Mets led third basemen. For double plays, Akinori Iwamura saved five runs in 152 games, two runs shy of Asdrubal Cabrera, who led second basemen in only 94 games. Baltimore's Nick Markakis led all outfielders with 17 throwing runs saved, helped by his 14 baserunner kills.

First Basemen

Name	Team	G	GS	Inn	PO	A	E	DP	Pct	Opps	Score	Grade	Runs Saved	Rank	Outs Made	To His Right	Straight On	To His Left	GB	Air	Total	Enhanced	Runs Saved	Rank
Marlon Anderson	NYM	6	3	26.0	22	4	0	4	1.000						5	+1	0	+1	+2	0	+2	+2	1	-
Garrett Atkins	Col	61	60	527.2	551	23	6	55	.990	6	.550	C	0	10	97	-5	-6	+1	-11	+1	-10	-9	-7	30
Michael Aubrey	Cle	12	11	94.1	99	6	0	14	1.000					-	21	0	0	-1	0	-1	-1	-1	-1	-
Rich Aurilia	SF	82	49	477.0	384	26	4	52	.990	4	.600	B-	1	6	90	-1	+3	-4	-1	0	-1	-1	-1	16
Brad Ausmus	Hou	2	0	4.0	5	0	0	0	1.000					-	0							0		
Willy Aybar	TB	19	18	155.0	144	11	0	10	1.000	1	1.000	A+	0	-	37	+1	+3	-1	+4	0	+4	+3	2	-
Jeff Bailey	Bos	12	7	67.0	77	3	0	10	1.000					-	13	-1	0	0	0	0	0	0	0	-
Jeff Baisley	Oak	4	4	33.0	37	1	1	3	.974					-	9	0	0	0	0	0	0	0	0	-
Jeff Baker	Col	22	13	128.2	143	5	0	14	1.000	1	.600	B-	0	-	25	+1	-2	0	-1	0	-1	-2	-1	-
Wes Bankston	Oak	13	12	108.0	104	6	1	10	.991	1	1.000	A+	0	-	23	0	0	-1	0	0	0	-1	-1	-
Rod Barajas	Tor	4	3	27.0	27	5	0	4	1.000	1	.600	B-	0	-	5	+1	-1	0	0	0	0	0	0	-
Brian Barden	StL	1	0	1.0	0	0	0	0	-					-	0		-1					-1	-1	-
Daric Barton	Oak	134	124	1121.2	1021	73	13	128	.988	10	.505	C-	-1	26	206	0	+2	+5	+7	-2	+5	+7	5	8
Jose Bautista	Tor	5	4	27.0	29	0	0	1	1.000					-	4	-1	0		-1	0	-1	-1	-1	-
Ronnie Belliard	Was	33	21	201.0	185	14	2	14	.990	2	.600	B-	0	-	43	0	+1	0	+1	0	+1	+1	1	-
Lance Berkman	Hou	152	151	1307.1	1240	132	5	122	.996	13	.592	C+	0	10	319	+5	+8	+4	+17	0	+17	+18	13	3
Wilson Betemit	NYY	36	21	207.0	191	13	1	23	.995	3	.367	F	-1	-	43	0	+2	-1	+1	0	+1	+1	1	-
Casey Blake	2 tms	29	19	177.0	198	10	2	22	.990	2	.250	F	0	-	36	+1	-1	+1	+1	0	+1	+1	0	-
Hank Blalock	Tex	34	34	296.0	262	13	1	24	.996	1	1.000	A+	0	-	62	+2	-3	-1	-2	0	-2	-2	-1	-
Henry Blanco	ChC	1	0	1.2	3	0	0	0	1.000					-	0							0		
Geoff Blum	Hou	5	2	24.2	17	1	0	1	1.000					-	4	+1	-1	-1	0	0	0	0	0	-
Aaron Boone	Was	54	35	342.0	313	17	1	32	.997	1	.600	B-	0	-	60	-2	+1	+2	+1	-1	0	+2	1	-
Jason Botts	Tex	8	5	41.0	51	2	2	7	.964					-	8	0	0	0	0	0	0	0	0	-
Rob Bowen	Oak	1	0	2.0	2	0	0	2	1.000					-	0				0	0	0	0	0	-
John Bowker	SF	71	67	550.1	448	39	6	43	.988	11	.614	B-	0	10	96	-1	+3	-4	-2	-1	-3	-4	-3	22
Russell Branyan	Mil	5	2	24.0	26	1	0	3	1.000					-	4	0	0	0	+1	0	+1	+1	1	-
Ben Broussard	Tex	26	23	204.0	202	22	3	32	.987	2	.425	D-	0	-	42	-2	-1	0	-3	0	-3	-3	-2	-
Emil Brown	Oak	1	0	0.1	1	0	0	0	1.000					-	0							0		
Eric Bruntlett	Phi	2	2	16.0	18	1	0	2	1.000					-	6	+1	0	0	+1	0	+1	+1	1	-
Chris Burke	Ari	9	6	63.0	67	4	0	6	1.000	1	1.000	A+	0	-	12	+1	-1	0	0	0	0	-1	-1	-
Jamie Burke	Sea	1	0	2.0	4	0	0	1	1.000					-	0							0		
Brian Buscher	Min	6	1	14.0	13	0	0	1	1.000					-	4	0	0	0	0	0	0	0	0	-
Billy Butler	KC	34	33	260.0	233	9	2	27	.992	1	1.000	A+	0	-	37	-5	+1	+1	-4	0	-4	-4	-3	-
Miguel Cabrera	Det	143	139	1204.0	1117	73	9	116	.992	5	.470	D+	-1	26	219	-4	-5	+3	-7	-1	-8	-6	-4	27
Miguel Cairo	Sea	70	37	394.0	414	23	1	43	.998	8	.341	F	2	3	77	-1	+2	0	+1	-1	0	0	0	13
Jorge Cantu	Fla	66	23	286.2	260	14	2	23	.993	3	.500	C-	-1	-	68	+1	0	+2	+2	0	+2	+3	2	-
Sean Casey	Bos	45	40	342.2	331	13	3	25	.991	2	1.125	A+	0	10	64	-2	-2	-1	-4	0	-4	-4	-3	23
Kory Casto	Was	23	20	175.2	149	13	2	13	.988	3	.250	F	-1	-	32	0	-2	-1	-3	0	-3	-3	-2	-
Frank Catalanotto	Tex	33	25	224.2	215	15	0	31	1.000	3	.617	B-	0	-	34	-1	-1	+1	-1	0	-1	-2	-1	-
Alex Cintron	Bal	2	0	3.0	3	1	0	1	1.000					-	1				0	0	0	0	0	-
Howie Clark	Min	2	0	5.0	3	1	0	0	1.000					-	1				0	0	0	0	0	-
Tony Clark	2 tms	26	13	155.0	165	15	2	19	.989	1	.600	B-	0	-	35	-1	-2	+2	0	0	0	0	0	-
Chris Coste	Phi	1	1	9.0	7	1	0	0	1.000	2	.625	B-	0	-	1	0			0	0	0	0	0	-
Michael Cuddyer	Min	2	2	18.0	22	1	1	5	.958					-	3	-1	+1	0	0	0	0	0	0	-
Johnny Damon	NYY	1	0	1.0	1	0	0	0	1.000					-	0							0		
Jamie D'Antona	Ari	2	1	7.0	7	2	0	2	1.000	1	.250	F	0	-	3	+1	-1	-1	-1	0	-1	-1	-1	-
Chris Davis	Tex	51	46	404.0	358	34	1	52	.997	3	.733	A	1	6	78	-2	0	-2	-3	+1	-2	-3	-2	21
Carlos Delgado	NYM	154	154	1376.1	1237	105	8	106	.994	28	.595	C+	2	3	281	-12	+3	-5	-14	-2	-16	-15	-11	33
Mark DeRosa	ChC	1	0	2.0	2	0	0	0	1.000					-	1				0	0	0	0	0	-
Joe Dillon	Mil	4	3	25.0	25	3	0	4	1.000	1	.250	F	0	-	7	0	0	-1	-1	0	-1	-1	-1	-
Greg Dobbs	Phi	2	1	8.0	6	2	0	1	1.000					-	0				0	0	0	0	0	-
Ryan Doumit	Pit	1	0	1.0	1	0	0	0	1.000					-	0							0		
Chris Duncan	StL	21	15	142.0	143	13	0	13	1.000	1	.600	B-	0	-	27	+1	0	-1	-1	0	-1	-1	-1	-
Shelley Duncan	NYY	16	12	107.0	98	5	3	8	.972					-	17	+2	0	-1	0	0	0	-1	-1	-
Adam Dunn	Ari	19	14	128.0	123	7	3	14	.977	4	.513	C-	0	-	20	-2	-2	0	-4	0	-4	-4	-3	-
Damion Easley	NYM	4	3	31.0	27	1	0	1	1.000					-	6	+1	+1	0	+2	0	+2	+2	1	-
Morgan Ensberg	NYY	7	3	35.0	38	1	0	1	1.000					-	4	-1	0	0	-1	0	-1	-1	-1	-
Darin Erstad	Hou	12	6	66.1	71	2	0	4	1.000					-	14	-1	0	0	-1	0	-1	-1	-1	-
Nick Evans	NYM	3	1	12.0	7	0	0	3	1.000					-	1				0	0	0	0	0	-
Sal Fasano	Cle	1	0	3.0	0	0	0	0	-					-	0	-1			-1	0	-1	-1	-1	-
Prince Fielder	Mil	155	155	1383.2	1369	89	17	132	.988	32	.567	C+	-1	26	257	-1	-4	-7	-12	-1	-13	-12	-9	32
Nomar Garciaparra	LAD	8	6	38.2	49	4	0	2	1.000					-	9	+1	0	0	0	0	0	0	0	-
Ryan Garko	Cle	121	121	1058.2	1039	80	4	123	.996	17	.474	D+	-3	33	193	-2	+3	-5	-4	+1	-3	-3	-2	20
Jason Giambi	NYY	113	112	898.0	870	36	9	77	.990	8	.563	C+	0	10	158	-6	-13	+2	-17	-1	-18	-18	-13	34
Troy Glaus	StL	4	3	28.2	29	2	0	5	1.000					-	7	0	0	0	+1	0	+1	+1	1	-
Ross Gload	KC	111	95	878.1	837	43	4	87	.995	6	.617	B-	0	10	159	-4	-1	0	-5	0	-5	-7	-5	28
Chris Gomez	Pit	5	4	35.0	39	4	0	6	1.000	2	.425	D-	0	-	6	+1			+1	+1	+2	+2	1	-
Adrian Gonzalez	SD	161	159	1417.1	1306	130	6	129	.996	31	.739	A	4	1	282	-1	-7	-1	-8	+2	-6	-6	-4	26
Andy Gonzalez	Cle	7	4	38.0	39	0	2	4	.951	1	.600	B-	0	-	7	0	0	0	0	0	0	0	0	-
Carlos Guillen	Det	24	18	162.0	142	11	2	22	.987	3	.483	D+	0	-	24	0	0	0	0	0	0	-1	-1	-
Jack Hannahan	Oak	10	10	80.0	82	5	2	7	.978					-	24	0	+1	+1	+2	0	+2	+3	2	-
Brendan Harris	Min	2	0	3.0	1	1	0	0	1.000	1	.600	B-	0	-	0				0	0	0	0	0	-
Scott Hatteberg	Cin	16	8	87.2	69	6	1	3	.987	2	.600	B-	0	-	12	0	+1	0	+1	-1	0	0	0	-
Wes Helms	Fla	42	18	209.1	185	13	2	19	.990	6	.617	B-	0	-	48	0	0	0	0	0	0	+1	1	-
Todd Helton	Col	81	81	715.1	830	57	3	79	.997	12	.517	C-	0	10	156	-3	+7	+2	+7	0	+7	+6	4	11
Ramon Hernandez	Bal	2	1	10.0	11	0	0	0	1.000					-	3	-1	0		-1	0	-1	-1	-1	-
Eric Hinske	TB	11	9	87.0	78	8	1	11	.989					-	16	+1	-1	+1	+1	0	+1	+1	1	-
Micah Hoffpauir	ChC	6	5	47.2	37	1	1	3	.974					-	4	-1	0		-1	-1	-2	-2	-1	-
Ryan Howard	Phi	159	156	1402.2	1408	101	19	128	.988	18	.572	C+	0	10	309	+1	-10	+5	-4	+2	-2	0	0	12
Aubrey Huff	Bal	24	23	194.1	177	16	0	16	1.000	7	.457	D	-1	-	39	-4	0	0	-4	+1	-3	-2	-1	-
Travis Ishikawa	SF	29	26	213.1	161	20	3	14	.984	2	.600	B-	0	-	51	+3	+1	-1	+3	0	+3	+4	3	-
Conor Jackson	Ari	68	66	571.2	533	30	4	34	.993	9	.611	B-	0	10	102	-1	-2	0	-3	-1	-4	-5	-4	24
Mike Jacobs	Fla	119	119	927.1	825	62	11	67	.988	21	.452	D	-3	33	163	-11	-8	-7	-26	-2	-28	-28	-20	35
Dan Johnson	TB	8	4	47.0	39	5	0	4	1.000	1	.250	F	0	-	11	0	+1	0	+2	0	+2	+2	1	-
Nick Johnson	Was	35	34	300.1	302	14	0	21	1.000	1	.250	F	0	-	62	-2	+2	+2	+2	0	+2	+3	2	-

		BASIC									BUNTS					PLUS/MINUS								
Name	Team	G	GS	Inn	PO	A	E	DP	Pct	Opps	Score	Grade	Runs Saved	Rank	Outs Made	To His Right	Straight On	To His Left	GB	Air	Total	Enhanced	Runs Saved	Rank
Kila Ka'aihue	KC	4	1	15.0	12	1	0	2	1.000					-	3	-1	0	0	-1	0	-1	-1	-1	-
Adam Kennedy	StL	3	2	18.0	23	3	1	4	.963					-	4	+1			0	0	0	0	0	-
Jeff Kent	LAD	1	1	4.0	7	1	0	0	1.000					-	3				0			0	0	-
Jeff Keppinger	Cin	3	2	18.2	15	1	0	1	1.000					-	2	0	0	0	0	0	0	0	0	-
Paul Konerko	CWS	116	116	995.2	1010	75	7	94	.994	10	.395	F	-3	33	209	+3	-2	+1	+2	0	+2	-2	-1	17
Joe Koshansky	Col	11	8	74.1	71	6	1	8	.987	1	.600	B-	0	-	18	+1	0	+1	+2	0	+2	+2	1	-
Casey Kotchman	2 tms	141	135	1210.1	1205	96	2	125	.998	10	.425	D-	-1	26	263	+2	+10	0	+11	+1	+12	+14	10	5
Mark Kotsay	Bos	6	4	39.0	35	3	1	7	.974					-	5	0	0	0	0	0	0	0	0	-
Bryan LaHair	Sea	36	33	273.0	277	18	2	37	.993	6	.367	F	-2	-	52	-1	+5	0	+4	-1	+3	+3	2	-
Mike Lamb	Min	9	5	52.1	46	8	0	4	1.000					-	10	+1	0	0	+1	0	+1	+1	1	-
Ryan Langerhans	Was	2	0	7.0	8	0	0	1	1.000					-	0				-1	0	-1	-1	-1	-
Jeff Larish	Det	8	2	38.0	41	3	0	9	1.000					-	9	0	+1	0	0	0	0	0	0	-
Adam LaRoche	Pit	129	128	1135.2	1130	81	8	121	.993	28	.625	B-	0	10	206	0	-1	-6	-7	+2	-5	-8	-6	29
Andy LaRoche	LAD	1	1	8.0	11	1	0	1	1.000					-	3	0			0	0	0	0	0	-
Jason LaRue	StL	3	0	7.1	7	1	0	1	1.000	1	1.000	A+	0	-	2				0	0	0	0	0	-
Derrek Lee	ChC	153	152	1339.1	1193	110	9	98	.993	26	.623	B-	1	6	304	+1	-6	+8	+3	0	+3	+6	4	9
Paul Lo Duca	2 tms	17	14	119.0	114	8	3	16	.976	3	.483	D+	0	-	26	-1	0	0	-1	-1	-2	-2	-1	-
James Loney	LAD	158	150	1362.2	1364	121	13	123	.991	25	.658	B	2	3	248	+2	-6	+2	-2	0	-2	-1	-1	14
Felipe Lopez	StL	1	0	1.0	2	0	0	0	1.000					-	0							0		-
Jose Lopez	Sea	13	12	100.0	100	11	1	5	.991	1	.600	B-	0	-	33	+2	+1	0	+3	0	+3	+4	3	-
Mark Loretta	Hou	2	2	17.0	14	0	0	1	1.000					-	5	0			+1	0	+1	+1	1	-
Matt Macri	Min	2	0	3.0	3	0	0	1	1.000					-	1				0	0	0	0	0	-
Andy Marte	Cle	1	0	1.0	2	1	0	1	1.000					-	1				0			0	0	-
Victor Martinez	Cle	10	9	82.0	82	4	1	9	.989	1	.250	F	0	-	17	0	0	0	0	0	0	0	0	-
Joe Mather	StL	4	0	13.0	9	1	0	1	1.000					-	3	+1			+1	0	+1	+1	1	-
Scott McClain	SF	4	3	28.1	26	2	0	1	1.000					-	9	+1	+1	0	+2	0	+2	+2	1	-
Doug Mientkiewicz	Pit	37	30	283.1	290	19	0	34	1.000	2	.250	F	-1	-	62	0	+3	+2	+4	0	+4	+4	3	-
Kevin Millar	Bal	130	128	1131.1	1099	110	6	128	.995	11	.482	D+	-2	30	259	+5	-1	-6	-1	-1	-2	-3	-2	19
Juan Miranda	NYY	5	3	32.2	30	2	0	1	1.000					-	8	+1	0	0	+1	0	+1	+1	1	-
Chad Moeller	NYY	2	0	3.0	4	0	0	1	1.000					-	1				0	0	0	0	0	-
Jose Molina	NYY	1	0	1.0	0	0	0	0	-					-	0				0	0	0	0	0	-
Yadier Molina	StL	2	1	11.0	13	3	0	1	1.000					-	6	-1	0	0	0	0	0	0	0	-
Kendry Morales	LAA	6	4	41.0	30	3	0	7	1.000					-	9	-1	0	-1	-1	0	-1	-1	-1	-
Justin Morneau	Min	155	155	1363.2	1316	89	4	149	.997	9	.406	F	-2	30	239	+1	-3	0	-2	0	-2	-1	-1	15
Brandon Moss	Bos	2	1	13.0	10	0	0	1	1.000					-	4				+1	0	+1	+1	1	-
Brian Myrow	SD	2	1	9.0	9	0	0	1	1.000					-	2	0			0	0	0	0	0	-
Xavier Nady	NYY	3	0	4.0	3	1	0	0	1.000					-	2	0	0	0	0	0	0	0	0	-
Brad Nelson	Mil	2	0	2.0	1	0	0	0	1.000					-	0				0			0		-
Greg Norton	2 tms	11	7	70.1	80	3	3	8	.965	1	.600	B-	0	-	12	-2	0	-2	-4	-1	-5	-5	-4	-
Dan Ortmeier	SF	13	4	52.0	41	6	0	3	1.000					-	13	+1	+1	-1	+1	0	+1	+1	1	-
Lyle Overbay	Tor	156	151	1354.2	1316	155	5	112	.997	13	.504	C-	-2	30	324	+7	+7	-1	+13	0	+13	+11	8	7
Carlos Pena	TB	132	131	1168.2	991	106	2	117	.998	16	.678	B+	1	6	262	+11	+8	0	+14	+1	+15	+14	10	6
Josh Phelps	StL	4	1	17.0	18	0	0	1	1.000					-	2				-1	0	-1	-1	-1	-
Andy Phillips	2 tms	5	4	31.2	35	0	1	3	.972					-	5	0	0	0	0	0	0	0	0	-
Jorge Posada	NYY	7	3	31.0	25	0	0	2	1.000					-	7	0	+1	-1	0	0	0	0	0	-
Martin Prado	Atl	17	14	124.1	123	11	1	10	.993	2	.600	B-	0	-	22	-1	+1	-1	-1	-1	-2	-2	-1	-
Albert Pujols	StL	144	140	1215.0	1297	135	6	119	.996	12	.617	B-	0	10	303	+9	+8	+4	+20	+1	+21	+20	15	2
Robb Quinlan	LAA	22	12	114.0	105	11	0	11	1.000	2	.600	B-	0	-	20	+2	0	0	+2	0	+2	+2	1	-
Max Ramirez	Tex	3	3	23.0	20	4	0	5	1.000	2	.425	D-	0	-	5	0	0	0	+1	0	+1	0	0	-
Cody Ransom	NYY	19	2	42.0	47	1	0	2	1.000					-	9	-1	-2	0	-3	0	-3	-3	-2	-
Jeremy Reed	Sea	1	0	1.0	2	0	1	0	.667					-	0				0			0		-
Mark Reynolds	Ari	1	0	2.0	1	0	1	0	.500					-	0				-1	0	-1	-1	-1	-
Juan Rivera	LAA	1	0	2.0	5	0	0	1	1.000					-	1	0	0		0	0	0	0	0	-
Mike Rivera	Mil	3	2	21.0	20	3	0	3	1.000	1	.600	B-	0	-	7	+1			+1	0	+1	+1	1	-
Luis Rodriguez	SD	2	1	10.0	3	2	0	0	1.000					-	2	0	0	0	0	0	0	0	0	-
Mark Saccomanno	Hou	2	0	6.0	6	0	0	0	1.000					-	1				0	0	0	0	0	-
Oscar Salazar	Bal	10	9	83.1	79	5	0	5	1.000	2	.250	F	-1	-	20	+1	+1	0	+2	0	+2	+2	1	-
Gaby Sanchez	Fla	3	1	11.0	13	1	0	1	1.000					-	1	-1	+1	0	0	0	0	0	0	-
Freddy Sandoval	LAA	1	0	1.0	0	0	0	0	-					-	0				0	0	0	0	0	-
Pablo Sandoval	SF	17	13	121.0	100	12	1	7	.991	4	1.050	A+	2	-	29	-1	+1	0	+1	0	+1	+1	1	-
Marco Scutaro	Tor	3	2	15.0	15	1	0	2	1.000					-	2	0	0	0	0	0	0	0	0	-
Richie Sexson	2 tms	92	78	684.0	646	56	2	58	.997	8	.619	B-	0	10	128	-3	-8	0	-11	0	-11	-11	-8	31
Ryan Shealy	KC	20	20	169.0	155	12	2	18	.988	1	1.000	A+	0	-	32	+1	-2	+1	0	-1	-1	-1	-1	-
Chris Shelton	Tex	39	26	247.1	241	20	3	21	.989	2	.625	B-	0	-	55	+4	0	+1	+5	0	+5	+5	4	-
Jason Smith	KC	1	0	2.0	2	0	0	0	1.000					-	2				+1	0	+1	+1	1	-
J.T. Snow	SF	0	0	0.0	0	0	0	0	-					-	0							0		-
Mark Sweeney	LAD	2	2	17.0	18	1	0	1	1.000					-	2	0	0		0	0	0	0	0	-
Mike Sweeney	Oak	13	11	90.0	89	11	0	9	1.000	2	.250	F	-1	-	19	+1	0	0	+2	0	+2	+3	2	-
Nick Swisher	CWS	71	47	462.0	447	32	2	52	.996	3	.750	A+	0	10	79	-7	-1	+1	-7	+1	-6	-5	-4	25
Fernando Tatis	NYM	6	1	18.0	16	1	2	0	.895	1	1.000	A+	0	-	4	+1	+1	0	+1	0	+1	+1	1	-
Mark Teahen	KC	14	13	121.1	130	10	1	13	.993	1	.600	B-	0	-	30	-1	+2	-2	-1	0	-1	-1	-1	-
Mark Teixeira	2 tms	153	153	1335.0	1394	99	5	131	.997	13	.550	C	0	10	312	+5	+11	+7	+23	+1	+24	+23	17	1
Marcus Thames	Det	9	3	41.0	34	1	0	10	1.000	3	.250	F	-1	-	3	-1	-1	0	-1	0	-1	-1	-1	-
Curtis Thigpen	Tor	1	0	3.0	1	0	0	0	1.000					-	0				0			0		-
Chad Tracy	Ari	65	62	523.0	528	26	4	49	.993	9	.572	C+	0	10	104	+2	-2	-2	-1	0	-1	-2	-1	18
Chase Utley	Phi	2	2	14.0	16	2	0	1	1.000					-	5	+1	0	0	+2	0	+2	+2	1	-
Javier Valentin	Cin	11	10	81.2	75	4	0	10	1.000	1	.600	B-	0	-	18	+1	0	0	0	0	0	0	0	-
Ramon Vazquez	Tex	1	0	2.0	2	0	0	0	1.000					-	0				0			0		-
Jose Vidro	Sea	9	7	55.1	54	5	1	6	.983	2	.625	B-	0	-	17	+1	0	+1	+2	0	+2	+2	1	-
Joey Votto	Cin	144	138	1223.2	1050	136	11	119	.991	26	.638	B	3	2	282	+6	+4	+7	+17	+1	+18	+18	13	4
Daryle Ward	ChC	13	4	60.0	54	4	0	4	1.000					-	12	+1	0	-1	0	0	0	0	0	-
Josh Whitesell	Ari	1	1	7.0	7	0	0	0	1.000					-	1				-1	0	-1	-1	-1	-
Brad Wilkerson	Tor	4	2	20.0	22	0	0	0	1.000					-	4	0			0	0	0	0	0	-
Kevin Youkilis	Bos	126	110	984.2	923	87	4	92	.996	12	.613	B-	0	10	203	+4	-2	+2	+4	+2	+6	+6	4	10
Dmitri Young	Was	38	37	290.0	275	15	7	10	.976	3	.483	D+	0	-	48	-4	-3	+1	-6	-1	-7	-7	-5	-
2008 MLB Averages									.993	582	.580	C+												

Second Basemen

		BASIC									GROUND DP					PLUS/MINUS								
Name	Team	G	GS	Inn	PO	A	E	DP	Pct	Rng	GDP Opps	GDP	Pct	Runs Saved	Rank	Outs Made	To His Right	Straight On	To His Left	GB	Air	Total	Runs Saved	Rank
Alfredo Amezaga	Fla	10	8	73.0	19	18	1	3	.974	4.56	8	2	.250	-1	-	24	+1	+1	+1	+3	0	+3	2	-
Marlon Anderson	NYM	1	0	4.0	1	2	0	0	1.000	6.75	2		-			2				0	0	0	0	
Robert Andino	Fla	15	9	89.2	30	31	2	7	.968	6.12	15	7	.467	0	-	39	+2	+1	0	+3	+1	+4	3	-
Matt Antonelli	SD	18	15	137.1	38	34	2	7	.973	4.72	21	7	.333	-1	-	42	-1	-1	-1	-3	0	-3	-2	-
Joaquin Arias	Tex	30	26	225.0	48	67	2	19	.983	4.60	32	17	.531	0	-	69	+2	0	-4	-2	0	-2	-2	-
Garrett Atkins	Col	1	0	8.1	3	5	0	2	1.000	8.64	4	2	.500	0	-	6	0	0	0	+1	0	+1	1	-
Rich Aurilia	SF	1	0	3.0	0	0	0	0	-	.00	0		-			0	-1		-1	-2	0	-2	-2	-
Brad Ausmus	Hou	1	0	1.0	0	0	0	0	-	.00	0		-			0				0	0	0	0	
Mike Aviles	KC	28	9	114.1	26	33	0	5	1.000	4.64	12	5	.417	0	-	42	-3	+2	0	-1	0	-1	-1	-
Erick Aybar	LAA	2	0	2.0	0	1	0	0	1.000	4.50	0		-			1	0			0	0	0	0	
Willy Aybar	TB	10	6	70.2	17	19	0	4	1.000	4.58	8	4	.500	0	-	21	0	+1	0	+1	0	+1	1	-
Jeff Baker	Col	49	47	369.2	71	131	4	31	.981	4.92	50	28	.560	1	-	139	+6	0	-10	-4	0	-4	-3	-
Brian Barden	StL	1	1	8.0	1	4	1	0	.833	5.63	0		-			4	0	0	-1	0	0	0	0	-
Josh Barfield	Cle	9	8	71.0	26	24	0	9	1.000	6.34	11	7	.636	0	-	27	-1	0	-1	-2	0	-2	-2	-
Clint Barmes	Col	61	54	486.0	91	178	6	35	.978	4.98	59	32	.542	1	11	185	+13	+1	-6	+8	+1	+9	7	8
Jose Bautista	Tor	2	2	16.0	2	6	0	2	1.000	4.50	3	2	.667	0	-	5	0	0	0	0	0	0	0	-
Ronnie Belliard	Was	29	27	229.2	53	60	3	20	.974	4.43	42	20	.476	0	-	59	+2	-5	-6	-9	+1	-8	-6	-
Doug Bernier	Col	2	1	11.0	5	2	0	0	1.000	5.73	2		-			4	0			0	0	0	0	-
Angel Berroa	LAD	5	1	12.0	1	4	0	0	1.000	3.75	0		-			5	+1		0	+1	0	+1	1	-
Wilson Betemit	NYY	3	3	24.0	4	8	1	2	.923	4.50	4	2	.500	0	-	10	0	0	-1	0	0	0	0	-
Casey Blake	LAD	1	0	1.0	0	0	0	0	-	.00	0		-			0				0	0	0	0	
Willie Bloomquist	Sea	7	4	37.0	8	15	0	7	1.000	5.59	9	7	.778	1	-	14	+1	0	-1	0	0	0	0	-
Geoff Blum	Hou	8	5	40.2	9	17	0	2	1.000	5.75	4	2	.500	0	-	18	-2	+1	-1	-2	0	-2	-2	-
Emilio Bonifacio	Was	37	37	325.0	78	82	7	25	.958	4.43	46	22	.478	0	-	100	-1	-2	+2	-1	+3	+2	2	-
Aaron Boone	Was	1	0	1.1	0	0	0	0	-	.00	0		-			0				0	0	0	0	
Jason Bourgeois	CWS	1	0	3.0	0	0	0	0	-	.00	0		-			0	0			0	0	0	0	
Matt Brown	LAA	1	0	2.0	1	1	0	0	1.000	9.00	0		-			1				0	0	0	0	
Eric Bruntlett	Phi	5	2	28.0	5	8	1	1	.929	4.18	5	1	.200	0	-	9	0	-1	0	0	0	0	0	-
Chris Burke	Ari	18	9	92.0	21	34	0	7	1.000	5.38	13	7	.538	0	-	37	+1	+1	+2	+3	0	+3	2	-
Emmanuel Burriss	SF	41	32	282.0	66	80	4	14	.973	4.66	30	13	.433	-1	-	90	+1	+2	+3	+5	0	+5	4	-
Brian Buscher	Min	1	0	1.0	0	0	0	0	-	.00	0		-			0				0	0	0	0	
Freddie Bynum	Bal	1	0	4.0	0	0	0	0	-	.00	0		-			0				0	0	0	0	
Asdrubal Cabrera	Cle	94	87	776.2	202	281	3	83	.994	5.60	112	79	.705	7	1	315	+12	+1	-6	+6	-2	+4	3	11
Jolbert Cabrera	Cin	3	2	15.0	4	6	0	3	1.000	6.00	4	3	.750	0	-	5	-1	0	-1	-1	0	-1	-1	-
Miguel Cairo	Sea	5	3	26.0	7	10	0	2	1.000	5.88	5	2	.400	0	-	10	+1	0	0	+1	-1	0	0	-
Alberto Callaspo	KC	46	42	365.2	74	119	0	36	1.000	4.75	44	32	.727	3	-	128	0	+4	-7	-3	-2	-5	-4	-
Robinson Cano	NYY	159	154	1376.2	305	482	13	103	.984	5.15	178	88	.494	0	15	530	-6	+1	-8	-13	-4	-17	-13	35
Jamey Carroll	Cle	74	66	580.1	105	192	3	46	.990	4.61	73	42	.575	2	8	203	+1	0	-1	0	-4	-4	-3	24
Alexi Casilla	Min	95	94	833.2	196	247	12	71	.974	4.78	125	66	.528	1	11	288	-11	-3	+9	-5	+1	-4	-3	23
Jose Castillo	2 tms	12	7	64.0	13	19	1	2	.970	4.50	7	2	.286	0	-	25	+1	+1	0	+2	0	+2	1	-
Luis Castillo	NYM	81	78	689.2	160	186	6	41	.983	4.52	91	38	.418	-2	26	219	+1	-1	-13	-14	0	-14	-11	32
Wilkin Castillo	Cin	2	2	16.0	5	2	0	2	1.000	3.94	3	2	.667	0	-	3	0	0	-1	-1	0	-1	-1	-
Juan Castro	Cin	2	0	2.0	1	2	0	0	1.000	13.50	0		-			3				-1	0	-1	-1	-
Ronny Cedeno	ChC	43	31	273.0	60	75	2	19	.985	4.45	34	18	.529	0	-	90	-2	-1	+2	-2	0	-2	-2	-
Alex Cintron	Bal	7	1	17.0	4	4	0	1	1.000	4.24	1	1	1.000	0	-	6	0			-2	0	-2	-2	-
Howie Clark	Min	1	0	3.0	0	2	0	1	1.000	6.00	1	1	1.000	0	-	2				0	0	0	0	
Brooks Conrad	Oak	2	2	17.0	4	3	0	1	1.000	3.71	0		-			5	0	0	0	0	0	0	0	-
Alex Cora	Bos	7	3	35.0	6	14	0	3	1.000	5.14	4	3	.750	0	-	14	0	+1	-1	0	0	0	0	-
Craig Counsell	Mil	19	11	112.0	16	42	0	5	1.000	4.66	16	5	.313	-1	-	44	-1	-1	+2	0	-1	-1	-1	-
Callix Crabbe	SD	5	3	29.2	4	7	3	1	.786	3.34	2	1	.500	0	-	8	+1	-1	-2	-2	0	-2	-2	-
Luis Cruz	Pit	2	2	17.0	6	5	0	2	1.000	5.82	3	2	.667	0	-	4	0	0		+1	0	+1	1	-
Rajai Davis	Oak	1	0	1.0	0	0	0	0	-	.00	0		-			0				0	0	0	0	
Travis Denker	SF	13	8	70.0	19	16	1	3	.972	4.50	10	3	.300	-1	-	19	0	0	0	0	0	0	0	-
Mark DeRosa	ChC	95	80	670.0	143	185	8	32	.976	4.41	77	30	.390	-3	32	231	-3	-4	-1	-8	0	-8	-6	28
Blake DeWitt	LAD	27	24	193.2	41	62	2	9	.981	4.79	22	9	.409	-1	-	69	0	-1	-2	-3	-1	-4	-3	-
Joe Dillon	Mil	6	5	43.2	9	18	1	5	.964	5.56	9	5	.556	0	-	21	0	-2		-2	0	-2	-2	-
German Duran	Tex	17	9	94.0	24	22	0	3	1.000	4.40	6	2	.333	0	-	39	-1	+1	0	0	+1	+1	1	-
Ray Durham	2 tms	95	85	738.0	188	190	3	53	.992	4.61	113	51	.451	-1	24	212	-10	+3	-1	-8	-3	-11	-8	31
Damion Easley	NYM	64	60	539.1	128	160	5	38	.983	4.81	89	36	.404	-3	32	170	0	+3	-12	-10	+3	-7	-5	26
David Eckstein	2 tms	24	23	197.0	37	79	0	18	1.000	5.30	33	16	.485	0	-	86	0	-1	+2	+1	0	+1	1	-
Mark Ellis	Oak	115	114	1011.2	228	336	4	88	.993	5.02	131	81	.618	5	2	373	+9	+7	+5	+22	+3	+25	19	2
Adam Everett	Min	1	0	1.0	0	0	0	0	-	.00	0		-			0				0	0	0	0	
Brandon Fahey	Bal	10	5	48.0	10	11	0	8	1.000	3.94	9	8	.889	1	-	5	0	0	-3	-2	0	-2	-2	-
Chone Figgins	LAA	9	7	63.0	10	19	0	4	1.000	4.14	8	4	.500	0	-	20	0	+1	+1	+2	-1	+1	1	-
Mike Fontenot	ChC	82	49	498.2	101	143	1	27	.996	4.40	48	25	.521	0	15	176	+2	+3	+6	+10	+1	+11	8	7
Ryan Freel	Cin	3	1	12.0	4	5	0	1	1.000	6.75	3		-			5				0	0	0	0	
Esteban German	KC	35	23	214.0	41	77	3	19	.975	4.96	31	17	.548	0	-	80	-4	0	-2	-5	0	-5	-4	-
Chris Getz	CWS	7	1	23.0	6	9	0	1	1.000	5.87	3	1	.333	0	-	11				0	0	0	0	
Chris Gomez	Pit	18	10	110.2	33	20	2	4	.964	4.31	12	4	.333	-1	-	32	0	0	-1	-2	0	-2	-2	-
Alberto Gonzalez	NYY	4	4	28.0	4	7	0	1	1.000	3.54	1	1	1.000	0	-	9	0	0	+1	+1	0	+1	1	-
Edgar Gonzalez	SD	72	66	559.2	92	189	4	35	.986	4.52	74	32	.432	-2	26	192	-2	-1	+6	+2	-1	+2	1	14
Ruben Gotay	Atl	3	3	26.0	3	10	0	2	1.000	4.50	3	2	.667	0	-	8	+1	0	+1	+2	0	+2	2	-
Mark Grudzielanek	KC	85	85	710.2	135	257	3	59	.990	4.96	87	52	.598	3	5	279	-2	+4	-7	-5	-2	-7	-5	25
Jerry Hairston	Cin	7	5	46.0	11	17	0	5	1.000	5.48	6	4	.667	0	-	19	+2	-1	0	+1	0	+1	1	-
Scott Hairston	SD	1	0	1.2	1	1	0	0	1.000	10.80	0		-			2	0			0	0	0	0	
Bill Hall	Mil	6	3	32.0	3	16	2	1	.905	5.34	5	1	.200	0	-	17	+1	0	-1	0	0	0	0	-
Brad Harman	Phi	4	4	17.0	2	3	0	0	1.000	2.65	1		-			4	0	0	0	0	0	0	0	-
Brendan Harris	Min	39	37	319.2	56	101	5	24	.969	4.42	41	20	.488	0	-	100	-2	+3	-1	+1	-1	0	0	-
Willie Harris	Was	14	11	86.1	29	30	1	9	.983	6.15	16	8	.500	0	-	34	+1	-1	+1	+2	-1	+1	1	-
Anderson Hernandez	Was	16	15	138.0	34	43	0	9	1.000	5.02	17	6	.353	-1	-	45	+2	+1	+2	+5	-1	+4	3	-
Luis Hernandez	Bal	5	2	21.0	3	9	0	2	1.000	5.14	3	1	.333	0	-	11	0	0	+1	+1	0	+1	1	-
Jonathan Herrera	Col	21	12	122.0	34	48	2	13	.976	6.05	20	13	.650	1	-	53	+6	-2	-2	+2	0	+2	2	-
Aaron Hill	Tor	55	53	479.0	87	150	1	27	.996	4.45	50	25	.500	0	-	164	-2	+2	0	0	-2	-2	-2	-
Michael Hollimon	Det	2	1	8.0	3	2	0	0	1.000	5.63	1		-			4				0	0	0	0	
Chin-lung Hu	LAD	30	7	108.2	15	28	1	4	.977	3.56	9	4	.444	0	-	30	0	-1	+2	+2	0	+2	2	-

		BASIC									GROUND DP					PLUS/MINUS								
Name	Team	G	GS	Inn	PO	A	E	DP	Pct	Rng	GDP Opps	GDP	Pct	Runs Saved	Rank	Outs Made	To His Right	Straight On	To His Left	GB	Air	Total	Runs Saved	Rank
Orlando Hudson	Ari	105	105	904.2	200	284	9	60	.982	4.82	106	53	.500	0	15	345	-11	0	+4	-7	+3	-4	-3	21
Tug Hulett	Sea	4	1	18.0	4	9	0	2	1.000	6.50	3	2	.667	0	-	8	0	0	+1	+1	-1	0	0	-
Tadahito Iguchi	2 tms	78	73	672.1	143	206	1	54	.997	4.67	94	52	.553	2	8	216	-8	+2	+5	0	0	0	0	17
Omar Infante	Atl	10	9	74.0	14	19	0	6	1.000	4.01	13	6	.462	0	-	19	+1	+1	0	+2	0	+2	2	-
Joe Inglett	Tor	66	62	541.1	123	176	5	38	.984	4.97	68	34	.500	0	15	206	-1	-4	+7	+2	+5	+7	5	9
Hernan Iribarren	Mil	2	1	9.1	1	3	0	1	1.000	3.86	2	1	.500	0	-	3	+1			+1	0	+1	1	-
Akinori Iwamura	TB	152	151	1337.0	284	397	7	109	.990	4.58	166	101	.608	5	2	434	-5	-6	+7	-4	+1	-3	-2	19
Maicer Izturis	LAA	23	20	183.2	49	61	2	15	.982	5.39	26	13	.500	0	-	65	0	-1	+2	0	+1	+1	1	-
Elliot Johnson	TB	1	1	9.0	3	5	0	1	1.000	8.00	1	1	1.000	0	-	5	+1	0	0	+1	+1	+2	2	-
Kelly Johnson	Atl	144	135	1198.2	262	425	14	89	.980	5.16	182	83	.456	-2	26	441	-3	-2	+5	0	-1	-1	-1	18
Sean Kazmar	SD	2	0	3.0	2	2	0	1	1.000	12.00	2	1	.500	0	-	1	0			0	0	0	0	-
Howie Kendrick	LAA	92	90	776.0	155	287	4	67	.991	5.13	99	61	.616	3	5	308	-13	-4	+13	-5	+1	-4	-3	22
Adam Kennedy	StL	84	74	635.2	144	224	7	56	.981	5.21	85	53	.624	3	5	245	+15	-1	+5	+18	0	+18	14	3
Jeff Kent	LAD	116	114	885.0	168	279	11	53	.976	4.55	128	53	.414	-3	32	291	-7	0	0	-7	-4	-11	-8	29
Jeff Keppinger	Cin	3	3	23.0	5	5	0	2	1.000	3.91	2	1	.500	0	-	3	-1	0		-1	0	-1	-1	-
Ian Kinsler	Tex	121	120	1064.0	292	390	18	123	.974	5.77	201	113	.562	4	4	412	-1	+2	-15	-13	-2	-15	-11	33
Andy LaRoche	LAD	3	2	13.0	7	2	0	3	1.000	6.23	5	3	.600	0	-	3				0	0	0	0	-
Felipe Lopez	2 tms	101	89	780.0	155	253	11	53	.974	4.71	103	45	.437	-2	26	267	-8	+1	-6	-12	-3	-15	-11	34
Jose Lopez	Sea	139	139	1229.1	259	468	12	99	.984	5.32	172	90	.523	1	11	532	-9	+1	+10	+2	-2	0	0	16
Mark Loretta	Hou	46	41	368.0	85	119	1	28	.995	4.99	42	26	.619	2	-	130	-4	+4	-4	-5	-1	-6	-5	-
Jed Lowrie	Bos	3	2	16.0	2	4	0	0	1.000	3.38	3				-	4	0			0	-1	-1	-1	-
Matt Macri	Min	2	1	10.0	1	6	0	1	1.000	6.30	1	1	1.000	0	-	4	0	0	0	0	0	0	0	-
Ramon Martinez	NYM	5	4	38.0	5	11	0	2	1.000	3.79	4	2	.500	0	-	15	0	+1	-3	-2	0	-2	-2	-
Kaz Matsui	Hou	94	94	806.0	190	219	12	56	.971	4.57	101	49	.485	0	15	267	-2	0	-7	-10	-1	-11	-8	30
Edwin Maysonet	Hou	3	0	4.0	2	0	0	0	1.000	4.50	0		-		-	2	0			0	0	0	0	-
Luis Maza	LAD	35	10	136.1	30	45	2	13	.974	4.95	22	12	.545	0	-	45	+1	-1	-1	-2	+1	-1	-1	-
John McDonald	Tor	1	0	3.0	0	0	0	0	-	.00	0		-		-	0				0	0	0	0	-
Aaron Miles	StL	85	49	499.2	91	165	3	47	.988	4.61	68	41	.603	2	8	171	+2	-1	-5	-4	+5	+1	1	15
Scott Moore	Bal	1	1	6.0	2	2	0	0	1.000	6.00	0		-		-	2				0	0	0	0	-
Donnie Murphy	Oak	10	7	61.0	12	20	0	3	1.000	4.72	7	3	.429	0	-	24	0	+1	0	+1	0	+1	1	-
David Newhan	Hou	28	19	177.2	33	39	1	11	.986	3.65	23	11	.478	0	-	40	-2	-1	-2	-4	0	-4	-3	-
Jayson Nix	Col	20	15	143.1	27	61	0	9	1.000	5.53	18	7	.389	-1	-	63	+2	+2	0	+4	0	+4	3	-
Ivan Ochoa	SF	8	5	48.0	8	14	1	2	.957	4.13	4	1	.250	0	-	17	0	0	+1	+1	-1	0	0	-
Augie Ojeda	Ari	44	30	286.0	70	92	6	26	1.000	5.10	41	24	.585	1	-	105	0	0	+3	+3	+3	+6	5	-
Pete Orr	Was	7	2	31.0	8	10	1	2	.947	5.23	5	2	.400	0	-	13	+2	0	-3	-1	0	-1	-1	-
Pablo Ozuna	2 tms	37	9	133.2	27	43	1	4	.986	4.71	15	2	.133	-1	-	50	-4	-1	+1	-3	-2	-5	-4	-
Eric Patterson	2 tms	22	20	177.1	51	49	4	15	.962	5.08	22	13	.591	1	-	60	0	-2	-2	-4	+2	-2	-2	-
Dustin Pedroia	Bos	157	155	1376.1	279	448	6	101	.992	4.75	176	90	.511	1	11	477	+1	+4	+9	+13	+2	+15	11	5
Cliff Pennington	Oak	16	15	136.0	33	44	0	17	1.000	5.10	18	16	.889	2	-	44	-2	-1	-2	-5	-1	-6	-5	-
Tomas Perez	Hou	5	1	15.0	2	2	0	2	1.000	2.40	2	2	1.000	0	-	2	0	-1	-2	-2	0	-2	-2	-
Gregorio Petit	Oak	4	4	39.0	7	14	0	1	1.000	4.85	5	1	.200	0	-	14	0	+1	+2	+3	0	+3	2	-
Andy Phillips	Cin	6	1	19.0	5	8	0	3	1.000	6.16	5	3	.600	0	-	8	0	0	+1	+2	0	+2	2	-
Brandon Phillips	Cin	140	140	1237.2	298	401	7	85	.990	5.08	183	80	.437	-3	32	429	+17	+4	0	+21	-4	+17	13	4
Placido Polanco	Det	141	136	1201.1	323	374	8	100	.989	5.22	178	89	.500	0	15	424	+5	-2	+10	+12	+2	+14	11	6
Martin Prado	Atl	17	15	142.0	33	55	3	7	.967	5.58	27	6	.222	-2	-	59	-2	-2	-2	-5	+2	-3	-2	-
Albert Pujols	StL	1	0	3.1	1	0	0	0	1.000	2.70	0		-		-	0				0	0	0	0	-
Nick Punto	Min	26	23	215.2	54	79	2	18	.985	5.55	30	16	.533	0	-	88	-1	-2	+4	+2	-1	+1	1	-
Omar Quintanilla	Col	40	21	212.2	40	72	1	24	.991	4.74	39	22	.564	1	-	74	+2	+1	-2	+1	-1	0	0	-
Ryan Raburn	Det	16	12	118.0	27	34	5	12	.924	4.65	17	12	.706	1	-	40	+2	-3	-1	-3	-1	-4	-3	-
Alexei Ramirez	CWS	121	117	1017.1	237	327	11	71	.981	4.99	135	67	.496	0	15	370	-10	+3	-6	-13	+5	-8	-6	27
Cody Ransom	NYY	2	1	13.0	3	3	1	0	.857	4.15	0		-		-	6	0	0	-1	-1	0	-1	-1	-
Argenis Reyes	NYM	27	20	193.1	48	59	0	17	1.000	4.98	30	16	.533	0	-	70	+3	+1	0	+4	+2	+6	5	-
Danny Richar	Cin	10	6	55.2	12	16	1	4	.966	4.53	9	4	.444	0	-	19	-1	0	0	-1	-1	-2	-2	-
Luis Rivas	Pit	29	19	191.2	51	68	1	22	.992	5.59	36	22	.611	1	-	62	+1	+1	-1	+1	0	+1	1	-
Juan Rivera	LAA	1	0	1.0	0	0	0	0	-	.00	0		-		-	0				0	0	0	0	-
Brian Roberts	Bal	154	151	1320.0	289	441	8	110	.989	4.98	211	105	.498	0	15	474	+13	+2	-15	-1	-3	-4	-3	20
Luis Rodriguez	SD	7	4	39.0	11	10	0	4	1.000	4.85	7	4	.571	0	-	12	0	0	-1	-1	0	-1	-1	-
Sean Rodriguez	LAA	51	45	423.2	97	127	2	36	.991	4.76	58	36	.621	2	-	149	-4	+1	+1	-2	0	-2	-2	-
Ryan Rohlinger	SF	3	2	3.0	0	0	0	0	-	.00	0		-		-	0				0	0	0	0	-
Adam Rosales	Cin	2	2	16.0	6	6	0	4	1.000	6.75	4	3	.750	0	-	4	+1	0	0	+1	0	+1	1	-
Brendan Ryan	StL	23	18	149.0	23	39	1	5	.984	3.74	16	5	.313	-1	-	42	-1	0	+1	-1	0	-1	-1	-
Freddy Sanchez	Pit	131	131	1135.2	291	355	7	104	.989	5.12	190	96	.505	0	15	369	+2	-2	+5	+5	-3	+2	2	12
Ramon Santiago	Det	21	13	117.2	30	36	0	13	1.000	5.05	20	13	.650	1	-	37	-1	0	-1	-2	+1	-1	-1	-
Marco Scutaro	Tor	50	39	354.1	60	126	1	19	.995	4.72	42	17	.405	-1	-	144	-3	-3	+6	0	+1	+1	1	-
Jason Smith	KC	9	3	41.0	5	16	0	2	1.000	4.61	5	2	.400	0	-	17	0	0	+1	+2	+1	+3	2	-
Alfonso Soriano	ChC	1	0	2.0	0	2	0	0	1.000	18.00	0		-		-	2				0	0	0	0	-
Craig Stansberry	SD	4	2	24.2	4	3	2	0	.778	2.55	4				-	4	0	-1	-2	-2	0	-2	-2	-
Ian Stewart	Col	12	12	93.0	16	38	1	5	.982	5.23	9	4	.444	0	-	42	+2	-1	+1	+2	0	+2	2	-
Matt Tolbert	Min	11	8	75.0	15	30	1	7	.978	5.40	10	6	.600	0	-	30	-4	0	+2	-2	0	-2	-2	-
Eider Torres	Bal	1	1	6.0	1	2	0	0	1.000	4.50	1				-	3	+1			+1	0	+1	1	-
Dan Uggla	Fla	144	144	1272.2	297	390	13	82	.981	4.86	154	74	.481	-1	24	464	+9	-5	0	+3	+1	+4	3	10
Juan Uribe	CWS	52	39	362.1	104	124	1	34	.996	5.66	56	33	.589	2	-	138	-3	+1	+1	-2	+1	-1	-1	-
Chase Utley	Phi	159	157	1395.2	340	463	13	102	.984	5.18	204	96	.471	-2	26	513	+8	+6	+32	+46	0	+46	35	1
Luis Valbuena	Sea	16	15	125.0	21	41	0	11	1.000	4.46	16	10	.625	1	-	39	-1	-2	-1	-4	-2	-6	-5	-
Ramon Vazquez	Tex	11	7	59.0	20	15	0	6	1.000	5.34	8	4	.500	0	-	18	-1	0	+2	+2	0	+2	2	-
Jorge Velandia	2 tms	2	2	17.0	4	4	0	1	1.000	4.24	1	1	1.000	0	-	5	0	0	0	0	0	0	0	-
Gil Velazquez	Bos	2	2	19.0	5	9	0	2	1.000	6.63	3	2	.667	0	-	9	0	-1	-1	-2	0	-2	-2	-
Eugenio Velez	SF	69	50	449.2	102	104	7	26	.967	4.12	58	22	.379	-2	-	129	-2	-3	-2	-7	+2	-5	-4	-
Rico Washington	StL	1	0	1.0	0	0	0	0	-	.00	0		-		-	0	0	0	0	0	0	0	0	-
Rickie Weeks	Mil	120	118	1056.0	256	333	15	84	.975	5.02	163	75	.460	-2	26	356	+3	-7	+4	+1	+1	+2	2	13
Delwyn Young	LAD	5	1	16.0	3	6	0	0	1.000	5.06	2				-	7	0	0	-1	-1	0	-1	-1	-
Ben Zobrist	TB	8	4	41.0	11	11	0	3	1.000	4.83	8	3	.375	0	-	11	+1	0	+1	+2	0	+2	2	-
2008 MLB Averages									.985	4.91	5995	3050	.509											

Third Basemen

		BASIC										BUNTS					PLUS/MINUS								
Name	Team	G	GS	Inn	PO	A	E	DP	Pct	Rng	Opps	Score	Grade	Runs Saved	Rank	Outs Made	To His Right	Straight On	To His Left	GB	Air	Total	Enhanced	Runs Saved	Rank
Alfredo Amezaga	Fla	15	0	25.2	2	5	0	0	1.000	2.45					-	7	0	+1	0	+2	0	+2	+2	2	-
Robert Andino	Fla	1	0	1.0	0	0	0	0	-	.00					-	0								0	-
Garrett Atkins	Col	94	92	797.0	47	197	9	21	.964	2.76	9	.494	C+	0	12	217	-1	-8	-3	-11	0	-11	-11	-8	32
Rich Aurilia	SF	63	50	427.2	31	67	5	4	.951	2.06	7	.650	A	1	-	89	-3	-2	0	-5	+1	-4	-4	-3	-
Brad Ausmus	Hou	1	0	1.0	0	0	1	0	.000	.00					-	0	-1			-1	0	-1	-1	-1	-
Mike Aviles	KC	7	3	29.2	3	3	0	0	1.000	1.82					-	5	-2	-1	+2	-1	0	-1	-1	-1	-
Willy Aybar	TB	41	40	358.1	29	84	5	12	.958	2.84	5	.920	A+	2	-	103	+1	-1	+2	+2	0	+2	+1	1	-
Jeff Baisley	Oak	10	10	79.0	6	14	0	1	1.000	2.28	1	.250	F	0	-	16	-1	-1	-1	-3	0	-3	-3	-2	-
Jeff Baker	Col	9	7	61.0	5	17	0	4	1.000	3.25	1	.600	B+	0	-	19	0	-2	+1	-1	0	-1	-1	-1	-
Brian Barden	StL	4	0	7.0	0	2	0	0	1.000	2.57					-	2	0			+1	0	+1	+1	1	-
Clint Barmes	Col	13	4	48.1	1	10	1	2	.917	2.05	1	.600	B+	0	-	9	+1	-1	-1	-1	0	-1	-1	-1	-
Daric Barton	Oak	1	0	2.0	1	1	0	1	1.000	9.00					-	1	0			0	0	0	0	0	-
Jose Bautista	2 tms	99	85	766.1	50	207	11	17	.959	3.02	16	.403	D+	-1	24	235	-2	-1	+1	-2	0	-2	-3	-2	21
Ronnie Belliard	Was	31	25	215.1	16	40	5	3	.918	2.34	1	.250	F	0	-	54	-1	-3	+1	-4	+1	-3	-3	-2	-
Adrian Beltre	Sea	139	137	1208.1	100	272	14	27	.964	2.77	16	.500	C+	0	12	328	+6	+3	+21	+30	+1	+31	+32	24	1
Wilson Betemit	NYY	21	9	100.0	4	21	3	4	.893	2.25	1	.250	F	0	-	24	-3	-1	0	-4	0	-4	-6	-5	-
Casey Blake	2 tms	133	130	1104.2	66	245	14	25	.957	2.53	16	.475	C	0	12	280	+7	-10	-3	-6	+1	-5	-4	-3	23
Hank Blalock	Tex	31	31	263.0	24	54	4	6	.951	2.67	7	.350	D-	-1	-	71	+2	-2	+2	+2	-1	+1	0	0	-
Willie Bloomquist	Sea	1	1	7.0	0	0	0	0	-	.00					-	0				0	0	0	0	0	-
Geoff Blum	Hou	75	68	599.2	43	144	3	8	.979	2.81	2	.425	C-	0	12	178	+5	-1	+3	+7	-1	+6	+7	5	12
Aaron Boone	Was	16	14	113.0	3	23	1	2	.963	2.07	4	.688	A+	0	-	25	-2	+1	0	-1	0	-1	-1	-1	-
Russell Branyan	Mil	35	33	276.0	22	63	4	6	.955	2.77	11	.414	D+	-1	-	75	0	+2	-1	+1	+1	+2	+2	2	-
Matt Brown	LAA	10	3	46.0	3	8	2	2	.846	2.15					-	11	-1	0	-1	-2	0	-2	-2	-2	-
Eric Bruntlett	Phi	27	1	132.0	16	26	2	1	.955	2.86	1	.250	F	0	-	39	+1	+1	0	+1	-1	0	+2	2	-
Chris Burke	Ari	4	2	20.0	2	5	0	0	1.000	3.15	2	.425	C-	0	-	6	0	-2		-1	0	-1	-1	-1	-
Jamie Burke	Sea	1	0	2.0	0	1	0	0	1.000	4.50					-	1		0		0	0	0	0	0	-
Brian Buscher	Min	64	60	519.1	37	113	10	9	.938	2.60	5	.470	C	0	12	139	-3	+3	-2	-3	0	-3	-3	-2	22
Jolbert Cabrera	Cin	3	1	9.1	1	2	0	0	1.000	2.89					-	3	-1	0	0	0	0	0	0	0	-
Miguel Cabrera	Det	14	14	116.0	15	30	5	4	.900	3.49	1	.250	F	0	-	37	-3	+1	-1	-4	0	-4	-4	-3	-
Miguel Cairo	Sea	19	12	112.0	13	21	1	5	.971	2.73	1	.600	B+	0	-	32	+2	-1	0	+1	0	+1	+1	1	-
Alberto Callaspo	KC	1	1	8.0	1	5	0	1	1.000	6.75	1	.250	F	0	-	5	0	+1	0	+1	0	+1	+1	1	-
Jorge Cantu	Fla	129	129	1066.2	83	214	20	21	.937	2.51	18	.536	B-	0	12	261	-3	-6	-2	-10	-1	-11	-11	-8	31
Jamey Carroll	Cle	43	18	199.2	12	55	6	5	.918	3.02					-	63	-1	+2	+4	+5	0	+5	+5	4	-
Kevin Cash	Bos	4	0	15.0	1	1	0	0	1.000	1.20	1	.250	F	0	-	2	0			0	0	0	0	0	-
Jose Castillo	2 tms	110	97	880.0	53	177	15	14	.939	2.35	20	.555	B	2	4	198	-2	-1	-1	-5	+1	-4	-5	-4	24
Kory Casto	Was	13	11	103.0	12	23	0	1	1.000	3.06	3	.367	D	0	-	32	+2	+1	+1	+4	0	+4	+4	3	-
Juan Castro	2 tms	5	0	8.0	1	4	0	0	1.000	5.63					-	5	0			-3	0	-3	-3	-2	-
Ronny Cedeno	ChC	7	0	12.0	1	1	0	0	1.000	1.50					-	2	+1	-1	0	0	0	0	+1	1	-
Mike Cervenak	Phi	2	1	10.0	0	0	0	0	-	.00					-	0							0	0	-
Eric Chavez	Oak	15	15	130.0	12	32	1	4	.978	3.05	1	.600	B+	0	-	42	0	0	-2	-1	+1	0	0	0	-
Alex Cintron	Bal	8	0	21.1	1	6	1	0	.875	2.95					-	7	0	+1	-1	0	0	0	0	0	-
Howie Clark	Min	1	1	8.0	3	2	0	1	1.000	5.63	1	.600	B+	0	-	3				0	0	0	0	0	-
Brooks Conrad	Oak	4	4	33.0	1	4	1	1	.833	1.36					-	5	0	0	0	0	0	0	0	0	-
Craig Counsell	Mil	38	30	268.1	23	54	1	6	.987	2.58	7	.707	A+	1	-	71	-1	+1	+3	+3	+1	+4	+4	3	-
Joe Crede	CWS	97	95	834.2	57	207	20	22	.930	2.85	14	.429	C-	-1	24	244	-8	+15	+7	+13	0	+13	+13	10	4
Chris Davis	Tex	32	31	276.0	31	44	3	5	.962	2.45	5	.550	B	0	-	66	-1	-3	-5	-9	0	-9	-9	-7	-
Travis Denker	SF	1	0	1.0	0	0	0	0	-	.00					-	0								0	-
Mark DeRosa	ChC	22	10	114.1	6	28	2	2	.944	2.68	2	.425	C-	0	-	32	+3	-2	+1	+1	-1	0	0	0	-
Blake DeWitt	LAD	95	77	727.2	58	193	8	19	.969	3.10	16	.634	A-	3	1	220	+3	+2	+9	+14	-2	+12	+11	8	7
Joe Dillon	Mil	1	1	9.0	0	2	0	0	1.000	2.00	1	.250	F	0	-	2				0	0	0	0	0	-
Greg Dobbs	Phi	52	42	327.1	34	67	3	7	.971	2.78	8	.625	A-	0	-	88	+1	-4	-2	-5	0	-5	-5	-4	-
German Duran	Tex	30	25	223.0	13	45	5	2	.921	2.34	7	.350	D-	-1	-	54	-2	-1	-2	-5	-1	-6	-7	-5	-
Damion Easley	NYM	1	1	9.0	3	0	0	0	1.000	3.00					-	3	0	-1	0	-1	0	-1	0	0	-
Edwin Encarnacion	Cin	143	141	1237.0	91	216	23	23	.930	2.23	21	.474	C	-1	24	278	-7	-6	-7	-20	-1	-21	-21	-16	35
Morgan Ensberg	NYY	21	13	133.0	8	32	1	2	.976	2.71	2	.425	C-	0	-	37	-1	-5	0	-6	0	-6	-5	-4	-
Pedro Feliz	Phi	129	106	978.1	73	223	8	19	.974	2.72	16	.522	B-	0	12	272	+16	-7	-6	+4	0	+4	+7	5	10
Josh Fields	CWS	12	6	61.2	6	16	2	3	.917	3.21	1	.250	F	0	-	20	0	-1	-1	-2	0	-2	-2	-2	-
Chone Figgins	LAA	105	105	914.1	84	185	6	15	.978	2.65	8	.569	B	1	7	243	+4	+6	-1	+9	0	+9	+11	8	6
Ryan Freel	Cin	4	4	33.0	4	4	1	0	.889	2.18					-	8	-1	0	-1	-2	0	-2	-2	-2	-
Mat Gamel	Mil	1	0	1.0	0	0	0	0	-	.00					-	0								0	-
Nomar Garciaparra	LAD	11	9	73.0	2	21	2	0	.920	2.84					-	23	-2	+2	0	+1	0	+1	+1	1	-
Esteban German	KC	6	5	43.0	2	5	0	2	1.000	1.47	1	.250	F	0	-	6	0	0	0	0	0	0	0	0	-
Conor Gillaspie	SF	2	0	4.0	1	0	0	0	1.000	2.25					-	0								0	-
Troy Glaus	StL	146	145	1243.1	99	279	7	27	.982	2.74	21	.648	A	2	4	339	+4	0	+4	+8	-1	+7	+6	5	13
Chris Gomez	Pit	20	6	85.2	5	17	1	1	.957	2.31					-	21	-2	+1	+1	+1	0	+1	+1	1	-
Alberto Gonzalez	2 tms	14	7	65.2	7	13	1	2	.952	2.74	1	.250	F	0	-	17	-1	-2	-1	-2	0	-2	-2	-2	-
Andy Gonzalez	Cle	2	1	12.0	1	1	1	0	.667	1.50					-	2	-2			-3	0	-3	-3	-2	-
Edgar Gonzalez	SD	4	2	23.0	1	3	1	0	.800	1.57					-	3				0	0	0	0	0	-
Alex Gordon	KC	133	133	1180.0	112	230	16	21	.955	2.61	16	.384	D	-2	30	311	+1	-2	-9	-10	-1	-11	-9	-7	26
Ruben Gotay	Atl	10	6	64.0	2	13	2	0	.882	2.11					-	13	0	-1	0	0	0	0	-1	-1	-
Carlos Guillen	Det	89	87	749.2	68	195	14	15	.949	3.16	17	.444	C-	-2	30	240	-1	-2	-6	-9	+2	-7	-9	-7	27
Jerry Hairston	Cin	1	0	2.0	0	0	0	0	-	.00					-	0	0	0	0	0	0	0	0	0	-
Bill Hall	Mil	113	98	899.1	69	193	17	24	.939	2.62	15	.367	D	-2	30	233	0	+4	-3	+1	0	+1	+1	1	18
Jack Hannahan	Oak	126	106	983.2	70	218	9	24	.970	2.64	15	.543	B-	0	12	261	+3	+10	+5	+18	+1	+19	+21	16	2
Brad Harman	Phi	1	0	1.0	0	0	0	0	-	.00					-	0				0	0	0	0	0	-
Brendan Harris	Min	34	28	256.1	18	48	2	4	.971	2.32	1	.250	F	0	-	56	+1	-1	-6	-6	0	-6	-5	-4	-
Willie Harris	Was	14	3	44.0	0	6	0	0	1.000	1.23					-	6	+1	0	0	+1	0	+1	+1	1	-
Chase Headley	SD	7	6	55.0	3	9	1	0	.923	1.96					-	11	+1	0	0	+1	0	+1	+1	1	-
Wes Helms	Fla	60	30	325.0	31	63	1	3	.989	2.60	6	.550	B	1	-	87	+2	+2	0	+4	0	+4	+5	4	-
Mike Hessman	Det	12	7	70.0	7	20	1	3	.964	3.47	1	.250	F	0	-	24	-1	0	-1	-2	0	-2	-3	-2	-
Eric Hinske	TB	8	4	49.0	1	6	0	0	1.000	1.29	1	.250	F	0	-	7	+1	+1	0	+1	0	+1	+1	1	-
Michael Hollimon	Det	2	0	2.0	1	0	0	0	1.000	4.50					-	1				0	0	0	0	0	-
Aubrey Huff	Bal	33	31	275.0	23	64	3	4	.967	2.85	6	.550	B	1	-	75	-1	+2	-1	0	-1	-1	-1	-1	-
Tug Hulett	Sea	1	0	1.0	0	0	0	0	-	.00					-	0								0	-
Chris Iannetta	Col	1	0	8.1	1	1	0	0	1.000	2.16					-	1	0	0	0	0	0	0	0	0	-

		BASIC										BUNTS					PLUS/MINUS									
Name	Team	G	GS	Inn	PO	A	E	DP	Pct	Rng	Opps	Score	Grade	Runs Saved	Rank	Outs Made	To His Right	Straight On	To His Left	GB	Air	Total	Enhanced	Runs Saved	Rank
Omar Infante	Atl	32	26	228.2	13	55	4	6	.944	2.68	2	.625	A-	0	-	62	+2	0	+1	+3	0	+3	+4	3	-
Brandon Inge	Det	51	33	324.1	38	80	1	14	.992	3.27	1	.250	F	0	-	112	+4	+1	-3	+2	-1	+1	+1	1	-
Joe Inglett	Tor	6	5	45.0	5	13	0	1	1.000	3.60	1	.600	B+	0	-	17	+1	0	+1	+3	0	+3	+3	2	-
Cesar Izturis	StL	8	1	15.2	3	3	0	0	1.000	3.45						6	0	0	0	0	0	0	0	0	-
Maicer Izturis	LAA	5	5	34.1	1	7	0	0	1.000	2.10						8	0	0	0	0	0	0	0	0	-
Chipper Jones	Atl	115	115	987.1	64	235	13	21	.958	2.73	14	.586	B+	2	4	264	+5	-3	+9	+11	-1	+10	+10	8	8
Jeff Keppinger	Cin	10	7	71.1	3	18	0	2	1.000	2.65						20	0	0	-2	-1	0	-1	-1	-1	-
Kevin Kouzmanoff	SD	154	154	1379.0	128	277	11	34	.974	2.64	22	.625	A-	1	7	358	+8	-8	-5	-5	+1	-4	-2	-2	20
Gerald Laird	Tex	2	1	10.0	0	3	0	0	1.000	2.70						3	-1	0	0	0	0	0	0	0	-
Mike Lamb	2 tms	56	51	460.2	41	90	5	8	.963	2.56	8	.575	B	0	12	112	-10	+2	+1	-7	-1	-8	-9	-7	28
Jeff Larish	Det	12	12	83.0	10	17	2	1	.931	2.93	4	.425	C-	-1	-	22	-1	-2	-1	-4	0	-4	-4	-3	-
Andy LaRoche	2 tms	59	57	502.1	25	136	10	20	.942	2.88	15	.483	C+	-1	24	146	+2	-2	0	+1	+1	+2	+1	1	19
Brent Lillibridge	Atl	1	0	2.0	0	1	0	0	1.000	4.50						1	0			0		0	0	0	-
Evan Longoria	TB	119	118	1045.0	86	230	12	26	.963	2.72	21	.526	B-	1	7	292	0	+5	+4	+10	-1	+9	+11	8	5
Felipe Lopez	StL	13	8	85.1	2	23	2	2	.926	2.64	2	.425	C-	0	-	24	+2	+1	-1	+2	0	+2	+2	2	-
Mark Loretta	Hou	17	12	110.2	7	31	1	1	.974	3.09	3	.733	A+	1	-	34	-2	+3	+2	+3	+1	+4	+4	3	-
Mike Lowell	Bos	110	108	935.2	80	217	10	20	.967	2.86	16	.525	B-	0	12	270	+3	+4	-2	+5	+2	+7	+7	5	11
Jed Lowrie	Bos	45	22	243.2	16	59	2	8	.974	2.77	6	.558	B	0	-	66	0	+1	0	+1	0	+1	0	0	-
Matt Macri	Min	11	8	64.1	3	14	1	3	.944	2.38						17	-3	0	+1	-2	0	-2	-3	-2	-
Andy Marte	Cle	76	68	581.1	43	155	6	19	.971	3.07	14	.382	D	-3	34	182	+3	+5	-2	+6	+1	+7	+6	5	14
Russell Martin	LAD	11	8	71.0	2	21	3	3	.885	2.92	3	.617	A-	0	-	20	-1	0	+1	+1	0	+1	+1	1	-
Joe Mather	StL	1	0	3.0	0	0	0	0	-	.00						0	-1			-1	0	-1	-1	-1	-
Scott McClain	SF	4	4	36.0	3	8	0	0	1.000	2.75						11	-1	0	-1	-2	0	-2	-2	-2	-
John McDonald	Tor	4	2	23.0	0	5	0	0	1.000	1.96						5	+1			+2	0	+2	+2	2	-
Casey McGehee	ChC	6	4	41.2	3	13	0	3	1.000	3.46						16	+1	0	+3	+3	0	+3	+3	2	-
Dallas McPherson	Fla	2	2	17.0	0	1	0	0	1.000	.53						1				0	0	0	0	0	-
Adam Melhuse	Tex	2	2	6.0	1	2	0	0	1.000	4.50	1	.600	B+	0	-	2	-1	0	0	0	0	0	0	0	-
Travis Metcalf	Tex	19	14	130.0	15	18	1	6	.971	2.28	3	.367	D	0	-	29	-1	-2	-2	-5	0	-5	-6	-5	-
Doug Mientkiewicz	Pit	33	30	244.2	24	54	7	5	.918	2.87	7	.564	B	0	-	69	-1	0	-3	-4	0	-4	-4	-3	-
Aaron Miles	StL	11	5	61.0	2	16	0	1	1.000	2.66						16	0	+1	+1	+2	0	+2	+1	1	-
Chad Moeller	NYY	3	0	3.2	0	0	0	0	-	.00						0				0	0	0	0	0	-
Scott Moore	Bal	1	1	9.0	0	2	0	0	1.000	2.00						2	0	0	0	0	0	0	0	0	-
Melvin Mora	Bal	124	124	1059.2	85	252	14	28	.960	2.86	17	.485	C+	-1	24	312	+7	-9	-12	-15	0	-15	-13	-10	34
Donnie Murphy	Oak	24	18	143.1	12	27	1	7	.975	2.45	1	.600	B+	0	-	36	0	+2	-3	-1	0	-1	-2	-2	-
Augie Ojeda	Ari	28	9	110.1	6	32	0	3	1.000	3.10	3	.367	D	0	-	34	+1	0	+1	+2	0	+2	+2	2	-
Pete Orr	Was	8	3	37.0	4	16	0	0	1.000	4.86	2	.425	C-	0	-	18	0	+1	0	+1	0	+1	+1	1	-
Pablo Ozuna	2 tms	17	10	101.0	8	29	4	4	.902	3.30						35	+1	0	-1	0	+1	+1	+2	2	-
Cliff Pennington	Oak	9	8	64.0	8	11	1	2	.950	2.67	3	.617	A-	0	-	14	+1	0	-1	0	-1	-1	-2	-2	-
Jhonny Peralta	Cle	1	1	9.0	1	2	0	1	1.000	3.00						3	0	0	0	+1	-1	0	0	0	-
Tomas Perez	Hou	1	0	2.0	0	0	0	0	-	.00						0				0		0	0	0	-
Andy Phillips	Cin	8	5	49.0	1	10	1	2	.917	2.02						11	0	-1	0	-1	-1	-2	-2	-2	-
Martin Prado	Atl	24	15	158.2	9	46	1	3	.982	3.12	2	.625	A-	0	-	52	0	+2	+2	+4	0	+4	+4	3	-
Nick Punto	Min	12	6	63.0	3	16	0	1	1.000	2.71	2	1.000	A+	1	-	16	+2	-1	0	+1	-1	0	0	0	-
Robb Quinlan	LAA	39	29	258.2	22	48	4	8	.946	2.44	3	.500	C+	0	-	64	-3	-2	-1	-6	0	-6	-5	-4	-
Ryan Raburn	Det	18	8	79.0	8	14	3	1	.880	2.51	1	.250	F	0	-	22	-1	0	-1	-2	-1	-3	-3	-2	-
Alexei Ramirez	CWS	1	1	1.0	0	1	0	0	1.000	9.00						1				0		0	0	0	-
Aramis Ramirez	ChC	147	147	1282.2	83	225	18	17	.945	2.16	21	.490	C+	0	12	279	-8	-2	-1	-11	-1	-12	-12	-9	33
Cody Ransom	NYY	4	3	24.0	1	6	0	0	1.000	2.63						6	+1	0	+1	+1	0	+1	+1	1	-
Mark Reynolds	Ari	150	149	1288.1	82	240	34	23	.904	2.25	22	.461	C	-1	24	293	-4	-6	-3	-13	0	-13	-11	-8	30
Luis Rivas	Pit	1	0	2.0	0	0	0	0	-	.00						0				0		0	0	0	-
Alex Rodriguez	NYY	131	131	1126.1	73	251	10	23	.970	2.59	19	.363	D	-3	34	292	-5	+6	+1	+2	+1	+3	+1	1	17
Luis Rodriguez	SD	1	0	1.1	1	1	0	1	1.000	13.50						1	0			0	0	0	0	0	-
Sean Rodriguez	LAA	1	0	1.0	0	0	0	0	-	.00						0				0		0	0	0	-
Ryan Rohlinger	SF	14	6	68.1	7	12	3	1	.864	2.50	2	.800	A+	1	-	17	-1	+1	0	0	0	0	0	0	-
Scott Rolen	Tor	115	115	1006.2	74	217	11	14	.964	2.60	15	.463	C	0	12	266	-7	+12	+8	+13	0	+13	+13	10	3
Adam Rosales	Cin	4	3	29.0	2	1	0	1	1.000	.93						3	-1	-1		-2	0	-2	-2	-2	-
Carlos Ruiz	Phi	1	0	1.0	0	0	0	0	-	.00						0				0		0	0	0	-
Brendan Ryan	StL	5	1	19.1	2	6	1	1	.889	3.72						7	-1	-1	0	-1	0	-1	-1	-1	-
Oscar Salazar	Bal	7	5	51.0	3	10	0	3	1.000	2.29	1	.250	F	0	-	11	0	0	+1	0	0	0	0	0	-
Freddy Sandoval	LAA	1	1	9.0	0	3	0	0	1.000	3.00	1	1.000	A+	0	-	2	0	0		0	0	0	0	0	-
Pablo Sandoval	SF	12	12	85.0	3	14	0	0	1.000	1.80	4	.338	D-	-1	-	16	+2	+1	-1	+2	-1	+1	+1	1	-
Ramon Santiago	Det	6	1	21.0	2	3	2	0	.714	2.14						5	-2	-2	0	-4	0	-4	-4	-3	-
Marco Scutaro	Tor	41	36	332.0	22	84	2	8	.981	2.87	5	.550	B	0	-	101	+2	+3	+11	+16	+1	+17	+17	13	-
Chris Shelton	Tex	1	0	1.0	0	0	0	0	-	.00						0				0		0	0	0	-
Jason Smith	KC	5	1	19.0	5	1	0	0	1.000	2.84						6				0	0	0	0	0	-
Ian Stewart	Col	65	59	531.1	40	127	10	15	.944	2.83	12	.554	B	1	7	153	+1	+3	0	+4	0	+4	+4	3	15
Fernando Tatis	NYM	4	2	22.0	2	2	0	0	1.000	1.64	1	1.000	A+	0	-	3	-2	-1	-1	-4	0	-4	-4	-3	-
Mark Teahen	KC	19	19	166.0	18	24	3	3	.933	2.28	4	.438	C-	-1	-	36	0	0	-2	-1	0	-1	-2	-2	-
Matt Tolbert	Min	17	9	89.1	9	24	4	4	.892	3.32	1	.250	F	0	-	31	-1	-2	0	-2	0	-2	-2	-2	-
Chad Tracy	Ari	2	2	16.0	2	2	0	0	1.000	2.25						4	0	0	0	0	0	0	0	0	-
Matt Tuiasosopo	Sea	13	12	105.0	11	23	2	4	.944	2.91	4	.338	D-	-1	-	30	0	-1	+2	+1	0	+1	+1	1	-
Juan Uribe	CWS	57	52	460.1	41	125	7	10	.960	3.25	9	.406	D+	-1	-	152	+6	-7	-2	-3	0	-3	-3	-2	-
Javier Valentin	Cin	4	1	9.2	0	0	0	0	-	.00						0				-1	0	-1	-1	-1	-
Ramon Vazquez	Tex	70	60	533.0	30	117	10	16	.936	2.48	8	.613	A-	1	7	133	0	-8	-3	-11	+1	-10	-10	-8	29
Rico Washington	StL	4	2	19.1	0	9	0	0	1.000	4.19						9	0	0	-1	-1	0	-1	-2	-2	-
Ty Wigginton	Hou	82	74	652.0	46	144	6	11	.969	2.62	11	.382	D	-2	30	172	-3	+2	+1	0	-1	-1	-5	-4	25
Brandon Wood	LAA	32	19	188.0	18	40	2	3	.967	2.78	7	.614	A-	1	-	50	0	0	0	0	0	0	0	0	-
David Wright	NYM	159	159	1433.1	114	286	16	21	.962	2.51	17	.674	A+	3	1	356	-2	+6	+1	+5	-2	+3	+2	2	16
Kevin Youkilis	Bos	36	32	252.0	23	70	3	5	.969	3.32	5	.530	B-	1	-	86	+1	+3	+4	+7	0	+7	+8	6	-
Ryan Zimmerman	Was	104	104	910.2	95	199	10	25	.967	2.91	16	.672	A+	3	1	263	-7	+10	+5	+8	+2	+10	+10	8	9
Ben Zobrist	TB	1	0	4.2	0	2	0	0	1.000	3.86						1	0			0	0	0	0	0	-
2008 MLB Averages									.957	2.66	724	.510	C+												

Shortstops

BASIC											GROUND DP					PLUS/MINUS								
Name	Team	G	GS	Inn	PO	A	E	DP	Pct	Rng	GDP Opps	GDP	Pct	Runs Saved	Rank	Outs Made	To His Right	Straight On	To His Left	GB	Air	Total	Runs Saved	Rank
Alfredo Amezaga	Fla	19	11	125.1	22	31	0	3	1.000	3.81	6	2	.333	0	-	43	+1	+1	+1	+2	0	+2	2	-
Robert Andino	Fla	4	0	8.0	0	2	0	0	1.000	2.25	0		-		-	2	+1			+1	0	+1	1	-
Mike Aviles	KC	91	89	747.2	141	238	10	66	.974	4.56	90	61	.678	2	3	273	-2	+6	+10	+14	+1	+15	11	6
Erick Aybar	LAA	96	91	784.2	140	276	18	63	.959	4.77	101	60	.594	0	15	304	+6	+3	-6	+3	+5	+8	6	10
Willy Aybar	TB	2	2	18.0	2	6	0	1	1.000	4.00	2	1	.500	0	-	6	0	+1	-1	0	0	0	0	-
Clint Barmes	Col	36	32	285.0	57	113	3	30	.983	5.37	41	25	.610	0	-	119	+2	-1	-1	0	0	0	0	-
Jason Bartlett	TB	125	122	1097.0	204	309	16	69	.970	4.21	113	62	.549	-1	24	381	+11	-4	-11	-4	+3	-1	-1	19
Ronnie Belliard	Was	5	4	33.0	6	11	1	3	.944	4.64	4	3	.750	0	-	14	0	-1	+3	+2	+1	+3	2	-
Angel Berroa	LAD	79	64	591.2	91	219	8	39	.975	4.72	67	38	.567	0	15	226	-6	+2	+6	+2	-2	0	0	18
Yuniesky Betancourt	Sea	153	150	1325.1	237	401	21	98	.968	4.33	150	93	.620	1	8	446	+7	-7	-21	-21	+2	-19	-14	35
Wilson Betemit	NYY	14	4	57.0	10	19	0	5	1.000	4.58	5	4	.800	0	-	20	0	+1	-1	-1	0	-1	-1	-
Brian Bixler	Pit	39	32	278.0	53	121	8	28	.956	5.63	37	25	.676	1	-	122	-1	-2	+5	+1	-3	-2	-2	-
Casey Blake	Cle	1	0	2.0	0	1	0	0	1.000	4.50	0		-		-	1	0			0	0	0	0	-
Willie Bloomquist	Sea	12	11	93.0	17	23	0	2	1.000	3.87	7	1	.143	-1	-	29	+2	-1	0	+1	+1	+2	2	-
Geoff Blum	Hou	4	3	26.0	2	7	0	0	1.000	3.12	0		-		-	7	0	0	0	+1	0	+1	1	-
Brian Bocock	SF	29	26	227.0	39	73	4	23	.966	4.44	31	20	.645	1	-	82	-1	0	0	-1	0	-1	-1	-
Reid Brignac	TB	4	2	21.1	4	7	2	3	.846	4.64	3	3	1.000	0	-	5	0	-1	-2	-2	-1	-3	-2	-
Eric Bruntlett	Phi	35	30	279.2	39	92	4	16	.970	4.22	25	14	.560	0	-	107	+1	-1	0	+1	0	+1	1	-
Chris Burke	Ari	2	2	13.2	2	4	1	2	.857	3.95	1	1	1.000	0	-	2	+1			0	0	0	0	-
Emmanuel Burriss	SF	47	34	315.0	50	93	5	11	.966	4.09	19	9	.474	-1	-	112	-7	-1	+1	-7	0	-7	-5	-
Freddie Bynum	Bal	37	32	283.1	56	81	5	28	.965	4.35	39	26	.667	1	-	99	-4	-1	+3	-2	+1	-1	-1	-
Asdrubal Cabrera	Cle	20	18	154.2	38	59	5	17	.951	5.64	22	16	.727	1	-	68	+1	-3	+1	-1	+2	+1	1	-
Jolbert Cabrera	Cin	9	7	60.1	7	14	0	5	1.000	3.13	7	5	.714	0	-	15	+1	+1	0	+2	-1	+1	1	-
Orlando Cabrera	CWS	161	160	1389.2	242	472	16	101	.978	4.62	146	93	.637	2	3	528	-3	-2	+8	+2	-1	+1	1	17
Miguel Cairo	Sea	1	0	2.0	0	1	0	0	1.000	4.50	0		-		-	1	0	-1	0	-1		-1	-1	-
Alberto Callaspo	KC	18	9	84.0	18	30	2	8	.960	5.14	8	6	.750	0	-	33	+1	0	-1	-1	-1	-2	-2	-
Andy Cannizaro	TB	1	0	1.0	1	0	0	0	1.000	9.00	0		-		-	0						0	0	-
Alexi Casilla	Min	2	1	10.0	2	3	0	0	1.000	4.50	0		-		-	5	0	0	0	0	0	0	0	-
Jose Castillo	SF	4	0	4.1	1	1	0	0	1.000	4.15	0		-		-	1	0			0	0	0	0	-
Juan Castro	2 tms	57	48	408.2	73	140	5	22	.977	4.69	44	18	.409	-2	31	152	+8	-4	-5	-2	-2	-4	-3	25
Ronny Cedeno	ChC	27	20	182.2	41	50	3	10	.968	4.48	16	8	.500	0	-	72	0	+1	-3	-2	+1	-1	-1	-
Alex Cintron	Bal	45	28	257.0	50	92	7	21	.953	4.97	38	20	.526	-1	-	103	-4	-6	-1	-11	-1	-12	-9	-
Alex Cora	Bos	69	38	386.0	74	136	6	39	.972	4.90	44	33	.750	2	-	141	-2	+1	-5	-5	+3	-2	-2	-
Craig Counsell	Mil	24	19	185.1	30	73	2	13	.981	5.00	23	12	.522	0	-	74	+1	+1	+3	+6	0	+6	5	-
Callix Crabbe	SD	3	2	18.0	3	4	0	1	1.000	3.50	2	1	.500	0	-	4	0	-1	0	-2	-1	-3	-2	-
Bobby Crosby	Oak	145	144	1263.0	202	384	17	99	.972	4.18	129	88	.682	4	1	423	-7	-2	-5	-13	0	-13	-10	32
Luis Cruz	Pit	20	18	163.1	32	61	1	14	.989	5.12	18	12	.667	0	-	65	0	+2	0	+2	0	+2	2	-
Mark DeRosa	ChC	1	0	1.0	0	1	0	0	1.000	9.00	0		-		-	1	0			0	0	0	0	-
Stephen Drew	Ari	151	147	1294.1	190	378	14	85	.976	3.95	128	78	.609	1	8	422	+6	-8	-7	-8	+3	-5	-4	26
German Duran	Tex	2	1	13.0	2	6	0	1	1.000	5.54	3	1	.333	0	-	5				0	0	0	0	-
Damion Easley	NYM	8	4	44.0	7	14	0	1	1.000	4.30	2	1	.500	0	-	18	0	-1	-1	-2	0	-2	-2	-
David Eckstein	Tor	57	56	484.1	69	146	9	33	.960	4.00	53	31	.585	0	15	150	-4	-1	-7	-12	-1	-13	-10	33
Alcides Escobar	Mil	2	0	2.0	0	0	0	0	-	.00	0		-		-	0					0	0	0	-
Yunel Escobar	Atl	126	125	1105.2	193	396	16	78	.974	4.79	145	74	.510	-3	34	439	0	+3	+19	+22	-2	+20	15	2
Adam Everett	Min	44	41	364.0	61	145	7	30	.967	5.09	48	27	.563	0	-	157	-2	-2	+3	-1	0	-1	-1	-
Brandon Fahey	Bal	46	27	248.0	43	87	5	19	.963	4.72	37	18	.486	-1	-	101	-1	-2	-5	-8	-1	-9	-7	-
Pedro Feliz	Phi	1	0	2.0	1	0	0	0	1.000	4.50	0		-		-	0					0	0	0	-
Mike Fontenot	ChC	1	0	1.0	0	0	0	0	-	.00	0		-		-	0						0	0	-
Rafael Furcal	LAD	36	35	296.0	46	92	4	17	.972	4.20	27	17	.630	0	-	102	+1	+2	-2	0	0	0	0	-
Nomar Garciaparra	LAD	31	29	238.0	29	89	4	14	.967	4.46	26	13	.500	-1	-	89	0	-2	+7	+5	-1	+4	3	-
Esteban German	KC	3	3	22.0	2	4	1	0	.857	2.45	3				-	5	0	-1	+1	0	0	0	0	-
Chris Gomez	Pit	13	10	94.1	16	34	3	7	.943	4.77	20	7	.350	-1	-	35	0	0	+1	+1	0	+1	1	-
Alberto Gonzalez	2 tms	26	15	156.0	25	43	0	9	1.000	3.92	14	9	.643	0	-	50	0	-1	+1	+2	0	+2	2	-
Edgar Gonzalez	SD	3	1	16.1	1	11	0	0	1.000	6.61	1				-	12	0	0	0	+1	0	+1	1	-
Khalil Greene	SD	105	103	934.0	146	289	8	66	.982	4.19	97	61	.629	1	8	327	+9	+2	-14	-2	-2	-4	-3	24
Cristian Guzman	Was	136	132	1174.0	192	394	17	75	.972	4.49	110	71	.645	2	3	442	-6	+2	+13	+9	+4	+13	10	7
Jerry Hairston	Cin	34	31	271.0	61	68	4	18	.970	4.28	27	17	.630	0	-	88	-2	0	0	-2	+1	-1	-1	-
J.J. Hardy	Mil	145	143	1268.1	202	430	15	86	.977	4.48	147	79	.537	-2	31	477	-1	-1	+18	+16	+3	+19	14	4
Brendan Harris	Min	55	51	464.1	84	159	6	42	.976	4.71	63	39	.619	1	8	160	+7	-1	-12	-7	-2	-9	-7	29
Willie Harris	Was	3	1	13.0	3	2	0	1	1.000	3.46	1	1	1.000	0	-	3				+1	-1	0	0	-
Anderson Hernandez	Was	3	3	24.0	3	3	3	0	.667	2.25	1				-	4	-4	-1	0	-5	+1	-4	-3	-
Luis Hernandez	Bal	30	26	223.0	52	75	3	19	.977	5.13	32	17	.531	-1	-	79	-1	-2	-2	-5	0	-5	-4	-
Jonathan Herrera	Col	2	1	9.0	2	4	0	0	1.000	6.00	0		-		-	6	+1	0		+1	0	+1	1	-
Michael Hollimon	Det	6	5	44.0	1	12	1	2	.929	2.66	4	2	.500	0	-	12	0	+1	-1	0	0	0	0	-
Chin-lung Hu	LAD	35	23	229.0	46	75	0	14	1.000	4.76	28	14	.500	-1	-	87	+1	+2	+1	+3	+1	+4	3	-
Tug Hulett	Sea	4	1	13.0	2	1	0	0	1.000	2.08	1				-	2				0	0	0	0	-
Omar Infante	Atl	20	15	138.0	27	45	5	12	.935	4.70	17	12	.706	1	-	50	-1	0	0	-1	+2	+1	1	-
Joe Inglett	Tor	2	0	2.0	0	2	0	0	1.000	9.00	0		-		-	2	0	0	0	0	0	0	0	-
Cesar Izturis	StL	130	110	1001.1	170	370	11	77	.980	4.85	128	73	.570	-1	24	408	+18	+4	-1	+22	-2	+20	15	3
Maicer Izturis	LAA	52	50	448.0	69	147	2	31	.991	4.34	46	30	.652	1	8	150	-4	+2	+7	+5	-3	+2	2	16
Paul Janish	Cin	36	20	204.1	31	78	3	13	.973	4.80	16	8	.500	0	-	84	-3	+2	0	-1	0	-1	-1	-
Derek Jeter	NYY	148	147	1258.2	220	347	12	69	.979	4.05	106	58	.547	-1	24	430	-18	+9	-1	-10	-1	-11	-8	31
Elliot Johnson	TB	2	2	18.0	4	6	1	3	.909	5.00	3	3	1.000	0	-	8	0	0	-1	-1	0	-1	-1	-
Sean Kazmar	SD	15	11	98.2	26	24	1	5	.980	4.56	11	3	.273	-1	-	34	-1	+1	0	0	+1	+1	1	-
Jeff Keppinger	Cin	108	101	880.2	145	246	8	72	.980	4.00	110	66	.600	0	15	274	-5	-1	-8	-14	0	-14	-11	34
Brent Lillibridge	Atl	23	20	182.0	39	61	6	13	.943	4.95	25	12	.480	-1	-	73	-3	-1	+5	0	0	0	0	-
Evan Longoria	TB	1	1	9.0	0	1	0	0	1.000	1.00	0		-		-	1	0			0	-1	-1	-1	-
Felipe Lopez	2 tms	13	10	79.0	6	28	0	5	1.000	3.87	9	5	.556	0	-	30	+1	0	-1	0	0	0	0	-
Mark Loretta	Hou	5	4	36.0	3	18	2	3	.913	5.25	6	3	.500	0	-	15	+2	0	-1	0	0	0	0	-
Jed Lowrie	Bos	49	45	386.0	46	109	0	21	1.000	3.61	35	21	.600	0	-	123	+3	+2	0	+6	+2	+8	6	-
Julio Lugo	Bos	81	79	671.1	100	176	16	34	.945	3.70	68	31	.456	-3	34	215	+5	-7	0	-2	0	-2	-2	22
Edwin Maysonet	Hou	4	0	9.0	0	6	1	0	.857	6.00	1				-	6	-1	0	0	0	0	0	0	-
Luis Maza	LAD	16	11	86.0	23	35	2	6	.967	6.07	14	6	.429	-1	-	41	-3	+2	0	-1	-1	-2	-2	-
John McDonald	Tor	67	52	478.0	80	134	9	33	.960	4.03	55	30	.545	-1	24	149	-2	+1	-1	-2	+1	-1	-1	20
Travis Metcalf	Tex	1	0	2.0	0	0	0	0	-	.00	0		-		-	0					0	0	0	-

		BASIC										GROUND DP					PLUS/MINUS								
Name	Team	G	GS	Inn	PO	A	E	DP	Pct	Rng	GDP Opps	GDP	Pct	Runs Saved	Rank	Outs Made	To His Right	Straight On	To His Left	GB	Air	Total	Runs Saved	Rank
Aaron Miles	StL	27	24	172.1	32	56	1	14	.989	4.60	24	14	.583	0	-	65	+2	+2	0	+5	0	+5	4	-
Melvin Mora	Bal	1	0	1.0	0	0	0	0	-	.00	0		-		-	0							0	-
Donnie Murphy	Oak	13	9	88.0	10	27	2	6	.949	3.78	8	6	.750	0	-	26	-1	0	-3	-4	-1	-5	-4	-
Ivan Ochoa	SF	35	26	238.0	45	71	3	20	.975	4.39	26	16	.615	0	-	87	0	+2	-2	0	-1	-1	-1	-
Augie Ojeda	Ari	22	13	126.2	17	39	3	6	.949	3.98	16	4	.250	-2	-	45	+2	+2	+2	+6	-1	+5	4	-
Pete Orr	Was	8	4	43.0	9	10	2	4	.905	3.98	8	4	.500	0	-	12	-1	-1	+1	-1	+1	0	0	-
Pablo Ozuna	LAD	4	0	6.2	0	4	0	0	1.000	5.40	0		-			3	+1	0	0	0	0	0	0	-
Tony F Pena	KC	94	61	592.0	74	180	9	35	.966	3.86	57	34	.596	0	15	199	-1	+1	+3	+3	-5	-2	-2	23
Cliff Pennington	Oak	10	6	56.0	10	16	4	5	.867	4.18	4	4	1.000	0	-	17	-4	-2	-1	-6	-3	-10	-8	-
Jhonny Peralta	Cle	146	143	1271.1	217	427	14	104	.979	4.56	153	97	.634	2	3	469	0	-6	-2	-7	-3	-10	-8	30
Gregorio Petit	Oak	8	2	28.0	7	12	2	5	.905	6.11	5	3	.600	0	-	11	-2	+1	0	-2	0	-2	-2	-
Martin Prado	Atl	2	2	15.0	2	2	1	1	.800	2.40	2	1	.500	0	-	2	+1	0		+1	0	+1	1	-
Nick Punto	Min	61	60	530.2	103	187	8	46	.973	4.92	60	44	.733	3	2	228	-6	+5	0	+3	-1	+2	3	14
Omar Quintanilla	Col	39	32	288.2	42	100	3	20	.979	4.43	28	19	.679	1	-	108	+6	0	-3	+3	-1	+2	2	-
Alexei Ramirez	CWS	16	2	53.0	8	15	1	4	.958	3.91	6	4	.667	0	-	18	-3	0	0	-2	-1	-3	-2	-
Hanley Ramirez	Fla	150	150	1302.0	236	401	22	89	.967	4.40	139	79	.568	-1	24	473	+10	-4	-1	+5	-2	+3	2	15
Cody Ransom	NYY	9	6	63.0	12	22	2	4	.944	4.86	7	4	.571	0	-	25	-2	-1	+2	-2	+1	-1	-1	-
Edgar Renteria	Det	138	134	1173.1	197	365	16	91	.972	4.31	150	88	.587	0	15	427	-11	-6	+7	-11	+2	-9	-7	28
Jose Reyes	NYM	158	158	1420.1	221	422	17	89	.974	4.07	149	86	.577	0	15	481	-3	+4	-1	0	-2	-2	-2	21
Danny Richar	Cin	1	1	8.0	1	1	0	0	1.000	2.25	1					2	0			0	0	0	0	-
Luis Rivas	Pit	31	22	223.0	37	70	6	24	.947	4.32	33	22	.667	1	-	71	+1	-2	-2	-3	-2	-5	-4	-
Luis Rodriguez	SD	52	45	391.1	79	121	3	33	.985	4.60	54	31	.574	0	-	143	-2	+2	-1	-1	-3	-4	-3	-
Sean Rodriguez	LAA	4	2	20.0	5	12	0	2	1.000	7.65	4	2	.500	0	-	12	0	0	+1	+2	0	+2	2	-
Jimmy Rollins	Phi	132	132	1168.0	193	393	7	71	.988	4.52	127	69	.543	-2	31	455	+2	+2	+16	+20	+3	+23	17	1
Brendan Ryan	StL	40	25	255.1	42	91	1	18	.993	4.69	30	17	.567	0	-	98	+1	+2	0	+4	-1	+3	2	-
Oscar Salazar	Bal	1	0	1.0	0	0	0	0	-	.00	0		-			0				0	0	0	0	-
Ramon Santiago	Det	33	23	227.2	45	70	3	15	.975	4.55	24	14	.583	0	-	79	-4	-2	+2	-5	-3	-8	-6	-
Marco Scutaro	Tor	56	53	472.1	71	165	5	30	.979	4.50	46	25	.543	-1	24	174	+1	+4	+6	+12	0	+12	9	8
Miguel Tejada	Hou	157	154	1354.1	187	442	11	97	.983	4.18	144	90	.625	2	3	472	+5	+7	-4	+7	0	+7	5	11
Ryan Theriot	ChC	149	141	1266.0	207	341	14	69	.975	3.90	107	64	.598	0	15	425	+2	-3	+1	+1	+5	+6	5	12
Matt Tolbert	Min	14	10	90.0	14	26	1	4	.976	4.00	8	4	.500	0	-	31	-1	0	-1	-2	0	-2	-2	-
Eider Torres	Bal	5	2	18.0	2	5	3	1	.700	3.50	3	1	.333	0	-	7	-1	0	0	-1	0	-1	-1	-
Troy Tulowitzki	Col	101	97	863.1	190	311	8	70	.984	5.22	114	62	.544	-1	24	355	-4	+4	+1	+1	+3	+4	3	13
Juan Uribe	CWS	4	1	15.0	2	2	0	0	1.000	2.40	0					3				0	0	0	0	-
Luis Valbuena	Sea	1	0	2.0	1	1	0	1	1.000	9.00	1	1	1.000	0	-	2				0	0	0	0	-
Ramon Vazquez	Tex	26	10	138.0	23	52	3	15	.962	4.89	25	14	.560	0	-	44	+1	+1	-2	0	0	0	0	-
Jorge Velandia	2 tms	4	2	19.0	2	5	0	2	1.000	3.32	2	2	1.000	0	-	5	+1			+1	0	+1	1	-
Gil Velazquez	Bos	1	0	3.0	0	1	0	0	1.000	3.00	0		-			1	0			0	0	0	0	-
Omar Vizquel	SF	84	76	657.2	108	179	2	43	.993	3.93	64	40	.625	1	8	210	+3	+2	+3	+8	+1	+9	7	9
Jack Wilson	Pit	80	80	696.1	115	277	5	52	.987	5.07	83	50	.602	0	15	285	+15	-1	+2	+16	0	+16	12	5
Brandon Wood	LAA	28	19	198.2	42	50	2	20	.979	4.17	26	18	.692	1	-	56	-6	0	-1	-7	-1	-8	-6	-
Michael Young	Tex	152	151	1289.0	193	465	11	113	.984	4.59	172	106	.616	1	8	488	-1	+2	-6	-6	-2	-8	-6	27
Ben Zobrist	TB	35	33	293.1	51	78	7	22	.949	3.96	41	22	.537	-1		90	0	-1	-7	-8	0	-8	-6	-
2008 MLB Averages									.974	4.41	4857	2859	.589											

Left Fielders

Name	Team	G	GS	Inn	PO	A	E	DP	Pct	Rng	Opps To Advance	Extra Bases	Pct	Kills	Runs Saved	Rank	Outs Made	Basic	Shallow	Medium	Deep	Enhanced	Runs Saved	Rank
Reggie Abercrombie	Hou	12	2	32.0	7	0	0	0	1.000	1.97	2	0	.000	0	0	-	7	0		0	-1	-1	-1	
Chris Aguila	NYM	6	2	26.0	5	1	0	0	1.000	2.08	4	3	.750	0	-1	-	5	0	0	0	+1	+1	1	
Moises Alou	NYM	13	13	92.1	18	0	0	0	1.000	1.75	8	4	.500	0	-1	-	18	0	0	+1	-1	0	0	
Brian Anderson	CWS	3	2	16.0	3	0	0	0	1.000	1.69	2	1	.500	0	0	-	3	0	0	+1	-1	0	0	
Garret Anderson	LAA	82	80	689.1	144	9	0	2	1.000	2.00	68	37	.544	5	-2	29	144	0	-4	+6	-1	+1	1	20
Josh Anderson	Atl	6	3	33.2	9	0	0	0	1.000	2.41	3	0	.000	0	1	-	9	+1	+1	0	0	0	0	
Marlon Anderson	NYM	25	20	165.2	45	1	2	1	.958	2.50	17	5	.294	0	0	-	45	+3	+2	+2	0	+5	3	
Rick Ankiel	StL	17	16	131.0	22	0	3	0	.880	1.51	15	4	.267	0	1	-	22	-1	+1	0	-2	-2	-1	
Jeff Bailey	Bos	5	2	23.0	3	0	0	0	1.000	1.17	2	0	.000	0	0	-	3	-2	-1	-2	0	-3	-2	
Rocco Baldelli	TB	1	0	7.0	1	0	0	0	1.000	1.29	1	0	.000	0	0	-	1	0		0		0	0	
Wladimir Balentien	Sea	5	5	43.0	13	1	0	0	1.000	2.93	4	1	.250	1	1	-	13	-1	-1	0	-1	-2	-1	
Brian Barton	StL	36	27	209.0	43	2	1	0	.978	1.94	19	8	.421	1	0	-	43	+1	+1	-1	+3	+3	2	
Jason Bay	2 tms	154	153	1344.2	254	8	4	0	.985	1.75	169	72	.426	5	-3	32	254	-11	-8	-7	+2	-12	-7	29
Roger Bernadina	Was	6	6	56.0	19	2	0	0	1.000	3.38	13	6	.462	1	0	-	19	+1	+1	+2	0	+3	2	
Gregor Blanco	Atl	77	55	512.2	86	3	2	0	.978	1.56	52	26	.500	2	-3	32	86	0	-1	0	+4	+3	2	18
Willie Bloomquist	Sea	8	1	17.2	3	0	0	0	1.000	1.53	2	0	.000	0	0	-	3	+1	+1	0	0	+1	1	
Brandon Boggs	Tex	76	59	579.0	131	7	3	2	.979	2.15	66	21	.318	3	4	5	131	+4	+1	+1	+3	+5	3	11
T.J. Bohn	Phi	12	0	22.0	6	1	1	0	.875	2.86	3	0	.000	1	2	-	6	+1	0	+1	0	+2	1	
Emilio Bonifacio	Ari	1	0	2.0	0	0	0	0	-	.00	0	0	-	0	0	-	0	0				0	0	
Jason Botts	Tex	4	1	14.0	3	0	0	0	1.000	1.93	1	0	.000	0	0	-	3	-1		0	0	-2	-2	-1	
John Bowker	SF	5	3	27.0	5	0	0	0	1.000	1.67	0	0	-	0	0	-	5	0	0	0	+1	0	0	
Milton Bradley	Tex	1	1	8.0	1	0	0	0	1.000	1.13	3	1	.333	0	0	-	1	-1		-2		-2	-1	
Ryan Braun	Mil	149	148	1310.1	275	9	0	0	1.000	1.95	123	46	.374	6	3	8	275	+4	+1	+1	+5	+7	4	8
Emil Brown	Oak	65	40	413.0	89	6	1	1	.990	2.07	37	20	.541	1	-3	32	89	+2	0	-1	+3	+2	1	19
Jay Bruce	Cin	11	4	41.0	3	0	0	0	1.000	.66	6	3	.500	0	-1	-	3	-2	0	-1	-1	-3	-2	
Eric Bruntlett	Phi	29	0	52.1	11	0	0	0	1.000	1.89	4	0	.000	0	1	-	11	+2	+2	+1	0	+3	2	
Travis Buck	Oak	12	3	47.0	11	1	0	0	1.000	2.30	5	2	.400	0	0	-	11	+1	-1	+1	+2	+2	1	
Chris Burke	Ari	18	13	116.1	43	1	0	0	1.000	3.40	17	8	.471	1	0	-	43	+3	0	+1	+4	+4	2	
Pat Burrell	Phi	155	154	1198.1	202	12	2	1	.991	1.61	133	40	.301	7	6	1	201	-10	+7	-3	-22	-19	-11	34
Marlon Byrd	Tex	31	30	236.0	61	0	0	0	1.000	2.33	27	10	.370	0	-1	-	61	-3	-6	-1	+3	-3	-2	
Eric Byrnes	Ari	51	50	419.2	76	1	1	0	.987	1.65	31	11	.355	0	-1	23	76	-1	-1	+2	-3	-2	-1	23
Jolbert Cabrera	Cin	17	15	124.0	21	2	1	0	.958	1.67	8	3	.375	1	1	-	21	+2	+1	+2	0	+2	1	
Melky Cabrera	NYY	8	1	18.0	4	0	0	0	1.000	2.00	2	1	.500	0	0	-	4	0	0	-1	+1	+1	1	
Miguel Cairo	Sea	2	0	4.0	0	0	0	0	-	.00	0	0	-	0	0	-	0	0				0	0	
Alberto Callaspo	KC	3	1	14.0	0	0	0	0	-	.00	1	1	1.000	0	0	-	0	0				0	0	
Brett Carroll	Fla	7	0	10.0	4	0	0	0	1.000	3.60	2	0	.000	0	0	-	4	0	0		+1	+1	1	
Jamey Carroll	Cle	1	0	3.0	0	0	0	0	-	.00	2	1	.500	0	0	-	0	-1	0			-1	-1	
Chris Carter	Bos	3	1	17.0	3	0	0	0	1.000	1.59	3	1	.333	0	0	-	3	0	0	0		0	0	
Wilkin Castillo	Cin	5	5	38.0	6	0	0	0	1.000	1.42	3	1	.333	0	0	-	6	+1	0	0	+1	+1	1	
Kory Casto	Was	8	6	53.2	11	0	0	0	1.000	1.84	3	1	.333	0	0	-	11	-1	0	0	-3	-3	-2	
Frank Catalanotto	Tex	26	20	168.1	29	0	1	0	.967	1.55	26	10	.385	0	0	-	29	-3	-1	-2	-1	-4	-2	
Ronny Cedeno	ChC	1	0	2.0	0	0	0	0	-	.00	1	0	.000	0	0	-	0	0				0	0	
Endy Chavez	NYM	54	13	197.1	62	2	0	0	1.000	2.92	17	5	.294	1	2	-	62	+6	+3	+1	+6	+10	6	
Shin-Soo Choo	Cle	26	25	223.0	40	3	1	0	.977	1.74	38	14	.368	3	3	-	40	+2	+2	0	+1	+2	1	
Justin Christian	NYY	9	6	53.0	5	0	1	0	.833	.85	7	2	.286	0	0	-	5	-1		-1	-1	-2	-1	
Brady Clark	NYM	2	2	14.2	2	0	0	0	1.000	1.23	1	1	1.000	0	0	-	2	0	0	0	0	0	0	
Brent Clevlen	Det	10	2	39.0	16	1	0	0	1.000	3.92	2	0	.000	1	1	-	16	+1	+1	0	+1	+2	1	
Buck Coats	Tor	7	1	23.0	6	0	0	0	1.000	2.35	2	0	.000	0	1	-	6	+1	0	0	+1	+1	1	
Callix Crabbe	SD	1	0	2.0	0	0	0	0	-	.00	0	0	-	0	0	-	0	0				0	0	
Carl Crawford	TB	108	103	920.2	231	2	4	0	.983	2.28	69	23	.333	0	0	19	231	+16	+10	+7	+6	+23	13	1
Jose Cruz	Hou	10	1	24.0	5	0	0	0	1.000	1.88	1	0	.000	0	0	-	5	0	0	-1	0	-1	-1	
Aaron Cunningham	Oak	18	18	150.0	41	1	3	0	.933	2.52	18	6	.333	1	2	-	41	+1	0	+1	0	+2	1	
Jack Cust	Oak	78	77	585.2	129	4	4	0	.971	2.04	63	28	.444	0	0	19	129	-7	+1	-7	-9	-15	-8	32
Johnny Damon	NYY	87	75	659.1	155	2	1	0	.994	2.14	63	19	.302	2	1	17	155	+6	+3	+2	+6	+7	4	9
Rajai Davis	SF	3	1	7.0	2	0	0	0	1.000	2.57	2	1	.500	0	0	-	2	0	0		+1	+1	1	
David DeJesus	KC	71	54	482.2	136	1	0	0	1.000	2.55	44	16	.364	0	-1	23	136	+4	-1	+1	+7	+8	4	7
David Dellucci	Cle	56	46	383.0	75	1	0	0	1.000	1.79	41	10	.244	0	1	-	75	-1	+1	0	-2	0	0	
Chris Denorfia	Oak	13	7	70.1	9	1	0	0	1.000	1.28	6	1	.167	1	1	-	9	0	0	0	-1	-1	-1	
Mark DeRosa	ChC	27	21	185.0	39	0	1	0	.975	1.90	21	9	.429	0	-2	-	39	0	+2	+2	-5	-1	-1	
Matt Diaz	Atl	37	33	288.2	59	2	1	1	.984	1.90	19	9	.474	1	-1	-	59	-1	0	+2	-5	-3	-2	
Chris Dickerson	Cin	28	19	182.2	38	0	0	0	1.000	1.87	23	5	.217	0	1	-	38	+2	0	0	+4	+4	2	
Joe Dillon	Mil	2	1	9.0	1	0	0	0	1.000	1.00	1	1	1.000	0	0	-	1	0	0	0		0	0	
Greg Dobbs	Phi	3	2	16.0	4	0	0	0	1.000	2.25	3	2	.667	0	0	-	4	+1	0	0		+1	1	
Elijah Dukes	Was	10	7	57.2	16	0	1	0	.941	2.50	3	0	.000	0	0	-	16	-1	0	-1	-1	-2	-1	
Chris Duncan	StL	43	40	321.1	73	1	2	0	.974	2.07	30	13	.433	1	-1	-	73	+1	-3	0	+7	+4	2	
Adam Dunn	2 tms	119	118	980.2	210	5	7	1	.968	1.97	108	41	.380	4	-1	23	210	-8	-2	-6	-7	-15	-9	31
German Duran	Tex	6	2	21.0	7	0	0	0	1.000	3.00	2	0	.000	0	0	-	7	+1	0	+1	0	+1	1	
Damion Easley	NYM	7	2	26.0	2	0	1	0	.667	.69	3	1	.333	0	0	-	2	0	-1			+1	1	
Jason Ellison	Tex	2	1	11.0	5	0	0	0	1.000	4.09	2	2	1.000	0	-1	-	5	0		0	+1	+1	1	
Jacoby Ellsbury	Bos	58	36	340.1	89	1	0	1	1.000	2.34	33	11	.333	1	1	-	89	+2	0	+4	+3	+7	4	
Darin Erstad	Hou	56	17	205.0	37	1	0	1	1.000	1.67	17	5	.294	1	0	-	37	+2	+1	+2	0	+3	2	
Andre Ethier	LAD	41	29	277.1	48	3	2	0	.962	1.66	34	17	.500	2	0	-	48	0	0	+1	0	+1	1	
Nick Evans	NYM	28	25	186.1	37	2	0	0	1.000	1.88	14	4	.286	2	2	-	37	+3	+3	0	0	+3	2	
Ben Francisco	Cle	83	71	643.0	150	7	2	2	.987	2.20	79	30	.380	6	4	5	150	+1	+1	-6	+9	+4	2	15
Ryan Freel	Cin	13	2	46.1	6	0	0	0	1.000	1.17	2	0	.000	0	0	-	6	-1	0	-2	0	-2	-1	
Brett Gardner	NYY	17	15	145.1	25	1	0	0	1.000	1.61	11	2	.182	1	1	-	25	-1	0	-2	0	-2	-1	
Joey Gathright	KC	3	0	9.0	2	0	0	0	1.000	2.00	1	1	1.000	0	0	-	2	0	0	0	0	0	0	
Esteban German	KC	39	25	235.0	54	0	2	0	.964	2.07	28	8	.286	0	0	-	54	-3	-3	+1	-1	-3	-2	
Ross Gload	KC	8	8	64.0	18	0	0	0	1.000	2.53	7	2	.286	0	0	-	18	+1	+1	-1	-1	-1	-1	
Jonny Gomes	TB	9	4	40.0	13	0	0	0	1.000	2.93	6	5	.833	0	-1	-	13	-1	0	-1	-1	-2	-1	
Edgar Gonzalez	SD	2	1	7.0	2	0	0	0	1.000	2.57	0	0	-	0	0	-	2	0		0	0	0	0	
Luis Gonzalez	Fla	64	60	503.2	105	0	4	0	.963	1.88	60	20	.333	0	0	19	105	-9	-6	0	-6	-12	-7	30
Gabe Gross	Mil	2	0	4.0	2	0	0	0	1.000	4.50	0	0	-	0	0	-	2	0		0	0	0	0	
Carlos Guillen	Det	2	2	17.0	6	0	0	0	1.000	3.18	3	1	.333	0	0	-	6	0	0	0	0	0	0	
Jose Guillen	KC	45	43	373.0	83	3	1	1	.989	2.08	37	15	.405	3	2	-	83	-7	-5	-2	-3	-10	-6	

		BASIC									THROWING						PLUS/MINUS							
Name	Team	G	GS	Inn	PO	A	E	DP	Pct	Rng	Opps To Advance	Extra Bases	Pct	Kills	Runs Saved	Rank	Outs Made	Basic	Shallow	Medium	Deep	Enhanced	Runs Saved	Rank
Franklin Gutierrez	Cle	11	8	78.0	14	0	0	0	1.000	1.62	11	5	.455	0	-1	-	14	0	0	-2	+3	+2	1	
Tony Gwynn	Mil	1	0	4.0	1	0	0	0	1.000	2.25	1	0	.000	0	0	-	1	0			+1	+1	1	
Jerry Hairston	Cin	24	4	63.1	10	0	0	0	1.000	1.42	5	1	.200	0	0	-	10	0	+1	-2	+1	-1	-1	
Scott Hairston	SD	49	30	310.0	70	2	0	0	1.000	2.09	26	6	.231	2	4	-	70	+1	0	+1	+1	+2	1	
Willie Harris	Was	86	58	562.0	145	4	2	2	.987	2.39	63	21	.333	2	2	13	145	+12	0	+5	+14	+20	11	2
Nathan Haynes	TB	2	1	12.0	2	0	0	0	1.000	1.50	0	0	-	0	0	-	2	0			0	0	0	
Chase Headley	SD	82	82	713.0	156	2	5	0	.969	1.99	77	31	.403	2	-2	29	156	+1	0	0	+4	+4	2	14
Wes Helms	Fla	1	0	1.0	0	0	0	0	-	.00	0	0	-	0	0	-	0	0				0	0	
Eric Hinske	TB	40	37	265.0	45	2	1	0	.979	1.60	26	10	.385	0	-1	-	45	+1	-1	+3	0	+2	1	
Micah Hoffpauir	ChC	7	3	38.0	6	0	1	0	.857	1.42	5	1	.200	0	0	-	6	0	0	+1	-1	0	0	
Matt Holliday	Col	139	139	1229.1	240	9	3	3	.988	1.82	163	54	.331	3	0	19	240	+3	-2	+5	+5	+9	5	5
Norris Hopper	Cin	8	3	31.1	5	0	0	0	1.000	1.44	4	2	.500	0	-1	-	5	0	0	0	0	0	0	
Brian Horwitz	SF	9	7	63.1	20	0	0	0	1.000	2.84	4	2	.500	0	-1	-	20	+1	+1	-1	-1	+1	1	
Justin Huber	SD	22	17	139.1	27	0	1	0	.964	1.74	12	5	.417	0	-1	-	27	+3	0	+4	+4	+7	4	
Raul Ibanez	Sea	153	153	1340.0	302	9	5	1	.984	2.09	160	54	.338	6	5	3	303	-10	-8	-8	-3	-19	-11	33
Omar Infante	Atl	34	26	225.0	44	0	1	0	.978	1.76	29	12	.414	0	0	-	44	+1	+1	0	+1	+3	2	
Brandon Inge	Det	2	0	6.0	0	0	0	0	-	.00	0	0	-	0	0	-	0	0				0	0	
Joe Inglett	Tor	22	5	73.0	15	0	0	0	1.000	1.85	6	2	.333	0	0	-	15	-1	0	0	-1	-1	-1	
Conor Jackson	Ari	77	75	656.0	146	5	3	3	.981	2.07	61	19	.311	4	3	8	146	+7	+2	+3	+6	+11	6	3
Charlton Jimerson	Sea	1	0	1.0	0	0	0	0	-	.00	0	0	-	0	0	-	0	0				0	0	
Dan Johnson	TB	1	1	6.0	3	0	0	0	1.000	4.50	0	0	-	0	0	-	3	0	0	0	0	0	0	
Reed Johnson	ChC	26	12	124.2	35	1	0	0	1.000	2.60	12	1	.083	1	2	-	35	+1	+1	0	+1	+2	1	
Brandon Jones	Atl	29	27	219.2	45	2	0	0	1.000	1.93	14	7	.500	0	-1	-	45	0	+3	-1	-5	-3	-2	
Jacque Jones	2 tms	27	24	192.1	42	1	1	0	.977	2.01	27	13	.481	0	-2	-	42	0	-1	0	-3	-3	-1	
Matt Joyce	Det	60	41	409.1	94	2	3	0	.970	2.11	54	15	.278	1	2	13	94	+1	0	+2	+2	+4	2	17
Gabe Kapler	Mil	17	12	118.1	22	1	0	0	1.000	1.75	9	0	.000	1	2	-	22	-2	0	-1	0	-2	-1	
Adam Kennedy	StL	1	0	1.0	0	0	0	0	-	.00	0	0	-	0	0	-	0	0				0	0	
Jason Kubel	Min	18	16	130.0	24	1	2	1	.926	1.73	19	5	.263	0	0	-	24	-3	-3	+1	-4	-6	-3	
Ryan Langerhans	Was	24	13	141.2	26	1	0	0	1.000	1.72	16	6	.375	0	-1	-	26	-1	-1	-2	+1	-2	-1	
Carlos Lee	Hou	110	110	915.1	187	4	1	0	.995	1.88	87	34	.391	1	-2	29	187	+4	+3	+3	-6	0	0	21
Fred Lewis	SF	112	101	905.2	178	11	6	1	.969	1.88	88	33	.375	3	3	8	177	+4	+6	+1	-4	+4	2	13
Adam Lind	Tor	71	71	590.2	113	2	0	1	1.000	1.75	49	20	.408	0	-1	23	113	-5	0	-2	-7	-9	-5	27
Paul Lo Duca	Was	5	4	23.2	11	0	1	0	.917	4.18	3	2	.667	0	0	-	11	0	-1	0	0	-1	-1	
Felipe Lopez	2 tms	16	13	107.0	12	2	0	0	1.000	1.18	9	4	.444	2	0	-	13	-1	-2	0	0	-2	-1	
Ryan Ludwick	StL	29	17	169.2	42	2	0	0	1.000	2.33	21	14	.667	0	-3	-	42	-3	-1	-2	-1	-5	-3	
Julio Lugo	Bos	1	0	1.0	0	0	0	0	-	.00	0	0	-	0	0	-	0	0				0	0	
Drew Macias	SD	4	2	21.0	7	0	0	0	1.000	3.00	5	1	.200	0	0	-	7	0	0	0	+1	+1	1	
Rob Mackowiak	Was	12	9	73.1	11	0	0	0	1.000	1.35	8	3	.375	0	0	-	11	-2	-1	-2	0	-3	-2	
Joe Mather	StL	25	12	124.2	30	1	0	0	1.000	2.24	16	6	.375	0	0	-	30	+1	-1	+1	+5	+4	2	
Hideki Matsui	NYY	21	20	176.1	40	2	1	1	.977	2.14	21	11	.524	2	0	-	40	0	+1	-1	-1	-1	-1	
Gary Matthews Jr.	LAA	37	36	313.1	57	1	2	0	.967	1.67	25	11	.440	1	0	-	57	-6	0	-1	-10	-12	-7	
Paul McAnulty	SD	35	30	266.0	48	1	0	0	1.000	1.66	33	17	.515	1	-1	-	48	-2	-1	-3	0	-4	-2	
Nate McLouth	Pit	4	1	18.0	2	0	0	0	1.000	1.00	0	0	-	0	0	-	2	0	0	0	0	0	0	
Kevin Mench	Tor	21	14	125.0	28	0	0	0	1.000	2.02	12	1	.083	0	0	-	28	-1	-1	0	0	-1	-1	
Jason Michaels	2 tms	34	24	225.2	52	2	0	0	1.000	2.15	36	10	.278	2	1	-	52	0	0	-2	+3	+1	0	
Aaron Miles	StL	4	3	26.0	3	0	0	0	1.000	1.04	2	1	.500	0	0	-	3	+1		0	+2	+2	1	
Craig Monroe	Min	1	0	1.0	0	0	0	0	-	.00	1	1	1.000	0	0	-	0	0		0		0	0	
Lou Montanez	Bal	26	20	174.1	30	1	2	0	.939	1.60	36	13	.361	0	0	-	30	+2	+3	+2	-2	+2	1	
Nyjer Morgan	Pit	23	18	166.2	40	2	1	0	.976	2.16	18	5	.278	0	0	-	40	0	-1	-1	+1	-1	0	
Brandon Moss	2 tms	36	33	294.1	60	2	1	1	.984	1.90	25	9	.360	0	-2	-	60	0	-1	-1	+1	-1	0	
Daniel Murphy	NYM	32	30	249.0	50	1	2	1	.962	1.84	21	7	.333	1	1	-	50	+4	+3	0	+2	+5	3	
David Murphy	Tex	54	48	404.2	86	3	1	0	.989	1.98	48	14	.292	2	3	8	86	-4	0	-1	-5	-6	-3	24
Donnie Murphy	Oak	1	0	2.0	0	0	0	0	-	.00	0	0	-	0	0	-	0	0				0	0	
Matt Murton	2 tms	17	13	123.0	40	1	0	1	1.000	3.00	7	3	.429	0	0	-	40	+2	+1	+2	-1	+3	2	
Xavier Nady	NYY	46	45	389.2	87	2	2	0	.978	2.06	44	12	.273	0	3	-	87	+2	+3	0	-1	+2	1	
David Newhan	Hou	2	0	2.0	2	0	0	0	-	.00	0	0	-	0	0	-		0				0	0	
Laynce Nix	Mil	2	1	10.0	4	0	0	0	1.000	3.60	1	0	.000	0	0	-	4	0	0	+1	0	0	0	
Trot Nixon	NYM	6	6	44.1	11	1	0	0	1.000	2.44	5	2	.400	0	0	-	11	+2	+1	+1	+2	+3	2	
Greg Norton	Atl	25	15	137.2	29	0	0	0	1.000	1.90	15	6	.400	0	-1	-	29	0	0	0	0	0	0	
Pete Orr	Was	2	1	9.0	2	0	0	0	1.000	2.00	1	0	.000	0	0	-	2	0				-1	-1	
Dan Ortmeier	SF	13	10	80.1	13	1	0	0	1.000	1.57	16	8	.500	0	-2	-	14	0	-1	+1	0	0	0	
Jerry Owens	CWS	7	1	25.0	3	0	0	0	1.000	1.08	1	0	.000	0	0	-	3	+1		0	+2	+2	1	
Pablo Ozuna	LAD	2	0	0.0	0	0	0	0	-	.00	0	0	-	0	0	-	0	0	0			0	0	
Angel Pagan	NYM	21	20	169.2	28	0	1	0	.966	1.49	17	5	.294	0	0	-	28	+3	+1	+1	+2	+4	2	
Eric Patterson	2 tms	17	15	131.0	28	1	4	0	.879	1.99	17	8	.471	1	0	-	28	+1	0	-1	+1	0	0	
Jay Payton	Bal	71	41	407.1	132	2	0	1	1.000	2.96	41	11	.268	1	2	13	132	+2	+2	-1	+3	+4	2	16
Steve Pearce	Pit	1	0	4.0	1	0	0	0	1.000	2.25	0	0	-	0	0	-	1	0			0	0	0	
Wily Mo Pena	Was	54	51	408.0	99	3	3	0	.971	2.25	50	20	.400	2	-1	23	99	+6	+6	-3	+4	+7	4	10
Fernando Perez	TB	8	2	32.2	5	0	0	0	1.000	1.38	2	0	.000	0	0	-	5	-1	0	0	-1	-1	-1	
Josh Phelps	StL	3	3	21.0	1	0	0	0	1.000	.43	4	3	.750	0	0	-	1	0	-1	0	0	-1	-1	
Andy Phillips	NYM	2	1	9.0	1	0	0	0	1.000	1.00	1	0	.000	0	0	-	1	0				0	0	
Felix Pie	ChC	1	1	8.2	3	0	0	0	1.000	3.12	2	0	.000	0	0	-	3	-1	0	-1	0	-1	-1	
Juan Pierre	LAD	84	71	622.2	125	0	3	0	.977	1.81	71	27	.380	0	-3	32	125	+3	+2	+1	+2	+5	3	12
Scott Podsednik	Col	10	2	30.0	7	0	0	0	1.000	2.10	3	1	.333	0	0	-	7	0		0	-1	-1	-1	
Martin Prado	Atl	3	3	23.0	7	0	0	0	1.000	2.74	1	0	.000	0	0	-	7	+1	+1	0	-1	+1	1	
Jason Pridie	Min	3	0	4.0	0	0	0	0	-	.00	0	0	-	0	0	-		0				0	0	
Carlos Quentin	CWS	130	130	1147.0	228	5	7	2	.971	1.83	113	32	.283	2	4	5	228	-3	+3	-4	-7	-7	-4	25
Robb Quinlan	LAA	3	0	7.1	1	0	0	0	1.000	1.23	0	0	-	0	0	-	1	+1		+1		+1	1	
Ryan Raburn	Det	30	9	127.2	29	2	1	0	.969	2.19	13	5	.385	1	1	-	29	0	0	-1	+2	+1	1	
Manny Ramirez	2 tms	119	119	974.0	190	7	3	2	.985	1.82	102	32	.314	3	2	13	190	-5	+2	-6	-5	-9	-5	26
Jeremy Reed	Sea	6	3	29.2	5	1	0	0	1.000	1.82	5	2	.400	0	0	-	5	-1	-1	0	-2	-2	-1	
Jason Repko	LAD	12	0	18.0	6	0	0	0	1.000	3.00	3	1	.333	0	0	-	6	+1	0	+1	0	+1	1	
Chris Resop	Atl	1	0	0.1	0	0	0	0	-	.00	0	0	-	0	0	-	0	0				0	0	
Shawn Riggans	TB	1	0	1.0	0	0	0	0	-	.00	0	0	-	0	0	-	0	0				0	0	
Juan Rivera	LAA	41	35	307.0	59	3	2	1	.969	1.82	20	7	.350	3	2	-	59	-2	-3	0	-1	-3	-2	
Dave Roberts	SF	32	23	205.2	54	3	0	2	1.000	2.49	18	5	.278	2	2	-	54	0	0	+1	-1	0	0	

		BASIC									THROWING						PLUS/MINUS							
Name	Team	G	GS	Inn	PO	A	E	DP	Pct	Rng	Opps To Advance	Extra Bases	Pct	Kills	Runs Saved	Rank	Outs Made	Basic	Shallow	Medium	Deep	Enhanced	Runs Saved	Rank
Alex Romero	Ari	13	3	42.1	5	0	0	0	1.000	1.06	4	2	.500	0	0	-	5	0	0	+1		+1	1	-
Cody Ross	Fla	17	2	45.0	10	1	0	0	1.000	2.20	8	1	.125	1	2	-	10	+1	+1	+1	0	+1	1	-
Justin Ruggiano	TB	26	6	94.0	23	0	0	0	1.000	2.20	6	0	.000	0	0	-	23	+2	0	0	+6	+5	3	-
Brendan Ryan	StL	1	0	1.0	1	0	0	0	1.000	9.00	0	0	-	0	0	-	1	0			0	+2	0	-
Jeff Salazar	Ari	27	13	133.1	17	2	0	0	1.000	1.28	17	10	.588	0	-2	-	17	0	-1	0	+2	+1	1	-
Skip Schumaker	StL	56	31	338.1	85	4	1	0	.989	2.37	47	14	.298	3	2	-	85	+5	+1	+4	+3	+8	4	-
Luke Scott	Bal	106	100	840.1	200	3	2	1	.990	2.17	105	37	.352	2	-1	23	200	+3	0	+3	+7	+10	6	4
Marco Scutaro	Tor	3	3	25.0	4	1	0	0	1.000	1.80	2	1	.500	1	1	-	4	0	0	0	-1	-1	-1	-
Gary Sheffield	Det	6	6	47.0	13	0	0	0	1.000	2.49	5	3	.600	0	-1	-	13	-1	0	0	-1	-1	-1	-
Jason Smith	KC	1	0	1.0	0	0	0	0	-	.00	0	0	-	0	0	-								
Seth Smith	Col	8	1	17.2	5	0	0	0	1.000	2.55	2	1	.500	0	0	-	5	-1	0	-1	0	-1	-1	-
Travis Snider	Tor	13	11	99.0	14	2	0	1	1.000	1.45	5	2	.400	2	1	-	14	-2	0	-1	-2	-3	-2	-
Alfonso Soriano	ChC	108	107	937.1	186	10	5	5	.975	1.88	63	19	.302	8	6	1	186	-1	0	+1	-2	-1	-1	22
Ryan Spilborghs	Col	22	20	166.2	30	0	0	0	1.000	1.62	15	8	.533	0	-1	-	30	-1	-1	+2	-1	-1	-1	-
Matt Stairs	Tor	9	8	62.0	10	0	0	0	1.000	1.45	7	4	.571	0	-1	-	10	-1	-2	+1	-1	-2	-1	-
Nick Stavinoha	StL	13	6	53.0	9	0	0	0	1.000	1.53	6	2	.333	0	0	-	9	0	+1	0	-1	0	0	-
Shannon Stewart	Tor	40	36	310.1	56	3	0	3	1.000	1.71	23	6	.261	3	3	-	56	+1	0	0	0	0	0	-
Cory Sullivan	Col	2	0	2.1	0	0	0	0	-	.00	1	0	.000	0	0	-	0	0			-1	-1	-1	-
Mark Sweeney	LAD	1	0	1.0	0	0	0	0	-	.00	0	0	-	0	0	-	0	0				0	0	-
Ryan Sweeney	Oak	13	2	43.0	12	0	0	0	1.000	2.51	6	3	.500	0	-1	-	12	0	0	0	-1	-1	-1	-
Nick Swisher	CWS	18	16	137.0	31	1	0	0	1.000	2.10	24	8	.333	1	1	-	31	0	+1	-1	+1	+1	1	-
So Taguchi	Phi	38	2	89.2	22	0	2	0	.917	2.21	9	3	.333	0	0	-	22	+1	+1	0	+2	+2	1	-
Fernando Tatis	NYM	51	28	284.0	47	0	2	0	.959	1.49	26	5	.192	0	0	-	47	+1	+2	-4	+5	+3	2	-
Mark Teahen	KC	31	31	267.0	75	3	0	1	1.000	2.63	32	14	.438	3	0	-	75	-3	+1	-3	-7	-9	-5	-
Marcus Thames	Det	73	69	488.0	120	3	5	1	.961	2.27	56	21	.375	1	1	17	120	-8	-5	-3	-1	-10	-6	28
Clete Thomas	Det	25	11	139.0	40	4	2	1	.957	2.85	22	10	.455	3	1	-	40	-1	-2	0	0	-1	-1	-
Joe Thurston	Bos	4	1	19.0	5	0	0	0	1.000	2.37	1	0	.000	0	0	-	5	0	0	+1	0	+1	1	-
Terry Tiffee	LAD	1	0	1.0	0	0	0	0	-	.00	0	0	-	0	0	-								
Clay Timpner	SF	1	0	2.0	0	0	0	0	-	.00	0	0	-	0	0	-								
Jason Tyner	Cle	1	1	10.0	0	0	0	0	-	.00	0	0	-	0	0	-	0	-1	-1			-1	-1	-
Jonathan Van Every	Bos	1	0	1.0	0	0	0	0	-	.00	0	0	-	0	0	-								
Eugenio Velez	SF	8	4	43.1	5	0	1	0	.833	1.04	2	1	.500	0	0	-	5	0	0	-2	+1	-2	-1	-
Daryle Ward	ChC	6	3	25.0	7	0	0	0	1.000	2.52	1	0	.000	0	0	-	7	+1	+1	0	+1	+2	1	-
Rico Washington	StL	1	0	0.0	0	0	0	0	-	-	0	0	-	0	0	-	0	0				0	0	-
Jayson Werth	Phi	28	4	71.1	15	0	0	0	1.000	1.89	9	2	.222	0	0	-	15	+1	0	+1	+1	+2	1	-
Ty Wigginton	Hou	31	31	247.0	46	2	0	0	1.000	1.75	35	9	.257	1	2	-	46	+5	+2	+4	0	+6	3	-
Brad Wilkerson	Tor	29	13	138.2	24	0	0	0	1.000	1.56	8	3	.375	0	0	-	24	-2	-1	+1	0	-1	-1	-
Josh Willingham	Fla	98	97	855.1	166	7	0	0	1.000	1.82	93	30	.323	7	5	3	166	+5	+3	+1	+4	+8	4	6
Reggie Willits	LAA	30	11	134.1	24	0	0	0	1.000	1.61	12	4	.333	0	0	-	24	-1	-3	+1	+1	-1	-1	-
Randy Winn	SF	15	13	107.2	30	1	0	0	1.000	2.59	15	6	.400	1	1	-	30	+1	+1	0	0	+1	1	-
Dewayne Wise	CWS	24	14	132.2	28	2	2	0	.938	2.04	11	4	.364	1	1	-	28	-1	0	0	-3	-2	-1	-
Delmon Young	Min	151	147	1324.0	282	11	8	2	.973	1.99	145	52	.359	7	3	8	282	-17	-11	+5	-20	-25	-14	35
Delwyn Young	LAD	15	9	86.0	16	2	0	0	1.000	1.88	10	3	.300	2	2	-	16	-2	0	-4	+1	-4	-2	-
Ben Zobrist	TB	14	8	79.1	21	1	0	0	1.000	2.50	8	2	.250	1	0	-	21	0	0	+1	0	+1	1	-
2008 MLB Averages									.983	1.97	4591	1647	.359	171	-	-								

Center Fielders

Name	Team	G	GS	Inn	PO	A	E	DP	Pct	Rng	Opps To Advance	Extra Bases	Pct	Kills	Runs Saved	Rank	Outs Made	Basic	Shallow	Medium	Deep	Enhanced	Runs Saved	Rank
Reggie Abercrombie	Hou	11	10	77.1	29	2	0	1	1.000	3.61	4	4	1.000	1	0	-	29	+2	0	+1	+4	+4	2	-
Chip Ambres	SD	3	3	22.1	3	0	0	0	1.000	1.21	2	1	.500	0	0	-	3	0	+1	0		+1	1	-
Alfredo Amezaga	Fla	79	48	457.1	144	6	1	1	.993	2.95	44	18	.409	3	4	-	146	+7	+1	+4	+7	+12	7	-
Brian Anderson	CWS	94	37	447.1	102	0	0	0	1.000	2.05	36	19	.528	0	1	-	102	+2	+5	0	-1	+3	2	-
Josh Anderson	Atl	30	27	236.0	55	0	1	2	.966	2.14	24	14	.583	0	0	-	55	+6	+2	+4	+4	+10	6	-
Robert Andino	Fla	1	0	6.0	2	0	0	0	1.000	3.00	1	1	1.000	0	0	-	2	0	0	0	0	0	0	-
Rick Ankiel	StL	89	84	766.1	213	4	5	1	.977	2.55	76	33	.434	4	7	2	213	-10	-5	-5	-9	-19	-11	33
Wladimir Balentien	Sea	29	25	218.2	60	0	0	0	1.000	2.47	24	10	.417	0	0	-	60	0	+2	+1	-3	0	0	-
Brian Barton	StL	2	0	2.0	0	0	0	0	-	.00	0	0	-	0	0	-								
Carlos Beltran	NYM	158	158	1407.1	418	8	3	1	.993	2.72	146	78	.534	6	4	10	418	+14	+10	+5	+10	+25	14	2
Roger Bernadina	Was	14	12	108.0	27	0	1	0	.964	2.25	15	10	.667	0	-1	-	27	+1	+1	0	0	+1	1	-
Gregor Blanco	Atl	69	54	494.1	128	4	0	0	1.000	2.40	53	26	.491	1	2	-	128	+1	+1	-1	+1	0	0	-
Willie Bloomquist	Sea	23	16	161.1	48	1	3	0	.942	2.73	19	6	.316	0	2	-	48	-1	0	+1	-3	-2	-1	-
Brandon Boggs	Tex	5	0	9.0	4	0	0	0	1.000	4.00	0	0	-	0	0	-	4	0	0	0	0	0	0	-
Michael Bourn	Hou	130	111	1009.0	291	9	5	2	.984	2.68	100	59	.590	4	0	20	291	-1	-9	+10	+2	+3	2	13
Emil Brown	Oak	1	0	1.0	0	0	0	0	-	.00	0	0	-	0	0	-	0	0	0	0	0	0	0	-
Jay Bruce	Cin	35	35	285.0	77	3	2	1	.976	2.53	31	15	.484	2	3	-	77	+2	0	+4	+1	+5	3	-
Marlon Byrd	Tex	57	46	433.0	149	4	3	0	.981	3.18	48	24	.500	3	3	-	149	0	-2	-1	+4	+1	1	-
Eric Byrnes	Ari	1	0	3.1	2	0	0	0	1.000	5.40	1	0	.000	0	0	-	2	0	0	0	0	0	0	-
Melky Cabrera	NYY	117	109	973.2	272	7	4	1	.986	2.58	88	46	.523	4	3	12	272	+1	-2	+7	-2	+3	2	14
Mike Cameron	Mil	119	119	1057.0	293	3	1	0	.997	2.52	86	42	.488	2	0	20	293	+7	+1	+4	+7	+12	7	7
Ronny Cedeno	ChC	1	0	1.0	0	0	0	0	-	.00	0	0	-	0	0	-	0	0						
Endy Chavez	NYM	10	2	38.1	9	1	0	0	1.000	2.35	7	5	.714	0	-1	-	9	0	0	0	+1	+1	1	-
Justin Christian	NYY	3	3	22.1	5	1	0	0	1.000	2.42	0	0	-	1	1	-	5	0	0	0	0	-1	-1	-
Brent Clevlen	Det	3	3	21.0	6	0	0	0	1.000	2.57	0	0	-	0	0	-	6	-1	0	-1	+1	-1	-1	-
Carl Crawford	TB	1	1	7.0	2	0	0	0	1.000	2.57	3	1	.333	0	0	-	2	0			0	0	0	-
Coco Crisp	Bos	114	98	886.0	234	4	2	1	.992	2.42	74	44	.595	1	-2	31	234	-2	-4	+1	+1	-2	-1	16
Jose Cruz	Hou	5	5	35.0	9	0	0	0	1.000	2.31	3	2	.667	0	0	-	9	0	+1	0	-3	-2	-1	-
Michael Cuddyer	Min	1	1	8.0	3	1	0	0	1.000	4.50	2	2	1.000	0	0	-	3	0			0	0	0	-
Johnny Damon	NYY	34	33	285.0	77	1	1	0	.987	2.46	34	21	.618	0	-1	-	77	-3	-2	+1	-2	-3	-2	-
Rajai Davis	2 tms	88	43	487.2	153	4	1	2	.994	2.90	61	29	.475	2	3	-	153	+5	+3	0	+5	+7	4	-
David DeJesus	KC	68	64	507.0	151	2	1	1	.994	2.72	49	35	.714	1	-3	34	151	-5	-5	+1	-6	-11	-6	26
Chris Denorfia	Oak	12	8	73.2	26	0	0	0	1.000	3.18	5	3	.600	0	0	-	26	+3	+2	-1	+4	+4	2	-
Chris Dickerson	Cin	7	6	45.0	10	0	0	0	1.000	2.00	4	3	.750	0	-1	-	10	+2	+1	+2		+3	2	-
J.D. Drew	Bos	1	0	5.2	0	0	0	0	-	.00	0	0	-	0	0	-	0	0				0	0	-
Elijah Dukes	Was	1	1	9.0	5	0	0	0	1.000	5.00	1	0	.000	0	0	-	5	+1	0	+1	0	+1	1	-
Jim Edmonds	2 tms	103	99	840.0	242	1	6	1	.976	2.60	61	34	.557	1	1	17	242	-7	+4	-8	-21	-25	-14	34
Jason Ellison	Tex	2	0	3.0	0	0	0	0	-	.00	0	0	-	0	0	-	0	0			0	0	0	-
Jacoby Ellsbury	Bos	66	63	546.2	171	3	0	1	1.000	2.86	62	34	.548	1	-1	27	171	+4	-2	+7	+3	+8	4	9
Darin Erstad	Hou	40	35	304.0	97	1	0	0	1.000	2.90	28	17	.607	1	-1	-	98	+4	+2	-1	+4	+5	3	-
Jeff Fiorentino	Oak	2	0	4.0	0	0	0	0	-	.00	0	0	-	0	0	-	0	0				0	0	-
Dexter Fowler	Col	9	5	49.2	12	1	0	1	1.000	2.36	4	4	1.000	1	0	-	12	+1	0	0	+2	+2	1	-
Ben Francisco	Cle	2	0	2.0	0	0	0	0	-	.00	0	0	-	0	0	-	0	0			-1	-1	-1	-
Ryan Freel	Cin	23	19	151.2	45	1	0	0	1.000	2.73	20	8	.400	0	0	-	45	-1	0	-1	-2	-3	-2	-
Kosuke Fukudome	ChC	12	5	59.0	10	0	0	0	1.000	1.53	4	3	.750	0	0	-	10	0	0	-1	-1	-2	-1	-
Brett Gardner	NYY	22	17	160.2	53	4	0	0	1.000	3.19	19	7	.368	3	4	-	53	+4	+1	+2	+5	+8	4	-
Joey Gathright	KC	100	75	720.0	197	5	1	0	.995	2.53	75	38	.507	2	0	20	197	-6	-8	+1	-3	-10	-6	24
Jody Gerut	SD	80	64	605.2	189	2	2	1	.990	2.84	54	30	.556	0	0	20	189	+8	+5	+2	+6	+13	7	6
Brian Giles	SD	2	0	2.0	0	0	0	0	-	.00	0	0	-	0	0	-	0	0				0	0	-
Greg Golson	Phi	2	1	9.0	4	0	0	0	.667	1.38	0	0	-	0	0	-	4	0		0	-1	-1	-1	-
Carlos Gomez	Min	151	143	1271.2	436	9	8	4	.982	3.15	135	73	.541	4	1	17	437	+14	-2	+8	+23	+29	16	1
Carlos Gonzalez	Oak	69	66	528.2	176	5	2	1	.989	3.08	50	26	.520	4	4	10	176	+4	+1	+1	+4	+6	3	12
Curtis Granderson	Det	140	131	1188.0	366	5	4	1	.989	2.81	123	67	.545	3	-1	27	366	-8	-6	0	-5	-11	-6	25
Ken Griffey Jr.	CWS	32	32	250.0	62	1	0	1	1.000	2.27	21	15	.714	1	0	-	62	+2	+2	-1	+4	+5	3	-
Gabe Gross	2 tms	18	17	128.2	34	2	1	0	.973	2.52	13	6	.462	1	2	-	34	-1	0	-3	+1	-2	-2	-
Franklin Gutierrez	Cle	12	11	97.0	30	1	1	0	.969	2.88	8	3	.375	1	2	-	30	-2	-2	-1	0	-3	-2	-
Tony Gwynn	Mil	7	5	46.0	14	0	0	0	1.000	2.74	1	0	.000	0	0	-	14	+1	0	0	+3	+3	2	-
Jerry Hairston	Cin	17	15	116.2	27	1	1	0	.966	2.16	10	5	.500	1	1	-	27	+1	+1	+1	0	+2	1	-
Scott Hairston	SD	51	45	378.0	114	2	2	0	.983	2.76	33	20	.606	2	1	-	114	-1	+2	-4	+4	+2	1	-
Josh Hamilton	Tex	111	107	912.0	268	3	5	3	.982	2.67	112	67	.598	1	0	20	268	-5	+5	-11	-7	-13	-7	29
Willie Harris	Was	17	14	131.1	46	0	1	0	.979	3.15	14	10	.714	0	-1	-	46	+2	0	+1	+2	+3	2	-
Nathan Haynes	TB	2	1	13.0	4	0	0	0	1.000	2.77	1	1	1.000	0	0	-	4	-2	0	-4	+1	-3	-2	-
Norris Hopper	Cin	7	5	46.0	12	0	0	0	1.000	2.35	9	3	.333	0	1	-	12	-1	-2	0	0	-2	-1	-
Torii Hunter	LAA	137	137	1193.1	350	4	0	0	1.000	2.67	120	68	.567	2	-1	27	350	-5	-3	+1	-6	-7	-4	20
Omar Infante	Atl	3	1	14.1	4	0	0	0	1.000	2.51	1	1	1.000	0	0	-	4	0	0	0	-1	0	0	-
Brandon Inge	Det	13	12	94.0	26	2	0	0	1.000	2.68	11	6	.545	1	2	-	26	+1	0	+2	-2	+1	1	-
Joe Inglett	Tor	1	1	7.0	1	0	0	0	1.000	1.29	0	0	-	0	0	-	1	0	0			0	0	-
Hernan Iribarren	Mil	1	0	3.0	1	0	0	0	1.000	3.00	0	0	-	0	0	-	1	0			0	0	0	-
Elliot Johnson	TB	1	0	3.0	1	0	0	0	1.000	3.00	0	0	-	0	0	-	1	0			+1	+1	1	-
Reed Johnson	ChC	78	64	563.2	144	2	1	1	.993	2.33	41	24	.585	2	0	20	144	-6	-2	-6	-3	-11	-6	27
Adam Jones	Bal	129	123	1102.0	336	4	3	1	.991	2.78	115	49	.426	4	7	2	337	+5	+5	+7	-5	+7	4	11
Andruw Jones	LAD	66	55	496.1	133	1	1	0	.993	2.43	55	28	.509	0	0	-	133	-2	+2	+2	-9	-5	-3	-
Jacque Jones	Fla	5	5	41.0	13	0	0	0	1.000	2.85	5	5	1.000	0	-1	-	13	+1	0	0	+1	+2	1	-
Gabe Kapler	Mil	36	25	251.0	70	0	1	0	.986	2.51	24	13	.542	0	1	-	70	+3	+2	+1	+3	+5	3	-
Matt Kemp	LAD	101	92	825.2	209	10	1	0	.995	2.39	76	40	.526	8	6	6	209	0	+7	-3	-6	-2	-1	17
Mark Kotsay	Atl	84	80	696.0	173	3	0	1	1.000	2.28	73	29	.397	3	7	2	173	-6	0	-4	-11	-15	-8	31
Fred Lewis	SF	14	5	69.0	16	0	0	0	1.000	2.09	7	5	.714	0	-1	-	16	-1	0	+1	-4	-3	-2	-
Ryan Ludwick	StL	14	10	64.0	20	0	1	0	.952	2.81	3	1	.333	0	0	-	20	0	0	0	-1	-1	-1	-
Mitch Maier	KC	33	23	217.2	69	0	1	0	.986	2.85	23	13	.565	0	0	-	69	+3	+1	+1	+2	+5	3	-
Joe Mather	StL	15	9	67.0	19	0	1	0	.950	2.55	7	4	.571	0	-1	-	19	0	0	+1	0	0	0	-
Gary Matthews Jr.	LAA	31	23	221.0	66	3	4	0	.945	2.81	25	12	.480	1	2	-	66	+2	+2	+1	+2	+5	3	-
Cameron Maybin	Fla	8	7	63.0	23	0	0	0	1.000	3.29	3	2	.667	0	0	-	23	+1	0	+1	0	+2	1	-
Nate McLouth	Pit	149	148	1300.1	380	5	1	1	.997	2.66	144	74	.514	2	2	14	380	-20	-5	+4	-36	-37	-21	35
Jason Michaels	Pit	8	6	57.1	22	0	0	0	1.000	3.45	1	0	.000	0	0	-	22	+1	-1	0	+2	+1	1	-
Aaron Miles	StL	1	0	2.0	0	0	0	0	-	.00	0	0	-	0	0	-								

108

		BASIC									THROWING						PLUS/MINUS							
Name	Team	G	GS	Inn	PO	A	E	DP	Pct	Rng	Opps To Advance	Extra Bases	Pct	Kills	Runs Saved	Rank	Outs Made	Basic	Shallow	Medium	Deep	Enhanced	Runs Saved	Rank
Lastings Milledge	Was	134	134	1185.2	348	1	5	0	.986	2.65	107	59	.551	0	0	20	348	-14	-8	-8	+6	-10	-6	23
Jai Miller	Fla	1	0	2.0	0	0	0	0	-	.00	0	0	-	0	0	-	0	0				0	0	-
Craig Monroe	Min	7	6	56.2	13	1	0	1	1.000	2.22	3	2	.667	1	1	-	13	-1	-2	0	+1	-1	-1	-
Lou Montanez	Bal	5	2	19.0	4	0	0	0	1.000	1.89	2	1	.500	0	0	-	4	0	0	0	+1	+1	1	-
Nyjer Morgan	Pit	17	8	97.1	31	0	0	0	1.000	2.87	8	5	.625	0	-1	-	31	+3	+2	-1	+2	+3	2	-
David Murphy	Tex	13	9	85.0	30	0	0	0	1.000	3.18	15	8	.533	0	1	-	30	-4	0	-1	-6	-8	-4	-
Jerry Owens	CWS	4	2	18.0	4	0	0	0	1.000	2.00	5	2	.400	0	0	-	4	0	0	0	0	0	0	-
Angel Pagan	NYM	2	2	18.2	8	0	0	0	1.000	3.86	1	1	1.000	0	0	-	8	0	-1	+1	0	0	0	-
Corey Patterson	Cin	124	82	798.0	242	3	3	1	.988	2.76	63	29	.460	3	2	14	242	+4	-1	0	+11	+10	6	8
Eric Patterson	ChC	1	0	2.0	0	0	0	0	-	.00	0	0	-	0	0	-	0	0				0	0	-
Jay Payton	Bal	38	36	301.0	99	6	0	0	1.000	3.14	38	15	.395	3	3	-	99	+6	+2	+2	+2	+6	3	-
Fernando Perez	TB	15	11	112.0	47	1	0	1	1.000	3.86	5	2	.400	0	0	-	47	+5	+3	+2	+1	+7	4	-
Felix Pie	ChC	39	17	197.1	58	1	0	0	1.000	2.69	19	11	.579	1	1	-	58	0	0	-2	+3	+1	1	-
Juan Pierre	LAD	18	14	116.1	28	1	0	1	1.000	2.24	9	5	.556	1	1	-	28	0	0	0	+1	+1	1	-
Scott Podsednik	Col	36	21	201.1	55	1	2	0	.966	2.50	22	13	.591	1	0	-	55	0	-1	-1	+4	+3	2	-
Nick Punto	Min	3	0	6.0	1	0	0	0	1.000	1.50	0	0	-	0	0	-	1	0		0	0	0	0	-
Ryan Raburn	Det	6	4	30.0	12	0	0	0	1.000	3.60	4	2	.500	0	0	-	12	+2	0	+1	+1	+3	2	-
Alexei Ramirez	CWS	11	6	63.0	16	1	1	0	.944	2.43	7	6	.857	1	0	-	16	-3	-2	-1	0	-4	-2	-
Jeremy Reed	Sea	58	52	453.2	132	1	1	0	.993	2.64	68	41	.603	0	-2	-	132	0	-3	+1	+6	+4	2	-
Jason Repko	LAD	2	1	9.0	7	0	0	0	1.000	7.00	2	1	.500	0	0	-	7	+1	+1	0	+1	+1	1	-
Alex Rios	Tor	62	59	522.2	156	10	3	1	.982	2.86	46	25	.543	7	6	6	156	+4	+1	+4	+3	+8	4	10
Juan Rivera	LAA	1	0	3.0	3	0	0	0	1.000	9.00	1	1	1.000	0	0	-	3	0	0	0		0	0	-
Alex Romero	Ari	2	2	13.2	4	0	0	0	1.000	2.63	1	0	.000	0	0	-	4	+1	+1	0		+1	1	-
Cody Ross	Fla	109	101	866.0	254	7	0	2	1.000	2.71	76	49	.645	5	3	12	254	+3	-7	+4	+16	+13	7	5
Aaron Rowand	SF	149	148	1275.1	412	6	4	0	.991	2.95	140	69	.493	4	5	9	411	-4	0	-3	-4	-8	-4	21
Justin Ruggiano	TB	5	1	17.0	5	2	0	1	1.000	3.71	3	2	.667	1	0	-	5	-1	-1	0	-2	-2	-1	-
Jeff Salazar	Ari	4	3	27.2	3	1	0	0	1.000	1.30	6	5	.833	0	-1	-	3	-2	-1	-1	-1	-3	-2	-
Skip Schumaker	StL	79	59	552.2	136	5	1	2	.993	2.30	63	38	.603	2	-2	31	136	-2	-2	-5	+3	-3	-2	18
Grady Sizemore	Cle	151	151	1338.0	382	2	2	1	.995	2.58	131	68	.519	2	1	17	382	-3	-8	+1	+8	+2	1	15
Seth Smith	Col	9	7	46.1	19	0	1	0	.950	3.69	5	3	.600	0	0	-	19	-1	0	0	-3	-3	-2	-
Denard Span	Min	19	13	116.2	34	1	1	0	.972	2.70	22	12	.545	1	1	-	34	-2	-2	0	0	-2	-1	-
Ryan Spilborghs	Col	17	16	130.2	34	0	0	0	1.000	2.34	15	9	.600	0	-1	-	34	-4	-3	0	-4	-7	-4	-
Cory Sullivan	Col	5	3	25.0	3	0	0	0	1.000	1.08	3	2	.667	0	0	-	3	-1	0	-1	-2	-3	-2	-
Ichiro Suzuki	Sea	69	69	601.2	195	4	1	1	.995	2.98	69	32	.464	4	6	6	195	-7	-5	-5	-4	-13	-7	30
Ryan Sweeney	Oak	51	46	362.2	95	0	0	0	1.000	2.36	27	17	.630	0	-1	-	95	-3	-3	-2	+3	-2	-1	-
Nick Swisher	CWS	70	69	535.1	138	2	4	0	.972	2.35	61	38	.623	1	-1	27	138	-4	0	-4	-6	-11	-6	28
So Taguchi	Phi	1	1	8.0	0	0	0	0	-	.00	1	0	.000	0	0	-	0	-1			-2	-2	-1	-
Willy Taveras	Col	124	110	993.0	282	6	7	2	.976	2.61	103	53	.515	3	2	14	282	0	+3	-9	+2	-4	-2	19
Mark Teahen	KC	1	0	1.0	0	0	0	0	-	.00	0	0	-	0	0	-	0	0				0	0	-
Clete Thomas	Det	16	12	112.0	40	0	2	0	.952	3.21	10	7	.700	0	-1	-	40	+1	0	+1	-1	+1	1	-
B.J. Upton	TB	143	141	1248.2	378	16	7	5	.983	2.84	121	72	.595	13	8	1	378	+3	+14	-7	-17	-10	-6	22
Jonathan Van Every	Bos	1	1	8.0	1	0	0	0	1.000	1.13	1	1	1.000	0	0	-	1	0	0		0	0	0	-
Eugenio Velez	SF	2	0	4.0	3	0	0	0	1.000	6.75	0	0	-	0	0	-	3	+1		+2	+1	+3	2	-
Will Venable	SD	27	26	238.0	84	1	0	0	1.000	3.21	21	16	.762	1	-1	-	84	+3	-1	+2	+5	+6	3	-
Shane Victorino	Phi	139	134	1195.1	314	7	2	2	.994	2.42	109	56	.514	6	7	2	314	+12	+14	-2	+2	+14	8	4
Vernon Wells	Tor	100	99	889.0	217	5	3	1	.987	2.25	77	50	.649	2	-2	31	217	-8	-2	-10	-6	-17	-10	32
Jayson Werth	Phi	31	26	233.1	73	2	2	1	.974	2.89	21	14	.667	2	0	-	73	+2	+5	-1	-2	+1	1	-
Brad Wilkerson	Tor	5	3	28.0	7	0	0	0	1.000	2.25	5	2	.400	0	0	-	7	-1	0	-1	0	-1	-1	-
Reggie Willits	LAA	9	2	34.0	10	0	0	0	1.000	2.65	1	1	1.000	0	0	-	10	-1	0	-1	0	-1	-1	-
Randy Winn	SF	10	7	71.0	18	1	0	0	1.000	2.41	13	8	.615	1	0	-	18	-1	-1	-1	-1	-2	-1	-
Dewayne Wise	CWS	23	17	144.0	40	0	0	0	1.000	2.50	14	7	.500	0	0	-	40	-1	+1	+1	-4	-3	-2	-
Chris Young	Ari	159	157	1390.0	393	5	3	2	.993	2.58	126	71	.563	2	-3	34	393	+6	-5	+10	+16	+21	12	3
Ben Zobrist	TB	5	3	27.0	8	0	0	0	1.000	2.67	5	1	.200	0	0	-	8	-1	-1	0	-1	-3	-2	-
2008 MLB Averages									.989	2.66	4307	2328	.541	155	-	-								

Right Fielders

Name	Team	G	GS	Inn	PO	A	E	DP	Pct	Rng	Opps To Advance	Extra Bases	Pct	Kills	Runs Saved	Rank	Outs Made	Basic	Shallow	Medium	Deep	Enhanced	Runs Saved	Rank
Bobby Abreu	NYY	150	148	1310.0	270	10	2	3	.993	1.92	145	65	.448	9	7	4	271	-14	-8	-10	-2	-20	-12	34
Chip Ambres	SD	7	6	50.0	16	0	1	0	.941	2.88	2	1	.500	0	0	-	16	0	0	0	+1	0	0	
Brian Anderson	CWS	2	0	6.0	0	0	0	0	-	.00	0	0	-	0	0	-	0	0				0	0	
Josh Anderson	Atl	1	0	0.1	0	0	0	0	-	.00	0	0	-	0	0	-								
Rick Ankiel	StL	1	0	2.0	1	0	0	0	1.000	4.50	0	0	-	0	0	-	1	+1		0		+1	1	
Jeff Bailey	Bos	1	0	1.0	0	0	0	0	-	.00	0	0	-	0	0	-	0	0				0	0	
Jeff Baker	Col	3	3	21.0	2	0	1	0	.667	.86	0	0	-	0	0	-	2	+1			+1	+1	1	
Rocco Baldelli	TB	6	3	29.2	5	0	1	0	.833	1.52	4	3	.750	0	0	-	5	+1	+1	0	0	+1	1	
Wladimir Balentien	Sea	35	32	293.0	76	5	2	0	.976	2.49	37	15	.405	2	3	-	76	+2	+4	0	-4	-1	-1	
Clint Barmes	Col	1	1	6.0	2	0	0	0	1.000	3.00	1	0	.000	0	0	-	2	0		0		0	0	
Brian Barton	StL	10	6	48.0	15	0	1	0	.938	2.81	8	4	.500	0	-1	-	15	+1	+1	0	0	+1	1	
Gregor Blanco	Atl	5	4	34.0	8	0	0	0	1.000	2.12	8	2	.250	0	-1	-	8	-1	-1	-1	+1	-2	-1	
Willie Bloomquist	Sea	13	7	74.1	14	0	0	0	1.000	1.70	5	3	.600	0	-1	-	14	-1	0	-2	0	-2	-1	
Brandon Boggs	Tex	3	1	11.1	3	0	0	0	1.000	2.38	2	1	.500	0	0	-	3	0	0	0	0	0		
Emilio Bonifacio	Ari	2	2	16.0	1	0	0	0	1.000	.56	2	1	.500	0	0	-	1	-1	0		-1	-1	-1	
John Bowker	SF	14	10	91.1	22	0	0	0	1.000	2.17	10	7	.700	0	-1	-	22	-2	-3	0	-1	-4	-2	
Milton Bradley	Tex	19	19	157.1	42	4	3	3	.939	2.63	24	6	.250	4	5	-	42	+1	-1	0	+2	+1	1	
Emil Brown	Oak	55	55	433.1	111	4	3	2	.975	2.39	42	18	.429	2	1	-	112	0	+2	+1	-2	+1	1	
Jay Bruce	Cin	78	64	590.0	143	5	9	3	.943	2.26	57	27	.474	5	3	15	143	+1	+3	+4	-11	-4	-2	24
Eric Bruntlett	Phi	7	1	12.2	3	0	0	0	1.000	2.13	2	1	.500	0	0	-	3	0	0	-1	-1	-1	-1	
Travis Buck	Oak	34	34	287.0	73	2	0	0	1.000	2.35	24	13	.542	2	0	-	74	+1	-2	0	+5	+3	2	
Chris Burke	Ari	9	7	62.2	9	0	0	0	1.000	1.29	6	3	.500	0	0	-	9	-1	0	-1	0	-1	-1	
Emmanuel Burriss	SF	1	0	2.1	0	0	0	0	-	.00	1	1	1.000	0	0	-								
Marlon Byrd	Tex	39	33	279.0	71	3	3	0	.961	2.39	45	23	.511	2	0	-	71	+4	+6	-2	+2	+6	3	
Jolbert Cabrera	Cin	3	2	17.0	1	0	0	0	1.000	.53	2	1	.500	0	0	-	1	-1	0		-1	-1	-1	
Melky Cabrera	NYY	5	2	23.2	8	0	0	0	1.000	3.04	1	0	.000	0	0	-	8	0	0	0	-1	0	0	
Miguel Cairo	Sea	1	0	2.0	0	0	0	0	-	.00	0	0	-	0	0	-								
Brett Carroll	Fla	4	3	28.1	9	2	0	0	1.000	3.49	3	3	1.000	2	1	-	9	+1	0	0	+1	+1	1	
Kory Casto	Was	1	1	9.0	4	1	0	1	1.000	5.00	0	0	-	0	0	-	4	+1	0	0	+2	+2	1	
Endy Chavez	NYM	60	41	400.0	109	4	1	2	.991	2.54	42	19	.452	3	2	-	110	+7	+4	0	+7	+11	6	
Shin-Soo Choo	Cle	51	45	398.1	88	1	1	0	.989	2.01	44	22	.500	1	-1	-	89	0	-7	0	+7	0	0	
Justin Christian	NYY	5	1	17.0	6	0	0	0	1.000	3.18	1	0	.000	0	0	-	6	0	0	0	0	0	0	
Ryan Church	NYM	83	81	724.0	180	7	1	1	.995	2.32	83	40	.482	4	0	24	180	+3	-1	+4	+5	+9	5	9
Brady Clark	NYM	2	0	2.0	0	0	0	0	-	.00	0	0	-	0	0	-								
Brent Clevlen	Det	1	1	9.0	1	0	0	0	1.000	1.00	0	0	-	0	0	-	1	-1			-1	-1	-1	
Callix Crabbe	SD	2	1	10.0	3	0	0	0	1.000	2.70	0	0	-	0	0	-	3	0	0	0	0	0	0	
Jose Cruz	Hou	3	1	11.0	4	0	0	0	1.000	3.27	0	0	-	0	0	-	4	0	-1	0	+3	+2	1	
Nelson Cruz	Tex	31	31	274.0	72	1	2	1	.973	2.40	42	17	.405	1	0	-	72	+2	+4	+1	-2	+4	2	
Michael Cuddyer	Min	58	57	501.2	123	6	1	4	.992	2.31	51	21	.412	5	5	8	123	-4	+2	-3	-7	-8	-5	28
Aaron Cunningham	Oak	2	2	18.1	6	0	0	0	1.000	2.95	3	0	.000	0	0	-	6	+1	0	+1	+1	+2	1	
Jack Cust	Oak	5	5	39.0	4	0	0	0	1.000	.92	4	1	.250	0	0	-	4	-3	-2	-1	0	-3	-2	
Rajai Davis	SF	1	0	2.0	1	0	0	0	1.000	4.50	0	0	-	0	0	-	1	0		0		0	0	
David DeJesus	KC	23	11	123.0	23	0	0	0	1.000	1.68	13	7	.538	0	0	-	23	0	0	-1	+2	+1	1	
Chris Denorfia	Oak	2	1	10.0	2	0	0	0	1.000	1.80	2	1	.500	0	0	-	2	-1		0	-1	-1	-1	
Mark DeRosa	ChC	38	32	266.2	72	0	0	0	1.000	2.43	29	12	.414	0	0	-	72	-4	+1	0		-3	-2	
Greg Dobbs	Phi	4	0	4.2	1	0	0	0	1.000	1.93	1	1	1.000	0	0	-	1	0		0	0	0	0	
J.D. Drew	Bos	106	105	886.0	184	6	4	1	.979	1.93	87	52	.598	4	-1	28	184	-5	0	-7	0	-7	-4	26
Elijah Dukes	Was	69	66	602.2	137	9	5	1	.967	2.18	70	42	.600	4	0	24	137	+4	0	0	+11	+11	6	8
Chris Duncan	StL	2	2	15.0	4	0	0	0	1.000	2.40	1	0	.000	0	0	-	4	+1	0	0	0	+1	1	
Shelley Duncan	NYY	4	3	23.0	4	0	0	0	1.000	1.57	1	0	.000	0	0	-	4	0	0	0	0	0	0	
Adam Dunn	Ari	23	22	182.2	29	0	1	0	.967	1.43	18	11	.611	0	0	-	29	-6	-2	-1	-7	-11	-6	
German Duran	Tex	2	1	9.0	4	0	0	0	1.000	4.00	1	0	.000	0	0	-	4	0	0	0	0	0	0	
Jermaine Dye	CWS	151	151	1312.2	266	5	1	0	.996	1.86	124	63	.508	3	-2	30	266	-5	+3	-9	-6	-12	-7	31
Jason Ellison	Tex	3	1	15.0	6	0	0	0	1.000	3.60	1	0	.000	0	0	-	6	0	0	0	0	0	0	
Jacoby Ellsbury	Bos	36	30	281.0	72	0	0	0	1.000	2.31	23	10	.435	0	0	-	72	+4	+1	+4	+2	+7	4	
Darin Erstad	Hou	6	6	48.0	12	0	0	0	1.000	2.25	5	2	.400	0	0	-	12	-1	0	0	-2	-2	-1	
Andre Ethier	LAD	109	102	881.0	171	8	0	0	1.000	1.83	90	46	.511	3	0	24	171	-13	-9	-4	-5	-19	-11	33
Dexter Fowler	Col	1	0	1.0	0	0	0	0	-	.00	1	0	.000	0	0	-	0	0				0	0	
Ben Francisco	Cle	32	27	230.0	46	5	2	1	.962	2.00	26	9	.346	4	4	-	46	-2	0	+1	-4	-3	-2	
Jeff Francoeur	Atl	152	151	1328.2	282	14	4	2	.987	2.01	115	50	.435	6	5	8	284	-3	-3	+4	-13	-12	-7	30
Ryan Freel	Cin	5	0	10.1	4	0	0	0	1.000	3.48	2	0	.000	0	1	-	4	0		0	+1	+1	1	
Kosuke Fukudome	ChC	137	121	1103.2	245	6	5	0	.980	2.05	104	49	.471	4	2	20	246	+2	+8	+2	-8	+1	1	14
Jody Gerut	SD	5	2	63.0	17	0	0	0	1.000	2.43	6	4	.667	0	0	-	17	+1	0	+1	+1	+2	1	
Brian Giles	SD	144	142	1263.0	276	3	7	1	.976	1.99	126	71	.563	2	-5	35	276	+9	-1	+7	+16	+22	13	2
Ross Gload	KC	3	1	13.0	3	0	0	0	1.000	2.08	2	1	.500	0	0	-	3	0	0	0		0	0	
Greg Golson	Phi	1	0	1.0	0	0	0	0	-	.00	0	0	-	0	0	-	0	0				0	0	
Jonny Gomes	TB	21	17	125.0	25	0	1	0	.962	1.80	9	5	.556	0	-1	-	25	-3	0	+1	-9	-8	-5	
Carlos Gonzalez	Oak	36	10	160.2	43	0	0	0	1.000	2.41	7	1	.143	0	1	-	43	+3	+2	+1	+3	+6	3	
Edgar Gonzalez	SD	3	1	16.2	5	1	0	1	1.000	3.24	1	1	1.000	1	0	-	5	0	0	0	0	0	0	
Luis Gonzalez	Fla	22	20	147.1	30	1	0	0	1.000	1.89	19	8	.421	0	0	-	30	0	0	0	-1	0	0	
Ken Griffey Jr.	2 tms	91	90	763.0	157	7	5	0	.970	1.93	83	38	.458	2	3	15	157	-10	-5	-5	-6	-16	-9	32
Gabe Gross	2 tms	121	75	768.1	186	6	1	0	.995	2.25	72	27	.375	3	4	14	186	+1	-5	+11	-5	+1	0	17
Vladimir Guerrero	LAA	99	99	839.0	180	8	4	2	.979	2.02	70	39	.557	3	-2	30	180	-4	-3	+1	-1	-4	-2	23
Jose Guillen	KC	67	65	539.1	121	7	3	1	.977	2.14	73	38	.521	4	2	20	121	-9	-10	+2	-3	-11	-6	29
Franklin Gutierrez	Cle	97	85	763.2	224	4	2	0	.991	2.69	91	35	.385	3	5	8	224	+16	+6	+6	+17	+29	17	1
Tony Gwynn	Mil	2	0	6.1	0	0	0	0	-	.00	0	0	-	0	0	-								
Jerry Hairston	Cin	12	5	47.0	17	0	0	0	1.000	3.26	3	2	.667	0	0	-	17	0	-3	+1	0	-2	-1	
Josh Hamilton	Tex	34	33	289.0	77	4	1	2	.988	2.52	37	16	.432	2	1	-	77	-1	+2	-3	+2	+1	1	
Corey Hart	Mil	156	156	1376.2	302	8	5	2	.984	2.03	122	64	.525	5	0	24	304	0	+7	-3	-3	0	0	18
Brad Hawpe	Col	133	132	1172.0	186	9	9	0	.956	1.50	150	78	.520	7	-1	28	188	-23	-12	-11	-14	-37	-21	35
Nathan Haynes	TB	15	8	83.0	19	0	1	0	.950	2.06	6	4	.667	0	-1	-	19	0	-1	-1	0	0	0	
Jeremy Hermida	Fla	132	124	1092.1	266	4	5	0	.982	2.22	122	65	.533	2	-3	32	266	-4	-9	+2	+9	+2	1	13
Eric Hinske	TB	49	47	339.1	88	2	1	0	.989	2.39	29	16	.552	1	0	-	88	0	-1	-1	+2	0	0	
Micah Hoffpauir	ChC	5	5	36.0	6	0	0	0	1.000	1.50	1	0	.000	0	0	-	6	-1	0	0	-1	-1	-1	
Norris Hopper	Cin	4	2	23.0	6	0	0	0	1.000	2.35	1	0	.000	0	0	-	6	+1	+1	0	0	+1	1	

Name	Team	G	GS	Inn	PO	A	E	DP	Pct	Rng	Opps To Advance	Extra Bases	Pct	Kills	Runs Saved	Rank	Outs Made	Basic	Shallow	Medium	Deep	Enhanced	Runs Saved	Rank
Brian Horwitz	SF	2	1	9.0	6	0	0	0	1.000	6.00	2	1	.500	0	0	-	6	+1	+1		0	+1	1	-
Joe Inglett	Tor	12	9	87.1	14	0	0	0	1.000	1.44	8	4	.500	0	-1	-	14	-1	0	0	+1	0	0	-
Geoff Jenkins	Phi	90	72	642.0	140	7	5	1	.967	2.06	54	22	.407	5	6	5	141	0	+2	+1	-5	-2	-1	21
Elliot Johnson	TB	1	1	8.0	3	0	0	0	1.000	3.38	3	2	.667	0	0	-	3	0	0	0		0	0	-
Reed Johnson	ChC	6	1	23.1	4	0	0	0	1.000	1.54	4	2	.500	0	0	-	4	+1	0		+3	+2	1	-
Brandon Jones	Atl	7	3	34.2	8	0	0	0	1.000	2.08	5	2	.400	0	0	-	8	0	-1	0	+1	0	0	-
Jacque Jones	Fla	3	1	13.2	3	0	0	0	1.000	1.98	0	0	-	0	0	-	3	-1		-1	0	-1	-1	-
Matt Joyce	Det	25	16	161.0	42	0	1	0	.977	2.35	21	10	.476	0	0	-	42	+2	0	+3	0	+3	2	-
Gabe Kapler	Mil	14	6	66.0	9	0	0	0	1.000	1.23	10	5	.500	0	0	-	9	-1	0	-1	-2	-2	-1	-
Austin Kearns	Was	85	83	734.0	187	3	4	0	.979	2.33	83	42	.506	1	-3	32	187	-2	-7	+3	+5	+1	1	16
Matt Kemp	LAD	63	52	478.2	97	6	2	0	.981	1.94	54	22	.407	3	5	-	98	0	+3	-4	+2	+1	1	-
Adam Kennedy	StL	9	6	55.0	15	0	0	0	1.000	2.45	3	0	.000	0	0	-	15	+2	+2	-1	0	+2	1	-
Mark Kotsay	Bos	19	18	151.2	32	0	0	0	1.000	1.90	8	5	.625	0	-1	-	32	0	0	-2	0	-2	-1	-
Jason Kubel	Min	32	26	238.2	74	1	1	0	.987	2.83	25	15	.600	0	-2	-	74	-1	-2	+3	-5	-5	-3	-
Ryan Langerhans	Was	12	9	74.1	23	1	0	1	1.000	2.91	8	3	.375	0	0	-	23	+3	0	+2	+4	+6	3	-
Fred Lewis	SF	2	2	18.0	5	0	0	0	1.000	2.50	2	1	.500	0	0	-	5	0	0	0	0	0	0	-
Felipe Lopez	StL	1	0	2.0	1	0	1	0	.500	4.50	1	1	1.000	0	0	-	1	0			+1	+1	1	-
Ryan Ludwick	StL	124	105	962.1	231	10	2	3	.992	2.25	92	34	.370	8	11	3	232	+2	+1	-5	+5	+1	1	15
Drew Macias	SD	3	0	7.1	4	0	0	0	1.000	4.91	0	0	-	0	0	-	4	0	0	0	0	0	0	-
Rob Mackowiak	Was	2	2	14.0	2	0	0	0	1.000	1.29	2	0	.000	0	0	-	2	0			+1	+1	1	-
Mitch Maier	KC	4	1	14.0	2	0	0	0	1.000	1.29	1	1	1.000	0	0	-	2	0		0	0	0	0	-
Nick Markakis	Bal	156	155	1367.0	327	17	3	3	.991	2.26	153	67	.438	14	14	1	329	+7	+10	+4	-4	+11	6	7
Joe Mather	StL	15	6	64.2	17	0	0	0	1.000	2.37	7	6	.857	0	-1	-	17	+3	+2	+1	+2	+5	3	-
Hideki Matsui	NYY	3	2	18.0	2	0	0	0	1.000	1.00	2	1	.500	0	0	-	2	0	0	0	0	0	0	-
Gary Matthews Jr.	LAA	43	36	344.0	77	2	2	0	.975	2.07	27	9	.333	1	1	-	77	-6	-1	-4	-4	-9	-5	-
Paul McAnulty	SD	15	5	48.1	18	0	0	0	1.000	3.35	3	0	.000	0	1	-	18	+1	+1	0	0	+1	1	-
Nate McLouth	Pit	2	1	12.0	2	0	0	0	1.000	1.50	2	0	.000	0	0	-	2	0		0	0	0	0	-
Kevin Mench	Tor	15	11	98.0	22	1	0	0	1.000	2.11	10	1	.100	1	2	-	22	+2	+1	+2	-1	+2	1	-
Jason Michaels	2 tms	43	30	293.0	88	2	4	0	.957	2.76	31	17	.548	1	-1	-	88	+1	+1	-2	+1	0	0	-
Doug Mientkiewicz	Pit	10	6	60.0	20	1	0	0	1.000	3.15	7	2	.286	0	1	-	20	0	0	0	-1	0	0	-
Aaron Miles	StL	1	0	3.2	3	0	0	0	1.000	7.36	0	0	-	0	0	-	3	0	0		0	0	0	-
Craig Monroe	Min	3	3	25.0	5	0	0	0	1.000	1.80	2	0	.000	0	0	-	5	-1	-1	0	-1	-2	-1	-
Lou Montanez	Bal	5	2	23.0	1	0	0	0	1.000	.39	3	2	.667	0	0	-	1	0		0	-1	-1	-1	-
Kendry Morales	LAA	12	4	60.0	19	0	0	0	1.000	2.85	9	5	.556	0	-1	-	19	-2	-1	-1	-1	-3	-2	-
Nyjer Morgan	Pit	6	5	47.0	14	0	0	0	1.000	2.68	3	1	.333	0	0	-	14	+1	0	+2	0	+2	1	-
Mike Morse	Sea	5	3	25.0	6	2	0	0	1.000	2.88	3	1	.333	1	1	-	6	0	0	-1	0	-1	-1	-
Brandon Moss	2 tms	32	24	234.0	58	6	0	1	1.000	2.46	36	18	.500	4	3	-	58	-4	0	-4	-3	-7	-4	-
David Murphy	Tex	56	43	407.1	107	1	1	1	.991	2.39	47	20	.426	1	-1	-	107	+7	+3	+4	+4	+11	6	-
Matt Murton	ChC	2	0	4.0	1	0	0	0	1.000	2.25	0	0	-	0	0	-	1	0	0			0	0	-
Xavier Nady	2 tms	89	88	763.2	199	10	2	5	.991	2.46	91	46	.505	7	3	15	199	-5	+1	-3	-3	-4	-2	22
Trot Nixon	NYM	5	4	37.2	9	0	0	0	1.000	2.15	8	6	.750	0	-1	-	9	0	0	0	+1	+1	1	-
Greg Norton	2 tms	2	1	5.0	0	0	0	0	-	.00	0	0	-	0	0	-	0	0				0	0	-
Magglio Ordonez	Det	135	134	1144.0	220	8	5	0	.979	1.79	143	72	.503	3	1	23	220	-5	-9	-3	+7	-5	-3	25
Dan Ortmeier	SF	2	0	5.0	1	0	0	0	1.000	1.80	1	0	.000	0	0	-	1	0		0		0	0	-
Angel Pagan	NYM	1	1	8.0	3	0	0	0	1.000	3.38	4	2	.500	0	0	-	3	+1	-1	+2		+1	1	-
Jay Payton	Bal	4	4	32.0	8	0	0	0	1.000	2.25	8	4	.500	0	0	-	8	0	0	+1	-1	0	0	-
Steve Pearce	Pit	29	27	226.1	49	1	2	0	.962	1.99	22	8	.364	1	2	-	49	-1	+1	+2	-6	-3	-2	-
Hunter Pence	Hou	156	154	1366.1	340	16	1	4	.997	2.34	116	46	.397	11	12	2	341	+5	+7	-2	-7	-2	-1	20
Fernando Perez	TB	2	2	17.0	1	0	0	0	1.000	.53	2	0	.000	0	1	-	1	-1	0			-1	-1	-
Jason Perry	Atl	4	3	41.0	13	0	0	0	1.000	2.85	4	3	.750	0	-1	-	13	-1	0	0	-1	-1	-1	-
Josh Phelps	StL	2	2	10.0	4	0	0	0	1.000	3.60	2	2	1.000	0	0	-	4	0	0	0	-2	-2	-1	-
Scott Podsednik	Col	1	0	3.0	1	0	0	0	1.000	3.00	0	0	-	0	0	-	1	+1	+1			+1	1	-
Jason Pridie	Min	3	0	7.0	3	0	1	0	.750	3.86	1	1	1.000	0	0	-	3	0	0	0	0	0	0	-
Robb Quinlan	LAA	3	0	5.1	1	0	0	0	1.000	1.69	1	1	1.000	0	0	-	1	0	0	0		0	0	-
Ryan Raburn	Det	22	6	84.0	22	0	1	0	.957	2.36	7	4	.571	0	0	-	22	-2	-1	-1	-1	-3	-2	-
Jeremy Reed	Sea	14	12	101.0	19	0	2	0	.905	1.69	10	5	.500	0	-1	-	19	0	0	0	0	+1	1	-
Jason Repko	LAD	7	0	15.0	2	0	0	0	1.000	1.20	0	0	-	0	0	-	2	+1	+1			+1	1	-
Alex Rios	Tor	93	92	820.0	170	4	1	2	.994	1.91	62	22	.355	3	5	8	170	+11	+7	+3	+6	+16	9	4
Juan Rivera	LAA	19	15	115.0	19	1	1	0	.952	1.57	18	9	.500	0	-2	-	19	-4	-2	-3	-1	-7	-4	-
Alex Romero	Ari	38	23	221.0	39	1	1	0	.976	1.63	30	12	.400	0	0	-	39	+1	0	0	+2	+2	1	-
Cody Ross	Fla	35	13	153.2	37	0	1	0	.974	2.17	10	3	.300	0	0	-	37	+3	+1	+1	+3	+6	3	-
Justin Ruggiano	TB	15	8	87.0	21	0	1	0	.955	2.17	9	1	.111	0	1	-	21	+1	0	+2	+2	+3	2	-
Brendan Ryan	StL	3	3	19.0	4	0	0	0	1.000	1.89	0	0	-	0	0	-	4	+1	+1	0	0	+1	1	-
Jeff Salazar	Ari	18	8	92.0	16	0	0	0	1.000	1.57	11	8	.727	0	-2	-	16	0	0	0	0	0	0	-
Nate Schierholtz	SF	19	18	161.2	40	1	0	0	1.000	2.28	17	12	.706	0	-1	-	40	+4	+2	+2	+5	+9	5	-
Skip Schumaker	StL	33	30	249.1	64	1	1	1	.985	2.35	25	10	.400	0	0	-	64	-1	+2	-3	0	-1	-1	-
Seth Smith	Col	14	11	86.0	18	1	0	0	1.000	1.99	14	8	.571	0	-1	-	18	-1	0	0	-1	-1	-1	-
Travis Snider	Tor	7	7	60.0	11	0	0	0	1.000	1.65	6	2	.333	0	0	-	11	+2	0	0	+4	+4	2	-
Denard Span	Min	85	77	686.2	192	5	3	2	.985	2.58	61	24	.393	5	6	5	192	+7	+4	0	+8	+12	7	6
Ryan Spilborghs	Col	22	15	146.0	37	0	2	0	.949	2.28	17	7	.412	0	0	-	37	-2	0	-1	-3	-5	-3	-
Matt Stairs	2 tms	10	9	61.2	14	0	0	0	1.000	2.04	10	6	.600	0	-1	-	14	-1	0	-1	0	-1	-1	-
Nick Stavinoha	StL	5	2	20.0	2	0	0	0	1.000	.90	4	2	.500	0	0	-	2	0	0		0	0	0	-
Cory Sullivan	Col	5	0	11.0	1	0	0	0	1.000	.82	0	0	-	0	0	-	1	0		0		0	0	-
Ichiro Suzuki	Sea	91	90	788.1	175	7	4	1	.978	2.08	93	39	.419	6	5	8	176	+7	+5	+6	+2	+13	8	5
Ryan Sweeney	Oak	75	54	486.2	136	6	1	0	.993	2.63	52	15	.288	3	6	5	136	+2	-2	0	+6	+5	3	11
Nick Swisher	CWS	18	11	118.0	25	0	1	0	.962	1.91	12	7	.583	0	-1	-	25	+1	+1	-1	+1	+1	1	-
So Taguchi	Phi	11	9	72.0	11	0	0	0	1.000	1.38	4	1	.250	0	0	-	11	0	0	0	0	+1	1	-
Fernando Tatis	NYM	39	35	292.2	55	2	0	0	1.000	1.75	21	10	.476	2	1	-	55	-2	0	-1	-3	-4	-2	-
Mark Teahen	KC	92	84	756.1	185	4	2	2	.990	2.25	77	48	.623	2	-3	32	185	-3	+1	-5	-3	-8	-5	27
Marcus Thames	Det	7	2	25.0	8	0	0	0	1.000	2.88	2	2	1.000	0	-1	-	8	0	0	-1	0	-1	-1	-
Clete Thomas	Det	3	3	22.0	8	0	0	0	1.000	3.27	2	1	.500	0	0	-	8	0	0	0	0	+1	1	-
Justin Upton	Ari	101	100	860.1	175	6	11	2	.943	1.89	82	38	.463	6	3	15	175	0	-2	+1	+4	+3	2	12
Jonathan Van Every	Bos	8	1	32.0	15	0	0	0	1.000	4.22	4	2	.500	0	0	-	15	+1	0	-1	+3	+2	1	-
Eugenio Velez	SF	7	4	44.1	8	1	0	0	1.000	1.83	3	1	.750	0	-1	-	8	-1	-1	0	0	-1	-1	-
Shane Victorino	Phi	5	4	40.0	14	0	0	0	1.000	3.15	3	1	.333	0	0	-	14	-1	-1	+1	-2	-1	-1	-
Daryle Ward	ChC	3	2	17.0	4	0	0	0	1.000	2.12	2	2	1.000	0	0	-	4	-1	0	0	-2	-2	-1	-

BASIC											THROWING						PLUS/MINUS							
Name	Team	G	GS	Inn	PO	A	E	DP	Pct	Rng	Opps To Advance	Extra Bases	Pct	Kills	Runs Saved	Rank	Outs Made	Basic	Shallow	Medium	Deep	Enhanced	Runs Saved	Rank
Rico Washington	StL	1	0	3.0	0	0	0	0	-	.00	0	0	-	0	0	-								
Jayson Werth	Phi	88	73	661.1	143	7	0	1	1.000	2.04	50	20	.400	6	5	8	143	+2	+3	+1	-4	0	0	19
Brad Wilkerson	2 tms	64	55	485.0	95	4	1	0	.990	1.84	46	22	.478	2	2	20	95	+5	+2	+3	+4	+9	5	10
Reggie Willits	LAA	22	8	88.0	12	0	0	0	1.000	1.23	10	2	.200	0	1	-	12	-1	-1	0	0	-1	-1	
Randy Winn	SF	133	127	1108.1	309	5	3	2	.991	2.55	96	43	.448	1	3	15	309	+12	+6	+5	+5	+16	9	3
Dewayne Wise	CWS	6	0	13.0	4	0	0	0	1.000	2.77	1	1	1.000	0	0	-	4	+1		+2		+2	1	-
Kevin Youkilis	Bos	2	0	8.2	3	0	0	0	1.000	3.12	0	0	-	0	0	-	3	0	0	0		0	0	
Delwyn Young	LAD	11	8	72.2	8	2	0	1	1.000	1.24	8	6	.750	0	-1	-	8	0	-1	0	+1	0	0	
Ben Zobrist	TB	2	1	7.0	0	0	0	0	-	.00	0	0	-	0	0	-	0	0				0	0	
2008 MLB Averages									.983	2.14	4459	2097	.470	204	-	-								

Catchers

BASIC												PITCHER HANDLING								STOLEN BASES							
Name	Team	G	GS	Inn	PO	A	E	WP	PB	DP	Pct	W	L	Pct	ER	CERA	ER Saved	Adj ER Saved	Rank	SBA	CCS	PCS	CPO	CS%	SB Saved	SB Runs Saved	Rank
Eliezer Alfonzo	SF	2	2	17.0	10	1	1	0	0	0	.917	0	2	.000	10	5.29	-1	0	-	3	0	0	0	.00	-1	-1	-
Danny Ardoin	LAD	24	17	145.1	126	11	1	8	2	4	.993	5	12	.294	61	3.78	1	0	-	13	3	0	0	.23	1	1	-
Brad Ausmus	Hou	77	62	569.2	428	33	2	9	4	4	.996	32	30	.516	235	3.71	18	2	12	24	4	1	0	.17	-2	-2	20
John Baker	Fla	59	54	496.0	402	22	4	15	3	0	.991	27	27	.500	233	4.23	-11	-1	25	48	6	2	0	.13	-4	-3	29
Paul Bako	Cin	96	88	770.2	679	39	5	27	9	7	.993	42	46	.477	373	4.36	0	0	21	77	20	2	1	.27	-3	-2	20
Rod Barajas	Tor	98	90	785.1	674	47	4	21	2	5	.994	54	36	.600	290	3.32	19	4	4	64	17	5	1	.29	2	1	8
Josh Bard	SD	49	47	416.2	329	20	3	12	1	1	.991	16	31	.340	197	4.26	2	0	-	63	9	1	1	.15	-2	-1	-
Michael Barrett	SD	30	29	252.1	205	16	2	8	3	0	.991	11	18	.379	125	4.46	-2	-1	-	49	5	1	0	.10	-4	-3	-
Edwin Bellorin	Col	2	0	6.0	4	0	0	0	0	0	1.000	0	0	-	4	6.00	0	0	-	0	0	0	0	-	0	0	-
Gary Bennett	LAD	10	6	54.0	43	3	1	4	1	0	.979	3	3	.500	27	4.50	-5	0	-	2	0	0	0	.00	-1	0	-
Henry Blanco	ChC	45	28	257.2	235	15	2	7	3	2	.992	16	12	.571	112	3.91	0	0	-	22	9	1	0	.43	2	2	-
Rob Bowen	Oak	31	25	220.0	147	9	2	7	3	1	.987	11	14	.440	119	4.87	-21	-1	-	24	5	4	0	.25	2	1	-
John Buck	KC	107	106	950.1	751	24	8	42	4	6	.990	49	57	.462	480	4.55	-1	-1	25	71	7	5	0	.11	-10	-7	35
Ryan Budde	LAA	7	1	17.0	13	2	0	2	0	0	1.000	0	1	.000	7	3.71	0	0	-	0	0	0	0	-	0	0	-
Jamie Burke	Sea	43	25	246.0	181	10	1	14	2	0	.995	9	16	.360	131	4.79	-4	0	-	20	5	3	0	.29	0	0	-
Robinson Cancel	NYM	15	9	93.0	81	1	0	3	1	0	1.000	5	4	.556	48	4.65	3	0	-	2	0	0	0	.00	0	0	-
Luke Carlin	SD	36	27	259.2	206	14	3	4	3	2	.987	14	13	.519	112	3.88	14	1	-	32	7	0	1	.22	1	1	-
Raul Casanova	NYM	13	13	118.0	89	7	0	6	1	0	1.000	6	7	.462	61	4.65	-5	0	-	5	2	0	0	.40	1	0	-
Kevin Cash	Bos	57	42	372.0	280	26	4	20	14	5	.987	22	20	.524	199	4.81	-16	-1	-	54	14	2	0	.27	3	2	-
Ramon Castro	NYM	47	40	354.1	286	19	4	8	1	2	.987	24	16	.600	145	3.68	9	1	-	23	5	0	0	.22	-1	-1	-
Francisco Cervelli	NYY	3	1	13.2	11	0	0	0	0	0	1.000	0	1	.000	12	7.90	-4	0	-	1	0	0	0	.00	0	0	-
Raul Chavez	Pit	35	31	278.0	188	23	1	11	3	2	.995	14	17	.452	147	4.76	0	0	-	25	8	4	3	.38	3	2	-
Jeff Clement	Sea	38	35	292.0	195	7	1	18	5	0	.995	16	19	.457	164	5.05	-7	0	-	20	0	2	0	.00	-5	-3	-
Chris Coste	Phi	78	69	612.2	488	23	3	15	1	6	.994	36	33	.522	270	3.97	9	1	17	57	8	5	0	.15	-4	-3	29
Robinzon Diaz	Pit	1	1	8.0	5	1	0	1	0	1	1.000	0	1	.000	8	9.00	-3	0	-	1	1	0	0	1.00	1	1	-
Mike DiFelice	TB	7	6	54.0	42	3	0	3	0	1	1.000	3	3	.500	22	3.67	4	0	-	6	2	0	0	.33	0	0	-
Ryan Doumit	Pit	106	103	909.0	596	59	8	44	9	8	.988	45	58	.437	512	5.07	1	0	21	93	15	10	0	.18	-3	-2	20
A.J. Ellis	LAD	3	1	10.0	7	1	0	0	0	0	1.000	0	1	.000	5	4.50	-1	0	-	0	0	0	0	-	0	0	-
Johnny Estrada	Was	14	12	94.1	78	8	2	2	0	0	.977	5	7	.417	54	5.15	-3	0	-	19	4	2	0	.24	0	0	-
Sal Fasano	Cle	15	14	117.0	102	9	2	4	3	1	.982	7	7	.500	74	5.69	-7	0	-	12	3	1	0	.27	0	0	-
Jesus Flores	Was	82	78	673.0	474	29	5	30	7	6	.990	27	51	.346	337	4.51	16	2	12	64	11	6	0	.19	-1	-1	14
Toby Hall	CWS	37	36	315.1	231	15	2	16	1	0	.992	22	14	.611	129	3.68	13	1	-	52	3	6	0	.07	-3	-2	-
Robby Hammock	Ari	15	11	107.1	92	3	0	3	0	0	1.000	6	5	.545	37	3.10	13	0	-	13	1	1	0	.08	-3	-2	-
Ryan Hanigan	Cin	30	25	229.1	186	19	1	8	1	4	.995	14	11	.560	106	4.16	10	1	-	23	8	0	0	.35	-1	-1	-
Michel Hernandez	TB	4	4	33.0	20	1	1	2	0	0	.955	2	2	.500	12	3.27	6	0	-	3	0	0	0	.00	0	0	-
Ramon Hernandez	Bal	127	119	1039.1	714	45	9	46	10	8	.988	57	62	.479	579	5.01	11	3	6	123	21	3	1	.18	-3	-2	20
Koyie Hill	ChC	9	2	42.2	40	1	1	1	0	0	.976	1	1	.500	26	5.48	-7	0	-	7	1	0	0	.14	-1	-1	-
Steve Holm	SF	42	19	210.1	190	5	0	18	1	0	1.000	8	11	.421	110	4.71	-11	-1	-	23	2	0	0	.09	-3	-2	-
Paul Hoover	Fla	13	12	104.1	84	8	0	9	2	0	1.000	4	8	.333	69	5.95	-14	0	-	8	3	0	0	.38	1	1	-
Nick Hundley	SD	59	55	486.1	366	32	4	15	4	4	.990	21	34	.382	257	4.76	-10	-1	-	56	13	1	0	.24	3	2	-
Chris Iannetta	Col	100	96	837.0	606	51	0	37	6	4	1.000	46	50	.479	429	4.61	3	2	12	53	8	4	1	.16	-2	-2	20
Brandon Inge	Det	60	56	493.2	370	33	0	20	11	4	1.000	25	31	.446	308	5.62	-37	-4	-	37	10	1	0	.28	1	0	-
John Jaso	TB	3	1	16.0	11	1	0	1	0	0	1.000	1	0	1.000	8	4.50	2	0	-	0	0	0	0	-	0	0	-
Kenji Johjima	Sea	100	95	833.1	632	34	8	24	7	8	.988	35	60	.368	423	4.57	12	2	12	77	18	7	1	.26	-2	-2	20
Mark Johnson	StL	10	4	40.0	34	0	0	4	0	0	1.000	3	1	.750	15	3.38	2	0	-	2	0	0	0	.00	-1	0	-
Rob Johnson	Sea	10	7	64.0	44	7	0	4	0	0	1.000	1	6	.143	36	5.06	-6	0	-	12	1	1	0	.09	-2	-1	-
Ryan Jorgensen	Min	2	0	3.0	1	0	0	0	0	0	1.000	0	0	-	0	0.00	1	0	-	0	0	0	0	-	0	0	-
Jason Kendall	Mil	149	149	1328.1	1025	95	6	45	4	13	.995	83	66	.557	568	3.85	15	4	4	96	36	5	0	.40	11	8	1
George Kottaras	Bos	2	0	8.0	5	0	0	0	0	0	1.000	0	0	-	7	7.88	-3	0	-	0	0	0	0	-	0	0	-
Gerald Laird	Tex	88	86	753.0	523	35	8	30	6	7	.986	43	43	.500	436	5.21	29	5	2	74	20	1	0	.27	2	1	8
Jason LaRue	StL	57	44	412.0	289	16	2	12	2	1	.993	22	22	.500	194	4.24	3	0	-	21	5	3	0	.28	0	0	-
Paul Lo Duca	2 tms	26	25	208.2	163	7	2	5	1	0	.988	12	13	.480	106	4.57	-1	0	-	20	1	1	0	.05	-3	-2	-
Lou Marson	Phi	1	1	9.0	9	1	0	0	0	0	1.000	1	0	1.000	3	3.00	2	0	-	1	1	0	0	1.00	0	0	-
Russell Martin	LAD	149	138	1238.0	1042	65	11	35	6	8	.990	76	62	.551	499	3.63	0	-2	27	93	17	6	1	.20	-2	-1	14
Victor Martinez	Cle	55	54	447.1	328	16	3	10	2	1	.991	24	30	.444	214	4.31	-3	0	-	35	10	3	0	.31	1	1	-
Jeff Mathis	LAA	94	90	793.1	624	57	13	21	3	5	.981	58	32	.644	323	3.66	17	3	6	77	16	4	3	.22	-4	-3	29
Joe Mauer	Min	139	135	1203.0	831	52	3	40	4	1	.997	73	62	.541	564	4.22	5	1	17	80	18	11	1	.26	-2	-1	14
Brian McCann	Atl	138	132	1143.1	879	70	9	33	7	9	.991	61	71	.462	540	4.25	28	7	1	120	21	6	2	.18	-1	-1	14
Adam Melhuse	2 tms	10	7	64.0	35	7	0	0	0	0	1.000	2	5	.286	34	4.78	9	0	-	6	4	0	0	.67	3	2	-
Corky Miller	Atl	29	17	164.1	129	18	3	2	4	0	.980	7	10	.412	70	3.83	10	0	-	15	6	0	0	.40	3	2	-
Chad Moeller	NYY	33	25	225.0	159	15	3	6	0	2	.983	16	9	.640	105	4.20	9	0	-	24	7	2	0	.32	-1	-1	-
Bengie Molina	SF	136	132	1128.1	987	71	5	54	5	6	.995	57	75	.432	539	4.30	5	1	17	104	32	4	1	.32	8	6	3
Gustavo Molina	NYM	2	2	18.0	19	0	0	1	0	0	1.000	1	1	.500	7	3.50	2	0	-	1	0	0	0	.00	0	0	-
Jose Molina	NYY	97	81	737.0	634	52	3	29	7	6	.996	43	38	.531	302	3.69	31	5	2	75	32	1	1	.43	11	7	2
Yadier Molina	StL	119	114	1002.0	653	70	10	34	5	7	.986	61	53	.535	470	4.22	-8	-2	27	52	16	2	7	.32	4	3	5
Miguel Montero	Ari	53	45	404.2	352	23	4	26	0	2	.989	17	28	.378	206	4.58	-24	-2	-	34	6	1	0	.18	-3	-2	-
Luke Montz	Was	8	6	56.0	44	4	1	3	1	1	.980	1	5	.167	32	5.14	-2	0	-	9	3	0	0	.33	1	0	-
Colt Morton	SD	7	4	43.1	26	5	0	4	0	0	1.000	1	3	.250	23	4.78	1	0	-	6	1	0	0	.17	0	0	-
Mike Napoli	LAA	75	71	625.0	469	21	3	27	7	3	.994	42	29	.592	309	4.45	-19	-3	32	63	9	2	0	.15	-5	-3	29
Dioner Navarro	TB	117	113	1011.1	837	55	5	35	6	10	.994	70	43	.619	438	3.90	-24	-5	34	73	25	3	0	.36	6	4	4
Wil Nieves	Was	61	46	449.2	359	31	3	20	3	4	.992	18	28	.391	230	4.60	0	0	-	49	9	1	1	.19	0	0	-
Miguel Olivo	KC	58	56	494.1	378	32	5	26	4	6	.988	26	30	.464	243	4.42	2	0	21	33	12	2	1	.39	4	3	5
Ronny Paulino	Pit	32	27	260.0	198	16	2	8	1	3	.991	8	19	.296	157	5.43	-1	0	-	31	8	0	0	.26	1	1	-
Paul Phillips	CWS	4	0	8.0	7	0	0	0	0	0	1.000	0	0	-	3	3.38	1	0	-	0	0	0	0	-	0	0	-
A.J. Pierzynski	CWS	131	127	1134.1	913	54	9	38	5	8	.991	67	60	.528	533	4.23	-21	-5	34	117	11	10	0	.10	-4	-3	29
Jorge Posada	NYY	30	28	234.1	197	7	1	12	2	1	.995	17	11	.607	121	4.65	-18	-1	-	41	3	4	0	.08	-6	-4	-
Humberto Quintero	Hou	59	52	447.0	373	26	1	5	1	3	.998	30	22	.577	243	4.89	-13	0	-	24	7	2	1	.32	1	1	-
Guillermo Quiroz	Bal	54	39	354.1	229	17	1	24	5	3	.996	11	28	.282	220	5.59	-16	-1	-	39	7	2	0	.19	0	0	-
Mike Rabelo	Fla	32	29	262.2	179	11	1	13	3	1	.995	18	11	.621	121	4.15	18	1	-	22	5	1	0	.24	0	0	-
Max Ramirez	Tex	12	8	82.0	56	5	1	8	0	2	.984	4	4	.500	72	7.90	-20	0	-	15	3	0	0	.20	-2	-1	-
Mike Redmond	Min	30	28	253.0	180	9	0	5	0	2	1.000	15	13	.536	113	4.02	0	0	-	23	3	2	0	.14	-3	-2	-
Shawn Riggans	TB	41	38	343.1	268	5	5	11	4	0	.982	21	17	.553	138	3.62	11	1	-	25	1	0	0	.04	-5	-4	-
Mike Rivera	Mil	17	13	127.1	112	11	3	8	1	2	.976	7	6	.538	58	4.10	1	0	-	20	2	2	0	.11	-3	-2	-
Ivan Rodriguez	2 tms	112	105	930.0	620	58	5	35	6	9	.993	52	53	.495	473	4.58	21	3	6	77	23	2	0	.31	0	0	12
David Ross	2 tms	54	43	399.2	346	29	3	11	6	4	.992	16	27	.372	227	5.11	-5	-1	-	36	10	0	0	.28	1	1	-

		BASIC										PITCHER HANDLING					ER Saved	Adj ER Saved	Rank	STOLEN BASES					SB Saved	SB Runs Saved	Rank
Name	Team	G	GS	Inn	PO	A	E	WP	PB	DP	Pct	W	L	Pct	ER	CERA				SBA	CCS	PCS	CPO	CS%			
Carlos Ruiz	Phi	110	92	828.0	623	58	5	19	4	2	.993	55	37	.598	354	3.85	-4	0	21	85	14	6	2	.18	-3	-2	20
Dusty Ryan	Det	15	14	122.1	99	5	0	14	1	0	1.000	3	11	.214	83	6.11	-18	0	-	13	4	2	0	.36	2	1	-
Jarrod Saltalamacchia	Tex	54	52	464.1	345	17	9	23	6	6	.976	26	26	.500	265	5.14	-3	0	-	49	7	2	0	.15	-6	-5	-
Clint Sammons	Atl	22	13	133.0	106	3	0	7	3	0	1.000	4	9	.308	105	7.11	-30	-1	-	13	0	2	0	.00	-2	-1	-
Pablo Sandoval	SF	11	9	86.1	76	6	0	5	2	1	1.000	7	2	.778	42	4.38	6	0	-	10	3	0	0	.30	0	0	-
Omir Santos	Bal	9	3	28.1	19	0	0	2	0	0	1.000	0	3	.000	15	4.76	4	0	-	1	0	0	0	.00	0	0	-
Dane Sardinha	Det	17	13	122.2	109	8	1	2	0	1	.992	7	6	.538	64	4.70	3	0	-	5	1	0	0	.20	0	0	-
Brian Schneider	NYM	109	98	881.0	741	41	5	37	4	3	.994	53	45	.541	402	4.11	-9	-2	27	63	16	5	0	.28	-3	-2	12
Kelly Shoppach	Cle	110	94	872.2	586	34	7	30	8	2	.989	50	44	.532	424	4.37	-5	-2	27	47	10	0	0	.21	-3	-2	20
Chris Snyder	Ari	112	106	922.2	777	69	0	30	7	5	1.000	59	47	.557	393	3.83	6	2	12	71	20	2	0	.29	2	1	8
Geovany Soto	ChC	136	131	1150.1	1011	55	5	40	5	9	.995	80	51	.611	486	3.80	5	3	6	94	18	7	0	.21	-6	-4	34
Chris Stewart	NYY	1	1	8.0	8	0	0	2	0	0	1.000	0	1	.000	6	6.75	0	0	-	1	0	0	0	.00	0	0	-
Kurt Suzuki	Oak	141	136	1215.0	927	53	6	23	5	4	.994	64	72	.471	521	3.86	16	3	6	87	16	16	0	.23	3	2	7
Taylor Teagarden	Tex	12	11	100.2	67	6	3	1	1	0	.961	5	6	.455	55	4.92	1	0	-	9	2	0	0	.22	0	0	-
Curtis Thigpen	Tor	9	5	49.0	36	3	0	1	0	2	1.000	3	2	.600	12	2.20	6	0	-	5	1	0	0	.20	0	0	-
Yorvit Torrealba	Col	67	64	581.0	433	26	2	24	4	4	.996	27	37	.422	331	5.13	-13	-2	27	61	12	4	0	.21	1	1	8
J.R. Towles	Hou	53	47	408.2	312	13	2	8	3	1	.994	24	23	.511	217	4.78	7	0	-	20	5	2	0	.28	-1	-1	-
Matt Treanor	Fla	65	60	524.2	453	29	8	21	2	3	.984	31	29	.517	269	4.61	4	1	17	59	12	3	0	.21	-1	-1	14
Matt Tupman	KC	1	0	1.0	0	0	0	0	0	0	-	0	0	-	0	0.00	1	0	-	0	0	0	0	-	0	0	-
Javier Valentin	Cin	17	6	67.2	67	5	0	6	1	0	1.000	2	4	.333	38	5.05	-4	0	-	1	0	0	0	.00	0	0	-
Jason Varitek	Bos	131	120	1041.1	903	42	4	23	4	7	.996	73	47	.608	424	3.66	14	3	6	72	13	3	0	.19	-3	-2	20
Bobby Wilson	LAA	7	0	16.0	15	1	0	0	0	0	1.000	0	0	-	6	3.38	2	0	-	0	0	0	0	-	0	0	-
Gregg Zaun	Tor	79	67	612.1	515	28	7	29	4	7	.987	29	38	.433	259	3.81	-25	-4	33	54	12	2	0	.23	-2	-1	14
2008 MLB Averages								303			.992					4.32								31			

Pitchers

BASIC						HOLDING					+/-					
Name	Tm	Inn	TC	E	Pct	SBA	CCS	PCS	PPO	CS%	Rght	Mid	Left	Tot	RS	Rnk
D Aardsma	Bos	49	9	0	1.000	2	0	0	0	.00	0	0	+1	+1	1	-
J Accardo	Tor	12	1	0	1.000	1	0	0	0	.00	0	-1	0	-1	-1	-
A Aceves	NYY	30	5	0	1.000	4	2	0	0	.50	-1	0		-1	-1	-
M Acosta	Atl	53	22	2	.909	7	0	0	0	.00	+2	+2	+1	+5	3	-
M Adams	SD	65	14	0	1.000	6	1	0	0	.17				0	0	-
N Adenhart	LAA	12	1	0	1.000	0	0	0	0	-	0	0		-1	-1	-
J Adkins	Cin	4	0	0	-									0		-
J Affeldt	Cin	78	30	1	.967	8	1	0	0	.13	+1	+2	0	+2	1	-
J Albaladejo	NYY	14	0	0	-									0		-
M Albers	Bal	49	11	0	1.000	4	1	0	0	.25	0	0	+1	+1	1	-
G Aquino	Bal	9	1	0	1.000									0		-
A Arias	2 tms	22	4	1	.750	1	0	0	0	.00				0	0	-
T Armas Jr.	NYM	8	3	0	1.000	1	0	0	0	.00	0	0		0	0	-
J Arredondo	LAA	61	3	0	1.000	5	2	0	0	.40	0	-1	0	-2	-2	-
B Arroyo	Cin	200	50	0	1.000	7	1	1	1	.29	0	0	+2	+2	3	23
J Ascanio	ChC	6	3	1	.667	0	0	0	0	-				0	0	-
L Ayala	2 tms	76	14	0	1.000	3	1	0	0	.33	0	0	+1	+1	1	-
B Backe	Hou	167	33	1	.970	10	5	1	0	.60	-1	-2	+1	-2	0	81
B Badenhop	Fla	47	12	0	1.000	7	3	0	0	.43	+3	0	0	+3	2	-
C Baek	2 tms	141	33	2	.939	14	4	1	1	.36	+1	-2	0	-2	-1	113
H Bailey	Cin	36	6	1	.833	9	1	0	0	.11	-1			-1	-2	-
S Baker	Min	172	22	1	.955	13	5	0	0	.38	-1	0	0	-1	0	81
J Bale	KC	27	9	0	1.000	4	0	1	0	.25	0	0	+1	+1	1	-
C Balester	Was	80	12	2	.833	6	3	0	1	.50	-1	-1	-1	-2	-1	113
G Balfour	TB	58	5	0	1.000	3	1	0	0	.33				0	0	-
J Banks	SD	85	23	0	1.000	20	3	0	0	.15	0	0	+2	+2	0	81
B Bannister	KC	183	42	2	.952	9	3	0	0	.33	0	+1	0	+1	2	31
J Barthmaier	Pit	10	0	0	-	2	1	0	0	.50	0			0	0	-
B Bass	2 tms	89	30	0	1.000	3	1	1	0	.67	0	-1	+4	+1	2	31
M Batista	Sea	115	25	1	.960	21	2	0	0	.10	-1	0	+1	0	-3	150
R Bauer	Cle	6	2	0	1.000	2	0	0	0	.00				0	0	-
D Bautista	2 tms	60	9	0	1.000	9	2	0	0	.22	0			0	-1	-
Y Bazardo	Det	3	2	0	1.000	1	1	0	0	1.00				0	0	-
T Beam	Pit	46	9	1	.889	4	1	0	0	.25	0	-1	0	-1	-1	-
J Beckett	Bos	174	35	2	.943	12	4	1	0	.42	0	0	0	-1	0	81
E Bedard	Sea	81	10	0	1.000	6	1	0	0	.17	+3	-1	0	+2	2	31
J Beimel	LAD	49	14	0	1.000	8	0	3	0	.38	0	0	0	0	1	-
M Belisle	Cin	30	8	1	.875	4	1	0	0	.25	-1			0	0	-
H Bell	SD	78	15	0	1.000	12	2	0	0	.17	-1	0	0	-1	-2	-
F Beltran	Det	13	1	0	1.000	0	0	0	0	-				0	0	-
A Benitez	Tor	6	0	0	-									0		-
J Bennett	Atl	97	17	2	.882	10	3	0	0	.30	-2	-2	0	-4	-3	150
J Benoit	Tex	45	7	0	1.000	2	1	0	0	.50	+1	0		+1	1	-
J Bergmann	Was	140	16	1	.938	10	1	0	0	.10	-1	0	-1	-2	-3	150
R Betancourt	Cle	71	9	1	.889	11	1	0	0	.09	-1	0	0	-2	-3	-
R Bierd	Bal	37	4	0	1.000	0	0	0	0	-	0			+1	1	-
C Billingsley	LAD	201	33	2	.939	12	4	0	0	.33	-1	+1	0	+1	2	31
K Birkins	TB	10	2	0	1.000	0	0	0	0	-	0	0		0	0	-
N Blackburn	Min	193	36	0	1.000	4	2	0	0	.50	0	-3	+3	-1	0	81
J Blanton	2 tms	198	42	1	.976	5	1	0	0	.20	-1	0	+2	+1	2	31
J Blevins	Oak	38	6	3	.500	4	0	2	0	.50	-1	0	-1	-1	0	-
M Boggs	StL	34	12	1	.917	2	0	0	0	.00	+1	0	0	+1	1	-
J Bonderman	Det	71	16	1	.938	7	5	0	0	.71	-1	-1	+2	0	1	-
E Bonine	Det	27	6	1	.833	3	1	0	0	.33	0			0	0	-
B Bonser	Min	118	25	3	.880	11	0	0	0	.00	0	-3	+1	-2	-3	150
C Bootcheck	LAA	16	0	0	-	1	0	0	0	.00	0			-1	-1	-
D Borkowski	Hou	36	9	0	1.000	0	0	0	0	-	0	+1	0	0	0	-
J Borowski	Cle	17	0	0	-	6	0	0	0	.00	0			-1	-2	-
M Bowden	Bos	5	2	0	1.000	0	0	0	0	-				0	0	-
C Bowers	Col	7	2	0	1.000	0	0	0	0	-	0	0	0	0	0	-
M Bowie	Col	8	1	0	1.000	0	0	0	0	-	0			0	0	-
B Boyer	Atl	72	9	0	1.000	10	2	0	0	.20	-1	0	0	-1	-2	-
D Braden	Oak	72	17	1	.941	3	2	0	7	.67	0	+1	-2	-1	3	-
C Bradford	2 tms	59	16	0	1.000	7	3	1	0	.57	0	-1	0	-1	0	-
B Bray	Cin	47	6	0	1.000	4	0	0	0	.00	-1	0	0	0	0	-
Y Brazoban	LAD	3	1	0	1.000	0	0	0	0	-				0	0	-
C Breslow	2 tms	47	12	0	1.000	7	2	3	0	.71	0	0	0	-1	1	-
C Britton	NYY	23	1	0	1.000	0	0	0	0	-	0			0	0	-
L Broadway	CWS	14	6	0	1.000	1	0	1	0	1.00	0	0		0	1	-
D Brocail	Hou	69	18	1	.944	4	1	0	0	.25	+1	0	+1	+1	1	-
A Brown	Oak	35	6	0	1.000	1	1	0	0	1.00	0	+1	0	0	0	-
J Broxton	LAD	69	7	1	.857	13	3	0	0	.23	-1	-1	-1	-4	-4	-
B Bruney	NYY	34	5	0	1.000	3	0	0	0	.00	+1	0	0	0	0	-
C Buchholz	Bos	76	9	0	1.000	5	2	0	1	.40	-1	-1	-1	-3	-1	-
T Buchholz	Col	66	15	1	.933	8	2	0	0	.25	0	0	0	0	0	-
B Buckner	Ari	14	0	0	-	0	0	0	0	-	0			0	0	-
M Buehrle	CWS	219	52	0	1.000	12	2	5	2	.58	+1	0	0	0	4	10
F Bueno	Atl	2	0	0	-	0	0	0	0	-				0	0	-
R Bukvich	Bal	5	0	0	-	0	0	0	0	-	0			0	0	-
J Bulger	LAA	16	3	0	1.000	1	0	0	0	.00	0	-1		-1	-1	-
B Bullington	Cle	15	1	0	1.000	2	0	0	0	.00				0	0	-
J Burke	Sea	1	0	0	-									0		-
A Burnett	Tor	221	54	7	.870	31	5	4	1	.29	-1	0	-1	-2	-2	133
S Burnett	Pit	57	17	0	1.000	8	1	2	0	.38	+1	0	-1	-1	-1	-
B Burres	Bal	130	26	1	.962	13	1	1	0	.15	+2	0	-1	+1	0	81
J Burton	Cin	59	16	1	.938	5	1	0	0	.20	+1	+1	+2	+4	3	-
D Bush	Mil	185	31	1	.968	26	9	0	0	.35	0	-1	+1	0	-1	113
P Byrd	2 tms	180	27	2	.926	10	5	0	3	.50	+1	-1	0	-1	2	31
T Byrdak	Hou	55	14	0	1.000	5	0	1	1	.20	0	0	+1	+1	1	-
D Cabrera	Bal	180	20	1	.950	31	4	0	0	.13	-3	-2	-1	-6	-8	175
F Cabrera	Bal	28	5	0	1.000	6	2	0	0	.33	0	-1	+1	0	0	-

BASIC						HOLDING					+/-					
Name	Tm	Inn	TC	E	Pct	SBA	CCS	PCS	PPO	CS%	Rght	Mid	Left	Tot	RS	Rnk
M Cain	SF	218	38	0	1.000	23	10	0	0	.43	+1	-2	-2	-2	-1	113
K Calero	Oak	5	0	0	-	0	0	0	0	-				0	0	-
K Cameron	SD	10	5	0	1.000	1	1	0	0	1.00	0			+1	1	-
S Camp	Tor	39	9	0	1.000	3	0	0	0	.00	+1	+2	0	+2	2	-
J Campillo	Atl	159	38	5	.868	10	2	0	0	.20	0	+1	-1	0	0	81
J Capellan	Col	2	0	0	-	0	0	0	0	-				0	0	-
M Capps	Pit	54	5	0	1.000	5	1	0	0	.20				-1	-1	-
J Carlson	Tor	60	10	0	1.000	4	1	2	0	.75	+1	+1	0	+2	3	-
B Carlyle	Atl	63	12	0	1.000	6	1	0	0	.17	+1	+1	-1	+1	1	-
F Carmona	Cle	121	32	2	.938	7	1	0	0	.14	0	+1	0	+2	2	31
A Carpenter	Phi	1	0	0	-									0		-
C Carpenter	StL	15	5	0	1.000	0	0	0	0	-	0	0	0	0	0	-
D Carrasco	CWS	39	5	1	.800	5	2	0	0	.40	0	0	0	+1	1	-
S Casilla	Oak	50	10	0	1.000	9	0	0	0	.00	0	-1	-2	-3	-3	-
J Cassel	Hou	30	8	1	.875	1	1	0	0	1.00	0	+1	0	+1	1	-
A Castillo	Bal	26	9	0	1.000	2	0	0	0	.00	0	0	0	+1	1	-
S Chacon	Hou	86	13	1	.923	5	2	1	1	.60	-1	-2	+1	-1	0	81
J Chamberlain	NYY	100	16	0	1.000	12	3	1	0	.33	0	0	-1	-1	-1	113
J Chavez	Pit	15	4	0	1.000	3	0	0	0	.00	0	0	0	0	0	-
R Cherry	Bal	17	3	1	.667	2	1	0	0	.50	0	0		+1	1	-
M Chico	Was	48	9	0	1.000	4	1	1	0	.50	+1	+1	0	+2	2	-
V Chulk	SF	32	7	0	1.000	1	0	0	0	.00	0	0	+1	0	0	-
T Clippard	Was	10	0	0	-	0	0	0	0	-				0	0	-
T Coffey	2 tms	27	7	0	1.000	3	1	0	0	.33	0	+1	0	0	0	-
P Coke	NYY	15	3	0	1.000	0	0	0	0	-	+1	0		+1	1	-
J Colome	Was	71	11	0	1.000	11	3	0	0	.27	0	+1	0	+1	0	-
B Colon	Bos	39	8	2	.750	0	0	0	0	-	-1	-1	0	-2	-2	-
C Condrey	Phi	69	16	0	1.000	6	3	0	0	.50	0	-1	0	-1	-1	-
J Contreras	CWS	121	19	0	1.000	17	0	1	0	.06	-1	0	0	0	-2	133
A Cook	Col	211	60	2	.967	13	8	0	4	.62	+1	+3	0	+4	7	3
R Corcoran	Sea	73	17	2	.882	1	0	0	0	.00	-1	0	-2	-3	-2	-
C Cordero	Was	4	0	0	-	0	0	0	0	-	0			0	0	-
F Cordero	Cin	70	8	1	.875	10	2	1	0	.30	0	-1	+2	0	0	-
B Corey	2 tms	45	11	1	.909	3	1	0	0	.33	-1	0	0	-1	-1	-
L Cormier	Bal	72	16	1	.938	8	2	0	0	.25	-2	0	+1	-1	-1	-
M Corpas	Col	80	15	0	1.000	2	0	0	0	.00	-1	0	+1	0	0	81
K Correia	SF	110	21	1	.952	11	6	1	0	.64	0	-2	0	-2	0	81
N Cotts	ChC	36	8	2	.750	3	0	0	0	.00	0	0	0	-1	-1	-
J Crain	Min	63	14	3	.786	7	1	0	0	.14	-1	-1	+2	+1	0	-
F Cruceta	Det	12	2	0	1.000	1	0	0	0	.00	0			0	0	-
J Cruz	Ari	52	8	2	.750	10	5	0	0	.50	+1			+1	1	-
J Cueto	Cin	174	34	3	.912	13	6	0	1	.46	+1	-2	+1	-1	0	81
J Danks	CWS	195	40	0	1.000	31	2	6	0	.26	+6	-1	-3	+2	2	31
K Davies	KC	113	15	1	.933	9	1	0	0	.11	-1	-2	0	-3	-3	150
D Davis	Ari	146	31	0	1.000	11	2	1	1	.27	+3	+2	-1	+4	4	10
J Davis	Pit	34	11	1	.909	6	1	0	0	.17	+1	0	+1	+2	1	-
F de la Cruz	Fla	9	5	0	1.000	3	0	0	0	.00	+1	0	+1	+2	1	-
J de la Rosa	Col	130	19	0	1.000	18	2	3	0	.28	+1	-1	-1	-1	-1	113
V de los Santos	Col	8	0	0	-	0	0	0	0	-				-1	-1	-
M Delcarmen	Bos	74	11	0	1.000	7	0	0	0	.00	+1	-1	0	0	-1	-
J Delgado	Fla	2	1	0	1.000									0		-
R Dempster	ChC	207	53	1	.981	15	4	0	0	.27	+1	+4	+1	+6	5	7
M DeSalvo	Atl	2	0	0	-	0	0	0	0	-	0			0	0	-
E Dessens	Atl	4	1	0	1.000	1	0	0	0	.00				0	0	-
J Devine	Oak	46	3	0	1.000	4	1	0	0	.25	0	-1		-1	-1	-
J Diaz	Tex	1	0	0	-									0		-
R Dickey	Sea	112	29	0	1.000	13	3	4	1	.54	+2	0	0	+2	4	10
M DiFelice	Mil	19	2	0	1.000	1	0	0	0	.00	0			0	0	-
T Dillard	Mil	14	2	0	1.000	1	1	0	0	1.00	0	0		0	0	-
L DiNardo	Oak	23	6	0	1.000	2	0	0	0	.00	0	0		0	0	-
S Dohmann	TB	15	2	0	1.000	4	0	0	0	.00				-1	-2	-
F Dolsi	Det	48	5	0	1.000	12	2	0	0	.17	0	0	-2	-2	-3	-
B Donnelly	Cle	14	3	0	1.000	2	1	0	0	.50	0	0	0	0	0	-
O Dotel	CWS	67	9	1	.889	17	1	0	0	.06				-1	-4	-
S Downs	Tor	71	25	1	.960	2	0	0	1	.00	+2	0	+1	+3	2	-
J Duchscherer	Oak	142	18	0	1.000	6	2	0	1	.33	0	+2	-1	+1	2	31
B Duckworth	KC	38	7	0	1.000	6	2	1	0	.50	0	+1	0	+1	1	-
Z Duke	Pit	185	52	2	.962	12	2	4	0	.50	+3	+3	-1	+5	6	5
P Dumatrait	Pit	79	13	0	1.000	4	2	0	0	.50	+1	+2	-1	+2	3	23
C Durbin	Phi	88	18	0	1.000	7	4	0	1	.57	0	+1	-2	-1	0	81
A Eaton	Phi	107	24	0	1.000	9	5	0	0	.56	+2	0	0	+1	2	31
M Ekstrom	SD	10	4	0	1.000	1	0	0	0	.00	0	0	0	0	0	-
S Elarton	Cle	15	5	0	1.000	1	0	0	0	.00				+1	1	-
S Elbert	LAD	6	1	0	1.000	2	0	0	0	.00	0			-1	-1	-
A Embree	Oak	62	8	0	1.000	7	0	1	0	.14	-1	0	0	-1	-1	-
G Espineli	SF	16	2	0	1.000	2	0	0	0	.00	0	0		-1	-1	-
S Estes	SD	44	10	0	1.000	7	1	0	0	.14	-1	0	0	0	-1	-
M Estrada	Was	13	3	0	1.000	1	1	0	0	1.00	0	0	0	0	0	-
D Eveland	Oak	168	23	0	1.000	17	2	2	0	.24	0	0	0	-1	-1	113
S Eyre	2 tms	26	1	0	1.000	3	0	0	0	.00				0	0	-
B Falkenborg	2 tms	22	6	0	1.000	2	0	0	0	.00	-1	-1		-1	-1	-
K Farnsworth	2 tms	60	9	0	1.000	13	7	0	0	.54	-1	-1	+1	-1	-1	-
R Feierabend	Sea	40	12	0	1.000	5	1	3	3	.80	+1	-1	0	0	3	-
S Feldman	Tex	151	36	2	.944	27	5	0	0	.19	+1	0	+3	+3	-1	113
P Feliciano	NYM	53	18	1	.944	0	0	0	0	-	-1	+1	+1	+1	1	-
N Figueroa	NYM	45	11	1	.909	3	0	0	0	.00	0	+1	-1	0	0	-
R Flores	StL	26	4	1	.750	4	0	0	0	.00	0	-1	-1	-2	-3	-
G Floyd	CWS	206	43	2	.953	42	4	1	0	.12	0	+2	-2	0	-5	170
J Fogg	Cin	78	17	2	.882	5	2	0	0	.40	0	0	0	0	0	-
C Fossum	Det	41	6	0	1.000	1	0	1	0	1.00	+1	0	0	+1	2	-
K Foulke	Oak	31	3	0	1.000	4	1	0	0	.25				0	0	-
C Fox	ChC	3	1	0	1.000									0		-
J Francis	Col	144	30	1	.967	11	1	1	0	.18	+2	+1	+1	+3	2	31

Name	Tm	Inn	TC	E	Pct	SBA	CCS	PCS	PPO	CS%	Rght	Mid	Left	Tot	RS	Rnk
BASIC						HOLDING					+/-					
F Francisco	Tex	63	4	1	.750	8	1	0	0	.13	0	-1	-1	-2	-3	-
R Franklin	StL	79	23	0	1.000	3	1	0	0	.33	-1	0	-1	-2	-2	133
J Frasor	Tor	47	10	0	1.000	7	2	0	0	.29	0	+1	+1	+2	2	-
B Fuentes	Col	63	10	0	1.000	5	0	1	1	.20	0	0		0	0	-
K Fukumori	Tex	4	0	0	-	1	0	0	0	.00				-1	-1	-
J Fulchino	KC	14	0	0	-	1	0	0	0	.00				0	0	-
K Gabbard	Tex	56	14	1	.929	2	0	0	0	.00	-1	+1	-2	-2	-2	-
E Gagne	Mil	46	9	0	1.000	0	0	0	0	-				0	0	-
A Galarraga	Det	179	26	2	.923	8	1	0	0	.13	0	+1	+1	+1	1	55
S Gallagher	2 tms	115	22	1	.955	9	4	0	0	.44	+3	0	0	+3	3	23
Y Gallardo	Mil	24	5	0	1.000	1	1	0	0	1.00	0	0	-1	0	0	-
F Garcia	Det	15	1	0	1.000	2	1	0	0	.50	+1			+1	1	-
J Garcia	StL	16	3	0	1.000	0	0	0	0	-	0	0	0	0	0	-
L Gardner	Fla	7	3	0	1.000	0	0	0	0	-				0	0	-
J Garland	LAA	197	52	1	.981	6	3	0	1	.50	0	+1	+2	+3	4	10
M Garza	TB	185	27	2	.926	6	1	0	0	.17	-2	-3	+1	-4	-3	150
C Gaudin	2 tms	90	22	5	.773	4	2	1	1	.75	-1	-1	+1	0	2	31
G Geary	Hou	64	11	0	1.000	0	0	0	0	-	0	0	0	-1	-1	-
J Geer	SD	27	4	0	1.000	2	1	0	0	.50	0			+1	1	-
F German	Tex	22	2	0	1.000	4	2	0	0	.50	0	-1	0	-1	-1	-
J Germano	SD	44	13	0	1.000	11	2	0	0	.18	-2	-1	+1	-2	-3	-
D Giese	NYY	43	5	2	.600	10	1	0	0	.10	0	-1	0	-1	-2	-
M Ginter	Cle	21	3	0	1.000	1	0	0	0	.00	0	0	0	0	0	-
T Glavine	Atl	63	20	0	1.000	5	1	3	0	.80	0	0	0	0	2	-
G Glover	2 tms	54	11	1	.909	1	1	0	0	1.00	-2	+1	0	-1	-1	-
J Gobble	KC	32	2	0	1.000	2	0	0	0	.00	0			0	0	-
E Gonzalez	Ari	48	10	0	1.000	3	1	0	0	.33	+1	+1	0	+1	1	-
E Gonzalez	SD	3	0	0	-									0		-
G Gonzalez	Oak	34	6	0	1.000	2	0	2	0	1.00	0	0	0	0	1	-
M Gonzalez	Atl	34	1	0	1.000	1	0	0	0	.00	0			0	0	-
B Gordon	Tex	4	2	0	1.000	0	0	0	0	-				0	0	-
T Gordon	Phi	30	6	2	.667	1	0	0	0	.00	0	0	0	0	0	-
T Gorzelanny	Pit	105	25	1	.960	20	2	2	1	.20	+1	0	0	+1	0	81
J Grabow	Pit	76	13	1	.923	5	1	1	0	.40	+1	-1	0	0	1	-
J Gray	Oak	5	2	0	1.000	0	0	0	0	-				0	0	-
S Green	Sea	79	11	2	.818	4	1	0	0	.25	-2	-2	-2	-5	-4	167
K Gregg	Fla	69	12	2	.833	8	2	0	0	.25	0	0	0	0	0	-
Z Greinke	KC	202	36	1	.972	6	3	1	2	.67	0	+3	+1	+4	6	5
J Grilli	2 tms	75	11	1	.909	6	2	0	0	.33	0	+1	0	0	0	-
E Guardado	2 tms	56	5	0	1.000	3	0	0	0	.00	0	-1	+1	0	0	-
M Guerrier	Min	76	16	1	.938	9	1	0	1	.11	-2	0	+1	-1	-1	-
C Guevara	SD	12	2	0	1.000	3	0	0	0	.00	0	+1		0	0	-
J Guthrie	Bal	191	43	3	.930	17	4	0	0	.24	+3	-1	+1	+3	1	55
A Guzman	ChC	10	2	0	1.000	0	0	0	0	-				0	0	-
C Haeger	SD	4	0	0	-									0		-
R Halladay	Tor	246	60	1	.983	20	5	0	0	.25	-1	+2	-2	-1	-2	133
C Hamels	Phi	227	47	3	.936	17	0	2	0	.12	-1	+2	+2	+3	1	55
J Hammel	TB	78	12	0	1.000	12	1	0	0	.08	-1			0	-1	-
J Hampson	SD	31	3	0	1.000	4	1	0	0	.25	0	0	-1	-1	-1	-
M Hampton	Atl	78	21	1	.952	8	3	1	1	.50	0	+1	+2	+3	3	-
J Hanrahan	Was	84	11	2	.818	11	0	0	0	.00	0	-1	0	-1	-3	150
D Hansack	Bos	7	1	1	.000	0	0	0	0	-				0	0	-
C Hansen	2 tms	46	7	0	1.000	5	1	0	0	.20	-2			-3	-2	-
J Happ	Phi	32	5	0	1.000	1	0	0	0	.00	0	0	+1	0	0	-
A Harang	Cin	184	28	1	.964	21	4	0	0	.19	-1	-1	-1	-4	-5	170
R Harden	2 tms	148	15	0	1.000	14	7	0	0	.50	-1	0	+2	+1	2	31
D Haren	Ari	216	29	0	1.000	11	2	0	0	.18	-1	-3	+2	-2	-2	133
M Harrison	Tex	84	9	0	1.000	6	3	0	0	.50	+1	0	-1	0	1	55
K Hart	ChC	28	10	0	1.000	4	0	0	0	.00	0	0	0	+1	0	-
L Hawkins	2 tms	62	8	0	1.000	4	2	0	0	.50	0	0	0	+1	1	-
D Hayhurst	SD	17	1	0	1.000	6	1	0	0	.17	0			0	-1	-
A Heilman	NYM	76	16	0	1.000	2	0	0	0	.00	0	+1	-1	+1	1	-
M Hendrickson	Fla	134	25	0	1.000	19	1	2	0	.16	+1	+1	-2	0	-1	113
S Henn	SD	9	3	0	1.000	0	0	0	0	-	+1			+1	1	-
B Hennessey	SF	40	10	0	1.000	7	3	0	0	.43	0	-2	+1	-2	-2	-
C Hensley	SD	39	7	0	1.000	4	0	0	0	.00	0	0	0	0	0	-
M Herges	Col	64	11	1	.909	3	2	0	0	.67	0	0	-1	-1	0	-
F Hernandez	Sea	201	46	1	.978	23	3	1	1	.17	0	-1	+5	+4	2	31
F Hernandez	Oak	3	1	0	1.000	0	0	0	0	-	+1			+1	1	-
L Hernandez	2 tms	180	40	1	.975	8	3	2	0	.63	+3	+1	-1	+2	4	10
R Hernandez	Hou	19	5	0	1.000	1	0	0	0	.00	-1	-1	+1	-1	-1	-
D Herrera	Cin	7	5	0	1.000	0	0	0	0	-				+1	1	-
Y Herrera	Pit	18	9	0	1.000	1	0	0	0	.00	0	+1	0	+1	1	-
R Hill	ChC	20	2	0	1.000									0		-
S Hill	Was	63	26	2	.923	11	3	0	0	.27	+4	+1	0	+5	3	-
M Hinckley	Was	14	2	0	1.000	1	0	0	0	.00	0			0	0	-
A Hinshaw	SF	40	7	1	.857	2	1	0	0	.50	0	0	-1	-1	-1	-
J Hirsh	Col	9	1	0	1.000	0	0	0	0	-				0	0	-
L Hochevar	KC	129	18	1	.944	18	4	0	0	.22	-1	-2	0	-2	-3	150
T Hoffman	SD	45	9	0	1.000	3	0	0	0	.00	0	-1	-1	-2	-2	-
J Howell	TB	89	17	1	.941	13	2	1	0	.23	+1	-2	-2	-3	-3	150
B Howry	ChC	71	8	0	1.000	5	0	0	0	.00	0	0	0	0	0	-
T Hudson	Atl	142	30	1	.967	10	4	0	0	.40	0	+1	+3	+4	3	23
P Hughes	NYY	34	5	0	1.000	8	0	0	0	.00	0	0		+1	0	-
P Humber	Min	12	2	0	1.000	0	0	0	0	-	0	0	-1	-1	-1	-
T Hunter	Tex	11	2	1	.500	2	0	1	0	.50				-1	-1	-
E Hurley	Tex	25	1	0	1.000	2	2	0	0	1.00				0	1	-
K Igawa	NYY	4	1	0	1.000									0		-
J Isringhausen	StL	43	19	1	.947	8	2	0	0	.25	+1	+1	-1	+2	1	-
E Jackson	TB	183	31	1	.968	18	6	0	1	.33	-2	-1	+1	-2	-1	113
Z Jackson	2 tms	58	21	2	.905	1	0	0	0	.00	0	0	-1	0	0	-
C James	Atl	30	4	0	1.000	5	0	0	0	.00	+1			0	-1	-
B Jenks	CWS	62	16	0	1.000	5	0	0	2	.00	-1	-1	+1	0	0	-

Name	Tm	Inn	TC	E	Pct	SBA	CCS	PCS	PPO	CS%	Rght	Mid	Left	Tot	RS	Rnk
BASIC						HOLDING					+/-					
J Jennings	Tex	27	8	1	.875	1	1	0	0	1.00	0	0	+1	0	0	-
K Jepsen	LAA	8	4	0	1.000	1	0	0	0	.00	0	+1	0	+1	1	-
C Jimenez	Sea	34	10	0	1.000	4	2	1	1	.75	0	0	0	0	1	-
K Jimenez	StL	24	8	0	1.000	2	0	0	0	.00	0	0	-1	0	0	-
U Jimenez	Col	199	52	4	.923	22	2	1	2	.14	+4	-1	-2	+1	0	81
J Johnson	LAD	29	5	0	1.000	1	0	0	0	.00	0	+1	0	+1	1	-
J Johnson	Bal	69	14	0	1.000	5	2	0	0	.40	+1	+1	-1	0	0	-
J Johnson	Fla	87	16	0	1.000	7	2	0	0	.29	0	-1	+1	0	0	81
R Johnson	Ari	184	17	3	.824	24	1	2	0	.13	-2	-3	-3	-7	-7	174
T Jones	Det	42	7	0	1.000	2	0	0	0	.00				0	0	-
J Julio	2 tms	30	2	0	1.000	3	0	0	0	.00	+1	0		+1	1	-
J Jurrjens	Atl	188	45	1	.978	31	3	0	0	.10	0	+1	-2	-1	-5	170
J Karstens	Pit	51	11	2	.818	6	2	1	0	.50	0	-1	0	-1	0	-
S Kazmir	TB	152	16	2	.875	10	1	2	2	.30	-1	0	-1	-2	0	81
K Kendrick	Phi	156	43	1	.977	20	4	1	0	.25	+2	+3	+2	+7	4	10
I Kennedy	NYY	40	7	0	1.000	7	2	0	1	.29	-1			+1	1	-
L Kensing	Fla	55	5	2	.600	11	0	0	0	.00	-1	-1	0	-1	-3	-
C Kershaw	LAD	108	20	1	.950	7	0	2	0	.29	+2	0	-2	0	1	55
R King	Was	6	3	1	.667	2	0	0	0	.00	0			-1	-1	-
J Kinney	StL	7	3	0	1.000	0	0	0	0	-	0	+1		+1	1	-
B Knight	NYM	12	3	0	1.000	0	0	0	0	-	0	0	0	0	0	-
M Kobayashi	Cle	56	11	0	1.000	2	0	0	0	.00	-1	-1	0	-2	-2	-
B Korecky	Min	18	6	0	1.000	2	0	0	0	.00	+1	0	-1	0	0	-
E Kunz	NYM	3	3	1	.667	0	0	0	0	-				0	0	-
H Kuo	LAD	80	10	1	.900	2	0	0	0	.00	+1	0	-1	0	0	81
H Kuroda	LAD	183	58	2	.966	9	2	0	2	.22	-1	+2	+3	+4	4	10
J Lackey	LAA	163	24	5	.792	14	2	1	0	.21	0	-1	-3	-4	-3	150
A Laffey	Cle	94	15	1	.933	4	2	0	0	.50	+1	0	-1	0	1	55
C Lambert	Det	21	4	0	1.000	7	0	0	0	.00	+1			+1	0	-
J Lannan	Was	182	43	2	.953	25	2	5	0	.28	-1	0	0	0	0	81
B League	Tor	33	12	0	1.000	0	0	0	0	-	+1	-1	-1	-1	-1	-
W LeBlanc	SD	21	5	0	1.000	1	0	0	0	.00				0	0	-
W Ledezma	2 tms	58	10	1	.900	14	2	0	0	.14	+1	-2	-1	-2	-4	-
C Lee	Cle	223	31	1	.968	3	0	0	0	.00	-2	-2	-1	-4	-2	133
J Lester	Bos	210	42	2	.952	13	2	3	0	.38	-2	+2	-1	-2	-1	113
J Lewis	Cle	66	15	0	1.000	2	1	0	0	.50	0	0	+1	0	0	-
S Lewis	Cle	24	6	0	1.000	1	1	0	0	1.00	0			+1	1	-
B Lidge	Phi	69	10	0	1.000	9	1	0	0	.11	0	0	+1	+1	0	-
J Lieber	ChC	47	7	0	1.000	0	0	0	0	-	0	-1	+1	0	0	-
T Lilly	ChC	205	27	0	1.000	20	2	6	0	.40	-1	-1	0	-1	1	55
T Lincecum	SF	227	26	0	1.000	23	3	0	0	.13	-1	-2	-1	-3	-4	167
M Lincoln	Cin	70	18	1	.944	2	1	0	0	.50	+1	0	-1	0	0	-
M Lindstrom	Fla	57	18	1	.944	2	1	0	0	.50	+1	0	+1	+2	2	-
S Linebrink	CWS	46	8	0	1.000	2	0	0	0	.00	0	0	0	-1	-1	-
F Liriano	Min	76	13	0	1.000	9	0	3	0	.33	0	-2	0	-2	-1	-
J Litsch	Tor	176	62	3	.952	9	6	0	1	.67	+5	-1	+3	+8	8	2
W Littleton	Tex	18	3	0	1.000	0	0	0	0	-	0	0	0	0	0	-
R Liz	Bal	84	13	3	.769	14	2	0	1	.14	-1	-1	0	-2	-3	150
E Loaiza	2 tms	27	5	0	1.000	0	0	0	0	-	0	0	0	0	0	-
K Loe	Tex	31	5	1	.800	0	0	0	1	-	0	0	0	0	1	-
A Loewen	Bal	21	4	0	1.000	5	1	1	0	.40	+2			+2	2	-
B Logan	CWS	42	9	0	1.000	4	0	1	0	.25	-1	0	0	-1	-1	-
K Lohse	StL	200	49	0	1.000	12	2	1	0	.25	0	-1	-1	-2	-2	133
B Looper	StL	199	35	0	1.000	1	0	0	0	.00	-1	-1	-1	-3	-1	113
A Lopez	Det	79	5	0	1.000	5	1	0	0	.20	-1	-1	0	-2	-2	133
J Lopez	Bos	59	21	4	.810	4	2	1	0	.75	-1	+1	+1	+1	2	-
S Loux	LAA	16	4	0	1.000	0	0	0	0	-	0			0	0	-
D Lowe	LAD	211	56	2	.964	17	3	0	0	.18	-1	-2	+4	+1	0	81
M Lowe	Sea	64	8	1	.875	5	0	0	0	.00	0	-1	0	-1	-2	-
D Lowery	KC	4	0	0	-	1	0	0	0	.00				0	0	-
B Lyon	Ari	59	8	0	1.000	2	1	0	0	.50	0	0	-3	-3	-2	-
M MacDougal	CWS	17	0	0	-	1	0	0	0	.00	-1			-1	-1	-
G Maddux	2 tms	194	77	3	.961	29	4	1	0	.17	+11	+3	0	+14	7	3
W Madrigal	Tex	36	7	0	1.000	6	2	0	0	.33	0	0	0	0	0	-
R Madson	Phi	83	16	0	1.000	8	1	0	0	.13	-2	0	+1	-1	-2	133
R Mahay	KC	65	9	1	.889	4	2	0	0	.50	0	-1	0	-1	-1	-
P Maholm	Pit	206	39	2	.949	12	4	3	0	.58	0	0	+2	+3	4	10
J Maine	NYM	140	25	1	.960	13	5	1	0	.46	0	-1	+1	0	1	55
G Majewski	Cin	40	5	0	1.000	1	0	0	0	.00	-1	-1	0	-2	-2	-
C Manning	Was	42	6	0	1.000	4	0	0	0	.00	0	0		0	-1	-
S Marcum	Tor	151	35	0	1.000	7	2	0	0	.29	-1	-1	+3	+1	1	55
C Marmol	ChC	87	15	1	.933	4	1	0	0	.25	+1	0	-1	0	0	81
J Marquis	ChC	167	46	1	.978	12	1	0	0	.08	+1	+3	0	+4	2	31
S Marshall	ChC	65	12	0	1.000	7	2	0	0	.29	0	+2	-1	+1	1	-
D Marte	2 tms	65	12	0	1.000	4	1	0	0	.25	0	+2	-1	+1	1	-
P Martinez	NYM	109	23	0	1.000	17	2	0	1	.12	+2	+1	0	+2	1	55
S Martis	Was	21	4	0	1.000	3	0	0	0	.00	+1	+1	0	+2	2	-
N Masset	2 tms	62	17	3	.824	3	1	0	1	.33	-1	0	-1	-2	-2	-
J Masterson	Bos	88	14	1	.929	10	1	0	0	.10	0	+1	+1	+2	1	55
T Mastny	Cle	20	5	0	1.000	1	0	0	0	.00				0	0	-
D Mathis	Tex	22	4	0	1.000	2	1	0	0	.50	0			0	0	-
O Matos	SF	21	4	1	.750	3	1	0	0	.33				0	0	-
D Matsuzaka	Bos	168	36	1	.972	20	5	0	0	.25	+2	+3	-2	+3	1	55
B McCarthy	Tex	22	1	0	1.000	7	1	0	0	.14	0	0		0	-1	-
K McClellan	StL	76	12	0	1.000	3	1	0	0	.33	0	-1	0	-1	-1	-
S McClung	Mil	105	15	1	.933	9	4	0	0	.44	-1	0	+1	0	1	55
B McCrory	Bal	6	1	0	1.000	0	0	0	0	-	0			0	0	-
J McDonald	LAD	6	2	0	1.000									0		-
D McGowan	Tor	111	25	3	.880	16	4	0	0	.25	-1	+1	-2	-1	-2	133
G Meche	KC	210	38	4	.895	14	2	0	0	.14	-1	0	+3	+3	1	55
B Medders	Ari	20	4	0	1.000	6	1	0	0	.17	0	0	0	0	-1	-
E Meek	Pit	13	6	1	.833	2	0	0	0	.00	+1	+1	0	+2	2	-
J Meloan	Cle	2	0	0	-									0		-

BASIC						HOLDING					+/-					
Name	Tm	Inn	TC	E	Pct	SBA	CCS	PCS	PPO	CS%	Rght	Mid	Left	Tot	RS	Rnk
L Mendoza	Tex	63	21	2	.905	9	1	1	0	.22	0	+2	-1	0	0	-
K Mercker	Cin	14	1	0	1.000									0		-
C Meredith	SD	70	22	2	.909	13	1	0	0	.08	0	-3	-1	-4	-5	-
R Messenger	Sea	13	3	1	.667	6	2	0	0	.33	0	0	-1	-1	-1	-
D Meyer	Oak	28	2	1	.500	2	1	0	1	.50	-1	0	-1	-2	-1	-
K Mickolio	Bal	8	2	0	1.000	1	0	0	0	.00	0			0	0	-
J Mijares	Min	10	2	0	1.000	0	0	0	0	-	+1			+1	1	-
A Miles	StL	1	1	0	1.000	0	0	0	0	-				0		-
A Miller	Fla	107	14	1	.929	16	2	1	0	.19	-1	-1	0	-2	-3	150
J Miller	Bal	8	4	2	.500	2	0	0	0	.00	0			0	0	-
J Miller	Fla	47	5	0	1.000	5	1	0	0	.20	-1	-1	0	-2	-2	-
T Miller	TB	43	6	0	1.000	2	2	0	0	1.00	0	+1	0	+1	2	-
K Millwood	Tex	169	34	2	.941	30	4	0	0	.13	-1	-2	+3	-1	-4	167
Z Miner	Det	118	22	0	1.000	12	4	0	0	.33	-1	0	+3	+1	1	55
P Misch	SF	52	5	0	1.000	5	0	0	0	.00	0	0	-1	-1	-2	-
G Mock	Was	41	5	1	.800	2	0	0	0	.00	0	0	-1	-1	-1	-
B Moehler	Hou	150	25	1	.960	9	0	0	0	.00	-1	0	-1	-2	-3	150
F Morales	Col	25	5	0	1.000	5	0	0	0	.00	+1	0	+1	+1	0	-
J Morillo	Col	1	0	0	-									0		-
M Morris	Pit	22	4	0	1.000	6	3	0	0	.50	0	-1	0	0	0	-
B Morrow	Sea	65	3	0	1.000	4	1	0	0	.25	0	-1	0	0	0	-
C Morton	Atl	75	10	0	1.000	9	1	1	0	.22	0	0	0	0	0	-
D Moseley	LAA	50	11	0	1.000	6	1	1	1	.33	0	-1	+1	0	1	-
G Mota	Mil	57	15	0	1.000	5	0	1	1	.20	+1	+2	0	+2	2	-
J Motte	StL	11	2	0	1.000	0	0	0	0	-	0			0	0	-
J Moyer	Phi	196	42	2	.952	19	2	4	0	.32	0	0	-1	-2	-1	113
P Moylan	Atl	6	1	0	1.000	1	0	0	0	.00				0	0	-
E Mujica	Cle	39	4	0	1.000	1	1	0	0	1.00	0	0	+1	+1	1	-
M Mulder	StL	2	0	0	-	1	0	0	0	.00				0	0	-
C Muniz	NYM	23	3	1	.667	0	0	0	1	-	0			0	1	-
A Murray	Tex	8	1	0	1.000	0	0	0	0	-				+1	1	-
N Musser	KC	1	0	0	-									0		-
M Mussina	NYY	200	42	1	.976	19	6	1	0	.37	0	+3	-1	+2	2	31
B Myers	Phi	190	38	0	1.000	20	2	1	0	.15	-1	0	+3	+2	0	81
J Nathan	Min	68	10	1	.900	5	0	0	0	.00	0	+1	0	0	-1	-
J Nelson	Fla	54	8	0	1.000	4	0	0	0	.00	0	+1	0	+1	0	-
P Neshek	Min	13	3	0	1.000	0	0	0	0	-	0	0		0	0	-
J Newman	2 tms	16	3	0	1.000	1	0	0	0	.00	0	0		0	0	-
J Niemann	TB	16	1	0	1.000	3	1	0	0	.33	-1			0	0	-
J Niese	NYM	14	4	0	1.000	0	0	0	0	-	0	0	0	0	0	-
F Nieve	Hou	11	2	0	1.000	0	0	0	0	-	0			0	0	-
D Nippert	Tex	72	10	1	.900	7	2	0	0	.29	0	0	-1	-1	-1	-
R Nolasco	Fla	212	29	0	1.000	12	5	0	0	.42	-1	-2	+1	-2	-1	113
H Nomo	KC	4	0	0	-	1	0	0	0	.00				0	0	-
L Nunez	KC	48	6	1	.833	2	0	1	0	.50	0	+1	-1	0	1	-
V Nunez	Atl	33	7	0	1.000	4	2	0	0	.50	0	0	0	0	0	-
M O'Connor	Was	9	1	0	1.000	1	0	0	0	.00				0	0	-
D O'Day	LAA	43	13	1	.923	3	1	0	0	.33	0	0	0	-1	-1	-
E O'Flaherty	Sea	7	4	0	1.000	4	0	1	0	.25	0	0	0	0	0	-
R Ohlendorf	2 tms	63	4	0	1.000	3	0	1	0	.33	0	-1	0	-1	-1	-
W Ohman	Atl	59	9	0	1.000	3	1	1	0	.67	0	0	-1	-1	0	-
H Okajima	Bos	62	7	0	1.000	1	1	0	0	1.00	0	-1	0	0	1	-
D Oliver	LAA	72	14	0	1.000	7	1	1	0	.29	+1	+2	-3	0	0	-
S Olsen	Fla	202	31	2	.935	15	4	3	1	.47	+4	-1	-1	+3	4	10
G Olson	Bal	133	25	4	.840	22	1	1	0	.09	-1	0	+1	-1	-3	150
F Osoria	Pit	61	14	2	.857	0	0	0	0	-	-1	0	-1	-2	-2	-
R Oswalt	Hou	209	54	0	1.000	2	1	0	0	.50	-2	+1	+4	+3	3	23
J Outman	Oak	26	4	1	.750	1	0	0	0	.00	+1			+1	1	-
M Owings	Ari	105	26	1	.962	5	2	0	0	.40	+2	+1	0	+3	3	23
V Padilla	Tex	171	34	4	.882	13	4	0	2	.31	-2	+2	+3	+2	3	23
M Palmer	SF	13	4	0	1.000	0	0	0	0	-	0	0	+1	+1	1	-
J Papelbon	Bos	69	13	3	.769	2	0	0	1	.00	-1	-2	-2	-5	-4	-
M Parisi	StL	23	8	0	1.000	1	1	0	0	1.00	0	0	0	0	0	-
C Park	LAD	95	31	0	1.000	6	1	0	0	.17	0	+2	-1	+1	1	55
B Parnell	NYM	5	1	0	1.000	0	0	0	0	-				+1	1	-
C Paronto	Hou	10	1	0	1.000	0	0	0	0	-				0	0	-
J Parr	Atl	22	3	0	1.000	1	0	1	0	1.00	0	0	-1	-1	0	-
M Parra	Mil	166	19	0	1.000	13	3	2	0	.38	0	0	-3	-3	-1	113
J Parrish	Tor	42	10	1	.900	3	1	0	2	.33	0	+1	0	+1	2	-
S Patterson	2 tms	5	0	0	-									0		-
D Pauley	Bos	12	1	0	1.000	2	0	0	0	.00				-1	-1	-
C Pavano	NYY	34	7	0	1.000	6	1	0	0	.17	+1	-1	-1	-1	-2	-
J Peavy	SD	174	40	2	.950	27	8	1	0	.33	+2	0	-2	0	-1	113
J Peguero	Ari	9	3	0	1.000	0	0	0	0	-	0	0	0	0	0	-
M Pelfrey	NYM	201	47	0	1.000	11	6	0	4	.55	-3	+3	-1	-1	2	31
T Pena	Ari	73	17	0	1.000	2	0	0	0	.00	+1	-2	+1	+1	1	-
T F Pena	KC	1	1	0	1.000	0	0	0	0	-	+1			+1		-
B Penny	LAD	95	24	1	.958	11	3	0	0	.27	-1	-2	0	-3	-2	133
J Peralta	KC	53	5	0	1.000	4	1	0	0	.25	-1			-2	-2	-
T Percival	TB	46	2	0	1.000	9	2	0	0	.22	0			0	-1	-
C Perez	StL	42	3	0	1.000	4	1	0	0	.25				0	0	-
O Perez	Was	160	35	0	1.000	20	3	4	0	.35	+3	-1	-3	-2	-1	113
O Perez	NYM	194	22	0	1.000	9	1	0	0	.11	+1	+1	-1	+1	1	55
R Perez	Cle	76	19	1	.947	5	3	0	0	.60	+2	-1	-1	0	1	-
G Perkins	Min	151	28	1	.964	7	1	3	0	.57	0	+3	0	+3	4	10
Y Petit	Ari	56	7	0	1.000	3	1	0	0	.33	0	-1	0	-1	-1	-
A Pettitte	NYY	204	38	2	.947	28	2	6	4	.29	-4	0	-3	-6	-3	150
A Pettyjohn	Cin	4	2	0	1.000									0		-
C Pignatiello	ChC	1	0	0	-	0	0	0	0	-				0	0	-
J Pineiro	StL	149	44	1	.977	9	3	1	1	.44	-1	+2	0	+1	2	31
R Pinto	Fla	65	13	2	.846	2	1	0	0	.50	-1	+1	0	0	0	-
S Ponson	2 tms	136	31	3	.903	8	4	1	0	.63	-2	+1	-2	-3	0	81
D Price	TB	14	1	0	1.000	0	0	0	0	-				0	0	-

BASIC						HOLDING					+/-					
Name	Tm	Inn	TC	E	Pct	SBA	CCS	PCS	PPO	CS%	Rght	Mid	Left	Tot	RS	Rnk
S Proctor	LAD	39	3	1	.667	2	1	0	0	.50				-2	-2	-
D Purcey	Tor	65	6	0	1.000	5	2	1	0	.60	0	-1	-2	-3	-1	-
J Putz	Sea	46	9	1	.889	3	1	1	0	.67	0	0	-1	0	1	-
C Qualls	Ari	74	13	2	.846	3	0	0	0	.00	0	0	-1	-1	-1	-
E Ramirez	NYY	55	7	0	1.000	6	4	0	0	.67	0			0	1	-
E Ramirez	Tex	3	0	0	-	0	0	0	0	-	0	0		0	0	-
H Ramirez	2 tms	37	13	0	1.000	5	0	0	0	.00	0	+1	+2	+3	2	-
R Ramirez	KC	72	11	1	.909	4	0	1	0	.25	0	+1	-1	0	0	-
R Ramirez	Cin	27	6	0	1.000	5	3	0	0	.60	0			0	0	-
C Rapada	Det	21	10	2	.800	1	0	1	1	1.00	0	0	-1	-1	0	-
D Rasner	NYY	113	24	0	1.000	6	3	0	0	.50	-1	+1	+1	+1	2	31
J Rauch	2 tms	72	9	0	1.000	4	1	0	0	.25	0	0	+1	0	0	-
T Redding	Was	182	27	2	.926	20	7	0	0	.35	-3	+2	+2	+1	1	55
M Redman	Col	45	9	0	1.000	2	0	0	0	.00	0	0	0	0	0	-
S Register	Col	10	0	0	-									0		-
C Reineke	SD	18	0	0	-	0	0	0	0	-				0	0	-
C Resop	Atl	18	3	0	1.000	1	0	0	0	.00				-2	-2	-
A Reyes	TB	23	2	0	1.000	2	0	0	0	.00	0	0	0	0	0	-
A Reyes	2 tms	49	9	0	1.000	4	1	0	0	.25	0	0	0	-1	-1	-
D Reyes	Min	46	8	0	1.000	8	0	2	0	.25	+1	0	-2	-1	-1	-
J Reyes	Atl	113	16	0	1.000	13	3	1	0	.31	+1	0	-1	0	0	81
G Reynolds	Col	62	10	0	1.000	3	0	0	0	.00	-1	0	-2	-3	-2	-
A Rhodes	2 tms	35	4	0	1.000	1	0	0	0	.00	0			0	0	-
C Richard	CWS	48	13	3	.769	6	0	0	0	.00	+2	0	-1	0	-1	-
S Richmond	Tor	27	2	0	1.000	2	1	0	0	.50	0			0	0	-
J Ridgway	Atl	10	3	0	1.000	0	0	0	0	-				0	0	-
J Rincon	2 tms	55	6	0	1.000	7	1	0	0	.14	0	-2	+1	-2	-2	-
R Rincon	NYM	4	0	0	-									0		-
R Ring	Atl	22	4	0	1.000	3	0	0	0	.00	0	0	0	0	0	-
D Riske	Mil	42	3	0	1.000	4	1	1	0	.50				0	1	-
M Rivera	NYY	71	14	0	1.000	7	1	0	0	.14	-1	0	+1	-1	-2	-
S Rivera	Was	84	29	0	1.000	13	0	0	0	.00	0	+2	+1	+3	0	81
C Robertson	Ari	7	2	0	1.000									0		-
D Robertson	NYY	30	4	0	1.000	7	3	0	0	.43	-1	-1	-1	-2	-2	-
N Robertson	Det	169	29	1	.966	11	3	1	0	.36	0	-1	-1	-1	0	81
F Rodney	Det	40	6	0	1.000	4	0	0	0	.00	0	0	+1	0	0	-
F Rodriguez	LAA	68	12	2	.833	8	0	0	0	.00	0	0	0	0	-1	-
W Rodriguez	Hou	137	23	0	1.000	7	2	1	0	.43	+1	0	-1	0	1	55
J Roenicke	Cin	3	0	0	-	0	0	0	0	-	0			0	0	-
K Rogers	Det	174	77	1	.987	3	2	0	3	.67	+4	+5	+6	+16	15	1
J Romero	Phi	59	22	0	1.000	12	0	2	1	.17	-1	0	+1	+1	1	-
S Romo	SF	34	7	0	1.000	5	1	0	0	.20	0	+1	0	+1	1	-
C Rosa	KC	3	0	0	-									0		-
L Rosales	Ari	30	5	1	.800	2	0	0	0	.00				0	0	-
R Rowland-Smith	Sea	118	11	1	.909	6	2	0	0	.33	+3	-1	-2	0	0	81
R Rundles	Cle	5	0	0	-	1	0	0	0	.00	0			0	0	-
J Rupe	Tex	89	15	0	1.000	1	1	0	0	1.00	0	-1	+2	+1	2	31
G Rusch	2 tms	84	11	0	1.000	3	0	0	0	.00	0	0	0	+1	1	55
A Russell	CWS	26	5	0	1.000	0	0	0	0	-	+1			0	0	-
B Ryan	Tor	58	5	0	1.000	4	0	0	0	.00	+1	+1	0	+1	1	-
J Ryu	TB	1	0	0	-									0		-
K Saarloos	Oak	26	5	0	1.000	1	0	0	0	.00	0	0	-1	-1	-1	-
C Sabathia	2 tms	253	34	1	.971	15	1	2	0	.20	-1	+2	-3	-2	-2	133
B Sadler	SF	44	6	0	1.000	6	3	0	0	.50	+1	0	0	+1	1	-
T Saito	LAD	47	6	0	1.000	2	0	1	0	.50	0	-1	0	-1	0	-
J Salas	TB	6	1	0	1.000									0		-
M Salas	Pit	17	1	0	1.000	0	0	0	0	-				-1	-1	-
J Samardzija	ChC	28	7	0	1.000	6	0	1	0	.17	0	0	0	0	0	-
C Sampson	Hou	117	23	1	.957	4	2	0	0	.50	-1	-1	-2	-3	-1	113
B Sanches	Was	11	1	0	1.000	1	0	0	0	.00				0	0	-
A Sanchez	Fla	52	11	4	.636	7	0	0	1	.00	0	+1	-1	-1	-2	-
D Sanchez	NYM	58	9	1	.889	4	0	0	0	.00	0	+1	0	+1	1	-
H Sanchez	NYY	2	1	0	1.000									0		-
J Sanchez	SF	158	17	0	1.000	22	2	1	0	.14	0	+1	-1	0	-2	133
R Sanchez	Pit	13	3	0	1.000	0	0	0	0	-	0	-1	+1	0	0	-
E Santana	LAA	219	32	0	1.000	20	4	0	0	.20	-1	-2	-3	-5	-5	170
J Santana	NYM	234	41	1	.976	11	3	2	0	.45	0	-1	-2	-3	0	81
D Sarfate	Bal	80	12	2	.833	8	2	0	1	.25	-1	-1	-1	-3	-2	133
J Saunders	LAA	198	41	0	1.000	25	4	3	0	.28	0	+3	0	+2	2	31
M Scherzer	Ari	56	10	1	.900	1	1	0	0	1.00	0	+1	0	0	1	-
S Schoeneweis	NYM	57	13	0	1.000	4	0	2	0	.50	0	0	-1	-1	0	-
C Schroder	Was	5	2	0	1.000	0	0	0	0	-	0			+1	1	-
R Seanez	Phi	43	9	2	.778	8	0	1	0	.13	-1	0	0	-1	-2	-
B Seay	Det	56	9	0	1.000	3	1	0	0	.33	+1	-1	-1	0	0	-
A Serrano	LAA	1	0	0	-									0		-
B Sheets	Mil	198	28	2	.929	20	7	0	2	.35	0	-2	+1	-1	0	81
S Shell	Was	50	10	0	1.000	3	1	0	0	.33	+1	+1	0	+1	1	-
G Sherrill	Bal	53	4	1	.750	3	0	0	0	.00	-1	-1	0	-2	-2	-
J Shields	TB	215	39	1	.974	13	6	0	1	.46	-1	-2	+2	-1	1	55
S Shields	LAA	63	9	0	1.000	9	1	0	0	.11	0	+2	-1	0	-1	-
B Shouse	Mil	51	20	1	.950	2	0	1	0	.50	0	0	+1	+2	3	-
C Silva	Sea	153	24	1	.958	10	2	0	0	.20	-1	-1	0	-2	-2	133
A Simon	Bal	13	7	0	1.000	1	0	0	0	.00				-1	-1	-
D Slaten	Ari	32	7	2	.714	0	0	0	0	-	+1	0	0	+1	1	-
B Slocum	Cle	2	0	0	-	0	0	0	0	-				0	0	-
K Slowey	Min	160	26	1	.962	8	4	0	1	.50	0	0	+1	+1	2	31
C Smith	Bos	18	5	0	1.000	0	0	0	1	-				0	1	-
G Smith	Oak	190	38	0	1.000	23	1	11	5	.52	0	-1	0	-2	4	10
J Smith	NYM	63	21	0	1.000	8	2	0	0	.25	+3	+2	-1	+4	3	-
J Smoltz	Atl	28	8	3	.625	1	0	0	0	.00	0	+1	0	0	0	-
I Snell	Pit	164	28	0	1.000	24	4	0	0	.17	-1	+2	-1	0	-2	133
K Snyder	Bos	2	0	0	-	0	0	0	0	-	0			0	0	-

Name	Tm	Inn	TC	E	Pct	SBA	CCS	PCS	PPO	CS%	Rght	Mid	Left	Tot	RS	Rnk
A Sonnanstine	TB	193	38	0	1.000	4	3	0	0	.75	-2	-2	+5	0	2	31
J Soria	KC	67	12	0	1.000	3	0	1	1	.33	-1	0	+1	0	1	-
R Soriano	Atl	14	2	0	1.000	2	1	0	0	.50				0	0	-
J Sosa	NYM	22	3	0	1.000	1	1	0	0	1.00	0			-1	-1	-
J Sowers	Cle	121	27	2	.926	15	5	1	0	.40	-1	+2	0	+2	2	31
J Speier	LAA	68	11	0	1.000	8	1	0	0	.13	0	0	-1	-2	-3	-
R Speier	Col	51	7	0	1.000	8	2	0	0	.25	0	0	-1	-1	-1	-
L Speigner	Was	8	3	0	1.000	2	2	0	0	1.00	+1			+1	1	-
R Springer	StL	50	11	2	.818	3	2	0	0	.67	0	0	0	-1	0	-
M Stetter	Mil	25	4	0	1.000	4	1	1	0	.50	0	0		0	0	-
P Stockman	Atl	7	1	0	1.000	1	0	0	0	.00	0			0	0	-
B Stokes	NYM	33	7	0	1.000	3	0	0	0	.00	0	0	0	0	0	-
H Street	Oak	70	11	0	1.000	9	2	1	0	.33	+1	0	+1	+2	2	-
E Stults	LAD	39	7	1	.857	3	1	0	0	.33	+1	0	0	0	0	-
T Sturtze	LAD	2	1	0	1.000	0	0	0	0	-				0	0	-
J Suppan	Mil	178	41	1	.976	11	6	1	1	.64	0	+3	+1	+4	5	7
R Swindle	Phi	5	0	0	-									0	0	-
M Talbot	TB	10	2	0	1.000	2	0	0	0	.00	0	0	0	0	0	-
B Tallet	Tor	56	7	1	.857	7	1	0	0	.14	0	-1	-2	-2	-3	-
T Tankersley	Fla	18	2	1	.500									0	0	-
J Taschner	SF	48	8	0	1.000	8	1	1	0	.25	+1	-1	-1	-1	-1	-
T Taubenheim	Pit	6	0	0	-									0	0	-
J Tavarez	3 tms	55	13	1	.923	5	0	0	0	.00	0	0	0	0	0	-
R Tejeda	2 tms	45	6	2	.667	5	0	1	1	.20				0	0	-
J Thatcher	SD	26	3	0	1.000	1	0	0	0	.00	+1	-1		0	0	-
J Thomas	Sea	4	1	0	1.000	0	0	0	0	-	0			0	0	-
B Thompson	StL	65	19	0	1.000	2	1	0	1	.50	0	+1	+1	+1	2	-
D Thompson	Cin	14	1	0	1.000	0	0	0	0	-	0	0	0	0	0	-
R Thompson	LAA	2	1	0	1.000	1	0	0	0	.00				+1	1	-
M Thornton	CWS	67	9	0	1.000	4	0	0	0	.00	0	0	0	0	0	-
E Threets	SF	10	1	0	1.000	1	0	0	0	.00	0			0	0	-
M Timlin	Bos	49	10	0	1.000	6	0	0	0	.00	0	+1	0	+1	0	-
B Tomko	2 tms	70	15	0	1.000	3	0	0	0	.00	0	+2	+1	+4	3	-
S Torres	Mil	80	22	0	1.000	3	2	0	0	.67	-2	-1	0	-3	-1	113
B Traber	NYY	17	4	0	1.000	4	1	0	0	.25				+1	1	-
S Trachsel	Bal	40	4	0	1.000	9	3	0	0	.33	0	-1	0	-1	-1	-
R Troncoso	LAD	38	8	0	1.000	5	0	0	0	.00	0	+1	+1	+1	0	-
R Tucker	Fla	37	7	0	1.000	3	1	0	0	.33	-1	+1	-1	-1	-1	-
D Turnbow	Mil	6	1	0	1.000	2	0	0	0	.00	0			0	0	-
M Valdez	SF	16	0	0	-	2	1	0	0	.50	0			0	0	-
J Valverde	Hou	72	10	1	.900	8	0	0	0	.00	0	-1	0	-1	-2	-
VanBenschoten	Pit	22	1	0	1.000	5	1	0	0	.20				+1	1	-
R VandenHurk	Fla	14	2	1	.500	0	0	0	0	-	0			0	0	-
C Vargas	NYM	37	10	0	1.000	3	1	0	0	.33	0	+1	+1	+1	1	-
J Vazquez	CWS	208	46	0	1.000	12	2	1	0	.25	+1	+2	+1	+5	4	10
J Veras	NYY	58	9	0	1.000	8	3	0	0	.38	+1	0	0	+1	1	-
J Verlander	Det	201	33	2	.939	17	8	1	1	.53	-1	0	+5	+4	5	7
C Villanueva	Mil	108	22	1	.955	7	2	0	0	.29	+1	-1	+1	+1	1	55
O Villarreal	Hou	38	8	0	1.000	3	1	0	0	.33	0	-1	0	0	0	-
R Villone	StL	50	13	1	.923	0	0	0	0	-	0	0	+1	+1	1	-
L Vizcaino	Col	46	7	0	1.000	2	0	0	0	.00	0	0	0	+1	1	-
E Volquez	Cin	196	35	1	.971	33	12	0	0	.36	+1	0	0	+1	0	81
C Volstad	Fla	84	13	0	1.000	14	2	0	0	.14	-2	0	0	-2	-3	150
C Wade	LAD	71	14	0	1.000	2	0	0	0	.00	0	-1	+1	0	0	-
D Waechter	Fla	63	4	1	.750	7	1	0	0	.14	0	0	0	0	-1	-
B Wagner	NYM	47	3	0	1.000	1	1	0	0	1.00	0	+1	0	0	0	-
A Wainwright	StL	132	28	1	.964	6	2	2	0	.67	0	0	+2	+2	4	10
T Wakefield	Bos	181	23	1	.957	37	10	0	1	.27	-1	+1	+2	+2	0	81
J Walker	Bal	38	10	0	1.000	3	0	1	0	.33	+1	-1	0	0	0	-
T Walker	SF	53	7	1	.857	3	1	0	0	.33	-1	0	0	-1	-1	-
L Walrond	Phi	10	7	0	1.000	1	1	0	0	1.00	0	0	0	0	0	-
C Wang	NYY	95	20	0	1.000	11	3	0	0	.27	+1	-1	-1	0	0	81
J Washburn	Sea	154	32	1	.969	9	2	2	0	.44	+1	0	0	1	1	55
E Wassermann	CWS	20	4	0	1.000	6	1	0	0	.17	0	-1	-1	-1	-1	-
C Waters	Bal	65	17	1	.941	3	0	0	0	.00	0	+1	0	+1	1	-
D Weathers	Cin	69	9	2	.778	3	0	0	0	.00	-1	+1	+1	+1	1	-
J Weaver	LAA	177	23	2	.913	25	5	0	2	.20	0	-1	-2	-2	-3	150
B Webb	Ari	227	74	2	.973	34	9	1	0	.29	+5	+2	-2	+5	3	23
T Wellemeyer	StL	192	36	2	.944	13	5	1	1	.46	-3	0	0	-3	0	81
J Wells	2 tms	8	3	0	1.000	2	0	0	0	.00	0			0	0	-
K Wells	2 tms	38	9	1	.889	3	1	1	0	.67	+1	0	0	+1	2	-
R Wells	2 tms	5	0	0	-									0	0	-
J Westbrook	Cle	35	12	1	.917	2	1	1	0	1.00	+1	0	+2	+3	3	-
D Wheeler	TB	66	7	1	.857	2	1	0	0	.50				-1	-1	-
B White	Tex	4	1	0	1.000									0		-
D Willis	Det	24	2	0	1.000	0	0	0	0	-	+1	-1	0	0	0	-
B Wilson	SF	62	9	0	1.000	3	1	0	0	.33	-1	+1	0	0	0	-
C Wilson	Tex	46	13	1	.923	2	1	0	0	.50	0	+2	-1	+1	1	-
M Wise	NYM	7	1	0	1.000	1	0	0	0	.00				0	0	-
R Wolf	2 tms	190	35	2	.943	13	4	1	1	.38	-1	-1	+1	-2	-1	113
B Wolfe	Tor	22	7	0	1.000	1	0	0	0	.00	0	0	0	0	0	-
K Wood	ChC	66	7	0	1.000	1	0	0	0	.00	0	-1	0	-1	-1	-
J Woods	Sea	19	2	0	1.000	0	0	0	0	-				0	0	-
M Worrell	StL	6	1	0	1.000									0		-
J Wright	Tex	84	35	2	.943	10	1	0	2	.10	-1	+2	+1	+1	1	55
W Wright	Hou	56	9	0	1.000	5	0	0	0	.00	+1	0	0	+1	0	-
M Wuertz	ChC	45	12	1	.917	7	3	0	0	.43	0	+1	-1	0	0	-
K Yabu	SF	68	15	3	.800	4	0	0	0	.00	0	-1	-1	-1	-1	-
Y Yabuta	KC	38	7	1	.857	4	0	0	0	.00	0	-1	-1	-2	-3	-
T Yates	Pit	73	15	1	.933	5	1	0	0	.20	-1	-2	+1	-2	-2	-
C Young	SD	102	16	1	.938	17	2	0	1	.12	-1	0	+1	0	-2	133
C Zambrano	ChC	189	45	3	.933	19	9	0	3	.47	-2	0	+1	-1	1	55

Name	Tm	Inn	TC	E	Pct	SBA	CCS	PCS	PPO	CS%	Rght	Mid	Left	Tot	RS	Rnk
B Ziegler	Oak	60	14	0	1.000	1	0	0	2	.00	+2	0	0	+2	3	-
C Zink	Bos	4	2	0	1.000	0	0	0	0	-				-1	-1	-
B Zito	SF	180	28	1	.964	10	3	1	1	.40	0	+1	-2	-1	1	55
J Zumaya	Det	23	1	0	1.000	1	0	0	0	.00	-1	0	0	-1	-1	-
2008 MLB Averages					.956											

Defensive Positioning System

Baseball Info Solutions sells something very special to Major League Baseball teams. We cannot show you all of it because of our team clients (plus it would be about fifty times the size of this book by itself), but we want to show you a bunch of cool examples.

We created infield and outfield charts by batter that help teams position their defense. These charts are not hit charts or spray charts or anything you have seen before.

The charts only include balls that an outfielder or infielder can potentially catch. To do this, we exclude from the charts batted balls that are going to be hits no matter what you do with your defense. For example, our infield chart doesn't include pop-ups, but does include short liners as well as groundballs. Pop-ups are normally easily caught in the infield regardless of the shift. We don't include bunts in the chart but we do indicate bunt frequency for each batter. We skip balls fielded by the catcher or pitcher, whether bunts or not. You cannot position catchers and pitchers, so they are not included.

Ground singles that go through the infield for a hit are not included in the outfield charts since no outfield shift can prevent those hits. The outfield chart doesn't include balls under 150 feet, doesn't include balls fielded by the infield (for example, a shortstop running into the outfield to catch a short fly), and doesn't include home runs that leave the park (inside-the-park homers are included). 99.9% of over-the-wall home runs are totally unplayable, of course.

We exclude line drives under 150 feet for the outfield, but include line drives up to 120 feet for the infield. We ignore line drives between 120 to 150 feet, considering them pretty much unplayable. Yes, there are always a few exceptions but we're looking for important tendencies, not the ability to defend hits that are basically indefensible.

For the infield, we divide the field into 12 slices, three for each normal infield position. We use colors on those slices to make an easy visual connection. The actual number of batted balls hit by a batter are shown on each slice.

For the outfield, we divide the field into 27 sections, nine for each normal outfield position. Each outfield position has a central area which is surrounded by eight additional areas representing shallow/average/deep going front to back and left/center/right going left to right within the position. We use colors on the 27 sections to make an easy visual connection. The actual number of batted balls hit by a batter are shown on each slice.

Finally, we use a coloring system that is weighted by a number of factors including the places on the field extra-base hits often occur. Red means it's a hot zone. Blue is a cold zone. More specifically:

Dark Red = Hot = places most in need of a fielder

Light Red (or Orange) = likely place for a fielder

Clear = average risk of a ball being hit here
Clear will look like green grass
and/or brown dirt

Light Blue (or Turquoise) = less important area to place a fielder

Dark Blue = Cold = a location least in need of a fielder

The formula for producing the colors includes a weighting of batted balls down or near both foul lines, balls hit in the gaps, and balls hit deep. Balls hit into these areas are more likely to go for extra bases and, in essence, count more than other batted balls. In addition, this color weighting includes how hard the ball is hit (harder hit balls getting greater weight). This means the raw batted ball counts shown on the charts will not always show the same color. Now that you have a fairly good understanding of our charts, let's have a look.

Chase Utley

Bats Left

Infield Chart

Updated October 30, 2008
Last 120 grounders and short liners

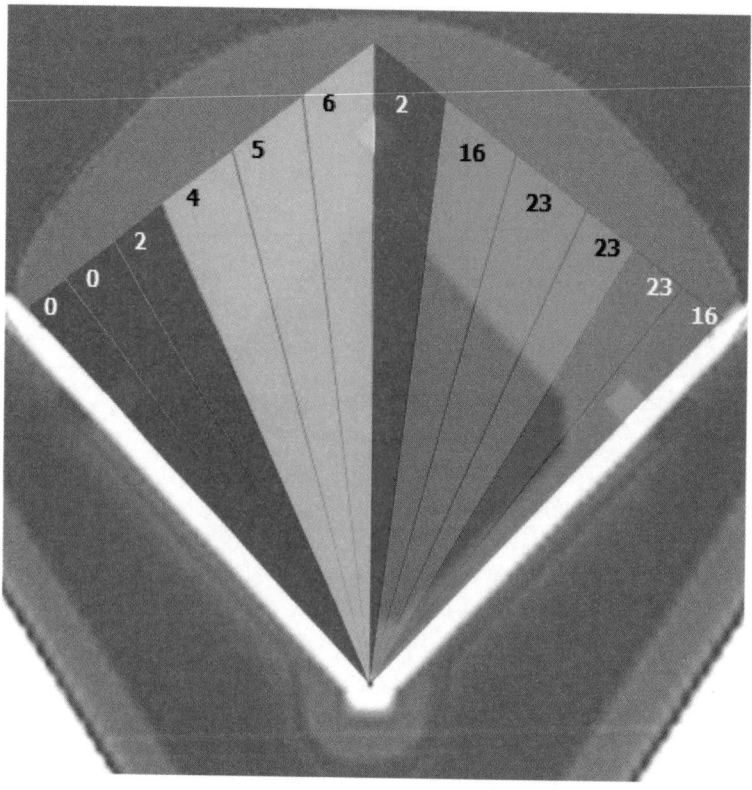

- Shift candidate! (86% right of 2B)

- 44% of last 250 were grounders and short liners.

- 2 bunt attempts in last 300 plate appearances.

Chase Utley is an extreme infield pull hitter having hit 86% of his last 250 grounders and short liners to the right of second base. Teams should consider playing a shift on him. In the World Series Tim McCarver and Joe Buck were surprised that the Tampa Bay Rays were shifting on him. And sure enough, Utley attempted a bunt. But that's a rare thing as he's only had two bunt attempts in his last 300 plate appearances. As you can see in the diagram, he just doesn't hit the ball down the third-base line, ever. Playing your third-baseman in the normal shortstop position makes sense. I'd make Utley beat me with a bunt once or twice before putting the third baseman back towards third base.

David Ortiz

Bats Left

Infield Chart

Updated October 30, 2008
Last 120 grounders and short liners

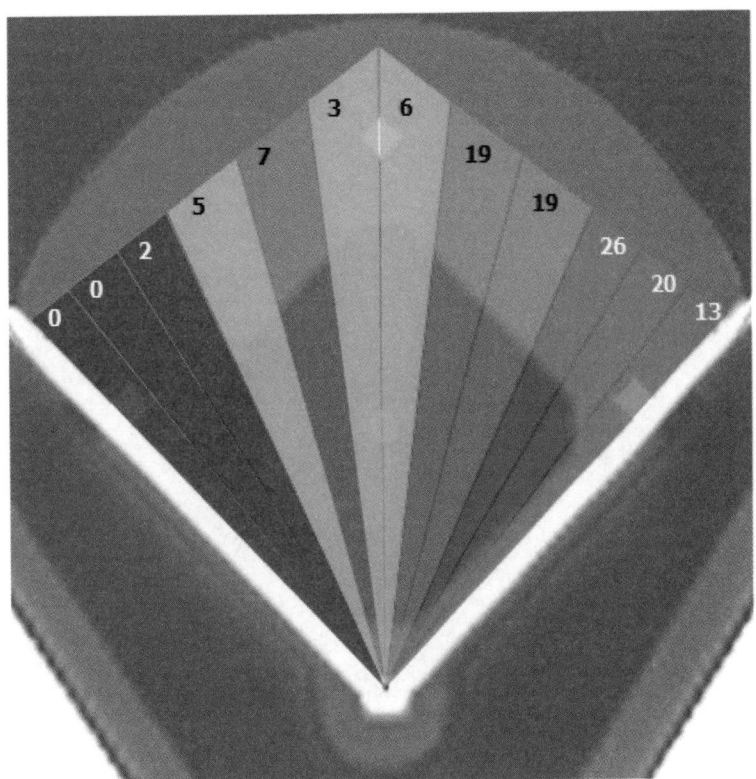

- Shift candidate! (86% right of 2B)

- 42% of last 250 were grounders and short liners.

- 2 bunt attempts in last 300 plate appearances.

Here's one of the guys that teams shift on all the time. David Ortiz. Like Utley he hits 86% of his grounders and short liners to the right side. Here's my rule of thumb: if a hitter hits significantly more than three out of every four balls in the infield (75%) on the right side, you should put three out of your four infielders on the right side. Let's look at a couple more players who get shifted.

Ryan Howard

Bats Left

Infield Chart

Updated October 30, 2008
Last 120 grounders and short liners

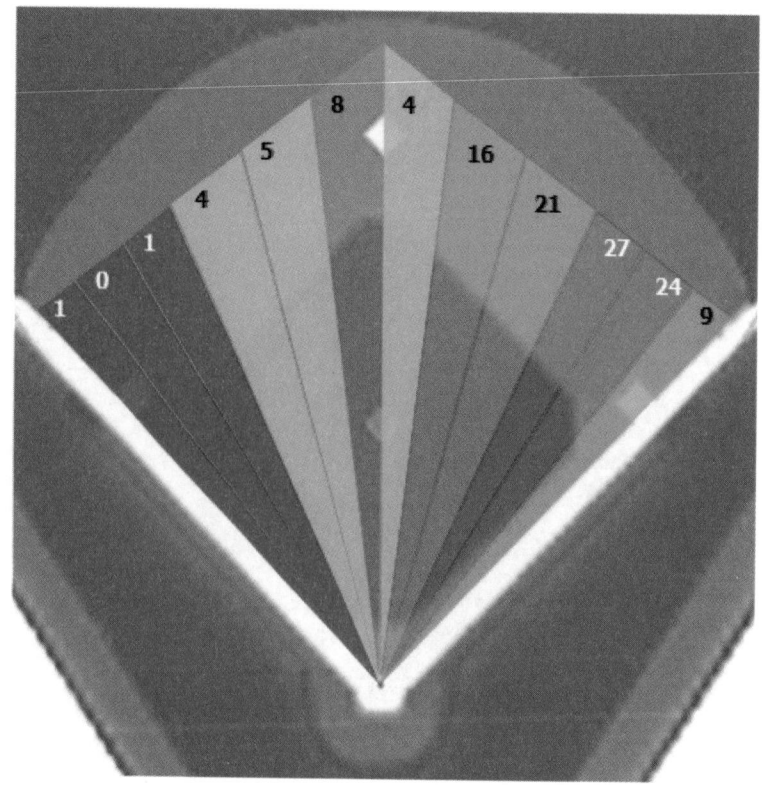

- Shift candidate! (84% right of 2B)

- 50% of last 250 were grounders and short liners.

- 0 bunt attempts in last 300 plate appearances.

Howard hits 84% grounders and short liners to the right side. Big Papi and Howard are two of seven guys in baseball for whom most teams play a shift, according to data from Baseball Info Solutions. The other five are Carlos Delgado, Jason Giambi, Ken Griffey Jr, Jim Thome, and the player on the next chart, Adam Dunn.

Adam Dunn

Bats Left

Infield Chart

Updated October 30, 2008
Last 120 grounders and short liners

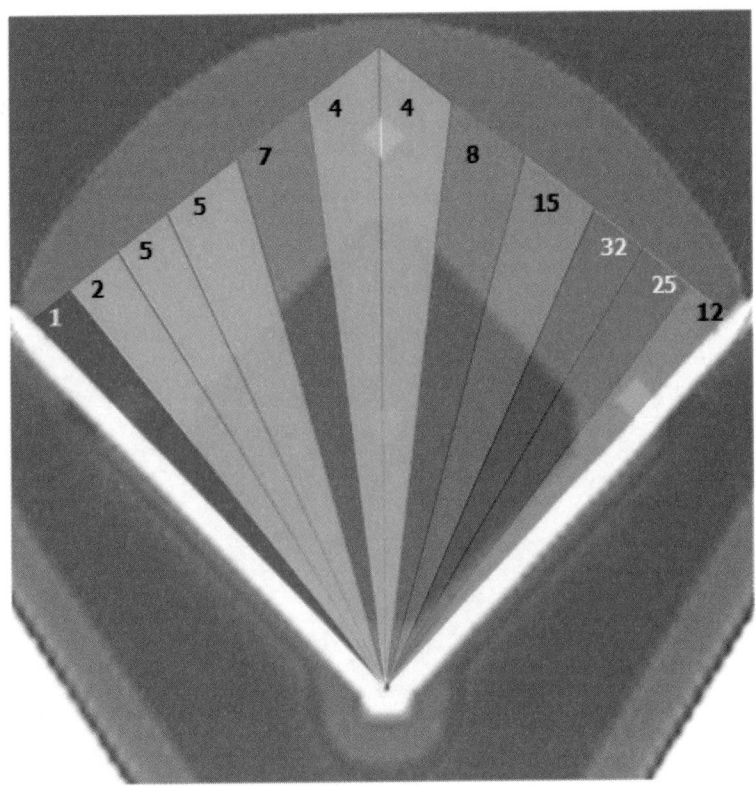

- Shift candidate! (80% right of 2B)

- 40% of last 250 were grounders and short liners.

- 0 bunt attempts in last 300 plate appearances.

At 80%, I consider shifting on Adam Dunn marginal. Here's why: The third baseman has a ton of ground to cover to handle 20% of the grounders, while each other fielder has a small amount of ground to cover to handle, theoretically, 26.7% apiece. The 20% compared to the 26.7% is too close. I'd like to see it more like 15% for the third basemen and almost double that for each of the other fielders. Plus, unlike some of the other hitters who get the shift, the 20% that Dunn hits to the left of second are pretty spread out.

Carlos Pena

Bats Left

Infield Chart

Updated October 30, 2008
Last 120 grounders and short liners

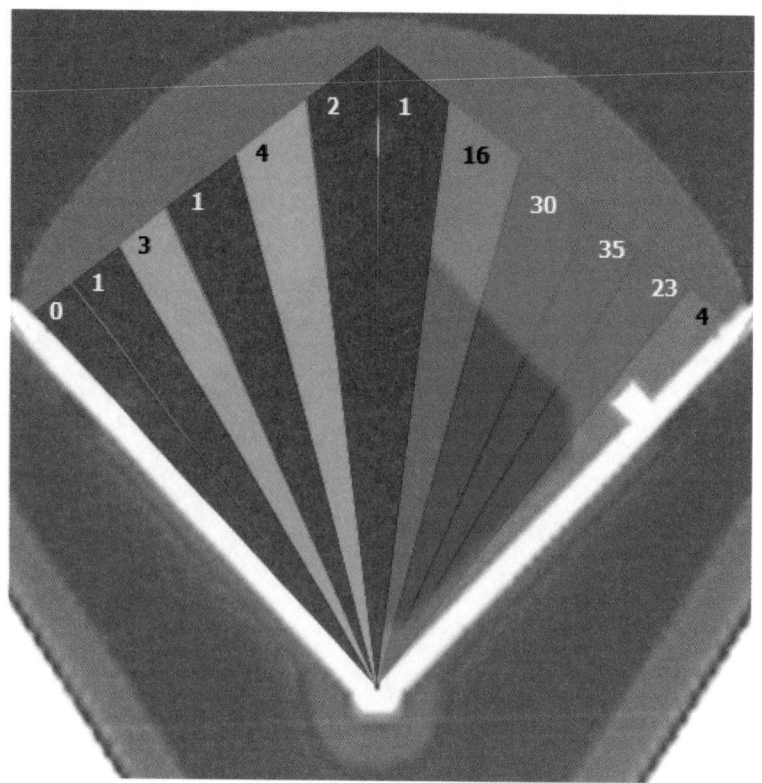

- Shift candidate! (91% right of 2B)

- 38% of last 250 were grounders and short liners.

- 6 bunt attempts in last 300 plate appearances.

A few teams play a shift on Carlos Pena, but not as many as shift for the big seven pull hitters previously mentioned. Those few teams have the right idea. Carlos Pena's 91% of his infield batted balls hit to the right side is the highest figure in baseball. But be careful. He will try a bunt once in a while.

Alex Gordon

Bats Left

Infield Chart

Updated October 30, 2008
Last 120 grounders and short liners

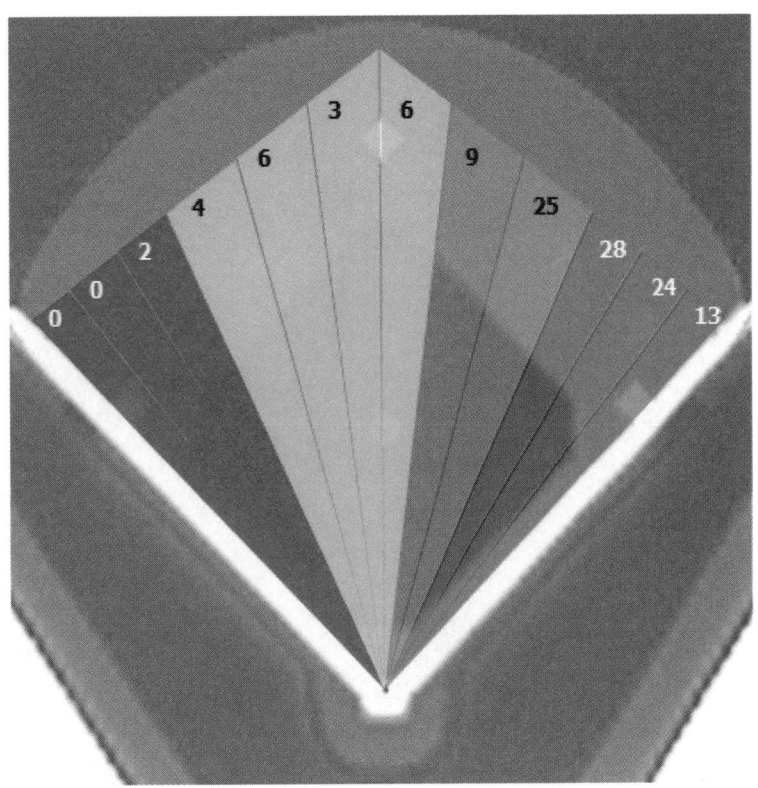

- Shift candidate! (88% right of 2B)
- 37% of last 250 were grounders and short liners.
- 3 bunt attempts in last 300 plate appearances.

Teams should *consider* shifting for Gordon.

Jim Thome

Bats Left

Infield Chart

Updated October 30, 2008
Last 120 grounders and short liners

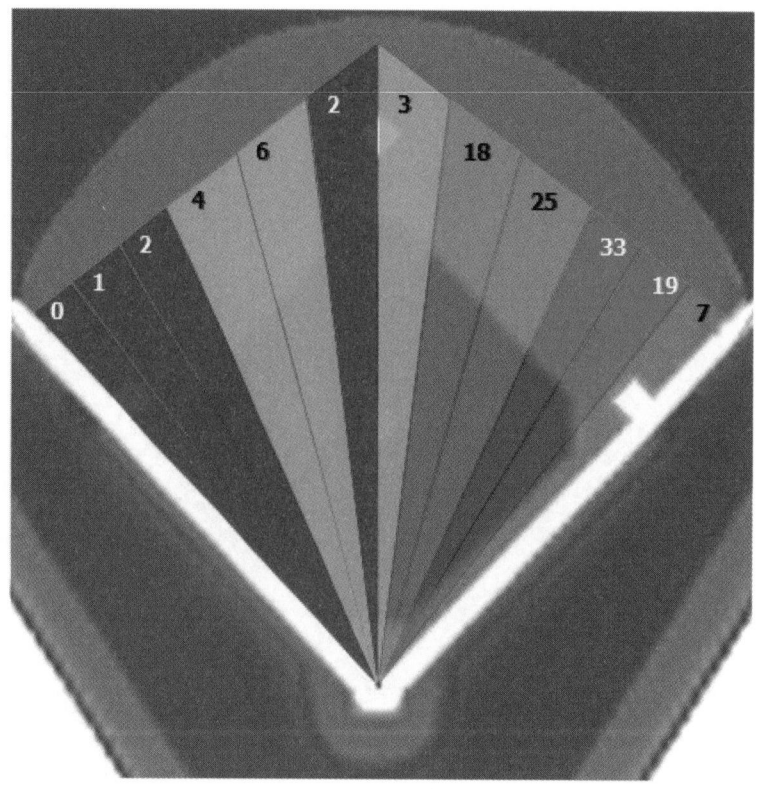

- Shift candidate! (88% right of 2B)
- 45% of last 250 were grounders and short liners.
- 0 bunt attempts in last 300 plate appearances.

As everyone knows, Thome is an extreme pull hitter on groundballs and nearly every team shifts on him. He never bunts, and he never hits the ball anywhere near third base. Putting the third baseman at the normal shortstop position is no problem at all.

Jim Thome

Bats Left

Outfield Chart

Updated October 30, 2008
Last 135 flies and line drives

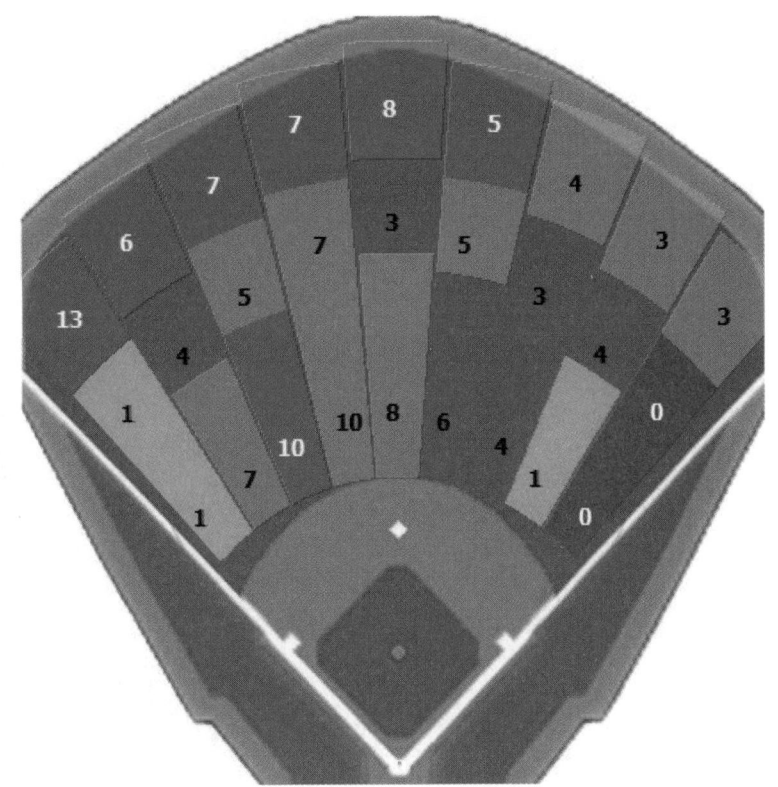

• 55% of last 250 were flies and line drives.

Here's what everyone doesn't know. Thome hits balls in the air to the outfield the opposite way. Hardly anything down the right field line. Here's one reason why this is surprising. Thome does pull a good number of home runs. But they are excluded from this chart because you can't play defense on a home run (well, that's true for the most part—the rare home-run saving catch is pretty awesome). Teams should play their outfielders shaded well towards left field (and deep!). Look at that "13" down the line in deep left field. It's the most common area in our diagram of where he hits the ball. How many teams know this?

Brian McCann

Bats Left

Infield Chart

Updated October 30, 2008
Last 120 grounders and short liners

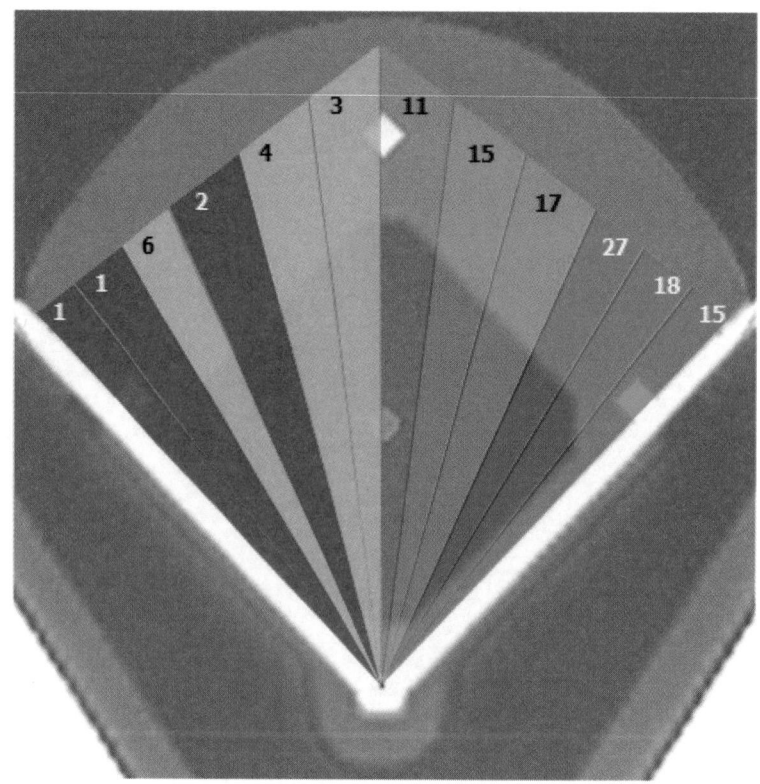

- Shift candidate! (86% right of 2B)
- 45% of last 250 were grounders and short liners.
- 1 bunt attempts in last 300 plate appearances.

McCann is another player who loves to pull the ball on the infield. There are about 30 left-hand hitting players in baseball for whom a shift might be in order, with infield pull percentages well over 80%.

Ichiro Suzuki

Bats Left

Infield Chart

Updated October 30, 2008
Last 120 grounders and short liners

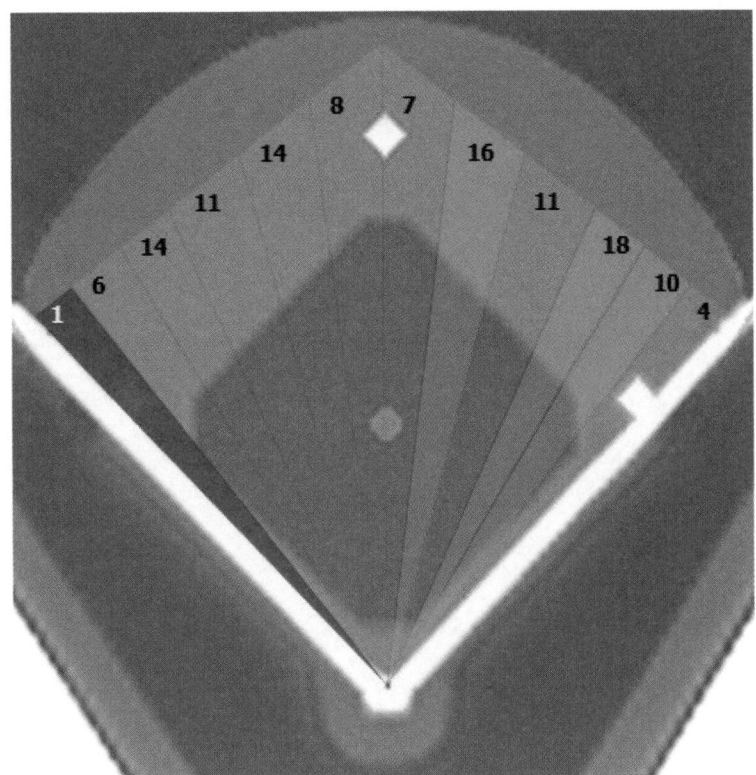

- 64% of last 250 were grounders and short liners.
- 7 bunt attempts in last 300 plate appearances.

Ichiro sprays the ball. The third baseman can play a bit more towards the shortstop position, but other than that, the infield should be at their normal positions.

Joey Gathright

Bats Left

Infield Chart

Updated October 30, 2008
Last 120 grounders and short liners

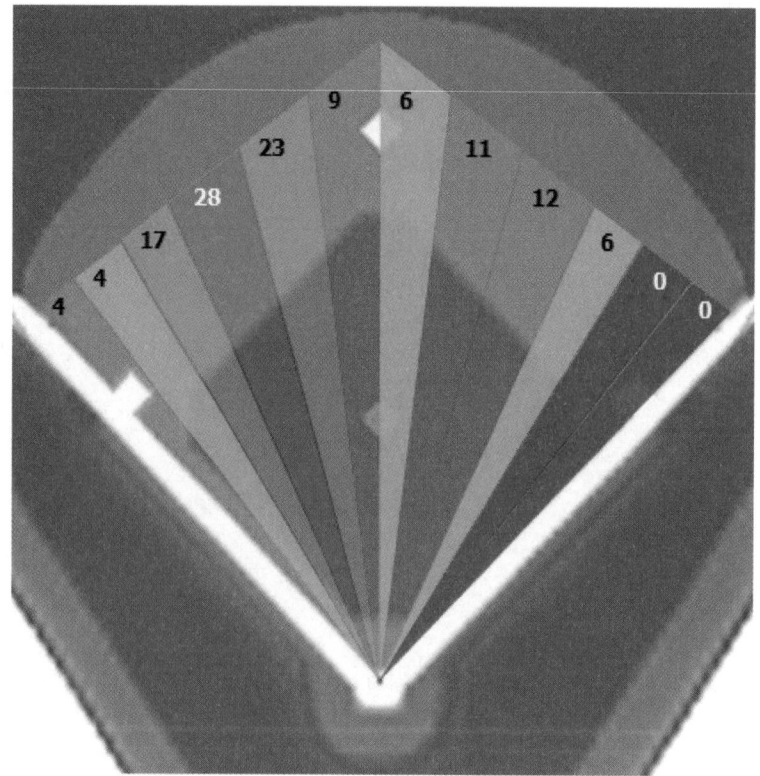

- 69% of last 250 were grounders and short liners.
- 52 bunt attempts in last 300 plate appearances.

Lefty-swinging Joey Gathright hits like a guy who was trained to hit the ball to the left side and outrun the infielder's arm. Given that the shortstop is typically the furthest from the plate Joey's aim looks pretty good (28 balls just to the right of the normal shortstop position). His distribution almost looks like that of a right-handed pull-hitter—except for those 52 bunts attempts!

Joey Gathright

Bats Left

Outfield Chart

Updated October 30, 2008
Last 135 flies and line drives

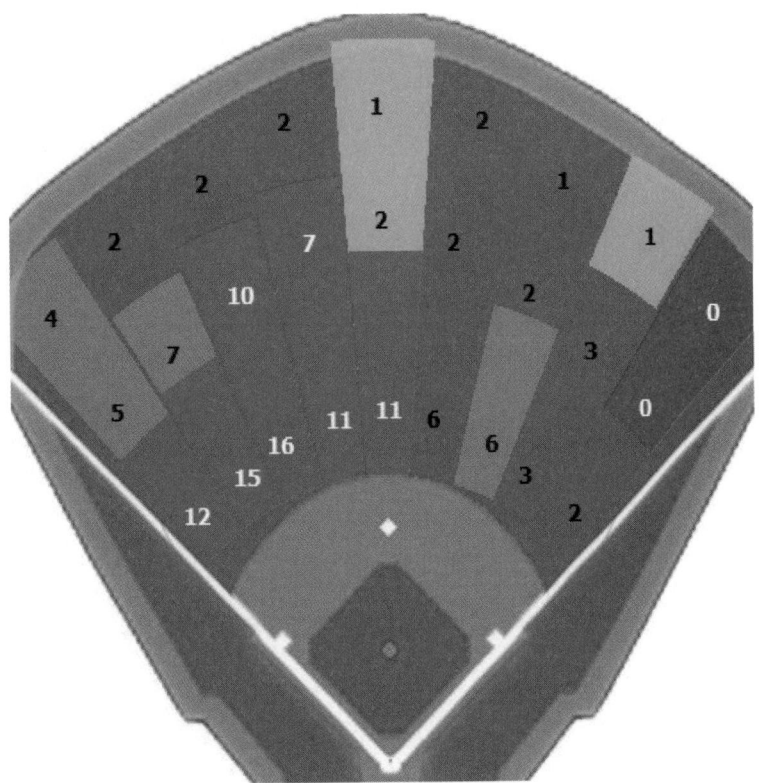

• 31% of last 250 were flies and line drives.

Joey's rather extreme left-facing distribution continues into the outfield. The left fielder should play very close to the line and very shallow. The center fielder should play in medium-shallow left center. The right fielder can take a nap.

Miguel Olivo

Bats Right

Outfield Chart

Updated October 30, 2008
Last 135 flies and line drives

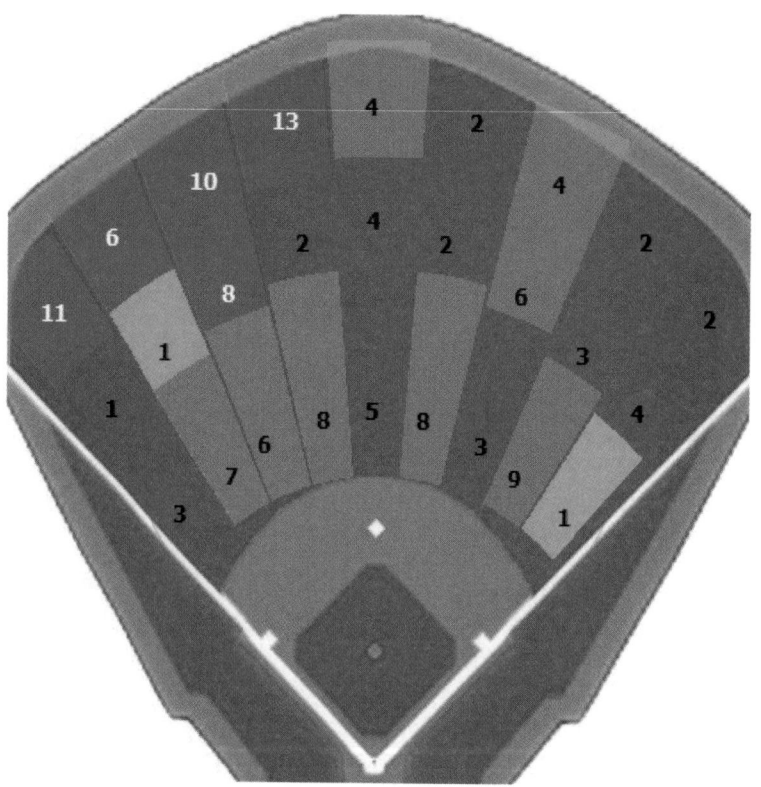

• 50% of last 250 were flies and line drives.

Miguel Olivo is an extreme pull hitter on balls hit in the air to the outfield. That's actually pretty rare. Play the left fielder deep towards the line, the center fielder deep in left-center, and the right-fielder at average depth in right-center (where the "6" is in the chart).

Jason Bay

Bats Right

Infield Chart

Updated October 30, 2008
Last 120 grounders and short liners

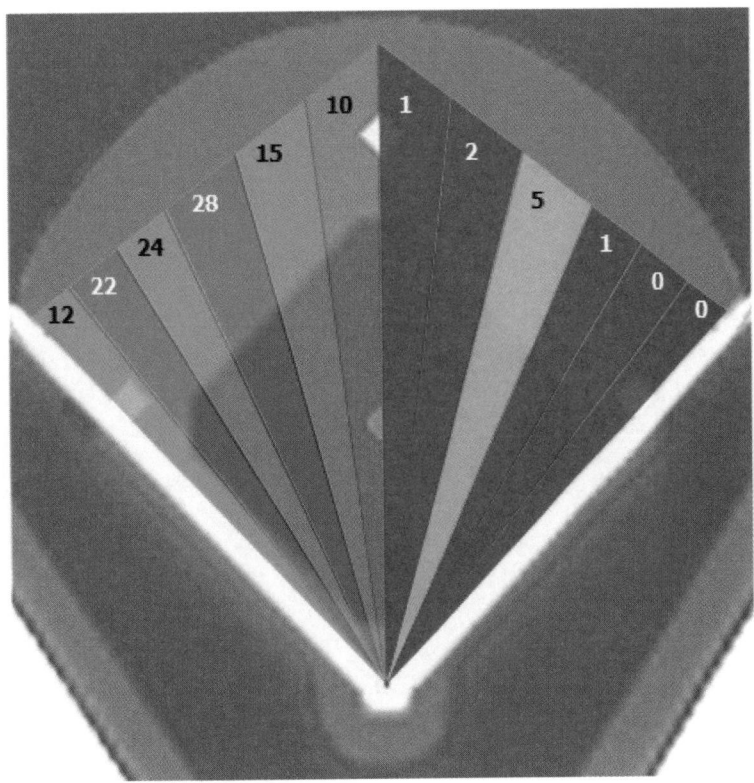

- Shift candidate! (93% left of 2B)
- 46% of last 250 were grounders and short liners.
- 0 bunt attempts in last 300 plate appearances.

As you can see, the right side of the infield doesn't have much to do against Bay. Here's the key question: How much shifting should take place on right-handed hitters? Right now, in baseball, you never see this. But if there ever was a guy for whom the infield should shift left, this is him. I would shift three guys left of second and play the first baseman as far off the line as possible that would allow him to easily return to first for a throw on a groundball to another infielder. On the next few pages are a few guys similar to Bay.

Garrett Atkins

Bats Right

Infield Chart

Updated October 30, 2008
Last 120 grounders and short liners

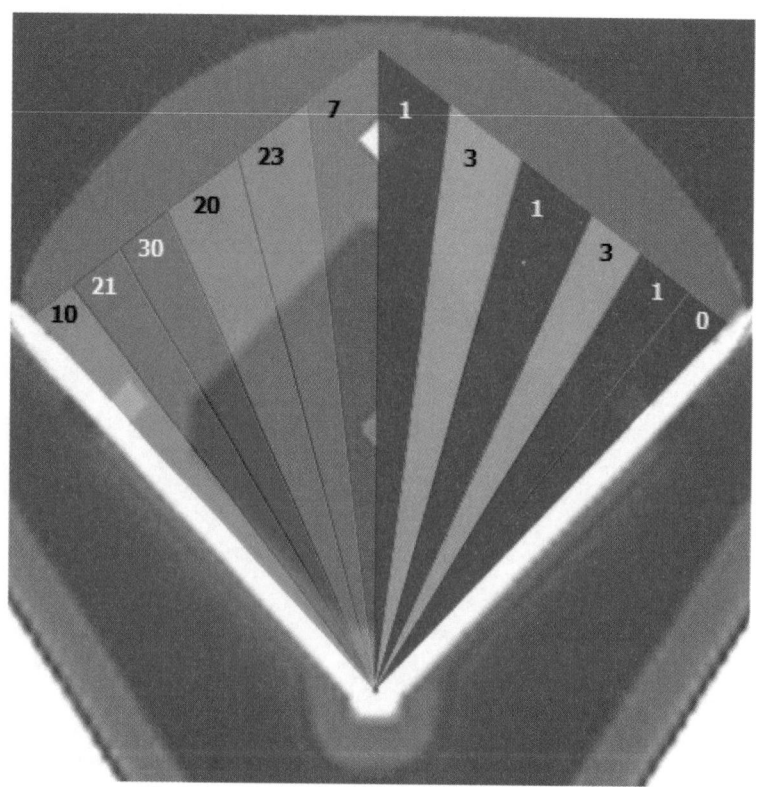

- Shift candidate! (93% left of 2B)

- 42% of last 250 were grounders and short liners.

- 0 bunt attempts in last 300 plate appearances.

Atkins is a lot like Bay.

Ben Francisco

Bats Right

Infield Chart

Updated October 30, 2008
Last 120 grounders and short liners

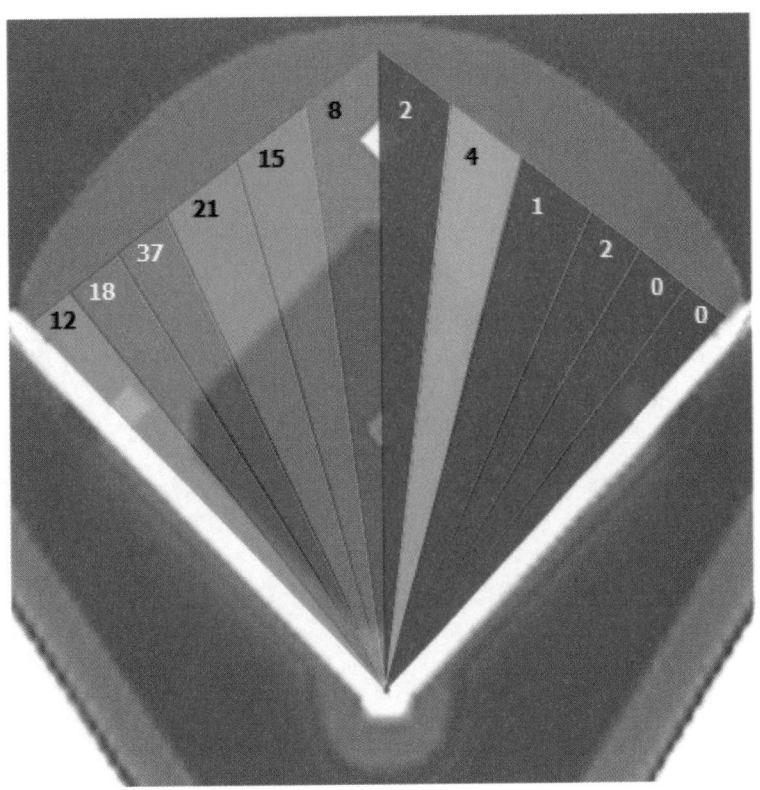

- Shift candidate! (93% left of 2B)

- 40% of last 250 were grounders and short liners.

- 5 bunt attempts in last 300 plate appearances.

So is Francisco.

Marcus Thames

Bats Right

Infield Chart

Updated October 30, 2008
Last 120 grounders and short liners

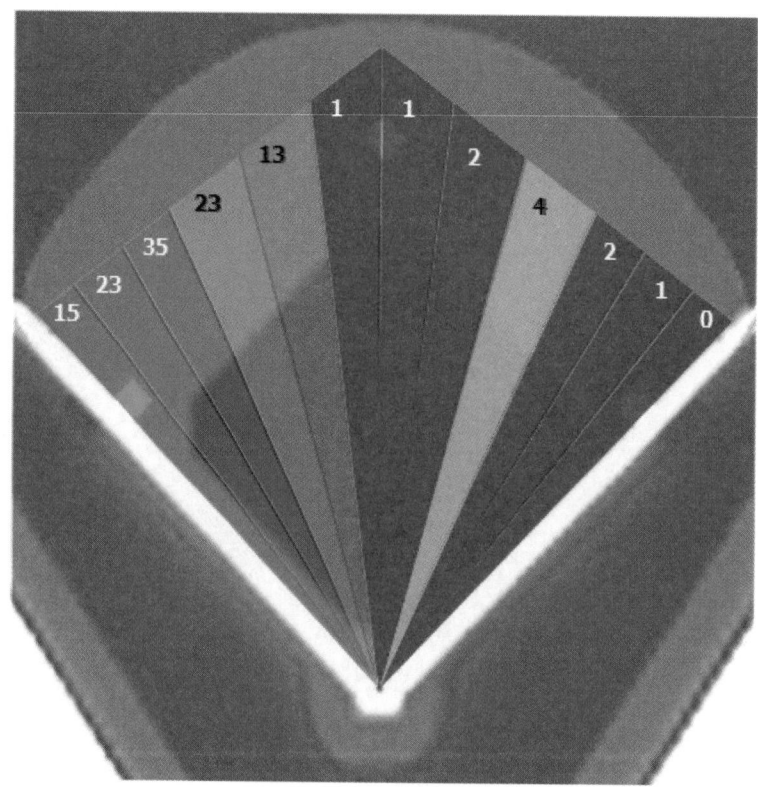

• Shift candidate! (92% left of 2B)

• 48% of last 250 were grounders and short liners.

• 0 bunt attempts in last 300 plate appearances.

And Thames.

Kevin Youkilis

Bats Right

Infield Chart

Updated October 30, 2008
Last 120 grounders and short liners

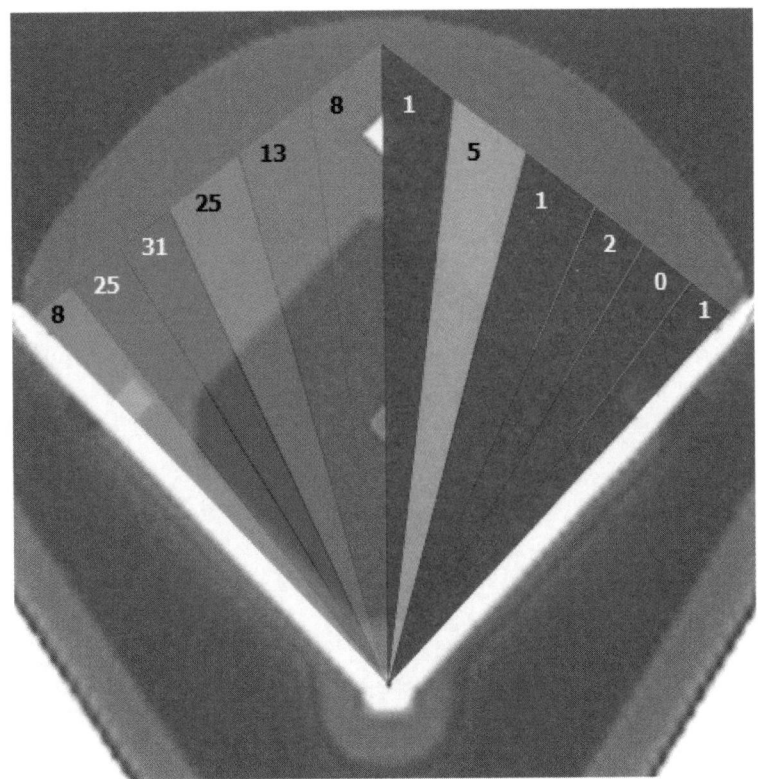

- Shift candidate! (92% left of 2B)

- 38% of last 250 were grounders and short liners.

- 0 bunt attempts in last 300 plate appearances.

For Youkilis—and the previous few—the first baseman has basically the same job as a Maytag repairman.

Norris Hopper

Bats Right

Infield Chart

Updated October 30, 2008
Last 120 grounders and short liners

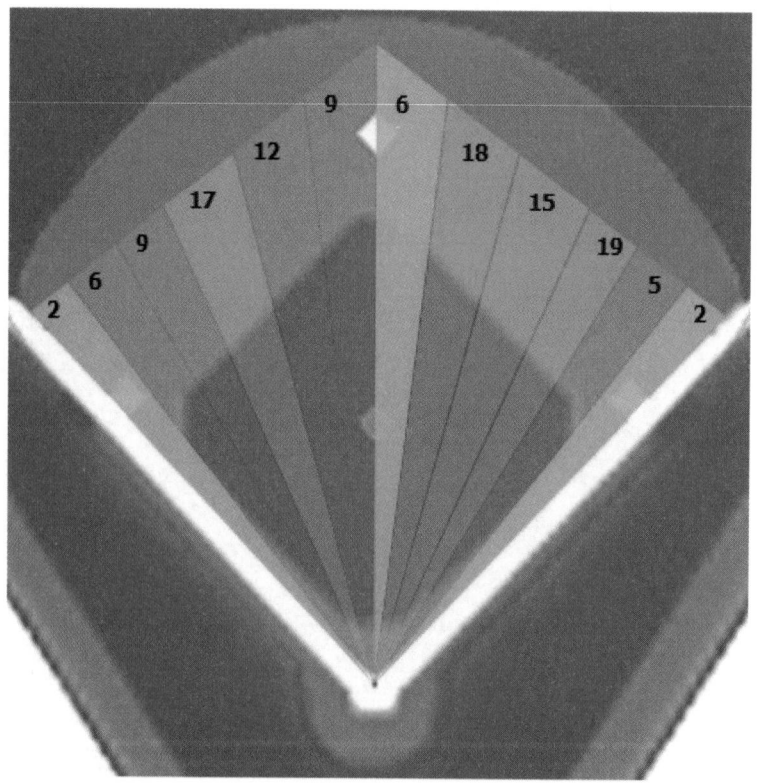

- 62% of last 250 were grounders and short liners.
- 32 bunt attempts in last 300 plate appearances.

Norris Hopper is the right-handed Joey Gathright. Most everything is hit the opposite way. Looking at his infield chart, he hits more grounders to the right than to the left side of the infield, but there is almost nothing you can do about it. The third baseman has to stay at home, and be ready for a bunt, given Hopper's tendency to bunt (32 bunt attempts in his last 300 PA). While a ton of grounders and short liners head over towards second, there's still plenty towards shortstop, and in fact, more towards the shortstop hole. The second baseman should be straight-away and the first baseman shaded towards second.

Norris Hopper

Bats Right

Outfield Chart

Updated October 30, 2008
Last 107 flies and line drives

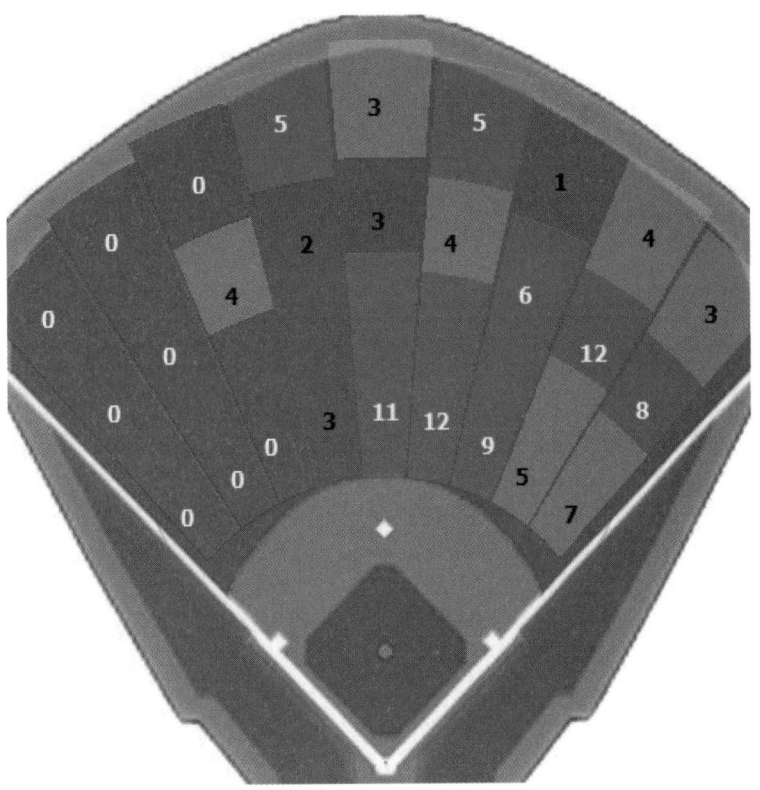

- 38% of last 250 were flies and line drives.

For Hopper—in the outfield—zero balls hit at or to the right of the left fielder. Amazing!

Derek Jeter

Bats Right

Outfield Chart

Updated October 30, 2008
Last 135 flies and line drives

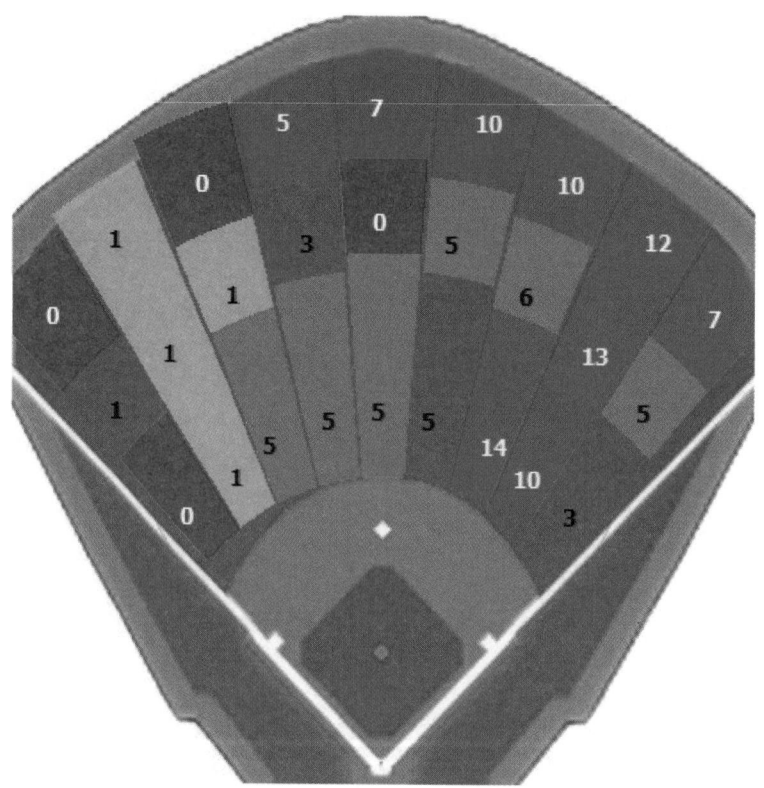

• 40% of last 250 were flies and line drives.

When he lifts the ball to the outfield, going the opposite way is standard operating procedure for Derek Jeter. The left fielder should be way off the line.

Delmon Young

Bats Right

Outfield Chart

Updated October 30, 2008
Last 135 flies and line drives

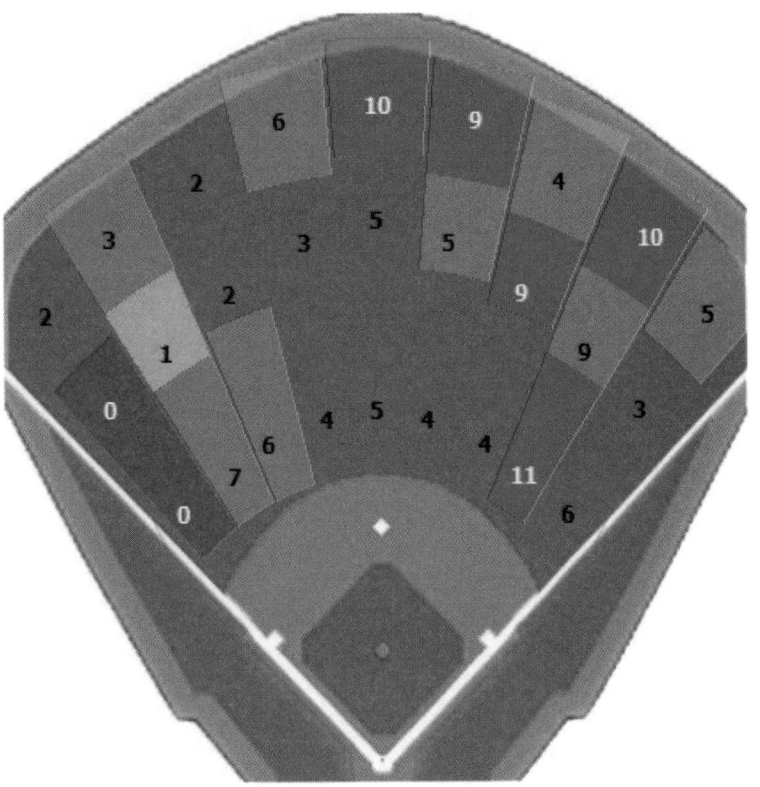

• 43% of last 250 were flies and line drives.

Hitting to the outfield, Delmon Young is somewhat similar to Jeter, but has his own tendencies. He hits with power the opposite way, but when he hits to left, it's generally shallow. Seems counter-intuitive, doesn't it? When he pulls the ball in the air, he hits it shallow (probably on a line). When he goes the opposite way, it's almost always deep.

Joe Mauer

Bats Left

Infield Chart

Updated October 30, 2008
Last 120 grounders and short liners

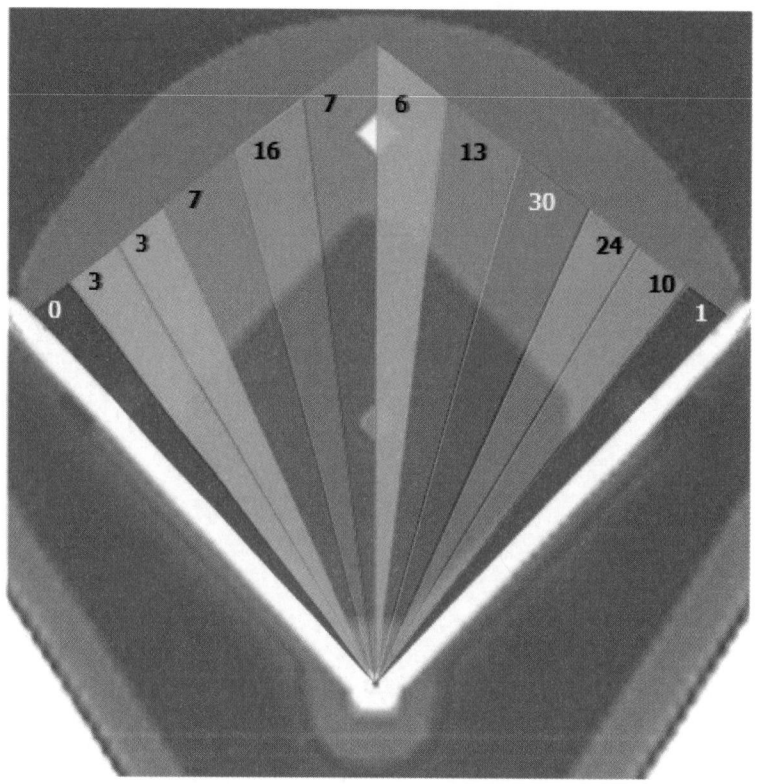

- 54% of last 250 were grounders and short liners.
- 1 bunt attempts in last 300 plate appearances.

Minnesota's still young (and probably still improving) catcher Joe Mauer hits the ball all over the infield with a small propensity to pull.

Joe Mauer

Bats Left

Outfield Chart

Updated October 30, 2008
Last 135 flies and line drives

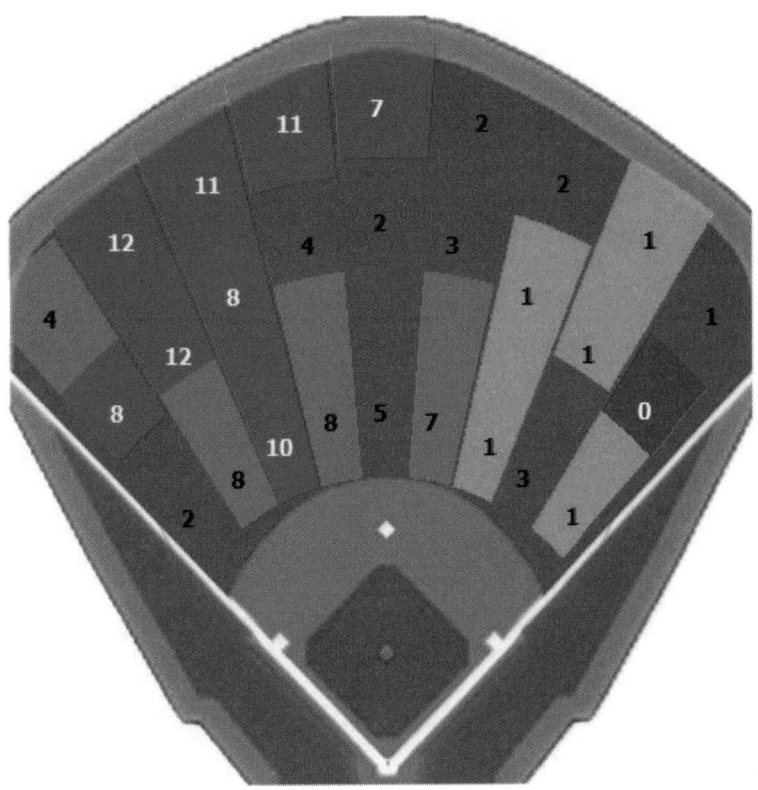

• 46% of last 250 were flies and line drives.

The outfield is a different story for the two-time batting champ. A total of 10 balls out of his last 135 flyballs and line drives to the outfield went to the nine sections of right field. If it weren't for groundball hits to right field that get through the infield, you could put the right fielder in left.

Jimmy Rollins

Switch Hitter When Batting Right

Infield Chart

Updated October 30, 2008
Last 120 grounders and short liners

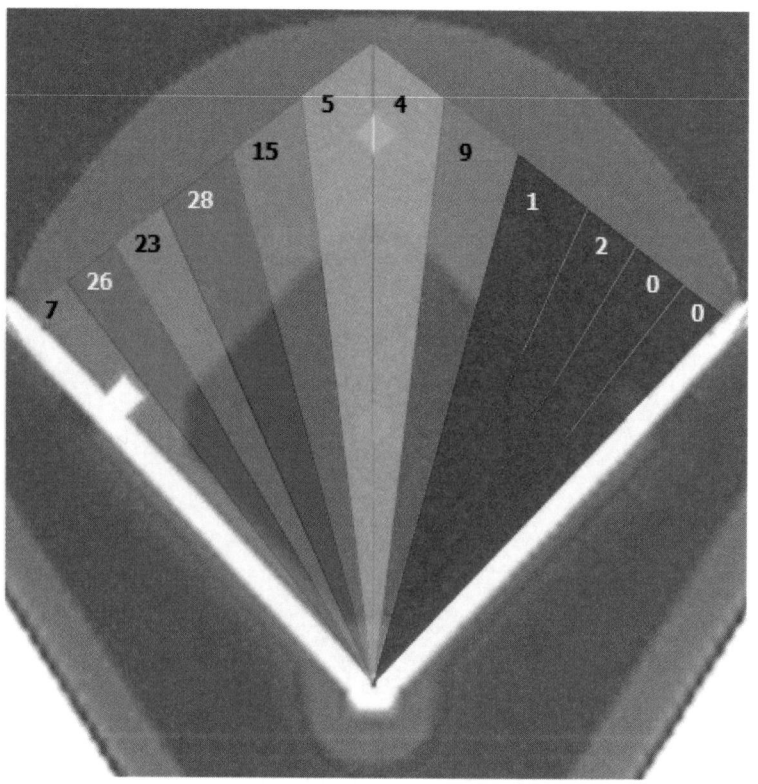

- 52% of last 250 were grounders and short liners.
- 5 bunt attempts in last 300 plate appearances.

Let's take a look at a switch-hitter. We'll use one of the best, Jimmy Rollins

Jimmy Rollins

Switch Hitter When Batting Left

Infield Chart

Updated October 30, 2008
Last 120 grounders and short liners

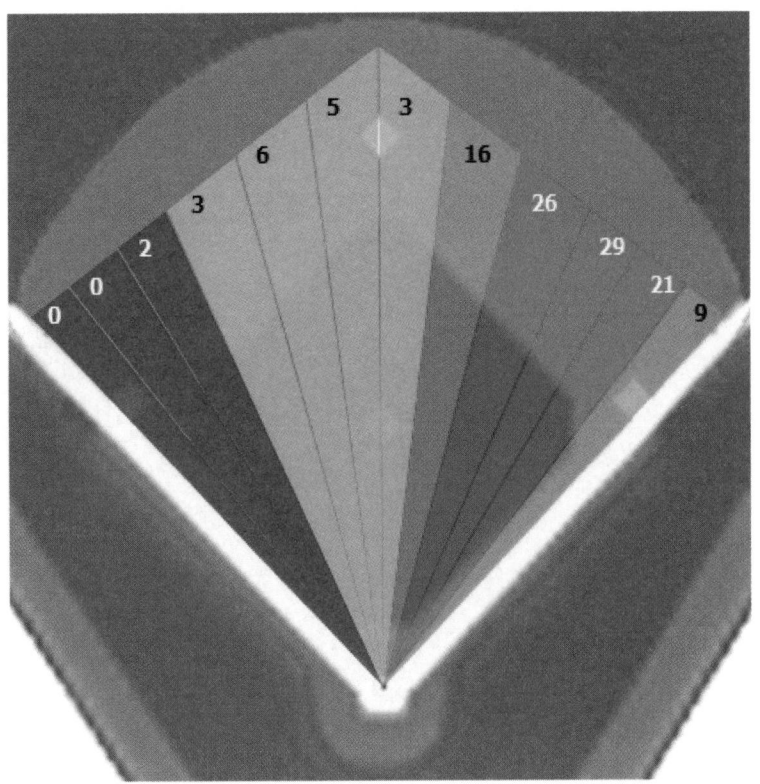

- Shift candidate! (87% right of 2B)
- 52% of last 250 were grounders and short liners.
- 5 bunt attempts in last 300 plate appearances.

No matter which way he bats, Rollins pulls the ball big time in the infield.

Jimmy Rollins

Switch Hitter When Batting Right

Outfield Chart

Updated October 30, 2008
Last 135 flies and line drives

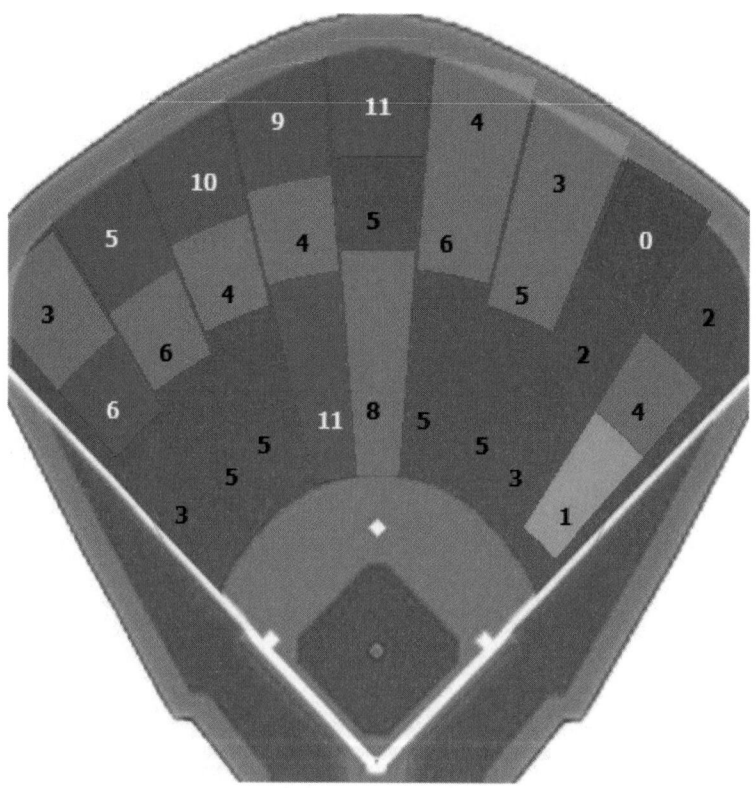

• 48% of last 250 were flies and line drives.

Batting righty Rollins hits deep and towards left-center, clearly showing a tendency to pull balls hit to the outfield.

Jimmy Rollins

Switch Hitter When Batting Left

Outfield Chart

Updated October 30, 2008
Last 135 flies and line drives

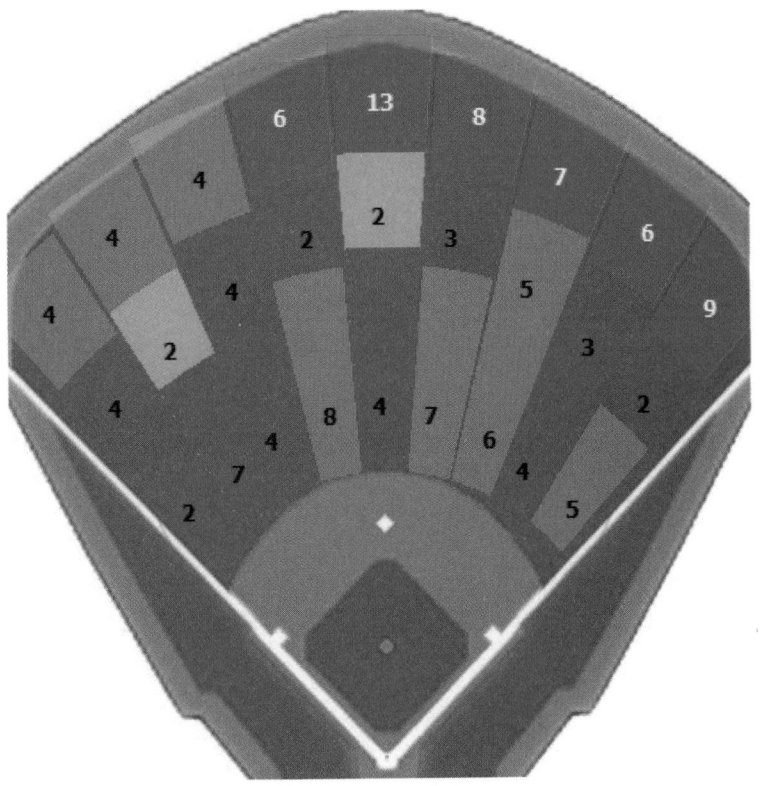

- 48% of last 250 were flies and line drives.

From the left side of the plate, Rollins uses the whole outfield, going deep frequently. Just a small tendency to pull.

Carlos Quentin

Bats Right

Outfield Chart

Updated October 30, 2008
Last 135 flies and line drives

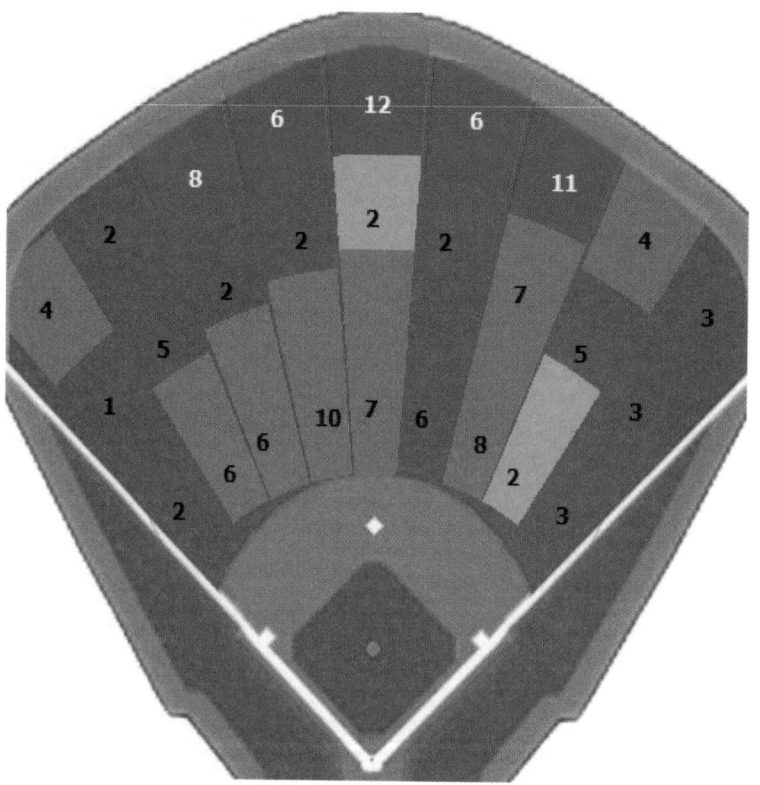

• 50% of last 250 were flies and line drives.

Carlos Quentin hits most of his outfield balls deep and to the middle of the field. Pinching both corner outfielders might generate defensively positive results.

What Makes Chase Utley So Good?

Before we talk a lot about Chase Utley, I want you to understand why Brandon Phillips won our Fielding Bible Award at second base in 2008. Go take a look at the player comment written by Bill James on page 273 and come back here when you're done.

Are you back yet? OK, good. So if Brandon Phillips is so good, why does Chase Utley have a plus/minus of +46 while Phillips "only" has +17 (or +21 if you only count groundballs)? On my Fielding Bible Award ballot I personally listed Utley first. In fact, Utley received more first place votes than Phillips, but Phillips was listed in one of the top three positions on all but one ballot while Utley had four voters who listed him from seventh to tenth place.

Most of the voters probably agree, however, that Phillips is more athletically talented. It shows up when you watch them on the field, and it shows up in our Misplays/Good Plays system. Phillips had more Good Plays in fewer chances than Utley (66 to 57) and fewer Defensive Misplays plus Errors by far (34 for Phillips vs. 48 for Utley). But, when I was voting, I looked at that plus/minus differential and couldn't justify voting for anyone but Utley. Let's take a closer look at how Utley's and Phillips' plus/minus numbers break down.

Left . . . Left . . . Left, Right, Left

Chase Utley's +46 means that if an average second baseman had all the same batted balls that Utley had, he'd have made 46 fewer plays. Looking at Utley's profile in the 2B Register in this book, we know he was +32 to his left, +6 straight on, and +8 to his right. He made 46 extra plays but he made four extra plays to his left for every one extra play to his right. The first thought that comes to mind is that Utley reacts better to his left. Not just better, amazingly better. But let's look further.

In working with this information over the years, one thing we've found out is that hitters generally pull balls hit on the infield. More specifically, when we isolate ground balls and catchable short liners on the infield we find that hitters pull the ball over 70% of the time. For flyballs, it's a different story, with less than half (45%)

being pulled. But we're dealing with infielders here, and with that pull ratio, shifting positions in the infield based on the handedness of the batter makes sense and is done all the time. As a result, we decided to analyze plus/minus based on bat side of the hitter.

Before we proceed, let me mention this. When we're measuring batted balls for second basemen and we're calling it "To His Left", "Straight On", and "To His Right", what we really mean is relative to the normal location for the second baseman. We looked at where all fieldable (by the second baseman) batted balls are hit and, in essence, broke it into thirds. But it is possible that a player could position himself in the area called "To His Left" and actually field the play as a ball hit right to him, or even slightly to his right.

Let's look at both Utley and Phillips. We'll ignore batted balls that are Straight On—these are the ones that are to the center of the second base position. When right-handed batters are at the plate, we find that there are about three times as many balls hit "To His Right" for both players.

Batted Balls Hit by Right-Handed Batters

In the Field	To His Left	To His Right
Utley	42	112
Phillips	28	90

How about with left-handed batters at the plate? Not surprisingly, it goes the other way. For Phillips there were twice as many balls To His Left, and for Utley about two-and-a-half times as many.

Batted Balls Hit by Left-Handed Batters

In the Field	To His Left	To His Right
Utley	185	68
Phillips	141	71

Based on this information, it's clear what needs to be done. Positioning. And it is done. Not just by Utley and Phillips, but by nearly every second baseman in baseball. However, what I'm trying to get at here is the extent. How much positioning is done? How much should be done?

Let's go deeper. Both Utley and Phillips have excellent plus/minus scores, but Utley is still higher. Can we see anything about positioning in the plus/minus numbers. Let's add plus/minus to the two charts we just did and put them side by side.

Batted Balls

In the Field	Right-Handed Batters		Left-Handed Batters	
	Left	Right	Left	Right
Utley	42	112	185	68
Phillips	28	90	141	71

Plus/Minus

In the Field	Right-Handed Batters		Left-Handed Batters	
	Left	Right	Left	Right
Utley	-6	+22	+37	-13
Phillips	-7	+18	+7	-2

What are these charts showing us? Against right-handed batters, Utley and Phillips look about the same. They both have minus plus/minus scores to their left. But their positive scores to their right more than make up for the difference. Both players appear to be shifting well over to the right when a right-handed batter is up. They have a harder time getting to the balls to their left, but there are fewer of those. They more than make up for the missed plays by making more plays on the greater number of balls to their right.

Now the Left-Handed Batters side of the chart. It's the whole key to Chase Utley. What appears to be clear from this chart is that both players are shifting left against left-handed batters, but Utley is going further. Phillips is missing plays to his right, but gets a few extra to his left. Utley is missing even more plays to his right, but is really making up for them on plays to his left. To the tune of +37, 30 more extra plays than even Brandon Phillips is making. That's huge.

So what makes Utley so good? Simple answer: Positioning. And more specifically, positioning against left-handed batters.

Now keep in mind that not all left-handed batters are created equal. If you look at the section on the Baseball Info Solutions Defensive Positioning System you'll see that. Utley has to vary his positioning by batter, even against different lefties, to maximize his performance. But, in general, the key appears to be that he is moving

closer to first base against lefties than virtually any other second baseman in baseball. BIS Video Scouts, who watch every game and chart nearly everything you can imagine, have said the same thing. Utley has a strong tendency to position himself towards hitters' pull side.

Some Players Besides Utley and Phillips

Another player who looks like a radical shifter at second base is Jose Lopez. We'll show his total positioning plus/minus:

Jose Lopez

	Left	Straight On	Right	Total
LHB	+20	-1	-17	+2
RHB	-11	+2	+9	-1
Total	+10	+1	-9	+2

Similar to Utley, Lopez is much better going to the pull side of the hitter. He's just not as good as Utley (no one is), with a plus/minus of +2 overall, about average.

Not all players are as straightforward as Utley or Lopez. Let's move across the second base bag and look at Yunel Escobar, a +22 shortstop:

Yunel Escobar

	Left	Straight On	Right	Total
LHB	+21	+1	-2	+20
RHB	-2	+2	+1	+2
Total	+19	+3	0	+22

It looks like the same story for Escobar—he's much better to his left against lefties. However, we might expect a similar strength to his right vs. RHB, but it's just not there. Somehow, Escobar was +20 against lefties and +2 against righties. Perhaps part of the problem is his positioning against right-handed hitters; maybe he positions much better against lefties. Or maybe he has a bizarre phobia of right-handed hitters.

Cesar Izturis appears to be one of the more radical-shifting shortstops, and just as good as Escobar (+22 overall):

Cesar Izturis

	Left	Straight On	Right	Total
LHB	+10	+2	-3	+9
RHB	-11	+2	+21	+13
Total	-1	+4	+18	+22

Like with Utley and Lopez (but not Escobar), notice how the shift is balanced Left/Right. Izturis is +10 to his left against lefties, but that drops to -11 vs. RHBs. The 21 play difference is opposite and nearly equal on the other side: he picks up a 24 play difference to his right between LHB and RHB. For Escobar, the differences were 23 and 3.

Escobar and Izturis were the strongest defensive shortstops in the Plus/Minus System on groundballs alone, so let's take a look at the other end of the spectrum, Yuniesky Betancourt:

Yuniesky Betancourt

	Left	Straight On	Right	Total
LHB	-4	-2	-1	-6
RHB	-17	-5	+8	-15
Total	-21	-7	+7	-21

The numbers are lower across the board, but Betancourt has fewer problems to his left against LHB than against RHB, and is actually above average to his right against righties.

The vast majority of infielders, both good and bad, are stronger to the hitter's pull side. But there are guys who fly in the face of convention. Take Adrian Beltre, the Fielding Bible Award winner at third base:

Adrian Beltre

	Left	Straight On	Right	Total
LHB	+3	+2	-1	+4
RHB	+17	+2	+7	+26
Total	+21	+3	+6	+30

There's no pattern here, other than the fact that Beltre seemed to handle right-handed batters stronger in both directions. But that's likely to be simply a matter of a lot more plays to handle with righties batting.

Plus/minus totals for first basemen and third basemen are the enhanced plus/minus numbers, which take into account extra-base hits.

Let's round out the infield with one of the worst defenders for all of 2008, Mike Jacobs:

Mike Jacobs

	Left	Straight On	Right	Total
LHB	-3	-5	-4	-12
RHB	-3	-4	-6	-13
Total	-6	-9	-11	-26

Jacobs was consistently bad no matter how you slice it. As you might expect, first basemen exhibit much smaller shift splits than other infield positions. Tethered to first base, they are not as free to shift far off the first base line. This makes them much less interesting to look at from this standpoint.

The Big Picture

So is it better for an infielder to shift drastically based on the handedness of the hitter? Rather than cherry-picking more examples, let's look at everyone.

Bear with me on the math here. We're going to come up with a "left shift" score to determine how much shifting left each player is doing, and a "right shift" score to see how much he is shifting right. A player's "left shift" score is measured by subtracting his plus/minus on balls to his left against right-handed hitters from his score to his left against lefties. For Chase Utley, this is 37 – (-6) = 43. His "right shift" is similar, subtract his plus/minus to his right against righties from his plus/minus to his right against lefties (Utley: 22 – (-13) = 35). The sum of these two is his Total Shift Score (Utley: 43 + 35 = 78, by far the highest in the majors).

Next, we'll limit our study to the regulars by taking the top 35 players at each position based on innings played. We split the players into three groups: biggest shifters, average shifters, and smallest shifters. Here is the combined plus/minus for each group:

Plus/Minus by Shift Group	1B	2B	SS	3B
12 Largest Shifters	+19	+87	+52	-41
11 Average Shifters	+4	+8	+29	+40
12 Smallest Shifters	-35	-57	-36	+34

Except for third base, the biggest shifters were the best fielders, and the smallest shifters were the worst. Third base is the exact opposite; in fact, three excellent defensive third basemen actually posted negative "shift scores": Joe Crede, Ryan Zimmerman, and Adrian Beltre.

(Interesting side note: since we are looking at 35 regulars at each position, the defensive replacements and backups are excluded. At second base, third base, and shortstop, the regulars posted an aggregate positive plus/minus score, indicating that the backups bring down the quality of fielding at each position. The opposite is true at first base, where poor defense is tolerable if the fielder's offense can adequately compensate.)

Aside from the three fielders at third base (who combine for a +51 plus/minus), we observe a general trend: the group of infielders with the largest LHB/RHB differences had a higher plus/minus score than the group that shifted the least. However, it is difficult to determine exactly how shifting one way or the other would benefit or hurt a specific player's defense. We *cannot* currently determine how a certain player would rate if he played a couple more steps to his left or right.

Caveats aside, the results are intriguing. The topic merits further study in the near future. For related discussion on this topic, check out the charts in the Defensive Positioning article on page 121.

McLouth vs. Gomez

Nate McLouth, the 35th ranked player out of 35 ranked center fielders throughout baseball in plus/minus, wins a Gold Glove. Carlos Gomez, the number one ranked center fielder, doesn't. What's up with that?

Let me start by sharing my Stat of the Week that I wrote right after the Gold Gloves were announced in November:

What about Nate McLouth's Gold Glove?

November 14, 2008

Well, I thought he was the worst outfielder in baseball.

Nate McLouth had a -40 plus/minus in center field. That means this:

- *Take every ball hit in the air anywhere in the vicinity of Nate McLouth when he played center field*
- *Replace McLouth with an average center fielder*
- *The average center fielder would have caught 20 more of them than McLouth did, allowing a total of 40 fewer bases taken on those 20 caught balls*

McLouth's -40 was the worst plus/minus figure for any center fielder in baseball last year. Not only that, it was the worst plus/minus figure for any outfielder in baseball. Not only that, it was the worst plus/minus figure for any player in baseball.

Is he that bad? No, absolutely not. The fact that there are a significant number of managers and coaches that think he's good definitely means something. There are aspects to being a good defensive outfielder that come into play other than catching balls hit in the air. They are lesser aspects, but important ones. I will get into more depth on these in The Fielding Bible—Volume II *coming out in February of 2009. For example, we are planning a video review of all McLouth's key fielding plays. But let me touch on a couple of things here.*

First, his throwing. While he only had two baserunner kills last year (direct throws to a base or home plate to nab a baserunner), he was the seventh best center fielder in preventing runners from taking an extra base on singles and doubles hit to centerfield.

Second, his Good Plays and Defensive Misplays. The Video Scouts at Baseball Info Solutions have 27 categories of Good Plays and 55 categories of Defensive Misplays. They review every play and decide if a play fits one of those categories. It sounds somewhat subjective, but because of the strict definitions of the categories, it actually becomes quite objective. For example, here's the definition of one of the 55 Defensive Misplays:

"Defensive Misplay Number 38, Failing to Anticipate the Wall: Outfielder goes to the outfield wall, allowing a ball to bounce over his head back toward the infield, allowing a runner or runners to take bases which they might not have been able to take had the fielder turned and played the ball off the wall."

It turns out that this happened to McLouth six times last year, tied for the most in baseball with right fielder Bobby Abreu, and more often than any other center fielder (Aaron Rowand and B.J. Upton were second in CF with five). This is another weakness for McLouth.

Overall, adding the six wall-difficulty plays to his other misplays, McLouth had a total of 24 defensive misplays and one error last season. That total of 25 is the ninth highest among all center fielders on the 30 teams last year. So, despite his low error total, McLouth is more prone to making poor plays in center field than the majority of other center fielders in baseball.

However, his good plays more than make up for the 25 misplays and errors. He had 31 good plays, good for third place among center fielders behind Carlos Gomez of the Twins (33) and B.J. Upton of the Rays (32). This is clearly what managers and coaches who vote for the Gold Gloves were seeing.

Net Plays are good plays minus defensive misplays and errors. McLouth had six more good plays than defensive misplays and errors, or six Net Plays. That was the seventh highest total in baseball among center fielders. Not bad.

All in all, I no longer think of McLouth as the worst center fielder in baseball. It means something that at least some of the managers and coaches think highly of him. And we see that two areas of his defense are above average: his ability to prevent baserunners from advancing on hits and his ability to make a play above and beyond the ordinary. But we also see that, despite this low error total, he has more than his share of defensive misplays. And the most important aspect of playing outfield defense is covering ground, and McLouth struggles here big time.

Here are some things we've learned since I wrote this.

Misplays, Good Plays, and Arms

In the Stat of the Week article, I misspoke. I said that McLouth is "more prone to making poor plays in center field than the majority of other center fielders in baseball." Not true. In fact, the opposite is true. Yes, McLouth's total of 25 misplays plus errors is the ninth highest among center fielders. But when you factor in opportunities (Touches), he has an above-average percentage.

McLouth had 777 touches in 2008. "Touches" are an estimate of the number of times a player touched the ball, whether they are balls hit to him in the air or on the ground. Taking all center fielders in baseball, the average rate of misplays plus errors is 3.7 per 100 touches. McLouth had 3.2 misplays/errors per 100 touches.

Gomez, young player that he is, was not as good. Gomez had the most touches of any center fielder in baseball (822), but he had 4.7 misplays/errors per 100 touches.

Based on McLouth's 777 touches and the misplay/error rates for each player, McLouth made about 12 fewer misplays/errors than Gomez.

On Good Plays, McLouth made 4.0 Good Plays per 100 touches compared to a league average of 3.4. Gomez had the most Good Plays among center fielders (33), but his average was the same as McLouth's at 4.0.

Comparing throwing arms, our numbers are also showing McLouth to be one run better than Gomez. In the Outfielder Arm chapter we show Nate McLouth as having saved two runs for Pittsburgh based on his throwing arm, while Gomez saved the Twins a run.

Video Review

The Baseball Info Solutions Video Scouts put together a DVD of 50 plays from 2008 for Nate McLouth. They had the 25 plays that most affected his plus/minus number in a positive direction, and the 25 plays that most affect his plus/minus negatively. First, we reviewed these 50 plays, plus about 600 other plays from around baseball for accuracy of coding. We do this Play Review every year to ensure the integrity of our data. As a result, McLouth's -40 "improved" to -37. Some corrections on his plays and some corrections on plays by other center fielders led to this change. Nevertheless, McLouth's plus/minus score remains the worst in all of baseball (tied with Brad Hawpe's -37).

What else did we learn from the video? Two things stood out:

- In the sample of 25 plays, McLouth had a lot of very nice plays. Good Plays, as we call them in our Misplay/Good Play system. Some Very Good Plays. Even some Excellent Plays. You can see why he impressed Gold Glove voters.

- On the other hand, a lot of balls went over his head. At first glance, it seems that many of these are just balls that he shouldn't be expected to handle. But upon further review. . . .

Batted Ball Charts

This is what led us to want to compare McLouth to Gomez. What about those balls hit over McLouth's head? Is Gomez getting to some of those? Are there other balls that Gomez is getting to that McLouth isn't? With the help of Baseball Info Solutions R&D staffer Ben Jedlovec, we put together batted ball charts for Gomez and McLouth. Here, I'll show them to you first and then explain them:

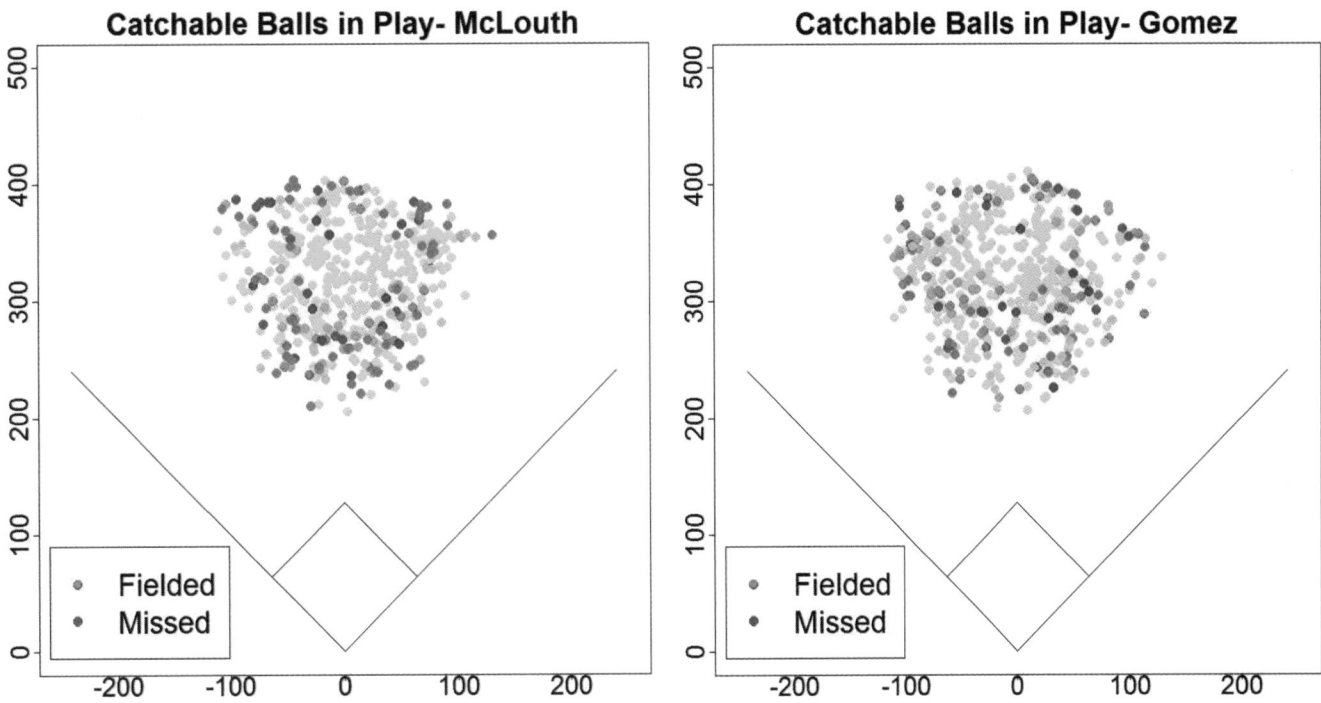

No, it's not an eye test. It's not just random dots. And you won't go blind if you stare at it too long, but it might flip between a picture of an old lady and a picture of young girl if you do. What we have here is the location of every fieldable ball that was hit to Gomez and McLouth last year. By fieldable, we mean each ball is hit to a location with the same velocity and hit type where at least one center fielder in baseball caught it in 2008. The red dots are balls that were caught and the blue dots are balls that dropped in. We took that one step further. If a ball was a difficult catch (had a high plus/ minus value), we colored the dot dark red. Medium red if it was average difficulty. If the ball was a relatively easy catch (caught by a high percentage of center fielders), but dropped in, we colored the dot dark blue. The balls that dropped in but were missed by most (but not all) other center fielders, we colored in light blue. This was designed to help bring out patterns more visually.

At first glance you can see that there is more blue in McLouth's charts. If you look closer, a lot of it appears to be in the upper left and upper right parts of the charts. That's deep center field towards the gaps. Those same areas on Gomez's charts are more red.

Based on this we decided to break the batted balls down into three areas: Deep, Medium and Shallow. Here are the same charts except that we're isolating the batted balls by depth.

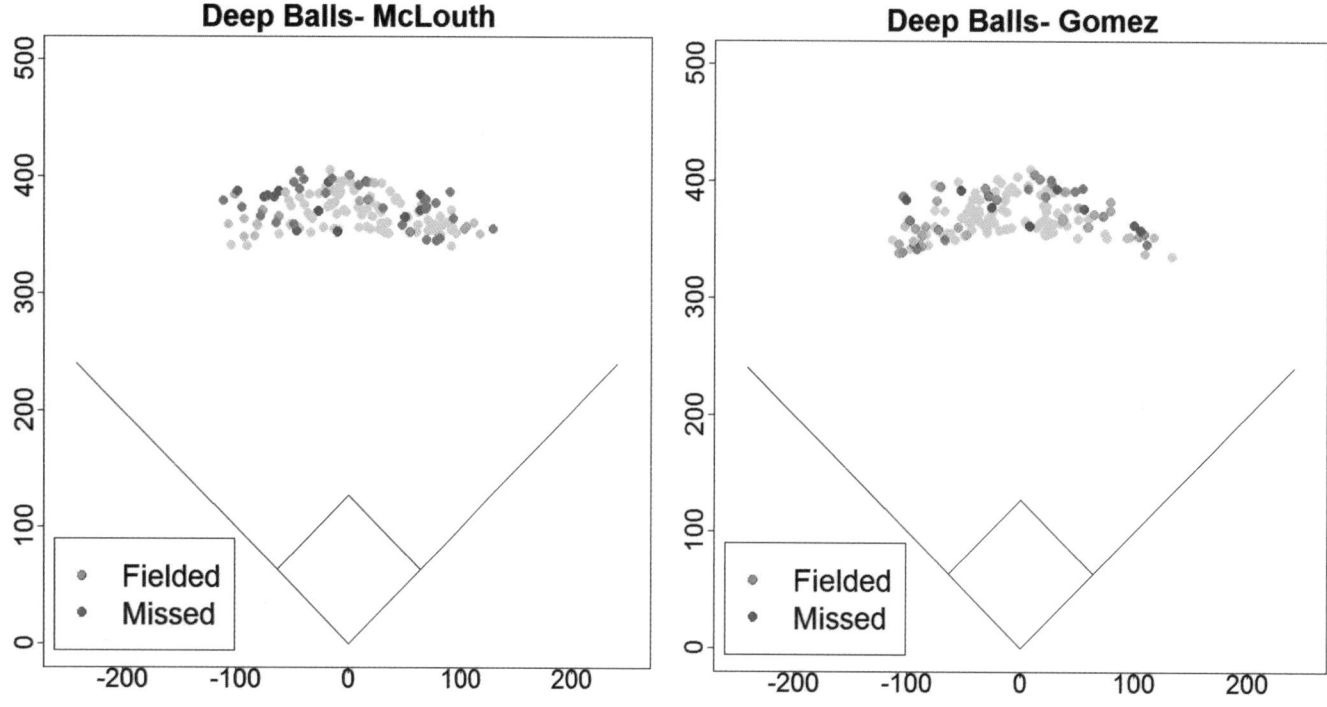

These are batted balls that travel at least 350 feet. The pattern becomes more clear. A lot more blue, a lot more missed balls, on McLouth's charts.

How about medium deep balls, between 300 and 350 feet?

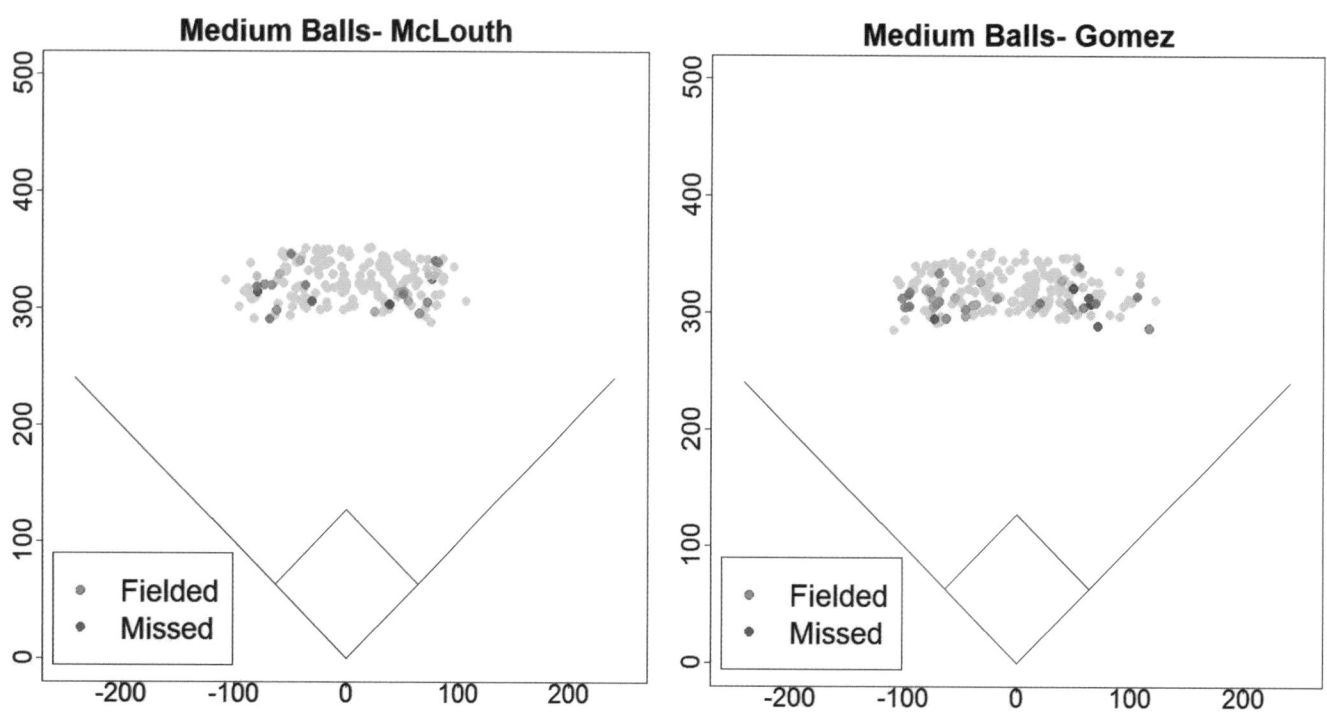

They don't look all that different. Am I seeing the area of red fielded balls on the Gomez chart to be a bit wider than McLouth's? Maybe. Let's just call it even for now.

Now shallow balls, under 300 feet.

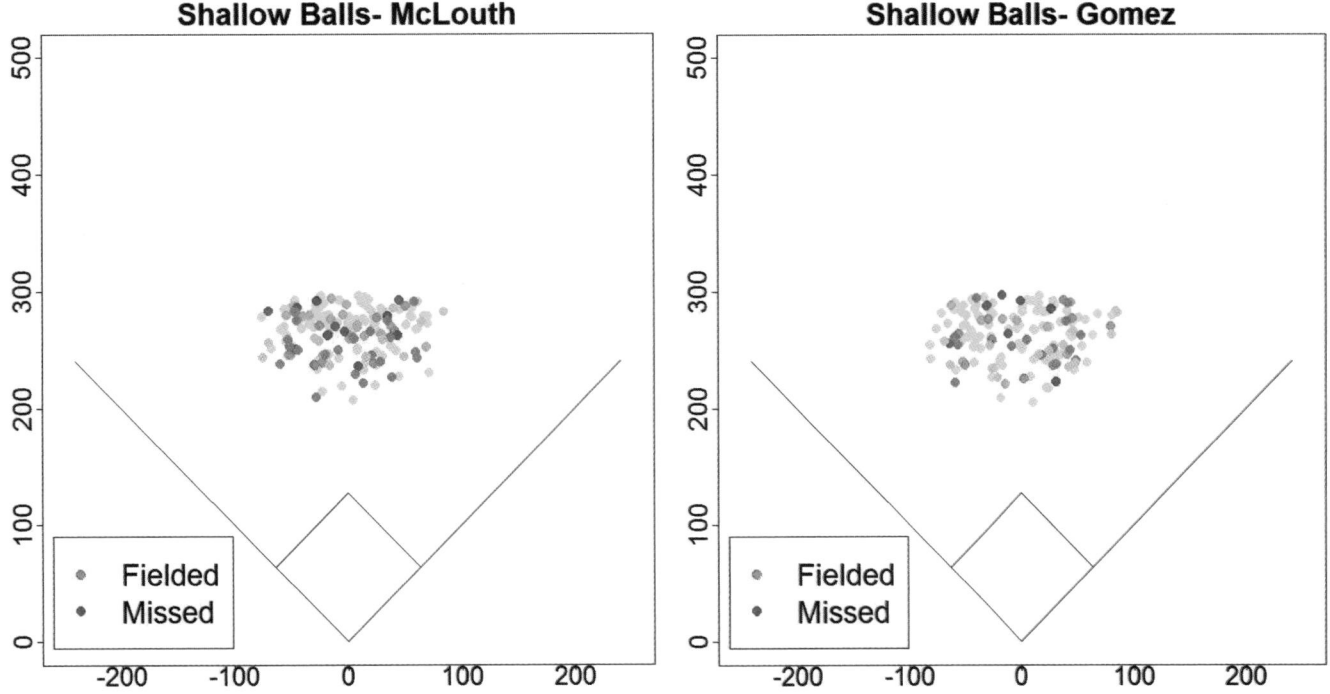

More blue on McLouth's chart. But not as pronounced as the deep outfield.

Looking at these charts led us to do further research on the depth of batted balls. In the infield, going all the way back to the first *Fielding Bible,* we looked at how plus/minus varies for each player as balls are hit to the left, straight on, or to the right of the normal location for that position.

Shallow, Medium, and Deep

The results are pretty dramatic. Here are the plus/minus figures for McLouth and Gomez broken down by depth of batted ball:

	Shallow	Medium	Deep	Total
McLouth	-5	+4	-36	-37
Gomez	-2	+8	+23	+29

Looking at balls that are hit shallow and medium, Gomez is slightly better than McLouth on each. Three plays on shallow hit balls, four on medium ones. It's the balls that are hit deep: There is a difference of 59 plus/minus points. (It's not actually plays on these deeply hit balls. The 59 difference also takes into account the extra bases that batters took on balls that were missed by McLouth).

Keep in mind that the batted ball eye-chart and the plus/minus figures by depth are measuring the same thing. We should see similar results. But it helps to confirm visually what the numbers are telling us. You can see the missed balls on the chart, and they are reflected in the numbers.

So that's the key. McLouth is having trouble on balls that are hit deep. Is it positioning? Is it difficulty getting a break on a ball hit over his head? Is it speed? Part of it is probably the Pittsburgh pitching staff. It looks like McLouth had a few more of the harder-to-field chances. We actually have one clue. McLouth doesn't have a lot of Misplays relative to his Touches, but there is one group of Misplays that he has more of than any other outfielder in baseball—Fences and Walls. Does he have some type of fear of the wall? He shared this problem with two other outfielders, Bobby Abreu and Brad Hawpe, both poor outfielders. I can't imagine it's a conscious thought. I'm sure they're not thinking, "I'm going to stay away from that deadly wall." But whatever it is, McLouth is not making those deep plays. I'm betting on simple positioning as the cause. Playing shallow in center field has been something that some of the best center fielders in the history of baseball have been known for. Maybe McLouth feels he can make more plays overall by playing shallow. The key problem is that when you miss a ball that's shallow, it's a single. When you miss a deep one, it's extra bases.

Defensive Runs Saved

Let's summarize using the Runs Saved numbers we've developed throughout this book.

Defensive Runs Saved

	Throwing	Plus/ Minus	Total
McLouth	2	-21	-19
Gomez	1	16	17
Difference			36 runs

We haven't yet measured the run value of Good Plays and Misplays. Gomez and McLouth had the same rate of Good Plays, but McLouth had 12 fewer Misplays and Errors after adjusting for opportunities. At the most, this might be worth 8 or 9 runs. That's probably a very high end estimate—a lot of these misplays/errors are already counted in the plus/minus system. But we'll be very conservative. That gives Gomez almost a 30-run advantage over McLouth defensively. Using the rule of thumb that 10 runs is worth about one victory, that's three wins better for a team with Gomez in center field rather than with McLouth.

Shallow, Medium, and Deep

It's clear from the McLouth/Gomez comparison in the previous article that some players are well above average on deep balls and others are well below average. Let's take a look at some other outfielders with interesting patterns by depth, starting with a regular on highlight reels a decade ago:

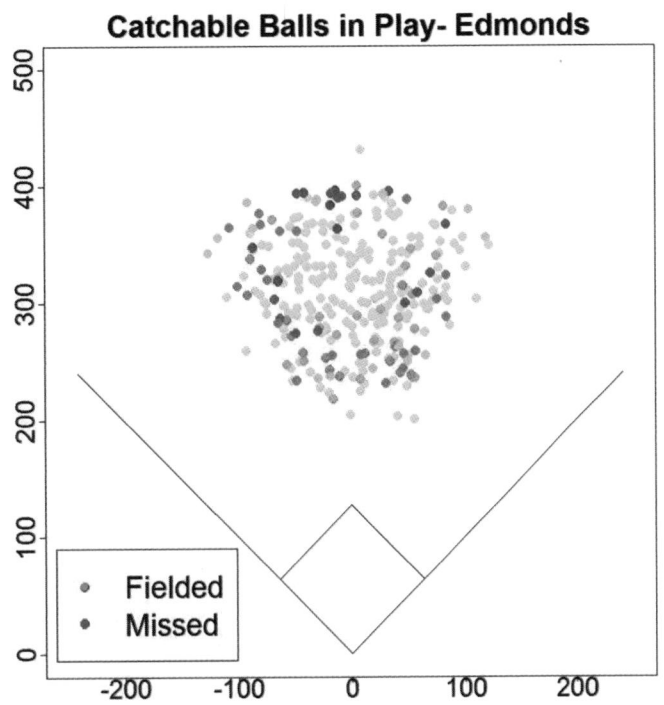

Back in the day, Jim Edmonds could probably afford to play shallow because he could get to most everything over his head. But in 2008, we can see from the chart that he missed a lot of balls behind him. There are many dark blue dots (balls that "should" have been caught) in the deeper parts of center field, and some dark red ones (difficult balls that "were" caught) very shallow, where center fielders don't normally cover.

Edmonds 2008

	Basic Plus/Minus	Enhanced Plus/Minus	Runs Saved
Deep	-10	-21	-12
Medium	-3	-8	-4
Shallow	+6	+4	2
Total	**-7**	**-25**	**-14**

It appears that Edmonds has not only lost a couple steps with age, but he hasn't adjusted his positioning, scoring only two runs saved on shallow balls and -12 runs on deep balls in 2008.

But is playing shallow a good thing? Here's how Edmonds' positioning helped or hurt his team over the past six seasons:

Edmonds 2003-2008

	Basic Plus/Minus	Enhanced Plus/Minus	Runs Saved
Deep	-50	-97	-54
Medium	-7	-21	-12
Shallow	+56	+59	33
Total	**-1**	**-58**	**-32**

Edmonds is a healthy 56 plays above average on shallow balls, good for 33 saved runs. While he has been 50 plays below average on deep balls, he still has about an average plus/minus score (-1). When we look at the enhanced plus/minus and the corresponding runs saved, we see that his -50 plays deep came out to a -97 enhanced plus/minus number (meaning 97 bases taken on those 50 plays), or a full 54 runs below average. His excellence on shallow balls did not compensate for his deep deficiency, and Edmonds actually cost his team 32 runs.

For corner outfielders, we change our deep/medium/shallow ranges. We call anything above 310 feet from home plate a deep ball and anything below 270 feet a shallow ball. (Center field is over 350 for deep balls and under 300 for shallow.) This splits all catchable balls roughly into thirds.

Let's take at look at two left fielders, one who is replacing the other on the World Champion Phillies:

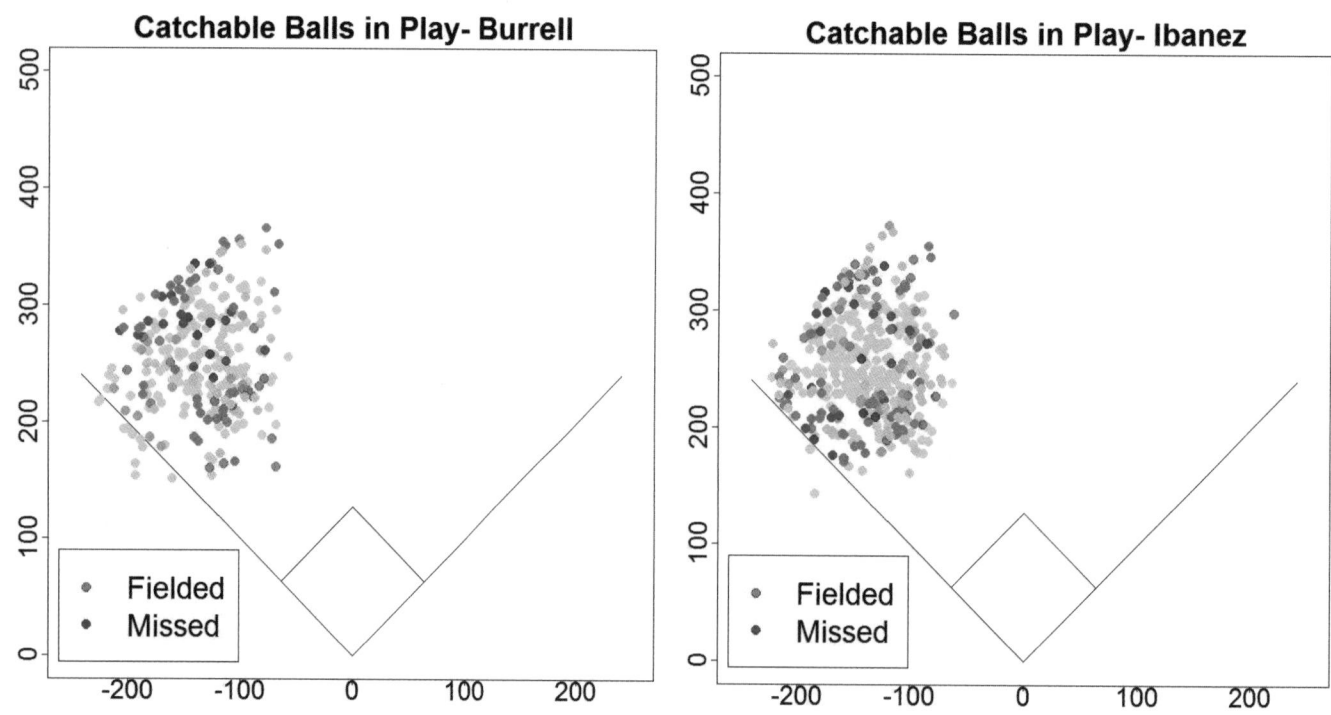

Pat Burrell is flat out atrocious on deep balls, but he somewhat compensates with an above average showing on shallow balls. His replacement, Raul Ibanez, was close to average on deep balls in 2008, but he was below average elsewhere. In fact, the two were equally poor defensively last season. Despite how much bad press Burrell's defense has received, Ibanez may not be the upgrade Philadelphians are expecting.

Burrell 2008			
	Basic Plus/Minus	Enhanced Plus/Minus	Runs Saved
Deep	-12	-22	-12
Medium	-3	-3	-2
Shallow	+5	+7	4
Total	**-10**	**-19**	**-11**

Ibanez 2008			
	Basic Plus/Minus	Enhanced Plus/Minus	Runs Saved
Deep	-1	-3	-2
Medium	-4	-8	-5
Shallow	-5	-8	-5
Total	**-10**	**-19**	**-11**

How about Willie Harris, the top enhanced plus/minus left fielder in the National League?

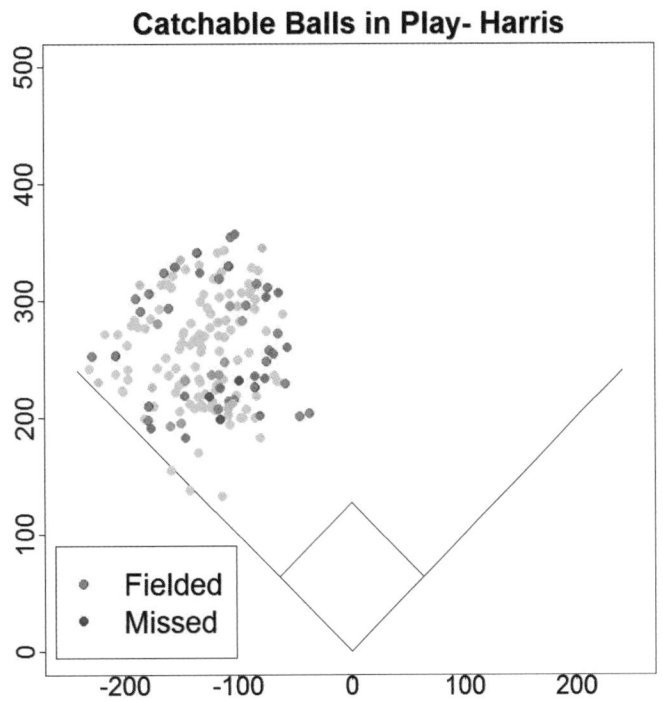

Catchable Balls in Play- Harris

Harris 2008			
	Basic Plus/Minus	Enhanced Plus/Minus	Runs Saved
Deep	+7	+14	8
Medium	+4	+5	3
Shallow	+1	0	0
Total	**+12**	**+20**	**11**

Harris is nothing special coming in on the ball, almost exactly average, but he shines on deep balls, exactly the opposite of Burrell.

On the other side of the outfield, we have a couple more players who are stronger on deep balls:

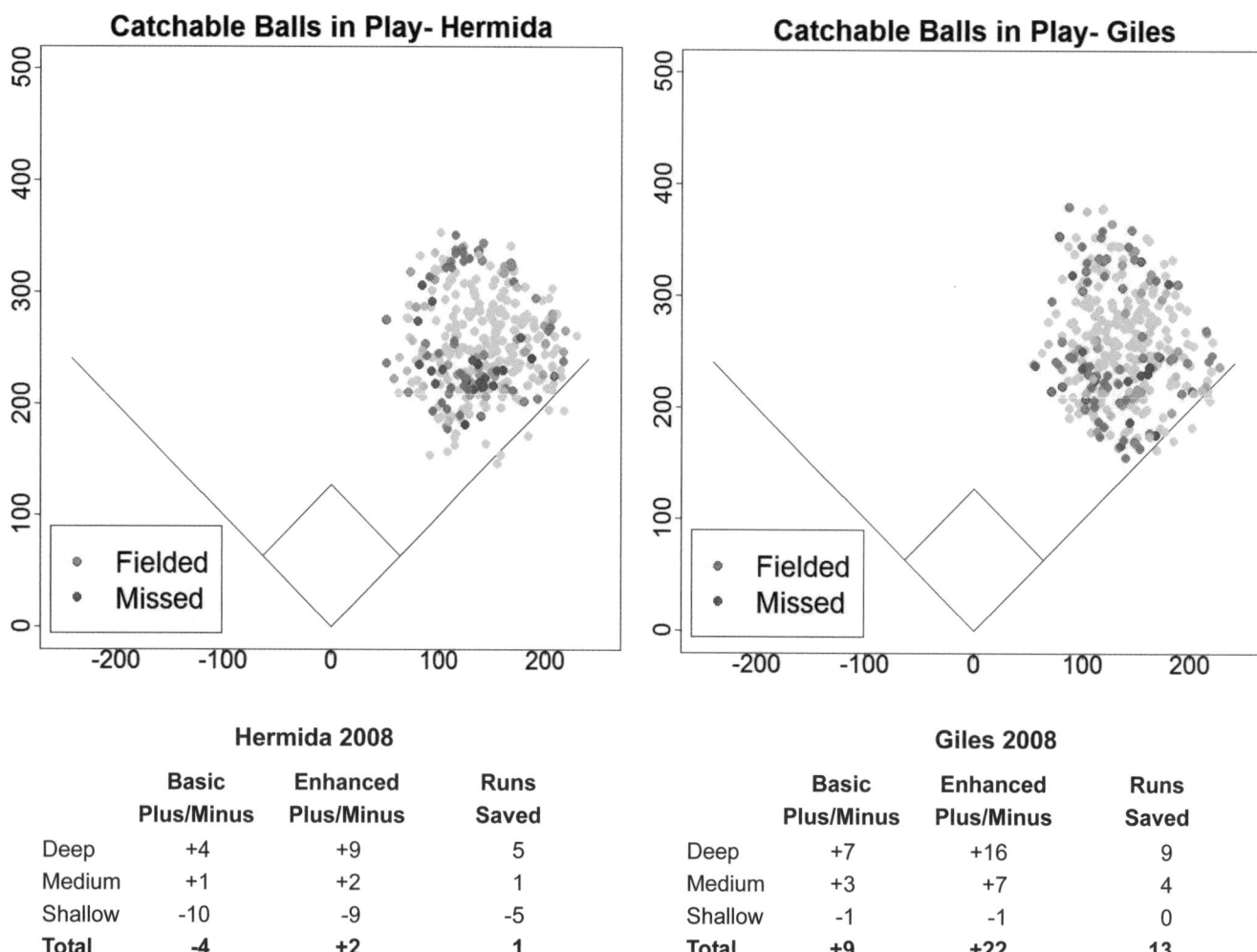

Hermida 2008			
	Basic Plus/Minus	Enhanced Plus/Minus	Runs Saved
Deep	+4	+9	5
Medium	+1	+2	1
Shallow	-10	-9	-5
Total	**-4**	**+2**	**1**

Giles 2008			
	Basic Plus/Minus	Enhanced Plus/Minus	Runs Saved
Deep	+7	+16	9
Medium	+3	+7	4
Shallow	-1	-1	0
Total	**+9**	**+22**	**13**

Jeremy Hermida, an average right fielder, is 10 plays below average on shallow balls, but saving just four deep balls above average fully compensates for the nine enhanced points and five runs he lost on shallow balls. Brian Giles was the top ranked National League right fielder in 2008 (by enhanced plus/minus), and it's all due to deep plays.

What is the difference between a shallow catch and a deep catch? Let's look back at Carlos Gomez, whom we found was especially good on deep balls.

Gomez 2008			
	Basic Plus/Minus	Enhanced Plus/Minus	Runs Saved
Deep	+10	+23	13
Medium	+5	+8	5
Shallow	-2	-2	-1
Total	**+14**	**+29**	**16**

His success came mostly on deep balls, which means he saved several extra-base hits. His 14 plays above average converted to an enhanced plus/minus score of +29 and a full 16 runs saved.

What if Gomez was reversed (we'll call him Zemog): +10 plays on shallow balls and -2 on deep balls? In other words, he makes the same number of plays, but he'll be above average on shallow balls instead of deep balls. The average plus/minus play in shallow center field was worth 1.2 enhanced points (or bases taken), while the average deep play was worth 2.1 enhanced points. Let's see how Zemog comes out:

Zemog 2008

	Basic Plus/Minus	Enhanced Plus/Minus	Runs Saved
Deep	-2	-5	-3
Medium	+5	+8	5
Shallow	+10	+12	7
Total	**+14**	**+16**	9

We see that Zemog's +14 plus/minus score is only worth 9 runs saved, compared to Gomez's 16. The same number of plays made, but a full seven run difference.

While playing shallow might rob a few singles, the trade off in doubles and triples are often more costly. With this in mind, a player like Edmonds may want to rethink where he stands before the pitch. That is, if he's standing on the field at all. At this writing he has not been signed.

Six-Year Register

Aside from being the term of office for a United States Senator, six years is the number of years we now have data for the following pages, formerly known as the Three-Year Register. I'm hoping that by doubling the data of the original *Fielding Bible* it will be even more difficult for the numbers to lie like. . .well. . .politicians.

With six years of solid data, this register enables you to more easily detect aberrations, such as Mark Teixeira's plus/minus score of -4 in 2007, and recognize talent, like Teixeira's six-year plus/minus score of +74. Recognize the fact that he ranked number one in all of baseball in plus/minus in four of those six years. And maybe realize that even in fielding, players can have slumps. While the One-Year Register helps you to compare a player's 2008 season to that of his peers, this multi-year register lets you develop a stronger assessment of a player through the examination of the last six years. Plain and simple, Jhonny Peralta is not good at getting to the ball to his left, as his six-year plus/minus score of -43 indicates. On the other hand, Peralta is better than most at getting to the ball to his right, as his +14 shows.

In keeping with the theme of this book, no discussion would be complete without relating all this data to runs saved—or in Manny Ramirez terms, runs lost. In the six years that span this register, Ramirez's runs saved score was -83. In fact the only year where Ramirez's runs saved wasn't double-digit negative was 2008, when he was -5.

Ramirez isn't alone at the bottom, he's joined by Derek Jeter, Adam Dunn, and reigning Gold Glover Michael Young (second to last to Jeter) as the players that have cost their teams the most runs, relative to position, over the six years of this register. However, as Bill James pointed out in his essay comparing Jeter to Adam Everett in the original *Fielding Bible*, just because a player is a bad *fielder* doesn't make him a bad *player*. In fact, the player must have unusual talent in other aspects of the game to maintain a spot in the lineup and an overall net positive contribution to his team, like all four of these players (three of them perennial All-Stars) do.

Because of page limitations, we don't list every player down to one inning in the Six-Year Register. For positions players, we include anyone who played at least 250 innings at a position in 2008. For pitchers, 75 innings pitched gets you in. Plus we threw in a few extra players that we wanted to see for good measure. The ranks shown in the six-year totals are based on the 175 pitchers who pitched in 2008 and had the most innings in the last six years.

For a more thorough explanation of all the chart headings, please take a look at the One-Year Register introduction on page 93.

First Basemen

Garrett Atkins

Year	Team	G	GS	Inn	PO	A	E	DP	Pct	Opps	Score	Grade	Runs Saved	Rank	Outs Made	To His Right	Straight On	To His Left	GB	Air	Total	Enhanced	Runs Saved	Rank
2004	Col	3	2	17.0	22	1	0	6	1.000					-	4	+1			0			0	0	-
2006	Col	3	0	5.0	5	0	0	1	1.000					-	0							0		
2007	Col	10	2	32.1	31	3	1	3	.971					-	11		+1	-1	0			0	0	-
2008	Col	61	60	527.2	551	23	6	55	.990	6	.550	C	0	10	97	-5	-6	+1	-11	+1	-10	-9	-7	30
		77	64	582.0	609	27	7	65	.989	6	.550	C	0	-	83	-4	-6	+1	-10	0	-10	-9	-7	

Rich Aurilia

Year	Team	G	GS	Inn	PO	A	E	DP	Pct	Opps	Score	Grade	Runs Saved	Rank	Outs Made	To His Right	Straight On	To His Left	GB	Air	Total	Enhanced	Runs Saved	Rank
2004	SD	1	0	3.0	7	0	0	0	1.000					-	0							0		
2006	Cin	47	37	329.2	302	26	2	34	.994	2	1.000	A+	1	-	69	+2	+4	-2	+4	0	+4	+5	4	
2007	SF	55	42	371.0	375	18	2	42	.995	2	.425	D-	0	-	69	+4	+2	+1	+6	+1	+7	+8	6	
2008	SF	82	49	477.0	384	26	4	52	.990	4	.600	B-	1	6	90	-1	+3	-4	-1	0	-1	-1	-1	16
		185	128	1180.2	1068	70	8	128	.993	8	.656	B	2	-	152	+5	+9	-5	+9	+1	+10	+12	9	

Daric Barton

Year	Team	G	GS	Inn	PO	A	E	DP	Pct	Opps	Score	Grade	Runs Saved	Rank	Outs Made	To His Right	Straight On	To His Left	GB	Air	Total	Enhanced	Runs Saved	Rank
2007	Oak	18	18	157.2	153	7	0	19	1.000	2	.425	D-	0	-	30	+2	+1	+1	+4	+1	+5	+5	4	-
2008	Oak	134	124	1121.2	1021	73	13	128	.988	10	.505	C-	-1	26	206	0	+2	+5	+7	-2	+5	+7	5	8
		152	142	1279.1	1174	80	13	147	.990	12	.492	D+	-1	-	166	+2	+3	+6	+11	-1	+10	+12	9	

Lance Berkman

Year	Team	G	GS	Inn	PO	A	E	DP	Pct	Opps	Score	Grade	Runs Saved	Rank	Outs Made	To His Right	Straight On	To His Left	GB	Air	Total	Enhanced	Runs Saved	Rank
2004	Hou	4	0	4.0	5	1	0	2	1.000					-	1	0			0			0	0	-
2005	Hou	96	84	737.2	772	49	6	77	.994	13	.758	A+	2	2	132	-1	-2	-3	-6	-1	-7	-7	-5	30
2006	Hou	112	105	923.0	964	69	6	95	.994	7	.514	C-	-1	22	195	+1	+4	0	+5	+1	+6	+7	5	8
2007	Hou	126	122	1066.1	1015	103	10	86	.991	15	.707	A-	1	8	216	+2	+1	-3	0	-2	-2	-3	-2	18
2008	Hou	152	151	1307.1	1240	132	5	122	.996	13	.592	C+	0	10	319	+5	+8	+4	+17	0	+17	+18	13	3
		490	462	4038.1	3996	354	26	382	.994	48	.661	B+	2	8	626	+7	+11	-2	+16	-2	+14	+15	11	8

Hank Blalock

Year	Team	G	GS	Inn	PO	A	E	DP	Pct	Opps	Score	Grade	Runs Saved	Rank	Outs Made	To His Right	Straight On	To His Left	GB	Air	Total	Enhanced	Runs Saved	Rank
2008	Tex	34	34	296.0	262	13	1	24	.996	1	1.000	A+	0	-	62	+2	-3	-1	-2	0	-2	-2	-1	-

Aaron Boone

Year	Team	G	GS	Inn	PO	A	E	DP	Pct	Opps	Score	Grade	Runs Saved	Rank	Outs Made	To His Right	Straight On	To His Left	GB	Air	Total	Enhanced	Runs Saved	Rank
2007	Fla	48	46	388.0	352	26	5	34	.987	4	.338	F	-1	-	85	+1	-7	-1	-6	0	-6	-5	-4	-
2008	Was	54	35	342.0	313	17	1	32	.997	1	.600	B-	0	-	60	-2	+1	+2	+1	-1	0	+2	1	-
		102	81	730.0	665	43	6	66	.992	5	.390	F	-1	-	106	-1	-6	+1	-5	-1	-6	-3	-3	-

John Bowker

Year	Team	G	GS	Inn	PO	A	E	DP	Pct	Opps	Score	Grade	Runs Saved	Rank	Outs Made	To His Right	Straight On	To His Left	GB	Air	Total	Enhanced	Runs Saved	Rank
2008	SF	71	67	550.1	448	39	6	43	.988	11	.614	B-	0	10	96	-1	+3	-4	-2	-1	-3	-4	-3	22

Ben Broussard

Year	Team	G	GS	Inn	PO	A	E	DP	Pct	Opps	Score	Grade	Runs Saved	Rank	Outs Made	To His Right	Straight On	To His Left	GB	Air	Total	Enhanced	Runs Saved	Rank
2003	Cle	114	101	925.0	957	63	9	86	.991	26	.600	B-	0	13	174	-2	0	-3	-5	+1	-4	-7	-5	26
2004	Cle	133	107	1019.1	991	77	6	106	.994	8	.713	A-	1	7	186	-1	+9	-3	+5	0	+5	+3	2	16
2005	Cle	138	112	1050.2	1082	60	9	112	.992	13	.485	D+	-2	31	214	-2	+2	+1	+1	-1	0	+1	1	19
2006	2 tms	90	69	641.2	652	59	9	70	.988	4	.525	C-	-1	22	146	-3	+4	-4	-3	0	-3	-5	-4	25
2007	Sea	52	36	337.0	281	21	2	39	.993	1	.600	B-	0	-	71	-5	+3	0	-3	-1	-4	-4	-3	-
2008	Tex	26	23	204.0	202	22	3	32	.987	2	.425	D-	0	-	42	-2	-1	0	-3	0	-3	-3	-2	
		553	448	4177.2	4165	302	38	445	.992	54	.577	C+	-2	22	578	-15	+17	-9	-8	-1	-9	-15	-11	25

First Basemen

Billy Butler

Year	Team	G	GS	Inn	PO	A	E	DP	Pct	Opps	Score	Grade	Runs Saved	Rank	Outs Made	To His Right	Straight On	To His Left	GB	Air	Total	Enhanced	Runs Saved	Rank
2007	KC	13	11	83.0	79	8	2	6	.978	1	.250	F	0	-	20	+1	+2	0	+3	0	+3	+3	2	-
2008	KC	34	33	260.0	233	9	2	27	.992	1	1.000	A+	0	-	37	-5	+1	+1	-4	0	-4	-4	-3	-
		47	44	343.0	312	17	4	33	.988	2	.625	B-	0	-	47	-4	+3	+1	-1	0	-1	-1	-1	-

Miguel Cabrera

Year	Team	G	GS	Inn	PO	A	E	DP	Pct	Opps	Score	Grade	Runs Saved	Rank	Outs Made	To His Right	Straight On	To His Left	GB	Air	Total	Enhanced	Runs Saved	Rank
2008	Det	143	139	1204.0	1117	73	9	116	.992	5	.470	D+	-1	26	219	-4	-5	+3	-7	-1	-8	-6	-4	27

Miguel Cairo

Year	Team	G	GS	Inn	PO	A	E	DP	Pct	Opps	Score	Grade	Runs Saved	Rank	Outs Made	To His Right	Straight On	To His Left	GB	Air	Total	Enhanced	Runs Saved	Rank
2003	StL	3	0	7.2	9	0	0	1	1.000					-	1		+1					+1	1	-
2004	NYY	1	0	3.0	2	0	0	0	1.000					-	0							0	0	-
2005	NYM	8	6	50.2	48	2	1	6	.980					-	12	-1	-1	+1	-1	0	-1	-1	-1	-
2006	NYY	16	6	71.2	60	5	0	5	1.000	2	.600	B-	0	-	17	+1	+1	0	+2	0	+2	+2	1	-
2007	2 tms	24	18	166.0	173	10	4	18	.979	5	.390	F	-1	-	36	0	0	+1	0	0	0	0	0	-
2008	Sea	70	37	394.0	414	23	1	43	.998	8	.931	A+	2	3	77	-1	+2	0	+1	-1	0	0	0	13
		122	67	693.0	706	40	6	73	.992	15	.707	A-	1	-	108	-1	+2	+2	+3	-1	+2	+2	1	-

Jorge Cantu

Year	Team	G	GS	Inn	PO	A	E	DP	Pct	Opps	Score	Grade	Runs Saved	Rank	Outs Made	To His Right	Straight On	To His Left	GB	Air	Total	Enhanced	Runs Saved	Rank
2007	2 tms	21	20	155.1	135	7	0	12	1.000	1	.250	F	0	-	24	-1	-2	0	-3	0	-3	-3	-2	-
2008	Fla	66	23	286.2	260	14	2	23	.993	3	.500	C-	-1	-	68	+1	0	+2	+2	0	+2	+3	2	-
		87	43	442.0	395	21	2	35	.995	4	.438	D-	-1	-	62	0	-2	+2	-1	0	-1	0	0	-

Sean Casey

Year	Team	G	GS	Inn	PO	A	E	DP	Pct	Opps	Score	Grade	Runs Saved	Rank	Outs Made	To His Right	Straight On	To His Left	GB	Air	Total	Enhanced	Runs Saved	Rank
2003	Cin	144	144	1251.2	1257	75	6	115	.996	20	.653	B	1	6	219	0	0	+4	+4	-1	+3	+3	2	12
2004	Cin	145	142	1245.2	1233	56	8	86	.994	24	.508	C-	-3	35	221	-1	-3	+4	0	+2	+2	+5	4	12
2005	Cin	134	132	1138.2	1153	55	2	91	.998	29	.614	B-	1	7	233	-2	-6	+1	-7	-1	-8	-6	-4	28
2006	2 tms	106	102	874.1	938	34	2	85	.998	15	.810	A+	2	3	156	-7	-4	-1	-12	0	-12	-12	-9	32
2007	Det	131	105	989.0	992	42	2	87	.998	9	.406	F	-2	35	194	0	-8	+4	-5	-1	-6	-3	-2	19
2008	Bos	45	40	342.2	331	13	3	25	.991	2	1.125	A+	0	10	64	-2	-2	-1	-4	0	-4	-4	-3	23
		705	665	5842.0	5904	275	23	489	.996	99	.617	B-	-1	20	750	-12	-23	+11	-24	-1	-25	-17	-12	26

Tony Clark

Year	Team	G	GS	Inn	PO	A	E	DP	Pct	Opps	Score	Grade	Runs Saved	Rank	Outs Made	To His Right	Straight On	To His Left	GB	Air	Total	Enhanced	Runs Saved	Rank
2003	NYM	80	50	499.2	465	25	4	43	.992	12	.550	C	0	13	78	-2	-5	-2	-9	-3	-12	-13	-9	35
2004	NYY	99	64	623.2	602	49	4	64	.994	3	.600	B-	1	7	137	-8	+5	-1	-4	+1	-3	-4	-3	25
2005	Ari	83	70	642.2	663	45	2	59	.997	7	.500	C-	0	11	119	-5	+6	0	0	+1	+1	+4	3	13
2006	2 tms	53	23	256.1	274	21	2	26	.993	2	.425	D-	0	-	50	-3	-1	-1	-5	0	-5	-6	-4	-
2007	Ari	83	43	452.2	432	32	2	50	.996	5	.540	C	0	15	95	+1	-1	-3	-3	0	-3	-4	-3	23
2008	2 tms	26	13	155.0	165	15	2	19	.989	1	.600	B-	0	-	35	-1	-2	+2	0	0	0	0	0	-
		424	263	2630.0	2601	187	16	261	.994	30	.535	C	1	10	351	-18	+2	-5	-21	-1	-22	-23	-16	28

Chris Davis

Year	Team	G	GS	Inn	PO	A	E	DP	Pct	Opps	Score	Grade	Runs Saved	Rank	Outs Made	To His Right	Straight On	To His Left	GB	Air	Total	Enhanced	Runs Saved	Rank
2008	Tex	51	46	404.0	358	34	1	52	.997	3	.733	A	1	6	78	-2	0	-2	-3	+1	-2	-3	-2	21

Carlos Delgado

Year	Team	G	GS	Inn	PO	A	E	DP	Pct	Opps	Score	Grade	Runs Saved	Rank	Outs Made	To His Right	Straight On	To His Left	GB	Air	Total	Enhanced	Runs Saved	Rank
2003	Tor	147	147	1278.0	1355	103	10	137	.993	10	.470	D+	-2	26	286	-5	+8	-8	-5	-1	-6	-8	-6	28
2004	Tor	120	120	1038.2	1041	89	5	96	.996	10	.465	D	-1	23	252	+5	-3	+3	+5	0	+5	+9	7	2
2005	Fla	141	140	1206.0	1147	83	14	133	.989	26	.525	C-	-1	21	239	-5	-5	-8	-18	0	-18	-23	-17	35
2006	NYM	141	141	1246.1	1199	70	8	94	.994	19	.611	B-	1	5	239	0	-9	+2	-7	+1	-6	-4	-3	23
2007	NYM	138	138	1219.1	1133	74	8	101	.993	23	.657	B	1	8	228	+4	-2	0	+2	0	+2	+1	1	14
2008	NYM	154	154	1376.1	1237	105	8	106	.994	28	.595	C+	2	3	281	-12	+3	-5	-14	-2	-16	-15	-11	33
		841	840	7364.2	7112	524	53	667	.993	116	.572	C+	0	13	1052	-13	-8	-16	-37	-2	-39	-40	-29	31

First Basemen

Darin Erstad

Year	Team	G	GS	Inn	PO	A	E	DP	Pct	Opps	Score	Grade	Runs Saved	Rank	Outs Made	To His Right	Straight On	To His Left	GB	Air	Total	Enhanced	Runs Saved	Rank
2004	Ana	124	124	1065.1	986	65	4	83	.996	10	.505	C-	-1	23	236	+6	+2	+1	+9	0	+9	+9	7	3
2005	LAA	147	144	1279.1	1218	79	4	109	.997	20	.505	C-	-3	35	294	+8	0	+2	+11	0	+11	+12	9	4
2006	LAA	13	0	28.0	31	1	0	1	1.000					-	6	+1	0	0	+1	0	+1	+1	1	-
2007	CWS	22	19	173.2	174	14	1	18	.995	4	.513	C-	0	-	44	+1	+2	0	+3	-1	+2	+2	1	-
2008	Hou	12	6	66.1	71	2	0	4	1.000					-	14	-1	0	0	-1	0	-1	-1	-1	-
		318	293	2612.2	2480	161	9	215	.997	34	.506	C-	-4	28	396	+15	+4	+3	+23	-1	+22	+23	17	7

Prince Fielder

Year	Team	G	GS	Inn	PO	A	E	DP	Pct	Opps	Score	Grade	Runs Saved	Rank	Outs Made	To His Right	Straight On	To His Left	GB	Air	Total	Enhanced	Runs Saved	Rank
2005	Mil	7	3	34.0	26	4	0	2	1.000	1	.600	B-	0	-	6				0	0	0	0	0	-
2006	Mil	152	151	1319.1	1259	88	11	113	.992	40	.610	B-	1	5	241	0	-6	-8	-15	-2	-17	-18	-13	35
2007	Mil	153	151	1338.0	1163	99	14	115	.989	20	.575	C+	0	15	252	-4	-8	-4	-16	+1	-15	-15	-11	32
2008	Mil	155	155	1383.2	1369	89	17	132	.988	32	.567	C+	-1	26	257	-1	-4	-7	-12	-1	-13	-12	-9	32
		467	460	4075.0	3817	280	42	362	.990	93	.588	C+	0	13	464	-5	-18	-19	-43	-2	-45	-45	-33	32

Ryan Garko

Year	Team	G	GS	Inn	PO	A	E	DP	Pct	Opps	Score	Grade	Runs Saved	Rank	Outs Made	To His Right	Straight On	To His Left	GB	Air	Total	Enhanced	Runs Saved	Rank
2006	Cle	45	45	396.0	398	30	6	50	.986	5	.620	B-	0	-	74	-1	+2	-1	-1	+1	0	0	0	-
2007	Cle	125	121	1066.1	1073	71	8	115	.993	19	.587	C+	-1	26	198	-6	-6	+1	-11	0	-11	-9	-7	29
2008	Cle	121	121	1058.2	1039	80	4	123	.996	17	.474	D+	-3	33	193	-2	+3	-5	-4	+1	-3	-3	-2	20
		291	287	2521.0	2510	181	18	288	.993	41	.544	C	-4	28	330	-9	-1	-5	-16	+2	-14	-12	-9	21

Jason Giambi

Year	Team	G	GS	Inn	PO	A	E	DP	Pct	Opps	Score	Grade	Runs Saved	Rank	Outs Made	To His Right	Straight On	To His Left	GB	Air	Total	Enhanced	Runs Saved	Rank
2003	NYY	85	85	742.2	747	19	4	62	.995	6	.575	C+	0	13	146	0	-8	+2	-6	0	-6	-6	-4	24
2004	NYY	47	47	375.0	372	14	4	30	.990	7	.614	B-	0	-	67	-2	+3	-2	-1	0	-1	-1	-1	-
2005	NYY	78	77	560.0	581	19	7	50	.988	7	.614	B-	0	11	90	-7	-3	+2	-8	0	-8	-8	-6	31
2006	NYY	68	64	480.0	459	11	7	43	.985	1	.250	F	0	11	71	-5	-6	-3	-14	-1	-15	-16	-12	34
2007	NYY	18	16	121.0	108	6	1	10	.991	1	.600	B-	0	-	25	+1	+3	-1	+3	+1	+4	+4	3	-
2008	NYY	113	112	898.0	870	36	9	77	.990	8	.563	C+	0	10	158	-6	-13	+2	-17	-1	-18	-18	-13	34
		409	401	3176.2	3137	105	32	272	.990	30	.580	C+	0	13	397	-19	-24	0	-43	-1	-44	-45	-33	33

Ross Gload

Year	Team	G	GS	Inn	PO	A	E	DP	Pct	Opps	Score	Grade	Runs Saved	Rank	Outs Made	To His Right	Straight On	To His Left	GB	Air	Total	Enhanced	Runs Saved	Rank
2004	CWS	42	21	218.1	219	12	0	15	1.000					-	57	-1	+1	-2	-2	0	-2	-3	-2	-
2005	CWS	24	6	89.0	72	4	1	9	.987					-	12	0	-2	0	-2	0	-2	-2	-1	-
2006	CWS	49	20	247.1	266	13	4	24	.986	1	.600	B-	0	-	49	-4	0	-1	-5	0	-5	-6	-4	-
2007	KC	89	74	675.2	623	45	3	78	.996	3	.867	A+	1	8	150	0	+8	-1	+8	-1	+7	+5	4	8
2008	KC	111	95	878.1	837	43	4	87	.995	6	.617	B-	0	10	159	-4	-1	0	-5	0	-5	-7	-5	28
		315	216	2108.2	2017	117	12	213	.994	10	.690	A-	1	10	296	-9	+6	-4	-6	-1	-7	-13	-8	24

Adrian Gonzalez

Year	Team	G	GS	Inn	PO	A	E	DP	Pct	Opps	Score	Grade	Runs Saved	Rank	Outs Made	To His Right	Straight On	To His Left	GB	Air	Total	Enhanced	Runs Saved	Rank
2004	Tex	11	10	89.0	93	6	1	13	.990	1	1.000	A+	0	-	15	0	+1	0	+1	0	+1	+1	1	-
2005	Tex	10	7	71.0	85	6	2	7	.978	1	.600	B-	0	-	15	+1	-1	-1	-1	0	-1	-1	-1	-
2006	SD	155	149	1341.0	1242	116	7	117	.995	25	.610	B-	2	3	286	-3	+4	0	+1	-1	0	0	0	18
2007	SD	161	161	1462.2	1470	140	10	134	.994	36	.671	B+	2	3	284	0	-5	0	-5	-1	-6	-7	-5	27
2008	SD	161	159	1417.1	1306	130	6	129	.996	31	.739	A	4	1	282	-1	-7	-1	-8	+2	-6	-6	-4	26
		498	486	4381.0	4196	398	26	400	.994	94	.680	B+	8	3	614	-3	-8	-2	-12	0	-12	-13	-9	22

Scott Hatteberg

Year	Team	G	GS	Inn	PO	A	E	DP	Pct	Opps	Score	Grade	Runs Saved	Rank	Outs Made	To His Right	Straight On	To His Left	GB	Air	Total	Enhanced	Runs Saved	Rank
2003	Oak	128	126	1111.1	1177	80	10	102	.992	22	.466	D	-4	31	176	+1	-3	+3	+1	-1	0	+2	1	14
2004	Oak	148	143	1280.0	1281	86	10	136	.993	12	.521	C-	-1	23	239	-12	-5	+2	-15	+3	-12	-8	-6	28
2005	Oak	53	50	436.2	423	38	7	47	.985	5	.970	A+	1	-	98	-3	-4	+1	-6	0	-6	-5	-4	-
2006	Cin	131	122	1088.2	1001	69	4	86	.996	19	.634	B	1	5	206	+3	-4	+4	+4	+2	+6	+8	6	5
2007	Cin	96	85	772.2	657	50	3	66	.996	11	.568	C+	1	8	135	-3	-10	+2	-11	+1	-10	-10	-7	31
2008	Cin	16	8	87.2	69	6	1	3	.987	2	.600	B-	0	-	12	0	+1	0	+1	-1	0	0	0	-
		572	534	4777.0	4608	329	35	440	.993	71	.575	C+	-2	22	574	-14	-25	+12	-26	+4	-22	-13	-10	23

First Basemen

Todd Helton

		BASIC								BUNTS					PLUS/MINUS									
Year	Team	G	GS	Inn	PO	A	E	DP	Pct	Opps	Score	Grade	Runs Saved	Rank	Outs Made	To His Right	Straight On	To His Left	GB	Air	Total	Enhanced	Runs Saved	Rank
2003	Col	159	159	1369.0	1419	156	11	153	.993	33	.671	B+	3	1	307	+1	-3	-2	-4	-5	-9	-11	-8	31
2004	Col	153	151	1320.2	1356	143	4	131	.997	42	.656	B	5	1	262	+10	+1	-2	+9	0	+9	+11	8	1
2005	Col	144	142	1229.2	1236	118	5	135	.996	24	.635	B	2	2	272	-3	+2	0	-1	+1	0	-1	-1	21
2006	Col	145	145	1272.1	1366	86	4	155	.997	18	.569	C+	0	11	256	-5	0	-2	-7	+1	-6	-7	-5	26
2007	Col	153	152	1337.0	1448	95	2	153	.999	19	.650	B	2	3	287	-1	+3	+5	+7	0	+7	+9	7	5
2008	Col	81	81	715.1	830	57	3	79	.997	12	.517	C-	0	10	156	-3	+7	+2	+7	0	+7	+6	4	11
		835	830	7244.0	7655	655	29	806	.997	148	.633	B	12	1	1117	-1	+10	+1	+11	-3	+8	+7	5	13

Ryan Howard

		BASIC								BUNTS					PLUS/MINUS									
Year	Team	G	GS	Inn	PO	A	E	DP	Pct	Opps	Score	Grade	Runs Saved	Rank	Outs Made	To His Right	Straight On	To His Left	GB	Air	Total	Enhanced	Runs Saved	Rank
2004	Phi	8	5	60.2	59	6	0	9	1.000					-	9	+1	+1	0	+2	0	+2	+2	1	-
2005	Phi	84	79	706.1	707	40	5	53	.993	7	.500	C-	0	11	149	+15	+6	-2	+19	0	+19	+16	12	2
2006	Phi	159	157	1412.0	1373	91	14	139	.991	27	.557	C	-1	22	257	-5	-5	-2	-6	-3	-9	-9	-7	28
2007	Phi	140	138	1241.0	1191	103	12	124	.991	27	.694	A-	2	1	240	-2	-2	-3	-8	0	-8	-5	-4	24
2008	Phi	159	156	1402.2	1408	101	19	128	.988	18	.572	C+	0	10	309	+1	-10	+5	-4	+2	-2	0	0	12
		550	535	4822.2	4738	341	50	453	.990	79	.603	B-	3	7	636	+10	-3	-3	+3	-1	+2	+4	2	17

Conor Jackson

		BASIC								BUNTS					PLUS/MINUS									
Year	Team	G	GS	Inn	PO	A	E	DP	Pct	Opps	Score	Grade	Runs Saved	Rank	Outs Made	To His Right	Straight On	To His Left	GB	Air	Total	Enhanced	Runs Saved	Rank
2005	Ari	20	20	161.0	171	11	5	19	.973	7	.500	C-	0	-	29	0	0	-2	-2	-1	-3	-4	-3	-
2006	Ari	129	127	1078.2	1109	81	12	111	.990	30	.535	C	0	11	210	-7	-9	+4	-11	0	-11	-11	-8	30
2007	Ari	108	107	867.2	859	48	11	86	.988	15	.563	C+	0	15	164	-4	+7	-8	-4	0	-4	-6	-4	25
2008	Ari	68	66	571.2	533	30	4	34	.993	9	.611	B-	0	10	102	-1	-2	0	-3	-1	-4	-5	-4	24
		325	320	2679.0	2672	170	32	250	.989	61	.549	C	0	13	370	-12	-4	-6	-20	-2	-22	-26	-19	29

Mike Jacobs

		BASIC								BUNTS					PLUS/MINUS									
Year	Team	G	GS	Inn	PO	A	E	DP	Pct	Opps	Score	Grade	Runs Saved	Rank	Outs Made	To His Right	Straight On	To His Left	GB	Air	Total	Enhanced	Runs Saved	Rank
2005	NYM	28	28	236.0	237	10	4	24	.984	4	.600	B-	1	-	41	-1	-1	-1	-2	0	-2	-3	-2	-
2006	Fla	124	120	972.0	931	57	7	101	.993	25	.670	B+	3	2	169	-4	-7	-1	-12	0	-12	-12	-9	31
2007	Fla	108	104	903.0	793	45	7	91	.992	16	.559	C	1	8	157	-8	-2	+2	-9	-2	-11	-10	-7	30
2008	Fla	119	119	927.1	825	62	11	67	.988	21	.452	D	-3	33	163	-11	-8	-7	-26	-2	-28	-28	-20	35
		379	371	3038.1	2786	174	29	283	.990	66	.570	C+	2	8	355	-24	-18	-7	-49	-4	-53	-53	-38	35

Dan Johnson

		BASIC								BUNTS					PLUS/MINUS									
Year	Team	G	GS	Inn	PO	A	E	DP	Pct	Opps	Score	Grade	Runs Saved	Rank	Outs Made	To His Right	Straight On	To His Left	GB	Air	Total	Enhanced	Runs Saved	Rank
2005	Oak	101	98	883.2	898	57	6	94	.994	6	.483	D+	0	11	187	-1	+1	0	0	+1	+1	+2	1	17
2006	Oak	85	77	714.2	688	63	4	97	.995	5	.550	C	-1	22	161	+3	0	+3	+6	0	+6	+6	4	12
2007	Oak	97	96	854.2	869	40	4	80	.996	4	.250	F	-1	26	166	-2	0	+2	0	-1	-1	-2	-1	16
2008	TB	8	4	47.0	39	5	0	4	1.000	1	.250	F	0	-	11	0	+1	0	+2	0	+2	+2	1	-
		291	275	2500.0	2494	165	14	275	.995	14	.457	D	-2	22	339	0	+2	+5	+8	0	+8	+8	5	12

Nick Johnson

		BASIC								BUNTS					PLUS/MINUS									
Year	Team	G	GS	Inn	PO	A	E	DP	Pct	Opps	Score	Grade	Runs Saved	Rank	Outs Made	To His Right	Straight On	To His Left	GB	Air	Total	Enhanced	Runs Saved	Rank
2003	NYY	60	60	529.0	512	34	5	45	.991	8	.475	D+	-1	22	111	0	0	-4	-4	+1	-3	-6	-4	25
2004	Mon	73	70	610.0	618	43	4	69	.994	5	.460	D	0	14	118	-1	+1	+2	+1	+1	+2	+2	1	17
2005	Was	129	126	1098.2	1017	95	5	109	.996	25	.662	B+	2	2	266	+4	-2	+3	+5	+1	+6	+6	4	10
2006	Was	147	143	1252.1	1163	93	15	91	.988	36	.744	A	6	1	288	+3	0	-3	0	+1	+1	0	0	17
2008	Was	35	34	300.1	302	14	0	21	1.000	1	.250	F	0	-	62	-2	+2	+2	+2	0	+2	+3	2	-
		444	433	3790.1	3612	279	29	335	.993	75	.663	B+	7	4	533	+4	+1	0	+4	+4	+8	+5	3	16

Paul Konerko

		BASIC								BUNTS					PLUS/MINUS									
Year	Team	G	GS	Inn	PO	A	E	DP	Pct	Opps	Score	Grade	Runs Saved	Rank	Outs Made	To His Right	Straight On	To His Left	GB	Air	Total	Enhanced	Runs Saved	Rank
2003	CWS	119	105	938.2	890	79	2	109	.998	17	.615	B-	0	13	204	-1	-3	+2	-2	+2	0	+4	3	11
2004	CWS	139	137	1177.2	1151	78	6	133	.995	18	.536	C	-2	31	208	-8	-6	+3	-11	-2	-13	-12	-9	33
2005	CWS	146	145	1272.2	1320	82	5	135	.996	19	.574	C+	0	11	275	-1	-1	+1	-1	-1	-2	-2	-1	24
2006	CWS	140	139	1181.0	1171	67	6	113	.995	15	.560	C+	-2	33	208	-6	-1	-2	-4	-1	-5	-5	-4	24
2007	CWS	141	140	1227.2	1180	71	5	131	.996	18	.619	B-	-1	26	245	+1	-7	+2	-3	0	-3	-3	-2	17
2008	CWS	116	116	995.2	1010	75	7	94	.994	10	.395	F	-3	33	209	+3	-2	+1	+2	0	+2	-2	-1	17
		801	782	6794.0	6722	452	31	715	.996	97	.562	C+	-8	35	894	-12	-20	+11	-19	-2	-21	-20	-14	27

First Basemen

Casey Kotchman

Year	Team	G	GS	Inn	PO	A	E	DP	Pct	Opps	Score	Grade	Runs Saved	Rank	Outs Made	To His Right	Straight On	To His Left	GB	Air	Total	Enhanced	Runs Saved	Rank
2004	Ana	34	27	270.1	231	15	3	17	.988	4	.425	D-	-1	-	45	0	-3	0	-2	0	-2	-2	-1	-
2005	LAA	20	13	131.0	111	7	0	10	1.000					-	24	0	0	-3	-2	0	-2	-5	-4	-
2006	LAA	26	22	197.0	180	15	0	12	1.000	1	.600	B-	0	-	44	+4	+1	+1	+5	0	+5	+5	4	-
2007	LAA	130	116	1033.0	978	68	3	103	.997	3	.617	B-	0	15	223	+9	+4	+7	+20	+1	+21	+24	18	2
2008	2 tms	141	135	1210.1	1205	96	2	125	.998	10	.425	D-	-1	26	263	+2	+10	0	+11	+1	+12	+14	10	5
		351	313	2841.2	2705	201	8	267	.997	18	.467	D	-2	22	423	+15	+12	+5	+32	+2	+34	+36	27	4

Bryan LaHair

Year	Team	G	GS	Inn	PO	A	E	DP	Pct	Opps	Score	Grade	Runs Saved	Rank	Outs Made	To His Right	Straight On	To His Left	GB	Air	Total	Enhanced	Runs Saved	Rank
2008	Sea	36	33	273.0	277	18	2	37	.993	6	.367	F	-2	-	52	-1	+5	0	+4	-1	+3	+3	2	-

Adam LaRoche

Year	Team	G	GS	Inn	PO	A	E	DP	Pct	Opps	Score	Grade	Runs Saved	Rank	Outs Made	To His Right	Straight On	To His Left	GB	Air	Total	Enhanced	Runs Saved	Rank
2004	Atl	98	82	720.0	739	40	5	87	.994	10	.575	C+	0	14	123	+2	-2	+1	+1	0	+1	+1	1	18
2005	Atl	125	117	1019.1	1070	77	7	105	.994	15	.513	C-	-1	21	232	0	-15	-3	-18	0	-18	-17	-12	34
2006	Atl	142	130	1153.1	1117	96	6	109	.994	29	.547	C	0	11	243	-10	-2	-3	-14	-1	-15	-14	-10	33
2007	Pit	151	148	1301.1	1296	81	6	154	.996	21	.693	A-	1	8	269	-4	+6	+1	+3	-1	+2	+3	2	11
2008	Pit	129	128	1135.2	1130	81	8	121	.993	28	.625	B-	0	10	206	0	-1	-6	-7	+2	-5	-8	-6	29
		645	605	5329.2	5352	375	31	576	.995	103	.596	C+	0	13	739	-12	-14	-10	-35	0	-35	-35	-25	30

Derrek Lee

Year	Team	G	GS	Inn	PO	A	E	DP	Pct	Opps	Score	Grade	Runs Saved	Rank	Outs Made	To His Right	Straight On	To His Left	GB	Air	Total	Enhanced	Runs Saved	Rank
2003	Fla	155	153	1353.2	1279	98	5	143	.996	23	.626	B-	2	2	259	-4	-8	-3	-15	+2	-13	-13	-9	34
2004	ChC	161	159	1432.0	1259	128	6	113	.996	35	.631	B	3	2	269	0	-4	+1	-3	0	-3	-2	-1	22
2005	ChC	158	158	1386.0	1323	122	6	118	.996	35	.736	A	6	1	256	0	-7	+6	-2	+2	0	+2	1	15
2006	ChC	47	44	393.2	370	26	5	34	.988	14	.582	C+	1	-	73	0	-1	+2	+1	+1	+2	+3	2	-
2007	ChC	147	146	1274.1	1165	87	7	99	.994	30	.550	C	-1	26	234	0	+1	-3	-3	-2	-5	-4	-3	21
2008	ChC	153	152	1339.1	1193	110	9	98	.993	26	.623	B-	1	6	304	+1	-6	+8	+3	0	+3	+6	4	9
		821	812	7179.0	6589	571	38	605	.995	163	.633	B	12	1	869	-3	-25	+11	-19	+3	-16	-8	-6	20

James Loney

Year	Team	G	GS	Inn	PO	A	E	DP	Pct	Opps	Score	Grade	Runs Saved	Rank	Outs Made	To His Right	Straight On	To His Left	GB	Air	Total	Enhanced	Runs Saved	Rank
2006	LAD	39	20	228.2	212	15	1	17	.996	2	.800	A+	0	-	36	-2	+3	+3	+4	-1	+3	+5	4	-
2007	LAD	93	85	774.2	748	42	3	87	.989	11	.768	A+	2	3	159	+5	-1	-1	+2	0	+2	+2	1	12
2008	LAD	158	150	1362.2	1364	121	13	123	.991	25	.658	B	2	3	248	+2	-6	+2	-2	0	-2	-1	-1	14
		290	255	2366.0	2301	197	23	227	.991	38	.697	A-	4	5	327	+5	-4	+4	+4	-1	+3	+6	4	15

Doug Mientkiewicz

Year	Team	G	GS	Inn	PO	A	E	DP	Pct	Opps	Score	Grade	Runs Saved	Rank	Outs Made	To His Right	Straight On	To His Left	GB	Air	Total	Enhanced	Runs Saved	Rank
2003	Min	139	133	1159.1	1091	68	4	86	.997	10	.610	B-	-1	22	252	+4	+7	+5	+16	+1	+17	+17	12	2
2004	2 tms	125	100	940.2	923	62	5	77	.995	13	.646	B	0	14	202	-3	+4	+2	+3	+1	+4	+6	4	10
2005	NYM	83	79	675.0	690	42	4	59	.995	16	.656	B	2	2	138	+5	+3	+1	+9	0	+9	+9	7	9
2006	KC	90	82	724.2	748	42	3	84	.996	5	.470	D+	-1	22	157	+7	+8	0	+15	+1	+16	+15	11	2
2007	NYY	70	48	458.0	482	23	2	59	.996	5	.620	B-	0	15	106	+4	+5	-1	+8	0	+8	+7	5	7
2008	Pit	37	30	283.1	290	19	0	34	1.000	2	.250	F	-1	-	62	0	+3	+2	+4	0	+4	+4	3	-
		544	472	4241.0	4224	256	18	399	.996	51	.607	B-	-1	20	604	+17	+30	+9	+55	+3	+58	+58	42	3

Kevin Millar

Year	Team	G	GS	Inn	PO	A	E	DP	Pct	Opps	Score	Grade	Runs Saved	Rank	Outs Made	To His Right	Straight On	To His Left	GB	Air	Total	Enhanced	Runs Saved	Rank
2003	Bos	101	96	853.0	858	81	4	82	.996	14	.482	D+	-2	26	202	-1	-8	+5	-4	+2	-2	+1	1	16
2004	Bos	69	66	512.0	466	57	6	45	.989	4	.800	A+	1	7	119	+3	+3	+2	+7	0	+7	+8	6	5
2005	Bos	110	102	796.1	799	86	7	67	.992	8	.475	D+	-2	31	216	-2	+3	+1	+1	+1	+2	+5	4	11
2006	Bal	98	97	792.1	765	62	4	74	.995	16	.547	C	-1	22	150	-3	-4	-1	-8	-1	-9	-10	-7	29
2007	Bal	101	101	873.0	852	66	1	94	.999	8	.519	C-	0	15	167	-1	-3	-1	-6	+1	-5	-7	-5	28
2008	Bal	130	128	1131.1	1099	110	6	128	.995	11	.482	D+	-2	30	259	+5	-1	-6	-1	-1	-2	-3	-2	19
		609	590	4958.0	4839	462	28	490	.995	61	.524	C-	-6	31	786	+1	-10	0	-11	+2	-9	-6	-3	19

First Basemen

Justin Morneau

		BASIC								BUNTS					PLUS/MINUS									
Year	Team	G	GS	Inn	PO	A	E	DP	Pct	Opps	Score	Grade	Runs Saved	Rank	Outs Made	To His Right	Straight On	To His Left	GB	Air	Total	Enhanced	Runs Saved	Rank
2003	Min	7	2	34.2	29	4	1	1	.971	1	1.000	A+	0	-	9	-1	-1	0	-2	0	-2	-3	-2	-
2004	Min	61	61	538.1	523	41	3	54	.995	5	.320	F	-2	31	90	-2	+1	-2	-2	-1	-3	-3	-2	23
2005	Min	138	128	1166.1	1191	91	8	123	.994	12	.742	A	1	7	246	-2	+7	+6	+11	0	+11	+13	9	3
2006	Min	153	152	1346.1	1296	111	8	111	.994	16	.613	B-	1	5	254	+1	-1	-1	0	+1	+1	+1	1	16
2007	Min	143	143	1259.1	1189	102	5	122	.996	12	.483	D+	-1	26	274	-6	+2	+1	-3	+3	0	0	0	15
2008	Min	155	155	1363.2	1316	89	4	149	.997	9	.406	F	-2	30	239	+1	-3	0	-2	0	-2	-1	-1	15
		657	641	5708.2	5544	438	29	560	.995	55	.559	C	-3	27	742	-9	+5	+4	+2	+3	+5	+7	5	14

Lyle Overbay

		BASIC								BUNTS					PLUS/MINUS									
Year	Team	G	GS	Inn	PO	A	E	DP	Pct	Opps	Score	Grade	Runs Saved	Rank	Outs Made	To His Right	Straight On	To His Left	GB	Air	Total	Enhanced	Runs Saved	Rank
2003	Ari	75	69	604.0	643	58	2	50	.997	11	.636	B	0	13	154	0	+4	+4	+8	-1	+7	+9	7	7
2004	Mil	158	150	1360.1	1310	113	11	110	.992	28	.668	B+	2	4	246	+2	-2	-9	-9	0	-9	-14	-10	34
2005	Mil	154	143	1265.0	1134	96	10	104	.992	28	.548	C	-2	31	247	+2	+6	-3	+5	0	+5	+4	3	12
2006	Tor	145	139	1233.0	1357	93	9	124	.994	13	.365	F	-5	35	305	+3	+3	-1	+5	+2	+7	+7	5	6
2007	Tor	119	107	972.1	1060	101	5	107	.996	6	.617	B-	0	15	218	+3	+5	+4	+12	-1	+11	+13	9	3
2008	Tor	156	151	1354.2	1316	155	5	112	.997	13	.504	C-	-2	30	324	+7	+7	-1	+13	0	+13	+11	8	7
		807	759	6789.1	6820	616	42	607	.994	99	.566	C+	-7	33	1075	+17	+23	-6	+34	0	+34	+30	22	5

Carlos Pena

		BASIC								BUNTS					PLUS/MINUS									
Year	Team	G	GS	Inn	PO	A	E	DP	Pct	Opps	Score	Grade	Runs Saved	Rank	Outs Made	To His Right	Straight On	To His Left	GB	Air	Total	Enhanced	Runs Saved	Rank
2003	Det	128	124	1094.2	1136	91	13	133	.990	17	.400	F	-4	31	206	+1	-3	-1	-3	0	-3	-5	-4	23
2004	Det	135	131	1159.1	1143	77	6	127	.995	14	.561	C+	-1	23	182	+4	+7	-2	+9	-1	+8	+4	3	13
2005	Det	51	49	429.1	418	35	3	46	.993	8	.431	D-	-2	-	94	-4	+1	-1	-3	0	-3	-5	-4	-
2006	Bos	17	8	80.0	81	5	1	15	.989						14	0	+1	0	+1	0	+1	+1	1	-
2007	TB	144	137	1221.0	1054	110	8	116	.993	22	.593	C+	-1	26	264	+8	+8	-5	+10	-1	+9	+4	3	10
2008	TB	132	131	1168.2	991	106	2	117	.998	16	.678	B+	1	6	262	+11	+8	-5	+14	+1	+15	+14	10	6
		607	580	5153.0	4823	444	33	554	.994	77	.545	C	-7	33	696	+20	+22	-14	+28	-1	+27	+13	9	9

Albert Pujols

		BASIC								BUNTS					PLUS/MINUS									
Year	Team	G	GS	Inn	PO	A	E	DP	Pct	Opps	Score	Grade	Runs Saved	Rank	Outs Made	To His Right	Straight On	To His Left	GB	Air	Total	Enhanced	Runs Saved	Rank
2003	StL	62	36	369.2	340	33	1	36	.997	3	.483	D+	0	-	76	+3	-1	+3	+5	+1	+6	+7	5	-
2004	StL	150	150	1338.2	1458	114	10	136	.994	13	.612	B-	1	7	300	-1	+1	+6	+6	-1	+5	+8	6	4
2005	StL	158	155	1358.2	1596	97	14	175	.992	18	.781	A+	2	2	304	+6	0	+3	+9	0	+9	+10	7	6
2006	StL	143	142	1244.1	1347	110	6	145	.996	25	.536	C	-1	22	287	+18	+5	+3	+26	+2	+28	+25	18	1
2007	StL	154	153	1324.2	1325	124	8	132	.995	17	.738	A	2	3	334	+13	+14	+6	+33	+1	+34	+37	27	1
2008	StL	144	140	1215.0	1297	135	6	119	.996	12	.617	B-	0	10	303	+9	+8	+4	+20	+1	+21	+20	15	2
		811	776	6851.0	7363	613	45	743	.994	88	.645	B	4	5	1194	+48	+27	+25	+99	+4	+103	+107	78	1

Richie Sexson

		BASIC								BUNTS					PLUS/MINUS									
Year	Team	G	GS	Inn	PO	A	E	DP	Pct	Opps	Score	Grade	Runs Saved	Rank	Outs Made	To His Right	Straight On	To His Left	GB	Air	Total	Enhanced	Runs Saved	Rank
2003	Mil	162	162	1452.0	1363	130	11	134	.993	38	.466	D	-5	34	297	+4	-3	-8	-7	+3	-4	-11	-8	32
2004	Ari	23	23	204.1	198	26	1	18	.996	7	.607	B-	1	-	49	0	+3	-2	+2	0	+2	-2	-1	-
2005	Sea	151	151	1302.0	1147	119	7	122	.995	19	.534	C	-1	21	257	-11	+7	-9	-13	0	-13	-15	-11	33
2006	Sea	150	149	1310.1	1234	110	4	115	.994	15	.617	B-	0	11	281	+5	+5	+1	+10	-1	+9	+5	4	13
2007	Sea	116	115	991.2	1000	72	2	102	.998	10	.465	D	-1	26	197	-3	-4	-7	-15	+1	-14	-15	-11	33
2008	2 tms	92	78	684.0	646	56	2	58	.997	8	.619	B-	0	10	128	-3	-8	0	-11	0	-11	-11	-8	31
		694	678	5944.1	5588	513	27	549	.996	97	.525	C-	-6	31	802	-8	0	-25	-34	+3	-31	-49	-35	34

Chris Shelton

		BASIC								BUNTS					PLUS/MINUS									
Year	Team	G	GS	Inn	PO	A	E	DP	Pct	Opps	Score	Grade	Runs Saved	Rank	Outs Made	To His Right	Straight On	To His Left	GB	Air	Total	Enhanced	Runs Saved	Rank
2004	Det	8	2	26.0	22	4	0	3	1.000					-	7	-1	0	0	0	0	0	0	0	-
2005	Det	84	83	738.1	778	60	6	88	.993	6	.683	B+	0	11	148	-3	-3	+1	-5	+1	-4	-2	-1	25
2006	Det	115	100	913.0	1003	55	6	93	.994	25	.550	C	0	11	176	+2	+4	+1	+8	0	+8	+7	5	10
2008	Tex	39	26	247.1	241	20	3	21	.989	2	.625	B-	0	-	55	+4	0	+1	+5	0	+5	+5	4	-
		246	211	1924.2	2044	139	15	205	.993	14	.618	B-	0	13	264	+2	+1	+3	+8	+1	+9	+10	8	10

First Basemen

J.T. Snow

	BASIC								BUNTS					PLUS/MINUS									
Year Team	G	GS	Inn	PO	A	E	DP	Pct	Opps	Score	Grade	Runs Saved	Rank	Outs Made	To His Right	Straight On	To His Left	GB	Air	Total	Enhanced	Runs Saved	Rank
2003 SF	98	94	812.1	814	74	5	81	.994	18	.633	B	1	6	159	+4	+5	0	+9	-1	+8	+9	7	6
2004 SF	100	88	793.0	801	56	4	69	.995	12	.521	C-	-1	23	166	+4	+3	-2	+4	0	+4	0	0	19
2005 SF	108	96	825.2	813	56	3	62	.997	15	.540	C	-1	21	188	-1	-1	+3	+1	0	+1	+2	1	16
2006 Bos	26	7	102.1	86	9	1	9	.990	2	1.000	A+	1	-	19	-1	-1	0	-2	+1	-1	-2	-1	-
2008 SF	0	0	0.0	0	0	0	0	-					-	0							0		
	332	285	2533.1	2514	195	13	221	.995	47	.590	C+	0	13	348	+6	+6	+1	+12	0	+12	+9	7	11

Nick Swisher

	BASIC								BUNTS					PLUS/MINUS									
Year Team	G	GS	Inn	PO	A	E	DP	Pct	Opps	Score	Grade	Runs Saved	Rank	Outs Made	To His Right	Straight On	To His Left	GB	Air	Total	Enhanced	Runs Saved	Rank
2004 Oak	3	2	18.0	19	0	0	3	1.000					-	1				0			0	0	-
2005 Oak	21	13	119.0	109	10	0	10	1.000	4	.525	C-	-1	-	25	+1	-1	0	+1	0	+1	+1	1	-
2006 Oak	90	80	700.0	665	42	5	55	.993	9	.578	C+	-1	22	148	+3	-2	-1	0	-2	-2	-1	-1	19
2007 Oak	44	39	346.2	391	25	3	31	.993	2	.800	A+	0	-	89	+4	+1	-5	+1	0	+1	-1	-1	-
2008 CWS	71	47	462.0	447	32	2	52	.996	3	.750	A+	0	10	79	-7	-1	+1	-7	+1	-6	-5	-4	25
	229	181	1645.2	1631	109	10	151	.994	18	.619	B-	-2	-	219	+1	-3	-5	-5	-1	-6	-6	-5	-

Mark Teixeira

	BASIC								BUNTS					PLUS/MINUS									
Year Team	G	GS	Inn	PO	A	E	DP	Pct	Opps	Score	Grade	Runs Saved	Rank	Outs Made	To His Right	Straight On	To His Left	GB	Air	Total	Enhanced	Runs Saved	Rank
2003 Tex	116	104	932.2	931	71	4	99	.996	17	.397	F	-4	31	208	+11	+16	+2	+29	+2	+31	+29	21	1
2004 Tex	142	138	1223.0	1209	98	10	114	.992	18	.531	C	-1	23	320	0	-1	+5	+4	-1	+3	+7	5	6
2005 Tex	155	154	1358.0	1378	101	3	127	.998	16	.569	C+	-1	21	337	+8	+2	+3	+13	+1	+14	+17	12	1
2006 Tex	159	159	1399.0	1480	88	4	158	.997	11	.645	B	-1	22	307	0	+2	+3	+5	-1	+4	+2	1	15
2007 2 tms	128	128	1098.0	1108	77	5	120	.996	15	.553	C	2	3	228	-2	-2	+2	-3	+1	-2	-4	-3	22
2008 2 tms	153	153	1335.0	1394	99	5	131	.997	13	.550	C	0	10	312	+5	+11	+7	+23	+1	+24	+23	17	1
	853	836	7345.2	7500	534	31	749	.996	90	.533	C	-5	30	1218	+22	+28	+22	+71	+3	+74	+74	53	2

Chad Tracy

	BASIC								BUNTS					PLUS/MINUS									
Year Team	G	GS	Inn	PO	A	E	DP	Pct	Opps	Score	Grade	Runs Saved	Rank	Outs Made	To His Right	Straight On	To His Left	GB	Air	Total	Enhanced	Runs Saved	Rank
2004 Ari	11	2	33.0	29	3	1	2	.970	1	.600	B-	0	-	7	-1	+2	0	+1	0	+1	+1	1	-
2005 Ari	80	72	652.2	706	47	3	75	.996	10	.690	A-	1	7	147	+3	+5	0	+9	+2	+11	+11	8	5
2006 Ari	6	2	21.1	23	1	1	2	.960					-	5	+1	0	-1	0	0	0	0	0	-
2007 Ari	18	12	114.2	122	5	1	9	.992						20	0	0	0	0	0	0	+1	1	-
2008 Ari	65	62	523.0	528	26	4	49	.993	9	.572	C+	0	10	104	+2	-2	-2	-1	0	-1	-2	-1	18
	180	150	1344.2	1408	82	10	137	.993	20	.633	B	1	-	195	+5	+5	-3	+9	+2	+11	+11	9	-

Joey Votto

	BASIC								BUNTS					PLUS/MINUS									
Year Team	G	GS	Inn	PO	A	E	DP	Pct	Opps	Score	Grade	Runs Saved	Rank	Outs Made	To His Right	Straight On	To His Left	GB	Air	Total	Enhanced	Runs Saved	Rank
2007 Cin	17	15	137.0	107	11	0	15	1.000	3	.367	F	-1	-	26	+2	-4	+1	-1	+1	0	0	0	-
2008 Cin	144	138	1223.2	1050	136	11	119	.991	26	.638	B	3	2	282	+6	+4	+7	+17	+1	+18	+18	13	4
	161	153	1360.2	1157	147	11	134	.992	29	.610	B-	2	-	212	+8	0	+8	+16	+2	+18	+18	13	-

Daryle Ward

	BASIC								BUNTS					PLUS/MINUS									
Year Team	G	GS	Inn	PO	A	E	DP	Pct	Opps	Score	Grade	Runs Saved	Rank	Outs Made	To His Right	Straight On	To His Left	GB	Air	Total	Enhanced	Runs Saved	Rank
2003 LA	13	11	95.1	108	10	1	14	.992	2	.425	D-	0	-	20	+1	-1	-1	-2	0	-2	-2	-1	-
2004 Pit	71	63	559.0	547	34	5	73	.991	12	.550	C	0	14	87	-3	+1	-1	-3	0	-3	-3	-2	24
2005 Pit	109	101	891.2	863	77	6	114	.994	14	.454	D	-2	31	164	-2	+5	-2	+2	0	+2	+3	2	14
2006 2 tms	10	6	61.0	55	3	1	4	.983	1	1.000	A+	0	-	13	0	-1	0	-1	0	-1	-1	0	-
2007 ChC	16	9	90.2	90	5	1	12	.990	1	.600	B-	0	-	15	-3	+1	0	-2	0	-2	-2	-1	-
2008 ChC	13	4	60.0	54	4	0	4	1.000						12	+1	0	-1	0	0	0	0	0	-
	232	194	1757.2	1717	133	14	221	.992	30	.513	C-	-2	22	217	-6	+5	-5	-6	0	-6	-5	-2	18

Kevin Youkilis

	BASIC								BUNTS					PLUS/MINUS									
Year Team	G	GS	Inn	PO	A	E	DP	Pct	Opps	Score	Grade	Runs Saved	Rank	Outs Made	To His Right	Straight On	To His Left	GB	Air	Total	Enhanced	Runs Saved	Rank
2005 Bos	9	5	47.0	48	0	0	4	1.000					-	7	0	0	0	0	0	0	0	0	-
2006 Bos	127	117	1030.0	1035	70	5	110	.995	11	.668	B+	0	11	225	+3	-4	+5	+4	+1	+5	+9	7	4
2007 Bos	135	124	1094.0	990	90	0	101	1.000	12	.675	B+	1	8	243	-2	+9	+3	+10	0	+10	+10	7	4
2008 Bos	126	110	984.2	923	87	4	92	.996	12	.613	B-	0	10	203	+4	-2	+2	+4	+2	+6	+6	4	10
	397	356	3155.2	2996	247	9	307	.997	35	.651	B	1	10	456	+5	+3	+10	+18	+3	+21	+25	18	6

First Basemen

Dmitri Young

		BASIC								BUNTS					PLUS/MINUS									
Year	Team	G	GS	Inn	PO	A	E	DP	Pct	Opps	Score	Grade	Runs Saved	Rank	Outs Made	To His Right	Straight On	To His Left	GB	Air	Total	Enhanced	Runs Saved	Rank
2003	Det	1	0	4.0	5	0	0	0	1.000					-	0							0	0	-
2004	Det	25	24	211.1	202	17	0	15	1.000	2	.425	D-	0	-	42	+2	+3	+1	+6	+1	+7	+7	5	-
2005	Det	30	30	257.0	265	22	3	25	.990	4	.425	D-	-1	-	58	-2	-1	+1	-2	0	-2	-1	-1	-
2006	Det	3	3	20.0	19	5	3	3	.889					-	5	+1	+1		+1	0	+1	+1	1	-
2007	Was	116	116	884.2	788	61	9	90	.990	11	.477	D+	-1	26	156	-7	-10	-4	-21	+1	-20	-22	-16	35
2008	Was	38	37	290.0	275	15	7	32	.976	3	.483	D+	0	-	48	-4	-3	+1	-6	-1	-7	-7	-5	-
		213	210	1667.0	1554	120	22	165	.987	20	.463	D	-2	-	205	-10	-10	-1	-22	+1	-21	-22	-16	-

Second Basemen

Jeff Baker

Year	Team	G	GS	Inn	PO	A	E	DP	Pct	Rng	GDP Opps	GDP	Pct	Runs Saved	Rank	Outs Made	To His Right	Straight On	To His Left	GB	Air	Total	Runs Saved	Rank
2008	Col	49	47	369.2	71	131	4	31	.981	4.92	50	28	.560	1	-	139	+6	0	-10	-4	0	-4	-3	-

Josh Barfield

Year	Team	G	GS	Inn	PO	A	E	DP	Pct	Rng	GDP Opps	GDP	Pct	Runs Saved	Rank	Outs Made	To His Right	Straight On	To His Left	GB	Air	Total	Runs Saved	Rank
2006	SD	147	138	1259.0	294	381	9	85	.987	4.83	164	79	.482	-1	25	442	-1	+2	+6	+7	+1	+8	6	11
2007	Cle	120	115	1032.0	242	338	15	73	.975	5.06	148	68	.459	-2	29	393	-5	-1	+12	+7	-2	+5	4	13
2008	Cle	9	8	71.0	26	24	0	9	1.000	6.34	11	7	.636	0	-	27	-1	0	-1	-2	0	-2	-2	-
		276	261	2362.0	562	743	24	167	.982	4.97	323	154	.477	-3	28	862	-7	+1	+17	+12	-1	+11	8	12

Clint Barmes

Year	Team	G	GS	Inn	PO	A	E	DP	Pct	Rng	GDP Opps	GDP	Pct	Runs Saved	Rank	Outs Made	To His Right	Straight On	To His Left	GB	Air	Total	Runs Saved	Rank
2004	Col	9	8	65.1	19	27	1	5	.979	6.34	12	4	.333	-1	-	25	+1	+1	+1	+3	-1	+2	2	-
2006	Col	4	0	14.0	2	9	0	1	1.000	7.07	1	1	1.000	0	-	9	0	0	+1	+1	0	+1	1	-
2007	Col	5	1	16.0	1	5	0	0	1.000	3.38	3			1	-	5	0	0	-1	-1	0	-1	-1	-
2008	Col	61	54	486.0	91	178	6	35	.978	4.98	59	32	.542	1	11	185	+13	+1	-6	+8	+1	+9	7	8
		79	63	581.1	113	219	7	41	.979	5.14	75	37	.493	0	-	224	+14	+2	-5	+11	0	+11	9	-

Ronnie Belliard

Year	Team	G	GS	Inn	PO	A	E	DP	Pct	Rng	GDP Opps	GDP	Pct	Runs Saved	Rank	Outs Made	To His Right	Straight On	To His Left	GB	Air	Total	Runs Saved	Rank
2003	Col	113	105	909.1	224	311	15	78	.973	5.30	143	72	.503	0	15	323	+8	-3	-9	-4	+1	-3	-2	21
2004	Cle	151	148	1320.2	278	426	14	86	.981	4.80	144	72	.500	0	13	444	+15	-1	-10	+5	-4	+1	1	14
2005	Cle	141	139	1243.2	259	413	13	95	.981	4.86	146	86	.589	4	3	463	+23	-2	-6	+15	+5	+20	15	4
2006	2 tms	145	141	1216.1	267	403	11	97	.984	4.96	148	88	.595	4	4	448	+13	-2	-16	-5	-1	-6	-5	25
2007	Was	115	113	1004.2	277	286	6	80	.989	5.04	148	73	.493	0	19	338	-1	0	-4	-5	+4	-1	-1	19
2008	Was	29	27	229.2	53	60	3	20	.974	4.43	42	20	.476	0	-	59	+2	-5	-6	-9	+1	-8	-6	-
		694	673	5924.1	1358	1899	62	456	.981	4.95	771	411	.533	8	9	2075	+60	-13	-51	-3	+6	+3	2	15

Emilio Bonifacio

Year	Team	G	GS	Inn	PO	A	E	DP	Pct	Rng	GDP Opps	GDP	Pct	Runs Saved	Rank	Outs Made	To His Right	Straight On	To His Left	GB	Air	Total	Runs Saved	Rank
2007	Ari	6	6	46.0	9	15	1	6	.960	4.70	8	6	.750	1	-	13	+1	0	-1	+1	0	+1	1	-
2008	Was	37	37	325.0	78	82	7	25	.958	4.43	46	22	.478	0	-	100	-1	-2	+2	-1	+3	+2	2	-
		43	43	371.0	87	97	8	31	.958	4.46	54	28	.519	1	-	113	0	-2	+1	0	+3	+3	3	-

Emmanuel Burriss

Year	Team	G	GS	Inn	PO	A	E	DP	Pct	Rng	GDP Opps	GDP	Pct	Runs Saved	Rank	Outs Made	To His Right	Straight On	To His Left	GB	Air	Total	Runs Saved	Rank
2008	SF	41	32	282.0	66	80	4	14	.973	4.66	30	13	.433	-1	-	90	+1	+2	+3	+5	0	+5	4	-

Asdrubal Cabrera

Year	Team	G	GS	Inn	PO	A	E	DP	Pct	Rng	GDP Opps	GDP	Pct	Runs Saved	Rank	Outs Made	To His Right	Straight On	To His Left	GB	Air	Total	Runs Saved	Rank
2007	Cle	40	34	321.0	70	119	1	28	.995	5.30	42	26	.619	2	-	122	+4	0	+1	+4	0	+4	3	-
2008	Cle	94	87	776.2	202	281	3	83	.994	5.60	112	79	.705	7	1	315	+12	+1	-6	+6	-2	+4	3	11
		134	121	1097.2	272	400	4	111	.994	5.51	154	105	.682	9	-	437	+16	+1	-5	+10	-2	+8	6	-

Miguel Cairo

Year	Team	G	GS	Inn	PO	A	E	DP	Pct	Rng	GDP Opps	GDP	Pct	Runs Saved	Rank	Outs Made	To His Right	Straight On	To His Left	GB	Air	Total	Runs Saved	Rank
2003	StL	40	33	294.2	58	88	2	17	.986	4.46	29	17	.586	1	-	106	0	+1	+1	+2	-1	+1	1	-
2004	NYY	113	96	856.0	195	274	6	58	.987	4.93	104	55	.529	1	6	310	-10	-1	-11	-22	+8	-14	-11	32
2005	NYM	82	74	657.1	151	212	6	58	.984	4.97	88	50	.568	2	7	242	-9	0	-1	-10	+2	-8	-6	27
2006	NYY	45	36	323.2	79	116	2	28	.990	5.42	37	26	.703	2	-	131	+4	+4	-1	+7	0	+7	5	-
2007	2 tms	12	7	65.2	15	20	0	1	1.000	4.80	6	1	.167	-1	-	27	0	0	+1	+2	-1	+1	1	-
2008	Sea	5	3	26.0	7	10	0	2	1.000	5.88	5	2	.400	0	-	10	+1	0	0	+1	-1	0	0	-
		297	249	2223.1	505	720	16	164	.987	4.96	269	151	.561	5	16	826	-14	+4	-11	-20	+7	-13	-10	24

Second Basemen

Alberto Callaspo

	BASIC										GROUND DP					PLUS/MINUS								
Year	Team	G	GS	Inn	PO	A	E	DP	Pct	Rng	GDP Opps	GDP	Pct	Runs Saved	Rank	Outs Made	To His Right	Straight On	To His Left	GB	Air	Total	Runs Saved	Rank
2006	Ari	3	3	26.0	7	11	1	2	.947	6.23	3	1	.333	0	-	14	0	0	0	0	0	0	0	-
2007	Ari	10	3	41.0	4	12	0	4	1.000	3.51	6	4	.667	0	-	14	0	+1	+1	+1	0	+1	1	-
2008	KC	46	42	365.2	74	119	0	36	1.000	4.75	44	32	.727	3	-	128	0	+4	-7	-3	-2	-5	-4	-
		59	48	432.2	85	142	1	42	.996	4.72	53	37	.698	3	-	156	0	+5	-6	-2	-2	-4	-3	-

Robinson Cano

	BASIC										GROUND DP					PLUS/MINUS								
Year	Team	G	GS	Inn	PO	A	E	DP	Pct	Rng	GDP Opps	GDP	Pct	Runs Saved	Rank	Outs Made	To His Right	Straight On	To His Left	GB	Air	Total	Runs Saved	Rank
2005	NYY	131	130	1142.2	258	391	17	77	.974	5.11	152	70	.461	-2	28	441	-16	-2	-15	-33	+6	-27	-21	35
2006	NYY	118	115	1009.0	230	333	9	73	.984	5.02	137	69	.504	0	19	387	-2	-3	-1	-5	+1	-4	-3	24
2007	NYY	159	157	1408.2	320	497	13	136	.984	5.22	187	122	.652	9	1	530	+6	+2	+9	+16	+1	+17	13	5
2008	NYY	159	154	1376.2	305	482	13	103	.984	5.15	178	88	.494	0	15	530	-6	+1	-8	-13	-4	-17	-13	35
		567	556	4937.0	1113	1703	52	389	.982	5.13	654	349	.534	7	10	1888	-18	-2	-15	-35	+4	-31	-24	29

Jamey Carroll

	BASIC										GROUND DP					PLUS/MINUS								
Year	Team	G	GS	Inn	PO	A	E	DP	Pct	Rng	GDP Opps	GDP	Pct	Runs Saved	Rank	Outs Made	To His Right	Straight On	To His Left	GB	Air	Total	Runs Saved	Rank
2003	Mon	11	5	51.1	12	15	0	5	1.000	4.73	11	5	.455	0	-	12	0	-2	0	-1	-1	-2	-2	-
2004	Mon	51	36	344.2	84	97	1	32	.995	4.73	45	28	.622	2	-	82	-2	+1	-7	-8	-1	-9	-7	-
2005	Was	63	44	427.2	96	145	5	33	.980	5.07	63	27	.429	-1	-	151	-4	-1	+10	+6	-1	+5	4	-
2006	Col	109	102	894.2	186	397	3	97	.995	5.86	139	91	.655	6	1	396	+4	+4	+8	+16	-3	+13	10	6
2007	Col	60	49	431.1	81	164	2	37	.992	5.11	68	35	.515	0	19	165	0	+1	+2	+2	-3	-1	-1	22
2008	Cle	74	66	580.1	105	192	3	46	.990	4.61	73	42	.575	2	8	203	+1	0	-1	0	-4	-4	-3	24
		368	302	2730.0	564	1010	14	250	.991	5.19	399	228	.571	9	4	1009	-1	+3	+12	+15	-13	+2	1	16

Alexi Casilla

	BASIC										GROUND DP					PLUS/MINUS								
Year	Team	G	GS	Inn	PO	A	E	DP	Pct	Rng	GDP Opps	GDP	Pct	Runs Saved	Rank	Outs Made	To His Right	Straight On	To His Left	GB	Air	Total	Runs Saved	Rank
2006	Min	4	1	13.0	5	8	0	4	1.000	9.00	5	4	.800	0	-	7				0	+1	+1	1	-
2007	Min	52	47	421.0	80	147	10	38	.958	4.85	67	36	.537	1	13	145	-5	-2	+4	-4	0	-4	-3	24
2008	Min	95	94	833.2	196	247	12	71	.974	4.78	125	66	.528	1	11	288	-11	-3	+9	-5	+1	-4	-3	23
		151	142	1267.2	281	402	22	113	.969	4.85	197	106	.538	2	-	440	-16	-5	+13	-9	+2	-7	-5	-

Jose Castillo

	BASIC										GROUND DP					PLUS/MINUS								
Year	Team	G	GS	Inn	PO	A	E	DP	Pct	Rng	GDP Opps	GDP	Pct	Runs Saved	Rank	Outs Made	To His Right	Straight On	To His Left	GB	Air	Total	Runs Saved	Rank
2004	Pit	123	105	951.0	229	301	11	79	.980	5.02	146	74	.507	0	13	288	-2	-2	0	-4	-2	-6	-5	26
2005	Pit	100	99	840.1	237	279	12	92	.977	5.53	131	82	.626	5	2	298	-5	-6	+1	-11	+3	-8	-6	26
2006	Pit	145	141	1235.0	344	350	18	107	.975	5.06	203	100	.493	0	19	386	-1	-2	-12	-15	0	-15	-11	32
2007	Pit	20	13	129.0	45	25	4	11	.946	4.88	19	9	.474	0	-	38	-2	0	-3	-4	0	-4	-3	-
2008	2 tms	12	7	64.0	13	19	1	2	.970	4.50	7	2	.286	0	-	25	+1	+1	0	+2	0	+2	1	-
		400	365	3219.1	868	974	46	291	.976	5.15	506	267	.528	5	16	1035	-9	-9	-14	-32	+1	-31	-24	30

Luis Castillo

	BASIC										GROUND DP					PLUS/MINUS								
Year	Team	G	GS	Inn	PO	A	E	DP	Pct	Rng	GDP Opps	GDP	Pct	Runs Saved	Rank	Outs Made	To His Right	Straight On	To His Left	GB	Air	Total	Runs Saved	Rank
2003	Fla	152	151	1312.1	286	433	10	99	.986	4.93	184	94	.511	1	8	472	+4	+6	-2	+7	+4	+11	8	8
2004	Fla	148	147	1274.1	275	405	6	96	.991	4.80	164	86	.524	1	6	423	+15	0	-8	+7	+1	+8	6	8
2005	Fla	120	116	1012.1	245	352	7	87	.988	5.31	172	79	.459	-2	28	387	+20	+3	-14	+9	0	+9	7	12
2006	Min	142	142	1239.1	267	378	6	78	.991	4.68	156	73	.468	-2	29	415	-5	+3	-1	-4	+1	-3	-2	21
2007	2 tms	135	133	1158.1	253	315	5	75	.991	4.41	159	68	.428	-4	34	369	-4	+3	0	-1	-2	-3	-2	25
2008	NYM	81	78	689.2	160	186	6	41	.983	4.52	91	38	.418	-2	26	219	+1	-1	-13	-14	0	-14	-11	32
		778	767	6686.1	1486	2069	40	476	.989	4.79	926	438	.473	-8	32	2285	+31	+14	-38	+4	+4	+8	6	14

Ronny Cedeno

	BASIC										GROUND DP					PLUS/MINUS								
Year	Team	G	GS	Inn	PO	A	E	DP	Pct	Rng	GDP Opps	GDP	Pct	Runs Saved	Rank	Outs Made	To His Right	Straight On	To His Left	GB	Air	Total	Runs Saved	Rank
2005	ChC	1	0	1.0	0	1	0	0	1.000	9.00	0		-		-	1	0			0	0	0	0	-
2006	ChC	15	14	126.2	35	37	2	7	.973	5.12	17	6	.353	-1	-	46	0	+1	-1	0	-2	-2	-2	-
2007	ChC	8	3	33.0	10	14	0	3	1.000	6.55	4	3	.750	0	-	15	+1	+1	-1	+1	0	+1	1	-
2008	ChC	43	31	273.0	60	75	2	19	.985	4.45	34	18	.529	0	-	90	-2	-1	+2	-2	0	-2	-2	-
		67	48	433.2	105	127	4	29	.983	4.81	55	27	.491	-1	-	152	-1	+1	0	-1	-2	-3	-3	-

Second Basemen

Alex Cora

Year	Team	G	GS	Inn	PO	A	E	DP	Pct	Rng	GDP Opps	GDP	Pct	Runs Saved	Rank	Outs Made	To His Right	Straight On	To His Left	GB	Air	Total	Runs Saved	Rank
				BASIC								**GROUND DP**						**PLUS/MINUS**						
2003	LA	141	122	1103.0	286	376	15	110	.978	5.40	178	99	.556	3	2	370	-4	0	+7	+3	-3	0	0	19
2004	LA	138	122	1091.1	261	343	8	90	.987	4.98	166	88	.530	2	2	354	-7	-1	-2	-8	0	-8	-6	28
2005	2 tms	50	35	328.1	76	107	2	29	.989	5.02	39	28	.718	2	-	125	+2	+1	+8	+11	-3	+8	6	-
2006	Bos	18	10	95.1	18	24	1	6	.977	3.97	8	6	.750	1	-	24	-3	-1	0	-4	0	-4	-3	-
2007	Bos	47	30	297.1	67	95	1	20	.994	4.90	36	20	.556	1	-	107	-3	+1	+4	+2	+2	+4	3	-
2008	Bos	7	3	35.0	6	14	0	3	1.000	5.14	4	3	.750	0	-	14	0	+1	-1	0	0	0	0	-
		401	322	2950.1	714	959	27	258	.984	5.10	431	244	.566	9	4	994	-15	+1	+16	+4	-4	0	0	17

Mark DeRosa

Year	Team	G	GS	Inn	PO	A	E	DP	Pct	Rng	GDP Opps	GDP	Pct	Runs Saved	Rank	Outs Made	To His Right	Straight On	To His Left	GB	Air	Total	Runs Saved	Rank
2003	Atl	29	25	229.1	49	78	2	20	.984	4.98	35	20	.571	1	-	84	+2	-2	0	0	0	0	0	-
2004	Atl	5	3	34.0	3	11	0	4	1.000	3.71	5	4	.800	0	-	9	0	+1	-2	-1		-1	-1	-
2005	Tex	17	8	78.0	13	20	1	3	.971	3.81	5	3	.600	0	-	25	+1	0	0	+1	0	+1	1	-
2006	Tex	26	26	222.2	50	86	1	16	.993	5.50	29	14	.483	0	-	87	+2	+2	-2	+1	-1	0	0	-
2007	ChC	93	88	708.2	168	193	6	45	.984	4.58	99	40	.404	-3	32	224	-2	0	+1	-1	+1	0	0	17
2008	ChC	95	80	670.0	143	185	8	32	.976	4.41	77	30	.390	-3	32	231	-3	-4	-1	-8	0	-8	-6	28
		265	230	1942.2	426	573	18	120	.982	4.63	250	111	.444	-5	-	660	0	-3	-4	-8	0	-8	-6	-

Ray Durham

Year	Team	G	GS	Inn	PO	A	E	DP	Pct	Rng	GDP Opps	GDP	Pct	Runs Saved	Rank	Outs Made	To His Right	Straight On	To His Left	GB	Air	Total	Runs Saved	Rank
2003	SF	105	101	867.2	186	309	5	65	.990	5.13	116	60	.517	1	8	338	-3	+4	+4	+4	+3	+7	5	11
2004	SF	118	115	990.1	243	314	16	75	.972	5.06	158	64	.405	-5	32	337	-5	-1	+3	-2	+2	0	0	15
2005	SF	133	131	1143.0	250	341	11	82	.982	4.65	148	66	.446	-2	28	378	-2	-1	+3	0	-4	-4	-3	20
2006	SF	133	132	1138.2	272	341	11	82	.982	4.85	162	77	.475	-1	25	391	-3	-1	+3	0	-6	-6	-5	26
2007	SF	124	117	1028.0	244	300	12	86	.978	4.76	157	80	.510	0	19	320	-7	-4	+2	-10	0	-10	-8	30
2008	2 tms	95	85	738.0	188	190	3	53	.992	4.61	113	51	.451	-1	24	212	-10	+3	-1	-8	-3	-11	-8	31
		708	681	5905.2	1383	1795	58	443	.982	4.84	854	398	.466	-8	32	1976	-30	0	+14	-16	-8	-24	-19	27

Damion Easley

Year	Team	G	GS	Inn	PO	A	E	DP	Pct	Rng	GDP Opps	GDP	Pct	Runs Saved	Rank	Outs Made	To His Right	Straight On	To His Left	GB	Air	Total	Runs Saved	Rank
2003	TB	4	3	24.2	4	7	0	1	1.000	4.01	2	1	.500	0	-	7	0	-1		-1	0	-1	-1	-
2004	Fla	25	15	158.1	28	53	3	11	.964	4.60	17	10	.588	0	-	56	+2	+2	0	+4	-2	+2	2	-
2005	Fla	46	34	324.0	80	98	4	26	.978	4.94	49	24	.490	0	-	123	-2	+1	-1	-1	+1	0	0	-
2006	Ari	9	5	46.2	16	16	0	7	1.000	6.17	10	7	.700	1	-	16	0	-1	-2	-3	0	-3	-2	-
2007	NYM	39	36	334.2	79	114	4	24	.980	5.19	41	23	.561	1	-	127	+4	0	-1	+2	+4	+6	5	-
2008	NYM	64	60	539.1	128	160	5	38	.983	4.81	89	36	.404	-3	32	170	0	+3	-12	-10	+3	-7	-5	26
		187	153	1427.2	335	448	16	107	.980	4.94	208	101	.486	-1	-	499	+4	+4	-16	-9	+6	-3	-1	-

Mark Ellis

Year	Team	G	GS	Inn	PO	A	E	DP	Pct	Rng	GDP Opps	GDP	Pct	Runs Saved	Rank	Outs Made	To His Right	Straight On	To His Left	GB	Air	Total	Runs Saved	Rank
2003	Oak	153	147	1297.2	324	455	14	94	.982	5.40	174	87	.500	0	15	535	-1	+1	+16	+17	+6	+23	17	2
2005	Oak	115	109	972.0	204	333	6	83	.989	4.97	134	74	.552	2	7	373	+2	+1	+5	+9	+2	+11	8	11
2006	Oak	123	121	1070.0	273	357	2	91	.997	5.30	152	89	.586	4	4	390	-3	+8	+5	+10	+3	+13	10	7
2007	Oak	150	149	1322.0	302	499	5	104	.994	5.45	177	95	.537	2	8	560	0	+5	+11	+16	+3	+19	14	4
2008	Oak	115	114	1011.2	228	336	4	88	.993	5.02	131	81	.618	5	2	373	+9	+7	+5	+22	+3	+25	19	2
		656	640	5673.1	1331	1980	31	460	.991	5.25	768	426	.555	13	2	2231	+7	+22	+42	+74	+17	+91	68	3

Mike Fontenot

Year	Team	G	GS	Inn	PO	A	E	DP	Pct	Rng	GDP Opps	GDP	Pct	Runs Saved	Rank	Outs Made	To His Right	Straight On	To His Left	GB	Air	Total	Runs Saved	Rank
2007	ChC	62	50	468.0	112	128	6	33	.976	4.62	63	32	.508	0	19	152	+1	+1	-3	-1	+1	0	0	18
2008	ChC	82	49	498.2	101	143	1	27	.996	4.40	48	25	.521	0	15	176	+2	+3	+6	+10	+1	+11	8	7
		144	99	966.2	213	271	7	60	.986	4.51	111	57	.514	0	-	328	+3	+4	+3	+9	+2	+11	8	-

Edgar Gonzalez

Year	Team	G	GS	Inn	PO	A	E	DP	Pct	Rng	GDP Opps	GDP	Pct	Runs Saved	Rank	Outs Made	To His Right	Straight On	To His Left	GB	Air	Total	Runs Saved	Rank
2008	SD	72	66	559.2	92	189	4	35	.986	4.52	74	32	.432	-2	26	192	-2	-1	+6	+2	-1	+1	1	14

Second Basemen

Mark Grudzielanek

		BASIC									GROUND DP					PLUS/MINUS								
Year	Team	G	GS	Inn	PO	A	E	DP	Pct	Rng	GDP Opps	GDP	Pct	Runs Saved	Rank	Outs Made	To His Right	Straight On	To His Left	GB	Air	Total	Runs Saved	Rank
2003	ChC	121	115	1011.2	231	331	8	92	.986	5.00	158	88	.557	3	2	342	+4	-1	-5	-1	-4	-5	-4	22
2004	ChC	76	61	568.0	136	186	5	30	.985	5.10	78	28	.359	-3	26	208	-5	+1	+5	+2	-2	0	0	18
2005	StL	137	132	1158.1	245	442	7	108	.990	5.34	166	104	.627	6	1	431	+15	+2	+3	+20	0	+20	15	5
2006	KC	132	130	1111.0	261	372	4	110	.994	5.13	173	107	.618	6	1	366	+13	+1	-3	+10	-1	+9	7	10
2007	KC	116	110	947.1	184	300	6	68	.988	4.60	113	62	.549	2	8	313	+7	+4	-1	+10	-3	+7	5	10
2008	KC	85	85	710.2	135	257	4	59	.990	4.96	87	52	.598	3	5	279	-2	+4	-7	-5	-2	-7	-5	25
		667	633	5507.0	1192	1888	34	467	.989	5.03	775	441	.569	17	1	1939	+32	+11	-8	+36	-12	+24	18	9

Brendan Harris

		BASIC									GROUND DP					PLUS/MINUS								
Year	Team	G	GS	Inn	PO	A	E	DP	Pct	Rng	GDP Opps	GDP	Pct	Runs Saved	Rank	Outs Made	To His Right	Straight On	To His Left	GB	Air	Total	Runs Saved	Rank
2004	Mon	11	10	82.0	15	20	1	3	.972	3.84	8	3	.375	0	-	22	0	0	+1	+1	0	+1	1	-
2005	Was	2	1	13.1	2	5	0	1	1.000	4.73	2	1	.500	0	-	4	0	0	0	0	0	0	0	-
2006	2 tms	7	3	34.0	9	7	0	2	1.000	4.24	2	1	.500	0	-	11	0	-1	0	-1	0	-1	-1	-
2007	TB	47	45	404.0	75	96	1	26	.994	3.81	37	24	.649	2	-	110	-5	0	0	-5	0	-5	-4	-
2008	Min	39	37	319.2	56	101	5	24	.969	4.42	41	20	.488	0	-	100	-2	+3	-1	+1	-1	0	0	-
		106	96	853.0	157	229	7	56	.982	4.07	90	49	.544	2	-	247	-7	+2	0	-4	-1	-5	-4	-

Aaron Hill

		BASIC									GROUND DP					PLUS/MINUS								
Year	Team	G	GS	Inn	PO	A	E	DP	Pct	Rng	GDP Opps	GDP	Pct	Runs Saved	Rank	Outs Made	To His Right	Straight On	To His Left	GB	Air	Total	Runs Saved	Rank
2005	Tor	22	19	177.2	33	77	1	15	.991	5.57	34	14	.412	-1	-	78	0	+1	+2	+3	-2	+1	1	-
2006	Tor	112	106	914.1	174	345	7	93	.987	5.11	132	86	.652	6	1	355	+15	+2	+11	+28	-3	+25	19	1
2007	Tor	160	158	1410.0	244	560	14	114	.983	5.13	193	110	.570	4	2	575	+7	+9	+7	+23	-1	+22	17	1
2008	Tor	55	53	479.0	87	150	1	27	.996	4.45	50	25	.500	0	-	164	-2	+2	0	0	-2	-2	-2	-
		349	336	2981.0	538	1132	23	249	.986	5.04	409	235	.575	9	4	1172	+20	+14	+20	+54	-8	+46	35	6

Orlando Hudson

		BASIC									GROUND DP					PLUS/MINUS								
Year	Team	G	GS	Inn	PO	A	E	DP	Pct	Rng	GDP Opps	GDP	Pct	Runs Saved	Rank	Outs Made	To His Right	Straight On	To His Left	GB	Air	Total	Runs Saved	Rank
2003	Tor	139	129	1146.2	267	477	12	98	.984	5.84	180	93	.517	1	8	513	-7	0	+24	+17	+5	+22	17	3
2004	Tor	133	128	1124.2	275	449	12	90	.984	5.79	162	79	.488	-1	19	486	+4	+7	+16	+26	+9	+35	27	1
2005	Tor	130	120	1067.2	302	390	6	80	.991	5.83	143	77	.538	2	7	487	-1	+1	+18	+17	+3	+20	15	3
2006	Ari	157	151	1349.0	311	510	13	116	.984	5.48	195	101	.518	1	15	550	-3	-11	+23	+8	+5	+13	10	5
2007	Ari	137	137	1183.1	258	387	10	96	.985	4.91	166	89	.536	2	8	433	-8	-5	+25	+11	+9	+20	15	3
2008	Ari	105	105	904.2	200	284	9	60	.982	4.82	106	53	.500	0	15	345	-11	0	+4	-7	+3	-4	-3	21
		801	770	6776.0	1613	2497	62	540	.985	5.46	952	492	.517	5	16	2814	-26	-8	+110	+72	+34	+106	81	2

Tadahito Iguchi

		BASIC									GROUND DP					PLUS/MINUS								
Year	Team	G	GS	Inn	PO	A	E	DP	Pct	Rng	GDP Opps	GDP	Pct	Runs Saved	Rank	Outs Made	To His Right	Straight On	To His Left	GB	Air	Total	Runs Saved	Rank
2005	CWS	133	129	1171.1	234	375	14	85	.978	4.68	141	79	.560	3	5	413	-9	+4	+3	-2	-1	-3	-2	19
2006	CWS	136	136	1209.1	270	371	8	76	.988	4.77	140	74	.529	1	15	428	-5	0	0	-6	-1	-7	-5	27
2007	2 tms	121	118	1043.1	260	337	6	96	.997	5.15	159	88	.553	3	4	360	-5	+1	-4	-9	0	-9	-7	29
2008	2 tms	78	73	672.1	143	206	1	54	.997	4.67	94	52	.553	2	8	216	-8	+2	+5	0	0	0	0	17
		468	456	4096.1	907	1289	29	311	.987	4.82	534	293	.549	9	4	1417	-27	+7	+4	-17	-2	-19	-14	26

Omar Infante

		BASIC									GROUND DP					PLUS/MINUS								
Year	Team	G	GS	Inn	PO	A	E	DP	Pct	Rng	GDP Opps	GDP	Pct	Runs Saved	Rank	Outs Made	To His Right	Straight On	To His Left	GB	Air	Total	Runs Saved	Rank
2003	Det	2	1	13.0	3	3	0	2	1.000	4.15	2	2	1.000	0	-	3				0	0	0	0	-
2004	Det	105	97	874.2	205	282	12	72	.976	5.01	124	71	.573	3	1	270	-6	-5	+3	-8	-1	-9	-7	29
2005	Det	69	65	591.2	153	186	4	51	.988	5.16	88	47	.534	1	12	190	-5	-2	0	-6	-1	-7	-5	25
2006	Det	37	34	307.1	65	108	4	30	.977	5.07	41	26	.634	2	-	110	+4	-1	+2	+5	0	+5	4	-
2007	Det	20	12	124.1	30	38	1	8	.986	4.92	15	6	.400	0	-	44	-1	0	+2	+1	0	+1	1	-
2008	Atl	10	9	74.0	14	19	0	6	1.000	4.01	13	6	.462	0	-	19	+1	+1	0	+2	0	+2	2	-
		243	218	1985.0	470	636	21	169	.981	5.01	283	158	.558	6	13	636	-7	-7	+7	-6	-2	-8	-5	21

Joe Inglett

		BASIC									GROUND DP					PLUS/MINUS								
Year	Team	G	GS	Inn	PO	A	E	DP	Pct	Rng	GDP Opps	GDP	Pct	Runs Saved	Rank	Outs Made	To His Right	Straight On	To His Left	GB	Air	Total	Runs Saved	Rank
2006	Cle	53	47	417.1	112	142	4	43	.984	5.48	66	38	.576	2	10	157	+6	0	-7	-1	+3	+2	2	14
2008	Tor	66	62	541.1	123	176	5	38	.984	4.97	68	34	.500	0	15	206	-1	-4	+7	+2	+5	+7	5	9
		119	109	958.2	235	318	9	81	.984	5.19	134	72	.537	2	-	363	+5	-4	0	+1	+8	+9	7	-

Second Basemen

Akinori Iwamura

Year	Team	G	GS	Inn	PO	A	E	DP	Pct	Rng	GDP Opps	GDP	Pct	Runs Saved	Rank	Outs Made	To His Right	Straight On	To His Left	GB	Air	Total	Runs Saved	Rank
2007	TB	1	1	9.0	2	2	0	1	1.000	4.00	1	1	1.000	0	-	2	0		0	0	0	0	0	-
2008	TB	152	151	1337.0	284	397	7	109	.990	4.58	166	101	.608	5	2	434	-5	-6	+7	-4	+1	-3	-2	19
		153	152	1346.0	286	399	7	110	.990	4.58	167	102	.611	5	-	436	-5	-6	+7	-4	+1	-3	-2	-

Kelly Johnson

Year	Team	G	GS	Inn	PO	A	E	DP	Pct	Rng	GDP Opps	GDP	Pct	Runs Saved	Rank	Outs Made	To His Right	Straight On	To His Left	GB	Air	Total	Runs Saved	Rank
2007	Atl	133	127	1153.1	227	383	14	83	.978	4.76	153	79	.516	1	13	412	+5	-4	-6	-5	+5	0	0	16
2008	Atl	144	135	1198.2	262	425	14	89	.980	5.16	182	83	.456	-2	26	441	-3	-2	+5	0	-1	-1	-1	18
		277	262	2352.0	489	808	28	172	.979	4.96	335	162	.484	-1	25	853	+2	-6	-1	-5	+4	-1	-1	18

Howie Kendrick

Year	Team	G	GS	Inn	PO	A	E	DP	Pct	Rng	GDP Opps	GDP	Pct	Runs Saved	Rank	Outs Made	To His Right	Straight On	To His Left	GB	Air	Total	Runs Saved	Rank
2006	LAA	28	25	220.0	48	67	0	24	1.000	4.70	33	23	.697	2	-	75	-4	+2	+4	+2	+1	+3	2	-
2007	LAA	86	85	751.1	146	254	9	54	.978	4.79	91	49	.538	1	13	275	-2	0	+9	+7	0	+7	5	11
2008	LAA	92	90	776.0	155	287	4	67	.991	5.13	99	61	.616	3	5	308	-13	-4	+13	-5	+1	-4	-3	22
		206	200	1747.1	349	608	13	145	.987	4.93	223	133	.596	6	-	658	-19	-2	+26	+4	+2	+6	4	-

Adam Kennedy

Year	Team	G	GS	Inn	PO	A	E	DP	Pct	Rng	GDP Opps	GDP	Pct	Runs Saved	Rank	Outs Made	To His Right	Straight On	To His Left	GB	Air	Total	Runs Saved	Rank
2003	Ana	140	125	1119.2	235	371	6	77	.990	4.87	131	70	.534	1	8	445	+6	0	+8	+15	0	+15	11	6
2004	Ana	144	138	1225.0	255	387	12	71	.982	4.72	133	62	.466	-1	19	438	+2	0	-3	-1	+8	+7	5	10
2005	LAA	127	123	1107.2	212	352	5	71	.991	4.58	110	65	.591	3	5	401	+11	-1	+8	+18	-2	+16	12	7
2006	LAA	133	127	1140.2	205	361	9	76	.984	4.47	127	70	.551	2	10	405	+3	-5	0	-3	+4	+1	1	15
2007	StL	79	74	630.1	156	211	7	46	.981	5.24	95	42	.442	-2	29	250	+2	-1	-1	+1	-2	-1	-1	20
2008	StL	84	74	635.2	144	224	7	56	.981	5.21	85	53	.624	3	5	245	+15	-1	+5	+18	0	+18	14	3
		707	661	5859.0	1207	1906	46	397	.985	4.78	681	362	.532	6	13	2184	+39	-8	+17	+48	+8	+56	42	5

Jeff Kent

Year	Team	G	GS	Inn	PO	A	E	DP	Pct	Rng	GDP Opps	GDP	Pct	Runs Saved	Rank	Outs Made	To His Right	Straight On	To His Left	GB	Air	Total	Runs Saved	Rank
2003	Hou	128	127	1113.0	278	354	11	82	.983	5.11	174	81	.466	-2	24	380	+1	-2	-4	-5	-3	-8	-6	24
2004	Hou	139	138	1189.1	276	374	7	73	.989	4.92	185	71	.384	-6	34	373	-3	+3	+19	+19	-4	+15	11	5
2005	LAD	140	138	1209.2	284	424	16	88	.978	5.27	177	78	.441	-3	34	438	-9	+6	-2	-6	+1	-5	-4	21
2006	LAD	108	107	887.2	217	313	8	73	.985	5.37	160	69	.431	-3	32	325	-11	-3	0	-14	-4	-18	-14	33
2007	LAD	133	132	1084.1	235	328	14	76	.976	4.67	174	76	.437	-3	32	355	-8	-2	+1	-8	-5	-13	-10	32
2008	LAD	116	114	885.0	168	279	11	53	.976	4.55	128	53	.414	-3	32	291	-7	0	0	-7	-4	-11	-8	29
		764	756	6369.0	1458	2072	67	445	.981	4.99	998	428	.429	-20	35	2162	-37	+2	+14	-21	-19	-40	-31	33

Ian Kinsler

Year	Team	G	GS	Inn	PO	A	E	DP	Pct	Rng	GDP Opps	GDP	Pct	Runs Saved	Rank	Outs Made	To His Right	Straight On	To His Left	GB	Air	Total	Runs Saved	Rank
2006	Tex	119	117	1032.0	247	393	18	94	.973	5.58	153	86	.562	3	8	424	-3	+1	-8	-10	+6	-4	-3	22
2007	Tex	130	129	1136.2	283	436	17	98	.977	5.69	163	88	.540	2	8	459	+7	-4	+1	+4	+3	+7	5	9
2008	Tex	121	120	1064.0	292	390	18	123	.974	5.77	201	113	.562	4	4	412	-1	+2	-15	-13	-2	-15	-11	33
		370	366	3232.2	822	1219	53	315	.975	5.68	517	287	.555	9	4	1295	+3	-1	-22	-19	+7	-12	-9	23

Felipe Lopez

Year	Team	G	GS	Inn	PO	A	E	DP	Pct	Rng	GDP Opps	GDP	Pct	Runs Saved	Rank	Outs Made	To His Right	Straight On	To His Left	GB	Air	Total	Runs Saved	Rank
2003	Cin	3	3	24.2	3	4	1	1	.875	2.55	3	1	.333	0	-	4	0	0	0	0		0	0	-
2004	Cin	2	0	5.0	1	1	1	1	.667	3.60	2	1	.500	0	-	0				-1		-1	-1	-
2005	Cin	7	5	48.0	15	11	0	4	1.000	4.88	7	4	.571	0	-	14	+1	0	0	+2	+1	+3	2	-
2007	Was	43	42	373.1	90	113	1	34	.995	4.89	50	33	.660	2	-	130	-2	+1	-3	-4	-2	-6	-5	-
2008	2 tms	101	89	780.0	155	253	11	53	.974	4.71	103	45	.437	-2	26	267	-8	+1	-6	-12	-3	-15	-11	34
		156	139	1231.0	264	382	14	93	.979	4.72	165	84	.509	0	-	415	-9	+2	-9	-15	-4	-19	-15	-

Second Basemen

Jose Lopez

Year	Team	G	GS	Inn	PO	A	E	DP	Pct	Rng	GDP Opps	GDP	Pct	Runs Saved	Rank	Outs Made	To His Right	Straight On	To His Left	GB	Air	Total	Runs Saved	Rank
2005	Sea	51	50	439.0	123	159	6	33	.979	5.78	61	32	.525	0	-	187	+1	+3	-3	0	-3	-3	-2	-
2006	Sea	150	148	1322.0	282	416	16	95	.978	4.75	162	89	.549	2	10	472	+15	0	-10	+5	+4	+9	7	9
2007	Sea	146	139	1231.1	280	423	8	105	.989	5.14	175	97	.554	3	11	487	+8	+2	-5	+5	0	+5	4	12
2008	Sea	139	139	1229.1	259	468	12	99	.984	5.32	172	90	.523	1	11	532	-9	+1	+10	+2	-2	0	0	16
		486	476	4221.2	944	1466	42	332	.983	5.14	570	308	.540	6	13	1678	+15	+6	-8	+12	-1	+11	9	11

Mark Loretta

Year	Team	G	GS	Inn	PO	A	E	DP	Pct	Rng	GDP Opps	GDP	Pct	Runs Saved	Rank	Outs Made	To His Right	Straight On	To His Left	GB	Air	Total	Runs Saved	Rank
2003	SD	150	144	1247.1	273	412	7	84	.990	4.94	160	77	.481	-1	25	450	+4	+4	+1	+9	0	+9	7	9
2004	SD	154	154	1339.0	289	451	10	100	.987	4.97	178	93	.522	1	6	477	-2	-2	-3	-7	0	-7	-5	27
2005	SD	105	105	910.1	201	261	6	61	.987	4.57	109	57	.523	1	12	307	-1	+1	-12	-12	+1	-11	-8	29
2006	Bos	138	133	1172.0	246	389	4	99	.994	4.88	156	91	.583	4	4	401	-18	-3	+10	-11	-4	-15	-11	31
2007	Hou	49	18	201.0	47	50	0	14	1.000	4.34	25	13	.520	1	-	59	0	+1	+1	+1	+1	+2	2	-
2008	Hou	46	41	368.0	85	119	1	28	.995	4.99	42	26	.619	2	-	130	-4	+4	-4	-5	-1	-6	-5	-
		642	595	5237.2	1141	1682	28	386	.990	4.85	670	357	.533	7	10	1824	-21	+5	-7	-25	-3	-28	-20	28

Kaz Matsui

Year	Team	G	GS	Inn	PO	A	E	DP	Pct	Rng	GDP Opps	GDP	Pct	Runs Saved	Rank	Outs Made	To His Right	Straight On	To His Left	GB	Air	Total	Runs Saved	Rank
2004	NYM	3	3	24.0	4	8	1	3	.923	4.50	4	3	.750	0	-	9	0	0	0	-1	0	-1	-1	-
2005	NYM	71	64	560.0	107	187	9	32	.970	4.73	64	31	.484	0	18	211	0	+2	-3	-1	0	-1	-1	15
2006	2 tms	52	51	463.0	120	158	3	48	.989	5.40	78	42	.538	1	15	169	+5	+4	-10	-2	0	-2	-1	19
2007	Col	102	96	863.1	200	311	4	84	.992	5.33	131	78	.595	4	2	335	+12	+6	-9	+9	+3	+12	9	6
2008	Hou	94	94	806.0	190	219	12	56	.971	4.57	101	49	.485	0	15	267	-2	0	-7	-10	-1	-11	-8	30
		322	308	2716.1	621	883	29	223	.981	4.98	378	203	.537	5	16	991	+15	+12	-29	-5	+2	-3	-2	19

Aaron Miles

Year	Team	G	GS	Inn	PO	A	E	DP	Pct	Rng	GDP Opps	GDP	Pct	Runs Saved	Rank	Outs Made	To His Right	Straight On	To His Left	GB	Air	Total	Runs Saved	Rank
2003	CWS	3	1	14.0	1	6	0	0	1.000	4.50	0		-			6	0	+1	0	0	0	0	0	-
2004	Col	128	116	1029.0	273	353	10	70	.984	5.48	169	63	.373	-6	34	371	-1	+5	+14	+18	+3	+21	16	2
2005	Col	79	69	602.0	154	207	6	48	.984	5.40	100	45	.450	-2	28	229	-6	0	+1	-5	-3	-8	-6	28
2006	StL	88	71	649.2	165	232	10	58	.975	5.50	109	55	.505	0	19	238	+1	-1	-2	+2	-2	0	0	17
2007	StL	85	63	590.2	152	160	5	39	.984	4.75	70	36	.514	0	19	184	+5	+2	-5	+1	-2	-1	-1	21
2008	StL	85	49	499.2	91	165	3	47	.988	4.61	68	41	.603	2	8	171	+2	-1	-5	-4	+5	+1	1	15
		468	369	3385.0	836	1123	34	262	.983	5.21	516	240	.465	-6	31	1199	+1	+6	+7	+12	+1	+13	10	10

Augie Ojeda

Year	Team	G	GS	Inn	PO	A	E	DP	Pct	Rng	GDP Opps	GDP	Pct	Runs Saved	Rank	Outs Made	To His Right	Straight On	To His Left	GB	Air	Total	Runs Saved	Rank
2003	ChC	5	4	37.0	8	9	0	2	1.000	4.14	2	1	.500	0	-	13	+1	0	-1	+1	0	+1	1	-
2004	Min	20	9	110.0	19	43	2	8	.969	5.07	12	8	.667	1	-	40	+3	-1	+1	+3	-1	+2	2	-
2007	Ari	26	16	164.2	29	70	0	18	1.000	5.41	26	18	.692	1	-	72	0	0	-2	-2	-1	-3	-2	-
2008	Ari	44	30	286.0	70	92	0	26	1.000	5.10	41	24	.585	1	-	105	0	0	+3	+3	+3	+6	5	-
		95	59	597.2	126	214	2	54	.994	5.12	81	51	.630	3	-	230	+4	-1	+1	+5	+1	+6	6	-

Dustin Pedroia

Year	Team	G	GS	Inn	PO	A	E	DP	Pct	Rng	GDP Opps	GDP	Pct	Runs Saved	Rank	Outs Made	To His Right	Straight On	To His Left	GB	Air	Total	Runs Saved	Rank
2006	Bos	27	19	172.0	45	73	3	17	.975	6.17	28	15	.536	0	-	82	-1	0	-2	-2	+1	-1	-1	-
2007	Bos	137	132	1141.1	259	360	6	78	.990	4.88	126	71	.563	2	8	417	-1	+3	-5	-4	-1	-5	-4	25
2008	Bos	157	155	1376.1	279	448	6	101	.992	4.75	176	90	.511	1	11	477	+1	+4	+9	+13	+2	+15	11	5
		321	306	2689.2	583	881	15	196	.990	4.90	330	176	.533	3	21	976	-1	+7	+2	+7	+2	+9	6	13

Brandon Phillips

Year	Team	G	GS	Inn	PO	A	E	DP	Pct	Rng	GDP Opps	GDP	Pct	Runs Saved	Rank	Outs Made	To His Right	Straight On	To His Left	GB	Air	Total	Runs Saved	Rank
2003	Cle	109	104	925.1	236	325	11	76	.981	5.46	144	73	.507	0	15	345	+8	+4	-5	+7	-1	+6	5	12
2004	Cle	6	6	56.2	17	19	1	4	.973	5.72	10	4	.400	0	-	16	0	-1	+1	0	0	0	0	-
2005	Cle	2	2	18.0	5	4	0	2	1.000	4.50	2	2	1.000	0	-	6	0	0	0	0	0	0	0	-
2006	Cin	142	136	1216.1	331	334	16	83	.977	4.92	170	76	.447	-3	32	403	+2	-5	-2	-5	+1	-4	-3	23
2007	Cin	156	154	1371.0	341	433	8	113	.990	5.08	198	101	.510	1	13	491	+3	+7	-2	+8	+3	+11	8	7
2008	Cin	140	140	1237.2	298	401	7	85	.990	5.08	183	80	.437	-3	32	429	+17	+4	0	+21	-4	+17	13	4
		555	542	4825.0	1228	1516	43	363	.985	5.12	707	336	.475	-5	30	1690	+30	+9	-8	+31	-1	+30	23	8

Second Basemen

Placido Polanco

Year	Team	G	GS	Inn	PO	A	E	DP	Pct	Rng	GDP Opps	GDP	Pct	Runs Saved	Rank	Outs Made	To His Right	Straight On	To His Left	GB	Air	Total	Runs Saved	Rank
2003	Phi	99	99	873.2	213	301	4	69	.992	5.29	130	67	.515	1	8	334	+8	+5	+5	+19	-1	+18	14	4
2004	Phi	109	105	944.0	264	304	3	76	.995	5.42	138	67	.486	-1	19	317	+11	-6	-12	-7	+3	-4	-3	23
2005	2 tms	113	109	945.2	244	322	3	95	.995	5.39	158	90	.570	4	3	336	+3	+7	+4	+14	-1	+13	10	9
2006	Det	108	107	943.0	224	325	6	81	.989	5.24	117	72	.615	4	4	372	+4	+5	-4	+5	0	+5	4	13
2007	Det	141	138	1209.0	294	389	0	101	1.000	5.08	172	95	.552	3	4	420	+4	0	+5	+9	+1	+10	8	8
2008	Det	141	136	1201.1	323	374	8	100	.989	5.22	178	89	.500	0	15	424	+5	-2	+10	+12	+2	+14	11	6
		711	694	6116.2	1562	2015	24	522	.993	5.26	893	480	.538	11	3	2203	+35	+9	+8	+52	+4	+56	44	4

Alexei Ramirez

Year	Team	G	GS	Inn	PO	A	E	DP	Pct	Rng	GDP Opps	GDP	Pct	Runs Saved	Rank	Outs Made	To His Right	Straight On	To His Left	GB	Air	Total	Runs Saved	Rank
2008	CWS	121	117	1017.1	237	327	11	71	.981	4.99	135	67	.496	0	15	370	-10	+3	-6	-13	+5	-8	-6	27

Luis Rivas

Year	Team	G	GS	Inn	PO	A	E	DP	Pct	Rng	GDP Opps	GDP	Pct	Runs Saved	Rank	Outs Made	To His Right	Straight On	To His Left	GB	Air	Total	Runs Saved	Rank
2003	Min	134	131	1144.0	218	325	10	64	.982	4.27	121	58	.479	-1	25	374	-13	+1	-11	-23	-2	-25	-19	35
2004	Min	109	95	860.1	176	317	3	75	.994	5.16	121	65	.537	1	6	303	-10	+1	+10	0	-5	-5	-4	25
2005	Min	53	40	360.0	77	112	1	26	.995	4.73	36	22	.611	1	-	124	-4	+1	-1	-4	-1	-5	-4	-
2007	Cle	2	2	15.0	3	4	0	0	1.000	4.20	1				-	6	+1	0	-1	0	-1	-1	-1	-
2008	Pit	29	19	191.2	51	68	1	22	.992	5.59	36	22	.611	1	-	62	+1	+1	-1	+1	0	+1	1	-
		327	287	2571.0	525	826	15	187	.989	4.73	315	167	.530	2	22	869	-25	+3	-4	-26	-9	-35	-27	31

Brian Roberts

Year	Team	G	GS	Inn	PO	A	E	DP	Pct	Rng	GDP Opps	GDP	Pct	Runs Saved	Rank	Outs Made	To His Right	Straight On	To His Left	GB	Air	Total	Runs Saved	Rank
2003	Bal	107	105	925.0	198	324	7	67	.987	5.08	120	63	.525	1	8	353	-3	+3	+13	+12	+4	+16	12	5
2004	Bal	150	148	1322.1	235	426	8	92	.988	4.50	167	89	.533	2	2	448	-1	-1	+3	-2	0	-2	-2	22
2005	Bal	141	138	1208.0	238	413	8	93	.988	4.85	152	84	.553	2	7	453	+8	+2	+6	+16	+2	+18	14	6
2006	Bal	137	135	1167.2	214	375	9	98	.985	4.54	156	85	.545	2	10	397	-4	+8	+4	+8	-1	+7	5	12
2007	Bal	154	151	1329.2	278	457	7	110	.991	4.97	205	101	.493	0	19	488	+1	+3	-2	+1	-1	0	0	15
2008	Bal	154	151	1320.0	289	441	8	110	.989	4.98	211	105	.498	0	15	474	+13	+2	-15	-1	-3	-4	-3	20
		843	828	7272.2	1452	2436	47	570	.988	4.81	1011	527	.521	7	10	2613	+14	+14	+9	+34	+1	+35	26	7

Sean Rodriguez

Year	Team	G	GS	Inn	PO	A	E	DP	Pct	Rng	GDP Opps	GDP	Pct	Runs Saved	Rank	Outs Made	To His Right	Straight On	To His Left	GB	Air	Total	Runs Saved	Rank
2008	LAA	51	45	423.2	97	127	2	36	.991	4.76	58	36	.621	2	-	149	-4	+1	+1	-2	0	-2	-2	-

Freddy Sanchez

Year	Team	G	GS	Inn	PO	A	E	DP	Pct	Rng	GDP Opps	GDP	Pct	Runs Saved	Rank	Outs Made	To His Right	Straight On	To His Left	GB	Air	Total	Runs Saved	Rank
2003	Bos	3	2	20.0	9	2	0	1	1.000	4.95	4	1	.250	0	-	4				0	0	0	0	-
2004	Pit	3	3	25.0	3	4	0	1	1.000	2.52	1	1	1.000	0	-	2	0		0	0	0	0	0	-
2005	Pit	58	39	387.1	108	117	2	40	.991	5.23	65	38	.585	2	-	125	-1	0	-3	-4	-2	-6	-5	-
2006	Pit	23	18	165.1	39	41	0	15	1.000	4.35	27	13	.481	0	-	46	-1	0	+1	-1	-1	-2	-2	-
2007	Pit	146	146	1272.2	313	379	9	121	.987	4.89	205	112	.546	3	4	378	+2	+2	-7	-3	-2	-5	-4	26
2008	Pit	131	131	1135.2	291	355	7	104	.989	5.12	190	96	.505	0	15	369	+2	-2	+5	+5	-3	+2	2	12
		364	339	3006.0	763	898	18	282	.989	4.97	492	261	.530	5	16	924	+2	0	-4	-3	-8	-11	-9	22

Marco Scutaro

Year	Team	G	GS	Inn	PO	A	E	DP	Pct	Rng	GDP Opps	GDP	Pct	Runs Saved	Rank	Outs Made	To His Right	Straight On	To His Left	GB	Air	Total	Runs Saved	Rank
2003	NYM	39	18	195.2	53	52	2	13	.981	4.83	30	12	.400	-1	-	59	-1	+1	0	-1	-1	-2	-2	-
2004	Oak	123	106	968.2	231	310	3	78	.994	5.03	136	72	.529	1	6	305	-7	-1	-4	-12	0	-12	-9	30
2005	Oak	30	29	267.2	56	92	1	19	.993	4.98	35	17	.486	0	-	104	+3	+2	+4	+9	-1	+8	6	-
2006	Oak	37	33	301.2	73	93	1	32	.994	4.95	48	32	.667	2	-	98	+1	+1	+1	+3	-1	+2	2	-
2007	Oak	13	12	110.0	19	44	0	10	1.000	5.15	16	10	.625	1	-	45	-2	0	+1	-1	0	-1	-1	-
2008	Tor	50	39	354.1	60	126	1	19	.995	4.72	42	17	.405	-1	-	144	-3	-3	+6	0	+1	+1	1	-
		292	237	2198.0	492	717	8	171	.993	4.95	307	160	.521	2	22	755	-9	0	+8	-2	-2	-4	-3	20

Second Basemen

Alfonso Soriano

		BASIC									GROUND DP					PLUS/MINUS							
Year	Team	G	GS	Inn	PO	A	E	DP	Pct	Rng	GDP Opps	GDP	Pct	Runs Saved	Rank	Outs Made	To His Right	Straight On	To His Left	GB	Air	Total	Runs Saved	Rank
2003	NYY	155	154	1376.0	293	444	19	87	.975	4.82	162	82	.506	0	15	502	-6	-6	+6	-5	+2	-3	-2	20
2004	Tex	142	142	1248.0	308	418	23	104	.969	5.24	198	100	.505	0	13	453	-7	-2	-6	-16	+1	-15	-11	33
2005	Tex	153	153	1351.0	284	447	21	101	.972	4.87	198	93	.470	-2	28	474	+2	+1	-23	-20	-2	-22	-17	33
2007	ChC	1	0	1.0	0	0	0	0	-	.00	0		-			0	0			0	0	0	0	-
2008	ChC	1	0	1.0	0	2	0	0	1.000	18.00	0		-			2		0		0	0	0	0	-
		452	449	3977.0	885	1311	63	292	.972	4.97	558	275	.493	-2	27	1431	-11	-7	-23	-41	+1	-40	-30	34

Dan Uggla

		BASIC									GROUND DP					PLUS/MINUS							
Year	Team	G	GS	Inn	PO	A	E	DP	Pct	Rng	GDP Opps	GDP	Pct	Runs Saved	Rank	Outs Made	To His Right	Straight On	To His Left	GB	Air	Total	Runs Saved	Rank
2006	Fla	151	150	1304.1	314	423	15	112	.980	5.09	206	107	.519	1	15	486	-6	+3	+5	+2	-2	0	0	16
2007	Fla	158	156	1383.2	323	402	11	111	.985	4.72	196	102	.520	1	13	438	-7	+4	-15	-18	-1	-19	-14	35
2008	Fla	144	144	1272.2	297	390	13	82	.981	4.86	154	74	.481	-1	24	464	+9	-5	0	+3	+1	+4	3	10
		453	450	3960.2	934	1215	39	305	.982	4.88	556	283	.509	1	24	1388	-4	+2	-10	-13	-2	-15	-11	25

Juan Uribe

		BASIC									GROUND DP					PLUS/MINUS							
Year	Team	G	GS	Inn	PO	A	E	DP	Pct	Rng	GDP Opps	GDP	Pct	Runs Saved	Rank	Outs Made	To His Right	Straight On	To His Left	GB	Air	Total	Runs Saved	Rank
2003	Col	11	10	89.0	25	40	1	10	.985	6.57	16	10	.625	1	-	44	0	+1	-1	0	0	0	0	-
2004	CWS	77	70	625.2	154	208	6	48	.984	5.21	88	46	.523	1	6	225	-1	+3	+1	+3	-3	0	0	16
2008	CWS	52	39	362.1	104	124	1	34	.996	5.66	56	33	.589	2	-	138	-3	+1	+1	-2	+1	-1	-1	-
		140	119	1077.0	283	372	8	92	.988	5.47	160	89	.556	4	-	407	-4	+5	+1	+1	-2	-1	-1	-

Chase Utley

		BASIC									GROUND DP					PLUS/MINUS							
Year	Team	G	GS	Inn	PO	A	E	DP	Pct	Rng	GDP Opps	GDP	Pct	Runs Saved	Rank	Outs Made	To His Right	Straight On	To His Left	GB	Air	Total	Runs Saved	Rank
2003	Phi	37	36	302.0	65	107	3	30	.983	5.13	47	29	.617	2	-	105	+6	0	-6	0	-1	-1	-1	-
2004	Phi	50	46	410.1	100	123	4	29	.982	4.89	54	26	.481	0	-	136	+6	-3	+2	+4	+3	+7	5	-
2005	Phi	135	135	1195.1	296	376	15	72	.978	5.06	144	64	.444	-2	28	456	+20	+1	+3	+23	+3	+26	20	2
2006	Phi	156	155	1367.1	357	425	18	115	.978	5.15	194	106	.546	3	8	474	+5	0	+9	+14	+2	+16	12	3
2007	Phi	132	130	1167.0	289	372	10	85	.985	5.10	172	80	.465	-2	26	407	+17	0	+4	+21	+1	+22	17	2
2008	Phi	159	157	1395.2	340	463	13	102	.984	5.18	204	96	.471	-2	26	513	+8	+6	+32	+46	0	+46	35	1
		669	659	5837.2	1447	1866	63	433	.981	5.11	815	401	.492	-1	25	2091	+62	+4	+44	+108	+8	+116	88	1

Eugenio Velez

		BASIC									GROUND DP					PLUS/MINUS							
Year	Team	G	GS	Inn	PO	A	E	DP	Pct	Rng	GDP Opps	GDP	Pct	Runs Saved	Rank	Outs Made	To His Right	Straight On	To His Left	GB	Air	Total	Runs Saved	Rank
2007	SF	4	1	12.0	5	4	1	2	.900	6.75	4	2	.500	0	-	3	-2	0	0	-2	-1	-3	-2	-
2008	SF	69	50	449.2	102	104	7	26	.967	4.12	58	22	.379	-2	-	129	-2	-3	-2	-7	+2	-5	-4	-
		73	51	461.2	107	108	8	28	.964	4.19	62	24	.387	-2	-	132	-4	-3	-2	-9	+1	-8	-6	-

Rickie Weeks

		BASIC									GROUND DP					PLUS/MINUS							
Year	Team	G	GS	Inn	PO	A	E	DP	Pct	Rng	GDP Opps	GDP	Pct	Runs Saved	Rank	Outs Made	To His Right	Straight On	To His Left	GB	Air	Total	Runs Saved	Rank
2003	Mil	4	2	21.0	1	1	1	0	.667	.86	1		-			1	-1			0	0	0	0	-
2005	Mil	95	94	837.1	178	233	21	60	.951	4.42	109	52	.477	-1	22	273	-3	-9	+4	-8	-3	-11	-8	30
2006	Mil	92	90	794.0	177	261	22	67	.952	4.96	141	65	.461	-2	29	265	-1	-8	-2	-10	-3	-13	-10	30
2007	Mil	115	111	984.0	232	286	13	73	.976	5.04	129	67	.519	1	13	301	-1	-5	-5	-12	-5	-17	-13	33
2008	Mil	120	118	1056.0	256	333	15	84	.975	5.02	163	75	.460	-2	26	356	+3	-7	+4	+1	+1	+2	2	13
		426	415	3692.1	844	1114	72	284	.965	4.77	543	259	.477	-4	29	1196	-3	-29	+1	-29	-10	-39	-29	32

Third Basemen

Garrett Atkins

Year	Team	G	GS	Inn	PO	A	E	DP	Pct	Rng	Opps	Score	Grade	Runs Saved	Rank	Outs Made	To His Right	Straight On	To His Left	GB	Air	Total	Enhanced	Runs Saved	Rank
2003	Col	19	16	134.0	9	25	6	0	.850	2.28	2	.625	A-	0	-	24	-1	-3	0	-5	+1	-4	-3	-2	-
2004	Col	4	3	27.0	2	4	0	1	1.000	2.00						5	+1	-1	0	0	0	0	0	0	-
2005	Col	136	136	1161.2	78	262	18	23	.950	2.63	24	.460	C	-1	27	303	+6	+1	-1	+6	0	+6	+10	8	11
2006	Col	157	157	1381.1	98	286	19	36	.953	2.50	21	.526	B-	1	12	347	-3	-8	+8	-4	+1	-3	-2	-2	18
2007	Col	154	153	1319.0	84	252	13	34	.963	2.29	24	.410	D+	-1	25	295	+2	-22	-5	-25	-3	-28	-29	-22	34
2008	Col	94	92	797.0	47	197	9	21	.964	2.76	9	.494	C+	0	12	217	-1	-8	-3	-11	0	-11	-11	-8	32
		564	557	4820.0	318	1026	65	115	.954	2.51	80	.471	C	-1	22	973	+4	-41	-1	-39	-1	-40	-35	-26	31

Rich Aurilia

Year	Team	G	GS	Inn	PO	A	E	DP	Pct	Rng	Opps	Score	Grade	Runs Saved	Rank	Outs Made	To His Right	Straight On	To His Left	GB	Air	Total	Enhanced	Runs Saved	Rank
2004	SD	29	28	231.2	16	41	5	2	.919	2.21	3	.367	D	0	-	45	0	+2	+3	+4	0	+4	+3	2	-
2005	Cin	18	14	129.1	12	33	1	4	.978	3.13	1	1.000	A+	0	-	40	0	-3	0	-3	0	-3	-4	-3	-
2006	Cin	52	39	356.0	24	78	5	7	.953	2.58	6	.483	C+	0	-	97	0	-3	-3	-6	0	-6	-7	-5	-
2007	SF	22	21	177.2	15	39	4	6	.931	2.74	4	.338	D-	-1	-	47	-1	+3	0	+2	-1	+1	+1	1	-
2008	SF	63	50	427.2	31	67	5	4	.951	2.06	7	.650	A	1	-	89	-3	-2	0	-5	+1	-4	-4	-3	-
		184	152	1322.1	98	258	20	23	.947	2.42	21	.519	C+	0	-	240	-4	-3	0	-8	0	-8	-11	-8	-

Willy Aybar

Year	Team	G	GS	Inn	PO	A	E	DP	Pct	Rng	Opps	Score	Grade	Runs Saved	Rank	Outs Made	To His Right	Straight On	To His Left	GB	Air	Total	Enhanced	Runs Saved	Rank
2005	LAD	20	20	174.0	16	35	2	3	.962	2.64	2	.800	A+	1	-	46	-2	+1	+3	+1	0	+1	+1	1	-
2006	2 tms	61	52	455.2	23	90	8	6	.934	2.23	5	.610	A-	1	12	102	-1	+4	-3	-2	0	-2	-1	-1	16
2008	TB	41	40	358.1	29	84	5	12	.958	2.84	5	.920	A+	2	-	103	+1	-1	+2	+2	0	+2	+1	1	-
		122	112	988.0	68	209	15	21	.949	2.52	12	.771	A+	4	-	194	-2	+4	+2	+1	0	+1	+1	1	-

Jose Bautista

Year	Team	G	GS	Inn	PO	A	E	DP	Pct	Rng	Opps	Score	Grade	Runs Saved	Rank	Outs Made	To His Right	Straight On	To His Left	GB	Air	Total	Enhanced	Runs Saved	Rank
2004	3 tms	17	6	67.0	5	19	1	2	.960	3.22	2	.250	F	-1	-	19	-1	0	0	+1	0	+1	0	0	-
2005	Pit	8	7	58.2	6	14	1	2	.952	3.07	3	.483	C+	0	-	16	0	+1	0	+1	0	+1	0	0	-
2006	Pit	33	31	267.1	22	54	6	5	.927	2.56	10	.545	B-	0	-	65	+1	-8	-4	-11	0	-11	-11	-8	-
2007	Pit	126	122	1064.2	95	251	15	16	.958	2.92	20	.500	C+	1	7	306	-2	-14	-7	-23	0	-23	-23	-17	32
2008	2 tms	99	85	766.1	50	207	11	17	.959	3.02	16	.403	D+	-1	24	235	-2	-1	+1	-2	0	-2	-3	-2	21
		283	251	2224.0	178	545	34	42	.955	2.93	51	.468	C	-1	22	509	-4	-22	-10	-34	0	-34	-37	-27	32

Adrian Beltre

Year	Team	G	GS	Inn	PO	A	E	DP	Pct	Rng	Opps	Score	Grade	Runs Saved	Rank	Outs Made	To His Right	Straight On	To His Left	GB	Air	Total	Enhanced	Runs Saved	Rank
2003	LA	157	150	1346.0	111	309	19	32	.957	2.81	20	.748	A+	2	4	350	+13	+11	+2	+26	-1	+25	+30	23	2
2004	LA	155	154	1340.1	120	322	10	32	.978	2.97	36	.551	B	3	2	381	+10	+18	+1	+30	-1	+29	+30	23	2
2005	Sea	155	155	1325.2	140	271	14	25	.967	2.79	21	.602	B+	1	4	364	+5	-3	+5	+7	+1	+8	+11	8	10
2006	Sea	155	155	1358.0	136	323	15	32	.968	3.04	21	.526	B-	1	12	404	+22	-7	+9	+23	-2	+21	+24	18	3
2007	Sea	147	146	1279.1	121	287	18	24	.958	2.87	13	.500	C+	0	12	370	+3	-2	+4	+4	-1	+3	+7	5	10
2008	Sea	139	137	1208.1	100	272	14	27	.964	2.77	16	.500	C+	0	12	328	+6	+3	+21	+30	+1	+31	+32	24	1
		908	897	7857.2	728	1784	90	172	.965	2.88	127	.575	B	7	4	1667	+59	+20	+42	+120	-3	+117	+134	101	1

Casey Blake

Year	Team	G	GS	Inn	PO	A	E	DP	Pct	Rng	Opps	Score	Grade	Runs Saved	Rank	Outs Made	To His Right	Straight On	To His Left	GB	Air	Total	Enhanced	Runs Saved	Rank
2003	Cle	140	136	1184.0	92	289	19	27	.953	2.90	24	.406	D+	-3	33	343	+8	+5	-1	+11	+5	+16	+18	14	4
2004	Cle	152	151	1352.1	121	275	26	24	.938	2.64	15	.390	D+	-1	27	345	-3	-7	-2	-10	+1	-9	-7	-5	26
2005	Cle	6	6	40.0	4	9	1	1	.929	2.93					-	13	+1	0	0	+1	0	+1	+1	1	-
2007	Cle	145	134	1209.0	99	258	14	24	.962	2.66	17	.485	C+	-1	25	316	+9	-4	-13	-8	0	-8	-5	-4	25
2008	2 tms	133	130	1104.2	66	245	14	25	.957	2.53	16	.475	C	0	12	280	+7	-10	-3	-6	+1	-5	-4	-3	23
		576	557	4890.0	382	1076	74	101	.952	2.68	72	.437	C-	-5	32	1013	+22	-16	-19	-12	+7	-5	+3	3	15

Hank Blalock

Year	Team	G	GS	Inn	PO	A	E	DP	Pct	Rng	Opps	Score	Grade	Runs Saved	Rank	Outs Made	To His Right	Straight On	To His Left	GB	Air	Total	Enhanced	Runs Saved	Rank
2003	Tex	141	131	1167.0	110	238	15	31	.959	2.68	17	.526	B-	1	9	302	+4	+29	+1	+34	+3	+37	+34	26	1
2004	Tex	159	154	1377.2	103	279	17	33	.957	2.50	19	.616	A-	2	4	348	-5	+14	0	+10	-2	+8	+5	4	13
2005	Tex	158	156	1374.0	96	304	11	23	.973	2.62	17	.509	C+	0	14	369	-6	-4	-6	-16	-1	-17	-21	-16	34
2006	Tex	122	120	1062.2	72	237	12	20	.963	2.62	13	.615	A-	2	3	284	-3	-1	+1	-3	0	-3	-4	-3	22
2007	Tex	39	39	339.1	18	69	6	9	.935	2.31	5	.530	B-	1	-	79	-2	-1	+1	-2	0	-2	-3	-2	-
2008	Tex	31	31	263.0	24	54	4	6	.951	2.67	7	.350	D-	-1	-	71	+2	-2	+2	+2	-1	+1	0	0	-
		650	631	5583.2	423	1181	65	122	.961	2.59	78	.544	B-	5	9	1116	-10	+35	-1	+25	-1	+24	+11	9	12

Third Basemen

Geoff Blum

Year Team	G	GS	Inn	PO	A	E	DP	Pct	Rng	Opps	Score	Grade	Runs Saved	Rank	Outs Made	To His Right	Straight On	To His Left	GB	Air	Total	Enhanced	Runs Saved	Rank
2003 Hou	83	72	617.0	32	135	5	18	.971	2.44	9	.411	D+	-1	25	150	+3	+2	+2	+7	-1	+6	+6	5	13
2004 TB	59	40	382.0	35	78	8	8	.934	2.66	2	.250	F	-1	-	101	0	-3	0	-2	+2	0	+1	1	-
2005 2 tms	46	35	316.2	24	91	6	9	.950	3.27	9	.489	C+	0	-	105	0	+5	+3	+8	0	+8	+9	7	-
2006 SD	34	17	200.1	18	36	0	1	1.000	2.43	6	.367	D	-1	-	50	+1	+2	+1	+4	-1	+3	+3	2	-
2007 SD	13	2	54.1	2	8	0	0	1.000	1.66					-	10	0	+1	0	+1	0	+1	+1	1	-
2008 Hou	75	68	599.2	43	144	4	8	.979	2.81	2	.425	C-	0	12	178	+5	-1	+3	+7	-1	+6	+7	5	12
	310	234	2170.0	154	492	23	44	.966	2.68	28	.416	D+	-3	27	465	+9	+6	+9	+25	-1	+24	+27	21	9

Aaron Boone

Year Team	G	GS	Inn	PO	A	E	DP	Pct	Rng	Opps	Score	Grade	Runs Saved	Rank	Outs Made	To His Right	Straight On	To His Left	GB	Air	Total	Enhanced	Runs Saved	Rank
2003 2 tms	137	133	1178.0	98	291	20	26	.951	2.97	22	.511	C+	1	9	330	-2	+5	+5	+7	+1	+8	+9	7	7
2005 Cle	142	139	1249.2	81	298	18	20	.955	2.73	22	.650	A	3	2	349	+1	-3	+1	-1	0	-1	+1	1	20
2006 Cle	101	97	842.2	56	186	16	16	.938	2.58	12	.546	B-	2	3	210	-9	-3	0	-12	-2	-14	-16	-12	34
2007 Fla	12	5	68.1	6	9	0	0	1.000	1.98	1	.600	B+	0	-	13	-1	-2	0	-3	0	-3	-3	-2	-
2008 Was	16	14	113.0	3	23	1	2	.963	2.07	4	.688	A+	0	-	25	-2	+1	0	-1	0	-1	-1	-1	-
	408	388	3451.2	244	807	55	64	.950	2.74	61	.581	B+	6	7	732	-13	-2	+6	-10	-1	-11	-10	-7	23

Russell Branyan

Year Team	G	GS	Inn	PO	A	E	DP	Pct	Rng	Opps	Score	Grade	Runs Saved	Rank	Outs Made	To His Right	Straight On	To His Left	GB	Air	Total	Enhanced	Runs Saved	Rank
2003 Cin	20	18	145.0	12	49	2	5	.968	3.79	7	.621	A-	0	-	43	0	+3	-1	+3	0	+3	+4	3	-
2004 Mil	44	40	361.0	35	91	5	6	.962	3.14	13	.508	C+	-1	-	103	-2	+2	+3	+3	-1	+2	+1	1	-
2005 Mil	59	56	456.2	40	82	7	10	.946	2.40	9	.617	A-	1	4	103	-6	-3	-3	-12	-1	-13	-16	-12	31
2006 2 tms	31	27	215.0	15	34	6	3	.891	2.05	5	.700	A+	1	-	43	-2	-1	-1	-4	-1	-5	-5	-4	-
2007 3 tms	34	24	210.2	17	60	1	14	.987	3.29	2	.425	C-	0	-	70	+2	+2	-1	+4	-1	+3	+3	3	-
2008 Mil	35	33	276.0	22	63	4	6	.955	2.77	11	.414	D+	-1	-	75	0	+2	-1	+1	+1	+2	+2	2	-
	223	198	1664.1	141	379	25	44	.954	2.81	47	.540	B-			341	-8	+5	-4	-5	-3	-8	-11	-7	-

Brian Buscher

Year Team	G	GS	Inn	PO	A	E	DP	Pct	Rng	Opps	Score	Grade	Runs Saved	Rank	Outs Made	To His Right	Straight On	To His Left	GB	Air	Total	Enhanced	Runs Saved	Rank
2007 Min	27	24	201.1	17	31	4	6	.923	2.15	6	.250	F	-2	-	41	-1	-2	0	-4	0	-4	-4	-3	-
2008 Min	64	60	519.1	37	113	10	9	.938	2.60	5	.470	C	0	12	139	-3	+3	-2	-3	0	-3	-3	-2	22
	91	84	720.2	54	144	14	15	.934	2.47	11	.350	D-	-2	-	142	-4	+1	-2	-7	0	-7	-7	-5	-

Miguel Cabrera

Year Team	G	GS	Inn	PO	A	E	DP	Pct	Rng	Opps	Score	Grade	Runs Saved	Rank	Outs Made	To His Right	Straight On	To His Left	GB	Air	Total	Enhanced	Runs Saved	Rank
2003 Fla	34	30	275.0	17	53	1	2	.986	2.29	3	.483	C+	0	-	63	+2	-4	0	-2	0	-2	-2	-2	-
2005 Fla	30	29	238.0	22	46	2	5	.971	2.57	7	.500	C+	1	-	59	0	-2	0	-1	0	-1	-1	-1	-
2006 Fla	157	157	1334.0	114	266	17	33	.957	2.56	20	.485	C+	0	21	339	-7	-1	-3	-10	-1	-11	-12	-9	31
2007 Fla	154	153	1310.2	100	266	23	33	.941	2.51	30	.537	B-	2	4	311	0	-14	-12	-27	+2	-25	-24	-18	33
2008 Det	14	14	116.0	15	30	5	4	.900	3.49	1	.250	F	0	-	37	-3	+1	-1	-4	0	-4	-4	-3	-
	389	383	3273.2	268	661	48	77	.951	2.55	61	.508	C+	3	11	620	-8	-20	-16	-44	+1	-43	-43	-33	33

Jorge Cantu

Year Team	G	GS	Inn	PO	A	E	DP	Pct	Rng	Opps	Score	Grade	Runs Saved	Rank	Outs Made	To His Right	Straight On	To His Left	GB	Air	Total	Enhanced	Runs Saved	Rank
2004 TB	11	11	94.1	9	26	3	1	.921	3.34	2	.800	A+	1	-	31	+1	0	+1	+2	0	+2	+3	2	-
2005 TB	62	58	496.0	31	93	12	7	.912	2.25	5	.540	B-	0	14	105	-8	-7	-3	-18	+1	-17	-19	-14	33
2007 Cin	1	0	4.0	0	0	0	0		.00					-	0				0		0		0	-
2008 Fla	129	129	1066.2	83	214	20	21	.937	2.51	18	.536	B-	0	12	261	-3	-6	-1	-10	-1	-11	-11	-8	31
	203	198	1661.0	123	333	35	29	.929	2.47	25	.558	B	1	-	313	-10	-13	-3	-26	0	-26	-27	-20	-

Jose Castillo

Year Team	G	GS	Inn	PO	A	E	DP	Pct	Rng	Opps	Score	Grade	Runs Saved	Rank	Outs Made	To His Right	Straight On	To His Left	GB	Air	Total	Enhanced	Runs Saved	Rank
2007 Pit	34	27	253.1	23	83	4	6	.964	3.77	9	.417	D+	-2	-	101	+1	0	+2	+2	+1	+3	+4	3	-
2008 2 tms	110	97	880.0	53	177	15	14	.939	2.35	20	.555	B	2	4	198	-2	-1	-1	-5	+1	-4	-5	-4	24
	144	124	1133.1	76	260	19	20	.946	2.67	29	.512	C+			242	-1	-1	+1	-3	+2	-1	-1	-1	

Third Basemen

Eric Chavez

Year	Team	G	GS	Inn	PO	A	E	DP	Pct	Rng	Opps	Score	Grade	Runs Saved	Rank	Outs Made	To His Right	Straight On	To His Left	GB	Air	Total	Enhanced	Runs Saved	Rank
2003	Oak	154	153	1333.1	125	343	14	33	.971	3.16	23	.528	B-	0	17	379	+3	-1	+3	+5	0	+5	+9	7	6
2004	Oak	125	125	1129.0	112	276	13	31	.968	3.09	22	.511	C+	1	10	314	+8	0	+2	+10	-1	+9	+13	10	7
2005	Oak	153	153	1348.1	121	301	15	28	.966	2.82	14	.671	A+	1	4	381	+16	-5	-1	+10	0	+10	+15	11	4
2006	Oak	134	133	1165.2	105	281	5	42	.987	2.98	11	.577	B	1	12	354	+16	-9	-9	-2	-1	-3	+2	2	14
2007	Oak	88	87	774.2	66	169	6	16	.975	2.73	12	.400	D+	-2	33	213	+6	-2	+3	+7	+1	+8	+10	8	8
2008	Oak	15	15	130.0	12	32	1	4	.978	3.05	1	.600	B+	0	-	42	0	0	-2	-1	+1	0	0	0	-
		669	666	5881.0	541	1402	54	154	.973	2.97	83	.537	B-	1	14	1288	+49	-17	-4	+29	0	+29	+49	38	6

Craig Counsell

Year	Team	G	GS	Inn	PO	A	E	DP	Pct	Rng	Opps	Score	Grade	Runs Saved	Rank	Outs Made	To His Right	Straight On	To His Left	GB	Air	Total	Enhanced	Runs Saved	Rank
2003	Ari	57	49	429.0	32	105	2	9	.986	2.87	13	.619	A-	1	9	108	+4	+2	+2	+9	0	+9	+9	7	8
2004	Mil	1	0	0.1	0	0	0	0	-	.00						0							0		
2006	Ari	7	2	23.0	2	6	0	0	1.000	3.13	1	.600	B+	0	-	6	+1	0	0	+1	0	+1	+2	2	-
2007	Mil	50	27	297.2	21	73	0	10	1.000	2.84	7	.621	A-	0	-	88	-2	+6	+3	+7	+2	+9	+8	6	-
2008	Mil	38	30	268.1	23	54	1	6	.987	2.58	7	.707	A+	1	-	71	-1	+1	+3	+3	+1	+4	+4	3	-
		153	108	1018.1	78	238	3	25	.991	2.79	28	.641	A	2	-	214	+2	+9	+8	+20	+3	+23	+23	18	-

Joe Crede

Year	Team	G	GS	Inn	PO	A	E	DP	Pct	Rng	Opps	Score	Grade	Runs Saved	Rank	Outs Made	To His Right	Straight On	To His Left	GB	Air	Total	Enhanced	Runs Saved	Rank
2003	CWS	151	149	1306.0	107	264	14	28	.964	2.56	24	.433	C-	-2	30	334	+10	-3	+5	+12	+2	+14	+16	12	5
2004	CWS	144	142	1235.0	90	243	12	21	.965	2.43	24	.460	C	-1	27	290	-3	-5	-2	-9	-1	-10	-11	-8	30
2005	CWS	130	122	1120.1	95	243	10	28	.971	2.72	21	.507	C+	1	4	311	-14	+16	+11	+12	-1	+11	+2	2	18
2006	CWS	149	146	1260.0	114	339	10	34	.978	3.24	17	.488	C+	-1	27	430	-4	+26	+8	+30	+1	+31	+31	24	1
2007	CWS	46	45	388.1	36	97	4	18	.971	3.08	8	.569	B	1	-	120	+4	+3	+2	+10	+1	+11	+11	8	-
2008	CWS	97	95	834.2	57	207	20	22	.930	2.85	14	.429	C-	-1	24	244	-8	+15	+7	+13	0	+13	+13	10	4
		717	699	6144.1	499	1393	70	151	.964	2.77	108	.472	C	-3	27	1330	-15	+52	+31	+68	+2	+70	+62	48	4

Chris Davis

Year	Team	G	GS	Inn	PO	A	E	DP	Pct	Rng	Opps	Score	Grade	Runs Saved	Rank	Outs Made	To His Right	Straight On	To His Left	GB	Air	Total	Enhanced	Runs Saved	Rank
2008	Tex	32	31	276.0	31	44	3	5	.962	2.45	5	.550	B	0	-	66	-1	-3	-5	-9	0	-9	-9	-7	-

Blake DeWitt

Year	Team	G	GS	Inn	PO	A	E	DP	Pct	Rng	Opps	Score	Grade	Runs Saved	Rank	Outs Made	To His Right	Straight On	To His Left	GB	Air	Total	Enhanced	Runs Saved	Rank
2008	LAD	95	77	727.2	58	193	8	19	.969	3.10	16	.634	A-	3	1	220	+3	+2	+9	+14	-2	+12	+11	8	7

Greg Dobbs

Year	Team	G	GS	Inn	PO	A	E	DP	Pct	Rng	Opps	Score	Grade	Runs Saved	Rank	Outs Made	To His Right	Straight On	To His Left	GB	Air	Total	Enhanced	Runs Saved	Rank
2004	Sea	14	12	108.2	5	21	2	3	.929	2.15					-	25	+1	-2	+1	0	0	0	0	0	-
2005	Sea	2	1	11.0	4	5	0	1	1.000	7.36					-	8	0	+1	-1	0	0	0	0	0	-
2006	Sea	2	0	2.0	1	0	0	0	1.000	4.50					-	1	0	0	0	0	0	0	0	0	-
2007	Phi	68	57	418.0	44	77	7	7	.945	2.61	7	.557	B	1	7	106	0	0	-4	-4	0	-4	-4	-3	24
2008	Phi	52	42	327.1	34	67	3	7	.971	2.78	8	.625	A-	0	-	88	+1	-4	-2	-5	0	-5	-5	-4	-
		138	112	867.0	88	170	12	18	.956	2.68	15	.593	B+	1	-	168	+2	-5	-6	-9	0	-9	-9	-7	-

Edwin Encarnacion

Year	Team	G	GS	Inn	PO	A	E	DP	Pct	Rng	Opps	Score	Grade	Runs Saved	Rank	Outs Made	To His Right	Straight On	To His Left	GB	Air	Total	Enhanced	Runs Saved	Rank
2005	Cin	56	55	478.0	54	116	10	9	.944	3.20	9	.450	C	-1	27	154	+4	-1	0	+2	0	+2	+5	4	15
2006	Cin	111	109	931.1	74	196	25	17	.915	2.61	18	.431	C-	-2	30	244	-1	-6	-10	-18	+2	-16	-15	-11	33
2007	Cin	137	134	1168.0	112	212	16	21	.953	2.50	24	.490	C+	-2	33	298	+1	-21	+4	-16	+3	-13	-15	-11	30
2008	Cin	143	141	1237.0	91	216	23	23	.930	2.23	21	.474	C	-1	24	278	-7	-6	-7	-20	-1	-21	-21	-16	35
		447	439	3814.1	331	740	74	70	.935	2.53	72	.465	C	-6	33	706	-3	-34	-13	-52	+4	-48	-46	-34	34

Third Basemen

Morgan Ensberg

		BASIC									BUNTS					PLUS/MINUS									
Year	Team	G	GS	Inn	PO	A	E	DP	Pct	Rng	Opps	Score	Grade	Runs Saved	Rank	Outs Made	To His Right	Straight On	To His Left	GB	Air	Total	Enhanced	Runs Saved	Rank
2003	Hou	111	89	818.0	77	184	9	16	.967	2.87	18	.553	B	1	9	218	+10	+9	0	+19	-1	+18	+19	14	3
2004	Hou	118	103	920.2	80	163	13	23	.949	2.38	15	.510	C+	1	10	207	-3	-7	+4	-6	0	-6	-8	-6	28
2005	Hou	148	147	1286.1	100	295	15	31	.963	2.76	20	.483	C+	0	14	362	+3	+6	+7	+16	-1	+15	+15	11	5
2006	Hou	117	106	975.0	80	230	12	25	.963	2.86	29	.521	B-	2	3	270	-2	+3	+11	+11	0	+11	+9	7	9
2007	2 tms	80	62	585.0	39	136	12	15	.936	2.69	9	.411	D+	-1	25	162	-6	-2	-1	-9	+2	-7	-8	-6	28
2008	NYY	21	13	133.0	8	32	1	2	.976	2.71	2	.425	C-	0	-	37	-1	-5	0	-6	0	-6	-5	-4	
		595	520	4718.0	384	1040	62	112	.958	2.72	93	.504	C+	3	11	978	+1	+4	+21	+25	0	+25	+22	16	10

Pedro Feliz

		BASIC									BUNTS					PLUS/MINUS									
Year	Team	G	GS	Inn	PO	A	E	DP	Pct	Rng	Opps	Score	Grade	Runs Saved	Rank	Outs Made	To His Right	Straight On	To His Left	GB	Air	Total	Enhanced	Runs Saved	Rank
2003	SF	49	28	293.0	24	82	3	8	.972	3.26	5	.320	F	-1	-	85	+2	+1	+4	+6	+1	+7	+7	5	-
2004	SF	51	37	339.1	32	85	3	7	.975	3.10	5	.610	A-	1	-	109	+7	+4	0	+11	0	+11	+13	10	-
2005	SF	79	67	591.2	47	144	6	17	.970	2.91	12	.792	A+	3	2	166	+2	+7	+5	+14	+2	+16	+16	12	2
2006	SF	159	154	1372.1	116	331	21	30	.955	2.93	32	.658	A	5	1	396	+3	+5	+9	+17	0	+17	+21	16	4
2007	SF	143	137	1220.0	93	302	11	28	.973	2.91	26	.640	A	3	2	355	+9	+8	+6	+22	+4	+26	+27	21	1
2008	Phi	129	106	978.1	73	223	8	19	.974	2.72	16	.522	B-	0	12	272	+16	-7	-6	+4	0	+4	+7	5	10
		610	529	4794.2	385	1167	52	109	.968	2.91	96	.627	A-	11	2	1083	+39	+18	+18	+74	+7	+81	+91	69	3

Chone Figgins

		BASIC									BUNTS					PLUS/MINUS									
Year	Team	G	GS	Inn	PO	A	E	DP	Pct	Rng	Opps	Score	Grade	Runs Saved	Rank	Outs Made	To His Right	Straight On	To His Left	GB	Air	Total	Enhanced	Runs Saved	Rank
2004	Ana	92	80	705.1	57	129	11	9	.944	2.37	13	.615	A-	2	4	161	-3	+1	+6	+4	-1	+3	+1	1	16
2005	LAA	56	48	437.2	34	95	3	8	.977	2.65	11	.482	C+	0	-	116	+3	+6	-5	+3	-1	+2	+4	3	-
2006	LAA	34	32	280.1	22	50	10	4	.878	2.31	6	.425	C-	0	-	65	-4	-4	-2	-10	0	-10	-9	-7	-
2007	LAA	99	96	836.2	52	165	13	14	.943	2.33	13	.500	C+	0	12	193	-4	+2	-1	-3	-1	-4	-3	-2	21
2008	LAA	105	105	914.1	84	185	6	15	.978	2.65	8	.569	B	1	7	243	+4	+6	-1	+9	-3	+9	+11	8	6
		386	361	3174.1	249	624	43	50	.953	2.48	51	.527	B-	3	11	591	-4	+11	-3	+3	-3	0	+4	3	14

Troy Glaus

		BASIC									BUNTS					PLUS/MINUS									
Year	Team	G	GS	Inn	PO	A	E	DP	Pct	Rng	Opps	Score	Grade	Runs Saved	Rank	Outs Made	To His Right	Straight On	To His Left	GB	Air	Total	Enhanced	Runs Saved	Rank
2003	Ana	87	86	732.1	56	136	16	10	.923	2.36	16	.528	B-	-1	25	152	-9	-5	-1	-14	+2	-12	-12	-9	33
2004	Ana	19	19	165.0	11	27	2	2	.950	2.07	2	.250	F	-1	-	33	-1	+1	0	0	-1	-1	-1	-1	-
2005	Ari	145	144	1264.0	113	310	24	25	.946	3.01	26	.485	C+	0	14	374	-2	-1	-11	-14	+2	-12	-12	-9	30
2006	Tor	145	135	1175.0	95	271	14	37	.963	2.80	19	.582	B+	0	21	315	+1	-4	+7	+4	+3	+7	+8	7	9
2007	Tor	114	110	928.0	63	197	9	24	.967	2.52	9	.400	D+	-2	33	238	0	+3	+4	+7	+1	+8	+9	5	13
2008	StL	146	145	1243.1	99	279	7	27	.982	2.74	21	.648	A	2	4	339	+4	0	+4	+8	-1	+7	+6	-1	18
		656	639	5507.2	437	1220	72	125	.958	2.71	93	.535	B-	-2	24	1147	-7	-6	+3	-9	+6	-3	-2		

Alex Gordon

		BASIC									BUNTS					PLUS/MINUS									
Year	Team	G	GS	Inn	PO	A	E	DP	Pct	Rng	Opps	Score	Grade	Runs Saved	Rank	Outs Made	To His Right	Straight On	To His Left	GB	Air	Total	Enhanced	Runs Saved	Rank
2007	KC	137	129	1135.0	99	247	14	22	.961	2.74	12	.425	C-	0	12	312	-2	+7	+5	+9	-3	+6	+6	5	12
2008	KC	133	133	1180.0	112	230	16	21	.955	2.61	16	.384	D	-2	30	311	+1	-2	-9	-10	-1	-11	-9	-7	26
		270	262	2315.0	211	477	30	43	.958	2.67	28	.402	D+	-2	24	462	-1	+5	-4	-1	-4	-5	-3	-2	19

Carlos Guillen

		BASIC									BUNTS					PLUS/MINUS									
Year	Team	G	GS	Inn	PO	A	E	DP	Pct	Rng	Opps	Score	Grade	Runs Saved	Rank	Outs Made	To His Right	Straight On	To His Left	GB	Air	Total	Enhanced	Runs Saved	Rank
2003	Sea	32	32	280.2	38	45	3	3	.965	2.66	2	.250	F	-1	-	79	-1	+2	+1	+2	0	+2	+1	1	-
2008	Det	89	87	749.2	68	195	14	15	.949	3.16	17	.444	C-	-2	30	240	-1	-2	-6	-9	+2	-7	-9	-7	27
		121	119	1030.1	106	240	17	18	.953	3.02	19	.424	C-	-3	-	228	-2	0	-5	-7	+2	-5	-8	-6	

Bill Hall

		BASIC									BUNTS					PLUS/MINUS									
Year	Team	G	GS	Inn	PO	A	E	DP	Pct	Rng	Opps	Score	Grade	Runs Saved	Rank	Outs Made	To His Right	Straight On	To His Left	GB	Air	Total	Enhanced	Runs Saved	Rank
2003	Mil	1	0	4.0	0	0	0	1	.000	.00						0				-1			-1	-1	-
2004	Mil	11	7	72.0	6	22	2	4	.933	3.50	3	.833	A+	0	-	25	+2	0	+1	+4	0	+4	+4	3	-
2005	Mil	59	49	435.1	39	84	6	11	.953	2.54	11	.618	A-	1	-	107	-2	0	+3	0	+1	+1	0	0	-
2006	Mil	11	10	86.0	5	15	2	2	.909	2.09	2	.250	F	0	-	18	-1	+1	0	+1	0	+1	+1	1	18
2008	Mil	113	98	899.1	69	193	17	24	.939	2.62	15	.367	D	-2	30	233	0	+4	-3	+1	0	+1	+1	1	18
		195	164	1496.2	119	314	28	41	.939	2.60	31	.494	C+	-2	-	300	-1	+5	+1	+5	+1	+6	+5	4	-

Third Basemen

Jack Hannahan

Year Team	G	GS	Inn	PO	A	E	DP	Pct	Rng	Opps	Score	Grade	Runs Saved	Rank	Outs Made	To His Right	Straight On	To His Left	GB	Air	Total	Enhanced	Runs Saved	Rank
2007 Oak	41	40	361.2	19	78	3	10	.970	2.41	10	.575	B	1	-	87	+2	0	0	+2	-2	0	0	0	-
2008 Oak	126	106	983.2	70	218	9	24	.970	2.64	15	.543	B-	0	12	261	+3	+10	+5	+18	+1	+19	+21	16	2
	167	146	1345.1	89	296	12	34	.970	2.58	25	.556	B	1	-	275	+5	+10	+5	+20	-1	+19	+21	16	-

Brendan Harris

Year Team	G	GS	Inn	PO	A	E	DP	Pct	Rng	Opps	Score	Grade	Runs Saved	Rank	Outs Made	To His Right	Straight On	To His Left	GB	Air	Total	Enhanced	Runs Saved	Rank
2004 2 tms	7	6	47.0	6	7	2	0	.867	2.49	2	.625	A-	0	-	11	-1	0	0	-1	-1	-2	-2	-2	-
2005 Was	1	1	8.0	1	4	0	0	1.000	5.63					-	5	0			0	0	0	0	0	-
2006 Was	3	2	20.0	1	5	0	0	1.000	2.70	1	.600	B+	0	-	5	+1	0	0	+1	0	+1	+1	1	-
2007 TB	4	2	24.2	2	1	1	0	.750	1.09	1	.250	F	0	-	2	0	-1	0	-1	0	-1	-1	-1	-
2008 Min	34	28	256.1	18	48	2	4	.971	2.32	1	.250	F	0	-	56	+1	-1	-6	-6	0	-6	-5	-4	-
	49	39	356.0	28	65	5	4	.949	2.35	5	.470	C	0	-	60	+1	-1	-6	-7	-1	-8	-7	-6	-

Wes Helms

Year Team	G	GS	Inn	PO	A	E	DP	Pct	Rng	Opps	Score	Grade	Runs Saved	Rank	Outs Made	To His Right	Straight On	To His Left	GB	Air	Total	Enhanced	Runs Saved	Rank
2003 Mil	130	130	1137.2	89	236	19	21	.945	2.57	35	.466	C	-3	33	274	-5	-4	0	-9	+2	-7	-11	-8	31
2004 Mil	67	66	546.0	45	105	16	10	.904	2.47	4	1.213	A+	2	4	128	-11	-3	-4	-19	-1	-20	-24	-18	35
2005 Mil	35	17	178.2	12	41	2	4	.964	2.67	3	.483	C+	0	-	50	0	-1	+2	+1	-1	0	0	0	-
2006 Fla	24	5	94.1	7	23	2	0	.938	2.86					-	30	-2	0	+2	0	+1	+1	+1	1	-
2007 Phi	68	53	441.2	27	97	9	3	.932	2.53	3	.500	C+	0	12	115	0	+1	+1	+2	+1	+3	+2	2	18
2008 Fla	60	30	325.0	31	63	1	3	.989	2.60	6	.550	B	1	-	87	+2	+2	0	+4	0	+4	+5	4	-
	384	301	2723.1	211	565	49	41	.941	2.56	51	.537	B-	0	18	512	-16	-5	+1	-21	+2	-19	-27	-19	29

Eric Hinske

Year Team	G	GS	Inn	PO	A	E	DP	Pct	Rng	Opps	Score	Grade	Runs Saved	Rank	Outs Made	To His Right	Straight On	To His Left	GB	Air	Total	Enhanced	Runs Saved	Rank
2003 Tor	124	120	1063.2	80	213	22	13	.930	2.48	22	.434	C-	-3	33	245	-5	-3	-2	-10	+1	-9	-5	-4	27
2004 Tor	153	148	1310.2	107	242	8	23	.978	2.40	22	.527	B-	1	10	297	-4	-10	-10	-23	+2	-21	-20	-15	34
2006 Tor	10	5	64.0	3	14	0	1	1.000	2.39					-	17	0	+2	0	+3	0	+3	+3	2	-
2008 TB	8	4	49.0	1	6	0	0	1.000	1.29	1	.250	F	0	-	7	+1	+1	0	+1	0	+1	+1	1	-
	295	277	2487.1	191	475	30	37	.957	2.41	45	.476	C	-2	24	423	-7	-10	-12	-29	+3	-26	-21	-16	27

Aubrey Huff

Year Team	G	GS	Inn	PO	A	E	DP	Pct	Rng	Opps	Score	Grade	Runs Saved	Rank	Outs Made	To His Right	Straight On	To His Left	GB	Air	Total	Enhanced	Runs Saved	Rank
2003 TB	8	7	71.0	7	8	3	2	.833	1.90					-	14	-1	-4	-1	-5	-1	-6	-7	-5	-
2004 TB	87	85	705.0	69	129	12	13	.943	2.53	12	.433	C-	-1	27	179	+3	-2	-4	-3	0	-3	0	0	17
2005 TB	4	2	21.0	2	2	0	1	1.000	1.71					-	3	0	-1	0	-1	0	-1	-1	-1	-
2006 2 tms	90	85	699.2	61	156	5	18	.977	2.79	14	.532	B-	1	12	183	+1	-6	-5	-11	0	-11	-9	-7	28
2007 Bal	15	15	122.0	9	24	1	1	.971	2.43	4	.425	C-	0	-	30	0	-2	-2	-4	-1	-5	-5	-4	-
2008 Bal	33	31	275.0	23	64	3	4	.967	2.85	6	.550	B	1	-	75	-1	+2	-1	0	-1	-1	-1	-1	-
	237	225	1893.2	171	383	24	39	.958	2.63	36	.490	C+	1	14	361	+2	-13	-13	-24	-3	-27	-23	-18	28

Brandon Inge

Year Team	G	GS	Inn	PO	A	E	DP	Pct	Rng	Opps	Score	Grade	Runs Saved	Rank	Outs Made	To His Right	Straight On	To His Left	GB	Air	Total	Enhanced	Runs Saved	Rank
2004 Det	73	58	524.2	42	131	12	12	.935	2.97	14	.539	B-	0	17	140	-4	-7	+6	-5	-1	-6	-8	-6	29
2005 Det	160	159	1399.2	128	378	23	41	.957	3.25	22	.477	C	0	14	462	+16	-6	-3	+7	-2	+5	+12	9	7
2006 Det	159	156	1392.0	135	398	22	34	.960	3.45	12	.558	B	0	21	501	+14	+15	-7	+23	+1	+24	+27	21	2
2007 Det	150	146	1309.2	91	325	18	25	.959	2.86	11	.536	B-	0	12	395	+9	+6	+5	+20	-2	+18	+22	17	2
2008 Det	51	33	324.1	38	80	1	14	.992	3.27	1	.250	F	0	-	112	+4	+1	-3	+2	-1	+1	+1	1	-
	593	552	4950.1	434	1312	76	126	.958	3.17	60	.515	C+	0	18	1283	+39	+9	-2	+47	-5	+42	+54	42	5

Chipper Jones

Year Team	G	GS	Inn	PO	A	E	DP	Pct	Rng	Opps	Score	Grade	Runs Saved	Rank	Outs Made	To His Right	Straight On	To His Left	GB	Air	Total	Enhanced	Runs Saved	Rank
2004 Atl	96	93	802.0	58	177	6	12	.975	2.64	18	.511	C+	0	17	211	+2	-4	+10	+8	0	+8	+8	6	9
2005 Atl	101	100	830.1	80	169	5	18	.980	2.70	21	.538	B-	0	14	209	+1	+1	-3	-1	0	-1	-2	-2	23
2006 Atl	105	104	888.1	87	177	18	22	.936	2.67	15	.667	A	2	3	234	-1	-12	-5	-18	-1	-19	-20	-15	35
2007 Atl	126	126	1080.2	75	226	9	17	.971	2.51	27	.554	B	2	4	262	+2	+4	-1	+4	-1	+3	+3	2	17
2008 Atl	115	115	987.1	64	235	13	21	.958	2.73	14	.586	B+	2	4	264	+5	-3	+9	+11	-1	+10	+10	8	8
	543	538	4588.2	364	984	51	90	.964	2.64	95	.565	B	6	7	904	+9	-14	+10	+4	-3	+1	-1	-1	17

Third Basemen

Kevin Kouzmanoff

	BASIC									BUNTS					PLUS/MINUS									
Year Team	G	GS	Inn	PO	A	E	DP	Pct	Rng	Opps	Score	Grade	Runs Saved	Rank	Outs Made	To His Right	Straight On	To His Left	GB	Air	Total	Enhanced	Runs Saved	Rank
2006 Cle	2	2	16.0	2	4	1	0	.857	3.38					-	6	0	-1	0	-1	0	-1	0	0	-
2007 SD	136	128	1135.1	91	209	22	12	.932	2.38	26	.573	B	0	12	267	-3	+4	-5	-4	+1	-3	-4	-3	22
2008 SD	154	154	1379.0	128	277	11	34	.974	2.64	22	.625	A-	1	7	358	+8	-8	-5	-5	+1	-4	-2	-2	20
	292	284	2530.1	221	490	34	46	.954	2.53	48	.597	B+	1	14	469	+5	-5	-10	-10	+2	-8	-6	-5	20

Mike Lamb

	BASIC									BUNTS					PLUS/MINUS									
Year Team	G	GS	Inn	PO	A	E	DP	Pct	Rng	Opps	Score	Grade	Runs Saved	Rank	Outs Made	To His Right	Straight On	To His Left	GB	Air	Total	Enhanced	Runs Saved	Rank
2003 Tex	1	0	1.2	0	0	0	0	-	.00						0							0		-
2004 Hou	57	53	453.2	41	106	13	9	.919	2.92	11	.568	B	1	10	95	-2	-1	0	-4	+1	-3	-3	-2	21
2005 Hou	15	12	103.1	16	34	1	0	.980	4.35	3	.600	B+	1	-	43	0	+2	+2	+4	0	+4	+5	4	-
2006 Hou	36	30	263.2	24	70	6	8	.940	3.21	10	.505	C+	0	-	83	0	+1	-1	0	0	0	-1	-1	-
2007 Hou	58	46	416.1	29	88	8	8	.936	2.53	10	.430	C-	-1	25	103	-5	+1	+6	+2	0	+2	0	0	19
2008 2 tms	56	51	460.2	41	90	5	8	.963	2.56	8	.575	B	0	12	112	-10	+2	+1	-7	-1	-8	-9	-7	28
	223	192	1699.1	151	388	33	33	.942	2.85	42	.524	B-	1	14	339	-17	+5	+8	-5	0	-5	-8	-6	22

Andy LaRoche

	BASIC									BUNTS					PLUS/MINUS									
Year Team	G	GS	Inn	PO	A	E	DP	Pct	Rng	Opps	Score	Grade	Runs Saved	Rank	Outs Made	To His Right	Straight On	To His Left	GB	Air	Total	Enhanced	Runs Saved	Rank
2007 LAD	30	28	237.0	22	48	3	8	.959	2.66	3	.367	D	0	-	64	+1	0	0	+1	0	+1	+1	1	-
2008 2 tms	59	57	502.1	25	136	10	20	.942	2.88	15	.483	C+	-1	24	146	+2	-2	0	+1	+1	+2	+1	1	19
	89	85	739.1	47	184	13	28	.947	2.81	18	.464	C	-1	-	176	+3	-2	0	+2	+1	+3	+2	2	-

Evan Longoria

	BASIC									BUNTS					PLUS/MINUS									
Year Team	G	GS	Inn	PO	A	E	DP	Pct	Rng	Opps	Score	Grade	Runs Saved	Rank	Outs Made	To His Right	Straight On	To His Left	GB	Air	Total	Enhanced	Runs Saved	Rank
2008 TB	119	118	1045.2	86	230	12	26	.963	2.72	21	.526	B-	1	7	292	0	+5	+4	+10	-1	+9	+11	8	5

Mike Lowell

	BASIC									BUNTS					PLUS/MINUS									
Year Team	G	GS	Inn	PO	A	E	DP	Pct	Rng	Opps	Score	Grade	Runs Saved	Rank	Outs Made	To His Right	Straight On	To His Left	GB	Air	Total	Enhanced	Runs Saved	Rank
2003 Fla	128	128	1109.2	84	243	9	27	.973	2.65	31	.681	A+	6	1	278	+2	-13	-2	-13	-1	-14	-12	-9	32
2004 Fla	154	153	1326.0	117	272	7	29	.982	2.64	34	.618	A-	4	1	309	+12	-13	-6	-7	+4	-3	-1	-1	18
2005 Fla	135	126	1126.2	107	243	6	34	.983	2.80	25	.670	A+	4	1	294	+16	-19	-7	-10	-3	-13	-8	-6	27
2006 Bos	153	148	1298.2	143	314	6	39	.987	3.17	17	.462	C	-1	27	419	+8	+4	-7	+5	+1	+6	+6	5	11
2007 Bos	154	150	1324.1	105	264	15	34	.961	2.51	15	.490	C+	0	12	334	+6	+4	-6	+4	+1	+5	+7	5	11
2008 Bos	110	108	935.2	80	217	10	20	.967	2.86	16	.525	B-	13	1	270	+3	+4	-2	+5	+2	+7	+7	5	11
	834	813	7121.0	636	1553	53	183	.976	2.77	138	.597	B+	13	1	1428	+47	-33	-30	-16	+4	-12	-1	-1	16

Andy Marte

	BASIC									BUNTS					PLUS/MINUS									
Year Team	G	GS	Inn	PO	A	E	DP	Pct	Rng	Opps	Score	Grade	Runs Saved	Rank	Outs Made	To His Right	Straight On	To His Left	GB	Air	Total	Enhanced	Runs Saved	Rank
2005 Atl	17	13	130.2	4	14	3	1	.857	1.24	2	.625	A-	0	-	16	-2	-2	-2	-6	0	-6	-8	-6	-
2006 Cle	50	49	428.0	32	118	6	14	.962	3.15	9	.617	A-	1	12	135	+2	+5	0	+7	+2	+9	+10	8	8
2007 Cle	19	16	135.2	16	27	4	2	.915	2.85	2	.625	A-	0	-	38	+1	0	0	+1	-1	0	0	0	-
2008 Cle	76	68	581.1	43	155	6	19	.971	3.07	14	.382	D	-3	34	182	+3	+5	-2	+6	+1	+7	+6	5	14
	162	146	1275.2	95	314	19	36	.956	2.89	27	.496	C+	-2	-	307	+4	+8	-4	+8	+2	+10	+8	7	-

Melvin Mora

	BASIC									BUNTS					PLUS/MINUS									
Year Team	G	GS	Inn	PO	A	E	DP	Pct	Rng	Opps	Score	Grade	Runs Saved	Rank	Outs Made	To His Right	Straight On	To His Left	GB	Air	Total	Enhanced	Runs Saved	Rank
2004 Bal	138	138	1210.1	122	258	21	21	.948	2.83	20	.450	C	-2	34	334	-4	-12	-1	-16	+2	-14	-15	-11	32
2005 Bal	148	148	1289.2	96	301	18	23	.957	2.77	18	.392	D+	-3	34	375	+2	+4	-2	+4	+1	+5	+6	5	13
2006 Bal	154	154	1323.0	100	296	17	18	.959	2.69	24	.313	F	-5	35	367	+1	-5	0	-4	+1	-3	-2	-2	17
2007 Bal	120	120	1051.1	79	260	10	18	.971	2.90	22	.493	C+	1	7	306	+5	-1	-1	+3	+1	+4	+6	5	13
2008 Bal	124	124	1059.2	85	252	14	28	.960	2.86	17	.485	C+	-1	24	312	+7	-9	-12	-15	0	-15	-13	-10	34
	684	684	5934.0	482	1367	80	108	.959	2.80	101	.422	C-	-10	34	1309	+11	-23	-16	-28	+5	-23	-18	-13	25

Third Basemen

Nick Punto

		BASIC									BUNTS					PLUS/MINUS								
Year	Team	G	GS	Inn	PO	A	E	DP	Pct	Rng	Opps	Score	Grade	Runs Saved	Rank	Outs Made	To His Right	Straight On	To His Left	GB	Air	Total	Enhanced	Runs Saved	Rank
2003	Phi	9	3	31.0	5	6	1	0	.917	3.19	1	1.000	A+	0	-	9	0	-1	+1	0	0	0	+1	1	-
2004	Min	2	0	4.0	0	0	0	0	-	.00	1	.250	F	0	-	0			-1				-1	-1	-
2005	Min	12	7	69.0	6	22	0	3	1.000	3.65	3	.367	D	0	-	22	+1	0	+1	+2	0	+2	+2	2	-
2006	Min	89	88	766.0	53	176	9	18	.962	2.69	13	.615	A-	2	3	208	+8	+6	-2	+12	+1	+13	+16	12	6
2007	Min	108	93	828.1	83	171	7	11	.973	2.76	7	.557	B	1	7	234	+2	+4	+2	+8	0	+8	+10	8	7
2008	Min	12	6	63.0	3	16	0	1	1.000	2.71	2	1.000	A+	1		16	+2	-1	0	+1	-1	0	0	0	-
		232	197	1761.1	150	391	17	33	.970	2.76	27	.602	B+	4	10	371	+13	+8	+2	+22	0	+22	+28	22	8

Robb Quinlan

		BASIC									BUNTS					PLUS/MINUS								
Year	Team	G	GS	Inn	PO	A	E	DP	Pct	Rng	Opps	Score	Grade	Runs Saved	Rank	Outs Made	To His Right	Straight On	To His Left	GB	Air	Total	Enhanced	Runs Saved	Rank
2004	Ana	32	28	218.0	13	44	1	1	.983	2.35	9	.722	A+	2	-	44	-5	-3	+2	-6	0	-6	-7	-5	-
2005	LAA	33	30	243.0	22	51	7	4	.913	2.70	5	.390	D+	0	-	66	-2	+1	+5	+4	+1	+5	+5	4	-
2006	LAA	18	16	130.0	11	24	1	1	.972	2.42	2	.625	A-	0	-	33	-1	-1	-1	-3	0	-3	-3	-2	-
2007	LAA	10	5	53.1	4	7	1	0	.917	1.86	1	.250	F	0	-	11	+1	-2	-1	-2	0	-2	-2	-2	-
2008	LAA	39	29	258.2	22	48	4	8	.946	2.44	3	.500	C+	0	-	64	-3	-2	-1	-6	0	-6	-5	-4	-
		132	108	903.0	72	174	14	14	.946	2.45	20	.573	B	2	-	159	-10	-7	+4	-13	+1	-12	-12	-9	-

Aramis Ramirez

		BASIC									BUNTS					PLUS/MINUS								
Year	Team	G	GS	Inn	PO	A	E	DP	Pct	Rng	Opps	Score	Grade	Runs Saved	Rank	Outs Made	To His Right	Straight On	To His Left	GB	Air	Total	Enhanced	Runs Saved	Rank
2003	2 tms	159	156	1397.2	97	336	33	24	.929	2.79	24	.490	C+	0	17	377	+1	-1	-4	-4	-3	-7	-4	-3	24
2004	ChC	144	141	1245.1	92	221	10	15	.969	2.26	25	.496	C+	0	17	272	+2	-9	-3	-10	-1	-11	-8	-6	27
2005	ChC	119	119	1020.1	70	218	16	14	.947	2.54	21	.417	D+	-1	27	257	-2	0	+3	+1	0	+1	0	0	21
2006	ChC	156	155	1353.0	110	252	13	17	.965	2.41	22	.475	C	1	12	321	-5	+3	-5	-7	0	-7	-6	-5	24
2007	ChC	126	126	1091.1	88	260	10	19	.972	2.87	24	.506	C+	0	12	316	+4	+8	+4	+16	-2	+14	+15	11	4
2008	ChC	147	147	1282.2	83	225	18	17	.945	2.16	21	.490	C+	0	12	279	-8	-2	-1	-11	-1	-12	-12	-9	33
		851	844	7390.1	540	1512	100	106	.954	2.50	137	.480	C+	0	18	1410	-8	-1	-6	-15	-7	-22	-15	-12	24

Mark Reynolds

		BASIC									BUNTS					PLUS/MINUS								
Year	Team	G	GS	Inn	PO	A	E	DP	Pct	Rng	Opps	Score	Grade	Runs Saved	Rank	Outs Made	To His Right	Straight On	To His Left	GB	Air	Total	Enhanced	Runs Saved	Rank
2007	Ari	104	97	842.1	55	157	11	21	.951	2.27	17	.600	B+	1	7	188	-6	-5	+3	-9	-1	-10	-8	-6	27
2008	Ari	150	149	1288.1	82	240	34	23	.904	2.25	22	.461	C	-1	24	293	-4	-6	-3	-13	0	-13	-11	-8	30
		254	246	2130.2	137	397	45	44	.922	2.26	39	.522	B-	0	18	368	-10	-11	0	-22	-1	-23	-19	-14	26

Alex Rodriguez

		BASIC									BUNTS					PLUS/MINUS								
Year	Team	G	GS	Inn	PO	A	E	DP	Pct	Rng	Opps	Score	Grade	Runs Saved	Rank	Outs Made	To His Right	Straight On	To His Left	GB	Air	Total	Enhanced	Runs Saved	Rank
2004	NYY	155	155	1364.1	100	262	13	23	.965	2.39	21	.336	D-	-5	35	317	-1	+19	+2	+21	+1	+22	+17	13	4
2005	NYY	161	161	1384.2	115	288	12	26	.971	2.62	17	.312	F	-4	35	371	-7	+13	+2	+4	+4	+6	+2	2	17
2006	NYY	151	148	1287.2	96	262	24	24	.937	2.50	14	.354	D-	-3	34	327	+3	-7	-7	-11	-2	-13	-12	-9	32
2007	NYY	154	154	1330.0	106	251	13	30	.965	2.42	21	.436	C-	-1	25	330	+3	+3	-4	+2	0	+2	+3	2	16
2008	NYY	131	131	1126.1	73	251	10	23	.970	2.59	19	.363	D	-3	34	292	-5	+6	+1	+2	+1	+3	+1	1	17
		752	749	6493.0	490	1314	72	126	.962	2.50	92	.363	D	-16	35	1280	-7	+34	-11	+16	+4	+20	+11	9	11

Scott Rolen

		BASIC									BUNTS					PLUS/MINUS								
Year	Team	G	GS	Inn	PO	A	E	DP	Pct	Rng	Opps	Score	Grade	Runs Saved	Rank	Outs Made	To His Right	Straight On	To His Left	GB	Air	Total	Enhanced	Runs Saved	Rank
2003	StL	153	152	1339.0	109	298	13	23	.969	2.74	15	.560	B	2	4	332	-2	+4	-4	-2	0	-2	-7	-5	29
2004	StL	142	140	1228.0	93	325	10	23	.977	3.06	18	.503	C+	0	17	375	+6	+13	+13	+32	+2	+34	+37	28	1
2005	StL	56	55	486.0	22	151	6	17	.966	3.20	7	.614	A-	1	4	156	+3	+3	+9	+15	0	+15	+16	12	3
2006	StL	142	141	1215.2	93	318	15	32	.965	3.04	21	.500	C+	2	3	376	-7	+25	+4	+22	+1	+23	+19	14	5
2007	StL	112	108	935.0	85	226	10	22	.969	2.99	12	.696	A+	2	4	286	+7	+3	+6	+16	-2	+14	+15	11	5
2008	Tor	115	115	1006.2	74	217	11	14	.964	2.60	15	.463	C	0	12	266	-7	+12	+8	+13	0	+13	+13	10	3
		720	711	6210.1	476	1535	65	131	.969	2.91	88	.540	B-	7	4	1412	0	+60	+36	+96	+1	+97	+93	70	2

Marco Scutaro

		BASIC									BUNTS					PLUS/MINUS								
Year	Team	G	GS	Inn	PO	A	E	DP	Pct	Rng	Opps	Score	Grade	Runs Saved	Rank	Outs Made	To His Right	Straight On	To His Left	GB	Air	Total	Enhanced	Runs Saved	Rank
2004	Oak	1	0	1.0	0	0	0	0	-	.00					-	0								0	-
2005	Oak	5	2	21.0	4	6	0	1	1.000	4.29					-	10	0	0		0	0	0	0	0	-
2006	Oak	12	8	78.0	4	21	3	1	.893	2.88	4	.338	D-	-1		22	+3	-2	+1	+2	0	+2	+2	2	-
2007	Oak	36	33	295.2	23	64	9	2	.906	2.65	4	.525	B-	0	-	81	0	-6	+3	-4	0	-4	-5	-4	-
2008	Tor	41	36	332.0	22	84	2	8	.981	2.87	5	.550	B	0	-	101	+2	+3	+11	+16	+1	+17	+17	13	-
		95	79	727.2	53	175	14	12	.942	2.82	13	.477	C	-1	-	170	+5	-5	+15	+14	+1	+15	+14	11	-

Third Basemen

Ian Stewart

	BASIC									BUNTS					PLUS/MINUS									
Year	Team	G	GS	Inn	PO	A	E	DP	Pct	Rng	Opps	Score	Grade	Runs Saved	Rank	Outs Made	To His Right	Straight On	To His Left	GB	Air	Total	Enhanced	Runs Saved	Rank
2007	Col	11	3	41.1	5	16	0	0	1.000	4.57					-	20	+1	+2	+2	+4	+1	+5	+5	4	-
2008	Col	65	59	531.1	40	127	10	15	.944	2.83	12	.554	B	1	7	153	+1	+3	0	+4	0	+4	+4	3	15
		76	62	572.2	45	143	10	15	.949	2.95	12	.554	B	1		137	+2	+5	+2	+8	+1	+9	+9	7	-

Mark Teahen

	BASIC									BUNTS					PLUS/MINUS									
Year	Team	G	GS	Inn	PO	A	E	DP	Pct	Rng	Opps	Score	Grade	Runs Saved	Rank	Outs Made	To His Right	Straight On	To His Left	GB	Air	Total	Enhanced	Runs Saved	Rank
2005	KC	128	122	1068.1	113	244	20	22	.947	3.01	19	.521	B-	0	14	311	-9	-6	-11	-25	+1	-24	-30	-23	35
2006	KC	109	104	923.2	79	237	14	33	.958	3.08	17	.421	C-	-2	30	280	-11	+5	+8	+2	+2	+4	0	0	15
2008	KC	19	19	166.0	18	24	3	3	.933	2.28	4	.438	C-	-1		36	0	0	-2	-1	0	-1	-2	-2	-
		256	245	2158.0	210	505	37	58	.951	2.98	40	.470	C	-3	27	474	-20	-1	-5	-24	+3	-21	-32	-25	30

Chad Tracy

	BASIC									BUNTS					PLUS/MINUS									
Year	Team	G	GS	Inn	PO	A	E	DP	Pct	Rng	Opps	Score	Grade	Runs Saved	Rank	Outs Made	To His Right	Straight On	To His Left	GB	Air	Total	Enhanced	Runs Saved	Rank
2004	Ari	135	120	1061.1	104	259	25	27	.936	3.08	15	.467	C	-1	27	308	+12	+3	-3	+12	+1	+13	+17	13	5
2006	Ari	147	143	1278.0	101	260	25	27	.935	2.54	11	.345	D-	-2	30	336	-4	+1	0	-4	+1	-3	-4	-3	21
2007	Ari	48	46	374.0	29	73	4	6	.962	2.45	3	.483	C+	0		95	+1	0	-3	-2	0	-2	-3	-2	-
2008	Ari	2	2	16.0	2	2	0	0	1.000	2.25						4	0	0	0	0	0	0	0	0	-
		332	311	2729.1	236	594	54	60	.939	2.74	29	.422	C-	-3	27	563	+9	+4	-6	+6	+2	+8	+10	8	13

Juan Uribe

	BASIC									BUNTS					PLUS/MINUS									
Year	Team	G	GS	Inn	PO	A	E	DP	Pct	Rng	Opps	Score	Grade	Runs Saved	Rank	Outs Made	To His Right	Straight On	To His Left	GB	Air	Total	Enhanced	Runs Saved	Rank
2004	CWS	27	19	181.1	14	41	2	5	.965	2.73	5	.320	F	-1		48	0	+3	+1	+3	0	+3	+3	2	-
2008	CWS	57	52	460.1	41	125	7	10	.960	3.25	9	.406	D+	-1		152	+6	-7	-2	-3	0	-3	-3	-2	-
		84	71	641.2	55	166	9	15	.961	3.10	14	.375	D	-2		159	+6	-4	-1	0	0	0	0	0	-

Ramon Vazquez

	BASIC									BUNTS					PLUS/MINUS									
Year	Team	G	GS	Inn	PO	A	E	DP	Pct	Rng	Opps	Score	Grade	Runs Saved	Rank	Outs Made	To His Right	Straight On	To His Left	GB	Air	Total	Enhanced	Runs Saved	Rank
2003	SD	4	3	27.0	2	3	1	0	.833	1.67					-	5	-2	-1		-3	-1	-4	-4	-3	-
2004	SD	9	5	54.0	8	6	0	2	1.000	2.33					-	11	0	0	+1	+1	-1	0	0	0	-
2005	Bos	8	6	56.0	6	11	0	3	1.000	2.73	2	.250	F	-1		13	0	-1	-1	-2	0	-2	-2	-2	-
2006	Cle	14	10	93.0	4	20	1	1	.960	2.32	2	.800	A+	1		20	-2	-1	-3	-5	0	-5	-5	-4	-
2007	Tex	71	61	540.1	46	123	7	17	.960	2.81	8	.381	D	-1	25	149	0	+1	+1	+1	-1	0	-2	-2	20
2008	Tex	70	60	533.0	30	117	10	16	.936	2.48	8	.613	A-	1	7	133	0	-8	-3	-11	+1	-10	-10	-8	29
		176	145	1303.1	96	280	19	39	.952	2.60	20	.503	C+	0		261	-4	-10	-7	-19	-2	-21	-23	-19	-

Ty Wigginton

	BASIC									BUNTS					PLUS/MINUS									
Year	Team	G	GS	Inn	PO	A	E	DP	Pct	Rng	Opps	Score	Grade	Runs Saved	Rank	Outs Made	To His Right	Straight On	To His Left	GB	Air	Total	Enhanced	Runs Saved	Rank
2003	NYM	155	153	1329.0	117	293	16	27	.962	2.78	28	.629	A-	2	4	360	-14	-8	+1	-21	-2	-23	-26	-20	35
2004	2 tms	122	104	931.1	63	208	18	15	.938	2.62	25	.420	C-	-1	27	236	-5	-1	+5	-1	-1	-2	-4	-4	22
2005	Pit	40	36	305.0	19	57	9	5	.894	2.24	6	.367	D	-1		65	-11	-5	+1	-15	0	-15	-18	-14	-
2006	TB	34	32	274.1	16	63	5	6	.940	2.59	4	.438	C-	-1		73	-2	-7	-1	-9	-1	-10	-11	-8	29
2007	2 tms	80	76	647.1	57	140	8	6	.961	2.74	15	.460	C	0	12	177	-6	-2	-1	-8	+1	-7	-11	-8	29
2008	Hou	82	74	652.0	46	144	6	11	.969	2.62	11	.382	D	-2	30	172	-3	+2	+1	0	-1	-1	-5	-4	25
		513	475	4139.0	318	905	62	70	.952	2.66	89	.485	C+	-3	27	837	-41	-21	+6	-54	-4	-58	-75	-58	35

David Wright

	BASIC									BUNTS					PLUS/MINUS									
Year	Team	G	GS	Inn	PO	A	E	DP	Pct	Rng	Opps	Score	Grade	Runs Saved	Rank	Outs Made	To His Right	Straight On	To His Left	GB	Air	Total	Enhanced	Runs Saved	Rank
2004	NYM	69	68	603.2	39	139	11	10	.942	2.65	9	.539	B-	0	17	155	-2	+14	-2	+10	-3	+7	+6	5	12
2005	NYM	160	160	1404.1	101	337	24	23	.948	2.81	32	.542	B-	1	4	396	-14	+2	0	-12	-2	-14	-17	-13	32
2006	NYM	153	153	1365.1	107	288	19	30	.954	2.60	23	.530	B-	2	3	339	-10	-6	+8	-12	-1	-11	-11	-8	29
2007	NYM	159	159	1418.1	107	324	21	24	.954	2.73	28	.582	B+	3	1	384	-11	+9	+18	+16	0	+16	+13	10	6
2008	NYM	159	159	1433.1	114	286	16	21	.962	2.51	17	.674	A+	3	1	356	-2	+6	+1	+5	-2	+3	+2	2	16
		700	699	6225.0	468	1374	91	108	.953	2.66	109	.570	B	9	3	1290	-39	+25	+25	+11	-9	+2	-7	-4	21

Third Basemen

Kevin Youkilis

		BASIC										BUNTS					PLUS/MINUS									
Year	Team	G	GS	Inn	PO	A	E	DP	Pct	Rng	Opps	Score	Grade	Runs Saved	Rank	Outs Made	To His Right	Straight On	To His Left	GB	Air	Total	Enhanced	Runs Saved	Rank
2004	Bos	65	54	506.0	47	106	5	7	.968	2.72	6	.550	B	1	10	145	-1	+6	+4	+8	-1	+7	+7	5	11
2005	Bos	24	14	139.0	10	29	0	3	1.000	2.53	1	.600	B+	0	-	37	-1	0	-1	-3	0	-3	-5	-4	-
2006	Bos	16	10	92.0	11	27	3	1	.927	3.72	1	1.000	A+	0	-	37	+2	-1	-2	-2	+1	-1	-1	-1	-
2007	Bos	13	12	108.0	5	30	3	4	.921	2.92	1	.250	F	0	-	33	-1	+1	0	0	0	0	+1	1	-
2008	Bos	36	32	252.0	23	70	3	5	.969	3.32	5	.530	B-	1	-	86	+1	+3	+4	+7	0	+7	+8	6	-
		154	122	1097.0	96	262	14	20	.962	2.94	14	.557	B	2	-	259	0	+9	+5	+10	0	+10	+10	7	-

Ryan Zimmerman

		BASIC										BUNTS					PLUS/MINUS									
Year	Team	G	GS	Inn	PO	A	E	DP	Pct	Rng	Opps	Score	Grade	Runs Saved	Rank	Outs Made	To His Right	Straight On	To His Left	GB	Air	Total	Enhanced	Runs Saved	Rank
2005	Was	14	11	111.0	6	26	0	5	1.000	2.59	4	.613	A-	1	-	26	+1	-1	0	0	0	0	+1	1	-
2006	Was	157	157	1368.1	152	260	15	30	.965	2.71	29	.502	C+	-1	27	368	+3	-1	0	+1	-1	0	+1	2	13
2007	Was	161	161	1431.2	140	348	23	39	.955	3.07	35	.581	B+	4	1	419	-4	+21	+2	+20	+4	+24	+21	16	3
2008	Was	104	104	910.2	95	199	10	25	.967	2.91	16	.672	A+	3	1	263	-7	+10	+5	+8	+2	+10	+10	8	9
		436	433	3821.2	393	833	48	99	.962	2.89	84	.573	B	7	4	767	-7	+29	+7	+29	+5	+34	+34	27	7

Shortstops

Mike Aviles

		BASIC									GROUND DP					PLUS/MINUS								
Year	Team	G	GS	Inn	PO	A	E	DP	Pct	Rng	GDP Opps	GDP	Pct	Runs Saved	Rank	Outs Made	To His Right	Straight On	To His Left	GB	Air	Total	Runs Saved	Rank
2008	KC	91	89	747.2	141	238	10	66	.974	4.56	90	61	.678	2	3	273	-2	+6	+10	+14	+1	+15	11	6

Erick Aybar

		BASIC									GROUND DP					PLUS/MINUS								
Year	Team	G	GS	Inn	PO	A	E	DP	Pct	Rng	GDP Opps	GDP	Pct	Runs Saved	Rank	Outs Made	To His Right	Straight On	To His Left	GB	Air	Total	Runs Saved	Rank
2006	LAA	19	6	76.0	13	22	4	6	.897	4.14	8	6	.750	0	-	23	-3	0	+2	-1	0	-1	-1	-
2007	LAA	20	7	79.0	14	24	3	2	.927	4.33	9	2	.222	-1	-	31	-1	-1	+2	0	-1	-1	-1	-
2008	LAA	96	91	784.2	140	276	18	63	.959	4.77	101	60	.594	0	15	304	+6	+3	-6	+3	+5	+8	6	10
		135	104	939.2	167	322	25	71	.951	4.68	118	68	.576	-1	-	358	+2	+2	-2	+2	+4	+6	4	-

Clint Barmes

		BASIC									GROUND DP					PLUS/MINUS								
Year	Team	G	GS	Inn	PO	A	E	DP	Pct	Rng	GDP Opps	GDP	Pct	Runs Saved	Rank	Outs Made	To His Right	Straight On	To His Left	GB	Air	Total	Runs Saved	Rank
2003	Col	12	8	75.0	19	27	2	7	.958	5.52	6	4	.667	0	-	24	-1	-1	-2	-4	0	-4	-3	-
2004	Col	9	9	76.0	17	36	1	7	.981	6.28	9	6	.667	0	-	20	+1	0	+2	+3	-1	+2	2	-
2005	Col	80	78	681.2	139	247	17	62	.958	5.10	105	59	.562	-1	22	277	+12	-5	+10	+17	0	+17	13	6
2006	Col	125	122	1072.2	193	371	18	88	.969	4.73	127	85	.669	3	2	405	+22	+2	+3	+27	0	+27	21	2
2007	Col	8	3	35.0	8	12	1	3	.952	5.14	4	3	.750	0	-	14	-1	+1	0	-1	0	-1	-1	-
2008	Col	36	32	285.0	57	113	3	30	.983	5.37	41	25	.610	0	-	119	+2	-1	-1	0	0	0	0	-
		270	252	2225.1	433	806	42	197	.967	5.01	292	182	.623	2	15	859	+35	-4	+12	+42	-1	+41	32	9

Jason Bartlett

		BASIC									GROUND DP					PLUS/MINUS								
Year	Team	G	GS	Inn	PO	A	E	DP	Pct	Rng	GDP Opps	GDP	Pct	Runs Saved	Rank	Outs Made	To His Right	Straight On	To His Left	GB	Air	Total	Runs Saved	Rank
2004	Min	5	2	22.0	5	11	2	3	.889	6.55	5	3	.600	0	-	11	+1	0	-1	0	+1	+1	1	-
2005	Min	68	65	585.2	95	227	7	45	.979	4.95	62	42	.677	2	6	257	+1	+3	+9	+12	+2	+14	11	7
2006	Min	99	99	879.2	131	298	13	45	.971	4.39	97	45	.464	-3	33	349	+1	+9	0	+9	+4	+13	10	7
2007	Min	138	135	1194.0	205	415	26	97	.960	4.67	136	83	.610	1	10	467	+11	-2	+4	+13	+5	+18	14	5
2008	TB	125	122	1097.0	204	309	16	69	.970	4.21	113	62	.549	-1	24	381	+11	-4	-11	-4	+3	-1	-1	19
		435	423	3778.1	640	1260	64	259	.967	4.53	413	235	.569	-1	24	1465	+25	+6	+1	+30	+15	+45	35	7

Angel Berroa

		BASIC									GROUND DP					PLUS/MINUS								
Year	Team	G	GS	Inn	PO	A	E	DP	Pct	Rng	GDP Opps	GDP	Pct	Runs Saved	Rank	Outs Made	To His Right	Straight On	To His Left	GB	Air	Total	Runs Saved	Rank
2003	KC	158	158	1381.2	264	473	24	106	.968	4.80	158	97	.614	1	6	509	-13	0	+2	-10	-3	-13	-10	33
2004	KC	133	132	1143.0	206	388	28	93	.955	4.68	133	84	.632	2	2	384	-4	-10	-2	-16	-4	-20	-15	34
2005	KC	159	159	1360.1	254	442	25	107	.965	4.47	161	102	.634	2	6	505	-23	-5	+4	-24	-2	-26	-20	33
2006	KC	131	129	1117.1	188	367	18	95	.969	4.47	136	86	.632	2	5	413	-7	-1	-2	-10	+2	-8	-6	25
2007	KC	4	2	21.2	4	11	0	6	1.000	6.23	5	5	1.000	1	-	7	0	+1	0	+1	0	+1	1	-
2008	LAD	79	64	591.2	91	219	8	39	.975	4.72	67	38	.567	0	15	226	-6	+2	+6	+2	-2	0	0	18
		664	644	5615.2	1007	1900	103	446	.966	4.66	660	412	.624	8	2	2044	-53	-13	+8	-57	-9	-66	-50	33

Yuniesky Betancourt

		BASIC									GROUND DP					PLUS/MINUS								
Year	Team	G	GS	Inn	PO	A	E	DP	Pct	Rng	GDP Opps	GDP	Pct	Runs Saved	Rank	Outs Made	To His Right	Straight On	To His Left	GB	Air	Total	Runs Saved	Rank
2005	Sea	53	52	454.0	82	136	5	34	.978	4.32	50	32	.640	1	12	161	-2	0	+1	-1	0	-1	-1	20
2006	Sea	157	156	1374.1	251	431	20	95	.972	4.47	141	88	.624	2	5	502	+4	0	-4	0	-3	-3	-2	22
2007	Sea	152	147	1302.1	239	435	23	110	.967	4.66	174	104	.598	1	10	463	-11	+6	-5	-10	0	-10	-8	27
2008	Sea	153	150	1325.1	237	401	21	98	.968	4.33	150	93	.620	1	8	446	+7	-7	-21	-21	+2	-19	-14	35
		515	505	4456.0	809	1403	69	337	.970	4.47	515	317	.616	5	6	1572	-2	-1	-29	-32	-1	-33	-25	29

Brian Bixler

		BASIC									GROUND DP					PLUS/MINUS								
Year	Team	G	GS	Inn	PO	A	E	DP	Pct	Rng	GDP Opps	GDP	Pct	Runs Saved	Rank	Outs Made	To His Right	Straight On	To His Left	GB	Air	Total	Runs Saved	Rank
2008	Pit	39	32	278.0	53	121	8	28	.956	5.63	37	25	.676	1	-	122	-1	-2	+5	+1	-3	-2	-2	-

Eric Bruntlett

		BASIC									GROUND DP					PLUS/MINUS								
Year	Team	G	GS	Inn	PO	A	E	DP	Pct	Rng	GDP Opps	GDP	Pct	Runs Saved	Rank	Outs Made	To His Right	Straight On	To His Left	GB	Air	Total	Runs Saved	Rank
2003	Hou	10	5	63.1	12	14	1	3	.963	3.69	5	2	.400	0	-	18	+1	-1	-2	-1	0	-1	-1	-
2004	Hou	33	10	127.0	17	28	3	9	.938	3.19	14	9	.643	0	-	29	+1	0	0	+1	0	+1	1	-
2005	Hou	10	4	49.0	9	21	0	4	1.000	5.51	5	4	.800	0	-	21	+1	0	+1	+2	0	+2	2	-
2006	Hou	21	13	144.2	20	57	4	9	.951	4.79	9	7	.778	0	-	57	+3	-2	+2	+3	-1	+2	2	-
2007	Hou	63	34	348.2	62	109	7	23	.961	4.41	40	21	.525	-1	-	131	+1	+1	-2	0	+2	+2	2	-
2008	Phi	35	30	279.2	39	92	4	16	.970	4.22	25	14	.560	0	-	107	+1	-1	0	+1	0	+1	1	-
		172	96	1012.1	159	321	19	64	.962	4.27	98	57	.582	-1		363	+8	-3	-1	+6	+1	+7	7	-

Shortstops

Emmanuel Burriss

	BASIC										GROUND DP					PLUS/MINUS								
Year	Team	G	GS	Inn	PO	A	E	DP	Pct	Rng	GDP Opps	GDP	Pct	Runs Saved	Rank	Outs Made	To His Right	Straight On	To His Left	GB	Air	Total	Runs Saved	Rank
2008	SF	47	34	315.0	50	93	5	11	.966	4.09	19	9	.474	-1		112	-7	-1	+1	-7	0	-7	-5	

Freddie Bynum

	BASIC										GROUND DP					PLUS/MINUS								
Year	Team	G	GS	Inn	PO	A	E	DP	Pct	Rng	GDP Opps	GDP	Pct	Runs Saved	Rank	Outs Made	To His Right	Straight On	To His Left	GB	Air	Total	Runs Saved	Rank
2007	Bal	15	7	66.0	13	16	1	2	.250	3.95	8	2	.250	-1	-	23	0	0	-1	0	0	0	0	-
2008	Bal	37	32	283.1	56	81	5	28	.965	4.35	39	26	.667	1	-	99	-4	-1	+3	-2	+1	-1	-1	-
		52	39	349.1	69	97	6	30	.965	4.28	47	28	.596	0	-	122	-4	-1	+2	-2	+1	-1	-1	-

Orlando Cabrera

	BASIC										GROUND DP					PLUS/MINUS								
Year	Team	G	GS	Inn	PO	A	E	DP	Pct	Rng	GDP Opps	GDP	Pct	Runs Saved	Rank	Outs Made	To His Right	Straight On	To His Left	GB	Air	Total	Runs Saved	Rank
2003	Mon	162	160	1385.2	258	456	18	100	.975	4.64	157	90	.573	-1	23	414	-1	+1	+7	+7	-2	+5	4	13
2004	2 tms	159	158	1358.2	226	437	15	93	.978	4.39	152	83	.546	-2	26	427	+2	+3	+4	+10	+3	+13	10	5
2005	LAA	141	140	1240.2	229	347	7	81	.988	4.18	128	75	.586	0	14	425	-8	0	+16	+7	0	+7	5	12
2006	LAA	152	152	1320.2	253	377	16	99	.975	4.29	150	91	.607	1	11	434	-18	-6	+13	-10	-2	-12	-9	31
2007	LAA	153	153	1330.2	239	415	11	104	.983	4.42	153	99	.647	3	2	462	-8	+4	+4	0	+2	+2	2	16
2008	CWS	161	160	1389.2	242	472	16	101	.978	4.62	146	93	.637	2	3	528	-3	-2	+8	+2	-1	+1	1	17
		928	923	8026.0	1447	2504	83	578	.979	4.43	886	531	.599	3	12	2690	-36	0	+52	+16	0	+16	13	15

Juan Castro

	BASIC										GROUND DP					PLUS/MINUS								
Year	Team	G	GS	Inn	PO	A	E	DP	Pct	Rng	GDP Opps	GDP	Pct	Runs Saved	Rank	Outs Made	To His Right	Straight On	To His Left	GB	Air	Total	Runs Saved	Rank
2003	Cin	24	18	154.0	28	43	0	14	1.000	4.15	15	11	.733	1	-	42	+2	0	+2	+4	0	+4	3	-
2004	Cin	31	21	190.1	32	72	2	16	.981	4.92	23	13	.565	0	-	69	-2	+1	0	0	+2	+2	2	-
2005	Min	73	66	568.2	98	231	5	49	.985	5.21	64	44	.688	2	6	246	0	+3	+5	+8	+1	+9	7	10
2006	2 tms	77	61	548.2	90	189	8	38	.972	4.58	59	36	.610	1	11	205	-4	+4	+3	+2	+3	+5	4	12
2007	Cin	16	11	89.1	10	27	0	5	1.000	3.73	8	5	.625	0	-	31	+1	0	-1	0	+1	+1	1	-
2008	2 tms	57	48	408.2	73	140	5	22	.977	4.69	44	18	.409	-2	31	152	+8	-4	-5	-2	-2	-4	-3	25
		278	225	1959.2	331	702	20	144	.981	4.74	213	127	.596	2	-	745	+5	+4	+4	+12	+5	+17	14	-

Alex Cintron

	BASIC										GROUND DP					PLUS/MINUS								
Year	Team	G	GS	Inn	PO	A	E	DP	Pct	Rng	GDP Opps	GDP	Pct	Runs Saved	Rank	Outs Made	To His Right	Straight On	To His Left	GB	Air	Total	Runs Saved	Rank
2003	Ari	93	90	795.2	138	234	8	56	.979	4.21	97	51	.526	-2	31	244	+5	+2	-8	0	-1	-1	-1	21
2004	Ari	133	125	1099.0	141	382	15	61	.972	4.28	119	57	.479	-4	35	385	+9	-2	-3	+5	-2	+3	2	17
2005	Ari	39	31	271.0	44	99	5	19	.966	4.75	30	17	.567	0	-	113	+3	+1	-3	+1	+1	+2	2	-
2006	CWS	41	35	319.0	50	94	4	19	.973	4.06	28	19	.679	1	-	108	-3	0	-2	-5	-2	-7	-5	-
2007	CWS	17	15	132.1	34	45	2	14	.975	5.37	26	12	.462	-1	-	50	-3	+1	-2	-3	-1	-4	-3	-
2008	Bal	45	28	257.0	50	92	7	21	.953	4.97	38	20	.526	-1	-	103	-4	-6	-1	-11	-1	-12	-9	-
		368	324	2874.0	457	946	41	190	.972	4.39	338	176	.521	-7	32	1003	+7	-4	-19	-13	-6	-19	-14	25

Alex Cora

	BASIC										GROUND DP					PLUS/MINUS								
Year	Team	G	GS	Inn	PO	A	E	DP	Pct	Rng	GDP Opps	GDP	Pct	Runs Saved	Rank	Outs Made	To His Right	Straight On	To His Left	GB	Air	Total	Runs Saved	Rank
2003	LA	15	5	55.1	10	18	0	4	1.000	4.55	8	4	.500	0	-	19	+2	0	+1	+3	+1	+4	3	-
2005	2 tms	35	27	245.2	37	107	3	16	.980	5.28	21	16	.762	1	-	122	+6	-1	+5	+9	-1	+8	6	-
2006	Bos	63	47	434.0	66	166	6	47	.975	4.81	60	42	.700	2	5	164	-5	+5	+6	+6	-2	+4	3	15
2007	Bos	33	22	202.1	25	69	3	18	.969	4.18	22	16	.727	1	-	66	-1	-1	+5	+3	0	+3	2	-
2008	Bos	69	38	386.0	74	136	6	39	.972	4.90	44	33	.750	2	-	141	-2	+1	-5	-5	+3	-2	-2	-
		215	139	1323.1	212	496	18	124	.975	4.82	155	111	.716	6	-	512	0	+4	+12	+16	+1	+17	12	-

Craig Counsell

	BASIC										GROUND DP					PLUS/MINUS								
Year	Team	G	GS	Inn	PO	A	E	DP	Pct	Rng	GDP Opps	GDP	Pct	Runs Saved	Rank	Outs Made	To His Right	Straight On	To His Left	GB	Air	Total	Runs Saved	Rank
2003	Ari	26	18	167.2	23	66	1	9	.989	4.78	15	9	.600	0	-	71	-2	0	+1	-1	0	-1	-1	-
2004	Mil	129	128	1130.2	164	358	9	69	.983	4.16	109	62	.569	-1	21	359	+7	-3	+2	+7	-1	+6	5	10
2005	Ari	1	0	1.0	0	0	0	0		.00	0				-	0				0		0	0	-
2006	Ari	88	83	736.2	127	296	9	75	.979	5.17	87	67	.770	5	1	309	+8	0	+12	+19	0	+19	14	4
2007	Mil	27	17	170.2	20	55	1	14	.987	3.96	17	13	.765	1	-	59	0	0	-1	-1	0	-1	-1	-
2008	Mil	24	19	185.1	30	73	2	13	.981	5.00	23	12	.522	0	-	74	+1	+1	+3	+6	0	+6	5	-
		295	265	2392.0	364	848	22	180	.982	4.56	251	163	.649	5	6	872	+14	-2	+17	+30	-1	+29	22	11

Shortstops

Bobby Crosby

		BASIC									GROUND DP					PLUS/MINUS								
Year	Team	G	GS	Inn	PO	A	E	DP	Pct	Rng	GDP Opps	GDP	Pct	Runs Saved	Rank	Outs Made	To His Right	Straight On	To His Left	GB	Air	Total	Runs Saved	Rank
2003	Oak	9	0	20.0	5	11	2	2	.889	7.20	9	2	.222	-1	-	11	-2	0	0	-2	0	-2	-2	-
2004	Oak	151	151	1356.0	241	505	19	107	.975	4.95	169	100	.592	0	12	525	+9	+6	-11	+3	+2	+5	4	12
2005	Oak	84	84	743.1	117	251	7	60	.981	4.46	85	57	.671	2	6	278	+3	+4	0	+8	0	+8	6	11
2006	Oak	95	95	828.0	145	268	12	59	.972	4.49	91	54	.593	0	17	307	-3	+1	-5	-7	-1	-8	-6	26
2007	Oak	92	92	813.2	131	282	14	61	.967	4.57	90	56	.622	1	10	314	-1	-1	+5	+3	-1	+2	2	17
2008	Oak	145	144	1263.0	202	384	17	99	.972	4.18	129	88	.682	4	1	423	-7	-2	-5	-13	0	-13	-10	32
		576	566	5024.0	841	1701	71	388	.973	4.55	573	357	.623	6	4	1858	-1	+8	-16	-8	0	-8	-6	22

Stephen Drew

		BASIC									GROUND DP					PLUS/MINUS								
Year	Team	G	GS	Inn	PO	A	E	DP	Pct	Rng	GDP Opps	GDP	Pct	Runs Saved	Rank	Outs Made	To His Right	Straight On	To His Left	GB	Air	Total	Runs Saved	Rank
2006	Ari	56	52	480.1	73	150	5	35	.978	4.18	55	32	.582	0	17	161	+5	0	-5	0	+2	+2	2	18
2007	Ari	147	143	1283.1	212	409	17	98	.973	4.36	145	90	.621	1	10	434	+17	-10	-15	-7	+6	-1	-1	19
2008	Ari	151	147	1294.1	190	378	14	85	.976	3.95	128	78	.609	1	8	422	+6	-8	-7	-8	+3	-5	-4	26
		354	342	3058.0	475	937	36	218	.975	4.16	328	200	.610	2	15	1017	+28	-18	-27	-15	+11	-4	-3	19

David Eckstein

		BASIC									GROUND DP					PLUS/MINUS								
Year	Team	G	GS	Inn	PO	A	E	DP	Pct	Rng	GDP Opps	GDP	Pct	Runs Saved	Rank	Outs Made	To His Right	Straight On	To His Left	GB	Air	Total	Runs Saved	Rank
2003	Ana	116	114	985.0	193	293	8	64	.984	4.44	101	59	.584	0	13	330	-4	+2	+4	+2	+2	+4	3	14
2004	Ana	139	137	1191.2	198	309	6	75	.988	3.83	125	68	.544	-2	26	349	+3	0	-2	+1	0	+1	1	20
2005	StL	156	154	1340.2	244	516	15	122	.981	5.10	188	118	.628	2	6	551	-6	+7	-1	0	-2	-2	-2	21
2006	StL	120	119	1029.0	178	363	6	87	.989	4.73	135	79	.585	0	17	385	+5	-1	+1	+6	-4	+2	2	17
2007	StL	114	112	943.2	164	310	20	59	.960	4.52	99	53	.535	-1	28	350	-1	-7	-1	-9	-5	-14	-11	30
2008	Tor	57	56	484.1	69	146	9	33	.960	4.00	53	31	.585	0	15	150	-4	-1	-7	-12	-1	-13	-10	33
		702	692	5974.1	1046	1937	64	440	.979	4.49	701	408	.582	-1	24	2115	-7	0	-6	-12	-10	-22	-17	26

Yunel Escobar

		BASIC									GROUND DP					PLUS/MINUS								
Year	Team	G	GS	Inn	PO	A	E	DP	Pct	Rng	GDP Opps	GDP	Pct	Runs Saved	Rank	Outs Made	To His Right	Straight On	To His Left	GB	Air	Total	Runs Saved	Rank
2007	Atl	53	36	363.0	59	113	4	22	.977	4.26	29	21	.724	1	-	135	-2	+3	+1	+2	-2	0	0	-
2008	Atl	126	125	1105.2	193	396	16	78	.974	4.79	145	74	.510	-3	34	439	0	+3	+19	+22	-2	+20	15	2
		179	161	1468.2	252	509	20	100	.974	4.66	174	95	.546	-2	-	574	-2	+6	+20	+24	-4	+20	15	-

Adam Everett

		BASIC									GROUND DP					PLUS/MINUS								
Year	Team	G	GS	Inn	PO	A	E	DP	Pct	Rng	GDP Opps	GDP	Pct	Runs Saved	Rank	Outs Made	To His Right	Straight On	To His Left	GB	Air	Total	Runs Saved	Rank
2003	Hou	128	116	1000.2	207	344	17	74	.970	4.96	109	63	.578	0	13	410	+13	+2	+5	+20	+1	+21	16	1
2004	Hou	99	97	842.0	137	278	10	55	.976	4.44	83	51	.614	1	4	306	+10	+5	+4	+19	+3	+22	17	1
2005	Hou	150	147	1291.2	209	420	14	96	.978	4.38	150	88	.587	0	14	470	+15	+4	+14	+34	-1	+33	25	1
2006	Hou	149	146	1292.1	202	479	7	104	.990	4.74	155	101	.652	3	2	500	+5	+5	+31	+42	-1	+41	31	1
2007	Hou	66	62	535.1	96	197	8	37	.973	4.93	60	37	.617	1	10	217	+3	+1	+13	+17	+1	+18	14	6
2008	Min	44	41	364.0	61	145	7	30	.967	5.09	48	27	.563	0	-	157	-2	-2	+3	-1	0	-1	-1	-
		636	609	5326.0	912	1863	63	396	.978	4.69	605	367	.607	5	6	2060	+44	+15	+70	+131	+3	+134	102	1

Rafael Furcal

		BASIC									GROUND DP					PLUS/MINUS								
Year	Team	G	GS	Inn	PO	A	E	DP	Pct	Rng	GDP Opps	GDP	Pct	Runs Saved	Rank	Outs Made	To His Right	Straight On	To His Left	GB	Air	Total	Runs Saved	Rank
2003	Atl	155	154	1350.0	237	481	31	107	.959	4.79	174	103	.592	0	13	510	+6	-8	+12	+10	0	+10	8	6
2004	Atl	131	130	1134.0	191	412	24	99	.962	4.79	160	95	.594	0	12	413	-1	-2	+5	+1	+1	+2	2	18
2005	Atl	152	152	1306.1	256	504	15	119	.981	5.24	172	110	.640	3	3	539	+14	0	+8	+22	+4	+26	20	3
2006	LAD	156	156	1371.0	269	492	27	117	.966	5.00	198	114	.576	-1	27	539	+6	+1	-4	+3	+1	+4	3	13
2007	LAD	138	138	1210.0	241	426	19	99	.972	4.96	151	94	.623	2	5	474	-8	+3	+12	+7	-1	+6	5	12
2008	LAD	36	35	296.0	46	92	4	17	.972	4.20	27	17	.630	0	-	102	+1	+2	-2	0	0	0	0	-
		768	765	6667.1	1240	2407	120	558	.968	4.92	882	533	.604	4	10	2577	+18	-4	+31	+43	+5	+48	38	5

Nomar Garciaparra

		BASIC									GROUND DP					PLUS/MINUS								
Year	Team	G	GS	Inn	PO	A	E	DP	Pct	Rng	GDP Opps	GDP	Pct	Runs Saved	Rank	Outs Made	To His Right	Straight On	To His Left	GB	Air	Total	Runs Saved	Rank
2003	Bos	156	155	1364.2	216	455	20	82	.971	4.43	155	78	.503	-4	35	492	-4	+3	+15	+14	-1	+13	10	2
2004	2 tms	79	78	676.0	121	176	9	34	.971	3.95	75	31	.413	-3	34	204	-2	-6	+1	-8	-4	-12	-9	30
2005	ChC	26	25	206.0	41	51	6	16	.939	4.02	24	15	.625	0	-	56	-4	+1	0	-3	+1	-2	-2	-
2008	LAD	31	29	238.0	29	89	4	14	.967	4.46	26	13	.500	-1	-	89	0	-2	+7	+5	-1	+4	3	-
		292	287	2484.2	407	771	39	146	.968	4.27	280	137	.489	-8	33	841	-10	-4	+23	+8	-5	+3	2	18

Shortstops

Alex Gonzalez

		BASIC									GROUND DP					PLUS/MINUS								
Year	Team	G	GS	Inn	PO	A	E	DP	Pct	Rng	GDP Opps	GDP	Pct	Runs Saved	Rank	Outs Made	To His Right	Straight On	To His Left	GB	Air	Total	Runs Saved	Rank
2003	Fla	150	150	1315.2	236	426	16	106	.976	4.53	143	99	.692	4	1	466	-6	0	-3	-8	-1	-9	-7	31
2004	Fla	158	155	1351.2	225	425	16	99	.976	4.33	144	88	.611	1	4	459	+8	-1	+3	+10	-1	+9	7	7
2005	Fla	124	124	1087.1	221	367	16	102	.974	4.87	138	90	.652	3	3	406	+2	0	-1	+1	-2	-1	-1	19
2006	Bos	111	110	966.1	163	305	7	68	.985	4.36	106	62	.585	0	17	352	-11	+3	+12	+5	-1	+4	3	14
2007	Cin	103	98	872.2	147	264	16	73	.963	4.24	98	66	.673	2	5	306	-4	+4	+1	+2	+2	+4	3	14
		646	637	5593.2	992	1787	71	448	.975	4.47	629	405	.644	10	-	1989	-11	+6	+12	+10	-3	+7	5	-

Khalil Greene

		BASIC									GROUND DP					PLUS/MINUS								
Year	Team	G	GS	Inn	PO	A	E	DP	Pct	Rng	GDP Opps	GDP	Pct	Runs Saved	Rank	Outs Made	To His Right	Straight On	To His Left	GB	Air	Total	Runs Saved	Rank
2003	SD	20	18	155.0	27	51	3	11	.963	4.53	17	10	.588	0	-	53	0	-1	+1	0	0	0	0	-
2004	SD	136	134	1189.2	177	380	20	80	.965	4.21	123	76	.618	1	4	404	-4	-3	+12	+4	0	+4	3	15
2005	SD	121	120	1028.2	161	312	14	64	.971	4.14	111	60	.541	-1	22	365	-7	-2	-5	-14	-2	-16	-12	31
2006	SD	113	111	997.2	138	309	9	61	.980	4.03	101	57	.564	-1	27	352	+20	+4	-10	+14	-1	+13	10	6
2007	SD	153	153	1396.1	218	461	11	98	.984	4.38	158	95	.601	1	10	503	+15	+3	-10	+8	-1	+7	5	10
2008	SD	105	103	934.0	146	289	8	66	.982	4.19	97	61	.629	1	8	327	+9	+2	-14	-2	-2	-4	-3	24
		648	639	5701.1	867	1802	65	380	.976	4.21	607	359	.591	1	20	2004	+33	+3	-26	+10	-6	+4	3	17

Cristian Guzman

		BASIC									GROUND DP					PLUS/MINUS								
Year	Team	G	GS	Inn	PO	A	E	DP	Pct	Rng	GDP Opps	GDP	Pct	Runs Saved	Rank	Outs Made	To His Right	Straight On	To His Left	GB	Air	Total	Runs Saved	Rank
2003	Min	141	137	1232.1	195	352	11	68	.980	3.99	109	61	.560	-1	23	395	-6	+3	-12	-15	-1	-16	-12	35
2004	Min	145	143	1304.2	234	440	12	103	.983	4.65	158	97	.614	1	4	456	+3	+2	-6	0	0	0	0	22
2005	Was	142	133	1161.0	217	327	15	85	.973	4.22	120	78	.650	2	6	382	-8	+2	+4	-2	-4	-6	-5	25
2007	Was	44	42	376.0	67	105	8	33	.956	4.12	49	32	.653	1	-	117	-4	-2	-1	-7	0	-7	-5	-
2008	Was	136	132	1174.0	192	394	17	75	.972	4.49	110	71	.645	2	3	442	-6	+2	+13	+9	+4	+13	10	7
		608	587	5248.0	905	1618	63	364	.976	4.33	546	339	.621	5	6	1792	-21	+7	-2	-15	-1	-16	-12	24

Jerry Hairston

		BASIC									GROUND DP					PLUS/MINUS								
Year	Team	G	GS	Inn	PO	A	E	DP	Pct	Rng	GDP Opps	GDP	Pct	Runs Saved	Rank	Outs Made	To His Right	Straight On	To His Left	GB	Air	Total	Runs Saved	Rank
2005	ChC	1	0	2.0	1	1	0	1	1.000	9.00	1	1	1.000	0	-	0					-1	-1	-1	-
2006	Tex	3	1	12.0	4	6	0	3	1.000	7.50	3	3	1.000	0	-	4	-1	0	+1	0	0	0	0	-
2007	Tex	2	0	3.0	1	0	0	0	1.000	3.00	0		-		-	1	0			0	0	0	0	-
2008	Cin	34	31	271.0	61	68	4	18	.970	4.28	27	17	.630	0	-	88	-2	0	0	-2	+1	-1	-1	-
		40	32	288.0	67	75	4	22	.973	4.44	31	21	.677	0	-	93	-3	0	+1	-2	0	-2	-2	-

J.J. Hardy

		BASIC									GROUND DP					PLUS/MINUS								
Year	Team	G	GS	Inn	PO	A	E	DP	Pct	Rng	GDP Opps	GDP	Pct	Runs Saved	Rank	Outs Made	To His Right	Straight On	To His Left	GB	Air	Total	Runs Saved	Rank
2005	Mil	119	104	937.2	133	259	10	52	.975	3.76	78	46	.590	0	14	316	+13	+1	-4	+9	+1	+10	8	8
2006	Mil	32	29	257.2	51	90	2	25	.986	4.92	39	25	.641	1	-	93	+5	0	+3	+8	-1	+7	5	-
2007	Mil	149	145	1271.2	168	397	13	83	.978	4.00	122	76	.623	1	10	443	-14	+4	+16	+6	+1	+7	5	11
2008	Mil	145	143	1268.1	202	430	15	86	.977	4.48	147	79	.537	-2	31	477	-1	-1	+18	+16	+3	+19	14	4
		445	421	3735.1	554	1176	40	246	.977	4.17	386	226	.585	0	21	1329	+3	+3	+33	+39	+4	+43	32	8

Brendan Harris

		BASIC									GROUND DP					PLUS/MINUS								
Year	Team	G	GS	Inn	PO	A	E	DP	Pct	Rng	GDP Opps	GDP	Pct	Runs Saved	Rank	Outs Made	To His Right	Straight On	To His Left	GB	Air	Total	Runs Saved	Rank
2006	Was	5	3	26.1	5	7	1	1	.923	4.10	4	1	.250	0	-	8	-1	+1	0	0	0	0	0	-
2007	TB	87	86	751.2	111	221	11	54	.968	3.98	92	49	.533	-1	28	235	-3	-4	-5	-12	-7	-19	-14	33
2008	Min	55	51	464.1	84	159	6	42	.976	4.71	63	39	.619	1	8	160	+7	-1	-12	-7	-2	-9	-7	29
		147	140	1242.1	200	387	18	97	.970	4.25	159	89	.560	0	-	403	+3	-4	-17	-19	-9	-28	-21	-

Cesar Izturis

		BASIC									GROUND DP					PLUS/MINUS								
Year	Team	G	GS	Inn	PO	A	E	DP	Pct	Rng	GDP Opps	GDP	Pct	Runs Saved	Rank	Outs Made	To His Right	Straight On	To His Left	GB	Air	Total	Runs Saved	Rank
2003	LA	158	154	1365.1	197	481	16	94	.977	4.47	149	87	.584	0	13	471	+19	+1	-11	+9	+1	+10	8	7
2004	LA	159	156	1386.0	234	430	10	96	.985	4.31	144	89	.618	1	4	491	+11	0	+4	+15	+4	+19	14	2
2005	LAD	106	105	918.0	146	325	11	62	.977	4.62	106	59	.557	-1	22	339	+5	+3	-2	+5	-1	+4	3	15
2006	2 tms	23	18	172.2	34	49	2	10	.976	4.33	19	10	.526	-1	-	63	-3	-1	+1	-3	-1	-4	-3	-
2007	2 tms	90	69	655.2	96	196	8	53	.973	4.01	72	51	.708	2	5	216	+1	+1	+1	+3	-4	-1	-1	21
2008	StL	130	110	1001.1	170	370	11	77	.980	4.85	128	73	.570	-1	24	408	+18	+4	-1	+22	-2	+20	15	3
		666	612	5499.0	877	1851	58	392	.979	4.46	618	369	.597	0	21	1988	+51	+8	-8	+51	-3	+48	36	6

Shortstops

Maicer Izturis

		BASIC										GROUND DP					PLUS/MINUS								
Year	Team	G	GS	Inn	PO	A	E	DP	Pct	Rng	GDP Opps	GDP	Pct	Runs Saved	Rank	Outs Made	To His Right	Straight On	To His Left	GB	Air	Total	Runs Saved	Rank
2004	Mon	23	20	187.0	33	71	7	15	.937	5.01	25	13	.520	0	-	67	-3	+1	0	-2	0	-2	-2	-
2005	LAA	29	21	212.2	44	55	2	8	.980	4.19	15	8	.533	0	-	73	-4	-2	+6	0	0	0	0	-
2006	LAA	10	4	53.0	9	13	1	7	.957	3.74	8	6	.750	0	-	14	0	0	-1	0	0	0	0	-
2007	LAA	3	2	19.0	8	3	1	1	.917	5.21	3	1	.333	0	-	7	0	-1		-1	0	-1	-1	-
2008	LAA	52	50	448.0	69	147	2	31	.991	4.34	46	30	.652	1	8	150	-4	+2	+7	+5	-3	+2	2	16
		117	97	919.2	163	289	13	62	.972	4.42	97	58	.598	1	-	311	-11	0	+12	+2	-3	-1	-1	-

Derek Jeter

		BASIC										GROUND DP					PLUS/MINUS								
Year	Team	G	GS	Inn	PO	A	E	DP	Pct	Rng	GDP Opps	GDP	Pct	Runs Saved	Rank	Outs Made	To His Right	Straight On	To His Left	GB	Air	Total	Runs Saved	Rank
2003	NYY	118	118	1033.2	159	271	14	51	.968	3.74	88	46	.523	-2	31	336	-12	+3	-6	-15	+1	-14	-11	34
2004	NYY	154	154	1341.2	273	392	13	95	.981	4.46	146	85	.582	0	12	456	-24	+5	-5	-25	+9	-16	-12	32
2005	NYY	157	157	1352.2	262	454	15	96	.979	4.76	156	84	.538	-2	31	526	-18	+3	-25	-39	+5	-34	-26	34
2006	NYY	150	149	1292.1	214	381	15	81	.975	4.14	131	75	.573	-1	27	450	-10	+1	-10	-19	-3	-22	-17	34
2007	NYY	155	153	1318.1	199	390	18	104	.970	4.02	152	98	.645	3	2	420	-14	-6	-14	-33	-1	-34	-26	34
2008	NYY	148	147	1258.2	220	347	12	69	.979	4.05	106	58	.547	-1	24	430	-18	+9	-1	-10	-1	-11	-8	31
		882	878	7597.1	1327	2235	87	496	.976	4.22	779	446	.573	-3	29	2618	-96	+15	-61	-141	+10	-131	-100	35

Jeff Keppinger

		BASIC										GROUND DP					PLUS/MINUS								
Year	Team	G	GS	Inn	PO	A	E	DP	Pct	Rng	GDP Opps	GDP	Pct	Runs Saved	Rank	Outs Made	To His Right	Straight On	To His Left	GB	Air	Total	Runs Saved	Rank
2007	Cin	47	43	390.2	62	124	2	27	.989	4.28	43	25	.581	0	23	130	0	-1	-4	-5	-1	-6	-5	24
2008	Cin	108	101	880.2	145	246	8	72	.980	4.00	110	66	.600	0	15	274	-5	-1	-8	-14	0	-14	-11	34
		155	144	1271.1	207	370	10	99	.983	4.08	153	91	.595	0	-	404	-5	-2	-12	-19	-1	-20	-16	-

Felipe Lopez

		BASIC										GROUND DP					PLUS/MINUS								
Year	Team	G	GS	Inn	PO	A	E	DP	Pct	Rng	GDP Opps	GDP	Pct	Runs Saved	Rank	Outs Made	To His Right	Straight On	To His Left	GB	Air	Total	Runs Saved	Rank
2003	Cin	50	42	397.1	60	132	15	20	.928	4.35	41	19	.463	-1	-	132	-4	-1	-2	-7	-1	-8	-6	-
2004	Cin	51	41	391.0	65	137	9	25	.957	4.65	51	24	.471	-2	-	126	-9	+2	+2	-5	-2	-7	-5	-
2005	Cin	140	133	1175.1	186	357	17	71	.970	4.16	127	69	.543	-2	31	418	-6	+4	+6	+3	-3	0	0	18
2006	2 tms	155	152	1337.0	187	389	28	79	.954	3.88	130	65	.500	-3	33	440	-7	-4	-9	-20	-1	-21	-16	33
2007	Was	111	104	927.0	154	289	20	56	.957	4.30	87	50	.575	0	23	362	-9	0	-7	-15	+2	-13	-10	29
2008	2 tms	13	10	79.0	6	28	0	5	1.000	3.87	9	5	.556	0	-	30	+1	0	-1	0	0	0	0	-
		520	482	4306.2	658	1332	89	256	.957	4.16	445	232	.521	-8	33	1508	-34	+1	-11	-44	-5	-49	-37	32

Jed Lowrie

		BASIC										GROUND DP					PLUS/MINUS								
Year	Team	G	GS	Inn	PO	A	E	DP	Pct	Rng	GDP Opps	GDP	Pct	Runs Saved	Rank	Outs Made	To His Right	Straight On	To His Left	GB	Air	Total	Runs Saved	Rank
2008	Bos	49	45	386.0	46	109	0	21	1.000	3.61	35	21	.600	0	-	123	+3	+2	0	+6	+2	+8	6	-

Julio Lugo

		BASIC										GROUND DP					PLUS/MINUS								
Year	Team	G	GS	Inn	PO	A	E	DP	Pct	Rng	GDP Opps	GDP	Pct	Runs Saved	Rank	Outs Made	To His Right	Straight On	To His Left	GB	Air	Total	Runs Saved	Rank
2003	2 tms	139	137	1198.0	241	391	20	83	.969	4.75	132	72	.545	-2	31	450	+1	-4	+2	0	+2	+2	1	17
2004	TB	143	142	1238.0	237	422	25	92	.963	4.79	138	86	.623	1	4	479	+2	-1	+6	+8	-3	+5	4	13
2005	TB	156	155	1338.2	311	424	24	94	.968	4.94	154	83	.539	-2	31	522	-4	-5	+6	-3	+1	-2	-2	22
2006	2 tms	81	74	647.2	116	212	16	42	.953	4.56	67	37	.552	0	17	253	+3	-10	0	-8	-2	-10	-8	30
2007	Bos	145	139	1228.1	214	360	19	70	.968	4.21	120	64	.533	-2	33	431	-2	-4	+10	+5	-4	+1	1	18
2008	Bos	81	79	671.1	100	176	16	34	.945	3.70	68	31	.456	-3	34	215	+5	-7	0	-2	0	-2	-2	22
		745	726	6322.0	1219	1985	120	415	.964	4.56	679	373	.549	-8	33	2350	+5	-31	+24	0	-6	-6	-6	20

John McDonald

		BASIC										GROUND DP					PLUS/MINUS								
Year	Team	G	GS	Inn	PO	A	E	DP	Pct	Rng	GDP Opps	GDP	Pct	Runs Saved	Rank	Outs Made	To His Right	Straight On	To His Left	GB	Air	Total	Runs Saved	Rank
2003	Cle	27	20	195.0	39	54	4	16	.959	4.29	22	15	.682	1	-	57	-3	0	0	-4	+1	-3	-2	-
2004	Cle	30	15	166.2	25	65	5	16	.947	4.86	20	15	.750	1	-	60	-1	-2	-1	-3	0	-3	-2	-
2005	2 tms	54	42	375.1	67	157	7	35	.966	5.37	49	32	.653	1	-	163	+3	+3	+1	+7	-1	+6	4	-
2006	Tor	90	76	661.2	105	231	14	57	.960	4.57	77	52	.675	2	5	238	+9	-2	-5	+1	0	+1	1	19
2007	Tor	102	93	799.1	148	294	8	66	.982	4.98	110	63	.573	0	23	312	+6	+6	+12	+25	+1	+26	20	2
2008	Tor	67	52	478.0	80	134	9	33	.960	4.03	55	30	.545	-1	24	149	-2	+1	-1	-2	+1	-1	-1	20
		370	298	2676.0	464	935	48	223	.967	4.71	333	207	.622	4	10	979	+12	+6	+6	+24	+2	+26	20	12

Shortstops

Tony F Pena

Year Team	G	GS	Inn	PO	A	E	DP	Pct	Rng	GDP Opps	GDP	Pct	Runs Saved	Rank	Outs Made	To His Right	Straight On	To His Left	GB	Air	Total	Runs Saved	Rank
2006 Atl	22	6	84.0	14	28	1	7	.977	4.50	10	7	.700	0	-	30	+1	0	+3	+4	-1	+3	2	-
2007 KC	150	145	1273.2	208	438	23	98	.966	4.56	145	92	.634	2	5	482	+3	+9	+4	+16	+2	+18	14	4
2008 KC	94	61	592.0	74	180	9	35	.966	3.86	57	34	.596	0	15	199	-1	+1	+3	+3	-5	-2	-2	23
	266	212	1949.2	296	646	33	140	.966	4.35	212	133	.627	2	-	711	+3	+10	+10	+23	-4	+19	14	-

Jhonny Peralta

Year Team	G	GS	Inn	PO	A	E	DP	Pct	Rng	GDP Opps	GDP	Pct	Runs Saved	Rank	Outs Made	To His Right	Straight On	To His Left	GB	Air	Total	Runs Saved	Rank
2003 Cle	72	69	624.0	104	222	8	41	.976	4.70	67	38	.567	0	13	222	+4	+2	-8	-1	+1	0	0	20
2004 Cle	7	6	55.0	7	17	3	2	.889	3.93	4	2	.500	0	-	15	0	-2	0	-2	+1	-1	-1	-
2005 Cle	141	138	1232.1	207	412	19	104	.970	4.52	132	94	.712	5	1	465	-5	+3	-10	-12	-2	-14	-11	29
2006 Cle	147	145	1275.1	235	459	16	95	.977	4.90	152	93	.612	1	11	535	+3	-1	-15	-13	+4	-9	-7	27
2007 Cle	152	149	1348.0	249	452	19	106	.974	4.68	164	95	.579	0	23	511	+12	-7	-8	-3	0	-3	-2	22
2008 Cle	146	143	1271.1	217	427	14	104	.979	4.56	153	97	.634	2	3	469	0	-6	-2	-7	-3	-10	-8	30
	665	650	5806.0	1019	1989	79	452	.974	4.66	672	419	.624	8	2	2217	+14	-11	-43	-38	+1	-37	-29	30

Nick Punto

Year Team	G	GS	Inn	PO	A	E	DP	Pct	Rng	GDP Opps	GDP	Pct	Runs Saved	Rank	Outs Made	To His Right	Straight On	To His Left	GB	Air	Total	Runs Saved	Rank
2003 Phi	7	5	52.0	5	17	0	2	1.000	3.81	5	2	.400	0	-	19	+1	0	0	+2	0	+2	2	-
2004 Min	11	10	88.0	16	33	0	9	1.000	5.01	15	7	.467	-1	-	30	+1	0	-2	0	-1	-1	-1	-
2005 Min	34	26	244.0	47	76	2	16	.984	4.54	25	14	.560	0	-	93	-2	0	+1	-1	+2	+1	1	-
2006 Min	26	15	146.2	14	50	2	7	.970	3.93	10	7	.700	0	-	54	+1	+2	+2	+5	-1	+4	3	-
2007 Min	27	24	210.2	44	70	3	17	.974	4.87	29	16	.552	0	-	80	+4	+1	-1	+4	+1	+5	4	-
2008 Min	61	60	530.2	103	187	8	46	.973	4.92	60	44	.733	3	2	228	-6	+5	0	-1	+5	+4	3	14
	166	140	1272.0	229	433	15	97	.978	4.68	144	90	.625	2	-	504	-1	+8	0	+9	+6	+15	12	-

Omar Quintanilla

Year Team	G	GS	Inn	PO	A	E	DP	Pct	Rng	GDP Opps	GDP	Pct	Runs Saved	Rank	Outs Made	To His Right	Straight On	To His Left	GB	Air	Total	Runs Saved	Rank
2005 Col	31	30	268.2	41	89	1	16	.992	4.35	31	15	.484	-1	-	100	0	+1	+6	+7	+1	+8	6	-
2006 Col	8	7	62.2	10	26	0	7	1.000	5.17	8	7	.875	1	-	28	0	+1	+1	+2	0	+2	2	-
2007 Col	2	0	5.0	1	2	0	0	1.000	5.40	0				-	3	0	0	0	0	0	0	0	-
2008 Col	39	32	288.2	42	100	3	20	.979	4.43	28	19	.679	1	-	108	+6	0	-3	+3	-1	+2	2	-
	80	69	625.0	94	217	4	43	.987	4.48	67	41	.612	1	-	239	+6	+2	+4	+12	0	+12	10	-

Hanley Ramirez

Year Team	G	GS	Inn	PO	A	E	DP	Pct	Rng	GDP Opps	GDP	Pct	Runs Saved	Rank	Outs Made	To His Right	Straight On	To His Left	GB	Air	Total	Runs Saved	Rank
2005 Bos	2	0	6.0	0	1	0	0	1.000	1.50	0				-	1				0		0	0	-
2006 Fla	154	153	1323.1	258	410	26	111	.963	4.54	163	103	.632	2	5	467	0	-4	+2	-3	-3	-6	-5	24
2007 Fla	151	150	1301.2	225	392	24	98	.963	4.27	150	90	.600	1	10	462	-21	-8	-6	-34	-3	-37	-28	35
2008 Fla	150	150	1302.0	236	401	22	89	.967	4.40	139	79	.568	-1	24	473	+10	-4	-1	+5	-2	+3	2	15
	457	453	3933.0	719	1204	72	298	.964	4.40	452	272	.602	2	15	1403	-11	-16	-5	-32	-8	-40	-31	31

Edgar Renteria

Year Team	G	GS	Inn	PO	A	E	DP	Pct	Rng	GDP Opps	GDP	Pct	Runs Saved	Rank	Outs Made	To His Right	Straight On	To His Left	GB	Air	Total	Runs Saved	Rank
2003 StL	156	154	1367.1	191	439	16	83	.975	4.15	124	76	.613	1	6	435	-6	+3	+5	+1	-3	-2	-2	23
2004 StL	149	148	1307.1	221	418	11	91	.983	4.40	147	83	.565	-1	21	436	-2	-1	+12	+9	0	+9	7	8
2005 Bos	153	150	1293.0	227	398	30	90	.954	4.35	154	82	.532	-2	31	451	+3	-14	+2	-9	-2	-11	-8	28
2006 Atl	146	146	1265.1	185	399	13	76	.978	4.15	128	73	.570	-1	27	447	-17	0	+18	+1	+5	+6	5	10
2007 Atl	121	121	1019.1	147	322	11	71	.977	4.14	111	70	.631	1	10	361	-19	-1	+18	-2	+1	-1	-1	20
2008 Det	138	134	1173.1	197	365	16	91	.972	4.31	150	88	.587	0	15	427	-11	-6	+7	-11	+2	-9	-7	28
	863	853	7425.2	1168	2341	97	502	.973	4.25	814	472	.580	-2	27	2557	-52	-19	+62	-11	+3	-8	-6	21

Jose Reyes

Year Team	G	GS	Inn	PO	A	E	DP	Pct	Rng	GDP Opps	GDP	Pct	Runs Saved	Rank	Outs Made	To His Right	Straight On	To His Left	GB	Air	Total	Runs Saved	Rank
2003 NYM	69	69	596.1	106	214	9	43	.973	4.83	73	39	.534	-1	23	248	+9	+3	-2	+9	+1	+10	8	8
2004 NYM	10	7	72.2	18	26	2	5	.957	5.45	9	5	.556	0	-	34	0	0	+1	+1	-3	-2	-2	-
2005 NYM	161	159	1398.1	237	427	18	105	.974	4.27	148	97	.655	3	3	481	-14	-1	+3	-13	+3	-10	-8	27
2006 NYM	149	148	1320.1	176	390	17	71	.971	3.86	121	68	.562	-1	27	444	+2	+10	+1	+14	+2	+16	12	5
2007 NYM	160	160	1431.1	203	445	12	88	.982	4.07	134	82	.612	1	10	500	+5	+5	+7	+16	-3	+13	10	7
2008 NYM	158	158	1420.1	221	422	17	89	.974	4.07	149	86	.577	0	15	481	-3	+4	-1	0	-2	-2	-2	21
	707	701	6239.1	961	1924	75	401	.975	4.16	634	377	.595	2	15	2188	-1	+21	+9	+27	-2	+25	18	13

Shortstops

Luis Rodriguez

		BASIC										GROUND DP					PLUS/MINUS								
Year	Team	G	GS	Inn	PO	A	E	DP	Pct	Rng	GDP Opps	GDP	Pct	Runs Saved	Rank	Outs Made	To His Right	Straight On	To His Left	GB	Air	Total	Runs Saved	Rank
2005	Min	10	3	44.0	8	14	0	4	1.000	4.50	5	3	.600	0	-	19	-1	-1	+2	0	-1	-1	-1	-
2006	Min	2	0	3.0	0	1	1	0	.500	3.00	0		-		-	1	0	-1	0	-1	0	-1	-1	-
2008	SD	52	45	391.1	79	121	3	33	.985	4.60	54	31	.574	0	-	143	-2	+2	-1	-1	-3	-4	-3	-
		64	48	438.1	87	136	4	37	.982	4.58	59	34	.576	0	-	163	-3	0	+1	-2	-4	-6	-5	-

Jimmy Rollins

		BASIC										GROUND DP					PLUS/MINUS								
Year	Team	G	GS	Inn	PO	A	E	DP	Pct	Rng	GDP Opps	GDP	Pct	Runs Saved	Rank	Outs Made	To His Right	Straight On	To His Left	GB	Air	Total	Runs Saved	Rank
2003	Phi	154	153	1357.2	203	463	14	92	.979	4.41	140	89	.636	2	2	511	+6	+5	0	+11	+1	+12	9	3
2004	Phi	154	153	1376.2	214	398	9	88	.986	4.00	130	82	.631	2	2	442	+2	+4	-1	+5	0	+5	4	14
2005	Phi	157	156	1356.0	208	411	12	80	.981	4.11	127	76	.598	0	14	473	+3	-2	+17	+19	+4	+23	17	4
2006	Phi	157	156	1378.0	213	446	11	96	.984	4.30	135	90	.667	3	2	500	-3	+4	+7	+8	+4	+12	9	8
2007	Phi	162	162	1441.1	227	479	11	110	.985	4.41	164	101	.616	1	10	529	+12	-6	-1	+5	+2	+7	5	9
2008	Phi	132	132	1168.0	193	393	7	71	.988	4.52	127	69	.543	-2	31	455	+2	+2	+16	+20	+3	+23	17	1
		916	912	8077.2	1258	2590	64	537	.984	4.29	823	507	.616	6	4	2910	+22	+7	+38	+68	+14	+82	61	2

Brendan Ryan

		BASIC										GROUND DP					PLUS/MINUS								
Year	Team	G	GS	Inn	PO	A	E	DP	Pct	Rng	GDP Opps	GDP	Pct	Runs Saved	Rank	Outs Made	To His Right	Straight On	To His Left	GB	Air	Total	Runs Saved	Rank
2007	StL	28	17	163.2	31	65	3	15	.970	5.28	22	15	.682	1	-	71	+2	-3	+3	+3	0	+3	2	-
2008	StL	40	25	255.1	42	91	1	18	.993	4.69	30	17	.567	0	-	98	+1	+2	+1	+4	-1	+3	2	-
		68	42	419.0	73	156	4	33	.983	4.92	52	32	.615	1	-	169	+3	-1	+4	+7	-1	+6	4	-

Marco Scutaro

		BASIC										GROUND DP					PLUS/MINUS								
Year	Team	G	GS	Inn	PO	A	E	DP	Pct	Rng	GDP Opps	GDP	Pct	Runs Saved	Rank	Outs Made	To His Right	Straight On	To His Left	GB	Air	Total	Runs Saved	Rank
2003	NYM	1	0	2.0	1	1	0	0	1.000	9.00	0		-		-	2				0	0	0	0	-
2004	Oak	16	11	113.1	25	42	2	9	.971	5.32	16	8	.500	0	-	46	-1	0	-1	-3	0	-3	-2	-
2005	Oak	81	73	663.0	115	213	8	50	.976	4.45	76	46	.605	0	14	239	-7	+2	-2	-8	0	-8	-6	26
2006	Oak	69	61	572.2	87	168	9	38	.966	4.01	57	35	.614	0	17	207	-10	-3	-10	-23	-3	-26	-20	35
2007	Oak	43	38	348.0	52	111	5	22	.970	4.22	36	22	.611	0	-	122	+1	-1	0	0	+1	+1	1	-
2008	Tor	56	53	472.1	71	165	5	30	.979	4.50	46	25	.543	-1	24	174	+1	+4	+6	+12	0	+12	9	8
		266	236	2171.1	351	700	29	149	.973	4.36	231	136	.589	-1	24	790	-16	+2	-7	-22	-2	-24	-18	27

Miguel Tejada

		BASIC										GROUND DP					PLUS/MINUS								
Year	Team	G	GS	Inn	PO	A	E	DP	Pct	Rng	GDP Opps	GDP	Pct	Runs Saved	Rank	Outs Made	To His Right	Straight On	To His Left	GB	Air	Total	Runs Saved	Rank
2003	Oak	162	162	1417.2	240	490	21	94	.972	4.63	151	85	.563	-1	23	481	-5	+2	-4	-7	+3	-4	-3	25
2004	Bal	162	162	1421.2	263	526	24	118	.970	4.99	191	105	.550	-2	26	561	+6	+7	+2	+15	-1	+14	11	4
2005	Bal	160	160	1394.2	252	480	22	105	.971	4.72	166	95	.572	-1	22	526	+25	-4	-17	+4	+1	+5	4	13
2006	Bal	150	150	1293.2	238	417	19	108	.972	4.56	158	96	.608	1	11	466	+1	0	-13	-12	-2	-14	-11	32
2007	Bal	124	122	1068.2	149	358	15	77	.971	4.27	135	73	.541	-2	33	362	+5	-4	-3	-2	-2	-4	-3	23
2008	Hou	157	154	1354.1	187	442	11	97	.983	4.18	144	90	.625	2	3	472	+5	+7	-4	+7	0	+7	5	11
		915	910	7950.2	1329	2713	112	599	.973	4.58	945	544	.576	-3	29	2868	+37	+8	-39	+5	-1	+4	3	16

Ryan Theriot

		BASIC										GROUND DP					PLUS/MINUS								
Year	Team	G	GS	Inn	PO	A	E	DP	Pct	Rng	GDP Opps	GDP	Pct	Runs Saved	Rank	Outs Made	To His Right	Straight On	To His Left	GB	Air	Total	Runs Saved	Rank
2006	ChC	2	2	17.0	3	4	1	1	.875	3.71	2	1	.500	0	-	5	-1	0	0	-1	-1	-2	-2	-
2007	ChC	108	101	859.0	126	260	8	56	.980	4.04	79	52	.658	2	5	301	+1	+2	+4	+6	-1	+5	4	13
2008	ChC	149	141	1266.0	207	341	14	69	.975	3.90	107	64	.598	0	15	425	+2	-3	+1	+1	+5	+6	5	12
		259	244	2142.0	336	605	23	126	.976	3.95	188	117	.622	2	-	731	+2	-1	+5	+6	+3	+9	7	-

Troy Tulowitzki

		BASIC										GROUND DP					PLUS/MINUS								
Year	Team	G	GS	Inn	PO	A	E	DP	Pct	Rng	GDP Opps	GDP	Pct	Runs Saved	Rank	Outs Made	To His Right	Straight On	To His Left	GB	Air	Total	Runs Saved	Rank
2006	Col	25	23	220.1	47	69	2	25	.983	4.74	34	23	.676	1	-	71	-1	-2	-3	-6	+1	-5	-4	-
2007	Col	155	155	1375.0	262	561	11	114	.987	5.39	167	108	.647	3	2	614	+24	+5	+6	+35	0	+35	27	1
2008	Col	101	97	863.1	190	311	8	70	.984	5.22	114	62	.544	-1	24	355	-4	+4	+1	+1	+3	+4	3	13
		281	275	2458.2	499	941	21	209	.986	5.27	315	193	.613	3	12	1040	+19	+7	+4	+30	+4	+34	26	10

Shortstops

Juan Uribe

Year	Team	G	GS	Inn	PO	A	E	DP	Pct	Rng	GDP Opps	GDP	Pct	Runs Saved	Rank	Outs Made	To His Right	Straight On	To His Left	GB	Air	Total	Runs Saved	Rank
2003	Col	74	69	598.1	143	242	11	57	.972	5.79	90	53	.589	0	13	257	+17	+1	-10	+8	-1	+7	5	11
2004	CWS	38	32	287.1	54	115	3	30	.983	5.29	44	30	.682	1	-	121	+11	-2	+1	+10	-1	+9	7	-
2005	CWS	146	143	1293.1	250	422	16	99	.977	4.68	149	89	.597	0	14	495	+12	-2	-7	+3	+6	+9	7	9
2006	CWS	132	127	1130.0	217	373	14	84	.977	4.70	130	77	.592	0	17	429	+10	+2	-12	0	+3	+3	2	16
2007	CWS	150	147	1305.1	245	443	17	102	.976	4.74	152	91	.599	1	10	513	-2	-5	-5	-12	+5	-7	-5	25
2008	CWS	4	1	15.0	2	2	0	0	1.000	2.40	0		-			3				0	0	0	0	-
		544	519	4629.1	911	1597	61	372	.976	4.88	565	340	.602	2	15	1818	+48	-6	-33	+9	+12	+21	16	14

Omar Vizquel

Year	Team	G	GS	Inn	PO	A	E	DP	Pct	Rng	GDP Opps	GDP	Pct	Runs Saved	Rank	Outs Made	To His Right	Straight On	To His Left	GB	Air	Total	Runs Saved	Rank
2003	Cle	64	63	551.1	114	203	7	58	.978	5.17	79	54	.684	2	2	233	+7	+2	-1	+9	+1	+10	8	9
2004	Cle	147	141	1245.0	200	395	11	90	.982	4.30	140	74	.529	-2	26	421	+5	+4	-4	+6	0	+6	5	9
2005	SF	150	144	1292.1	234	426	8	80	.988	4.60	142	75	.528	-2	31	501	-7	+16	-5	-9	+4	-5	3	14
2006	SF	152	148	1281.1	205	389	4	87	.993	4.17	134	79	.590	0	17	441	+3	+6	+1	+9	-2	+7	5	9
2007	SF	143	136	1219.1	198	444	9	90	.986	4.74	135	84	.622	1	10	503	-1	+15	+1	+15	+5	+20	15	3
2008	SF	84	76	657.2	108	179	2	43	.993	3.93	64	40	.625	1	8	210	+3	+2	+3	+8	+1	+9	7	9
		740	708	6247.0	1059	2036	41	448	.987	4.46	694	406	.585	0	21	2309	+10	+45	-5	+51	+5	+56	43	4

Jack Wilson

Year	Team	G	GS	Inn	PO	A	E	DP	Pct	Rng	GDP Opps	GDP	Pct	Runs Saved	Rank	Outs Made	To His Right	Straight On	To His Left	GB	Air	Total	Runs Saved	Rank
2003	Pit	149	148	1294.2	218	454	17	104	.975	4.67	161	96	.596	0	13	434	+3	0	+2	+5	+3	+8	6	10
2004	Pit	156	155	1355.2	235	491	17	128	.977	4.82	177	118	.667	4	4	491	+14	0	-6	+9	+2	+11	8	6
2005	Pit	157	155	1360.0	246	522	14	126	.982	5.08	184	120	.652	4	2	544	+27	+8	-9	+26	+5	+31	24	2
2006	Pit	131	129	1130.0	198	425	18	88	.972	4.96	132	82	.621	1	11	454	+8	-3	-8	-3	+3	0	0	20
2007	Pit	131	131	1142.0	177	452	11	112	.983	4.96	162	109	.673	4	1	470	+28	-5	-14	+9	+1	+10	8	8
2008	Pit	80	80	696.1	115	277	5	52	.987	5.07	83	50	.602	0	15	285	+15	-1	+2	+16	0	+16	12	5
		804	798	6978.2	1189	2621	82	610	.979	4.91	899	575	.640	13	1	2678	+95	-1	-33	+62	+14	+76	58	3

Michael Young

Year	Team	G	GS	Inn	PO	A	E	DP	Pct	Rng	GDP Opps	GDP	Pct	Runs Saved	Rank	Outs Made	To His Right	Straight On	To His Left	GB	Air	Total	Runs Saved	Rank
2003	Tex	7	1	17.0	4	5	0	1	1.000	4.76	2	1	.500	0	-	8				0	0	0	0	-
2004	Tex	158	158	1386.2	225	422	19	98	.971	4.20	167	92	.551	-2	26	478	+1	-3	-27	-30	-4	-34	-26	35
2005	Tex	155	155	1356.0	239	426	18	95	.974	4.41	157	88	.561	-1	22	489	-15	-2	-19	-36	-3	-39	-30	35
2006	Tex	155	155	1356.1	241	492	14	113	.981	4.86	177	107	.605	1	11	536	-4	+6	-12	-9	-1	-10	-8	28
2007	Tex	150	150	1291.1	211	446	19	107	.972	4.58	166	94	.566	-1	28	478	-1	+3	-13	-11	-4	-15	-11	32
2008	Tex	152	151	1289.0	193	465	11	113	.984	4.59	172	106	.616	1	8	488	-1	+2	-6	-6	-2	-8	-6	27
		777	770	6696.1	1113	2256	81	527	.977	4.53	841	488	.580	-2	27	2477	-20	+6	-77	-92	-14	-106	-81	34

Ben Zobrist

Year	Team	G	GS	Inn	PO	A	E	DP	Pct	Rng	GDP Opps	GDP	Pct	Runs Saved	Rank	Outs Made	To His Right	Straight On	To His Left	GB	Air	Total	Runs Saved	Rank
2006	TB	52	50	440.2	86	147	9	31	.963	4.76	52	30	.577	0	17	173	-1	-2	-2	-5	0	-5	-4	23
2007	TB	30	26	224.2	37	63	6	17	.943	4.01	25	14	.560	0	-	71	-2	-4	-1	-7	0	-7	-5	-
2008	TB	35	33	293.1	51	78	7	22	.949	3.96	41	22	.537	-1	-	90	0	-1	-7	-8	0	-8	-6	-
		117	109	958.2	174	288	22	70	.955	4.34	118	66	.559	-1	-	334	-3	-7	-10	-20	0	-20	-15	-

Left Fielders

Moises Alou

		BASIC									THROWING						PLUS/MINUS						
											Opps To	Extra			Runs		Outs						Runs	
Year	Team	G	GS	Inn	PO	A	E	DP	Pct	Rng	Advance	Bases	Pct	Kills	Saved	Rank	Made	Basic	Shallow	Medium	Deep	Enhanced	Saved	Rank
2003	ChC	142	140	1219.0	203	4	6	1	.972	1.53	108	48	.444	4	0	24	199	-1	-3	+4	-4	-3	-2	23
2004	ChC	154	152	1338.1	240	7	8	2	.969	1.66	99	34	.343	4	3	13	236	-1	-5	+2	+3	0	0	18
2005	SF	74	66	576.0	132	1	4	0	.971	2.08	62	19	.306	1	1	17	132	+2	0	-2	+6	+4	2	12
2006	SF	11	10	79.0	19	0	0	0	1.000	2.16	3	2	.667	0	0	-	19	0	+3	-2	-2	0	0	-
2007	NYM	84	84	703.0	138	7	7	0	.973	1.86	81	33	.407	4	1	13	138	+2	-3	+2	+2	+2	1	16
2008	NYM	13	13	92.1	18	0	0	0	1.000	1.75	8	4	.500	0	-1	-	18	0	0	+1	-1	0	0	-
		478	465	4007.2	750	19	22	3	.972	1.73	361	140	.388	13	4	21	742	+2	-8	+6	+5	+3	1	18

Garret Anderson

		BASIC									THROWING						PLUS/MINUS						
											Opps To	Extra			Runs		Outs						Runs	
Year	Team	G	GS	Inn	PO	A	E	DP	Pct	Rng	Advance	Bases	Pct	Kills	Saved	Rank	Made	Basic	Shallow	Medium	Deep	Enhanced	Saved	Rank
2003	Ana	144	144	1241.1	326	14	1	2	.997	2.47	134	52	.388	7	1	19	302	-4	-7	-6	+14	+2	1	12
2005	LAA	106	106	920.0	201	4	5	1	.976	2.01	85	32	.376	3	0	25	201	-7	-13	+1	+4	-8	-4	31
2006	LAA	94	94	812.2	192	1	0	0	1.000	2.14	74	35	.473	1	-4	33	192	-2	-2	+6	-4	0	0	22
2007	LAA	85	85	724.1	143	7	2	0	.987	1.86	78	26	.333	4	2	7	143	-6	-3	+2	-3	-4	-2	24
2008	LAA	82	80	689.1	144	9	0	2	1.000	2.00	68	37	.544	5	-2	29	144	0	-4	+6	-1	+1	1	20
		511	509	4387.2	1006	35	8	5	.992	2.14	439	182	.415	20	-3	29	982	-19	-29	+9	+11	-9	-4	23

Jason Bay

		BASIC									THROWING						PLUS/MINUS						
											Opps To	Extra			Runs		Outs						Runs	
Year	Team	G	GS	Inn	PO	A	E	DP	Pct	Rng	Advance	Bases	Pct	Kills	Saved	Rank	Made	Basic	Shallow	Medium	Deep	Enhanced	Saved	Rank
2003	Pit	24	20	180.1	34	0	1	0	.971	1.70	16	7	.438	0	0	-	29	0	-1	0	+1	0	0	-
2004	Pit	116	107	959.0	208	3	2	0	.991	1.98	101	40	.396	2	0	20	179	+1	+2	+1	0	+3	2	13
2005	Pit	146	133	1185.2	264	3	1	1	.996	2.03	121	49	.405	3	-4	34	266	-2	-5	-5	+9	-1	-1	18
2006	Pit	157	157	1373.0	316	10	3	1	.991	2.14	176	72	.409	4	-5	35	316	+4	-5	-1	+18	+12	7	5
2007	Pit	142	142	1237.0	265	13	8	3	.972	2.02	172	63	.366	7	1	13	266	-14	-8	-14	+3	-19	-11	31
2008	2 tms	154	153	1344.2	254	8	4	0	.985	1.75	169	72	.426	5	-3	32	254	-11	-8	-7	+2	-12	-7	29
		739	712	6279.2	1341	37	19	5	.986	1.97	755	303	.401	21	-11	34	1310	-22	-25	-26	+33	-17	-10	27

Gregor Blanco

		BASIC									THROWING						PLUS/MINUS						
											Opps To	Extra			Runs		Outs						Runs	
Year	Team	G	GS	Inn	PO	A	E	DP	Pct	Rng	Advance	Bases	Pct	Kills	Saved	Rank	Made	Basic	Shallow	Medium	Deep	Enhanced	Saved	Rank
2008	Atl	77	55	512.2	86	3	2	0	.978	1.56	52	26	.500	2	-3	32	86	0	-1	0	+4	+3	2	18

Brandon Boggs

		BASIC									THROWING						PLUS/MINUS						
											Opps To	Extra			Runs		Outs						Runs	
Year	Team	G	GS	Inn	PO	A	E	DP	Pct	Rng	Advance	Bases	Pct	Kills	Saved	Rank	Made	Basic	Shallow	Medium	Deep	Enhanced	Saved	Rank
2008	Tex	76	59	579.0	131	7	3	2	.979	2.15	66	21	.318	3	4	5	131	+4	+1	+1	+3	+5	3	11

Ryan Braun

		BASIC									THROWING						PLUS/MINUS						
											Opps To	Extra			Runs		Outs						Runs	
Year	Team	G	GS	Inn	PO	A	E	DP	Pct	Rng	Advance	Bases	Pct	Kills	Saved	Rank	Made	Basic	Shallow	Medium	Deep	Enhanced	Saved	Rank
2008	Mil	149	148	1310.1	275	9	0	0	1.000	1.95	123	46	.374	6	3	8	275	+4	+1	+1	+5	+7	4	8

Emil Brown

		BASIC									THROWING						PLUS/MINUS						
											Opps To	Extra			Runs		Outs						Runs	
Year	Team	G	GS	Inn	PO	A	E	DP	Pct	Rng	Advance	Bases	Pct	Kills	Saved	Rank	Made	Basic	Shallow	Medium	Deep	Enhanced	Saved	Rank
2005	KC	11	9	82.1	21	2	1	0	.958	2.51	11	4	.364	1	1	-	21	+1	+2	-3	+1	0	0	-
2006	KC	87	84	719.1	163	7	1	2	.994	2.13	110	35	.318	6	5	7	163	+2	-1	+1	+3	+3	2	15
2007	KC	78	66	606.1	155	7	6	2	.964	2.40	57	21	.368	4	2	7	155	+4	+3	0	+2	+5	3	12
2008	Oak	65	40	413.0	89	6	1	1	.990	2.07	37	20	.541	1	-3	32	89	+2	0	-1	+3	+2	1	19
		241	199	1821.0	428	22	9	5	.980	2.22	215	80	.372	12	5	17	428	+9	+4	-3	+9	+10	6	14

Pat Burrell

		BASIC									THROWING						PLUS/MINUS						
											Opps To	Extra			Runs		Outs						Runs	
Year	Team	G	GS	Inn	PO	A	E	DP	Pct	Rng	Advance	Bases	Pct	Kills	Saved	Rank	Made	Basic	Shallow	Medium	Deep	Enhanced	Saved	Rank
2003	Phi	140	138	1186.2	234	7	6	0	.976	1.83	113	37	.327	4	5	3	229	+7	+6	+4	-3	+7	4	4
2004	Phi	122	121	1060.0	217	9	4	1	.983	1.92	104	29	.279	7	6	4	207	-3	-8	+5	-4	-7	-4	28
2005	Phi	153	153	1296.2	236	10	7	2	.972	1.71	149	50	.336	9	7	4	236	+3	+5	+8	-13	0	0	17
2006	Phi	126	126	987.2	204	8	3	1	.986	1.93	100	40	.400	6	3	12	205	-14	-2	-6	-18	-26	-15	34
2007	Phi	138	138	1028.1	176	8	10	2	.948	1.61	112	42	.375	6	2	7	176	-14	+3	-4	-26	-27	-15	34
2008	Phi	155	154	1198.1	202	12	2	1	.991	1.61	133	40	.301	7	6	1	201	-10	+7	-3	-22	-19	-11	34
		834	830	6757.2	1269	54	32	7	.976	1.76	711	238	.335	39	29	2	1254	-31	+10	+4	-85	-72	-41	33

Left Fielders

Eric Byrnes

		BASIC									THROWING						PLUS/MINUS						
Year	Team	G	GS	Inn	PO	A	E	DP	Pct	Rng	Opps To Advance	Extra Bases	Pct	Kills	Runs Saved	Rank	Outs Made	Basic	Shallow	Medium	Deep	Enhanced	Runs Saved	Rank
2003	Oak	44	31	283.1	49	3	0	0	1.000	1.65	28	7	.250	1	2	-	40	0	+1	+2	-2	+1	1	-
2004	Oak	109	98	871.1	172	7	2	2	.989	1.85	90	27	.300	3	2	16	165	+4	+4	+2	-5	+1	1	16
2005	3 tms	106	90	803.0	209	5	4	1	.982	2.40	74	28	.378	4	1	17	209	+3	+5	+4	-3	+6	4	10
2006	Ari	12	3	43.1	10	0	0	0	1.000	2.08	1	0	.000	0	0	-	10	0	0	0	0	0	0	-
2007	Ari	123	113	970.2	239	9	4	0	.984	2.30	83	36	.434	6	1	13	239	+15	+8	+6	+11	+25	14	1
2008	Ari	51	50	419.2	76	1	1	0	.987	1.65	31	11	.355	0	-1	23	76	-1	-1	+2	-3	-2	-1	23
		445	385	3391.1	755	25	11	3	.986	2.07	307	109	.355	14	5	17	739	+21	+18	+16	-3	+31	19	4

Frank Catalanotto

		BASIC									THROWING						PLUS/MINUS						
Year	Team	G	GS	Inn	PO	A	E	DP	Pct	Rng	Opps To Advance	Extra Bases	Pct	Kills	Runs Saved	Rank	Outs Made	Basic	Shallow	Medium	Deep	Enhanced	Runs Saved	Rank
2003	Tor	61	55	460.1	91	4	1	0	.990	1.86	51	16	.314	3	1	19	84	+2	+4	0	-4	0	0	18
2004	Tor	41	34	309.2	66	1	2	1	.971	1.95	33	12	.364	1	0	-	62	+2	+1	+2	-1	+2	1	-
2005	Tor	111	99	761.0	163	4	0	0	1.000	1.98	55	13	.236	3	6	7	163	-3	+3	-1	-8	-6	-3	30
2006	Tor	101	94	760.0	140	10	0	3	1.000	1.78	83	38	.458	6	-1	21	140	+2	+2	+1	-1	+2	1	17
2007	Tex	64	60	483.1	98	2	0	0	1.000	1.86	52	21	.404	1	-1	26	98	-2	+1	-3	0	-2	-1	22
2008	Tex	26	20	168.1	29	0	1	0	.967	1.55	26	10	.385	0	0	-	29	-3	-1	-2	-1	-4	-2	-
		404	362	2942.2	587	21	4	4	.993	1.86	300	110	.367	14	5	17	576	-2	+9	-3	-14	-8	-4	22

Carl Crawford

		BASIC									THROWING						PLUS/MINUS						
Year	Team	G	GS	Inn	PO	A	E	DP	Pct	Rng	Opps To Advance	Extra Bases	Pct	Kills	Runs Saved	Rank	Outs Made	Basic	Shallow	Medium	Deep	Enhanced	Runs Saved	Rank
2003	TB	137	131	1159.1	317	10	3	1	.991	2.54	134	47	.351	5	4	7	294	+9	+5	+1	+8	+14	8	2
2004	TB	123	116	1010.0	274	5	1	1	.996	2.49	107	30	.280	3	5	6	270	+14	+9	+5	+8	+22	12	1
2005	TB	147	142	1246.2	341	3	2	1	.994	2.48	159	38	.239	3	7	4	341	+15	+5	+2	+12	+19	11	2
2006	TB	148	144	1252.1	302	9	3	0	.990	2.24	156	60	.385	7	2	14	302	+6	+3	+3	+4	+10	6	7
2007	TB	139	136	1186.1	286	3	4	1	.986	2.19	143	45	.315	2	1	13	286	0	+1	+2	-3	0	0	19
2008	TB	108	103	920.2	231	2	4	0	.983	2.28	69	23	.333	0	0	19	231	+16	+10	+7	+6	+23	13	1
		802	772	6775.1	1751	32	17	4	.991	2.37	768	243	.316	20	19	6	1724	+60	+32	+20	+36	+88	50	1

Jack Cust

		BASIC									THROWING						PLUS/MINUS						
Year	Team	G	GS	Inn	PO	A	E	DP	Pct	Rng	Opps To Advance	Extra Bases	Pct	Kills	Runs Saved	Rank	Outs Made	Basic	Shallow	Medium	Deep	Enhanced	Runs Saved	Rank
2003	Bal	1	0	4.2	3	0	0	0	1.000	5.79	1	1	1.000	0	0	-	3	0	0	0		0	0	-
2006	SD	1	0	2.0	0	0	0	0		.00	0	0	.000	0	0	-	0	0				0	0	-
2007	Oak	14	12	81.2	14	0	1	0	.933	1.54	7	1	.143	0	0	-	14	0	-1	0	+1	0	0	-
2008	Oak	78	77	585.2	129	4	4	0	.971	2.04	63	28	.444	4	0	19	129	-7	+1	-7	-9	-15	-8	32
		94	89	674.0	146	4	5	0	.968	2.00	71	30	.423	4	0		146	-7	+1	-7	-8	-15	-8	

Johnny Damon

		BASIC									THROWING						PLUS/MINUS						
Year	Team	G	GS	Inn	PO	A	E	DP	Pct	Rng	Opps To Advance	Extra Bases	Pct	Kills	Runs Saved	Rank	Outs Made	Basic	Shallow	Medium	Deep	Enhanced	Runs Saved	Rank
2007	NYY	32	31	271.0	71	2	2	0	.973	2.42	27	13	.481	1	-2	-	71	+5	+3	+2	+2	+7	4	-
2008	NYY	87	75	659.1	155	2	1	0	.994	2.14	63	19	.302	2	1	17	155	+6	+3	-2	+6	+7	4	9
		119	106	930.1	226	4	3	0	.987	2.23	90	32	.356	3	-1	-	226	+11	+6	0	+9	+14	8	

David DeJesus

		BASIC									THROWING						PLUS/MINUS						
Year	Team	G	GS	Inn	PO	A	E	DP	Pct	Rng	Opps To Advance	Extra Bases	Pct	Kills	Runs Saved	Rank	Outs Made	Basic	Shallow	Medium	Deep	Enhanced	Runs Saved	Rank
2004	KC	4	4	32.0	9	0	0	0	1.000	2.53	4	1	.250	0	0	-	7	+1		+1	+2	+2	1	-
2006	KC	73	60	544.2	138	5	2	0	.986	2.36	90	27	.300	3	2	14	138	-2	0	-5	+3	-2	-1	23
2008	KC	71	54	482.2	136	1	0	0	1.000	2.55	44	16	.364	0	-1	23	136	+4	-1	+1	+7	+8	4	7
		148	118	1059.1	283	6	2	0	.993	2.46	138	44	.319	3	1	-	281	+3	0	-3	+12	+8	4	

David Dellucci

		BASIC									THROWING						PLUS/MINUS						
Year	Team	G	GS	Inn	PO	A	E	DP	Pct	Rng	Opps To Advance	Extra Bases	Pct	Kills	Runs Saved	Rank	Outs Made	Basic	Shallow	Medium	Deep	Enhanced	Runs Saved	Rank
2003	2 tms	6	2	21.1	2	0	0	0	1.000	.84	2	1	.500	0	0	-	2	+1	+1	0		+1	1	-
2004	Tex	84	77	648.2	152	0	2	0	.987	2.11	60	28	.467	0	-5	33	147	-1	0	-1	-4	-5	-3	26
2005	Tex	47	44	378.2	84	4	2	1	.978	2.09	40	14	.350	1	0	-	84	-1	+3	+1	-7	-3	-2	-
2006	Phi	45	31	279.2	59	1	0	0	1.000	1.93	32	8	.250	1	2	-	59	0	+1	0	-1	-1	-1	-
2007	Cle	51	44	382.1	97	3	0	0	1.000	2.35	54	21	.389	1	1	-	97	-3	-5	0	+3	-2	-1	-
2008	Cle	56	46	383.0	75	1	0	0	1.000	1.79	41	10	.244	0	1	-	75	-1	+1	0	-2	0	0	-
		289	244	2093.2	469	9	4	1	.992	2.05	229	82	.358	3	-1	26	464	-5	+1	0	-12	-10	-6	24

Left Fielders

Matt Diaz

		BASIC									THROWING						PLUS/MINUS							
Year	Team	G	GS	Inn	PO	A	E	DP	Pct	Rng	Opps To Advance	Extra Bases	Pct	Kills	Runs Saved	Rank	Outs Made	Basic	Shallow	Medium	Deep	Enhanced	Runs Saved	Rank
2003	TB	1	1	9.0	6	0	1	0	.857	6.00	0	0	-	0	0	-	6	0	0	0	0	0	0	-
2004	TB	3	3	20.0	8	0	0	0	1.000	3.60	5	0	.000	0	1	-	6	-1	+1	0	-1	-1	-1	-
2005	KC	19	16	136.0	34	0	2	0	.944	2.25	14	8	.571	0	-2	-	34	-2	-4	-1	+3	-3	-2	-
2006	Atl	95	62	587.1	163	5	4	1	.977	2.57	62	22	.355	5	1	17	163	+4	+4	+3	+3	+10	6	9
2007	Atl	95	77	678.1	155	4	2	1	.988	2.11	68	31	.456	4	1	13	155	+3	-2	+1	+10	+10	6	6
2008	Atl	37	33	288.2	59	2	1	1	.984	1.90	19	9	.474	1	-1	-	59	-1	0	+2	-5	-3	-2	-
		250	192	1719.1	425	11	10	3	.978	2.28	168	70	.417	10	0	24	423	+3	-2	+4	+11	+13	7	12

Chris Duncan

		BASIC									THROWING						PLUS/MINUS							
Year	Team	G	GS	Inn	PO	A	E	DP	Pct	Rng	Opps To Advance	Extra Bases	Pct	Kills	Runs Saved	Rank	Outs Made	Basic	Shallow	Medium	Deep	Enhanced	Runs Saved	Rank
2006	StL	49	40	327.1	66	2	3	0	.958	1.87	30	9	.300	1	1	-	66	-3	-4	-1	0	-5	-3	-
2007	StL	99	90	747.0	158	5	2	0	.988	1.96	108	39	.361	4	2	7	158	-5	-4	-6	+6	-4	-2	23
2008	StL	43	40	321.1	73	1	2	0	.974	2.07	30	13	.433	1	-1	-	73	+1	-3	0	+7	+4	2	-
		191	170	1395.2	297	8	7	0	.978	1.97	168	61	.363	6	2	-	297	-7	-11	-7	+13	-5	-3	-

Adam Dunn

		BASIC									THROWING						PLUS/MINUS							
Year	Team	G	GS	Inn	PO	A	E	DP	Pct	Rng	Opps To Advance	Extra Bases	Pct	Kills	Runs Saved	Rank	Outs Made	Basic	Shallow	Medium	Deep	Enhanced	Runs Saved	Rank
2003	Cin	99	98	828.2	205	5	9	2	.959	2.28	107	38	.355	3	2	16	184	-3	-2	0	-1	-3	-2	24
2004	Cin	156	146	1327.1	250	10	8	1	.970	1.76	134	35	.261	2	10	1	225	-5	+9	+6	-33	-18	-10	32
2005	Cin	133	126	1090.2	246	6	5	0	.981	2.08	119	39	.328	2	3	10	246	-5	+5	+6	-27	-16	-9	33
2006	Cin	156	156	1321.0	279	7	12	1	.960	1.95	147	60	.408	6	-1	21	279	-9	-5	-1	-12	-18	-10	33
2007	Cin	144	142	1189.2	244	4	6	0	.976	1.88	132	47	.356	2	-2	32	245	-14	-2	-3	-24	-28	-16	35
2008	2 tms	119	118	980.2	210	5	7	1	.968	1.97	108	41	.380	4	-1	23	210	-8	-2	-6	-7	-15	-9	31
		807	786	6738.0	1434	37	47	5	.969	1.96	747	260	.348	24	11	12	1389	-44	+4	+2	-104	-98	-56	34

Jacoby Ellsbury

		BASIC									THROWING						PLUS/MINUS							
Year	Team	G	GS	Inn	PO	A	E	DP	Pct	Rng	Opps To Advance	Extra Bases	Pct	Kills	Runs Saved	Rank	Outs Made	Basic	Shallow	Medium	Deep	Enhanced	Runs Saved	Rank
2007	Bos	22	15	144.0	37	0	0	0	1.000	2.31	15	9	.600	0	-2	-	37	-2	-1	+2	-3	-2	-1	-
2008	Bos	58	36	346.1	89	1	0	1	1.000	2.34	33	11	.333	1	1	-	89	+2	0	+4	+3	+7	4	-
		80	51	490.1	126	1	0	1	1.000	2.33	48	20	.417	1	-1	-	126	0	0	+6	0	+5	3	-

Andre Ethier

		BASIC									THROWING						PLUS/MINUS							
Year	Team	G	GS	Inn	PO	A	E	DP	Pct	Rng	Opps To Advance	Extra Bases	Pct	Kills	Runs Saved	Rank	Outs Made	Basic	Shallow	Medium	Deep	Enhanced	Runs Saved	Rank
2006	LAD	109	99	895.2	172	9	6	1	.968	1.82	99	29	.293	0	5	7	172	+2	-3	+2	+4	+3	2	14
2007	LAD	60	26	306.0	73	2	1	0	.987	2.21	36	16	.444	0	-2	-	73	0	+1	-1	+2	+2	1	-
2008	LAD	41	29	277.1	48	3	2	0	.962	1.66	34	17	.500	2	0	-	48	0	0	+1	0	+1	1	-
		210	154	1479.0	293	14	9	1	.972	1.87	169	62	.367	8	3	-	293	+2	-2	+2	+5	+6	4	-

Ben Francisco

		BASIC									THROWING						PLUS/MINUS							
Year	Team	G	GS	Inn	PO	A	E	DP	Pct	Rng	Opps To Advance	Extra Bases	Pct	Kills	Runs Saved	Rank	Outs Made	Basic	Shallow	Medium	Deep	Enhanced	Runs Saved	Rank
2007	Cle	14	11	102.1	26	0	0	0	1.000	2.29	14	3	.214	0	1	-	26	+2	0	+2	+1	+3	2	-
2008	Cle	83	71	643.0	150	7	2	2	.987	2.20	79	30	.380	6	4	5	150	+1	+1	-6	+9	+4	2	15
		97	82	745.1	176	7	2	2	.989	2.21	93	33	.355	6	5	-	176	+3	+1	-4	+10	+7	4	-

Luis Gonzalez

		BASIC									THROWING						PLUS/MINUS							
Year	Team	G	GS	Inn	PO	A	E	DP	Pct	Rng	Opps To Advance	Extra Bases	Pct	Kills	Runs Saved	Rank	Outs Made	Basic	Shallow	Medium	Deep	Enhanced	Runs Saved	Rank
2003	Ari	154	154	1359.1	249	9	3	0	.989	1.71	122	49	.402	2	-2	29	235	-2	+3	-4	-1	-2	-1	20
2004	Ari	104	103	900.1	162	2	6	0	.965	1.64	88	32	.364	2	-1	22	157	-1	+1	-1	0	0	0	19
2005	Ari	152	149	1318.1	270	7	3	1	.989	1.89	154	60	.390	0	-4	34	270	+6	-4	+3	+13	+12	7	5
2006	Ari	150	149	1315.0	256	3	1	1	.996	1.77	125	48	.384	3	-1	21	256	0	-1	-1	+3	+1	1	20
2007	LAD	127	126	996.0	192	4	1	0	.995	1.77	99	44	.444	0	-5	34	192	-8	-2	-6	-5	-13	-7	29
2008	Fla	64	60	503.2	105	0	4	0	.963	1.88	60	20	.333	0	0	19	105	-9	-6	0	-6	-12	-7	30
		751	741	6392.2	1234	25	18	2	.986	1.77	648	253	.390	7	-13	35	1215	-14	-9	-8	+4	-14	-7	25

Left Fielders

Jose Guillen

Year	Team	G	GS	Inn	PO	A	E	DP	Pct	Rng	Opps To Advance	Extra Bases	Pct	Kills	Runs Saved	Rank	Outs Made	Basic	Shallow	Medium	Deep	Enhanced	Runs Saved	Rank
2003	2 tms	32	21	194.1	46	0	4	0	.920	2.13	20	5	.250	0	0	-	43	+3	+2	+1	-1	+2	1	-
2004	Ana	135	135	1157.0	266	9	6	1	.979	2.14	115	39	.339	7	7	2	256	-10	-9	-11	+7	-13	-7	30
2005	Was	2	2	17.0	2	0	0	0	1.000	1.06	1	1	1.000	0	0	-	2	+1	+1	0		+1	1	-
2008	KC	45	43	373.0	83	3	1	1	.989	2.08	37	15	.405	3	2	-	83	-7	-5	-2	-3	-10	-6	-
		214	201	1741.1	397	12	11	2	.974	2.11	173	60	.347	10	9	14	384	-13	-12	-11	+3	-20	-11	29

Scott Hairston

Year	Team	G	GS	Inn	PO	A	E	DP	Pct	Rng	Opps To Advance	Extra Bases	Pct	Kills	Runs Saved	Rank	Outs Made	Basic	Shallow	Medium	Deep	Enhanced	Runs Saved	Rank
2004	Ari	2	0	4.0	0	0	0	0	-	.00	0	0	.	0	0	-						0	0	-
2005	Ari	4	1	13.1	3	0	0	0	1.000	2.03	2	0	.000	0	0	-	3	0	0	0	0	0	0	-
2006	Ari	5	3	24.1	8	0	0	0	1.000	2.96	2	1	.500	0	0	-	8	0	0	+1	+1	+1	1	-
2007	2 tms	77	60	560.1	114	4	3	1	.975	1.90	66	24	.364	3	1	13	115	+7	+2	+3	+7	+12	7	4
2008	SD	49	30	310.0	70	2	0	0	1.000	2.09	26	6	.231	2	4	-	70	+1	0	+1	+1	+2	1	-
		137	94	912.0	195	6	3	1	.985	1.98	96	31	.323	5	5	-	196	+8	+1	+5	+9	+15	9	-

Willie Harris

Year	Team	G	GS	Inn	PO	A	E	DP	Pct	Rng	Opps To Advance	Extra Bases	Pct	Kills	Runs Saved	Rank	Outs Made	Basic	Shallow	Medium	Deep	Enhanced	Runs Saved	Rank
2004	CWS	1	0	2.0	2	0	0	0	1.000	9.00	0	0	.	0	0	-	2	-1	0		0	-1	-1	-
2006	Bos	11	2	33.0	10	1	0	0	1.000	3.00	3	1	.333	1	1	-	10	-3	0	-1	-4	-5	-3	-
2007	Atl	85	69	620.1	138	4	3	1	.979	2.06	71	27	.380	4	0	22	138	+10	0	+4	+14	+18	10	3
2008	Was	86	58	562.0	145	4	2	2	.987	2.39	63	21	.333	2	2	13	145	+12	0	+5	+14	+20	11	2
		183	129	1217.1	295	9	5	3	.984	2.25	137	49	.358	7	3	-	295	+18	0	+8	+24	+32	17	-

Chase Headley

Year	Team	G	GS	Inn	PO	A	E	DP	Pct	Rng	Opps To Advance	Extra Bases	Pct	Kills	Runs Saved	Rank	Outs Made	Basic	Shallow	Medium	Deep	Enhanced	Runs Saved	Rank
2008	SD	82	82	713.0	156	2	5	0	.969	1.99	77	31	.403	2	-2	29	156	+1	0	0	+4	+4	2	14

Eric Hinske

Year	Team	G	GS	Inn	PO	A	E	DP	Pct	Rng	Opps To Advance	Extra Bases	Pct	Kills	Runs Saved	Rank	Outs Made	Basic	Shallow	Medium	Deep	Enhanced	Runs Saved	Rank
2006	2 tms	6	3	24.0	5	0	0	0	1.000	1.88	2	0	.000	0	0	-	5	0	+1	-1	-1	-1	-1	-
2007	Bos	24	10	101.0	26	1	0	0	1.000	2.41	10	1	.100	0	1	-	26	-1	0	+1	-2	-1	-1	-
2008	TB	40	37	265.0	45	2	1	0	.979	1.60	26	10	.385	0	-1	-	45	+1	-1	+3	0	+2	1	-
		70	50	390.0	76	3	1	0	.988	1.82	38	11	.289	0	0	-	76	0	0	+2	-3	0	-1	-

Matt Holliday

Year	Team	G	GS	Inn	PO	A	E	DP	Pct	Rng	Opps To Advance	Extra Bases	Pct	Kills	Runs Saved	Rank	Outs Made	Basic	Shallow	Medium	Deep	Enhanced	Runs Saved	Rank
2004	Col	115	109	917.0	177	4	7	1	.963	1.78	110	42	.382	1	-4	31	168	0	+2	-4	0	-2	-1	22
2005	Col	123	121	1049.2	236	5	7	2	.972	2.07	117	40	.342	3	0	25	236	+8	+8	-1	+5	+12	7	6
2006	Col	153	153	1334.1	277	8	6	2	.979	1.92	138	60	.435	3	-3	31	277	-3	+2	+2	-16	-12	-7	32
2007	Col	157	157	1383.2	296	7	3	0	.990	1.97	144	46	.319	3	1	13	296	+3	-3	+2	+5	+4	2	13
2008	Col	139	139	1229.1	240	9	3	3	.988	1.82	163	54	.331	3	0	19	240	+3	-2	+5	+5	+9	5	5
		687	679	5914.0	1226	33	26	8	.980	1.92	672	242	.360	13	-6	33	1217	+11	+7	+5	-1	+11	6	13

Raul Ibanez

Year	Team	G	GS	Inn	PO	A	E	DP	Pct	Rng	Opps To Advance	Extra Bases	Pct	Kills	Runs Saved	Rank	Outs Made	Basic	Shallow	Medium	Deep	Enhanced	Runs Saved	Rank
2003	KC	128	119	1042.0	231	8	3	1	.988	2.06	104	34	.327	6	4	7	215	-5	-14	-1	+14	-2	-1	21
2004	Sea	110	106	949.1	227	10	4	3	.983	2.25	93	31	.333	6	5	6	216	+6	+6	0	+2	+8	4	5
2005	Sea	55	54	463.2	105	6	2	3	.982	2.15	59	18	.305	5	5	8	106	+3	-1	+2	+7	+8	4	9
2006	Sea	157	157	1396.2	301	10	2	0	.994	2.01	171	52	.304	9	7	3	301	-1	-3	-3	+9	+2	1	16
2007	Sea	131	131	1114.1	224	10	6	2	.975	1.89	143	56	.392	4	0	22	224	-13	-3	-5	-17	-25	-14	33
2008	Sea	153	153	1340.0	302	9	5	1	.984	2.09	160	54	.338	6	5	3	303	-10	-8	-8	-3	-19	-11	33
		734	720	6306.0	1390	54	22	10	.985	2.06	730	245	.336	36	26	3	1365	-20	-24	-16	+12	-28	-17	30

Conor Jackson

Year	Team	G	GS	Inn	PO	A	E	DP	Pct	Rng	Opps To Advance	Extra Bases	Pct	Kills	Runs Saved	Rank	Outs Made	Basic	Shallow	Medium	Deep	Enhanced	Runs Saved	Rank
2005	Ari	1	1	9.0	0	0	0	0	-	.00	2	2	1.000	0	-1	-		-1	0			-1	-1	-
2007	Ari	2	1	9.0	3	0	0	0	1.000	3.00	0	0	.	0	0	-	3	0	0	0	0	0	0	-
2008	Ari	77	75	656.0	146	5	3	3	.981	2.07	61	19	.311	4	3	8	146	+7	+2	+3	+6	+11	6	3
		80	77	674.0	149	5	3	3	.981	2.06	63	21	.333	4	2	-	149	+6	+2	+3	+6	+10	5	-

Left Fielders

Reed Johnson

	BASIC										THROWING						PLUS/MINUS							
Year	Team	G	GS	Inn	PO	A	E	DP	Pct	Rng	Opps To Advance	Extra Bases	Pct	Kills	Runs Saved	Rank	Outs Made	Basic	Shallow	Medium	Deep	Enhanced	Runs Saved	Rank
2003	Tor	53	33	326.2	74	2	1	0	.987	2.09	29	12	.414	2		-	61	+1	+5	-3	+1	+3	2	-
2004	Tor	57	53	461.1	96	5	2	1	.981	1.97	47	15	.319	4	2	16	94	+5	+5	+2	+2	+10	6	4
2005	Tor	118	55	590.2	134	4	1	1	.993	2.10	49	15	.306	2	2	13	134	+10	+8	+6	+3	+17	10	4
2006	Tor	100	64	635.1	129	7	1	0	.993	1.93	51	11	.216	6	8	2	129	+8	+4	+4	+4	+11	6	6
2007	Tor	70	54	503.0	108	2	0	0	1.000	1.97	49	15	.306	2	2	7	108	-1	+5	-5	+2	+2	1	18
2008	ChC	26	12	124.2	35	1	0	0	1.000	2.60	12	1	.083	1	2	-	35	+1	+1	0	+1	+2	1	-
		424	271	2641.2	576	21	5	2	.992	2.03	237	69	.291	17	16	7	561	+24	+28	+4	+14	+45	26	3

Matt Joyce

	BASIC										THROWING						PLUS/MINUS							
Year	Team	G	GS	Inn	PO	A	E	DP	Pct	Rng	Opps To Advance	Extra Bases	Pct	Kills	Runs Saved	Rank	Outs Made	Basic	Shallow	Medium	Deep	Enhanced	Runs Saved	Rank
2008	Det	60	41	409.1	94	2	3	0	.970	2.11	54	15	.278	1	2	13	94	+1	0	+2	+2	+4	2	17

Carlos Lee

	BASIC										THROWING						PLUS/MINUS							
Year	Team	G	GS	Inn	PO	A	E	DP	Pct	Rng	Opps To Advance	Extra Bases	Pct	Kills	Runs Saved	Rank	Outs Made	Basic	Shallow	Medium	Deep	Enhanced	Runs Saved	Rank
2003	CWS	156	155	1328.2	307	8	7	1	.978	2.13	129	57	.442	4	-5	35	303	+6	+4	+2	+9	+15	8	1
2004	CWS	148	148	1277.2	282	11	0	2	1.000	2.06	118	43	.364	8	5	6	277	-1	-3	-1	+10	+6	3	10
2005	Mil	162	161	1404.0	307	8	6	3	.981	2.02	138	48	.348	5	1	17	307	-8	-16	+1	+5	-9	-5	32
2006	2 tms	149	148	1259.1	227	5	6	0	.975	1.66	138	48	.348	2	-2	28	227	-11	-7	-8	+6	-8	-4	29
2007	Hou	157	157	1369.1	261	8	4	2	.985	1.77	151	59	.391	6	0	22	261	+2	0	-1	+3	+2	1	15
2008	Hou	110	110	915.1	187	4	1	0	.995	1.88	87	34	.391	1	-2	29	187	+4	+3	+3	-6	0	0	21
		882	879	7554.1	1571	44	24	8	.985	1.92	761	289	.380	26	-3	29	1562	-8	-19	-4	+28	+6	3	15

Fred Lewis

	BASIC										THROWING						PLUS/MINUS							
Year	Team	G	GS	Inn	PO	A	E	DP	Pct	Rng	Opps To Advance	Extra Bases	Pct	Kills	Runs Saved	Rank	Outs Made	Basic	Shallow	Medium	Deep	Enhanced	Runs Saved	Rank
2006	SF	6	1	18.0	7	0	1	0	.875	3.50	3	1	.333	0	0	-	7	0	0	0	0	0	0	-
2007	SF	24	10	115.0	32	0	1	0	.970	2.50	18	4	.222	0	1	-	32	+3	+2	+1	+1	+4	2	-
2008	SF	112	101	905.2	178	11	6	1	.969	1.88	88	33	.375	3	3	8	177	+4	+6	+1	-4	+4	2	13
		142	112	1038.2	217	11	8	1	.966	1.98	109	38	.349	3	4	-	216	+7	+8	+3	-3	+8	4	-

Adam Lind

	BASIC										THROWING						PLUS/MINUS							
Year	Team	G	GS	Inn	PO	A	E	DP	Pct	Rng	Opps To Advance	Extra Bases	Pct	Kills	Runs Saved	Rank	Outs Made	Basic	Shallow	Medium	Deep	Enhanced	Runs Saved	Rank
2006	Tor	2	2	17.0	4	0	0	0	1.000	2.12	1	0	.000	0	0	-	4	0	0	0	0	0	0	-
2007	Tor	80	72	651.2	137	5	0	0	1.000	1.96	58	25	.431	4	-1	26	137	+4	-2	0	+11	+9	5	7
2008	Tor	71	71	590.2	113	2	0	1	1.000	1.75	49	20	.408	0	-1	23	113	-5	0	-2	-7	-9	-5	27
		153	145	1259.1	254	7	0	1	1.000	1.87	108	45	.417	4	-2	-	254	-1	-2	-2	+4	0	0	-

Hideki Matsui

	BASIC										THROWING						PLUS/MINUS							
Year	Team	G	GS	Inn	PO	A	E	DP	Pct	Rng	Opps To Advance	Extra Bases	Pct	Kills	Runs Saved	Rank	Outs Made	Basic	Shallow	Medium	Deep	Enhanced	Runs Saved	Rank
2003	NYY	118	110	997.1	210	11	7	3	.969	1.99	121	47	.388	4	0	24	210	-10	-12	-4	+3	-12	-7	32
2004	NYY	162	160	1388.0	303	8	7	2	.978	2.02	136	36	.265	5	7	2	289	-15	-11	-7	-2	-20	-11	33
2005	NYY	115	110	977.1	219	7	3	1	.987	2.08	119	41	.345	4	3	10	219	-2	-6	-1	+11	+4	2	11
2006	NYY	36	36	289.0	82	1	1	1	.988	2.58	43	19	.442	1	-2	-	82	0	+2	0	-4	-1	-1	-
2007	NYY	112	111	980.0	213	6	3	0	.986	2.01	105	33	.314	5	6	3	214	0	+4	-2	-11	-9	-5	26
2008	NYY	21	20	176.1	40	2	1	1	.977	2.14	21	11	.524	2	0	-	40	0	+1	-1	-1	-1	-1	-
		564	547	4808.0	1067	35	22	8	.980	2.06	545	187	.343	21	14	9	1054	-27	-22	-15	-3	-39	-23	32

Gary Matthews Jr.

	BASIC										THROWING						PLUS/MINUS							
Year	Team	G	GS	Inn	PO	A	E	DP	Pct	Rng	Opps To Advance	Extra Bases	Pct	Kills	Runs Saved	Rank	Outs Made	Basic	Shallow	Medium	Deep	Enhanced	Runs Saved	Rank
2003	SD	33	20	195.2	37	0	1	0	.974	1.70	24	6	.250	0	0	-	37	+2	+3	+1	-1	+3	2	-
2004	Tex	3	1	11.0	7	1	0	0	1.000	6.55	0	0	-	1	1	-	7	+1	+1	0	+1	+1	1	-
2005	Tex	5	5	40.0	8	0	0	0	1.000	1.80	6	0	.000	0	1	-	8	0	0	+1	-2	-1	-1	-
2008	LAA	37	36	313.1	57	1	2	0	.967	1.67	25	11	.440	1	0	-	57	-6	0	-1	-10	-12	-7	-
		78	62	560.0	109	2	3	0	.974	1.78	55	17	.309	2	2	-	109	-3	+3	0	-12	-9	-5	-

Left Fielders

Paul McAnulty

Year	Team	G	GS	Inn	PO	A	E	DP	Pct	Rng	Opps To Advance	Extra Bases	Pct	Kills	Runs Saved	Rank	Outs Made	Basic	Shallow	Medium	Deep	Enhanced	Runs Saved	Rank
2005	SD	6	2	29.0	5	0	0	0	1.000	1.55	2	0	.000	0	0	-	5	0	0	0	0	+1	1	-
2007	SD	4	2	22.2	5	0	0	0	1.000	1.99	3	2	.667	0	0	-	5	+1	+1	0	0	+1	1	-
2008	SD	35	30	266.0	48	1	0	0	1.000	1.66	33	17	.515	1	-1	-	48	-2	-1	-3	0	-4	-2	-
		45	34	317.2	58	1	0	0	1.000	1.67	38	19	.500	1	-1	-	58	-1	+1	-3	0	-2	0	-

Kevin Mench

Year	Team	G	GS	Inn	PO	A	E	DP	Pct	Rng	Opps To Advance	Extra Bases	Pct	Kills	Runs Saved	Rank	Outs Made	Basic	Shallow	Medium	Deep	Enhanced	Runs Saved	Rank
2003	Tex	34	30	267.0	56	1	1	0	.983	1.92	41	15	.366	0	-1	-	54	-3	-2	-1	-1	-4	-2	-
2004	Tex	53	37	362.2	73	1	1	1	.987	1.84	29	8	.276	0	0	17	73	+2	+7	-4	-2	0	0	-
2005	Tex	119	108	978.1	230	8	2	3	.992	2.19	123	51	.415	7	1	17	231	+3	+8	-2	-8	-3	-2	24
2006	2 tms	55	46	407.2	80	2	2	0	.976	1.81	42	19	.452	0	-2	28	79	0	-1	0	+2	+2	1	19
2007	Mil	51	44	377.2	55	3	0	1	1.000	1.38	44	22	.500	3	-1	-	55	+2	+1	-1	+2	+3	2	-
2008	Tor	21	14	125.0	28	0	0	0	1.000	2.02	12	1	.083	0	0	-	28	-1	-1	0	0	-1	-1	-
		333	279	2518.1	522	15	6	5	.989	1.92	291	116	.399	10	-3	29	520	+3	+12	-7	-7	-3	-2	19

Jason Michaels

Year	Team	G	GS	Inn	PO	A	E	DP	Pct	Rng	Opps To Advance	Extra Bases	Pct	Kills	Runs Saved	Rank	Outs Made	Basic	Shallow	Medium	Deep	Enhanced	Runs Saved	Rank
2003	Phi	23	5	82.1	13	3	0	0	1.000	1.75	7	1	.143	2	3	-	13	-2	-4	0	+1	-3	-2	-
2004	Phi	39	23	227.1	49	3	0	2	1.000	2.06	25	8	.320	0	0	-	45	-1	-1	-1	-2	-4	-2	-
2005	Phi	22	2	46.1	11	1	0	1	1.000	2.33	2	0	.000	1	1	-	11	+1	+1	0	-1	0	0	-
2006	Cle	117	115	1009.1	214	6	2	2	.991	1.96	118	47	.398	3	-3	31	214	+9	+8	-1	+3	+10	6	8
2007	Cle	74	55	499.2	117	4	0	0	1.000	2.18	64	20	.313	3	3	5	117	+3	+3	-1	0	+2	1	17
2008	2 tms	34	24	225.2	52	2	0	0	1.000	2.15	36	10	.278	2	1	-	52	0	0	-2	+3	+1	0	-
		309	224	2090.2	456	19	2	5	.996	2.04	252	86	.341	11	5	17	452	+10	+6	-4	+4	+6	3	17

Craig Monroe

Year	Team	G	GS	Inn	PO	A	E	DP	Pct	Rng	Opps To Advance	Extra Bases	Pct	Kills	Runs Saved	Rank	Outs Made	Basic	Shallow	Medium	Deep	Enhanced	Runs Saved	Rank
2003	Det	75	70	602.2	148	6	4	1	.975	2.30	71	29	.408	5	2	16	138	-4	-2	-8	+4	-5	-3	26
2004	Det	65	50	446.0	102	1	8	0	.928	2.08	46	18	.391	0	-1	22	80	+3	-1	-2	+10	+7	4	9
2005	Det	69	56	501.2	99	6	1	4	.991	1.88	53	20	.377	3	1	17	99	+1	-2	-2	+6	+2	1	14
2006	Det	113	105	927.1	168	12	3	2	.984	1.75	93	36	.387	10	6	4	168	-8	-5	-5	0	-10	-6	31
2007	2 tms	102	88	805.2	166	4	3	1	.983	1.92	82	30	.366	4	3	5	166	-3	-3	-4	+5	-2	-1	21
2008	Min	1	0	1.0	0	0	0	0	-	.00	1	1	1.000	0	0	-	0	0	0	0	0	0	-
		425	369	3284.1	683	31	19	8	.974	1.96	346	134	.387	22	11	12	651	-11	-12	-21	+25	-8	-5	21

Brandon Moss

Year	Team	G	GS	Inn	PO	A	E	DP	Pct	Rng	Opps To Advance	Extra Bases	Pct	Kills	Runs Saved	Rank	Outs Made	Basic	Shallow	Medium	Deep	Enhanced	Runs Saved	Rank
2007	Bos	13	4	52.0	11	1	0	0	1.000	2.08	6	1	.167	0	0	-	11	0	0	0	0	0	0	-
2008	2 tms	36	33	294.1	60	2	1	1	.984	1.90	25	9	.360	0	-2	-	60	0	-1	-1	+1	-1	0	-
		49	37	346.1	71	3	1	1	.987	1.92	31	10	.323	0	-2	-	71	0	-2	-1	+2	-1	0	-

David Murphy

Year	Team	G	GS	Inn	PO	A	E	DP	Pct	Rng	Opps To Advance	Extra Bases	Pct	Kills	Runs Saved	Rank	Outs Made	Basic	Shallow	Medium	Deep	Enhanced	Runs Saved	Rank
2006	Bos	6	1	20.0	1	0	0	0	1.000	.45	2	1	.500	0	0	-	1	-1	-1	0	-1	-2	-1	-
2007	2 tms	32	5	95.1	26	0	1	0	.963	2.45	13	4	.308	0	0	-	26	0	0	-1	+2	+1	1	-
2008	Tex	54	48	404.2	86	3	1	0	.989	1.98	48	14	.292	2	3	8	86	-4	0	-1	-5	-6	-3	24
		92	54	520.0	113	3	2	0	.983	2.01	63	19	.302	2	3	-	113	-5	-1	-2	-4	-7	-3	-

Xavier Nady

Year	Team	G	GS	Inn	PO	A	E	DP	Pct	Rng	Opps To Advance	Extra Bases	Pct	Kills	Runs Saved	Rank	Outs Made	Basic	Shallow	Medium	Deep	Enhanced	Runs Saved	Rank
2004	SD	18	10	105.0	16	1	2	0	.895	1.46	9	2	.222	1	1	-	14	-1	0	-1	-1	-2	-1	-
2005	SD	26	6	100.0	18	0	1	0	.947	1.62	6	5	.833	0	-1	-	18	+1	+1	0	0	+1	1	-
2007	Pit	10	9	76.2	14	0	0	0	1.000	1.64	11	4	.364	0	-1	-	14	-1	0	-1	-1	-2	-1	-
2008	NYY	46	45	389.2	87	2	2	0	.978	2.06	44	12	.273	0	3	-	87	+2	+3	0	-1	+2	1	-
		100	70	671.1	135	3	5	0	.965	1.85	70	23	.329	1	2	-	133	+1	+3	-1	-4	-1	0	-

Left Fielders

Jay Payton

		BASIC									THROWING						PLUS/MINUS							
Year	Team	G	GS	Inn	PO	A	E	DP	Pct	Rng	Opps To Advance	Extra Bases	Pct	Kills	Runs Saved	Rank	Outs Made	Basic	Shallow	Medium	Deep	Enhanced	Runs Saved	Rank
2003	Col	149	143	1230.0	298	6	3	1	.990	2.22	152	38	.250	3	4	7	273	-4	+2	+2	-11	-6	-3	28
2004	SD	9	4	48.0	8	0	0	0	1.000	1.50	3	1	.333	0	0	-	8	+1	0	+2	0	+2	1	-
2005	2 tms	60	50	465.1	107	1	0	0	1.000	2.09	34	9	.265	1	1	17	107	+1	+3	0	-3	+1	1	15
2006	Oak	62	51	454.0	118	3	2	0	.984	2.40	63	13	.206	3	5	7	119	-2	-2	0	-3	-5	-3	26
2007	Bal	123	100	904.0	232	2	5	1	.979	2.33	117	39	.333	1	1	13	231	-7	-3	-4	-3	-10	-6	27
2008	Bal	71	41	407.1	132	2	0	1	1.000	2.96	41	11	.268	1	2	13	132	+2	+2	-1	+3	+4	2	16
		474	389	3508.2	895	14	10	3	.989	2.33	410	111	.271	9	13	10	870	-9	+2	0	-16	-14	-8	26

Wily Mo Pena

		BASIC									THROWING						PLUS/MINUS							
Year	Team	G	GS	Inn	PO	A	E	DP	Pct	Rng	Opps To Advance	Extra Bases	Pct	Kills	Runs Saved	Rank	Outs Made	Basic	Shallow	Medium	Deep	Enhanced	Runs Saved	Rank
2003	Cin	8	4	38.2	6	0	0	0	1.000	1.40	3	3	1.000	0	-1	-	6	-2	0	-1	-2	-3	-2	-
2004	Cin	1	0	0.0	0	0	0	0	-	-	0	0	-	0	0	-								
2005	Cin	10	9	73.2	12	0	2	0	.857	1.47	11	5	.455	0	0	-	12	-3	-1	-1	-4	-6	-3	-
2006	Bos	18	11	113.0	24	3	1	0	.964	2.15	15	5	.333	3	3	-	24	-1	+1	-2	-2	-3	-2	-
2007	2 tms	55	41	363.1	68	1	0	0	1.000	1.71	33	12	.364	0	-1	-	68	+2	+4	-1	+1	+4	3	-
2008	Was	54	51	408.0	99	3	3	0	.971	2.25	50	20	.400	2	-1	23	99	+6	+6	-3	+4	+7	4	10
		146	116	996.2	209	7	6	0	.973	1.95	112	45	.402	5	0	-	209	+2	+10	-8	-4	-1	0	-

Juan Pierre

		BASIC									THROWING						PLUS/MINUS							
Year	Team	G	GS	Inn	PO	A	E	DP	Pct	Rng	Opps To Advance	Extra Bases	Pct	Kills	Runs Saved	Rank	Outs Made	Basic	Shallow	Medium	Deep	Enhanced	Runs Saved	Rank
2008	LAD	84	71	622.2	125	0	3	0	.977	1.81	71	27	.380	0	-3	32	125	+3	+2	+1	+2	+5	3	12

Scott Podsednik

		BASIC									THROWING						PLUS/MINUS							
Year	Team	G	GS	Inn	PO	A	E	DP	Pct	Rng	Opps To Advance	Extra Bases	Pct	Kills	Runs Saved	Rank	Outs Made	Basic	Shallow	Medium	Deep	Enhanced	Runs Saved	Rank
2003	Mil	3	0	8.1	0	0	0	0	-	.00	0	0	-	0	0	-	0	0				0	0	-
2005	CWS	124	118	1061.2	260	3	3	1	.989	2.23	96	31	.323	3	1	17	260	+11	+4	-3	+15	+17	10	3
2006	CWS	135	121	1086.2	245	4	8	0	.969	2.06	98	36	.367	3	-1	21	245	+3	+5	+6	-2	+8	4	10
2007	CWS	54	52	460.1	108	4	4	1	.966	2.19	64	20	.313	2	2	7	108	+5	+3	+1	+2	+7	4	9
2008	Col	10	2	30.0	7	0	0	0	1.000	2.10	3	1	.333	0	0	-	7	0		0	-1	-1	-1	-
		326	293	2647.0	620	11	15	2	.977	2.15	261	88	.337	8	2	22	620	+19	+12	+4	+14	+31	17	5

Carlos Quentin

		BASIC									THROWING						PLUS/MINUS							
Year	Team	G	GS	Inn	PO	A	E	DP	Pct	Rng	Opps To Advance	Extra Bases	Pct	Kills	Runs Saved	Rank	Outs Made	Basic	Shallow	Medium	Deep	Enhanced	Runs Saved	Rank
2006	Ari	2	1	11.0	1	0	0	0	1.000	.82	0	0	-	0	0	-	1	0	0		0	0	0	-
2007	Ari	3	1	7.1	3	0	0	0	1.000	3.68	2	1	.500	0	0	-	3	0		0	0	0	0	-
2008	CWS	130	130	1147.0	228	5	7	2	.971	1.83	113	32	.283	2	4	5	228	-3	+3	-4	-7	-7	-4	25
		135	132	1165.1	232	5	7	2	.971	1.83	115	33	.287	2	4	-	232	-3	+3	-3	-7	-7	-4	-

Manny Ramirez

		BASIC									THROWING						PLUS/MINUS							
Year	Team	G	GS	Inn	PO	A	E	DP	Pct	Rng	Opps To Advance	Extra Bases	Pct	Kills	Runs Saved	Rank	Outs Made	Basic	Shallow	Medium	Deep	Enhanced	Runs Saved	Rank
2003	Bos	128	126	1073.0	207	11	4	1	.982	1.83	124	41	.331	5	7	1	207	-9	+4	-15	-14	-25	-14	35
2004	Bos	132	132	1087.2	198	4	7	0	.967	1.67	123	51	.415	2	-1	22	197	-12	+5	-2	-24	-21	-12	34
2005	Bos	149	147	1225.0	243	17	7	0	.974	1.91	154	51	.331	13	10	2	243	-19	+12	-13	-39	-40	-22	35
2006	Bos	123	123	1031.1	175	7	2	0	.989	1.59	112	36	.321	4	6	4	175	-17	+10	-8	-33	-31	-17	35
2007	Bos	120	120	994.2	182	8	2	0	.990	1.72	102	45	.441	6	-1	26	182	-10	+4	-7	-22	-24	-13	32
2008	2 tms	119	119	974.0	190	7	3	2	.985	1.82	102	32	.314	3	2	13	190	-5	+2	-6	-5	-9	-5	26
		771	767	6385.2	1195	54	25	3	.980	1.76	717	256	.357	33	23	4	1194	-72	+38	-51	-137	-150	-83	35

Juan Rivera

		BASIC									THROWING						PLUS/MINUS							
Year	Team	G	GS	Inn	PO	A	E	DP	Pct	Rng	Opps To Advance	Extra Bases	Pct	Kills	Runs Saved	Rank	Outs Made	Basic	Shallow	Medium	Deep	Enhanced	Runs Saved	Rank
2003	NYY	34	30	289.2	65	0	2	0	.970	2.02	30	11	.367	0	-1	-	58	+2	+3	-2	+1	+2	1	-
2004	Mon	10	9	71.0	17	1	0	0	1.000	2.28	11	6	.545	1	0	-	14	+1	-2	-1	+4	+1	1	-
2005	LAA	33	32	297.2	72	3	0	0	1.000	2.27	28	10	.357	3	1	-	72	+5	+4	0	+5	+9	5	-
2006	LAA	56	54	478.1	126	7	3	1	.978	2.50	37	10	.270	5	6	4	126	-1	-5	+1	-1	-5	-3	25
2007	LAA	2	2	15.0	0	0	0	0	-	.00	1	0	.000	0	0	-	0	0				0	0	-
2008	LAA	41	35	307.0	59	3	2	1	.969	1.82	20	7	.350	3	2	-	59	-2	-2	-3	+8	+4	2	-
		176	162	1458.2	339	14	7	2	.981	2.18	127	44	.346	12	8	-	329	+5	-2	-3	+8	+4	2	-

Left Fielders

Dave Roberts

Year	Team	G	GS	Inn	PO	A	E	DP	Pct	Rng	Opps To Advance	Extra Bases	Pct	Kills	Runs Saved	Rank	Outs Made	Basic	Shallow	Medium	Deep	Enhanced	Runs Saved	Rank
2004	2 tms	66	47	428.2	87	0	2	0	.978	1.83	33	11	.333	0	0	20	87	+3	+3	0	-1	+2	1	15
2006	SD	116	108	970.0	239	0	0	0	1.000	2.22	69	30	.435	0	-4	33	239	+12	+5	+2	+9	+16	9	2
2007	SF	20	7	83.1	24	0	0	0	1.000	2.59	7	1	.143	0	0	-	24	-2	-1	0	-2	-4	-2	-
2008	SF	32	23	205.2	54	3	0	2	1.000	2.49	18	5	.278	2	2	-	54	0	0	+1	-1	0	0	-
		234	185	1687.2	404	3	2	2	.995	2.17	127	47	.370	2	-2	28	404	+13	+7	+2	+5	+14	8	10

Skip Schumaker

Year	Team	G	GS	Inn	PO	A	E	DP	Pct	Rng	Opps To Advance	Extra Bases	Pct	Kills	Runs Saved	Rank	Outs Made	Basic	Shallow	Medium	Deep	Enhanced	Runs Saved	Rank
2005	StL	14	0	22.1	6	0	0	0	1.000	2.42	4	2	.500	0	0	-	6	-1	-1	0	-1	-1	-1	-
2006	StL	13	5	63.0	13	0	0	0	1.000	1.86	4	0	.000	0	0	-	13	-1	-1	-3	+1	-3	-2	-
2007	StL	23	10	122.2	20	0	1	0	.952	1.47	10	6	.600	0	-1	-	20	-1	0	0	-1	-1	-1	-
2008	StL	56	31	338.1	85	4	1	0	.989	2.37	47	14	.298	3	2	-	85	+5	+1	+4	+3	+8	4	-
		106	46	546.1	124	4	2	0	.985	2.11	65	22	.338	3	2	-	124	+2	0	+1	+2	+3	0	-

Luke Scott

Year	Team	G	GS	Inn	PO	A	E	DP	Pct	Rng	Opps To Advance	Extra Bases	Pct	Kills	Runs Saved	Rank	Outs Made	Basic	Shallow	Medium	Deep	Enhanced	Runs Saved	Rank
2005	Hou	21	18	151.1	22	2	1	0	.960	1.43	13	3	.231	2	1	-	22	+1	-1	+2	+1	+2	1	-
2006	Hou	50	48	417.0	81	1	0	1	1.000	1.77	37	12	.324	1	0	19	81	+5	+3	+3	+2	+8	4	12
2007	Hou	5	1	18.0	4	0	0	0	1.000	2.00	1	0	.000	0	0	-	4	0	+1	0		+1	1	-
2008	Bal	106	100	840.1	200	3	2	1	.990	2.17	105	37	.352	2	-1	23	200	+3	0	+3	+7	+10	6	4
		182	167	1426.2	307	6	3	2	.991	1.97	156	52	.333	5	0	-	307	+9	+2	+9	+10	+21	12	-

Alfonso Soriano

Year	Team	G	GS	Inn	PO	A	E	DP	Pct	Rng	Opps To Advance	Extra Bases	Pct	Kills	Runs Saved	Rank	Outs Made	Basic	Shallow	Medium	Deep	Enhanced	Runs Saved	Rank
2006	Was	158	158	1373.2	326	22	11	9	.969	2.28	154	59	.383	15	10	1	326	+6	-10	+3	+26	+19	11	1
2007	ChC	122	122	1064.0	244	19	6	4	.978	2.22	124	41	.331	19	17	1	245	-2	-4	+2	0	-2	-1	20
2008	ChC	108	107	937.1	186	10	5	5	.975	1.88	63	19	.302	8	6	1	186	-1	0	+1	-2	-1	-1	22
		388	387	3375.0	756	51	22	18	.973	2.15	341	119	.349	42	33	1	757	+3	-14	+6	+24	+16	9	9

Shannon Stewart

Year	Team	G	GS	Inn	PO	A	E	DP	Pct	Rng	Opps To Advance	Extra Bases	Pct	Kills	Runs Saved	Rank	Outs Made	Basic	Shallow	Medium	Deep	Enhanced	Runs Saved	Rank
2003	2 tms	115	113	986.1	247	7	4	0	.984	2.32	100	37	.370	5	1	19	233	+2	-2	+4	+1	+3	2	10
2004	Min	71	71	639.1	103	2	3	0	.972	1.48	60	23	.383	0	-1	22	96	-1	-1	-3	+4	0	0	20
2005	Min	125	125	1107.0	249	7	4	2	.985	2.08	106	34	.321	3	3	10	249	0	+3	-1	-2	-1	-1	19
2006	Min	34	34	286.0	58	3	1	1	.984	1.92	30	9	.300	0	-1	-	58	+4	+1	-1	+5	+5	3	-
2007	Oak	139	128	1154.0	277	4	3	2	.989	2.19	123	55	.447	3	-5	34	277	+4	+5	+3	-2	+6	3	10
2008	Tor	40	36	310.1	56	3	0	3	1.000	1.71	23	6	.261	3	3	-	56	+1	0	0	0	0	0	-
		524	507	4483.0	990	26	15	8	.985	2.04	442	164	.371	14	0	24	969	+10	+6	+1	+6	+13	7	11

Fernando Tatis

Year	Team	G	GS	Inn	PO	A	E	DP	Pct	Rng	Opps To Advance	Extra Bases	Pct	Kills	Runs Saved	Rank	Outs Made	Basic	Shallow	Medium	Deep	Enhanced	Runs Saved	Rank
2006	Bal	3	3	22.0	3	1	0	0	1.000	1.64	4	2	.500	0	0	-	3	-1	0		-4	-3	-2	-
2008	NYM	51	28	284.0	47	0	2	0	.959	1.49	26	5	.192	0	0	-	47	+1	+2	-4	+5	+3	2	-
		54	31	306.0	50	1	2	0	.962	1.50	30	7	.233	0	0	-	50	0	+2	-4	+2	0	0	-

Mark Teahen

Year	Team	G	GS	Inn	PO	A	E	DP	Pct	Rng	Opps To Advance	Extra Bases	Pct	Kills	Runs Saved	Rank	Outs Made	Basic	Shallow	Medium	Deep	Enhanced	Runs Saved	Rank
2008	KC	31	31	267.0	75	3	0	1	1.000	2.63	32	14	.438	3	0	-	75	-3	+1	-3	-7	-9	-5	-

Marcus Thames

Year	Team	G	GS	Inn	PO	A	E	DP	Pct	Rng	Opps To Advance	Extra Bases	Pct	Kills	Runs Saved	Rank	Outs Made	Basic	Shallow	Medium	Deep	Enhanced	Runs Saved	Rank
2003	Tex	4	2	19.0	5	0	0	0	1.000	2.37	0	0	-	0	0	-	5	0	-1	0	0	-1	-1	-
2004	Det	40	31	298.2	78	3	0	1	1.000	2.44	34	12	.353	3	1	-	65	+4	-1	0	+11	+9	5	-
2005	Det	21	16	153.0	31	0	0	0	1.000	1.82	19	9	.474	0	-1	-	31	-3	-1	-4	0	-5	-3	-
2006	Det	54	52	400.2	70	1	2	0	.973	1.59	33	11	.333	0	-1	-	70	-6	-6	0	-2	-8	-4	-
2007	Det	37	32	276.2	67	1	2	1	.971	2.21	25	8	.320	1	1	-	67	0	+1	-1	+4	+4	2	-
2008	Det	73	69	488.0	120	3	5	1	.961	2.27	56	21	.375	1	1	17	120	-8	-5	-3	-1	-10	-6	28
		229	202	1636.0	371	8	9	3	.977	2.08	167	61	.365	5	1	-	358	-13	-13	-10	+12	-11	-7	-

Left Fielders

Brad Wilkerson

		BASIC									THROWING						PLUS/MINUS							
Year	Team	G	GS	Inn	PO	A	E	DP	Pct	Rng	Opps To Advance	Extra Bases	Pct	Kills	Runs Saved	Rank	Outs Made	Basic	Shallow	Medium	Deep	Enhanced	Runs Saved	Rank
2003	Mon	95	80	702.1	167	8	4	1	.978	2.24	75	25	.333	7	5	3	128	+2	-1	+2	+6	+7	4	6
2004	Mon	59	51	439.1	94	4	2	2	.980	2.01	39	7	.179	4	6	4	75	+2	+1	0	+5	+6	3	11
2005	Was	38	31	288.1	67	0	1	0	.985	2.09	28	7	.250	0	0	-	67	+4	+2	-2	+6	+6	3	-
2006	Tex	80	76	664.1	139	7	1	3	.993	1.98	90	33	.367	5	1	17	139	0	-1	+2	+2	+2	1	18
2007	Tex	36	33	275.1	73	2	2	0	.974	2.45	39	16	.410	2	0	-	73	+1	+2	+3	-6	-1	-1	-
2008	Tor	29	13	138.2	24	0	0	0	1.000	1.56	8	3	.375	0	0	-	24	-2	-1	+1	0	-1	-1	-
		337	284	2508.1	564	21	10	6	.983	2.10	279	91	.326	18	12	11	506	+7	+2	+4	+13	+19	9	7

Josh Willingham

		BASIC									THROWING						PLUS/MINUS							
Year	Team	G	GS	Inn	PO	A	E	DP	Pct	Rng	Opps To Advance	Extra Bases	Pct	Kills	Runs Saved	Rank	Outs Made	Basic	Shallow	Medium	Deep	Enhanced	Runs Saved	Rank
2004	Fla	3	3	21.0	6	0	0	0	1.000	2.57	1	0	.000	0	0	-	6	-1	0	0	-1	-1	-1	-
2005	Fla	1	0	1.0	0	0	0	0	-	.00	0	0	-	0	0	-								
2006	Fla	132	129	1069.2	206	5	7	0	.968	1.78	107	33	.308	3	4	11	206	-2	+1	-2	-5	-6	-3	27
2007	Fla	137	137	1176.1	211	9	3	0	.987	1.68	151	40	.265	5	7	2	211	-14	-7	+5	-16	-18	-10	30
2008	Fla	98	97	855.1	166	7	0	0	1.000	1.82	93	30	.323	7	5	3	166	+5	+3	+1	+4	+8	4	6
		371	366	3123.1	589	21	10	0	.984	1.76	352	103	.293	15	16	7	589	-12	-2	+3	-17	-17	-10	28

Randy Winn

		BASIC									THROWING						PLUS/MINUS							
Year	Team	G	GS	Inn	PO	A	E	DP	Pct	Rng	Opps To Advance	Extra Bases	Pct	Kills	Runs Saved	Rank	Outs Made	Basic	Shallow	Medium	Deep	Enhanced	Runs Saved	Rank
2003	Sea	139	134	1188.0	299	3	3	1	.990	2.29	100	39	.390	1	-4	34	290	+7	+7	+4	+1	+12	7	3
2004	Sea	40	32	288.0	74	0	0	0	1.000	2.31	36	11	.306	0	0	-	70	+1	-1	+4	-2	0	0	-
2005	Sea	92	90	795.2	226	2	0	0	1.000	2.58	85	28	.329	2	-1	27	226	+1	+4	+5	-11	-2	-1	22
2006	SF	20	10	100.2	27	0	0	0	1.000	2.41	12	2	.167	0	1	-	27	0	0	0	-1	-1	-1	-
2007	SF	23	14	137.2	27	2	0	0	1.000	1.90	18	6	.333	0	0	-	27	-2	0	-1	-3	-4	-2	-
2008	SF	15	13	107.2	30	1	0	0	1.000	2.59	15	6	.400	1	1	-	30	+1	+1	0	0	+1	1	-
		329	293	2617.2	683	8	3	1	.996	2.38	266	92	.346	4	-3	29	670	+8	+12	+12	-17	+6	4	16

Delmon Young

		BASIC									THROWING						PLUS/MINUS							
Year	Team	G	GS	Inn	PO	A	E	DP	Pct	Rng	Opps To Advance	Extra Bases	Pct	Kills	Runs Saved	Rank	Outs Made	Basic	Shallow	Medium	Deep	Enhanced	Runs Saved	Rank
2008	Min	151	147	1324.0	282	11	8	2	.973	1.99	145	52	.359	7	3	8	282	-17	-11	+5	-20	-25	-14	35

Center Fielders

Alfredo Amezaga

Year	Team	G	GS	Inn	PO	A	E	DP	Pct	Rng	Opps To Advance	Extra Bases	Pct	Kills	Runs Saved	Rank	Outs Made	Basic	Shallow	Medium	Deep	Enhanced	Runs Saved	Rank
2006	Fla	75	64	529.0	155	2	4	0	.975	2.67	61	33	.541	1	7	15	155	+3	+1	0	+5	+6	3	14
2007	Fla	87	71	643.2	208	8	5	1	.977	3.02	66	34	.515	7	7	3	208	+8	-2	+4	+13	+15	8	6
2008	Fla	79	48	457.1	144	6	1	1	.993	2.95	44	18	.409	3	4	-	146	+7	+1	+4	+7	+12	7	-
		241	183	1630.0	507	16	10	2	.981	2.89	171	85	.497	11	11	-	509	+18	+1	+8	+25	+33	18	

Brian Anderson

Year	Team	G	GS	Inn	PO	A	E	DP	Pct	Rng	Opps To Advance	Extra Bases	Pct	Kills	Runs Saved	Rank	Outs Made	Basic	Shallow	Medium	Deep	Enhanced	Runs Saved	Rank
2005	CWS	5	3	36.0	7	0	0	0	1.000	1.75	2	1	.500	0	0	-	7	0	+1	-1	+1	+1	1	-
2006	CWS	134	106	966.0	305	3	2	1	.994	2.87	112	61	.545	1	0	15	305	+6	+6	-2	0	+4	2	17
2007	CWS	3	3	24.0	8	0	1	0	.889	3.00	1	1	1.000	0	0	-	8	0	+1	0	-2	-1	-1	-
2008	CWS	94	37	447.1	102	0	0	0	1.000	2.05	36	19	.528	0	1	-	102	+2	+5	0	-1	+3	2	-
		236	149	1473.1	422	3	3	1	.993	2.60	151	82	.543	1	1	-	422	+8	+12	-3	-2	+7	4	-

Rick Ankiel

Year	Team	G	GS	Inn	PO	A	E	DP	Pct	Rng	Opps To Advance	Extra Bases	Pct	Kills	Runs Saved	Rank	Outs Made	Basic	Shallow	Medium	Deep	Enhanced	Runs Saved	Rank
2007	StL	22	14	137.0	27	0	0	0	1.000	1.77	9	5	.556	0	0	-	27	-1	-1	-2	+1	-1	-1	-
2008	StL	89	84	766.1	213	4	5	1	.977	2.55	76	33	.434	4	7	2	213	-10	-5	-5	-9	-19	-11	33
		111	98	903.1	240	4	5	1	.980	2.43	85	38	.447	4	7	-	240	-11	-6	-7	-8	-20	-12	-

Rocco Baldelli

Year	Team	G	GS	Inn	PO	A	E	DP	Pct	Rng	Opps To Advance	Extra Bases	Pct	Kills	Runs Saved	Rank	Outs Made	Basic	Shallow	Medium	Deep	Enhanced	Runs Saved	Rank
2003	TB	154	149	1322.2	438	14	5	4	.989	3.08	146	69	.473	5	9	1	415	-6	-1	+1	-9	-9	-5	29
2004	TB	124	120	1047.0	341	11	8	2	.978	3.03	110	54	.491	9	9	3	327	-1	-7	-5	+5	-7	-4	26
2006	TB	91	85	749.1	228	6	5	3	.979	2.81	87	49	.563	3	0	15	228	0	-4	-5	+12	+4	2	19
2007	TB	20	20	162.0	62	3	0	1	1.000	3.61	33	21	.636	2	0	-	62	+1	-2	+2	+3	+3	2	-
		389	374	3281.0	1069	34	18	10	.984	3.03	376	193	.513	19	18	7	1032	-6	-13	-6	+10	-9	-5	24

Carlos Beltran

Year	Team	G	GS	Inn	PO	A	E	DP	Pct	Rng	Opps To Advance	Extra Bases	Pct	Kills	Runs Saved	Rank	Outs Made	Basic	Shallow	Medium	Deep	Enhanced	Runs Saved	Rank
2003	KC	130	129	1123.0	371	10	5	1	.987	3.05	111	62	.559	6	4	7	338	-2	-1	+4	-6	-3	-2	24
2004	2 tms	158	157	1369.1	398	13	8	4	.981	2.70	144	81	.563	6	0	18	332	0	+2	+1	+8	+10	6	7
2005	NYM	150	149	1289.1	378	5	4	1	.990	2.67	128	80	.625	4	-3	33	378	-1	-6	0	+10	+4	2	15
2006	NYM	136	136	1184.0	357	13	2	6	.995	2.81	111	65	.586	4	3	4	357	+5	-4	-3	+18	+11	6	8
2007	NYM	141	141	1240.1	389	6	5	2	.988	2.87	121	73	.603	4	-1	28	389	+5	+5	+1	+18	+24	13	2
2008	NYM	158	158	1407.1	418	8	3	1	.993	2.72	146	78	.534	6	4	10	418	+14	+10	+5	+10	+25	14	2
		873	870	7613.1	2311	55	27	15	.989	2.80	761	439	.577	34	7	11	2212	+29	+5	+8	+58	+71	39	2

Gregor Blanco

Year	Team	G	GS	Inn	PO	A	E	DP	Pct	Rng	Opps To Advance	Extra Bases	Pct	Kills	Runs Saved	Rank	Outs Made	Basic	Shallow	Medium	Deep	Enhanced	Runs Saved	Rank
2008	Atl	69	54	494.1	128	4	0	0	1.000	2.40	53	26	.491	1	2	-	128	+1	+1	-1	+1	0	0	-

Michael Bourn

Year	Team	G	GS	Inn	PO	A	E	DP	Pct	Rng	Opps To Advance	Extra Bases	Pct	Kills	Runs Saved	Rank	Outs Made	Basic	Shallow	Medium	Deep	Enhanced	Runs Saved	Rank
2007	Phi	12	6	56.2	16	0	0	0	1.000	2.54	7	4	.571	0	0	-	16	+3	+2	0	+4	+6	3	-
2008	Hou	130	111	1009.0	291	9	5	2	.984	2.68	100	59	.590	4	0	20	291	-1	-9	+10	+2	+3	2	13
		142	117	1065.2	307	9	5	2	.984	2.67	107	63	.589	4	0	-	307	+2	-7	+10	+6	+9	5	-

Jay Bruce

Year	Team	G	GS	Inn	PO	A	E	DP	Pct	Rng	Opps To Advance	Extra Bases	Pct	Kills	Runs Saved	Rank	Outs Made	Basic	Shallow	Medium	Deep	Enhanced	Runs Saved	Rank
2008	Cin	35	35	285.0	77	3	2	1	.976	2.53	31	15	.484	2	3	-	77	+2	0	+4	+1	+5	3	-

Center Fielders

Marlon Byrd

	BASIC										THROWING						PLUS/MINUS						
Year	Team	G	GS	Inn	PO	A	E	DP	Pct	Rng	Opps To Advance	Extra Bases	Pct	Kills	Runs Saved	Rank	Outs Made	Basic	Shallow	Medium	Deep	Enhanced	Runs Saved	Rank
2003	Phi	131	124	1100.1	295	5	5	1	.984	2.45	99	53	.535	3	2	9	288	+1	+2	-2	0	0	0	20
2004	Phi	92	86	753.1	195	4	2	1	.990	2.38	62	37	.597	1	-2	24	181	-7	+2	+6	-27	-19	-11	31
2005	2 tms	16	10	95.0	20	0	0	0	1.000	1.89	3	1	.333	0	1	-	20	-1	0	+1	-2	-1	-1	-
2006	Was	57	44	393.1	125	1	1	0	.992	2.88	58	29	.500	1	1	-	125	+3	-2	+3	+7	+8	4	-
2007	Tex	63	54	496.1	114	4	2	1	.983	2.14	44	29	.659	2	2	14	114	-3	-3	-2	+2	-3	-2	25
2008	Tex	57	46	433.0	149	4	3	0	.981	3.18	48	24	.500	3	3	-	149	0	-2	-1	+4	+1	1	-
		416	364	3271.1	898	18	13	3	.986	2.52	314	173	.551	10	7	11	877	-7	-3	+4	-15	-14	-9	26

Eric Byrnes

	BASIC										THROWING						PLUS/MINUS						
Year	Team	G	GS	Inn	PO	A	E	DP	Pct	Rng	Opps To Advance	Extra Bases	Pct	Kills	Runs Saved	Rank	Outs Made	Basic	Shallow	Medium	Deep	Enhanced	Runs Saved	Rank
2003	Oak	82	77	672.1	163	2	2	1	.988	2.21	61	34	.557	2	1	13	147	0	+4	0	-8	-5	-3	26
2004	Oak	33	22	215.1	62	3	1	0	.985	2.72	16	7	.438	2	2	-	54	+4	+6	-1	-1	+4	2	-
2005	3 tms	7	5	42.0	14	1	0	1	1.000	3.21	2	1	.500	1	1	-	14	+1	+1	+1	+1	+3	2	-
2006	Ari	123	117	1051.0	270	5	1	1	.996	2.35	93	52	.559	2	0	15	270	+2	-1	-1	+6	+4	2	18
2007	Ari	23	17	169.0	50	0	0	0	1.000	2.66	16	7	.438	0	1	-	50	+2	+1	+1	+2	+4	2	-
2008	Ari	1	0	3.1	2	0	0	0	1.000	5.40	1	0	.000	0	0	-	2	0	0	0	0	0	0	-
		269	238	2153.0	561	11	4	3	.993	2.39	189	101	.534	7	5	17	537	+9	+10	0	0	+10	5	20

Melky Cabrera

	BASIC										THROWING						PLUS/MINUS						
Year	Team	G	GS	Inn	PO	A	E	DP	Pct	Rng	Opps To Advance	Extra Bases	Pct	Kills	Runs Saved	Rank	Outs Made	Basic	Shallow	Medium	Deep	Enhanced	Runs Saved	Rank
2005	NYY	6	6	49.0	9	0	0	0	1.000	1.65	8	5	.625	0	0	-	9	-3	+1	-4	-4	-7	-4	-
2006	NYY	4	1	23.0	8	0	0	0	1.000	3.13	3	2	.667	0	0	-	8	-2	-1	0	-3	-4	-2	-
2007	NYY	131	117	1072.2	346	14	4	1	.989	3.02	132	72	.545	13	9	2	347	-10	-2	-7	-12	-21	-12	34
2008	NYY	117	109	973.2	272	7	4	1	.986	2.58	88	46	.523	4	3	12	272	+1	-2	+7	-2	+3	2	14
		258	233	2118.1	635	21	8	2	.988	2.79	231	125	.541	17	12	9	636	-14	-4	-4	-21	-29	-16	31

Mike Cameron

	BASIC										THROWING						PLUS/MINUS						
Year	Team	G	GS	Inn	PO	A	E	DP	Pct	Rng	Opps To Advance	Extra Bases	Pct	Kills	Runs Saved	Rank	Outs Made	Basic	Shallow	Medium	Deep	Enhanced	Runs Saved	Rank
2003	Sea	147	145	1284.0	485	3	4	2	.992	3.42	119	73	.613	2	-1	22	475	+13	+5	+1	+17	+23	13	2
2004	NYM	135	132	1184.0	354	7	8	2	.978	2.74	135	68	.504	0	1	15	349	0	+5	+2	-15	-8	-4	27
2005	NYM	10	9	79.0	15	1	0	0	1.000	1.82	7	5	.714	0	-1	-	15	0	0	+1	0	+1	1	-
2006	SD	141	139	1244.0	367	6	6	2	.984	2.70	106	68	.642	3	-2	24	367	+5	-4	+7	+5	+9	5	9
2007	SD	150	148	1329.0	365	7	5	2	.987	2.52	144	83	.576	4	1	18	365	-2	-7	+1	+7	+2	1	14
2008	Mil	119	119	1057.0	293	3	1	0	.997	2.52	86	42	.488	2	0	20	293	+7	+1	+4	+7	+12	7	7
		702	692	6177.0	1879	27	24	8	.988	2.78	597	339	.568	11	-2	29	1864	+23	+1	+16	+22	+39	23	5

Endy Chavez

	BASIC										THROWING						PLUS/MINUS						
Year	Team	G	GS	Inn	PO	A	E	DP	Pct	Rng	Opps To Advance	Extra Bases	Pct	Kills	Runs Saved	Rank	Outs Made	Basic	Shallow	Medium	Deep	Enhanced	Runs Saved	Rank
2003	Mon	135	112	1033.1	279	9	3	2	.990	2.51	85	34	.400	6	9	1	214	-4	0	+2	-13	-12	-7	33
2004	Mon	127	122	1081.2	301	9	5	5	.984	2.58	96	54	.563	6	4	5	258	+12	+9	+4	+2	+15	8	4
2005	2 tms	34	10	137.0	32	3	1	1	.972	2.30	8	3	.375	1	2	-	32	+1	+1	-2	0	-1	-1	-
2006	NYM	39	25	264.1	83	2	0	2	1.000	2.89	15	8	.533	1	1	-	83	+5	+4	+1	+1	+6	3	-
2007	NYM	10	5	58.0	24	0	0	0	1.000	3.72	3	3	1.000	0	0	-	24	+3	+1	+1	+3	+5	3	-
2008	NYM	10	2	38.1	9	1	0	0	1.000	2.35	7	5	.714	0	-1	-	9	0	0	0	+1	+1	1	-
		355	276	2612.2	728	24	9	10	.988	2.59	214	107	.500	14	15	8	620	+17	+14	+6	-6	+14	7	15

Coco Crisp

	BASIC										THROWING						PLUS/MINUS						
Year	Team	G	GS	Inn	PO	A	E	DP	Pct	Rng	Opps To Advance	Extra Bases	Pct	Kills	Runs Saved	Rank	Outs Made	Basic	Shallow	Medium	Deep	Enhanced	Runs Saved	Rank
2003	Cle	53	51	462.0	125	1	0	2	1.000	2.45	34	18	.529	1	0	19	112	+1	0	-1	+3	+3	2	14
2004	Cle	94	90	807.1	205	3	4	0	.981	2.32	85	48	.565	0	-2	24	199	+2	-3	-1	+7	+3	2	14
2005	Cle	10	10	79.2	21	0	1	0	.955	2.37	5	3	.600	0	0	-	21	-1	-1	0	-2	-3	-2	-
2006	Bos	103	100	900.2	246	3	1	3	.996	2.49	98	55	.561	1	-1	20	246	-5	+1	-3	-5	-7	-4	29
2007	Bos	144	137	1216.1	408	7	1	4	.998	3.07	108	55	.509	4	1	18	408	+18	+9	+1	+16	+26	15	1
2008	Bos	114	98	886.0	234	4	2	1	.992	2.42	74	44	.595	7	-2	31	234	-2	-4	+1	+1	-2	-1	16
		518	486	4352.0	1239	18	9	10	.993	2.60	404	223	.552		-4	31	1220	+13	+1	-1	+20	+20	12	11

Center Fielders

Johnny Damon

Year Team	G	GS	Inn	PO	A	E	DP	Pct	Rng	Opps To Advance	Extra Bases	Pct	Kills	Runs Saved	Rank	Outs Made	Basic	Shallow	Medium	Deep	Enhanced	Runs Saved	Rank
2003 Bos	144	141	1265.0	362	7	1	1	.997	2.63	130	81	.623	3	-4	31	363	+8	+3	+1	+9	+13	7	6
2004 Bos	148	145	1256.1	349	5	5	2	.986	2.54	113	64	.566	4	2	11	346	-9	-9	-3	-8	-20	-11	32
2005 Bos	147	144	1225.0	394	5	6	0	.985	2.93	114	62	.544	4	1	17	396	-7	-7	+1	-6	-11	-6	29
2006 NYY	131	129	1086.2	306	3	3	1	.990	2.56	110	68	.618	1	-5	34	306	+2	+8	+1	-11	-2	-1	24
2007 NYY	48	45	377.0	121	1	0	0	1.000	2.91	37	18	.486	0	0	-	121	-2	0	-1	-1	-2	-1	-
2008 NYY	34	33	285.0	77	1	1	0	.987	2.46	34	21	.618	0	-1	-	77	-3	-2	+1	-2	-3	-2	-
	652	637	5495.0	1609	22	16	4	.990	2.67	538	314	.584	12	-7	34	1609	-11	-6	+1	-20	-25	-14	30

Rajai Davis

Year Team	G	GS	Inn	PO	A	E	DP	Pct	Rng	Opps To Advance	Extra Bases	Pct	Kills	Runs Saved	Rank	Outs Made	Basic	Shallow	Medium	Deep	Enhanced	Runs Saved	Rank
2007 2 tms	58	43	379.1	124	3	0	0	1.000	3.01	44	23	.523	2	3	-	124	-1	+2	+9	-15	-4	-2	-
2008 2 tms	88	43	487.2	153	4	1	2	.994	2.90	61	29	.475	2	3	-	153	+5	+3	0	+5	+7	4	-
	146	86	867.0	277	7	1	2	.996	2.95	105	52	.495	4	6	-	277	+4	+4	+9	-10	+3	2	-

David DeJesus

Year Team	G	GS	Inn	PO	A	E	DP	Pct	Rng	Opps To Advance	Extra Bases	Pct	Kills	Runs Saved	Rank	Outs Made	Basic	Shallow	Medium	Deep	Enhanced	Runs Saved	Rank
2003 KC	8	0	21.0	2	0	0	0	1.000	.86	4	4	1.000	0	-1	-	2	-1	-1	0	0	-1	-1	-
2004 KC	85	85	732.1	231	3	4	0	.983	2.88	86	53	.616	3	-2	24	206	+5	+4	-2	+8	+10	6	8
2005 KC	119	118	1005.1	306	7	4	3	.987	2.80	115	60	.522	7	5	6	306	+8	+12	-5	0	+7	4	10
2006 KC	61	58	479.2	149	7	1	1	.994	2.93	45	29	.644	4	5	6	149	-1	-8	0	+9	+1	1	22
2007 KC	156	153	1351.1	401	5	4	1	.990	2.70	135	75	.556	2	1	18	400	-1	-3	+6	-3	-1	-1	19
2008 KC	68	64	507.0	151	2	1	1	.994	2.72	49	35	.714	1	-3	34	151	-5	-5	+1	-6	-11	-6	26
	497	478	4096.2	1240	24	14	5	.989	2.78	434	256	.590	17	2	22	1214	+5	-2	0	+7	+5	3	22

Jim Edmonds

Year Team	G	GS	Inn	PO	A	E	DP	Pct	Rng	Opps To Advance	Extra Bases	Pct	Kills	Runs Saved	Rank	Outs Made	Basic	Shallow	Medium	Deep	Enhanced	Runs Saved	Rank
2003 StL	128	118	1017.1	334	12	5	4	.986	3.06	107	55	.514	8	5	3	305	+7	+13	+1	-6	+7	4	9
2004 StL	146	141	1241.2	314	11	4	2	.988	2.36	118	49	.415	9	12	1	305	-7	+12	-8	-29	-25	-14	34
2005 StL	139	132	1153.1	318	5	2	1	.994	2.52	115	46	.400	2	7	3	319	+1	+8	-1	-13	-6	-3	24
2006 StL	99	92	792.1	223	4	3	0	.987	2.58	83	49	.590	1	-2	24	223	+3	+9	-1	-6	+2	1	20
2007 StL	103	99	828.1	244	8	5	4	.981	2.74	88	43	.489	5	5	5	244	+2	+14	-4	-21	-11	-6	31
2008 2 tms	103	99	840.0	242	1	6	1	.976	2.60	61	34	.557	1	1	17	242	-7	+4	-8	-21	-25	-14	34
	718	681	5873.0	1675	41	25	12	.986	2.63	572	276	.483	26	28	1	1638	-1	+59	-21	-97	-58	-32	34

Jacoby Ellsbury

Year Team	G	GS	Inn	PO	A	E	DP	Pct	Rng	Opps To Advance	Extra Bases	Pct	Kills	Runs Saved	Rank	Outs Made	Basic	Shallow	Medium	Deep	Enhanced	Runs Saved	Rank
2007 Bos	16	12	107.0	38	0	0	0	1.000	3.20	9	4	.444	0	0	-	38	-1	0	0	-1	-2	-1	-
2008 Bos	66	63	546.2	171	3	0	1	1.000	2.86	62	34	.548	1	-1	27	171	+4	-2	+7	+3	+8	4	9
	82	75	653.2	209	3	0	1	1.000	2.92	71	38	.535	1	-1	-	209	+3	-3	+7	+1	+6	3	-

Darin Erstad

Year Team	G	GS	Inn	PO	A	E	DP	Pct	Rng	Opps To Advance	Extra Bases	Pct	Kills	Runs Saved	Rank	Outs Made	Basic	Shallow	Medium	Deep	Enhanced	Runs Saved	Rank
2003 Ana	66	66	559.1	190	2	0	0	1.000	3.09	61	30	.492	1	1	13	188	+5	+2	0	+6	+9	5	8
2006 LAA	27	25	219.2	71	1	0	0	1.000	2.95	20	14	.700	1	-1	-	71	+1	+1	+1	-1	+2	1	-
2007 CWS	45	43	371.1	105	1	1	0	.991	2.57	41	23	.561	0	0	-	105	+4	+4	-1	+3	+6	3	-
2008 Hou	40	35	304.0	97	1	0	0	1.000	2.90	28	17	.607	1	-1	-	98	+4	+2	-1	+4	+5	3	-
	178	169	1454.1	463	5	1	0	.998	2.90	150	84	.560	3	-1	-	462	+14	+10	0	+12	+22	12	-

Joey Gathright

Year Team	G	GS	Inn	PO	A	E	DP	Pct	Rng	Opps To Advance	Extra Bases	Pct	Kills	Runs Saved	Rank	Outs Made	Basic	Shallow	Medium	Deep	Enhanced	Runs Saved	Rank
2004 TB	11	11	96.0	27	0	0	0	1.000	2.53	14	7	.500	0	0	-	27	-1	+1	-1	-3	-3	-2	-
2005 TB	70	56	505.2	180	3	3	2	.984	3.26	54	30	.556	3	2	13	181	+12	+2	+1	+23	+26	15	4
2006 2 tms	130	112	1016.2	341	6	3	4	.991	3.07	115	75	.652	4	-3	31	341	+5	+3	+1	+4	+8	5	10
2007 KC	10	5	56.0	16	0	1	0	.941	2.57	5	3	.600	0	0	-	16	-1	0	0	-1	-1	-1	-
2008 KC	100	75	720.0	197	5	1	0	.995	2.53	75	38	.507	2	0	20	197	-6	-8	+1	-3	-10	-6	24
	321	259	2394.1	761	14	8	6	.990	2.91	263	153	.582	9	-1	26	762	+9	-2	+2	+19	+20	11	12

Center Fielders

Jody Gerut

Year	Team	G	GS	Inn	PO	A	E	DP	Pct	Rng	Opps To Advance	Extra Bases	Pct	Kills	Runs Saved	Rank	Outs Made	Basic	Shallow	Medium	Deep	Enhanced	Runs Saved	Rank
2003	Cle	14	12	110.2	29	1	0	0	1.000	2.44	15	8	.533	1	1	-	29	0	0	0	+1	0	0	-
2004	Cle	12	11	100.0	25	0	0	0	1.000	2.25	9	4	.444	0	0	-	25	-1	-1	-1	+2	0	0	-
2008	SD	80	64	605.2	189	2	2	1	.990	2.84	54	30	.556	2	0	20	189	+8	+5	+2	+6	+13	7	6
		106	87	816.1	243	3	2	1	.992	2.71	78	42	.538	3	1	-	243	+7	+4	0	+9	+13	7	-

Carlos Gomez

Year	Team	G	GS	Inn	PO	A	E	DP	Pct	Rng	Opps To Advance	Extra Bases	Pct	Kills	Runs Saved	Rank	Outs Made	Basic	Shallow	Medium	Deep	Enhanced	Runs Saved	Rank
2007	NYM	4	0	12.0	4	0	0	0	1.000	3.00	0	0	-	0	0	-	4	+1	0		+3	+3	2	-
2008	Min	151	143	1271.2	436	9	8	4	.982	3.15	135	73	.541	4	1	17	437	+14	-2	+8	+23	+29	16	1
		155	143	1283.2	440	9	8	4	.982	3.15	135	73	.541	4	1		441	+15	-2	+8	+26	+32	18	-

Carlos Gonzalez

Year	Team	G	GS	Inn	PO	A	E	DP	Pct	Rng	Opps To Advance	Extra Bases	Pct	Kills	Runs Saved	Rank	Outs Made	Basic	Shallow	Medium	Deep	Enhanced	Runs Saved	Rank
2008	Oak	69	66	528.2	176	5	2	1	.989	3.08	50	26	.520	4	4	10	176	+4	+1	+1	+4	+6	3	12

Curtis Granderson

Year	Team	G	GS	Inn	PO	A	E	DP	Pct	Rng	Opps To Advance	Extra Bases	Pct	Kills	Runs Saved	Rank	Outs Made	Basic	Shallow	Medium	Deep	Enhanced	Runs Saved	Rank
2004	Det	8	7	61.0	16	1	0	0	1.000	2.51	7	5	.714	1	0	-	16	-1	-1	0	-1	-2	-1	-
2005	Det	41	39	320.0	119	2	0	0	1.000	3.40	34	17	.500	1	1	-	119	+7	+1	+3	+8	+12	7	-
2006	Det	157	143	1312.0	385	3	1	0	.997	2.66	120	64	.533	0	-2	24	385	+8	+5	+3	+4	+12	7	6
2007	Det	157	140	1285.0	424	10	5	4	.989	3.04	154	82	.532	8	3	11	424	+11	+2	+6	+12	+20	11	4
2008	Det	140	131	1188.0	366	5	4	1	.989	2.81	123	67	.545	13	-1	27	366	-8	-6	0	-5	-11	-6	25
		503	460	4166.0	1310	21	10	5	.993	2.88	438	235	.537	13	1	23	1310	+17	+2	+11	+17	+31	18	8

Ken Griffey Jr.

Year	Team	G	GS	Inn	PO	A	E	DP	Pct	Rng	Opps To Advance	Extra Bases	Pct	Kills	Runs Saved	Rank	Outs Made	Basic	Shallow	Medium	Deep	Enhanced	Runs Saved	Rank
2003	Cin	43	43	355.2	89	3	1	0	.989	2.33	37	23	.622	2	1	-	87	-5	0	-1	-9	-10	-6	-
2004	Cin	76	76	656.1	173	4	1	1	.994	2.43	73	38	.521	1	1	15	168	-9	+5	-6	-24	-24	-13	33
2005	Cin	124	124	1065.2	285	6	3	1	.990	2.46	127	66	.520	4	3	9	286	-11	+1	-5	-20	-24	-13	33
2006	Cin	100	100	870.1	229	6	5	0	.979	2.43	103	56	.544	3	1	11	229	-18	-8	-5	-16	-29	-16	35
2008	CWS	32	32	250.0	62	1	0	1	1.000	2.27	21	15	.714	1	0	-	62	+2	+2	-1	+4	+5	3	-
		375	375	3198.0	838	20	10	3	.988	2.41	361	198	.548	11	6	14	832	-41	+1	-18	-65	-82	-45	35

Scott Hairston

Year	Team	G	GS	Inn	PO	A	E	DP	Pct	Rng	Opps To Advance	Extra Bases	Pct	Kills	Runs Saved	Rank	Outs Made	Basic	Shallow	Medium	Deep	Enhanced	Runs Saved	Rank
2005	Ari	1	0	0.2	0	0	0	0		.00	0	0	-	0	0	-	0				-1	-1	-1	-
2007	2 tms	3	0	6.0	1	0	0	0	1.000	1.50	0	0	-	0	0	-	1	+1			+2	+2	1	-
2008	SD	51	45	378.0	114	2	2	0	.983	2.76	33	20	.606	2	1	-	114	-1	+2	-4	+4	+2	1	-
		55	45	384.2	115	2	2	0	.983	2.74	33	20	.606	2	1	-	115	0	+2	-4	+5	+3	1	-

Josh Hamilton

Year	Team	G	GS	Inn	PO	A	E	DP	Pct	Rng	Opps To Advance	Extra Bases	Pct	Kills	Runs Saved	Rank	Outs Made	Basic	Shallow	Medium	Deep	Enhanced	Runs Saved	Rank
2007	Cin	71	64	555.2	168	6	4	2	.978	2.82	50	28	.560	4	2	14	168	+1	+1	+1	-4	-2	-1	22
2008	Tex	111	107	912.0	268	3	5	3	.982	2.67	112	67	.598	1	0	20	268	-5	+5	-11	-7	-13	-7	29
		182	171	1467.2	436	9	9	5	.980	2.73	162	95	.586	5	2	-	436	-4	+6	-10	-11	-15	-8	-

Torii Hunter

Year	Team	G	GS	Inn	PO	A	E	DP	Pct	Rng	Opps To Advance	Extra Bases	Pct	Kills	Runs Saved	Rank	Outs Made	Basic	Shallow	Medium	Deep	Enhanced	Runs Saved	Rank
2003	Min	151	149	1299.1	425	5	4	1	.991	2.98	148	82	.554	4	1	13	390	+10	-9	0	+37	+28	16	1
2004	Min	126	124	1100.0	311	5	4	0	.988	2.59	130	61	.469	5	4	5	301	+7	-5	+11	+15	+21	12	2
2005	Min	93	92	813.1	218	9	3	4	.987	2.51	85	49	.576	7	3	9	218	+3	-1	+1	+8	+7	4	11
2006	Min	143	143	1232.1	343	8	4	4	.989	2.56	120	72	.600	3	-3	31	343	-4	-7	-8	+13	-2	-1	23
2007	Min	155	155	1314.2	387	5	2	0	.995	2.68	132	72	.545	3	0	24	389	-3	-5	-1	+6	0	0	18
2008	LAA	137	137	1193.1	350	4	0	0	1.000	2.67	120	68	.567	2	-1	27	350	-5	-3	+1	-6	-7	-4	20
		805	800	6953.0	2034	36	17	9	.992	2.68	735	404	.550	24	4	19	1991	+8	-30	+4	+72	+47	27	4

Center Fielders

Reed Johnson

Year	Team	G	GS	Inn	PO	A	E	DP	Pct	Rng	Opps To Advance	Extra Bases	Pct	Kills	Runs Saved	Rank	Outs Made	Basic	Shallow	Medium	Deep	Enhanced	Runs Saved	Rank
2003	Tor	5	0	8.0	1	0	0	0	1.000	1.13	0	0	-	0	0	-	1	0	0			0	0	-
2004	Tor	33	29	265.0	82	1	0	0	1.000	2.82	35	21	.600	1	-2	-	82	+1	-1	0	+1	0	0	-
2005	Tor	9	5	53.0	11	0	0	0	1.000	1.87	7	4	.571	0	0	-	11	0	0	0	-1	-2	-1	-
2006	Tor	16	11	106.0	20	2	0	1	1.000	1.87	13	6	.462	2	2	-	20	-5	-1	+1	-6	-7	-4	-
2007	Tor	1	1	8.0	1	0	0	0	1.000	1.13	1	1	1.000	0	0	-	1	0	0	0	0	0	0	-
2008	ChC	78	64	563.2	144	2	1	1	.993	2.33	41	24	.585	2	0	20	144	-6	-2	-6	-3	-11	-6	27
		142	110	1003.2	259	5	1	2	.996	2.37	97	56	.577	5	0	-	259	-10	-5	-5	-10	-20	-11	-

Adam Jones

Year	Team	G	GS	Inn	PO	A	E	DP	Pct	Rng	Opps To Advance	Extra Bases	Pct	Kills	Runs Saved	Rank	Outs Made	Basic	Shallow	Medium	Deep	Enhanced	Runs Saved	Rank
2006	Sea	26	23	193.0	67	5	3	1	.960	3.36	20	10	.500	3	3	-	67	-1	-2	0	+1	0	0	-
2007	Sea	7	3	34.0	10	0	1	0	.909	2.65	0	0	-	0	0	-	10	+2	0	0	+3	+3	2	-
2008	Bal	129	123	1102.0	336	4	3	1	.991	2.78	115	49	.426	4	7	2	337	+5	+5	+7	-5	+7	4	11
		162	149	1329.0	413	9	7	2	.984	2.86	135	59	.437	7	10	-	414	+6	+4	+7	-1	+10	6	-

Andruw Jones

Year	Team	G	GS	Inn	PO	A	E	DP	Pct	Rng	Opps To Advance	Extra Bases	Pct	Kills	Runs Saved	Rank	Outs Made	Basic	Shallow	Medium	Deep	Enhanced	Runs Saved	Rank
2003	Atl	155	153	1329.0	390	8	3	1	.993	2.70	148	77	.520	3	5	3	387	+16	+19	+1	-3	+17	10	4
2004	Atl	154	153	1347.0	389	10	3	3	.993	2.67	155	80	.516	6	3	9	382	+7	+8	+2	-4	+6	3	10
2005	Atl	159	158	1366.1	365	11	2	1	.995	2.48	136	67	.493	6	9	1	365	+8	+11	+5	-4	+12	7	7
2006	Atl	153	152	1317.1	378	4	2	1	.995	2.61	133	82	.617	2	-1	20	377	+17	+12	0	+15	+27	15	1
2007	Atl	154	153	1346.0	396	3	2	1	.995	2.67	138	60	.435	2	7	3	396	+15	+8	+9	+5	+22	12	3
2008	LAD	66	55	496.1	133	1	1	0	.993	2.43	55	28	.509	0	0	-	133	-2	+2	+2	-9	-5	-3	-
		841	824	7202.0	2051	37	13	7	.994	2.61	765	394	.515	19	23	3	2040	+61	+60	+19	0	+79	44	1

Gabe Kapler

Year	Team	G	GS	Inn	PO	A	E	DP	Pct	Rng	Opps To Advance	Extra Bases	Pct	Kills	Runs Saved	Rank	Outs Made	Basic	Shallow	Medium	Deep	Enhanced	Runs Saved	Rank
2003	2 tms	10	9	78.2	22	2	2	0	.923	2.75	6	4	.667	1	1	-	23	-1	0	-1	-1	-2	-1	-
2004	Bos	17	9	92.0	24	1	2	0	.926	2.45	19	12	.632	0	-1	-	24	-2	+1	0	-4	-3	-2	-
2005	Bos	12	9	80.0	19	0	0	0	1.000	2.14	7	4	.571	0	-1	-	19	-1	0	0	-2	-2	-1	-
2006	Bos	14	11	95.0	17	0	0	0	1.000	1.61	9	7	.778	0	-1	-	17	-3	0	-2	-3	-6	-3	-
2008	Mil	36	25	251.0	70	0	1	0	.986	2.51	24	13	.542	0	1	-	70	+3	+2	+1	+3	+5	3	-
		89	63	596.2	152	3	5	0	.969	2.34	65	40	.615	1	0	-	153	-4	+3	-3	-8	-8	-4	-

Matt Kemp

Year	Team	G	GS	Inn	PO	A	E	DP	Pct	Rng	Opps To Advance	Extra Bases	Pct	Kills	Runs Saved	Rank	Outs Made	Basic	Shallow	Medium	Deep	Enhanced	Runs Saved	Rank
2006	LAD	29	19	189.2	37	0	3	0	.925	1.76	21	13	.619	0	0	-	37	-2	-1	-2	-1	-4	-2	-
2007	LAD	6	0	17.1	8	0	0	0	1.000	4.15	1	0	.000	0	0	-	8	0	0	0	+1	+1	1	-
2008	LAD	101	92	825.2	209	10	1	3	.995	2.39	76	40	.526	8	6	6	209	0	+7	-3	-6	-2	-1	17
		136	111	1032.2	254	10	4	3	.985	2.30	98	53	.541	8	6	-	254	-2	+6	-6	-6	-5	-2	-

Mark Kotsay

Year	Team	G	GS	Inn	PO	A	E	DP	Pct	Rng	Opps To Advance	Extra Bases	Pct	Kills	Runs Saved	Rank	Outs Made	Basic	Shallow	Medium	Deep	Enhanced	Runs Saved	Rank
2003	SD	127	121	1055.1	324	13	3	3	.991	2.87	129	70	.543	6	5	3	315	+2	0	+2	-2	0	0	19
2004	Oak	145	140	1255.0	347	11	6	3	.984	2.57	123	64	.520	6	4	5	331	+4	+13	+1	-12	+2	1	15
2005	Oak	137	137	1184.1	298	7	4	2	.987	2.32	102	47	.461	6	6	4	300	-1	+1	-1	0	0	0	20
2006	Oak	127	116	1047.0	281	6	2	2	.993	2.47	105	62	.590	4	-1	20	281	-5	+2	-1	-13	-11	-6	32
2007	Oak	56	53	472.2	141	5	2	3	.986	2.78	57	28	.491	3	4	7	141	-3	-3	0	-3	-7	-4	27
2008	Atl	84	80	696.0	173	3	0	1	1.000	2.28	73	29	.397	3	2	7	173	-6	0	-4	-11	-15	-8	31
		676	647	5710.1	1564	45	17	14	.990	2.54	589	300	.509	28	25	2	1541	-9	+13	-3	-41	-31	-17	32

Gary Matthews Jr.

Year	Team	G	GS	Inn	PO	A	E	DP	Pct	Rng	Opps To Advance	Extra Bases	Pct	Kills	Runs Saved	Rank	Outs Made	Basic	Shallow	Medium	Deep	Enhanced	Runs Saved	Rank
2003	2 tms	75	65	593.2	165	3	0	0	1.000	2.55	64	36	.563	1	0	19	158	+4	-1	+2	+4	+5	2	12
2004	Tex	30	25	221.2	69	3	0	0	1.000	2.92	24	14	.583	3	1	-	69	+4	0	-1	+10	+8	4	-
2005	Tex	97	95	846.0	257	5	5	2	.981	2.79	127	72	.567	3	0	21	258	+4	-1	+10	+1	+10	6	9
2006	Tex	142	141	1227.0	331	8	7	2	.980	2.49	146	81	.555	7	2	6	333	+1	+1	+5	+1	+7	4	12
2007	LAA	135	133	1144.2	362	7	5	2	.987	2.90	114	69	.605	5	0	24	362	-13	0	0	-23	-24	-13	35
2008	LAA	31	23	221.0	66	3	4	0	.945	2.81	25	12	.480	1	2	-	66	+2	+2	+1	+2	+5	3	-
		510	482	4254.0	1250	29	21	6	.984	2.71	500	284	.568	20	5	17	1246	+2	0	+17	-6	+11	6	18

Center Fielders

Nate McLouth

		BASIC									THROWING						PLUS/MINUS						
Year	Team	G	GS	Inn	PO	A	E	DP	Pct	Rng	Opps To Advance	Extra Bases	Pct	Kills	Runs Saved	Rank	Outs Made	Basic	Shallow	Medium	Deep	Enhanced	Runs Saved	Rank
2005	Pit	21	19	166.0	36	0	0	0	1.000	1.95	14	8	.571	0	0	-	36	0	+1	0	-3	-2	-1	-
2006	Pit	42	41	345.0	84	1	1	1	.988	2.22	45	24	.533	1	0	-	84	0	-1	+3	-2	0	0	-
2007	Pit	66	53	495.1	142	2	2	1	.986	2.62	69	39	.565	2	-1	28	142	-6	-4	+2	-7	-9	-5	30
2008	Pit	149	148	1300.1	380	5	1	1	.997	2.66	144	74	.514	2	2	14	380	-20	-5	+4	-36	-37	-21	35
		278	261	2306.2	642	8	4	3	.994	2.54	272	145	.533	5	1	23	642	-26	-9	+9	-48	-48	-27	33

Lastings Milledge

		BASIC									THROWING						PLUS/MINUS						
Year	Team	G	GS	Inn	PO	A	E	DP	Pct	Rng	Opps To Advance	Extra Bases	Pct	Kills	Runs Saved	Rank	Outs Made	Basic	Shallow	Medium	Deep	Enhanced	Runs Saved	Rank
2007	NYM	14	13	120.0	41	2	1	0	.977	3.23	8	4	.500	2	1	-	41	0	-1	0	+2	+2	1	-
2008	Was	134	134	1185.2	348	1	5	0	.986	2.65	107	59	.551	0	0	20	348	-14	-8	-8	+6	-10	-6	23
		148	147	1305.2	389	3	6	0	.985	2.70	115	63	.548	2	1	-	389	-14	-9	-7	+8	-8	-5	

Corey Patterson

		BASIC									THROWING						PLUS/MINUS						
Year	Team	G	GS	Inn	PO	A	E	DP	Pct	Rng	Opps To Advance	Extra Bases	Pct	Kills	Runs Saved	Rank	Outs Made	Basic	Shallow	Medium	Deep	Enhanced	Runs Saved	Rank
2003	ChC	82	79	710.1	152	3	4	1	.975	1.96	71	48	.676	1	-3	30	150	0	0	-3	+3	0	0	21
2004	ChC	157	152	1367.2	324	8	1	5	.997	2.18	104	54	.519	6	5	4	321	+6	+4	+3	0	+7	4	9
2005	ChC	122	111	986.2	239	6	5	2	.980	2.23	88	50	.568	5	1	17	240	0	+1	+9	-5	+4	2	17
2006	Bal	133	122	1076.2	345	7	4	4	.989	2.94	111	63	.568	5	1	11	345	+13	+3	+5	+19	+27	15	2
2007	Bal	132	118	1057.1	281	8	3	1	.990	2.46	102	56	.549	3	1	18	281	-3	-6	-7	+15	+2	1	15
2008	Cin	124	82	798.0	242	3	1	1	.988	2.76	63	29	.460	3	2	14	242	+4	-1	0	+11	+10	6	8
		750	664	5996.2	1583	35	20	14	.988	2.43	539	300	.557	23	7	11	1579	+20	0	+7	+43	+50	28	3

Jay Payton

		BASIC									THROWING						PLUS/MINUS						
Year	Team	G	GS	Inn	PO	A	E	DP	Pct	Rng	Opps To Advance	Extra Bases	Pct	Kills	Runs Saved	Rank	Outs Made	Basic	Shallow	Medium	Deep	Enhanced	Runs Saved	Rank
2003	Col	8	4	45.0	8	0	0	0	1.000	1.60	3	1	.333	0	0	-	6	+1	+1	-1	-1	0	0	-
2004	SD	128	111	1027.0	334	11	4	2	.989	3.02	88	36	.409	7	10	2	318	+6	+10	-6	-3	+1	1	17
2005	2 tms	41	28	290.0	74	2	0	0	1.000	2.36	28	10	.357	1	3	-	73	+4	+2	+1	+4	+7	4	-
2006	Oak	46	44	380.2	104	1	3	0	.972	2.48	35	14	.400	1	3	-	104	-5	-5	+1	-3	-7	-4	-
2007	Bal	17	14	107.1	41	1	2	1	.955	3.52	8	4	.500	1	1	-	41	+1	0	+1	+1	+2	1	-
2008	Bal	38	36	301.0	99	6	0	0	1.000	3.14	38	15	.395	3	3	-	99	+6	+2	+2	+2	+6	3	-
		278	237	2151.0	660	21	9	3	.987	2.85	200	80	.400	13	20	5	641	+13	+11	-2	-1	+9	5	21

Juan Pierre

		BASIC									THROWING						PLUS/MINUS						
Year	Team	G	GS	Inn	PO	A	E	DP	Pct	Rng	Opps To Advance	Extra Bases	Pct	Kills	Runs Saved	Rank	Outs Made	Basic	Shallow	Medium	Deep	Enhanced	Runs Saved	Rank
2003	Fla	161	161	1433.1	402	6	3	5	.993	2.56	143	85	.594	5	-2	25	391	+10	-1	-1	+22	+20	11	3
2004	Fla	162	162	1439.0	364	3	2	1	.995	2.30	112	73	.652	1	-6	34	345	+9	+8	+2	+1	+12	7	5
2005	Fla	160	155	1383.0	332	7	4	3	.988	2.21	142	87	.613	5	-2	33	332	-5	+2	-7	-13	-19	-11	32
2006	ChC	162	162	1426.0	379	5	0	0	1.000	2.42	124	72	.581	1	-4	33	379	+7	+3	+6	+3	+12	7	7
2007	LAD	162	160	1416.2	366	4	5	0	.987	2.35	142	91	.641	2	-4	35	366	+5	0	+2	+7	+9	5	9
2008	LAD	18	14	116.1	28	1	0	1	1.000	2.24	9	5	.556	1	1	-	28	0	0	0	+1	+1	1	-
		825	814	7214.1	1871	26	14	10	.993	2.37	672	413	.615	15	-17	35	1841	+26	+12	+3	+20	+35	20	6

Scott Podsednik

		BASIC									THROWING						PLUS/MINUS						
Year	Team	G	GS	Inn	PO	A	E	DP	Pct	Rng	Opps To Advance	Extra Bases	Pct	Kills	Runs Saved	Rank	Outs Made	Basic	Shallow	Medium	Deep	Enhanced	Runs Saved	Rank
2003	Mil	123	122	1090.0	315	3	3	1	.991	2.63	99	46	.465	3	2	9	293	-6	+2	-2	-18	-18	-10	35
2004	Mil	153	152	1361.0	392	5	4	2	.990	2.63	119	66	.555	3	2	11	367	+4	+8	+2	-12	-2	-1	19
2005	CWS	7	6	55.0	14	0	0	0	1.000	2.29	2	1	.500	0	0	-	14	+1	+5	0	-4	+1	1	-
2007	CWS	3	2	20.0	2	0	0	0	1.000	.90	1	1	1.000	0	0	-	2	0	0	-1	0	-1	-1	-
2008	Col	36	21	201.1	55	1	2	0	.966	2.50	22	13	.591	1	0	-	55	0	-1	-1	+4	+3	2	-
		322	303	2727.1	778	9	9	3	.989	2.60	243	127	.523	7	4	19	731	-1	+14	-1	-30	-17	-9	27

Jeremy Reed

		BASIC									THROWING						PLUS/MINUS						
Year	Team	G	GS	Inn	PO	A	E	DP	Pct	Rng	Opps To Advance	Extra Bases	Pct	Kills	Runs Saved	Rank	Outs Made	Basic	Shallow	Medium	Deep	Enhanced	Runs Saved	Rank
2004	Sea	16	14	123.1	50	0	1	0	.980	3.65	7	4	.571	0	0	-	50	+2	+4	+3	-5	+2	1	-
2005	Sea	137	129	1149.2	383	7	3	1	.992	3.05	120	72	.600	4	-4	35	384	+11	+1	+6	+19	+26	15	3
2006	Sea	64	55	507.1	129	3	1	0	.992	2.34	52	27	.519	0	1	11	129	0	0	0	+2	+2	1	21
2008	Sea	58	52	453.2	132	1	1	0	.993	2.64	68	41	.603	0	-2	-	132	0	-3	+1	+6	+4	2	-
		275	250	2234.0	694	11	6	1	.992	2.84	247	144	.583	4	-5	33	695	+13	+2	+10	+22	+34	19	7

Center Fielders

Alex Rios

		BASIC										THROWING						PLUS/MINUS						
Year	Team	G	GS	Inn	PO	A	E	DP	Pct	Rng	Opps To Advance	Extra Bases	Pct	Kills	Runs Saved	Rank	Outs Made	Basic	Shallow	Medium	Deep	Enhanced	Runs Saved	Rank
2004	Tor	3	2	21.0	1	0	0	0	1.000	.43	3	3	1.000	0	0	-	1	-1	-1	-1	-1	-3	-2	-
2005	Tor	5	4	36.0	12	0	0	0	1.000	3.00	2	0	.000	0	0	-	12	+1	+1	+1	0	+2	1	-
2006	Tor	6	4	32.0	6	1	0	0	1.000	1.97	3	2	.667	0	0	-	6	+1	+1	0	-1	0	0	-
2007	Tor	22	18	161.2	44	1	2	0	.957	2.51	18	8	.444	0	1	-	44	-1	0	-2	0	-2	-1	-
2008	Tor	62	59	522.2	156	10	3	1	.982	2.86	46	25	.543	7	6	6	156	+4	+1	+4	+3	+8	4	10
		98	87	773.1	219	12	5	1	.979	2.69	72	38	.528	7	7	-	219	+4	+2	+2	+1	+5	2	-

Cody Ross

		BASIC										THROWING						PLUS/MINUS						
Year	Team	G	GS	Inn	PO	A	E	DP	Pct	Rng	Opps To Advance	Extra Bases	Pct	Kills	Runs Saved	Rank	Outs Made	Basic	Shallow	Medium	Deep	Enhanced	Runs Saved	Rank
2006	Fla	21	18	145.0	40	1	1	0	.976	2.54	16	8	.500	1	0	-	40	-1	-1	-1	+2	+1	1	-
2007	Fla	36	28	239.1	63	2	1	1	.985	2.44	34	21	.618	2	0	-	63	0	0	+1	-1	0	0	-
2008	Fla	109	101	866.0	254	7	0	2	1.000	2.71	76	49	.645	5	3	12	254	+3	-7	+4	+16	+13	7	5
		166	147	1250.1	357	10	2	3	.995	2.64	126	78	.619	8	3	-	357	+2	-8	+4	+18	+14	8	-

Aaron Rowand

		BASIC										THROWING						PLUS/MINUS						
Year	Team	G	GS	Inn	PO	A	E	DP	Pct	Rng	Opps To Advance	Extra Bases	Pct	Kills	Runs Saved	Rank	Outs Made	Basic	Shallow	Medium	Deep	Enhanced	Runs Saved	Rank
2003	CWS	65	39	378.2	101	6	0	0	1.000	2.54	32	18	.563	3	3	8	98	-2	-2	-2	+2	-3	-2	25
2004	CWS	126	114	1018.2	290	8	6	1	.980	2.63	100	53	.530	6	3	9	289	-2	-8	+5	+8	+5	3	12
2005	CWS	157	151	1367.2	388	8	3	1	.992	2.57	113	56	.496	1	-1	24	388	+19	-1	+11	+24	+34	19	1
2006	Phi	107	102	900.2	251	6	5	2	.981	2.57	94	54	.574	2	1	11	250	-4	+4	+4	-19	-11	-6	33
2007	Phi	161	155	1373.2	392	11	2	2	.995	2.64	153	81	.529	9	11	1	392	+1	+4	-5	-3	-4	-2	26
2008	SF	149	148	1275.1	412	6	4	0	.991	2.95	140	69	.493	4	5	9	411	-4	0	-3	-4	-8	-4	21
		765	709	6314.2	1834	40	20	6	.989	2.67	632	331	.524	25	22	4	1828	+8	-4	+9	+7	+13	8	16

Skip Schumaker

		BASIC										THROWING						PLUS/MINUS						
Year	Team	G	GS	Inn	PO	A	E	DP	Pct	Rng	Opps To Advance	Extra Bases	Pct	Kills	Runs Saved	Rank	Outs Made	Basic	Shallow	Medium	Deep	Enhanced	Runs Saved	Rank
2005	StL	4	1	12.1	4	0	0	0	1.000	2.92	0	0	-	0	0	-	4	0	0	-1	0	-1	-1	-
2006	StL	5	3	25.0	10	0	0	0	1.000	3.60	3	2	.667	0	0	-	10	0	0	-1	+2	+1	1	-
2007	StL	15	5	64.1	20	1	0	0	1.000	2.94	8	5	.625	1	1	-	20	-1	0	-2	+1	-1	-1	-
2008	StL	79	59	552.2	136	5	1	2	.993	2.30	63	38	.603	2	-2	31	136	-2	-2	-5	+3	-3	-2	18
		103	68	654.1	170	6	1	2	.994	2.42	74	45	.608	3	-1	-	170	-3	-3	-9	+7	-4	-3	-

Grady Sizemore

		BASIC										THROWING						PLUS/MINUS						
Year	Team	G	GS	Inn	PO	A	E	DP	Pct	Rng	Opps To Advance	Extra Bases	Pct	Kills	Runs Saved	Rank	Outs Made	Basic	Shallow	Medium	Deep	Enhanced	Runs Saved	Rank
2004	Cle	42	38	348.1	105	0	1	0	.991	2.71	34	14	.412	0	2	-	95	+1	-1	-3	+6	+2	1	-
2005	Cle	155	152	1370.0	373	3	3	1	.992	2.47	113	53	.469	2	1	17	373	+5	0	+5	+9	+14	8	5
2006	Cle	160	159	1379.1	409	7	3	1	.993	2.71	170	93	.547	2	-2	24	409	-1	-4	+4	+5	+4	2	16
2007	Cle	160	157	1408.2	399	4	2	2	.995	2.57	138	80	.580	2	-1	28	399	-2	-6	0	+6	0	0	17
2008	Cle	151	151	1338.0	382	2	2	1	.995	2.58	131	68	.519	2	1	17	382	-3	-8	+1	+8	+2	1	15
		668	657	5844.1	1668	16	11	5	.994	2.59	586	308	.526	8	1	23	1658	0	-19	+7	+34	+22	12	10

Ichiro Suzuki

		BASIC										THROWING						PLUS/MINUS						
Year	Team	G	GS	Inn	PO	A	E	DP	Pct	Rng	Opps To Advance	Extra Bases	Pct	Kills	Runs Saved	Rank	Outs Made	Basic	Shallow	Medium	Deep	Enhanced	Runs Saved	Rank
2006	Sea	39	38	338.0	114	1	1	0	.991	3.06	23	12	.522	1	0	-	114	+4	-1	+6	+2	+6	3	-
2007	Sea	155	155	1339.1	424	8	1	3	.998	2.90	134	69	.515	4	3	11	424	+4	+3	-5	+6	+4	2	12
2008	Sea	69	69	601.2	195	4	1	1	.995	2.98	69	32	.464	4	6	6	195	-7	-5	-5	-4	-13	-7	30
		263	262	2279.0	733	13	3	4	.996	2.95	226	113	.500	9	9	10	733	+1	-3	-4	+4	-3	-2	23

Ryan Sweeney

		BASIC										THROWING						PLUS/MINUS						
Year	Team	G	GS	Inn	PO	A	E	DP	Pct	Rng	Opps To Advance	Extra Bases	Pct	Kills	Runs Saved	Rank	Outs Made	Basic	Shallow	Medium	Deep	Enhanced	Runs Saved	Rank
2006	CWS	7	3	35.0	8	0	0	0	1.000	2.06	2	2	1.000	0	0	-	8	-1	-2	-1	0	-3	-2	-
2007	CWS	3	3	26.0	6	0	0	0	1.000	2.08	1	0	.000	0	0	-	6	+1	+1	0	+1	+2	1	-
2008	Oak	51	46	362.2	95	0	0	0	1.000	2.36	27	17	.630	0	-1	-	95	-3	-3	-2	+3	-2	-1	-
		61	52	423.2	109	0	0	0	1.000	2.32	30	19	.633	0	-1	-	109	-3	-4	-3	+4	-3	-2	-

Center Fielders

Nick Swisher

		BASIC									THROWING						PLUS/MINUS							
Year	Team	G	GS	Inn	PO	A	E	DP	Pct	Rng	Opps To Advance	Extra Bases	Pct	Kills	Runs Saved	Rank	Outs Made	Basic	Shallow	Medium	Deep	Enhanced	Runs Saved	Rank
2004	Oak	1	0	1.0	0	0	0	0	-	.00	0	0	-	0	0	-								
2006	Oak	1	0	2.0	3	0	0	0	1.000	13.50	0	0	-	0	0	-	3	+1	+1			+1	1	-
2007	Oak	59	56	481.0	139	1	2	0	.986	2.62	58	32	.552	1	1	18	139	+3	+4	+3	-3	+4	2	13
2008	CWS	70	69	535.1	138	2	4	0	.972	2.35	61	38	.623	1	-1	27	138	-4	0	-4	-6	-11	-6	28
		131	125	1019.1	280	3	6	0	.979	2.50	119	70	.588	2	0		280	0	+5	-2	-9	-6	-3	

Willy Taveras

		BASIC									THROWING						PLUS/MINUS							
Year	Team	G	GS	Inn	PO	A	E	DP	Pct	Rng	Opps To Advance	Extra Bases	Pct	Kills	Runs Saved	Rank	Outs Made	Basic	Shallow	Medium	Deep	Enhanced	Runs Saved	Rank
2004	Hou	4	0	6.0	1	0	0	0	1.000	1.50	1	1	1.000	0	0	-	1	-1			-1	-2	-1	-
2005	Hou	148	144	1254.0	332	10	3	2	.991	2.45	93	48	.516	8	6	4	332	+5	+3	+6	+6	+14	8	6
2006	Hou	138	120	1116.2	335	9	5	3	.986	2.77	84	45	.536	7	7	1	335	+9	+2	+12	+6	+20	11	3
2007	Col	86	85	714.0	212	7	4	0	.982	2.76	74	37	.500	2	4	7	212	-5	0	-7	-2	-9	-5	29
2008	Col	124	110	993.0	282	6	7	2	.976	2.61	103	53	.515	3	2	14	282	0	+3	-9	-4	-4	-2	19
		500	459	4083.2	1162	32	19	7	.984	2.63	355	184	.518	20	19	6	1162	+8	+7	+2	+11	+19	11	13

B.J. Upton

		BASIC									THROWING						PLUS/MINUS							
Year	Team	G	GS	Inn	PO	A	E	DP	Pct	Rng	Opps To Advance	Extra Bases	Pct	Kills	Runs Saved	Rank	Outs Made	Basic	Shallow	Medium	Deep	Enhanced	Runs Saved	Rank
2007	TB	78	74	664.2	204	11	2	2	.991	2.91	84	48	.571	7	4	7	204	+1	-1	+3	-1	+1	1	16
2008	TB	143	141	1248.2	378	16	7	5	.983	2.84	121	72	.595	13	8	1	378	+3	+14	-7	-17	-10	-6	22
		221	215	1913.1	582	27	9	7	.985	2.86	205	120	.585	20	12		582	+4	+13	-4	-18	-9	-5	

Shane Victorino

		BASIC									THROWING						PLUS/MINUS							
Year	Team	G	GS	Inn	PO	A	E	DP	Pct	Rng	Opps To Advance	Extra Bases	Pct	Kills	Runs Saved	Rank	Outs Made	Basic	Shallow	Medium	Deep	Enhanced	Runs Saved	Rank
2003	SD	16	11	110.0	22	1	0	0	1.000	1.88	15	5	.333	1	2	-	20	-1	-2	0	-1	-3	-2	-
2005	Phi	5	0	7.0	0	0	0	0	-	.00	0	0	-	0	0	-							0	-
2006	Phi	67	60	557.2	161	6	0	2	1.000	2.70	58	32	.552	4	3	4	161	+8	+11	-2	-2	+6	3	13
2007	Phi	4	1	16.0	3	0	0	0	1.000	1.69	4	2	.500	0	0	-	3	-1	-1	0	-1	-2	-1	-
2008	Phi	139	134	1195.1	314	7	2	2	.994	2.42	109	56	.514	6	7	2	314	+12	+14	-2	+2	+14	8	4
		231	206	1886.0	500	14	2	4	.996	2.45	186	95	.511	11	12		498	+18	+22	-4	-3	+15	8	

Vernon Wells

		BASIC									THROWING						PLUS/MINUS							
Year	Team	G	GS	Inn	PO	A	E	DP	Pct	Rng	Opps To Advance	Extra Bases	Pct	Kills	Runs Saved	Rank	Outs Made	Basic	Shallow	Medium	Deep	Enhanced	Runs Saved	Rank
2003	Tor	161	161	1416.0	383	3	4	0	.990	2.45	142	91	.641	3	-5	34	351	-6	-1	-3	-7	-12	-7	32
2004	Tor	131	130	1135.0	327	5	1	0	-	2.63	111	63	.568	4	2	11	313	+3	-13	+1	+27	+15	8	3
2005	Tor	155	153	1358.0	351	12	0	4	1.000	2.41	139	79	.568	7	4	7	351	0	-10	+6	+8	+4	2	16
2006	Tor	150	147	1290.1	332	4	4	3	.988	2.34	122	59	.484	3	6	2	332	+9	-1	+7	+8	+14	8	4
2007	Tor	148	143	1279.0	321	5	3	0	.991	2.29	102	61	.598	3	1	18	321	+5	+1	-4	+10	+7	4	10
2008	Tor	100	99	889.0	217	5	3	1	.987	2.25	77	50	.649	2	-2	31	217	-8	-2	-10	-6	-17	-10	32
		845	833	7367.1	1931	34	15	8	.992	2.40	693	403	.582	22	6	14	1885	+3	-26	-3	+40	+11	5	17

Chris Young

		BASIC									THROWING						PLUS/MINUS							
Year	Team	G	GS	Inn	PO	A	E	DP	Pct	Rng	Opps To Advance	Extra Bases	Pct	Kills	Runs Saved	Rank	Outs Made	Basic	Shallow	Medium	Deep	Enhanced	Runs Saved	Rank
2006	Ari	24	15	149.1	50	1	0	0	1.000	3.07	16	11	.688	0	-1	-	50	+3	+1	+1	+3	+5	3	-
2007	Ari	146	144	1263.0	354	6	6	2	.984	2.57	123	70	.569	2	0	24	354	-1	+1	+6	-10	-3	-2	23
2008	Ari	159	157	1390.0	393	5	3	2	.993	2.58	126	71	.563	2	-3	34	393	+6	-5	+10	+16	+21	12	3
		329	316	2802.1	797	12	9	4	.989	2.60	265	152	.574	4	-4	31	797	+8	-3	+17	+9	+23	13	9

Right Fielders

Bobby Abreu

Year	Team	G	GS	Inn	PO	A	E	DP	Pct	Rng	Opps To Advance	Extra Bases	Pct	Kills	Runs Saved	Rank	Outs Made	Basic	Shallow	Medium	Deep	Enhanced	Runs Saved	Rank
					BASIC								THROWING							PLUS/MINUS				
2003	Phi	158	156	1373.1	304	6	6	0	.981	2.03	122	46	.377	5	5	5	302	+5	-1	+2	+3	+5	3	8
2004	Phi	158	157	1394.2	311	13	6	4	.982	2.09	127	65	.512	9	2	13	295	0	+8	-4	-7	-3	-2	20
2005	Phi	158	158	1364.0	266	7	4	0	.986	1.80	117	55	.470	4	4	8	267	-5	-1	0	-13	-14	-8	32
2006	2 tms	154	149	1293.0	291	10	3	0	.990	2.10	143	76	.531	6	1	17	293	-7	-1	-4	-9	-14	-8	32
2007	NYY	157	150	1333.0	313	6	4	1	.988	2.15	131	54	.412	2	1	13	313	-7	-5	-4	-5	-14	-8	32
2008	NYY	150	148	1310.0	270	10	2	3	.993	1.92	145	65	.448	9	7	4	271	-14	-8	-10	-2	-20	-12	34
		935	918	8068.0	1755	52	25	8	.986	2.02	785	361	.460	33	20	6	1741	-28	-8	-19	-33	-60	-35	33

Wladimir Balentien

Year	Team	G	GS	Inn	PO	A	E	DP	Pct	Rng	Opps To Advance	Extra Bases	Pct	Kills	Runs Saved	Rank	Outs Made	Basic	Shallow	Medium	Deep	Enhanced	Runs Saved	Rank
2007	Sea	2	0	4.0	0	0	0	0	-	.00	1	0	.000	0	0	-	0	-1	-1			-1	-1	-
2008	Sea	35	32	293.0	76	5	2	0	.976	2.49	37	15	.405	2	3	-	76	+2	+4	0	-4	-1	-1	-
		37	32	297.0	76	5	2	0	.976	2.45	38	15	.395	2	3	-	76	+1	+3	0	-4	-2	-2	-

Milton Bradley

Year	Team	G	GS	Inn	PO	A	E	DP	Pct	Rng	Opps To Advance	Extra Bases	Pct	Kills	Runs Saved	Rank	Outs Made	Basic	Shallow	Medium	Deep	Enhanced	Runs Saved	Rank
2004	LA	31	31	267.2	66	5	4	0	.947	2.39	33	20	.606	1	-1	-	61	+6	+3	+5	0	+9	5	-
2006	Oak	94	94	802.2	191	4	4	0	.980	2.19	84	41	.488	2	1	17	191	-5	-3	-3	-1	-7	-4	25
2007	2 tms	4	3	29.0	6	0	0	0	1.000	1.86	0	0	-	0	0	-	6	+1	+1	0		+1	1	-
2008	Tex	19	19	157.1	42	4	3	0	.939	2.63	24	6	.250	4	5	-	42	+1	-1	0	+2	+1	1	-
		148	147	1256.2	305	13	11	3	.967	2.28	141	67	.475	7	5	-	300	+3	0	+3	+1	+4	3	-

Emil Brown

Year	Team	G	GS	Inn	PO	A	E	DP	Pct	Rng	Opps To Advance	Extra Bases	Pct	Kills	Runs Saved	Rank	Outs Made	Basic	Shallow	Medium	Deep	Enhanced	Runs Saved	Rank
2005	KC	129	126	1097.1	243	7	11	0	.958	2.05	145	82	.566	1	-8	35	243	-7	-7	-1	-4	-12	-7	29
2006	KC	54	46	414.0	110	3	2	0	.983	2.46	38	25	.658	0	-3	32	110	-1	-2	-1	+2	-1	-1	20
2007	KC	21	17	150.2	42	1	0	0	1.000	2.57	13	6	.462	0	0	-	42	0	-1	0	-1	-2	-1	-
2008	Oak	55	55	433.1	111	4	3	2	.975	2.39	42	18	.429	2	1	-	112	0	+2	+1	-2	+1	1	-
		259	244	2095.1	506	15	16	2	.970	2.24	238	131	.550	3	-10	35	507	-8	-8	-1	-4	-14	-8	27

Jay Bruce

Year	Team	G	GS	Inn	PO	A	E	DP	Pct	Rng	Opps To Advance	Extra Bases	Pct	Kills	Runs Saved	Rank	Outs Made	Basic	Shallow	Medium	Deep	Enhanced	Runs Saved	Rank
2008	Cin	78	64	590.0	143	5	9	3	.943	2.26	57	27	.474	5	3	15	143	+1	+3	+4	-11	-4	-2	24

Travis Buck

Year	Team	G	GS	Inn	PO	A	E	DP	Pct	Rng	Opps To Advance	Extra Bases	Pct	Kills	Runs Saved	Rank	Outs Made	Basic	Shallow	Medium	Deep	Enhanced	Runs Saved	Rank
2007	Oak	65	56	509.1	110	2	0	0	1.000	1.98	37	25	.676	1	-2	28	110	+2	+1	0	+2	+3	2	17
2008	Oak	34	34	287.0	73	2	0	0	1.000	2.35	24	13	.542	2	0	-	74	+1	-2	0	+5	+3	2	-
		99	90	796.1	183	4	0	0	1.000	2.11	61	38	.623	3	-2	-	184	+3	-2	0	+7	+6	4	-

Marlon Byrd

Year	Team	G	GS	Inn	PO	A	E	DP	Pct	Rng	Opps To Advance	Extra Bases	Pct	Kills	Runs Saved	Rank	Outs Made	Basic	Shallow	Medium	Deep	Enhanced	Runs Saved	Rank
2005	Was	4	3	34.0	10	0	0	0	1.000	2.65	2	1	.500	0	0	-	10	+1	+1	0	+1	+2	1	-
2006	Was	18	7	83.0	23	0	1	0	.958	2.49	5	2	.400	0	0	-	23	-1	-1	0	-2	-2	-1	-
2007	Tex	40	36	304.1	78	5	1	4	.988	2.45	44	16	.364	4	5	-	78	+1	-1	-1	+2	0	0	-
2008	Tex	39	33	279.0	71	3	3	0	.961	2.39	45	23	.511	2	0	-	71	+4	+6	-2	+2	+6	3	-
		101	79	700.1	182	8	5	4	.974	2.44	96	42	.438	6	5	-	182	+5	+5	-2	+3	+6	3	-

Endy Chavez

Year	Team	G	GS	Inn	PO	A	E	DP	Pct	Rng	Opps To Advance	Extra Bases	Pct	Kills	Runs Saved	Rank	Outs Made	Basic	Shallow	Medium	Deep	Enhanced	Runs Saved	Rank
2005	Phi	5	0	10.0	2	0	0	0	1.000	1.80	0	0	-	0	0	-	2	-1	-1	0	0	-1	-1	-
2006	NYM	45	32	310.2	71	3	0	1	1.000	2.14	23	13	.565	1	0	-	71	-1	+3	0	-7	-4	-2	-
2007	NYM	24	8	100.0	31	0	0	0	1.000	2.79	8	6	.750	0	-1	-	31	+3	+1	0	+4	+5	3	-
2008	NYM	60	41	400.0	109	4	1	2	.991	2.54	42	19	.452	3	2	-	110	+7	+4	0	+7	+11	6	-
		134	81	820.2	213	7	1	3	.995	2.41	73	38	.521	4	1	-	214	+8	+7	0	+4	+11	6	-

Right Fielders

Shin-Soo Choo

		BASIC									THROWING						PLUS/MINUS							
Year	Team	G	GS	Inn	PO	A	E	DP	Pct	Rng	Opps To Advance	Extra Bases	Pct	Kills	Runs Saved	Rank	Outs Made	Basic	Shallow	Medium	Deep	Enhanced	Runs Saved	Rank
2006	Cle	30	29	256.2	67	2	1	1	.986	2.42	22	7	.318	1	2	-	67	+3	+2	-1	+6	+7	4	-
2007	Cle	2	1	11.0	0	0	0	0	-	.00	0	0	-	0	0	-	0	0				0	0	-
2008	Cle	51	45	398.1	88	1	1	0	.989	2.01	44	22	.500	1	-1	-	89	0	-7	0	+7	0	0	-
		83	75	666.0	155	3	2	1	.988	2.14	66	29	.439	2	1	-	156	+3	-5	-1	+13	+7	4	-

Ryan Church

		BASIC									THROWING						PLUS/MINUS							
Year	Team	G	GS	Inn	PO	A	E	DP	Pct	Rng	Opps To Advance	Extra Bases	Pct	Kills	Runs Saved	Rank	Outs Made	Basic	Shallow	Medium	Deep	Enhanced	Runs Saved	Rank
2004	Mon	6	3	38.0	12	1	0	0	1.000	3.08	5	3	.600	1	0	-	12	+1	+1	+1	+1	+2	1	-
2005	Was	21	14	135.2	43	0	0	0	1.000	2.85	12	5	.417	0	-2	-	43	-1	0	-2	+1	-1	-1	-
2006	Was	14	10	97.0	20	0	0	0	1.000	1.86	6	4	.667	0	-1	-	20	+1	0	-1	+2	+1	1	-
2008	NYM	83	81	724.0	180	7	1	1	.995	2.32	83	40	.482	4	0	24	180	+3	-1	+4	+5	+9	5	9
		124	108	994.2	255	8	1	1	.996	2.38	106	52	.491	5	-1	-	255	+4	-1	+2	+9	+11	6	-

Jose Cruz

		BASIC									THROWING						PLUS/MINUS							
Year	Team	G	GS	Inn	PO	A	E	DP	Pct	Rng	Opps To Advance	Extra Bases	Pct	Kills	Runs Saved	Rank	Outs Made	Basic	Shallow	Medium	Deep	Enhanced	Runs Saved	Rank
2003	SF	157	151	1332.2	336	18	2	7	.994	2.39	130	53	.408	13	11	2	307	+4	+5	+6	-2	+9	5	6
2004	TB	151	147	1301.2	312	10	10	0	.970	2.23	142	61	.430	8	6	6	307	-6	+4	-4	-10	-10	-6	29
2005	3 tms	55	51	433.0	110	4	5	0	.958	2.37	45	22	.489	4	1	20	110	+5	+4	+1	+4	+9	5	8
2006	LAD	24	14	144.1	37	0	0	0	1.000	2.31	14	4	.286	0	0	-	37	+1	+1	-1	+2	+2	1	-
2007	SD	23	20	178.1	54	1	0	1	1.000	2.78	12	5	.417	1	0	-	54	+1	+2	-2	+1	+1	1	-
2008	Hou	3	1	11.0	4	0	0	0	1.000	3.27	0	0	-	0	0	-	4	0	-1	0	+3	+2	1	-
		413	384	3401.0	853	33	17	8	.981	2.34	343	145	.423	26	18	7	819	+5	+15	0	-2	+13	7	12

Nelson Cruz

		BASIC									THROWING						PLUS/MINUS							
Year	Team	G	GS	Inn	PO	A	E	DP	Pct	Rng	Opps To Advance	Extra Bases	Pct	Kills	Runs Saved	Rank	Outs Made	Basic	Shallow	Medium	Deep	Enhanced	Runs Saved	Rank
2005	Mil	6	1	16.0	4	0	0	0	1.000	2.25	3	1	.333	0	0	-	4	0	0	0	+1	0	0	-
2006	Tex	38	35	307.1	69	4	0	1	1.000	2.14	33	14	.424	3	3	-	69	+2	-1	0	+5	+4	2	-
2007	Tex	82	65	604.1	148	5	5	1	.968	2.28	73	38	.521	1	0	19	148	+3	-3	+3	+6	+7	4	10
2008	Tex	31	31	274.0	72	1	2	1	.973	2.40	42	17	.405	1	0	-	72	+2	+4	+1	-2	+4	2	-
		157	132	1201.2	293	10	7	3	.977	2.27	151	70	.464	5	3	-	293	+7	0	+5	+10	+15	8	-

Michael Cuddyer

		BASIC									THROWING						PLUS/MINUS							
Year	Team	G	GS	Inn	PO	A	E	DP	Pct	Rng	Opps To Advance	Extra Bases	Pct	Kills	Runs Saved	Rank	Outs Made	Basic	Shallow	Medium	Deep	Enhanced	Runs Saved	Rank
2003	Min	17	16	139.0	24	1	0	0	1.000	1.62	7	5	.714	0	-1	-	21	-1	0	+1	-2	-1	-1	-
2004	Min	8	5	49.0	13	0	0	0	1.000	2.39	4	2	.500	0	0	-	10	0	0	0	0	-1	-1	-
2005	Min	20	18	159.0	35	0	0	0	1.000	1.98	7	3	.429	0	0	-	35	+3	+1	0	+4	+6	3	-
2006	Min	142	137	1227.1	244	11	5	2	.981	1.87	113	45	.398	7	7	4	245	-13	+4	+2	-34	-28	-16	35
2007	Min	140	140	1224.1	256	19	4	2	.986	2.02	129	50	.388	12	13	1	256	-12	+1	-4	-19	-22	-13	34
2008	Min	58	57	501.2	123	6	1	4	.992	2.31	51	21	.412	5	5	8	123	-4	+2	-3	-7	-8	-5	28
		385	373	3300.1	695	37	10	8	.987	2.00	311	126	.405	24	24	3	690	-27	+7	-5	-56	-54	-33	32

Mark DeRosa

		BASIC									THROWING						PLUS/MINUS							
Year	Team	G	GS	Inn	PO	A	E	DP	Pct	Rng	Opps To Advance	Extra Bases	Pct	Kills	Runs Saved	Rank	Outs Made	Basic	Shallow	Medium	Deep	Enhanced	Runs Saved	Rank
2005	Tex	25	21	185.0	46	1	0	0	1.000	2.29	17	6	.353	1	1	-	46	+5	+4	0	0	+5	3	-
2006	Tex	60	59	512.0	125	4	1	1	.992	2.27	60	25	.417	2	2	11	125	+6		+3	+8	+10	6	9
2007	ChC	22	13	138.2	28	1	0	0	1.000	1.88	10	3	.300	1	1	-	28	0	0	+1	-3	-2	-1	-
2008	ChC	38	32	266.2	72	0	0	0	1.000	2.43	29	12	.414	0	0	-	72	0	-4	+1	0	-3	-2	-
		145	125	1102.1	271	6	1	1	.996	2.26	116	46	.397	4	4	-	271	+11	0	+5	+5	+10	6	-

J.D. Drew

		BASIC									THROWING						PLUS/MINUS							
Year	Team	G	GS	Inn	PO	A	E	DP	Pct	Rng	Opps To Advance	Extra Bases	Pct	Kills	Runs Saved	Rank	Outs Made	Basic	Shallow	Medium	Deep	Enhanced	Runs Saved	Rank
2003	StL	53	47	391.0	101	5	1	1	.991	2.44	35	22	.629	3	0	-	90	+1	-1	+5	-2	+2	1	-
2004	Atl	138	137	1193.0	277	11	3	0	.990	2.17	123	61	.496	5	1	17	272	+10	+6	+8	+9	+24	14	3
2005	LAD	44	44	382.0	83	3	2	0	.977	2.03	53	24	.453	2	1	-	83	-1	-6	+3	+6	+3	2	-
2006	LAD	135	131	1118.0	284	3	5	0	.983	2.31	104	48	.462	2	1	17	284	+6	-4	+1	+15	+12	7	6
2007	Bos	133	123	1062.0	212	3	5	1	.977	1.82	84	43	.512	2	0	19	212	0	-5	+5	+5	+5	3	13
2008	Bos	106	105	886.0	184	6	4	1	.979	1.93	87	52	.598	4	-1	28	184	-5	0	-7	0	-7	-4	26
		609	587	5032.0	1141	31	20	3	.983	2.10	486	250	.514	18	2	23	1125	+11	-10	+15	+33	+39	23	7

Right Fielders

Elijah Dukes

Year	Team	G	GS	Inn	PO	A	E	DP	Pct	Rng	Opps To Advance	Extra Bases	Pct	Kills	Runs Saved	Rank	Outs Made	Basic	Shallow	Medium	Deep	Enhanced	Runs Saved	Rank
2007	TB	1	0	1.1	0	0	0	0	-	.00	0	0	-	0	0	-	0	0				0	0	-
2008	Was	69	66	602.2	137	9	5	1	.967	2.18	70	42	.600	4	0	24	137	+4	0	0	+11	+11	6	8
		70	66	604.0	137	9	5	1	.967	2.18	70	42	.600	4	0	-	137	+4	0	0	+11	+11	6	-

Jermaine Dye

Year	Team	G	GS	Inn	PO	A	E	DP	Pct	Rng	Opps To Advance	Extra Bases	Pct	Kills	Runs Saved	Rank	Outs Made	Basic	Shallow	Medium	Deep	Enhanced	Runs Saved	Rank
2003	Oak	60	59	500.1	102	1	0	0	1.000	1.85	53	31	.585	0	-3	32	91	+1	+2	-1	-1	+1	1	16
2004	Oak	134	132	1178.0	257	3	2	2	.992	1.99	118	65	.551	3	-3	29	234	+5	0	+2	0	+2	1	13
2005	CWS	140	137	1235.1	259	9	8	2	.971	1.95	123	53	.431	5	3	13	259	-7	-9	+3	0	-6	-3	24
2006	CWS	146	145	1245.0	305	4	6	2	.981	2.23	131	62	.473	2	0	22	305	-6	0	+1	-15	-14	-8	31
2007	CWS	135	135	1156.0	284	9	3	3	.990	2.28	137	77	.562	5	-2	28	284	-16	-8	-6	-27	-41	-24	35
2008	CWS	151	151	1312.2	266	5	1	0	.996	1.86	124	63	.508	3	-2	30	266	-5	+3	-9	-6	-12	-7	31
		766	759	6627.1	1473	31	20	9	.987	2.04	686	351	.512	18	-7	34	1439	-28	-11	-9	-49	-70	-40	34

Jacoby Ellsbury

Year	Team	G	GS	Inn	PO	A	E	DP	Pct	Rng	Opps To Advance	Extra Bases	Pct	Kills	Runs Saved	Rank	Outs Made	Basic	Shallow	Medium	Deep	Enhanced	Runs Saved	Rank
2007	Bos	1	1	6.0	0	0	0	0	-	.00	1	0	.000	0	0	-	0	0				0	0	-
2008	Bos	36	30	281.0	72	0	0	0	1.000	2.31	23	10	.435	0	0	-	72	+4	+1	+4	+2	+7	4	-
		37	31	287.0	72	0	0	0	1.000	2.26	24	10	.417	0	0	-	72	+4	+1	+4	+2	+7	4	-

Andre Ethier

Year	Team	G	GS	Inn	PO	A	E	DP	Pct	Rng	Opps To Advance	Extra Bases	Pct	Kills	Runs Saved	Rank	Outs Made	Basic	Shallow	Medium	Deep	Enhanced	Runs Saved	Rank
2007	LAD	102	91	779.2	176	8	4	1	.979	2.12	90	55	.611	6	-2	28	177	+7	-1	+5	+12	+16	9	3
2008	LAD	109	102	881.0	171	8	0	0	1.000	1.83	90	46	.511	3	0	24	171	-13	-9	-4	-5	-19	-11	33
		211	193	1660.2	347	16	4	1	.989	1.97	180	101	.561	9	-2	29	348	-6	-10	+1	+7	-3	-2	23

Jeff Francoeur

Year	Team	G	GS	Inn	PO	A	E	DP	Pct	Rng	Opps To Advance	Extra Bases	Pct	Kills	Runs Saved	Rank	Outs Made	Basic	Shallow	Medium	Deep	Enhanced	Runs Saved	Rank
2005	Atl	67	65	589.0	131	13	5	3	.966	2.20	65	28	.431	10	9	1	131	+6	0	+1	+9	+11	6	5
2006	Atl	162	162	1421.2	316	13	9	4	.973	2.08	169	77	.456	9	7	4	317	+3	+4	+4	-5	+3	2	13
2007	Atl	162	162	1440.2	327	19	5	2	.986	2.16	129	53	.411	11	13	1	328	+7	+5	+6	-2	+10	6	6
2008	Atl	152	151	1328.2	282	14	4	2	.987	2.01	115	50	.435	6	5	8	284	-3	-3	+4	-13	-12	-7	30
		543	540	4780.0	1056	59	23	11	.980	2.10	478	208	.435	36	34	2	1060	+13	+7	+16	-10	+12	7	13

Kosuke Fukudome

Year	Team	G	GS	Inn	PO	A	E	DP	Pct	Rng	Opps To Advance	Extra Bases	Pct	Kills	Runs Saved	Rank	Outs Made	Basic	Shallow	Medium	Deep	Enhanced	Runs Saved	Rank
2008	ChC	137	121	1103.2	245	6	5	0	.980	2.05	104	49	.471	4	2	20	246	+2	+8	+2	-8	+1	1	14

Jody Gerut

Year	Team	G	GS	Inn	PO	A	E	DP	Pct	Rng	Opps To Advance	Extra Bases	Pct	Kills	Runs Saved	Rank	Outs Made	Basic	Shallow	Medium	Deep	Enhanced	Runs Saved	Rank
2003	Cle	63	61	542.2	125	6	1	2	.992	2.17	53	28	.528	5	3	8	108	+1	0	+2	+1	+3	2	13
2004	Cle	118	109	1009.1	242	7	4	2	.984	2.22	111	58	.523	6	1	17	226	-9	-1	-9	-5	-14	-8	33
2005	3 tms	26	25	217.1	40	0	0	0	1.000	1.66	23	12	.522	0	-1	-	40	-2	0	-4	0	-4	-2	-
2008	SD	9	7	63.0	17	0	0	0	1.000	2.43	6	4	.667	0	0	-	17	+1	0	+1	+1	+2	1	-
		216	202	1832.1	424	13	5	4	.989	2.15	193	102	.528	11	3	22	391	-9	-1	-9	-3	-13	-7	26

Brian Giles

Year	Team	G	GS	Inn	PO	A	E	DP	Pct	Rng	Opps To Advance	Extra Bases	Pct	Kills	Runs Saved	Rank	Outs Made	Basic	Shallow	Medium	Deep	Enhanced	Runs Saved	Rank
2004	SD	159	158	1383.0	322	8	7	3	.979	2.15	153	82	.536	5	-3	29	314	-3	-10	+6	+6	+2	1	12
2005	SD	143	140	1220.0	295	6	4	1	.987	2.22	138	70	.507	4	2	17	295	-1	-2	+4	-5	-2	-1	19
2006	SD	158	158	1398.2	299	7	7	2	.978	1.97	134	64	.478	4	3	10	298	+6	-2	-7	+24	+16	9	2
2007	SD	120	119	1062.2	216	2	5	1	.978	1.85	102	53	.520	2	-3	34	216	+1	-3	-4	+8	+2	1	18
2008	SD	144	142	1263.0	276	3	7	1	.976	1.99	126	71	.563	2	-5	35	276	+9	-1	+7	+16	+22	13	2
		724	717	6327.1	1408	26	30	8	.980	2.04	653	340	.521	17	-6	33	1399	+12	-17	+7	+50	+40	23	5

Right Fielders

Ken Griffey Jr.

		BASIC									THROWING						PLUS/MINUS							
Year	Team	G	GS	Inn	PO	A	E	DP	Pct	Rng	Opps To Advance	Extra Bases	Pct	Kills	Runs Saved	Rank	Outs Made	Basic	Shallow	Medium	Deep	Enhanced	Runs Saved	Rank
2004	Cin	1	1	4.0	0	0	0	0	-	.00	1	0	.000	0	0	-						0	0	-
2007	Cin	133	131	1163.0	291	5	8	2	.974	2.29	116	67	.578	3	-3	34	291	-4	+4	-8	-4	-8	-5	28
2008	2 tms	91	90	763.0	157	7	5	0	.970	1.93	83	38	.458	2	3	15	157	-10	-5	-5	-6	-16	-9	32
		225	222	1930.0	448	12	13	2	.973	2.15	200	105	.525	5	0	28	448	-14	-1	-13	-10	-24	-14	29

Gabe Gross

		BASIC									THROWING						PLUS/MINUS							
Year	Team	G	GS	Inn	PO	A	E	DP	Pct	Rng	Opps To Advance	Extra Bases	Pct	Kills	Runs Saved	Rank	Outs Made	Basic	Shallow	Medium	Deep	Enhanced	Runs Saved	Rank
2005	Tor	20	16	143.1	32	1	1	0	.971	2.07	14	10	.714	0	-1	-	32	0	0	+2	0	+2	1	-
2006	Mil	8	3	38.1	13	0	0	0	1.000	3.05	3	1	.333	0	0	-	13	+1	0	+2	0	+2	1	-
2007	Mil	45	39	288.2	70	2	2	0	.973	2.24	25	7	.280	1	2	-	70	-2	0	0	-1	-2	-1	-
2008	2 tms	121	75	768.1	186	6	1	0	.995	2.25	72	27	.375	3	4	14	186	+1	-5	+11	-5	+1	0	17
		194	133	1238.2	301	9	4	0	.987	2.25	114	45	.395	4	5	-	301	0	-5	+14	-6	+3	1	-

Vladimir Guerrero

		BASIC									THROWING						PLUS/MINUS							
Year	Team	G	GS	Inn	PO	A	E	DP	Pct	Rng	Opps To Advance	Extra Bases	Pct	Kills	Runs Saved	Rank	Outs Made	Basic	Shallow	Medium	Deep	Enhanced	Runs Saved	Rank
2003	Mon	112	112	949.2	217	10	7	0	.970	2.15	94	52	.553	7	1	14	170	-5	-5	-3	+1	-7	-4	33
2004	Ana	143	143	1234.0	308	13	9	2	.973	2.34	122	60	.492	8	3	11	299	-14	-15	-9	+10	-15	-9	34
2005	LAA	120	120	1040.0	242	8	3	2	.988	2.16	79	32	.405	6	4	8	245	+6	+1	+3	+6	+10	6	7
2006	LAA	126	126	1090.0	251	7	11	3	.959	2.13	113	48	.425	7	6	6	253	-6	0	+4	-14	-10	-6	27
2007	LAA	108	108	930.2	208	5	9	3	.959	2.06	92	39	.424	3	3	10	208	-6	-5	+2	-3	-6	-3	25
2008	LAA	99	99	839.0	180	8	4	2	.979	2.02	70	39	.557	3	-2	30	180	-4	-3	+1	-1	-4	-2	23
		708	708	6083.1	1406	51	43	11	.971	2.16	570	270	.474	34	15	10	1355	-29	-27	-3	-1	-32	-18	30

Jose Guillen

		BASIC									THROWING						PLUS/MINUS							
Year	Team	G	GS	Inn	PO	A	E	DP	Pct	Rng	Opps To Advance	Extra Bases	Pct	Kills	Runs Saved	Rank	Outs Made	Basic	Shallow	Medium	Deep	Enhanced	Runs Saved	Rank
2003	2 tms	96	92	802.2	183	9	8	1	.960	2.15	68	36	.529	7	3	8	161	+7	+2	+3	+7	+11	7	4
2004	Ana	4	1	22.0	4	0	0	0	1.000	1.64	1	1	1.000	0	0	-	4	0	-1	+1	-1	0	0	-
2005	Was	140	135	1189.2	299	10	7	4	.978	2.34	134	65	.485	7	5	5	299	+4	+3	+6	+5	+13	8	3
2006	Was	68	64	537.2	163	3	2	0	.988	2.78	51	31	.608	3	-1	26	164	-1	+4	0	-5	-1	-1	19
2007	Sea	150	150	1273.2	268	9	8	3	.972	1.96	170	71	.418	6	7	6	268	-3	+1	+1	-9	-7	-4	26
2008	KC	67	65	539.1	121	7	3	1	.977	2.14	73	38	.521	4	2	20	121	-9	-10	+2	-3	-11	-6	29
		525	507	4365.0	1038	38	28	9	.975	2.22	497	242	.487	27	16	8	1017	-2	-2	+13	-6	+5	4	20

Franklin Gutierrez

		BASIC									THROWING						PLUS/MINUS							
Year	Team	G	GS	Inn	PO	A	E	DP	Pct	Rng	Opps To Advance	Extra Bases	Pct	Kills	Runs Saved	Rank	Outs Made	Basic	Shallow	Medium	Deep	Enhanced	Runs Saved	Rank
2006	Cle	28	24	212.0	50	1	2	0	.962	2.17	33	18	.545	1	-1	-	50	+3	-1	+4	+3	+6	3	-
2007	Cle	88	59	578.2	136	3	1	1	.993	2.16	63	36	.571	1	-2	28	136	+8	-1	+3	+19	+20	12	1
2008	Cle	97	85	763.2	224	4	2	0	.991	2.69	91	35	.385	3	5	8	224	+16	+6	+6	+17	+29	17	1
		213	168	1554.1	410	8	5	1	.988	2.42	187	89	.476	5	2	23	410	+27	+3	+13	+39	+55	32	3

Josh Hamilton

		BASIC									THROWING						PLUS/MINUS							
Year	Team	G	GS	Inn	PO	A	E	DP	Pct	Rng	Opps To Advance	Extra Bases	Pct	Kills	Runs Saved	Rank	Outs Made	Basic	Shallow	Medium	Deep	Enhanced	Runs Saved	Rank
2007	Cin	10	9	81.0	27	1	0	0	1.000	3.11	10	3	.300	1	2	-	27	0	0	+1	-1	0	0	-
2008	Tex	34	33	289.0	77	4	1	2	.988	2.52	37	16	.432	2	1	-	77	-1	+2	-3	+2	+1	1	-
		44	42	370.0	104	5	1	2	.991	2.65	47	19	.404	3	3	-	104	-1	+2	-2	0	+1	1	-

Corey Hart

		BASIC									THROWING						PLUS/MINUS							
Year	Team	G	GS	Inn	PO	A	E	DP	Pct	Rng	Opps To Advance	Extra Bases	Pct	Kills	Runs Saved	Rank	Outs Made	Basic	Shallow	Medium	Deep	Enhanced	Runs Saved	Rank
2005	Mil	3	3	27.0	8	1	1	0	.900	3.00	4	2	.500	1	0	-	8	0	0	-1	+1	0	0	-
2006	Mil	37	32	266.0	63	2	0	0	1.000	2.20	30	21	.700	0	-2	-	63	+1	0	+3	-1	+2	1	-
2007	Mil	113	94	864.1	253	3	1	0	.996	2.67	105	52	.495	0	-2	28	253	+6	-1	+1	+10	+10	6	7
2008	Mil	156	156	1376.2	302	8	5	2	.984	2.03	122	64	.525	5	0	24	304	0	+7	-3	-3	0	0	18
		309	285	2534.0	626	14	7	2	.989	2.27	261	139	.533	6	-4	31	628	+7	+5	0	+8	+12	7	14

Right Fielders

Brad Hawpe

	BASIC										THROWING						PLUS/MINUS							
Year	Team	G	GS	Inn	PO	A	E	DP	Pct	Rng	Opps To Advance	Extra Bases	Pct	Kills	Runs Saved	Rank	Outs Made	Basic	Shallow	Medium	Deep	Enhanced	Runs Saved	Rank
2004	Col	32	29	233.0	52	1	1	1	.981	2.05	29	17	.586	1	0	-	48	-1	+2	-3	-3	-3	-2	-
2005	Col	89	79	693.0	148	10	3	2	.981	2.05	103	53	.515	6	3	13	148	-2	0	+8	-12	-4	-2	22
2006	Col	145	134	1197.2	280	16	4	3	.987	2.22	142	55	.387	12	12	1	280	-6	+3	-5	-10	-11	-6	30
2007	Col	142	137	1236.2	246	6	6	1	.977	1.83	114	60	.526	4	-1	22	247	-12	-5	-3	-10	-18	-10	33
2008	Col	133	132	1172.0	186	9	9	0	.956	1.50	150	78	.520	7	-1	28	188	-23	-12	-11	-14	-37	-21	35
		541	511	4532.1	912	42	23	7	.976	1.89	538	263	.489	30	13	11	911	-44	-12	-13	-48	-73	-41	35

Jeremy Hermida

	BASIC										THROWING						PLUS/MINUS							
Year	Team	G	GS	Inn	PO	A	E	DP	Pct	Rng	Opps To Advance	Extra Bases	Pct	Kills	Runs Saved	Rank	Outs Made	Basic	Shallow	Medium	Deep	Enhanced	Runs Saved	Rank
2005	Fla	10	6	58.2	17	0	0	0	1.000	2.61	5	3	.600	0	0	-	17	+1	+1	+1	+1	+3	2	-
2006	Fla	85	78	683.2	157	1	8	0	.952	2.08	73	34	.466	1	0	22	157	-3	-6	+2	+2	-3	-2	21
2007	Fla	116	114	985.2	247	7	9	1	.966	2.32	110	56	.509	3	1	13	247	+1	+2	-3	+8	+7	4	9
2008	Fla	132	124	1092.1	266	4	5	0	.982	2.22	122	65	.533	2	-3	32	266	-4	-9	+2	+9	+2	1	13
		343	322	2820.1	687	12	22	1	.969	2.23	310	158	.510	6	-2	29	687	-5	-13	+2	+20	+9	5	17

Eric Hinske

	BASIC										THROWING						PLUS/MINUS							
Year	Team	G	GS	Inn	PO	A	E	DP	Pct	Rng	Opps To Advance	Extra Bases	Pct	Kills	Runs Saved	Rank	Outs Made	Basic	Shallow	Medium	Deep	Enhanced	Runs Saved	Rank
2006	2 tms	40	35	275.0	51	3	0	1	1.000	1.77	33	15	.455	0	0	-	51	0	-1	+2	+1	+1	1	-
2007	Bos	12	9	82.1	16	0	0	0	1.000	1.75	8	3	.375	0	0	-	16	0	-2	-1	+2	0	0	-
2008	TB	49	47	339.1	88	2	1	0	.989	2.39	29	16	.552	1	0	-	88	0	-1	-1	+2	0	0	-
		101	91	696.2	155	5	1	1	.994	2.07	70	34	.486	1	0	-	155	0	-4	+1	+4	+1	1	-

Geoff Jenkins

	BASIC										THROWING						PLUS/MINUS							
Year	Team	G	GS	Inn	PO	A	E	DP	Pct	Rng	Opps To Advance	Extra Bases	Pct	Kills	Runs Saved	Rank	Outs Made	Basic	Shallow	Medium	Deep	Enhanced	Runs Saved	Rank
2005	Mil	144	144	1241.1	307	10	5	7	.984	2.30	117	59	.504	10	5	5	307	+6	+1	+5	+7	+13	8	2
2006	Mil	133	126	1101.0	247	6	6	2	.977	2.07	93	45	.484	4	0	22	247	+3	0	0	+6	+6	3	11
2008	Phi	90	72	642.0	140	7	5	1	.967	2.06	54	22	.407	5	6	5	141	0	+2	+1	-5	-2	-1	21
		367	342	2984.1	694	23	16	10	.978	2.16	264	126	.477	19	11	13	695	+9	+2	+7	+8	+17	10	10

Jacque Jones

	BASIC										THROWING						PLUS/MINUS							
Year	Team	G	GS	Inn	PO	A	E	DP	Pct	Rng	Opps To Advance	Extra Bases	Pct	Kills	Runs Saved	Rank	Outs Made	Basic	Shallow	Medium	Deep	Enhanced	Runs Saved	Rank
2003	Min	11	10	81.0	23	0	0	0	1.000	2.56	7	4	.571	0	0	-	18	-1	0	0	-1	-1	-1	-
2004	Min	141	138	1237.0	314	5	2	2	.994	2.32	131	59	.450	1	2	13	285	-9	-1	+4	-16	-13	-8	31
2005	Min	123	121	1080.1	261	9	4	2	.985	2.25	92	39	.424	7	4	8	262	-4	+1	0	-9	-8	-5	27
2006	ChC	143	139	1205.0	275	5	7	2	.976	2.09	115	53	.461	3	2	11	275	0	+4	0	-6	-1	-1	18
2007	ChC	67	32	349.0	75	0	0	0	1.000	1.93	33	19	.576	0	-2	-	75	+1	+1	-1	+2	+2	1	-
2008	Fla	3	1	13.2	3	0	0	0	1.000	1.98	0	0	-	0	0	-	3	-1		-1	0	-1	-1	-
		488	441	3966.0	951	19	13	6	.987	2.20	378	174	.460	11	6	19	918	-14	+5	+2	-30	-22	-15	28

Austin Kearns

	BASIC										THROWING						PLUS/MINUS							
Year	Team	G	GS	Inn	PO	A	E	DP	Pct	Rng	Opps To Advance	Extra Bases	Pct	Kills	Runs Saved	Rank	Outs Made	Basic	Shallow	Medium	Deep	Enhanced	Runs Saved	Rank
2003	Cin	50	40	365.0	96	2	1	0	.990	2.42	35	17	.486	2	1	-	93	+2	+1	0	0	+2	1	-
2004	Cin	60	59	508.1	118	1	3	0	.975	2.11	44	21	.477	1	-1	24	106	+4	0	+5	0	+5	3	9
2005	Cin	107	103	890.0	237	8	3	3	.988	2.48	97	43	.443	8	5	5	238	+7	+9	0	-3	+7	4	11
2006	2 tms	144	139	1228.2	346	7	7	2	.981	2.59	141	61	.433	5	6	6	346	+13	+15	+7	-11	+11	6	8
2007	Was	158	156	1376.1	374	9	2	4	.995	2.50	151	78	.517	6	-1	22	375	+7	-1	+3	+15	+17	10	2
2008	Was	85	83	734.0	187	3	4	0	.979	2.33	83	42	.506	1	-3	32	187	-2	-7	+3	+5	+1	1	16
		604	580	5102.1	1358	30	20	9	.986	2.45	551	262	.475	23	7	17	1345	+31	+17	+18	+7	+43	25	4

Matt Kemp

	BASIC										THROWING						PLUS/MINUS							
Year	Team	G	GS	Inn	PO	A	E	DP	Pct	Rng	Opps To Advance	Extra Bases	Pct	Kills	Runs Saved	Rank	Outs Made	Basic	Shallow	Medium	Deep	Enhanced	Runs Saved	Rank
2006	LAD	10	6	71.2	8	1	1	0	.900	1.13	10	2	.200	1	2	-	8	0	-1	0	+1	0	0	-
2007	LAD	88	66	619.2	129	2	4	1	.970	1.90	53	27	.509	1	-1	22	129	0	0	+3	-4	-1	-1	21
2008	LAD	63	52	478.2	97	6	2	0	.981	1.94	54	22	.407	3	5	-	98	0	+3	-4	+2	+1	1	-
		161	124	1170.0	234	9	7	1	.972	1.87	117	51	.436	5	6	-	235	0	+2	-2	-1	0	0	-

Right Fielders

Ryan Ludwick

		BASIC									THROWING						PLUS/MINUS							
Year	Team	G	GS	Inn	PO	A	E	DP	Pct	Rng	Opps To Advance	Extra Bases	Pct	Kills	Runs Saved	Rank	Outs Made	Basic	Shallow	Medium	Deep	Enhanced	Runs Saved	Rank
2003	2 tms	25	23	215.0	51	2	0	0	1.000	2.22	18	10	.556	1	-1	-	51	+6	+1	+2	+4	+7	4	-
2004	Cle	15	13	119.2	32	0	1	0	.970	2.41	8	4	.500	0	0	-	31	+3	+2	+2	+1	+5	3	-
2005	Cle	6	3	34.0	6	0	0	0	1.000	1.59	3	2	.667	0	0	-	6	0	0	+1	0	+1	1	-
2007	StL	41	25	252.1	60	0	1	0	.984	2.14	21	7	.333	0	1	-	60	0	0	0	+1	+1	1	-
2008	StL	124	105	962.1	231	10	2	3	.992	2.25	92	34	.370	8	11	3	232	+2	+1	-5	+5	+1	1	15
		211	169	1583.1	380	12	4	3	.990	2.23	142	57	.401	9	11	13	380	+11	+4	0	+11	+15	10	11

Nick Markakis

		BASIC									THROWING						PLUS/MINUS							
Year	Team	G	GS	Inn	PO	A	E	DP	Pct	Rng	Opps To Advance	Extra Bases	Pct	Kills	Runs Saved	Rank	Outs Made	Basic	Shallow	Medium	Deep	Enhanced	Runs Saved	Rank
2006	Bal	126	100	913.1	240	7	1	0	.996	2.43	102	50	.490	5	2	11	240	+1	-3	+5	+2	+3	2	14
2007	Bal	161	158	1399.2	303	13	2	4	.994	2.03	157	75	.478	10	5	8	303	-6	-1	+2	-6	-5	-3	24
2008	Bal	156	155	1367.0	327	17	3	3	.991	2.26	153	67	.438	14	14	1	329	+7	+10	+4	-4	+11	6	7
		443	413	3680.0	870	37	6	7	.993	2.22	412	192	.466	29	21	5	872	+2	+6	+11	-8	+9	5	16

Gary Matthews Jr.

		BASIC									THROWING						PLUS/MINUS							
Year	Team	G	GS	Inn	PO	A	E	DP	Pct	Rng	Opps To Advance	Extra Bases	Pct	Kills	Runs Saved	Rank	Outs Made	Basic	Shallow	Medium	Deep	Enhanced	Runs Saved	Rank
2003	SD	35	22	215.0	47	1	0	0	1.000	2.01	17	3	.176	1	2	-	44	0	+2	0	-1	+1	1	-
2004	Tex	66	51	476.1	119	4	2	1	.984	2.32	47	21	.447	3	2	13	119	-2	-6	+5	+2	+1	1	16
2005	Tex	22	21	189.2	51	2	1	2	.981	2.51	20	10	.500	2	1	-	51	+5	+1	0	+7	+9	5	-
2006	Tex	3	3	26.0	9	0	0	0	1.000	3.12	3	0	.000	0	1	-	9	-2	-1	-1	-1	-3	-2	-
2008	LAA	43	36	344.0	77	2	2	0	.975	2.07	27	9	.333	1	1	-	77	-6	-1	-4	-4	-9	-5	-
		169	133	1251.0	303	9	5	3	.984	2.24	114	43	.377	7	7	-	300	-5	-5	+1	+3	-1	0	-

Kevin Mench

		BASIC									THROWING						PLUS/MINUS							
Year	Team	G	GS	Inn	PO	A	E	DP	Pct	Rng	Opps To Advance	Extra Bases	Pct	Kills	Runs Saved	Rank	Outs Made	Basic	Shallow	Medium	Deep	Enhanced	Runs Saved	Rank
2003	Tex	2	0	3.0	0	0	0	0	-	.00	1	0	.000	0	0	-							0	-
2004	Tex	62	60	500.2	127	5	0	2	1.000	2.37	53	20	.377	4	4	10	123	+2	+6	+1	-4	+2	1	14
2005	Tex	41	36	311.1	60	0	2	0	.968	1.73	36	12	.333	0	2	-	60	+3	+1	-1	+9	+9	5	-
2006	Tex	57	57	488.2	112	2	0	1	1.000	2.10	54	21	.389	1	1	17	112	-5	-4	-1	-3	-8	-5	26
2007	Mil	33	21	219.2	56	3	2	1	.967	2.42	24	13	.542	2	0	-	56	+3	+2	0	+3	+5	3	-
2008	Tor	15	11	98.0	22	1	0	0	1.000	2.11	10	1	.100	1	2	-	22	+2	+1	+2	-1	+2	1	-
		210	185	1621.1	377	11	4	4	.990	2.15	178	67	.376	8	9	15	373	+5	+6	+1	+4	+10	5	15

Jason Michaels

		BASIC									THROWING						PLUS/MINUS							
Year	Team	G	GS	Inn	PO	A	E	DP	Pct	Rng	Opps To Advance	Extra Bases	Pct	Kills	Runs Saved	Rank	Outs Made	Basic	Shallow	Medium	Deep	Enhanced	Runs Saved	Rank
2003	Phi	13	6	68.1	16	0	1	0	.941	2.11	8	2	.250	0	1	-	16	+1	+1	+1	0	+2	1	-
2004	Phi	12	5	67.0	22	1	0	0	1.000	3.09	6	3	.500	1	1	-	22	+3	+3	0	+1	+4	2	-
2005	Phi	13	4	53.0	13	2	0	0	1.000	2.55	7	4	.571	1	0	-	14	+2	+1	+1	+1	+3	2	-
2006	Cle	1	1	9.0	2	0	0	0	1.000	2.00	2	1	.500	0	0	-	2	+1			+1	+1	1	-
2007	Cle	27	10	116.0	29	0	1	0	.967	2.25	9	5	.556	0	0	-	29	-1	0	0	0	-1	-1	-
2008	2 tms	43	30	293.0	88	2	4	0	.957	2.76	31	17	.548	1	-1	-	88	+1	+1	-2	+1	0	0	-
		109	56	606.1	170	5	6	0	.967	2.60	63	32	.508	3	1	-	171	+7	+4	0	+4	+9	5	-

David Murphy

		BASIC									THROWING						PLUS/MINUS							
Year	Team	G	GS	Inn	PO	A	E	DP	Pct	Rng	Opps To Advance	Extra Bases	Pct	Kills	Runs Saved	Rank	Outs Made	Basic	Shallow	Medium	Deep	Enhanced	Runs Saved	Rank
2006	Bos	2	1	9.1	2	0	0	0	1.000	1.93	0	0	-	0	0	-	2	0		0	0	0	0	-
2007	2 tms	15	10	80.0	14	4	0	1	1.000	2.03	9	4	.444	2	1	-	14	0	0	-1	+1	0	0	-
2008	Tex	56	43	407.1	107	1	1	1	.991	2.39	47	20	.426	1	-1	-	107	+7	+3	+4	+4	+11	6	-
		73	54	496.2	123	5	1	2	.992	2.32	56	24	.429	3	0	-	123	+7	+3	+3	+5	+11	6	-

Xavier Nady

		BASIC									THROWING						PLUS/MINUS							
Year	Team	G	GS	Inn	PO	A	E	DP	Pct	Rng	Opps To Advance	Extra Bases	Pct	Kills	Runs Saved	Rank	Outs Made	Basic	Shallow	Medium	Deep	Enhanced	Runs Saved	Rank
2003	SD	105	98	846.2	170	12	6	2	.968	1.93	79	42	.532	8	1	14	159	+9	+7	+8	-5	+10	6	5
2004	SD	2	2	14.0	2	0	0	0	1.000	1.29	2	0	.000	0	0	-	2	0	0	0	-1	-1	-1	-
2005	SD	13	7	82.0	11	0	0	0	1.000	1.21	13	6	.462	0	0	-	11	0	+1	-1	-1	-1	-1	-
2006	2 tms	99	97	854.2	187	6	4	0	.980	2.03	86	51	.593	6	-1	26	187	-4	-6	-5	+6	-5	-3	23
2007	Pit	94	89	748.0	161	4	0	0	1.000	1.99	65	36	.554	3	1	13	162	-2	-3	-3	+7	+1	1	19
2008	2 tms	89	88	763.2	199	10	2	5	.991	2.46	91	46	.505	7	3	15	199	-5	+1	-3	-3	-4	-2	22
		402	381	3309.0	730	32	12	7	.984	2.07	336	181	.539	24	4	21	720	-2	0	-4	+3	0	0	21

Right Fielders

Trot Nixon

Year	Team	G	GS	Inn	PO	A	E	DP	Pct	Rng	Opps To Advance	Extra Bases	Pct	Kills	Runs Saved	Rank	Outs Made	Basic	Shallow	Medium	Deep	Enhanced	Runs Saved	Rank
2003	Bos	129	119	1078.2	230	4	4	0	.983	1.95	120	55	.458	2	0	19	231	+4	+2	-2	+8	+8	5	7
2004	Bos	40	36	306.0	63	1	1	0	.985	1.88	33	24	.727	0	-3	-	63	+2	+3	-4	+4	+3	2	-
2005	Bos	118	107	935.1	240	8	1	3	.996	2.39	107	57	.533	5	3	13	240	+11	+2	+2	+13	+17	10	1
2006	Bos	110	100	891.1	212	6	1	2	.995	2.20	70	42	.600	2	-3	32	212	-1	-4	0	+6	+2	1	15
2007	Cle	87	82	675.0	129	4	4	2	.971	1.77	63	34	.540	2	-1	22	129	-5	-1	-2	-4	-8	-5	29
2008	NYM	5	4	37.2	9	0	0	0	1.000	2.15	8	6	.750	0	-1	-	9	0	0	0	+1	+1	1	-
		489	448	3924.0	883	23	11	7	.988	2.08	401	218	.544	11	-5	32	884	+11	+2	-6	+27	+23	14	8

Magglio Ordonez

Year	Team	G	GS	Inn	PO	A	E	DP	Pct	Rng	Opps To Advance	Extra Bases	Pct	Kills	Runs Saved	Rank	Outs Made	Basic	Shallow	Medium	Deep	Enhanced	Runs Saved	Rank
2003	CWS	154	154	1324.2	316	7	2	1	.994	2.19	129	59	.457	7	4	7	311	0	-7	+4	+14	+11	6	3
2004	CWS	43	43	364.0	95	0	1	0	.990	2.35	38	22	.579	0	-1	-	94	-6	-9	0	+6	-3	-2	-
2005	Det	81	79	672.1	139	5	1	0	.993	1.93	86	47	.547	2	1	20	139	+2	0	+2	+1	+4	2	13
2006	Det	148	147	1268.0	258	9	7	1	.974	1.90	113	45	.398	6	8	3	258	-11	-2	-2	-11	-16	-9	33
2007	Det	143	142	1221.0	261	4	1	2	.996	1.95	105	44	.419	3	3	10	261	+3	+5	+3	-5	+3	2	15
2008	Det	135	134	1144.0	220	8	5	0	.979	1.79	143	72	.503	3	1	23	220	-5	-9	-3	+7	-5	-3	25
		704	699	5994.0	1289	33	17	4	.987	1.98	614	289	.471	21	16	8	1283	-17	-22	+4	+11	-6	-4	24

Hunter Pence

Year	Team	G	GS	Inn	PO	A	E	DP	Pct	Rng	Opps To Advance	Extra Bases	Pct	Kills	Runs Saved	Rank	Outs Made	Basic	Shallow	Medium	Deep	Enhanced	Runs Saved	Rank
2007	Hou	14	13	115.2	36	0	2	0	.947	2.80	11	6	.545	0	0	-	36	+1	0	0	+1	+1	1	-
2008	Hou	156	154	1366.1	340	16	1	4	.997	2.34	116	46	.397	11	12	2	341	+5	+7	-2	-7	-2	-1	20
		170	167	1482.0	376	16	3	4	.992	2.38	127	52	.409	11	12	-	377	+6	+7	-2	-6	-1	0	-

Alex Rios

Year	Team	G	GS	Inn	PO	A	E	DP	Pct	Rng	Opps To Advance	Extra Bases	Pct	Kills	Runs Saved	Rank	Outs Made	Basic	Shallow	Medium	Deep	Enhanced	Runs Saved	Rank
2004	Tor	108	107	943.2	217	11	2	4	.991	2.17	103	41	.398	8	9	3	209	+9	+10	+2	0	+12	7	4
2005	Tor	138	116	1056.2	245	7	2	1	.992	2.15	113	42	.372	4	6	2	246	+1	+1	+2	-2	+1	1	14
2006	Tor	124	104	953.0	218	7	1	2	.996	2.12	92	27	.293	5	10	4	218	+11	+8	+3	+5	+16	9	3
2007	Tor	147	139	1250.0	243	10	5	1	.981	1.82	123	48	.390	6	9	5	243	+4	-1	+5	+8	+12	7	4
2008	Tor	93	92	820.0	170	4	1	2	.994	1.91	62	22	.355	3	5	8	170	+11	+7	+3	+6	+16	9	4
		610	558	5023.1	1093	39	11	10	.990	2.03	493	180	.365	26	39	1	1086	+36	+24	+15	+17	+57	33	2

Denard Span

Year	Team	G	GS	Inn	PO	A	E	DP	Pct	Rng	Opps To Advance	Extra Bases	Pct	Kills	Runs Saved	Rank	Outs Made	Basic	Shallow	Medium	Deep	Enhanced	Runs Saved	Rank
2008	Min	85	77	686.2	192	5	3	2	.985	2.58	61	24	.393	5	6	5	192	+7	+4	0	+8	+12	7	6

Ichiro Suzuki

Year	Team	G	GS	Inn	PO	A	E	DP	Pct	Rng	Opps To Advance	Extra Bases	Pct	Kills	Runs Saved	Rank	Outs Made	Basic	Shallow	Medium	Deep	Enhanced	Runs Saved	Rank
2003	Sea	159	156	1367.0	337	12	2	4	.994	2.30	140	53	.379	8	8	4	333	+7	+2	+4	+10	+15	9	1
2004	Sea	158	158	1405.1	372	12	3	2	.992	2.46	146	55	.377	7	8	4	367	+22	+18	+6	+8	+32	19	1
2005	Sea	158	158	1388.1	381	9	2	2	.995	2.53	168	88	.524	6	-2	31	383	+7	+4	+7	-1	+10	6	6
2006	Sea	121	120	1061.2	250	8	2	3	.992	2.19	119	55	.462	4	4	9	250	+7	+1	0	+13	+14	8	4
2008	Sea	91	90	788.1	175	7	4	1	.978	2.08	93	39	.419	6	5	8	176	+7	+5	+6	+2	+13	8	5
		687	682	6010.2	1515	48	13	12	.992	2.34	666	290	.435	31	23	4	1509	+50	+30	+22	+31	+84	50	1

Ryan Sweeney

Year	Team	G	GS	Inn	PO	A	E	DP	Pct	Rng	Opps To Advance	Extra Bases	Pct	Kills	Runs Saved	Rank	Outs Made	Basic	Shallow	Medium	Deep	Enhanced	Runs Saved	Rank
2006	CWS	6	3	28.0	13	0	0	0	1.000	4.18	2	1	.500	0	0	-	13	0	-1	0	+1	0	0	-
2008	Oak	75	54	486.2	136	6	1	0	.993	2.63	52	15	.288	3	6	5	136	+2	-2	0	+6	+5	3	11
		81	57	514.2	149	6	1	0	.994	2.71	54	16	.296	3	6	-	149	+2	-3	+1	+7	+5	3	-

Right Fielders

Nick Swisher

Year	Team	G	GS	Inn	PO	A	E	DP	Pct	Rng	Opps To Advance	Extra Bases	Pct	Kills	Runs Saved	Rank	Outs Made	Basic	Shallow	Medium	Deep	Enhanced	Runs Saved	Rank
											THROWING						PLUS/MINUS							
2004	Oak	4	3	28.0	5	0	2	0	.714	1.61	5	2	.400	0	1	-	5	0	0	0	-1	-1	-1	-
2005	Oak	121	115	1027.1	196	6	2	2	.990	1.77	83	41	.494	4	0	25	197	+7	+2	-5	+7	+4	2	12
2006	Oak	1	0	3.0	1	0	0	0	1.000	3.00	0	0	-	0	0	-	1	0	0	0	0	0	0	-
2007	Oak	57	46	413.2	107	2	0	0	1.000	2.37	36	19	.528	2	1	13	109	+6	+5	+2	-2	+5	3	14
2008	CWS	18	11	118.0	25	0	1	0	.962	1.91	12	7	.583	0	-1	-	25	+1	+1	-1	+1	+1	1	-
		201	175	1590.0	334	8	5	2	.986	1.94	136	69	.507	6	1	27	337	+14	+8	-4	+5	+9	5	19

Fernando Tatis

Year	Team	G	GS	Inn	PO	A	E	DP	Pct	Rng	Opps To Advance	Extra Bases	Pct	Kills	Runs Saved	Rank	Outs Made	Basic	Shallow	Medium	Deep	Enhanced	Runs Saved	Rank
2006	Bal	1	1	8.0	4	0	0	0	1.000	4.50	3	1	.333	0	0	-	4	0	0	0		0	0	-
2008	NYM	39	35	292.2	55	2	0	0	1.000	1.75	21	10	.476	2	1	-	55	-2	0	-1	-3	-4	-2	-
		40	36	300.2	59	2	0	0	1.000	1.83	24	11	.458	2	1	-	59	-2	0	-1	-3	-4	-2	-

Mark Teahen

Year	Team	G	GS	Inn	PO	A	E	DP	Pct	Rng	Opps To Advance	Extra Bases	Pct	Kills	Runs Saved	Rank	Outs Made	Basic	Shallow	Medium	Deep	Enhanced	Runs Saved	Rank
2007	KC	137	130	1150.2	318	17	6	7	.982	2.62	132	65	.492	12	5	8	318	+4	+6	+8	-9	+5	3	12
2008	KC	92	84	756.1	185	4	2	2	.990	2.25	77	48	.623	2	-3	32	185	-3	+1	-5	-3	-8	-5	27
		229	214	1907.0	503	21	8	9	.985	2.47	209	113	.541	14	2	23	503	+1	+7	+3	-12	-3	-2	22

Justin Upton

Year	Team	G	GS	Inn	PO	A	E	DP	Pct	Rng	Opps To Advance	Extra Bases	Pct	Kills	Runs Saved	Rank	Outs Made	Basic	Shallow	Medium	Deep	Enhanced	Runs Saved	Rank
2007	Ari	42	38	315.1	65	1	5	0	.930	1.88	29	16	.552	1	0	-	65	+2	0	0	+3	+3	2	-
2008	Ari	101	100	860.1	175	6	11	2	.943	1.89	82	38	.463	6	3	15	175	0	-2	+1	+4	+3	2	12
		143	138	1175.2	240	7	16	2	.939	1.89	111	54	.486	7	3	-	240	+2	-2	0	+8	+6	4	-

Jayson Werth

Year	Team	G	GS	Inn	PO	A	E	DP	Pct	Rng	Opps To Advance	Extra Bases	Pct	Kills	Runs Saved	Rank	Outs Made	Basic	Shallow	Medium	Deep	Enhanced	Runs Saved	Rank
2003	Tor	19	10	99.0	21	1	0	0	1.000	2.00	14	7	.500	1	1	-	16	-1	-1	0	0	-1	-1	-
2004	LA	14	8	74.0	19	0	0	0	1.000	2.31	2	2	1.000	0	-1	-	19	+1	-1	+1	+1	+1	1	-
2005	LAD	43	37	291.0	71	3	0	2	1.000	2.29	24	11	.458	3	2	-	71	+3	+4	-1	-1	+2	1	-
2007	Phi	58	55	446.0	109	7	2	1	.983	2.34	47	13	.277	3	6	7	109	+3	+1	+2	+4	+7	4	11
2008	Phi	88	73	661.1	143	7	0	1	1.000	2.04	50	20	.400	6	5	8	143	+2	+3	+1	-4	0	0	19
		222	183	1571.1	363	18	2	4	.995	2.18	137	53	.387	13	13	11	358	+8	+6	+4	-1	+9	5	18

Brad Wilkerson

Year	Team	G	GS	Inn	PO	A	E	DP	Pct	Rng	Opps To Advance	Extra Bases	Pct	Kills	Runs Saved	Rank	Outs Made	Basic	Shallow	Medium	Deep	Enhanced	Runs Saved	Rank
2003	Mon	16	9	95.0	19	1	0	0	1.000	1.89	11	4	.364	0	0	-	17	-1	+1	-2	-2	-2	-1	-
2004	Mon	10	9	76.0	19	1	0	1	1.000	2.37	9	4	.444	1	1	-	15	-2	0	-3	+1	-2	-1	-
2005	Was	6	5	45.2	12	0	1	0	.923	2.36	3	1	.333	0	0	-	12	0	-1	+1	+1	+1	0	-
2006	Tex	3	2	21.0	4	0	0	0	1.000	1.71	0	0	-	0	0	-	4	0	0	0	0	0	0	-
2007	Tex	19	12	111.0	27	0	0	0	1.000	2.19	12	6	.500	0	0	-	27	+2	+1	+1	0	+2	1	-
2008	2 tms	64	55	485.0	95	4	1	0	.990	1.84	46	22	.478	2	2	20	95	+5	+2	+3	+4	+9	5	10
		118	92	833.2	176	6	2	1	.989	1.96	81	37	.457	3	3	-	170	+4	+2	+1	+5	+8	5	-

Randy Winn

Year	Team	G	GS	Inn	PO	A	E	DP	Pct	Rng	Opps To Advance	Extra Bases	Pct	Kills	Runs Saved	Rank	Outs Made	Basic	Shallow	Medium	Deep	Enhanced	Runs Saved	Rank
2003	Sea	4	3	24.0	4	0	0	0	1.000	1.50	1	0	.000	0	0	-	4	-2	-1	0	-1	-2	-1	-
2006	SF	89	69	652.2	184	6	3	1	.984	2.62	65	31	.477	5	2	11	184	+7	+4	+2	+8	+14	8	5
2007	SF	104	98	869.0	209	3	2	0	.991	2.20	86	37	.430	3	2	12	209	+9	+4	+4	+4	+12	7	5
2008	SF	133	127	1108.1	309	5	3	2	.991	2.55	96	43	.448	1	3	15	309	+12	+6	+5	+5	+16	9	3
		330	297	2654.0	706	14	8	3	.989	2.44	248	111	.448	9	7	17	706	+26	+13	+11	+16	+40	23	6

Catchers

Danny Ardoin

		BASIC										PITCHER HANDLING								STOLEN BASES							
Year	Team	G	GS	Inn	PO	A	E	WP	PB	DP	Pct	W	L	Pct	ER	CERA	ER Saved	Adj ER Saved	Rank	SBA	CCS	PCS	CPO	CS%	SB Saved	SB Runs Saved	Rank
2004	Tex	6	2	25.0	21	2	1	1	1	0	.958	1	1	.500	10	3.60	-2	0	-	4	0	0	0	.00	-1	-1	-
2005	Col	80	66	591.0	452	48	6	22	6	4	.988	28	38	.424	322	4.90	7	1	11	45	18	4	4	.44	9	6	2
2006	2 tms	40	37	323.1	239	16	3	9	2	1	.988	21	16	.568	147	4.09	25	2	-	28	7	0	0	.25	1	1	-
2008	LAD	24	17	145.1	126	11	1	8	2	4	.993	5	12	.294	61	3.78	1	0	-	13	3	0	0	.23	1	1	-
		150	122	1084.2	838	77	11	40	11	9	.988	55	67	.451	540	4.48	31	3	-	90	28	4	4	.33	10	7	-

Brad Ausmus

		BASIC										PITCHER HANDLING								STOLEN BASES							
Year	Team	G	GS	Inn	PO	A	E	WP	PB	DP	Pct	W	L	Pct	ER	CERA	ER Saved	Adj ER Saved	Rank	SBA	CCS	PCS	CPO	CS%	SB Saved	SB Runs Saved	Rank
2003	Hou	143	129	1158.0	982	76	3	34	3	12	.997	66	63	.512	471	3.66	6	2	10	105	31	6	1	.31	6	4	4
2004	Hou	128	114	1018.1	920	61	5	29	4	11	.995	63	51	.553	462	4.08	2	1	12	106	23	5	1	.23	-6	-4	31
2005	Hou	134	118	1065.2	884	65	1	26	5	6	.999	68	50	.576	374	3.16	-4	-1	20	57	13	5	2	.25	-4	-3	26
2006	Hou	138	124	1124.2	932	61	2	25	1	8	.998	66	58	.532	477	3.82	10	3	6	77	12	5	1	.17	-8	-5	32
2007	Hou	114	101	906.2	763	47	4	15	2	5	.995	48	53	.475	432	4.29	16	4	8	64	9	8	2	.16	-9	-6	31
2008	Hou	77	62	569.2	428	33	2	9	4	4	.996	32	30	.516	235	3.71	18	2	12	24	4	1	0	.17	-2	-2	20
		734	648	5843.0	4909	343	17	138	17	46	.997	343	305	.529	2451	3.78	47	11	6	433	92	30	7	.23	-23	-16	32

John Baker

		BASIC										PITCHER HANDLING								STOLEN BASES							
Year	Team	G	GS	Inn	PO	A	E	WP	PB	DP	Pct	W	L	Pct	ER	CERA	ER Saved	Adj ER Saved	Rank	SBA	CCS	PCS	CPO	CS%	SB Saved	SB Runs Saved	Rank
2008	Fla	59	54	496.0	402	22	4	15	3	0	.991	27	27	.500	233	4.23	-11	-1	25	48	6	2	0	.13	-4	-3	29

Paul Bako

		BASIC										PITCHER HANDLING								STOLEN BASES							
Year	Team	G	GS	Inn	PO	A	E	WP	PB	DP	Pct	W	L	Pct	ER	CERA	ER Saved	Adj ER Saved	Rank	SBA	CCS	PCS	CPO	CS%	SB Saved	SB Runs Saved	Rank
2003	ChC	69	57	507.2	440	33	6	24	4	2	.987	28	29	.491	215	3.81	15	2	-	40	11	2	2	.29	0	0	-
2004	ChC	47	43	377.2	332	30	4	9	1	2	.989	26	17	.605	149	3.55	24	2	-	51	15	0	0	.29	2	1	-
2005	LAD	13	13	107.0	61	6	1	5	1	0	.985	6	7	.462	64	5.38	-7	0	-	4	2	1	2	.67	1	1	-
2006	KC	53	44	392.0	258	19	2	20	4	3	.993	18	26	.409	250	5.74	3	0	-	29	8	1	1	.29	2	1	-
2007	Bal	57	47	421.0	324	24	4	16	8	5	.989	20	27	.426	232	4.96	0	0	-	35	6	1	1	.18	-3	-2	-
2008	Cin	96	88	770.2	679	39	5	27	9	7	.993	42	46	.477	373	4.36	0	0	21	77	20	2	1	.27	-3	-2	20
		335	292	2576.0	2094	151	22	101	27	19	.990	140	152	.479	1283	4.48	35	4	15	236	62	7	7	.27	-1	-1	20

Rod Barajas

		BASIC										PITCHER HANDLING								STOLEN BASES							
Year	Team	G	GS	Inn	PO	A	E	WP	PB	DP	Pct	W	L	Pct	ER	CERA	ER Saved	Adj ER Saved	Rank	SBA	CCS	PCS	CPO	CS%	SB Saved	SB Runs Saved	Rank
2003	Ari	79	65	595.0	543	40	0	16	7	5	1.000	36	29	.554	239	3.62	6	0	18	43	16	1	1	.38	2	1	14
2004	Tex	105	102	908.2	656	23	7	17	7	2	.990	61	41	.598	454	4.50	0	0	15	64	16	6	0	.28	-1	-1	15
2005	Tex	119	117	1025.1	689	41	9	32	7	5	.988	57	60	.487	567	4.98	-14	-2	25	67	21	2	0	.32	2	1	7
2006	Tex	94	94	825.0	591	35	10	19	5	2	.984	48	46	.511	434	4.73	-10	-1	20	57	15	4	1	.28	2	2	10
2007	Phi	38	37	303.0	252	14	0	16	1	3	1.000	17	20	.459	174	5.17	-2	0	-	19	6	1	0	.33	1	1	-
2008	Tor	98	90	785.1	674	47	4	21	2	5	.994	54	36	.600	290	3.32	19	4	4	64	17	5	1	.29	2	1	8
		533	505	4442.1	3405	200	30	121	29	22	.992	273	232	.541	2158	4.37	-1	1	21	314	91	19	3	.31	8	5	12

Josh Bard

		BASIC										PITCHER HANDLING								STOLEN BASES							
Year	Team	G	GS	Inn	PO	A	E	WP	PB	DP	Pct	W	L	Pct	ER	CERA	ER Saved	Adj ER Saved	Rank	SBA	CCS	PCS	CPO	CS%	SB Saved	SB Runs Saved	Rank
2003	Cle	87	80	715.2	486	55	5	23	4	7	.991	35	45	.438	343	4.31	1	-2	24	64	19	4	0	.32	5	3	6
2004	Cle	7	6	53.0	47	4	0	4	0	1	1.000	4	2	.667	23	3.91	11	0	-	6	2	0	0	.33	0	0	-
2005	Cle	31	23	219.2	164	10	3	3	3	2	.983	15	8	.652	78	3.20	11	1	-	11	2	2	1	.22	0	0	-
2006	2 tms	78	56	547.2	417	37	3	12	10	7	.993	26	30	.464	266	4.37	-24	-4	31	64	9	2	2	.15	-3	-2	25
2007	SD	108	103	927.1	751	39	3	27	3	4	.996	62	41	.602	354	3.44	18	2	13	131	8	2	0	.06	-12	-9	34
2008	SD	49	47	416.2	329	20	3	12	1	1	.991	16	31	.340	197	4.26	2	0	-	63	9	1	1	.15	-2	-1	-
		360	315	2880.0	2194	165	17	81	21	22	.993	158	157	.502	1261	3.94	18	-3	27	339	49	11	4	.15	-13	-9	26

Michael Barrett

		BASIC										PITCHER HANDLING								STOLEN BASES							
Year	Team	G	GS	Inn	PO	A	E	WP	PB	DP	Pct	W	L	Pct	ER	CERA	ER Saved	Adj ER Saved	Rank	SBA	CCS	PCS	CPO	CS%	SB Saved	SB Runs Saved	Rank
2003	Mon	68	63	562.2	391	21	1	38	7	4	.998	33	30	.524	266	4.25	-3	-1	21	26	10	0	1	.38	1	1	14
2004	ChC	130	119	1081.1	1035	47	6	41	8	9	.994	63	56	.529	467	3.89	-17	-3	25	96	18	6	1	.20	-8	-5	33
2005	ChC	122	114	1017.2	870	51	6	45	4	8	.994	52	62	.456	503	4.45	-4	-1	20	91	20	1	1	.22	-2	-1	17
2006	ChC	102	96	852.0	727	42	5	45	10	7	.994	40	56	.417	435	4.60	10	2	7	110	16	5	0	.15	-10	-7	34
2007	2 tms	95	83	768.0	613	34	6	21	12	2	.991	35	48	.422	355	4.16	-18	-5	31	86	8	6	0	.10	-5	-3	25
2008	SD	30	29	252.1	205	16	2	8	3	0	.991	11	18	.379	125	4.46	-2	-1	-	49	5	1	0	.10	-4	-3	-
		547	504	4534.0	3841	211	26	198	44	30	.994	234	270	.464	2151	4.27	-35	-9	31	458	77	19	3	.18	-28	-18	34

Catchers

Gary Bennett

		BASIC										PITCHER HANDLING					ER Saved	Adj ER Saved	Rank	STOLEN BASES					SB Saved	SB Runs Saved	Rank
Year	Team	G	GS	Inn	PO	A	E	WP	PB	DP	Pct	W	L	Pct	ER	CERA				SBA	CCS	PCS	CPO	CS%			
2003	SD	91	87	747.0	536	24	2	25	6	4	.996	45	42	.517	322	3.88	43	7	3	60	11	1	0	.19	-5	-4	30
2004	Mil	75	65	584.0	379	32	3	20	3	2	.993	25	40	.385	332	5.12	-10	-1	19	44	9	2	0	.21	-2	-2	20
2005	Was	64	57	523.1	384	25	6	14	4	1	.986	29	28	.509	225	3.87	-9	-2	25	34	6	3	0	.19	-3	-2	21
2006	StL	56	43	385.1	243	14	3	9	1	1	.988	22	21	.512	196	4.58	13	1		29	3	0	0	.10	-6	-4	
2007	StL	52	41	370.1	244	9	1	8	2	1	.996	21	20	.512	215	5.23	-18	-2		28	2	2	0	.08	-6	-4	
2008	LAD	10	6	54.0	43	3	1	4	1	0	.979	3	3	.500	27	4.50	-5	0		2	0	0	0	.00	-1	0	
		348	299	2664.0	1829	107	16	80	17	9	.992	145	154	.485	1317	4.45	14	3	18	197	31	8	0	.16	-23	-16	32

Henry Blanco

		BASIC										PITCHER HANDLING					ER Saved	Adj ER Saved	Rank	STOLEN BASES					SB Saved	SB Runs Saved	Rank
Year	Team	G	GS	Inn	PO	A	E	WP	PB	DP	Pct	W	L	Pct	ER	CERA				SBA	CCS	PCS	CPO	CS%			
2003	Atl	52	42	388.0	255	25	1	17	1	2	.996	23	19	.548	193	4.48	-15	-1		44	10	1	0	.23	-1	-1	
2004	Min	114	95	872.1	686	44	7	31	5	8	.991	52	43	.547	424	4.25	-28	-6	32	61	25	5	0	.45	7	5	2
2005	ChC	54	48	422.1	407	31	1	12	2	2	.998	27	21	.563	168	3.58	13	1		39	19	0	0	.49	6	4	
2006	ChC	69	59	526.0	467	34	1	21	2	9	.998	24	35	.407	289	4.94	-15	-2	26	42	15	3	0	.38	5	3	6
2007	ChC	14	13	109.0	102	4	0	6	2	1	1.000	3	10	.231	58	4.79	-4	0		11	2	1	0	.20	-1	-1	
2008	ChC	45	28	257.2	235	15	2	7	3	2	.992	16	12	.571	112	3.91	0	0		22	9	1	0	.43	2	2	
		348	285	2575.1	2152	153	12	94	15	24	.995	145	140	.509	1232	4.31	-49	-8	29	219	80	11	0	.38	18	12	5

Rob Bowen

		BASIC										PITCHER HANDLING					ER Saved	Adj ER Saved	Rank	STOLEN BASES					SB Saved	SB Runs Saved	Rank
Year	Team	G	GS	Inn	PO	A	E	WP	PB	DP	Pct	W	L	Pct	ER	CERA				SBA	CCS	PCS	CPO	CS%			
2003	Min	7	0	23.0	14	2	1	4	1	0	.941				17	6.65	0	0		8	0	0	0	.00	-1	-1	
2004	Min	15	8	81.2	65	1	1	2	0	1	.985	4	4	.500	36	3.97	5	0		7	1	0	0	.14	-1	-1	
2006	SD	65	8	202.0	144	14	1	11	3	1	.994	5	3	.625	76	3.39	2	0		9	1	0	0	.11	-1	0	
2007	3 tms	56	45	415.0	306	20	5	13	3	3	.985	26	19	.578	193	4.19	6	0		39	4	1	0	.11	-3	-2	
2008	Oak	31	25	220.0	147	9	2	7	3	1	.987	11	14	.440	119	4.87	-21	-1		24	5	4	0	.25	2	1	
		174	86	941.2	676	46	10	37	10	6	.986	46	40	.535	441	4.21	-8	-1		87	11	5	0	.13	-4	-3	

John Buck

		BASIC										PITCHER HANDLING					ER Saved	Adj ER Saved	Rank	STOLEN BASES					SB Saved	SB Runs Saved	Rank
Year	Team	G	GS	Inn	PO	A	E	WP	PB	DP	Pct	W	L	Pct	ER	CERA				SBA	CCS	PCS	CPO	CS%			
2004	KC	68	66	575.0	376	14	3	26	7	5	.992	24	42	.364	339	5.31	-9	-2	10	44	7	7	0	.19	-1	0	10
2005	KC	117	112	976.2	638	57	3	51	3	4	.996	36	76	.321	615	5.67	-10	-2	25	91	27	4	3	.31	-2	-2	21
2006	KC	112	107	930.1	615	37	6	56	5	6	.991	41	66	.383	590	5.71	2	1	11	50	13	4	1	.28	0	0	17
2007	KC	112	104	924.1	697	29	8	31	3	6	.989	43	61	.413	455	4.43	-21	-4	30	56	9	3	0	.17	-5	-4	29
2008	KC	107	106	950.1	751	24	8	42	4	6	.990	49	57	.462	480	4.55	-1	-1	25	71	7	5	0	.11	-10	-7	35
		516	495	4356.2	3077	161	28	206	22	27	.991	193	302	.390	2479	5.12	-40	-8	29	312	63	23	4	.22	-18	-13	30

Jamie Burke

		BASIC										PITCHER HANDLING					ER Saved	Adj ER Saved	Rank	STOLEN BASES					SB Saved	SB Runs Saved	Rank
Year	Team	G	GS	Inn	PO	A	E	WP	PB	DP	Pct	W	L	Pct	ER	CERA				SBA	CCS	PCS	CPO	CS%			
2003	CWS	4	2	18.0	7	1	0	1	1	0	1.000	0	2	.000	14	7.00	-4	0		2	0	0	0	.00	0	0	
2004	CWS	45	32	292.0	215	11	3	3	1	1	.987	18	14	.563	155	4.78	4	0		19	7	1	0	.39	1	1	
2007	Sea	48	34	321.2	259	9	1	20	3	0	.996	20	14	.588	134	3.75	34	2		28	3	2	0	.12	-5	-4	
2008	Sea	43	25	246.0	181	10	1	14	2	0	.995	9	16	.360	131	4.79	-4	0		20	5	3	0	.29	0	0	
		140	93	877.2	662	31	5	38	7	1	.993	47	46	.505	434	4.45	30	2		69	15	6	0	.24	-5	-3	

Robinson Cancel

		BASIC										PITCHER HANDLING					ER Saved	Adj ER Saved	Rank	STOLEN BASES					SB Saved	SB Runs Saved	Rank
Year	Team	G	GS	Inn	PO	A	E	WP	PB	DP	Pct	W	L	Pct	ER	CERA				SBA	CCS	PCS	CPO	CS%			
2008	NYM	15	9	93.0	81	1	0	3	1	0	1.000	5	4	.556	48	4.65	3	0		2	0	0	0	.00	0	0	

Luke Carlin

		BASIC										PITCHER HANDLING					ER Saved	Adj ER Saved	Rank	STOLEN BASES					SB Saved	SB Runs Saved	Rank
Year	Team	G	GS	Inn	PO	A	E	WP	PB	DP	Pct	W	L	Pct	ER	CERA				SBA	CCS	PCS	CPO	CS%			
2008	SD	36	27	259.2	206	14	3	4	3	2	.987	14	13	.519	112	3.88	14	1		32	7	0	1	.22	1	1	

Raul Casanova

		BASIC										PITCHER HANDLING					ER Saved	Adj ER Saved	Rank	STOLEN BASES					SB Saved	SB Runs Saved	Rank
Year	Team	G	GS	Inn	PO	A	E	WP	PB	DP	Pct	W	L	Pct	ER	CERA				SBA	CCS	PCS	CPO	CS%			
2005	CWS	6	0	14.0	9	0	0	1	0	0	1.000	0	0	-	2	1.29	5	0		0	0	0	0	-	0	0	
2007	TB	23	19	168.2	138	9	3	7	4	3	.980	4	15	.211	131	6.99	-21	-1		14	4	1	0	.31	-2	-1	
2008	NYM	13	13	118.0	89	7	0	6	1	0	1.000	6	7	.462	61	4.65	-5	0		5	2	0	0	.40	1	0	
		42	32	300.2	236	16	3	14	5	3	.988	10	22	.313	194	5.81	-21	-1		19	6	1	0	.33	-1	-1	

Catchers

Kevin Cash

Year	Team	G	GS	Inn	PO	A	E	WP	PB	DP	Pct	W	L	Pct	ER	CERA	ER Saved	Adj ER Saved	Rank	SBA	CCS	PCS	CPO	CS%	SB Saved	SB Runs Saved	Rank
2003	Tor	34	31	278.0	179	13	1	10	1	0	.995	24	7	.774	129	4.18	7	0	-	20	5	1	0	.26	1	0	-
2004	Tor	60	50	460.1	317	35	2	22	5	4	.994	17	33	.340	260	5.08	-2	0	-	34	14	1	2	.42	6	4	-
2005	TB	13	10	89.0	56	8	0	2	4	1	1.000	1	9	.100	69	6.98	-14	0	-	6	3	0	0	.50	1	1	-
2007	Bos	12	8	82.0	56	8	1	1	0	2	.985	5	3	.625	36	3.95	0	0	-	11	2	0	0	.18	-1	0	-
2008	Bos	57	42	372.0	280	26	4	20	14	5	.987	22	20	.524	199	4.81	-16	-1	-	54	14	2	0	.27	3	2	-
		176	141	1281.1	888	90	8	55	24	12	.992	69	72	.489	693	4.87	-26	-1	-	125	38	4	2	.31	10	7	-

Ramon Castro

Year	Team	G	GS	Inn	PO	A	E	WP	PB	DP	Pct	W	L	Pct	ER	CERA	ER Saved	Adj ER Saved	Rank	SBA	CCS	PCS	CPO	CS%	SB Saved	SB Runs Saved	Rank
2003	Fla	18	2	65.2	51	2	1	2	1	0	.981	1	1	.500	23	3.15	13	0	-	2	0	0	0	.00	-1	0	-
2004	Fla	31	27	243.0	193	11	2	7	0	2	.990	17	10	.630	96	3.56	7	0	-	14	5	0	0	.36	1	1	-
2005	NYM	99	57	576.1	402	22	3	9	2	3	.993	30	27	.526	203	3.59	1	0	14	35	9	2	1	.27	0	0	11
2006	NYM	37	32	307.1	267	16	1	6	1	3	.996	19	13	.594	144	4.22	5	0	-	26	9	0	1	.35	3	2	-
2007	NYM	50	35	330.2	303	12	4	9	1	1	.987	21	14	.600	157	4.27	3	1	-	30	2	1	0	.07	-4	-2	-
2008	NYM	47	40	354.1	286	19	4	8	1	2	.987	24	16	.600	145	3.68	9	1	-	23	5	0	0	.22	-1	-1	-
		282	193	1877.1	1502	82	15	41	6	11	.991	112	81	.580	795	3.81	38	2	-	130	30	3	2	.24	-1	0	-

Raul Chavez

Year	Team	G	GS	Inn	PO	A	E	WP	PB	DP	Pct	W	L	Pct	ER	CERA	ER Saved	Adj ER Saved	Rank	SBA	CCS	PCS	CPO	CS%	SB Saved	SB Runs Saved	Rank
2003	Hou	16	7	77.2	55	3	0	1	0	0	1.000	4	3	.571	38	4.40	2	0	-	5	2	1	0	.50	0	0	-
2004	Hou	61	48	423.2	396	28	4	16	2	3	.990	29	19	.604	187	3.97	6	0	-	34	10	1	1	.30	0	0	-
2005	Hou	36	30	253.1	213	19	2	9	1	2	.991	12	17	.414	136	4.83	-8	0	-	18	11	0	0	.61	5	3	-
2006	Bal	15	8	75.0	60	5	1	3	0	1	.985	0	8	.000	62	7.44	-2	0	-	5	2	1	0	.50	1	1	-
2008	Pit	35	31	278.0	188	23	1	11	3	2	.995	14	17	.452	147	4.76	0	0	-	25	8	4	3	.38	3	2	-
		163	124	1107.2	912	78	8	40	6	8	.992	59	64	.480	570	4.63	-1	0	-	87	33	7	4	.41	9	6	-

Jeff Clement

Year	Team	G	GS	Inn	PO	A	E	WP	PB	DP	Pct	W	L	Pct	ER	CERA	ER Saved	Adj ER Saved	Rank	SBA	CCS	PCS	CPO	CS%	SB Saved	SB Runs Saved	Rank
2008	Sea	38	35	292.0	195	7	1	18	5	0	.995	16	19	.457	164	5.05	-7	0	-	20	0	2	0	.00	-5	-3	-

Chris Coste

Year	Team	G	GS	Inn	PO	A	E	WP	PB	DP	Pct	W	L	Pct	ER	CERA	ER Saved	Adj ER Saved	Rank	SBA	CCS	PCS	CPO	CS%	SB Saved	SB Runs Saved	Rank
2006	Phi	54	46	434.1	328	12	4	9	4	0	.988	27	19	.587	215	4.46	-1	0	-	31	6	0	0	.19	-4	-2	-
2007	Phi	31	25	242.2	157	12	0	3	2	3	1.000	14	11	.560	133	4.93	3	0	-	21	6	0	1	.29	0	0	-
2008	Phi	78	69	612.2	488	23	3	15	1	6	.994	36	33	.522	270	3.97	9	1	17	57	8	5	0	.15	-4	-3	29
		163	140	1289.2	973	47	7	27	7	9	.993	77	63	.550	618	4.31	11	1	-	109	20	5	1	.19	-7	-5	-

Ryan Doumit

Year	Team	G	GS	Inn	PO	A	E	WP	PB	DP	Pct	W	L	Pct	ER	CERA	ER Saved	Adj ER Saved	Rank	SBA	CCS	PCS	CPO	CS%	SB Saved	SB Runs Saved	Rank
2005	Pit	50	48	422.0	286	29	8	16	4	1	.975	19	29	.396	217	4.63	-12	-1	-	35	10	4	0	.32	0	0	-
2006	Pit	11	10	91.2	66	12	1	4	2	0	.987	4	6	.400	62	6.09	-13	0	-	15	2	2	0	.15	-1	-1	-
2007	Pit	28	28	223.2	149	7	2	8	5	2	.987	6	22	.214	137	5.51	5	0	-	27	4	2	0	.16	0	0	-
2008	Pit	106	103	909.0	596	59	8	44	9	8	.988	45	58	.437	512	5.07	1	0	21	93	15	10	0	.18	-3	-2	20
		195	189	1646.1	1097	107	19	72	20	11	.984	74	115	.392	928	5.07	-18	-1	-	170	31	18	0	.20	-4	-3	-

Johnny Estrada

Year	Team	G	GS	Inn	PO	A	E	WP	PB	DP	Pct	W	L	Pct	ER	CERA	ER Saved	Adj ER Saved	Rank	SBA	CCS	PCS	CPO	CS%	SB Saved	SB Runs Saved	Rank
2003	Atl	14	6	76.1	47	1	0	2	0	0	1.000	4	2	.667	34	4.01	4	0	-	6	0	0	0	.00	-2	-1	-
2004	Atl	133	120	1042.0	776	44	9	31	8	8	.989	70	50	.583	436	3.77	0	0	15	86	15	1	2	.18	-8	-5	33
2005	Atl	104	97	826.1	574	51	2	25	2	6	.997	48	49	.495	366	3.99	14	2	9	84	21	5	1	.27	0	0	11
2006	Ari	108	103	924.2	684	49	3	32	4	10	.996	51	52	.495	457	4.45	6	1	11	93	21	6	2	.24	-5	-3	28
2007	Mil	113	111	961.0	803	37	6	36	5	6	.993	57	54	.514	474	4.44	-1	0	17	84	6	5	0	.08	-13	-9	34
2008	Was	14	12	94.1	78	8	2	2	0	0	.977	5	7	.417	54	5.15	-3	0	-	19	4	2	0	.24	0	0	-
		486	449	3924.2	2962	190	22	128	19	30	.993	235	214	.523	1821	4.18	19	3	18	372	67	19	5	.19	-26	-18	34

Catchers

Sal Fasano

Year	Team	G	GS	Inn	PO	A	E	WP	PB	DP	Pct	W	L	Pct	ER	CERA	ER Saved	Adj ER Saved	Rank	SBA	CCS	PCS	CPO	CS%	SB Saved	SB Runs Saved	Rank
2005	Bal	60	47	417.0	284	25	4	19	6	1	.987	16	31	.340	236	5.09	-22	-2	-	44	5	2	1	.12	-5	-3	-
2006	2 tms	77	58	518.1	369	35	4	21	4	2	.990	24	34	.414	279	4.84	1	0	-	46	10	1	0	.22	-1	-1	-
2007	Tor	16	14	120.1	93	5	3	5	1	0	.970	6	8	.429	79	5.91	-23	-1	-	14	3	0	0	.21	0	0	-
2008	Cle	15	14	117.0	102	9	2	4	3	1	.982	7	7	.500	74	5.69	-7	0	-	12	3	1	0	.27	0	0	-
		168	133	1172.2	848	74	13	49	14	4	.986	53	80	.398	668	5.13	-51	-3	-	116	21	4	1	.19	-6	-4	-

Jesus Flores

Year	Team	G	GS	Inn	PO	A	E	WP	PB	DP	Pct	W	L	Pct	ER	CERA	ER Saved	Adj ER Saved	Rank	SBA	CCS	PCS	CPO	CS%	SB Saved	SB Runs Saved	Rank
2007	Was	55	42	395.1	262	30	4	14	4	1	.986	21	21	.500	176	4.01	23	3	-	40	11	2	0	.29	0	0	-
2008	Was	82	78	673.0	474	29	5	30	7	6	.990	27	51	.346	337	4.51	16	2	12	64	11	6	0	.19	-1	-1	14
		137	120	1068.1	736	59	9	44	11	7	.989	48	72	.400	513	4.32	39	5	-	104	22	8	0	.23	-1	-1	-

Toby Hall

Year	Team	G	GS	Inn	PO	A	E	WP	PB	DP	Pct	W	L	Pct	ER	CERA	ER Saved	Adj ER Saved	Rank	SBA	CCS	PCS	CPO	CS%	SB Saved	SB Runs Saved	Rank
2003	TB	130	126	1107.0	685	60	9	53	7	8	.988	53	73	.421	614	4.99	-11	-2	24	78	31	3	0	.41	8	6	2
2004	TB	119	115	1011.1	686	38	6	40	7	5	.992	51	64	.443	530	4.72	12	4	3	67	17	6	1	.28	2	1	7
2005	TB	135	122	1061.2	759	51	9	43	8	6	.989	53	69	.434	608	5.15	17	5	4	79	28	5	3	.38	4	3	5
2006	2 tms	82	69	628.0	394	31	4	23	3	3	.991	31	38	.449	357	5.12	-20	-3	28	58	12	4	0	.22	-4	-3	28
2007	CWS	37	35	292.2	187	10	3	10	5	1	.985	13	22	.371	199	6.12	-43	-3	-	29	3	0	0	.10	-1	-1	-
2008	CWS	37	36	315.1	231	15	2	16	1	0	.992	22	14	.611	129	3.68	13	1	-	52	3	6	0	.07	-3	-2	-
		540	503	4416.0	2942	205	33	185	31	23	.990	223	280	.443	2437	4.97	-31	2	20	363	94	24	4	.28	6	4	15

Robby Hammock

Year	Team	G	GS	Inn	PO	A	E	WP	PB	DP	Pct	W	L	Pct	ER	CERA	ER Saved	Adj ER Saved	Rank	SBA	CCS	PCS	CPO	CS%	SB Saved	SB Runs Saved	Rank
2003	Ari	36	28	264.0	263	18	2	9	4	1	.993	16	12	.571	120	4.09	-9	0	-	25	6	1	0	.25	0	0	-
2004	Ari	46	42	376.2	313	21	1	13	5	7	.997	17	25	.405	165	3.94	34	3	-	39	10	2	0	.27	-2	-1	-
2007	Ari	12	2	39.0	41	6	0	2	1	0	1.000	1	1	.500	20	4.62	-2	0	-	4	3	0	0	.75	1	1	-
2008	Ari	15	11	107.1	92	3	0	3	0	0	1.000	6	5	.545	37	3.10	13	0	-	13	1	1	0	.08	-3	-2	-
		109	83	787.0	709	48	3	27	10	8	.996	40	43	.482	342	3.91	36	3	-	81	20	4	0	.26	-3	-2	-

Ryan Hanigan

Year	Team	G	GS	Inn	PO	A	E	WP	PB	DP	Pct	W	L	Pct	ER	CERA	ER Saved	Adj ER Saved	Rank	SBA	CCS	PCS	CPO	CS%	SB Saved	SB Runs Saved	Rank
2007	Cin	3	2	20.0	16	0	0	1	0	0	1.000	2	0	1.000	9	4.05	4	0	-	1	0	0	0	.00	0	0	-
2008	Cin	30	25	229.1	186	19	1	8	1	4	.995	14	11	.560	106	4.16	10	1	-	23	8	0	0	.35	-1	-1	-
		33	27	249.1	202	19	1	9	1	4	.995	16	11	.593	115	4.15	14	1	-	24	8	0	0	.33	-1	-1	-

Ramon Hernandez

Year	Team	G	GS	Inn	PO	A	E	WP	PB	DP	Pct	W	L	Pct	ER	CERA	ER Saved	Adj ER Saved	Rank	SBA	CCS	PCS	CPO	CS%	SB Saved	SB Runs Saved	Rank
2003	Oak	139	133	1172.2	864	54	8	25	8	8	.991	84	49	.632	453	3.48	6	1	12	109	24	12	0	.25	3	2	9
2004	SD	108	106	925.1	753	35	6	18	7	7	.992	51	55	.481	412	4.01	-12	-2	22	74	18	3	0	.25	2	1	7
2005	SD	97	94	806.0	640	36	8	17	6	4	.988	52	42	.553	362	4.04	23	6	2	70	18	0	0	.26	1	1	7
2006	Bal	135	126	1094.1	793	69	13	47	13	5	.985	58	68	.460	637	5.24	-14	-3	28	97	35	7	4	.39	10	7	1
2007	Bal	104	97	855.0	636	44	7	27	9	4	.990	43	54	.443	494	5.20	-6	0	17	88	17	3	0	.20	-5	-3	25
2008	Bal	127	119	1039.1	714	45	9	46	10	8	.988	57	62	.479	579	5.01	11	3	6	123	21	3	1	.18	-3	-2	20
		710	675	5892.2	4400	283	51	180	53	36	.989	345	330	.511	2937	4.49	8	5	13	561	133	28	5	.25	8	6	8

Steve Holm

Year	Team	G	GS	Inn	PO	A	E	WP	PB	DP	Pct	W	L	Pct	ER	CERA	ER Saved	Adj ER Saved	Rank	SBA	CCS	PCS	CPO	CS%	SB Saved	SB Runs Saved	Rank
2008	SF	42	19	210.1	190	5	0	18	1	0	1.000	8	11	.421	110	4.71	-11	-1	-	23	2	0	0	.09	-3	-2	-

Paul Hoover

Year	Team	G	GS	Inn	PO	A	E	WP	PB	DP	Pct	W	L	Pct	ER	CERA	ER Saved	Adj ER Saved	Rank	SBA	CCS	PCS	CPO	CS%	SB Saved	SB Runs Saved	Rank
2006	Fla	3	1	8.1	7	0	1	1	1	0	.875	0	1	.000	3	3.24	1	0	-	1	0	0	0	.00	0	0	-
2007	Fla	2	1	12.2	12	0	0	0	0	0	1.000	1	0	1.000	10	7.11	-1	0	-	2	0	1	0	.00	0	0	-
2008	Fla	13	12	104.1	84	8	0	9	2	0	1.000	4	8	.333	69	5.95	-14	0	-	8	3	0	0	.38	1	1	-
		18	14	125.1	103	8	1	10	3	0	.991	5	9	.357	82	5.89	-14	0	-	11	3	1	0	.30	1	1	-

Catchers

Nick Hundley

Year Team	G	GS	Inn	PO	A	E	WP	PB	DP	Pct	W	L	Pct	ER	CERA	ER Saved	Adj ER Saved	Rank	SBA	CCS	PCS	CPO	CS%	SB Saved	SB Runs Saved	Rank
2008 SD	59	55	486.1	366	32	4	15	4	4	.990	21	34	.382	257	4.76	-10	-1	-	56	13	1	0	.24	3	2	-

Chris Iannetta

Year Team	G	GS	Inn	PO	A	E	WP	PB	DP	Pct	W	L	Pct	ER	CERA	ER Saved	Adj ER Saved	Rank	SBA	CCS	PCS	CPO	CS%	SB Saved	SB Runs Saved	Rank
2006 Col	21	20	191.2	139	8	0	13	2	3	1.000	12	8	.600	130	6.10	-30	-1	-	21	3	0	0	.14	-1	-1	-
2007 Col	60	54	496.2	301	27	1	9	4	1	.997	31	23	.574	260	4.71	-17	-2	26	43	8	2	1	.20	-1	-1	18
2008 Col	100	96	837.0	606	51	0	37	6	4	1.000	46	50	.479	429	4.61	3	2	12	53	8	4	1	.16	-2	-2	20
	181	170	1525.1	1046	86	1	59	12	8	.999	89	81	.524	819	4.83	-44	-1	-	117	19	6	2	.17	-4	-4	-

Brandon Inge

Year Team	G	GS	Inn	PO	A	E	WP	PB	DP	Pct	W	L	Pct	ER	CERA	ER Saved	Adj ER Saved	Rank	SBA	CCS	PCS	CPO	CS%	SB Saved	SB Runs Saved	Rank
2003 Det	104	98	867.1	500	67	2	35	5	6	.996	26	72	.265	499	5.18	12	1	12	110	30	10	1	.30	6	4	4
2004 Det	39	34	312.2	209	30	3	16	4	1	.988	12	22	.353	177	5.09	-6	-1	-	51	18	3	0	.38	2	2	-
2008 Det	60	56	493.2	370	33	0	20	11	4	1.000	25	31	.446	308	5.62	-37	-4	-	37	10	1	0	.28	1	0	-
	203	188	1673.2	1079	130	5	71	20	11	.996	63	125	.335	984	5.29	-31	-4	-	198	58	14	1	.32	9	6	-

Kenji Johjima

Year Team	G	GS	Inn	PO	A	E	WP	PB	DP	Pct	W	L	Pct	ER	CERA	ER Saved	Adj ER Saved	Rank	SBA	CCS	PCS	CPO	CS%	SB Saved	SB Runs Saved	Rank
2006 Sea	144	131	1172.2	882	58	7	39	10	9	.993	64	67	.489	627	4.81	-39	-11	35	86	22	7	1	.28	0	0	17
2007 Sea	133	128	1106.2	805	56	2	39	5	15	.998	68	60	.531	624	5.07	-38	-10	35	86	30	10	3	.39	4	3	5
2008 Sea	100	95	833.1	632	34	8	24	7	8	.988	35	60	.368	423	4.57	12	2	12	77	18	7	1	.26	-2	-2	20
	377	354	3112.2	2319	148	17	102	22	32	.993	167	187	.472	1674	4.84	-66	-19	35	249	70	24	5	.31	2	1	17

Jason Kendall

Year Team	G	GS	Inn	PO	A	E	WP	PB	DP	Pct	W	L	Pct	ER	CERA	ER Saved	Adj ER Saved	Rank	SBA	CCS	PCS	CPO	CS%	SB Saved	SB Runs Saved	Rank
2003 Pit	146	145	1278.1	841	48	10	44	9	2	.989	68	77	.469	635	4.47	31	9	2	86	15	8	1	.19	-7	-5	32
2004 Pit	146	145	1259.0	998	78	10	40	2	13	.991	66	79	.455	627	4.48	-20	-6	32	102	31	6	0	.32	3	2	5
2005 Oak	147	146	1286.0	985	52	7	39	4	5	.993	79	67	.541	542	3.79	-9	-3	30	123	18	4	0	.15	-6	-4	29
2006 Oak	141	141	1254.0	924	53	5	41	7	9	.995	85	56	.603	570	4.09	16	5	3	102	23	8	1	.24	5	4	2
2007 2 tms	132	130	1146.0	847	58	9	38	12	6	.990	66	64	.508	476	3.74	44	14	1	131	13	7	0	.10	-12	-8	33
2008 Mil	149	149	1328.1	1025	95	6	45	4	13	.995	83	66	.557	568	3.85	15	4	4	96	36	5	0	.40	11	8	1
	861	856	7551.2	5620	384	47	247	38	48	.992	447	409	.522	3418	4.07	77	23	1	640	136	38	2	.23	-5	-3	22

Gerald Laird

Year Team	G	GS	Inn	PO	A	E	WP	PB	DP	Pct	W	L	Pct	ER	CERA	ER Saved	Adj ER Saved	Rank	SBA	CCS	PCS	CPO	CS%	SB Saved	SB Runs Saved	Rank
2003 Tex	16	12	111.0	65	8	1	4	1	2	.986	5	7	.417	71	5.76	3	0	-	7	3	0	0	.43	0	0	-
2004 Tex	49	46	397.0	276	18	5	11	6	6	.983	23	23	.500	194	4.40	17	2	-	31	12	2	0	.41	3	2	-
2005 Tex	13	11	99.0	61	5	3	3	1	2	.957	5	6	.455	55	5.00	-2	0	-	11	3	0	0	.27	-1	-1	-
2006 Tex	71	65	578.1	392	30	5	15	5	5	.988	31	34	.477	282	4.39	8	0	17	46	19	2	1	.43	5	3	6
2007 Tex	119	114	987.1	675	75	12	33	9	13	.984	53	61	.465	524	4.78	-5	0	17	98	39	0	1	.40	9	6	2
2008 Tex	88	86	753.0	523	35	8	30	6	7	.986	43	43	.500	436	5.21	29	5	2	74	20	1	0	.27	2	1	8
	356	334	2925.2	1992	171	34	96	28	35	.985	160	174	.479	1562	4.81	51	7	11	267	96	5	2	.37	17	11	6

Jason LaRue

Year Team	G	GS	Inn	PO	A	E	WP	PB	DP	Pct	W	L	Pct	ER	CERA	ER Saved	Adj ER Saved	Rank	SBA	CCS	PCS	CPO	CS%	SB Saved	SB Runs Saved	Rank
2003 Cin	114	109	954.1	649	45	11	27	6	6	.984	44	65	.404	541	5.10	5	1	12	64	16	1	2	.25	0	0	21
2004 Cin	111	106	930.0	648	59	8	41	15	7	.989	54	52	.509	512	4.95	22	4	3	54	16	0	1	.30	4	3	4
2005 Cin	109	104	914.2	646	52	5	33	6	2	.993	46	58	.442	539	5.30	-1	0	14	76	22	3	0	.30	2	1	7
2006 Cin	63	57	512.1	375	37	2	12	3	9	.995	32	25	.561	252	4.43	10	1	-	36	11	2	0	.32	-1	-1	-
2007 KC	65	55	474.1	311	24	5	22	2	3	.985	24	31	.436	251	4.76	3	0	-	40	13	1	0	.33	4	3	-
2008 StL	57	44	412.0	289	16	2	12	2	1	.993	22	22	.500	194	4.24	3	0	-	21	5	3	0	.28	0	0	-
	519	475	4197.2	2918	233	33	147	34	28	.990	222	253	.467	2289	4.91	41	6	12	291	83	10	3	.30	9	6	8

Catchers

Paul Lo Duca

BASIC												PITCHER HANDLING					ER Saved	Adj ER Saved	Rank	STOLEN BASES					SB Saved	SB Runs Saved	Rank
Year	Team	G	GS	Inn	PO	A	E	WP	PB	DP	Pct	W	L	Pct	ER	CERA				SBA	CCS	PCS	CPO	CS%			
2003	LA	123	120	1080.0	1014	100	15	37	6	8	.987	66	54	.550	327	2.73	42	10	1	140	43	14	2	.34	11	8	1
2004	2 tms	130	125	1104.2	844	65	4	36	12	9	.996	76	49	.608	470	3.83	25	9	2	129	29	7	2	.24	0	0	10
2005	Fla	128	118	1033.1	817	61	8	31	4	8	.991	61	57	.517	436	3.80	19	4	5	118	24	5	1	.21	-3	-2	21
2006	NYM	118	117	1027.0	802	59	11	31	9	4	.987	70	47	.598	495	4.34	-14	-5	32	111	22	5	0	.21	-2	-1	21
2007	NYM	113	112	974.0	754	34	9	24	2	5	.989	59	53	.527	447	4.13	4	0	17	94	17	5	1	.19	-3	-2	21
2008	2 tms	26	25	208.2	163	7	2	5	1	0	.988	12	13	.480	106	4.57	-1	0	-	20	1	1	0	.05	-3	-2	-
		638	617	5427.2	4394	326	49	164	34	34	.990	344	273	.558	2281	3.78	75	18	2	612	136	37	6	.24	-1	1	17

Russell Martin

BASIC												PITCHER HANDLING					ER Saved	Adj ER Saved	Rank	STOLEN BASES					SB Saved	SB Runs Saved	Rank
Year	Team	G	GS	Inn	PO	A	E	WP	PB	DP	Pct	W	L	Pct	ER	CERA				SBA	CCS	PCS	CPO	CS%			
2006	LAD	117	114	1015.0	788	62	6	41	5	8	.993	71	43	.623	443	3.93	7	2	7	103	25	7	0	.26	1	0	17
2007	LAD	145	143	1254.0	1065	85	14	40	5	11	.988	78	65	.545	550	3.95	15	4	8	123	33	8	4	.29	7	5	3
2008	LAD	149	138	1238.0	1042	65	11	35	6	8	.990	76	62	.551	499	3.63	0	-2	27	93	17	6	1	.20	-2	-1	14
		411	395	3507.0	2895	212	31	116	16	27	.990	225	170	.570	1492	3.83	21	4	15	319	75	21	5	.25	6	4	15

Victor Martinez

BASIC												PITCHER HANDLING					ER Saved	Adj ER Saved	Rank	STOLEN BASES					SB Saved	SB Runs Saved	Rank
Year	Team	G	GS	Inn	PO	A	E	WP	PB	DP	Pct	W	L	Pct	ER	CERA				SBA	CCS	PCS	CPO	CS%			
2003	Cle	40	40	342.0	231	23	1	10	3	2	.996	14	26	.350	160	4.21	-3	0	-	29	8	1	0	.29	0	0	-
2004	Cle	132	124	1108.0	865	62	6	35	9	14	.994	59	65	.476	614	4.99	-19	-7	27	119	26	4	0	.23	-4	-3	27
2005	Cle	142	139	1233.0	904	58	5	23	3	6	.995	78	61	.561	504	3.68	-11	-3	30	125	25	4	2	.21	-2	-2	21
2006	Cle	133	127	1110.0	753	45	8	34	4	7	.990	65	62	.512	556	4.51	-23	-6	33	122	16	6	0	.14	-12	-9	35
2007	Cle	121	118	1042.2	779	53	4	27	6	8	.995	70	48	.593	465	4.01	-7	-2	26	103	30	3	1	.30	2	2	7
2008	Cle	55	54	447.1	328	16	3	10	2	1	.991	24	30	.444	214	4.31	-3	0	-	35	10	3	0	.31	1	1	-
		623	602	5283.0	3860	257	27	139	27	38	.993	310	292	.515	2513	4.28	-66	-18	34	533	115	21	3	.22	-16	-11	28

Jeff Mathis

BASIC												PITCHER HANDLING					ER Saved	Adj ER Saved	Rank	STOLEN BASES					SB Saved	SB Runs Saved	Rank
Year	Team	G	GS	Inn	PO	A	E	WP	PB	DP	Pct	W	L	Pct	ER	CERA				SBA	CCS	PCS	CPO	CS%			
2005	LAA	3	0	5.0	4	0	0	0	0	0	1.000	0	0	-	0	0.00	2	0	-	0	0	0	0	-	0	0	-
2006	LAA	20	14	133.0	92	6	3	6	1	0	.970	4	10	.286	86	5.82	-19	-1	-	15	2	1	0	.14	-1	-1	-
2007	LAA	57	52	467.0	383	42	4	24	5	2	.991	34	18	.654	202	3.89	4	0	-	48	8	0	7	.17	-4	-2	-
2008	LAA	94	90	793.1	624	57	13	21	3	5	.981	58	32	.644	323	3.66	17	3	6	77	16	4	3	.22	-4	-3	29
		174	156	1398.1	1103	105	20	51	9	8	.984	96	60	.615	611	3.93	4	2	-	140	26	5	10	.19	-9	-6	-

Joe Mauer

BASIC												PITCHER HANDLING					ER Saved	Adj ER Saved	Rank	STOLEN BASES					SB Saved	SB Runs Saved	Rank
Year	Team	G	GS	Inn	PO	A	E	WP	PB	DP	Pct	W	L	Pct	ER	CERA				SBA	CCS	PCS	CPO	CS%			
2004	Min	32	29	257.0	212	10	2	5	0	0	.991	19	10	.655	97	3.40	12	1	-	18	5	2	0	.31	0	0	-
2005	Min	116	110	999.2	692	46	5	26	6	6	.993	53	57	.482	410	3.69	-6	-1	20	54	18	5	0	.37	0	0	11
2006	Min	120	119	1059.1	867	43	4	31	5	7	.996	71	48	.597	461	3.92	-2	-1	20	58	17	5	0	.32	-1	-1	21
2007	Min	91	88	777.2	598	35	1	29	4	5	.998	44	44	.500	327	3.78	29	5	6	45	19	5	0	.48	4	3	5
2008	Min	139	135	1203.0	831	52	3	40	4	1	.997	73	62	.541	564	4.22	5	1	17	80	18	11	1	.26	-2	-1	14
		498	481	4296.2	3200	186	15	131	19	19	.996	260	221	.541	1859	3.89	39	5	13	255	77	28	1	.34	1	1	17

Brian McCann

BASIC												PITCHER HANDLING					ER Saved	Adj ER Saved	Rank	STOLEN BASES					SB Saved	SB Runs Saved	Rank
Year	Team	G	GS	Inn	PO	A	E	WP	PB	DP	Pct	W	L	Pct	ER	CERA				SBA	CCS	PCS	CPO	CS%			
2005	Atl	57	49	449.1	310	21	3	10	5	1	.991	33	16	.673	195	3.91	-9	-1	-	27	5	0	1	.19	-2	-1	-
2006	Atl	124	118	1016.1	778	39	9	29	5	5	.989	62	56	.525	498	4.41	13	2	7	91	20	1	0	.22	-1	-1	21
2007	Atl	132	130	1139.0	907	53	13	36	6	9	.987	70	60	.538	492	3.89	4	1	16	89	17	2	0	.20	-3	-2	21
2008	Atl	138	132	1143.1	879	70	9	33	7	9	.991	61	71	.462	540	4.25	28	7	1	120	21	6	2	.18	-1	-1	14
		451	429	3748.0	2874	183	34	108	23	24	.989	226	203	.527	1725	4.14	37	9	8	327	63	9	3	.20	-6	-5	23

Corky Miller

BASIC												PITCHER HANDLING					ER Saved	Adj ER Saved	Rank	STOLEN BASES					SB Saved	SB Runs Saved	Rank
Year	Team	G	GS	Inn	PO	A	E	WP	PB	DP	Pct	W	L	Pct	ER	CERA				SBA	CCS	PCS	CPO	CS%			
2003	Cin	11	9	78.2	60	5	0	3	0	0	1.000	5	4	.556	39	4.46	9	0	-	12	1	1	0	.09	-1	-1	-
2004	Cin	12	12	104.0	84	5	1	7	1	1	.989	5	7	.417	73	6.32	-13	0	-	3	1	0	0	.33	0	0	-
2005	Min	4	3	27.1	24	2	0	3	2	0	1.000	2	1	.667	8	2.63	3	0	-	3	2	0	0	.67	1	1	-
2006	Bos	1	1	9.0	6	0	0	0	0	0	1.000	0	0	1.000	5	5.00	0	0	-	0	0	0	0	-	0	0	-
2007	Atl	11	6	62.0	49	3	0	2	1	1	1.000	4	2	.667	31	4.50	0	0	-	3	1	0	0	.33	1	0	-
2008	Atl	29	17	164.1	129	18	3	2	4	0	.980	7	10	.412	70	3.83	10	0	-	15	6	0	0	.40	3	2	-
		68	48	445.1	352	33	4	17	8	2	.990	23	25	.479	226	4.57	9	0	-	36	11	1	0	.31	3	2	-

Catchers

Chad Moeller

Year	Team	G	GS	Inn	PO	A	E	WP	PB	DP	Pct	W	L	Pct	ER	CERA	ER Saved	Adj ER Saved	Rank	SBA	CCS	PCS	CPO	CS%	SB Saved	SB Runs Saved	Rank
2003	Ari	76	69	596.0	490	37	7	27	3	2	.987	32	37	.464	262	3.96	2	0	18	54	12	2	0	.23	0	0	21
2004	Mil	100	92	827.0	718	47	1	38	4	4	.999	42	50	.457	337	3.67	6	1	12	69	13	4	1	.20	-4	-3	27
2005	Mil	65	58	520.2	454	32	3	32	4	6	.994	30	28	.517	226	3.91	-3	0	14	44	6	4	0	.15	-4	-3	26
2006	Mil	29	25	231.0	192	15	1	8	0	0	.995	8	17	.320	139	5.42	-3	0	-	28	3	3	0	.12	-1	0	-
2007	2 tms	24	11	115.2	97	6	0	4	0	0	1.000	3	8	.273	82	6.38	-20	0	-	12	1	0	0	.08	-2	-1	-
2008	NYY	33	25	225.0	159	15	3	6	0	2	.983	16	9	.640	105	4.20	9	0	-	24	7	2	0	.32	-1	-1	-
		327	280	2515.1	2110	152	15	115	11	14	.993	131	149	.468	1151	4.12	-8	1	21	231	42	15	1	.19	-12	-8	24

Bengie Molina

Year	Team	G	GS	Inn	PO	A	E	WP	PB	DP	Pct	W	L	Pct	ER	CERA	ER Saved	Adj ER Saved	Rank	SBA	CCS	PCS	CPO	CS%	SB Saved	SB Runs Saved	Rank
2003	Ana	117	109	949.2	672	62	5	40	4	2	.993	53	56	.486	456	4.32	-9	-3	29	81	31	5	2	.41	7	5	3
2004	Ana	89	89	762.0	597	56	3	39	6	5	.995	51	38	.573	365	4.31	-8	-1	19	69	17	1	0	.25	-2	-1	15
2005	LAA	105	100	873.1	641	48	10	40	10	5	.996	57	43	.570	344	3.55	19	4	5	64	18	2	0	.29	-1	-1	17
2006	Tor	99	98	842.0	614	48	2	29	11	6	.997	51	47	.520	412	4.40	-4	-1	20	83	13	2	1	.16	-5	-3	28
2007	SF	129	125	1104.0	808	61	8	41	16	4	.991	55	70	.440	504	4.11	13	4	8	76	17	6	2	.24	-1	-1	18
2008	SF	136	132	1128.1	987	71	5	54	5	6	.995	57	75	.432	539	4.30	5	1	17	104	32	4	1	.32	8	6	3
		675	653	5659.1	4319	346	26	243	52	28	.994	324	329	.496	2620	4.17	15	4	15	477	128	20	6	.28	6	5	12

Jose Molina

Year	Team	G	GS	Inn	PO	A	E	WP	PB	DP	Pct	W	L	Pct	ER	CERA	ER Saved	Adj ER Saved	Rank	SBA	CCS	PCS	CPO	CS%	SB Saved	SB Runs Saved	Rank
2003	Ana	53	39	332.0	221	17	1	9	3	0	.996	17	22	.436	150	4.07	13	1	-	25	6	1	1	.25	-2	-1	-
2004	Ana	70	57	524.1	441	37	3	17	3	4	.994	34	23	.596	251	4.31	5	1	12	45	19	3	5	.45	5	4	3
2005	LAA	65	53	480.1	409	40	3	26	1	6	.993	33	20	.623	195	3.65	-4	0	-	39	18	2	3	.49	8	6	-
2006	LAA	76	71	603.1	502	50	8	42	5	4	.986	38	33	.535	267	3.98	7	1	11	47	19	1	4	.41	5	3	6
2007	2 tms	69	53	492.1	436	30	4	18	4	3	.991	31	22	.585	252	4.61	-4	0	17	44	12	1	1	.28	0	0	13
2008	NYY	97	81	737.0	634	52	3	29	7	6	.996	43	38	.531	302	3.69	31	5	2	75	32	1	1	.43	11	7	2
		430	354	3169.1	2643	226	22	141	25	23	.992	196	158	.554	1417	4.02	49	8	10	275	106	9	15	.40	26	19	2

Yadier Molina

Year	Team	G	GS	Inn	PO	A	E	WP	PB	DP	Pct	W	L	Pct	ER	CERA	ER Saved	Adj ER Saved	Rank	SBA	CCS	PCS	CPO	CS%	SB Saved	SB Runs Saved	Rank
2004	StL	51	39	344.0	256	16	2	11	4	1	.993	24	15	.615	139	3.64	7	1	-	17	8	0	1	.47	3	2	-
2005	StL	114	111	959.1	684	66	7	26	8	4	.991	73	38	.658	361	3.39	11	3	7	39	17	8	9	.55	7	5	3
2006	StL	127	118	1037.1	734	79	4	25	7	6	.995	61	57	.517	522	4.53	0	1	11	66	26	3	1	.41	6	4	2
2007	StL	107	101	861.1	582	63	6	24	7	8	.991	46	55	.455	414	4.33	27	6	4	50	23	4	2	.50	10	7	1
2008	StL	119	114	1002.0	653	70	10	34	5	7	.986	61	53	.535	470	4.22	-8	-2	27	52	16	2	7	.32	4	3	5
		518	483	4204.0	2909	294	29	120	31	26	.991	265	218	.549	1906	4.08	37	9	8	224	90	17	26	.43	30	21	1

Miguel Montero

Year	Team	G	GS	Inn	PO	A	E	WP	PB	DP	Pct	W	L	Pct	ER	CERA	ER Saved	Adj ER Saved	Rank	SBA	CCS	PCS	CPO	CS%	SB Saved	SB Runs Saved	Rank
2006	Ari	5	4	40.0	36	4	0	2	1	0	1.000	1	3	.250	21	4.73	-2	0	-	4	1	0	0	.25	0	0	-
2007	Ari	73	57	510.2	340	30	6	18	5	5	.984	26	31	.456	273	4.81	-22	-3	29	45	9	1	0	.20	-5	-4	29
2008	Ari	53	45	404.2	352	23	4	26	0	2	.989	17	28	.378	206	4.58	-24	-2	-	34	6	1	0	.18	-3	-2	-
		131	106	955.1	728	57	10	46	6	7	.987	44	62	.415	500	4.71	-49	-5	-	83	16	2	0	.20	-8	-6	-

Mike Napoli

Year	Team	G	GS	Inn	PO	A	E	WP	PB	DP	Pct	W	L	Pct	ER	CERA	ER Saved	Adj ER Saved	Rank	SBA	CCS	PCS	CPO	CS%	SB Saved	SB Runs Saved	Rank
2006	LAA	94	77	716.1	575	48	8	37	2	2	.987	47	30	.610	299	3.76	3	1	11	55	16	1	0	.30	1	1	13
2007	LAA	75	68	598.2	460	32	7	28	1	2	.986	38	30	.559	285	4.28	-7	-1	23	64	13	2	1	.21	-3	-2	21
2008	LAA	75	71	625.0	469	21	3	27	7	3	.994	42	29	.592	309	4.45	-19	-3	32	63	9	2	0	.15	-5	-3	29
		244	216	1940.0	1504	101	18	92	10	7	.989	127	89	.588	893	4.14	-23	-3	-	182	38	5	1	.21	-7	-4	-

Dioner Navarro

Year	Team	G	GS	Inn	PO	A	E	WP	PB	DP	Pct	W	L	Pct	ER	CERA	ER Saved	Adj ER Saved	Rank	SBA	CCS	PCS	CPO	CS%	SB Saved	SB Runs Saved	Rank
2004	NYY	4	1	13.0	9	0	0	0	0	0	1.000	1	0	1.000	2	1.38	6	0	-	0	0	0	0	-	0	0	-
2005	LAD	50	49	435.2	336	29	2	8	3	1	.995	24	25	.490	210	4.34	1	0	-	42	8	1	0	.20	-1	-1	-
2006	2 tms	78	75	653.2	479	37	8	34	6	3	.985	28	47	.373	355	4.89	4	0	17	68	18	2	0	.27	-2	-1	21
2007	TB	112	110	956.1	814	67	14	33	6	11	.984	47	63	.427	584	5.50	1	0	17	101	24	6	0	.25	-4	-3	25
2008	TB	117	113	1011.1	837	55	5	35	6	10	.994	70	43	.619	438	3.90	-24	-5	34	73	25	3	0	.36	6	4	4
		361	348	3070.0	2475	188	29	110	21	25	.989	170	178	.489	1589	4.66	-12	-5	28	284	75	12	0	.28	-1	-1	20

Catchers

Wil Nieves

		BASIC										PITCHER HANDLING					ER Saved	Adj ER Saved	Rank	STOLEN BASES					SB Saved	SB Runs Saved	Rank
Year	Team	G	GS	Inn	PO	A	E	WP	PB	DP	Pct	W	L	Pct	ER	CERA				SBA	CCS	PCS	CPO	CS%			
2005	NYY	3	0	9.0	11	0	0	0	0	0	1.000	0	0		4	4.00	2	0	-	0	0	0	0		0	0	-
2006	NYY	6	1	19.0	15	1	0	2	1	0	1.000	0	1	.000	10	4.74	0	0	-	3	1	0	0	.33	0	0	-
2007	NYY	25	21	169.0	111	6	2	3	1	1	.983	12	9	.571	82	4.37	12	1	-	27	6	0	0	.22	-1	-1	-
2008	Was	61	46	449.2	359	31	3	20	3	4	.992	18	28	.391	230	4.60	0	0	-	49	9	1	1	.19	0	0	-
		95	68	646.2	496	38	5	25	5	5	.991	30	38	.441	326	4.54	15	1	-	79	16	1	1	.21	-1	-1	-

Miguel Olivo

		BASIC										PITCHER HANDLING					ER Saved	Adj ER Saved	Rank	STOLEN BASES					SB Saved	SB Runs Saved	Rank
Year	Team	G	GS	Inn	PO	A	E	WP	PB	DP	Pct	W	L	Pct	ER	CERA				SBA	CCS	PCS	CPO	CS%			
2003	CWS	113	98	848.0	692	39	9	24	8	4	.988	54	44	.551	358	3.80	7	1	12	53	19	0	3	.36	2	2	9
2004	2 tms	95	83	760.1	510	29	5	32	12	8	.991	42	41	.506	383	4.53	27	4	3	49	11	6	3	.26	-3	-2	20
2005	2 tms	91	77	690.0	505	29	9	28	7	3	.983	34	43	.442	326	4.25	12	1	11	46	12	2	2	.27	-1	0	11
2006	Fla	124	109	971.1	732	65	7	37	10	11	.991	52	57	.477	476	4.41	-6	-1	20	78	25	5	2	.34	3	2	10
2007	Fla	119	111	990.1	787	64	12	51	16	9	.986	47	64	.423	555	5.04	-16	-5	31	76	20	5	8	.28	1	1	10
2008	KC	58	56	494.1	378	32	5	26	4	6	.988	26	30	.464	243	4.42	2	0	21	33	12	2	1	.39	4	3	5
		600	534	4754.1	3604	258	47	198	57	41	.988	255	279	.478	2341	4.43	26	0	23	335	99	20	19	.31	7	6	8

Ronny Paulino

		BASIC										PITCHER HANDLING					ER Saved	Adj ER Saved	Rank	STOLEN BASES					SB Saved	SB Runs Saved	Rank
Year	Team	G	GS	Inn	PO	A	E	WP	PB	DP	Pct	W	L	Pct	ER	CERA				SBA	CCS	PCS	CPO	CS%			
2005	Pit	2	1	11.0	10	0	0	0	0	0	1.000	1	0	1.000	2	1.64	1	0	-	1	0	0	0	.00	0	0	-
2006	Pit	124	117	1047.0	799	72	11	45	9	4	.988	53	64	.453	488	4.19	40	9	1	105	24	14	3	.26	2	1	13
2007	Pit	129	119	1088.0	784	58	7	31	8	9	.992	58	61	.487	557	4.61	8	2	13	101	19	8	1	.20	-2	-1	18
2008	Pit	32	27	260.0	198	16	2	8	1	3	.991	8	19	.296	157	5.43	-1	0	-	31	8	0	0	.26	1	1	-
		287	264	2406.0	1791	146	20	84	18	16	.990	120	144	.455	1204	4.50	48	11	-	238	51	22	4	.24	1	1	-

A.J. Pierzynski

		BASIC										PITCHER HANDLING					ER Saved	Adj ER Saved	Rank	STOLEN BASES					SB Saved	SB Runs Saved	Rank
Year	Team	G	GS	Inn	PO	A	E	WP	PB	DP	Pct	W	L	Pct	ER	CERA				SBA	CCS	PCS	CPO	CS%			
2003	Min	135	131	1165.2	844	45	6	48	5	6	.993	75	56	.573	537	4.15	21	6	4	66	17	3	0	.27	-2	-1	26
2004	SF	118	117	1022.0	697	56	1	36	9	6	.999	65	52	.556	488	4.30	7	2	6	66	11	4	0	.18	-5	-3	27
2005	CWS	128	124	1117.2	803	48	1	45	7	8	.998	77	47	.621	464	3.74	-22	-5	32	102	20	3	1	.20	-1	0	11
2006	CWS	132	126	1125.0	797	60	3	44	10	4	.997	74	52	.587	559	4.47	18	5	3	115	21	4	0	.19	-2	-2	25
2007	CWS	130	116	1058.0	796	46	2	32	14	6	.998	54	62	.466	519	4.41	30	7	2	82	12	8	0	.16	1	0	13
2008	CWS	131	127	1134.1	913	54	9	38	5	8	.991	67	60	.528	533	4.23	-21	-5	34	117	11	10	0	.10	-4	-3	29
		774	741	6622.2	4850	309	22	243	50	38	.996	412	329	.556	3100	4.21	33	10	7	548	92	32	1	.18	-13	-9	26

Jorge Posada

		BASIC										PITCHER HANDLING					ER Saved	Adj ER Saved	Rank	STOLEN BASES					SB Saved	SB Runs Saved	Rank
Year	Team	G	GS	Inn	PO	A	E	WP	PB	DP	Pct	W	L	Pct	ER	CERA				SBA	CCS	PCS	CPO	CS%			
2003	NYY	137	131	1165.0	933	75	6	30	13	2	.994	81	50	.618	535	4.13	-20	-5	33	100	26	2	4	.27	1	1	14
2004	NYY	134	126	1102.1	835	53	9	50	9	12	.990	80	46	.635	570	4.65	-17	-3	25	92	23	2	1	.26	-3	-2	20
2005	NYY	133	123	1076.2	718	76	3	33	8	6	.996	69	54	.561	559	4.67	-11	-2	25	129	35	4	1	.28	0	0	11
2006	NYY	134	121	1050.1	787	68	9	37	13	7	.990	76	45	.628	510	4.37	-12	-3	28	102	34	4	2	.35	5	3	6
2007	NYY	138	125	1111.1	799	54	5	52	13	6	.994	71	54	.568	556	4.50	0	-1	23	134	28	4	0	.22	-8	-6	31
2008	NYY	30	28	234.1	197	7	1	12	2	1	.995	17	11	.607	121	4.65	-18	-1	-	41	3	4	0	.08	-6	-4	-
		706	654	5740.0	4269	333	33	214	58	34	.993	394	260	.602	2851	4.47	-78	-15	32	598	149	20	8	.26	-11	-8	24

Humberto Quintero

		BASIC										PITCHER HANDLING					ER Saved	Adj ER Saved	Rank	STOLEN BASES					SB Saved	SB Runs Saved	Rank
Year	Team	G	GS	Inn	PO	A	E	WP	PB	DP	Pct	W	L	Pct	ER	CERA				SBA	CCS	PCS	CPO	CS%			
2003	SD	11	7	58.1	52	2	1	1	2	1	.982	0	7	.000	42	6.48	-10	0	-	3	0	1	1	.00	0	0	-
2004	SD	21	19	171.2	130	10	0	4	0	0	1.000	14	5	.737	70	3.67	5	0	-	9	1	0	0	.11	-1	0	-
2005	Hou	16	15	124.0	86	5	1	3	0	0	.989	9	6	.600	54	3.92	13	0	-	9	1	1	1	.13	-3	-2	-
2006	Hou	10	7	56.2	42	6	0	2	1	3	1.000	2	5	.286	35	5.56	-8	0	-	5	3	0	1	.60	2	1	-
2007	Hou	26	15	151.2	97	13	2	4	1	0	.982	5	10	.333	86	5.10	0	0	-	13	5	0	0	.38	2	1	-
2008	Hou	59	52	447.0	373	26	1	5	1	3	.998	30	22	.577	243	4.89	-13	0	-	24	7	2	1	.32	1	1	-
		143	115	1009.1	780	62	5	19	5	7	.994	60	55	.522	530	4.73	-13	0	-	63	17	4	4	.29	1	1	-

Guillermo Quiroz

		BASIC										PITCHER HANDLING					ER Saved	Adj ER Saved	Rank	STOLEN BASES					SB Saved	SB Runs Saved	Rank
Year	Team	G	GS	Inn	PO	A	E	WP	PB	DP	Pct	W	L	Pct	ER	CERA				SBA	CCS	PCS	CPO	CS%			
2004	Tor	15	13	114.2	76	6	2	7	3	3	.976	5	8	.385	68	5.34	-11	0	-	7	2	0	0	.29	0	0	-
2005	Tor	10	10	85.0	56	5	0	3	0	1	1.000	4	6	.400	47	4.98	-6	0	-	14	2	1	0	.15	-1	0	-
2006	Sea	1	1	8.0	5	0	0	0	0	0	1.000	0	1	.000	5	5.63	1	0	-	0	0	0	0	.00	0	0	-
2007	Tex	8	2	28.2	25	0	2	1	0	0	.926	0	2	.000	20	6.28	-7	0	-	5	0	0	0	.00	-1	-1	-
2008	Bal	54	39	354.1	229	17	1	24	5	3	.996	11	28	.282	220	5.59	-16	-1	-	39	7	2	0	.19	0	0	-
		88	65	590.2	391	28	5	35	8	7	.988	20	45	.308	360	5.49	-38	-1	-	65	11	3	0	.18	-2	-1	-

Catchers

Mike Rabelo

Year	Team	G	GS	Inn	PO	A	E	WP	PB	DP	Pct	W	L	Pct	ER	CERA	ER Saved	Adj ER Saved	Rank	SBA	CCS	PCS	CPO	CS%	SB Saved	SB Runs Saved	Rank
2007	Det	49	43	394.2	246	21	5	22	3	5	.982	21	22	.488	222	5.06	-12	-1	-	36	8	2	0	.24	-2	-2	-
2008	Fla	32	29	262.2	179	11	1	13	3	1	.995	18	11	.621	121	4.15	18	1	-	22	5	1	0	.24	0	0	-
		81	72	657.1	425	32	6	35	6	6	.987	39	33	.542	343	4.70	6	0	-	58	13	3	0	.24	-2	-2	-

Mike Redmond

Year	Team	G	GS	Inn	PO	A	E	WP	PB	DP	Pct	W	L	Pct	ER	CERA	ER Saved	Adj ER Saved	Rank	SBA	CCS	PCS	CPO	CS%	SB Saved	SB Runs Saved	Rank
2003	Fla	37	26	247.1	195	10	1	3	0	1	.995	10	16	.385	143	5.20	-18	-1	-	33	4	1	1	.13	-5	-3	-
2004	Fla	79	71	604.1	488	33	2	15	4	7	.996	32	39	.451	308	4.59	-18	-3	25	65	11	3	0	.18	-6	-4	31
2005	Min	45	43	376.1	230	13	0	6	1	2	1.000	24	19	.558	162	3.87	0	0	-	19	9	1	0	.50	2	2	-
2006	Min	43	43	378.0	317	21	0	9	0	2	1.000	25	18	.581	170	4.05	-7	-1	-	27	8	1	0	.31	-1	0	-
2007	Min	56	55	482.2	385	24	0	8	0	4	1.000	29	26	.527	235	4.38	-7	-1	23	39	13	3	0	.36	0	0	13
2008	Min	30	28	253.0	180	9	0	5	0	2	1.000	15	13	.536	113	4.02	0	0	-	23	3	2	0	.14	-3	-2	-
		290	266	2341.2	1795	110	3	46	5	18	.998	135	131	.508	1131	4.35	-50	-6	-	206	48	11	1	.25	-13	-7	-

Shawn Riggans

Year	Team	G	GS	Inn	PO	A	E	WP	PB	DP	Pct	W	L	Pct	ER	CERA	ER Saved	Adj ER Saved	Rank	SBA	CCS	PCS	CPO	CS%	SB Saved	SB Runs Saved	Rank
2006	TB	8	8	67.1	56	4	0	4	0	1	1.000	1	7	.125	32	4.28	9	0	-	3	3	0	0	1.00	1	1	-
2007	TB	3	3	27.0	31	1	2	2	0	0	.941	2	1	.667	13	4.33	1	0	-	3	0	0	0	.00	-1	0	-
2008	TB	41	38	343.1	268	5	5	11	4	0	.982	21	17	.553	138	3.62	11	1	-	25	1	0	0	.04	-5	-4	-
		52	49	437.2	355	10	7	17	4	1	.981	24	25	.490	183	3.76	21	1	-	31	4	0	0	.13	-5	-3	-

Mike Rivera

Year	Team	G	GS	Inn	PO	A	E	WP	PB	DP	Pct	W	L	Pct	ER	CERA	ER Saved	Adj ER Saved	Rank	SBA	CCS	PCS	CPO	CS%	SB Saved	SB Runs Saved	Rank
2003	SD	19	16	139.0	133	7	2	15	2	0	.986	4	12	.250	88	5.70	-8	0	-	13	2	1	0	.17	-1	-1	-
2006	Mil	44	39	352.2	299	31	4	14	0	2	.988	18	21	.462	197	5.03	-22	-2	-	47	8	0	0	.17	-4	-3	-
2007	Mil	11	1	37.0	33	2	0	2	0	0	1.000	1	0	1.000	18	4.38	0	0	-	3	1	0	0	.33	0	0	-
2008	Mil	17	13	127.1	112	11	3	8	1	2	.976	7	6	.538	58	4.10	1	0	-	20	2	2	0	.11	-3	-2	-
		91	69	656.0	577	51	9	39	3	4	.986	30	39	.435	361	4.95	-28	-2	-	83	13	3	0	.16	-8	-6	-

Ivan Rodriguez

Year	Team	G	GS	Inn	PO	A	E	WP	PB	DP	Pct	W	L	Pct	ER	CERA	ER Saved	Adj ER Saved	Rank	SBA	CCS	PCS	CPO	CS%	SB Saved	SB Runs Saved	Rank
2003	Fla	138	134	1132.1	915	46	8	46	10	6	.992	80	54	.597	483	3.84	22	5	6	60	19	1	2	.32	0	0	21
2004	Det	125	124	1051.0	770	52	11	50	3	6	.987	58	66	.468	568	4.86	7	2	6	59	16	3	1	.29	-2	-1	15
2005	Det	123	121	1032.2	702	60	4	40	4	4	.995	56	65	.463	511	4.45	6	1	11	68	26	9	6	.44	11	8	1
2006	Det	123	121	1054.1	741	58	2	34	4	4	.998	73	48	.603	449	3.83	2	1	11	51	21	5	1	.46	6	4	2
2007	Det	127	119	1052.2	834	50	6	53	7	7	.993	67	52	.563	515	4.40	20	5	6	68	19	2	2	.29	3	2	7
2008	2 tms	112	105	930.0	620	58	5	35	6	9	.993	52	53	.495	473	4.58	21	3	6	77	23	2	0	.31	0	0	12
		748	724	6253.0	4582	324	36	258	34	39	.993	386	338	.533	2999	4.32	77	17	3	383	124	22	12	.34	18	13	4

David Ross

Year	Team	G	GS	Inn	PO	A	E	WP	PB	DP	Pct	W	L	Pct	ER	CERA	ER Saved	Adj ER Saved	Rank	SBA	CCS	PCS	CPO	CS%	SB Saved	SB Runs Saved	Rank
2003	LA	38	35	314.0	259	26	4	12	2	2	.986	16	19	.457	160	4.59	-38	-3	-	45	13	3	0	.31	4	3	-
2004	LA	67	51	451.2	356	20	3	13	6	0	.992	25	26	.490	213	4.24	-8	-1	-	39	11	1	2	.29	-1	0	-
2005	2 tms	42	33	304.0	211	23	3	12	4	5	.987	14	19	.424	140	4.14	15	1	-	15	7	2	0	.54	3	2	-
2006	Cin	75	73	620.2	480	33	8	23	4	5	.985	34	39	.466	294	4.26	12	2	7	31	12	2	1	.41	2	1	13
2007	Cin	108	98	837.1	662	50	5	32	6	7	.993	38	60	.388	425	4.57	18	2	13	61	23	2	1	.39	6	4	4
2008	2 tms	54	43	399.2	346	29	3	11	6	4	.992	16	27	.372	227	5.11	-5	-1	-	36	10	0	0	.28	1	1	-
		384	333	2927.1	2314	181	26	103	28	23	.990	143	190	.429	1459	4.49	-6	0	23	227	76	10	4	.35	15	11	6

Carlos Ruiz

Year	Team	G	GS	Inn	PO	A	E	WP	PB	DP	Pct	W	L	Pct	ER	CERA	ER Saved	Adj ER Saved	Rank	SBA	CCS	PCS	CPO	CS%	SB Saved	SB Runs Saved	Rank
2006	Phi	24	18	176.1	147	11	3	10	1	1	.981	9	9	.500	81	4.13	7	0	-	14	2	1	1	.15	-1	-1	-
2007	Phi	111	100	912.2	688	54	2	27	5	4	.997	58	42	.580	465	4.59	15	3	11	83	19	7	4	.25	1	1	10
2008	Phi	110	92	828.0	623	58	5	19	4	2	.993	55	37	.598	354	3.85	-4	0	21	85	14	6	2	.18	-3	-2	20
		245	210	1917.0	1458	123	10	56	10	7	.994	122	88	.581	900	4.23	18	3	-	182	35	14	7	.21	-3	-2	-

Dusty Ryan

Year	Team	G	GS	Inn	PO	A	E	WP	PB	DP	Pct	W	L	Pct	ER	CERA	ER Saved	Adj ER Saved	Rank	SBA	CCS	PCS	CPO	CS%	SB Saved	SB Runs Saved	Rank
2008	Det	15	14	122.1	99	5	0	14	1	0	1.000	3	11	.214	83	6.11	-18	0	-	13	4	2	0	.36	2	1	-

Catchers

Jarrod Saltalamacchia

Year	Team	G	GS	Inn	PO	A	E	WP	PB	DP	Pct	W	L	Pct	ER	CERA	ER Saved	Adj ER Saved	Rank	SBA	CCS	PCS	CPO	CS%	SB Saved	SB Runs Saved	Rank
2007	2 tms	47	42	372.2	265	17	3	19	2	4	.989	19	23	.452	197	4.76	0	-1	-	45	6	2	0	.14	-3	-2	-
2008	Tex	54	52	464.1	345	17	9	23	6	6	.976	26	26	.500	265	5.14	-3	0	-	49	7	2	0	.15	-6	-5	-
		101	94	837.0	610	34	12	42	8	10	.982	45	49	.479	462	4.97	-3	-1	-	94	13	4	0	.14	-10	-7	-

Clint Sammons

Year	Team	G	GS	Inn	PO	A	E	WP	PB	DP	Pct	W	L	Pct	ER	CERA	ER Saved	Adj ER Saved	Rank	SBA	CCS	PCS	CPO	CS%	SB Saved	SB Runs Saved	Rank
2007	Atl	2	1	9.0	5	1	0	0	0	0	1.000	0	1	.000	4	4.00	0	0	-	2	1	0	0	.50	1	0	-
2008	Atl	22	13	133.0	106	3	0	7	3	0	1.000	4	9	.308	105	7.11	-30	-1	-	13	0	2	0	.00	-2	-1	-
		24	14	142.0	111	4	0	7	3	0	1.000	4	10	.286	109	6.91	-30	-1	-	15	1	2	0	.08	-1	-1	-

Pablo Sandoval

Year	Team	G	GS	Inn	PO	A	E	WP	PB	DP	Pct	W	L	Pct	ER	CERA	ER Saved	Adj ER Saved	Rank	SBA	CCS	PCS	CPO	CS%	SB Saved	SB Runs Saved	Rank
2008	SF	11	9	86.1	76	6	0	5	2	1	1.000	7	2	.778	42	4.38	6	0	-	10	3	0	0	.30	0	0	-

Dane Sardinha

Year	Team	G	GS	Inn	PO	A	E	WP	PB	DP	Pct	W	L	Pct	ER	CERA	ER Saved	Adj ER Saved	Rank	SBA	CCS	PCS	CPO	CS%	SB Saved	SB Runs Saved	Rank
2003	Cin	1	0	4.0	2	0	0	0	0	0	1.000	0	0	-	3	6.75	0	0	-	0	0	0	0	-	0	0	-
2005	Cin	1	1	8.0	7	0	0	0	0	0	1.000	0	1	.000	7	7.88	-2	0	-	0	0	0	0	-	0	0	-
2008	Det	17	13	122.2	109	8	1	2	0	1	.992	7	6	.538	64	4.70	3	0	-	5	1	0	0	.20	0	0	-
		19	14	134.2	118	8	1	2	0	1	.992	7	7	.500	74	4.95	1	0	-	5	1	0	0	.20	0	0	-

Brian Schneider

Year	Team	G	GS	Inn	PO	A	E	WP	PB	DP	Pct	W	L	Pct	ER	CERA	ER Saved	Adj ER Saved	Rank	SBA	CCS	PCS	CPO	CS%	SB Saved	SB Runs Saved	Rank
2003	Mon	98	95	841.0	661	45	3	29	3	9	.996	49	46	.516	351	3.76	7	2	10	51	21	6	0	.47	3	2	9
2004	Mon	133	125	1114.0	814	59	2	28	4	16	.998	52	73	.416	478	3.86	43	11	1	72	33	3	4	.48	10	7	1
2005	Was	113	105	926.2	654	52	5	35	3	10	.993	52	53	.495	400	3.88	14	3	7	80	29	3	4	.38	5	4	4
2006	Was	123	111	990.1	692	55	5	28	5	8	.993	45	66	.405	581	5.28	-29	-7	34	83	21	4	0	.27	1	1	13
2007	Was	122	120	1051.1	702	53	6	38	5	4	.992	52	68	.433	560	4.79	-22	-7	33	77	22	2	0	.29	2	1	10
2008	NYM	109	98	881.0	741	41	5	37	4	3	.994	53	45	.541	402	4.11	-9	-2	27	63	16	5	0	.28	0	0	12
		698	654	5804.1	4264	305	26	195	24	50	.994	303	351	.463	2772	4.30	4	0	23	426	142	23	8	.35	21	15	3

Kelly Shoppach

Year	Team	G	GS	Inn	PO	A	E	WP	PB	DP	Pct	W	L	Pct	ER	CERA	ER Saved	Adj ER Saved	Rank	SBA	CCS	PCS	CPO	CS%	SB Saved	SB Runs Saved	Rank
2005	Bos	7	2	29.0	14	0	0	3	0	0	1.000	1	1	.500	16	4.97	-2	0	-	2	0	0	0	.00	0	0	-
2006	Cle	40	31	280.1	208	20	2	11	3	5	.991	12	19	.387	128	4.11	9	1	-	30	10	1	1	.34	3	2	-
2007	Cle	58	44	420.0	287	28	4	15	2	6	.987	26	18	.591	194	4.16	15	2	-	36	13	0	0	.36	3	2	-
2008	Cle	110	94	872.2	586	34	7	30	8	2	.989	50	44	.532	424	4.37	-5	-2	27	47	10	0	0	.21	-3	-2	20
		215	171	1602.0	1095	82	13	59	13	13	.989	89	82	.520	762	4.28	17	1	-	115	33	1	1	.29	2	2	-

Chris Snyder

Year	Team	G	GS	Inn	PO	A	E	WP	PB	DP	Pct	W	L	Pct	ER	CERA	ER Saved	Adj ER Saved	Rank	SBA	CCS	PCS	CPO	CS%	SB Saved	SB Runs Saved	Rank
2004	Ari	29	27	247.1	213	19	0	10	3	2	1.000	11	16	.407	119	4.33	19	1	-	19	6	0	0	.32	1	1	-
2005	Ari	113	105	915.2	679	44	2	41	7	0	.997	50	55	.476	462	4.54	30	6	2	63	12	5	0	.21	1	1	7
2006	Ari	60	55	495.0	394	35	2	19	6	6	.995	24	31	.436	250	4.55	-5	0	-	38	13	4	0	.38	2	1	-
2007	Ari	106	103	891.1	722	58	1	28	9	9	.999	63	40	.612	369	3.73	10	3	11	81	18	11	1	.26	2	2	7
2008	Ari	112	106	922.2	777	69	0	30	7	5	1.000	59	47	.557	393	3.83	6	2	12	71	20	2	0	.29	2	1	8
		420	396	3472.0	2785	225	5	128	32	22	.998	207	189	.523	1593	4.13	60	12	4	272	69	22	1	.28	8	6	8

Geovany Soto

Year	Team	G	GS	Inn	PO	A	E	WP	PB	DP	Pct	W	L	Pct	ER	CERA	ER Saved	Adj ER Saved	Rank	SBA	CCS	PCS	CPO	CS%	SB Saved	SB Runs Saved	Rank
2006	ChC	7	7	55.0	66	4	1	2	0	0	.986	2	5	.286	32	5.24	-3	0	-	5	0	0	0	.00	-1	0	-
2007	ChC	16	13	122.0	109	10	0	2	0	0	1.000	10	3	.769	49	3.61	1	0	-	14	4	0	0	.29	0	0	-
2008	ChC	136	131	1150.1	1011	55	5	40	5	9	.995	80	51	.611	486	3.80	5	3	6	94	18	7	0	.21	-6	-4	34
		159	151	1327.1	1186	69	6	44	5	9	.995	92	59	.609	567	3.84	3	3	-	113	22	7	0	.21	-6	-4	-

Catchers

Kurt Suzuki

Year	Team	G	GS	Inn	PO	A	E	WP	PB	DP	Pct	W	L	Pct	ER	CERA	ER Saved	Adj ER Saved	Rank	SBA	CCS	PCS	CPO	CS%	SB Saved	SB Runs Saved	Rank
2007	Oak	66	61	539.0	431	32	2	21	7	0	.996	27	34	.443	318	5.31	-52	-7	33	36	7	0	0	.19	0	0	13
2008	Oak	141	136	1215.0	927	53	6	23	5	4	.994	64	72	.471	521	3.86	16	3	6	87	16	16	0	.23	3	2	7
		207	197	1754.0	1358	85	8	44	12	4	.994	91	106	.462	839	4.31	-36	-4		123	23	16	0	.21	3	2	

Taylor Teagarden

Year	Team	G	GS	Inn	PO	A	E	WP	PB	DP	Pct	W	L	Pct	ER	CERA	ER Saved	Adj ER Saved	Rank	SBA	CCS	PCS	CPO	CS%	SB Saved	SB Runs Saved	Rank
2008	Tex	12	11	100.2	67	6	3	1	1	0	.961	5	6	.455	55	4.92	1	0	-	9	2	0	0	.22	0	0	-

Yorvit Torrealba

Year	Team	G	GS	Inn	PO	A	E	WP	PB	DP	Pct	W	L	Pct	ER	CERA	ER Saved	Adj ER Saved	Rank	SBA	CCS	PCS	CPO	CS%	SB Saved	SB Runs Saved	Rank
2003	SF	66	52	495.2	365	29	1	17	0	1	.997	31	21	.596	228	4.14	-13	-2	-	41	14	5	1	.39	3	2	-
2004	SF	59	45	433.0	349	18	2	16	2	5	.995	26	19	.578	215	4.47	-11	-1	-	30	6	3	0	.22	-1	-1	-
2005	2 tms	68	60	536.2	372	34	0	8	1	2	1.000	25	35	.417	271	4.54	-13	-1	20	56	15	5	0	.29	-1	-1	17
2006	Col	63	61	530.0	337	34	5	7	4	7	.987	20	41	.328	277	4.70	-11	-2	26	52	16	5	0	.34	6	4	2
2007	Col	112	105	935.1	679	56	7	23	4	7	.991	56	49	.533	428	4.12	26	6	4	76	13	2	1	.18	0	0	13
2008	Col	67	64	581.0	433	26	2	24	4	4	.996	27	37	.422	331	5.13	-13	-2	27	61	12	4	0	.21	1	1	8
		435	387	3511.2	2535	197	17	95	15	26	.994	185	202	.478	1750	4.49	-35	-2	26	316	76	24	2	.26	7	5	12

J.R. Towles

Year	Team	G	GS	Inn	PO	A	E	WP	PB	DP	Pct	W	L	Pct	ER	CERA	ER Saved	Adj ER Saved	Rank	SBA	CCS	PCS	CPO	CS%	SB Saved	SB Runs Saved	Rank
2007	Hou	14	9	95.0	65	6	0	5	1	1	1.000	7	2	.778	45	4.26	7	0	-	6	3	0	0	.50	1	1	-
2008	Hou	53	47	408.2	312	13	2	8	3	1	.994	24	23	.511	217	4.78	7	0	-	20	5	2	0	.28	-1	-1	-
		67	56	503.2	377	19	2	13	4	2	.995	31	25	.554	262	4.68	13	0	-	26	8	2	0	.33	0	0	-

Matt Treanor

Year	Team	G	GS	Inn	PO	A	E	WP	PB	DP	Pct	W	L	Pct	ER	CERA	ER Saved	Adj ER Saved	Rank	SBA	CCS	PCS	CPO	CS%	SB Saved	SB Runs Saved	Rank
2004	Fla	27	14	147.2	117	6	3	4	0	0	.976	6	8	.429	72	4.39	0	0	-	14	3	0	0	.21	-1	0	-
2005	Fla	55	41	366.2	309	14	5	12	4	4	.985	21	20	.512	195	4.79	-15	-1	-	33	9	0	0	.27	2	1	-
2006	Fla	61	50	439.2	374	26	3	9	2	2	.993	26	24	.520	205	4.20	5	0	-	34	13	3	0	.42	4	3	-
2007	Fla	53	50	440.2	385	16	3	16	3	2	.993	23	27	.460	230	4.70	20	2	-	49	6	1	1	.13	-3	-2	-
2008	Fla	65	60	524.2	453	29	8	21	2	3	.984	31	29	.517	269	4.61	4	1	17	59	12	3	0	.21	-1	-1	14
		261	215	1919.1	1638	91	22	62	11	11	.987	107	108	.498	971	4.55	15	2	-	189	43	7	1	.24	1	1	

Jason Varitek

Year	Team	G	GS	Inn	PO	A	E	WP	PB	DP	Pct	W	L	Pct	ER	CERA	ER Saved	Adj ER Saved	Rank	SBA	CCS	PCS	CPO	CS%	SB Saved	SB Runs Saved	Rank
2003	Bos	137	119	1075.1	854	43	9	28	6	6	.990	73	46	.613	539	4.51	-18	-5	33	84	19	4	0	.24	1	1	14
2004	Bos	130	121	1062.0	880	49	2	20	5	11	.998	73	48	.603	494	4.18	-15	-3	25	100	20	3	2	.21	-3	-2	20
2005	Bos	130	127	1089.0	783	33	8	43	7	4	.990	73	54	.575	609	5.03	-40	-10	35	86	16	5	1	.20	-9	-6	33
2006	Bos	99	94	822.1	647	28	4	24	1	3	.994	58	36	.617	442	4.84	0	0	17	59	10	3	0	.18	-4	-3	28
2007	Bos	125	121	1064.0	937	39	6	16	4	8	.994	73	48	.603	449	3.80	-9	-2	26	83	19	1	0	.23	-3	-2	21
2008	Bos	131	120	1041.1	903	42	4	23	4	7	.996	73	47	.608	424	3.66	14	3	6	72	13	3	0	.19	-3	-2	20
		752	702	6154.2	5004	234	33	154	27	39	.994	423	279	.603	2957	4.32	-68	-17	33	484	97	19	3	.21	-20	-14	31

Gregg Zaun

Year	Team	G	GS	Inn	PO	A	E	WP	PB	DP	Pct	W	L	Pct	ER	CERA	ER Saved	Adj ER Saved	Rank	SBA	CCS	PCS	CPO	CS%	SB Saved	SB Runs Saved	Rank
2003	2 tms	45	38	320.1	223	10	6	9	2	0	.975	21	17	.553	184	5.17	-8	0	-	34	4	7	0	.15	-2	-2	-
2004	Tor	97	91	789.0	547	46	8	28	3	5	.987	44	47	.484	420	4.79	13	2	6	83	21	2	0	.26	2	2	5
2005	Tor	132	121	1088.0	761	49	8	27	5	3	.990	64	57	.529	458	3.79	32	8	1	93	17	4	2	.19	-7	-5	31
2006	Tor	72	59	541.1	437	32	3	22	4	2	.994	32	27	.542	261	4.34	-10	-1	20	72	12	5	0	.18	-3	-2	25
2007	Tor	103	93	838.1	590	41	8	23	4	7	.987	53	40	.570	331	3.55	33	7	3	86	12	1	1	.14	-3	-3	25
2008	Tor	79	67	612.1	515	28	7	29	4	7	.987	29	38	.433	259	3.81	-25	-4	33	54	12	2	0	.23	-2	-1	14
		528	469	4189.1	3073	206	40	138	20	21	.988	243	226	.518	1913	4.11	35	12	4	422	78	21	3	.19	-16	-11	28

Pitchers

Tony Armas Jr.

Year	Tm	G	Inn	TC	E	Pct	SBA	CCS	PCS	PPO	CS%	Rght	Mid	Left	Tot	RS	Rnk
		BASIC					HOLDING					+/-					
2003	Mon	5	31	4	0	1.000	1	0	0	0	.00	+1	0	0	+1	1	-
2004	Mon	16	72	15	0	1.000	8	2	1	0	.38	+3	0	+1	+3	2	-
2005	Was	19	101	21	2	.913	7	3	1	0	.57	0	0	+1	+1	2	36
2006	Was	30	154	27	0	1.000	13	2	0	0	.15	0	+1	-1	0	-1	108
2007	Pit	31	97	13	0	1.000	13	2	0	0	.15	-2	0	0	-2	-3	153
2008	NYM	3	8	3	0	1.000	1	0	0	0	.00	0	0	0	0	0	-
		104	463	85	2	.976	43	9	2	0	.26	+2	+1	+1	+3	1	84

Josh Beckett

Year	Tm	G	Inn	TC	E	Pct	SBA	CCS	PCS	PPO	CS%	Rght	Mid	Left	Tot	RS	Rnk
		BASIC					HOLDING					+/-					
2003	Fla	24	142	24	1	.960	10	5	0	0	.50	-2	-2	+2	-2	-1	113
2004	Fla	26	157	21	2	.913	10	5	0	0	.50	-1	+2	+1	+1	2	38
2005	Fla	29	179	37	1	.974	13	6	1	0	.54	-2	0	+1	-1	0	81
2006	Bos	33	205	38	0	1.000	16	1	0	0	.06	-2	+1	0	-2	-4	170
2007	Bos	30	201	30	2	.938	20	6	0	1	.30	0	0	-2	-3	-2	129
2008	Bos	27	174	33	2	.943	12	4	1	0	.42	0	0	0	-1	0	81
		169	1057	191	8	.958	81	27	2	1	.36	-7	+1	+2	-8	-5	132

Bronson Arroyo

Year	Tm	G	Inn	TC	E	Pct	SBA	CCS	PCS	PPO	CS%	Rght	Mid	Left	Tot	RS	Rnk
		BASIC					HOLDING					+/-					
2003	Bos	6	17	2	0	1.000									0		-
2004	Bos	32	179	40	2	.952	9	5	0	0	.56	-1	0	-1	-3	-1	104
2005	Bos	35	205	42	2	.955	7	3	0	1	.43	-2	-1	-1	-4	-2	134
2006	Cin	35	241	62	0	1.000	10	5	0	0	.50	-1	0	+1	0	1	56
2007	Cin	34	211	38	1	.974	9	6	0	2	.67	0	-1	+2	+1	4	10
2008	Cin	34	200	50	0	1.000	7	1	1	1	.29	0	0	+2	+2	3	23
		176	1052	239	5	.979	42	20	1	4	.50	-4	-2	+3	-4	5	52

Joaquin Benoit

Year	Tm	G	Inn	TC	E	Pct	SBA	CCS	PCS	PPO	CS%	Rght	Mid	Left	Tot	RS	Rnk
		BASIC					HOLDING					+/-					
2003	Tex	25	105	22	1	.957	9	5	0	0	.56	+1	0	+1	+3	3	14
2004	Tex	28	103	12	1	.923	5	1	0	0	.20	0	0	-1	-1	-1	104
2005	Tex	32	87	9	0	1.000	7	2	0	0	.29	+2	0	-1	+2	2	36
2006	Tex	56	80	8	0	1.000	1	0	0	0	.00	0	0	-1	-1	-1	-
2007	Tex	70	82	12	0	1.000	4	2	0	0	.50	-1	+1	0	0	1	57
2008	Tex	44	45	7	0	1.000	2	1	0	0	.50	+1	0	0	+1	1	-
		255	501	72	2	.972	28	11	0	0	.39	+3	+1	-1	+4	5	52

Brandon Backe

Year	Tm	G	Inn	TC	E	Pct	SBA	CCS	PCS	PPO	CS%	Rght	Mid	Left	Tot	RS	Rnk
		BASIC					HOLDING					+/-					
2003	TB	28	45	6	0	1.000	4	4	0	0	1.00	0	0	0	0	1	-
2004	Hou	33	67	14	0	1.000	5	3	0	0	.60	0	-1	0	-1	0	-
2005	Hou	26	149	27	0	1.000	8	4	0	0	.50	+1	-2	-1	-2	-1	115
2006	Hou	8	43	14	0	1.000	1	1	0	1	1.00	0	0	+2	+1	2	-
2007	Hou	5	29	8	0	1.000	1	1	0	0	1.00	0	+1	0	+1	1	-
2008	Hou	31	167	32	1	.970	10	5	1	0	.60	-1	-2	+1	-2	0	81
		131	499	102	1	.990	29	18	1	1	.66	0	-4	+2	-3	3	73

Jason Bergmann

Year	Tm	G	Inn	TC	E	Pct	SBA	CCS	PCS	PPO	CS%	Rght	Mid	Left	Tot	RS	Rnk
		BASIC					HOLDING					+/-					
2005	Was	15	20	3	0	1.000	4	1	0	0	.25	0			0	0	-
2006	Was	29	65	9	0	1.000	2	1	0	0	.50	-1	-1	+1	-1	-1	-
2007	Was	21	115	16	1	.941	11	3	0	2	.27	-1	-1	-1	-3	-2	129
2008	Was	30	140	15	1	.938	10	1	0	0	.10	-1	0	-1	-2	-3	150
		95	339	45	2	.956	27	6	0	2	.22	-3	-2	-1	-6	-6	-

Rafael Betancourt

Year	Tm	G	Inn	TC	E	Pct	SBA	CCS	PCS	PPO	CS%	Rght	Mid	Left	Tot	RS	Rnk
		BASIC					HOLDING					+/-					
2003	Cle	33	38	3	0	1.000	3	0	0	0	.00	0	-1	0	-1	-1	-
2004	Cle	68	67	5	0	1.000	9	2	0	0	.22	-1	0	+1	0	-1	-
2005	Cle	54	68	6	0	1.000	7	4	0	0	.57	0	-1	-1	-1	0	-
2006	Cle	50	57	3	0	1.000	10	2	0	0	.20	0	-1	0	-1	-2	-
2007	Cle	68	79	6	0	1.000	8	4	0	0	.50	0	0	0	0	0	-
2008	Cle	69	71	8	1	.889	11	1	0	0	.09	-1	0	0	-2	-3	-
		342	379	32	1	.969	48	13	0	0	.27	-2	-3	0	-5	-7	150

Scott Baker

Year	Tm	G	Inn	TC	E	Pct	SBA	CCS	PCS	PPO	CS%	Rght	Mid	Left	Tot	RS	Rnk
		BASIC					HOLDING					+/-					
2005	Min	10	54	11	0	1.000	3	3	0	1	1.00	0	-1	-1	-1	0	-
2006	Min	16	83	11	0	1.000	8	3	0	0	.38	0	0	0	-1	-1	108
2007	Min	24	144	19	2	.905	15	4	0	0	.27	-1	0	+1	0	-1	105
2008	Min	28	172	21	1	.955	13	5	0	0	.38	-1	0	0	-1	0	81
		78	453	65	3	.954	39	15	0	0	.38	-2	-1	0	-3	-2	110

Chad Billingsley

Year	Tm	G	Inn	TC	E	Pct	SBA	CCS	PCS	PPO	CS%	Rght	Mid	Left	Tot	RS	Rnk
		BASIC					HOLDING					+/-					
2006	LAD	18	90	9	0	1.000	10	5	0	1	.50	+1	0	-2	-1	0	81
2007	LAD	43	147	25	0	1.000	11	4	2	0	.55	-1	-1	+2	0	2	36
2008	LAD	35	201	31	2	.970	12	4	0	0	.33	-1	+1	0	+1	2	31
		96	437	67	2	.970	33	13	2	1	.45	-1	0	0	0	4	64

Brian Bannister

Year	Tm	G	Inn	TC	E	Pct	SBA	CCS	PCS	PPO	CS%	Rght	Mid	Left	Tot	RS	Rnk
		BASIC					HOLDING					+/-					
2006	NYM	8	38	5	0	1.000	8	1	0	0	.13	0			0	-1	-
2007	KC	27	165	33	0	1.000	12	5	0	2	.42	-1	+1	+1	+1	3	18
2008	KC	32	183	40	2	.952	9	3	0	0	.33	0	+1	0	+1	2	31
		67	385	80	2	.975	29	9	0	2	.31	-1	+2	+2	+2	4	64

Nick Blackburn

Year	Tm	G	Inn	TC	E	Pct	SBA	CCS	PCS	PPO	CS%	Rght	Mid	Left	Tot	RS	Rnk
		BASIC					HOLDING					+/-					
2007	Min	6	12	0	0	-	1	1	0	0	1.00	-1			-1	-1	-
2008	Min	33	193	36	0	1.000	4	2	0	0	.50	0	-3	+3	-1	0	81
		39	205	36	0	1.000	5	3	0	0	.60	-1	-3	+3	-2	-1	-

Joe Blanton

Year	Tm	G	Inn	TC	E	Pct	SBA	CCS	PCS	PPO	CS%	Rght	Mid	Left	Tot	RS	Rnk
		BASIC					HOLDING					+/-					
2004	Oak	3	8	1	0	1.000	1	1	0	0	1.00	0	0	0	0	0	-
2005	Oak	33	201	33	1	.971	9	0	1	1	.11	0	0	-1	-1	-1	115
2006	Oak	32	194	27	4	.871	18	4	1	0	.28	0	-2	0	-3	-2	136
2007	Oak	34	230	42	0	1.000	23	3	1	1	.17	-1	-2	0	-2	-3	153
2008	2 tms	33	198	41	1	.976	5	1	0	0	.20	-1	0	+2	+1	2	31
		135	831	150	6	.960	56	9	3	2	.21	-2	-4	0	-5	-4	126

Miguel Batista

Year	Tm	G	Inn	TC	E	Pct	SBA	CCS	PCS	PPO	CS%	Rght	Mid	Left	Tot	RS	Rnk
		BASIC					HOLDING					+/-					
2003	Ari	36	193	41	3	.932	16	7	1	0	.50	+1	+2	-4	0	2	28
2004	Tor	38	199	48	1	.980	20	11	0	0	.55	+1	+2	-1	+2	4	14
2005	Tor	71	75	8	1	.889	2	0	0	0	.00	-1	0	-4	-4	-3	-
2006	Ari	34	206	46	4	.920	22	5	2	0	.32	+2	+4	-3	+2	2	36
2007	Sea	33	193	41	2	.953	23	8	1	0	.39	0	+1	-3	-1	0	82
2008	Sea	44	115	24	1	.960	21	2	0	0	.10	-1	0	+1	0	-3	150
		256	981	220	12	.945	104	33	4	0	.36	+2	+9	-14	-1	2	79

Jeremy Bonderman

Year	Tm	G	Inn	TC	E	Pct	SBA	CCS	PCS	PPO	CS%	Rght	Mid	Left	Tot	RS	Rnk
		BASIC					HOLDING					+/-					
2003	Det	33	162	38	1	.974	34	9	0	1	.26	-2	+1	-2	-3	-4	167
2004	Det	33	184	29	3	.906	15	2	0	0	.13	-3	-3	-1	-7	-6	174
2005	Det	29	189	29	5	.853	9	5	0	0	.56	-2	-3	+1	-4	-2	134
2006	Det	34	214	30	1	.968	16	1	1	0	.13	-3	-1	0	-4	-4	170
2007	Det	28	174	32	3	.914	23	4	0	1	.17	-3	-3	+2	-3	-4	164
2008	Det	12	71	15	1	.938	7	5	0	0	.71	-1	-1	+2	0	1	-
		169	994	187	14	.925	104	26	1	2	.26	-14	-10	+1	-21	-19	173

237

Pitchers

Boof Bonser

Year	Tm	G	Inn	TC	E	Pct	SBA	CCS	PCS	PPO	CS%	Rght	Mid	Left	Tot	RS	Rnk
2006	Min	18	100	13	0		7	3	0	2	.43	-2			0	1	56
2007	Min	31	173	29	3	.906	18	6	1	0	.39	-1	-3	+1	-4	-2	129
2008	Min	47	118	22	3	.880	11	0	0	0	.00	0	-3	+1	-2	-3	150
		96	391	70	6	.914	36	9	1	2	.28	-3	-6	+2	-6	-4	126

Mark Buehrle

Year	Tm	G	Inn	TC	E	Pct	SBA	CCS	PCS	PPO	CS%	Rght	Mid	Left	Tot	RS	Rnk
2003	CWS	35	230	53	0	1.000	5	2	2	3	.80	0	-2	0	-3	2	28
2004	CWS	35	245	68	4	.944	13	2	6	4	.62	+3	+4	0	+7	10	2
2005	CWS	33	237	58	2	.967	11	1	2	3	.27	0	+2	0	+2	4	11
2006	CWS	32	204	44	1	.978	11	3	4	6	.64	+3	0	+2	+5	9	2
2007	CWS	30	201	47	1	.979	5	0	3	2	.60	0	+2	0	+2	5	4
2008	CWS	34	219	52	0	1.000	12	2	5	2	.58	+1	0	0	0	4	10
		199	1336	330	8	.976	57	10	22	20	.56	+7	+6	+2	+13	34	2

A.J. Burnett

Year	Tm	G	Inn	TC	E	Pct	SBA	CCS	PCS	PPO	CS%	Rght	Mid	Left	Tot	RS	Rnk
2003	Fla	4	23	7	0	1.000	2	1	0	0	.50				0	0	-
2004	Fla	20	120	28	0	1.000	19	4	1	1	.26	+1	+2	-1	+3	1	53
2005	Fla	32	209	29	2	.935	30	6	0	1	.20	-4	-1	+2	-3	-4	169
2006	Tor	21	136	22	1	.957	22	4	0	1	.18	0	0	-2	-2	-4	170
2007	Tor	25	166	32	2	.941	31	0	0	0	.00	-1	+1	-1	-1	-6	170
2008	Tor	35	221	47	7	.870	31	5	4	1	.29	-1	0	-1	-2	-2	133
		137	874	177	12	.932	135	20	5	4	.19	-5	+2	-3	-5	-15	167

Brian Burres

Year	Tm	G	Inn	TC	E	Pct	SBA	CCS	PCS	PPO	CS%	Rght	Mid	Left	Tot	RS	Rnk
2006	Bal	11	8	1	0	1.000	2	0	0	0	.00				0	0	-
2007	Bal	37	121	12	1	.923	16	4	1	0	.31	-1	0	+1	-1	-1	105
2008	Bal	31	130	25	1	.962	13	1	1	0	.15	+2	0	-1	+1	0	81
		79	258	40	2	.950	31	5	2	0	.23	+1	0	0	0	-1	

David Bush

Year	Tm	G	Inn	TC	E	Pct	SBA	CCS	PCS	PPO	CS%	Rght	Mid	Left	Tot	RS	Rnk
2004	Tor	16	98	14	0	1.000	9	2	1	0	.33	-2	-1	+1	-2	-2	132
2005	Tor	25	136	38	0	1.000	20	4	0	0	.20	+1	0	+1	+2	0	81
2006	Mil	34	210	45	1	.978	26	7	1	0	.31	0	+1	0	+1	0	81
2007	Mil	33	186	41	1	.976	22	7	0	0	.32	0	0	+1	+1	0	82
2008	Mil	31	185	30	1	.968	26	9	0	0	.35	0	-1	+1	0	-1	113
		139	815	171	3	.982	103	29	2	0	.30	-1	-1	+4	+2	-3	118

Paul Byrd

Year	Tm	G	Inn	TC	E	Pct	SBA	CCS	PCS	PPO	CS%	Rght	Mid	Left	Tot	RS	Rnk
2004	Atl	19	114	21	3	.875	11	3	0	0	.27	-2	+1	0	-1	-1	104
2005	LAA	31	204	36	2	.947	19	6	0	0	.32	-1	+1	-1	0	0	81
2006	Cle	31	179	26	5	.839	23	5	0	1	.22	+2	-1	-3	-2	-3	157
2007	Cle	31	192	35	0	1.000	13	2	0	2	.15	-1	0	-2	-3	-2	129
2008	2 tms	30	180	25	2	.926	10	5	0	3	.50	+1	-1	0	0	2	31
		142	870	155	12	.923	76	21	0	6	.28	-1	0	-6	-7	-4	126

Daniel Cabrera

Year	Tm	G	Inn	TC	E	Pct	SBA	CCS	PCS	PPO	CS%	Rght	Mid	Left	Tot	RS	Rnk
2004	Bal	28	148	15	1	.938	11	4	0	0	.36	-2	-2	-3	-7	-5	170
2005	Bal	29	161	23	1	.958	23	7	0	0	.30	-2	-3	0	-5	-5	172
2006	Bal	26	148	17	0	1.000	16	5	0	0	.31	-1	+1	0	0	0	81
2007	Bal	34	204	17	1	.944	28	4	0	0	.14	-3	-3	-2	-9	-10	175
2008	Bal	30	180	19	1	.950	31	4	0	0	.13	-3	-2	-1	-6	-8	175
		147	841	95	4	.958	109	24	0	0	.22	-11	-9	-6	-27	-28	175

Matt Cain

Year	Tm	G	Inn	TC	E	Pct	SBA	CCS	PCS	PPO	CS%	Rght	Mid	Left	Tot	RS	Rnk
2005	SF	7	46	3	1	.750	2	1	0	0	.50				0	0	-
2006	SF	32	191	32	3	.914	18	3	0	0	.17	-2	+1	-1	-2	-3	157
2007	SF	32	200	31	0	1.000	13	5	0	0	.38	-1	0	-1	-2	-1	105
2008	SF	34	218	38	0	1.000	23	10	0	0	.43	+1	-2	-2	-2	-1	113
		105	654	108	4	.963	56	19	0	0	.34	-2	-1	-4	-6	-5	132

Jorge Campillo

Year	Tm	G	Inn	TC	E	Pct	SBA	CCS	PCS	PPO	CS%	Rght	Mid	Left	Tot	RS	Rnk
2005	Sea	2	2	0	0										0		-
2006	Sea	1	2	1	0	1.000									0	0	-
2007	Sea	5	13	2	0	1.000	3	1	0	0	.33	-1	0		0	0	-
2008	Atl	39	159	33	5	.868	10	2	0	0	.20	0	+1	-1	0	0	81
		47	176	41	5	.878	13	3	0	0	.23	-1	+1	-1	0	0	-

Fausto Carmona

Year	Tm	G	Inn	TC	E	Pct	SBA	CCS	PCS	PPO	CS%	Rght	Mid	Left	Tot	RS	Rnk
2006	Cle	38	75	24	0	1.000	12	1	1	0	.17	0	+1	+1	+2	1	-
2007	Cle	32	215	62	2	.969	18	5	0	2	.28	-3	0	+2	0	0	82
2008	Cle	22	121	30	2	.938	7	1	0	0	.14	0	+1	0	+2	2	31
		92	410	120	4	.967	37	7	1	2	.22	-3	+2	+3	+4	3	73

Chris Carpenter

Year	Tm	G	Inn	TC	E	Pct	SBA	CCS	PCS	PPO	CS%	Rght	Mid	Left	Tot	RS	Rnk
2004	StL	28	182	45	1	.978	3	3	0	1	1.00	+1	+2	0	+3	3	21
2005	StL	33	242	55	1	.982	6	4	1	1	.83	0	+2	0	+2	5	7
2006	StL	32	222	36	0	1.000	10	7	0	0	.70	-2	+2	+4	+3	4	10
2007	StL	1	6	2	0	1.000	0	0	0	0	-				0	0	-
2008	StL	4	15	5	0	1.000	0	0	0	0	-	0	0	0	0	0	-
		98	666	145	2	.986	19	14	1	1	.79	-1	+6	+4	+8	12	15

Joba Chamberlain

Year	Tm	G	Inn	TC	E	Pct	SBA	CCS	PCS	PPO	CS%	Rght	Mid	Left	Tot	RS	Rnk
2007	NYY	19	24	1	0	1.000	1	0	0	0	.00				0	0	-
2008	NYY	42	100	16	0	1.000	12	3	1	0	.33	0	0	-1	-1	-1	113
		61	124	17	0	1.000	13	3	1	0	.31	0	0	-1	-1	-1	-

Bartolo Colon

Year	Tm	G	Inn	TC	E	Pct	SBA	CCS	PCS	PPO	CS%	Rght	Mid	Left	Tot	RS	Rnk
2003	CWS	34	242	28	3	.903	7	6	0	1	.86	0	-1	-1	-2	1	58
2004	Ana	34	208	38	3	.927	9	6	0	1	.67	0	0	0	-1	1	53
2005	LAA	33	223	24	0	1.000	6	4	0	0	.67	-1	0	-2	-3	-1	115
2006	LAA	10	56	11	1	.917	4	3	0	0	.75	-1	0	0	0	1	-
2007	LAA	19	99	11	1	.917	4	2	0	0	.50	0	-3	-1	-4	-2	129
2008	Bos	7	39	6	2	.750	0	0	0	0	-	-1	-1	0	-2	-2	110
		137	867	128	10	.922	30	21	0	2	.70	-2	-6	-4	-12	-2	110

Jose Contreras

Year	Tm	G	Inn	TC	E	Pct	SBA	CCS	PCS	PPO	CS%	Rght	Mid	Left	Tot	RS	Rnk
2003	NYY	18	71	10	1	.909	7	0	0	0	.00	-1	0	+1	-1	-2	-
2004	2 tms	31	170	19	2	.905	40	10	1	1	.28	-2	+1	0	-1	-3	150
2005	CWS	32	205	36	2	.947	30	2	0	2	.07	-1	+2	0	+1	-2	134
2006	CWS	30	196	29	2	.935	27	6	0	0	.22	+1	+2	-1	+2	0	81
2007	CWS	32	189	27	6	.818	31	5	1	0	.19	-1	-1	-3	-5	-6	170
2008	CWS	20	121	19	0	1.000	17	0	1	0	.06	-1	0	0	0	-2	133
		163	952	153	13	.915	152	23	3	3	.17	-5	+4	-3	-4	-15	167

Aaron Cook

Year	Tm	G	Inn	TC	E	Pct	SBA	CCS	PCS	PPO	CS%	Rght	Mid	Left	Tot	RS	Rnk
2003	Col	43	124	37	1	.974	9	1	0	1	.11	-1	0	0	-1	-1	113
2004	Col	16	97	32	1	1.000	5	1	0	1	.20	0	+2	+1	+3	2	38
2005	Col	13	83	19	2	.905	3	0	0	0	.00	0	-1	-2	-3	-2	134
2006	Col	32	213	67	2	.971	12	4	1	1	.42	+3	+1	-2	+2	4	10
2007	Col	25	166	47	0	1.000	10	2	0	0	.20	+2	+2	+1	+6	7	3
2008	Col	32	211	58	2	.967	13	8	0	4	.62	+1	+3	0	+4	7	3
		161	894	267	7	.974	52	16	1	7	.33	+5	+7	-2	+11	15	12

Francisco Cordero

Year	Tm	G	Inn	TC	E	Pct	SBA	CCS	PCS	PPO	CS%	Rght	Mid	Left	Tot	RS	Rnk
2003	Tex	73	83	18	1	.947	10	4	1	1	.50	0	+1	0	+2	3	-
2004	Tex	67	72	14	0	1.000	7	1	1	1	.29	-1	+1	0	-1	1	-
2005	Tex	69	69	12	0	1.000	4	0	0	0	.00	-1	+1	0	0	0	-
2006	2 tms	77	75	11	0	1.000	6	2	0	0	.33	0	0	0	0	0	-
2007	Mil	66	63	8	0	1.000	3	0	0	0	.00	0	+1	-1	-1	-1	-
2008	Cin	72	70	7	1	.875	10	2	1	0	.30	0	-1	+2	0	0	-
		424	432	72	2	.972	40	9	3	2	.30	-2	+3	+1	+1	3	73

Pitchers

Kevin Correia

Year	Tm	G	Inn	TC	E	Pct	SBA	CCS	PCS	PPO	CS%	Rght	Mid	Left	Tot	RS	Rnk
				BASIC					HOLDING					+/-			
2003	SF	10	39	7	0	1.000	6	2	0	0	.33	+1	-1	0	0	0	-
2004	SF	12	19	3	0	1.000	3	0	0	0	.00	0	0	-1	-1	-1	-
2005	SF	16	58	4	0	1.000	6	2	0	0	.33	0	-1		-2	-2	-
2006	SF	48	70	6	0	1.000	6	2	1	0	.50	0	-1	0	-1	0	-
2007	SF	59	102	17	0	1.000	13	3	0	0	.23	0	-2	0	-2	-3	153
2008	SF	25	110	20	1	.952	11	6	1	0	.64	0	-2	0	-2	0	81
		170	398	58	1	.983	45	15	2	0	.38	+1	-7	-1	-8	-6	141

Johnny Cueto

Year	Tm	G	Inn	TC	E	Pct	SBA	CCS	PCS	PPO	CS%	Rght	Mid	Left	Tot	RS	Rnk
				BASIC					HOLDING					+/-			
2008	Cin	31	174	31	3	.912	13	6	0	1	.46	+1	-2	+1	-1	0	81

John Danks

Year	Tm	G	Inn	TC	E	Pct	SBA	CCS	PCS	PPO	CS%	Rght	Mid	Left	Tot	RS	Rnk
				BASIC					HOLDING					+/-			
2007	CWS	26	139	22	1	.957	11	0	1	1	.09	0	+2	0	+2	2	36
2008	CWS	33	195	40	0	1.000	31	3	6	0	.26	+6	-1	-3	+2	2	31
		59	334	63	1	.984	42	2	7	1	.21	+6	+1	-3	+4	4	31

Kyle Davies

Year	Tm	G	Inn	TC	E	Pct	SBA	CCS	PCS	PPO	CS%	Rght	Mid	Left	Tot	RS	Rnk
				BASIC					HOLDING					+/-			
2005	Atl	21	88	16	1	.941	4	2	2	0	1.00	0	0	-1	-1	1	63
2006	Atl	14	63	8	0	1.000	5	1	0	1	.20	0	-1	0	0		-
2007	2 tms	28	136	24	2	.923	17	3	0	0	.18	+1	+1	0	+2	1	57
2008	KC	21	113	14	1	.933	9	1	0	0	.11	-1	-2	0	-3	-3	150
		84	400	66	4	.939	35	7	2	1	.26	0	-1	-2	-2	-1	100

Doug Davis

Year	Tm	G	Inn	TC	E	Pct	SBA	CCS	PCS	PPO	CS%	Rght	Mid	Left	Tot	RS	Rnk
				BASIC					HOLDING					+/-			
2003	3 tms	21	109	16	0	1.000	7	2	1	0	.43	-1	-1	-1	-3	-3	161
2004	Mil	34	207	41	1	.976	21	3	3	1	.29	+1	0	0	+1	2	38
2005	Mil	35	223	44	2	.957	18	3	4	1	.39	+1	-1	+1	0	2	36
2006	Mil	34	203	32	1	.970	19	1	3	0	.21	+1	0	-3	-2	-2	136
2007	Ari	33	193	43	2	.956	12	0	6	2	.50	0	+2	-3	-1	3	18
2008	Ari	26	146	31	0	1.000	11	2	1	1	.27	+3	+2	-1	+4	4	10
		183	1081	213	6	.972	88	11	18	5	.33	+5	+2	-7	-1	6	44

Jason Davis

Year	Tm	G	Inn	TC	E	Pct	SBA	CCS	PCS	PPO	CS%	Rght	Mid	Left	Tot	RS	Rnk
				BASIC					HOLDING					+/-			
2003	Cle	27	165	37	6	.860	11	7	1	3	.73	-5	0	+1	-3	1	58
2004	Cle	26	114	30	3	.909	21	2	1	1	.14	-1	+1	0	0	-1	104
2005	Cle	11	40	4	0	1.000	8	1	0	0	.13	0	-1		-1	-2	-
2006	Cle	39	55	10	1	.909	5	1	0	0	.20	-3	+1	-1	-4	-3	-
2007	2 tms	24	37	7	1	.875	2	0	0	0	.00	-1	0	0	-3	-2	-
2008	Pit	14	34	10	1	.909	6	1	0	0	.17	+1	0	+1	+2	1	-
		141	446	110	12	.891	53	12	2	4	.26	-9	+1	+1	-9	-6	141

Jorge de la Rosa

Year	Tm	G	Inn	TC	E	Pct	SBA	CCS	PCS	PPO	CS%	Rght	Mid	Left	Tot	RS	Rnk
				BASIC					HOLDING					+/-			
2004	Mil	5	23	4	1	.800	3	1	0	0	.33	+1	0	0	+1	1	-
2005	Mil	38	42	7	1	.875	4	0	0	0	.00	0	0	-2	-1	-1	-
2006	2 tms	28	79	9	1	.900	11	0	1	0	.09	+1	-1	0	0	-1	-
2007	KC	26	130	16	1	.941	10	2	2	0	.40	-1	+1	-1	-1	0	82
2008	Col	28	130	19	0	1.000	18	2	3	0	.28	+1	-1	-1	-1	-1	113
		125	404	59	4	.932	46	5	6	0	.24	+2	-1	-4	-2	-2	110

Ryan Dempster

Year	Tm	G	Inn	TC	E	Pct	SBA	CCS	PCS	PPO	CS%	Rght	Mid	Left	Tot	RS	Rnk
				BASIC					HOLDING					+/-			
2003	Cin	22	116	18	3	.857	4	2	1	0	.75	-1	0	0	-1	0	85
2004	ChC	23	21	6	0	1.000	2	0	0	0	.00	+1			+1	1	-
2005	ChC	63	92	20	0	1.000	8	2	0	0	.25	+1	+1	-2	0	0	81
2006	ChC	74	75	11	1	.917	5	0	0	0	.00	-1	-1	+1	-1	-1	-
2007	ChC	66	67	11	0	1.000	4	0	0	0	.00	-1	0	-1	0	-1	-
2008	ChC	33	207	52	1	.981	15	4	0	0	.27	+1	+4	+1	+6	5	7
		281	576	123	5	.959	43	8	1	0	.21	+1	+5	-1	+5	4	64

Elmer Dessens

Year	Tm	G	Inn	TC	E	Pct	SBA	CCS	PCS	PPO	CS%	Rght	Mid	Left	Tot	RS	Rnk
				BASIC					HOLDING					+/-			
2003	Ari	34	176	27	0	1.000	11	4	0	0	.36	-2	-2	-2	-6	-4	167
2004	2 tms	50	105	19	1	.950	5	1	0	1	.20	-1	+1	-1	-1	0	74
2005	LAD	28	66	17	0	1.000	6	1	0	0	.17	+1	0	0	+1	1	-
2006	2 tms	62	77	16	0	1.000	5	2	0	0	.40	0	-2	+3	+2	2	-
2007	2 tms	17	34	10	0	1.000	1	0	0	0	.00	0	0	+1	+3	3	-
2008	Atl	4	4	1	0	1.000	0	0	0	0	-				0	0	-
		195	461	91	1	.989	29	8	0	1	.28	-2	-3	+1	-1	2	79

R.A. Dickey

Year	Tm	G	Inn	TC	E	Pct	SBA	CCS	PCS	PPO	CS%	Rght	Mid	Left	Tot	RS	Rnk
				BASIC					HOLDING					+/-			
2003	Tex	38	117	20	0	1.000	9	2	0	1	.22	+2	0	+1	+3	2	28
2004	Tex	25	104	29	2	.935	11	5	0	4	.45	0	0	-1	-1	1	53
2005	Tex	9	30	10	0	1.000	3	0	0	0	.00	+1	+1	+1	+3	2	-
2006	Tex	1	3	0	0	-									0		-
2008	Sea	32	112	29	0	.978	13	3	4	1	.54	+2	0	0	+2	4	10
		105	366	90	2	.978	36	10	4	6	.39	+5	+1	+1	+7	9	-

Justin Duchscherer

Year	Tm	G	Inn	TC	E	Pct	SBA	CCS	PCS	PPO	CS%	Rght	Mid	Left	Tot	RS	Rnk
				BASIC					HOLDING					+/-			
2003	Oak	4	16	3	0	1.000	2	0	0	0	.00	0	0	0	0	0	-
2004	Oak	53	96	24	0	1.000	8	3	1	1	.50	+1	0	0	+1	2	38
2005	Oak	65	86	15	3	.833	8	2	0	1	.25	+1	0	+1	+2	2	36
2006	Oak	53	56	16	0	1.000	6	1	0	2	.17	0	0	0	+1	1	-
2007	Oak	17	16	6	0	1.000	3	0	0	0	.00	+1	0	0	+1	1	-
2008	Oak	22	142	18	0	1.000	6	2	0	1	.33	0	+2	-1	+1	2	31
		214	412	85	3	.965	33	8	1	5	.27	+3	+2	0	+6	8	38

Zach Duke

Year	Tm	G	Inn	TC	E	Pct	SBA	CCS	PCS	PPO	CS%	Rght	Mid	Left	Tot	RS	Rnk
				BASIC					HOLDING					+/-			
2005	Pit	14	85	19	0	1.000	4	1	2	0	.75	-1	0	+2	+1	2	36
2006	Pit	34	215	60	1	.984	25	5	7	0	.48	+4	+1	+2	+7	8	3
2007	Pit	20	107	24	0	1.000	10	3	2	0	.50	0	0	+1	+1	2	36
2008	Pit	31	185	50	2	.962	12	2	4	0	.50	+3	+3	-1	+5	6	5
		99	592	156	3	.981	51	11	15	0	.51	+6	+5	+3	+14	18	10

Adam Eaton

Year	Tm	G	Inn	TC	E	Pct	SBA	CCS	PCS	PPO	CS%	Rght	Mid	Left	Tot	RS	Rnk
				BASIC					HOLDING					+/-			
2003	SD	31	183	47	3	.940	12	2	0	0	.17	+1	+1	+1	+3	1	58
2004	SD	33	199	35	2	.946	11	5	0	0	.45	0	+1	-3	-1	0	74
2005	SD	24	129	23	1	.958	9	1	0	0	.11	+1	0	0	-1	-1	115
2006	Tex	13	65	9	0	1.000	7	5	0	0	.71	0	+1	0	0	1	-
2007	Phi	30	162	36	2	.947	15	8	1	0	.60	-1	-1	+2	0	2	36
2008	Phi	21	107	24	0	1.000	9	5	0	0	.56	+2	0	0	+1	2	31
		152	845	182	8	.956	63	26	1	0	.43	+3	+2	-1	+3	5	52

Scott Elarton

Year	Tm	G	Inn	TC	E	Pct	SBA	CCS	PCS	PPO	CS%	Rght	Mid	Left	Tot	RS	Rnk
				BASIC					HOLDING					+/-			
2003	Col	11	52	14	0	1.000	5	0	0	0	.00	0	0	0	-1	-2	-
2004	2 tms	29	159	20	1	.952	12	2	0	1	.17	+1	-2	-1	-3	-3	150
2005	Cle	31	182	18	2	.900	8	4	0	1	.50	+2	-1	-2	-1	0	81
2006	KC	20	115	16	0	1.000	7	3	0	2	.43	+1	+1	+2	+3	3	20
2007	KC	9	37	3	0	1.000	2	0	0	0	.00	0	+1		+1	1	-
2008	Cle	8	15	5	0	1.000	1	0	0	0	-				+1	1	-
		108	559	79	3	.962	35	9	0	4	.26	+4	-1	-1	0	0	93

Shawn Estes

Year	Tm	G	Inn	TC	E	Pct	SBA	CCS	PCS	PPO	CS%	Rght	Mid	Left	Tot	RS	Rnk
				BASIC					HOLDING					+/-			
2003	ChC	29	152	39	3	.929	16	3	1	0	.25	+3	+2	0	+4	3	14
2004	Col	34	202	41	1	.976	18	2	5	0	.39	+1	+1	-1	+1	3	21
2005	Ari	21	124	40	2	.952	5	1	0	0	.20	0	0	0	0	0	81
2006	SD	1	6	0	0	-	0	0	0	0	-	0	-1		-1	-1	-
2008	SD	9	44	10	0	1.000	7	1	0	0	.14	-1	0	0	0	-1	-
		94	527	136	6	.956	46	6	7	0	.28	+3	+2	-1	+4	4	64

Pitchers

Dana Eveland

BASIC							HOLDING					+/-					
Year	Tm	G	Inn	TC	E	Pct	SBA	CCS	PCS	PPO	CS%	Rght	Mid	Left	Tot	RS	Rnk
2005	Mil	27	32	5	0	1.000	0	0	0	0	-	-1	0	-1	-2	-2	-
2006	Mil	9	28	2	0	1.000	7	1	1	0	.29	-1			-1	-1	-
2007	Ari	5	5	2	0	1.000	1	0	0	0	.00	0			0	0	-
2008	Oak	29	168	23	0	1.000	17	2	2	0	.24	0	0	0	-1	-1	113
		70	232	32	0	1.000	25	3	3	0	.24	-2	0	-1	-4	-4	-

Kyle Farnsworth

BASIC							HOLDING					+/-					
Year	Tm	G	Inn	TC	E	Pct	SBA	CCS	PCS	PPO	CS%	Rght	Mid	Left	Tot	RS	Rnk
2003	ChC	77	76	17	0	1.000	12	4	0	0	.33	-1	+1	+1	+1	1	-
2004	ChC	72	67	16	1	.941	9	3	1	0	.44	-1	-1	0	-2	-1	-
2005	2 tms	72	70	11	1	.917	10	2	0	0	.20	-1	+1	0	0	0	-
2006	NYY	72	66	10	0	1.000	8	2	0	0	.25	-1	0	0	0	0	-
2007	NYY	64	60	10	3	.769	11	2	0	0	.18	0	+1	-1	-1	-2	-
2008	2 tms	61	60	9	0	1.000	13	7	0	0	.54	-1	-1	+1	-1	-1	-
		418	399	78	5	.936	63	20	1	0	.33	-5	+1	+1	-3	-3	118

Scott Feldman

BASIC							HOLDING					+/-					
Year	Tm	G	Inn	TC	E	Pct	SBA	CCS	PCS	PPO	CS%	Rght	Mid	Left	Tot	RS	Rnk
2005	Tex	8	9	2	0	1.000	1	1	0	0	1.00	+1			+1	1	-
2006	Tex	36	41	12	3	.800	3	1	0	0	.33	+1	+1	-1	+1	1	-
2007	Tex	29	39	8	0	1.000	8	2	0	0	.25	0	0	+1	+1	0	-
2008	Tex	28	151	34	2	.944	27	5	0	0	.19	+1	0	+3	+3	-1	113
		101	241	61	5	.918	39	9	0	0	.23	+3	+1	+3	+6	1	-

Gavin Floyd

BASIC							HOLDING					+/-					
Year	Tm	G	Inn	TC	E	Pct	SBA	CCS	PCS	PPO	CS%	Rght	Mid	Left	Tot	RS	Rnk
2004	Phi	6	28	4	0	1.000	8	1	0	0	.13	0	0	0	0	-1	-
2005	Phi	7	26	5	0	1.000	2	0	0	0	.00	0	-2		-2	-2	-
2006	Phi	11	54	10	1	.909	13	1	1	0	.15	0	0	0	0	-1	-
2007	CWS	16	70	11	1	.917	12	0	0	0	.00	-1	-1	+1	-1	-3	-
2008	CWS	33	206	41	2	.953	42	4	1	0	.12	0	+2	-2	0	-5	170
		73	385	75	4	.947	77	6	2	0	.10	-1	-1	-1	-3	-12	165

Casey Fossum

BASIC							HOLDING					+/-					
Year	Tm	G	Inn	TC	E	Pct	SBA	CCS	PCS	PPO	CS%	Rght	Mid	Left	Tot	RS	Rnk
2003	Bos	19	79	9	0	1.000	11	3	3	0	.55	-1	0	0	0	1	-
2004	Ari	27	142	24	0	1.000	23	4	4	0	.35	0	-2	0	-2	-2	132
2005	TB	36	163	27	1	.964	14	3	1	0	.29	-2	-1	0	-3	-2	134
2006	TB	25	130	27	1	.964	15	1	2	0	.20	+3	+2	-1	+4	3	20
2007	TB	40	76	19	0	1.000	10	0	0	0	.00	+2	+1	+1	+4	2	-
2008	Det	31	41	6	0	1.000	1	0	1	0	1.00	+1	0	0	+1	2	-
		178	631	114	2	.982	74	11	11	0	.30	+3	0	0	+4	4	64

Jeff Francis

BASIC							HOLDING					+/-					
Year	Tm	G	Inn	TC	E	Pct	SBA	CCS	PCS	PPO	CS%	Rght	Mid	Left	Tot	RS	Rnk
2004	Col	7	37	8	0	1.000	2	0	0	0	.00	0			-1	-1	-
2005	Col	33	184	25	0	1.000	30	6	5	0	.37	-2	-1	+2	-1	0	81
2006	Col	32	199	42	0	1.000	28	3	4	1	.25	0	+1	0	+2	2	36
2007	Col	34	215	45	0	1.000	13	1	3	1	.31	+2	+2	+1	+5	6	1
2008	Col	24	144	29	1	.967	11	1	1	0	.18	+2	+1	+1	+3	2	31
		130	778	150	1	.993	84	11	13	2	.29	+2	+3	+4	+8	9	33

Brian Fuentes

BASIC							HOLDING					+/-					
Year	Tm	G	Inn	TC	E	Pct	SBA	CCS	PCS	PPO	CS%	Rght	Mid	Left	Tot	RS	Rnk
2003	Col	75	75	12	1	.923	5	0	4	0	.80	+1	-2		-1	1	-
2004	Col	47	45	6	1	.857	1	0	0	0	.00	+1	0	+1	+1	1	-
2005	Col	78	74	8	0	1.000	3	0	1	0	.33	0	-1	0	-1	-1	-
2006	Col	66	65	7	1	.875	4	1	0	0	.25	+1	-1	0	0	0	-
2007	Col	64	61	6	1	.857	2	0	1	0	.50	0	+1	-1	-1	0	-
2008	Col	67	63	10	0	1.000	5	0	1	1	.20	0	0		0	0	-
		397	383	53	4	.925	20	1	7	1	.40	+3	-3	0	-2	1	84

Armando Galarraga

BASIC							HOLDING					+/-					
Year	Tm	G	Inn	TC	E	Pct	SBA	CCS	PCS	PPO	CS%	Rght	Mid	Left	Tot	RS	Rnk
2007	Tex	3	9	1	0	1.000									0		-
2008	Det	30	179	24	2	.923	8	1	0	0	.13	0	+1	+1	+1	1	55
		33	187	27	2	.926	8	1	0	0	.13	0	+1	+1	+1	1	-

Sean Gallagher

BASIC							HOLDING					+/-					
Year	Tm	G	Inn	TC	E	Pct	SBA	CCS	PCS	PPO	CS%	Rght	Mid	Left	Tot	RS	Rnk
2007	ChC	8	15	1	0	1.000	0	0	0	0	-	0	0	0	-1	-1	-
2008	2 tms	23	115	21	1	.955	9	4	0	0	.44	+3	0	0	+3	3	23
		31	130	23	1	.957	9	4	0	0	.44	+3	0	0	+2	2	-

Freddy Garcia

BASIC							HOLDING					+/-					
Year	Tm	G	Inn	TC	E	Pct	SBA	CCS	PCS	PPO	CS%	Rght	Mid	Left	Tot	RS	Rnk
2003	Sea	33	203	43	1	.977	13	5	2	1	.54	+1	-1	0	-1	1	58
2004	2 tms	31	210	49	0	1.000	17	4	1	1	.29	+2	+2	0	+5	5	8
2005	CWS	33	228	47	0	1.000	24	5	0	1	.21	0	0	0	0	-1	115
2006	CWS	33	216	30	2	.938	42	2	0	0	.05	-1	0	0	-1	-7	174
2007	Phi	11	58	10	0	1.000	5	0	0	1	.00	0	0	0	0	0	-
2008	Det	3	15	1	0	1.000	2	1	0	0	.50	+1			+1	1	-
		144	930	183	3	.984	103	17	3	4	.19	+3	+1	0	+4	-1	100

Jon Garland

BASIC							HOLDING					+/-					
Year	Tm	G	Inn	TC	E	Pct	SBA	CCS	PCS	PPO	CS%	Rght	Mid	Left	Tot	RS	Rnk
2003	CWS	32	192	44	0	1.000	15	6	0	1	.40	0	0	+1	+1	2	28
2004	CWS	34	217	56	2	.966	11	3	0	0	.27	+1	+4	0	+4	3	21
2005	CWS	32	221	47	1	.979	9	6	0	0	.67	+4	-1	-4	-1	1	63
2006	CWS	33	211	46	3	.939	13	7	0	0	.54	0	+2	-1	+1	3	20
2007	CWS	32	208	48	1	.980	8	5	1	1	.75	+2	+1	+1	+4	6	1
2008	LAA	32	197	51	1	.981	6	3	0	1	.50	0	+1	+2	+3	4	10
		195	1246	300	8	.973	62	30	1	3	.50	+7	+7	-1	+12	19	9

Matt Garza

BASIC							HOLDING					+/-					
Year	Tm	G	Inn	TC	E	Pct	SBA	CCS	PCS	PPO	CS%	Rght	Mid	Left	Tot	RS	Rnk
2006	Min	10	50	6	0	1.000	2	0	0	0	.00	0	0	-1	-2	-2	-
2007	Min	16	83	11	2	.846	4	2	1	0	.75	-1	-3	+2	-2	-1	105
2008	TB	30	185	25	2	.926	6	1	0	0	.17	-2	-3	+1	-4	-3	150
		56	317	46	4	.913	12	3	1	0	.33	-3	-6	+2	-8	-6	-

Tom Glavine

BASIC							HOLDING					+/-					
Year	Tm	G	Inn	TC	E	Pct	SBA	CCS	PCS	PPO	CS%	Rght	Mid	Left	Tot	RS	Rnk
2003	NYM	32	183	48	2	.960	20	3	5	1	.40	+2	+1	+2	+5	6	5
2004	NYM	33	212	59	1	.983	15	5	3	0	.53	+5	+3	+3	+11	10	2
2005	NYM	33	211	55	0	1.000	9	3	2	0	.56	0	+1	0	0	2	36
2006	NYM	32	198	54	4	.931	15	7	2	0	.60	+3	+2	0	+5	6	5
2007	NYM	34	200	32	1	.970	13	6	2	0	.62	+1	+3	-1	+2	4	10
2008	Atl	13	63	20	0	1.000	5	1	3	0	.80	0	0	0	0	2	-
		177	1068	276	8	.971	77	25	17	1	.55	+11	+10	+4	+23	30	3

Jimmy Gobble

BASIC							HOLDING					+/-					
Year	Tm	G	Inn	TC	E	Pct	SBA	CCS	PCS	PPO	CS%	Rght	Mid	Left	Tot	RS	Rnk
2003	KC	9	53	7	0	1.000	6	1	0	0	.17	0	0	0	-1	-2	-
2004	KC	25	148	17	3	.850	13	3	0	0	.23	0	-1	-1	-2	-3	150
2005	KC	28	54	6	2	.750	6	1	0	0	.17				-1	-1	-
2006	KC	60	84	14	0	1.000	6	1	1	0	.33	0	0	-3	-4	-3	157
2007	KC	74	54	11	1	.917	3	1	0	0	.33	+2	+1	-1	+2	2	-
2008	KC	39	32	2	0	1.000	2	0	0	0	.00	0			0	0	-
		235	424	63	6	.905	36	7	1	0	.22	+2	0	-5	-6	-7	150

Tom Gordon

BASIC							HOLDING					+/-					
Year	Tm	G	Inn	TC	E	Pct	SBA	CCS	PCS	PPO	CS%	Rght	Mid	Left	Tot	RS	Rnk
2003	CWS	66	74	16	0	1.000	1	0	0	0	.00	+3	0	0	+3	2	-
2004	NYY	80	90	19	1	.950	3	0	1	0	.33	0	+2	+1	+2	2	38
2005	NYY	79	81	20	1	.952	4	1	0	0	.25	+1	+3	-1	+2	2	-
2006	Phi	59	59	13	0	1.000	6	0	0	0	.00	-1	+1	0	+1	0	-
2007	Phi	44	40	13	0	1.000	2	1	0	0	.50	0	+1	0	+1	1	-
2008	Phi	34	30	4	2	.667	1	0	0	0	.00	0	0	0	0	0	-
		362	373	89	4	.955	17	2	1	0	.18	+3	+7	0	+9	7	43

Tom Gorzelanny

BASIC							HOLDING					+/-					
Year	Tm	G	Inn	TC	E	Pct	SBA	CCS	PCS	PPO	CS%	Rght	Mid	Left	Tot	RS	Rnk
2005	Pit	3	6	3	0	1.000	0	0	0	0	-	0			0	0	-
2006	Pit	11	62	21	3	.875	6	0	2	0	.33	0	0	0	0	1	-
2007	Pit	32	202	34	1	.971	22	3	2	1	.23	+1	-4	+1	-1	-1	105
2008	Pit	21	105	24	1	.960	20	2	2	1	.20	+1	0	0	+1	0	81
		67	374	87	5	.943	48	5	6	2	.23	+2	-4	+1	0	0	93

Pitchers

Kevin Gregg

Year	Tm	G	Inn	TC	E	Pct	SBA	CCS	PCS	PPO	CS%	Rght	Mid	Left	Tot	RS	Rnk
2003	Ana	5	25	2	0	1.000	3	2	0	0	.67				0	0	-
2004	Ana	55	88	7	0	1.000	7	2	0	0	.29	-1	-2	-1	-4	-3	150
2005	LAA	33	64	10	0	1.000	6	0	0	0	.00	0	-1	0	-1	-2	-
2006	LAA	32	78	6	2	.750	5	0	0	1	.00	-1	-2	-2	-5	-4	-
2007	Fla	74	84	12	0	1.000	3	0	1	0	1.00	0	0	0	+1	1	57
2008	Fla	72	69	10	2	.833	8	2	0	0	.25	0	0	0	0	0	-
		271	407	51	4	.922	32	6	0	2	.19	-2	-5	-3	-9	-8	154

Zack Greinke

Year	Tm	G	Inn	TC	E	Pct	SBA	CCS	PCS	PPO	CS%	Rght	Mid	Left	Tot	RS	Rnk
2004	KC	24	145	28	0	1.000	8	3	0	0	.38	0	+1	+2	+3	2	38
2005	KC	33	183	43	1	.977	8	3	0	1	.38	0	0	+3	+2	3	24
2006	KC	3	6	1	0	1.000	0	0	0	0	-				0	0	-
2007	KC	52	122	18	0	1.000	10	3	0	1	.30	0	-1	+1	0	0	82
2008	KC	32	202	35	1	.972	6	3	1	2	.67	0	+3	+1	+4	6	5
		144	658	127	2	.984	32	12	1	4	.41	0	+3	+7	+9	11	20

Jeremy Guthrie

Year	Tm	G	Inn	TC	E	Pct	SBA	CCS	PCS	PPO	CS%	Rght	Mid	Left	Tot	RS	Rnk
2004	Cle	6	12	2	0	1.000	1	0	0	0	.00				0	0	-
2005	Cle	1	6	3	0	1.000											
2006	Cle	9	19	5	0	1.000	3	1	0	0	.33	+1	0	+1	+2	2	-
2007	Bal	32	175	37	1	.974	9	5	0	1	.56	+1	0	0	+1	3	18
2008	Bal	30	191	40	3	.930	17	4	0	0	.24	+3	-1	+1	+3	1	55
		78	403	91	4	.956	30	10	0	1	.33	+5	-1	+2	+6	6	44

Roy Halladay

Year	Tm	G	Inn	TC	E	Pct	SBA	CCS	PCS	PPO	CS%	Rght	Mid	Left	Tot	RS	Rnk
2003	Tor	36	266	73	1	.986	27	4	0	0	.15	+2	+1	0	+4	0	85
2004	Tor	21	133	30	1	.968	9	2	0	0	.22	-1	-3	+2	-3	-2	132
2005	Tor	19	142	35	1	.971	18	2	0	0	.11	+2	+3	-4	0	-2	134
2006	Tor	32	220	56	1	.982	25	5	0	0	.20	+2	+3	-1	+3	0	81
2007	Tor	31	225	55	2	.965	27	6	1	0	.26	0	-1	0	-1	-2	129
2008	Tor	34	246	59	1	.983	20	5	0	0	.20	-1	+2	-2	-1	-2	133
		173	1232	313	7	.978	126	24	1	0	.20	+4	+5	-5	+2	-8	154

Cole Hamels

Year	Tm	G	Inn	TC	E	Pct	SBA	CCS	PCS	PPO	CS%	Rght	Mid	Left	Tot	RS	Rnk
2006	Phi	23	132	24	0	1.000	11	2	0	0	.18	+2	+1	+1	+4	2	36
2007	Phi	28	183	28	1	.966	16	0	2	0	.13	+1	-1	-2	-1	-2	129
2008	Phi	33	227	44	3	.936	17	0	2	0	.12	-1	+2	+2	+3	1	55
		84	543	100	4	.960	44	2	4	0	.14	+2	+2	+1	+6	1	84

Aaron Harang

Year	Tm	G	Inn	TC	E	Pct	SBA	CCS	PCS	PPO	CS%	Rght	Mid	Left	Tot	RS	Rnk
2003	2 tms	16	76	9	0	1.000	10	2	0	0	.20	+1	0	+1	+1	0	-
2004	Cin	28	161	31	0	1.000	12	5	0	0	.42	0	0	+1	0	0	74
2005	Cin	32	212	30	0	1.000	18	9	0	0	.50	0	0	+1	+1	2	36
2006	Cin	36	234	44	2	.957	24	7	1	0	.33	-1	-1	-2	-4	-3	157
2007	Cin	34	232	31	0	1.000	21	8	0	0	.38	+2	-2	0	0	0	82
2008	Cin	30	184	27	1	.964	21	4	0	0	.19	-1	-1	-1	-4	-5	170
		176	1099	175	3	.983	106	35	1	0	.34	+1	-4	-2	-6	-6	141

Rich Harden

Year	Tm	G	Inn	TC	E	Pct	SBA	CCS	PCS	PPO	CS%	Rght	Mid	Left	Tot	RS	Rnk
2003	Oak	15	75	16	1	.941	11	2	0	1	.18	0	+1	+1	+1	1	-
2004	Oak	31	190	33	1	.971	17	5	1	1	.35	-3	-1	0	-4	-2	132
2005	Oak	22	128	20	1	.952	8	4	0	0	.50	-1	-1	+1	0	1	63
2006	Oak	9	47	13	0	1.000	5	3	0	0	.60	0	0	+1	+1	1	-
2007	Oak	7	26	3	0	1.000	2	1	0	0	.50				-1	-1	-
2008	2 tms	25	148	15	0	1.000	14	7	0	0	.50	-1	0	+2	+1	2	31
		109	612	103	3	.971	57	22	1	2	.40	-5	-1	+5	-2	2	79

Dan Haren

Year	Tm	G	Inn	TC	E	Pct	SBA	CCS	PCS	PPO	CS%	Rght	Mid	Left	Tot	RS	Rnk
2003	StL	14	73	8	0	1.000	3	1	0	0	.33	0	0	-1	-1	-1	-
2004	StL	14	46	9	1	.900	3	0	0	0	.00	-1	0	+1	0	0	-
2005	Oak	34	217	40	2	.952	24	4	1	0	.21	-1	-1	0	-2	-3	161
2006	Oak	34	223	43	1	.977	14	4	0	1	.29	-3	-1	+7	+3	3	20
2007	Oak	34	223	29	1	.967	26	6	0	0	.23	-1	-6	+1	-5	-6	170
2008	Ari	33	216	29	1	.967	11	2	0	0	.18	-1	-3	+2	-2	-2	133
		163	997	163	5	.969	81	17	1	1	.22	-7	-11	+10	-7	-9	161

LaTroy Hawkins

Year	Tm	G	Inn	TC	E	Pct	SBA	CCS	PCS	PPO	CS%	Rght	Mid	Left	Tot	RS	Rnk
2003	Min	74	77	10	0	1.000	4	2	0	0	.50	0	-1	0	-1	-1	-
2004	ChC	77	82	11	0	1.000	4	2	1	0	.75	0	+1	0	+1	0	-
2005	2 tms	66	56	11	2	.846	1	0	0	0	.00	0	0	0	0	0	-
2006	Bal	60	60	11	1	.917	9	2	0	0	.22	0	+1	-1	0	-1	-
2007	Col	62	55	21	0	1.000	3	1	0	0	.33	+1	+1	0	+2	2	-
2008	2 tms	57	62	8	0	1.000	4	2	0	0	.50	0	0	0	+1	1	-
		396	393	75	3	.960	25	9	1	0	.40	+1	+2	-1	+3	3	73

Mark Hendrickson

Year	Tm	G	Inn	TC	E	Pct	SBA	CCS	PCS	PPO	CS%	Rght	Mid	Left	Tot	RS	Rnk
2003	Tor	30	158	30	2	.938	28	5	3	0	.29	0	+2	0	+1	-1	113
2004	TB	32	183	39	0	1.000	13	2	0	0	.15	+3	-1	0	+2	1	53
2005	TB	31	178	39	1	.975	9	1	5	0	.67	-2	0	0	-1	2	36
2006	TB	31	165	26	3	.897	12	1	2	0	.25	0	-1	-3	-3	-3	157
2007	LAD	39	123	25	0	1.000	13	0	2	0	.15	-1	-2	0	-2	-2	129
2008	Fla	36	134	25	0	1.000	19	1	2	0	.16	+1	+1	-2	0	-1	113
		199	941	190	6	.968	94	10	14	0	.26	+1	-3	-4	-5	-4	126

Felix Hernandez

Year	Tm	G	Inn	TC	E	Pct	SBA	CCS	PCS	PPO	CS%	Rght	Mid	Left	Tot	RS	Rnk
2005	Sea	12	84	27	0	1.000	5	1	1	1	.40	0	+1	+3	+2	3	24
2006	Sea	31	191	41	0	1.000	19	4	1	0	.26	-1	0	+5	+6	5	8
2007	Sea	30	190	37	1	.974	15	5	0	1	.33	-1	-4	+3	-1	0	82
2008	Sea	31	201	45	1	.978	23	3	1	1	.17	0	-1	+5	+4	2	31
		104	666	152	2	.987	62	13	3	3	.26	-3	-4	+16	+11	10	24

Livan Hernandez

Year	Tm	G	Inn	TC	E	Pct	SBA	CCS	PCS	PPO	CS%	Rght	Mid	Left	Tot	RS	Rnk
2003	Mon	33	233	62	1	.984	12	4	1	1	.42	+6	+5	0	+10	9	1
2004	Mon	35	255	82	2	.976	25	9	0	2	.36	+8	+2	-1	+9	8	5
2005	Was	35	246	61	1	.984	25	10	1	1	.44	+3	+3	-1	+4	5	7
2006	2 tms	34	216	49	4	.925	18	3	1	1	.22	+1	+2	-3	0	0	81
2007	Ari	33	204	52	0	1.000	25	5	0	2	.20	+2	0	0	+1	1	57
2008	2 tms	31	180	39	1	.975	8	3	2	0	.63	+3	+1	-1	+2	4	10
		201	1335	354	9	.975	113	34	5	7	.35	+23	+13	-6	+28	27	4

Runelvys Hernandez

Year	Tm	G	Inn	TC	E	Pct	SBA	CCS	PCS	PPO	CS%	Rght	Mid	Left	Tot	RS	Rnk
2003	KC	16	92	16	0	1.000	11	7	0	0	.64	+2	0	0	+3	3	14
2005	KC	29	160	26	4	.867	21	6	0	1	.29	+1	0	+1	+3	2	36
2006	KC	21	110	15	1	.938	4	2	0	0	.50	0	0	+1	+1	2	36
2008	Hou	4	19	5	0	1.000	1	0	0	0	.00	-1	-1	+1	-1	-1	-
		70	380	67	5	.925	37	15	0	1	.41	+2	-1	+3	+6	6	44

Luke Hochevar

Year	Tm	G	Inn	TC	E	Pct	SBA	CCS	PCS	PPO	CS%	Rght	Mid	Left	Tot	RS	Rnk
2007	KC	4	13	5	0	1.000	0	0	0	0	-	0	0	-1	-1	-1	-
2008	KC	22	129	17	1	.944	18	4	0	0	.22	-1	-2	0	-2	-3	150
		26	141	23	1	.957	18	4	0	0	.22	-1	-2	-1	-3	-4	

Tim Hudson

Year	Tm	G	Inn	TC	E	Pct	SBA	CCS	PCS	PPO	CS%	Rght	Mid	Left	Tot	RS	Rnk
2003	Oak	34	240	72	2	.973	13	6	0	2	.46	-1	+1	+3	+3	4	10
2004	Oak	27	189	48	1	.980	12	4	0	1	.33	-1	-3	+1	-3	-1	104
2005	Atl	29	192	63	1	.984	17	6	1	1	.41	0	-1	+2	+1	2	36
2006	Atl	35	218	47	0	1.000	27	3	1	1	.15	-1	-4	+4	-1	-3	157
2007	Atl	34	224	70	0	1.000	13	4	0	2	.31	-1	+2	+4	+5	5	4
2008	Atl	23	142	29	1	.967	10	4	0	0	.40	0	+1	+3	+4	3	23
		182	1205	334	5	.985	92	27	2	7	.32	-4	-4	+17	+9	10	24

241

Pitchers

Edwin Jackson

Year	Tm	G	Inn	TC	E	Pct	SBA	CCS	PCS	PPO	CS%	Rght	Mid	Left	Tot	RS	Rnk
2003	LA	4	22	3	0	1.000	1	0	0	0	.00	-1	+1	+1	+1	1	-
2004	LA	8	25	8	0	1.000	2	0	0	1	1.00	+2	+1	-1	+1	1	-
2005	LAD	7	29	2	0	1.000	3	1	0	0	.33	0	0	0	0	0	-
2006	TB	23	36	6	0	1.000	3	0	0	0	.00	0	0	0	0	0	-
2007	TB	32	161	25	2	.926	22	4	1	0	.23	-2	-3	-1	-6	-6	170
2008	TB	32	183	30	1	.968	18	6	0	1	.33	-2	-1	+1	-2	-1	113
		106	456	77	3	.961	49	11	1	1	.24	-3	-2	0	-6	-5	132

Jason Jennings

Year	Tm	G	Inn	TC	E	Pct	SBA	CCS	PCS	PPO	CS%	Rght	Mid	Left	Tot	RS	Rnk
2003	Col	32	181	31	2	.939	15	5	1	0	.40	-1	-1	+2	0	1	58
2004	Col	33	201	43	1	.977	22	8	0	0	.36	-1	-4	+2	-3	-2	132
2005	Col	20	122	31	2	.939	9	0	1	0	.11	0	0	-1	0	0	81
2006	Col	32	212	39	1	.975	23	7	0	0	.30	-2	-1	0	-2	-3	157
2007	Hou	19	99	11	0	1.000	18	2	1	0	.17	0	0	0	0	-1	105
2008	Tex	6	27	7	1	.875	1	1	0	0	1.00	0	0	+1	0	0	-
		142	842	169	7	.959	88	23	3	0	.30	-4	-6	+4	-5	-5	132

Ubaldo Jimenez

Year	Tm	G	Inn	TC	E	Pct	SBA	CCS	PCS	PPO	CS%	Rght	Mid	Left	Tot	RS	Rnk
2006	Col	2	8	2	0	1.000	3	1	0	0	.33				0	0	-
2007	Col	15	82	22	3	.880	16	0	0	0	.00	0	+1	0	+1	-2	129
2008	Col	34	199	48	4	.923	22	2	1	2	.14	+4	-1	-2	+1	0	81
		51	288	79	7	.911	41	3	1	2	.10	+4	0	-2	+2	-2	-

Jason Johnson

Year	Tm	G	Inn	TC	E	Pct	SBA	CCS	PCS	PPO	CS%	Rght	Mid	Left	Tot	RS	Rnk
2003	Bal	32	190	32	3	.914	38	6	0	0	.16	+1	-1	+1	+1	-5	172
2004	Det	33	197	27	3	.900	14	3	0	0	.21	-2	-1	-2	-4	-3	150
2005	Det	33	210	42	4	.913	19	8	0	0	.42	-1	0	+3	+2	3	24
2006	3 tms	24	115	16	1	.941	19	0	0	0	.00	-4	-4	-1	-9	-10	176
2008	LAD	16	29	5	0	1.000	1	0	0	0	.00	0	+1	0	+1	1	-
		138	740	133	11	.917	91	17	0	0	.19	-6	-5	-1	-11	-14	166

Randy Johnson

Year	Tm	G	Inn	TC	E	Pct	SBA	CCS	PCS	PPO	CS%	Rght	Mid	Left	Tot	RS	Rnk
2003	Ari	18	114	15	0	1.000	19	5	1	0	.32	-1	-3	+1	-3	-3	161
2004	Ari	35	246	24	0	1.000	27	10	0	0	.37	-1	-1	-1	-3	-3	150
2005	NYY	34	226	28	2	.933	37	10	4	0	.38	0	-1	-2	-3	-2	134
2006	NYY	33	205	28	1	.966	31	9	1	0	.32	0	+4	-5	0	-1	108
2007	Ari	10	57	8	0	1.000	8	2	2	0	.50	0	0	-1	-1	0	-
2008	Ari	30	184	14	3	.824	24	1	2	0	.13	-2	-3	-3	-7	-7	174
		160	1031	123	6	.951	146	37	10	0	.32	-4	-4	-11	-17	-16	171

Todd Jones

Year	Tm	G	Inn	TC	E	Pct	SBA	CCS	PCS	PPO	CS%	Rght	Mid	Left	Tot	RS	Rnk
2003	2 tms	59	69	16	1	.941	8	3	0	0	.38	0	-1	0	0	0	-
2004	2 tms	78	82	11	2	.846	7	2	0	0	.29	-1	-1	0	-3	0	-
2005	Fla	68	73	18	1	.947	4	1	0	0	.25	+1	0	+2	+3	2	-
2006	Det	62	64	12	0	1.000	0	0	0	0	-	0	0	0	0	-1	-
2007	Det	63	61	9	1	.900	1	0	0	0	.00	+1	-1	+1	+1	1	-
2008	Det	45	42	7	0	1.000	2	0	0	0	.00	0	0	0	0	0	-
		375	391	78	5	.936	22	6	0	0	.27	+1	-4	+3	0	-1	100

Jair Jurrjens

Year	Tm	G	Inn	TC	E	Pct	SBA	CCS	PCS	PPO	CS%	Rght	Mid	Left	Tot	RS	Rnk
2007	Det	7	31	4	0	1.000	2	0	0	0	.00	0	0	0	+1	1	-
2008	Atl	31	188	44	1	.978	31	3	0	0	.10	0	+1	-2	-1	-5	170
		38	219	49	1	.980	33	3	0	0	.09	0	+1	-2	0	-4	-

Scott Kazmir

Year	Tm	G	Inn	TC	E	Pct	SBA	CCS	PCS	PPO	CS%	Rght	Mid	Left	Tot	RS	Rnk
2004	TB	8	33	5	1	.833	8	2	1	1	.38	0	0	0	0	0	-
2005	TB	32	186	24	3	.889	16	8	1	1	.56	-1	0	-1	-2	0	81
2006	TB	24	145	16	1	.941	18	1	2	3	.17	-1	-1	-1	-2	-2	136
2007	TB	34	207	25	3	.893	20	6	2	1	.40	-2	-2	-2	-6	-3	153
2008	TB	27	152	14	2	.875	10	1	2	2	.30	-1	0	-1	-2	0	81
		125	723	94	10	.894	72	18	8	8	.36	-5	-3	-5	-12	-5	132

Kyle Kendrick

Year	Tm	G	Inn	TC	E	Pct	SBA	CCS	PCS	PPO	CS%	Rght	Mid	Left	Tot	RS	Rnk
2007	Phi	20	121	27	0	1.000	10	2	0	0	.20	+1	+1	-1	+1	1	57
2008	Phi	31	156	42	1	.977	20	4	1	0	.25	+2	+3	+2	+7	4	10
		51	276	70	1	.986	30	6	1	0	.23	+3	+4	+1	+8	5	-

Clayton Kershaw

Year	Tm	G	Inn	TC	E	Pct	SBA	CCS	PCS	PPO	CS%	Rght	Mid	Left	Tot	RS	Rnk
2008	LAD	22	108	19	1	.950	7	0	2	0	.29	+2	0	-2	0	1	55

Hiroki Kuroda

Year	Tm	G	Inn	TC	E	Pct	SBA	CCS	PCS	PPO	CS%	Rght	Mid	Left	Tot	RS	Rnk
2008	LAD	31	183	56	2	.966	9	2	0	2	.22	-1	+2	+3	+4	4	10

John Lackey

Year	Tm	G	Inn	TC	E	Pct	SBA	CCS	PCS	PPO	CS%	Rght	Mid	Left	Tot	RS	Rnk
2003	Ana	33	204	35	3	.921	22	7	1	0	.36	-2	+1	0	0	0	85
2004	Ana	33	198	38	0	1.000	23	7	0	1	.32	-5	+1	+2	-2	-2	132
2005	LAA	33	209	30	3	.909	19	7	1	1	.42	-2	-3	+1	-3	-1	115
2006	LAA	33	218	35	0	1.000	16	4	0	0	.25	-1	+2	+5	+5	4	10
2007	LAA	33	224	47	2	.959	25	5	1	1	.24	-1	-1	-1	-3	-3	153
2008	LAA	24	163	19	5	.792	14	2	1	0	.21	0	-1	-3	-4	-3	150
		189	1216	217	13	.940	118	32	4	3	.31	-11	-1	+4	-7	-5	132

John Lannan

Year	Tm	G	Inn	TC	E	Pct	SBA	CCS	PCS	PPO	CS%	Rght	Mid	Left	Tot	RS	Rnk
2007	Was	6	35	8	0	1.000	6	1	1	0	.33	0	+1	0	+1	1	-
2008	Was	31	182	41	2	.953	25	2	5	0	.28	-1	0	0	0	0	81
		37	216	51	2	.961	31	3	6	0	.29	-1	+1	0	+1	1	-

Cliff Lee

Year	Tm	G	Inn	TC	E	Pct	SBA	CCS	PCS	PPO	CS%	Rght	Mid	Left	Tot	RS	Rnk
2003	Cle	9	52	6	1	.857	6	2	0	0	.33	0	0	0	0	0	-
2004	Cle	33	179	12	0	1.000	14	4	1	0	.36	0	-2	0	-2	-1	104
2005	Cle	32	202	15	3	.833	11	4	0	0	.36	-1	-2	-1	-4	-2	134
2006	Cle	33	201	22	1	.957	10	1	2	0	.30	0	-1	-1	-2	-1	108
2007	Cle	20	97	12	1	.923	5	1	0	0	.20	-1	-1	-1	-3	-2	129
2008	Cle	31	223	30	1	.968	3	0	0	0	.00	-2	-2	-1	-4	-2	133
		158	954	104	7	.933	49	12	3	0	.31	-4	-8	-4	-15	-8	154

Jon Lester

Year	Tm	G	Inn	TC	E	Pct	SBA	CCS	PCS	PPO	CS%	Rght	Mid	Left	Tot	RS	Rnk
2006	Bos	15	81	11	0	1.000	15	1	5	1	.40	0	0	-1	-1	1	56
2007	Bos	12	63	10	1	.909	6	1	0	0	.33	0	-1	-1	-2	-2	-
2008	Bos	33	210	40	2	.952	13	2	3	0	.38	-2	+2	-1	-2	-1	113
		60	354	64	3	.953	34	4	9	1	.38	-2	+1	-3	-5	-2	-

Brad Lidge

Year	Tm	G	Inn	TC	E	Pct	SBA	CCS	PCS	PPO	CS%	Rght	Mid	Left	Tot	RS	Rnk
2003	Hou	78	85	6	0	1.000	11	6	0	0	.55	0	-1	-1	-1	0	85
2004	Hou	80	95	4	0	1.000	7	5	0	0	.71	0	-1	0	-1	0	74
2005	Hou	70	71	6	1	.857	7	2	0	1	.29	0	-2	0	-2	-2	-
2006	Hou	78	75	11	2	.846	7	0	0	0	.00	0	0	0	0	-2	-
2007	Hou	66	67	7	0	1.000	3	0	0	0	.00	0	0	-2	-2	-2	-
2008	Phi	72	69	10	0	1.000	9	1	0	0	.11	0	0	+1	+1	0	-
		444	461	47	3	.936	44	14	0	1	.32	0	-4	-2	-5	-5	132

Jon Lieber

Year	Tm	G	Inn	TC	E	Pct	SBA	CCS	PCS	PPO	CS%	Rght	Mid	Left	Tot	RS	Rnk
2004	NYY	27	177	29	4	.879	3	1	0	0	.33	+1	+1	-5	-3	-1	104
2005	Phi	35	218	40	4	.909	16	5	0	0	.31	0	-1	+1	0	0	81
2006	Phi	27	168	34	3	.919	11	3	0	0	.27	-2	-1	+1	-2	-2	136
2007	Phi	14	78	10	2	.833	2	0	0	0	.00	-2	-3	+1	-4	-3	-
2008	ChC	26	47	7	0	1.000	0	0	0	0	-	0	-1	+1	0	0	-
		129	687	133	13	.902	32	9	0	0	.28	-3	-5	-1	-9	-6	141

Pitchers

Ted Lilly

BASIC						HOLDING					+/-					
Year Tm	G	Inn	TC	E	Pct	SBA	CCS	PCS	PPO	CS%	Rght	Mid	Left	Tot	RS	Rnk
2003 Oak	32	178	19	0	1.000	25	0	1	0	.04	0	0	-2	-1	-4	167
2004 Tor	32	197	20	2	.909	8	1	0	0	.13	-1	-3	0	-4	-3	150
2005 Tor	25	126	15	0	1.000	11	0	1	0	.09	-2	+1	0	-1	-2	134
2006 Tor	32	182	31	1	.969	17	1	2	0	.18	-1	0	+1	0	-1	108
2007 ChC	34	207	30	2	.938	18	2	2	0	.22	+1	0	0	+1	1	57
2008 ChC	34	205	27	0	1.000	20	2	6	0	.40	-1	-1	0	-1	1	55
	189	1095	147	5	.966	99	6	12	0	.18	-4	-3	-1	-6	-8	154

Tim Lincecum

BASIC						HOLDING					+/-					
Year Tm	G	Inn	TC	E	Pct	SBA	CCS	PCS	PPO	CS%	Rght	Mid	Left	Tot	RS	Rnk
2007 SF	24	146	24	0	1.000	12	2	0	0	.17	-1	-1	0	-2	-3	153
2008 SF	34	227	26	0	1.000	23	3	0	0	.13	-1	-2	-1	-3	-4	167
	58	373	50	0	1.000	35	5	0	0	.14	-2	-3	-1	-5	-7	150

Scott Linebrink

BASIC						HOLDING					+/-					
Year Tm	G	Inn	TC	E	Pct	SBA	CCS	PCS	PPO	CS%	Rght	Mid	Left	Tot	RS	Rnk
2003 2 tms	52	92	10	0	1.000	13	4	0	0	.31	-2	0	0	-2	-2	144
2004 SD	73	84	9	2	.818	7	2	0	0	.29	-2	+1	-1	-2	-2	132
2005 SD	73	74	4	2	.667	9	1	0	0	.11	-1	0	-1	-1	-2	-
2006 SD	73	76	13	0	1.000	9	1	0	0	.11	-1	0	+1	-1	-2	-
2007 2 tms	71	70	14	2	.875	9	3	0	0	.33	-1	-2	+1	-1	-1	-
2008 CWS	50	46	8	0	1.000	2	0	0	0	.00	0	0	0	-1	-1	-
	392	442	64	6	.906	49	11	0	0	.22	-7	-1	0	-8	-10	162

Jesse Litsch

BASIC						HOLDING					+/-					
Year Tm	G	Inn	TC	E	Pct	SBA	CCS	PCS	PPO	CS%	Rght	Mid	Left	Tot	RS	Rnk
2007 Tor	20	111	31	0	1.000	9	3	0	0	.33	+1	0	+3	+3	2	36
2008 Tor	29	176	59	3	.952	9	6	0	1	.67	+5	-1	+3	+8	8	2
	49	287	93	3	.968	18	9	0	1	.50	+6	-1	+6	+11	10	-

Esteban Loaiza

BASIC						HOLDING					+/-					
Year Tm	G	Inn	TC	E	Pct	SBA	CCS	PCS	PPO	CS%	Rght	Mid	Left	Tot	RS	Rnk
2003 CWS	34	226	47	2	.959	15	9	0	1	.60	0	+2	-1	+1	3	14
2004 2 tms	31	183	42	0	1.000	18	8	0	0	.44	+5	+2	-1	+5	5	8
2005 Was	34	217	43	1	.977	6	2	0	0	.33	-1	0	-2	-2	-1	115
2006 Oak	26	155	20	1	.952	13	3	0	0	.23	-2	-2	+2	-2	-2	136
2007 2 tms	7	37	3	0	1.000	1	0	0	0	.00	0	0		0	0	-
2008 2 tms	10	27	5	0	1.000	0	0	0	0	-	0	0	0	0	0	-
	142	845	164	4	.976	53	22	0	1	.42	+2	+2	-2	+2	5	52

Kyle Lohse

BASIC						HOLDING					+/-					
Year Tm	G	Inn	TC	E	Pct	SBA	CCS	PCS	PPO	CS%	Rght	Mid	Left	Tot	RS	Rnk
2003 Min	33	201	37	1	.974	15	3	0	1	.20	-2	+1	-2	-3	-2	144
2004 Min	35	194	34	0	1.000	24	5	3	1	.33	0	0	-1	-1	0	74
2005 Min	31	179	40	0	1.000	9	3	3	1	.67	-2	0	0	-2	1	63
2006 2 tms	34	127	36	0	1.000	5	2	1	1	.60	0	-1	0	0	2	36
2007 2 tms	34	193	33	1	.971	20	8	0	1	.40	-1	+2	0	+1	2	36
2008 StL	33	200	49	0	1.000	12	2	1	0	.25	0	-1	-1	-2	-2	133
	200	1093	231	2	.991	85	23	8	5	.36	-5	+1	-4	-7	1	84

Braden Looper

BASIC						HOLDING					+/-					
Year Tm	G	Inn	TC	E	Pct	SBA	CCS	PCS	PPO	CS%	Rght	Mid	Left	Tot	RS	Rnk
2003 Fla	74	81	11	0	1.000	2	0	0	0	.00	-1	-1	-1	-2	-2	-
2004 NYM	71	83	17	0	1.000	8	2	0	0	.25	-1	0	0	0	0	74
2005 NYM	60	59	8	1	.889	3	1	0	0	.33	+1	+1	0	+2	2	-
2006 StL	69	73	16	0	1.000	4	1	0	0	.25	+1	0	0	0	0	-
2007 StL	31	175	29	0	1.000	6	1	0	0	.17	-1	-1	-1	-3	-2	129
2008 StL	33	199	35	0	1.000	1	0	0	0	.00	-1	-1	-1	-3	-1	113
	338	670	117	1	.991	24	5	0	0	.21	-2	-2	-3	-6	-3	118

Derek Lowe

BASIC						HOLDING					+/-					
Year Tm	G	Inn	TC	E	Pct	SBA	CCS	PCS	PPO	CS%	Rght	Mid	Left	Tot	RS	Rnk
2003 Bos	33	203	64	0	1.000	17	2	1	0	.18	+2	+1	-1	+2	1	58
2004 Bos	33	183	61	3	.953	36	1	1	1	.06	-1	0	+1	0	-4	164
2005 LAD	35	222	69	1	.986	25	6	0	0	.24	0	0	+2	+3	1	63
2006 LAD	35	218	67	3	.957	30	3	1	0	.13	0	+2	-1	+1	-2	136
2007 LAD	33	199	39	0	1.000	26	12	0	0	.46	-1	+2	+1	+2	3	18
2008 LAD	34	211	54	2	.964	17	3	0	0	.18	-1	-2	+4	+1	0	81
	203	1236	363	9	.975	151	27	3	1	.20	-1	+3	+6	+9	-1	100

Greg Maddux

BASIC						HOLDING					+/-					
Year Tm	G	Inn	TC	E	Pct	SBA	CCS	PCS	PPO	CS%	Rght	Mid	Left	Tot	RS	Rnk
2003 Atl	36	218	71	2	.973	34	8	0	1	.24	+1	+4	+2	+6	3	14
2004 ChC	33	213	76	1	.987	38	12	0	0	.32	+5	+4	0	+9	5	8
2005 ChC	35	225	68	3	.958	40	8	0	0	.20	+8	+1	-4	+5	0	81
2006 2 tms	34	210	66	0	1.000	31	5	1	0	.19	+7	+2	+2	+10	4	10
2007 SD	34	198	70	1	.986	39	2	0	1	.05	+7	+2	+1	+10	3	18
2008 2 tms	33	194	74	3	.961	29	4	1	0	.17	+11	+3	0	+14	7	3
	205	1258	435	10	.977	211	39	2	2	.19	+39	+16	+1	+54	22	5

Paul Maholm

BASIC						HOLDING					+/-					
Year Tm	G	Inn	TC	E	Pct	SBA	CCS	PCS	PPO	CS%	Rght	Mid	Left	Tot	RS	Rnk
2005 Pit	6	41	7	0	1.000	4	2	0	0	.50	+1	0	+1	+2	2	-
2006 Pit	30	176	51	2	.962	24	3	8	1	.46	0	+1	0	+1	4	10
2007 Pit	29	178	36	1	.973	17	5	1	0	.35	-2	+1	+1	0	0	82
2008 Pit	31	206	37	2	.949	12	4	3	0	.58	0	0	+2	+3	4	10
	96	601	136	5	.963	57	14	12	1	.46	-1	+2	+4	+6	10	24

John Maine

BASIC						HOLDING					+/-					
Year Tm	G	Inn	TC	E	Pct	SBA	CCS	PCS	PPO	CS%	Rght	Mid	Left	Tot	RS	Rnk
2004 Bal	1	4	1	0	1.000	1	1	0	0	1.00				0	0	-
2005 Bal	10	40	7	1	.875	5	0	0	0	.00	0	-1	0	-1	-2	-
2006 NYM	16	90	14	0	1.000	9	3	0	0	.33	0	+2	0	+1	1	56
2007 NYM	32	191	21	0	1.000	17	5	0	1	.29	-1	+1	0	-1	-1	105
2008 NYM	25	140	24	1	.960	13	5	1	0	.46	0	-1	+1	0	1	55
	84	464	69	2	.971	45	14	1	1	.33	-1	+1	+1	-1	-1	100

Shaun Marcum

BASIC						HOLDING					+/-					
Year Tm	G	Inn	TC	E	Pct	SBA	CCS	PCS	PPO	CS%	Rght	Mid	Left	Tot	RS	Rnk
2005 Tor	5	8	0	0	-									0		-
2006 Tor	21	78	12	0	1.000	3	1	0	0	.33	0	-2	+2	0	0	-
2007 Tor	38	159	46	0	1.000	8	2	0	1	.25	0	+2	+1	+3	3	18
2008 Tor	25	151	35	0	1.000	7	2	0	0	.29	-1	-1	+3	+1	1	55
	89	396	93	0	1.000	18	5	0	1	.28	-1	-1	+6	+4	4	64

Jason Marquis

BASIC						HOLDING					+/-					
Year Tm	G	Inn	TC	E	Pct	SBA	CCS	PCS	PPO	CS%	Rght	Mid	Left	Tot	RS	Rnk
2003 Atl	21	41	11	1	.917	1	0	0	0	.00	-1	0	+1	+1	1	-
2004 StL	32	201	52	3	.945	11	4	0	1	.36	+2	-1	+1	+2	3	21
2005 StL	33	207	41	2	.953	9	6	0	0	.67	0	+1	-1	0	2	36
2006 StL	33	194	43	1	.977	15	5	0	0	.33	-1	-1	-1	-2	-2	136
2007 ChC	34	192	42	2	.955	22	2	0	0	.09	-1	0	+4	+3	0	82
2008 ChC	29	167	45	1	.978	12	1	0	0	.08	+1	+3	0	+4	2	31
	182	1002	244	10	.959	70	18	0	1	.26	0	+2	+4	+8	6	44

Pedro Martinez

BASIC						HOLDING					+/-					
Year Tm	G	Inn	TC	E	Pct	SBA	CCS	PCS	PPO	CS%	Rght	Mid	Left	Tot	RS	Rnk
2003 Bos	29	187	33	0	1.000	8	3	0	0	.38	-1	+2	0	+1	1	58
2004 Bos	33	217	32	1	.970	24	5	0	1	.21	-1	-4	0	-4	-4	164
2005 NYM	31	217	25	0	1.000	18	4	0	0	.22	+2	+1	+1	+4	2	36
2006 NYM	23	133	20	5	.800	14	1	0	0	.07	0	0	-2	-2	-4	170
2007 NYM	5	28	1	0	1.000	3	0	0	0	.00	-1	-1	0	-2	-2	-
2008 NYM	20	109	23	0	1.000	17	2	0	1	.12	+2	+1	0	+2	1	55
	141	890	140	6	.957	84	15	0	2	.18	+1	-1	-1	-1	-6	141

Daisuke Matsuzaka

BASIC						HOLDING					+/-					
Year Tm	G	Inn	TC	E	Pct	SBA	CCS	PCS	PPO	CS%	Rght	Mid	Left	Tot	RS	Rnk
2007 Bos	32	205	34	0	1.000	25	7	0	0	.28	+1	+2	-3	0	-1	105
2008 Bos	29	168	35	1	.972	20	5	0	0	.25	+2	+3	-2	+3	1	55
	61	372	70	1	.986	45	12	0	0	.27	+3	+5	-5	+3	0	-

Seth McClung

BASIC						HOLDING					+/-					
Year Tm	G	Inn	TC	E	Pct	SBA	CCS	PCS	PPO	CS%	Rght	Mid	Left	Tot	RS	Rnk
2003 TB	12	39	5	0	1.000	3	3	0	0	1.00	0	0	0	0	1	-
2005 TB	34	109	13	0	1.000	10	4	0	0	.40	-1	0	0	0	0	81
2006 TB	39	103	12	3	.800	20	4	1	0	.25	0	-1	-1	-1	-2	136
2007 Mil	14	12	1	0	1.000	0	0	0	0	-				-1	-1	-
2008 Mil	37	105	14	1	.933	9	4	0	0	.44	-1	0	+1	0	1	55
	136	368	49	4	.918	42	15	1	0	.38	-2	-1	0	-2	-1	-

Pitchers

Dustin McGowan

Year	Tm	G	Inn	TC	E	Pct	SBA	CCS	PCS	PPO	CS%	Rght	Mid	Left	Tot	RS	Rnk
2005	Tor	13	45	7	1	.875	10	2	1	0	.30	-1	0	+1	0	0	-
2006	Tor	16	27	4	0	1.000	4	1	0	0	.25	0	-1	0	-1	-1	-
2007	Tor	27	170	46	4	.920	30	1	0	0	.03	+1	+3	+1	+5	-1	105
2008	Tor	19	111	22	3	.880	16	4	0	0	.25	-1	+1	-2	-1	-2	133
		75	353	87	8	.908	60	8	1	0	.15	-1	+3	0	+3	-4	-

Gil Meche

Year	Tm	G	Inn	TC	E	Pct	SBA	CCS	PCS	PPO	CS%	Rght	Mid	Left	Tot	RS	Rnk
2003	Sea	32	186	35	1	.972	8	4	0	0	.50	-1	+2	0	+1	2	28
2004	Sea	23	128	12	1	.923	8	4	1	0	.63	-3	0	0	-3	-1	104
2005	Sea	29	143	30	1	.968	16	8	0	2	.50	0	0	+1	+1	3	24
2006	Sea	32	187	31	1	.969	12	6	1	1	.58	-1	-3	+3	0	2	36
2007	KC	34	216	37	3	.925	9	4	1	1	.56	-1	0	+1	-1	1	57
2008	KC	34	210	34	4	.895	14	2	0	0	.14	-1	0	+3	+3	1	55
		184	1070	190	11	.942	67	28	3	4	.46	-7	-1	+8	+1	8	38

Andrew Miller

Year	Tm	G	Inn	TC	E	Pct	SBA	CCS	PCS	PPO	CS%	Rght	Mid	Left	Tot	RS	Rnk
2006	Det	8	10	1	0	1.000	0	0	0	0	-	0		0	0	0	-
2007	Det	13	64	10	2	.833	11	1	0	0	.09	-1	0	-2	-2	-3	-
2008	Fla	29	107	13	1	.929	16	2	1	0	.19	-1	-1	0	-2	-3	150
		50	181	27	3	.889	27	3	1	0	.15	-2	-1	-2	-4	-6	-

Kevin Millwood

Year	Tm	G	Inn	TC	E	Pct	SBA	CCS	PCS	PPO	CS%	Rght	Mid	Left	Tot	RS	Rnk
2003	Phi	35	222	33	2	.943	45	4	0	0	.09	-1	+2	+1	+2	-4	167
2004	Phi	25	141	29	0	1.000	13	1	0	0	.08	-2	+1	0	-1	-2	132
2005	Cle	30	192	25	0	1.000	39	6	0	0	.15	-2	-2	0	-4	-7	176
2006	Tex	34	215	42	0	1.000	13	3	0	0	.23	0	+1	0	+1	1	56
2007	Tex	31	173	17	3	.850	19	5	0	0	.26	-3	-2	0	-5	-5	168
2008	Tex	29	169	32	2	.941	30	4	0	0	.13	-1	-2	+3	-1	-4	167
		184	1111	185	7	.962	159	23	0	0	.14	-9	-2	+4	-8	-21	174

Zach Miner

Year	Tm	G	Inn	TC	E	Pct	SBA	CCS	PCS	PPO	CS%	Rght	Mid	Left	Tot	RS	Rnk
2006	Det	27	93	9	0	1.000	13	4	1	0	.38	0	0	0	-1	-1	108
2007	Det	34	54	9	2	.818	10	6	0	0	.60	-1	-1	+1	-1	0	-
2008	Det	45	118	22	0	1.000	12	4	0	0	.33	-1	0	+3	+1	1	55
		106	264	42	2	.952	35	14	1	0	.43	-2	-1	+4	-1	0	-

Brian Moehler

Year	Tm	G	Inn	TC	E	Pct	SBA	CCS	PCS	PPO	CS%	Rght	Mid	Left	Tot	RS	Rnk
2003	Hou	3	14	5	0	1.000	0	0	0	0	-	0	0	+1		1	-
2005	Fla	37	158	47	1	.979	21	4	1	0	.24	+1	-1	-2	-2	-3	161
2006	Fla	29	122	26	1	.963	11	5	1	1	.55	0	+1	0	+1	3	20
2007	Hou	42	60	15	0	1.000	3	0	0	0	.00	0	-2	-1	-3	-2	-
2008	Hou	31	150	24	1	.960	9	0	0	0	.00	-1	0	-1	-2	-3	150
		142	503	120	3	.975	44	9	2	1	.25	0	-2	-3	-5	-4	126

Matt Morris

Year	Tm	G	Inn	TC	E	Pct	SBA	CCS	PCS	PPO	CS%	Rght	Mid	Left	Tot	RS	Rnk
2003	StL	27	172	32	0	1.000	6	3	0	0	.50	-2	0	+1	-1	0	85
2004	StL	32	202	46	1	.979	14	3	0	1	.21	-2	0	+1	0	0	74
2005	StL	31	193	33	1	.971	6	1	0	0	.17	-1	+1	0	0	0	81
2006	SF	33	208	48	3	.941	16	1	2	1	.19	-2	-1	+2	-1	-1	108
2007	2 tms	32	199	44	1	.978	17	2	0	0	.12	0	+1	+1	+2	1	57
2008	Pit	5	22	4	0	1.000	6	3	0	0	.50	0	-1	0	0	0	-
		160	995	213	6	.972	65	13	2	2	.23	-7	0	+5	0	0	93

Guillermo Mota

Year	Tm	G	Inn	TC	E	Pct	SBA	CCS	PCS	PPO	CS%	Rght	Mid	Left	Tot	RS	Rnk
2003	LA	76	105	20	1	.952	13	5	0	0	.38	+5	0	-1	+4	3	14
2004	2 tms	78	97	16	0	1.000	24	2	1	0	.13	-1	0	+1	+1	-1	104
2005	Fla	56	67	7	0	1.000	13	3	0	0	.23	0	+1	0	+1	0	-
2006	2 tms	52	56	4	0	1.000	10	1	0	0	.10	0	0	0	0	-1	-
2007	NYM	52	59	15	1	.938	9	0	0	0	.00	+1	+1	+2	+4	2	-
2008	Mil	58	57	15	0	1.000	5	0	1	1	.20	+1	+2	0	+2	2	-
		372	440	79	2	.975	74	11	2	1	.18	+7	+4	+2	+12	5	52

Jamie Moyer

Year	Tm	G	Inn	TC	E	Pct	SBA	CCS	PCS	PPO	CS%	Rght	Mid	Left	Tot	RS	Rnk
2003	Sea	33	215	48	1	.980	17	2	4	0	.35	-2	0	+1	-1	0	85
2004	Sea	34	202	38	0	1.000	13	2	2	0	.31	-1	0	+3	+2	3	21
2005	Sea	32	200	46	0	1.000	34	3	4	0	.21	+1	-1	0	0	-2	134
2006	2 tms	33	211	48	2	.960	19	3	5	0	.42	0	+1	+2	+3	4	10
2007	Phi	33	199	46	1	.979	15	2	4	0	.40	0	+2	0	+2	4	10
2008	Phi	33	196	40	2	.952	19	2	4	0	.32	0	0	-1	-1	-1	113
		198	1224	272	6	.978	117	14	23	0	.32	-2	+2	+5	+4	8	38

Mark Mulder

Year	Tm	G	Inn	TC	E	Pct	SBA	CCS	PCS	PPO	CS%	Rght	Mid	Left	Tot	RS	Rnk
2003	Oak	26	187	45	0	1.000	20	4	6	1	.50	-2	-2	0	-3	1	58
2004	Oak	33	226	57	3	.950	27	5	8	1	.48	+1	+3	-1	+3	5	8
2005	StL	32	205	57	2	.966	10	3	5	0	.80	-1	+7	+2	+8	9	1
2006	StL	17	93	29	0	1.000	6	1	0	0	.17	+3	0	0	+3	2	36
2007	StL	3	11	3	0	1.000	1	0	1	0	1.00	-1				1	-
2008	StL	3	2	0	0	-	1	0	0	0	.00					0	-
		114	723	196	5	.974	65	13	20	2	.51	0	+8	+1	+11	18	10

Mike Mussina

Year	Tm	G	Inn	TC	E	Pct	SBA	CCS	PCS	PPO	CS%	Rght	Mid	Left	Tot	RS	Rnk
2003	NYY	31	193	47	0	1.000	19	10	0	0	.53	+3	+3	+1	+7	6	5
2004	NYY	27	165	39	2	.951	13	3	0	0	.23	+3	+2	0	+3	2	38
2005	NYY	30	180	33	4	.892	22	7	0	0	.32	+2	+1	+1	+4	3	36
2006	NYY	32	197	25	0	1.000	19	4	0	0	.21	+4	-1	0	+4	2	36
2007	NYY	28	152	36	0	1.000	27	3	0	0	.11	0	+1	0	+1	-2	129
2008	NYY	34	200	41	1	.976	19	6	0	0	.37	0	+3	-1	+2	2	31
		182	1108	228	7	.969	119	33	1	0	.29	+12	+9	-1	+21	12	15

Brett Myers

Year	Tm	G	Inn	TC	E	Pct	SBA	CCS	PCS	PPO	CS%	Rght	Mid	Left	Tot	RS	Rnk
2003	Phi	32	193	40	2	.952	21	5	0	0	.24	-1	0	+3	+4	2	28
2004	Phi	32	176	38	0	1.000	21	3	0	0	.14	+1	-3	-1	-1	-3	150
2005	Phi	34	215	48	2	.960	19	4	0	2	.21	-1	+5	+1	+4	3	24
2006	Phi	31	198	38	0	1.000	18	3	2	0	.28	-1	-1	+3	0	0	81
2007	Phi	51	69	16	0	1.000	7	1	0	0	.14	-2	+1	0	-1	-1	-
2008	Phi	30	190	38	0	1.000	20	2	1	0	.15	-1	0	+3	+2	0	81
		210	1041	222	4	.982	106	18	3	2	.20	-4	+3	+12	+9	1	84

Joe Nathan

Year	Tm	G	Inn	TC	E	Pct	SBA	CCS	PCS	PPO	CS%	Rght	Mid	Left	Tot	RS	Rnk
2003	SF	78	79	9	0	1.000	6	1	0	0	.17	-1	-1	-1	-3	-2	-
2004	Min	73	72	7	0	1.000	7	3	0	0	.43	-1	0	0	0	0	-
2005	Min	69	70	8	1	.889	3	1	0	0	.33	0	0	0	0	0	-
2006	Min	64	68	8	2	.800	2	0	0	0	.00	+1	0	0	+1	1	-
2007	Min	68	72	4	1	.800	7	0	0	0	.00	0	0	0	0	-1	-
2008	Min	68	68	9	1	.900	5	0	0	0	.00	0	+1	0	0	0	-
		420	429	50	5	.900	30	5	0	0	.17	-1	0	-1	-2	-3	118

Ricky Nolasco

Year	Tm	G	Inn	TC	E	Pct	SBA	CCS	PCS	PPO	CS%	Rght	Mid	Left	Tot	RS	Rnk
2006	Fla	35	140	21	4	.840	12	6	0	0	.50	-1	-1	+2	-1	0	81
2007	Fla	5	21	2	0	1.000	3	1	0	0	.33	0	-1	-1	-2	-2	-
2008	Fla	34	212	29	0	1.000	12	5	0	0	.42	-1	-2	+1	-2	-1	113
		74	373	56	4	.929	27	12	0	0	.44	-2	-4	+2	-5	-3	118

Hideo Nomo

Year	Tm	G	Inn	TC	E	Pct	SBA	CCS	PCS	PPO	CS%	Rght	Mid	Left	Tot	RS	Rnk
2003	LA	33	218	43	1	.977	33	14	0	0	.42	-1	-1	+1	-1	-1	113
2004	LA	18	84	19	0	1.000	19	4	0	0	.21	0	+2	0	+2	0	74
2005	TB	19	101	18	0	1.000	10	3	0	0	.30	-1	+1	0	0	0	81
2008	KC	3	4	0	0	-	1	0	0	0	.00					0	-
		73	407	81	1	.988	63	21	0	0	.33	-2	+2	+1	+1	-1	100

Pitchers

Darren Oliver

Year	Tm	G	Inn	TC	E	Pct	SBA	CCS	PCS	PPO	CS%	Rght	Mid	Left	Tot	RS	Rnk
2003	Col	33	180	34	0	1.000	20	2	4	0	.30	-1	+1	-1	-1	-1	113
2004	2 tms	27	73	13	0	1.000	7	4	0	0	.57	+1	0	+1	+2	2	-
2006	NYM	45	81	14	0	1.000	4	1	0	0	.25	0	-1	+1	0	0	81
2007	LAA	61	64	13	1	.929	3	0	0	0	.00	+1	-1	-2	-2	-2	-
2008	LAA	54	72	14	0	1.000	7	1	1	0	.29	+1	+2	-3	0	0	-
		220	470	89	1	.989	41	8	5	0	.32	+2	+1	-4	-1	-1	100

Scott Olsen

Year	Tm	G	Inn	TC	E	Pct	SBA	CCS	PCS	PPO	CS%	Rght	Mid	Left	Tot	RS	Rnk
2005	Fla	5	20	3	1	.750	4	1	1	0	.50	0	0		0	0	-
2006	Fla	31	181	28	1	.966	16	5	3	0	.50	+2	+1	-2	+1	3	20
2007	Fla	33	177	24	0	1.000	16	4	2	0	.38	0	-2	0	-2	-3	-
2008	Fla	33	202	29	2	.935	15	4	3	1	.47	+4	-1	-1	+3	4	149
		102	579	88	4	.955	51	14	9	1	.45	+6	-2	-7	-2	3	73

Garrett Olson

Year	Tm	G	Inn	TC	E	Pct	SBA	CCS	PCS	PPO	CS%	Rght	Mid	Left	Tot	RS	Rnk
2007	Bal	7	32	5	2	.714	4	0	1	0	.25	+1	0	-1	-1	-1	-
2008	Bal	26	133	21	4	.840	22	1	1	0	.09	-1	0	+1	-1	-3	150
		33	165	32	6	.813	26	1	2	0	.12	0	0	0	-2	-4	-

Roy Oswalt

Year	Tm	G	Inn	TC	E	Pct	SBA	CCS	PCS	PPO	CS%	Rght	Mid	Left	Tot	RS	Rnk
2003	Hou	21	127	23	0	1.000	6	4	1	0	.83	-1	-3	0	-4	-1	113
2004	Hou	36	237	46	3	.939	11	4	1	0	.45	+4	-4	+2	+2	3	21
2005	Hou	35	242	50	0	1.000	7	4	0	1	.57	0	0	-1	-1	1	63
2006	Hou	33	221	43	1	.977	11	5	1	0	.55	-3	-1	+3	-1	1	56
2007	Hou	33	212	56	0	1.000	6	1	0	0	.17	-1	0	+2	+1	2	36
2008	Hou	32	209	54	0	1.000	2	1	0	0	.50	-2	+1	+4	+3	3	23
		190	1247	276	4	.986	43	19	3	1	.51	-3	-7	+10	0	9	33

Micah Owings

Year	Tm	G	Inn	TC	E	Pct	SBA	CCS	PCS	PPO	CS%	Rght	Mid	Left	Tot	RS	Rnk
2007	Ari	29	153	26	2	.929	7	3	0	0	.43	+1	0	-1	0	0	82
2008	Ari	22	105	25	1	.962	5	2	0	0	.40	+2	+1	0	+3	3	23
		51	257	54	3	.944	12	5	0	0	.42	+2	+2	-2	+2	3	-

Vicente Padilla

Year	Tm	G	Inn	TC	E	Pct	SBA	CCS	PCS	PPO	CS%	Rght	Mid	Left	Tot	RS	Rnk
2003	Phi	32	209	47	4	.922	9	4	0	0	.44	0	0	+2	+1	2	28
2004	Phi	20	115	24	0	1.000	7	2	0	0	.29	-1	-2	+1	-1	-1	104
2005	Phi	27	147	27	1	.964	3	1	0	1	.33	-1	+2	-1	-1	0	81
2006	Tex	33	200	34	1	.971	11	2	1	1	.27	-3	-1	+2	-1	0	81
2007	Tex	23	120	18	1	.947	6	2	1	0	.50	-2	0	-1	-2	-1	105
2008	Tex	29	171	30	4	.882	13	4	0	2	.31	-2	+2	+3	+2	3	23
		164	962	191	11	.942	49	15	2	4	.35	-9	+1	+6	-2	3	73

Manny Parra

Year	Tm	G	Inn	TC	E	Pct	SBA	CCS	PCS	PPO	CS%	Rght	Mid	Left	Tot	RS	Rnk
2007	Mil	9	26	3	0	1.000	0	0	0	0	-	0	0	-1	-1	-1	-
2008	Mil	32	166	19	0	1.000	13	3	2	0	.38	0	0	-3	-3	-1	113
		41	192	22	0	1.000	13	3	2	0	.38	0	0	-4	-4	-2	-

Carl Pavano

Year	Tm	G	Inn	TC	E	Pct	SBA	CCS	PCS	PPO	CS%	Rght	Mid	Left	Tot	RS	Rnk
2003	Fla	33	201	40	0	1.000	20	3	0	0	.15	0	+1	+1	+2	0	85
2004	Fla	31	222	40	0	1.000	21	5	0	0	.24	-2	0	+1	-1	-2	132
2005	NYY	17	100	13	0	1.000	15	4	0	0	.27	0	-1	-2	-2	-3	161
2007	NYY	2	11	3	0	1.000	3	0	0	0	.00	-1	+1		0	-1	-
2008	NYY	7	34	7	0	1.000	6	1	0	0	.17	+1	-1	-1	-1	-2	-
		90	569	103	0	1.000	65	13	0	0	.20	-2	0	-1	-2	-8	154

Jake Peavy

Year	Tm	G	Inn	TC	E	Pct	SBA	CCS	PCS	PPO	CS%	Rght	Mid	Left	Tot	RS	Rnk
2003	SD	32	195	37	3	.925	8	1	0	0	.13	0	-2	+1	-1	-1	113
2004	SD	27	166	34	1	.971	17	1	0	0	.06	0	0	+1	+1	-1	104
2005	SD	30	203	34	1	.971	24	5	0	1	.21	+2	+1	0	+2	0	81
2006	SD	32	202	42	2	.955	31	6	0	0	.19	0	0	+1	+1	-2	136
2007	SD	34	223	48	0	1.000	23	2	0	1	.09	+3	+1	+1	+5	2	36
2008	SD	27	174	38	2	.950	27	8	1	0	.33	+2	0	-2	0	-1	113
		182	1163	242	9	.963	130	23	1	2	.18	+7	0	+2	+8	-3	118

Mike Pelfrey

Year	Tm	G	Inn	TC	E	Pct	SBA	CCS	PCS	PPO	CS%	Rght	Mid	Left	Tot	RS	Rnk
2006	NYM	4	21	4	0	1.000	3	1	0	0	.33	0				0	-
2007	NYM	15	73	8	0	1.000	8	0	1	0	1.00	0	-2	0	-2	-3	-
2008	NYM	32	201	47	0	1.000	11	6	0	4	.55	-3	+3	-1	-1	2	31
		51	294	59	0	1.000	22	7	0	5	.32	-3	+1		-3	-1	-

Odalis Perez

Year	Tm	G	Inn	TC	E	Pct	SBA	CCS	PCS	PPO	CS%	Rght	Mid	Left	Tot	RS	Rnk
2003	LA	34	185	46	1	.979	34	2	7	0	.26	+1	0	-1	+1	1	58
2004	LA	31	196	49	1	.980	19	1	4	0	.26	+1	+2	0	+2	2	38
2005	LAD	19	109	17	0	1.000	16	0	2	0	.13	+2	-2	0	-1	-2	134
2006	2 tms	32	126	27	1	.964	12	2	1	0	.25	+2	-1	-1	0	0	81
2007	KC	26	137	24	0	1.000	12	2	1	0	.25	-1	+2	+1	+2	2	36
2008	Was	30	160	35	0	1.000	20	3	4	0	.35	+3	-1	-3	-2	-1	113
		168	913	201	3	.985	113	10	19	0	.26	+7	+2	-4	+3	2	79

Oliver Perez

Year	Tm	G	Inn	TC	E	Pct	SBA	CCS	PCS	PPO	CS%	Rght	Mid	Left	Tot	RS	Rnk
2003	2 tms	24	127	16	1	.941	2	0	1	0	.50	+1	-1	0	0	1	58
2004	Pit	30	196	28	0	1.000	8	4	0	0	.50	+2	-1	0	+2	3	21
2005	Pit	20	103	12	1	.923	8	3	2	0	.63	+1	-2	-3	-3	0	81
2006	2 tms	22	113	14	2	.875	6	0	1	0	.17	0	0	-1	0	-1	108
2007	NYM	29	177	15	3	.833	16	1	2	1	.19	+1	0	-2	0	0	82
2008	NYM	34	194	22	0	1.000	9	1	0	0	.11	+1	+1	-1	+1	1	55
		159	909	114	7	.939	49	9	6	1	.31	+6	-3	-6	-1	4	64

Glen Perkins

Year	Tm	G	Inn	TC	E	Pct	SBA	CCS	PCS	PPO	CS%	Rght	Mid	Left	Tot	RS	Rnk
2006	Min	4	6	1	0	1.000									0	0	-
2007	Min	19	29	3	0	1.000	2	1	0	0	.50	0	-1	0	0	0	-
2008	Min	26	151	27	1	.964	7	1	3	0	.57	0	+3	0	+3	4	10
		49	185	32	1	.969	9	2	3	0	.56	0	+2	0	+3	4	-

Andy Pettitte

Year	Tm	G	Inn	TC	E	Pct	SBA	CCS	PCS	PPO	CS%	Rght	Mid	Left	Tot	RS	Rnk
2003	NYY	33	208	36	6	.857	14	1	0	0	.07	+1	-1	0	0	-1	113
2004	Hou	15	83	23	1	.958	5	1	1	0	.40	+1	+2	+1	+2	3	-
2005	Hou	33	222	52	1	.981	9	1	1	1	.44	+2	+3	+1	+6	7	4
2006	Hou	36	214	33	2	.943	13	0	3	1	.23	0	-1	+2	+1	2	36
2007	NYY	36	215	41	1	.976	26	4	4	1	.31	+2	+1	-1	+2	3	18
2008	NYY	33	204	36	2	.947	28	2	6	4	.29	-4	0	-3	-6	-3	150
		186	1147	234	13	.944	95	9	17	7	.27	+2	+4	0	+6	10	24

Joel Pineiro

Year	Tm	G	Inn	TC	E	Pct	SBA	CCS	PCS	PPO	CS%	Rght	Mid	Left	Tot	RS	Rnk
2003	Sea	32	212	44	1	.978	13	2	0	0	.15	+3	-1	+2	+4	2	28
2004	Sea	21	141	23	1	.958	14	3	0	0	.21	0	0	+1	0	-1	104
2005	Sea	30	189	41	1	.976	9	2	0	0	.22	0	0	0	0	0	81
2006	Sea	40	166	36	0	1.000	11	3	0	0	.27	-1	+1	+4	+4	1	56
2007	2 tms	42	98	26	2	.929	8	1	1	0	.33	0	+1	+1	+1	5	4
2008	StL	26	149	43	1	.977	9	3	1	1	.44	-1	+2	0	+1	2	31
		191	953	219	6	.973	62	15	1	1	.26	+1	+3	+8	+12	9	33

Pitchers

Sidney Ponson

Year	Tm	G	Inn	TC	E	Pct	SBA	CCS	PCS	PPO	CS%	Rght	Mid	Left	Tot	RS	Rnk
2003	2 tms	31	216	48	1	.980	16	3	1	0	.25	+1	-1	0	+1	1	58
2004	Bal	33	216	49	1	.980	12	3	0	0	.25	-3	0	-3	-6	-5	170
2005	Bal	23	130	28	2	.933	10	1	0	0	.10	-2	-1	+1	-3	-3	161
2006	2 tms	19	85	14	1	.933	8	2	1	1	.38	-1	-2	0	-4	-2	136
2007	Min	7	38	7	1	.875	3	2	0	0	.67	0	0	0	0	1	-
2008	2 tms	25	136	28	3	.903	8	4	1	0	.63	-2	+1	-2	-3	0	81
		138	820	183	9	.951	57	15	3	1	.32	-7	-3	-4	-15	-8	154

David Riske

Year	Tm	G	Inn	TC	E	Pct	SBA	CCS	PCS	PPO	CS%	Rght	Mid	Left	Tot	RS	Rnk
2003	Cle	68	75	7	0	1.000	6	2	0	0	.33	-1	0	0	-1	-1	-
2004	Cle	72	77	11	0	1.000	2	0	0	0	.00	0	0	0	-1	-1	-
2005	Cle	58	73	9	0	1.000	3	1	0	0	.33	-1	-1	-1	-3	-2	-
2006	2 tms	41	44	4	1	.800	4	1	0	0	.25	0	0	0	-1	-1	-
2007	KC	65	70	16	0	1.000	5	1	0	0	.20	0	0	-1	-2	-2	-
2008	Mil	45	42	3	0	1.000	4	1	0	0	.50				0	1	-
		349	380	51	1	.980	24	6	1	0	.29	-2	-1	-2	-8	-6	141

Horacio Ramirez

Year	Tm	G	Inn	TC	E	Pct	SBA	CCS	PCS	PPO	CS%	Rght	Mid	Left	Tot	RS	Rnk
2003	Atl	29	182	39	3	.929	17	3	1	0	.24	0	0	0	-1	-2	144
2004	Atl	10	60	20	0	1.000	4	1	0	1	.25	0	+1	+1	+2	2	-
2005	Atl	33	202	50	2	.962	18	4	2	1	.33	+2	0	+3	+4	4	11
2006	Atl	14	76	30	1	.968	6	1	0	0	.17	+1	+2	+1	+4	3	-
2007	Sea	20	98	30	0	1.000	14	2	3	0	.36	+3	+1	-1	+3	3	18
2008	2 tms	32	37	13	0	1.000	5	0	0	0	.00	0	+1	+2	+3	2	-
		138	656	188	6	.968	64	11	6	2	.27	+6	+5	+6	+15	12	15

Mariano Rivera

Year	Tm	G	Inn	TC	E	Pct	SBA	CCS	PCS	PPO	CS%	Rght	Mid	Left	Tot	RS	Rnk
2003	NYY	64	70	19	2	.905	5	2	0	0	.40	+2	0	-1	0	0	-
2004	NYY	74	79	41	1	.976	6	1	0	0	.17	+2	0	+1	+4	4	-
2005	NYY	71	78	29	0	1.000	9	3	0	0	.33	+2	0	+1	+3	2	-
2006	NYY	63	75	25	0	1.000	6	3	0	0	.50	0	+3	+1	+3	2	-
2007	NYY	67	71	16	0	1.000	3	1	0	0	.33	+1	0	0	0	0	-
2008	NYY	64	71	14	0	1.000	7	1	0	0	.14	-1	0	+1	-1	-2	-
		403	444	146	3	.979	36	11	0	0	.31	+6	+3	+3	+9	5	52

Darrell Rasner

Year	Tm	G	Inn	TC	E	Pct	SBA	CCS	PCS	PPO	CS%	Rght	Mid	Left	Tot	RS	Rnk
2005	Was	5	7	0	0											0	-
2006	NYY	6	20	4	0	1.000	0	0	0	0	-	0	0	+1	+1	1	-
2007	NYY	6	25	3	0	1.000	4	1	0	0	.25				0	0	-
2008	NYY	24	113	24	0	1.000	6	3	0	0	.50	-1	+1	+1	+1	2	31
		41	165	31	0	1.000	10	4	0	0	.40	-1	+1	+2	+2	3	-

Tim Redding

Year	Tm	G	Inn	TC	E	Pct	SBA	CCS	PCS	PPO	CS%	Rght	Mid	Left	Tot	RS	Rnk
2003	Hou	33	176	35	2	.946	19	2	0	0	.11	0	+2	0	+2	0	85
2004	Hou	27	101	25	1	.962	9	1	0	0	.11	0	0	-1	-1	-2	132
2005	2 tms	10	31	7	1	.875	1	0	0	0	.00			-1	-1	-1	-
2007	Was	15	84	16	1	.941	8	3	0	0	.38	0	0	+2	+1	1	57
2008	Was	33	182	25	2	.926	20	7	0	0	.35	-3	+2	+2	+1	1	55
		118	573	115	7	.939	57	13	0	0	.23	-3	+4	+3	+2	-1	100

Mark Redman

Year	Tm	G	Inn	TC	E	Pct	SBA	CCS	PCS	PPO	CS%	Rght	Mid	Left	Tot	RS	Rnk
2003	Fla	29	192	29	1	.967	4	1	0	0	.25	-2	+1	+2	+1	2	28
2004	Oak	32	191	34	1	.971	13	1	7	2	.62	-3	0	-2	-4	1	53
2005	Pit	30	178	49	1	.980	10	3	1	0	.40	0	+1	+3	+5	5	7
2006	KC	29	167	33	3	.917	11	5	1	0	.55	-1	+2	0	0	2	36
2007	2 tms	11	41	3	0	1.000	2	1	0	0	.50	0	0	-2	-2	-2	-
2008	Col	10	45	9	0	1.000	2	0	0	0	.00	0	0	0	0	0	-
		141	814	163	6	.963	42	11	9	3	.48	-6	+4	+1	0	8	38

Jo-Jo Reyes

Year	Tm	G	Inn	TC	E	Pct	SBA	CCS	PCS	PPO	CS%	Rght	Mid	Left	Tot	RS	Rnk
2007	Atl	11	51	8	0	1.000	3	0	1	0	.33	+1	0	0	+1	1	-
2008	Atl	23	113	16	0	1.000	13	3	1	0	.31	+1	0	-1	0	0	81
		34	163	24	0	1.000	16	3	2	0	.31	+2	0	-1	+1	1	-

Juan Rincon

Year	Tm	G	Inn	TC	E	Pct	SBA	CCS	PCS	PPO	CS%	Rght	Mid	Left	Tot	RS	Rnk
2003	Min	58	87	25	0	1.000	9	1	0	0	.11	-1	+1	-2	-2	-3	161
2004	Min	77	82	9	3	.750	6	2	0	0	.33	-1	0	+1	-1	-1	-
2005	Min	75	77	17	1	.944	4	1	1	1	.50	+1	0	0	0	1	-
2006	Min	75	74	13	0	1.000	3	0	0	0	.00	-1	-1	0	-2	-2	-
2007	Min	63	60	14	1	.933	4	1	0	0	.25	0	+1	0	+1	1	-
2008	2 tms	47	55	6	0	1.000	7	1	0	0	.14	0	-2	+1	0	-2	-
		395	435	89	5	.944	33	6	1	1	.21	-2	-1	0	-6	-6	141

Nate Robertson

Year	Tm	G	Inn	TC	E	Pct	SBA	CCS	PCS	PPO	CS%	Rght	Mid	Left	Tot	RS	Rnk
2003	Det	8	44	7	0	1.000	4	2	1	0	.75	-1	0	0	-1	1	-
2004	Det	34	197	29	5	.853	12	6	0	1	.50	+1	-1	-2	-2	0	74
2005	Det	32	197	32	3	.914	13	4	1	0	.38	-1	+1	+1	+1	2	36
2006	Det	32	209	31	3	.912	14	4	1	0	.36	-1	0	-4	-5	-3	157
2007	Det	30	178	32	2	.941	11	3	1	0	.36	0	+1	-1	0	0	82
2008	Det	32	169	28	1	.966	11	3	1	0	.36	0	-1	-1	-1	0	81
		168	992	173	14	.919	65	22	5	1	.42	-2	+1	-8	-8	0	93

Francisco Rodriguez

Year	Tm	G	Inn	TC	E	Pct	SBA	CCS	PCS	PPO	CS%	Rght	Mid	Left	Tot	RS	Rnk
2003	Ana	59	86	15	0	1.000	10	3	1	0	.40	0	0	-1	0	0	85
2004	Ana	69	84	14	0	1.000	6	2	0	0	.33	0	+1	-1	0	0	74
2005	LAA	66	67	11	1	.917	2	0	0	0	.00	-1			-1	-1	-
2006	LAA	69	73	10	0	1.000	3	1	0	1	.33	0	0	+1	+1	2	-
2007	LAA	64	67	6	0	1.000	13	1	0	0	.08	0	0	-1	-1	-3	-
2008	LAA	76	68	10	2	.833	8	0	0	0	.00	0	0	0	0	-1	-
		403	446	69	3	.957	42	7	1	1	.19	-1	+1	-2	-1	-3	118

Wandy Rodriguez

Year	Tm	G	Inn	TC	E	Pct	SBA	CCS	PCS	PPO	CS%	Rght	Mid	Left	Tot	RS	Rnk
2005	Hou	25	129	29	2	.935	11	4	2	0	.55	+1	+1	+1	+3	3	24
2006	Hou	30	136	21	1	.955	12	2	4	0	.50	0	0	-1	-1	1	56
2007	Hou	31	183	36	1	.973	22	3	6	0	.41	0	+1	0	+2	4	10
2008	Hou	25	137	23	0	1.000	7	2	1	0	.43	+1	0	-1	0	1	55
		111	584	113	4	.965	52	11	13	0	.46	+2	+2	-1	+4	9	33

Kenny Rogers

Year	Tm	G	Inn	TC	E	Pct	SBA	CCS	PCS	PPO	CS%	Rght	Mid	Left	Tot	RS	Rnk
2003	Min	33	195	56	1	.966	6	1	1	3	.33	+1	+2	+2	+5	6	5
2004	Tex	35	212	64	1	.985	7	2	3	3	.71	+5	+2	+2	+9	11	1
2005	Tex	30	195	65	1	.985	3	0	0	0	.00	+1	+2	+4	+7	6	4
2006	Det	34	204	52	5	.912	7	5	1	1	.86	+3	+3	+2	+9	10	1
2007	Det	11	63	17	1	.944	0	0	0	2	-	0	+1	0	+1	2	-
2008	Det	30	174	76	1	.987	3	2	0	3	.67	+4	+5	+6	+16	15	1
		173	1042	341	11	.968	26	10	5	12	.58	+14	+15	+16	+47	50	1

Ryan Rowland-Smith

Year	Tm	G	Inn	TC	E	Pct	SBA	CCS	PCS	PPO	CS%	Rght	Mid	Left	Tot	RS	Rnk
2007	Sea	26	39	6	1	.857	2	1	1	1	1.00	+1			0	1	-
2008	Sea	47	118	10	1	.909	6	2	0	0	.33	+3	-1	-2	0	0	81
		73	157	18	2	.889	8	3	1	1	.50	+4	-1	-2	0	1	-

Pitchers

Kirk Saarloos

Year	Tm	G	Inn	TC	E	Pct	SBA	CCS	PCS	PPO	CS%	Rght	Mid	Left	Tot	RS	Rnk
2003	Hou	36	49	8	2	.800	5	1	0	0	.20	-1	0	0	0	0	-
2004	Oak	6	24	11	0	1.000	2	0	0	0	.00	+1	+1	-1	+1	1	-
2005	Oak	29	160	55	2	.965	19	5	0	0	.26	+6	+2	-1	+7	4	11
2006	Oak	35	121	36	0	1.000	12	5	0	0	.42	+3	+3	-1	+5	4	10
2007	Cin	34	43	13	1	.929	2	0	0	0	.00	+2	+1	0	+2	2	-
2008	Oak	8	26	5	0	1.000	1	0	0	0	.00	0	0	-1	-1	-1	-
		148	423	133	5	.962	41	11	0	0	.27	+11	+7	-4	+14	10	24

CC Sabathia

Year	Tm	G	Inn	TC	E	Pct	SBA	CCS	PCS	PPO	CS%	Rght	Mid	Left	Tot	RS	Rnk
2003	Cle	30	198	26	2	.929	14	7	2	0	.64	0	0	0	0	2	28
2004	Cle	30	188	18	0	1.000	23	5	1	0	.26	+1	-1	0	0	-2	132
2005	Cle	31	197	19	2	.905	18	5	2	0	.39	-2	-2	-1	-5	-3	161
2006	Cle	28	193	22	3	.880	19	5	0	0	.26	0	-1	-2	-2	-3	157
2007	Cle	34	241	25	1	.962	20	9	1	0	.50	+1	+1	0	+1	3	18
2008	2 tms	35	253	33	1	.971	15	1	2	0	.20	-1	+2	-3	-2	-2	133
		188	1269	152	9	.941	109	32	8	0	.37	-1	-1	-7	-9	-5	132

Chris Sampson

Year	Tm	G	Inn	TC	E	Pct	SBA	CCS	PCS	PPO	CS%	Rght	Mid	Left	Tot	RS	Rnk
2006	Hou	12	34	15	0	1.000	0	0	0	0	-	0	-1	+1	0	0	-
2007	Hou	24	122	50	0	1.000	4	1	0	1	.25	+1	+2	+1	+4	4	10
2008	Hou	54	117	22	1	.957	4	2	0	0	.50	-1	-1	-2	-3	-1	113
		90	273	88	1	.989	8	3	0	1	.38	0	0	0	+1	3	-

Jonathan Sanchez

Year	Tm	G	Inn	TC	E	Pct	SBA	CCS	PCS	PPO	CS%	Rght	Mid	Left	Tot	RS	Rnk
2006	SF	27	40	2	0	1.000	9	0	0	0	.00	+1				-1	-
2007	SF	33	52	6	0	1.000	5	3	1	0	.80	0	-2	0	-2	-1	-
2008	SF	29	158	17	0	1.000	22	2	1	0	.14	0	+1	-1	0	-2	133
		89	250	25	0	1.000	36	5	2	0	.19	+1	-1	-1	-2	-4	-

Ervin Santana

Year	Tm	G	Inn	TC	E	Pct	SBA	CCS	PCS	PPO	CS%	Rght	Mid	Left	Tot	RS	Rnk
2005	LAA	23	134	20	0	1.000	13	4	1	0	.38	0	-1	+1	0	0	81
2006	LAA	33	204	25	2	.926	14	8	1	0	.64	-1	-1	-1	-2	0	81
2007	LAA	28	150	19	0	1.000	14	3	0	0	.21	-2	+1	0	-1	-1	105
2008	LAA	32	219	32	0	1.000	20	4	0	0	.20	-1	-2	-3	-5	-5	170
		116	706	98	2	.980	61	19	2	0	.34	-4	-3	-3	-8	-6	141

Johan Santana

Year	Tm	G	Inn	TC	E	Pct	SBA	CCS	PCS	PPO	CS%	Rght	Mid	Left	Tot	RS	Rnk
2003	Min	44	155	12	3	.800	6	1	1	1	.33	0	-1	-1	-2	-1	113
2004	Min	34	228	33	4	.892	13	3	4	0	.54	+1	-1	0	+1	3	21
2005	Min	33	232	37	2	.949	9	5	0	0	.56	+3	0	+1	+4	4	11
2006	Min	34	234	43	1	.977	9	5	0	0	.56	+6	+1	+2	+9	8	3
2007	Min	33	219	40	0	1.000	11	2	3	1	.45	+3	+1	0	+5	6	1
2008	NYM	34	234	40	1	.976	11	3	2	0	.45	0	-1	-2	-3	0	81
		212	1302	216	11	.949	59	19	10	2	.49	+13	-1	0	+14	20	8

Joe Saunders

Year	Tm	G	Inn	TC	E	Pct	SBA	CCS	PCS	PPO	CS%	Rght	Mid	Left	Tot	RS	Rnk
2005	LAA	2	9	0	0	-										0	-
2006	LAA	13	71	11	0	1.000	4	2	1	0	.75	0	-1	-1	-2	-1	-
2007	LAA	18	107	17	0	1.000	11	2	2	0	.36	+1	-2	+1	-1	0	82
2008	LAA	31	198	41	0	1.000	25	4	3	0	.28	0	+3	0	+2	2	31
		64	385	69	0	1.000	40	8	6	0	.35	+1	0	0	-1	1	84

Scott Schoeneweis

Year	Tm	G	Inn	TC	E	Pct	SBA	CCS	PCS	PPO	CS%	Rght	Mid	Left	Tot	RS	Rnk
2003	2 tms	59	65	11	2	.846	3	0	1	0	.33	0	-2	-2	-3	-3	-
2004	CWS	20	113	28	0	1.000	20	4	6	0	.50	+1	-1	0	0	2	38
2005	Tor	80	57	22	1	.957	9	0	1	0	.11	0	+1	0	+2	1	-
2006	2 tms	71	52	13	0	1.000	6	1	0	0	.17	0	-2	0	-2	-2	-
2007	NYM	70	59	9	1	.900	7	0	1	0	.14	-1	-1	0	-2	-2	-
2008	NYM	73	57	13	0	1.000	4	0	2	0	.50	0	0	-1	-1	0	-
		373	401	100	4	.960	49	5	11	0	.33	0	-5	-3	-6	-4	126

Ben Sheets

Year	Tm	G	Inn	TC	E	Pct	SBA	CCS	PCS	PPO	CS%	Rght	Mid	Left	Tot	RS	Rnk
2003	Mil	34	221	41	2	.953	18	4	0	1	.22	0	-3	-2	-5	-4	167
2004	Mil	34	237	37	2	.949	20	5	0	1	.25	0	0	+2	+1	0	74
2005	Mil	22	157	13	3	.813	16	2	0	0	.13	-1	-3	-2	-5	-6	174
2006	Mil	17	106	13	0	1.000	12	2	0	2	.17	-1	0	-1	-2	-2	136
2007	Mil	24	141	19	0	1.000	21	0	0	1	.00	-2	0	+1	0	-3	153
2008	Mil	31	198	26	2	.929	20	7	0	2	.35	0	-2	+1	-1	0	81
		162	1060	158	9	.943	107	20	0	7	.19	-4	-8	-1	-12	-15	167

James Shields

Year	Tm	G	Inn	TC	E	Pct	SBA	CCS	PCS	PPO	CS%	Rght	Mid	Left	Tot	RS	Rnk
2006	TB	21	125	29	0	1.000	11	2	2	2	.36	0	-1	+1	0	1	56
2007	TB	31	215	54	1	.982	15	6	0	0	.40	+1	-1	+2	+2	3	18
2008	TB	33	215	38	1	.974	13	6	0	1	.46	-1	-2	+2	-1	1	55
		85	554	123	2	.984	39	14	2	3	.41	0	-4	+5	+1	5	52

Scot Shields

Year	Tm	G	Inn	TC	E	Pct	SBA	CCS	PCS	PPO	CS%	Rght	Mid	Left	Tot	RS	Rnk
2003	Ana	44	148	44	1	.978	17	6	2	1	.47	+1	+1	+1	+2	3	18
2004	Ana	60	105	19	1	.950	4	0	0	0	.00	-1	-3	0	-4	-4	164
2005	LAA	78	92	22	2	.917	8	2	0	0	.25	0	+1	+1	+1	1	63
2006	LAA	74	88	23	1	.958	10	0	0	0	.00	-1	+1	+1	+1	0	81
2007	LAA	71	77	14	2	.875	4	1	0	0	.25	0	+1	-1	0	-1	-
2008	LAA	64	63	9	0	1.000	9	1	0	0	.11	0	+2	-1	0	-1	-
		391	573	138	7	.949	54	10	2	2	.22	-1	+3	+1	-1	-1	100

Carlos Silva

Year	Tm	G	Inn	TC	E	Pct	SBA	CCS	PCS	PPO	CS%	Rght	Mid	Left	Tot	RS	Rnk
2003	Phi	62	87	21	1	.955	5	1	0	0	.20	-2	+1	0	-1	-1	113
2004	Min	33	203	36	2	.947	13	6	0	0	.46	-1	+1	-1	-2	-1	104
2005	Min	27	188	40	0	1.000	11	4	0	0	.36	-1	+2	-2	-1	-1	115
2006	Min	36	180	33	0	1.000	12	2	0	0	.17	-1	-2	+1	-2	-2	136
2007	Min	33	202	40	0	1.000	15	7	0	0	.47	-1	0	0	-1	0	82
2008	Sea	28	153	23	1	.958	10	2	0	0	.20	-1	0	0	-2	-2	133
		219	1014	197	4	.980	66	22	0	0	.33	-8	+1	-2	-9	-7	150

Kevin Slowey

Year	Tm	G	Inn	TC	E	Pct	SBA	CCS	PCS	PPO	CS%	Rght	Mid	Left	Tot	RS	Rnk
2007	Min	13	67	6	0	1.000	0	0	0	0	-	+1	0	-1	0	0	-
2008	Min	27	160	25	1	.962	8	4	0	1	.50	0	0	+1	+1	2	31
		40	227	32	1	.969	8	4	0	1	.50	+1	0	0	+1	2	-

Greg Smith

Year	Tm	G	Inn	TC	E	Pct	SBA	CCS	PCS	PPO	CS%	Rght	Mid	Left	Tot	RS	Rnk
2008	Oak	32	190	38	0	1.000	23	1	11	5	.52	0	-1	0	-2	4	10

John Smoltz

Year	Tm	G	Inn	TC	E	Pct	SBA	CCS	PCS	PPO	CS%	Rght	Mid	Left	Tot	RS	Rnk
2003	Atl	61	63	10	0	1.000	2	1	0	0	.50	+1	0	0	0	0	-
2004	Atl	73	82	18	0	1.000	3	1	0	0	.33	-1	+1	+1	+1	1	-
2005	Atl	33	230	53	0	1.000	16	6	0	0	.38	-1	-1	+5	+2	2	36
2006	Atl	35	232	53	2	.964	14	4	0	0	.29	0	-1	+2	+1	1	56
2007	Atl	32	206	48	3	.941	15	4	0	1	.27	+1	+2	-1	+2	2	36
2008	Atl	6	28	5	3	.625	1	0	0	0	.00	0	+1	0	0	0	-
		240	840	195	8	.959	51	16	0	1	.31	0	+2	+7	+6	6	44

Ian Snell

Year	Tm	G	Inn	TC	E	Pct	SBA	CCS	PCS	PPO	CS%	Rght	Mid	Left	Tot	RS	Rnk
2004	Pit	3	12	4	0	1.000	1	0	0	0	.00				+1	1	-
2005	Pit	15	42	4	0	1.000	2	1	0	0	.50	0	-1	0	-1	-1	-
2006	Pit	32	186	33	0	1.000	21	5	0	0	.24	0	-1	+4	+3	1	56
2007	Pit	32	208	26	0	1.000	20	6	0	0	.30	-1	-1	+1	-1	-1	105
2008	Pit	31	164	28	0	1.000	24	4	0	0	.17	-1	+2	-1	0	-2	133
		113	612	95	0	1.000	68	16	0	0	.24	-2	-1	+4	+2	-2	110

Pitchers

Andy Sonnanstine

		BASIC					HOLDING					+/-					
Year	Tm	G	Inn	TC	E	Pct	SBA	CCS	PCS	PPO	CS%	Rght	Mid	Left	Tot	RS	Rnk
2007	TB	22	131	29	2	.935	9	8	0	0	.89	-1	-1	0	-2	0	82
2008	TB	32	193	38	0	1.000	4	3	0	0	.75	-2	-2	+5	0	2	31
		54	324	69	2	.971	13	11	0	0	.85	-3	-3	+5	-2	2	-

Jorge Sosa

		BASIC					HOLDING					+/-					
Year	Tm	G	Inn	TC	E	Pct	SBA	CCS	PCS	PPO	CS%	Rght	Mid	Left	Tot	RS	Rnk
2003	TB	29	129	13	0	1.000	9	4	0	0	.44	-2	0	0	-1	0	85
2004	TB	43	99	9	0	1.000	5	0	0	0	.00	0	0	0	0	0	74
2005	Atl	44	134	11	3	.786	21	1	0	0	.05	-2	-1	-1	-4	-6	174
2006	2 tms	45	118	11	0	1.000	4	1	1	0	.50	-1	0	-3	-3	-1	108
2007	NYM	42	113	10	0	1.000	6	2	0	0	.33	0	-1	0	-2	-2	129
2008	NYM	20	22	3	0	1.000	1	1	0	0	1.00	0				-1	-
		223	614	60	3	.950	46	9	1	0	.22	-5	-2	-4	-11	-10	162

Jeremy Sowers

		BASIC					HOLDING					+/-					
Year	Tm	G	Inn	TC	E	Pct	SBA	CCS	PCS	PPO	CS%	Rght	Mid	Left	Tot	RS	Rnk
2006	Cle	14	88	11	1	.917	9	3	0	0	.33	0	0	-1	-1	-1	108
2007	Cle	13	67	12	0	1.000	12	2	0	0	.17	0	0	0	0	-1	-
2008	Cle	22	121	25	2	.926	15	5	1	0	.40	-1	+2	0	+2	2	31
		49	276	51	3	.941	36	10	1	0	.31	-1	+2	-1	+1	0	-

Justin Speier

		BASIC					HOLDING					+/-					
Year	Tm	G	Inn	TC	E	Pct	SBA	CCS	PCS	PPO	CS%	Rght	Mid	Left	Tot	RS	Rnk
2003	Col	72	73	9	0	1.000	8	3	0	0	.38	0	0	0	+1	1	-
2004	Tor	62	69	6	2	.750	9	4	0	0	.44	+1	0	+2	+2	2	-
2005	Tor	65	67	7	0	1.000	4	2	0	0	.50	0	0	0	0	0	-
2006	Tor	58	51	9	0	1.000	10	0	1	0	.10	-1	+1	0	0	-1	-
2007	LAA	51	50	7	1	.875	5	3	0	0	.60	0	-1	0	-1	-1	-
2008	LAA	62	68	11	0	1.000	8	1	0	0	.13	0	0	-1	-2	-3	-
		370	378	52	3	.942	44	13	1	0	.32	0	0	+1	0	-2	110

Jeff Suppan

		BASIC					HOLDING					+/-					
Year	Tm	G	Inn	TC	E	Pct	SBA	CCS	PCS	PPO	CS%	Rght	Mid	Left	Tot	RS	Rnk
2003	2 tms	32	204	48	1	.980	13	1	1	0	.31	+2	-3	+1	-1	-1	113
2004	StL	31	188	40	1	.976	14	3	0	1	.21	+2	-1	0	+1	1	53
2005	StL	32	194	40	1	.976	10	4	1	0	.50	-2	0	0	-1	0	81
2006	StL	32	190	33	0	1.000	15	3	0	1	.20	+1	+1	+4	+4	3	20
2007	Mil	34	207	49	1	.980	7	0	0	0	.00	+1	+1	0	+3	2	36
2008	Mil	31	178	40	1	.976	11	6	1	1	.64	0	+3	+1	+4	5	7
		192	1160	255	5	.980	70	19	3	3	.31	+5	+1	+3	+10	10	24

Julian Tavarez

		BASIC					HOLDING					+/-					
Year	Tm	G	Inn	TC	E	Pct	SBA	CCS	PCS	PPO	CS%	Rght	Mid	Left	Tot	RS	Rnk
2003	Pit	64	84	26	0	1.000	0	0	0	0	-	+2	-3	+1	-1	-1	85
2004	StL	77	64	16	0	1.000	6	2	0	0	.33	+1	0	+1	+1	1	-
2005	StL	74	66	10	0	1.000	3	1	0	0	.33	0	-2	0	-2	-2	-
2006	Bos	58	99	23	2	.920	2	0	0	0	.00	0	+1	-1	0	0	81
2007	Bos	34	135	20	1	.952	0	0	0	0	-	0	-1	-1	-2	-1	105
2008	3 tms	52	55	12	1	.923	5	0	0	0	.00	0	0	0	0	0	-
		359	502	111	4	.964	16	3	0	0	.19	+1	-2	-1	-3	-2	110

Brett Tomko

		BASIC					HOLDING					+/-					
Year	Tm	G	Inn	TC	E	Pct	SBA	CCS	PCS	PPO	CS%	Rght	Mid	Left	Tot	RS	Rnk
2003	StL	33	203	48	0	1.000	9	4	1	0	.56	0	-1	0	-2	0	85
2004	SF	32	194	38	2	.950	7	3	0	0	.43	0	+2	+1	+3	3	21
2005	SF	33	191	32	1	.970	8	3	0	0	.38	-1	-1	+2	0	1	63
2006	LAD	44	112	18	0	1.000	5	1	0	0	.20	+1	-1	0	0	0	81
2007	2 tms	40	131	22	2	.917	13	5	0	0	.38	+1	+1	-1	+4	4	10
2008	2 tms	22	70	15	0	1.000	3	0	0	0	.00	0	+2	+1	+4	3	-
		204	901	178	5	.972	45	16	1	0	.38	+1	+2	+3	+9	11	20

Steve Trachsel

		BASIC					HOLDING					+/-					
Year	Tm	G	Inn	TC	E	Pct	SBA	CCS	PCS	PPO	CS%	Rght	Mid	Left	Tot	RS	Rnk
2003	NYM	33	205	46	2	.958	25	6	2	3	.32	+1	+1	-1	+1	2	28
2004	NYM	33	203	50	0	1.000	26	7	0	1	.27	+1	+1	+7	+9	6	7
2005	NYM	6	37	10	1	.909	4	0	0	0	.00	-2	0	+2	0	-1	-
2006	NYM	30	165	35	1	.972	19	7	0	1	.37	+1	0	+3	+4	3	20
2007	2 tms	29	158	52	0	1.000	26	4	3	1	.27	0	+2	0	+3	2	36
2008	Bal	10	40	4	0	1.000	9	3	0	0	.33	0	-1	0	-1	-1	-
		141	806	201	4	.980	109	27	5	6	.29	+1	+3	+11	+16	11	20

Claudio Vargas

		BASIC					HOLDING					+/-					
Year	Tm	G	Inn	TC	E	Pct	SBA	CCS	PCS	PPO	CS%	Rght	Mid	Left	Tot	RS	Rnk
2003	Mon	23	114	18	1	.947	14	5	0	0	.36	0	-1	0	-1	-1	113
2004	Mon	45	118	21	0	1.000	7	5	0	1	.71	-2	0	0	-2	0	74
2005	2 tms	25	132	17	0	1.000	9	3	0	0	.33	-1	-2	+1	-2	-2	134
2006	Ari	31	168	31	2	.939	17	2	3	0	.29	0	-1	+4	+3	2	36
2007	Mil	29	134	21	2	.913	16	3	2	0	.31	-1	0	-2	-3	-2	129
2008	NYM	11	37	10	0	1.000	3	1	0	0	.33	0	+1	+1	+1	1	-
		164	703	123	5	.959	66	19	5	1	.36	-4	-3	+4	-4	-2	110

Javier Vazquez

		BASIC					HOLDING					+/-					
Year	Tm	G	Inn	TC	E	Pct	SBA	CCS	PCS	PPO	CS%	Rght	Mid	Left	Tot	RS	Rnk
2003	Mon	34	231	43	2	.956	5	1	1	0	.40	0	+1	0	0	1	58
2004	NYY	32	198	46	2	.958	7	4	1	2	.71	+1	+2	0	+3	5	8
2005	Ari	33	216	42	3	.933	8	1	1	0	.25	-1	-1	-1	-2	-2	134
2006	CWS	33	203	36	0	1.000	14	2	2	0	.29	-3	+2	0	0	1	56
2007	CWS	32	217	38	2	.950	10	4	0	0	.40	0	0	+2	+2	3	18
2008	CWS	33	208	46	0	1.000	12	2	1	0	.25	+1	+2	+1	+5	4	10
		197	1272	260	9	.965	56	14	6	2	.36	-2	+8	+2	+8	12	15

Justin Verlander

		BASIC					HOLDING					+/-					
Year	Tm	G	Inn	TC	E	Pct	SBA	CCS	PCS	PPO	CS%	Rght	Mid	Left	Tot	RS	Rnk
2005	Det	2	11	4	1	.800	1	0	0	0	.00					0	-
2006	Det	30	186	35	3	.921	6	4	1	7	.83	-1	0	+2	+1	6	5
2007	Det	32	202	24	0	1.000	5	1	0	2	.20	-3	-1	+1	-2	0	82
2008	Det	33	201	31	2	.939	17	8	1	1	.53	-1	0	+5	+4	5	7
		97	600	100	6	.940	29	13	2	10	.52	-5	-1	+8	+3	11	20

Carlos Villanueva

		BASIC					HOLDING					+/-					
Year	Tm	G	Inn	TC	E	Pct	SBA	CCS	PCS	PPO	CS%	Rght	Mid	Left	Tot	RS	Rnk
2006	Mil	10	54	11	0	1.000	2	0	0	0	.00	+2	+1	0	+3	2	-
2007	Mil	59	114	11	0	1.000	9	2	1	0	.33	0	0	-2	-2	-2	129
2008	Mil	47	108	21	1	.955	7	2	0	0	.29	+1	-1	+1	+1	1	55
		116	276	44	1	.977	18	4	1	0	.28	+3	0	-1	+2	1	-

Ron Villone

		BASIC					HOLDING					+/-					
Year	Tm	G	Inn	TC	E	Pct	SBA	CCS	PCS	PPO	CS%	Rght	Mid	Left	Tot	RS	Rnk
2003	Hou	19	107	30	0	1.000	5	4	0	3	.80	+1	-1	0	0	2	28
2004	Sea	56	117	23	4	.852	6	0	2	1	.33	0	0	-1	-1	0	74
2005	2 tms	79	64	18	1	.947	2	1	0	0	.50	0	+1	0	+1	2	-
2006	NYY	70	80	21	1	.955	4	1	2	1	.75	0	+2	0	+2	4	10
2007	NYY	37	42	5	0	1.000	0	0	0	0	-	+1	0	0	+1	1	-
2008	StL	74	50	12	1	.923	0	0	0	0	-	0	0	+1	+1	1	-
		335	460	116	7	.940	17	6	4	6	.59	+2	+2	0	+4	10	24

Luis Vizcaino

		BASIC					HOLDING					+/-					
Year	Tm	G	Inn	TC	E	Pct	SBA	CCS	PCS	PPO	CS%	Rght	Mid	Left	Tot	RS	Rnk
2003	Mil	75	62	11	0	1.000	4	1	0	0	.25	0	0	-1	-1	-1	-
2004	Mil	73	72	7	0	1.000	4	0	0	0	.00	-1	0	0	-1	-1	-
2005	CWS	65	70	13	0	1.000	5	2	0	0	.40	0	0	+1	+1	1	-
2006	Ari	70	65	11	0	1.000	4	2	0	0	.50	0	+1	-1	0	0	-
2007	NYY	77	75	14	0	1.000	7	2	0	0	.29	0	0	0	+1	1	-
2008	Col	43	46	7	0	1.000	2	0	0	0	.00	0	0	0	+1	1	-
		403	390	63	0	1.000	26	7	0	0	.27	-1	+1	-1	0	0	93

Pitchers

Edinson Volquez

Year	Tm	G	Inn	TC	E	Pct	SBA	CCS	PCS	PPO	CS%	Rght	Mid	Left	Tot	RS	Rnk
2005	Tex	6	13	1	0	1.000	1	0	0	0	.00	0	0	0	-1	-1	-
2006	Tex	8	33	6	0	1.000	5	1	0	0	.20	0	-1	+1	0	0	-
2007	Tex	6	34	2	0	1.000	2	0	0	0	.00	-1	0	-2	-2	-2	-
2008	Cin	33	196	34	1	.971	33	12	0	0	.36	+1	0	0	+1	0	81
		53	276	44	1	.977	41	13	0	0	.32	0	-1	-1	-2	-3	-

Doug Waechter

Year	Tm	G	Inn	TC	E	Pct	SBA	CCS	PCS	PPO	CS%	Rght	Mid	Left	Tot	RS	Rnk
2003	TB	6	35	3	0	1.000	2	0	0	0	.00	-1				-1	-
2004	TB	14	70	10	1	.909	8	3	1	0	.50	0	0	+1	+1	2	-
2005	TB	29	157	19	3	.864	9	4	0	0	.44	-1	-1	+1	-1	0	81
2006	TB	11	53	4	1	.800	1	0	0	0	.67	0	-1	+1	0	1	-
2008	Fla	48	63	3	1	.750	7	1	0	0	.14	0			0		-
		108	379	45	6	.867	29	10	1	0	.38	-2	-2	+3	-1	1	84

Billy Wagner

Year	Tm	G	Inn	TC	E	Pct	SBA	CCS	PCS	PPO	CS%	Rght	Mid	Left	Tot	RS	Rnk
2003	Hou	78	86	16	0	1.000	6	1	1	0	.33	+2	+1	+1	+4	3	14
2004	Phi	45	48	10	0	1.000	2	0	1	0	.50	+2	0	0	+1	1	-
2005	Phi	75	78	10	0	1.000	11	2	0	0	.18	+3	-1	0	+2	1	-
2006	NYM	70	72	12	0	1.000	9	3	1	0	.44	+1	0	0	+2	2	-
2007	NYM	66	68	8	1	.889	6	0	0	0	.00	0	-1	-2	-2	-3	-
2008	NYM	45	47	3	0	1.000	1	1	0	0	1.00	0	+1	0	0	0	-
		379	399	60	1	.983	35	7	3	0	.29	+8	+1	-1	+7	4	64

Adam Wainwright

Year	Tm	G	Inn	TC	E	Pct	SBA	CCS	PCS	PPO	CS%	Rght	Mid	Left	Tot	RS	Rnk
2005	StL	2	2	0	0	-									0	0	-
2006	StL	61	75	10	1	.909	3	0	0	0	.00	-1			0	0	-
2007	StL	32	202	41	2	.953	14	7	1	0	.57	-3	+1	+1	-1	1	57
2008	StL	20	132	27	1	.964	6	2	2	0	.67	0	0	+2	+2	4	10
		115	411	82	4	.951	23	9	3	0	.52	-4	+1	+3	+1	5	52

Tim Wakefield

Year	Tm	G	Inn	TC	E	Pct	SBA	CCS	PCS	PPO	CS%	Rght	Mid	Left	Tot	RS	Rnk
2003	Bos	35	202	36	1	.973	31	8	0	0	.26	+1	+1	-1	+2	0	85
2004	Bos	32	188	38	4	.905	41	7	1	2	.20	-2	+1	-1	-2	-5	170
2005	Bos	33	225	50	2	.962	25	6	1	0	.28	-3	+2	+2	+1	0	81
2006	Bos	23	140	25	0	1.000	28	4	0	2	.14	+1	0	0	+2	0	81
2007	Bos	31	189	36	0	1.000	49	8	0	0	.16	-1	+2	+1	+1	-5	168
2008	Bos	30	181	22	1	.957	37	10	0	1	.27	-1	+1	+2	+2	0	81
		184	1126	215	8	.963	211	43	2	5	.21	-5	+7	+3	+6	-10	162

Jarrod Washburn

Year	Tm	G	Inn	TC	E	Pct	SBA	CCS	PCS	PPO	CS%	Rght	Mid	Left	Tot	RS	Rnk
2003	Ana	32	207	23	1	.958	17	3	0	1	.71	0	+1	-1	0	1	58
2004	Ana	25	149	25	1	.962	7	2	2	1	.57	+2	+1	0	+4	5	8
2005	LAA	29	177	21	4	.840	6	5	1	0	1.00	0	-2	0	-2	0	81
2006	Sea	31	187	31	0	1.000	12	3	2	0	.50	0	+1	0	+1	3	20
2007	Sea	32	194	31	1	.969	11	1	4	0	.45	+1	+2	0	+4	5	4
2008	Sea	28	154	31	1	.969	9	2	2	0	.44	+1	0	0	0	1	55
		177	1068	170	8	.953	60	16	14	1	.50	+4	+3	-1	+7	15	12

David Weathers

Year	Tm	G	Inn	TC	E	Pct	SBA	CCS	PCS	PPO	CS%	Rght	Mid	Left	Tot	RS	Rnk
2003	NYM	77	88	16	4	.800	7	5	0	1	.71	-2	-1	-1	-4	-1	113
2004	3 tms	66	82	10	0	1.000	7	3	0	0	.43	-1	0	0	-1	-3	-
2005	Cin	73	78	6	0	1.000	7	3	0	0	.43	-1	0	0	-1	-1	-
2006	Cin	67	74	5	1	.833	4	1	0	0	.25	0	-1	-3	-2	-1	-
2007	Cin	70	78	11	0	1.000	6	1	0	0	.17	+1	0	0	+1	1	-
2008	Cin	72	69	7	2	.778	3	0	0	0	.00	-1	+1	+1	+1	-1	-
		425	468	62	7	.887	34	13	0	1	.38	-4	-1	-1	-10	-5	132

Jered Weaver

Year	Tm	G	Inn	TC	E	Pct	SBA	CCS	PCS	PPO	CS%	Rght	Mid	Left	Tot	RS	Rnk
2006	LAA	19	123	15	2	.882	14	3	0	0	.21	0	0	-1	0	-1	108
2007	LAA	28	161	27	2	.931	21	2	0	1	.10	0	-1	-1	-3	-4	164
2008	LAA	30	177	21	2	.913	25	5	0	2	.20	0	-1	-2	-2	-3	150
		77	460	69	6	.913	60	10	0	3	.17	0	-2	-4	-5	-8	154

Brandon Webb

Year	Tm	G	Inn	TC	E	Pct	SBA	CCS	PCS	PPO	CS%	Rght	Mid	Left	Tot	RS	Rnk
2003	Ari	29	181	47	3	.940	14	3	0	0	.21	+1	0	-1	0	-1	113
2004	Ari	35	208	54	5	.915	41	7	3	0	.24	-1	+1	+1	+1	-1	104
2005	Ari	33	229	62	2	.969	30	3	1	1	.13	+4	0	0	+4	1	63
2006	Ari	33	235	63	3	.955	33	7	2	0	.27	+4	+4	-1	+7	4	10
2007	Ari	34	236	70	5	.933	35	7	2	0	.26	0	+2	+2	+3	0	82
2008	Ari	34	227	72	2	.973	34	9	1	0	.29	+5	+2	-2	+5	3	23
		198	1315	388	20	.948	187	36	9	1	.24	+13	+9	-1	+20	6	44

Todd Wellemeyer

Year	Tm	G	Inn	TC	E	Pct	SBA	CCS	PCS	PPO	CS%	Rght	Mid	Left	Tot	RS	Rnk
2003	ChC	15	28	3	0	1.000	1	1	0	0	1.00	0				0	-
2004	ChC	20	24	2	0	1.000	2	0	0	0	.00	0	0	-1	-2	-2	-
2005	ChC	22	32	3	0	1.000	1	0	0	0	.00	0	0	0	0	0	-
2006	2 tms	46	78	14	0	1.000	7	0	1	0	.14	0	+1	+1	+2	2	-
2007	2 tms	32	79	8	0	1.000	5	1	0	0	.20	0	0	0	+1	1	-
2008	StL	32	192	34	2	.944	13	5	1	1	.46	-3	0	0	-3	0	81
		167	433	66	2	.970	29	7	2	1	.31	-3	+1	0	-2	1	84

Kip Wells

Year	Tm	G	Inn	TC	E	Pct	SBA	CCS	PCS	PPO	CS%	Rght	Mid	Left	Tot	RS	Rnk
2003	Pit	31	197	38	5	.884	16	1	1	2	.13	-2	+1	0	-2	-2	144
2004	Pit	24	138	25	3	.893	14	6	0	0	.43	+2	-4	+3	+1	1	53
2005	Pit	33	182	39	2	.951	18	3	0	0	.17	+3	+1	-1	+2	1	63
2006	2 tms	9	44	4	0	1.000	6	4	0	0	.67	0	0	0	-1	-1	-
2007	StL	34	163	31	4	.886	22	4	1	1	.23	0	0	+1	+2	1	57
2008	2 tms	25	38	8	1	.889	3	1	0	0	.67	+1	0	0	+1	2	-
		156	762	160	15	.906	79	19	3	3	.28	+4	-2	+3	+3	2	79

Jake Westbrook

Year	Tm	G	Inn	TC	E	Pct	SBA	CCS	PCS	PPO	CS%	Rght	Mid	Left	Tot	RS	Rnk
2003	Cle	34	133	29	1	.967	15	4	0	1	.27	+2	+1	0	+3	2	28
2004	Cle	33	216	73	3	.961	14	6	0	3	.43	+5	+4	+2	+11	9	4
2005	Cle	34	211	82	2	.976	17	2	2	0	.24	+1	+2	+3	+5	4	11
2006	Cle	32	211	73	1	.986	19	1	2	1	.16	-1	+2	+2	+3	2	36
2007	Cle	25	152	48	0	1.000	21	7	0	2	.33	+2	+2	-2	+2	2	36
2008	Cle	5	35	11	1	.917	2	1	1	0	1.00	+1	0	+2	+3	3	-
		163	957	322	8	.975	88	21	5	5	.30	+10	+11	+7	+27	22	5

Dan Wheeler

Year	Tm	G	Inn	TC	E	Pct	SBA	CCS	PCS	PPO	CS%	Rght	Mid	Left	Tot	RS	Rnk
2003	NYM	35	51	5	0	1.000	7	2	2	0	.57	-1	-1	0	-2	-1	-
2004	2 tms	46	65	10	2	.833	3	0	0	0	.00	0	-1	-1	-2	-2	-
2005	Hou	71	71	14	0	1.000	6	0	0	0	.00	0	+1	0	+1	0	-
2006	Hou	75	71	9	0	1.000	4	1	0	0	.25	0	0	+1	+1	1	-
2007	2 tms	70	75	15	0	1.000	4	0	0	0	.00	0	-1	-1	-3	-3	-
2008	TB	70	66	6	1	.857	2	1	0	0	.50			-1		-1	-
		367	401	62	3	.952	26	4	2	0	.23	-1	-2	-1	-6	-6	141

Dontrelle Willis

Year	Tm	G	Inn	TC	E	Pct	SBA	CCS	PCS	PPO	CS%	Rght	Mid	Left	Tot	RS	Rnk
2003	Fla	27	161	19	4	.826	6	3	0	3	.50	0	+1	-1	0	2	28
2004	Fla	32	197	49	2	.961	19	4	3	2	.37	0	+2	0	+2	4	14
2005	Fla	34	236	45	3	.938	6	4	1	0	.83	+5	+1	+2	+7	7	2
2006	Fla	34	223	55	5	.917	11	4	1	1	.45	+6	-1	-1	+4	5	8
2007	Fla	35	205	43	5	.896	7	1	0	1	.14	+5	+1	-3	+3	3	18
2008	Det	8	24	2	0	1.000	0	0	0	0		+1	-1	0	0	0	-
		170	1046	232	19	.918	49	16	5	7	.43	+17	+3	-3	+16	21	7

Randy Wolf

Year	Tm	G	Inn	TC	E	Pct	SBA	CCS	PCS	PPO	CS%	Rght	Mid	Left	Tot	RS	Rnk
2003	Phi	33	201	37	3	.925	10	2	0	0	.20	-2	0	+2	+1	1	58
2004	Phi	23	136	22	2	.917	6	0	0	0	.00	+1	-1	0	+1	0	74
2005	Phi	13	80	11	0	1.000	2	0	1	0	.50	0	0	0	0	1	-
2006	Phi	12	57	12	0	1.000	5	2	0	0	.40	+1	0	+1	+2	2	-
2007	LAD	18	103	17	0	1.000	7	3	0	0	.43	0	0	+1	+1	2	36
2008	2 tms	33	190	33	2	.943	13	4	1	1	.38	-1	-1	+1	-2	-1	113
		132	767	139	7	.950	43	11	2	1	.30	-1	-2	+5	+3	5	52

Pitchers

Kerry Wood

Year	Tm	BASIC					HOLDING					+/-				RS	Rnk
		G	Inn	TC	E	Pct	SBA	CCS	PCS	PPO	CS%	Rght	Mid	Left	Tot	RS	Rnk
2003	ChC	32	211	36	1	.973	13	8	0	3	.62	-1	-1	+1	0	3	14
2004	ChC	22	140	17	1	.944	17	1	2	1	.18	-2	-1	0	-3	-2	132
2005	ChC	21	66	6	2	.750	7	3	1	0	.57	-2			-1	0	-
2006	ChC	4	20	2	1	.667	3	1	0	0	.33	0		+1	+1	1	-
2007	ChC	22	24	0	0	-	1	1	0	0	1.00	0			0	0	-
2008	ChC	65	66	7	0	1.000	1	0	0	0	.00	0	-1	0	-1	-1	-
		166	527	73	5	.932	42	14	3	4	.40	-5	-3	+1	-4	1	84

Chris Young

Year	Tm	BASIC					HOLDING					+/-				RS	Rnk
		G	Inn	TC	E	Pct	SBA	CCS	PCS	PPO	CS%	Rght	Mid	Left	Tot	RS	Rnk
2004	Tex	7	36	5	1	.833	5	0	1	0	.20	-1	0	0	0	0	-
2005	Tex	31	165	20	0	1.000	19	6	0	0	.32	0	+1	+2	+2	2	36
2006	SD	31	179	20	0	1.000	45	4	0	1	.09	0	-2	+1	-2	-8	175
2007	SD	30	173	20	1	.952	44	0	0	2	.00	0	0	-1	-1	-8	174
2008	SD	18	102	15	1	.938	17	2	0	1	.12	-1	0	+1	0	-2	133
		117	655	83	3	.964	130	12	1	4	.10	-2	-1	+2	-1	-16	171

Carlos Zambrano

Year	Tm	BASIC					HOLDING					+/-				RS	Rnk
		G	Inn	TC	E	Pct	SBA	CCS	PCS	PPO	CS%	Rght	Mid	Left	Tot	RS	Rnk
2003	ChC	32	214	64	4	.941	8	5	0	1	.63	-3	0	+2	0	2	28
2004	ChC	31	210	47	2	.959	11	3	1	0	.36	-1	-2	+3	0	1	53
2005	ChC	33	223	55	2	.965	10	9	0	3	.90	+2	-2	+1	+1	5	7
2006	ChC	33	214	45	4	.918	5	3	0	1	.60	-1	0	-1	-2	0	81
2007	ChC	34	216	48	1	.980	7	3	0	1	.43	0	-3	+2	-1	1	57
2008	ChC	30	189	42	3	.933	19	9	0	3	.47	-2	0	+1	-1	1	55
		193	1266	317	16	.950	60	32	1	9	.55	-5	-7	+8	-3	10	24

Barry Zito

Year	Tm	BASIC					HOLDING					+/-				RS	Rnk
		G	Inn	TC	E	Pct	SBA	CCS	PCS	PPO	CS%	Rght	Mid	Left	Tot	RS	Rnk
2003	Oak	35	233	41	1	.976	20	4	3	0	.35	-1	0	0	-1	0	85
2004	Oak	34	213	35	2	.946	23	3	5	0	.35	0	-1	-1	-2	-1	104
2005	Oak	35	228	46	0	1.000	26	2	2	0	.15	+5	-1	+2	+7	3	24
2006	Oak	34	221	25	1	.962	20	10	2	0	.60	+1	-1	-3	-4	0	81
2007	SF	34	197	24	0	1.000	6	0	1	0	.17	+1	0	-1	+1	2	36
2008	SF	32	180	27	1	.964	10	3	1	1	.40	0	+1	-2	-1	1	55
		204	1271	203	5	.975	105	22	14	1	.34	+6	-2	-5	0	5	52

Uribe vs. Tulowitzki

Juan Uribe and Troy Tulowitzki aren't that different, really. The former signed as a 17-year-old in the Dominican Republic and broke into the majors four years later as Colorado's shortstop. Over eight seasons and two teams, he's posted a sub-.300 on-base percentage but popped over 20 home runs three times. The latter was drafted seventh overall out of Long Beach State in 2005, breezed through one season of minor league seasoning, then broke through with a .291 batting average, .359 on-base percentage, 24 home run season as Colorado's shortstop and finished runner-up to Ryan Braun in the Rookie of the Year voting.

Ok, so maybe they're a little different offensively. But this is *The Fielding Bible*—we focus on defense. Both started their careers as shortstops in Colorado and earned reputations as good, if not excellent, defensive shortstops with strong arms. Additionally, both posted strong plus/minus numbers for pennant winning teams just two seasons apart. Uribe's defensive reputation was cemented by the last two plays of the 2005 World Series, diving into the stands for the second out and throwing on the run from behind the mound on the subsequent play to clinch the series. Here are the plus/minus numbers for both shortstops:

SS Plus/Minus Totals

	Uribe	Tulowitzki
2003	+7	-
2004	+9	-
2005	+9	-
2006	+3	-5
2007	-7	+35
2008	0	+4
Total	+21	+34

SS Plus/Minus on Grounders

	Uribe	Tulowitzki
2003	+8	-
2004	+10	-
2005	+3	-
2006	0	-6
2007	-12	+35
2008	0	+1
Total	+9	+30

While both saw limited action at short last season (Uribe spent time at second and third base while Tulo was injured), the 2007 season stands out for both players. The White Sox shortstop experienced a significant drop off, particularly on groundballs, and the Rockies infielder posted easily the best defensive season of any shortstop that year and won a Fielding Bible Award as a result.

We'll take a look at the two shortstops to see if we can isolate what Uribe might have been doing wrong and Tulowitzki doing right in 2007, and maybe we'll learn something in the process.

If you check out the Six-Year Register section, you'll see that Tulowitzki was +24 plays on balls hit to his right, while Uribe was -2 plays in 2007. Both players were better going to their right than on balls hit straight on or balls hit up the middle, but the difference of 26 plays seems like a good place to start looking for differences. Was Tulowitzki a spectacular defender ranging deep into the hole and showing off his rocket arm? Has Uribe lost a couple steps of quickness to his right? Maybe Uribe plays up the middle more?

In an attempt to answer these questions, we chose a sample set of plays, watching all plays hit to Vector 203 when Uribe or Tulowitzki was on the field. Vector 203 is slightly to the shortstop side of the "5-6 hole", the place just between the typical third baseman and shortstop position. On a slow grounder to Vector 203, the shortstop will typically charge in and to his right and make the throw to first on the run. As it turns out, on these slow rollers the shortstop fielded the ball and got the out 58% of the time in 2007. The shortstop can't charge a medium groundball to Vector 203—he has to range a few steps to his right, field the ball, then get rid of it in time for the out, which shortstops did 81% of the time that year. Hard grounders to Vector 203 are the ones where a shortstop has to range close to the outfield grass, which the shortstop converted 43% of the time.

Uribe had 20 grounders to Vector 203 and got the out on 12 of them, yielding a -1 plus/minus score in the process. Tulowitzki, on the other hand, converted 20 of 23, good for a +3 plus/minus.

In reviewing the video of each play we found that both shortstops exhibited solid fundamentals, squared the ball up and set their feet, and showed off strong arms. In fact, the one time the Rockies shortstop leapt into the air Jeter-style to make the throw to first, the throw was off line and the runner beat it out. Uribe forgot his fundamentals once and side-armed a throw to first on the run, and he fielded more than one ball off to the side that he could have squared up (he still got the outs, which is the bottom line). Tulo and Uribe each had one play where they brought their glove up too early and the grounder went directly underneath. All in all, not much of a discrepancy in mechanics.

So what's the big difference? With these 43 plays we have a limited sample size to work with, and as a result, we have a limited number of differences we could find. But we did find some:

- Tulowitzki made 20 of the 23 plays. Of the three he missed, two of them could have been made but not without extraordinary effort. The third was not playable.

- Uribe only made 12 of 20 plays.

- One ball went through his legs (and not ruled an error).

- One of them he underestimated the speed of the runner (Jayson Werth), took a little stutter step before the throw and just missed him at first.

- On another play, Coco Crisp was batting right-handed against the lefty Boone Logan. Uribe was playing deep towards second (clearly out of position) and couldn't get to the slow chopper quick enough to make the play.

- On four different plays against left-handed hitters, Uribe was positioned too close to second base to

make the play. Tulo successfully fielded all four of his plays against lefty swingers, while Uribe only made one out of five.

- Like Tulo, Uribe had one play that was completely unplayable (aside from the four plays against lefties).

In summary, Uribe had three plays on which he clearly made mistakes. One was through his legs, one he underestimated the baserunner, and on the third he was out of position. Three is not a lot but in a small sample, relative to 43 total plays, it may be.

The other thing that came through in the small sample was positioning against lefty hitters. Tulowitzki was four-for-four on groundballs hit by lefties, but Uribe only converted one out of five. To be fair, three of those four hits were well out of Uribe's reach because he was shading up the middle with the lefty at the plate. But was he shading too much?

If we had just seen these 43 plays, you might think we're picking on Uribe unfairly because he shifts up the middle on lefties. I'm sure he compensates and fields a few extra balls up the middle against lefties, right?

Let's dig a little deeper and break down all groundballs (all vectors) as we did in the Chase Utley article, looking at each player's plus/minus score to his left, straight on, and to his right—split up against right-handed and left-handed hitters:

Tulowitzki 2007

	Left	Straight On	Right	Total
LHB	+11	-1	0	+9
RHB	-4	+6	+24	+26
Total	+6	+5	+24	+35

Uribe 2007

	Left	Straight On	Right	Total
LHB	+3	-3	-12	-12
RHB	-8	-2	+10	0
Total	-5	-5	-2	-12

Both players follow the traditional pattern of faring better to the hitter's pull side. You can see that Tulowitzki gets a huge boost on balls to his right against right-handed batters (RHB) and a less significant boost to his left versus lefties. Uribe is also stronger to the hitter's pull side. But in Uribe's case his -12 against lefties to his right is not made up for by his +3 to his left. Against lefties Uribe does not reach enough balls to his left to compensate for the balls he misses to his right. It appears that he may be positioning too far left against lefties and flat out doesn't have the range of Tulowitzki, despite his reputation.

Moreover, we see that Tulowitzki was stronger than Uribe in every category—to his right, left, straight on, against lefties and righties.

When we watched the video, we caught some subtle positioning differences, those three plays that Uribe missed, and the plays against lefties which may or may not suggest a pattern. But it just doesn't seem like this should add up to the 47 plus/minus discrepancy by Uribe over the course of the 2007 season. But maybe it does.

Soriano: More Like Manny or More Like Carl?

Alfonso Soriano is a baseball enigma. He does so many things on the baseball field so well, yet he does so many things so poorly. He has tremendous athleticism, yet he was a horrible second baseman. He's built like a string bean, yet he has prodigious home run power. He's a great hitter, yet he has no patience at the plate.

Now it's his outfield defense. Since moving to left field in 2006 he's posted some pretty decent numbers, based on both his plus/minus scores and on his throwing results. However, there are times he looks clueless in the field. We decided to try to see if we could crack the code by comparing him to the best left fielder in baseball, Carl Crawford, and the worst left fielder in baseball, Manny Ramirez.

You can say this much about Manny's defense: he's a great hitter. Ramirez isn't known for his defense, but he does get attention for his behavior on the field. In some ways he's covered more ground than a typical left fielder, what with going to the top of the wall to high-five a fan after making a play, or paying a visit *inside* the Green Monster on another occasion. Carl Crawford is a two-time winner of the Fielding Bible Award and should have a few Gold Gloves (if the voters could understand that non-center fielders can win that award). With his great speed, he covers a lot of ground and can track down any ball hit anywhere near him. Soriano has the best and worst qualities of both men, it seems. He has the same great speed that Crawford has. Everything else seems to be more like Manny.

Video Review

We undertook this project last July. At that time the numbers suggested that Soriano was doing pretty well for himself, while Carl and Manny were up to their usual performances:

**Plus/Minus Scores
as of mid-July, 2008**

Carl Crawford	+15
Manny Ramirez	-14
Alfonso Soriano	+5

Those of us watching Alfonso here in Chicago were surprised by this. There were some really bonehead plays that he had pulled thus far in the season, and it was hard to believe that he came out this well in plus/minus. In order to get a better idea of what was going on we decided to do a video review of Alfonso Soriano plays. We would also review Carl Crawford and Manny Ramirez plays for comparison. We limited our play reviews to those plays that had the most effect on the plus/minus scores of each player. Specifically, we chose plays that had an enhanced plus/minus of +.5 or greater (Plus Plays), and plays that had a plus/minus of -.5 or less (Minus Plays). The Plus Plays would be those situations where they made a play on a relatively difficult ball. The Minus Plays are misses on relatively easy plays. This would give us, in general, the best and worst plays of each player.

We then had one of our scouts grade the plays. The scale will remind you of your school days. An "A" is an absolutely great play, a "C" is an average play, and an "F" is a disaster. Plus Plays could be graded no lower than a C, and Minus Plays no higher than a C. Here are the grade results of the plays.

Number of plays scored "B" or better

Carl	18 of 63 plays (29%)
Manny	7 of 40 (18%)
Alfonso	5 of 37 (14%)

In making above-average plays, Alfonso was more like Manny. Actually, not even as "good" as Manny.

How about the other end of the spectrum?

Number of plays scored "D" or worse

Carl	6 of 63 plays (10%)
Manny	5 of 40 (13%)
Alfonso	7 of 37 (19%)

Once again, Soriano was worse than even Manny Ramirez. Soriano had more than his share of balls where he simply looked bad.

However, when we summarize the plays in another way, a more bottom-line oriented way, our results point more to Soriano's similarity to Crawford. We chose plays based on specific and objective criteria: plays above or at +.5 plus/minus and plays below or at - .5 plus/minus. How many of those plays were Plus Plays for each player?

Number of Plus Plays

Carl	46 of 63 plays (73%)
Manny	14 of 40 (35%)
Alfonso	22 of 37 (59%)

Alfonso is between the two players, but closer to Carl.

What it comes down to, it seems, is that Soriano makes more than his share of plays, but when he misses them, he misses badly.

Let's go one step further.

Taking Risks

There is a big difference between risk-taking and acting recklessly, and that was evident from looking at the video. Carl Crawford was a calculated risk-taker in that he would sprint towards a ball that no ordinary fielder would ever have a shot at catching. He'd dive and, more often than not, come up with a great catch. In fact, Crawford would rarely lay out and let a ball get by him. Plus/minus scores for the full year 2008 confirm how good Crawford is. He was at his best getting to the ball in front of him (+10). But he was no slouch getting to balls hit relatively in his direction (+7 on medium hit balls) or over his head (+6 on deep balls). One of his strengths (which we don't measure right now) is that he's excellent at going left or right and was seen going a long way to make a diving play in foul territory on numerous occasions.

If Crawford is a calculated risk-taker, Manny Ramirez seems to fall on the other end of the spectrum. Everyone's favorite lackadaisical left fielder doesn't chase balls hit past him in the gap or down the line with nearly the tenacity that Crawford does. In fact, if a ball is hit to left-center field, Ramirez is perfectly content watching the center fielder chase the ball down and throw it in. He slows up dramatically on these plays, often resulting in a runner taking an extra base. Although, aside from the infamous play where the ball fell in front of Manny and he rolled on top of it like a playful puppy-dog, he is very good at getting to balls in front of him. His +34 over the past six years on balls hit shallow trails the speedy Crawford by only one. On balls hit medium or deep, however, Ramirez is woeful. He is -54 on medium balls over the past six years and an alarming -141 on deep balls. It would be easy to blame the Green Monster for Ramirez's -141 on deep balls, but even with the Manny Adjustment that accounts for the Fenway wall in the Plus/Minus System, his plus/minus numbers are still significantly negative on medium and deep balls. On balls hit off the wall, the video shows that Manny is actually quite good—if he is positioned properly. While balls hit higher off the wall may give him more trouble, Ramirez plays balls hit lower on the wall well, often bare-handing the ball and getting it in quickly.

Somewhere between Crawford's calculated risk-taking and Ramirez's lack of hustle is Alfonso Soriano. After watching video of Soriano, it was clear that the former infielder rarely takes a risk, unless you count staring into the sun or the lights for a flyball as risky. But saying Soriano rarely takes a risk doesn't mean he's a bad outfielder. From the limited sample of the video, lack of risk meant that most of the time he was well positioned. Of the 37 plays reviewed of Soriano, only about 8 required him to sprint to make the play. Crawford, on the other hand, was constantly sprinting to cover ground.

Soriano remains an enigma as an outfielder. He makes more than his share of the plays, yet at other times he can look so bad you wonder why the Cubs ever put him on the field.

Separating the Man from the Boys

When you consider his throwing however, Soriano's identity as a fielder changes drastically. In the past three seasons, Soriano has saved 33 runs with his arm, 26 more than Ramirez and 30 more than Crawford. Combine those 33 throwing runs saved with his 9 plus/minus runs saved and Soriano has saved 42 total runs over the past three seasons. Ramirez has cost his teams 28 runs over the past three seasons thanks to -35 plus/minus runs. While Ramirez has a good arm for a left fielder, it's no match for Soriano's, and his range pales by comparison. As for Carl Crawford, the reigning Fielding Bible Award winner has saved 22 total runs over the past three seasons. Surprisingly, that's 20 less than Soriano. When making this comparison, Soriano suddenly sheds his reputation as a poor fielder. The results speak. No left fielder has saved as many runs for his team as Soriano.

Does that mean Alfonso Soriano is a better fielder than Carl Crawford? Not at all. Yes, Soriano has saved more runs in the last three years, but it was the surprise element that caused a lot of it. They thought they could run on the converted middle infielder. Soriano snuck up on prospective challengers on the basepaths, but now his arm is getting more respect and they're running less often. In 2008, Soriano's kills were cut more than half from his 2007 total of 19 to 8, and his throwing runs saved dropped from a superhuman 17 in 2007 to a more pedestrian 6 in 2008 (that still tied for the left field throwing lead).

We add throwing runs saved to plus/minus runs saved to get total runs saved. In 2008 total runs saved better reflected the abilities of Carl Crawford, Alfonso Soriano and Manny Ramirez. Crawford had the most left field runs saved in baseball at 13 (tied with Willie Harris). Soriano was above average with a total of five runs saved. Manny had one of his better years but still finished with -3 runs saved.

Defensive Scouting Reports

This section contains defensive scouting reports on over 250 position players who played baseball last year. The Video Scouts at Baseball Info Solutions viewed, reviewed, analyzed, and tabulated every facet of every pitch of every play that occurred in Major League Baseball last year. When it comes to understanding the defensive strengths and weaknesses of each player, there could be no more thorough source. I asked Steve Moyer, president of Baseball Info Solutions, if the Video Scouts might be available to put together these defensive scouting reports. He was happy to oblige.

Gold Gloves That Should Have Been

The first part of the section for each position is a continuation from the first volume of *The Fielding Bible,* where I shared my choices, based on the work from the book, as to who should have been the Gold Glove winners at each position. Players have up and down years from a defensive standpoint, just as they do hitting and pitching. Other than players getting injured, Gold Glove voters don't recognize this very well. It's a little like All-Star voting. In All-Star voting the players who are more well-known often wind up winning the vote ahead of the guy having the great year. Gold Glove voters go a bit overboard sticking with the better known players. As a player, it's difficult to get that first Gold Glove, but once a player gets it, he's part of the club. As a result, some players get more awards than they should, hanging on when the voters should have passed them by. Some examples of this in recent years are Torii Hunter, Omar Vizquel, Derek Jeter, Greg Maddux, and Bret Boone. The other side of the same coin is that players don't get recognized until a year or two after they should have won the award, such as Yadier Molina, Albert Pujols, and Orlando Hudson. Or worst of all, some deserving players can't break into the club at all (Adam Everett, Carl Crawford, and Alex Rios).

Having said that, I am in general agreement with a good number of the awards given out each year. In the first volume, I agreed with 26 out of 42 awards I reviewed, well over half. In the last three years, as we've learned still more about defense, the percentage is not quite as high. I've only agreed with 22 of the last 55 awards given out. Here's the year-by-year chart.

Year	Gold Glove Winners Reviewed	Agree	Disagree
2003	14	9	5
2004	14	11	3
2005	14	6	8
2006	18	9	9
2007	19	6	13
2008	18	7	11

In the outfield, Gold Glove voters generally vote for the three best outfielders, regardless of position. As it turns out, they almost always come up with three center fielders in the National League. In the last six years the only exceptions were Jeff Francoeur in 2007 and Jose Cruz in 2003. When I came up with my "Gold Gloves That Should Have Been," I followed the same format. For example, in the National League in 2008, Gold Gloves went to Carlos Beltran, Shane Victorino and Nate McLouth. I agreed with the first two choices, but chose a third winner based on my personal assessment of who was the next best outfielder. It happened to be a left fielder, Willie Harris.

My Personal Ratings

After the Gold Gloves That Should Have Been, I show my personal ratings, listing in order the top ten and the bottom five defensive players at each position. Only players who played in 2008 are considered. The players that I list as the best defensive players in baseball match the 2008 Fielding Bible Awards with one exception: I chose Chase Utley over Brandon Phillips at second base. My ratings are developed while analyzing the defensive numbers presented in this book, but I am a strong believer that visual observation is essential. That's what the Video Scouts brought to the table. Their reports were vital to my considerations, as well as my own observations.

Player Data Blocks

Each report has a "data block" along with it. Each data block has the player's defensive runs saved for 2008 and his defensive runs saved for the three-year period from 2006 to 2008. The reports as a whole are sorted by three-year runs saved within each position, from the player who had the most runs saved to the least. If there is any one number that gives you the best idea of who the best defensive players in baseball are, regardless of anything else, it's the three-year total of runs saved for each player. That's why we chose it for sorting the players.

The second part of the data block is for good plays and misplays (and errors). Good plays and misplays are discussed in Bill James' article called "Defensive Misplays" on page 27. For each player we show you how many good plays he had for the 2008 season. Based on the number of touches each player had, and the league average of good plays per touch, we tell you how many good plays the average player at his position would have had with the same number of touches. For the other side of the ledger, we add misplays and errors together. Similarly, the number of misplays and errors that an average fielder at that position with the same number of touches would make is shown on this side.

The final item in the data block is Good Play/ Misplay Percentage. This is a percentage that can be viewed like a winning percentage. If it's around .500 the combination of the player's good plays, misplays, and errors is about average compared to others at his position. If it's over .500, it's good. If it's under .500, not so good. This percentage is helpful when, for example, a player has fewer good plays than average, but also fewer misplays and errors than average.

Take Khalil Greene, for instance. He has 32 good plays, a little less than the 34 expected by an average shortstop with the same number of touches. He also had fewer misplays and errors than average (24, compared to the average of 29). This translates to a .531 percentage, a slightly above-average good play/misplay percentage.

When analyzing the data to do my own personal evaluations, I factored in the misplays/good plays information hand-in-hand with defensive runs saved. The number of good plays relative to average, the number of misplays and errors relative to average, and the good play/misplay percentage were all key considerations.

Scouting Reports

As mentioned above, the Video Scouts at Baseball Info Solutions prepared the Defensive Scouting Reports in the final section of each position. Players were assigned to each scout early in the season. Then each scout made a point of reviewing plays for their assigned players as the season transpired. Any player with 500 or more defensive innings (plus a few others) has a report. For other players with more than 250 defensive innings at a position, the player data block is shown without a report.

The Video Scouts who scouted the players and wrote the reports are: Jake Argue, Dan Casey, Austin Diamond, Jeremy Gordon, Matthew Kelliher-Gibson, Mike Piekarski, Brian Powalish, Mike Wolverton, and J.D. Wyborny.

Once the reports were prepared, they went through three layers of review. Baseball analyst and blogger Eric Ferguson did the first review, providing his own insight into the process. Steve Moyer did the next review. The final review was done by me.

First Basemen Evaluations

Year	League	Gold Glove Winners	Should Have Been
2003	AL	John Olerud	John Olerud
	NL	Derrek Lee	J.T. Snow
2004	AL	Darin Erstad	Darin Erstad
	NL	Todd Helton	Todd Helton
2005	AL	Mark Teixeira	Mark Teixeira
	NL	Derrek Lee	Albert Pujols
2006	AL	Mark Teixeira	Doug Mientkiewicz
	NL	Albert Pujols	Albert Pujols
2007	AL	Kevin Youkilis	Casey Kotchman
	NL	Derrek Lee	Albert Pujols
2008	AL	Carlos Pena	Carlos Pena
	NL	Adrian Gonzalez	Albert Pujols

My Personal Ratings

Top Ten

1 Albert Pujols, StL
2 Mark Teixeira, NYY
3 Casey Kotchman, Atl
4 Doug Mientkiewicz, FA
5 Kevin Youkilis, Bos
6 Lance Berkman, Hou
7 Carlos Pena, TB
8 Todd Helton, Col
9 Derrek Lee, ChC
10 Adrian Gonzalez, SD

Bottom Five

26 Richie Sexson, FA
27 Jason Giambi, Oak
28 Dmitri Young, Was
29 Prince Fielder, Mil
30 Mike Jacobs, KC

Player teams based on transactions through February 11, 2009

First Basemen

Albert Pujols

	Innings	Runs Saved
2008	1215	15
2006-2008	3784	61

	Good Plays	Misplays and Errors
Pujols 2008	62	22
Avg First Baseman	62	33
Good Play/Misplay Pct		.598

The only three-time winner of the Fielding Bible Award, Albert Pujols continues to make it look easy, whether at the plate or in the field. His superlative hand-eye coordination allows him to snag even the most difficult throws, which gives his infielders the confidence to attempt plays they otherwise wouldn't. Most of Pujols' miscues occurred on extremely hard-hit balls or when he was unable to get his body in front of the ball. Known for his superior offensive abilities, Pujols also deserves props for his defensive prowess. He has saved an estimated 61 runs defensively for the Cardinals in the last three years. That's exactly twice as many as the second best first baseman in this category, Casey Kotchman.

Casey Kotchman

	Innings	Runs Saved
2008	1210	9
2006-2008	2440	31

	Good Plays	Misplays and Errors
Kotchman 2008	76	18
Avg First Baseman	57	30
Good Play/Misplay Pct		.690

Kotchman is an elite first baseman. The smooth fielder only committed two errors in 2008, thanks in part to his sure hands and quick reflexes. He has good feet around the bag and picks the majority of throws in the dirt. He had 45 Good Fielding Plays on throws last year, second only to Justin Morneau's 47 for first basemen in all of baseball. Kotchman has room to improve on bunts, but he charges the ball well. He has average range on pop-ups and reads them well, although he can get lost when he has to run straight back on them.

Kevin Youkilis

	Innings	Runs Saved
2008	985	4
2006-2008	3109	19

	Good Plays	Misplays and Errors
Youkilis 2008	40	14
Avg First Baseman	44	23
Good Play/Misplay Pct		.601

While Youkilis did not go through the 2008 season errorless at first base like he did in 2007, he is still an above-average first baseman with no glaring weakness and very good instincts. Youkilis' range allows him to make a lot of plays in the hole between first and second, and his hands are reliable on groundballs and throws in the dirt. His arm is accurate and leads the pitcher to the bag well. Youkilis has good feet around the bag, charges hard on bunts, and tracks pop-ups well.

Doug Mientkiewicz

	Innings	Runs Saved
2008	283	2
2006-2008	1466	17

	Good Plays	Misplays and Errors
Mientkiewicz 2008	12	5
Avg First Baseman	13	7
Good Play/Misplay Pct		.558

Mark Teixeira

	Innings	Runs Saved
2008	1335	17
2006-2008	3832	16

	Good Plays	Misplays and Errors
Teixeira 2008	93	22
Avg First Baseman	65	34
Good Play/Misplay Pct		.690

Making all the average plays, most of the difficult plays, and some of the impossible ones, Teixeira is among the game's premier defensive first basemen. In 2008 he had a tremendous year with the most runs saved (17) by any first baseman, the most Good Fielding Plays by a wide margin (93, Kotchman second with 76), and the highest plus/minus as well (+23). Playing in both leagues put him out of the running for a Gold Glove. He fell one vote short of winning the Fielding Bible Award over Albert Pujols. Teixeira has outstanding footwork around the bag, allowing him to prepare for throws of any variety, and he shows excellent range to both his glove and throwing sides. He fields flyballs with the ease

First Basemen

of a natural-born outfielder. He also has great baseball instincts and a good arm for a first baseman, which he uses to cut down advancing baserunners. We recorded seven Good Fielding Plays on throws for Mark in 2008; the average first baseman had one or two. Everyone recognizes his talent as a slugging switch-hitter, but it's his combination of offensive firepower and slick fielding that makes him truly remarkable.

Lance Berkman

	Innings	Runs Saved
2008	1307	13
2006-2008	3297	16

	Good Plays	Misplays and Errors
Berkman 2008	64	22
Avg First Baseman	59	31
Good Play/Misplay Pct		.605

Since moving from the outfield, Big Puma has become a quality first baseman. He doesn't have a quick first step, but the former center fielder's athleticism shows in his instincts on pop-ups and his ability to range to his right. Berkman has soft hands for fielding groundballs and handling throws from his infielders, giving them confidence to make the tough throw. He has quick feet and sound fundamentals around the bag that permit him to adjust to wild throws. Entering his mid-30s, Berkman continues to put up All-Star numbers each year, and playing first base instead of the outfield should keep the wear and tear to a minimum.

Joey Votto

	Innings	Runs Saved
2008	1224	16
2006-2008	1361	15

	Good Plays	Misplays and Errors
Votto 2008	57	44
Avg First Baseman	53	28
Good Play/Misplay Pct		.406

Among first basemen, Votto ranked near the bottom in fielding percentage (.991) and errors (11). That's more of a reflection on those metrics, not Votto. He is one of the best fielding first basemen in terms of groundballs hit within his reach and his reactions and footwork compare favorably with those of any other first baseman. It's the throws that he has trouble with, both receiving them and making them. He had the most Defensive Misplays and Errors in each category among first baseman. He had 16 misplays/errors catching throws and 11 making them. His struggles begin when receiving throws, mostly those in the dirt. He tends to use too much wrist motion, which

often knocks the ball out of his glove. When making throws many of them were simply wild. If he improves his ability to handle throws at first base, his skills will be more accurately reflected in less sophisticated metrics.

Lyle Overbay

	Innings	Runs Saved
2008	1355	6
2006-2008	3560	15

	Good Plays	Misplays and Errors
Overbay 2008	38	26
Avg First Baseman	64	34
Good Play/Misplay Pct		.435

Overbay's defensive ability goes largely unnoticed, possibly because he doesn't put up the flashy home run and RBI totals that other first basemen do. But also because he doesn't put up the flashy plays. He had a surprisingly low total of Good Fielding Plays compared to other first baseman, but he makes all the routine plays and has the range to cover the line or snag balls that are hit to his right. He doesn't make very many mistakes, but he is not especially adept at handling bunts. Taking all things into account, Overbay is a very good defensive first baseman.

Carlos Pena

	Innings	Runs Saved
2008	1169	11
2006-2008	2470	14

	Good Plays	Misplays and Errors
Pena 2008	64	24
Avg First Baseman	48	25
Good Play/Misplay Pct		.584

Pena has quietly asserted himself as one of the best first basemen in the American League. He pairs excellent footwork with the quick reflexes necessary to man the position. Factor in his gritty style of play, and you have a recipe for success. When holding a runner on base, he will quickly leap off the bag to try and take away the hole to his right. This contributes to his ability to make good fielding plays moving to his right. He is not quite as good moving to his throwing side, but overall he fields groundballs and line drives well. Pena also is adept at going back on pop-ups, taking good angles and hustling to the spot to snag balls many first basemen wouldn't reach. Pena's sharpest skill, though, is snagging the errant throw. Pena successfully received a throw of unusual difficulty thirty-eight times in 2008, producing outs and keeping baserunners from advancing. Only twice did he fail to catch a throw that he "should" have caught. He was rewarded for his efforts in 2008 with his first Gold Glove award.

263

First Basemen

Rich Aurilia

	Innings	Runs Saved
2008	477	0
2006-2008	1178	11

	Good Plays	Misplays and Errors
Aurilia 2008	20	15
Avg First Baseman	18	10
Good Play/Misplay Pct		.413

Daric Barton

	Innings	Runs Saved
2008	1122	4
2006-2008	1279	8

	Good Plays	Misplays and Errors
Barton 2008	51	33
Avg First Baseman	48	25
Good Play/Misplay Pct		.449

A former catcher, Barton can make the easy plays. While his 225-pound frame suggests he might have limited mobility, he has done well going to his right and to his left when compared to other first basemen using the Plus/Minus System. His footwork when turning double plays needs improvement, as it takes him awhile to get into position to throw. Like others converted from catcher to first base, he has a natural capacity to pick balls from the dirt, even though he occasionally puts himself in a bad position to receive the throw. There is no doubt that, with more reps, Barton can become a solid fielder at first base. He may already be there.

Todd Helton

	Innings	Runs Saved
2008	715	4
2006-2008	3325	8

	Good Plays	Misplays and Errors
Helton 2008	60	10
Avg First Baseman	38	20
Good Play/Misplay Pct		.760

Before hitting the disabled list with a back injury, Helton showed that he remains one of the most sure-handed first basemen in the majors. He didn't commit an error on a groundball in 2008 and had the fewest Defensive Misplays (seven) among qualifying first basemen, thanks in part to his excellent reaction time. Despite his advanced age, Helton has solid range on grounders and displays great hands on throws in the dirt. In fact, no one in baseball was better than Helton handling errant throws from his fellow infielders in 2008.

The major league leader at first base was Justin Morneau with 47, but Helton had almost as many (42) while playing barely over half as many innings. His arm isn't strong, but it's generally accurate.

Nick Johnson

	Innings	Runs Saved
2008	300	2
2006-2008	1552	8

	Good Plays	Misplays and Errors
Johnson 2008	5	5
Avg First Baseman	14	7
Good Play/Misplay Pct		.345

James Loney

	Innings	Runs Saved
2008	1363	1
2006-2008	2366	8

	Good Plays	Misplays and Errors
Loney 2008	69	30
Avg First Baseman	65	34
Good Play/Misplay Pct		.548

Loney is great with his glove, scooping throws in the dirt or fielding tough hops. He can be indecisive in ranging off the bag to his right, perhaps due to Jeff Kent's tendency to play toward the first-base hole. Loney's mistakes usually occur on balls hit right at him. He is one of the majors' best when it comes to fielding bunts, thanks to his physical and mental quickness.

Derrek Lee

	Innings	Runs Saved
2008	1339	5
2006-2008	3007	4

	Good Plays	Misplays and Errors
Lee 2008	55	21
Avg First Baseman	57	30
Good Play/Misplay Pct		.580

The tall and athletic Lee had an above-average year defensively. He has great hand-eye coordination, which leads to many backhanded dives for outs. He has a good ability to get to wild throws. His flexibility allows him to stretch for balls and make scoops to prevent singles and errors. At times, he has trouble fielding hard-hit balls hit right at him. He also needs to work on his glove-to-hand transfer on balls deep in the first-base hole. Overall, Lee is a solid defender who makes his other fielders better.

First Basemen

Miguel Cairo

	Innings	Runs Saved
2008	394	2
2006-2008	632	2

	Good Plays	Misplays and Errors
Cairo 2008	20	5
Avg First Baseman	19	10
Good Play/Misplay Pct		.678

Hank Blalock

	Innings	Runs Saved
2008	296	-1
2006-2008	296	-1

	Good Plays	Misplays and Errors
Blalock 2008	8	7
Avg First Baseman	12	6
Good Play/Misplay Pct		.376

Bryan LaHair

	Innings	Runs Saved
2008	273	0
2006-2008	273	0

	Good Plays	Misplays and Errors
LaHair 2008	13	5
Avg First Baseman	13	7
Good Play/Misplay Pct		.578

Chris Davis

	Innings	Runs Saved
2008	404	-1
2006-2008	404	-1

	Good Plays	Misplays and Errors
Davis 2008	22	11
Avg First Baseman	17	9
Good Play/Misplay Pct		.513

Chad Tracy

	Innings	Runs Saved
2008	523	-1
2006-2008	659	0

	Good Plays	Misplays and Errors
Tracy 2008	18	15
Avg First Baseman	24	13
Good Play/Misplay Pct		.387

Billy Butler

	Innings	Runs Saved
2008	260	-3
2006-2008	343	-1

	Good Plays	Misplays and Errors
Butler 2008	9	8
Avg First Baseman	11	6
Good Play/Misplay Pct		.372

Tracy is an average first baseman who doesn't do anything terrific or terrible. He has average range for the position, but he isn't sure-handed when he is on the move. He displays an accurate throwing arm when throwing to second or leading the pitcher on plays at first. He can handle balls in the dirt, and he moves his feet well around the bag on off-line throws. He also shows good feet when throwing to second on double-play opportunities.

Jorge Cantu

	Innings	Runs Saved
2008	287	1
2006-2008	442	-1

	Good Plays	Misplays and Errors
Cantu 2008	9	6
Avg First Baseman	12	6
Good Play/Misplay Pct		.441

Adrian Gonzalez

	Innings	Runs Saved
2008	1417	0
2006-2008	4221	-1

	Good Plays	Misplays and Errors
Gonzalez 2008	53	27
Avg First Baseman	63	33
Good Play/Misplay Pct		.508

Gonzalez is a smart player who has a good idea of where he wants to go with the ball when it is hit to him. He also has good hands on groundballs and low throws, especially on the backhand, and is as good as they come at fielding bunts. Gonzalez's arm is below-average, but he is accurate on force plays to second and always hits the pitcher in stride on plays at first. He can get sloppy transferring the ball from his glove to his hand when he has to rush. He has decent feet around the bag and acceptable range. He won a National League Gold Glove in 2008, but Fielding Bible Award voters thought of him as only a slightly above-average first baseman.

First Basemen

Justin Morneau

	Innings	Runs Saved
2008	1364	-3
2006-2008	3969	-2

	Good Plays	Misplays and Errors
Morneau 2008	70	29
Avg First Baseman	61	32
Good Play/Misplay Pct		.560

Morneau makes a lot of great scoops to convert putouts at first base. He led MLB first basemen in handling bad throws with 47 in 2008. He also plays satisfactory defense on grounders hit to either side of him, although he tends to come up empty on hard-hit balls when holding runners on base. Bunt grounders seem to give him the most problems. He needs to work on fielding them and then throwing on the run. Still, he doesn't embarrass himself. The Twins will take his mediocre defense as long as he keeps hitting.

John Bowker

	Innings	Runs Saved
2008	550	-3
2006-2008	550	-3

	Good Plays	Misplays and Errors
Bowker 2008	21	19
Avg First Baseman	22	11
Good Play/Misplay Pct		.368

Normally an outfielder, Bowker saw playing time at first base due to Rich Aurilia's lack of production. Forced to learn a new trade on the big stage, Bowker improved as the season progressed. There's nothing flashy about him, but he at least has the ability to make the routine plays look routine.

Aaron Boone

	Innings	Runs Saved
2008	342	1
2006-2008	730	-4

	Good Plays	Misplays and Errors
Boone 2008	16	9
Avg First Baseman	14	8
Good Play/Misplay Pct		.484

Ross Gload

	Innings	Runs Saved
2008	878	-5
2006-2008	1801	-4

	Good Plays	Misplays and Errors
Gload 2008	55	12
Avg First Baseman	38	20
Good Play/Misplay Pct		.707

Gload was the Royals' primary first baseman in 2008. Defensively, he rarely makes a mistake, committing only four errors while also having the fewest Defensive Misplays among first basemen who played more than 850 innings at the position. Gload displays below-average range but has very good hands. He makes his share of diving plays and is exceptional at handling difficult throws in the dirt, although he makes some plays look harder than they need to be. He has an accurate arm, good instincts, and a feel for fielding bunts well. If he has a weakness, it is fielding hard groundballs hit right at him.

Miguel Cabrera

	Innings	Runs Saved
2008	1204	-5
2006-2008	1204	-5

	Good Plays	Misplays and Errors
Cabrera 2008	38	33
Avg First Baseman	52	28
Good Play/Misplay Pct		.378

Still just a youngster, Cabrera already has slid to the lowest end of the defensive spectrum. Playing first base for the first time in his career, Cabrera took a while to adjust to the role. He showed decent range around the bag and benefited from his previous experience at third base. He occasionally struggled with his footwork and tended to short-arm throws in the dirt. At times, he was indecisive when coming in on a ball or covering the bag in certain fielding situations. He had five misplays involving covering the first base bag; no one else had more than three. These are problems that should be remedied with more experience, however.

First Basemen

Nick Swisher

	Innings	Runs Saved
2008	462	-4
2006-2008	1509	-7

	Good Plays	Misplays and Errors
Swisher 2008	32	5
Avg First Baseman	21	11
Good Play/Misplay Pct		.771

Overall, Swisher is very solid at first base without any glaring weaknesses. He has very good footwork around the bag and is quick to move in catching errant throws. However, standing at only six feet tall, he is unable to stretch as well as taller first basemen. Swisher has very good hands fielding ground balls and handling throws in the dirt. He possesses only an average arm, but he is accurate throwing the ball around the diamond. He has very good instincts and fields bunts well.

Garrett Atkins

	Innings	Runs Saved
2008	528	-7
2006-2008	565	-7

	Good Plays	Misplays and Errors
Atkins 2008	19	12
Avg First Baseman	25	13
Good Play/Misplay Pct		.455

Atkins received his first extended playing time at first base in 2008 after Todd Helton went down with an injury. Immediately after the switch, Atkins looked uncomfortable, but he improved as the season progressed. That being said, "first baseman Garrett Atkins" is a work in progress. He has an inaccurate arm to go with inconsistent hands and footwork. Still, we're grading on a curve here: Atkins' range is subpar for a third baseman, but it is not far off from average for a first baseman.

Ryan Howard

	Innings	Runs Saved
2008	1403	0
2006-2008	4056	-8

	Good Plays	Misplays and Errors
Howard 2008	64	56
Avg First Baseman	67	35
Good Play/Misplay Pct		.376

Howard is agile for his size but has below-average speed. He makes the routine plays, but his poor reactions hurt him on hard-hit balls. He lacks flexibility, which limits his ability to stretch for errant throws, and his throwing isn't always accurate. He makes more than his share of misplays and errors as he led all MLB first basemen with 56. On the plus side, he has a knack for running down pop-ups, both fair and foul.

Carlos Delgado

	Innings	Runs Saved
2008	1376	-9
2006-2008	3842	-9

	Good Plays	Misplays and Errors
Delgado 2008	54	29
Avg First Baseman	59	31
Good Play/Misplay Pct		.495

Delgado lacks range and has a slow first step that limits him even more. His iron glove makes every play an adventure and impairs his ability to field throws from infielders, especially short hops and off-target throws. Delgado has never been a solid first baseman. At this point in his career, improvement is highly unlikely.

Paul Konerko

	Innings	Runs Saved
2008	996	-4
2006-2008	3405	-13

	Good Plays	Misplays and Errors
Konerko 2008	54	22
Avg First Baseman	48	25
Good Play/Misplay Pct		.564

Konerko gets the job done at first base by showing good hands, both in fielding grounders and handling throws in the dirt. He isn't very mobile, but he displays good footwork around the bag and reacts well to hard-hit balls in his vicinity. Still, the White Sox recognized his limitations in 2008, (or was it recognizing Nick Swisher's strengths) as they often replaced Paulie with Swisher late in games to shore up the defense.

Ryan Garko

	Innings	Runs Saved
2008	1059	-5
2006-2008	2521	-13

	Good Plays	Misplays and Errors
Garko 2008	51	18
Avg First Baseman	49	26
Good Play/Misplay Pct		.599

Garko is a dependable first baseman, even though he doesn't always look graceful. He has limited range, but he doesn't make very many mistakes. He's very good at scoops, especially backhanded. He has a strong, accurate arm with a good touch on throws to the pitcher covering. Hitters who have bunted on Garko have chosen wisely.

First Basemen

Adam LaRoche

	Innings	Runs Saved
2008	1136	-6
2006-2008	3590	-13

	Good Plays	Misplays and Errors
LaRoche 2008	39	22
Avg First Baseman	53	28
Good Play/Misplay Pct		.483

The elder LaRoche makes some nifty scoops at first base, saving his infield brethren from throwing errors. He is good at tracking foul pop-ups down the right field line, smoothly making those over-the-shoulder grabs. However, he simply doesn't cover much ground at first base and makes far less than his fair share of plays. He has trouble with throws to second base when there is a runner in the baseline, and he can be nonchalant when applying a tag. This has allowed some runners to evade him. On the whole, though, LaRoche provides acceptable defense.

Sean Casey

	Innings	Runs Saved
2008	343	-3
2006-2008	2206	-14

	Good Plays	Misplays and Errors
Casey 2008	12	7
Avg First Baseman	15	8
Good Play/Misplay Pct		.475

Conor Jackson

	Innings	Runs Saved
2008	572	-4
2006-2008	2518	-16

	Good Plays	Misplays and Errors
Jackson 2008	18	20
Avg First Baseman	25	13
Good Play/Misplay Pct		.322

Jackson started off the year as a first baseman and played an average first base at best. With some athleticism and quickness, he moved around the right side of the infield fairly well. He showed some good glove work on balls hit right to him and made a couple of diving catches to prevent extra bases. But he made a lot of mistakes and the good plays are fewer than you'd like to see. He was prone to failing to catch throws from his infielders. Sometimes it was due to lack of balance or scoops that he failed to execute. When the opposition bunted, Jackson was an active fielder, normally converting the out.

Richie Sexson

	Innings	Runs Saved
2008	684	-8
2006-2008	2986	-16

	Good Plays	Misplays and Errors
Sexson 2008	21	10
Avg First Baseman	31	16
Good Play/Misplay Pct		.525

Once highly regarded, Sexson is now a disappointment in all areas of the game. When fielding groundballs, he lacks a quick first step and quick reactions in general. He has average range to his left and toward the second base hole but is not a guarantee to field the balls he reaches. He has trouble scooping throws in the dirt and stretching to his full potential, both metaphorically and literally. We'd say his future looks bleak, but he has made millions. He'll be just fine.

Kevin Millar

	Innings	Runs Saved
2008	1131	-4
2006-2008	2797	-17

	Good Plays	Misplays and Errors
Millar 2008	64	22
Avg First Baseman	53	28
Good Play/Misplay Pct		.605

Millar made the transition to first base in 2003 and was decent for a converted outfielder. Five years later, not much has changed. He still has poor footwork around the bag and has trouble scooping the ball. Unlike a good first baseman, Millar actually makes his fielders look worse than they are. He never squares up to his fielder before stretching, preferring to stretch before the play and then dive for throws not directly at him. Even one of his strengths, ranging to his right, can be a fault; he sometimes abandons first to cut off the second baseman on groundballs.

Dmitri Young

	Innings	Runs Saved
2008	290	-5
2006-2008	1195	-21

	Good Plays	Misplays and Errors
Young 2008	10	14
Avg First Baseman	13	7
Good Play/Misplay Pct		.273

First Basemen

Jason Giambi

	Innings	Runs Saved
2008	898	-13
2006-2008	1499	-22

	Good Plays	Misplays and Errors
Giambi 2008	52	28
Avg First Baseman	40	21
Good Play/Misplay Pct		.495

Lacking athleticism and mobility, Giambi tends to go for flashy scoops at first base. While he converts many of them, he also allows many of them to pass him completely. He will make the occasional great stop to his left, but he struggles to his right and on balls that are hit right at him. He also is infamous for his wild throws. You won't see a lot of 3-6-3s when the Giambino is on the field.

Mike Jacobs

	Innings	Runs Saved
2008	927	-23
2006-2008	2802	-35

	Good Plays	Misplays and Errors
Jacobs 2008	33	36
Avg First Baseman	40	21
Good Play/Misplay Pct		.326

As a first baseman, Jacobs makes a great designated hitter. His footwork is rough, his hands are inconsistent, and his range doesn't measure up to the relatively low standards of his position. We estimate that his defense cost his team about 23 runs in 2008, a huge number. His limited fielding positives are his decent (if erratic) arm and that he does a good job scooping balls out of the dirt.

Prince Fielder

	Innings	Runs Saved
2008	1384	-10
2006-2008	4041	-33

	Good Plays	Misplays and Errors
Fielder 2008	54	47
Avg First Baseman	65	34
Good Play/Misplay Pct		.377

Fielder is an odd case. He can move quickly at times, but more often plays at the speed his body type would indicate. He is better to his right than to his left, but that's a pretty low standard. Simply put, he's terrible to his left. With his physique and lack of defensive skill, it's only a matter of time before he falls off the defensive spectrum and fulfills his destiny a designated hitter.

Second Basemen Evaluations

Year	League	Gold Glove Winners	Should Have Been
2003	AL	Bret Boone	Orlando Hudson
	NL	Luis Castillo	Luis Castillo
2004	AL	Bret Boone	Orlando Hudson
	NL	Luis Castillo	Luis Castillo
2005	AL	Orlando Hudson	Orlando Hudson
	NL	Luis Castillo	Craig Counsell
2006	AL	Mark Grudzielanek	Mark Ellis
	NL	Orlando Hudson	Orlando Hudson
2007	AL	Placido Polanco	Aaron Hill
	NL	Orlando Hudson	Orlando Hudson
2008	AL	Dustin Pedroia	Mark Ellis
	NL	Brandon Phillips	Chase Utley

My Personal Ratings

Top Ten

1 Chase Utley, Phi
2 Mark Ellis, Oak
3 Brandon Phillips, Cin
4 Orlando Hudson, FA
5 Placido Polanco, Det
6 Dustin Pedroia, Bos
7 Aaron Hill, Tor
8 Adam Kennedy, FA
9 Asdrubal Cabrera, Cle
10 Jose Lopez, Sea

Bottom Five

26 Felipe Lopez, Ari
27 Luis Castillo, NYM
28 Ray Durham, FA
29 Jeff Kent, retired
30 Rickie Weeks, Mil

Player teams based on transactions through February 11, 2009

Second Basemen

Chase Utley

	Innings	Runs Saved
2008	1396	33
2006-2008	3930	63

	Good Plays	Misplays and Errors
Utley 2008	57	48
Avg Second Baseman	54	41
Good Play/Misplay Pct		.475

Utley has proven again and again that he's excellent on balls to his left. Is it ultra-positioning? Take a look at the article, "What Makes Chase Utley So Good?" on page 151. He charges softly hit balls with superb glove-to-hand transfer. He possesses an above-average arm at second base, throwing on the run with ease thanks to a nice side-flick throw. He also has improved on the double play. He can be inconsistent on balls to his right, booting some easy outs. He also has made a couple of bad throws that allowed extra bases on occasion. Michael Jordan missed a free throw every now and then, too.

Mark Ellis

	Innings	Runs Saved
2008	1012	24
2006-2008	3404	54

	Good Plays	Misplays and Errors
Ellis 2008	29	22
Avg Second Baseman	37	28
Good Play/Misplay Pct		.501

Ellis is an excellent second baseman, without a Gold Glove or Fielding Bible Award to show for it. Perhaps his athleticism is a notch below that of some of his peers, as is his average throwing arm. He has difficulty getting much mustard on throws when he doesn't have a chance to set himself. That said, Ellis gobbles up most everything that comes near him and rarely makes mistakes. Showing superb positional awareness and instincts, Ellis always seems to get a good jump on the ball. He is particularly strong to his right. He's as good as they come on the double play. If Fielding Bible Award voters could have chosen the 2008 American League Gold Glove winner, it would have been Ellis. He was the highest ranked American Leaguer in the final vote tabulation, finishing second overall to Brandon Phillips.

Aaron Hill

	Innings	Runs Saved
2008	479	-2
2006-2008	2803	44

	Good Plays	Misplays and Errors
Hill 2008	17	9
Avg Second Baseman	17	13
Good Play/Misplay Pct		.590

Hill had a defensive year of historic excellence in 2007 when he had the second highest assist total (560) for a second baseman in the last 77 years (topped only by Ryne Sandberg's 571 assists in 1983). He won the 2007 Fielding Bible Award for second basemen as he led all second basemen in baseball for the second year in a row with a +22 plus/minus. His 2008 season got cut short after a nasty collision with David Eckstein on a shallow pop fly in late May that resulted in post-concussion syndrome. He'll be back for the start of the 2009 season.

Hill is a solid, yet not flashy, second baseman with very good range. He's excellent at dropping back and going after shallow fly balls in the outfield, and his lateral range is above average. At times, he has trouble with soft grounders, where a single "catch-and-throw" motion is needed. His arm strength is average, but accurate.

Placido Polanco

	Innings	Runs Saved
2008	1201	11
2006-2008	3353	30

	Good Plays	Misplays and Errors
Polanco 2008	42	24
Avg Second Baseman	46	35
Good Play/Misplay Pct		.571

Polanco is as smooth as they come at second base. He always seems to be in position and makes every play look routine. He ranges back on soft flyballs as well as anyone and is especially good at making the barehanded play. Based on Bill James' Universal Fielding Percentage, Polanco is the most sure-handed second baseman of all time. See page 345.

Second Basemen

Orlando Hudson

	Innings	Runs Saved
2008	905	-3
2006-2008	3437	25

	Good Plays	Misplays and Errors
Hudson 2008	48	18
Avg Second Baseman	33	25
Good Play/Misplay Pct		.670

O-Dog's season-ending wrist injury in early August likely cost him a fourth consecutive Gold Glove, but he doesn't need the added hardware to confirm his status as one of the top second basemen in baseball. He's fantastic going back on pop-ups, often making running catches in the outfield that few, if any other second basemen could execute. He has excellent range, makes diving plays, and fires accurate throws even when his feet aren't set. Athletic and smooth, he can improvise when necessary, fielding and flipping the ball with his glove in one motion. He excels even in unfamiliar situations, such as scooping low throws while covering first base. Although Hudson will be 31 entering the 2009 season, he'll shine for several years to come.

Mark Grudzielanek

	Innings	Runs Saved
2008	711	-2
2006-2008	2769	18

	Good Plays	Misplays and Errors
Grudzielanek 2008	27	23
Avg Second Baseman	27	20
Good Play/Misplay Pct		.472

Grudzielanek is playing fewer and fewer games as he approaches the big 4-0. Although he had a late-career revival as a defensive player after he learned how to position himself better, his physical tools are not what they used to be. His quickness and speed have diminished his range, while injuries have often kept him off the field entirely. His arm is average, but he still turns the double play with the best of them. With Grudzielanek's focus on playing smarter, he is perfectly suited to mentor a young second baseman just breaking into the bigs.

Adam Kennedy

	Innings	Runs Saved
2008	636	17
2006-2008	2407	17

	Good Plays	Misplays and Errors
Kennedy 2008	27	10
Avg Second Baseman	24	18
Good Play/Misplay Pct		.673

Kennedy is an underrated second baseman. He gets good jumps on balls, which allows him to make more plays than the average second baseman. His arm is average at best, but he is an accurate thrower even when he is on the run or in a hurry. Kennedy has very good hands on short hops, as well as when he moves to his right or left. He also has good feet around the bag and is quick to pivot when starting the double play on grounders to his left. His error/misplay rate is very low. On balls in the air, Kennedy has above-average range and takes good routes.

Jose Lopez

	Innings	Runs Saved
2008	1229	1
2006-2008	3783	17

	Good Plays	Misplays and Errors
Lopez 2008	41	41
Avg Second Baseman	50	38
Good Play/Misplay Pct		.432

On a disappointing Mariners team, Lopez's defense was a relative bright spot. He showed average range up the middle and great range to his left in 2008, to the point that he even backed up the first baseman on some plays. Excellent positioning was the key. He sports a plus arm that helps him complete the double play, and his quick feet enable him to avoid incoming runners. By the end of the season, the lack of viable defensive options forced Lopez to move to first base for the last few weeks of the season.

Asdrubal Cabrera

	Innings	Runs Saved
2008	777	10
2006-2008	1098	15

	Good Plays	Misplays and Errors
Cabrera 2008	31	12
Avg Second Baseman	31	24
Good Play/Misplay Pct		.663

Cabrera's midseason demotion to the minors wasn't a reflection of his defense. He has great range up the

Second Basemen

middle and a strong arm that helps him turn the double play. He has a long arm action that can slow his release, though. Cabrera's first full season mirrored Cleveland's disappointing season but, just like the Indians, Cabrera bounced back in the end, after everyone had stopped paying attention.

Jamey Carroll

	Innings	Runs Saved
2008	580	-1
2006-2008	1906	14

	Good Plays	Misplays and Errors
Carroll 2008	23	15
Avg Second Baseman	20	15
Good Play/Misplay Pct		.539

Carroll filled in at second and third base for the Indians in 2008, displaying average range to his right and left. His arm suffices at second but doesn't cut it at third. He is aggressive on slowly hit balls and has a quick release. He is very good on the double play. Asdrubal Cabrera's demotion to the minors and numerous injuries resulted in Carroll playing in more than 100 games. He won't hurt you at all defensively, but overall he is strictly bench material.

Brandon Phillips

	Innings	Runs Saved
2008	1238	10
2006-2008	3825	13

	Good Plays	Misplays and Errors
Phillips 2008	66	34
Avg Second Baseman	48	36
Good Play/Misplay Pct		.597

I saw Cincinnati in just one series last year, but Brandon Phillips was probably the most impressive defensive player that I saw. I had always thought of him as being a kind of a talented hitter/moody player who wasn't really into the game from the defensive standpoint, about which I couldn't have been more wrong. I remember two plays that he made, neither of which ultimately amounted to anything, but which were memorable anyway. One was a pop up that he caught in short right field, racing away from second base, with a runner on second. In that situation, because the second baseman's momentum is so strongly away from the play, a lot of times you can tag up at second and go to third. The Red Sox had Kevin Youkilis on second, who is very alert to things like that, but Phillips caught the ball, sprang in the air, pivoted 180 degrees in the air to stop his momentum, and then fired a rocket to third base. It

wouldn't show up in the plus/minus rankings, but he'd have been out by 50 feet if he had tried.

The other was a stolen base play, Jacoby Ellsbury stealing second, on which the throw came in a little bit to the first base side of second and a little bit high. Phillips caught the throw but faked like he hadn't, and started gearing up like he was going to chase the ball into center field. Jacoby jumped to his feet, and you could see he was that close to breaking off the bag, seeing if he could make third, but fortunately he didn't take his foot off the bag. Phillips faked for just a second, very convincingly, and then slapped a tag on Ellsbury, who was still on the base. It wouldn't show up in the books because nothing happened, but if Jacoby hadn't been alert it would have been an inning spoiler for sure, taking a runner off of second base.

Phillips was so alert, so "into" the game, that he made the other team nervous. You felt like you had to watch yourself every second around second base, because you never knew what he was up to. I noticed that he was leading second basemen in Good Fielding Plays with a couple of weeks left in the season, and I would bet, over the course of the season, that he really caught some people napping, and I would bet also that some people didn't move up who could have moved up, because Phillips made them so nervous that they were tentative about moving.

- Bill James

Howie Kendrick

	Innings	Runs Saved
2008	776	0
2006-2008	1747	10

	Good Plays	Misplays and Errors
Kendrick 2008	28	11
Avg Second Baseman	30	23
Good Play/Misplay Pct		.660

Kendrick is sound defensively, even if he doesn't always look like a natural. He has plenty of arm for a second baseman and turns a fine double play. He needs to improve his footwork, as he sometimes ends up making an off-balance throw when he has enough time to set himself. He's not as smooth as some other second basemen, and the time he takes to transfer the ball from glove to hand occasionally gets him in trouble. He is capable of outstanding diving plays and does show quickness getting back to his feet. Kendrick is athletic and still young, so some improvement should be expected.

Second Basemen

Dustin Pedroia

	Innings	Runs Saved
2008	1376	12
2006-2008	2690	9

	Good Plays	Misplays and Errors
Pedroia 2008	66	31
Avg Second Baseman	49	38
Good Play/Misplay Pct		.619

Never regarded as a great athlete, Pedroia gets good jumps and has above-average range. He has great hands and fields the balls that are hit to him. He makes some spectacular plays, especially going to his right, and is quick to get up and make a strong and accurate throw when diving up the middle. Pedroia is very quick and accurate throwing to second when starting the double play, but he is less adept when making the pivot. Similarly, he is quick when his feet are set at the bag, but he is less accurate and gets less on the throw when he comes across it. Notoriously scrappy, he hangs in well when the runner slides hard into second. If he isn't dirty, he isn't playing. Pedroia was recognized for his defense with a Gold Glove in 2008.

Joe Inglett

	Innings	Runs Saved
2008	541	5
2006-2008	959	9

	Good Plays	Misplays and Errors
Inglett 2008	21	14
Avg Second Baseman	20	15
Good Play/Misplay Pct		.533

Inglett's versatility was put to good use in 2008, splitting time between the corner outfield positions (mainly as a late-inning defensive replacement) and second base. But when Aaron Hill went out with an injury in late May, Inglett was inserted as Toronto's primary second baseman for the rest of the season. He has a quick first step and excellent range up the middle. His strong arm and ability to set himself quickly has taken quite a few potential base hits away. On balls hit to his glove side, however, he tends to have a little more difficulty. At times he lets the ball play him and fades deeper into the hole than most second basemen, perhaps knowing his arm can bail him out most of the time.

Mike Fontenot

	Innings	Runs Saved
2008	499	8
2006-2008	967	8

	Good Plays	Misplays and Errors
Fontenot 2008	12	9
Avg Second Baseman	16	12
Good Play/Misplay Pct		.504

When Mark DeRosa is off gallivanting at third base or in the outfield, Fontenot fills in at second base. He is a solid, sure-handed defender who doesn't do anything flashy. He's as good or better than DeRosa. Despite limited innings in 2008, Fontenot didn't look rusty when he found his way off the bench. With DeRosa gone, he'll have an opportunity to show his stuff in 2009.

Clint Barmes

	Innings	Runs Saved
2008	486	8
2006-2008	516	8

	Good Plays	Misplays and Errors
Barmes 2008	23	17
Avg Second Baseman	19	14
Good Play/Misplay Pct		.508

Barmes gets forced over to second base while Troy Tulowitzki is in the lineup, but Barmes is no slouch with the glove. He possesses great range and excellent hands to either side, tracking down balls up the middle or in the hole. He also has an arm that is sufficient at shortstop and great at second base. His great instincts allow him to make plays on baserunners that would be "ill-advised" if he didn't get the job done. Barmes' weakness, relatively speaking, is flagging down shallow flyballs. In a system that focuses on developing groundball pitchers, it helps to have a guy like Barmes who can play either shortstop or second base with aplomb.

Robinson Cano

	Innings	Runs Saved
2008	1377	-13
2006-2008	3794	6

	Good Plays	Misplays and Errors
Cano 2008	69	42
Avg Second Baseman	54	41
Good Play/Misplay Pct		.556

Cano took a step back defensively in 2008. Granted, he made some flashy plays on the run, going side to side or charging softly hit balls. He also possesses an above-average arm and features a nifty sidearm flick that helps on the double play. With all his flashes of brilliance, though, Cano still had a hard time fielding simple groundballs. On balls not hit particularly hard, Cano stabs too quickly at the ball or botches the play entirely. He also can seem lackadaisical. As time passes, 2007 is looking more like the exception than the rule.

Augie Ojeda

	Innings	Runs Saved
2008	286	6
2006-2008	451	5

	Good Plays	Misplays and Errors
Ojeda 2008	13	3
Avg Second Baseman	10	8
Good Play/Misplay Pct		.767

Kaz Matsui

	Innings	Runs Saved
2008	806	-8
2006-2008	2132	5

	Good Plays	Misplays and Errors
Matsui 2008	24	27
Avg Second Baseman	28	21
Good Play/Misplay Pct		.404

Matsui just missed the plus/minus trailer list making 11 fewer plays than an average second baseman including 12 errors in only 806 innings. Balls hit up the middle gave him problems in 2008, but he has done well with them in the past. Even when he reaches the ball, he doesn't always field it cleanly and looks uncomfortable using his backhand. It's hard to point to one specific strength that Matsui possesses. As Harry Doyle once said, "Let's give him credit. At least he didn't spike himself."

Emilio Bonifacio

	Innings	Runs Saved
2008	325	2
2006-2008	371	4

	Good Plays	Misplays and Errors
Bonifacio 2008	10	20
Avg Second Baseman	12	9
Good Play/Misplay Pct		.276

Marco Scutaro

	Innings	Runs Saved
2008	354	0
2006-2008	766	4

	Good Plays	Misplays and Errors
Scutaro 2008	16	4
Avg Second Baseman	13	10
Good Play/Misplay Pct		.753

Brian Roberts

	Innings	Runs Saved
2008	1320	-3
2006-2008	3817	4

	Good Plays	Misplays and Errors
Roberts 2008	57	37
Avg Second Baseman	50	38
Good Play/Misplay Pct		.540

Roberts is one of the few bright spots on a perennially disappointing team. He is sound in all aspects of the game, from groundballs and pop-ups to turning the double play, and he features a strong arm. His speed and quick first step give him above-average range, especially up the middle. His work on the double play is worth noting. Good Fielding Play type 13 is called "Double play despite aggressive slide". We recorded one or two for most second basemen in 2008. Gold Glovers Dustin Pedroia and Brandon Phillips had five apiece. Roberts had the most in baseball among second basemen with six.

Emmanuel Burriss

	Innings	Runs Saved
2008	282	3
2006-2008	282	3

	Good Plays	Misplays and Errors
Burriss 2008	15	9
Avg Second Baseman	10	8
Good Play/Misplay Pct		.559

Second Basemen

Akinori Iwamura

	Innings	Runs Saved
2008	1337	3
2006-2008	1346	3

	Good Plays	Misplays and Errors
Iwamura 2008	37	34
Avg Second Baseman	46	35
Good Play/Misplay Pct		.453

The arrival of Evan Longoria forced Iwamura from third base to second base in 2008. While not a complete success, Iwamura's transition wasn't a disaster either. He struggled with turning two early in the year, but he improved as the season progressed. Most of Iwamura's problems (wasted throws, miscues on hard-hit balls to his glove side) were the natural result of his inexperience at the position. Given time, Iwamura has the athletic ability to develop into an above-average defensive second baseman.

Aaron Miles

	Innings	Runs Saved
2008	500	3
2006-2008	1740	2

	Good Plays	Misplays and Errors
Miles 2008	17	16
Avg Second Baseman	17	13
Good Play/Misplay Pct		.447

Miles is below average athletically, but he is a solid second baseman. He is intelligent on the diamond and always seems to know where to go with the ball given the situation. He can play multiple positions, but his below-average arm makes him best suited for second base. Miles displays good footwork and gets his body in position to quickly start the double play. He hangs in well on aggressive slides, but he loses pace and accuracy when off balance. Miles has average range and also tracks balls well in the air. He has decent hands, but they suffer when he is on the run.

Juan Uribe

	Innings	Runs Saved
2008	362	1
2006-2008	362	1

	Good Plays	Misplays and Errors
Uribe 2008	13	7
Avg Second Baseman	15	11
Good Play/Misplay Pct		.586

Sean Rodriguez

	Innings	Runs Saved
2008	424	0
2006-2008	424	0

	Good Plays	Misplays and Errors
Rodriguez 2008	14	9
Avg Second Baseman	16	12
Good Play/Misplay Pct		.542

Alberto Callaspo

	Innings	Runs Saved
2008	366	-1
2006-2008	433	0

	Good Plays	Misplays and Errors
Callaspo 2008	9	2
Avg Second Baseman	12	9
Good Play/Misplay Pct		.774

Ian Kinsler

	Innings	Runs Saved
2008	1064	-7
2006-2008	3233	0

	Good Plays	Misplays and Errors
Kinsler 2008	38	33
Avg Second Baseman	45	34
Good Play/Misplay Pct		.467

Kinsler possesses great range at second base with solid first-step quickness. He made a lot of diving catches going to his right, throwing off-balance to execute plays to first base. With plus footwork and arm strength, Kinsler is very good at turning the double play as either the pivot man or the lead man. Kinsler's glaring weakness is his inability to make plays to his left. He struggles with his glove-to-hand transfer on balls to his glove side, often botching grounders that an average second baseman would easily convert. He also has trouble fielding softly hit groundballs cleanly. Still, Kinsler has the tools (and time) to become an average defensive second baseman.

Second Basemen

Freddy Sanchez

	Innings	Runs Saved
2008	1136	2
2006-2008	2574	-1

	Good Plays	Misplays and Errors
Sanchez 2008	37	30
Avg Second Baseman	43	32
Good Play/Misplay Pct		.484

Sanchez' fielding suffered due to injuries in 2008. He was plagued by both an inflamed rotator cuff and blurred vision due to getting a sliver of metal in his eye in 2007. When healthy, Sanchez uses his quickness and good instincts to field balls to his left and right. He holds his own turning the double play, possessing sound footwork and a good, accurate arm. However, he has struggled with flyballs long enough that it has become a fact of life rather than a phase. He often misreads balls in the shallow outfield, turning outs into hits.

Edgar Gonzalez

	Innings	Runs Saved
2008	560	-1
2006-2008	560	-1

	Good Plays	Misplays and Errors
Gonzalez 2008	12	18
Avg Second Baseman	19	15
Good Play/Misplay Pct		.337

While his brother Adrian has long had a reputation as a solid defensive first baseman, it was not known what the 30-year-old Edgar would bring to the table. Despite not being fleet of foot, Gonzalez covers ground well and takes good routes to the ball. This allows him to have above-average range, especially to his left. He also has an exceptionally quick release, which allows his somewhat below-average arm to play up. He can get sloppy with his footwork, though, almost as if he is trying to throw the ball before catching it. This causes him to mishandle some balls or make wild throws. He also isn't the best option for turning the double play. By and large, Gonzalez is a good fielder, but his consistent mistakes show why it took him so long to join his little brother in the Bigs.

Kelly Johnson

	Innings	Runs Saved
2008	1199	-3
2006-2008	2352	-2

	Good Plays	Misplays and Errors
Johnson 2008	37	45
Avg Second Baseman	47	36
Good Play/Misplay Pct		.385

Johnson is an average second baseman but continues to make strides with experience. With good positioning he showed improved range to his left in 2008, though it might have cost him a bit to his right. He especially struggles with backhanding the ball in the hole. On the plus side, he has a strong arm and turns two quickly.

Jeff Baker

	Innings	Runs Saved
2008	370	-2
2006-2008	370	-2

	Good Plays	Misplays and Errors
Baker 2008	9	9
Avg Second Baseman	14	10
Good Play/Misplay Pct		.432

Brendan Harris

	Innings	Runs Saved
2008	320	0
2006-2008	758	-3

	Good Plays	Misplays and Errors
Harris 2008	13	10
Avg Second Baseman	11	8
Good Play/Misplay Pct		.498

Alexi Casilla

	Innings	Runs Saved
2008	834	-2
2006-2008	1268	-3

	Good Plays	Misplays and Errors
Casilla 2008	47	27
Avg Second Baseman	30	23
Good Play/Misplay Pct		.570

Defensively speaking, Casilla suffers from a kind of home-field disadvantage. About half of his Defensive Misplays were groundballs. All but two of these misplays came at home on a surface that could be better used as a basketball court, and the other two came on the turface at

Second Basemen

Tropicana Field. Still, the slick surface is no match for Casilla's natural ability as a defender. He takes great angles to grounders and flyballs of every variety and flags them down with his impressive range. He combines that speed with excellent footwork around second base and gives the Twins one-half of an excellent double-play combination for years to come. If he can deal with the turf until the Twins move into their new ballpark, he could be one of the better defenders in the league.

Damion Easley

	Innings	Runs Saved
2008	539	-8
2006-2008	921	-3

	Good Plays	Misplays and Errors
Easley 2008	19	14
Avg Second Baseman	19	15
Good Play/Misplay Pct		.508

Easley saw more playing time than expected in 2008, due to Luis Castillo's injury woes. Like Castillo, Easley doesn't have the speed or agility that he once did, struggling with balls hit to the first base hole in particular. His lack of agility also cost him on the double play, as evidenced by his paltry GDP percentage. If we see Easley playing second base in the future, it will be by accident rather than design.

Ronny Cedeno

	Innings	Runs Saved
2008	273	-2
2006-2008	433	-4

	Good Plays	Misplays and Errors
Cedeno 2008	7	6
Avg Second Baseman	9	7
Good Play/Misplay Pct		.471

Tadahito Iguchi

	Innings	Runs Saved
2008	672	2
2006-2008	2925	-6

	Good Plays	Misplays and Errors
Iguchi 2008	15	8
Avg Second Baseman	23	17
Good Play/Misplay Pct		.588

Iguchi's inability to hit cost him playing time in 2008. He doesn't have spectacular range, but he has excellent mechanics and great footwork that enable him to make a variety of plays. His soft hands and quick release make him an asset on the double play.

Alexei Ramirez

	Innings	Runs Saved
2008	1017	-6
2006-2008	1017	-6

	Good Plays	Misplays and Errors
Ramirez 2008	40	27
Avg Second Baseman	39	29
Good Play/Misplay Pct		.530

Ramirez's ability to play outfield, shortstop, or second base gives the White Sox valuable flexibility. When defensive specialist Juan Uribe stopped hitting, Ramirez stepped in at second base and never looked back. He is exciting to watch, with incredible range on pop-ups that allows him to track them down behind first base and down the right field line. That range might decrease as he fills out his extraordinarily lean frame, but right now he reaches a lot of balls that most second baseman wouldn't, even if he doesn't always convert those opportunities into outs. He is fluid on the double-play pivot and possesses above-average accuracy and arm strength. Alexei has raw talent but a lot to learn playing second base. It's not likely he'll get the chance. He says shortstop is his natural position and, with Orlando Cabrera gone from the team, it looks like he'll be able to demonstrate his skills at short for the White Sox in 2009.

Eugenio Velez

	Innings	Runs Saved
2008	450	-6
2006-2008	462	-8

	Good Plays	Misplays and Errors
Velez 2008	15	23
Avg Second Baseman	15	11
Good Play/Misplay Pct		.332

Mark Loretta

	Innings	Runs Saved
2008	368	-3
2006-2008	1741	-8

	Good Plays	Misplays and Errors
Loretta 2008	6	8
Avg Second Baseman	13	10
Good Play/Misplay Pct		.364

Second Basemen

Dan Uggla

	Innings	Runs Saved
2008	1273	2
2006-2008	3961	-10

	Good Plays	Misplays and Errors
Uggla 2008	62	40
Avg Second Baseman	48	36
Good Play/Misplay Pct		.541

Infamous for his three-error performance at the All-Star game, Uggla's defense isn't quite as ugly as one would think. Granted, he has below-average range and occasionally boots balls hit right at him, but he is good at judging pop-ups and is willing to go deep into the outfield to get them. He makes more good plays than the average second baseman. His arm also allows him to make all the necessary throws. His worst crime might be having a really bad night in an exhibition game.

Mark DeRosa

	Innings	Runs Saved
2008	670	-9
2006-2008	1601	-12

	Good Plays	Misplays and Errors
DeRosa 2008	13	21
Avg Second Baseman	23	18
Good Play/Misplay Pct		.320

A defensive Swiss Army knife, DeRosa sees regular time at second base (his primary position), third base, and in the outfield. He has average range to both sides and fields almost everything he can reach. His arm is strong for second base but only average when he moves across the diamond. He is slow starting double plays. As an outfielder, he lacks the foot speed and quickness to be anything better than average. His ability to move around the field makes any manager's job easier when filling out the lineup card.

Felipe Lopez

	Innings	Runs Saved
2008	780	-13
2006-2008	1153	-16

	Good Plays	Misplays and Errors
Lopez 2008	20	27
Avg Second Baseman	28	22
Good Play/Misplay Pct		.361

Lopez's tools, including a very strong throwing arm, make him a viable option at second base, shortstop, or third base. After moving to the Cardinals, manager/mad scientist Tony LaRussa even used him in left field.

Lopez can be frustrating, though. He makes some tough plays and can improvise, using backhand flips, "touch" throws over runners in the baseline, and even bounce-throws from his belly (admittedly, some of these creative attempts are ill-advised). But he also botches much easier plays, occasionally appearing indecisive. Base on his plus/minus figures, he lacks range both right and left. He garnered "Worst Defensive Play of the Year – Nonchalance Category" honors on August 23 when he triple-hesitated on a Martin Prado grounder and failed to get an easy out. Still, underneath the miscues lies the potential to be a good defender.

Ray Durham

	Innings	Runs Saved
2008	738	-9
2006-2008	2905	-23

	Good Plays	Misplays and Errors
Durham 2008	11	21
Avg Second Baseman	26	20
Good Play/Misplay Pct		.285

Durham is a sure-handed fielder, but he no longer has the range he once had and looks stiff when he is on the run. His arm is below average, but it's accurate. He does lose some accuracy, however, when the runner slides hard into second. He transfers the ball quickly on the double play and shows good footwork when delivering the ball to second. Overall, defensively there are better options than Durham.

Luis Castillo

	Innings	Runs Saved
2008	690	-13
2006-2008	3087	-23

	Good Plays	Misplays and Errors
Castillo 2008	21	14
Avg Second Baseman	24	18
Good Play/Misplay Pct		.533

Once blessed with great speed and agility, Castillo's defensive abilities have been ravaged by injury. He struggles fielding any balls at the edge of his range, especially to his left. His poor showing on the double play in recent years is likely attributable to his reduced mobility as well. However, his throwing arm remains strong and helps him on the balls up the middle that he does reach.

Second Basemen

Rickie Weeks

	Innings	Runs Saved
2008	1056	0
2006-2008	2834	-24

	Good Plays	Misplays and Errors
Weeks 2008	36	59
Avg Second Baseman	42	32
Good Play/Misplay Pct		.317

Where to begin? We can start with the good: He is excellent at moving to his right for balls up the middle and making Jeterian jump-throws to first. He is also good at fielding throws from the catcher on stolen base attempts and quickly applying the tag.

Jeff Kent

	Innings	Runs Saved
2008	885	-11
2006-2008	2857	-41

	Good Plays	Misplays and Errors
Kent 2008	32	24
Avg Second Baseman	31	24
Good Play/Misplay Pct		.504

Kent never had exceptional speed or agility, and he had even less in 2008, the final season of his career. Still, he played a stiff-but-steady second base, relying on his instincts and over-shifting to compensate for his lack of range. He played especially close to the first base hole on lefties, which would explain the gap in his plus/minus numbers to his right and left. Due to his poor agility and throwing arm, Kent regularly ranked among the game's worst at turning the double play.

Third Basemen Evaluations

Year	League	Gold Glove Winners	Should Have Been
2003	AL	Eric Chavez	Eric Chavez
	NL	Scott Rolen	Adrian Beltre
2004	AL	Eric Chavez	Eric Chavez
	NL	Scott Rolen	Scott Rolen
2005	AL	Eric Chavez	Eric Chavez
	NL	Mike Lowell	David Bell
2006	AL	Eric Chavez	Adrian Beltre
	NL	Scott Rolen	Scott Rolen
2007	AL	Adrian Beltre	Brandon Inge
	NL	David Wright	Pedro Feliz
2008	AL	Adrian Beltre	Adrian Beltre
	NL	David Wright	David Wright

My Personal Ratings

Top Ten

1 Adrian Beltre, Sea
2 Pedro Feliz, Phi
3 Joe Crede, FA
4 David Wright, NYM
5 Scott Rolen, Tor
6 Evan Longoria, TB
7 Brandon Inge, Det
8 Mike Lowell, Bos
9 Jack Hannahan, Oak
10 Ryan Zimmerman, Was

Bottom Five

26 Melvin Mora, Bal
27 Ty Wigginton, Bal
28 Garrett Atkins, Col
29 Edwin Encarnacion, Cin
30 Mark Reynolds, Ari

Player teams based on transactions through February 11, 2009

Third Basemen

Pedro Feliz

	Innings	Runs Saved
2008	978	5
2006-2008	3571	50

	Good Plays	Misplays and Errors
Feliz 2008	30	27
Avg Third Baseman	37	33
Good Play/Misplay Pct		.494

Hall of Fame Broadcaster Harry Kalas sometimes refers to Feliz as "the Glove." This may sound like homerism, but consider that Kalas has seen Mike Schmidt and Scott Rolen play. He knows what good defense looks like. We estimate that Feliz has saved more runs playing third base in the last three years (50) than any other player in baseball. His great year in 2007 (24 runs saved) earned him a Fielding Bible Award.

Feliz plays in more often than most third basemen do, which allows him to field many soft hits and choppers but costs him a few groundballs in the hole. He doesn't always come up with balls you think he should, but only three of his 27 Defensive Misplays (a low total compared to an average third baseman) came on a throw. Add that to the fact that he made only eight errors in his nearly 980 innings in 2008, and you have a sure-handed third baseman with a golden arm.

Adrian Beltre

	Innings	Runs Saved
2008	1208	24
2006-2008	3846	48

	Good Plays	Misplays and Errors
Beltre 2008	62	29
Avg Third Baseman	45	40
Good Play/Misplay Pct		.653

Another season, another Gold Glove-caliber performance from Beltre. He was his second Gold Glove and his second Fielding Bible Award in 2008. Possessing outstanding balance and composure after fielding the ball, he is aware of the runner's speed and sets himself accordingly. His arm is above average in both its strength and accuracy. Scott Rolen sometimes gets more props, but no one plays better defense at third than Beltre.

Joe Crede

	Innings	Runs Saved
2008	835	9
2006-2008	2483	41

	Good Plays	Misplays and Errors
Crede 2008	52	31
Avg Third Baseman	34	30
Good Play/Misplay Pct		.596

The American Chiropractic Association's favorite player again fought through chronic back issues in 2008, spending a month on the disabled list. When healthy, he is one of the game's best third basemen. He has outstanding reflexes on hot shots down the line and fields in-between hops cleanly. Featuring a strong, accurate arm, the only thing Crede lacks is the ability to stay on the field.

Scott Rolen

	Innings	Runs Saved
2008	1007	10
2006-2008	3157	39

	Good Plays	Misplays and Errors
Rolen 2008	32	22
Avg Third Baseman	35	31
Good Play/Misplay Pct		.561

When healthy, Rolen remains a great third baseman, although it wouldn't kill broadcasters to ease off the "vacuum cleaner" schtick. The switch to the Rogers Centre's turf didn't bother him defensively. He still has incredible range and soft hands for his size (or anyone else's), and his throws are consistently strong and accurate. His reflexes also allow him to snare any hard-hit balls that come his way.

Brandon Inge

	Innings	Runs Saved
2008	324	1
2006-2008	3026	39

	Good Plays	Misplays and Errors
Inge 2008	18	7
Avg Third Baseman	14	12
Good Play/Misplay Pct		.694

Third Basemen

Ryan Zimmerman

	Innings	Runs Saved
2008	911	11
2006-2008	3711	32

	Good Plays	Misplays and Errors
Zimmerman 2008	48	32
Avg Third Baseman	36	32
Good Play/Misplay Pct		.569

First the good news: Zimmerman shows good awareness and anticipation, especially on bunts. Although he makes his share of diving stops, he sometimes allows routine grounders to clank off his glove. He has a habit of waving his glove at balls low to his left, like a first baseman scooping a throw, a maneuver that gets mixed results. His arm is his biggest weakness, though. Too often, he just doesn't get enough zip on his throws, sending loopy tosses to first base. He also tends to sidearm throws when it's not necessary. Yes, he had a bad shoulder in 2008, but it was his non-throwing shoulder. Zimmerman entered the league with a sterling defensive reputation and does a very good job, but he's not Fielding Bible Award caliber just yet.

Troy Glaus

	Innings	Runs Saved
2008	1243	7
2006-2008	3346	18

	Good Plays	Misplays and Errors
Glaus 2008	26	31
Avg Third Baseman	45	40
Good Play/Misplay Pct		.425

Traded to St. Louis over the winter, Glaus avoided the foot injuries that plagued him on Toronto's artificial turf. He sets his body well before throwing and tends to play shallow in order to discourage players from bunting on him. His arm strength is above average, but having Albert Pujols at first base might make Glaus look a little more accurate than he really is. Glaus has done a nice job to overcome his injuries from a few years ago to settle back into being an above-average third sacker.

Jack Hannahan

	Innings	Runs Saved
2008	984	16
2006-2008	1345	17

	Good Plays	Misplays and Errors
Hannahan 2008	53	33
Avg Third Baseman	35	31
Good Play/Misplay Pct		.586

Hannahan moved into a full-time role when Eric Chavez went down with an injury once again. His bat didn't cut it, but his glove did. He features an above-average arm and the ability to handle balls down the line. He covers plenty of ground in foul territory and has good field awareness. After his season ended abruptly on a diving catch, he will struggle to find playing time unless he starts hitting or Chavez gets hurt or moves to the designated hitter role.

Mike Lowell

	Innings	Runs Saved
2008	936	5
2006-2008	3559	14

	Good Plays	Misplays and Errors
Lowell 2008	27	16
Avg Third Baseman	36	31
Good Play/Misplay Pct		.598

If every play were a slow roller, Lowell would be the best third baseman around. Of course, he's not too shabby at the other stuff, either. Lowell guards the line quite well and has the arm strength to throw any runner out from his backhand. His biggest problem is with balls hit directly at him: He tries to play everything to his side, which causes hard-hit balls to sneak by his glove. Lowell remains a solid defensive third baseman.

Craig Counsell

	Innings	Runs Saved
2008	268	4
2006-2008	589	12

	Good Plays	Misplays and Errors
Counsell 2008	5	11
Avg Third Baseman	10	9
Good Play/Misplay Pct		.286

Counsell is versatile, handling second base, shortstop, or third base. At this point, that adaptability is his top defensive attribute. He doesn't make many errors, but he doesn't make all the plays either. His arm may no longer be strong enough to suffice at shortstop. When he's on, Counsell is smooth and quick on the release. Despite his age, he still shows good range.

Third Basemen

David Wright

	Innings	Runs Saved
2008	1433	5
2006-2008	4217	12

	Good Plays	Misplays and Errors
Wright 2008	78	40
Avg Third Baseman	50	44
Good Play/Misplay Pct		.632

One of the most durable players over the last four years, Wright continues to show why he is one of the best third basemen in the majors. Toss Wright's name in a hat with Adrian Beltre, Pedro Feliz, Joe Crede and Scott Rolen. If you pull any one of them out, you have a tremendous defensive third baseman pretty much indistinguishable from the others. Wright reacts very quickly to soft hits and bunts, and has a fluid motion on barehanded plays. He possesses above-average arm strength, although his accuracy is not always consistent. Wright's lateral range is also above average, and on diving plays he displays good footwork to set himself before the throw. He won his second straight Gold Glove in 2008.

Blake DeWitt

	Innings	Runs Saved
2008	728	11
2006-2008	728	11

	Good Plays	Misplays and Errors
DeWitt 2008	27	32
Avg Third Baseman	30	27
Good Play/Misplay Pct		.426

In his first major league season, DeWitt established himself as an excellent, versatile defender. He started the season at the hot corner and was exceptional with the glove. He was particularly strong to his backhand side and handled all his routine chances. DeWitt didn't hit, though, and was sent down to the minors after the acquisition of Casey Blake. DeWitt played second base in the minors (he had played second base earlier in his career), and he got the call back to Los Angeles when Jeff Kent went down. He proved just as proficient at second as he was at third.

DeWitt has a good arm but not a rocket, suggesting his future may be at second. He vacuums up many difficult chances, and most of his mistakes stem from a lack of experience rather than skill.

Andy Marte

	Innings	Runs Saved
2008	581	2
2006-2008	1145	11

	Good Plays	Misplays and Errors
Marte 2008	17	17
Avg Third Baseman	24	21
Good Play/Misplay Pct		.468

The midseason trade of Casey Blake made Marte the Indians' third baseman by default. While improving his hitting (relatively speaking), Marte also proved himself a capable defender. With quicker feet than one would expect, he plays well off the line and moves aggressively to his left. He has a strong, accurate arm despite a tendency to throw somewhat sidearm. Still only 25-years-old, Marte could contribute for the Indians if his bat can catch up with his glove.

Marco Scutaro

	Innings	Runs Saved
2008	332	13
2006-2008	706	10

	Good Plays	Misplays and Errors
Scutaro 2008	13	10
Avg Third Baseman	13	11
Good Play/Misplay Pct		.534

Evan Longoria

	Innings	Runs Saved
2008	1046	9
2006-2008	1046	9

	Good Plays	Misplays and Errors
Longoria 2008	49	27
Avg Third Baseman	40	35
Good Play/Misplay Pct		.615

The American League Rookie of the Year quickly established himself as one of the best defensive third basemen in the league. He is solid on bunts, making the running play toward the infield grass. With his quickness and excellent hands, he can make very difficult plays to his left. He also pairs a plus arm with great accuracy. Only 23, Longoria does make some mental errors. He lost some balls in the Trop's dome and overthrew the ball or misfired when he had opportunities to make plays down the line. Look for Longoria to follow his strong rookie campaign with continued success.

Third Basemen

Wes Helms

	Innings	Runs Saved
2008	325	5
2006-2008	861	8

	Good Plays	Misplays and Errors
Helms 2008	17	9
Avg Third Baseman	12	10
Good Play/Misplay Pct		.624

Ian Stewart

	Innings	Runs Saved
2008	531	4
2006-2008	573	8

	Good Plays	Misplays and Errors
Stewart 2008	27	18
Avg Third Baseman	21	18
Good Play/Misplay Pct		.569

Stewart is still a bit raw defensively, but he appears to have the tools to develop into a top third baseman. He got an extended look in 2008 when Todd Helton spent time on the DL, moving Garret Atkins over to first. He has a strong arm, yet can be wild at times. Stewart possesses soft hands and has good athleticism, which enables him to excel at fielding bunts and softly hit balls.

Kevin Youkilis

	Innings	Runs Saved
2008	252	7
2006-2008	452	7

	Good Plays	Misplays and Errors
Youkilis 2008	5	8
Avg Third Baseman	11	10
Good Play/Misplay Pct		.355

Geoff Blum

	Innings	Runs Saved
2008	600	5
2006-2008	854	7

	Good Plays	Misplays and Errors
Blum 2008	18	14
Avg Third Baseman	23	20
Good Play/Misplay Pct		.531

Blum spent the majority of the 2008 season at third base, but he's a versatile fielder who can play all of the infield positions. He is a solid defender, displaying decent range to both sides, and has an average throwing arm. Blum profiles better at either first base or third base, but he will likely return to being a utility guy, just filling in whenever and wherever he's needed.

Willy Aybar

	Innings	Runs Saved
2008	358	3
2006-2008	814	3

	Good Plays	Misplays and Errors
Aybar 2008	17	13
Avg Third Baseman	14	12
Good Play/Misplay Pct		.535

Chipper Jones

	Innings	Runs Saved
2008	987	10
2006-2008	2956	1

	Good Plays	Misplays and Errors
Jones 2008	29	27
Avg Third Baseman	36	32
Good Play/Misplay Pct		.486

Jones is a good defender, but he lacks the range he once had. Still, he looks comfortable charging bunts or slow-rolling grounders. Chipper positions himself well but seems to have a delayed reaction at times, especially on balls hit down the line. His arm remains strong and accurate.

Russell Branyan

	Innings	Runs Saved
2008	276	1
2006-2008	702	1

	Good Plays	Misplays and Errors
Branyan 2008	4	11
Avg Third Baseman	11	10
Good Play/Misplay Pct		.242

Andy LaRoche

	Innings	Runs Saved
2008	502	0
2006-2008	739	1

	Good Plays	Misplays and Errors
LaRoche 2008	21	16
Avg Third Baseman	21	18
Good Play/Misplay Pct		.536

LaRoche has an adequate arm for his position, although his throws sometimes lack accuracy. He can make the brilliant diving play, but more often than not he'll knock it down rather than pick it and get the out. Lacking great defensive instincts, LaRoche grades out slightly below average.

Chone Figgins

	Innings	Runs Saved
2008	914	9
2006-2008	2031	0

	Good Plays	Misplays and Errors
Figgins 2008	32	33
Avg Third Baseman	33	29
Good Play/Misplay Pct		.460

Figgins uses his quick reflexes and speed to make the most difficult plays seem routine, causing many people to overlook his ability. His horizontal range might be his biggest strength, but he also handles bunts and slowly hit grounders well. His only real problem is his tendency to hold on to the ball too long. This hesitation causes him to over-think and can lead to erratic throws. He isn't your prototypical third baseman, but Figgins might be the most athletic one in the game today.

Bill Hall

	Innings	Runs Saved
2008	899	-1
2006-2008	985	-1

	Good Plays	Misplays and Errors
Hall 2008	40	36
Avg Third Baseman	34	30
Good Play/Misplay Pct		.494

The Brewers have never seemed to like Hall's defense, but he turned in a solid campaign in 2008. He makes some diving stops and is adept at barehanded pickups and off-balance throws. Still, he can be inconsistent, as some routine balls get past him. Hall's arm is strong enough to consistently make good throws to first base from his knees. He played a handful of games at second base and looked less comfortable there. If he stays at third, he'll need to work on fielding bunts.

Jose Castillo

	Innings	Runs Saved
2008	880	-2
2006-2008	1133	-1

	Good Plays	Misplays and Errors
Castillo 2008	31	31
Avg Third Baseman	28	25
Good Play/Misplay Pct		.468

Castillo is not a terrible fielder, but he is a below-

average third baseman. He has decent range, covering a bit more ground to his left. He makes the routine plays, but his hands are inconsistent on the move or when balls are hit hard right at him. Although often erratic, his arm is strong enough for third base. He is quick on his throws to second base to get the double play rolling.

Aramis Ramirez

	Innings	Runs Saved
2008	1283	-9
2006-2008	3727	-2

	Good Plays	Misplays and Errors
Ramirez 2008	39	39
Avg Third Baseman	39	35
Good Play/Misplay Pct		.468

After showing flashes of brilliance in 2007, Ramirez seemed to regress in 2008. He struggled with glove-side balls hit more than a step away. He had the same number of misplays plus errors as good plays (39). For a third baseman that's not a good ratio, though not horrible. On a more positive note, Ramirez continues to have one of the strongest and most accurate arms in the league. He just needs to put himself in better position to use it.

Hank Blalock

	Innings	Runs Saved
2008	263	-1
2006-2008	1665	-3

	Good Plays	Misplays and Errors
Blalock 2008	9	6
Avg Third Baseman	9	8
Good Play/Misplay Pct		.569

Juan Uribe

	Innings	Runs Saved
2008	460	-3
2006-2008	460	-3

	Good Plays	Misplays and Errors
Uribe 2008	18	21
Avg Third Baseman	20	18
Good Play/Misplay Pct		.430

Third Basemen

Kevin Kouzmanoff

	Innings	Runs Saved
2008	1379	-1
2006-2008	2530	-4

	Good Plays	Misplays and Errors
Kouzmanoff 2008	49	37
Avg Third Baseman	49	43
Good Play/Misplay Pct		.538

The Mashin' Macedonian's glovework was mostly lost in San Diego's disappointing season, but he showed some improvement. Although not a fast man, he anticipates the ball well, and he uses this ability to snag a ton of hard-hit balls, particularly to his right. His strong arm also allows him to make spectacular plays from the far reaches of his territory. What is particularly disappointing about Kouzmanoff is that he doesn't make a wide variety of good defensive plays. Thirty-eight of his 49 good fielding plays were acrobatic plays on groundballs or line drives. Although quick as a cat, Kouzmanoff has some struggles. He has trouble coming up with reachable pop-ups, and he also struggles with the catch-and-tag. As long as Kouzmanoff continues to stop bullets headed to the left field corner, however, the Padres will take the good with the bad.

Brendan Harris

	Innings	Runs Saved
2008	256	-4
2006-2008	301	-4

	Good Plays	Misplays and Errors
Harris 2008	14	4
Avg Third Baseman	8	7
Good Play/Misplay Pct		.755

Alex Gordon

	Innings	Runs Saved
2008	1180	-9
2006-2008	2315	-4

	Good Plays	Misplays and Errors
Gordon 2008	34	46
Avg Third Baseman	43	38
Good Play/Misplay Pct		.394

Gordon has good reflexes and looks best on plays that require quickness, such as line drives and diving stops. He's also adept at barehanding slow rollers and firing quickly. But the more time he has to make the throw, the worse the results. He has a very strong arm but needs to work on his accuracy. Gordon saw his share of one-hoppers ricochet off his glove in 2008 and fared much worse on balls hit to his left than he did in his rookie campaign. He had 46 misplays and errors compared to 34 good fielding plays, a ratio that needs to improve.

Greg Dobbs

	Innings	Runs Saved
2008	327	-4
2006-2008	747	-6

	Good Plays	Misplays and Errors
Dobbs 2008	18	16
Avg Third Baseman	13	12
Good Play/Misplay Pct		.498

Brian Buscher

	Innings	Runs Saved
2008	519	-2
2006-2008	721	-7

	Good Plays	Misplays and Errors
Buscher 2008	14	22
Avg Third Baseman	20	17
Good Play/Misplay Pct		.359

Prior to the 2008 season, Buscher focused on his footwork and fielding to help his chances of locking down the Twins' third base job. He stepped up, especially offensively, earning himself playing time over the team's other third base options. That's not to say he didn't have his issues with the glove, but he has decent reflexes, a good arm, and enough range to make the plays he should.

Rich Aurilia

	Innings	Runs Saved
2008	428	-2
2006-2008	961	-7

	Good Plays	Misplays and Errors
Aurilia 2008	14	12
Avg Third Baseman	12	11
Good Play/Misplay Pct		.507

Third Basemen

Chris Davis

	Innings	Runs Saved
2008	276	-7
2006-2008	276	-7

	Good Plays	Misplays and Errors
Davis 2008	5	12
Avg Third Baseman	10	9
Good Play/Misplay Pct		.268

Casey Blake

	Innings	Runs Saved
2008	1105	-3
2006-2008	2314	-8

	Good Plays	Misplays and Errors
Blake 2008	45	30
Avg Third Baseman	38	34
Good Play/Misplay Pct		.569

Blake is the definition of a steady defender. He tends to play deep off the third base line, allowing him to cover the most ground, especially toward the shortstop hole. He has the quick first step that is necessary for any corner infielder, and his arm is accurate even when he's on the run. He has not handled the bunt well.

Robb Quinlan

	Innings	Runs Saved
2008	259	-4
2006-2008	442	-8

	Good Plays	Misplays and Errors
Quinlan 2008	9	11
Avg Third Baseman	10	8
Good Play/Misplay Pct		.419

Jorge Cantu

	Innings	Runs Saved
2008	1067	-8
2006-2008	1071	-8

	Good Plays	Misplays and Errors
Cantu 2008	32	38
Avg Third Baseman	37	33
Good Play/Misplay Pct		.426

A former second baseman, Cantu played a sub-par third base in 2008. His first-step quickness and excellent footwork enable him to convert softly hit grounders into outs, and his above-average to plus arm comes in handy when charging bunts and throwing out the runner at first.

However, he has trouble reacting to balls hit hard right at him. He also struggles with getting in position to catch hard-hit line drives. At the hot corner, Cantu will need to improve his reactions in order to become an average defender.

Mike Lamb

	Innings	Runs Saved
2008	461	-7
2006-2008	1141	-9

	Good Plays	Misplays and Errors
Lamb 2008	17	14
Avg Third Baseman	17	15
Good Play/Misplay Pct		.517

Carlos Guillen

	Innings	Runs Saved
2008	750	-9
2006-2008	750	-9

	Good Plays	Misplays and Errors
Guillen 2008	24	28
Avg Third Baseman	32	28
Good Play/Misplay Pct		.430

Guillen started the season at first base but soon switched positions with third baseman Miguel Cabrera when it became clear that neither player could handle his original position. Guillen came up as a shortstop but was moved to first (and then third) by the Tigers in an effort to keep him healthy. He brings soft hands and above-average range to his right to third. Guillen initially had some trouble with the throw to first base, but his arm proved sound once he had time to stretch it out. Although the move from shortstop was supposed to keep Guillen healthy, he only played 115 games in the field in 2008. He will be an asset whenever he's on the field, but how often that will be is uncertain.

Aubrey Huff

	Innings	Runs Saved
2008	275	0
2006-2008	1097	-10

	Good Plays	Misplays and Errors
Huff 2008	14	10
Avg Third Baseman	11	9
Good Play/Misplay Pct		.552

Third Basemen

Melvin Mora

	Innings	Runs Saved
2008	1060	-11
2006-2008	3434	-12

	Good Plays	Misplays and Errors
Mora 2008	39	34
Avg Third Baseman	43	37
Good Play/Misplay Pct		.502

Mora has tended to play more toward the line recently. This, combined with his declining range, helps explain his poor numbers to his left. Injuries (knee and hamstring) and age also might have factored into his defensive struggles.

Alex Rodriguez

	Innings	Runs Saved
2008	1126	-2
2006-2008	3744	-13

	Good Plays	Misplays and Errors
Rodriguez 2008	39	23
Avg Third Baseman	40	35
Good Play/Misplay Pct		.599

The Yankee should-be shortstop remains stuck at the hot corner, where his athletic ability and fantastic hand-eye coordination have helped him become a better-than-average third baseman. When playing behind the bag, Rodriguez gets to behave like the Gold Glove shortstop he once was and field balls that most third basemen wouldn't reach.

He does have his issues, though. Bunts continue to give him fits. In particular, he struggles with bunts that require him to barehand the ball and throw quickly to first. This can no longer be excused as inexperience—he just hasn't improved in this facet of the game. Also, his glove hand is slow vertically, which proves problematic when a ball is hit between his legs. You have to protect those wickets, A-Rod.

Ramon Vazquez

	Innings	Runs Saved
2008	533	-7
2006-2008	1166	-13

	Good Plays	Misplays and Errors
Vazquez 2008	15	18
Avg Third Baseman	19	17
Good Play/Misplay Pct		.423

Vazquez's .936 fielding percentage at third base is Betty-ugly, but it doesn't tell the whole story. He failed to come up with a few balls that he should have, and he struggled at times to make easy throws, but he displayed solid range and impressive quickness for a journeyman utility infielder. He also has shown that his arm can play at third base. While he hasn't made a convincing case for full-time status, Vazquez has proven to be an acceptable short-term replacement.

Mark Reynolds

	Innings	Runs Saved
2008	1288	-9
2006-2008	2131	-14

	Good Plays	Misplays and Errors
Reynolds 2008	46	67
Avg Third Baseman	44	39
Good Play/Misplay Pct		.377

Reynolds has the raw ability to make outstanding plays, but his inconsistency makes him one of the worst third basemen in the game. He has a strong arm but—you can guess where this is going—needs to improve his accuracy. He had 67 misplays and errors last year, the most in baseball at all positions and 20 more than the next highest at the hot corner. Twenty-four of them involved throwing. If Reynolds' works at his issues, they are fixable. He has the tools to be a dependable defender.

Ty Wigginton

	Innings	Runs Saved
2008	652	-6
2006-2008	1574	-23

	Good Plays	Misplays and Errors
Wigginton 2008	22	21
Avg Third Baseman	23	20
Good Play/Misplay Pct		.480

The Astros' Opening Day third baseman moved to left field when Carlos Lee went down. Wigginton is not a good third baseman and has a ton of problems with balls hit to his right. Maybe they were doing him a favor moving him to left field, but he didn't look comfortable in the outfield, often misreading balls hit over his head and lacking the mobility to make up for it. He has a strong arm, suggesting that third base might be the spot where he can cause the least damage.

Third Basemen

Jose Bautista

	Innings	Runs Saved
2008	766	-3
2006-2008	2098	-27

	Good Plays	Misplays and Errors
Bautista 2008	39	32
Avg Third Baseman	34	30
Good Play/Misplay Pct		.518

Bautista has the tools to be a decent third baseman, but he is inconsistent. He combines good range with an above-average, accurate arm. He reacts well when moving to his right and can get up quickly and make a strong throw when he dives in that direction. It's Bautista's hands that are problematic. When a ball is hit to his glove side or right at him, it can leave him flat-footed and victimized. He charges groundballs well and throws accurately on the run, but he is less accurate on long throws.

Garrett Atkins

	Innings	Runs Saved
2008	797	-8
2006-2008	3497	-32

	Good Plays	Misplays and Errors
Atkins 2008	27	20
Avg Third Baseman	29	26
Good Play/Misplay Pct		.543

Atkins has regressed defensively at third base. He has adequate hands and a strong arm, but he lacks range and quickness, diving for balls that better defenders would be able to handle on their feet. He doesn't make a lot of mistakes, but he just doesn't get to balls that most other third basemen do.

Edwin Encarnacion

	Innings	Runs Saved
2008	1237	-17
2006-2008	3336	-43

	Good Plays	Misplays and Errors
Encarnacion 2008	37	47
Avg Third Baseman	41	36
Good Play/Misplay Pct		.409

Encarnacion is to third base what the bull is to the china shop. In his last three years he has posted plus/minus totals of -15, -15 and -21. Suffice it to say, he is a work in progress. His strong arm could be a weapon if he could learn to control it. With time, Encarnacion should improve in all areas of his game. There's nowhere to go but up.

Shortstops Evaluations

Year	League	Gold Glove Winners	Should Have Been
2003	AL	Alex Rodriguez	Alex Rodriguez
	NL	Edgar Renteria	Adam Everett
2004	AL	Derek Jeter	Miguel Tejada
	NL	Cesar Izturis	Cesar Izturis
2005	AL	Derek Jeter	Juan Uribe
	NL	Omar Vizquel	Adam Everett
2006	AL	Derek Jeter	Alex Gonzalez
	NL	Omar Vizquel	Adam Everett
2007	AL	Orlando Cabrera	John McDonald
	NL	Jimmy Rollins	Troy Tulowitzki
2008	AL	Michael Young	Erick Aybar
	NL	Jimmy Rollins	Jimmy Rollins

My Personal Ratings

Top Ten

1 Jimmy Rollins, Phi
2 Troy Tulowitzki, Col
3 Jack Wilson, Pit
4 Adam Everett, Det
5 Erick Aybar, LAA
6 Yunel Escobar, Atl
7 Cesar Izturis, Bal
8 Omar Vizquel, Tex
9 J.J. Hardy, Mil
10 John McDonald, Tor

Bottom Five

26 Derek Jeter, NYY
27 Yuniesky Betancourt, Sea
28 Julio Lugo, Bos
29 David Eckstein, SD
30 Jeff Keppinger, Cin

Player teams based on transactions through February 11, 2009

Shortstops

Adam Everett

	Innings	Runs Saved
2008	364	-1
2006-2008	2191	48

	Good Plays	Misplays and Errors
Everett 2008	19	13
Avg Shortstop	17	15
Good Play/Misplay Pct		.554

From 2003 through 2007, Everett was the best shortstop in the game. It wasn't even close. Even in his partial season of 2007, when he was injured and only played in 66 games, he had the fourth highest plus/minus score (+18) at shortstop. How many Gold Gloves did he win in that time period? None. It was a crime. Why did it happen? Because he didn't hit well enough to get on the radar screen. He should have won at least three or four Gold Gloves.

Adam, here at *The Fielding Bible* we recognize and applaud you.

Jimmy Rollins

	Innings	Runs Saved
2008	1168	15
2006-2008	3987	33

	Good Plays	Misplays and Errors
Rollins 2008	65	33
Avg Shortstop	48	40
Good Play/Misplay Pct		.626

Rollins might be the only shortstop who possesses every single skill necessary to be a great fielder. Not only does he have great reactions, but his range is second to none. Add in his arm strength and throwing accuracy, and you have the best defensive shortstops in the game right now. While we believe that Rollins was second best to Troy Tulowitzki when he won his 2007 Gold Glove, he definitely earned it in 2008. And he received his first Fielding Bible Award as well.

Omar Vizquel

	Innings	Runs Saved
2008	658	8
2006-2008	3158	29

	Good Plays	Misplays and Errors
Vizquel 2008	25	10
Avg Shortstop	22	19
Good Play/Misplay Pct		.680

Vizquel is a shadow of his former self, but most 41-year-olds are. Recognizing that he has lost a step or two, he positions himself well according to the situation. He is as dependable as ever, refusing to make mistakes. More than anything else, his arm strength has declined, which occasionally causes him to rush plays and make errant throws. Even if Vizquel is 75 percent of what he used to be, that's still pretty good.

Troy Tulowitzki

	Innings	Runs Saved
2008	863	2
2006-2008	2458	29

	Good Plays	Misplays and Errors
Tulowitzki 2008	39	26
Avg Shortstop	38	32
Good Play/Misplay Pct		.560

Tulowitzki failed to live up to the lofty expectations his rookie season created, but it is hard to call him a disappointment considering how well he played despite missing six weeks with a torn quadricep muscle. He made every kind of play you could ask from an elite shortstop, while making few mistakes. Once Tulowitzki was fully healthy, you could see why scouts drool over him. He has great range, often fielding balls the third baseman or second baseman would be expected to handle. His arm is as strong and accurate as any other shortstop's. He also possesses great quickness, which helps him turn more forceouts into double plays than just about anybody. A down year from Tulo is still better than a good year from many other shortstops. For a better look at his great 2007 season, take a look at the article on page 251.

Jack Wilson

	Innings	Runs Saved
2008	696	12
2006-2008	2968	25

	Good Plays	Misplays and Errors
Wilson 2008	41	22
Avg Shortstop	31	27
Good Play/Misplay Pct		.613

Wilson is an exceptional shortstop who makes all the plays. He has a quick release but lacks the big arm that many shortstops have, occasionally giving first basemen trouble with low throws. Overall, he's a smart player who always hustles and backs up his teammates. Wilson has traditionally been stronger to his right than to his left, a trend that continued in 2008.

Shortstops

J.J. Hardy

	Innings	Runs Saved
2008	1268	12
2006-2008	2798	24

	Good Plays	Misplays and Errors
Hardy 2008	52	34
Avg Shortstop	49	42
Good Play/Misplay Pct		.565

Hardy has above-average range, good hands, and a strong arm. He reaches most balls to his right, but he is better going to his left. His arm is stronger and more accurate when moving in that direction. He loses some accuracy and has a slower release when he fields grounders in the hole. Hardy's release can be slow turning the double play, but he delivers accurate and strong throws while avoiding the oncoming runner. He also is accurate in delivering the ball to the second baseman. Hardy will occasionally misplay groundballs when he has to rush.

Clint Barmes

	Innings	Runs Saved
2008	285	0
2006-2008	1393	23

	Good Plays	Misplays and Errors
Barmes 2008	12	7
Avg Shortstop	13	11
Good Play/Misplay Pct		.593

John McDonald

	Innings	Runs Saved
2008	478	-2
2006-2008	1939	21

	Good Plays	Misplays and Errors
McDonald 2008	21	16
Avg Shortstop	17	14
Good Play/Misplay Pct		.527

Jason Bartlett

	Innings	Runs Saved
2008	1097	-2
2006-2008	3171	20

	Good Plays	Misplays and Errors
Bartlett 2008	43	42
Avg Shortstop	42	35
Good Play/Misplay Pct		.465

An auxiliary piece of the Great Garza-for-Young

Swindle, Bartlett stabilized a Rays infield that included a rookie at third base and a former third baseman at second. Epitomizing the shortstop role as commander of the infield, Bartlett took charge of any ball near him, always making the aggressive play. He has a quick first step, great range up the middle, and a strong arm that turns seemingly impossible plays into outs. He is fearless on pop-ups, not giving up until an outfielder calls him off. Although he might have gone from underrated to overrated faster than you can say "David Eckstein," Bartlett brings confidence to an otherwise inexperienced infield and looks effortless in the process.

Jose Reyes

	Innings	Runs Saved
2008	1420	-2
2006-2008	4171	20

	Good Plays	Misplays and Errors
Reyes 2008	51	40
Avg Shortstop	51	43
Good Play/Misplay Pct		.520

Reyes had a high error total at 17, but that is partly because of his aggressiveness. His quick reactions complement his speed, giving him great range to his right and up the middle. He turns the double play with a quick release and a willingness to hang in against aggressive slides. His arm is top of the line, allowing him to recover from bobbles and make the play deep in the hole. Expect Reyes to continue to improve in all facets of the game as he enters his prime.

Tony F. Pena

	Innings	Runs Saved
2008	592	-2
2006-2008	1950	16

	Good Plays	Misplays and Errors
Pena 2008	24	25
Avg Shortstop	22	18
Good Play/Misplay Pct		.449

Pena's fielding doesn't come close to outweighing his paltry offensive contributions. What he has going for him is an arm so strong that he should pitch mop-up duty. Pena always sets himself quickly and throws on target. He can make some amazing plays deep in the hole and throws well on the run. On the downside, he's not the greatest ball-stopper, and pop-ups behind short can lead to communication problems and drops.

293

Shortstops

Yunel Escobar

	Innings	Runs Saved
2008	1106	12
2006-2008	1469	13

	Good Plays	Misplays and Errors
Escobar 2008	44	43
Avg Shortstop	47	40
Good Play/Misplay Pct		.465

Able to make 360-degree turns on the run, Escobar converts plays with high degrees of difficulty. He has great quickness and reaction skills, and his plus-plus arm strength is recognized throughout the league. He still needs to improve in some aspects of the game, though. He sometimes stabs at balls to his left. He needs to let his speed and athletic ability guide him to balls and then field them cleanly. Overall, Escobar performed as an elite shortstop and gives the Braves a valuable asset at a key defensive position.

Mike Aviles

	Innings	Runs Saved
2008	748	13
2006-2008	748	13

	Good Plays	Misplays and Errors
Aviles 2008	38	27
Avg Shortstop	30	25
Good Play/Misplay Pct		.545

Aviles doesn't look like your typical shortstop, as he has a thicker build than many of his counterparts. He hit very well after bursting onto the scene as a 27-year-old in 2008, so the assumption might be that he is a lousy fielder. . .otherwise, where has he been? Truth is, Aviles gets the job done at shortstop. He can make the diving stops, has the reflexes to handle bad hops, and has a good enough arm. He does have his weaknesses, though. He is not always smooth, his throws can be wild, and his footwork needs improvement.

Nick Punto

	Innings	Runs Saved
2008	531	6
2006-2008	889	13

	Good Plays	Misplays and Errors
Punto 2008	24	16
Avg Shortstop	23	20
Good Play/Misplay Pct		.560

After playing mostly second and third base in previous years, Punto did a great job at shortstop in 2008. He seems to do everything well. He displays great range to both sides, possesses a strong arm, runs a smooth double play (leading major-league shortstops in GDP percentage), and is exceptionally quick with his pivot. He also gets good reads on soft flyballs hit down the line, in foul territory, and in the shallow outfield.

Khalil Greene

	Innings	Runs Saved
2008	934	-2
2006-2008	3328	13

	Good Plays	Misplays and Errors
Greene 2008	32	24
Avg Shortstop	34	29
Good Play/Misplay Pct		.531

Greene plays up the middle on lefties and deep in the hole on righties. His outstanding footwork when charging or surrounding balls and his quick release are the keys to his game. A smooth, somewhat flashy player, Greene gets the job done on the double play.

Cesar Izturis

	Innings	Runs Saved
2008	1001	14
2006-2008	1830	11

	Good Plays	Misplays and Errors
Izturis 2008	40	28
Avg Shortstop	43	36
Good Play/Misplay Pct		.548

The prototypical good field/no hit shortstop, Izturis shows good footwork, especially on balls in the hole between third base and shortstop. He also has an accurate arm with a quick release. Izturis had his best year defensively since his Gold Glove year in 2004 and he still ranks among the game's best defensive shortstops.

Ryan Theriot

	Innings	Runs Saved
2008	1266	5
2006-2008	2142	9

	Good Plays	Misplays and Errors
Theriot 2008	48	44
Avg Shortstop	45	39
Good Play/Misplay Pct		.481

Theriot has strong range up the middle and good hands, but he has occasional trouble when he backs up on groundballs instead of attacking them. His arm is an asset when turning two or completing a tough play. He is tremendous on any kind of ball hit in the air, both line drives and pop-ups. His plus/minus was +5 on balls in the air, and he had the most good fielding plays on flies and liners with 15 by a wide margin (Jason Barlett was

Shortstops

second with 9). A favorite of veterans and rookies alike, Theriot brings a steady glove to the Cubs infield.

Rafael Furcal

	Innings	Runs Saved
2008	296	0
2006-2008	2877	9

	Good Plays	Misplays and Errors
Furcal 2008	12	6
Avg Shortstop	11	9
Good Play/Misplay Pct		.629

Furcal missed a majority of the 2008 season with a herniated disk, and he did not move nearly as fluidly upon his return. Before the injury, Furcal displayed excellent range and one of the strongest throwing arms at the position. He is accurate throwing the ball over the top, but he loses accuracy when he throws sidearm. While he makes a lot of outstanding plays, he also shows a lack of concentration at times, which can lead to errors on routine plays. He attacks groundballs well on double-play opportunities and has a quick release around the bag, using his athleticism to avoid aggressive baserunners.

Cristian Guzman

	Innings	Runs Saved
2008	1174	12
2006-2008	1550	8

	Good Plays	Misplays and Errors
Guzman 2008	33	37
Avg Shortstop	47	40
Good Play/Misplay Pct		.431

Guzman is one of the most fundamentally sound shortstops around. He is always prepared for the next action he has to take. He doesn't have the best range, but he positions himself well and takes great angles on groundballs, which allows him to maximize his abilities. He has a very accurate arm and a quick release, which makes his arm appear stronger than it is. The biggest problem with Guzman is that he doesn't always consider the baserunner, leading to rushed or delayed throws and runners reaching base when they shouldn't. Overall, Guzman combines his talent with his intelligence and positively impacts his team.

Alex Cora

	Innings	Runs Saved
2008	386	0
2006-2008	1022	8

	Good Plays	Misplays and Errors
Cora 2008	19	12
Avg Shortstop	16	13
Good Play/Misplay Pct		.574

Jed Lowrie

	Innings	Runs Saved
2008	386	6
2006-2008	386	6

	Good Plays	Misplays and Errors
Lowrie 2008	9	6
Avg Shortstop	12	10
Good Play/Misplay Pct		.560

Omar Quintanilla

	Innings	Runs Saved
2008	289	3
2006-2008	357	6

	Good Plays	Misplays and Errors
Quintanilla 2008	10	8
Avg Shortstop	12	10
Good Play/Misplay Pct		.515

Brendan Ryan

	Innings	Runs Saved
2008	255	2
2006-2008	419	5

	Good Plays	Misplays and Errors
Ryan 2008	6	5
Avg Shortstop	10	9
Good Play/Misplay Pct		.505

Eric Bruntlett

	Innings	Runs Saved
2008	280	1
2006-2008	774	4

	Good Plays	Misplays and Errors
Bruntlett 2008	19	11
Avg Shortstop	11	9
Good Play/Misplay Pct		.595

Shortstops

Erick Aybar

	Innings	Runs Saved
2008	785	6
2006-2008	939	3

	Good Plays	Misplays and Errors
Aybar 2008	55	35
Avg Shortstop	34	29
Good Play/Misplay Pct		.572

All Aybar's defensive game lacks is consistency. At times, he can be absolutely brilliant, making plays he has no right to make. He has an extremely strong throwing arm, which enables him to get outs from deep in the hole. His arm is so strong that he manages to get plenty of velocity on his throws even when he doesn't get a chance to set himself, and his superb range allows him to get to more balls than most shortstops. He doesn't panic when something goes wrong, like a bobbled ball or when another infielder fails to cover the bag. Aybar's weakness is that he makes too many careless mistakes, letting balls skip off or under his glove. If he can demonstrate more consistency, Aybar will join the defensive elite at shortstop.

Maicer Izturis

	Innings	Runs Saved
2008	448	3
2006-2008	520	2

	Good Plays	Misplays and Errors
Izturis 2008	20	7
Avg Shortstop	16	13
Good Play/Misplay Pct		.708

Izturis is Erick Aybar-lite. He can make most of the same plays as the other Angels shortstop and might be a better ball-stopper. The big advantage Aybar has over Izturis is his throwing arm. Izturis's arm is acceptable for a shortstop but not strong. He shows good instincts and reflexes but is prone to the occasional mental lapse. He is very quick, both in getting to his feet after diving and transferring the ball from his glove to his throwing hand. Izturis also can handle second base and third base. His lack of a cannon arm is less noticeable at those positions.

Juan Castro

	Innings	Runs Saved
2008	409	-5
2006-2008	1047	1

	Good Plays	Misplays and Errors
Castro 2008	20	15
Avg Shortstop	17	15
Good Play/Misplay Pct		.531

A utility player by trade, Castro stepped into the black hole at shortstop for the Orioles after the All-Star break. In a word, he's decent. He doesn't have an especially strong arm, but his positioning and footwork made him especially effective on balls hit to his right.

Orlando Cabrera

	Innings	Runs Saved
2008	1390	3
2006-2008	4042	0

	Good Plays	Misplays and Errors
Cabrera 2008	55	56
Avg Shortstop	59	50
Good Play/Misplay Pct		.455

Cabrera is a fundamentally sound shortstop who plays with a lot of energy and does everything well. He has above-average range and makes a lot of sliding plays, but he also led all shortstops in 2008 in defensive misplays (56). He has a quick release and is good on double-play opportunities, delivering the ball accurately to second base. He also has good feet around the bag when making the turn. Cabrera won a Gold Glove in 2007.

Jerry Hairston

	Innings	Runs Saved
2008	271	-1
2006-2008	286	-1

	Good Plays	Misplays and Errors
Hairston 2008	18	7
Avg Shortstop	10	9
Good Play/Misplay Pct		.686

Hairston began his career as a second baseman before seeing more and more time in the outfield in recent years. Thus it was surprising that half of Hairston's innings in 2008 came at shortstop, a development necessitated by injuries to Alex Gonzalez and Jeff Keppinger. Usually, a 32-year-old switches from shortstop to second base rather than the other way around, but Hairston held his own at the tougher defensive position. He doesn't have the arm of an ideal shortstop, and often looks like he's slinging the ball, but most of his throws get where they need to go. Hairston was particularly strong fielding balls to his backhand side. In the outfield, he showed good hustle if not textbook reads. Insert your jack-of-all-trades cliche here.

Freddie Bynum

	Innings	Runs Saved
2008	283	0
2006-2008	349	-1

	Good Plays	Misplays and Errors
Bynum 2008	7	16
Avg Shortstop	12	10
Good Play/Misplay Pct		.271

Brian Bixler

	Innings	Runs Saved
2008	278	-1
2006-2008	278	-1

	Good Plays	Misplays and Errors
Bixler 2008	18	18
Avg Shortstop	14	12
Good Play/Misplay Pct		.459

Stephen Drew

	Innings	Runs Saved
2008	1294	-3
2006-2008	3057	-1

	Good Plays	Misplays and Errors
Drew 2008	40	37
Avg Shortstop	47	40
Good Play/Misplay Pct		.479

Drew positions himself toward the third-base hole, especially against right-handed hitters. Due to this positioning and his quickness, he makes a lot of plays on balls hit into the hole but costs himself chances up the middle. His excellent footwork on the pivot allows him to avoid baserunners, and his plus arm helps him seal the deal.

Angel Berroa

	Innings	Runs Saved
2008	592	0
2006-2008	1731	-2

	Good Plays	Misplays and Errors
Berroa 2008	26	21
Avg Shortstop	25	21
Good Play/Misplay Pct		.513

Back by popular demand (cough), Berroa filled in as a capable defensive replacement for Rafael Furcal in 2008. He does not excel in any one aspect in the field, but he has good hands and range to his right and left. Berroa's arm is nothing special, and he can be erratic with his throws due to inconsistent mechanics and/or throwing off-balance. On double-play balls, Berroa doesn't always charge the ball, which costs him some opportunities. He has good range and takes good routes on flyballs, but he struggles if he has to go straight back.

Edgar Renteria

	Innings	Runs Saved
2008	1173	-7
2006-2008	3457	-3

	Good Plays	Misplays and Errors
Renteria 2008	38	41
Avg Shortstop	45	39
Good Play/Misplay Pct		.441

Renteria likes to shade up the middle to increase coverage to that side, but this also reduces his range to his right. He can make the tough play up the middle or in the hole but will also misplay balls hit straight at him. He does a good job at feeding the second baseman and turning the double play, but his tendency to double-clutch before throwing to first costs him on close plays.

Luis Rodriguez

	Innings	Runs Saved
2008	391	-3
2006-2008	394	-4

	Good Plays	Misplays and Errors
Rodriguez 2008	22	8
Avg Shortstop	16	13
Good Play/Misplay Pct		.700

Emmanuel Burriss

	Innings	Runs Saved
2008	315	-6
2006-2008	315	-6

	Good Plays	Misplays and Errors
Burriss 2008	14	13
Avg Shortstop	12	10
Good Play/Misplay Pct		.478

Shortstops

Miguel Tejada

	Innings	Runs Saved
2008	1354	7
2006-2008	3717	-8

	Good Plays	Misplays and Errors
Tejada 2008	49	41
Avg Shortstop	50	43
Good Play/Misplay Pct		.504

The 34-year-old Tejada has aged better than most shortstops, as he still possesses superior range and a rocket arm. His arm and quick release permit him to stay back on balls that many shortstops are forced to charge, giving him time to position himself in the best manner possible to make the correct play. Tejada's only struggles occur when he trusts his arm too much and plays the ball to his backhand, even though it would be easier to just get in front of it. Tejada has made a name for himself as one of the top defensive shortstops in the game, but the data suggests this reputation might now be a bit overblown.

Bobby Crosby

	Innings	Runs Saved
2008	1263	-6
2006-2008	2905	-9

	Good Plays	Misplays and Errors
Crosby 2008	42	36
Avg Shortstop	47	40
Good Play/Misplay Pct		.498

Crosby's well publicized string of injuries has reduced his range, quickness, and agility, although he can show flashes of former glory with the occasional acrobatic play. He does have a rocket arm, which helped him rank as one of the majors' best shortstops at turning the double play in 2008.

Marco Scutaro

	Innings	Runs Saved
2008	472	8
2006-2008	1393	-11

	Good Plays	Misplays and Errors
Scutaro 2008	20	14
Avg Shortstop	19	16
Good Play/Misplay Pct		.548

Julio Lugo

	Innings	Runs Saved
2008	671	-5
2006-2008	2546	-14

	Good Plays	Misplays and Errors
Lugo 2008	24	24
Avg Shortstop	23	19
Good Play/Misplay Pct		.459

Lugo often seems to lack concentration, committing mental errors such as making ill-advised throws with his outstanding but erratic arm. He also is fighting a losing battle with his arch-nemesis, the double play. He consistently ranks among the worst shortstops at turning two, because he is inconsistent with the timing and accuracy of his feeds, and doesn't take contact well from aggressive slides on the pivot.

Jhonny Peralta

	Innings	Runs Saved
2008	1271	-6
2006-2008	3894	-14

	Good Plays	Misplays and Errors
Peralta 2008	34	34
Avg Shortstop	51	43
Good Play/Misplay Pct		.459

Peralta's fielding skills are often derided, but there are more deserving targets for this kind of scorn. Peralta makes most of the routine plays and ranked in the top five in assists with 427 (granted, the Indians' staff was a groundball staff). He can make accurate throws from almost any position and does a nice job on the double play. His biggest flaw is more mental than physical: he has a tendency to panic and rush his throws when he doesn't field the ball cleanly. There's a chance that he could move to third base in 2009, but he isn't the American League shortstop most in need of a position change.

Ben Zobrist

	Innings	Runs Saved
2008	293	-7
2006-2008	959	-16

	Good Plays	Misplays and Errors
Zobrist 2008	14	15
Avg Shortstop	11	9
Good Play/Misplay Pct		.442

Shortstops

Jeff Keppinger

	Innings	Runs Saved
2008	881	-11
2006-2008	1272	-16

	Good Plays	Misplays and Errors
Keppinger 2008	21	21
Avg Shortstop	31	27
Good Play/Misplay Pct		.459

On good days, Keppinger is solid but not spectacular. His arm, although average, is prone to low throws. He lets some easy grounders get by him, but he makes most of the plays and shows good positional awareness. The bottom line is, if he's going to last in the bigs, he will need to hit better. He won't make it on defense alone.

Alex Cintron

	Innings	Runs Saved
2008	257	-10
2006-2008	708	-18

	Good Plays	Misplays and Errors
Cintron 2008	11	19
Avg Shortstop	12	10
Good Play/Misplay Pct		.330

David Eckstein

	Innings	Runs Saved
2008	484	-10
2006-2008	2457	-20

	Good Plays	Misplays and Errors
Eckstein 2008	13	16
Avg Shortstop	17	14
Good Play/Misplay Pct		.408

Yuniesky Betancourt

	Innings	Runs Saved
2008	1325	-13
2006-2008	4001	-20

	Good Plays	Misplays and Errors
Betancourt 2008	49	46
Avg Shortstop	49	42
Good Play/Misplay Pct		.475

Betancourt has a great deal of talent as a defender, but his ability to reach balls with ease makes you scratch your head sometimes when he can't seal the deal. Two plays from 2008 illustrate this point. The first was a grounder up the middle off the bat of the fleet-footed Rajai Davis. Betancourt snared the ball destined for center field and threw a missile slightly off target to first from shallow right-center. Although Miguel Cairo appeared to have his foot on the bag as he dove to catch the off-target throw, Davis was credited with a single. The second play was a hard-hit grounder from Franklin Gutierrez that bounced off Adrian Beltre's glove. Somehow, Betancourt had anticipated this, fielded the ball, and again sent a bullet slightly astray towards first. Cairo appeared to tag Gutierrez, but Gutierrez was called safe and Betancourt received an error for his trouble.

Despite his talent, Betancourt has yet to post a positive plus/minus season, that is, a season where he has converted as many outs as the average shortstop. This part makes you scratch your head as well. Maybe there are simply too many "close, but no cigar" plays.

Brendan Harris

	Innings	Runs Saved
2008	464	-6
2006-2008	1242	-21

	Good Plays	Misplays and Errors
Harris 2008	18	15
Avg Shortstop	19	16
Good Play/Misplay Pct		.505

Michael Young

	Innings	Runs Saved
2008	1289	-5
2006-2008	3936	-24

	Good Plays	Misplays and Errors
Young 2008	51	41
Avg Shortstop	52	45
Good Play/Misplay Pct		.514

Michael Young was the other big surprise winner of a Gold Glove in 2008 (with Nate McLouth). Here's what we had to say about Young in the first volume of *The Fielding Bible* three years ago:

"Before switching over to shortstop, Young had a reputation as an excellent defensive second basemen. However, his 2003 plus/minus figure of -16 suggests otherwise. We reviewed videotape of many of his plays that year to try to figure out the discrepancy, because his basic tools are superb. The problem became apparent very quickly. He simply was playing too close to second base and missed hit after hit to his left. His plus/minus figure was -22 to his left that year and +10 to his right. Now, after having moved to shortstop in 2004, he continues to have problems to his left with a cumulative

-46 over the last two seasons. He has a very strong arm and it seems pretty likely at this point that he shades too far to his right to try and take advantage of that arm. In 2005 the average Major League team allowed 292 hits up the middle or in the shortstop hole. The Rangers allowed 374. That was the most in baseball. So, in only two years of work as a shortstop, Young claims last place in three-year plus/minus, three-year zone ratings, team hits allowed near the shortstop position in 2005, and he's second to last in Bill James' new relative range plus/minus. Not good."

Three years ago Young was one of the worst shortstops in baseball. Has he improved to the point where he's the best in the American League?

He is better. But frankly, that's not saying much. His 2003 and 2004 plus/minus figures were -34 and -39. He has "improved" to -10, -15, and -8 over the last three years. And he still had problems going to his left.

In 2008 there is one area in which he excelled: double plays. Out of 172 ground balls hit Young's way with a man on first and less than two out, 106 (62%) were turned into outs. That was the eighth highest percentage in baseball out of the 35 shortstops who played the most all year. In addition, he also had 14 good fielding plays involving double plays with zero misplays or errors—the best net figure (+14) on double plays in all of baseball. His forte is standing in on an aggressive slide to turn the double play. We recorded him with nine good plays on aggressive slides; most other shortstops had one or two. The next best were Erick Aybar (7), Orlando Cabrera (4), and Jose Reyes (4).

However, in addition to his poor plus/minus number, Young was also weak in another key area for shortstops—throwing. While his arm may be strong, he clearly has problems in this area. His 15 misplays and errors on thrown balls with zero good plays (net -15) was the fourth worst total in baseball. By contrast, National League Gold Glover and Fielding Bible Award winner Jimmy Rollins had a net of -3 with five throwing good plays and only eight misplays or errors.

One of the key reasons Young won the American League award was lack of competition. In the voting for the Fielding Bible Awards, eight of the top ten shortstops in baseball were from the National League. Young, in fact, came in 11th in the voting. But the guy that should have beaten him for the AL Gold Glove came in fourth in the Fielding Bible Awards voting (the other American Leaguer was White Sox shortstop Orlando Cabrera, who came in sixth). The fourth place finisher was Erick Aybar of the Los Angeles Angels. The key reason that Aybar didn't win a Gold Glove is that he only played in 98 games. Nevertheless, his plus/minus was +8 and he

turned in more good fielding plays than Young (55 to 51) and had fewer defensive misplays (35 to Young's 41).

Hanley Ramirez

	Innings	Runs Saved
2008	1302	1
2006-2008	3927	-29

	Good Plays	Misplays and Errors
Ramirez 2008	48	47
Avg Shortstop	51	43
Good Play/Misplay Pct		.465

In 2007, Ramirez was one the worst defensive shortstops in the league. He improved dramatically in 2008, thanks in large part to his quick reflexes. On hard-hit balls to his left, Hanley does a great job of handling the ball and making strong throws. Softly hit groundballs aren't quite as easy for him. He is prone to double-clutching his glove before fielding the ball, which leads to mistakes. A smoother approach will help him convert the double play more effectively and gun down more runners at first (air mailing fewer balls over the first baseman's head would also be a good idea). Ramirez's newfound mediocrity at shortstop makes his bat that much more valuable.

Derek Jeter

	Innings	Runs Saved
2008	1259	-9
2006-2008	3869	-50

	Good Plays	Misplays and Errors
Jeter 2008	35	29
Avg Shortstop	45	38
Good Play/Misplay Pct		.506

Jeter has made some outstanding defensive plays in his career, many of them in crucial playoff situations. This has helped him build a reputation that outstrips his actual ability. He does some things extremely well, such as using his good athleticism to jump and snare line drives. Then there is the signature Jeter play, when he fields a backhander in the hole and makes his patented jump-throw. Jeter still excels at this play, but it disguises the fact that he does it because he lacks the arm strength to plant his feet and throw. His arm also causes him to play more shallow than other shortstops, cutting down on his range. The good plays do not come as often as they used to. Only 35 of them last year compared to the expected 45 from an average shortstop. The Captain is an intelligent player, but he'll need to play even smarter as he gets older in order to compensate for his declining skills.

Left Fielders Evaluations

Year	League	Gold Glove Winners	Should Have Been
2003	AL	none	none
	NL	none	none
2004	AL	none	none
	NL	none	none
2005	AL	none	almost: Carl Crawford
	NL	none	none
2006	AL	none	none
	NL	none	none
2007	AL	none	none
	NL	none	none
2008	AL	none	none
	NL	none	Willie Harris

My Personal Ratings

Top Ten

1 Carl Crawford, TB
2 Willie Harris, Was
3 Eric Byrnes, Ari
4 Reed Johnson, ChC
5 Brandon Boggs, Tex
6 Jay Payton, FA
7 Matt Holliday, Oak
8 Alfonso Soriano, ChC
9 Conor Jackson, Ari
10 Johnny Damon, NYY

Bottom Five

26 Jack Cust, Oak
27 Delmon Young, Min
28 Manny Ramirez, FA
29 Pat Burrell, TB
30 Adam Dunn, Was

Player teams based on transactions through February 11, 2009

Left Fielders

Alfonso Soriano

	Innings	Runs Saved
2008	937	5
2006-2008	3375	42

	Good Plays	Misplays and Errors
Soriano 2008	14	29
Avg Left Fielder	15	18
Good Play/Misplay Pct		.361

See the article, "Soriano: More like Manny or More like Carl?" on page 255. Soriano has saved more runs with his throwing arm over the last three years than any other outfielder in baseball, by a wide margin. If there are any other baserunners or third base coaches who think they can still test his arm, they are sadly mistaken and will pay the price in the long run. Soriano covers a lot of ground in left field, but when he misses a play, he misses badly and the whole stadium knows it. He made 29 misplays and errors in 2008, about 50% more than you would expect from an average left fielder. His annoying little "bunny hop" before routine catches has yet to result in an error (although it may have resulted in an injury), but the baseball world won't let him hear the end of it when it does. He still struggles with his routes and angles, but all in all, the complete Soriano defensive package is a big positive.

Carl Crawford

	Innings	Runs Saved
2008	921	13
2006-2008	3359	22

	Good Plays	Misplays and Errors
Crawford 2008	20	15
Avg Left Fielder	16	18
Good Play/Misplay Pct		.609

Crawford is the best left fielder playing today. He has great range and takes good routes on balls in all directions. He judges line drives well and gets good jumps, catching liners hit in front of him that most left fielders would let drop. His only weakness on flyballs is that he sometimes loses track of how far away he is from the wall. He often jumps when he doesn't have to, causing him to miss an occasional ball he should catch. With average arm strength and accuracy, Crawford puts himself in a good position to throw by charging grounders. He won his second Fielding Bible Award in 2008.

Willie Harris

	Innings	Runs Saved
2008	562	13
2006-2008	1215	21

	Good Plays	Misplays and Errors
Harris 2008	16	12
Avg Left Fielder	11	13
Good Play/Misplay Pct		.609

Harris played a remarkable left field in 2008. After having played a remarkable left field in 2007. At a position not known for defensive wizardry, Harris' plus quickness and speed made him a nightly "Web Gems" nominee. He takes great routes on line drives and flyballs. His Web Gem-iness sometimes causes problems, though. Whenever a hard-hit line drive comes his way, he always wants to make the diving catch rather than take the better-safe-than-sorry approach. Other than some failed dives for balls, Harris is one of the top left fielders in baseball.

Scott Hairston

	Innings	Runs Saved
2008	310	5
2006-2008	894	14

	Good Plays	Misplays and Errors
Hairston 2008	4	7
Avg Left Fielder	6	7
Good Play/Misplay Pct		.401

Eric Byrnes

	Innings	Runs Saved
2008	420	-2
2006-2008	1434	13

	Good Plays	Misplays and Errors
Byrnes 2008	7	3
Avg Left Fielder	6	7
Good Play/Misplay Pct		.732

Emil Brown

	Innings	Runs Saved
2008	413	-2
2006-2008	1738	12

	Good Plays	Misplays and Errors
Brown 2008	5	9
Avg Left Fielder	7	9
Good Play/Misplay Pct		.394

Left Fielders

Matt Diaz

	Innings	Runs Saved
2008	289	-3
2006-2008	1554	11

	Good Plays	Misplays and Errors
Diaz 2008	4	7
Avg Left Fielder	5	6
Good Play/Misplay Pct		.401

Luke Scott

	Innings	Runs Saved
2008	840	5
2006-2008	1275	10

	Good Plays	Misplays and Errors
Scott 2008	9	12
Avg Left Fielder	16	19
Good Play/Misplay Pct		.467

Scott is defensive milquetoast. He can be hesitant and often does not read the ball well off the bat. He'll try to make a play on a ball that should instead, be played off the wall. Then he'll give up on a catchable pop-up. That said, given the position's lax requirements, he is pretty good. He will make an occasional eye-popping catch and has a decent throwing arm. Scott's effort can't be faulted, but his instincts can.

Conor Jackson

	Innings	Runs Saved
2008	656	9
2006-2008	665	9

	Good Plays	Misplays and Errors
Jackson 2008	9	14
Avg Left Fielder	12	14
Good Play/Misplay Pct		.429

Jackson moved from first base to left field when Eric Byrnes went on the disabled list, and the change suited Jackson nicely. He looks more comfortable in the outfield than he did at first base (not coincidentally, he came up as an outfielder). For the most part, he has been solid and can handle the routine plays. He shows decent range, has a relatively strong and accurate arm, and will surprise you by making a great play every now and then.

Johnny Damon

	Innings	Runs Saved
2008	659	7
2006-2008	930	9

	Good Plays	Misplays and Errors
Damon 2008	11	13
Avg Left Fielder	12	14
Good Play/Misplay Pct		.497

Now a *de facto* left fielder, the former center fielder still has good range, although age and injuries have caught up with him. To counteract the decline in speed, Damon takes more risks. Once known for rarely needing to dive for a ball, it has now become a regular occurrence. He has never had a strong arm, but it's less of a problem in left field. Placed on the disabled list for the first time in his career in 2008, Damon will continue to start in left field, or the DH spot in an effort to keep him as healthy and productive as possible.

Ben Francisco

	Innings	Runs Saved
2008	643	6
2006-2008	745	9

	Good Plays	Misplays and Errors
Francisco 2008	11	12
Avg Left Fielder	13	16
Good Play/Misplay Pct		.517

Francisco's defense is still a work in progress, but he will continue to improve with experience. He plays either corner outfield position well and doesn't make many mistakes. He has shown decent speed, good arm strength, and the ability to keep his mistakes to a minimum.

Fred Lewis

	Innings	Runs Saved
2008	906	5
2006-2008	1039	8

	Good Plays	Misplays and Errors
Lewis 2008	21	26
Avg Left Fielder	16	19
Good Play/Misplay Pct		.486

Lewis is a gifted athlete who has good speed, a good first step, and a playable arm. But having tools doesn't make you a good player, and Lewis definitely has room for improvement. This is not to say that he is a liability in the outfield, because he makes more than his fair share of impressive catches. To be a better outfielder, though, he'll need to cut down on his mistakes. Far too often, he allows balls to bounce off his glove or eat him up after falling safely for a hit. Given his athletic ability, he simply doesn't come close to catching as many balls as he should. His best skill currently is his ability to create outs with his arm. He doesn't have the strongest arm in the world, but he plays it up by getting rid of the ball quickly and accurately. He also is prepared to throw on every play, preventing runners from advancing by throwing the ball to the correct base. Lewis has above-average talent for a left fielder. If he puts that talent to better use, he could be a superb defender.

Josh Willingham

	Innings	Runs Saved
2008	855	9
2006-2008	3101	7

	Good Plays	Misplays and Errors
Willingham 2008	18	17
Avg Left Fielder	15	17
Good Play/Misplay Pct		.553

A former catcher, Willingham has the tools and skills to play the outfield. He is quicker than he looks when pursuing balls. He has good range to the line and in the gap as he aggressively tracks flyballs. He has some trouble judging flies, which can cause him to take a bad route or be caught too close to the wall. When he gets to the ball, he has no trouble completing the catch. His arm is strong but gets away from him, especially in overthrowing the cutoff man. Injuries kept Willingham out of the lineup, slowing his development as an outfielder. With more time in the field, Willingham's ability to judge flyballs and the routes he takes to the ball will improve, making him an asset in the field.

Ryan Braun

	Innings	Runs Saved
2008	1310	7
2006-2008	1310	7

	Good Plays	Misplays and Errors
Braun 2008	24	25
Avg Left Fielder	23	27
Good Play/Misplay Pct		.529

Braun is at his best when he keeps it simple. He plays a deep left field, which prevents most balls from getting past him but also allows more hits to fall in front of him. He gets into trouble when he tries to dive for balls or take an overly aggressive route. He has an average arm but does not take major chances with it. He is aware of his limitations and minimizes his mistakes. After his horrible rookie year misadventures at third base in 2007, Braun may have found his true defensive calling in left

field. With less negative publicity for his glovework, Braun's hitting will continue to be the real story.

Brandon Boggs

	Innings	Runs Saved
2008	579	7
2006-2008	579	7

	Good Plays	Misplays and Errors
Boggs 2008	14	22
Avg Left Fielder	12	14
Good Play/Misplay Pct		.427

Boggs, a natural center fielder, turned in a great performance in left for the Rangers in 2008. He had a bit of trouble adapting to the position and made more than his share of misplays, but he is a good athlete capable of playing all three outfield positions. He has a very strong arm, reads the ball well, and covers a lot of ground. Given Boggs' struggles with the bat, his future likely is in center field (or on the bench).

Andre Ethier

	Innings	Runs Saved
2008	277	1
2006-2008	1479	7

	Good Plays	Misplays and Errors
Ethier 2008	4	5
Avg Left Fielder	5	5
Good Play/Misplay Pct		.483

David DeJesus

	Innings	Runs Saved
2008	483	3
2006-2008	1028	6

	Good Plays	Misplays and Errors
DeJesus 2008	10	6
Avg Left Fielder	9	11
Good Play/Misplay Pct		.661

Wily Mo Pena

	Innings	Runs Saved
2008	408	3
2006-2008	884	6

	Good Plays	Misplays and Errors
Pena 2008	5	9
Avg Left Fielder	8	9
Good Play/Misplay Pct		.394

Left Fielders

Matt Joyce

	Innings	Runs Saved
2008	409	4
2006-2008	409	4

	Good Plays	Misplays and Errors
Joyce 2008	6	10
Avg Left Fielder	8	10
Good Play/Misplay Pct		.412

Joyce has the makings of a solid defensive outfielder. He's not very flashy, but he covers ground pretty well and has a solid arm. The biggest problems that he had this season seemed to be the result of inexperience. Generally speaking, Joyce took very good routes to the ball, allowing him to maximize his range. Every now and then, however, he would get tangled up and cost himself the chance for an out. He occasionally allowed baserunners to tag up and advance from first base, a byproduct of not knowing the players and/or the situation. He is capable of making some great catches and plays balls off the fence well. With more experience, Joyce could soon become an above-average left fielder.

Jay Payton

	Innings	Runs Saved
2008	407	7
2006-2008	1765	4

	Good Plays	Misplays and Errors
Payton 2008	12	11
Avg Left Fielder	9	10
Good Play/Misplay Pct		.561

Payton entered 2008 as a platoon left fielder but saw plenty of time in center field after Adam Jones went down. Payton is dependable in either spot and finished the season without making an error. He gets good reads and can still run. He makes the sliding plays that elude many of his left field counterparts, but he becomes less assured the closer he gets to the wall. His eight outfield assists (in fewer than 750 innings in 2008), and his eight runs saved with his arm in the last three years, testify to his above-average arm.

Skip Schumaker

	Innings	Runs Saved
2008	338	6
2006-2008	524	3

	Good Plays	Misplays and Errors
Schumaker 2008	9	4
Avg Left Fielder	7	8
Good Play/Misplay Pct		.725

Shannon Stewart

	Innings	Runs Saved
2008	310	3
2006-2008	1750	3

	Good Plays	Misplays and Errors
Stewart 2008	6	2
Avg Left Fielder	5	5
Good Play/Misplay Pct		.778

Juan Rivera

	Innings	Runs Saved
2008	307	0
2006-2008	800	3

	Good Plays	Misplays and Errors
Rivera 2008	3	7
Avg Left Fielder	5	6
Good Play/Misplay Pct		.334

Jacoby Ellsbury

	Innings	Runs Saved
2008	346	5
2006-2008	490	2

	Good Plays	Misplays and Errors
Ellsbury 2008	15	2
Avg Left Fielder	7	8
Good Play/Misplay Pct		.898

Juan Pierre

	Innings	Runs Saved
2008	623	2
2006-2008	623	2

	Good Plays	Misplays and Errors
Pierre 2008	11	12
Avg Left Fielder	11	12
Good Play/Misplay Pct		.517

Left Fielders

The scrappy outfielder provided a positive spark to the Dodgers outfield in 2008. Playing left field for the first time in his career, Pierre became one of the fastest left fielders in the game. His wheels are in the same league as speedy outfielders Carl Crawford and Willie Harris. Pierre has a below-average arm, even for left field. Although his arm allows some runs, his range and outfield savvy make up for it. Before games, Pierre is known to take a stroll through his opponent's outfield to see the dimensions.

Xavier Nady

	Innings	Runs Saved
2008	390	4
2006-2008	467	2

	Good Plays	Misplays and Errors
Nady 2008	5	7
Avg Left Fielder	8	9
Good Play/Misplay Pct		.455

David Dellucci

	Innings	Runs Saved
2008	383	1
2006-2008	1045	2

	Good Plays	Misplays and Errors
Dellucci 2008	10	5
Avg Left Fielder	7	8
Good Play/Misplay Pct		.700

Matt Holliday

	Innings	Runs Saved
2008	1229	5
2006-2008	3947	1

	Good Plays	Misplays and Errors
Holliday 2008	24	19
Avg Left Fielder	23	27
Good Play/Misplay Pct		.596

Holliday is the rare slugging left fielder who also does well defensively. . .even if he doesn't give himself the credit he deserves. Holliday has stated that he needs to improve in the field and puts a lot of time and effort into doing so. Whatever he's doing, he should keep it up. He is exceptional at playing caroms off the wall, plays angles effectively, and has a quick release and strong arm on throws back to infield. The athletic Holliday can look uncomfortable at times, but his plus/minus total has increased in each of the last two seasons.

Chase Headley

	Innings	Runs Saved
2008	713	0
2006-2008	713	0

	Good Plays	Misplays and Errors
Headley 2008	10	17
Avg Left Fielder	13	15
Good Play/Misplay Pct		.407

Making his big-league debut, Headley transitioned from third base to the outfield so the Padres could get his bat into the lineup. He has power potential at the plate but remains something of a question mark on defense. He can handle the routine plays, but he also misjudged balls at times. Most likely, this can be fixed with experience. However, you can't teach the speed necessary to cover Petco's gaps, and Headley doesn't have it.

Fernando Tatis

	Innings	Runs Saved
2008	284	2
2006-2008	306	0

	Good Plays	Misplays and Errors
Tatis 2008	4	5
Avg Left Fielder	4	5
Good Play/Misplay Pct		.483

David Murphy

	Innings	Runs Saved
2008	405	0
2006-2008	520	0

	Good Plays	Misplays and Errors
Murphy 2008	6	7
Avg Left Fielder	8	9
Good Play/Misplay Pct		.501

Carlos Quentin

	Innings	Runs Saved
2008	1147	0
2006-2008	1165	0

	Good Plays	Misplays and Errors
Quentin 2008	18	24
Avg Left Fielder	20	24
Good Play/Misplay Pct		.467

While Quentin made the most noise on offense, he still was a reliable outfielder. He possesses an above-average, accurate arm with great awareness of runners on

Left Fielders

the basepaths. He also thrived playing hard-hit balls toward the wall. His below-average speed means he can't cover as much ground as an outfielder like Carl Crawford does. Quentin sometimes made unwarranted dives for line drives, resulting in extra bases for the opponent. Overall, though, Quentin was an average left fielder with more improvement to come.

Chris Duncan

	Innings	Runs Saved
2008	321	1
2006-2008	1395	-1

	Good Plays	Misplays and Errors
Duncan 2008	4	6
Avg Left Fielder	6	7
Good Play/Misplay Pct		.438

Gregor Blanco

	Innings	Runs Saved
2008	513	-1
2006-2008	513	-1

	Good Plays	Misplays and Errors
Blanco 2008	7	11
Avg Left Fielder	8	9
Good Play/Misplay Pct		.427

A center fielder by trade, the rookie played left field until Mark Kotsay's departure in 2008. Blanco has a quick first step and great range to either side. His arm is strong for any outfield position, but he can be overly aggressive with it, allowing runners to take an extra base. With increased playing time, Blanco could assert himself as one of the league's top center fielders.

Eric Hinske

	Innings	Runs Saved
2008	265	0
2006-2008	389	-1

	Good Plays	Misplays and Errors
Hinske 2008	4	4
Avg Left Fielder	4	5
Good Play/Misplay Pct		.539

Brandon Moss

	Innings	Runs Saved
2008	294	-2
2006-2008	346	-2

	Good Plays	Misplays and Errors
Moss 2008	2	5
Avg Left Fielder	6	7
Good Play/Misplay Pct		.319

Paul McAnulty

	Innings	Runs Saved
2008	266	-3
2006-2008	289	-2

	Good Plays	Misplays and Errors
McAnulty 2008	7	9
Avg Left Fielder	5	5
Good Play/Misplay Pct		.476

Adam Lind

	Innings	Runs Saved
2008	591	-6
2006-2008	1260	-2

	Good Plays	Misplays and Errors
Lind 2008	6	10
Avg Left Fielder	9	10
Good Play/Misplay Pct		.412

Lind struggled in left field, especially after his return from the minors in late June. He took bad routes, fumbled the ball after base hits on occasion, and sometimes looked uncomfortable on the plays he did make. He managed a few nice running catches toward the left field corner and has a decent arm. Lind improved his defense in September, and one can imagine that some of his mistakes were due to nerves as he tried to stick in the majors. Look for some improvement in 2009.

Jose Guillen

	Innings	Runs Saved
2008	373	-4
2006-2008	373	-4

	Good Plays	Misplays and Errors
Guillen 2008	5	13
Avg Left Fielder	7	8
Good Play/Misplay Pct		.310

Left Fielders

Garret Anderson

	Innings	Runs Saved
2008	689	-1
2006-2008	2226	-5

	Good Plays	Misplays and Errors
Anderson 2008	15	12
Avg Left Fielder	12	14
Good Play/Misplay Pct		.594

Anderson's intelligence and baseball instincts make him a dependable fielder despite his declining range and increasing age. His arm remains strong and accurate, but baserunners aren't afraid to run on him.

Carlos Lee

	Innings	Runs Saved
2008	915	-2
2006-2008	3543	-5

	Good Plays	Misplays and Errors
Lee 2008	9	21
Avg Left Fielder	18	21
Good Play/Misplay Pct		.334

Lee appears to be a designated hitter masquerading as a left fielder. In 2008 he made about half the number of good plays you would expect from an average left fielder. On the other hand, his misplay rate was average in 2008, and so was his plus/minus number. His speed has declined, which does not bode well for his defensive future. Over the years Lee has covered up his deficiencies by playing deep, but in 2008 he did a better job on balls hit in front of him. He has a habit of throwing the ball around, allowing runners to take extra bases. Taken all together, Lee is a below-average outfielder who has gotten the most from his abilities.

Mark Teahen

	Innings	Runs Saved
2008	267	-5
2006-2008	267	-5

	Good Plays	Misplays and Errors
Teahen 2008	10	7
Avg Left Fielder	5	6
Good Play/Misplay Pct		.626

Marcus Thames

	Innings	Runs Saved
2008	488	-5
2006-2008	1166	-7

	Good Plays	Misplays and Errors
Thames 2008	11	14
Avg Left Fielder	10	12
Good Play/Misplay Pct		.479

There's a reason why Thames isn't an everyday left fielder: he is a defensive liability. He does have a knack for making great catches, though. Less impressive is that most of these catches resulted from his lack of ability as a defender. He simply does not have much range, gets bad reads on flyballs, takes circuitous routes, and ends up diving for balls he should have caught easily. Four times this season, Thames cost his team an extra base by diving for a flyball he had no chance of catching, and there are countless other times when his lack of prowess cost his team outs. With that said, Thames does have a playable arm, and he could work as a stopgap if he limited his mistakes.

Gary Matthews Jr.

	Innings	Runs Saved
2008	313	-7
2006-2008	313	-7

	Good Plays	Misplays and Errors
Matthews Jr. 2008	4	11
Avg Left Fielder	5	6
Good Play/Misplay Pct		.298

Jack Cust

	Innings	Runs Saved
2008	586	-8
2006-2008	670	-8

	Good Plays	Misplays and Errors
Cust 2008	14	15
Avg Left Fielder	11	13
Good Play/Misplay Pct		.522

Cust, who apparently can only bend at the waist, never makes a play look easy. His lack of speed allows softly hit balls to drop in front of him, but he gets surprisingly good reads on most balls. He rarely camps under flyballs, always standing a step or two off and staggering into the catch. He is tentative when charging balls and struggles with caroms off the wall. He's not a total loss in the outfield, but he's close.

Left Fielders

Raul Ibanez

	Innings	Runs Saved
2008	1340	-6
2006-2008	3851	-8

	Good Plays	Misplays and Errors
Ibanez 2008	30	33
Avg Left Fielder	27	31
Good Play/Misplay Pct		.515

On the long list of things that could have gone better for the Mariners in 2008, you'll find Ibanez's play in left field. Ibanez's most glaring weakness is his utter lack of range. Many of his good fielding plays resulted from flyballs that an average outfielder would have caught easily. To be fair, he does take good routes to the balls he does reach. Range aside, he routinely makes errant throws or throws to the wrong base, allowing teams to take further advantage of his declining skills.

His only real strength is his awareness of his limitations. This allowed him to hold six hits to singles when extra-base hits seemed imminent. He also unloads the ball quickly, which allows him to throw out baserunners with a below-average arm. His habit of playing deep has helped him. For more on this, see the article called Shallow, Medium, and Deep on page 161.

Delmon Young

	Innings	Runs Saved
2008	1324	-11
2006-2008	1324	-11

	Good Plays	Misplays and Errors
Young 2008	27	37
Avg Left Fielder	26	30
Good Play/Misplay Pct		.460

It is surprising how awkward Young looks in left field. He has good speed and an excellent throwing arm, but that's the end of the defensive compliments. He normally plays deep and often fails to get a good read on the ball, letting numerous hits drop in front of him. Yet he still has difficulty in the deep zone of left field (plus/minus of -20 in deep left field in 2008). He mishandles some routine hits, which calls his concentration into question. Young takes some poor angles, is prone to the occasional bad decision, doesn't leap very well, and doesn't seem to do anything particularly quickly. Even when he makes a play, he can look clumsy doing so. In fairness, Young was dealing with a position change from right to left field. He has youth on his side, so improvement is likely. He has a long way to go.

Jason Bay

	Innings	Runs Saved
2008	1344	-8
2006-2008	3954	-14

	Good Plays	Misplays and Errors
Bay 2008	23	13
Avg Left Fielder	26	30
Good Play/Misplay Pct		.674

Bay doesn't have the superior athleticism of some outfielders, but he has enough speed and awareness to be an average left fielder at the very least. He reads the ball off the bat well and usually gets to line drives in left-center. He also does a good job of gauging how much room he has every time he goes back on a ball. Softly hit flyballs in shallow left field pose more of a problem. Lacking first-step quickness and speed, Bay tends to let those balls drop. He also isn't as quick as others when it comes to cutting off hard line drives down the left field line. Once he gets to the ball, he has a slightly above-average, but extremely accurate throwing arm. With more experience in front of the Green Monster, Bay will increase his assist totals and his overall level of play.

Luis Gonzalez

	Innings	Runs Saved
2008	504	-7
2006-2008	2815	-17

	Good Plays	Misplays and Errors
Gonzalez 2008	6	9
Avg Left Fielder	9	11
Good Play/Misplay Pct		.438

Gonzalez plays defense like he's in his 40s because he is. He lacks a quick first step but limits his mistakes by playing deep and cautiously. He can catch the balls he reaches, but his range has never been great. His injury-ravaged arm, which occasionally requires double cutoffs on throws to home plate, is not as big a liability in left field, but the Marlins moved him to right field late in the season in an attempt to keep his bat in the lineup. This gave runners the green light to go first to third on all hits to him. Even as a part-time player, Gonzalez doesn't have much time left.

Left Fielders

Manny Ramirez

	Innings	Runs Saved
2008	974	-3
2006-2008	3000	-28

	Good Plays	Misplays and Errors
Ramirez 2008	14	20
Avg Left Fielder	16	19
Good Play/Misplay Pct		.450

Want to start a fight at your next SABR rendezvous? Start with this: Manny Ramirez isn't the worst left fielder in the game today. Although he doesn't possess extraordinary range, he makes good reads on balls hit within his vicinity. His arm is also better than he gets credit for, as it can deter baserunners from taking the extra base. Of course, Manny occasionally makes a bonehead play, whether it be letting a ball drop in front of him or failing to make an effort on a routine play. All in all, Manny's defense depends on the effort he is willing to exert. We'll get a better sense of his skills now that he has left Boston, but indications are that Manny being Manny doesn't always mean defensive ineptitude. For more on Manny, see "Soriano: More like Manny or More like Carl?" on page 255.

Pat Burrell

	Innings	Runs Saved
2008	1198	-5
2006-2008	3214	-30

	Good Plays	Misplays and Errors
Burrell 2008	32	23
Avg Left Fielder	21	24
Good Play/Misplay Pct		.619

There's regular slow, and then there's Pat Burrell slow. Any balls hit out of his limited range will roll for days or until they hit a wall, whichever comes first. With the Phillies, he positioned himself slightly toward the line to give himself a better shot on balls hit hard to his right, and he relied on speedy former teammates Jimmy Rollins and Shane Victorino to cover for him on balls to his left. He recently took over the crown of "Worst Three-Year Plus/Minus Score" from Manny Ramirez. Not good. It's not all bad news, though. Burrell's tremendous throwing arm and quick release make him one of the toughest left fielders on which to run.

Adam Dunn

	Innings	Runs Saved
2008	981	-10
2006-2008	3492	-39

	Good Plays	Misplays and Errors
Dunn 2008	14	21
Avg Left Fielder	18	22
Good Play/Misplay Pct		.438

It's a scientific fact: Dunn is a designated hitter trapped in the National League. Due to his size, he is simply unable to track down balls that most outfielders would reach. He'll occasionally turn in a good fielding play, but most of them result from a bad route or his overall lack of speed. A change of position (next stop: first base) or a move to the American League is in everyone's best interests. Too bad he just signed a two-year deal with the Nats.

Center Fielders Evaluations

Year	League	Gold Glove Winners	Should Have Been
2003	AL	Mike Cameron Torii Hunter	Mike Cameron Torii Hunter
	NL	Andruw Jones Jim Edmonds	Andruw Jones Jim Edmonds
2004	AL	Torii Hunter Vernon Wells	Torii Hunter Vernon Wells
	NL	Andruw Jones Steve Finley Jim Edmonds	Andruw Jones Steve Finley
2005	AL	Torii Hunter Vernon Wells	Torii Hunter Aaron Rowand
	NL	Andruw Jones Jim Edmonds	Andruw Jones Willy Taveras
2006	AL	Torii Hunter Vernon Wells	Vernon Wells
	NL	Andruw Jones Carlos Beltran Mike Cameron	Andruw Jones Carlos Beltran Willy Taveras
2007	AL	Torii Hunter Grady Sizemore Ichiro Suzuki	Ichiro Suzuki Coco Crisp
	NL	Andruw Jones Carlos Beltran Aaron Rowand	Andruw Jones Carlos Beltran
2008	AL	Torii Hunter Grady Sizemore	Carlos Gomez
	NL	Carlos Beltran Shane Victorino Nate McLouth	Carlos Beltran Shane Victorino

My Personal Ratings

Top Ten

1 Carlos Beltran, NYM
2 Carlos Gomez, Min
3 Shane Victorino, Phi
4 Corey Patterson, Was
5 Mike Cameron, Mil
6 Adam Jones, Bal
7 Willy Taveras, Cin
8 Cody Ross, Fla
9 Andruw Jones, Tex
10 Carlos Gonzalez, Col

Bottom Five

26 Nick Swisher, NYY
27 Johnny Damon, NYY
28 Mark Kotsay, Bos
29 Ken Griffey Jr., FA
30 Jim Edmonds, FA

Player teams based on transactions through February 11, 2009

Center Fielders

Carlos Beltran

	Innings	Runs Saved
2008	1407	21
2006-2008	3832	44

	Good Plays	Misplays and Errors
Beltran 2008	25	23
Avg Center Fielder	28	30
Good Play/Misplay Pct		.541

Beltran still has speed, even if he doesn't run as well as he used to. His excellent range is a product of reading balls well off the bat and taking direct routes, while his high baserunner kills totals result from a combination of charging the ball and throwing it on target. Beltran isn't a flawless center fielder, but he is the best. He won his second Fielding Bible award in 2008 and his third straight Gold Glove.

Andruw Jones

	Innings	Runs Saved
2008	496	-3
2006-2008	3160	35

	Good Plays	Misplays and Errors
Jones 2008	8	11
Avg Center Fielder	10	10
Good Play/Misplay Pct		.441

Jones started the season a good 30 pounds heavier than usual, and it showed in his plus/minus numbers. Prior to 2008 he averaged +17 per season. In 2009 he came in at -5 in only 496 innings. But he still looked good. He always has played with a casual nonchalance, making even the most difficult catches look easy. Lack of dedication and work ethic questions have been raised, but all the tools are still there when he wants them to be: a very strong and accurate arm, excellent reads off the bat and above-average speed. Jones still has the quick reaction time and first step, but it appears that the extra weight may be just the difference between one of the best center fielders in the game and an average one.

Corey Patterson

	Innings	Runs Saved
2008	798	11
2006-2008	2932	32

	Good Plays	Misplays and Errors
Patterson 2008	17	15
Avg Center Fielder	16	17
Good Play/Misplay Pct		.551

Patterson's greatest asset is his speed, which he uses to cover a great deal of ground in center field. He usually reads the ball well off the bat and gets good jumps. His throwing arm is decent for a center fielder. Over the past six years he's had an excellent +50 plus/minus score. He is average on balls that are hit shallow (a plus/minus of 0). He is phenomenal on deep ones (+43).

Alfredo Amezaga

	Innings	Runs Saved
2008	457	11
2006-2008	1630	29

	Good Plays	Misplays and Errors
Amezaga 2008	13	11
Avg Center Fielder	10	10
Good Play/Misplay Pct		.562

Shane Victorino

	Innings	Runs Saved
2008	1195	15
2006-2008	1769	20

	Good Plays	Misplays and Errors
Victorino 2008	21	29
Avg Center Fielder	22	24
Good Play/Misplay Pct		.440

This was Victorino's first full season in center, and he struggled a bit early. In fact, after he botched four plays in three days early in the season, the Phillies briefly considered moving him back to right field and replacing him with Jayson Werth. As Victorino adjusted to his new position, however, he cut down on his mistakes.

The Flyin' Hawaiian lives up to his nickname with great speed and a quick first step as he runs down all types of flyballs. He uses his speed well, rarely coming up short when he leaves his feet. Despite his diminutive size, he has a big arm, which grades near the top of the list of major league center fielders. His arm is also incredibly accurate, but he could use better judgment deciding when to use it. He struggles at times with his routes, and he's never been that good at fielding balls off the wall. He won his first Gold Glove in 2008, and it was well deserved. But he still has room for improvement.

Center Fielders

Carlos Gomez

	Innings	Runs Saved
2008	1272	17
2006-2008	1284	19

	Good Plays	Misplays and Errors
Gomez 2008	34	40
Avg Center Fielder	29	31
Good Play/Misplay Pct		.480

Gomez was a rookie this past year and he already is the best center fielder in the American League. The scary part is that he will get better. Gomez produced an impressive 2008 campaign defensively. He made an assortment of highlight-reel catches, and they weren't the type during which the outfielder hangs back then slides to make it look good. Granted, he didn't make all the catches, but no one in the league is quicker to his feet to scramble after a loose ball. Gomez has great speed, gets good jumps, takes good routes, covers a ton of ground, and has a decent arm. Did I say he covers a ton of ground? It should be said more than once because it's incredible. The place where he'll improve is the number of misplays. He had 40 misplays, highest among AL center fielders. Ten of those misplays involved allowing runners to take extra bases after a safe hit. That will go down as he gains experience. With Torii Hunter in decline and Carlos Beltran getting older, the title of "Best Defensive Center Fielder" may soon belong to Gomez.

Willy Taveras

	Innings	Runs Saved
2008	993	0
2006-2008	2824	19

	Good Plays	Misplays and Errors
Taveras 2008	21	27
Avg Center Fielder	19	20
Good Play/Misplay Pct		.457

In 2005 and 2006 Taveras rated as one of the best center fielders in baseball, but he has since slipped based on the Plus/Minus system. That being said, he is still in his athletic prime and possesses all the tools that make up an outstanding center fielder. His routes can be shaky at times, but he gets very good jumps off the bat and is in elite company when it comes to covering the outfield and running down flyballs. However, Taveras is not as comfortable on line drives hit in front of him. He can be too aggressive and take poor angles, often turning a routine single into extra bases. Taveras also does not charge balls particularly well, taking too long to set up, but he possesses a very strong and accurate arm.

Adam Jones

	Innings	Runs Saved
2008	1102	11
2006-2008	1329	16

	Good Plays	Misplays and Errors
Jones 2008	18	23
Avg Center Fielder	22	23
Good Play/Misplay Pct		.459

The cornerstone of the Erik Bedard trade, Jones has a tall, lean, athletic body and terrific speed. He usually gets great reads, and even when he misjudges the flight of the ball he can close in with his long strides. He has a knack for making terrific dives on hard-hit balls to the gaps and on shallow flyballs. He also possesses a plus arm, preventing baserunner advancement. Jones profiles as an above-average to plus defender in center field.

Mike Cameron

	Innings	Runs Saved
2008	1057	7
2006-2008	3630	15

	Good Plays	Misplays and Errors
Cameron 2008	26	22
Avg Center Fielder	19	21
Good Play/Misplay Pct		.562

Still one of the better center fielders in baseball, Cameron is the epitome of consistency in the Brewers' outfield. He ranges effortlessly through the outfield with a sneaky-quick first step. Although he does not cover as much ground as he used to, Cameron still catches almost everything he can get to. His arm is accurate and stronger than the average center fielder's. He should continue to be an asset in the field.

Curtis Granderson

	Innings	Runs Saved
2008	1188	-7
2006-2008	3785	14

	Good Plays	Misplays and Errors
Granderson 2008	22	18
Avg Center Fielder	23	25
Good Play/Misplay Pct		.570

Granderson missed the first three weeks of the season with a hand injury, but his feet are his best assets on defense. He has a lot of room to roam in Comerica Park's center field, and he takes full advantage of it. His routes on flyballs are sound, and he plays shallow at times because. . .well, he's fast enough to get away with it. Although his arm isn't particularly strong, it isn't a liability. It's a bit of a mystery why his plus/minus score for 2008 was so low (-11). Could it be that playing shallow hurt him? In the past he made up for mediocre plus/minus scores on shallow balls (+7 prior to 2008) with excellent coverage on balls hit deep (+23 before 2008). But in 2008 he was an uncharacteristic -5 in deep center field.

Marlon Byrd

	Innings	Runs Saved
2008	433	4
2006-2008	1323	12

	Good Plays	Misplays and Errors
Byrd 2008	9	12
Avg Center Fielder	10	10
Good Play/Misplay Pct		.448

Chris Young

	Innings	Runs Saved
2008	1390	9
2006-2008	2802	11

	Good Plays	Misplays and Errors
Young 2008	9	34
Avg Center Fielder	28	30
Good Play/Misplay Pct		.223

Young is a talented player who covers a lot of ground in center field but is generally unspectacular. He had an excellent plus/minus score of +21 last year, but he only had nine good fielding plays when the average center fielder had 28. He also had some problems preventing runners from taking an extra base in 2008. Nevertheless, his main asset is his speed, and he bolsters it with a great first step. Young should keep improving with age.

Cody Ross

	Innings	Runs Saved
2008	866	10
2006-2008	1250	11

	Good Plays	Misplays and Errors
Ross 2008	17	9
Avg Center Fielder	16	18
Good Play/Misplay Pct		.672

You wouldn't know it to look at him, but Ross plays above-average defense at a tough defensive position. He is surprisingly quick for his body type and can cover a lot of ground, especially in Dolphin Stadium's odd dimensions. He displays good instincts and hustle, which earned him regular playing time after many considered

him to be more of a fourth outfielder. He is sure-handed and keeps his misplays and errors to a minimum.

Alex Rios

	Innings	Runs Saved
2008	523	10
2006-2008	716	10

	Good Plays	Misplays and Errors
Rios 2008	11	9
Avg Center Fielder	11	12
Good Play/Misplay Pct		.570

Coco Crisp

	Innings	Runs Saved
2008	886	-3
2006-2008	3003	10

	Good Plays	Misplays and Errors
Crisp 2008	9	16
Avg Center Fielder	16	18
Good Play/Misplay Pct		.379

Formerly one-half of Boston's Jacoco Crispbury tag team, Crisp now takes his outstanding range to Kansas City. He plays balls off the wall well and has above-average speed, although he seems to slow down when approaching flyballs, preferring to make diving catches whenever possible. Crisp had a spectacular season for Boston in their championship year of 2007 and should have won a Gold Glove, but last year his defense regressed back to the norm.

Jay Payton

	Innings	Runs Saved
2008	301	8
2006-2008	789	9

	Good Plays	Misplays and Errors
Payton 2008	7	5
Avg Center Fielder	7	7
Good Play/Misplay Pct		.603

Rajai Davis

	Innings	Runs Saved
2008	488	7
2006-2008	867	8

	Good Plays	Misplays and Errors
Davis 2008	12	9
Avg Center Fielder	11	12
Good Play/Misplay Pct		.591

Center Fielders

Jody Gerut

	Innings	Runs Saved
2008	606	7
2006-2008	606	7

	Good Plays	Misplays and Errors
Gerut 2008	15	9
Avg Center Fielder	12	13
Good Play/Misplay Pct		.644

Defense is definitely Gerut's strength. He did a great job in his first extended stint as a major league center fielder in 2008. He is a solid player who always hustles and gets the job done. He used to be able to chase down anything, but he has lost a few steps due to knee injuries. His reactions and good reads off the bat still help him make some pretty nice grabs. He also has a good arm.

Carlos Gonzalez

	Innings	Runs Saved
2008	529	7
2006-2008	529	7

	Good Plays	Misplays and Errors
Gonzalez 2008	11	14
Avg Center Fielder	11	12
Good Play/Misplay Pct		.460

The centerpiece of the Dan Haren deal looked right at home in center field for the A's. Although Gonzalez spent a few weeks in the minors in the second half, his days as a regular could come quickly. He features a very strong arm but produced mixed results when tested, occasionally shooting for the lead runner only to allow the trail runner to advance. He usually gets good reads off the bat and has the speed to make up for it when he doesn't.

Michael Bourn

	Innings	Runs Saved
2008	1009	4
2006-2008	1066	7

	Good Plays	Misplays and Errors
Bourn 2008	24	24
Avg Center Fielder	20	22
Good Play/Misplay Pct		.520

Speed is Bourn's identity. Being fast certainly comes in handy when roaming Minute Maid Park's spacious center field (as well as on the basepaths). His range allows him to close in on shots in the gap or over his head. Of course, it might also cause him to take unnecessary risks when the wiser choice would be to play it safe. Live by the wheels, die by the wheels. . . .

B.J. Upton

	Innings	Runs Saved
2008	1249	2
2006-2008	1913	7

	Good Plays	Misplays and Errors
Upton 2008	32	41
Avg Center Fielder	26	28
Good Play/Misplay Pct		.458

Originally a middle infielder, Upton moved to center field in 2007. He has amazing athletic ability along with top-notch speed, but he has yet to put it all together. He takes bad routes to balls in the right- and left-center gaps and has a little trouble on balls hit to the wall. At times, Upton tries to make an almost impossible catch on a ball hit off the wall and ends up losing a base for his team. He needs to better understand his boundaries and pick his spots for attempting the implausible. He led all major league center fielders with 41 misplays, but that should improve with experience. Unless it simply runs in the family; his brother Justin had 38 misplays in right fielder for Arizona, second most in right. B.J. possesses one of the best center-field arms in the game. He saved an estimated eight runs with his arm last year, the highest total for center fielders. He still uses the same three-quarters throwing motion he had as a shortstop, but it doesn't hurt his accuracy.

Ichiro Suzuki

	Innings	Runs Saved
2008	602	-1
2006-2008	2279	7

	Good Plays	Misplays and Errors
Suzuki 2008	11	12
Avg Center Fielder	13	14
Good Play/Misplay Pct		.498

Vernon Wells

	Innings	Runs Saved
2008	889	-12
2006-2008	3458	7

	Good Plays	Misplays and Errors
Wells 2008	18	11
Avg Center Fielder	16	18
Good Play/Misplay Pct		.639

Wells is a former Gold Glove center fielder coming off a down year for him. He gets good jumps and has speed, as well as experience. His throwing arm is better than the typical center fielder's. He makes quite a few

Center Fielders

plays diving or sliding on balls in front of him, but he can also get back to the wall for deep drives. Wells will occasionally slide for a ball when he doesn't need to.

Jay Bruce

	Innings	Runs Saved
2008	285	6
2006-2008	285	6

	Good Plays	Misplays and Errors
Bruce 2008	6	6
Avg Center Fielder	5	6
Good Play/Misplay Pct		.520

Matt Kemp

	Innings	Runs Saved
2008	826	5
2006-2008	1033	6

	Good Plays	Misplays and Errors
Kemp 2008	22	14
Avg Center Fielder	15	16
Good Play/Misplay Pct		.630

Kemp lacks a quick first step, but he has above-average speed once he gets going. He reads line drives hit in front of him well, either catching them or at least keeping them in front of him. His arm is strong, but he might like it a little too much. He is prone to allowing the trail runner to advance while making a play on the lead runner. All in all, Kemp is not spectacular, but he gets the job done.

Darin Erstad

	Innings	Runs Saved
2008	304	2
2006-2008	895	5

	Good Plays	Misplays and Errors
Erstad 2008	5	4
Avg Center Fielder	6	7
Good Play/Misplay Pct		.575

Aaron Rowand

	Innings	Runs Saved
2008	1275	1
2006-2008	3550	5

	Good Plays	Misplays and Errors
Rowand 2008	19	38
Avg Center Fielder	27	30
Good Play/Misplay Pct		.351

When watching Rowand play, you get the feeling that he doesn't quite know his limits. He is still adept at reading the ball off the bat and taking great routes to the ball, using his above-average range, but at times he just doesn't put it together. While his ability to track down balls and make the highlight-reel catch won him a Gold Glove in the postage stamp yard in Philadelphia, he has more area to cover in a weaker defensive outfield in San Francisco. This caused Rowand to take more bad angles and come up short more often. He also consistently throws balls to the wrong base or throws inaccurately to a base, which allows baserunners to advance. Rowand still is a good center fielder, but he needs to rein it in to better exploit his ability.

Brian Anderson

	Innings	Runs Saved
2008	447	3
2006-2008	1437	4

	Good Plays	Misplays and Errors
Anderson 2008	6	10
Avg Center Fielder	7	8
Good Play/Misplay Pct		.394

Grady Sizemore

	Innings	Runs Saved
2008	1338	2
2006-2008	4126	4

	Good Plays	Misplays and Errors
Sizemore 2008	28	24
Avg Center Fielder	26	28
Good Play/Misplay Pct		.558

There is no doubt that Sizemore is one of the most exciting players in the game. And he has two consecutive Gold Gloves to show for it. It seems he always makes the highlight reels by laying out, crashing into a wall, or stealing a home run. Still, it's possible that his defensive abilities might be slightly exaggerated. Don't misunderstand: Sizemore is an above-average defender who has great range, a fantastic first step, and a

Center Fielders

noteworthy arm. But making the highlight reel isn't everything.

Scott Hairston

	Innings	Runs Saved
2008	378	2
2006-2008	384	3

	Good Plays	Misplays and Errors
Hairston 2008	10	13
Avg Center Fielder	7	8
Good Play/Misplay Pct		.455

Jacoby Ellsbury

	Innings	Runs Saved
2008	547	3
2006-2008	654	2

	Good Plays	Misplays and Errors
Ellsbury 2008	19	9
Avg Center Fielder	11	12
Good Play/Misplay Pct		.696

Ellsbury is versatile enough to play any outfield position, and he saw substantial time at each spot in 2008. He covers a lot of ground but still needs to learn the intricacies of playing in front of Fenway's walls. When playing in parks with more room to run, he gets to show off a little more. Skilled at reaching the diving liners that most outfielders let fall for singles, Ellsbury also features an above-average, accurate arm. He almost never makes a mistake. Read about that in Bill James' article, Defensive Misplays, on page 27.

Jeremy Reed

	Innings	Runs Saved
2008	454	0
2006-2008	961	2

	Good Plays	Misplays and Errors
Reed 2008	11	5
Avg Center Fielder	10	11
Good Play/Misplay Pct		.705

Gregor Blanco

	Innings	Runs Saved
2008	494	2
2006-2008	494	2

	Good Plays	Misplays and Errors
Blanco 2008	10	6
Avg Center Fielder	9	10
Good Play/Misplay Pct		.644

Torii Hunter

	Innings	Runs Saved
2008	1193	-2
2006-2008	3740	2

	Good Plays	Misplays and Errors
Hunter 2008	18	19
Avg Center Fielder	25	27
Good Play/Misplay Pct		.507

Known as one of the most exciting center fielders in the game, Hunter is well removed from his defensive prime. Nevertheless he won his eighth consecutive Gold Glove in 2008. He still plays center field well going side to side. When he is shifted to deep left-center field and needs to run to deep right-center, he can cover a lot of ground with smooth strides that make it look like he's gliding. He also possesses an above-average arm with good accuracy. He robbed two more home runs in 2008, giving him seven in the last three years. The next most is five (Gary Mathews Jr.).

However, some of Hunter's routes have become problematic. He was fooled numerous times on hard-hit line drives that either went over his head or bounced off his glove. He also tended to miss some soft, catchable flyballs. He would sometimes try to basket-catch balls or misread them, leading to base hits. Even with these fielding woes, Hunter still plays acceptable defense. But an "oh-ver-ray-ted" chant might not be out of line.

Gabe Kapler

	Innings	Runs Saved
2008	251	4
2006-2008	346	0

	Good Plays	Misplays and Errors
Kapler 2008	4	4
Avg Center Fielder	5	5
Good Play/Misplay Pct		.520

Melky Cabrera

	Innings	Runs Saved
2008	974	5
2006-2008	2069	0

	Good Plays	Misplays and Errors
Cabrera 2008	22	17
Avg Center Fielder	18	20
Good Play/Misplay Pct		.584

Cabrera struggled mightily at the plate in 2008, but he improved his defense to become an effective center fielder. Prone to taking bad routes in the past, he started

Center Fielders

getting better reads on the ball. He has great first-step quickness, which gives his speed a boost. He also possesses a plus arm for a center fielder. He consistently throws runners out and holds some doubles to singles, although he also overthrows sometimes. His attempts to make difficult dives on hard-hit balls often result in multiple-base losses.

Ryan Sweeney

	Innings	Runs Saved
2008	363	-2
2006-2008	424	-3

	Good Plays	Misplays and Errors
Sweeney 2008	2	9
Avg Center Fielder	7	7
Good Play/Misplay Pct		.194

Skip Schumaker

	Innings	Runs Saved
2008	553	-4
2006-2008	642	-3

	Good Plays	Misplays and Errors
Schumaker 2008	11	8
Avg Center Fielder	10	11
Good Play/Misplay Pct		.598

Schumaker split time among all three outfield spots in 2008, playing more than 240 innings at each position. He played the most innings in center field, but he is probably best-suited defensively for a corner position, especially right field considering his strong arm. He gets good jumps and has good range, but he also takes circuitous routes to a lot of flyballs. He isn't afraid to lay out for a ball, but he also is prone to failure on those diving attempts. Schumaker's tendency to overrun balls that hit off the wall doesn't help.

Nick Swisher

	Innings	Runs Saved
2008	535	-7
2006-2008	1018	-3

	Good Plays	Misplays and Errors
Swisher 2008	11	15
Avg Center Fielder	10	11
Good Play/Misplay Pct		.443

Swisher saw equal time at first base and in center field in 2008, a rare combination. Unfortunately, he just doesn't have the wheels for center. He takes good routes but lacks the speed to track down hard-hit balls. He also has difficulty with balls in the right-center gap, as he routinely takes rounded paths to the ball rather than direct ones. You can't fault and you can't teach Swisher's hustle, but you also can't deny that it occasionally causes him to over-pursue balls and make unnecessary dives. A solid defender in the corner outfield positions, Swisher's true calling is as a first baseman, where scouts believe he could take home a Gold Glove or two someday.

Rick Ankiel

	Innings	Runs Saved
2008	766	-2
2006-2008	903	-3

	Good Plays	Misplays and Errors
Ankiel 2008	20	26
Avg Center Fielder	15	16
Good Play/Misplay Pct		.455

The athleticism that allowed Ankiel to transition from a power pitcher to a power hitter is on full display in center field. He has only been playing outfield for a couple years, though, so he is still rough around the edges. He has trouble judging flyballs, specifically ones directly at him or over his head, but his great speed covers for some of his mistakes. His best asset is his accurate arm, a carryover from his pitching days and one of the strongest in the league. Ankiel didn't play much in the last few months of the season because of injuries, but with more experience his skills will catch up to his immense raw talent.

Lastings Milledge

	Innings	Runs Saved
2008	1186	-6
2006-2008	1306	-4

	Good Plays	Misplays and Errors
Milledge 2008	17	39
Avg Center Fielder	23	25
Good Play/Misplay Pct		.321

The talented center fielder had his ups and downs in 2008. He has great speed, along with superb athleticism to get to balls in the gaps. On some occasions, Milledge would show amazing range going back to his right, making exceptional diving plays. He also possesses an above-average arm that prevents baserunner advancement. With all of this ability, Milledge still isn't the total package as a center fielder. He sometimes has trouble reading hard-hit line drives and consistently mishandles base hits, giving up extra bases. He needs to get better reads, which will help him get in better position to make the play. Expect Milledge to correct some of these weaknesses in 2009.

Center Fielders

David DeJesus

	Innings	Runs Saved
2008	507	-9
2006-2008	2338	-4

	Good Plays	Misplays and Errors
DeJesus 2008	7	11
Avg Center Fielder	10	11
Good Play/Misplay Pct		.408

DeJesus originally was called up by the Royals to replace Carlos Beltran in center field, but in 2008 he split time between left and center. His speed, enhanced by his quick first step and ability to read flyballs, allows him to cover ground from the left-field line to the left-center gap. Sometimes he is too aggressive, attempting to cut off balls in the gap only to over-pursue and misplay them instead. His arm is a better fit for left field, but DeJesus can play in either left or center.

Josh Hamilton

	Innings	Runs Saved
2008	912	-5
2006-2008	1468	-4

	Good Plays	Misplays and Errors
Hamilton 2008	21	24
Avg Center Fielder	19	21
Good Play/Misplay Pct		.487

Hamilton possesses all the raw tools one would look for in a center fielder. He has great arm strength, along with above-average speed and quickness, but he had some problems reading the ball off the bat on softly hit flyballs. These balls often dropped for hits. Hamilton also was inconsistent running to hard-hit balls to his left or right. His great range and plus arm sometimes produced difficult flyouts as well as outfield assists. However, Hamilton sometimes failed to convert outs on occasions when he misread the ball's trajectory or simply didn't time his slide well enough. While Hamilton has significant room for improvement, he has shown that he can't ever be counted out.

Joey Gathright

	Innings	Runs Saved
2008	720	-6
2006-2008	1793	-5

	Good Plays	Misplays and Errors
Gathright 2008	22	18
Avg Center Fielder	14	15
Good Play/Misplay Pct		.570

One of the game's premier athletes, it's entirely possible that Gathright just isn't very good at baseball. There's no denying his incredible speed and agility. His range is tremendous, but he is held back by bad routes and angles. He doesn't have a great arm, but his speed allows him to reach balls quicker than other outfielders would, which keeps baserunners from advancing. As time goes by, Gathright's defensive ceiling gets lower and lower.

Johnny Damon

	Innings	Runs Saved
2008	285	-3
2006-2008	1749	-8

	Good Plays	Misplays and Errors
Damon 2008	2	5
Avg Center Fielder	6	6
Good Play/Misplay Pct		.302

Reed Johnson

	Innings	Runs Saved
2008	564	-6
2006-2008	678	-8

	Good Plays	Misplays and Errors
Johnson 2008	6	6
Avg Center Fielder	10	11
Good Play/Misplay Pct		.520

Johnson can track down balls deep in the gaps and has an uncanny knack for taking direct routes to the ball. Although his arm isn't the strongest, he still makes accurate throws and deters runners from advancing. Like most outfielders, he has problems with balls hit directly over his head, but he was a better defensive option for the Cubs in 2008 than Jim Edmonds. He is a tremendous left fielder who is a bit out of place in center.

Center Fielders

Mark Kotsay

	Innings	Runs Saved
2008	696	-1
2006-2008	2216	-8

	Good Plays	Misplays and Errors
Kotsay 2008	7	5
Avg Center Fielder	13	14
Good Play/Misplay Pct		.603

A midseason trade to the Red Sox gave Kotsay the chance to show his athleticism, playing multiple outfield positions and an impressive first base. Kotsay's playing time has been limited because of injuries, especially chronic back problems, but he is still an above-average defender when healthy. He has always had a quick first step and a knack for reading the ball off the bat. Although he isn't as fast as he used to be, his range to the gaps is very good. His arm remains strong and accurate, allowing him to play right field when the need arises. Right field and first base are now his best positions, as his best days as a center fielder have been curtailed by his injuries. He might not be (OK, he just plain isn't) durable enough to be a full-time starter anymore, but Kotsay might rejuvenate his career as one of the best bench players in baseball.

Ken Griffey Jr.

	Innings	Runs Saved
2008	250	3
2006-2008	1120	-10

	Good Plays	Misplays and Errors
Griffey Jr. 2008	4	5
Avg Center Fielder	4	5
Good Play/Misplay Pct		.464

Jim Edmonds

	Innings	Runs Saved
2008	840	-13
2006-2008	2461	-15

	Good Plays	Misplays and Errors
Edmonds 2008	15	21
Avg Center Fielder	16	17
Good Play/Misplay Pct		.436

It's hell getting old. Long gone are the days when Edmonds made acrobatic plays in center field. His age-induced lack of range and inability to recover from bad routes cause him to dive more frequently than most center fielders. Unfortunately, diving only looks cool if you catch the ball. Edmonds' failed diving attempts amount to a lowlight reel. Given that Edmonds still has the ability to throw out almost any runner at any time, a move to a corner spot would be a great idea.

Nate McLouth

	Innings	Runs Saved
2008	1300	-19
2006-2008	2141	-25

	Good Plays	Misplays and Errors
McLouth 2008	31	25
Avg Center Fielder	27	29
Good Play/Misplay Pct		.573

McLouth has the range you want in a center fielder, but it didn't show up in his numbers (-37 plus/minus) in 2008, because he simply plays too shallow. See McLouth vs. Gomez on page 155. He reads the ball well off the bat and takes great routes to the ball, making quite a few impressive catches in the process. He struggles with anticipating the wall. On multiple occasions, his misplays on caroms allowed baserunners to advance, as did his tendency to get sloppy when picking up balls that fell safely for hits. If McLouth can improve in these areas, and not play quite so shallow, he might win a Gold Glove. . .and actually deserve it.

Right Fielders Evaluations

Year	League	Gold Glove Winners	Should Have Been
2003	AL	Ichiro Suzuki	Ichiro Suzuki
	NL	Jose Cruz	Richard Hidalgo
2004	AL	Ichiro Suzuki	Ichiro Suzuki
	NL	none	Richard Hidalgo
2005	AL	Ichiro Suzuki	Ichiro Suzuki
	NL	Bobby Abreu	Geoff Jenkins
2006	AL	Ichiro Suzuki	Ichiro Suzuki
			Alex Rios
	NL	none	none
2007	AL	none	Alex Rios
	NL	Jeff Francoeur	Jeff Francoeur
2008	AL	Ichiro Suzuki	Franklin Gutierrez
			Nick Markakis
	NL	none	none

My Personal Ratings

Top Ten

1 Franklin Gutierrez, Cle
2 Alex Rios, Tor
3 Nick Markakis, Bal
4 Ichiro Suzuki, Sea
5 Denard Span, Min
6 Jeff Francoeur, Atl
7 Randy Winn, SF
8 Hunter Pence, Hou
9 Ryan Ludwick, StL
10 Brian Giles, SD

Bottom Five

26 Vladimir Guerrero, LAA
27 Bobby Abreu, LAA
28 Jermaine Dye, CWS
29 Ken Griffey Jr., FA
30 Brad Hawpe, Col

Player teams based on transactions through February 11, 2009

Right Fielders

Alex Rios

	Innings	Runs Saved
2008	820	14
2006-2008	3023	49

	Good Plays	Misplays and Errors
Rios 2008	11	15
Avg Right Fielder	15	16
Good Play/Misplay Pct		.449

One of baseball's best defensive outfielders, Rios should have had a Gold Glove or two by now. He was the Fielding Bible Award winner in right field in 2007. He has great speed and a laser arm with pinpoint precision. He played center field while Vernon Wells was hurt, proving himself a superb defender at that position as well. His combined +24 plus/minus score (+8 in center, +16 in right) trailed only Franklin Gutierrez, Carlos Gomez and Carlos Beltran in the outfield in 2008. His three-year total of 49 defensive runs saved in right field is the highest total of any outfielder. And that doesn't even count the 10 runs Rios saved playing center field last year.

Franklin Gutierrez

	Innings	Runs Saved
2008	764	22
2006-2008	1554	34

	Good Plays	Misplays and Errors
Gutierrez 2008	22	8
Avg Right Fielder	17	19
Good Play/Misplay Pct		.754

Gutierrez is a classic right fielder with a rocket arm that discourages runners from trying to take extra bases. He is smooth and graceful in right and doesn't make many mistakes. His timing is excellent when he leaves his feet, and he covers plenty of ground. His MLB-leading right field plus/minus totals of +29 and +20 in the last two years were posted while playing only 97 and 88 games, respectively. Gutierrez was voted the best right fielder in baseball last year, winning his first Fielding Bible Award.

Randy Winn

	Innings	Runs Saved
2008	1108	12
2006-2008	2630	31

	Good Plays	Misplays and Errors
Winn 2008	20	13
Avg Right Fielder	23	25
Good Play/Misplay Pct		.631

Winn has been one of the more consistent right fielders in baseball, finishing in the top five in the Plus/Minus System for the last three seasons. He does not have elite range, but he can still run, gets good jumps, and takes good routes to flyballs. Winn is comfortable going straight back on flyballs, and he is tremendous reading line drives off the bat, often making sliding catches that normally would drop in for base hits. Winn's only weakness is that his arm strength is below average for a right fielder, but he charges balls well and is very accurate with his throws, thus limiting the extra bases runners would normally take. Winn also rarely makes mistakes, further cementing his value as a defensive asset in the field, despite his age.

Nick Markakis

	Innings	Runs Saved
2008	1367	20
2006-2008	3680	30

	Good Plays	Misplays and Errors
Markakis 2008	41	15
Avg Right Fielder	28	31
Good Play/Misplay Pct		.753

Sporting a cannon for an arm, Markakis is one of the best young right fielders in the game. He takes great routes to the ball, and he has developed a heightened awareness of the big right field wall in Camden Yards. He has enough quickness to get great jumps on the ball and make smart plays when the ball is out of reach. Of course, he isn't infallible. He isn't always in the best position to field balls off the wall, which leads to extra bases. And he makes an occasional overthrow. These faults don't outweigh his strengths. His 14 runs saved with his throwing arm last year was the highest mark in three years of tabulating this new statistic for right fielders. Markakis's arm and instincts make him one of the game's top right fielders, and he is only going to get better.

Right Fielders

Ichiro Suzuki

	Innings	Runs Saved
2008	788	15
2006-2008	1850	27

	Good Plays	Misplays and Errors
Suzuki 2008	24	18
Avg Right Fielder	15	17
Good Play/Misplay Pct		.597

Whether playing center field early in the season or right field for the remainder, Ichiro's superb range and direct routes put him among the game's best outfielders. He has great body control and leaping ability, and he isn't wall-shy. In addition, his arm strength and accuracy prove valuable not just in terms of throwing out baserunners, but in deterring aggressive baserunning in the first place. His assist totals might be down, but it's more an indication of the respect he commands from baserunners than an indication of declining skills. He has won an American League Gold Glove in each of the eight years he's been in Major League Baseball, and a Fielding Bible Award in 2006 as the best right fielder in baseball to boot.

Jeff Francoeur

	Innings	Runs Saved
2008	1329	-2
2006-2008	4191	26

	Good Plays	Misplays and Errors
Francoeur 2008	16	22
Avg Right Fielder	25	28
Good Play/Misplay Pct		.447

Fresh off a Gold Glove, Francoeur took a step back in 2008. He struggled at the plate and might have taken these struggles with him into the field. It's no secret that Francoeur has one of the best outfield arms in the game. In 2008, however, he had more wasted throws than ever before (although he still prevented more runners from advancing than the average right fielder). He also had a problem overrunning balls in attempts to throw out advancing baserunners. Francoeur needs to improve on his glove-to-hand transfer to execute more baserunner kills. Still one of the quicker, more athletic right fielders in the game, he made some great running catches, along with some diving plays. But he had his troubles in 2008. After posting plus/minus scores totaling +24 the previous three years, he dropped to -12 last year. Francoeur's hustle, great attitude, and athleticism make him a great asset in right field and a comeback is a near certainty.

Brian Giles

	Innings	Runs Saved
2008	1263	8
2006-2008	3724	20

	Good Plays	Misplays and Errors
Giles 2008	23	22
Avg Right Fielder	24	27
Good Play/Misplay Pct		.538

Giles isn't fast, and he knows it. He relies on tremendous jumps and solid routes to make up for his lack of speed. He takes good angles on grounders and charges them aggressively, but his arm has weakened over time. Baserunners recognize this; they took 71 extra bases on him last year, costing the Padres an estimated five runs. But he more than made up for it with the ground he covered, saving 13 runs based on his plus/minus score of +22 in 2008.

Austin Kearns

	Innings	Runs Saved
2008	734	-2
2006-2008	3339	19

	Good Plays	Misplays and Errors
Kearns 2008	8	19
Avg Right Fielder	16	17
Good Play/Misplay Pct		.319

Normally a superb fielder, Kearns was hampered by injuries in 2008, logging just 734 innings in the field and only three outfield assists. While he still flashed his cannon arm on occasion, his injuries limited his ability to impact the opposition's running game. He was slower getting to balls and seemed a little too deliberate in his throwing, which resulted in many off-target throws and the resultant runs and extra bases. As long as he gets healthy, Kearns should bounce back to his previous skill level, a level recognized by Fielding Bible Award voters in 2007 when they voted him in a tie with Jeff Francoeur as the second best right fielder in baseball (Alex Rios was first).

Right Fielders

Denard Span

	Innings	Runs Saved
2008	687	15
2006-2008	687	15

	Good Plays	Misplays and Errors
Span 2008	18	14
Avg Right Fielder	14	16
Good Play/Misplay Pct		.589

Span emerged in 2008 as one of the best right fielders in baseball. He is very aggressive, has outstanding range, and possesses a strong, accurate arm. He fears no wall and generally gets there early enough to time his jump. He takes good routes, but he sometimes gets turned around when he has to run back on hard-hit balls. His aggressiveness can hurt him at times, as he is prone to overrunning balls that hit off the wall or overthrowing the cutoff man in an attempt to throw out a runner. Span's defense will be a bright spot for the Twins for years to come.

Jayson Werth

	Innings	Runs Saved
2008	661	5
2006-2008	1107	15

	Good Plays	Misplays and Errors
Werth 2008	12	10
Avg Right Fielder	11	12
Good Play/Misplay Pct		.572

Werth played all three outfield positions in 2008 for the Phillies, but he spent most of his time in right. He is not a spectacular outfielder, but he is a good athlete who minimizes mistakes, gets good jumps, and tracks flyballs well. Werth's arm is average, but he has outstanding accuracy and positions himself well to throw.

Ryan Ludwick

	Innings	Runs Saved
2008	962	12
2006-2008	1215	14

	Good Plays	Misplays and Errors
Ludwick 2008	22	19
Avg Right Fielder	20	22
Good Play/Misplay Pct		.563

An overnight sensation six years in the making, Ludwick has emerged as a solid corner outfielder. Despite his lanky appearance, he gets quick jumps that allow him to track down difficult flyballs in right field. His arm was a highlight in 2008. He had eight baserunner kills and allowed the fewest extra bases on singles and doubles per attempt of any National League right fielder. His arm saved an estimated 11 runs for the Cardinals, third best in MLB for any outfielder.

Hunter Pence

	Innings	Runs Saved
2008	1366	11
2006-2008	1482	12

	Good Plays	Misplays and Errors
Pence 2008	27	28
Avg Right Fielder	27	30
Good Play/Misplay Pct		.518

Pence is an all-out, all-the-time guy. He isn't afraid to be aggressive and will sacrifice his body to make a play. His arm can victimize runners who try to advance without the proper caution. He had 11 baserunner kills, the highest total in the National League. Due to his lanky build, he never looks particularly graceful, but he gets the job done.

Nelson Cruz

	Innings	Runs Saved
2008	274	2
2006-2008	1186	11

	Good Plays	Misplays and Errors
Cruz 2008	5	7
Avg Right Fielder	6	7
Good Play/Misplay Pct		.443

Ryan Sweeney

	Innings	Runs Saved
2008	487	9
2006-2008	515	9

	Good Plays	Misplays and Errors
Sweeney 2008	12	11
Avg Right Fielder	10	11
Good Play/Misplay Pct		.548

Sweeney is an excellent right fielder, especially for a guy his size. He has a very strong arm and makes accurate throws. What's surprising is how smooth and quick Sweeney looks. He made numerous diving and sliding catches in 2008, several after long runs into the vast foul territory in Oakland. He can be counted on to make jumping catches at or near the wall and shows no fear when approaching the fence. Sweeney could patrol right field for years.

Right Fielders

Endy Chavez

	Innings	Runs Saved
2008	400	8
2006-2008	811	8

	Good Plays	Misplays and Errors
Chavez 2008	13	6
Avg Right Fielder	8	9
Good Play/Misplay Pct		.707

Chavez has outstanding speed in the outfield, and plays all three positions well. He is the defensive specialist for the Mets, entering into any outfield position to replace anyone not named Beltran. His plus/minus figures over his three years with the Mets are +10 or better at each outfield position. In 2008 he played primarily right field, posting a +11 in one partial year by itself. He has an occasional problem where he takes a bad route or misjudges a ball. He is better at tracking down balls in front of him than over his head, but he does do a good job playing base hits off the wall. Chavez has an above-average arm but it's nothing to write home about.

Brad Wilkerson

	Innings	Runs Saved
2008	485	7
2006-2008	617	8

	Good Plays	Misplays and Errors
Wilkerson 2008	10	10
Avg Right Fielder	8	9
Good Play/Misplay Pct		.527

Corey Hart

	Innings	Runs Saved
2008	1377	2
2006-2008	2507	8

	Good Plays	Misplays and Errors
Hart 2008	22	32
Avg Right Fielder	25	28
Good Play/Misplay Pct		.433

Hart has above-average speed in right field. Being tall and lanky gives him great extension stretching out for balls on the run. His speed should normally allow him to get to balls others can't, but at times he struggles with his routes, especially if he has a lot of ground to cover. Hart possesses an average throwing arm, but is inconsistent with his release, resulting in throws often coming in too low. All things considered, he is the role model for being an average outfielder.

Geoff Jenkins

	Innings	Runs Saved
2008	642	5
2006-2008	1743	8

	Good Plays	Misplays and Errors
Jenkins 2008	17	21
Avg Right Fielder	12	13
Good Play/Misplay Pct		.474

Jenkins lost his starting job in the middle of 2008 due to poor production at the plate, but he is a capable right fielder. He has good range but can struggle with reading the ball off the bat. He charges the ball aggressively in the air and on the ground, but he tends to pull up when he approaches a wall. Jenkins possesses an extremely accurate throwing arm, which contributed to his seven assists in 2008. Five of those assists were direct baserunner kills as he accounted for an estimated six runs saved with his arm.

Marlon Byrd

	Innings	Runs Saved
2008	279	3
2006-2008	666	7

	Good Plays	Misplays and Errors
Byrd 2008	8	12
Avg Right Fielder	6	7
Good Play/Misplay Pct		.426

Justin Upton

	Innings	Runs Saved
2008	860	5
2006-2008	1176	7

	Good Plays	Misplays and Errors
Upton 2008	11	38
Avg Right Fielder	15	17
Good Play/Misplay Pct		.244

Only 21-years-old, Upton is adjusting to playing right field in the majors. He has one of the stronger outfield arms in the game, along with great speed. His flair for the dramatic led to failed dives and extra bases for the opposition, and he consistently tried to catch hard-hit line drives that should've been fielded for singles instead. Upton also had a tough time playing the wall, sometimes allowing the ball to get past him on the carom. He did show good range in right field to go with his athleticism and quickness, making some great plays in shallow right field. Upton also used his strong arm to convert six baserunner kills. His 38 misplays and errors

Right Fielders

was the second-highest outfield total in all of baseball (Brad Hawpe, 42). With plenty of lessons left to learn, Upton has the potential to be a defensive asset.

David Murphy

	Innings	Runs Saved
2008	407	5
2006-2008	497	6

	Good Plays	Misplays and Errors
Murphy 2008	6	6
Avg Right Fielder	8	9
Good Play/Misplay Pct		.527

A versatile fielder who can play all three outfield positions, Murphy mainly split time between left and right in 2008. He has above-average range and a very strong throwing arm. He does a good job of squaring up his body on flyballs before the throw, but his confidence in his arm has resulted in several extra bases being taken when trying to gun down the lead runner. When ranging back to the wall, Murphy is aware of how much room he has to work with and adjusts well.

Elijah Dukes

	Innings	Runs Saved
2008	603	6
2006-2008	604	6

	Good Plays	Misplays and Errors
Dukes 2008	14	15
Avg Right Fielder	12	13
Good Play/Misplay Pct		.509

Despite his sordid past (multiple run-ins with the law), Dukes has found a home in Washington because of his immense talent. While most people will tell you about his potential as a slugger, he also has the potential to be a great outfielder. He has an absolute rocket arm, and he knows how to take advantage of it. He understands when he cannot make a play on a ball in the air and prepares himself well to keep the batter from taking an extra base. He doesn't always take the best routes to flyballs, but he does adjust well. Dukes played about a third of the time in center field in 2008, but he probably won't see much time there going forward. That's not necessarily a bad thing. His powerful arm and good instincts make him a weapon in right.

Jacoby Ellsbury

	Innings	Runs Saved
2008	281	6
2006-2008	287	6

	Good Plays	Misplays and Errors
Ellsbury 2008	6	0
Avg Right Fielder	5	6
Good Play/Misplay Pct		1.000

Matt Kemp

	Innings	Runs Saved
2008	479	6
2006-2008	1170	6

	Good Plays	Misplays and Errors
Kemp 2008	9	12
Avg Right Fielder	9	10
Good Play/Misplay Pct		.455

Gabe Gross

	Innings	Runs Saved
2008	769	4
2006-2008	1095	6

	Good Plays	Misplays and Errors
Gross 2008	10	10
Avg Right Fielder	14	16
Good Play/Misplay Pct		.527

Although not a great athlete, Gross makes all the plays needed from a right fielder. He has average range and charges balls aggressively in the air and on the ground. Gross reads balls well off the bat, but he tends to drift on flyballs hit over his head. He plays balls well off the wall and in the corner, giving him a chance to hold runners from advancing. Gross has an accurate arm, if not an especially strong one. Baserunners didn't advance very often on singles and doubles, helping him save four runs for his team.

Mark DeRosa

	Innings	Runs Saved
2008	267	-2
2006-2008	917	6

	Good Plays	Misplays and Errors
DeRosa 2008	9	6
Avg Right Fielder	5	6
Good Play/Misplay Pct		.625

Right Fielders

J.D. Drew

	Innings	Runs Saved
2008	886	-5
2006-2008	3066	6

	Good Plays	Misplays and Errors
Drew 2008	13	17
Avg Right Fielder	15	17
Good Play/Misplay Pct		.460

Drew has above-average speed but lacks aggression on balls in the gap, a fault he makes up for by taking good angles. His arm is strong and true, rarely overthrowing the cutoff man or throwing to the wrong base. Assigned the tricky task of playing right field in Fenway Park, Drew has acquitted himself well, rarely allowing extra bases on caroms off the wall. He had an off-year defensively in 2008, posting a -7 plus/minus rating after five years all above zero. He should bounce back in 2009.

Ryan Church

	Innings	Runs Saved
2008	724	5
2006-2008	821	5

	Good Plays	Misplays and Errors
Church 2008	19	15
Avg Right Fielder	15	17
Good Play/Misplay Pct		.585

Church lost playing time due to a concussion suffered in May while attempting to break up a double play. When healthy, he can play all three outfield positions, but he should serve as the Mets' everyday right fielder in 2009. His arm isn't the best, but he has the range to make plays one wouldn't expect him to make. He is an above-average right fielder.

Shin-Soo Choo

	Innings	Runs Saved
2008	398	-1
2006-2008	666	5

	Good Plays	Misplays and Errors
Choo 2008	5	14
Avg Right Fielder	8	9
Good Play/Misplay Pct		.284

Choo made some miscues in 2008, but most were related to his judgment rather than his skills. Too often he would go to the wall instead of turning and playing the ball off the carom, allowing runners to take additional bases in the process. He tried to be a hero sometimes, throwing home in a lost cause when a throw to second base would have been smarter. He does have a very strong arm but registered only one kill, in part because of his decision-making. With better judgment, Choo should become an improved defender.

Josh Hamilton

	Innings	Runs Saved
2008	289	2
2006-2008	370	4

	Good Plays	Misplays and Errors
Hamilton 2008	10	7
Avg Right Fielder	7	7
Good Play/Misplay Pct		.614

Jeremy Hermida

	Innings	Runs Saved
2008	1092	-2
2006-2008	2762	3

	Good Plays	Misplays and Errors
Hermida 2008	10	17
Avg Right Fielder	23	25
Good Play/Misplay Pct		.396

Hermida has the speed and arm necessary to handle the responsibilities in right. He is much better coming in on balls than going back on them. He had some trouble holding down baserunner advancement in 2008, costing his team three runs. Already a dependable, if unspectacular, right fielder, Hermida has the talent to be even better.

Kosuke Fukudome

	Innings	Runs Saved
2008	1104	3
2006-2008	1104	3

	Good Plays	Misplays and Errors
Fukudome 2008	25	17
Avg Right Fielder	20	22
Good Play/Misplay Pct		.621

Fukudome came into the major leagues as a four-time Gold Glover in Japan. Although he did not perform well at the plate, his defense compared well with that of his counterparts.

Fukudome takes great routes to balls in right field, and he always seems to be in position to make a diving catch. He possesses an above-average to plus throwing arm with great accuracy. At times, he hogs right-center field, failing to yield to the center fielder when necessary. But with great instincts and good range in right field, Fukudome did a great job of converting difficult outs and preventing baserunner advancement with his arm.

Right Fielders

Travis Buck

	Innings	Runs Saved
2008	287	2
2006-2008	796	2

	Good Plays	Misplays and Errors
Buck 2008	9	8
Avg Right Fielder	6	6
Good Play/Misplay Pct		.556

Eric Hinske

	Innings	Runs Saved
2008	339	0
2006-2008	697	1

	Good Plays	Misplays and Errors
Hinske 2008	5	12
Avg Right Fielder	7	7
Good Play/Misplay Pct		.317

Magglio Ordonez

	Innings	Runs Saved
2008	1144	-2
2006-2008	3633	2

	Good Plays	Misplays and Errors
Ordonez 2008	10	23
Avg Right Fielder	21	24
Good Play/Misplay Pct		.326

Wladimir Balentien

	Innings	Runs Saved
2008	293	2
2006-2008	297	1

	Good Plays	Misplays and Errors
Balentien 2008	6	7
Avg Right Fielder	7	8
Good Play/Misplay Pct		.488

None of us are getting any younger, but some of us are getting less young than others. Like Magglio Ordonez, for example. His range and mobility continue to decline, but he'll be in the field for at least one more year, given Gary Sheffield's lock on the Tigers' designated hitter job. Ordonez's strength is knowing when to say when. By playing it safe, he prevents opposing baserunners from taking extra bases on ill-advised throws or would-be Web Gems.

Jay Bruce

	Innings	Runs Saved
2008	590	1
2006-2008	590	1

	Good Plays	Misplays and Errors
Bruce 2008	15	21
Avg Right Fielder	12	13
Good Play/Misplay Pct		.443

Mark Teahen

	Innings	Runs Saved
2008	756	-6
2006-2008	1907	2

	Good Plays	Misplays and Errors
Teahen 2008	13	17
Avg Right Fielder	16	18
Good Play/Misplay Pct		.460

Teahen still looks uncomfortable in the outfield two seasons after his transition from third base. Even though he has an above-average arm, he doesn't get himself in effective throwing positions and appears overly cautious when running down hits to his left or right. As a result, baserunners run on him like an indoor track.

In his rookie campaign, Bruce moved around the outfield before settling in as the everyday right fielder. He seemed hesitant to take control on shallow flyballs, deferring to back-pedaling infielders instead. This should improve as he gets more comfortable, both as a right fielder and as a major leaguer. He has a strong arm, average speed, and makes good plays on balls hit over his head, either catching them or playing them correctly off the wall. Bruce had five baserunner kills, a respectable total in his half-season in right field.

Jason Michaels

	Innings	Runs Saved
2008	293	-1
2006-2008	418	-1

	Good Plays	Misplays and Errors
Michaels 2008	7	10
Avg Right Fielder	6	7
Good Play/Misplay Pct		.438

Right Fielders

Fernando Tatis

	Innings	Runs Saved
2008	293	-1
2006-2008	301	-1

	Good Plays	Misplays and Errors
Tatis 2008	6	6
Avg Right Fielder	5	5
Good Play/Misplay Pct		.527

Xavier Nady

	Innings	Runs Saved
2008	764	1
2006-2008	2366	-1

	Good Plays	Misplays and Errors
Nady 2008	19	15
Avg Right Fielder	16	18
Good Play/Misplay Pct		.585

Nady's unpredictable arm is his biggest challenge. Seven of his defensive misplays this year resulted from throwing poorly—to the wrong base, or to no one in particular. However, he also made seven good fielding plays and seven baserunner kills with his arm, so it's actually a net positive. Nady doesn't have the best range, but he rarely takes a bad route or comes up short when he dives for balls. He seems well prepared for every batter because he doesn't make many mental mistakes. Every once in a while, though, he'll just plain miss a catch. He isn't a particularly good corner outfielder, but he's good enough.

Vladimir Guerrero

	Innings	Runs Saved
2008	839	-2
2006-2008	2860	-2

	Good Plays	Misplays and Errors
Guerrero 2008	10	23
Avg Right Fielder	15	16
Good Play/Misplay Pct		.326

Guerrero is a veteran who still has a cannon arm that deters runners from advancing, although runners seemed to fear him less in 2008. He has shown some ability getting to balls down the right-field line and has even caught a few balls in the stands. However, at age 33, his speed is fading fast. Vlad struggles getting to balls in the right-center gap and making plays on shallow flyballs. He also has consistently mishandled balls off the wall due to poor awareness of the ball's flight. Despite a great arm, the aging Guerrero might see increased time at DH in the near future.

Andre Ethier

	Innings	Runs Saved
2008	881	-11
2006-2008	1661	-2

	Good Plays	Misplays and Errors
Ethier 2008	11	14
Avg Right Fielder	16	18
Good Play/Misplay Pct		.466

Ethier used his bat and Andruw Jones' struggles to wedge his way into a crowded Dodger outfield. He can play either corner spot but stuck to right field once Manny Ramirez arrived. He struggled there, posting a -19 plus/minus score over the course of the season. There is nothing particularly noteworthy about Ethier's abilities, and he's best served as a left fielder.

Emil Brown

	Innings	Runs Saved
2008	433	2
2006-2008	998	-3

	Good Plays	Misplays and Errors
Brown 2008	4	12
Avg Right Fielder	8	9
Good Play/Misplay Pct		.271

Right Fielders

Jose Guillen

	Innings	Runs Saved
2008	539	-4
2006-2008	2351	-3

	Good Plays	Misplays and Errors
Guillen 2008	10	13
Avg Right Fielder	11	13
Good Play/Misplay Pct		.461

Guillen played through groin and leg injuries that made him slower and more tentative last season. The injuries even affected his well-regarded arm, leaving him unable to attack groundballs and get his entire body behind his throws. He looked like a shell of his former self in the second half.

Gary Matthews Jr.

	Innings	Runs Saved
2008	344	-4
2006-2008	370	-5

	Good Plays	Misplays and Errors
Matthews Jr. 2008	8	10
Avg Right Fielder	6	7
Good Play/Misplay Pct		.471

Michael Cuddyer

	Innings	Runs Saved
2008	502	0
2006-2008	2953	-9

	Good Plays	Misplays and Errors
Cuddyer 2008	18	15
Avg Right Fielder	10	11
Good Play/Misplay Pct		.572

Cuddyer has been the starting right fielder for the Twins for the last couple of seasons, but he missed significant time in 2008 due to injury. He reads balls well off the bat, but he occasionally struggles with routes when he has to run back for flyballs. Cuddyer's best tool is his strong, accurate arm. He throws well when charging in and is adept at fielding balls off the Metrodome's right field tarp. Over the last three years, Cuddyer's arm has saved the Twins an estimated 25 runs, but he's given all of that back, and then some, before costing them 34 runs with his lack of range.

Ken Griffey Jr.

	Innings	Runs Saved
2008	763	-6
2006-2008	1926	-14

	Good Plays	Misplays and Errors
Griffey Jr. 2008	20	15
Avg Right Fielder	14	16
Good Play/Misplay Pct		.597

At this point, Junior is a lot of things—first-ballot Hall of Famer, one-time guest star on "The Simpsons," etc.—but a solid defensive outfielder is no longer one of them. He started 2008 as the Reds' right fielder but moved back to center field after his trade to the White Sox for the stretch run. The years have not been kind to Griffey's range, arm, or speed. He still gets good reads, but now he only prevents the occasional extra-base opportunity instead of stealing hits. His arm is still accurate, and he is smart with his throws.

Bobby Abreu

	Innings	Runs Saved
2008	1310	-5
2006-2008	3936	-19

	Good Plays	Misplays and Errors
Abreu 2008	16	34
Avg Right Fielder	26	29
Good Play/Misplay Pct		.344

Father Time must get sick of spending so much time in the Yankee clubhouse. The 35-year-old Abreu's range, quickness, and overall speed have declined, causing him to alter his playing style. In an effort to keep balls in front of him, he plays an extremely deep right field. This means, essentially, that he is playing a no-doubles defense at all times, limiting the number of extra-base hits. It also means that Abreu allows more hits to fall in front of him and that runners have a better chance to take the extra base, thanks to his weakening arm. Abreu might have to consider a position change with the Angels if he wants to maintain his everyday player status.

Right Fielders

Brad Hawpe

	Innings	Runs Saved
2008	1172	-22
2006-2008	3606	-27

	Good Plays	Misplays and Errors
Hawpe 2008	19	42
Avg Right Fielder	22	24
Good Play/Misplay Pct		.335

Hawpe has average range but takes some questionable routes. He tends to misread the ball off the bat and thus fails to make the play, especially with balls hit over his head. He always seems cautious to dive and either pulls up or slides awkwardly on balls that appear to be catchable. He led all major league outfielders in two categories that he'd prefer not to. He was tied with Nate McLouth with the worst plus/minus figure in all of baseball (-37) and he had the most outfielder defensive misplays and errors as well (42). Hawpe's best asset is his arm.

Jermaine Dye

	Innings	Runs Saved
2008	1313	-9
2006-2008	3714	-39

	Good Plays	Misplays and Errors
Dye 2008	30	18
Avg Right Fielder	23	26
Good Play/Misplay Pct		.650

Dye is not the athletic, speedy player he was in the 90's, but he shows flashes of brilliance. He still has a plus arm, great accuracy, and good instincts in right field. However, he has had some trouble dealing with hard-hit line drives. On multiple occasions, line drives deflected off Dye's glove because of a bad route or a mistimed slide. With his lack of first-step quickness, his range has decreased, which leads to fewer outs. Over the last three years he has the lowest plus/minus total of any right fielder (-67). He still makes great running plays along the foul line, though. Overall, Dye remains a threat with his arm, but his time as a legitimate right fielder has passed.

Catchers Evaluations

Year	League	Gold Glove Winners	Should Have Been
2006	AL	Ivan Rodriguez	Ivan Rodriguez
	NL	Brad Ausmus	Yadier Molina
2007	AL	Ivan Rodriguez	Joe Mauer
	NL	Russell Martin	Yadier Molina
2008	AL	Joe Mauer	Jose Molina
	NL	Yadier Molina	Bengie Molina

My Personal Ratings

Top Ten

1 Yadier Molina, StL
2 Jose Molina, NYY
3 Jason Kendall, Mil
4 Rod Barajas, Tor
5 Bengie Molina, SF
6 Ivan Rodriguez, FA
7 Gerald Laird, Det
8 Joe Mauer, Min
9 Kurt Suzuki, Oak
10 Chris Snyder, Ari

Bottom Five

26 Ramon Hernandez, Cin
27 Mike Napoli, LAA
28 Victor Martinez, Cle
29 John Buck, KC
30 Michael Barrett, Tor

Player teams based on transactions through February 11, 2009

Catchers

Jason Kendall

	Innings	Runs Saved
2008	1328	12
2006-2008	3728	27

	Good Plays	Misplays and Errors
Kendall 2008	16	15
Avg Catcher	10	17
Good Play/Misplay Pct		.634

In the past, scouts and fans alike mocked Kendall's inability to throw out baserunners. The ridicule took a breather in 2008. Kendall drastically improved his arm strength and quickened his release, which allowed him to throw out a league-leading (among qualifiers) 42.7 % of basestealers. While the Brewers' pitching staff deserves some of the credit, Kendall's arm strength and footwork shouldn't be overlooked. In the past, Kendall struggled with his ability to re-place his feet, which allows catchers to get into position to make accurate throws. Last season, though, Kendall possessed arguably the quickest footwork of any catcher in the league. He also continued to excel at receiving the ball, performing particularly well when framing a low strike.

In 2008, Kendall was the most improved defensive player in the game. Add his newly found ability to thwart baserunners to his ability to handle pitchers and you now have one of the best defensive catchers in the game. Over the last three years we credit Kendall with having saved 23 earned runs for his pitchers. The second-best catcher saved 11 earned runs in that time frame. In recognition for his defense in 2008, Fielding Bible Award voters placed him second overall (in a tie with Jose Molina) to Yadier Molina.

Yadier Molina

	Innings	Runs Saved
2008	1002	1
2006-2008	2901	19

	Good Plays	Misplays and Errors
Molina 2008	20	19
Avg Catcher	8	12
Good Play/Misplay Pct		.631

The baby Molina, Yadier won his second Fielding Bible Award and his first Gold Glove in 2008, even though it wasn't his best year defensively. Like his older brothers, he has excellent hand-eye coordination, although he can rely on it too much sometimes at the expense of proper footwork on balls in the dirt. As a general rule, though, Molina blocks everything near him with quick feet and sound blocking technique. His pitchers have total confidence in his ability to catch and

frame any pitch at any time. What makes Molina really fun to watch is his gunslinger attitude; possessing a strong arm and the guts to use it, he will throw behind runners at any base. He had the most Good Fielding Plays (not involving pitches) of any catcher in baseball in 2008.

Jose Molina

	Innings	Runs Saved
2008	737	12
2006-2008	1833	16

	Good Plays	Misplays and Errors
Molina 2008	5	10
Avg Catcher	6	10
Good Play/Misplay Pct		.449

Widely perceived as the "other" Molina brother, Jose is a force to be reckoned with. He has a rocket arm and extremely quick feet despite his size. These attributes allowed him to post a 43% caught-stealing percentage in 2008. His glovework is solid, as there is little movement when he receives the pitch. The only problem he has is with blocking balls in the dirt. Molina allowed seven passed balls last season, ranking in the bottom quartile of catchers. His size likely prevents him from moving well enough horizontally to block balls to his left and right. But his pitchers swear by him (take a look at the article on page 75), and he was particularly effective in 2008 working with them, saving seven earned runs. He was tied with Jason Kendall as the runner-up to his brother Yadier for the 2008 Fielding Bible Award for catchers.

Gerald Laird

	Innings	Runs Saved
2008	753	6
2006-2008	2319	15

	Good Plays	Misplays and Errors
Laird 2008	2	11
Avg Catcher	6	10
Good Play/Misplay Pct		.228

The Rangers used a plethora of catchers in 2008, but Laird caught the most innings. Judging by his runs saved, they could have done much worse. Laird is a good athlete who moves well behind the plate and blocks balls in the dirt. His receiving skills could use some work, as his glovework takes low pitches or pitches away from his body further from the strike zone. He has a quick release and sets up quickly on stolen base attempts. While his arm may look below average, Laird gets the job done, having saved ten stolen bases for the Rangers over the last three years. All in all, Laird looks like an average catcher, but performs at an above-average level.

Catchers

Ivan Rodriguez

	Innings	Runs Saved
2008	930	3
2006-2008	3037	15

	Good Plays	Misplays and Errors
Rodriguez 2008	7	13
Avg Catcher	8	13
Good Play/Misplay Pct		.467

Pudge has been a great catcher for a long time, but his reign as "Best Catcher in the Game" has passed. Rodriguez used to be the best at every defensive aspect of catching: throwing, blocking balls in the dirt, blocking the plate, fielding balls in play, etc. He just isn't that guy anymore. He still fields balls well, and his laser-like arm helps him eliminate baserunners, but his accuracy has diminished greatly.

The best way to gauge Rodriguez's play behind the plate is to watch his body language. Always a fiery competitor, he consistently shows frustration and disappointment with himself throughout the course of a game. He knows that he's no longer as accurate with his throws as he once was, and he knows that he struggles to block balls in the dirt with anything less than maximum effort.

Nevertheless, he is still in a battle with Jason Kendall and maybe a few others for a different title: "Best Catcher in the Game Not Named Molina".

Ronny Paulino

	Innings	Runs Saved
2008	260	1
2006-2008	2395	12

	Good Plays	Misplays and Errors
Paulino 2008	1	4
Avg Catcher	2	4
Good Play/Misplay Pct		.289

David Ross

	Innings	Runs Saved
2008	400	0
2006-2008	1858	9

	Good Plays	Misplays and Errors
Ross 2008	7	10
Avg Catcher	4	6
Good Play/Misplay Pct		.532

Chris Snyder

	Innings	Runs Saved
2008	923	3
2006-2008	2309	9

	Good Plays	Misplays and Errors
Snyder 2008	3	7
Avg Catcher	8	12
Good Play/Misplay Pct		.411

Snyder is a top-10 backstop who continues to develop with the bat as well. He logged the most innings of any catcher who didn't make an error in 2008. Limiting the running game with his quality arm, he threw out close to 30% of potential basestealers. Opportunities for improvement: blocking balls in the dirt and locating popups behind home plate.

Russell Martin

	Innings	Runs Saved
2008	1238	-3
2006-2008	3507	8

	Good Plays	Misplays and Errors
Martin 2008	11	17
Avg Catcher	9	14
Good Play/Misplay Pct		.513

Only Jason Kendall logged more innings behind the dish in 2008, thus Martin ranks high in many defensive categories, both good and bad. He led all catchers not named Jeff Mathis in errors (11), but also ranked third in catcher blocks. Martin threw out just 20% of attempted basestealers, but he possesses a good arm. He also gets out from behind the plate quickly to field weak tappers. Martin took a step backward in 2008 in terms of blocking balls in the dirt and preventing wild pitches. He made his first big-league appearances at third base in 2008, starting there eight times. He made some nice plays charging in on slow rollers, but did make three errors in 11 games. With Brad Ausmus on board, Martin will probably see more time at third base. That would be too bad, because Martin is a better catcher than Ausmus overall. Defensively they're similar, but offensively Martin crushes the 40-year-old Ausmus.

Catchers

Yorvit Torrealba

	Innings	Runs Saved
2008	581	-1
2006-2008	2046	7

	Good Plays	Misplays and Errors
Torrealba 2008	0	5
Avg Catcher	5	8
Good Play/Misplay Pct		.000

Sharing time with Chris Iannetta in 2008, Torrealba is a good receiver with a strong arm. Sometimes he takes too long to set his feet on stolen base attempts, and then loses some accuracy as he tries to speed things up, but the overall results are above average. He struggles with blocking pitches in the dirt, trying to use his glove rather than blocking the ball with his chest.

Rod Barajas

	Innings	Runs Saved
2008	785	5
2006-2008	1913	7

	Good Plays	Misplays and Errors
Barajas 2008	16	9
Avg Catcher	7	11
Good Play/Misplay Pct		.743

Splitting time with Gregg Zaun as the Blue Jays backstop in 2008, Barajas proved to be the superior defensive option. He receives pitches well, framing borderline pitches for the benefit of his hurlers. He drops to his knees quickly on balls in the dirt and minimizes the space in which a ball can get by him. His arm is below average but accurate, and he sets his feet and releases the ball quickly on stolen base attempts. On balls in play, Barajas gets out of his stance smoothly to field bunts and track popups well into foul territory. He makes more than his share of good plays and keeps his misplays down to a minimum. An excellent catcher.

Joe Mauer

	Innings	Runs Saved
2008	1203	0
2006-2008	3040	6

	Good Plays	Misplays and Errors
Mauer 2008	7	10
Avg Catcher	8	12
Good Play/Misplay Pct		.532

Other than his raw caught-stealing numbers (34% caught stealing in his career), Mauer's stats are pretty average. He's still a good catcher, though. He won his first Gold Glove in 2008, though our Fielding Bible Award voters thought two other AL catchers, Jose Molina and Kurt Suzuki, were better.

He does struggle with blocking balls in the dirt, occasionally getting lazy and trying to scoop balls up instead of blocking them. Of course, a lot of his wild pitch misplays happened when he tried to block the ball but couldn't get square.

This might be because Mauer is tall for a catcher. At 6-5, he dwarfs most of his catching competition. His unusual height makes it difficult for him to get to pitches in the dirt on the opposite side of the plate.

That doesn't mean he doesn't have good technique behind the plate. His catch-and-throw skills are nearly unmatched, thanks to his exceptional footwork. He also is a smooth fielder, making some difficult plays look easy. He might not blow you away with his catching ability, but he's a plus defender that any team would love to have as their backstop.

Brian McCann

	Innings	Runs Saved
2008	1143	6
2006-2008	3299	6

	Good Plays	Misplays and Errors
McCann 2008	10	21
Avg Catcher	11	17
Good Play/Misplay Pct		.437

Widely known as one of the best hitting catchers in the game today, McCann just might become one of the best all-around catchers—period. A few years ago, McCann was one of those players you tolerated behind the plate, but he now is a solid defender. With a few improvements, he could be a great one.

His biggest problems are mechanical issues that aren't terribly hard to fix. First, he tends not to close up on balls in the dirt, allowing more balls to go five-hole than he should. Despite having good footwork and getting his body squared in front of the ball, McCann sometimes tries to catch the ball. That's risky business after the ball hits the dirt.

He also needs to address his throwing. You can't entirely fault a catcher for allowing 93 stolen bases in a season; the inability of Atlanta pitchers to hold runners definitely comes into play. However, you can blame a catcher for (a) not transferring the ball to his throwing hand cleanly and (b) consistently trying to throw the ball into right-center field.

These are fixable issues. McCann has worked hard in the past to become a good catcher. He already calls a good game for his pitchers, and continued overall improvement shouldn't surprise anyone.

Catchers

Bengie Molina

	Innings	Runs Saved
2008	1128	7
2006-2008	3074	6

	Good Plays	Misplays and Errors
Molina 2008	11	8
Avg Catcher	9	15
Good Play/Misplay Pct		.691

The founding member of the Brotherhood of Catching Molinas, Bengie is fundamentally sound. His defensive abilities continue to wane as time passes, though. He doesn't have the reactions he once did, as shown by his difficulty handling pitches thrown out of the zone. He had the most misplays on pitcher wild pitches in baseball last year with 41. In the past, he handled balls in the dirt well, but he let some blockable balls pass in 2008. Despite his advancing age, he still features the standard Molina throwing arm that can gun down would-be basestealers, and 2008 was his best year in this department for quite some time.

Jesus Flores

	Innings	Runs Saved
2008	673	1
2006-2008	1068	4

	Good Plays	Misplays and Errors
Flores 2008	7	9
Avg Catcher	5	8
Good Play/Misplay Pct		.559

Flores took over the Nationals' starting job in 2008 and held his own. Despite his relative inexperience, Flores worked well with his pitchers and proved to be a good defender with an above-average arm and a quick release. He possesses good lateral movement, which helps with blocking balls in the dirt, but he has a tendency to allow some blockable balls to skip past him.

Raul Chavez

	Innings	Runs Saved
2008	278	2
2006-2008	353	3

	Good Plays	Misplays and Errors
Chavez 2008	5	2
Avg Catcher	2	4
Good Play/Misplay Pct		.803

Humberto Quintero

	Innings	Runs Saved
2008	447	1
2006-2008	655	3

	Good Plays	Misplays and Errors
Quintero 2008	5	4
Avg Catcher	3	5
Good Play/Misplay Pct		.670

Kelly Shoppach

	Innings	Runs Saved
2008	873	-4
2006-2008	1573	3

	Good Plays	Misplays and Errors
Shoppach 2008	9	10
Avg Catcher	5	9
Good Play/Misplay Pct		.594

Shoppach has the perfect build for a catcher, but his defensive abilities don't live up to the promise. He not only struggles with throwing out runners, but he also has problems with routine plays in the field. There is no question that he has the arm strength to make such plays, but he lacks the proper footwork and throwing accuracy. When fielding bunts, Shoppach often can't get his feet into proper position to throw. His poor footwork also creeps up during stolen-base situations, leading to poor throws to second base. Shoppach might be a better defensive catcher than teammate Victor Martinez, but that's not saying much.

Matt Treanor

	Innings	Runs Saved
2008	525	0
2006-2008	1405	3

	Good Plays	Misplays and Errors
Treanor 2008	7	10
Avg Catcher	5	8
Good Play/Misplay Pct		.532

Treanor signed with the Tigers after serving as the primary backstop in the Marlins' "college of catchers" in 2008. While he is below-average with the bat, Treanor is a good receiver and possesses an average arm for the position. He can be a little slow with his release on stolen base attempts, but he is generally accurate. Quick to get out of his crouch on balls hit in front of the plate, his accuracy suffers when he moves too quickly and rushes his throws. Treanor's greatest strength is his ability to block balls in the dirt, as he moves his feet well and uses proper technique by blocking balls with his chest.

Catchers

Jason LaRue

	Innings	Runs Saved
2008	412	0
2006-2008	1399	3

	Good Plays	Misplays and Errors
LaRue 2008	1	3
Avg Catcher	2	4
Good Play/Misplay Pct		.352

Luke Carlin

	Innings	Runs Saved
2008	260	2
2006-2008	260	2

	Good Plays	Misplays and Errors
Carlin 2008	5	4
Avg Catcher	3	4
Good Play/Misplay Pct		.670

Ramon Hernandez

	Innings	Runs Saved
2008	1039	1
2006-2008	2989	2

	Good Plays	Misplays and Errors
Hernandez 2008	11	24
Avg Catcher	10	16
Good Play/Misplay Pct		.427

Hernandez was a defensive liability for the Orioles in 2008. He failed to corral wild pitch after wild pitch, often looking lazy in the process. On numerous occasions, Hernandez fumbled the ball while getting it out of his glove on stolen base attempts, and the throws he did make were erratic. Sometimes he wouldn't even stand up to throw, choosing instead to just chuck it to second base from his knees. You can guess how well that worked out. Unafraid to block the plate to prevent a run, he is just as likely to mishandle the throw home. Only three catchers had more errors than Hernandez (nine), and no other catcher allowed more steals than Ramon's 99. Hernandez even led the league in passed balls with 10. Improvement is needed, both in effort and results.

A.J. Pierzynski

	Innings	Runs Saved
2008	1134	-8
2006-2008	3317	2

	Good Plays	Misplays and Errors
Pierzynski 2008	5	13
Avg Catcher	10	16
Good Play/Misplay Pct		.385

It's been suggested of Pierzynski that he might "handle the staff well" and "call a smart game." Our numbers over the last six years suggest this could be true. He has 10 adjusted earned runs saved in that time, good for seventh among the 35 most active catchers. A.J. moves around well for a big man, which helps him block balls in the dirt. Despite possessing a good arm, he doesn't deter many baserunners. This is partly due to his inaccuracy, but the White Sox pitchers (other than Mark Buehrle) also bear some of the blame.

Henry Blanco

	Innings	Runs Saved
2008	258	2
2006-2008	893	2

	Good Plays	Misplays and Errors
Blanco 2008	1	3
Avg Catcher	2	3
Good Play/Misplay Pct		.352

Kevin Cash

	Innings	Runs Saved
2008	372	1
2006-2008	454	1

	Good Plays	Misplays and Errors
Cash 2008	3	11
Avg Catcher	5	8
Good Play/Misplay Pct		.307

Nick Hundley

	Innings	Runs Saved
2008	486	1
2006-2008	486	1

	Good Plays	Misplays and Errors
Hundley 2008	7	10
Avg Catcher	5	8
Good Play/Misplay Pct		.532

Catchers

Carlos Ruiz

	Innings	Runs Saved
2008	828	-2
2006-2008	1917	1

	Good Plays	Misplays and Errors
Ruiz 2008	9	13
Avg Catcher	8	13
Good Play/Misplay Pct		.530

Ruiz receives the ball smoothly and blocks most pitches thrown within his vicinity. His biggest problem in 2008 was his inability to throw out baserunners. He compiled an 18% caught-stealing percentage, costing the Phillies two runs as a result. Despite this flaw, many people argue that Ruiz's ability to handle a pitching staff makes him a valuable asset. This remains to be seen as he gets more experience under his belt.

Ramon Castro

	Innings	Runs Saved
2008	354	0
2006-2008	992	1

	Good Plays	Misplays and Errors
Castro 2008	2	5
Avg Catcher	2	4
Good Play/Misplay Pct		.394

Wil Nieves

	Innings	Runs Saved
2008	450	0
2006-2008	638	0

	Good Plays	Misplays and Errors
Nieves 2008	5	4
Avg Catcher	4	7
Good Play/Misplay Pct		.670

Miguel Olivo

	Innings	Runs Saved
2008	494	3
2006-2008	2456	0

	Good Plays	Misplays and Errors
Olivo 2008	4	10
Avg Catcher	4	7
Good Play/Misplay Pct		.394

J.R. Towles

	Innings	Runs Saved
2008	409	-1
2006-2008	504	0

	Good Plays	Misplays and Errors
Towles 2008	2	5
Avg Catcher	2	3
Good Play/Misplay Pct		.394

Geovany Soto

	Innings	Runs Saved
2008	1150	-1
2006-2008	1327	-1

	Good Plays	Misplays and Errors
Soto 2008	5	9
Avg Catcher	9	14
Good Play/Misplay Pct		.475

Although Soto's National League Rookie of the Year award probably had more to do with his bat than his glove, he did show dexterity at blocking balls in the dirt, which benefited a Cubs staff prone to wildness. Soto employs good footwork and a quick release, but his middling arm made him struggle to contain basestealers in 2008. He did a good job handling the Cubs pitching staff in his first full year, and he might win a Gold Glove, or even a Fielding Bible Award, someday if he improves against the running game.

Guillermo Quiroz

	Innings	Runs Saved
2008	354	-1
2006-2008	391	-2

	Good Plays	Misplays and Errors
Quiroz 2008	1	3
Avg Catcher	3	5
Good Play/Misplay Pct		.352

Mike Rabelo

	Innings	Runs Saved
2008	263	1
2006-2008	657	-2

	Good Plays	Misplays and Errors
Rabelo 2008	1	4
Avg Catcher	2	4
Good Play/Misplay Pct		.289

Catchers

Shawn Riggans

	Innings	Runs Saved
2008	343	-3
2006-2008	438	-2

	Good Plays	Misplays and Errors
Riggans 2008	0	7
Avg Catcher	2	4
Good Play/Misplay Pct		.000

Kurt Suzuki

	Innings	Runs Saved
2008	1215	5
2006-2008	1754	-2

	Good Plays	Misplays and Errors
Suzuki 2008	9	11
Avg Catcher	8	12
Good Play/Misplay Pct		.571

In the summer of 2007, when it was clear the A's were in full rebuilding mode, they traded away proven veteran Jason Kendall and threw a rookie (Suzuki) into the fire. Earning the everyday job in 2008, Suzuki proved durable and led American League catchers in innings logged. Still young at 25, Suzuki is mobile behind the plate and blocks balls in the dirt well. His youth might also help him when it comes to handling Oakland's young pitching staff. An asset against the running game, Suzuki makes up in accuracy what he lacks in arm strength.

Paul Bako

	Innings	Runs Saved
2008	771	-2
2006-2008	1584	-3

	Good Plays	Misplays and Errors
Bako 2008	6	10
Avg Catcher	6	11
Good Play/Misplay Pct		.494

A dime-a-dozen catcher, Bako doesn't curtail the opponents' running game, he isn't that impressive on blocking balls in the dirt, and he doesn't have any one thing that he does better than most other catchers. He does always manage to land a job.

Ryan Doumit

	Innings	Runs Saved
2008	909	-2
2006-2008	1224	-3

	Good Plays	Misplays and Errors
Doumit 2008	3	14
Avg Catcher	9	14
Good Play/Misplay Pct		.259

Doumit is one of those rare "offense-first" catchers. Although his catching skills improved as last year progressed, he still has a long way to go. He is a poor receiver who often turns borderline pitches into balls, and his arm is inaccurate (but strong—he has seen time in right field). In particular, he tends to sail his throws to third base. His footwork could use some help, whether on stolen base attempts or on balls in the dirt. Despite his flaws, he seems to block balls in the dirt well, and he gets out of his stance quickly on grounders in front of the plate.

Jeff Clement

	Innings	Runs Saved
2008	292	-3
2006-2008	292	-3

	Good Plays	Misplays and Errors
Clement 2008	2	3
Avg Catcher	2	3
Good Play/Misplay Pct		.520

Brandon Inge

	Innings	Runs Saved
2008	494	-4
2006-2008	494	-4

	Good Plays	Misplays and Errors
Inge 2008	5	4
Avg Catcher	5	8
Good Play/Misplay Pct		.670

Entering last season, Inge hadn't caught a game since 2004, serving as the Tigers' everyday third baseman in the interim. He was game enough last season to don the tools of ignorance after a four-year layoff, but the results were borderline. He handled opponent baserunners fairly well and he managed to do a decent job blocking balls in the dirt (other than the 11 passed balls). But the rust in his game showed as every pitcher he caught for 30 innings or more had a worse ERA with Inge catching than with other Tiger catchers. (See article on page 75.) Expected to return to the hot corner in 2009, Inge showed that he can man the dish when the Tigers are desperate, but that's about it.

Catchers

John Baker

	Innings	Runs Saved
2008	496	-4
2006-2008	496	-4

	Good Plays	Misplays and Errors
Baker 2008	2	10
Avg Catcher	4	7
Good Play/Misplay Pct		.246

Brad Ausmus

	Innings	Runs Saved
2008	570	0
2006-2008	2601	-4

	Good Plays	Misplays and Errors
Ausmus 2008	4	6
Avg Catcher	4	6
Good Play/Misplay Pct		.520

Ausmus is the proverbial veteran catcher who knows how to handle a pitching staff. He still shows decent mobility, but his arm isn't what it used to be. At this point, he's not an everyday catcher, but he'll be a serviceable backup for Russell Martin in Los Angeles.

Gregg Zaun

	Innings	Runs Saved
2008	612	-5
2006-2008	1992	-4

	Good Plays	Misplays and Errors
Zaun 2008	6	8
Avg Catcher	5	9
Good Play/Misplay Pct		.550

Zaun lost his everyday duties in Toronto last season after a brief DL stint in late May. His experience and pitcher-handling abilities are his calling cards, but his arm is average at best. At times, he has trouble with wild pitches, choosing to trap balls in the dirt rather than get out of his crouch. After signing with Baltimore in December, Zaun will keep the dish warm until uber-prospect Matt Wieters is ready. Time is not on Zaun's side (he'll turn 38 this season).

Jeff Mathis

	Innings	Runs Saved
2008	793	0
2006-2008	1393	-4

	Good Plays	Misplays and Errors
Mathis 2008	10	13
Avg Catcher	7	12
Good Play/Misplay Pct		.556

Mathis excels at blocking balls in the dirt and consistently uses his chest to keep balls in front of him. He also is one of the best catchers in the league fielding soft grounders and bunts in front of the plate, aggressively attacking the ball. And he's not shy when attempting to pick off runners on first and third. Although a decent receiver, he struggles when he catches the pitch across his body. He has an average arm and a quick release, but he is arguably the most inconsistent throwing catcher in the league. He led all catchers last season with 13 errors, almost all of which were on throwing errors on stolen base attempts.

Chris Coste

	Innings	Runs Saved
2008	613	-2
2006-2008	1290	-4

	Good Plays	Misplays and Errors
Coste 2008	3	5
Avg Catcher	5	8
Good Play/Misplay Pct		.494

If you've already read Carlos Ruiz's entry, this will seem like deja vu. Coste receives the ball well and seems to be good at blocking pitches in the dirt, but he has a difficult time throwing out baserunners. His arm is average at best, and his feet are a bit slow, which causes his throws to be either late or in the dirt. The key difference is that Ruiz is considerably younger than Coste and makes more sense as the Phillies' primary catcher.

Mike Redmond

	Innings	Runs Saved
2008	253	-2
2006-2008	1114	-4

	Good Plays	Misplays and Errors
Redmond 2008	2	2
Avg Catcher	2	3
Good Play/Misplay Pct		.619

Catchers

Chris Iannetta

	Innings	Runs Saved
2008	837	0
2006-2008	1525	-5

	Good Plays	Misplays and Errors
Iannetta 2008	6	7
Avg Catcher	7	11
Good Play/Misplay Pct		.582

Improving with both the bat and the glove, Iannetta became the Rockies' primary catcher as the 2008 season progressed. Although he didn't commit an error (in the Henry Chadwick sense) all season, he still showed some weaknesses. At times he looks like he's fighting the ball, despite being a good receiver overall. While he is decent at blocking balls in the dirt, he gets caught between trying to catch the ball with his glove and dropping to block it with his chest. He has an above-average arm with good accuracy, but he is slow setting his feet to throw on stolen base attempts and has yet to post an above-average caught stealing percentage in parts of three different seasons. Iannetta is quick to get out of his crouch on bunts and soft grounders in front of the plate.

Dioner Navarro

	Innings	Runs Saved
2008	1011	-1
2006-2008	2621	-5

	Good Plays	Misplays and Errors
Navarro 2008	8	9
Avg Catcher	8	12
Good Play/Misplay Pct		.591

Navarro can anticipate balls in the dirt, has good footwork and a quick release to control the basepaths, and he's comfortable fielding balls in play. He saved four runs for the Rays with his throwing arm over the season on stolen base attempts. Simply put, he can play his position just about as well as he wants to.

The problem is that he doesn't always seem to want to play the position well. The most obvious evidence of this is his tendency to attempt to catch everything. Navarro has a body built for blocking baseballs; he's not tall, and he's fairly athletic given his stocky build. Despite the amount of area his body takes up, he often refuses to take balls off his chest. Frequently, these balls skip away due to carelessness.

Other than that, Navarro makes very few mistakes. In fact, all but four of his Misplays last season involved a pitched ball, and he never repeated a mistake. If Navarro can buckle down and take a few shots off the chest protector, he could be a revelation behind the dish.

Jason Varitek

	Innings	Runs Saved
2008	1041	1
2006-2008	2928	-6

	Good Plays	Misplays and Errors
Varitek 2008	4	9
Avg Catcher	7	12
Good Play/Misplay Pct		.420

A case study in the intangibles vs. statistics debate, Varitek is world-renowned for his leadership abilities but less impressive on a scoresheet or a spreadsheet. Despite an accurate arm, he has never had great numbers throwing out basestealers, as he is a bit slow on his release. He is effective at blocking balls in the dirt overall, but he has a dangerous tendency to slide his knees back as he drops down rather than attacking the ball. This leaves him more exposed to bad hops and balls skipping off the plate. Finally, our numbers question his pitch calling and his pitcher handling, with 17 adjusted earned runs lost for his pitchers over the last six years.

Mike Napoli

	Innings	Runs Saved
2008	625	-6
2006-2008	1940	-7

	Good Plays	Misplays and Errors
Napoli 2008	2	9
Avg Catcher	5	8
Good Play/Misplay Pct		.266

Napoli saw significant time at catcher in 2008 for the Angels despite sharing duties with Jeff Mathis. Possessing an average (at best) arm, he exits his crouch reasonably well on stolen-base attempts and has a quick release. But the results are below average. He is very good at blocking balls in the dirt but occasionally has trouble controlling the ball off his chest. He is quick to go after bunts, but he struggles on balls in the air

Jarrod Saltalamacchia

	Innings	Runs Saved
2008	464	-5
2006-2008	837	-8

	Good Plays	Misplays and Errors
Saltalamacchia 2008	3	14
Avg Catcher	5	7
Good Play/Misplay Pct		.259

Catchers

Miguel Montero

	Innings	Runs Saved
2008	405	-4
2006-2008	955	-11

	Good Plays	Misplays and Errors
Montero 2008	4	5
Avg Catcher	3	5
Good Play/Misplay Pct		.566

Josh Bard

	Innings	Runs Saved
2008	417	-1
2006-2008	1892	-14

	Good Plays	Misplays and Errors
Bard 2008	5	4
Avg Catcher	5	7
Good Play/Misplay Pct		.670

Toby Hall

	Innings	Runs Saved
2008	315	-1
2006-2008	1236	-11

	Good Plays	Misplays and Errors
Hall 2008	5	5
Avg Catcher	3	5
Good Play/Misplay Pct		.619

John Buck

	Innings	Runs Saved
2008	950	-8
2006-2008	2805	-15

	Good Plays	Misplays and Errors
Buck 2008	3	10
Avg Catcher	6	10
Good Play/Misplay Pct		.328

Buck has been the Royals' primary catcher for the past four seasons. Like most of the Royals' decisions over the last 20 years, this is ill-advised. Buck is a well-below-average defensive catcher who cost the team an estimated eight runs last season alone. Although he has a strong arm, he has a slow release and his accuracy comes and goes. He also struggles with balls in the dirt and has below-average lateral quickness. For those of you who desperately need something nice to say about him: Buck is excellent at coming out of his crouch to track popups.

Victor Martinez

	Innings	Runs Saved
2008	447	1
2006-2008	2600	-14

	Good Plays	Misplays and Errors
Martinez 2008	5	7
Avg Catcher	3	5
Good Play/Misplay Pct		.538

Michael Barrett

	Innings	Runs Saved
2008	252	-4
2006-2008	1872	-17

	Good Plays	Misplays and Errors
Barrett 2008	1	7
Avg Catcher	4	6
Good Play/Misplay Pct		.189

Brian Schneider

	Innings	Runs Saved
2008	881	-2
2006-2008	2923	-14

	Good Plays	Misplays and Errors
Schneider 2008	11	12
Avg Catcher	6	10
Good Play/Misplay Pct		.599

Schneider shows good fundamentals behind the plate, which makes him good on balls in the dirt and helps him control the running game. The only things that really stand out about him are his talents for effectively blocking the plate and receiving throws. He also shows quick reactions to balls that are batted near him, be they weakly hit grounders or pop-ups. Our numbers suggest he may not be the best at handling pitchers. His -16 adjusted earned runs saved over the last three years is the second worst we have on record during that time period.

Catchers

Kenji Johjima

	Innings	Runs Saved
2008	833	0
2006-2008	3113	-18

	Good Plays	Misplays and Errors
Johjima 2008	6	15
Avg Catcher	6	11
Good Play/Misplay Pct		.394

Johjima has a very quick release, but he might be more accurate if he slowed things down. He excels at blocking balls in the dirt. Johjima's playing time has decreased steadily since his arrival in the majors in 2006, and his future with the M's depends on the defensive progress of prospect Jeff Clement, who was given a shot at regular playing time last season but struggled.

Universal Fielding Percentages

Putting Fielding Percentages on a Common Scale

Bill James

There is a unique problem with reading fielding percentages, which is the multiplicity of standards. We interpret baseball statistics in casual conversation by the use of standards—he's a 17-game winner with a 3.80 ERA, or he's a .270 hitter with 80-90 RBI a year. The existence of universally understood standards makes sense of all of the numbers, not merely those that meet or exceed the standard.

Fielding percentages are different, because

a) there are no magic numbers, and

b) the standards are so different from position to position that nobody can carry a full set of them around in his head.

A .988 fielding percentage for an outfielder. . .is that good or bad? It's tremendous for a shortstop, outstanding for a second baseman, bad for a first baseman. . .what is it for a catcher? .964 for a third baseman in the 1950s. . .good or bad? No peeking. .978 for a shortstop in 2007. . .above average or below? No peeking.

Not only are there different standards for each position, but these standards have changed tremendously over time. Yes, it is true that there are different expectations for hitters at different positions; yes, it is true that standards of batting and pitching excellence change somewhat over time. Not to the same level. 200 strikeouts for a pitcher was outstanding in 1940, it was outstanding in 1950, it was outstanding in 1960, it is outstanding today. There was a period in the 1960s when it was a little less outstanding. 90 RBI was a middle-of-the-order hitter in 1940; it's a middle-of-the-order hitter today. Seventeen wins was a quality starting pitcher in 1930 or 1960 or 2007. ERA norms may be 3.70 in one decade and 4.70 in another, but they're not 1.70 or 6.70.

There are some people who have a pretty good grasp on fielding percentages, of course, and there are many people who are very good baseball fans and have been for many years and can tell you who won the NL batting title in 1970 and the American League MVP Award in 1984, but who can't tell you whether a .951 fielding percentage for a shortstop will get you bronzed or get you benched. It's very hard to compare one to another. One might know that .986 is not a good fielding percentage for a first baseman and .941 is not a good fielding percentage for a shortstop, but. . .which is worse? One might know that .997 is a good fielding percentage for a catcher and .986 is good for a second baseman, but which is better?

I have a method to deal with this problem. . .it's actually a very good method and I've had it for a long time, but I just realized (because of a letter in "Hey Bill" on BillJamesOnline.com) that I had never explained it to the public. The method scores everyone on a zero-to-one scale with an average player at .500, good fielders over .500 and poor fielders under .500. It enables you to easily and meaningfully combine fielding percentages from different positions so that if a player played 400 games at first base in his career, 350 at first base, 275 in the outfield and 4 at second base, you can give him a career fielding percentage which is a meaningful number to the extent that fielding percentage is a meaningful concept. You can combine all the positions into one—or, if you prefer, you can get a separate number for each position.

This is how it works:

A player's expected errors are the number of errors he would have had if he had had an average fielding percentage at the position, and the number of total chances he actually had.

We will call his expected errors X, and his actual errors E.

The formula is

$$\frac{2X - E}{2X}$$

That's all.

Let's take Bill Russell, Dodger shortstop of the 1970s/1980s, famous for being not the best shortstop ever. In 1974 Russell made 39 errors and fielded .946 at shortstop. The fielding percentage for National League shortstops in 1974 was .961, and Russell had 724 fielding chances. He thus had 28.02 expected errors. He exceeded his expected errors by 10.98, resulting in a Universal Fielding Percentage Score of .304 for the season—well below average:

$$(56.04 - 39) / 56.04 = .304$$

In his career as a shortstop Russell was below average more often than above average, although he was rarely as error-prone as he was in 1974. He was actually over .500—over the league average—in both 1973 and 1975, and in three other seasons. In his career he had 339 errors as a shortstop, with 301.53 expected errors—a Fielding Percentage Score at shortstop of .438:

$$(603.06 - 339) / 603.06 = .438$$

He also played 62 games in his career at second base, with a score there of .212, and 299 games in the outfield, with a score of .545. He had one fielding chance at third base, and handled that cleanly for a score of 1.000. Adding it up, he has a Universal Fielding Percentage Score of .436:

Shortstop	Expected Errors	301.53	Actual Errors	339
Second Base	Expected Errors	5.71	Actual Errors	9
Outfield	Expected Errors	7.69	Actual Errors	7
Third Base	Expected Errors	.05	Actual Errors	0
Total	Expected Errors	314.98	Actual Errors	355

Universal Fielding Percentage Score .436

For players with limited playing time, you might occasionally get numbers less than zero. I would just enter them as zero, but I guess I'll leave that up to you.

Here's a Whitman's Sample of Universal Fielding Percentage Scores for some other players:

Omar Vizquel at shortstop   .713
(Never played any other position)

Brooks Robinson at third base   .696
Brooks Robinson overall   .695

Ozzie Smith at shortstop   .684
(Never played any other position)

Al Kaline in the outfield   .652
Al Kaline, all positions   .640

Alan Trammell as a shortstop   .645
Alan Trammell, all positions   .639

Sherm Lollar at catcher   .630
Sherm Lollar overall   .634

Orlando Cabrera at shortstop   .638
Orlando Cabrera all positions   .632

Bill Freehan at catcher   .613
Bill Freehan at first base   .642
Bill Freehan overall   .616

Bobby Grich at second base   .619
Bobby Grich at shortstop   .408
Bobby Grich all positions   .599

Stan Hack at third base   .598
Stan Hack overall   .597

Bill Dickey at catcher   .570
(Never played any other position)

Juan Uribe at shortstop   .568
Juan Uribe all positions   .560

Robin Yount at shortstop   .506
Robin Yount in the outfield   .742
Robin Yount all positions   .549

Ray Schalk at catcher   .548
(Never played any other position)

Derek Jeter at shortstop   .548
(Has not played another position)

Jim Hegan at catcher   .535
(Never played any other position)

Travis Jackson at shortstop   .531
Travis Jackson at third base   .569
Travis Jackson all positions   .535

Darrell Porter at catcher   .531
Darrell Porter overall   .531

Gabby Hartnett at catcher	.521	Wally Schang at catcher	.464
Gabby Hartnett overall	.518	Wally Schang in the outfield	.245
		Wally Schang all positions	.434
Bobby Abreu in the outfield	.516		
(Has not played another position)		Rod Carew at second base	.392
		Rod Carew at first base	.455
Ernie Lombardi at catcher	.505	Rod Carew all positions	.421
(Never played any other position)			
		Roberto Clemente in the outfield	.414
Bob Elliott at third base	.496	Roberto Clemente all positions	.407
Bob Elliott overall	.499		
		Reggie Jackson in the outfield	.166
Bill Russell at shortstop	.438	(Never played any other position)	
Bill Russell in the outfield	.545		
Bill Russell all positions	.436	George Bell in the outfield	.053
		George Bell all positions	.057

Editor's note: This article was originally published in the Bill James Online (BillJamesOnline.com) in April 2007.

Universal Fielding Percentage Leaders

UFP - 1B			UFP - 2B			UFP - 3B			UFP - SS	
Lee, Travis	.767		Polanco, Placido	.747		Lowell, Mike	.717		Vizquel, Omar	.716
Garvey, Steve	.756		Sandberg, Ryne	.726		Turner, Terry	.705		Bowa, Larry	.712
Parker, Wes	.754		Herr, Tom	.716		Reitz, Ken	.697		Scott, Everett	.701
Mattingly, Don	.737		Fletcher, Scott	.715		Groh, Heinie	.696		Boudreau, Lou	.700
Mientkiewicz, Doug	.729		Morandini, Mickey	.693		Robinson, Brooks	.696		Miller, Eddie	.691
Helton, Todd	.727		Lind, Jose	.690		Cross, Lave	.687		Sanchez, Rey	.690
McCormick, Frank	.726		Loretta, Mark	.685		Buechele, Steve	.685		Duffy, Frank	.684
McGann, Dan	.707		Dauer, Rich	.680		Kamm, Willie	.681		Smith, Ozzie	.684
Teixeira, Mark	.705		Flynn, Doug	.670		Money, Don	.680		Bordick, Mike	.680
Gandil, Chick	.701		Ellis, Mark	.670		Petrocelli, Rico	.675		Rollins, Jimmy	.677

UFP - LF (1996-on)			UFP - CF (1996-on)			UFP - RF (1996-on)			UFP - OF	
Surhoff, B.J.	.742		Sizemore, Grady	.711		Suzuki, Ichiro	.786		Downing, Brian	.877
Anderson, Garret	.723		Winn, Randy	.705		Jordan, Brian	.718		Bigbie, Larry	.862
Crawford, Carl	.695		Glanville, Doug	.693		Rios, Alex	.704		Jefferies, Gregg	.846
Vaughn, Greg	.689		Jones, Andruw	.687		Tucker, Michael	.657		Hamilton, Darryl	.840
Gonzalez, Luis	.681		Anderson, Brady	.681		Walker, Larry	.651		Puhl, Terry	.833
Jenkins, Geoff	.661		Williams, Bernie	.665		O'Neill, Paul	.650		Gallagher, Dave	.833
White, Rondell	.632		Wells, Vernon	.660		Sanders, Reggie	.644		Lewis, Darren	.833
Bay, Jason	.611		Hunter, Torii	.659		Green, Shawn	.644		Erstad, Darin	.822
O'Leary, Troy	.593		Goodwin, Tom	.652		Ordonez, Magglio	.614		Rose, Pete	.808
Bonds, Barry	.589		Damon, Johnny	.643		Kearns, Austin	.608		Butler, Brett	.800

UFP - P			UFP - C	
Nolan, Gary	.889		Rosar, Buddy	.768
Mossi, Don	.887		Pytlak, Frankie	.759
Rhoden, Rick	.887		Sundberg, Jim	.745
Fryman, Woodie	.872		Freehan, Bill	.735
Wilson, Jim	.861		Miller, Damian	.721
Ortiz, Russ	.859		Wilson, Dan	.710
Rueter, Kirk	.854		Hassey, Ron	.708
Radke, Brad	.852		Hoiles, Chris	.706
Warneke, Lon	.850		Desautels, Gene	.705
Gura, Larry	.843		Mueller, Ray	.700

Universal Fielding Percentage Trailers

UFP - 1B	
Stuart, Dick	.089
Vaughn, Mo	.215
Perry, Gerald	.263
Morgan, Ed	.284
Hassett, Buddy	.292
McCovey, Willie	.303
Fournier, Jack	.316
Chase, Hal	.347
Allen, Dick	.348
Clendenon, Donn	.349

UFP - 2B	
Soriano, Alfonso	.223
Cora, Joey	.257
Samuel, Juan	.280
Grantham, George	.299
Anderson, Marlon	.343
Young, Eric	.349
Alicea, Luis	.350
Baerga, Carlos	.355
Kolloway, Don	.361
Robinson, Yank	.361

UFP - 3B	
Hobson, Butch	.207
Allen, Dick	.292
Hart, James	.305
Hollins, Dave	.317
Johnson, Howard	.320
Bonilla, Bobby	.336
Palmer, Dean	.337
Freese, Gene	.349
Lewis, Buddy	.354
Killebrew, Harmon	.369

UFP - SS	
Offerman, Jose	.144
Valentin, Jose	.272
Jackson, Sonny	.303
Stillwell, Kurt	.304
Ramirez, Rafael	.324
Smalley, Roy	.339
Hamner, Granny	.340
Taveras, Frank	.342
Rivera, Luis	.347
Koenig, Mark	.365

UFP - LF (1996-on)	
Dunn, Adam	.177
Martin, Al	.202
Ramirez, Manny	.339
Burrell, Pat	.390
Floyd, Cliff	.400
Alou, Moises	.407
Greer, Rusty	.414
Holliday, Matt	.419
Giles, Brian	.457
Henderson, Rickey	.487

UFP - CF (1996-on)	
Matthews, Gary Jr.	.207
Everett, Carl	.262
Wilson, Preston	.309
Beltran, Carlos	.400
Lofton, Kenny	.437
Griffey Jr., Ken	.444
Cameron, Mike	.446
Patterson, Corey	.471
Edmonds, Jim	.472
Rowand, Aaron	.529

UFP - RF (1996-on)	
Guerrero, Vladimir	.027
Guillen, Jose	.280
Ramirez, Manny	.369
Salmon, Tim	.411
Sosa, Sammy	.425
Burnitz, Jeromy	.437
Mondesi, Raul	.445
Giles, Brian	.481
Dye, Jermaine	.494
Encarnacion, Juan	.496

UFP - OF	
Sanchez, Alex	.000
Johnson, Alex	.000
Kingman, Dave	.000
Meyer, Dan	.000
Johnson, Roy	.019
Throneberry, Faye	.020
Turner, Jerry	.024
Braggs, Glenn	.026
Guerrero, Vladimir	.028
Lemon, Jim	.032

UFP - P	
Sadecki, Ray	.000
Sothoron, Allen	.000
Ramsey, Toad	.000
Johnson, Randy	.000
Underwood, Tom	.000
Ryan, Nolan	.000
Wight, Bill	.000
Finley, Chuck	.000
Kirby, Clay	.000
Mulholland, Terry	.000
Odom, Johnny	.000

UFP - C	
Stinnett, Kelly	.105
Heath, Mike	.233
Zaun, Greg	.244
Bateman, John	.259
Moss, Les	.264
Harper, Brian	.278
Cannizzaro, Chris	.292
Trevino, Alex	.305
Wingo, Ivey	.306
Moore, Charlie	.307

Revised Zone Ratings

Dave Studenmund

There is more than one way to tell a story. Writers like to play with things like character development and plot. Sometimes they'll speed to the conclusion; other times they'll slowly develop the story. Their approaches often depend on what they're trying to say and what they think you, the reader, want to hear.

So it is with baseball stats. The Plus/Minus System is terrific because it gives you a straightforward conclusion ("Forget the details, just give me the answer, now!"). There are details to be mined, but most people don't bother. And the plus/minus perspective is what it is—plays above and below average.

Revised zone ratings are a different way to tell the fielding story. Instead of telling you the number of runs a player was above or below average, these ratings tell you the proportion of "fieldable" balls each fielder cleanly handled (fieldable balls are defined as balls that fall within an area in which 50% of balls are caught by fielders at that position, on average). In addition, revised zone ratings tell you the number of balls each fielder reached that were outside of his zone.

There's value in telling the fielding story this way. For example, let's look at Chase Utley, who led all second basemen in the plus/minus system with a remarkable +46 plays. When you find him in the following leaderboards, you'll see that Utley actually finished seventh in fielding balls within his zone, behind the likes of Mark Ellis and Adam Kennedy.

However, nobody got to as many balls outside the zone. Utley cleanly fielded 66 balls outside of the second baseman's zone—a figure much higher than any other second baseman. Seattle's Jose Lopez fielded 51 balls out of zone, but he also played more innings in the field.

You now know a bit more than when you just knew that Utley was +46 plays above average. You know that Utley shows outstanding range and/or positioning anticipation, but he's not as much of a "sure thing" within the zone. Mark Ellis, on the other hand, is the standard "sure thing" at second base, but he doesn't have Utley's range/positioning. Is this valuable information? For those who want the more complete story, sure.

Hitting and pitching are relatively clear parts of the game of baseball. Their outcomes are discernable and their impact is clear. Fielding is much more complex, difficult to judge and measure. Its mysteries are deep and nearly unfathomable. That's why we're able to produce an entire book about it.

If you're interested in fielding, be sure to avoid the "one stat fits all" mentality. At the Hardball Times (HardballTimes.com), we'll continue to post Baseball Info Solutions' revised zone ratings on a daily basis during the season.

First Basemen - 3-Year Zone Ratings

Player		Balls In Zone	Plays Made	Zone Rating	Plays Out Of Zone
Doug Mientkiewicz		191	159	.832	56
Albert Pujols		625	516	.826	164
Lyle Overbay		642	515	.802	115
Casey Kotchman		359	287	.799	83
Todd Helton		512	403	.787	105
Mark Teixeira		624	489	.784	115
Daric Barton		170	133	.782	33
Dan Johnson		238	186	.782	37
Lance Berkman		541	421	.778	105
Kevin Youkilis		485	372	.767	77
Nomar Garciaparra		244	185	.758	41
Miguel Cabrera		177	134	.757	25
Carlos Pena		363	273	.752	84
Nick Johnson		234	175	.748	40
Ross Gload		287	214	.746	34
Ryan Howard		615	455	.740	73
Adam LaRoche		553	407	.736	88
Derek Lee		392	288	.735	71
Adrian Gonzalez		658	482	.733	111
Sean Casey		328	240	.732	39
Carlos Delgado		559	409	.732	83
Joey Votto		207	151	.729	61
Justin Morneau		590	430	.729	78
James Loney		334	243	.728	84
Paul Konerko		521	378	.726	69
Nick Swisher		225	163	.724	41
Scott Hatteberg		268	194	.724	41
Ryan Garko		379	274	.723	56
Richie Sexson		460	330	.717	87
Kevin Millar		435	309	.710	88
Conor Jackson		424	300	.708	48
Prince Fielder		536	364	.679	95
Jason Giambi		248	168	.677	27
Mike Jacobs		405	270	.667	56
Dmitri Young		161	105	.652	25

First Basemen - 2007 Zone Ratings

Player	Tm	Balls In Zone	Plays Made	Zone Rating	Plays Out Of Zone
Albert Pujols	StL	235	198	.843	51
Doug Mientkiewicz	NYY	55	46	.836	19
Kevin Youkilis	Bos	176	147	.835	22
Lyle Overbay	Tor	173	140	.809	26
Casey Kotchman	LAA	152	123	.809	32
Todd Helton	Col	203	164	.808	42
Andy Phillips	NYY	67	54	.806	16
Ross Gload	KC	117	94	.803	15
Adam LaRoche	Pit	192	150	.781	23
Carlos Pena	TB	182	140	.769	38
Justin Morneau	Min	223	171	.767	18
Dan Johnson	Oak	120	92	.767	14
Mark Teixeira	2 tms	165	124	.752	32
Ryan Klesko	SF	124	92	.742	14
Ryan Garko	Cle	166	121	.729	17
Conor Jackson	Ari	139	101	.727	14
Derek Lee	ChC	145	105	.724	24
Ryan Howard	Phi	188	136	.723	21
Adrian Gonzalez	SD	237	171	.722	46
Tony Clark	Ari	86	62	.721	8
Scott Thorman	Atl	100	72	.720	23
Lance Berkman	Hou	170	122	.718	27
Paul Konerko	CWS	198	140	.707	25
Sean Casey	Det	157	111	.707	22
Kevin Millar	Bal	133	94	.707	22
Carlos Delgado	NYM	170	120	.706	25
Brad Wilkerson	Tex	74	52	.703	10
James Loney	LAD	125	87	.696	21
Nomar Garciaparra	LAD	97	67	.691	12
Mike Jacobs	Fla	125	86	.688	23
Scott Hatteberg	Cin	117	79	.675	12
Prince Fielder	Mil	187	125	.668	29
Jeff Conine	2 tms	74	49	.662	11
Richie Sexson	Sea	165	108	.655	24
Dmitri Young	Was	122	78	.639	19

First Basemen - 2008 Zone Ratings

Player	Tm	Balls In Zone	Plays Made	Zone Rating	Plays Out Of Zone
Albert Pujols	StL	200	168	.840	52
Lance Berkman	Hou	224	184	.821	53
Todd Helton	Col	105	86	.819	30
Mark Teixeira	2 tms	230	186	.809	50
Casey Kotchman	2 tms	183	147	.803	40
Lyle Overbay	Tor	264	210	.795	46
Daric Barton	Oak	147	114	.776	28
Miguel Cairo	Sea	61	47	.770	9
Nick Swisher	CWS	58	44	.759	3
Paul Konerko	CWS	153	116	.758	27
Miguel Cabrera	Det	177	134	.757	25
Sean Casey	Bos	53	40	.755	5
Joey Votto	Cin	192	144	.750	57
Carlos Delgado	NYM	196	147	.750	38
Ryan Howard	Phi	226	168	.743	32
John Bowker	SF	66	49	.742	13
Derek Lee	ChC	195	144	.738	43
Carlos Pena	TB	170	124	.729	44
James Loney	LAD	185	134	.724	58
Rich Aurilia	SF	64	46	.719	12
Ryan Garko	Cle	161	115	.714	29
Kevin Youkilis	Bos	139	99	.712	28
Ross Gload	KC	134	95	.709	16
Kevin Millar	Bal	190	134	.705	44
Adam LaRoche	Pit	141	99	.702	34
Justin Morneau	Min	183	128	.699	22
Adrian Gonzalez	SD	208	145	.697	35
Chad Tracy	Ari	81	56	.691	16
Prince Fielder	Mil	196	134	.684	37
Garrett Atkins	Col	91	62	.681	9
Jason Giambi	NYY	159	108	.679	22
Conor Jackson	Ari	95	64	.674	16
Chris Davis	Tex	67	45	.672	15
Richie Sexson	2 tms	98	65	.663	25
Mike Jacobs	Fla	141	88	.624	15

First Basemen - 2006 Zone Ratings

Player	Tm	Balls In Zone	Plays Made	Zone Rating	Plays Out Of Zone
Kendry Morales	LAA	82	70	.854	15
Ryan Shealy	2 tms	58	49	.845	10
Chris Shelton	Det	111	92	.829	20
Doug Mientkiewicz	KC	93	77	.828	30
Nomar Garciaparra	LAD	137	112	.818	27
Shea Hillenbrand	2 tms	98	79	.806	20
Lyle Overbay	Tor	205	165	.805	43
Richie Sexson	Sea	197	157	.797	38
Albert Pujols	StL	190	150	.789	61
Dan Johnson	Oak	112	88	.786	21
Lance Berkman	Hou	147	115	.782	25
Mark Teixeira	Tex	229	179	.782	33
Adrian Gonzalez	SD	213	166	.779	30
Mike Lamb	Hou	72	56	.778	12
Scott Hatteberg	Cin	143	108	.755	28
Sean Casey	2 tms	118	89	.754	12
Andy Phillips	NYY	69	52	.754	14
Ryan Howard	Phi	201	151	.751	20
Todd Helton	Col	204	153	.750	33
Travis Lee	TB	128	95	.742	26
Kevin Youkilis	Bos	170	126	.741	27
Carlos Delgado	NYM	193	142	.736	20
Nick Johnson	Was	190	139	.732	32
Ben Broussard	2 tms	107	78	.729	26
Kevin Millar	Bal	112	81	.723	22
Nick Swisher	Oak	103	74	.718	22
Adam LaRoche	Atl	220	158	.718	31
Paul Konerko	CWS	170	122	.718	17
Justin Morneau	Min	184	131	.712	38
Conor Jackson	Ari	190	135	.711	18
Mike Jacobs	Fla	139	96	.691	18
Craig Wilson	2 tms	71	49	.690	11
Prince Fielder	Mil	153	105	.686	29
Jason Giambi	NYY	69	45	.652	3
Jeff Conine	Bal	71	46	.648	16

Second Basemen - 3-Year Zone Ratings

Player		Balls In Zone	Plays Made	Zone Rating	Plays Out Of Zone
Mark Ellis		994	874	.879	109
Placido Polanco		907	789	.870	102
Jamey Carroll		669	577	.862	55
Aaron Hill		916	787	.859	109
Brian Roberts		1117	949	.850	112
Brandon Phillips		1000	846	.846	118
Mark Grudzielanek		802	675	.842	64
Kaz Matsui		618	520	.841	46
Chase Utley		1052	883	.839	162
Adam Kennedy		698	582	.834	88
Mark DeRosa		429	357	.832	37
Freddy Sanchez		659	547	.830	56
Jose Lopez		1209	998	.825	132
Asdrubal Cabrera		360	297	.825	41
Ian Kinsler		1107	913	.825	93
Howie Kendrick		541	446	.824	59
Tadahito Iguchi		784	646	.824	85
Dustin Pedroia		810	667	.823	74
Mark Loretta		501	412	.822	34
Felipe Lopez		348	286	.822	18
Kelly Johnson		768	629	.819	62
Robinson Cano		1223	999	.817	108
Aaron Miles		504	411	.815	46
Jeff Kent		894	729	.815	63
Dan Uggla		1078	870	.807	138
Ray Durham		757	610	.806	68
Josh Barfield		677	544	.804	78
Luis Castillo		807	647	.802	83
Alexi Casilla		363	289	.796	28
Ronnie Belliard		671	533	.794	74
Orlando Hudson		1063	841	.791	151
Alexei Ramirez		319	252	.790	16
Akinori Iwamura		348	274	.787	44
Rickie Weeks		793	624	.787	98
Jose Castillo		349	269	.771	32

Second Basemen - 2007 Zone Ratings

Player	Tm	Balls In Zone	Plays Made	Zone Rating	Plays Out Of Zone
Mark Ellis	Oak	431	381	.884	45
Geoff Blum	SD	144	127	.882	14
Kaz Matsui	Col	277	241	.870	22
Jamey Carroll	Col	146	127	.870	14
Mark DeRosa	ChC	168	146	.869	15
Placido Polanco	Det	319	277	.868	39
Aaron Hill	Tor	490	424	.865	57
Brandon Phillips	Cin	351	303	.863	49
Marcus Giles	SD	301	259	.860	24
Chase Utley	Phi	306	263	.859	53
Mark Grudzielanek	KC	252	214	.849	31
Ian Kinsler	Tex	362	306	.845	53
Brian Roberts	Bal	393	330	.840	47
Jose Lopez	Sea	385	323	.839	44
Jeff Kent	LAD	301	251	.834	28
Freddy Sanchez	Pit	313	261	.834	23
Robinson Cano	NYY	420	350	.833	53
Howie Kendrick	LAA	217	179	.825	33
Dustin Pedroia	Bos	330	272	.824	34
Tadahito Iguchi	2 tms	271	223	.823	34
Adam Kennedy	StL	184	151	.821	26
Aaron Miles	StL	139	114	.820	16
Mike Fontenot	ChC	118	96	.814	9
Kelly Johnson	Atl	364	296	.813	34
Danny Richar	CWS	126	101	.802	14
Ray Durham	SF	266	213	.801	26
Luis Castillo	2 tms	280	224	.800	38
Ronnie Belliard	Was	240	192	.800	31
Orlando Hudson	Ari	332	265	.798	58
Rickie Weeks	Mil	246	193	.785	35
Josh Barfield	Cle	320	251	.784	41
Alexi Casilla	Min	134	105	.784	13
B.J. Upton	TB	129	101	.783	13
Craig Biggio	Hou	256	199	.777	32
Dan Uggla	Fla	348	270	.776	55

Second Basemen - 2008 Zone Ratings

Player	Tm	Balls In Zone	Plays Made	Zone Rating	Plays Out Of Zone
Mark Ellis	Oak	274	246	.898	31
Clint Barmes	Col	156	139	.891	12
Adam Kennedy	StL	176	155	.881	30
Mike Fontenot	ChC	121	105	.868	17
Tadahito Iguchi	2 tms	176	152	.864	16
Brandon Phillips	Cin	349	300	.860	35
Placido Polanco	Det	310	266	.858	39
Edgar Gonzalez	SD	177	149	.842	16
Chase Utley	Phi	379	318	.839	66
Mark Grudzielanek	KC	248	206	.831	8
Jamey Carroll	Cle	177	147	.831	11
Brian Roberts	Bal	398	330	.829	41
Dustin Pedroia	Bos	408	337	.826	37
Joe Inglett	Tor	166	137	.825	12
Kelly Johnson	Atl	404	333	.824	28
Felipe Lopez	2 tms	255	210	.824	7
Jose Lopez	Sea	448	368	.821	51
Jeff Kent	LAD	284	233	.820	21
Howie Kendrick	LAA	265	217	.819	22
Freddy Sanchez	Pit	314	257	.818	30
Asdrubal Cabrera	Cle	260	212	.815	28
Dan Uggla	Fla	346	281	.812	44
Aaron Miles	StL	158	128	.810	10
Robinson Cano	NYY	472	382	.809	30
Rickie Weeks	Mil	296	239	.807	40
Mark DeRosa	ChC	186	150	.806	13
Ian Kinsler	Tex	357	286	.801	20
Alexi Casilla	Min	225	180	.800	15
Kaz Matsui	Hou	209	167	.799	14
Damion Easley	NYM	156	124	.795	4
Alexei Ramirez	CWS	319	252	.790	16
Ray Durham	2 tms	180	142	.789	14
Akinori Iwamura	TB	347	273	.787	44
Orlando Hudson	Ari	274	215	.785	27
Luis Castillo	NYM	189	142	.751	16

Second Basemen - 2006 Zone Ratings

Player	Tm	Balls In Zone	Plays Made	Zone Rating	Plays Out Of Zone
Jose Valentin	NYM	250	222	.888	23
Brian Roberts	Bal	326	289	.887	24
Placido Polanco	Det	278	246	.885	24
Jamey Carroll	Col	346	303	.876	30
Aaron Hill	Tor	285	245	.860	37
Mark Ellis	Oak	289	247	.855	33
Tony Graffanino	2 tms	116	99	.853	23
Kaz Matsui	2 tms	132	112	.848	10
Mark Grudzielanek	KC	302	255	.844	25
Craig Biggio	Hou	313	263	.840	25
Neifi Perez	2 tms	124	104	.839	22
Luis Castillo	Min	338	281	.831	29
Dan Uggla	Fla	384	319	.831	39
Ian Kinsler	Tex	388	321	.827	20
Chase Utley	Phi	367	302	.823	43
Josh Barfield	SD	337	277	.822	37
Ray Durham	SF	311	255	.820	28
Marcus Giles	Atl	349	285	.817	32
Adam Kennedy	LAA	338	276	.817	32
Jose Lopez	Sea	376	307	.816	37
Aaron Miles	StL	207	169	.816	20
Todd Walker	2 tms	108	88	.815	17
Brandon Phillips	Cin	300	243	.810	34
Robinson Cano	NYY	331	267	.807	25
Mark Loretta	Bos	353	284	.805	28
Tadahito Iguchi	CWS	337	271	.804	35
Ronnie Belliard	2 tms	373	297	.796	41
Jeff Kent	LAD	309	245	.793	14
Orlando Hudson	Ari	457	361	.790	66
Jose Castillo	Pit	309	240	.777	26
Jose Vidro	Was	251	193	.769	22
Joe Inglett	Cle	124	95	.766	15
Rickie Weeks	Mil	251	192	.765	23
Hector Luna	2 tms	143	108	.755	10
Jorge Cantu	TB	249	187	.751	22

Third Basemen - 3-Year Zone Ratings

Player	Balls In Zone	Plays Made	Zone Rating	Plays Out Of Zone
Joe Crede	665	504	.758	121
Mike Lowell	878	660	.752	98
Scott Rolen	756	568	.751	153
Brandon Inge	907	680	.750	125
Jack Hannahan	293	219	.747	56
Andy Marte	338	252	.746	43
Nick Punto	393	290	.738	55
Pedro Feliz	897	654	.729	145
Maicer Izturis	264	188	.712	39
Ryan Zimmerman	811	576	.710	169
Casey Blake	613	432	.705	54
Chad Tracy	387	272	.703	54
Morgan Ensberg	433	304	.702	74
Adrian Beltre	924	647	.700	203
Alex Gordon	570	398	.698	64
Troy Glaus	833	580	.696	136
Kevin Kouzmanoff	562	390	.694	79
David Wright	936	647	.691	196
Eric Chavez	554	382	.690	81
Aramis Ramirez	825	568	.688	126
Alex Rodriguez	873	599	.686	151
Jose Castillo	295	202	.685	40
Ty Wigginton	389	266	.684	62
Melvin Mora	943	642	.681	132
Chone Figgins	447	301	.673	87
Ramon Vazquez	291	195	.670	48
Chipper Jones	653	436	.668	150
Hank Blalock	406	271	.667	78
Mark Reynolds	455	303	.666	65
Garrett Atkins	882	587	.666	114
Miguel Cabrera	676	439	.649	91
Wilson Betemit	253	164	.648	40
Jose Bautista	624	401	.643	81
Mike Lamb	301	192	.638	46
Edwin Encarnacion	786	494	.628	102

Third Basemen - 2007 Zone Ratings

Player	Tm	Balls In Zone	Plays Made	Zone Rating	Plays Out Of Zone
Pedro Feliz	SF	293	219	.747	62
Maicer Izturis	LAA	93	69	.742	15
Scott Rolen	StL	240	178	.742	39
Mike Lowell	Bos	310	227	.732	27
Ryan Zimmerman	Was	342	245	.716	71
Aramis Ramirez	ChC	291	208	.715	37
Brandon Inge	Det	368	262	.712	63
Abraham Nunez	Phi	197	140	.711	26
Casey Blake	Cle	319	226	.708	27
Nick Punto	Min	192	136	.708	29
Troy Glaus	Tor	204	144	.706	48
Alex Gordon	KC	284	200	.704	41
Ramon Vazquez	Tex	131	92	.702	25
Wes Helms	Phi	114	80	.702	17
Travis Metcalf	Tex	103	72	.699	12
David Wright	NYM	312	215	.689	88
Melvin Mora	Bal	289	199	.689	48
Ty Wigginton	2 tms	149	102	.685	26
Kevin Kouzmanoff	SD	244	166	.680	36
Chone Figgins	LAA	182	123	.676	31
Josh Fields	CWS	205	137	.668	15
Adrian Beltre	Sea	319	213	.668	64
Morgan Ensberg	2 tms	161	107	.665	26
Chipper Jones	Atl	225	149	.662	57
Alex Rodriguez	NYY	296	196	.662	47
Mark Reynolds	Ari	172	113	.657	30
Eric Chavez	Oak	190	123	.647	37
Greg Dobbs	Phi	104	67	.644	10
Miguel Cabrera	Fla	311	195	.627	50
Akinori Iwamura	TB	246	154	.626	40
Mike Lamb	Hou	97	60	.619	23
Garrett Atkins	Col	323	198	.613	40
Jose Bautista	Pit	322	197	.612	36
Edwin Encarnacion	Cin	275	165	.600	39
Ryan Braun	Mil	225	127	.564	21

Third Basemen - 2008 Zone Ratings

Player	Tm	Balls In Zone	Plays Made	Zone Rating	Plays Out Of Zone
Jack Hannahan	Oak	212	161	.759	43
Mike Lowell	Bos	232	176	.759	28
Andy Marte	Cle	177	132	.746	23
Scott Rolen	Tor	216	160	.741	48
Andy LaRoche	2 tms	146	107	.733	21
Ty Wigginton	Hou	157	115	.732	25
Evan Longoria	TB	234	171	.731	43
Joe Crede	CWS	221	161	.729	39
Bill Hall	Mil	216	156	.722	28
Ian Stewart	Col	149	107	.718	14
Geoff Blum	Hou	158	113	.715	29
David Wright	NYM	308	220	.714	56
Pedro Feliz	Phi	262	187	.714	27
Ryan Zimmerman	Was	198	141	.712	42
Blake DeWitt	LAD	201	143	.711	42
Kevin Kouzmanoff	SD	311	220	.707	42
Chone Figgins	LAA	193	136	.705	49
Alex Rodriguez	NYY	266	187	.703	57
Casey Blake	2 tms	294	206	.701	27
Carlos Guillen	Det	217	152	.700	32
Adrian Beltre	Sea	263	184	.700	78
Jose Bautista	2 tms	233	163	.700	36
Garrett Atkins	Col	226	158	.699	27
Troy Glaus	StL	329	230	.699	37
Chipper Jones	Atl	225	157	.698	59
Alex Gordon	KC	286	198	.692	23
Brian Buscher	Min	138	95	.688	16
Jose Castillo	2 tms	196	132	.673	28
Mark Reynolds	Ari	283	190	.671	35
Melvin Mora	Bal	329	219	.666	26
Jorge Cantu	Fla	266	176	.662	29
Aramis Ramirez	ChC	246	162	.659	51
Ramon Vazquez	Tex	138	89	.645	21
Edwin Encarnacion	Cin	277	174	.628	34
Mike Lamb	2 tms	120	72	.600	15

Third Basemen - 2006 Zone Ratings

Player	Tm	Balls In Zone	Plays Made	Zone Rating	Plays Out Of Zone
Brandon Inge	Det	451	352	.780	49
Nick Punto	Min	185	143	.773	24
Scott Rolen	StL	300	230	.767	66
Mike Lowell	Bos	336	257	.765	43
Andy Marte	Cle	129	98	.760	15
Joe Crede	CWS	362	275	.760	57
Morgan Ensberg	Hou	228	171	.750	43
Corey Koskie	Mil	162	121	.747	17
Freddy Sanchez	Pit	244	180	.738	40
Adrian Beltre	Sea	342	250	.731	61
Pedro Feliz	SF	342	248	.725	56
Eric Chavez	Oak	325	233	.717	37
Vinny Castilla	2 tms	123	88	.715	15
David Bell	2 tms	306	216	.706	57
Ryan Zimmerman	Was	271	190	.701	56
Willy Aybar	2 tms	96	67	.698	16
Maicer Izturis	LAA	162	113	.698	23
Hank Blalock	Tex	256	178	.695	52
Alex Rodriguez	NYY	311	216	.695	47
Garrett Atkins	Col	333	231	.694	47
Chad Tracy	Ari	299	207	.692	46
Melvin Mora	Bal	325	224	.689	58
Aramis Ramirez	ChC	288	198	.688	38
Troy Glaus	Tor	300	206	.687	51
B.J. Upton	TB	110	75	.682	8
Miguel Cabrera	Fla	325	220	.677	39
Mark Teahen	KC	265	179	.675	45
David Wright	NYM	316	212	.671	52
Abraham Nunez	Phi	171	114	.667	27
Aubrey Huff	2 tms	187	124	.663	19
Edwin Encarnacion	Cin	234	155	.662	29
Aaron Boone	Cle	210	137	.652	33
Wilson Betemit	2 tms	131	85	.649	27
Chipper Jones	Atl	203	130	.640	34
Tony Batista	Min	123	74	.602	15

Shortstops - 3-Year Zone Ratings

Player		Balls In Zone	Plays Made	Zone Rating	Plays Out Of Zone
Adam Everett		688	605	.879	108
Omar Vizquel		898	787	.876	108
Troy Tulowitzki		813	703	.865	110
Cesar Izturis		536	459	.856	89
Jose Reyes		1153	985	.854	138
Yunel Escobar		463	391	.844	71
Clint Barmes		436	367	.842	62
Tony F Pena		549	461	.840	105
Khalil Greene		953	800	.839	132
Miguel Tejada		1100	923	.839	135
John McDonald		542	452	.834	101
Ryan Theriot		572	477	.834	64
Jack Wilson		1039	859	.827	163
Cristian Guzman		461	381	.826	61
Jimmy Rollins		1210	1000	.826	168
Michael Young		1303	1076	.826	139
Jason Bartlett		951	783	.823	137
Ronny Cedeno		410	337	.822	62
Marco Scutaro		417	342	.820	55
Rafael Furcal		927	760	.820	122
Bobby Crosby		868	711	.819	107
Edgar Renteria		1020	835	.819	146
Juan Uribe		751	613	.816	89
Angel Berroa		557	454	.815	62
J.J. Hardy		801	652	.814	160
Orlando Cabrera		1147	927	.808	152
Carlos Guillen		747	603	.807	85
Derek Jeter		1106	891	.806	92
David Eckstein		758	610	.805	104
Yuniesky Betancourt		1176	944	.803	134
Hanley Ramirez		1125	900	.800	154
Julio Lugo		727	577	.794	103
Felipe Lopez		712	564	.792	71
Jhonny Peralta		1287	1016	.789	152
Stephen Drew		873	687	.787	125

Shortstops - 2007 Zone Ratings

Player	Tm	Balls In Zone	Plays Made	Zone Rating	Plays Out Of Zone
Omar Vizquel	SF	395	350	.886	47
Adam Everett	Hou	155	135	.871	35
Jose Reyes	NYM	394	343	.871	58
Alex Gonzalez	Cin	246	212	.862	32
Troy Tulowitzki	Col	467	402	.861	87
Cesar Izturis	2 tms	171	147	.860	25
Ryan Theriot	ChC	239	205	.858	28
Khalil Greene	SD	401	340	.848	59
Tony F Pena	KC	368	312	.848	70
John McDonald	Tor	232	196	.845	51
Jeff Keppinger	Cin	116	98	.845	11
Bobby Crosby	Oak	253	211	.834	40
Miguel Tejada	Bal	317	263	.830	48
Rafael Furcal	LAD	385	317	.823	53
Jack Wilson	Pit	396	323	.816	76
Edgar Renteria	Atl	297	242	.815	49
Michael Young	Tex	419	339	.809	45
Jimmy Rollins	Phi	447	361	.808	65
Orlando Cabrera	LAA	374	302	.807	51
Julio Lugo	Bos	332	268	.807	55
J.J. Hardy	Mil	362	292	.807	64
Royce Clayton	2 tms	164	132	.805	27
Jason Bartlett	Min	373	300	.804	67
Yuniesky Betancourt	Sea	399	320	.802	46
Carlos Guillen	Det	341	273	.801	36
Juan Uribe	CWS	416	331	.796	49
Felipe Lopez	Was	296	232	.784	30
David Eckstein	StL	295	231	.783	46
Brendan Harris	TB	202	157	.777	37
Derek Jeter	NYY	386	300	.777	35
Stephen Drew	Ari	376	292	.777	57
Mark Loretta	Hou	152	118	.776	21
Hanley Ramirez	Fla	388	300	.773	45
Jhonny Peralta	Cle	427	326	.763	65
Josh Wilson	2 tms	127	93	.732	18

Shortstops - 2008 Zone Ratings

Player	Tm	Balls In Zone	Plays Made	Zone Rating	Plays Out Of Zone
Troy Tulowitzki	Col	285	252	.884	18
Miguel Tejada	Hou	389	342	.879	43
Marco Scutaro	Tor	143	125	.874	21
Angel Berroa	LAD	186	162	.871	26
Cesar Izturis	StL	314	273	.869	58
Omar Vizquel	SF	151	131	.868	25
Nick Punto	Min	172	148	.860	15
Mike Aviles	KC	202	173	.856	31
Erick Aybar	LAA	237	202	.852	30
Jack Wilson	Pit	242	206	.851	39
Michael Young	Tex	426	362	.850	41
Jimmy Rollins	Phi	350	297	.849	57
Maicer Izturis	LAA	124	105	.847	21
Yunel Escobar	Atl	358	302	.844	60
Hanley Ramirez	Fla	369	310	.840	48
Derek Jeter	NYY	335	281	.839	29
Cristian Guzman	Was	358	300	.838	50
Jose Reyes	NYM	400	334	.835	40
Khalil Greene	SD	266	222	.835	37
Orlando Cabrera	CWS	422	352	.834	57
J.J. Hardy	Mil	374	309	.826	72
Ryan Theriot	ChC	327	269	.823	36
Tony F Pena	KC	162	133	.821	28
Bobby Crosby	Oak	349	285	.817	43
Jhonny Peralta	Cle	401	326	.813	41
Jason Bartlett	TB	285	230	.807	44
John McDonald	Tor	114	92	.807	19
Edgar Renteria	Det	355	284	.800	42
Yuniesky Betancourt	Sea	378	302	.799	33
Jeff Keppinger	Cin	237	189	.797	27
Stephen Drew	Ari	359	283	.788	51
Julio Lugo	Bos	182	143	.786	23
Juan Castro	2 tms	135	106	.785	18
Brendan Harris	Min	145	113	.779	17
David Eckstein	Tor	143	110	.769	15

Shortstops - 2006 Zone Ratings

Player	Tm	Balls In Zone	Plays Made	Zone Rating	Plays Out Of Zone
Adam Everett	Hou	396	353	.891	60
Omar Vizquel	SF	352	306	.869	36
Jason Bartlett	Min	293	253	.863	26
Alex Cora	Bos	142	122	.859	19
Jose Reyes	NYM	359	308	.858	40
Alex Gonzalez	Bos	269	230	.855	42
Clint Barmes	Col	315	269	.854	51
Craig Counsell	Ari	246	210	.854	47
Juan Uribe	CWS	333	280	.841	40
David Eckstein	StL	320	269	.841	43
Edgar Renteria	Atl	368	309	.840	55
Juan Castro	2 tms	166	139	.837	24
John McDonald	Tor	196	164	.837	31
Khalil Greene	SD	286	238	.832	36
Jimmy Rollins	Phi	413	342	.828	46
Ronny Cedeno	ChC	322	265	.823	54
Jack Wilson	Pit	401	330	.823	48
Michael Young	Tex	458	375	.819	53
Carlos Guillen	Det	406	330	.813	49
Rafael Furcal	LAD	458	372	.812	57
Stephen Drew	Ari	138	112	.812	17
Bobby Crosby	Oak	266	215	.808	24
Miguel Tejada	Bal	394	318	.807	44
Yuniesky Betancourt	Sea	399	322	.807	55
Derek Jeter	NYY	385	310	.805	28
Bill Hall	Mil	294	234	.796	66
Jhonny Peralta	Cle	459	364	.793	46
Felipe Lopez	2 tms	388	307	.791	39
Ben Zobrist	TB	147	116	.789	15
Marco Scutaro	Oak	180	142	.789	14
Hanley Ramirez	Fla	368	290	.788	61
Angel Berroa	KC	364	286	.786	36
Julio Lugo	2 tms	213	166	.779	25
Orlando Cabrera	LAA	351	273	.778	44
Royce Clayton	2 tms	333	258	.775	48

Left Fielders - 3-Year Zone Ratings

Player		Balls In Zone	Plays Made	Zone Rating	Plays Out Of Zone
Eric Byrnes		283	263	.929	62
Dave Roberts		286	265	.927	52
Andre Ethier		278	254	.914	39
Matt Murton		292	266	.911	64
Melky Cabrera		232	210	.905	45
Scott Podsednik		339	305	.900	55
Hideki Matsui		326	292	.896	44
Willie Harris		244	218	.893	75
Ryan Braun		233	208	.893	67
Adam Lind		241	215	.892	39
Matt Diaz		323	288	.892	89
Matt Holliday		746	663	.889	150
Shannon Stewart		368	327	.889	64
Reed Johnson		246	217	.882	55
Alfonso Soriano		714	629	.881	128
Carl Crawford		774	681	.880	138
Luke Scott		260	228	.877	57
Emil Brown		362	317	.876	90
Adam Dunn		718	626	.872	108
Jay Payton		469	408	.870	74
Raul Ibanez		805	695	.863	133
Jason Michaels		347	298	.859	85
Carlos Quentin		224	192	.857	40
Jason Bay		797	683	.857	153
Josh Willingham		580	497	.857	86
Luis Gonzalez		548	468	.854	85
Delmon Young		275	234	.851	48
Carlos Lee		641	544	.849	131
Marcus Thames		242	205	.847	52
Garret Anderson		467	390	.835	89
Pat Burrell		593	490	.826	92
Craig Monroe		316	261	.826	73
Frank Catalanotto		279	229	.821	38
Chris Duncan		304	249	.819	48
Manny Ramirez		584	438	.750	109

Left Fielders - 2007 Zone Ratings

Player	Tm	Balls In Zone	Plays Made	Zone Rating	Plays Out Of Zone
Eric Byrnes	Ari	206	191	.927	48
Moises Alou	NYM	130	119	.915	19
Scott Podsednik	CWS	109	99	.908	9
Shannon Stewart	Oak	261	235	.900	42
Adam Lind	Tor	128	115	.898	22
Geoff Jenkins	Mil	225	202	.898	41
Joey Gathright	KC	134	120	.896	34
Reggie Willits	LAA	143	128	.895	23
Matt Holliday	Col	279	249	.892	47
Ryan Church	Was	183	163	.891	33
Rob Mackowiak	2 tms	100	89	.890	9
Hideki Matsui	NYY	209	186	.890	28
Scott Hairston	2 tms	99	88	.889	27
Alfonso Soriano	ChC	233	205	.880	40
Jason Kubel	Min	157	138	.879	21
Carl Crawford	TB	280	246	.879	40
Jason Michaels	Cle	103	90	.874	27
Carlos Lee	Hou	258	225	.872	36
Willie Harris	Atl	125	109	.872	29
Matt Diaz	Atl	130	113	.869	42
Josh Willingham	Fla	218	188	.862	23
Craig Monroe	2 tms	154	132	.857	34
Reed Johnson	Tor	105	90	.857	18
Jason Bay	Pit	257	219	.852	47
Emil Brown	KC	139	118	.849	37
Jay Payton	Bal	233	197	.845	34
Adam Dunn	Cin	255	214	.839	31
Garret Anderson	LAA	147	123	.837	20
Frank Catalanotto	Tex	98	82	.837	16
Luis Gonzalez	LAD	192	160	.833	32
Barry Bonds	SF	160	133	.831	29
Raul Ibanez	Sea	225	183	.813	41
Pat Burrell	Phi	193	155	.803	21
Chris Duncan	StL	168	132	.786	26
Manny Ramirez	Bos	191	147	.770	35

Left Fielders - 2008 Zone Ratings

Player	Tm	Balls In Zone	Plays Made	Zone Rating	Plays Out Of Zone
Willie Harris	Was	106	100	.943	45
Jay Payton	Bal	121	113	.934	19
Conor Jackson	Ari	127	118	.929	28
Eric Byrnes	Ari	69	64	.928	12
David DeJesus	KC	114	105	.921	31
David Murphy	Tex	76	70	.921	16
Johnny Damon	NYY	134	123	.918	32
Chase Headley	SD	131	120	.916	36
Carl Crawford	TB	201	184	.915	47
Fred Lewis	SF	151	137	.907	40
Adam Dunn	2 tms	193	175	.907	35
Matt Holliday	Col	211	191	.905	49
Josh Willingham	Fla	147	133	.905	33
Matt Joyce	Det	84	76	.905	18
Ben Francisco	Cle	135	122	.904	28
Gregor Blanco	Atl	70	63	.900	23
Raul Ibanez	Sea	292	262	.897	41
Juan Pierre	LAD	105	94	.895	31
Ryan Braun	Mil	233	208	.893	67
Wily Mo Pena	Was	83	74	.892	25
Adam Lind	Tor	108	96	.889	17
Alfonso Soriano	ChC	171	151	.883	35
Brandon Boggs	Tex	112	98	.875	33
Luke Scott	Bal	188	164	.872	36
Luis Gonzalez	Fla	107	93	.869	12
Manny Ramirez	2 tms	180	154	.856	36
Carlos Quentin	CWS	220	188	.855	40
Emil Brown	Oak	81	69	.852	20
Delmon Young	Min	275	234	.851	48
Carlos Lee	Hou	167	142	.850	45
Jason Bay	2 tms	240	204	.850	50
Jack Cust	Oak	127	107	.843	22
Garret Anderson	LAA	137	115	.839	29
Pat Burrell	Phi	188	156	.830	45
Marcus Thames	Det	115	95	.826	25

Left Fielders - 2006 Zone Ratings

Player	Tm	Balls In Zone	Plays Made	Zone Rating	Plays Out Of Zone
Dave Roberts	SD	220	205	.932	34
Ryan Langerhans	Atl	136	126	.926	30
Andre Ethier	LAD	162	149	.920	23
Matt Diaz	Atl	135	124	.919	39
Emil Brown	KC	142	130	.915	33
Melky Cabrera	NYY	199	182	.915	35
Juan Rivera	LAA	116	106	.914	20
Matt Murton	ChC	218	197	.904	43
Nick Swisher	Oak	158	142	.899	28
Scott Podsednik	CWS	222	199	.896	46
Reed Johnson	Tor	110	98	.891	31
Luke Scott	Hou	68	60	.882	21
Alfonso Soriano	Was	310	273	.881	53
Adam Dunn	Cin	270	237	.878	42
David DeJesus	KC	133	116	.872	22
Matt Holliday	Col	256	223	.871	54
Raul Ibanez	Sea	288	250	.868	51
Jason Bay	Pit	300	260	.867	56
Cliff Floyd	NYM	148	128	.865	20
Luis Gonzalez	Ari	249	215	.863	41
Jason Michaels	Cle	200	172	.860	42
Carl Crawford	TB	293	251	.857	51
Barry Bonds	SF	179	153	.855	35
Jay Payton	Oak	115	98	.852	21
Jeff Conine	2 tms	92	78	.848	10
Preston Wilson	2 tms	151	128	.848	28
Pat Burrell	Phi	212	179	.844	26
Frank Catalanotto	Tor	145	122	.841	18
Brad Wilkerson	Tex	138	116	.841	23
Garret Anderson	LAA	183	152	.831	40
Carlos Lee	2 tms	216	177	.819	50
Josh Willingham	Fla	215	176	.819	30
Kevin Mench	2 tms	70	56	.800	23
Craig Monroe	Det	162	129	.796	39
Manny Ramirez	Bos	213	137	.643	38

Center Fielders - 3-Year Zone Ratings

Player	Balls In Zone	Plays Made	Zone Rating	Plays Out Of Zone
Carlos Gomez	354	336	.949	105
Adam Jones	351	330	.940	84
Corey Patterson	782	730	.934	138
Cody Ross	311	289	.929	68
Johnny Damon	453	419	.925	85
Eric Byrnes	289	267	.924	55
Melky Cabrera	577	533	.924	94
Alfredo Amezaga	440	405	.920	104
Curtis Granderson	1018	937	.920	238
Juan Pierre	710	652	.918	121
Andruw Jones	777	713	.918	193
David DeJesus	672	616	.917	84
Carlos Beltran	1026	940	.916	224
Mike Cameron	928	848	.914	177
Chris Young	688	628	.913	169
Brian Anderson	358	326	.911	89
Shane Victorino	390	354	.908	124
Ichiro Suzuki	634	574	.905	159
B.J. Upton	506	458	.905	124
Grady Sizemore	1104	999	.905	191
Coco Crisp	825	744	.902	144
Joey Gathright	498	449	.902	105
Aaron Rowand	974	876	.899	177
Marlon Byrd	352	316	.898	72
Willy Taveras	712	639	.897	190
Torii Hunter	1003	897	.894	185
Vernon Wells	839	750	.894	120
Josh Hamilton	386	345	.894	91
Jim Edmonds	638	568	.890	141
Mark Kotsay	554	491	.886	104
Cory Sullivan	283	250	.883	54
Nate McLouth	555	490	.883	116
Gary Matthews Jr.	716	630	.880	131
Lastings Milledge	349	304	.871	85
Ken Griffey Jr.	284	241	.849	50

Center Fielders - 2007 Zone Ratings

Player	Tm	Balls In Zone	Plays Made	Zone Rating	Plays Out Of Zone
Felix Pie	ChC	110	104	.945	16
Jacque Jones	ChC	173	160	.925	35
Jerry Owens	CWS	199	184	.925	24
Curtis Granderson	Det	367	339	.924	85
Alfredo Amezaga	Fla	182	168	.923	40
Andruw Jones	Atl	343	316	.921	80
Coco Crisp	Bos	382	350	.916	58
Carlos Beltran	NYM	355	325	.915	64
Corey Patterson	Bal	267	244	.914	37
Melky Cabrera	NYY	344	314	.913	33
Nook Logan	Was	226	206	.912	42
David DeJesus	KC	389	354	.910	46
Juan Pierre	LAD	334	303	.907	63
Chris Duffy	Pit	164	148	.902	24
Mark Kotsay	Oak	138	124	.899	17
Josh Hamilton	Cin	167	150	.898	18
Ichiro Suzuki	Sea	365	327	.896	97
Mike Cameron	SD	349	312	.894	53
Torii Hunter	Min	384	342	.891	47
Grady Sizemore	Cle	399	354	.887	45
Marlon Byrd	Tex	115	102	.887	12
Vernon Wells	Tor	326	289	.887	32
Hunter Pence	Hou	243	215	.885	45
Nick Swisher	Oak	138	122	.884	17
Willy Taveras	Col	198	175	.884	37
Chris Young	Ari	329	288	.875	66
B.J. Upton	TB	191	167	.874	37
Nate McLouth	Pit	138	119	.862	23
Aaron Rowand	Phi	375	323	.861	69
Dave Roberts	SF	219	188	.858	36
Kenny Lofton	2 tms	180	154	.856	34
Gary Matthews Jr.	LAA	351	300	.855	62
Jim Edmonds	StL	230	196	.852	48
Bill Hall	Mil	285	241	.846	54
Ryan Freel	Cin	125	103	.824	33

Center Fielders - 2008 Zone Ratings

Player	Tm	Balls In Zone	Plays Made	Zone Rating	Plays Out Of Zone
Alex Rios	Tor	132	127	.962	29
Adam Jones	Bal	278	267	.960	70
Carlos Gonzalez	Oak	143	137	.958	39
Cody Ross	Fla	207	197	.952	57
Aaron Rowand	SF	362	344	.950	67
Carlos Gomez	Min	352	334	.949	103
Chris Young	Ari	318	301	.947	92
Mike Cameron	Mil	242	229	.946	64
Jacoby Ellsbury	Bos	147	139	.946	32
Melky Cabrera	NYY	227	213	.938	59
Corey Patterson	Cin	200	187	.935	55
David DeJesus	KC	137	128	.934	23
Reed Johnson	ChC	119	111	.933	33
Grady Sizemore	Cle	311	290	.932	92
Jody Gerut	SD	161	150	.932	39
Skip Schumaker	StL	112	104	.929	32
Carlos Beltran	NYM	332	308	.928	110
Coco Crisp	Bos	206	191	.927	43
Jim Edmonds	2 tms	202	187	.926	55
Michael Bourn	Hou	226	209	.925	82
Curtis Granderson	Det	304	281	.924	85
B.J. Upton	TB	315	291	.924	87
Rick Ankiel	StL	191	176	.921	37
Shane Victorino	Phi	253	232	.917	82
Nick Swisher	CWS	114	104	.912	34
Willy Taveras	Col	230	209	.909	73
Matt Kemp	LAD	184	167	.908	42
Ichiro Suzuki	Sea	173	157	.908	38
Torii Hunter	LAA	289	260	.900	90
Josh Hamilton	Tex	219	195	.890	73
Joey Gathright	KC	173	154	.890	43
Nate McLouth	Pit	339	301	.888	79
Mark Kotsay	Atl	151	134	.887	39
Vernon Wells	Tor	201	177	.881	40
Lastings Milledge	Was	307	267	.870	81

Center Fielders - 2006 Zone Ratings

Player	Tm	Balls In Zone	Plays Made	Zone Rating	Plays Out Of Zone
Corey Patterson	Bal	315	299	.949	46
Brady Clark	Mil	221	207	.937	43
Steve Finley	SF	279	261	.935	26
Juan Pierre	ChC	353	327	.926	52
Andruw Jones	Atl	329	304	.924	73
Johnny Damon	NYY	274	252	.920	54
David DeJesus	KC	146	134	.918	15
Eric Byrnes	Ari	242	222	.917	48
Randy Winn	SF	131	120	.916	17
Jeremy Reed	Sea	118	108	.915	21
Curtis Granderson	Det	347	317	.914	68
Mike Cameron	SD	337	307	.911	60
Vernon Wells	Tor	312	284	.910	48
Joey Gathright	2 tms	309	281	.909	60
Carlos Beltran	NYM	339	307	.906	50
Brian Anderson	CWS	274	248	.905	57
Chris Duffy	Pit	163	147	.902	19
Shane Victorino	Phi	132	119	.902	42
Rocco Baldelli	TB	213	192	.901	36
Grady Sizemore	Cle	394	355	.901	54
Jim Edmonds	StL	206	185	.898	38
Willy Taveras	Hou	284	255	.898	80
Cory Sullivan	Col	202	181	.896	43
Torii Hunter	Min	330	295	.894	48
Gary Matthews Jr.	Tex	310	277	.894	56
Reggie Abercrombie	Fla	149	133	.893	39
Alfredo Amezaga	Fla	139	124	.892	31
Aaron Rowand	Phi	237	209	.882	41
Mark Kotsay	Oak	265	233	.879	48
Chone Figgins	LAA	236	207	.877	35
Kenny Lofton	LAD	239	208	.870	33
Jose Bautista	Pit	119	102	.857	12
Coco Crisp	Bos	237	203	.857	43
Rob Mackowiak	CWS	115	97	.843	22
Ken Griffey Jr.	Cin	238	198	.832	31

Right Fielders - 3-Year Zone Ratings

Player		Balls In Zone	Plays Made	Zone Rating	Plays Out Of Zone
Franklin Gutierrez		339	318	.938	92
Randy Winn		596	556	.933	146
Kosuke Fukudome		191	178	.932	68
Gabe Gross		234	217	.927	52
Ichiro Suzuki		364	336	.923	90
Hunter Pence		331	302	.912	75
Austin Kearns		807	735	.911	173
Jayson Werth		211	192	.910	60
Ryan Ludwick		262	238	.908	54
Jacque Jones		319	289	.906	64
Alex Rios		539	488	.905	143
Shane Victorino		234	211	.902	70
Nick Markakis		824	740	.898	132
Jeff Francoeur		823	738	.897	191
J.D. Drew		626	561	.896	119
Andre Ethier		323	289	.895	59
Mark Teahen		473	423	.894	80
Trot Nixon		326	291	.893	59
Corey Hart		575	512	.890	108
Jeremy Hermida		616	548	.890	122
Geoff Jenkins		347	308	.888	80
Xavier Nady		519	460	.886	88
Nelson Cruz		261	231	.885	58
Delmon Young		287	254	.885	48
Magglio Ordonez		729	644	.883	95
Brian Giles		701	619	.883	171
Bobby Abreu		893	783	.877	94
Jose Guillen		543	475	.875	78
Justin Upton		215	187	.870	53
Vladimir Guerrero		639	555	.869	86
Brad Hawpe		696	604	.868	111
Ken Griffey Jr.		454	392	.863	56
Matt Kemp		229	197	.860	38
Michael Cuddyer		609	522	.857	102
Jermaine Dye		850	723	.851	132

Right Fielders - 2007 Zone Ratings

Player	Tm	Balls In Zone	Plays Made	Zone Rating	Plays Out Of Zone
Nick Swisher	Oak	97	90	.928	19
Jayson Werth	Phi	93	86	.925	23
Andre Ethier	LAD	158	146	.924	31
Randy Winn	SF	190	175	.921	34
Travis Buck	Oak	98	90	.918	20
Luke Scott	Hou	183	168	.918	29
Alex Rios	Tor	218	200	.917	43
Magglio Ordonez	Det	254	232	.913	29
Austin Kearns	Was	338	307	.908	68
Franklin Gutierrez	Cle	119	108	.908	28
Shane Victorino	Phi	192	174	.906	55
Carlos Quentin	Ari	127	114	.898	24
Jeff Francoeur	Atl	297	266	.896	62
Bobby Abreu	NYY	322	288	.894	25
Shawn Green	NYM	198	177	.894	26
Corey Hart	Mil	241	214	.888	39
Brad Hawpe	Col	237	210	.886	37
Trot Nixon	Cle	130	115	.885	14
Xavier Nady	Pit	155	137	.884	25
Jeremy Hermida	Fla	231	204	.883	43
Ken Griffey Jr.	Cin	298	263	.883	28
Delmon Young	TB	246	217	.882	35
Juan Encarnacion	StL	125	110	.880	15
Mark Teahen	KC	307	270	.879	48
J.D. Drew	Bos	210	184	.876	28
Nelson Cruz	Tex	144	126	.875	22
Jack Cust	Oak	82	71	.866	8
Jose Guillen	Sea	271	234	.863	34
Matt Kemp	LAD	131	113	.863	16
Nick Markakis	Bal	300	258	.860	45
Michael Cuddyer	Min	254	218	.858	38
Brian Giles	SD	197	169	.858	47
Vladimir Guerrero	LAA	217	182	.839	26
Cliff Floyd	ChC	77	64	.831	5
Jermaine Dye	CWS	303	246	.812	38

Right Fielders - 2008 Zone Ratings

Player	Tm	Balls In Zone	Plays Made	Zone Rating	Plays Out Of Zone
Franklin Gutierrez	Cle	177	169	.955	55
Randy Winn	SF	253	240	.949	69
Gabe Gross	2 tms	160	151	.944	35
Brad Wilkerson	2 tms	80	75	.938	20
J.D. Drew	Bos	157	147	.936	37
Denard Span	Min	165	154	.933	38
Kosuke Fukudome	ChC	191	178	.932	68
Nick Markakis	Bal	295	273	.925	56
Ryan Ludwick	StL	207	191	.923	41
Mark Teahen	KC	166	153	.922	32
Ryan Sweeney	Oak	115	105	.913	31
Jeff Francoeur	Atl	243	221	.909	63
Hunter Pence	Hou	298	270	.906	71
Brian Giles	SD	226	204	.903	72
Michael Cuddyer	Min	111	100	.901	23
Ichiro Suzuki	Sea	140	126	.900	50
Jayson Werth	Phi	118	106	.898	37
Xavier Nady	2 tms	186	167	.898	32
Jeremy Hermida	Fla	244	219	.898	47
Elijah Dukes	Was	117	105	.897	32
Alex Rios	Tor	134	120	.896	50
Vladimir Guerrero	LAA	161	144	.894	36
Austin Kearns	Was	159	142	.893	45
Jermaine Dye	CWS	237	211	.890	55
Corey Hart	Mil	272	242	.890	62
Jay Bruce	Cin	121	107	.884	36
Bobby Abreu	NYY	273	239	.875	32
Ryan Church	NYM	150	131	.873	49
Andre Ethier	LAD	165	143	.867	28
Magglio Ordonez	Det	211	182	.863	38
Brad Hawpe	Col	187	161	.861	27
Justin Upton	Ari	151	130	.861	45
Geoff Jenkins	Phi	121	104	.860	37
Jose Guillen	KC	127	109	.858	12
Ken Griffey Jr.	2 tms	156	129	.827	28

Right Fielders - 2006 Zone Ratings

Player	Tm	Balls In Zone	Plays Made	Zone Rating	Plays Out Of Zone
Mark DeRosa	Tex	109	103	.945	22
Reggie Sanders	KC	154	145	.942	25
Ichiro Suzuki	Sea	224	210	.938	40
Austin Kearns	2 tms	310	286	.923	60
Randy Winn	SF	153	141	.922	43
Juan Encarnacion	StL	196	180	.918	39
Emil Brown	KC	104	95	.913	15
Nick Markakis	Bal	229	209	.913	31
Jason Lane	Hou	146	133	.911	22
Damon Hollins	TB	112	102	.911	32
Jose Guillen	Was	145	132	.910	32
Milton Bradley	Oak	170	154	.906	37
Geoff Jenkins	Mil	226	204	.903	43
Jacque Jones	ChC	251	226	.900	49
Moises Alou	SF	150	135	.900	19
Jay Payton	Oak	80	72	.900	17
Trot Nixon	Bos	188	169	.899	43
Alex Rios	Tor	187	168	.898	50
Carlos Quentin	Ari	87	78	.897	18
Shawn Green	2 tms	218	195	.894	25
J.D. Drew	LAD	259	230	.888	54
Jeff Francoeur	Atl	283	251	.887	66
Jeremy Hermida	Fla	141	125	.887	32
Brian Giles	SD	278	246	.885	52
Casey Blake	Cle	193	170	.881	40
Vladimir Guerrero	LAA	261	229	.877	24
Xavier Nady	2 tms	178	156	.876	31
Kevin Mench	Tex	111	97	.874	15
Magglio Ordonez	Det	264	230	.871	28
Bobby Abreu	2 tms	298	256	.859	37
Jermaine Dye	CWS	310	266	.858	39
Brad Hawpe	Col	272	233	.857	47
Michael Cuddyer	Min	244	204	.836	41
Bernie Williams	NYY	108	89	.824	9
Jeromy Burnitz	Pit	123	98	.797	22

Three-Year Revised Zone Rating Leaders by Position

First base – Doug Mientkiewicz

Second base – Mark Ellis

Third base – Joe Crede

Shortstop – Adam Everett

Left field – Eric Byrnes

Center field – Carlos Gomez

Right field – Franklin Gutierrez

These are the unsung heroes of defense. All of them should
have won a Gold Glove. Only one has (Mientkiewicz - 2001).

Defensive Replacements

One way of getting factual information about a player's defense is simply to look at how many times he was put into the game for defense, and how many times he was taken out of the game for defense. The chart on the next page gives all players who were used as defensive substitutes five or more times in 2008, or who were removed for substitutes five or more times.

Gabe Gross was used as a defensive substitute 19 times last year for Tampa Bay, and was never removed from the game for another rightfielder. On the other hand, well, on several other hands, we have Pat Burrell, Eric Hinske, Mike Jacobs, Jeff Kent, Jason Giambi, John Bowker, Wily Mo Pena, Jack Cust, Luke Scott, Emil Brown, Adam Lind, Jeff Baker, Marcus Thames, and Carlos Lee, each of whom was substituted for on defense at least 10 times without ever being used as a defensive substitute.

We also have the multi-position players Jorge Cantu and Nick Swisher. Cantu was subbed for 19 times at third base without ever being a defensive sub but he appeared 15 times as a defensive sub at first base without ever being removed for a replacement. Swisher was brought in at first base seven times without being removed but was removed 10 times from center field without ever being brought in. What the Marlins and the White Sox were doing is apparent from the chart. In the late innings Cantu moved from third base to first base replacing Mike Jacobs. Wes Helms or Alfredo Amezaga came in at third. At other times Amezaga came in to play center field replacing Cody Ross, with Ross moving over to right to replace Jeremy Hermida in right field. For the White Sox, a typical change was to move Swisher from center field to first base, replacing Paul Konerko, while Brian Anderson came in to play center.

Then there's the seemingly strange case of Mark DeRosa and Mike Fontenot (or maybe Sweet Lou). DeRosa was a defensive sub six times and was removed for a defensive sub seven times. Fontenot was a defensive sub six times and was removed for a defensive sub four times. Was Lou having difficulty making up his mind which was better? More likely, it had something to do with offense, rather than defense, since DeRosa bats right and Fontenot left.

Overall, this data gives you an idea of what the managers of these folks believed. If we take a quick look at the plus/minus values of these substitutions maybe the data will reinforce the choices made by the managers.

We split the defensive replacements into two groups; one group that served as a defensive sub more often, one group that was replaced more often. We found that the average plus/minus of players removed is -2.6 and the average plus/minus of the players brought in is 2.3. As a whole, the Plus/Minus System backs up the defensive choices made by the managers.

2008 Defensive Replacements

Team	Position	Player	Def In	Def Out
Arizona Diamondbacks	Third Base	Augie Ojeda	7	0
Arizona Diamondbacks	Third Base	Mark Reynolds	0	7
Arizona Diamondbacks	Right Field	Justin Upton	0	5
Atlanta Braves	Left Field	Gregor Blanco	8	0
Baltimore Orioles	Left Field	Jay Payton	10	0
Baltimore Orioles	Left Field	Luke Scott	0	11
Boston Red Sox	Shortstop	Alex Cora	9	0
Boston Red Sox	Shortstop	Julio Lugo	0	6
Boston Red Sox	Left Field	Jacoby Ellsbury	5	0
Chicago Cubs	Second Base	Mark DeRosa	6	7
Chicago Cubs	Second Base	Mike Fontenot	6	4
Chicago Cubs	Left Field	Reed Johnson	7	0
Chicago Cubs	Center Field	Felix Pie	8	0
Chicago Cubs	Center Field	Reed Johnson	0	9
Chicago Cubs	Right Field	Kosuke Fukudome	6	2
Chicago White Sox	First Base	Nick Swisher	7	0
Chicago White Sox	First Base	Paul Konerko	0	7
Chicago White Sox	Second Base	Juan Uribe	5	0
Chicago White Sox	Center Field	Brian Anderson	12	0
Chicago White Sox	Center Field	Nick Swisher	0	10
Cincinnati Reds	Left Field	Adam Dunn	0	7
Cincinnati Reds	Center Field	Corey Patterson	9	1
Cincinnati Reds	Right Field	Ken Griffey Jr.	0	5
Colorado Rockies	Second Base	Omar Quintanilla	8	0
Colorado Rockies	Second Base	Clint Barmes	2	5
Colorado Rockies	Second Base	Jeff Baker	0	10
Detroit Tigers	Third Base	Brandon Inge	6	0
Detroit Tigers	Left Field	Matt Joyce	5	0
Detroit Tigers	Left Field	Marcus Thames	0	10
Florida Marlins	First Base	Jorge Cantu	15	0
Florida Marlins	First Base	Mike Jacobs	0	17
Florida Marlins	Third Base	Wes Helms	11	0
Florida Marlins	Third Base	Alfredo Amezaga	9	1
Florida Marlins	Third Base	Jorge Cantu	0	19
Florida Marlins	Center Field	Alfredo Amezaga	8	3
Florida Marlins	Center Field	Cody Ross	3	8
Florida Marlins	Right Field	Cody Ross	12	0
Florida Marlins	Right Field	Jeremy Hermida	0	9
Houston Astros	Left Field	Darin Erstad	12	0
Houston Astros	Left Field	Carlos Lee	0	10
Kansas City Royals	First Base	Ross Gload	7	0
Kansas City Royals	First Base	Billy Butler	0	6
Kansas City Royals	Second Base	Mike Aviles	5	0
Kansas City Royals	Shortstop	Tony F. Pena	10	0
Kansas City Royals	Shortstop	Mike Aviles	0	9
Kansas City Royals	Left Field	David DeJesus	5	1
Kansas City Royals	Center Field	Joey Gathright	6	0
Kansas City Royals	Center Field	David DeJesus	0	5
Los Angeles Angels	Left Field	Reggie Willits	8	0
Los Angeles Angels	Left Field	Juan Rivera	1	7
Los Angeles Dodgers	Second Base	Luis Maza	7	0
Los Angeles Dodgers	Second Base	Pablo Ozuna	5	1
Los Angeles Dodgers	Second Base	Chin-lung Hu	5	0
Los Angeles Dodgers	Second Base	Jeff Kent	0	15
Los Angeles Dodgers	Third Base	Blake DeWitt	5	0
Los Angeles Dodgers	Shortstop	Angel Berroa	5	1
Los Angeles Dodgers	Shortstop	Nomar Garciaparra	0	5
Los Angeles Dodgers	Left Field	Andre Ethier	5	0
Los Angeles Dodgers	Left Field	Juan Pierre	1	5
Los Angeles Dodgers	Center Field	Matt Kemp	1	5
Los Angeles Dodgers	Right Field	Matt Kemp	6	0
Los Angeles Dodgers	Right Field	Andre Ethier	0	7
New York Mets	Left Field	Endy Chavez	11	0
New York Mets	Left Field	Fernando Tatis	5	3
New York Mets	Left Field	Nick Evans	0	9
New York Mets	Right Field	Endy Chavez	7	0
New York Mets	Right Field	Fernando Tatis	0	7
New York Yankees	First Base	Cody Ransom	7	0
New York Yankees	First Base	Jason Giambi	0	13

Team	Position	Player	Def In	Def Out
Oakland Athletics	Left Field	Emil Brown	7	1
Oakland Athletics	Left Field	Jack Cust	0	12
Oakland Athletics	Center Field	Rajai Davis	9	0
Oakland Athletics	Center Field	Ryan Sweeney	1	5
Oakland Athletics	Center Field	Carlos Gonzalez	1	5
Oakland Athletics	Right Field	Carlos Gonzalez	11	0
Oakland Athletics	Right Field	Ryan Sweeney	11	5
Oakland Athletics	Right Field	Emil Brown	0	11
Oakland Athletics	Right Field	Travis Buck	0	6
Philadelphia Phillies	Catcher	Carlos Ruiz	6	1
Philadelphia Phillies	Catcher	Chris Coste	1	6
Philadelphia Phillies	Third Base	Greg Dobbs	1	8
Philadelphia Phillies	Left Field	Eric Bruntlett	8	0
Philadelphia Phillies	Left Field	Jayson Werth	8	2
Philadelphia Phillies	Left Field	So Taguchi	7	0
Philadelphia Phillies	Left Field	Pat Burrell	0	23
Philadelphia Phillies	Right Field	Geoff Jenkins	7	3
Philadelphia Phillies	Right Field	Jayson Werth	2	7
San Diego Padres	Second Base	Edgar Gonzalez	1	7
San Diego Padres	Left Field	Scott Hairston	5	1
San Diego Padres	Center Field	Jody Gerut	5	0
San Diego Padres	Center Field	Scott Hairston	2	6
San Francisco Giants	First Base	Rich Aurilia	14	0
San Francisco Giants	First Base	John Bowker	0	13
San Francisco Giants	Third Base	Jose Castillo	6	0
San Francisco Giants	Third Base	Rich Aurilia	2	6
Seattle Mariners	Catcher	Jamie Burke	6	1
Seattle Mariners	Catcher	Jeff Clement	1	6
Seattle Mariners	First Base	Miguel Cairo	5	0
St Louis Cardinals	Second Base	Aaron Miles	15	3
St Louis Cardinals	Second Base	Adam Kennedy	3	15
St Louis Cardinals	Shortstop	Cesar Izturis	5	4
St Louis Cardinals	Shortstop	Aaron Miles	1	5
St Louis Cardinals	Left Field	Ryan Ludwick	5	0
St Louis Cardinals	Left Field	Brian Barton	1	5
St Louis Cardinals	Center Field	Skip Schumaker	5	0
St Louis Cardinals	Right Field	Ryan Ludwick	5	3
Tampa Bay Rays	Left Field	Justin Ruggiano	8	0
Tampa Bay Rays	Left Field	Eric Hinske	0	6
Tampa Bay Rays	Right Field	Gabe Gross	19	0
Tampa Bay Rays	Right Field	Eric Hinske	0	18
Toronto Blue Jays	Second Base	Marco Scutaro	7	1
Toronto Blue Jays	Second Base	Joe Inglett	1	6
Toronto Blue Jays	Shortstop	John McDonald	10	1
Toronto Blue Jays	Shortstop	Marco Scutaro	1	5
Toronto Blue Jays	Shortstop	David Eckstein	0	5
Toronto Blue Jays	Left Field	Joe Inglett	10	0
Toronto Blue Jays	Left Field	Brad Wilkerson	5	1
Toronto Blue Jays	Left Field	Adam Lind	0	11
Toronto Blue Jays	Left Field	Shannon Stewart	0	5
Washington Nationals	Catcher	Wil Nieves	5	0
Washington Nationals	First Base	Aaron Boone	9	0
Washington Nationals	First Base	Dmitri Young	0	8
Washington Nationals	Second Base	Willie Harris	1	5
Washington Nationals	Left Field	Willie Harris	16	3
Washington Nationals	Left Field	Ryan Langerhans	5	0
Washington Nationals	Left Field	Wily Mo Pena	0	13

Note: Includes players who were used as defensive substitutes 5 or more times in 2008, or who were removed for substitutes 5 or more times

Fielding Bunts

In this section of the original *Fielding Bible*, Bill James introduced a system to rate corner infielders on fielding bunts. Bill's method categorizes each bunt as a Sacrifice, Base Hit, Pure Out (no base advancement), Error, or a Double Play. A point value is assigned to each outcome, and the average of the point values gives the Bunt Score. The average Bunt Score is around .500. To give you an idea how to interpret the Bunt Score (or to remind you of your middle school report card), each was awarded a letter grade from A+ to F.

We made a couple of improvements to Bill's system. Keeping with the theme of *Volume II*, we put bunt fielding on a scale based on runs saved. And we incorporated an adjustment into the system to recognize that a bunt is a bit of a more difficult play for a third baseman than a first baseman. See the end of this article for the technical details.

Lowell vs. A-Rod

As you might expect, most players didn't field enough bunts to have a significant impact on their team. Three years ago, Bill found the best third sacker was Mike Lowell, and the new runs saved technique agrees, to the tune of +13 runs (above positional average) on 138 bunts from 2003 to 2008.

Mike Lowell

Season	Chances	Bunt Runs Saved
2003	31	6
2004	34	4
2005	25	4
2006	17	-1
2007	15	0
2008	16	0

Interestingly, Lowell's bunt numbers dropped off when he moved to Boston and the American League in 2006. As Bill suggested, there is a slight league difference due to the pitcher/DH factor. Lowell's lowest bunt total (all opportunities) pre-2006 was 25; since then, he hasn't broken 17. If the difference in opportunities is due to sacrifice bunt attempts laid down by slow-footed pitchers, it is easy to see why his numbers aren't as impressive as they once were. I'm sure age and injuries have taken their toll on his effectiveness as well.

Guess who finishes dead last? Everyone's favorite 30 million dollar player: Alex Rodriguez. He's even worse than Lowell is good, -16 runs on 92 chances since he moved to third. Using data from 2003 to 2005, the first Fielding Bible ranked A-Rod dead last among 3B. Looking only at the three seasons since, he again occupies the cellar. Subtract that from his monster offensive production and you get. . .well, a perennial MVP candidate nonetheless.

Looking at first base over the last three years, Adrian Gonzalez (+8) saved a handful of runs for his team, while Lyle Overbay (-7) cost the Blue Jays a handful of runs in a division where every run counts. As you can see in the charts on the following pages, Overbay allowed 20 base hits on only 32 bunt attempts while Gonzalez allowed only 22 hits in 92 bunt attempts.

Perhaps unsurprisingly, the better plus/minus fielders also tend to be stronger when it comes to fielding bunts. Pedro Feliz (+8) and Ryan Zimmerman (+5) are among the leaders in Bunt Runs Saved, and they are among the better plus/minus fielders as well. Edwin Encarnacion hit the bottom of the plus/minus standings and has trouble with bunts as well (-5). Over at first base, we find some interesting counterexamples. Mike Jacobs has terrible plus/minus numbers, but is slightly above average at handling bunts (+1), while Overbay is the exact opposite.

In 2008, David Wright, Ryan Zimmerman, and Blake DeWitt (all +3 runs at third base) and Adrian Gonzalez (+4 at first base) led their respective positions. Five players were tied at -3 runs apiece as the worst in 2008. The best single seasons in our sample were Nick Johnson's 2006 (+6) and Lowell's 2003 (+6); the worst were Richie Sexson's -5 in 2003 and Melvin Mora's -5 in 2006.

One final note on bunts as a strategic tool: oftentimes, a hitter will bunt in a particularly crucial situation within the game, and the impact of the play is magnified by the inning and the score. As a result, a fielder's ability (or lack thereof) to turn a bunt into an out may have a disproportionately large impact on the outcome of the game. While A-Rod's weakness on bunts may seem trivial compared to his offensive production, Yankee opponents may want to exploit this flaw, particularly in a crucial, late-September game.

Turning Bunt Data into Runs Saved

Our first mission was to determine the run value of each bunt outcome, and then "award" these run values to the appropriate fielder. Using the run matrix table, we compared before and after base-out states and found the change in run expectancy for each outcome. For example, a sacrifice bunt to the third baseman converted into an out at first base (allowing the runners to advance) actually lowered the batting teams expected number of runs scored by 0.17 runs. We give the third baseman a +0.17 for his effort.

A second important change is the separation of first basemen and third basemen, rating them on a positional average scale. The batter was much more likely to leg out a base hit on a bunt to third than a bunt to first, and on top of that, third basemen are more likely to throw the ball away and allow runners to advance extra bases. In short, third basemen have a much more difficult play. In fact, the average bunt to third increased the offense's run expectancy by 0.10 runs, while a bunt to first decreased their potential 0.02 runs. So on top of the +0.17 runs we gave the third baseman in the previous example, we give him a +0.10 positional adjustment and his Runs Saved for the play becomes +0.27.

Here are the values for each outcome, by position:

	1B	3B
Bunt DP	.90	.90
Pure Outs	.29	.39
Sac Hits	.17	.27
Bunt Hits	-.48	-.34
Errors	-.74	-.70

The Bunt Score and Grade System

Bill's original method categorizes each bunt and assigns a point value to each outcome as follows:

1) If the bunt try results in a double play, we give the fielder 2 points.

2) If the bunt try results in a pure out, with no base advancement, we give the fielder 1 point.

3) If the bunt try results in a sacrifice bunt, we give the fielder 6/10 of one point.

4) If the bunt try results in a base hit, no out recorded, we give the fielder one-quarter of a point.

5) If the fielder makes an error on the play, we give him no points.

We total this up and then average it per opportunity to get the "Bunt Score" with .500 as the average.

We made up a chart to convert the stat into a letter grade, in case this would help you interpret the performance. . . For third basemen, .58 to .61 is a 'B+', .61 to .64 is an 'A-', .33 to .36 is a 'D-', etc. For first baseman, the scale is shifted up by .08.

In the Register section of this book, you will find a Bunts section for all first and third basemen that lists the following:

- The number of bunts the fielder has been challenged to field (Opps),
- The average scores we have assigned him for the results of these bunts (Score),
- A letter grade corresponding to the score (Grade),
- The number of runs saved by the fielder on balls bunted to him (Runs Saved), and
- His Bunt Runs Saved rank among regulars at his position (Rank).

First Basemen - 3-Year Bunt Defense

Player	Opps	Bunt DP	Pure Outs	Sac Hits	Bunt Hits	Errors	Score	Grade	Runs Saved
Adrian Gonzalez	92	5	21	43	22	0	.677	B+	8
Nick Johnson	37	3	6	23	5	0	.731	A	6
James Loney	38	1	11	20	6	0	.697	A-	4
Carlos Delgado	70	1	13	41	15	0	.619	B-	4
Ryan Howard	72	0	18	36	18	0	.613	B-	3
Joey Votto	29	0	6	17	6	0	.610	B-	2
Scott Hatteberg	32	0	6	20	6	0	.609	B-	2
Todd Helton	49	0	9	28	12	0	.588	C+	2
Ross Gload	10	0	4	4	2	0	.690	A-	1
Kevin Youkilis	35	0	13	13	8	1	.651	B	1
Nomar Garciaparra	19	0	4	12	3	0	.629	B-	1
Albert Pujols	54	1	12	26	15	0	.618	B-	1
Adam LaRoche	78	3	15	34	26	0	.614	B-	1
Derrek Lee	70	1	12	36	21	0	.584	C+	1
Mark Teixeira	39	1	4	23	11	0	.578	C+	1
Mike Jacobs	62	0	9	37	16	0	.568	C+	1
Sean Casey	26	2	7	8	9	0	.694	A-	0
Carlos Pena	38	2	8	14	14	0	.629	B-	0
Lance Berkman	35	1	9	14	10	1	.626	B-	0
Prince Fielder	92	1	19	43	29	0	.588	C+	0
Conor Jackson	54	0	8	30	16	0	.556	C	0
Jason Giambi	10	0	1	6	3	0	.535	C	0
Nick Swisher	14	0	6	3	5	0	.646	B	-1
Richie Sexson	33	0	9	11	13	0	.571	C+	-1
Daric Barton	12	0	2	4	6	0	.492	D+	-1
Casey Kotchman	14	0	1	7	6	0	.479	D+	-1
Dmitri Young	14	0	1	7	6	0	.479	D+	-1
Miguel Cabrera	5	0	1	1	3	0	.470	D+	-1
Justin Morneau	37	0	4	20	13	0	.520	C-	-2
Doug Mientkiewicz	12	0	3	2	7	0	.496	D+	-2
Dan Johnson	8	0	2	0	6	0	.438	D-	-2
Kevin Millar	35	0	7	12	16	0	.520	C-	-3
Ryan Garko	41	0	13	8	18	2	.544	C	-4
Paul Konerko	43	1	10	10	22	0	.547	C	-6
Lyle Overbay	32	0	7	5	20	0	.469	D	-7

First Basemen - 2008 Bunt Defense

Player	Tm	Opps	Bunt DP	Pure Outs	Sac Hits	Bunt Hits	Errors	Score	Grade	Runs Saved
Adrian Gonzalez	SD	31	2	9	14	6	0	.739	A	4
Joey Votto	Cin	26	0	6	16	4	0	.638	B	3
Miguel Cairo	Sea	8	1	4	2	1	0	.931	A+	2
James Loney	LAD	25	0	8	12	5	0	.658	B	2
Carlos Delgado	NYM	28	0	4	19	5	0	.595	C+	2
Chris Davis	Tex	3	0	1	2	0	0	.733	A	1
Carlos Pena	TB	16	1	4	6	5	0	.678	B+	1
Derrek Lee	ChC	26	1	5	12	8	0	.623	B-	1
Rich Aurilia	SF	4	0	0	4	0	0	.600	B-	1
Sean Casey	Bos	2	1	0	0	1	0	1.125	A+	0
Nick Swisher	CWS	3	0	2	0	1	0	.750	A+	0
Adam LaRoche	Pit	28	1	7	10	10	0	.625	B-	0
Richie Sexson	2 tms	8	0	3	2	3	0	.619	B-	0
Albert Pujols	StL	12	0	4	4	4	0	.617	B-	0
Ross Gload	KC	6	0	2	2	2	0	.617	B-	0
John Bowker	SF	11	0	3	5	3	0	.614	B-	0
Kevin Youkilis	Bos	12	0	3	6	3	0	.613	B-	0
Conor Jackson	Ari	9	0	2	5	2	0	.611	B-	0
Lance Berkman	Hou	13	0	3	7	2	1	.592	C+	0
Chad Tracy	Ari	9	0	2	4	3	0	.572	C+	0
Ryan Howard	Phi	18	0	4	8	6	0	.572	C+	0
Jason Giambi	NYY	8	0	1	5	2	0	.563	C+	0
Mark Teixeira	2 tms	13	0	1	9	3	0	.550	C	0
Garrett Atkins	Col	6	0	1	3	2	0	.550	C	0
Todd Helton	Col	12	0	1	7	4	0	.517	C-	0
Prince Fielder	Mil	32	0	7	14	11	0	.567	C+	-1
Daric Barton	Oak	10	0	2	3	5	0	.505	C-	-1
Miguel Cabrera	Det	5	0	1	1	3	0	.470	D+	-1
Casey Kotchman	2 tms	10	0	0	5	5	0	.425	D-	-1
Lyle Overbay	Tor	13	0	3	3	7	0	.504	C-	-2
Kevin Millar	Bal	11	0	2	3	6	0	.482	D+	-2
Justin Morneau	Min	9	0	0	4	5	0	.406	F	-2
Ryan Garko	Cle	17	0	4	3	9	1	.474	D+	-3
Mike Jacobs	Fla	21	0	1	10	10	0	.452	D	-3
Paul Konerko	CWS	10	0	1	2	7	0	.395	F	-3

First Basemen - 2007 Bunt Defense

Player	Tm	Opps	Bunt DP	Pure Outs	Sac Hits	Bunt Hits	Errors	Score	Grade	Runs Saved
Ryan Howard	Phi	27	0	9	15	3	0	.694	A-	4
Ryan Klesko	SF	23	0	7	13	3	0	.676	B+	3
James Loney	LAD	11	1	2	7	1	0	.768	A+	2
Albert Pujols	StL	17	1	5	8	3	0	.738	A	2
Adrian Gonzalez	SD	36	3	7	14	11	0	.671	B+	2
Todd Helton	Col	19	0	5	11	3	0	.650	B	2
Mark Teixeira	2 tms	15	0	0	13	2	0	.553	C	2
Ross Gload	KC	3	0	2	1	0	0	.867	A+	1
Lance Berkman	Hou	15	1	4	6	4	0	.707	A-	1
Adam LaRoche	Pit	21	2	4	8	7	0	.693	A-	1
Kevin Youkilis	Bos	12	0	4	6	2	0	.675	B+	1
Carlos Delgado	NYM	23	1	5	11	6	0	.657	B	1
Scott Hatteberg	Cin	11	0	0	10	1	0	.568	C+	1
Mike Jacobs	Fla	16	0	1	12	3	0	.559	C	1
Nomar Garciaparra	LAD	5	0	2	2	1	0	.690	A-	0
Doug Mientkiewicz	NYY	5	0	2	1	2	0	.620	B-	0
Scott Thorman	Atl	5	0	2	1	2	0	.620	B-	0
Lyle Overbay	Tor	6	0	2	2	2	0	.617	B-	0
Casey Kotchman	LAA	3	0	1	1	1	0	.617	B-	0
Jeff Conine	2 tms	4	0	1	2	1	0	.613	B-	0
Prince Fielder	Mil	20	0	4	10	6	0	.575	C+	0
Conor Jackson	Ari	15	0	3	7	5	0	.563	C+	0
Tony Clark	Ari	5	0	1	2	2	0	.540	C	0
Kevin Millar	Bal	8	0	1	4	3	0	.519	C-	0
Brad Wilkerson	Tex	4	0	0	3	1	0	.513	C-	0
Paul Konerko	CWS	18	0	7	4	7	0	.619	B-	-1
Carlos Pena	TB	22	1	4	8	9	0	.593	C+	-1
Ryan Garko	Cle	19	0	7	4	7	1	.587	C+	-1
Derrek Lee	ChC	30	0	5	15	10	0	.550	C	-1
Justin Morneau	Min	12	0	0	8	4	0	.483	D+	-1
Dmitri Young	Was	11	0	1	5	5	0	.477	D+	-1
Richie Sexson	Sea	10	0	1	4	5	0	.465	D	-1
Andy Phillips	NYY	3	0	0	1	2	0	.367	F	-1
Dan Johnson	Oak	2	0	0	0	2	0	.250	F	-1
Sean Casey	Det	9	0	0	4	5	0	.406	F	-2

First Basemen - 2006 Bunt Defense

Player	Tm	Opps	Bunt DP	Pure Outs	Sac Hits	Bunt Hits	Errors	Score	Grade	Runs Saved
Nick Johnson	Was	36	3	6	23	4	0	.744	A	6
Mike Jacobs	Fla	25	0	7	15	3	0	.670	B+	3
Sean Casey	2 tms	15	1	7	4	3	0	.810	A+	2
Adrian Gonzalez	SD	25	0	5	15	5	0	.610	B-	2
Travis Lee	TB	9	0	3	4	2	0	.656	B	1
Scott Hatteberg	Cin	19	0	6	8	5	0	.634	B	1
Justin Morneau	Min	16	0	4	8	4	0	.613	B-	1
Carlos Delgado	NYM	19	0	4	11	4	0	.611	B-	1
Prince Fielder	Mil	40	1	8	19	12	0	.610	B-	1
Nomar Garciaparra	LAD	14	0	2	10	2	0	.607	B-	1
Kevin Youkilis	Bos	11	0	6	1	3	1	.668	B+	0
Richie Sexson	Sea	15	0	5	5	5	0	.617	B-	0
Craig Wilson	2 tms	6	0	2	2	2	0	.617	B-	0
Mike Lamb	Hou	10	0	3	4	3	0	.615	B-	0
Kendry Morales	LAA	8	0	2	4	2	0	.613	B-	0
Todd Helton	Col	18	0	3	10	5	0	.569	C+	0
Chris Shelton	Det	6	0	1	3	2	0	.550	C	0
Adam LaRoche	Atl	29	0	4	16	9	0	.547	C	0
Conor Jackson	Ari	30	0	3	18	9	0	.535	C	0
Jeff Conine	Bal	6	0	0	4	2	0	.483	D+	0
Jason Giambi	NYY	1	0	0	0	1	0	.250	F	0
Mark Teixeira	Tex	11	1	3	1	6	0	.645	B	-1
Nick Swisher	Oak	9	0	3	2	4	0	.578	C+	-1
Ryan Howard	Phi	27	0	5	13	9	0	.557	C	-1
Dan Johnson	Oak	5	0	2	0	3	0	.550	C	-1
Kevin Millar	Bal	16	0	4	5	7	0	.547	C	-1
Albert Pujols	StL	25	0	3	14	8	0	.536	C	-1
Andy Phillips	NYY	4	0	1	1	2	0	.525	C-	-1
Ben Broussard	2 tms	4	0	1	1	2	0	.525	C-	-1
Lance Berkman	Hou	7	0	2	1	4	0	.514	C-	-1
Doug Mientkiewicz	KC	5	0	1	1	3	0	.470	D+	-1
Ryan Shealy	2 tms	4	0	1	0	3	0	.438	D-	-1
Paul Konerko	CWS	15	1	2	4	8	0	.560	C+	-2
Shea Hillenbrand	2 tms	15	0	1	8	6	0	.487	D+	-2
Lyle Overbay	Tor	13	0	2	0	11	0	.365	F	-5

Third Basemen - 3-Year Bunt Defense

Player	Opps	Bunt DP	Pure Outs	Sac Hits	Bunt Hits	Errors	Score	Grade	Runs Saved
Pedro Feliz	74	2	19	28	25	0	.622	A-	8
David Wright	68	2	11	32	23	0	.588	B+	8
Chipper Jones	56	1	12	24	19	0	.592	B+	6
Ryan Zimmerman	80	1	16	34	29	0	.571	B	6
Nick Punto	22	0	7	9	6	0	.632	A-	4
Scott Rolen	48	1	3	28	16	0	.538	B-	4
Hank Blalock	25	0	4	11	10	0	.524	B-	2
Miguel Cabrera	51	0	7	23	21	0	.511	C+	2
Kevin Kouzmanoff	48	3	11	9	25	0	.597	B+	1
Jack Hannahan	25	0	6	9	10	0	.556	B	1
Ramon Vazquez	18	0	3	8	7	0	.531	B-	1
Adrian Beltre	50	0	9	18	23	0	.511	C+	1
Chone Figgins	27	0	4	11	12	0	.504	C+	1
Morgan Ensberg	40	0	4	19	17	0	.491	C+	1
Aramis Ramirez	67	0	8	29	30	0	.491	C+	1
Troy Glaus	49	2	12	10	25	0	.577	B	0
Brandon Inge	24	1	4	6	13	0	.535	B-	0
Mark Reynolds	39	2	2	16	19	0	.522	B-	0
Wilson Betemit	21	1	2	7	11	0	.521	B-	0
Jose Castillo	29	0	5	11	13	0	.512	C+	0
Jose Bautista	46	0	5	19	22	0	.476	C	0
Garrett Atkins	54	0	6	21	27	0	.469	C	0
Maicer Izturis	14	0	0	7	7	0	.425	C-	0
Mike Lamb	28	0	6	7	15	0	.498	C+	-1
Mike Lowell	48	0	8	16	24	0	.492	C+	-1
Eric Chavez	24	0	3	10	11	0	.490	C+	-1
Joe Crede	39	0	7	11	21	0	.483	C+	-1
Casey Blake	33	0	5	11	17	0	.480	C+	-1
Andy Marte	25	0	6	4	15	0	.486	C+	-2
Alex Gordon	28	0	1	10	17	0	.402	D+	-2
Chad Tracy	14	0	0	5	9	0	.375	D	-2
Ty Wigginton	30	0	2	11	17	0	.428	C-	-3
Edwin Encarnacion	63	1	8	17	37	0	.467	C	-5
Melvin Mora	63	0	5	21	36	1	.422	C-	-5
Alex Rodriguez	54	0	3	15	36	0	.389	D	-7

Third Basemen - 2008 Bunt Defense

Player	Tm	Opps	Bunt DP	Pure Outs	Sac Hits	Bunt Hits	Errors	Score	Grade	Runs Saved
David Wright	NYM	17	1	4	7	5	0	.674	A+	3
Ryan Zimmerman	Was	16	1	2	10	3	0	.672	A+	3
Blake DeWitt	LAD	16	0	4	9	3	0	.634	A-	3
Troy Glaus	StL	21	1	6	6	8	0	.648	A	2
Chipper Jones	Atl	14	0	3	7	4	0	.586	B+	2
Jose Castillo	2 tms	20	0	3	11	6	0	.555	B	2
Kevin Kouzmanoff	SD	22	2	4	5	11	0	.625	A-	1
Ramon Vazquez	Tex	8	0	2	4	2	0	.613	A-	1
Chone Figgins	LAA	8	0	2	3	3	0	.569	B	1
Ian Stewart	Col	12	0	3	4	5	0	.554	B	1
Evan Longoria	TB	21	0	4	8	9	0	.526	B-	1
Mike Lamb	2 tms	8	0	3	1	4	0	.575	B	0
Jack Hannahan	Oak	15	0	4	4	7	0	.543	B-	0
Jorge Cantu	Fla	18	0	5	4	9	0	.536	B-	0
Mike Lowell	Bos	16	0	4	4	8	0	.525	B-	0
Pedro Feliz	Phi	16	0	3	6	7	0	.522	B-	0
Adrian Beltre	Sea	16	0	3	5	8	0	.500	C+	0
Garrett Atkins	Col	9	0	2	2	5	0	.494	C+	0
Aramis Ramirez	ChC	21	0	3	8	10	0	.490	C+	0
Casey Blake	2 tms	16	0	2	6	8	0	.475	C	0
Brian Buscher	Min	5	0	1	1	3	0	.470	C	0
Scott Rolen	Tor	15	0	1	7	7	0	.463	C	0
Geoff Blum	Hou	2	0	0	1	1	0	.425	C-	0
Melvin Mora	Bal	17	0	3	5	9	0	.485	C+	-1
Andy LaRoche	2 tms	15	1	0	5	9	0	.483	C+	-1
Edwin Encarnacion	Cin	21	0	3	7	11	0	.474	C	-1
Mark Reynolds	Ari	22	0	2	9	11	0	.461	C	-1
Joe Crede	CWS	14	0	1	5	8	0	.429	C-	-1
Jose Bautista	2 tms	16	0	0	7	9	0	.403	D+	-1
Carlos Guillen	Det	17	0	3	3	11	0	.444	C-	-2
Alex Gordon	KC	16	0	1	4	11	0	.384	D	-2
Ty Wigginton	Hou	11	0	1	2	8	0	.382	D	-2
Bill Hall	Mil	15	0	0	5	10	0	.367	D	-2
Andy Marte	Cle	14	0	2	1	11	0	.382	D	-3
Alex Rodriguez	NYY	19	0	1	4	14	0	.363	D	-3

Third Basemen - 2007 Bunt Defense

Player	Tm	Opps	Bunt DP	Pure Outs	Sac Hits	Bunt Hits	Errors	Score	Grade	Runs Saved
Ryan Zimmerman	Was	35	0	8	16	11	0	.581	B+	4
Pedro Feliz	SF	26	1	7	9	9	0	.640	A	3
David Wright	NYM	28	1	4	13	10	0	.582	B+	3
Scott Rolen	StL	12	1	2	6	3	0	.696	A+	2
Chipper Jones	Atl	27	1	3	12	11	0	.554	B	2
Miguel Cabrera	Fla	30	0	4	16	10	0	.537	B-	2
Mark Reynolds	Ari	17	2	0	7	8	0	.600	B+	1
Greg Dobbs	Phi	7	0	1	4	2	0	.557	B	1
Nick Punto	Min	7	0	1	4	2	0	.557	B	1
Jose Bautista	Pit	20	0	2	10	8	0	.500	C+	1
Melvin Mora	Bal	22	0	2	11	9	0	.493	C+	1
Kevin Kouzmanoff	SD	26	1	7	4	14	0	.573	B	0
Brandon Inge	Det	11	1	0	4	6	0	.536	B-	0
Josh Fields	CWS	15	0	4	3	8	0	.520	B-	0
Aramis Ramirez	ChC	24	0	4	9	11	0	.506	C+	0
Adrian Beltre	Sea	13	0	2	5	6	0	.500	C+	0
Chone Figgins	LAA	13	0	2	5	6	0	.500	C+	0
Wes Helms	Phi	3	0	1	0	2	0	.500	C+	0
Travis Metcalf	Tex	13	0	2	5	6	0	.500	C+	0
Abraham Nunez	Phi	15	0	3	4	8	0	.493	C+	0
Mike Lowell	Bos	15	0	2	6	7	0	.490	C+	0
Ty Wigginton	2 tms	15	0	0	9	6	0	.460	C	0
Alex Gordon	KC	12	0	0	6	6	0	.425	C-	0
Maicer Izturis	LAA	5	0	0	2	3	0	.390	D+	0
Casey Blake	Cle	17	0	3	5	9	0	.485	C+	-1
Ryan Braun	Mil	21	0	4	6	10	1	.481	C+	-1
Alex Rodriguez	NYY	21	0	1	9	11	0	.436	C-	-1
Mike Lamb	Hou	10	0	1	3	6	0	.430	C-	-1
Akinori Iwamura	TB	18	0	1	7	10	0	.428	C-	-1
Morgan Ensberg	2 tms	9	0	1	2	6	0	.411	D+	-1
Garrett Atkins	Col	24	0	0	11	13	0	.410	D+	-1
Ramon Vazquez	Tex	8	0	0	3	5	0	.381	D	-1
Edwin Encarnacion	Cin	24	1	3	5	15	0	.490	C+	-2
Troy Glaus	Tor	9	1	-1	1	8	0	.400	D+	-2
Eric Chavez	Oak	12	0	1	3	8	0	.400	D+	-2

Third Basemen - 2006 Bunt Defense

Player	Tm	Opps	Bunt DP	Pure Outs	Sac Hits	Bunt Hits	Errors	Score	Grade	Runs Saved
Pedro Feliz	SF	32	1	9	13	9	0	.658	A	5
Freddy Sanchez	Pit	29	2	7	8	12	0	.648	A	3
Chipper Jones	Atl	15	0	6	5	4	0	.667	A	2
Vinny Castilla	2 tms	11	0	3	6	2	0	.645	A	2
Nick Punto	Min	13	0	4	5	4	0	.615	A-	2
Hank Blalock	Tex	13	0	4	5	4	0	.615	A-	2
Corey Koskie	Mil	18	0	4	8	6	0	.572	B	2
Aaron Boone	Cle	12	0	1	8	3	0	.546	B-	2
David Wright	NYM	23	0	3	12	8	0	.530	B-	2
Morgan Ensberg	Hou	29	0	3	16	10	0	.521	B-	2
Scott Rolen	StL	21	0	0	15	6	0	.500	C+	2
Wilson Betemit	2 tms	10	1	1	5	3	0	.675	A+	1
Andy Marte	Cle	9	0	3	3	3	0	.617	A-	1
Willy Aybar	2 tms	5	0	1	3	1	0	.610	A-	1
Eric Chavez	Oak	11	0	2	6	3	0	.577	B	1
Aubrey Huff	2 tms	14	0	2	7	5	0	.532	B-	1
Adrian Beltre	Sea	21	0	4	8	9	0	.526	B-	1
Garrett Atkins	Col	21	0	4	8	9	0	.526	B-	1
Abraham Nunez	Phi	17	0	2	8	7	0	.503	C+	1
Aramis Ramirez	ChC	22	0	1	12	9	0	.475	C	1
Troy Glaus	Tor	19	0	7	3	9	0	.582	B+	0
Brandon Inge	Det	12	0	4	2	6	0	.558	B	0
Miguel Cabrera	Fla	20	0	3	7	10	0	.485	C+	0
Tony Batista	Min	3	0	0	2	1	0	.483	C+	0
Maicer Izturis	LAA	9	0	0	5	4	0	.444	C-	0
B.J. Upton	TB	8	0	0	4	4	0	.425	C-	0
Ryan Zimmerman	Was	29	0	6	8	15	0	.502	C+	-1
Joe Crede	CWS	17	0	4	3	10	0	.488	C+	-1
Mike Lowell	Bos	17	0	2	6	9	0	.462	C	-1
David Bell	2 tms	25	0	2	9	14	0	.436	C-	-2
Edwin Encarnacion	Cin	18	0	2	5	11	0	.431	C-	-2
Mark Teahen	KC	17	0	2	4	11	0	.421	C-	-2
Chad Tracy	Ari	11	0	0	3	8	0	.345	D-	-2
Alex Rodriguez	NYY	14	0	1	2	11	0	.354	D-	-3
Melvin Mora	Bal	24	0	0	5	18	1	.313	F	-5

Groundball Double Plays and Pivots

Another aspect of fielding that the Plus/Minus System does not account for is the double play. When a groundball is hit with a runner on first base and less than two outs, the Plus/Minus System rewards a fielder if he records an out on the play, but does not give him any extra credit for turning a double play. We need to reward those players who completed the twin-killings (and penalize them if they failed to turn double plays).

We found the run values for completed and failed double plays and awarded credit appropriately. You can read about the details of the calculation below. Here are some interesting tidbits on double plays over the past six seasons:

- Jeff Kent recently retired, but not in time to prevent himself from costing his teams 9 runs on double-play opportunities in the last three years, and 20 runs over the past six years. The second worst second baseman was Luis Castillo at -8 runs over 2006-2008. Five of Kent's six seasons were among the 20 worst seasons since 2003.

- Oakland's Mark Ellis ranked as the top second baseman since 2006 with 11 runs saved to go with his superb plus/minus rating. Mark Grudzielanek also added 11 runs above the average second baseman on double plays.

- Orlando Cabrera topped shortstops at 6 runs saved. Expanding our sample back to 2003, Jack Wilson has three of the top six single seasons, saving five runs each.

- Asdrubal Cabrera's 2008 year was worth seven runs saved, the second highest single season total for a second baseman. Cabrera combines with Jhonny Peralta for a strong double-play tandem for the Tribe. Peralta's 2005 (before Cabrera arrived in Cleveland) ranks as the top single season for a shortstop.

There is an undeniable teammate effect that is virtually impossible to remove from the data. For instance, Rafael Furcal can flip the ball to Jeff Kent, but if Kent doesn't pivot and toss to first base quickly enough, it will reflect as a missed opportunity for Furcal. However, a few examples suggest that the technique we are using can separate teammates to some extent: Mark Grudzielanek had four of the top 35 single seasons over the six years, including stints with three different teams. Adam Kennedy had seasons in the top 25 with two different teams, while Julio Lugo, Felipe Lopez, Royce Clayton, and Omar Vizquel all had multiple single seasons in the bottom 25 with two different teams. Changing uniforms and teammates didn't change their abilities (or inabilities) to convert double plays.

Calculating GDP Runs Saved

Using the definitions from the original *Fielding Bible*:

GDPs: How many times the player was involved in a groundball double play, either starting the double play or as the "pivot" man.

GDP Opps: How many times the player was involved in a fielding play on a groundball in a double play situation (man on first with less than two outs). This includes DPs, force outs, errors, etc.

Pivots: How many times the player made the double play pivot (for second basemen: 6-4-3 DP or 5-4-3 DP or 1-4-3 or 3-4-3 or 2-4-3).

Pivot Opps: How many times the player accepted a force out at second in a situation that could have been a double play (for second basemen: 6-4, 5-4, 1-4, or 3-4).

Pivots and Pivot Opps are included in GDPs and GDP Opps, but are also listed separately because of the different set of skills required. We include a pivot rating for shortstops as well (yeah, I know, a shortstop doesn't usually pivot physically like a second basemen does, but you get the idea).

Now we need to determine the run value of the successful and unsuccessful double play. It turns out the changes in base-out run expectancies (from 2003 to 2008) are very close for both positions:

Run Expectancy Changes

	SS	2B
DP	0.80	0.81
Missed DP	0.23	0.21
DP%	59%	51%
Avg RE Change	0.57	0.51

By Run Expectancy Change (RE), we mean, for example, that on a completed double play involving the shortstop the number of expected runs that the offense will score in the inning has dropped by .80 runs. If the fielder doesn't get the double play and only gets a force (or the occasional error), RE only drops by .23 runs.

Note that shortstops converted a higher percentage of DP Opps into double plays. For shortstops then, the offense's run expectancy based on all GDP Opps (whether completed or not) drops by .80*.59 + .23*(1-.59) = .57 runs on a GDP Opp fielded by an average shortstop, but only .51 runs when fielded by an average

second baseman. Since we are putting Runs Saved on an above average scale, the run value awarded to each play will subtract out the average run expectancy change on GDP Opps. For shortstops, a completed DP will be worth .80 - .57 = .23, and a Missed DP is .23 - .57 = -.34.

Run Values Above Average

	SS	2B
DP	0.23	0.29
Missed DP	-0.34	-0.30

However, we're not quite through. A typical double play involves more than one fielder to complete. A 6-4-3 double play requires both the shortstop and the second baseman. In fact, we're double-counting all such double plays. How much credit should we give to each? Who knows? Let's split it 50/50 and call it even:

GDP Run Values

	SS	2B
DP	0.12	0.15
Missed DP	-0.17	-0.15

These are the values we apply to each player's DPs and Missed DPs to find out how many runs each middle infielder helped or hurt his team on double play opportunities. That is how we can say with confidence that you'd rather have Jack Wilson or Aaron Hill trying to turn a double play than Julio Lugo or, heaven forbid, Jeff Kent.

Second Basemen - 3-Year GDPs & Pivots

Player	GDP Opps	GDP	GDP Pct	Rank	Pivot Opps	Pivots	Pivot Pct	Rank	Runs Saved
Mark Grudzielanek	373	221	.592	5	219	150	.685	10	11
Mark Ellis	460	265	.576	8	276	188	.681	13	11
Aaron Hill	375	221	.589	6	198	135	.682	12	10
Asdrubal Cabrera	154	105	.682	1	85	68	.800	1	9
Robinson Cano	502	279	.556	9	278	185	.665	20	9
Ian Kinsler	517	287	.555	10	284	187	.658	22	9
Jamey Carroll	280	168	.600	3	132	96	.727	5	8
Placido Polanco	467	256	.548	11	282	172	.610	32	7
Howie Kendrick	223	133	.596	4	116	82	.707	7	6
Mark Loretta	223	130	.583	7	137	100	.730	4	6
Tadahito Iguchi	393	214	.545	13	220	150	.682	11	6
Jose Lopez	509	276	.542	14	245	165	.673	15	6
Akinori Iwamura	167	102	.611	2	103	73	.709	6	5
Kaz Matsui	310	169	.545	12	159	104	.654	26	5
Ronnie Belliard	338	181	.536	17	177	130	.734	3	4
Adam Kennedy	307	165	.537	16	153	103	.673	16	3
Dustin Pedroia	330	176	.533	19	173	114	.659	21	3
Freddy Sanchez	422	221	.524	20	220	143	.650	27	3
Orlando Hudson	467	243	.520	21	221	167	.756	2	3
Alexi Casilla	197	106	.538	15	99	67	.677	14	2
Aaron Miles	247	132	.534	18	134	90	.672	18	2
Brian Roberts	572	291	.509	24	291	174	.598	33	2
Dan Uggla	556	283	.509	23	273	190	.696	9	1
Felipe Lopez	153	78	.510	22	76	49	.645	29	0
Alexei Ramirez	135	67	.496	25	76	50	.658	23	0
Jose Castillo	229	111	.485	27	115	77	.670	19	0
Chase Utley	570	282	.495	26	312	205	.657	25	-1
Kelly Johnson	335	162	.484	28	159	103	.648	28	-1
Ray Durham	432	208	.481	29	216	142	.657	24	-2
Rickie Weeks	433	207	.478	30	230	141	.613	31	-3
Josh Barfield	323	154	.477	31	164	105	.640	30	-3
Brandon Phillips	551	257	.466	32	259	174	.672	17	-5
Mark DeRosa	205	84	.410	35	89	62	.697	8	-6
Luis Castillo	406	179	.441	33	205	119	.580	34	-8
Jeff Kent	462	198	.429	34	214	124	.579	35	-9

Second Basemen - 2008 GDPs & Pivots

Player	Tm	GDP Opps	GDP	GDP Pct	Rank	Pivot Opps	Pivots	Pivot Pct	Rank	Runs Saved
Asdrubal Cabrera	Cle	112	79	.705	1	65	51	.785	1	7
Mark Ellis	Oak	131	81	.618	3	75	53	.707	7	5
Akinori Iwamura	TB	166	101	.608	5	102	72	.706	8	5
Ian Kinsler	Tex	201	113	.562	9	109	72	.661	17	4
Adam Kennedy	StL	85	53	.624	2	47	36	.766	3	3
Howie Kendrick	LAA	99	61	.616	4	51	36	.706	9	3
Mark Grudzielanek	KC	87	52	.598	7	49	35	.714	6	3
Aaron Miles	StL	68	41	.603	6	34	23	.676	13	2
Jamey Carroll	Cle	73	42	.575	8	34	21	.618	26	2
Tadahito Iguchi	2 tms	94	52	.553	10	47	36	.766	3	2
Clint Barmes	Col	59	32	.542	11	30	21	.700	11	1
Alexi Casilla	Min	125	66	.528	12	62	40	.645	21	1
Jose Lopez	Sea	172	90	.523	13	77	51	.662	16	1
Dustin Pedroia	Bos	176	90	.511	15	93	60	.645	20	1
Mike Fontenot	ChC	48	25	.521	14	22	17	.773	2	0
Freddy Sanchez	Pit	190	96	.505	16	98	58	.592	30	0
Placido Polanco	Det	178	89	.500	17	117	64	.547	34	0
Orlando Hudson	Ari	106	53	.500	18	54	39	.722	5	0
Joe Inglett	Tor	68	34	.500	19	40	24	.600	28	0
Brian Roberts	Bal	211	105	.498	20	115	66	.574	32	0
Alexei Ramirez	CWS	135	67	.496	21	76	50	.658	19	0
Robinson Cano	NYY	178	88	.494	22	93	59	.634	23	0
Kaz Matsui	Hou	101	49	.485	23	49	30	.612	27	0
Dan Uggla	Fla	154	74	.481	24	73	49	.671	15	-1
Ray Durham	2 tms	113	51	.451	28	51	32	.627	25	-1
Chase Utley	Phi	204	96	.471	25	114	75	.658	18	-2
Rickie Weeks	Mil	163	75	.460	26	88	49	.557	33	-2
Kelly Johnson	Atl	182	83	.456	27	86	54	.628	24	-2
Felipe Lopez	2 tms	103	45	.437	30	48	28	.583	31	-2
Edgar Gonzalez	SD	74	32	.432	31	27	16	.593	29	-2
Luis Castillo	NYM	91	38	.418	32	34	24	.706	10	-2
Brandon Phillips	Cin	183	80	.437	29	87	56	.644	22	-3
Jeff Kent	LAD	128	53	.414	33	52	27	.519	35	-3
Damion Easley	NYM	89	36	.404	34	37	25	.676	14	-3
Mark DeRosa	ChC	77	30	.390	35	32	22	.688	12	-3

Second Basemen - 2007 GDPs & Pivots

Player	Tm	GDP Opps	GDP	GDP Pct	Rank	Pivot Opps	Pivots	Pivot Pct	Rank	Runs Saved
Robinson Cano	NYY	187	122	.652	1	110	80	.727	3	9
Kaz Matsui	Col	131	78	.595	2	71	47	.662	20	4
Aaron Hill	Tor	193	110	.570	3	102	66	.647	21	4
Jose Lopez	Sea	175	97	.554	5	85	55	.647	22	3
Tadahito Iguchi	2 tms	159	88	.553	6	94	65	.691	12	3
Placido Polanco	Det	172	95	.552	7	100	63	.630	23	3
Freddy Sanchez	Pit	205	112	.546	9	114	79	.693	11	3
Dustin Pedroia	Bos	126	71	.563	4	65	44	.677	14	2
Mark Grudzielanek	KC	113	62	.549	8	62	38	.613	27	2
Ian Kinsler	Tex	163	88	.540	10	94	64	.681	13	2
Mark Ellis	Oak	177	95	.537	13	97	61	.629	24	2
Orlando Hudson	Ari	166	89	.536	14	80	60	.750	1	2
Howie Kendrick	LAA	91	49	.538	11	47	33	.702	10	1
Alexi Casilla	Min	67	36	.537	12	34	24	.706	9	1
Dan Uggla	Fla	196	102	.520	15	101	73	.723	6	1
Rickie Weeks	Mil	129	67	.519	16	74	49	.662	19	1
Kelly Johnson	Atl	153	79	.516	17	73	49	.671	15	1
Brandon Phillips	Cin	198	101	.510	20	97	70	.722	7	1
Jamey Carroll	Col	68	35	.515	18	30	20	.667	16	0
Aaron Miles	StL	70	36	.514	19	45	28	.622	25	0
Ray Durham	SF	157	80	.510	21	86	57	.663	18	0
Mike Fontenot	ChC	63	32	.508	22	33	24	.727	4	0
Danny Richar	CWS	70	35	.500	23	34	21	.618	26	0
Ronnie Belliard	Was	148	73	.493	24	74	55	.743	2	0
Brian Roberts	Bal	205	101	.493	25	99	59	.596	28	0
Marcus Giles	SD	139	68	.489	26	62	45	.726	5	0
Geoff Blum	SD	55	26	.473	27	24	16	.667	17	0
B.J. Upton	TB	51	22	.431	32	27	13	.481	34	-1
Chase Utley	Phi	172	80	.465	28	92	54	.587	30	-2
Josh Barfield	Cle	148	68	.459	29	78	43	.551	32	-2
Adam Kennedy	StL	95	42	.442	30	44	26	.591	29	-2
Jeff Kent	LAD	174	76	.437	31	81	46	.568	31	-3
Mark DeRosa	ChC	99	40	.404	34	41	29	.707	8	-3
Luis Castillo	2 tms	159	68	.428	33	84	44	.524	33	-4
Craig Biggio	Hou	138	54	.391	35	70	33	.471	35	-5

Second Basemen - 2006 GDPs & Pivots

Player	Tm	GDP Opps	GDP	GDP Pct	Rank	Pivot Opps	Pivots	Pivot Pct	Rank	Runs Saved
Jamey Carroll	Col	139	91	.655	1	68	55	.809	1	6
Aaron Hill	Tor	132	86	.652	2	71	54	.761	4	6
Mark Grudzielanek	KC	173	107	.618	3	108	77	.713	7	6
Placido Polanco	Det	117	72	.615	4	65	45	.692	13	4
Ronnie Belliard	2 tms	148	88	.595	5	80	61	.763	3	4
Mark Ellis	Oak	152	89	.586	7	104	74	.712	8	4
Mark Loretta	Bos	156	91	.583	8	98	69	.704	12	4
Ian Kinsler	Tex	153	86	.562	10	81	51	.630	26	3
Chase Utley	Phi	194	106	.546	13	106	76	.717	6	3
Neifi Perez	2 tms	54	32	.593	6	30	20	.667	21	2
Joe Inglett	Cle	66	38	.576	9	38	28	.737	5	2
Adam Kennedy	LAA	127	70	.551	11	62	41	.661	22	2
Jose Lopez	Sea	162	89	.549	12	83	59	.711	9	2
Brian Roberts	Bal	156	85	.545	14	77	49	.636	24	2
Kaz Matsui	2 tms	78	42	.538	15	39	27	.692	14	1
Tadahito Iguchi	CWS	140	74	.529	16	79	49	.620	29	1
Dan Uggla	Fla	206	107	.519	17	99	68	.687	18	1
Orlando Hudson	Ari	195	101	.518	18	87	68	.782	2	1
Craig Biggio	Hou	150	76	.507	19	72	42	.583	35	0
Aaron Miles	StL	109	55	.505	20	55	39	.709	10	0
Robinson Cano	NYY	137	69	.504	21	75	46	.613	32	0
Hector Luna	2 tms	70	35	.500	22	44	27	.614	31	0
Marcus Giles	Atl	159	79	.497	23	79	53	.671	19	0
Jose Castillo	Pit	203	100	.493	24	103	71	.689	17	0
Josh Barfield	SD	164	79	.482	25	79	56	.709	11	-1
Jorge Cantu	TB	122	58	.475	26	65	40	.615	30	-1
Todd Walker	2 tms	61	29	.475	27	29	20	.690	16	-1
Ray Durham	SF	162	77	.475	28	79	53	.671	19	-1
Luis Castillo	Min	156	73	.468	29	87	51	.586	34	-2
Rickie Weeks	Mil	141	65	.461	30	68	43	.632	25	-2
Jose Valentin	NYM	105	45	.429	33	51	32	.627	28	-2
Brandon Phillips	Cin	170	76	.447	31	75	48	.640	23	-3
Jeff Kent	LAD	160	69	.431	32	81	51	.630	26	-3
Tony Graffanino	2 tms	66	25	.379	34	26	18	.692	15	-3
Jose Vidro	Was	130	46	.354	35	51	31	.608	33	-6

Shortstops - 3-Year GDPs & Pivots

Player	GDP Opps	GDP	GDP Pct	Rank	Pivot Opps	Pivots	Pivot Pct	Rank	Runs Saved
Orlando Cabrera	449	283	.630	5	267	172	.644	8	6
Jack Wilson	377	241	.639	3	208	127	.611	21	5
Bobby Crosby	310	198	.639	4	162	99	.611	20	5
Adam Everett	263	165	.627	6	157	108	.688	3	4
Yuniesky Betancourt	465	285	.613	10	274	176	.642	10	4
Clint Barmes	172	113	.657	1	103	66	.641	12	3
Cristian Guzman	159	103	.648	2	89	64	.719	2	3
Angel Berroa	208	129	.620	9	109	68	.624	17	3
Troy Tulowitzki	315	193	.613	11	192	123	.641	13	3
Jhonny Peralta	469	285	.608	16	271	175	.646	7	3
Tony F Pena	212	133	.627	7	111	82	.739	1	2
Ryan Theriot	188	117	.622	8	99	64	.646	5	2
Jimmy Rollins	426	260	.610	13	222	143	.644	9	2
Stephen Drew	328	200	.610	14	180	111	.617	18	2
Omar Vizquel	333	203	.610	15	169	99	.586	28	2
Hanley Ramirez	452	272	.602	17	235	138	.587	27	2
Carlos Guillen	258	155	.601	18	130	84	.646	6	1
John McDonald	242	145	.599	19	140	91	.650	4	1
Rafael Furcal	376	225	.598	20	237	151	.637	15	1
Khalil Greene	356	213	.598	21	193	114	.591	26	1
Michael Young	515	307	.596	22	275	163	.593	25	1
Juan Uribe	282	168	.596	23	162	104	.642	11	1
Derek Jeter	389	231	.594	24	217	138	.636	16	1
Miguel Tejada	437	259	.593	26	247	144	.583	29	1
Cesar Izturis	219	134	.612	12	118	71	.602	24	0
Edgar Renteria	389	231	.594	24	203	123	.606	22	0
J.J. Hardy	308	180	.584	28	164	105	.640	14	0
Jose Reyes	404	236	.584	29	204	123	.603	23	0
Ronny Cedeno	117	68	.581	30	57	35	.614	19	0
Marco Scutaro	139	82	.590	27	75	42	.560	33	-1
David Eckstein	287	163	.568	31	175	99	.566	32	-1
Yunel Escobar	174	95	.546	33	95	55	.579	31	-2
Jason Bartlett	346	190	.549	32	176	102	.580	30	-3
Felipe Lopez	226	120	.531	34	102	55	.539	34	-3
Julio Lugo	255	132	.518	35	144	73	.507	35	-5

Shortstops - 2008 GDPs & Pivots

Player	Tm	GDP Opps	GDP	GDP Pct	Rank	Pivot Opps	Pivots	Pivot Pct	Rank	Runs Saved
Bobby Crosby	Oak	129	88	.682	2	65	43	.662	5	4
Nick Punto	Min	60	44	.733	1	26	23	.885	1	3
Mike Aviles	KC	90	61	.678	3	48	31	.646	6	2
Cristian Guzman	Was	110	71	.645	5	62	45	.726	2	2
Orlando Cabrera	CWS	146	93	.637	6	80	50	.625	11	2
Jhonny Peralta	Cle	153	97	.634	7	93	59	.634	8	2
Miguel Tejada	Hou	144	90	.625	9	81	49	.605	16	2
Maicer Izturis	LAA	46	30	.652	4	32	23	.719	3	1
Khalil Greene	SD	97	61	.629	8	58	36	.621	12	1
Omar Vizquel	SF	64	40	.625	10	36	23	.639	7	1
Yuniesky Betancourt	Sea	150	93	.620	11	94	59	.628	9	1
Brendan Harris	Min	63	39	.619	12	42	28	.667	4	1
Michael Young	Tex	172	106	.616	13	88	53	.602	18	1
Stephen Drew	Ari	128	78	.609	14	63	39	.619	13	1
Jack Wilson	Pit	83	50	.602	15	49	28	.571	25	0
Jeff Keppinger	Cin	110	66	.600	16	55	30	.545	29	0
Ryan Theriot	ChC	107	64	.598	17	62	37	.597	20	0
Tony F Pena	KC	57	34	.596	18	30	18	.600	19	0
Erick Aybar	LAA	101	60	.594	19	52	32	.615	14	0
Edgar Renteria	Det	150	88	.587	20	75	47	.627	10	0
David Eckstein	Tor	53	31	.585	21	34	20	.588	22	0
Jose Reyes	NYM	149	86	.577	22	80	47	.588	23	0
Angel Berroa	LAD	67	38	.567	25	38	23	.605	15	0
Cesar Izturis	StL	128	73	.570	23	70	40	.571	24	-1
Hanley Ramirez	Fla	139	79	.568	24	70	37	.529	33	-1
Jason Bartlett	TB	113	62	.549	26	63	34	.540	30	-1
Derek Jeter	NYY	106	58	.547	27	67	37	.552	27	-1
John McDonald	Tor	55	30	.545	28	32	18	.563	26	-1
Troy Tulowitzki	Col	114	62	.544	29	73	43	.589	21	-1
Marco Scutaro	Tor	46	25	.543	30	28	15	.536	31	-1
Jimmy Rollins	Phi	127	69	.543	31	67	37	.552	27	-2
J.J. Hardy	Mil	147	79	.537	32	81	49	.605	16	-2
Juan Castro	2 tms	44	18	.409	35	29	12	.414	34	-2
Yunel Escobar	Atl	145	74	.510	33	77	41	.532	32	-3
Julio Lugo	Bos	68	31	.456	34	35	13	.371	35	-3

Shortstops - 2007 GDPs & Pivots

Player	Tm	GDP Opps	GDP	GDP Pct	Rank	Pivot Opps	Pivots	Pivot Pct	Rank	Runs Saved
Jack Wilson	Pit	162	109	.673	3	84	54	.643	15	4
Orlando Cabrera	LAA	153	99	.647	5	91	62	.681	7	3
Troy Tulowitzki	Col	167	108	.647	6	95	64	.674	9	3
Derek Jeter	NYY	152	98	.645	7	82	59	.720	5	3
Cesar Izturis	2 tms	72	51	.708	1	37	26	.703	6	2
Alex Gonzalez	Cin	98	66	.673	2	48	31	.646	14	2
Ryan Theriot	ChC	79	52	.658	4	36	27	.750	2	2
Tony F Pena	KC	145	92	.634	8	76	59	.776	1	2
Rafael Furcal	LAD	151	94	.623	11	99	65	.657	12	2
Edgar Renteria	Atl	111	70	.631	9	56	35	.625	19	1
J.J. Hardy	Mil	122	76	.623	10	58	39	.672	10	1
Omar Vizquel	SF	135	84	.622	12	63	38	.603	24	1
Bobby Crosby	Oak	90	56	.622	13	45	28	.622	22	1
Stephen Drew	Ari	145	90	.621	14	87	55	.632	17	1
Adam Everett	Hou	60	37	.617	15	39	29	.744	3	1
Jimmy Rollins	Phi	164	101	.616	16	81	55	.679	8	1
Jose Reyes	NYM	134	82	.612	17	72	46	.639	16	1
Jason Bartlett	Min	136	83	.610	18	64	47	.734	4	1
Khalil Greene	SD	158	95	.601	19	90	53	.589	25	1
Hanley Ramirez	Fla	150	90	.600	20	74	42	.568	28	1
Juan Uribe	CWS	152	91	.599	21	84	53	.631	18	1
Yuniesky Betancourt	Sea	174	104	.598	22	98	65	.663	11	1
Josh Wilson	2 tms	49	29	.592	23	28	16	.571	27	0
Jeff Keppinger	Cin	43	25	.581	24	26	14	.538	32	0
Jhonny Peralta	Cle	164	95	.579	25	98	61	.622	21	0
Felipe Lopez	Was	87	50	.575	26	38	20	.526	34	0
John McDonald	Tor	110	63	.573	27	63	41	.651	13	0
Michael Young	Tex	166	94	.566	28	90	49	.544	31	-1
Carlos Guillen	Det	124	70	.565	29	61	38	.623	20	-1
David Eckstein	StL	99	53	.535	31	64	33	.516	35	-1
Brendan Harris	TB	92	49	.533	33	48	29	.604	23	-1
Royce Clayton	2 tms	55	29	.527	34	31	18	.581	26	-1
Miguel Tejada	Bal	135	73	.541	30	78	43	.551	30	-2
Julio Lugo	Bos	120	64	.533	32	74	41	.554	29	-2
Mark Loretta	Hou	57	27	.474	35	30	16	.533	33	-2

Shortstops - 2006 GDPs & Pivots

Player	Tm	GDP Opps	GDP	GDP Pct	Rank	Pivot Opps	Pivots	Pivot Pct	Rank	Runs Saved
Craig Counsell	Ari	87	67	.770	1	50	41	.820	1	5
Clint Barmes	Col	127	85	.669	4	76	49	.645	11	3
Jimmy Rollins	Phi	135	90	.667	5	74	51	.689	5	3
Adam Everett	Hou	155	101	.652	6	94	66	.702	3	3
Alex Cora	Bos	60	42	.700	2	30	21	.700	4	2
John McDonald	Tor	77	52	.675	3	45	32	.711	2	2
Carlos Guillen	Det	134	85	.634	7	69	46	.667	7	2
Angel Berroa	KC	136	86	.632	8	67	41	.612	18	2
Hanley Ramirez	Fla	163	103	.632	9	91	59	.648	10	2
Yuniesky Betancourt	Sea	141	88	.624	10	82	52	.634	13	2
Jack Wilson	Pit	132	82	.621	11	75	45	.600	19	1
Jhonny Peralta	Cle	152	93	.612	13	80	55	.688	6	1
Juan Castro	2 tms	59	36	.610	14	35	23	.657	8	1
Miguel Tejada	Bal	158	96	.608	15	88	52	.591	21	1
Orlando Cabrera	LAA	150	91	.607	16	96	60	.625	15	1
Michael Young	Tex	177	107	.605	17	97	61	.629	14	1
Marco Scutaro	Oak	57	35	.614	12	27	14	.519	34	0
Bobby Crosby	Oak	91	54	.593	18	52	28	.538	33	0
Juan Uribe	CWS	130	77	.592	19	78	51	.654	9	0
Omar Vizquel	SF	134	79	.590	20	70	38	.543	31	0
David Eckstein	StL	135	79	.585	21	77	46	.597	20	0
Alex Gonzalez	Bos	106	62	.585	22	60	33	.550	29	0
Stephen Drew	Ari	55	32	.582	23	30	17	.567	25	0
Ronny Cedeno	ChC	95	55	.579	24	44	28	.636	12	0
Ben Zobrist	TB	52	30	.577	25	29	16	.552	28	0
Julio Lugo	2 tms	67	37	.552	31	35	19	.543	32	0
Rafael Furcal	LAD	198	114	.576	26	118	73	.619	16	-1
Derek Jeter	NYY	131	75	.573	27	68	42	.618	17	-1
Edgar Renteria	Atl	128	73	.570	28	72	41	.569	24	-1
Khalil Greene	SD	101	57	.564	29	45	25	.556	26	-1
Jose Reyes	NYM	121	68	.562	30	52	30	.577	23	-1
Bill Hall	Mil	102	54	.529	32	47	26	.553	27	-2
Felipe Lopez	2 tms	130	65	.500	33	62	34	.548	30	-3
Royce Clayton	2 tms	94	46	.489	34	51	30	.588	22	-3
Jason Bartlett	Min	97	45	.464	35	49	21	.429	35	-3

Outfielder Throwing Arms

We all know that when there's a hit to the outfield, a runner on base has a decision to make. *"Do I go for the extra base or do I settle for what the hit will give me?"* The factors that go into this instantaneous decision are many and complex. Is there another runner in front? How hard was the ball hit? How far will the fielder have to go to grab the ball and make a throw? Will he have to throw across his body? How strong is his throwing arm? How quick is his release? What's the relative risk of the extra base versus being thrown out? What's the coach signaling? For some, I'm sure the last question might be the key one, allowing the coach to worry about the rest.

All that must be considered in an instant based upon the experience of the runner and/or the coach. The fielder, on the other hand, needs only to consider preventing the extra base, or when the extra base is home, preventing a run—the ultimate defensive play. For this Outfielder Arms section of the book we want to quantify the effect of outfielders on baserunners trying to advance on the basepaths (or not). In addition to listing their "counting" statistics, we'll show the number of runs the outfielder saved his team, or cost his team. For example we've calculated it to be worth almost half a run if a runner on second stops at third on a single to the outfield. Just because a fielder doesn't throw a runner out doesn't mean he hasn't saved his team a run.

Noodle Arm? Not!

Alfonso Soriano isn't generally considered to have a strong arm for an outfielder, but look at which left fielder has saved the most runs by stopping baserunners over the last three years. By a wide margin. He's thrown out 42 baserunners (that's direct throws to a base to get the out with no other assist; we call them "kills"). In 2007 alone he "killed" 19 baserunners and saved 17 runs. The top of this leaderboard is mixed with fielders known for their throwing and others not so much. Manny Ramirez is tied for eight most runs saved over the last three years. Yes, Manny. We also measure the percentage of times runners take an extra base, and Manny holds his own with his ranking right in the middle of the pack. In total, he was above average in outfielder throwing runs saved in 2008 among left fielders. In 2009, his replacement in left field is Jason Bay. Jason is generally considered to be a fair outfielder, but the throwing numbers certainly don't back that up. Jason is all by himself at the bottom over the last three years in left fielder throwing runs saved. Not only has he allowed many more runs than the average left fielder, he's also near the bottom in allowing the extra base. It will be very interesting to see what Fenway Park does to these numbers.

Having the great fielder Torii Hunter near the bottom of the list of three-year center field throwers seems out of place, nevertheless he's consistently near the bottom of all three years. Throwing is not Torii's shtick.

Baltimore's Nick Markakis shows why he's an up and coming, well-rounded star, leading 2008 right fielders in throwing runs saved and kills. St. Louis' Ryan Ludwick and Houston's Hunter Pence appear to be well suited to stopping runners from advancing and otherwise throwing them out from right field. One of the two fielders tied for the lead in outfield arms runs saved in right field since 2006 comes as no surprise—Atlanta's Jeff Francoeur with 25 runs saved and 26 kills. That, my friends, is a lot of runs. But look who's tied with him at the top. Michael Cuddyer. This is the Michael Cuddyer who was been moved all over the field, at least that was true earlier in his career. He didn't really settle in right field until 2006. As recently as 2005 he played over 900 innings in the infield and only 159 in the outfield.

It's with a very sad heart I bring your attention towards the bottom of the 2008 right field chart. Thirteen years have taken their toll on the body of Vlad (The Impaler) Guerrero. This formerly most-feared thrower is a shadow of his former cannon-armed self. In 2008, he's in the bottom five in throwing runs allowed and in percentage of extra bases taken. His three kills put him only slightly below average, but his reputation is no longer holding runners. Long live The Impaler. It was a great run (or throw).

Runs Saved

All the outfielder throwing metrics from the last book are here. Now we've added outfielder arm runs saved. Wins are made up of runs and that's what we really want to measure. We compare fielders only to their peers at the same position.

In this section, first we specifically look at only three sets of circumstances; single to the outfield with a runner on first base (second unoccupied), single to the outfield with a runner on second base, and double to the outfield with a runner on first base. We then separately examine any other direct kill by an outfielder not included in the first three circumstances.

To turn outfield throwing into runs saved (or allowed) versus the average at the same position, we count the number of times all outfielders at the same position are presented with one of the first three circumstances above. For each, we measure the run expectancy change before and after all those opportunities. If a runner does station to station, the expectancy change is defined to be zero. If he takes the extra base or is thrown out at the next base, we measure that expectancy change. We sum up all those changes for the league and determine the number of runs for each play every time a runner moved up, doesn't move up, or is thrown out. We then multiply those league-wide factors by each outcome for each fielder and total the results for "runs saved" versus the average.

The catch-all category that we call "other kills" includes the batter himself being thrown out or any other runner trying to move up on an out. It's impossible to determine what an "opportunity" is here, since you could say any hit is an opportunity for the batter to stretch for an extra base, but we all know that's not true and there's no way to define those opportunities from the data. We assigned an average run value to other kills.

The columns in the charts are "Opps", "Extra Bases", "Pct", "Kills", and "Runs Saved". Opps is the number of opportunities to take an extra base. Extra Bases are those extra bases taken. Pct is Extra Bases divided by Opps. Kills is any runner thrown out with no other intervening fielder (i.e. no other assist).

Left Fielders - 3-Year Throwing

Player	Opps	Extra Bases	Pct	Kills	Runs Saved
Alfonso Soriano	341	119	.349	42	33
Josh Willingham	351	103	.293	15	16
Reed Johnson	112	27	.241	9	12
Raul Ibanez	474	162	.342	19	12
Pat Burrell	345	122	.354	19	11
Craig Monroe	176	67	.381	14	9
Jay Payton	221	63	.285	5	8
Melky Cabrera	136	48	.353	11	7
Manny Ramirez	316	113	.358	13	7
Carlos Quentin	115	33	.287	2	4
Emil Brown	204	76	.373	11	4
Hideki Matsui	169	63	.373	8	4
Carl Crawford	368	128	.348	9	3
Willie Harris	137	49	.358	7	3
Delmon Young	145	52	.359	7	3
Andre Ethier	169	62	.367	8	3
Ryan Braun	123	46	.374	6	3
Matt Murton	131	45	.344	3	2
Chris Duncan	168	61	.363	6	2
Scott Podsednik	165	57	.345	5	1
Marcus Thames	114	40	.351	2	1
Jason Michaels	218	77	.353	8	1
Matt Diaz	149	62	.416	10	1
Eric Byrnes	115	47	.409	6	0
Luke Scott	143	49	.343	3	-1
Matt Holliday	445	160	.360	9	-2
Dave Roberts	94	36	.383	2	-2
Adam Lind	108	45	.417	4	-2
Frank Catalanotto	161	69	.429	7	-2
Shannon Stewart	176	70	.398	6	-3
Carlos Lee	376	141	.375	9	-4
Adam Dunn	387	148	.382	12	-4
Garret Anderson	220	98	.445	10	-4
Luis Gonzalez	284	112	.394	3	-6
Jason Bay	517	207	.400	16	-7

Left Fielders - 2007 Throwing

Player	Tm	Opps	Extra Bases	Pct	Kills	Runs Saved
Alfonso Soriano	ChC	124	41	.331	19	17
Josh Willingham	Fla	151	40	.265	5	7
Hideki Matsui	NYY	105	33	.314	5	6
Ryan Church	Was	82	25	.305	3	4
Jason Michaels	Cle	64	20	.313	3	3
Craig Monroe	2 tms	82	30	.366	4	3
Reed Johnson	Tor	49	15	.306	2	2
Scott Podsednik	CWS	64	20	.313	2	2
Garret Anderson	LAA	78	26	.333	4	2
Chris Duncan	StL	108	39	.361	4	2
Emil Brown	KC	57	21	.368	4	2
Pat Burrell	Phi	112	42	.375	6	2
Carl Crawford	TB	143	45	.315	2	1
Matt Holliday	Col	144	46	.319	3	1
Jay Payton	Bal	117	39	.333	1	1
Reggie Willits	LAA	61	22	.361	1	1
Scott Hairston	2 tms	66	24	.364	3	1
Jason Bay	Pit	172	63	.366	7	1
Moises Alou	NYM	81	33	.407	4	1
Eric Byrnes	Ari	83	36	.434	6	1
Matt Diaz	Atl	68	31	.456	4	1
Willie Harris	Atl	71	27	.380	4	0
Carlos Lee	Hou	151	59	.391	6	0
Raul Ibanez	Sea	143	56	.392	4	0
Geoff Jenkins	Mil	110	44	.400	5	0
Joey Gathright	KC	56	20	.357	1	-1
Barry Bonds	SF	69	26	.377	1	-1
Rob Mackowiak	2 tms	50	19	.380	1	-1
Frank Catalanotto	Tex	52	21	.404	1	-1
Adam Lind	Tor	58	25	.431	4	-1
Manny Ramirez	Bos	102	45	.441	6	-1
Adam Dunn	Cin	132	47	.356	2	-2
Jason Kubel	Min	69	27	.391	1	-3
Luis Gonzalez	LAD	99	44	.444	4	-5
Shannon Stewart	Oak	123	55	.447	3	-5

Left Fielders - 2008 Throwing

Player	Tm	Opps	Extra Bases	Pct	Kills	Runs Saved
Pat Burrell	Phi	133	40	.301	7	6
Alfonso Soriano	ChC	63	19	.302	8	6
Josh Willingham	Fla	93	30	.323	7	5
Raul Ibanez	Sea	160	54	.338	6	5
Carlos Quentin	CWS	113	32	.283	2	4
Brandon Boggs	Tex	66	21	.318	3	4
Ben Francisco	Cle	79	30	.380	6	4
David Murphy	Tex	48	14	.292	2	3
Conor Jackson	Ari	61	19	.311	4	3
Delmon Young	Min	145	52	.359	7	3
Ryan Braun	Mil	123	46	.374	6	3
Fred Lewis	SF	88	33	.375	3	3
Jay Payton	Bal	41	11	.268	1	2
Matt Joyce	Det	54	15	.278	1	2
Manny Ramirez	2 tms	102	32	.314	3	2
Willie Harris	Was	63	21	.333	2	2
Johnny Damon	NYY	63	19	.302	2	1
Marcus Thames	Det	56	21	.375	1	1
Matt Holliday	Col	163	54	.331	3	0
Carl Crawford	TB	69	23	.333	0	0
Luis Gonzalez	Fla	60	20	.333	0	0
Jack Cust	Oak	63	28	.444	4	0
Luke Scott	Bal	105	37	.352	2	-1
Eric Byrnes	Ari	31	11	.355	0	-1
David DeJesus	KC	44	16	.364	0	-1
Adam Dunn	2 tms	108	41	.380	4	-1
Wily Mo Pena	Was	50	20	.400	2	-1
Adam Lind	Tor	49	20	.408	0	-1
Carlos Lee	Hou	87	34	.391	1	-2
Chase Headley	SD	77	31	.403	2	-2
Garret Anderson	LAA	68	37	.544	5	-2
Juan Pierre	LAD	71	27	.380	0	-3
Jason Bay	2 tms	169	72	.426	5	-3
Gregor Blanco	Atl	52	26	.500	2	-3
Emil Brown	Oak	37	20	.541	1	-3

Left Fielders - 2006 Throwing

Player	Tm	Opps	Extra Bases	Pct	Kills	Runs Saved
Alfonso Soriano	Was	154	59	.383	15	10
Reed Johnson	Tor	51	11	.216	6	8
Raul Ibanez	Sea	171	52	.304	9	7
Juan Rivera	LAA	37	10	.270	5	6
Manny Ramirez	Bos	112	36	.321	4	6
Craig Monroe	Det	93	36	.387	10	6
Jay Payton	Oak	63	13	.206	3	5
Andre Ethier	LAD	99	29	.293	6	5
Emil Brown	KC	110	35	.318	6	5
Melky Cabrera	NYY	121	44	.364	9	5
Josh Willingham	Fla	107	33	.308	3	4
Jeff Conine	2 tms	56	17	.304	2	3
Pat Burrell	Phi	100	40	.400	6	3
David DeJesus	KC	90	27	.300	3	2
Matt Murton	ChC	101	34	.337	2	2
Carl Crawford	TB	156	60	.385	7	2
Matt Diaz	Atl	62	22	.355	5	1
Brad Wilkerson	Tex	90	33	.367	5	1
Luke Scott	Hou	37	12	.324	1	0
Nick Swisher	Oak	82	29	.354	3	0
Scott Podsednik	CWS	98	36	.367	3	-1
Preston Wilson	2 tms	81	30	.370	2	-1
Luis Gonzalez	Ari	125	48	.384	3	-1
Cliff Floyd	NYM	78	30	.385	2	-1
Ryan Langerhans	Atl	75	29	.387	2	-1
Adam Dunn	Cin	147	60	.408	6	-1
Frank Catalanotto	Tor	83	38	.458	6	-1
Carlos Lee	2 tms	138	48	.348	2	-2
Kevin Mench	2 tms	42	19	.452	0	-2
Barry Bonds	SF	66	31	.470	3	-2
Jason Michaels	Cle	118	47	.398	3	-3
Matt Holliday	Col	138	60	.435	3	-3
Dave Roberts	SD	69	30	.435	0	-4
Garret Anderson	LAA	74	35	.473	1	-4
Jason Bay	Pit	176	72	.409	4	-5

Center Fielders - 3-Year Throwing

Player	Opps	Extra Bases	Pct	Kills	Runs Saved
Aaron Rowand	387	204	.527	15	17
Willy Taveras	261	135	.517	12	13
Melky Cabrera	223	120	.538	17	12
B.J. Upton	205	120	.585	20	12
Alfredo Amezaga	171	85	.497	11	11
Adam Jones	135	59	.437	7	10
Mark Kotsay	235	119	.506	10	10
Shane Victorino	171	90	.526	10	10
Ichiro Suzuki	226	113	.500	9	9
Andruw Jones	326	170	.521	4	6
Marlon Byrd	150	82	.547	6	6
Carlos Beltran	378	216	.571	18	6
Vernon Wells	301	170	.565	8	5
Corey Patterson	276	148	.536	11	4
Jim Edmonds	232	126	.543	7	4
Gary Matthews Jr.	285	162	.568	13	4
Cory Sullivan	124	73	.589	5	3
Cody Ross	126	78	.619	8	3
Josh Hamilton	162	95	.586	5	2
Nate McLouth	258	137	.531	5	1
Eric Byrnes	110	59	.536	2	1
Carlos Gomez	135	73	.541	4	1
Brian Anderson	149	81	.544	1	1
Lastings Milledge	115	63	.548	2	1
Ken Griffey Jr.	124	71	.573	4	1
Curtis Granderson	397	213	.537	11	0
David DeJesus	229	139	.607	7	0
Mike Cameron	336	193	.574	9	-1
Grady Sizemore	439	241	.549	6	-2
Coco Crisp	280	154	.550	6	-2
Joey Gathright	195	116	.595	6	-3
Torii Hunter	372	212	.570	8	-4
Chris Young	265	152	.574	4	-4
Johnny Damon	181	107	.591	1	-6
Juan Pierre	275	168	.611	4	-7

Center Fielders - 2007 Throwing

Player	Tm	Opps	Extra Bases	Pct	Kills	Runs Saved
Aaron Rowand	Phi	153	81	.529	9	11
Melky Cabrera	NYY	132	72	.545	13	9
Andruw Jones	Atl	138	60	.435	2	7
Alfredo Amezaga	Fla	66	34	.515	7	7
Bill Hall	Mil	114	51	.447	2	5
Jim Edmonds	StL	88	43	.489	5	5
Mark Kotsay	Oak	57	28	.491	3	4
Willy Taveras	Col	74	37	.500	2	4
Ryan Freel	Cin	60	33	.550	3	4
B.J. Upton	TB	84	48	.571	7	4
Ichiro Suzuki	Sea	134	69	.515	4	3
Curtis Granderson	Det	154	82	.532	8	3
Hunter Pence	Hou	78	44	.564	4	3
Jacque Jones	ChC	54	29	.537	1	2
Chris Duffy	Pit	56	31	.554	2	2
Josh Hamilton	Cin	50	28	.560	4	2
Marlon Byrd	Tex	44	29	.659	2	2
Coco Crisp	Bos	108	55	.509	4	1
Corey Patterson	Bal	102	56	.549	3	1
Nick Swisher	Oak	58	32	.552	1	1
David DeJesus	KC	135	75	.556	2	1
Mike Cameron	SD	144	83	.576	4	1
Vernon Wells	Tor	102	61	.598	3	1
Felix Pie	ChC	28	14	.500	1	0
Torii Hunter	Min	132	72	.545	3	0
Chris Young	Ari	123	70	.569	2	0
Gary Matthews Jr.	LAA	114	69	.605	5	0
Jerry Owens	CWS	75	40	.533	0	-1
Nate McLouth	Pit	69	39	.565	2	-1
Grady Sizemore	Cle	138	80	.580	2	-1
Dave Roberts	SF	72	42	.583	1	-1
Kenny Lofton	2 tms	73	44	.603	2	-1
Carlos Beltran	NYM	121	73	.603	4	-1
Nook Logan	Was	70	44	.629	1	-3
Juan Pierre	LAD	142	91	.641	2	-4

Center Fielders - 2008 Throwing

Player	Tm	Opps	Extra Bases	Pct	Kills	Runs Saved
B.J. Upton	TB	121	72	.595	13	8
Mark Kotsay	Atl	73	29	.397	3	7
Adam Jones	Bal	115	49	.426	4	7
Rick Ankiel	StL	76	33	.434	4	7
Shane Victorino	Phi	109	56	.514	6	7
Ichiro Suzuki	Sea	69	32	.464	4	6
Matt Kemp	LAD	76	40	.526	8	6
Alex Rios	Tor	46	25	.543	7	6
Aaron Rowand	SF	140	69	.493	4	5
Carlos Gonzalez	Oak	50	26	.520	4	4
Carlos Beltran	NYM	146	78	.534	6	4
Melky Cabrera	NYY	88	46	.523	4	3
Cody Ross	Fla	76	49	.645	5	3
Corey Patterson	Cin	63	29	.460	3	2
Nate McLouth	Pit	144	74	.514	2	2
Willy Taveras	Col	103	53	.515	3	2
Grady Sizemore	Cle	131	68	.519	2	1
Carlos Gomez	Min	135	73	.541	4	1
Jim Edmonds	2 tms	61	34	.557	1	1
Mike Cameron	Mil	86	42	.488	2	0
Joey Gathright	KC	75	38	.507	2	0
Lastings Milledge	Was	107	59	.551	0	0
Jody Gerut	SD	54	30	.556	2	0
Reed Johnson	ChC	41	24	.585	2	0
Michael Bourn	Hou	100	59	.590	4	0
Josh Hamilton	Tex	112	67	.598	1	0
Curtis Granderson	Det	123	67	.545	3	-1
Jacoby Ellsbury	Bos	62	34	.548	1	-1
Torii Hunter	LAA	120	68	.567	2	-1
Nick Swisher	CWS	61	38	.623	1	-1
Coco Crisp	Bos	74	44	.595	1	-2
Skip Schumaker	StL	63	38	.603	2	-2
Vernon Wells	Tor	77	50	.649	2	-2
Chris Young	Ari	126	71	.563	2	-3
David DeJesus	KC	49	35	.714	1	-3

Center Fielders - 2006 Throwing

Player	Tm	Opps	Extra Bases	Pct	Kills	Runs Saved
Willy Taveras	Hou	84	45	.536	7	7
Vernon Wells	Tor	122	59	.484	3	6
Cory Sullivan	Col	91	53	.582	4	4
Shane Victorino	Phi	58	32	.552	4	3
Carlos Beltran	NYM	111	65	.586	8	3
Reggie Abercrombie	Fla	67	34	.507	2	2
Jose Bautista	Pit	58	30	.517	2	2
Gary Matthews Jr.	Tex	146	81	.555	7	2
Chone Figgins	LAA	73	42	.575	4	2
David DeJesus	KC	45	29	.644	4	2
Jeremy Reed	Sea	52	27	.519	0	1
Ken Griffey Jr.	Cin	103	56	.544	3	1
Corey Patterson	Bal	111	63	.568	5	1
Aaron Rowand	Phi	94	54	.574	2	1
Alfredo Amezaga	Fla	61	33	.541	1	0
Rob Mackowiak	CWS	46	25	.543	0	0
Brian Anderson	CWS	112	61	.545	1	0
Eric Byrnes	Ari	93	52	.559	2	0
Rocco Baldelli	TB	87	49	.563	3	0
Coco Crisp	Bos	98	55	.561	1	-1
Chris Duffy	Pit	68	40	.588	2	-1
Mark Kotsay	Oak	105	62	.590	4	-1
Andruw Jones	Atl	133	82	.617	2	-1
Curtis Granderson	Det	120	64	.533	0	-2
Grady Sizemore	Cle	170	93	.547	2	-2
Steve Finley	SF	105	60	.571	3	-2
Brady Clark	Mil	96	56	.583	0	-2
Jim Edmonds	StL	83	49	.590	1	-2
Mike Cameron	SD	106	68	.642	3	-2
Randy Winn	SF	48	33	.688	2	-2
Torii Hunter	Min	120	72	.600	3	-3
Joey Gathright	2 tms	115	75	.652	4	-3
Juan Pierre	ChC	124	72	.581	2	-4
Johnny Damon	NYY	110	68	.618	1	-5
Kenny Lofton	LAD	108	70	.648	2	-6

Right Fielders - 3-Year Throwing

Player	Opps	Extra Bases	Pct	Kills	Runs Saved
Michael Cuddyer	293	116	.396	24	25
Jeff Francoeur	413	180	.436	26	25
Alex Rios	277	97	.350	14	24
Nick Markakis	412	192	.466	29	21
Shane Victorino	109	38	.349	12	15
Delmon Young	170	63	.371	14	14
Ryan Ludwick	113	41	.363	8	12
Hunter Pence	127	52	.409	11	12
Magglio Ordonez	361	161	.446	12	12
Jayson Werth	97	33	.340	9	11
Brad Hawpe	406	193	.475	23	10
Ichiro Suzuki	212	94	.443	10	9
Bobby Abreu	419	195	.465	17	9
Jose Guillen	294	140	.476	13	8
Randy Winn	247	111	.449	9	7
Vladimir Guerrero	275	126	.458	13	7
Gabe Gross	100	35	.350	4	6
Matt Kemp	117	51	.436	5	6
Geoff Jenkins	147	67	.456	9	6
Nelson Cruz	148	69	.466	5	3
Justin Upton	111	54	.486	7	3
Xavier Nady	242	133	.550	16	3
Kosuke Fukudome	104	49	.471	4	2
Franklin Gutierrez	187	89	.476	5	2
Austin Kearns	375	181	.483	12	2
Mark Teahen	209	113	.541	14	2
Jacque Jones	148	72	.486	3	0
J.D. Drew	275	143	.520	8	0
Ken Griffey Jr.	199	105	.528	5	0
Jeremy Hermida	305	155	.508	6	-2
Andre Ethier	180	101	.561	9	-2
Jermaine Dye	392	202	.515	10	-4
Corey Hart	257	137	.533	5	-4
Brian Giles	362	188	.519	8	-5
Trot Nixon	141	82	.582	4	-5

Right Fielders - 2007 Throwing

Player	Tm	Opps	Extra Bases	Pct	Kills	Runs Saved
Shane Victorino	Phi	95	31	.326	9	13
Michael Cuddyer	Min	129	50	.388	12	13
Jeff Francoeur	Atl	129	53	.411	11	13
Delmon Young	TB	128	45	.352	11	11
Alex Rios	Tor	123	48	.390	6	9
Jose Guillen	Sea	170	71	.418	6	7
Jayson Werth	Phi	47	13	.277	3	6
Nick Markakis	Bal	157	75	.478	10	5
Mark Teahen	KC	132	65	.492	12	5
Magglio Ordonez	Det	105	44	.419	3	3
Vladimir Guerrero	LAA	92	39	.424	3	3
Randy Winn	SF	86	37	.430	3	2
Bobby Abreu	NYY	131	54	.412	2	1
Carlos Quentin	Ari	55	23	.418	1	1
Jeremy Hermida	Fla	110	56	.509	3	1
Nick Swisher	Oak	36	19	.528	2	1
Xavier Nady	Pit	65	36	.554	3	1
Luke Scott	Hou	74	41	.554	6	1
Juan Encarnacion	StL	65	29	.446	2	0
J.D. Drew	Bos	84	43	.512	2	0
Nelson Cruz	Tex	73	38	.521	1	0
Matt Kemp	LAD	53	27	.509	1	-1
Austin Kearns	Was	151	78	.517	6	-1
Cliff Floyd	ChC	23	12	.522	1	-1
Jack Cust	Oak	40	21	.525	1	-1
Brad Hawpe	Col	114	60	.526	4	-1
Trot Nixon	Cle	63	34	.540	2	-1
Corey Hart	Mil	105	52	.495	0	-2
Shawn Green	NYM	67	34	.507	2	-2
Jermaine Dye	CWS	137	77	.562	5	-2
Franklin Gutierrez	Cle	63	36	.571	1	-2
Andre Ethier	LAD	90	55	.611	6	-2
Travis Buck	Oak	37	25	.676	1	-2
Brian Giles	SD	102	53	.520	2	-3
Ken Griffey Jr.	Cin	116	67	.578	3	-3

Right Fielders - 2008 Throwing

Player	Tm	Opps	Extra Bases	Pct	Kills	Runs Saved
Nick Markakis	Bal	153	67	.438	14	14
Hunter Pence	Hou	116	46	.397	11	12
Ryan Ludwick	StL	92	34	.370	8	11
Bobby Abreu	NYY	145	65	.448	9	7
Ryan Sweeney	Oak	52	15	.288	3	6
Denard Span	Min	61	24	.393	5	6
Geoff Jenkins	Phi	54	22	.407	5	6
Alex Rios	Tor	62	22	.355	3	5
Franklin Gutierrez	Cle	91	35	.385	3	5
Jayson Werth	Phi	50	20	.400	6	5
Michael Cuddyer	Min	51	21	.412	5	5
Ichiro Suzuki	Sea	93	39	.419	6	5
Jeff Francoeur	Atl	115	50	.435	6	5
Gabe Gross	2 tms	72	27	.375	3	4
Randy Winn	SF	96	43	.448	1	3
Ken Griffey Jr.	2 tms	83	38	.458	2	3
Justin Upton	Ari	82	38	.463	6	3
Jay Bruce	Cin	57	27	.474	5	3
Xavier Nady	2 tms	91	46	.505	7	3
Kosuke Fukudome	ChC	104	49	.471	4	2
Brad Wilkerson	2 tms	46	22	.478	2	2
Jose Guillen	KC	73	38	.521	4	2
Magglio Ordonez	Det	143	72	.503	3	1
Ryan Church	NYM	83	40	.482	4	0
Andre Ethier	LAD	90	46	.511	3	0
Corey Hart	Mil	122	64	.525	5	0
Elijah Dukes	Was	70	42	.600	4	0
Brad Hawpe	Col	150	78	.520	7	-1
J.D. Drew	Bos	87	52	.598	4	-1
Jermaine Dye	CWS	124	63	.508	3	-2
Vladimir Guerrero	LAA	70	39	.557	3	-2
Austin Kearns	Was	83	42	.506	1	-3
Jeremy Hermida	Fla	122	65	.533	2	-3
Mark Teahen	KC	77	48	.623	2	-3
Brian Giles	SD	126	71	.563	2	-5

Right Fielders - 2006 Throwing

Player	Tm	Opps	Extra Bases	Pct	Kills	Runs Saved
Brad Hawpe	Col	142	55	.387	12	12
Alex Rios	Tor	92	27	.293	5	10
Magglio Ordonez	Det	113	45	.398	6	8
Michael Cuddyer	Min	113	45	.398	7	7
Jeff Francoeur	Atl	169	77	.456	9	7
Vladimir Guerrero	LAA	113	48	.425	7	6
Austin Kearns	2 tms	141	61	.433	5	6
Jeromy Burnitz	Pit	65	19	.292	1	5
Ichiro Suzuki	Sea	119	55	.462	4	4
Brian Giles	SD	134	64	.478	4	3
Jason Lane	Hou	67	27	.403	1	2
Mark DeRosa	Tex	60	25	.417	2	2
Jacque Jones	ChC	115	53	.461	3	2
Randy Winn	SF	65	31	.477	5	2
Nick Markakis	Bal	102	50	.490	5	2
Casey Blake	Cle	84	42	.500	4	2
Kevin Mench	Tex	54	21	.389	1	1
J.D. Drew	LAD	104	48	.462	2	1
Milton Bradley	Oak	84	41	.488	2	1
Carlos Quentin	Ari	47	23	.489	2	1
Bobby Abreu	2 tms	143	76	.531	6	1
Jeremy Hermida	Fla	73	34	.466	1	0
Jermaine Dye	CWS	131	62	.473	2	0
Geoff Jenkins	Mil	93	45	.484	4	0
Jay Payton	Oak	30	17	.567	1	0
Reggie Sanders	KC	61	29	.475	0	-1
Damon Hollins	TB	57	28	.491	1	-1
Bernie Williams	NYY	46	25	.543	0	-1
Xavier Nady	2 tms	86	51	.593	6	-1
Jose Guillen	Was	51	31	.608	0	-1
Moises Alou	SF	53	28	.528	0	-2
Juan Encarnacion	StL	102	51	.500	1	-3
Trot Nixon	Bos	70	42	.600	2	-3
Emil Brown	KC	38	25	.658	0	-3
Shawn Green	2 tms	113	68	.602	1	-5

379

Team Defense

Now that we've looked at individual players, who are the best and worst defensive *teams*?

As you might expect, the best defensive team of 2008 was the World Champion Philadelphia Phillies. Led by an exceptional season from Chase Utley, the Phillies posted the highest defensive runs saved total (78) of the past three years and the second highest over six seasons. The only team to beat the Phillies were the Phillies. The 2005 Phillies (featuring Ryan Howard, Utley, and Jimmy Rollins as well as David Bell) earned praise in the first Fielding Bible, and their 104 runs saved ranks as the top by any team over the past six years.

The Phillies' counterpart in the 2008 World Series also featured a strong defense, though not where some might expect. Tampa Bay exorcised the Devil from their name following their 2007 last place finish in team defense (71 runs lost defensively) and improved to ninth (26 runs saved) en route to the franchise's first playoff appearance. If you listened to the media during the World Series, you probably heard that Jason Bartlett was a big part of that improvement. Actually, Bartlett turned in a -2 runs saved (or two runs lost) at shortstop, while his backups (most notably, Ben Zobrist at seven runs lost) combined for another 11 runs below average. The chart points to three positions where the Rays excelled at defense: 1) First base, with Gold Glover Carlos Pena, 2) Left field with baseball's best left fielder, Carl Crawford, and 3) Third base, where future-Gold Glover Evan Longoria plays.

The 2007 Devil Rays were the worst defensive team in any year from 2006 through 2008, but the 2005 Yankees have them beat. The '05 Bronx Bombers lost 118 runs defensively, also featuring the worst outfield defense at 54 runs below average. Combining Andruw Jones's range with Jeff Francoeur's rifle arm, the mid-2000's Braves teams provided the top three defensive outfields in recent history, with the 2005 version leading the way at 64 runs saved. The Ichiro Suzuki/Mike Cameron/Randy Winn Mariners and the Reed Johnson/Vernon Wells/Alex Rios Blue Jays outfields also rate well.

You might notice that the St. Louis Cardinals rank near the top in each season. The Cardinals, at 177 runs saved defensively over three years, rank as the best defensive team. The 2005 White Sox rode pitching and defense to the World Series, but their defense collapsed shortly thereafter and ranks as the worst defense in that time. Jermaine Dye's defense in right field (or lack thereof) has weighed the team down the most. How much of the White Sox pitching staff's drop-off since that World Series is due to poor defense behind them? The 100 runs below average over three seasons is roughly 10 wins due to below-average defense, more than enough to make an impact on the standings.

The following charts show team Defensive Runs Saved by position for 2006 through 2008. Charts showing more detail follow.

Team Defensive Runs by Position - 2008

Team	Pitcher	Catcher	First Base	Second Base	Third Base	Shortstop	Left Field	Center Field	Right Field	Total
Philadelphia Phillies	1	-4	2	33	3	16	4	14	9	78
St Louis Cardinals	3	1	14	16	7	20	2	-10	18	71
Oakland Athletics	14	5	6	23	10	-17	-9	17	15	64
Toronto Blue Jays	9	0	5	3	29	-4	-7	-3	21	53
Milwaukee Brewers	8	10	-9	-3	3	17	9	14	0	49
New York Mets	13	-2	-6	-18	2	-4	25	18	13	41
Atlanta Braves	-2	6	5	-3	15	14	-4	7	-5	33
Cleveland Indians	1	-3	-6	7	-4	-3	12	1	24	29
Tampa Bay Rays	-8	-4	15	8	13	-13	14	1	0	26
Washington Nationals	2	0	-6	-13	11	12	10	-4	10	22
Houston Astros	-2	0	13	-19	3	8	3	5	11	22
Boston Red Sox	-5	2	2	9	12	1	0	0	-3	18
Seattle Mariners	-1	-4	0	-2	25	-13	-6	0	15	14
Florida Marlins	-8	-3	-21	6	-1	4	7	22	3	9
Chicago Cubs	13	0	4	-3	-6	4	8	-13	0	7
Los Angeles Dodgers	3	-2	0	-17	14	1	3	5	-5	2
Arizona Diamondbacks	0	-3	-12	6	-8	-1	11	7	-4	-4
San Diego Padres	-14	-2	0	-7	0	-6	6	7	11	-5
San Francisco Giants	-12	3	5	-13	-6	1	7	-4	12	-7
Colorado Rockies	9	0	-3	15	-6	6	0	-6	-25	-10
Minnesota Twins	4	-2	-2	-3	-15	-3	-14	17	7	-11
Pittsburgh Pirates	9	2	-3	2	-3	10	-13	-17	2	-11
Cincinnati Reds	-1	-2	16	9	-25	-11	-12	15	-4	-15
Detroit Tigers	20	8	-8	9	-21	-13	-3	-3	-4	-15
Los Angeles Angels	-13	-6	16	2	4	6	-8	-1	-15	-15
Baltimore Orioles	-13	0	-7	-3	-13	-30	8	18	19	-21
Texas Rangers	-5	1	-1	-6	-26	-5	1	-6	18	-29
Chicago White Sox	-7	-9	-8	-7	6	1	3	-5	-8	-34
New York Yankees	-2	-2	-18	-13	-10	-10	8	10	-6	-43
Kansas City Royals	8	-5	-10	-6	-12	9	-9	-12	-11	-48

Team Totals and Rankings - 2008

Team	PLUS/MINUS Middle Infield	Corner Infield	Outfield	Total	Rank	GROUND DP GDP Opps	GDP	Pct	Rank	BUNTS Opps	Score	Grade	Rank	THROWING Opps To Advance	Extra Bases	Kills	Pct	Rank
Philadelphia Phillies	+70	+7	0	+77	1	338	127	.376	22	45	.559	B-	11	406	163	27	.401	2
St Louis Cardinals	+43	+26	-3	+66	2	330	135	.409	11	37	.634	A-	3	456	202	20	.443	8
Toronto Blue Jays	+4	+47	0	+51	3	293	111	.379	21	35	.499	C	24	373	167	21	.448	12
New York Mets	-21	-12	+79	+46	4	341	113	.331	29	47	.640	A-	2	446	203	20	.455	16
Oakland Athletics	-5	+26	+24	+45	5	273	142	.520	1	34	.529	C+	17	419	188	20	.449	13
Milwaukee Brewers	+25	-5	+25	+45	5	374	132	.353	25	68	.504	C+	23	389	175	15	.450	15
Washington Nationals	-1	+3	+35	+37	7	310	119	.384	19	39	.549	B-	14	465	227	12	.488	27
Tampa Bay Rays	-12	+33	+11	+32	8	303	134	.442	8	45	.622	B+	4	392	179	19	.457	17
Atlanta Braves	+22	+24	-19	+27	9	390	132	.338	28	34	.566	B-	10	416	187	13	.450	14
Boston Red Sox	+16	+18	-8	+26	10	299	119	.398	15	42	.577	B	7	422	202	14	.479	25
Florida Marlins	+17	-28	+36	+25	11	313	100	.319	30	54	.512	C+	20	448	207	20	.462	19
San Diego Padres	-16	-7	+46	+23	12	324	127	.392	17	53	.692	A+	1	424	216	14	.509	29
Houston Astros	-18	+24	+15	+21	13	296	120	.405	12	30	.532	C+	16	398	178	20	.447	11
Cleveland Indians	-10	-5	+33	+18	14	330	159	.482	2	47	.447	C-	27	489	203	23	.415	3
Arizona Diamondbacks	+6	-25	+30	+11	15	324	114	.352	26	52	.513	C+	19	415	199	13	.480	26
San Francisco Giants	-10	-8	+10	-8	16	283	104	.367	23	53	.607	B+	6	441	207	12	.469	22
Seattle Mariners	-23	+35	-20	-8	16	336	138	.411	10	44	.572	B	8	510	215	20	.422	4
Los Angeles Angels	0	+28	-41	-13	18	315	141	.448	4	31	.555	B-	13	407	206	16	.506	28
Los Angeles Dodgers	-11	+12	-14	-13	18	362	124	.343	27	50	.613	B+	5	452	210	19	.465	21
Baltimore Orioles	-38	-21	+37	-22	20	368	142	.386	18	44	.473	C	26	501	199	24	.397	1
Chicago Cubs	+6	-4	-26	-24	21	266	97	.365	24	49	.558	B-	12	361	161	17	.446	10
Cincinnati Reds	+2	-11	-24	-33	22	340	130	.382	20	50	.567	B-	9	442	187	18	.423	5
Chicago White Sox	-13	+3	-25	-35	23	311	138	.444	6	37	.435	D+	28	432	203	10	.470	23
Colorado Rockies	+21	-12	-48	-39	24	359	144	.401	14	43	.535	C+	15	519	241	15	.464	20
Minnesota Twins	-13	-21	-8	-42	25	327	142	.434	9	28	.511	C+	21	467	208	23	.445	9
Pittsburgh Pirates	+14	-4	-53	-43	26	391	157	.402	13	68	.524	C+	18	505	233	15	.461	18
Detroit Tigers	-8	-34	-22	-64	27	341	153	.449	3	36	.411	D+	30	503	237	14	.471	24
Texas Rangers	-22	-37	-7	-66	28	361	160	.443	7	44	.506	C+	22	549	240	19	.437	7
New York Yankees	-29	-33	-8	-70	29	280	110	.393	16	36	.419	D+	29	447	191	22	.427	6
Kansas City Royals	-4	-24	-49	-77	30	301	134	.445	5	31	.474	C	25	463	238	15	.514	30

Team Defensive Runs by Position - 2007

Team	Pitcher	Catcher	First Base	Second Base	Third Base	Shortstop	Left Field	Center Field	Right Field	Total
Toronto Blue Jays	-10	-1	9	22	5	23	7	5	10	70
Atlanta Braves	9	-1	-2	-3	4	0	18	20	20	65
Philadelphia Phillies	5	5	-1	14	4	5	-9	12	29	64
St Louis Cardinals	12	6	28	-1	22	-15	3	-4	4	55
Detroit Tigers	5	4	1	10	20	-5	1	14	4	54
Kansas City Royals	-1	-5	15	9	2	16	5	-2	11	50
Colorado Rockies	21	3	8	12	-19	31	1	-4	-12	41
Arizona Diamondbacks	-1	-1	-6	19	-5	0	21	1	10	38
New York Mets	-5	-1	-1	-4	14	12	8	18	-3	38
Minnesota Twins	6	1	-1	-8	12	19	-3	-2	1	25
Oakland Athletics	-9	10	2	16	3	0	1	0	2	25
San Francisco Giants	-6	4	17	-13	23	12	-8	-17	10	22
Chicago Cubs	-14	-15	-6	-1	16	5	21	15	-4	17
Cleveland Indians	3	4	-8	1	-4	1	13	-1	7	16
Texas Rangers	4	1	1	3	-10	-9	17	-6	11	12
San Diego Padres	3	-13	-3	-3	2	4	6	7	2	5
Washington Nationals	4	-3	-22	-5	20	-17	8	9	6	0
New York Yankees	4	-7	7	21	3	-25	5	-4	-5	-1
Boston Red Sox	-12	-4	4	2	7	2	-16	10	4	-3
Los Angeles Angels	-20	-5	22	9	-2	2	7	-16	-5	-8
Baltimore Orioles	-11	-4	-6	0	3	0	3	2	2	-11
Milwaukee Brewers	-1	-7	-11	-6	-21	6	12	2	6	-16
Los Angeles Dodgers	-1	8	-11	-15	-1	9	-14	6	0	-21
Seattle Mariners	11	-9	-16	1	4	-7	-11	6	0	-22
Pittsburgh Pirates	-6	0	4	-6	-18	10	-13	-7	14	-22
Houston Astros	9	-6	2	-19	-16	8	6	-7	-9	-32
Cincinnati Reds	-4	2	-9	8	-14	-1	-18	3	0	-33
Chicago White Sox	4	3	-3	-21	-11	-8	7	8	-27	-48
Florida Marlins	-10	-4	-10	-11	-20	-27	4	22	6	-50
Tampa Bay Devil Rays	-14	-3	-1	-9	-15	-29	-3	-1	4	-71

Team Totals and Rankings - 2007

Team	PLUS/MINUS Middle Infield	Corner Infield	Outfield	Total	Rank	GROUND DP GDP Opps	GDP	Pct	Rank	BUNTS Opps	Score	Grade	Rank	THROWING Opps To Advance	Extra Bases	Kills	Pct	Rank
Toronto Blue Jays	+56	+25	+16	+97	1	348	148	.425	8	22	.461	C-	30	416	187	18	.450	13
New York Mets	+15	+11	+42	+68	2	319	110	.345	29	54	.622	B+	2	400	203	16	.508	29
Kansas City Royals	+25	+24	+14	+63	3	296	139	.470	1	25	.466	C-	26	448	211	21	.471	22
Atlanta Braves	-5	+4	+62	+61	4	334	123	.368	27	59	.529	C+	17	432	179	21	.414	2
Arizona Diamondbacks	+19	-18	+43	+44	5	330	141	.427	6	41	.562	B-	10	409	191	18	.467	20
Detroit Tigers	0	+29	+15	+44	5	297	125	.421	10	24	.515	C+	19	452	203	18	.449	12
Chicago Cubs	+3	+13	+23	+39	7	303	117	.386	26	61	.534	C+	14	402	173	27	.430	6
St Louis Cardinals	-17	+58	-11	+30	8	338	135	.399	22	35	.734	A+	1	477	211	19	.442	9
Oakland Athletics	+14	+8	-1	+21	9	318	135	.425	9	33	.480	C	22	453	222	12	.490	26
San Diego Padres	0	-6	+25	+19	10	326	128	.393	24	67	.612	B+	4	418	207	14	.495	27
Philadelphia Phillies	+25	-2	-5	+18	11	341	137	.402	21	55	.589	B	6	473	192	29	.406	1
Cleveland Indians	+5	-9	+22	+18	11	335	137	.409	17	49	.530	C+	16	458	214	14	.467	21
San Francisco Giants	+1	+46	-34	+13	13	328	130	.396	23	63	.618	B+	3	445	201	9	.452	15
Boston Red Sox	+3	+14	-4	+13	13	278	117	.421	11	31	.577	B	8	380	180	13	.474	23
Minnesota Twins	+14	+16	-23	+7	15	298	127	.426	7	29	.469	C-	25	426	182	18	.427	4
Texas Rangers	-9	-14	+25	+2	16	366	143	.391	25	37	.470	C	24	487	232	20	.476	24
Washington Nationals	-33	-8	+40	-1	17	318	132	.415	14	55	.580	B	7	442	199	12	.450	14
Colorado Rockies	+46	-16	-33	-3	18	346	156	.451	4	44	.518	C+	18	449	204	18	.454	16
Los Angeles Angels	+8	+27	-40	-5	19	296	135	.456	3	30	.465	C-	27	508	227	19	.447	10
Baltimore Orioles	+3	-5	-6	-8	20	333	135	.405	19	49	.462	C-	28	468	207	16	.443	19
Milwaukee Brewers	-5	-41	+36	-10	21	298	124	.416	13	51	.545	B-	12	479	220	15	.459	18
Los Angeles Dodgers	-8	-20	+14	-14	22	338	142	.420	12	46	.593	B	5	439	242	9	.551	30
New York Yankees	-20	+17	-39	-42	23	333	153	.459	2	39	.462	C-	29	458	196	25	.428	5
Pittsburgh Pirates	-4	-18	-26	-48	24	369	164	.444	5	52	.575	B	9	514	235	21	.457	17
Houston Astros	-5	-17	-28	-50	25	334	114	.341	30	52	.547	B-	11	436	219	19	.502	28
Seattle Mariners	-11	-14	-28	-53	26	339	140	.413	16	34	.472	C	23	498	215	16	.432	7
Cincinnati Reds	+7	-29	-41	-63	27	319	132	.414	15	49	.490	C	21	476	213	17	.447	11
Florida Marlins	-54	-44	+18	-80	28	346	127	.367	28	56	.530	C+	15	545	237	26	.435	8
Chicago White Sox	-38	-15	-29	-82	29	345	139	.403	20	49	.491	C	20	528	220	24	.417	3
Tampa Bay Devil Rays	-51	-17	-39	-107	30	314	128	.408	18	49	.491	C	20	495	215	20	.434	25

Team Defensive Runs by Position - 2006

Team	Pitcher	Catcher	First Base	Second Base	Third Base	Shortstop	Left Field	Center Field	Right Field	Total
Seattle Mariners	12	-9	4	9	19	2	8	8	12	65
Detroit Tigers	10	4	4	18	19	3	-1	0	-1	56
Houston Astros	5	-1	4	0	5	35	-4	14	-4	54
St Louis Cardinals	7	2	16	1	20	1	-2	1	5	51
Kansas City Royals	9	3	16	11	-6	-2	9	-5	6	41
New York Mets	2	-4	-2	20	-1	15	-1	11	0	40
San Diego Padres	-9	-6	4	6	8	16	4	6	10	39
Toronto Blue Jays	-16	-8	3	23	4	-15	12	12	23	38
San Francisco Giants	-5	-3	11	-8	21	2	0	6	7	31
Colorado Rockies	7	2	-6	9	-1	25	-9	-4	4	27
Milwaukee Brewers	-8	2	-12	-2	6	21	11	-3	3	18
Arizona Diamondbacks	7	-1	-10	10	-3	19	2	3	-13	14
Minnesota Twins	2	-3	1	-5	6	8	18	-8	-6	13
Florida Marlins	18	3	-10	1	-8	-2	2	10	-2	12
Texas Rangers	1	3	0	-2	-2	-7	-5	12	9	9
Los Angeles Angels	0	4	14	6	-14	-9	3	4	0	8
Chicago Cubs	-1	-4	8	-3	-4	-1	4	6	1	6
Philadelphia Phillies	12	-3	-7	14	-8	10	-7	1	-7	5
Oakland Athletics	1	10	0	17	3	-25	1	-8	5	4
Baltimore Orioles	0	4	-10	6	-6	-11	4	12	1	0
Atlanta Braves	-5	-2	-10	-12	-17	1	15	14	10	-6
Los Angeles Dodgers	-6	-3	4	-21	1	1	7	-11	11	-17
Tampa Bay Devil Rays	-2	-7	3	-9	-18	-6	11	1	9	-18
Chicago White Sox	3	2	-10	-8	22	-2	-6	-5	-14	-18
Cincinnati Reds	1	4	11	-6	-18	-13	-12	-11	20	-24
Pittsburgh Pirates	11	6	-9	-13	-5	-1	1	-12	-10	-32
New York Yankees	16	-2	-16	5	-8	-18	7	-12	-9	-37
Washington Nationals	-10	-12	6	-27	1	-25	26	-3	5	-39
Cleveland Indians	-14	-14	-13	-5	-6	-16	10	3	11	-44
Boston Red Sox	-19	-8	9	-10	2	6	-20	-16	7	-49

Team Totals and Rankings - 2006

Team	PLUS/MINUS Middle Infield	Corner Infield	Outfield	Total	Rank	GROUND DP GDP Opps	GDP	Pct	Rank	BUNTS Opps	Score	Grade	Rank	THROWING Opps To Advance	Extra Bases	Kills	Pct	Rank
San Diego Padres	+33	+11	+42	+86	1	318	121	.381	22	53	.586	B	8	386	193	8	.500	29
St Louis Cardinals	0	+48	+17	+65	2	380	154	.405	18	52	.530	C+	20	438	210	4	.479	22
Toronto Blue Jays	+7	+18	+40	+65	2	308	129	.419	12	39	.487	C	26	411	166	24	.404	1
Seattle Mariners	+9	+30	+25	+64	4	297	130	.438	8	37	.565	B-	13	474	202	19	.426	2
San Francisco Giants	-3	+32	+34	+63	5	317	110	.347	27	62	.662	A	1	412	216	16	.524	30
Milwaukee Brewers	+34	-13	+28	+49	6	315	113	.359	25	86	.585	B	9	416	207	12	.498	27
Houston Astros	+42	+11	-5	+48	7	331	145	.438	7	61	.539	C+	19	379	176	16	.464	12
New York Mets	+49	-11	0	+38	8	315	104	.330	29	49	.558	B-	15	408	203	28	.498	26
Kansas City Royals	-2	+22	+6	+26	9	357	161	.451	5	36	.401	D	30	523	245	18	.468	15
Chicago Cubs	+4	-1	+20	+23	10	283	96	.339	28	62	.555	B-	16	416	187	8	.450	11
Detroit Tigers	+14	+30	-29	+15	11	301	139	.462	3	27	.620	B+	4	402	175	19	.435	6
Arizona Diamondbacks	+30	-16	-4	+10	12	346	142	.410	16	45	.496	C	25	427	213	8	.499	28
Minnesota Twins	+11	+4	-7	+8	13	296	111	.375	23	35	.603	B+	6	415	186	18	.448	10
Atlanta Braves	-12	-39	+57	+6	14	355	133	.375	24	58	.574	B	11	469	220	18	.469	16
Los Angeles Dodgers	-18	+10	+11	+3	15	375	155	.413	14	43	.584	B	10	455	214	14	.470	17
Baltimore Orioles	-10	-14	+8	-16	16	314	129	.411	15	46	.416	D+	28	479	207	20	.432	3
Cleveland Indians	-33	-27	+40	-20	17	330	144	.436	9	40	.559	B-	14	493	232	14	.471	18
Texas Rangers	-17	-4	-3	-24	18	359	146	.407	17	30	.613	B+	5	510	221	29	.433	4
Tampa Bay Devil Rays	-26	-20	+19	-27	19	324	130	.401	20	37	.505	C+	24	514	245	24	.477	20
Washington Nationals	-49	-1	+23	-27	19	324	88	.272	30	71	.634	A-	3	495	241	27	.487	24
Colorado Rockies	+30	-12	-47	-29	21	362	164	.453	4	43	.551	B-	17	480	224	23	.467	13
Los Angeles Angels	-11	+1	-20	-30	22	296	128	.432	10	44	.486	C	27	411	183	26	.445	8
Oakland Athletics	-19	+7	-19	-31	23	319	151	.473	2	33	.515	C+	22	466	202	15	.433	5
Florida Marlins	-4	-27	0	-31	23	367	148	.403	19	53	.571	B	12	454	202	13	.445	7
Chicago White Sox	-16	+18	-39	-37	25	283	127	.449	6	39	.529	C+	21	445	213	8	.479	21
Philadelphia Phillies	+25	-17	-45	-37	25	319	134	.420	11	56	.513	C+	23	437	207	21	.474	19
Boston Red Sox	-14	+13	-62	-63	27	307	149	.485	1	32	.588	B	7	452	220	15	.487	23
Cincinnati Reds	-18	-11	-37	-66	28	318	112	.352	26	47	.551	B-	18	457	204	27	.446	9
New York Yankees	-18	-28	-21	-67	29	302	126	.417	13	25	.410	D+	29	485	238	17	.491	25
Pittsburgh Pirates	-20	-27	-36	-83	30	382	146	.382	21	80	.639	A-	2	495	231	12	.467	13

Crossing Positions

Bill James

(Editors's Note: This article was written by Bill James in September, 2008 and published on the Bill James Online—BillJamesOnline.com—on December 8, 2008. Published with permission)

In one of the profiles in the Statistics section of the Bill James Online, we rank players in specific skills. Marcus (Scoot Scoot) Scutaro, for example, ranks low in power among all players—at the 20th percentile—but in the middle of the pack among shortstops, at the 46th percentile. Todd Helton ranks low in speed—21st percentile among all players—but in the middle of the pack among first basemen (47th percentile).

One of the skills assessed is Fielding; Orlando Hudson ranks at the 92nd percentile among second basemen in terms of fielding, but where does that rank among all players? There appears to be no obvious way to answer the question. Who ranks first—a shortstop who is at the 41st pecentile among shortstops, or a third baseman who is at the 99th percentile among third basemen? How do we approach that question?

That is the purpose of this article—to propose a methodology to answer that question.

The first question we have to ask is "How many runs are 'saved' by the players at each position?" If we knew that shortstops save 50 runs a year and third basemen save 35 runs a year, then a third baseman who was +8 runs would rank ahead of a shortstop who was –8:

Crappy shortstop	50 – 8 = 42
Good third baseman	35 + 8 = 43

The problem is, we don't know what the base is. We don't know how many runs are being "saved" by each position.

Well, how many runs are being "saved" overall?

If we assume that offense and defense are the same thing, merely seen from a different perspective, then it must be true that Runs Saved equal Runs Scored, right? Therefore, if an average major league team scores 769 runs per season—which is the average over the years 2005-2007—then an average team must also SAVE 769 runs per season.

Of those runs, some are "saved" by the pitchers, and some are saved by the fielders (and some, of course, are Saved by the Bell.) How do we split them?

It is apparent for various reasons that I don't want to get into right now that the lion's share of these Runs Saved must be attributable to pitchers. What *exactly* the percentage is I don't know and don't believe that you know, but the Runs Saved by pitchers must be somewhere between 2/3 and 3/4 of all Runs Saved. Let us assume, for the purpose of moving toward an answer, that 72% of Runs Saved are saved by pitchers, and 28% by fielders.

If Runs Saved equal Runs Scored and 72% of Runs Saved are saved by pitchers, then that leaves 215.432 runs to be "saved" by fielders at the other eight positions. Let's call it 216, since

a) there is a certain amount of guesswork involved here, and

b) 216 is a much easier number to work with than 215.432.

How, then, do we allocate these 216 runs to each of the eight defensive positions?

We can do that by assuming that the defensive differences are equal to the offensive differences. Let us assume that the an average major league team's catchers

385

create 70 runs per season—which is the actual average of all major league teams over the three seasons, 2005-2007—and that an average major league team's first basemen create 99 runs per season (which they have). Let us assume that the number of outs made by the first basemen is the same as the number of outs made by the catchers (which it is, basically—466 outs by the first basemen, 463 by the catchers.)

If catchers create 70 runs per season and first basemen create 99, then either

   a) first basemen are better players than catchers, or
   b) catchers must be "saving" 29 more runs a year than first basemen.

By simply choosing option (b), we can figure out how many runs to attribute to each fielding position, as a base. These are the Runs Created by the players at each position, 2005-2007 (thank you, Retrosheet):

Catcher	70
First Base	99
Second Base	85
Third Base	90
Shortstop	81
Left Field	96
Center Field	89
Right Field	94

Let's leave designated hitters out of this, since we can assume that their Runs Saved are zero. If

   a) those are their Runs Created,
   b) Runs Created + Runs Saved must balance by position, and
   c) Runs Saved must total 216, then we can calculate how many runs are "saved" at each position:

	Created	Saved
Catcher	70	45
First Base	99	16
Second Base	85	30
Third Base	90	25
Shortstop	81	34
Left Field	96	19
Center Field	89	26
Right Field	94	21
Total		**216**

These are almost the numbers that I will propose we use, but not quite. For purposes of making a simple explanation, I assumed that outs were the same at each

position. They aren't, of course; center fielders made an average of 493 outs over the three seasons, and catchers an average of 463. The average Runs Created/Out at all eight positions was .184 (.183 923). If you multiply the outs by the runs created/out and save decimals, catchers are not 19 runs behind center fielders, but actually only 13. Our adjusted values, then, look like this:

	Created	Outs	Saved
Catcher	70	463	45
First Base	99	466	16
Second Base	85	487	30
Third Base	90	474	25
Shortstop	81	490	34
Left Field	96	477	19
Center Field	89	493	26
Right Field	94	474	21
Total			**216**

216 runs at eight positions is 27 runs per position. If a team is saving 27 runs per position in 1,444 innings, then (an average major league team plays 1,443.5+ innings a year in the field), that comes to 1 run every 53.5 innings, or .01874 runs per inning.

OK, let's import some actual players here. I'll list players from 2007, maybe one per team. Here's a list:

Arizona	C	Chris Snyder
Atlanta	1B	Scott Thorman
Baltimore	2B	Brian Roberts
Boston	3B	Mike Lowell
Chicago AL	SS	Juan Uribe
Chicago NL	LF	Alfonso Soriano
Cincinnati	CF	Josh Hamilton
Cleveland	RF	Trot Nixon
Colorado	C	Yorvit Torrealba
Detroit	1B	Sean Casey
Florida	2B	Dan Uggla
Houston	3B	Morgan Ensberg
Kansas City	SS	Tony Pena
LA Angels	LF	Garrett Anderson
LA Dodgers	CF	Juan Pierre
Milwaukee	RF	Corey Hart
Minnesota	C	Joe Mauer
New York A	1B	Andy Phillips
New York N	2B	Luis Castillo
Oakland	3B	Eric Chavez
Philadelphia	SS	Jimmy Rollins

Pittsburgh	LF	Jason Bay	
San Diego	CF	Mike Cameron	
San Francisco	RF	Randy Winn	
Seattle	C	Kenji Johjima	
St. Louis	1B	Albert Pujols	
Tampa Bay	2B	Ty Wigginton	
Texas	3B	Ramon Vazquez	
Toronto	SS	John McDonald	
Washington	LF	Ryan Church	

Pos	Player	Innings	Base
CF	Mike Cameron	1329.0	26.69
RF	Randy Winn	869.0	12.04
C	Kenji Johjima	1106.2	32.19
1B	Albert Pujols	1324.2	11.93
2B	Ty Wigginton	321.0	7.11
3B	Ramon Vazquez	540.1	9.35
SS	John McDonald	799.1	19.93
LF	Ryan Church	719.1	9.46

The first thing we have to do is figure a "base" for each player. For purposes of this study I am going to use only the player's defensive numbers at the position, ignoring any fielding contributions he may have made at some other position or with some other team. Several of the players we happened to pick switched teams; we're only using Morgan Ensberg's numbers with Houston and Luis Castillo's numbers with the Mets. Chris Snyder played 891.1 innings at catcher for Arizona in 2007. We credit catchers with 42 Runs Saved per 1,444 innings, so that comes to 25.93 Runs Saved for Snyder, if he is an exactly average defensive catcher. That data for these 30 players:

Pos	Player	Innings	Base
C	Chris Snyder	891.1	25.93
1B	Scott Thorman	608.1	5.48
2B	Brian Roberts	1329.2	29.47
3B	Mike Lowell	1324.1	22.93
SS	Juan Uribe	1305.1	32.55
LF	Alfonso Soriano	1064.0	14.00
CF	Josh Hamilton	555.2	11.16
RF	Trot Nixon	675.0	9.35
C	Yorvit Torrealba	935.1	27.20
1B	Sean Casey	989.0	8.90
2B	Dan Uggla	1383.2	30.66
3B	Morgan Ensberg	492.1	8.52
SS	Tony Pena	1273.2	31.75
LF	Garrett Anderson	724.1	9.53
CF	Juan Pierre	1416.1	28.45
RF	Corey Hart	1096.2	15.19
C	Joe Mauer	777.2	22.62
1B	Andy Phillips	431.0	3.88
2B	Luis Castillo	432.0	9.57
3B	Eric Chavez	774.2	13.41
SS	Jimmy Rollins	1441.1	35.93
LF	Jason Bay	1237.0	16.28

This is the number of runs the player will be credited with saving *if he is an average defender at the position.* If he is a good fielder, we will move him up from here; if he is below-average at the position, he goes down.

Is Chris Snyder an above-average catcher or a below-average catcher? There is a lot that we don't know about catchers' defense, but we can't worry about what we don't know. What we are trying to figure out is how to rank the players based on the information that we do have.

National League catchers in 2007 allowed 1,562 stolen bases in 23,247.1 innings. Snyder allowed 52 stolen bases in 891.1 innings. An average NL catcher would have allowed 59.89 stolen bases in that number of innings. Snyder allowed 7.89 fewer steals than an average catcher. Valuing a stolen base at .20 runs, this makes Snyder 1.578 runs better than average.

NL catchers caught 510 runners stealing. Pro-rated to Snyder's innings, we expect him to gun down 19.554 runners (18, plus Prince Fielder.) He actually threw out 29 baserunners, making him +9.446 in this area. Valuing a caught stealing at .35 runs, this makes Snyder 3.306 runs better than an average catcher.

Snyder had a fielding percentage of .999 (1 error in 780 chances)—the best fielding percentage in the major leagues at his position. The major league average fielding percentage by a catcher was .991 (309 errors in 35,689 chances.) Snyder thus made 5.75 fewer errors than an average catcher. Valuing an error by a catcher at .25 runs (assuming that most E-2, but not all, are on stolen base attempts), we can estimate the value of this at 1.4375 runs. (I am using major league data for fielding percentage but league data for stolen bases, on the theory that stolen base totals are league-specific, but fielding stats are in general not.)

Major league catchers had 335 Passed Balls in 43,425.2 innings. Pro-rated to Snyder's innings, we would expect him to have 6.87 Passed Balls. He actually had 9 Passed Balls, so in this respect he was below average, negative 2.13. Valuing each of those at 0.20 runs, that is a negative .426.

Adding these four things together (Stolen Bases, Caught Stealing, Errors and Passed Balls), we estimate that Snyder is 5.90 runs better than an average catcher, based on what we know. Adding that to his 25.93 "base", we credit him with saving 31.82 runs in 891.1 innings.

Now that I look at it, we have a problem here. Our arbitrary selection criteria picked four catchers, all of whom are pretty good defensive catchers. This is going to screw up our charts later on. Since "catcher" is the highest-valued defensive position anyway, it's going to look like all catchers rank better than all players at any other position. I'd better throw in a couple of not-so-good catchers as well. . .let's say, John Buck and Johnny Estrada.

While I'm expanding the field, let's put Orlando Hudson in there, too, just because I brought up his name earlier. . .when I pose the question "Where does Orlando Hudson rank?", I should suggest some sort of answer.

OK, following through that procedure for the catchers listed here, we have totals of +9.69 for Joe Mauer (who had the best catcher-throwing data in the American League), +12.56 for Kenji Johjima, +0.62 for John Buck, -0.84 for Yorvit Torrealba, and -4.21 for Johnny Estrada. So actually, Buck comes in a hair better than average, and Torrealba a little below average. You learn something every day.

Moving on to the first basemen. . .for first basemen we seem to have two things we can work with: The Fielding +/-, and the Fielding Percentage. Scott Thorman was +3 plays in 2007, according to the Fielding Bible Plus/Minus system. We'll credit him with .400 Runs Saved for each play above average, making him +1.20 on that. His fielding percentage was .991. The major league average at first base was .994. Thorman was two plays worse-than-average (2.06), so he comes out +.94 plays, which is +.376 runs (actually +.378 if you work the decimals):

Pos	Player	Innings	Base	Individual Credits	Total
C	Chris Snyder	891.1	25.93	+5.90	31.83
1B	Scott Thorman	608.1	5.48	-0.38	5.85

I hope you understand. . .my main focus here is not in determining how good a first baseman Scott Thorman is, or how bad a catcher Johnny Estrada is. It is necessary to the process that I am trying to outline that I have some system to say whether a player is +3 (three runs better

than average) or -7 (seven runs worse than average), so I am dutifully going through the process of outlining how that might be done, with a little bit of actual data. I am well aware that there are probably better ways to do this, and that's fine. . .It's just that this question is standing in my pathway and I'm trying to climb over it to get to the finish line. If you have a better system to determine how many runs a fielder is above or below average, by all means use it.

Anyway, my system for third basemen is the same as for first basemen. . .+.40 runs saved for each +/- play, and -.40 for each error above the major league norm for the position. For second basemen and shortstops, we'll need to add something for the ability to turn the double play. The norm for second basemen turning a double play is about .515 Double Plays per opportunity, so we'll credit the second basemen with .30 Runs Saved for each Double Play above .515 times GIDP Opportunities (Data from the Fielding Bible Plus/Minus in the Bill James Online.)

Orlando Hudson in 2007 was +20 plays made, meaning that he made 20 more plays than one would expect an average second baseman to make. That makes him +8.00 runs. His fielding percentage was .985 against a major league for second basemen of .984, so he's almost average there, +0.28 plays. He had 166 Double Play Opportunities and turned 89 Double Plays, whereas an average second baseman would have turned 85.5, so he's 3.5 Double Plays above average.

I give a little less weight to a Double Play because there are more people involved in it, so that it gives a less clear or less certain indication of the player's individual performance. Anyway, adding those together, Hudson is +9.17 Runs Saved, above his base, which is 26.22. We thus credit him with saving 35.39 runs.

The norm for Double Plays per opportunity at shortstop is higher than at second base, probably because there are more 5-4-3 double play attempts than 3-6-3. Anyway, the norm for shortstops is about .615; otherwise the process is the same.

John McDonald, Toronto's magic-fingered shortstop, fielded .982 against a major league norm of .972; that made him 4.465 plays better than average. According to *The Fielding Bible* he was +26 plays. He turned 63 double plays in 110 double play opportunities, a below-average figure; he's 4.65 plays below average. Adding these together, McDonald is about 10.79 Runs better than an average shortstop:

$$(4.465 * .4) + (26 * .4) - (4.65 * .30) = 10.79$$

Adding that to his "position base", which was 19.93 runs, we credit McDonald with saving 30.72 runs in 799.1 innings.

Some people will object that Fielding Percentages (errors) and the Fielding Bible's +/- measure the same plays, thus that our calculation is redundant. It is true that it *can be* redundant, sometimes.

But I think the better arguments are on the other side of the issue.

1) "Errors" were not a great idea and are not a good way to evaluate a fielder by themselves, but they are a very *specific* observation. A player who is charged with an error has, in almost all cases, made a clearly observable mistake. A fielder who is "+" a play may simply be benefiting from team positioning decisions, or he may be benefiting from some poorly-understood wrinkle in the +/- range evaluation system. It's not really the same thing.

2) An event which is observed twice, by different evaluation systems, is more concrete than an event which is observed by one system but missed by another. Assuming that this *is* a redundant measure—which it is sometimes—that's OK, because an event which can be observed by both systems is more tangible and more certain than an event which appears in only one.

3) In many cases or perhaps most cases, errors actually are *not* plays that would show up in the fielder's plus/minus range. Certainly many of them would not—overthrows allowing advancement, errors made in receiving throws from another fielder, etc.

For outfielders, we have the two elements we had for first and third basemen--+.40 for a "plus" play in the Fielding Bible, -.40 for an error (or +.40 for an error not made.) Also, for outfielders, we have "throwing" data. . .what do we do with that?

A left fielder "allows advancement" on about 40% of advancement opportunities. We'll credit him with .15 runs saved for each base not advanced below. 400, and charge him with .15 for bases advanced beyond .400. Center Fielders and Right Fielders the same, except that the norm is about .55. (Runners don't go first-to-third on balls hit to left.)

OK, I figured the "Individual Plus/Minus Run Elements" for each of the 33 fielders now in our study. This is the data, added to the chart above:

Pos	Player	Innings	Base	Individual Credits	Total
C	Chris Snyder	891.1	25.93	+5.90	31.83
1B	Scott Thorman	608.1	5.48	-0.38	5.85
2B	Brian Roberts	1329.2	29.47	+0.49	29.95
3B	Mike Lowell	1324.1	22.93	+2.79	25.72
SS	Juan Uribe	1305.1	32.55	-2.53	30.01
LF	Alfonso Soriano	1064.0	14.00	-1.23	12.77
CF	Josh Hamilton	555.2	11.16	-0.73	10.43
RF	Trot Nixon	675.0	9.35	-2.97	6.38
C	Yorvit Torrealba	935.1	27.20	-0.84	26.36
1B	Sean Casey	989.0	8.90	-0.62	8.28
2B	Dan Uggla	1383.2	30.66	-7.06	23.60
3B	Morgan Ensberg	492.1	8.52	-4.08	4.45
SS	Tony Pena	1273.2	31.75	+6.26	38.01
LF	Garrett Anderson	724.1	9.53	-1.75	7.78
CF	Juan Pierre	1416.1	28.45	+0.55	29.00
RF	Corey Hart	1096.2	15.19	+3.58	18.77
C	Joe Mauer	777.2	22.62	+9.69	32.31
1B	Andy Phillips	431.0	3.88	+3.82	7.70
2B	Luis Castillo	432.0	9.57	-1.52	8.05
3B	Eric Chavez	774.2	13.41	+3.06	16.47
SS	Jimmy Rollins	1441.1	35.93	+6.39	42.32
LF	Jason Bay	1237.0	16.28	-9.00	7.28
CF	Mike Cameron	1329.0	26.69	-2.54	24.15
RF	Randy Winn	869.0	12.04	+5.25	17.29
C	Kenji Johjima	1106.2	32.19	+12.56	44.75
1B	Albert Pujols	1324.2	11.93	+14.03	25.96
2B	Ty Wigginton	321.0	7.11	-1.66	5.45
3B	Ramon Vazquez	540.1	9.35	+0.31	9.67
SS	John McDonald	799.1	19.93	+10.79	30.72
LF	Ryan Church	719.1	9.46	+5.38	14.85
C	John Buck	924.1	26.88	+0.62	27.50
C	Johnny Estrada	961.0	27.95	-4.21	23.74
2B	Orlando Hudson	1183.1	26.22	9.17	35.39

So Kenji Johjima and NL MVP Jimmy Rollins are listed now as the players who saved the most runs.

These numbers, however, are raw totals, rather than per-inning averages. In order to compare players on a level playing field, we have to convert these into per-inning averages. For cosmetic reasons I'll list them per 1000 innings.

By this analysis, the highest-rated defensive player among these 33, in the year 2007, would be Joe Mauer of the Twins. Mauer, playing a critical defensive position with outstanding defensive numbers, is credited with 32.31 Runs Saved in 777.2 innings, which is 41.5 Runs Saved per 1000 innings:

	Position	Player	Innings	Runs Saved	Runs Saved Per 1000 Innings
1	Catcher	Joe Mauer	777.2	32.31	41.50
2	Catcher	Kenji Johjima	1106.2	44.75	40.40
3	Shortstop	John McDonald	799.1	30.72	38.40
4	Catcher	Chris Snyder	891.1	31.82	35.70
5	Second	Orlando Hudson	1183.1	35.39	29.90
6	Shortstop	Tony Pena	1273.2	38.01	29.80
7	Catcher	John Buck	924.1	27.50	29.80
8	Shortstop	Jimmy Rollins	1441.1	42.32	29.40
9	Catcher	Yorvit Torrealba	935.1	26.36	28.20
10	Catcher	Johnny Estrada	961.0	23.74	24.70
11	Shortstop	Juan Uribe	1305.1	30.01	23.00
12	Second	Brian Roberts	1329.2	29.95	22.50
13	Third	Eric Chavez	774.2	16.47	21.30
14	Left	Ryan Church	719.1	14.85	20.60
15	Center	Juan Pierre	1416.2	29.00	20.50
16	Right	Randy Winn	869.0	17.29	19.90
17	First	Albert Pujols	1324.2	25.96	19.60
18	Third	Mike Lowell	1324.1	25.72	19.40
19	Center	Josh Hamilton	555.2	10.43	18.80
20	Second	Luis Castillo	432.0	8.05	18.60
21	Center	Mike Cameron	1329.0	24.15	18.20
22	Third	Ramon Vazquez	540.1	9.67	17.90
23	First	Andy Phillips	431.0	7.70	17.90
24	Right	Corey Hart	1096.2	18.77	17.10
25	Second	Dan Uggla	1383.2	23.60	17.10
26	Second	Ty Wigginton	321.0	5.45	17.00
27	Left	Alfonso Soriano	1064.0	12.77	12.00
28	Left	Garret Anderson	724.1	7.78	10.70
29	First	Scott Thorman	608.1	5.85	9.60
30	Right	Trot Nixon	675.0	6.38	9.50
31	Third	Morgan Ensberg	492.1	4.45	9.00
32	First	Sean Casey	989.0	8.28	8.40
33	Left	Jason Bay	1237.0	7.28	5.90

So we have reached our goal line. These are the numbers by which we can give a reasonable answer to the question: *Where does Orlando Hudson's defense rank him, among all major league players?* He ranks at about the 85th profile, if this group of players is representative of all major league players.

I'm a little surprised that the number isn't higher. If Hudson ranks at the 92nd percentile among second basemen, and second base is a relatively high-value defensive position, one might guess intuitively that he would rank higher than the 92nd percentile among all players. But having gone through this exercise, I see why this cannot be true. Second basemen in general cannot rank ahead of catchers and shortstops. If Hudson ranked ahead of all other second basemen, but below the catchers and shortstops, that would put him at about the 75th percentile—ahead of the first basemen, third basemen, the outfielders and all of the other second basemen, thus ahead of six positions but behind two. Because the numbers spread out, he does rank ahead of a good many of the shortstops and some of the catchers, and he ranks higher than the 75th percentile—but not back up to the 92nd.

Total Runs

Total Runs is kind of the culmination of everything, thus it is appropriate that it is the last thing introduced in this book. It gives us one number to recognize the total contribution of each player in baseball. It's not the end-all-be-all of sabermetrics, not a Unified Theory of Eveything, by any stretch of the imagination, but it is kind of an end-all for this book. (In case you don't get to end of this article—warning: heavy math, but only in the last section of this article—thank you for reading!)

The theme of this book has been Defensive Runs Saved. We've converted nearly every one of our defensive measurements into the key element of every baseball game: runs. In the Defensive Runs chapter, we compared every player at every position within each position. But is there a way to compare players across positions including both offense and defense? We know that players are more valuable the farther left that they go on the defensive spectrum. Is there a way to measure that?

Bill James's "Crossing Positions" article, right before this one, gives us the framework to compare the defensive contributions of players at different positions. So now, with Bill's few assumptions, we can assemble the pieces of the puzzle and determine the position players who contributed the most to their teams in 2008.

We have four main components of what we call "Total Runs": Positional Average, Defensive Runs Saved, Baserunning Runs, and Offensive Runs. We'll save the detailed explanation for the end of the article; let's get right into the results.

Utley for MVP

Chase Utley had an excellent season at a premium defensive position. He is ranked number one in all of baseball, at the top of the 2008 Total Runs chart we have in the following pages. We give Utley a Positional Average of 31 runs for playing close to a full season of innings at second base (and a handful at first base). By comparison, Albert Pujols only gets 11 positional runs for playing the easiest defensive position, first base. On top of the runs for playing second base, Utley had 34 Runs Saved, or 34 runs above an average second baseman defensively. Add in a strong offensive season (122 Runs Created) and above average baserunning (two Baserunning runs), and you get a runaway NL MVP winner, especially since his team did pretty well.

What's that? Utley finished 14th in the MVP voting? Albert Pujols isn't a *bad* choice—he edged out Carlos Beltran for second place in our Total Runs list. He had the best offensive season in baseball last season, and was among the best defenders at his position. Utley leapfrogs him in Total Runs because he plays a much more difficult position and was even more brilliant defensively.

Ryan Howard shared the right side of the Phillies infield with Utley but, based on this analysis, doesn't belong in the same MVP discussion. Howard, who finished second to Pujols in the MVP balloting, knocked 48 home runs and drove in 146 runs (thanks, in part, to Utley's .380 on-base percentage batting in front of him). However, he only managed 108 runs created (his low totals in the non-power categories pulled him down), average defense at the least demanding position on the field, and below-average baserunning. In fact, Howard finished tied for 50th in Total Runs, behind three Phillies teammates (Utley, Shane Victorino-136 runs, and Jimmy Rollins-135 runs).

Over in the American League, the MVP voters got the winner right according to Total Runs. Similar to Utley, Dustin Pedroia posted above average defense at second base and an excellent offensive season (118 runs created). His 162 total runs edged out Grady Sizemore

(157 total runs, 10th in AL MVP voting) for the top player in the junior circuit. Close behind Sizemore are three excellent defensive right fielders who aren't bad at the plate either: Nick Markakis, Ichiro Suzuki and Alex Rios. Other than Utley, these might be the most underrated players in the game today; combined, the trio collected exactly one tenth-place MVP vote.

As in the National League, the AL runner-up probably doesn't merit MVP candidacy. Justin Morneau collected seven first-place MVP votes, but played below average defense at first base. His 121 Total Runs placed him tied for 44th in the majors.

Other interesting observations

- J.J. Hardy, Placido Polanco, Adrian Beltre, Cristian Guzman, and Chris Young (the Arizona outfielder) finish in the top 40 in Total Runs on the strength of good or excellent defense at a premium position. Very few players are capable of playing above average defense at difficult positions. Considering only their offensive production seriously underestimates their value.

- Brad Hawpe and Mike Jacobs seem to do more harm than good by taking the field regularly. Their Positional Average, the run contribution of an average fielder with the same number of innings on the field, is completely erased by their ineptitude with the glove. The same is true to a lesser extent for Jason Giambi, Adam Dunn, and Jack Cust. Unless their defense improves significantly, their teams should seriously consider a full-time designated hitter role in order to help the team. For more information on Positional Average, keep reading or refer back to Bill James' "Crossing Positions" article preceding this one.

Calculating Total Runs—Positional Average

For starters, Bill puts a player's defensive contributions on the same scale as other positions. If teams are efficient at balancing offensive abilities with defensive abilities, we would expect that the average player at each position contributes the same amount to his team's success or failure. For instance, a player may be drafted as a shortstop but not be adequate defensively to play there everyday in the majors. If he is a strong offensive player, his organization might try to shift him to third base. He will only survive at third if his offensive production, combined with his defensive contributions, stands out from all other players his organization can replace him with. If the player is going to be in the majors for long, his team will have to balance his offensive and defensive contributions and decide where his skills help the team the most.

Whether they make this decision consciously or not, every team faces this same issue with every player in their organization. As Bill illustrates in detail, we can assume that any difference in offensive production has an equal and opposite difference in defensive production. (You didn't think we'd squeeze Isaac Newton into the discussion, did you?) We aren't saying that Chase Utley is just as valuable as Sean Casey, but we are saying that if you put together the offensive and defensive contributions, the average second baseman and the average first baseman are equally important to their teams.

Here are the Positional Averages—the values awarded to a full-time player at each position to put them on the same scale for comparison:

Position	Positional Adjustment
Catcher	42
First Base	13
Second Base	32
Third Base	25
Shortstop	36
Left Field	19
Center Field	29
Right Field	20

As Bill explains, we give each player a fraction of the Positional Adjustment based on how many innings they played at each position. Chase Utley played 96.7% of a full season of innings at second base and 0.97% at first. Applying the Positional Averages, we get $.967*32 + .0097*13 = 30.9 + 0.1 = 31$.

Calculating Total Runs—Defensive Runs

Each component of Defensive Runs is explained somewhere in this book. For more information, refer to the Defensive Runs article on page 11.

Calculating Total Runs—Runs Created

"Runs Created" is an estimate of the number of a team's runs created by each individual hitter. The Philadelphia Phillies scored 799 runs last year. How many of those were created by Ryan Howard? How many by Chase Utley? How many by Carlos Ruiz?

There are many different formulas for estimating runs created...we'll use one customized to the 2008 run environment. There are three factors:

A = Hits + Total Walks + Hit-by-Pitch – Caught Stealing – Ground into Double Play

B = Total Bases + 0.20*(Unintentional Walks + Hit-by-Pitch) +0.48*(Stolen Bases + Sac Hits + Sac Flies)

C = At Bats + Total Walks + Hit-by-Pitch + Sac Hits + Sac Flies

The typical Runs Created formula takes A, multiplies by B, and divides by C. However, this assumes that a hitter is in a lineup of eight hitters identical to the given player. To counter this, we put the hitter in the context of a lineup of eight slightly below average hitters:

$$newA = A + 2.4*C$$
$$newB = B + 3*C$$
$$newC = 9*C$$

$$Runs\ Created = (newA)*(newB)/(newC) - 0.9*C$$

The Bill James Handbook includes an adjustment for situational, or "clutch", hitting. We have been extremely careful to remove the situational components from our Defensive Runs calculations, so we will exclude this portion of the calculation for our purposes in this book.

The highest Runs Created totals for 2008 are Albert Pujols (142), Manny Ramirez (131), David Wright (127), Lance Berkman (126), and Hanley Ramirez (126).

Calculating Total Runs—Baserunning Runs

Estimating the run impact of baserunning is similar to the outfield arms method on page 375. We have already included Stolen Bases, Caught Stealing, and Double Plays in our Runs Created calculations, but we need to include several other aspects of baserunning.

The key concept here is at some time baserunners have a decision point when they choose to try to take an extra base or not. Where is the ball hit? Where is the fielder throwing from and how good is his arm? What kind of jump did the runner get and how fast is he? How do the runner's legs feel that day? All these things must be considered in an instant and a decision made. Our method attempts to capture the ramifications of each decision and objectively assess the cost or benefit of the result. It's appropriate to reward the runner for taking the extra base and penalize him for being thrown out at the next base or being too conservative and *not* taking the base. It's a classic risk-reward scenario.

To calculate the run impact of baserunning let's take the example of a runner on first with a single hit to the outfield (and no runner on second). Actually let's take the entire league of runners in this example. We calculate the run expectancy change (the run matrix) after the three most common outcomes on every play of this type; runner stops at second, runner makes it to third, runner is thrown out at third. We assume that the run expectancy change for moving only to second has a change of zero. We sum all the expectancy changes for all the outcomes and calculate the average run expectancy change for each opportunity (decision point). We then compare each individual's performance, play-by-play to the league average for that play to get the cost or benefit to his team in runs above or below average.

We take exactly the same approach for runners going from second to home on a single and first to home on a double. We also look at all the other "bases taken" or outs run into on wild pitches, balks, passed balls, defensive indifference, sacrifice flies, any runner out at their original base at the start of the play on a ball caught in the air or any runner—or batter—out trying to advance on any of the following that do not fall into any other category: a ball hit to the outfield, a base hit, or a ball caught in the air.

The best baserunner in 2008 according to our method was Curtis Granderson at 9 runs above average, while the worst was Dioner Navarro at -8 runs.

Total Runs

So there we have the four pieces to the puzzle: offense, defense, baserunning, and an adjustment that allows us to compare across positions. What's left? Just add them up. In the following chart, you'll find a list of the best 260 position players in baseball last year with 50 or more Total Runs, led by a certain Phillies second baseman.

By no means is this the final answer. We've already made numerous changes to the various components, and by the time you pick up this book, we'll already be working on the next one. Baseball Info Solutions tracks Good Fielding Plays and Defensive Misplays, some of which we've accounted for and others we haven't touched yet. As the BIS staff continues to analyze and track new aspects of each play, we'll continue to improve our estimates and bring you better answers—so you can impress your friends, win those bar arguments, or simply understand and enjoy the game of baseball a little bit more than you did before.

2008 Total Runs

Player	Team	DEFENSIVE Positional Average	DEFENSIVE Runs Saved	OFFENSIVE Baserunning	OFFENSIVE Runs Created	TOTAL Runs
Chase Utley	Phi	31	34	2	122	189
Albert Pujols	StL	11	15	0	142	168
Carlos Beltran	NYM	28	21	3	115	167
Hanley Ramirez	Fla	32	1	4	126	163
Dustin Pedroia	Bos	31	12	1	118	162
Grady Sizemore	Cle	27	2	5	123	157
Lance Berkman	Hou	12	13	4	126	155
David Wright	NYM	25	5	-2	127	155
Nick Markakis	Bal	19	20	-1	116	154
Mark Teixeira	2 Tms	12	17	0	124	153
Jose Reyes	NYM	35	-2	3	117	153
Ichiro Suzuki	Sea	23	14	7	101	145
Matt Holliday	Col	16	5	7	117	145
Alex Rios	Tor	22	24	2	94	142
Josh Hamilton	Tex	22	-3	3	120	142
Joe Mauer	Min	35	0	7	97	139
Manny Ramirez	2 Tms	13	-3	-2	131	139
Chipper Jones	Atl	17	10	0	111	138
Ryan Ludwick	StL	17	5	3	113	138
Kevin Youkilis	Bos	13	11	1	112	137
Shane Victorino	Phi	25	14	8	89	136
Jimmy Rollins	Phi	29	15	2	89	135
Ryan Braun	Mil	17	7	3	108	135
Brian Roberts	Bal	29	-3	2	107	135
Randy Winn	SF	18	13	2	97	130
Matt Kemp	LAD	23	11	2	92	128
Brian Giles	SD	18	8	3	99	128
Alex Rodriguez	NYY	20	-2	2	108	128
J.J. Hardy	Mil	32	12	-4	87	127
Placido Polanco	Det	27	11	5	83	126
Stephen Drew	Ari	32	-3	-3	100	126
Brian McCann	Atl	33	6	-8	94	125
Curtis Granderson	Det	24	-7	9	99	125
Adrian Beltre	Sea	21	24	-2	81	124
Dan Uggla	Fla	28	2	-1	95	124
Ian Kinsler	Tex	24	-7	8	99	124
Jason Bay	2 Tms	18	-8	1	113	124
Cristian Guzman	Was	29	12	-2	84	123
Chris Young	Ari	28	9	0	86	123
Troy Glaus	StL	22	8	-3	95	122
Ryan Theriot	ChC	32	5	6	79	122
Russell Martin	LAD	37	-2	2	85	122
Aubrey Huff	Bal	7	-2	2	115	122
Justin Morneau	Min	12	-3	2	110	121
Nate McLouth	Pit	27	-19	5	108	121
Joey Votto	Cin	11	16	-1	94	120
Orlando Cabrera	CWS	35	3	1	81	120
Michael Young	Tex	32	-5	7	86	120
Akinori Iwamura	TB	30	3	0	86	119
Carlos Quentin	CWS	15	0	2	101	118
Ryan Howard	Phi	13	0	-3	108	118
Raul Ibanez	Sea	18	-6	2	104	118
Jose Lopez	Sea	28	4	-3	88	117
Aramis Ramirez	ChC	22	-9	-1	105	117
Bobby Abreu	NYY	18	-5	0	102	115
Conor Jackson	Ari	14	5	6	89	114
Carlos Pena	TB	11	11	-3	94	113
Hunter Pence	Hou	19	11	1	82	113
Adrian Gonzalez	SD	13	0	-4	104	113
Geovany Soto	ChC	33	-1	-6	87	113
Kelly Johnson	Atl	27	-3	3	86	113
Brandon Phillips	Cin	27	10	1	74	112
Xavier Nady	2 Tms	16	5	-4	95	112
Johnny Damon	NYY	14	4	-3	97	112
B.J. Upton	TB	25	2	0	85	112
Jhonny Peralta	Cle	32	-6	0	86	112
Jacoby Ellsbury	Bos	19	14	3	75	111
Yunel Escobar	Atl	28	12	2	69	111
Miguel Tejada	Hou	34	7	0	70	111
Jorge Cantu	Fla	21	-7	2	95	111
Derek Lee	ChC	12	5	-3	96	110
Jermaine Dye	CWS	18	-9	-1	102	110
Marco Scutaro	Tor	26	21	-4	66	109
Evan Longoria	TB	18	8	2	81	109

Player	Team	DEFENSIVE		OFFENSIVE		TOTAL
		Positional Average	Runs Saved	Baserunning	Runs Created	Runs
Pat Burrell	Phi	16	-5	-2	100	109
Torii Hunter	LAA	24	-2	1	85	108
Miguel Cabrera	Det	13	-8	-7	110	108
Andre Ethier	LAD	16	-10	3	99	108
Carlos Gomez	Min	26	17	3	61	107
Cody Ross	Fla	20	16	0	71	107
Jason Kendall	Mil	39	12	-2	58	107
Mike Aviles	KC	22	11	6	66	105
Bengie Molina	SF	33	7	-4	69	105
Derek Jeter	NYY	31	-9	0	83	105
Corey Hart	Mil	19	2	2	81	104
Carlos Delgado	NYM	12	-9	-3	104	104
Kurt Suzuki	Oak	35	5	0	63	103
Prince Fielder	Mil	12	-10	-7	108	103
Jayson Werth	Phi	15	7	1	79	102
Mark DeRosa	ChC	23	-14	1	92	102
Adam Dunn	2 Tms	17	-19	0	104	102
Milton Bradley	Tex	2	5	-3	97	101
Magglio Ordonez	Det	16	-2	-5	92	101
Casey Blake	2 Tms	21	-3	0	83	101
Vladimir Guerrero	LAA	12	-2	-1	91	100
Mark Ellis	Oak	22	24	-1	54	99
Mike Cameron	Mil	21	7	0	71	99
Rickie Weeks	Mil	23	0	7	69	99
Kevin Kouzmanoff	SD	24	-1	-1	77	99
Alfonso Soriano	ChC	12	5	-1	81	97
Skip Schumaker	StL	19	1	2	75	97
Ryan Doumit	Pit	26	-2	1	72	97
Kosuke Fukudome	ChC	16	2	5	72	95
Aaron Rowand	SF	26	1	-2	70	95
David DeJesus	KC	18	-5	0	82	95
Lyle Overbay	Tor	12	6	-1	77	94
Alex Gordon	KC	20	-9	7	76	94
Marlon Byrd	Tex	16	4	3	69	92
James Loney	LAD	12	1	-1	80	92
Adam Jones	Bal	22	11	1	57	91
Fred Lewis	SF	14	2	3	72	91
Mark Reynolds	Ari	22	-10	0	79	91
Garrett Atkins	Col	19	-14	1	85	91
Carlos Lee	Hou	12	-2	-7	87	90
Chris Iannetta	Col	24	0	-1	66	89
Luke Scott	Bal	11	5	-2	74	88
Freddy Sanchez	Pit	25	2	1	60	88
J.D. Drew	Bos	12	-5	4	77	88
Robinson Cano	NYY	31	-13	2	68	88
Denard Span	Min	12	15	0	60	87
Ryan Zimmerman	Was	16	11	0	60	87
Ben Francisco	Cle	12	7	5	63	87
Jack Cust	Oak	8	-10	1	88	87
Melvin Mora	Bal	18	-11	1	79	87
Chone Figgins	LAA	17	10	2	57	86
Adam LaRoche	Pit	10	-6	0	82	86
Brad Hawpe	Col	16	-22	1	91	86
Carl Crawford	TB	12	13	4	56	85
Scott Rolen	Tor	17	10	-3	61	85
Clint Barmes	Col	19	7	3	56	85
Shin-Soo Choo	Cle	8	3	8	66	85
Jim Thome	CWS	0	0	-3	88	85
Garret Anderson	LAA	9	-1	2	75	85
A.J. Pierzynski	CWS	33	-8	-6	66	85
Franklin Gutierrez	Cle	14	24	1	45	84
Jack Hannahan	Oak	18	18	1	47	84
Willie Harris	Was	13	16	2	53	84
Ramon Hernandez	Bal	30	0	-4	57	83
Rick Ankiel	StL	17	-1	-1	68	83
Kelly Shoppach	Cle	25	-4	1	61	83
Orlando Hudson	Ari	20	-3	3	62	82
Ken Griffey Jr.	2 Tms	16	-3	-3	72	82
Lastings Milledge	Was	24	-6	-2	66	82
Bobby Crosby	Oak	31	-6	4	53	82
Alexei Ramirez	CWS	25	-10	1	66	82
Chris Snyder	Ari	27	3	-2	53	81
Yadier Molina	StL	29	1	-4	55	81
Edwin Encarnacion	Cin	21	-17	-2	79	81
Casey Kotchman	2 Tms	11	9	-6	66	80
Delmon Young	Min	17	-11	1	73	80

Player	Team	DEFENSIVE Positional Average	DEFENSIVE Runs Saved	OFFENSIVE Baserunning	OFFENSIVE Runs Created	TOTAL Runs
Cesar Izturis	StL	25	14	-3	43	79
Josh Willingham	Fla	11	9	-1	60	79
Ty Wigginton	Hou	15	-1	-1	66	79
Jason Bartlett	TB	27	-2	0	54	79
Jason Giambi	NYY	8	-13	-4	88	79
Jody Gerut	SD	13	8	1	56	78
Justin Upton	Ari	12	5	3	58	78
Jeremy Hermida	Fla	15	-2	1	64	78
Edgar Renteria	Det	29	-7	0	56	78
Ivan Rodriguez	2 Tms	27	3	0	47	77
David Murphy	Tex	13	2	1	61	77
Carlos Guillen	Det	15	-10	3	69	77
Asdrubal Cabrera	Cle	21	12	-2	45	76
Aaron Miles	StL	17	9	1	49	76
Jay Bruce	Cin	14	4	3	55	76
Willy Taveras	Col	20	0	4	52	76
Dioner Navarro	TB	29	-1	-8	56	76
Jeff Francoeur	Atl	18	-2	2	58	76
Nick Swisher	CWS	18	-9	0	67	76
Yuniesky Betancourt	Sea	33	-13	-2	58	76
Blake DeWitt	LAD	17	7	1	50	75
Mike Lowell	Bos	16	5	-8	62	75
Adam Kennedy	StL	15	19	2	38	74
Ryan Sweeney	Oak	15	5	2	52	74
Gregor Blanco	Atl	17	0	1	56	74
Ryan Garko	Cle	10	-5	-1	70	74
Joe Inglett	Tor	15	5	3	50	73
David Ortiz	Bos	0	0	-3	76	73
Mark Teahen	KC	18	-15	-1	71	73
Nick Punto	Min	19	8	2	43	72
Erick Aybar	LAA	20	6	3	43	72
Jose Guillen	KC	12	-8	-3	71	72
Kaz Matsui	Hou	18	-8	3	59	72
Vernon Wells	Tor	18	-12	-1	67	72
Gerald Laird	Tex	22	6	-1	44	71
Daric Barton	Oak	10	4	4	53	71
Joe Crede	CWS	14	9	2	45	70
Mike Fontenot	ChC	11	8	0	50	69
Eric Hinske	TB	10	2	1	56	69
Jamey Carroll	Cle	16	2	5	46	69
Jason Varitek	Bos	30	1	-7	45	69
Kevin Millar	Bal	10	-4	-6	69	69
Ray Durham	2 Tms	16	-9	1	61	69
Felipe Lopez	2 Tms	22	-11	-3	61	69
Pedro Feliz	Phi	17	5	-2	48	68
Troy Tulowitzki	Col	22	2	0	44	68
Alexi Casilla	Min	19	-2	3	48	68
Coco Crisp	Bos	18	-3	2	51	68
Jason Kubel	Min	5	-8	1	70	68
Alfredo Amezaga	Fla	14	16	2	35	67
Michael Bourn	Hou	20	4	0	43	67
Gabe Gross	2 Tms	13	4	2	48	67
Brendan Harris	Min	23	-10	0	54	67
Omar Infante	Atl	12	11	-1	44	66
Scott Hairston	SD	12	7	-2	49	66
Melky Cabrera	NYY	20	6	-1	41	66
Paul Konerko	CWS	9	-4	-3	64	66
Elijah Dukes	Was	9	6	0	50	65
Howie Kendrick	LAA	17	0	3	45	65
Jerry Hairston	Cin	12	0	3	50	65
Jeff Kent	LAD	20	-11	0	56	65
Bill Hall	Mil	16	-1	4	45	64
Mark Kotsay	2 Tms	16	-3	3	48	64
Jay Payton	Bal	12	15	3	33	63
Ryan Church	NYM	10	5	2	46	63
Rod Barajas	Tor	23	5	-5	40	63
Reed Johnson	ChC	13	-2	3	49	63
Brandon Inge	Det	22	0	0	40	62
Brian Schneider	NYM	26	-2	-3	40	61
Jack Wilson	Pit	17	12	-1	32	60
Mike Napoli	LAA	18	-6	-1	49	60
Juan Pierre	LAD	11	4	1	43	59
Mark Grudzielanek	KC	16	-2	1	44	59
Jim Edmonds	2 Tms	17	-13	0	55	59
Ian Stewart	Col	11	6	-1	42	58
Rich Aurilia	SF	12	-4	-3	53	58

Player	Team	DEFENSIVE		OFFENSIVE		TOTAL
		Positional Average	Runs Saved	Baserunning	Runs Created	Runs
Chase Headley	SD	10	1	-1	47	57
Jeff Keppinger	Cin	24	-13	-1	47	57
Corey Patterson	Cin	16	11	1	28	56
Ronnie Belliard	Was	11	-5	0	50	56
Ramon Vazquez	Tex	14	-5	-1	48	56
John Buck	KC	28	-8	-2	38	56
Matt Joyce	Det	8	6	1	40	55
Jed Lowrie	Bos	14	5	0	36	55
Kenji Johjima	Sea	24	0	-1	32	55
Jose Castillo	2 Tms	17	-1	-2	41	55
Jeff Baker	Col	11	-3	2	45	55
Brandon Boggs	Tex	8	7	0	39	54
Willy Aybar	TB	10	6	-4	42	54
Todd Helton	Col	6	4	-2	46	54
Maicer Izturis	LAA	16	4	0	34	54
Hideki Matsui	NYY	3	-1	1	51	54
Mike Jacobs	Fla	8	-23	-3	72	54
Geoff Blum	Hou	12	4	-1	38	53
Endy Chavez	NYM	9	16	0	27	52
Jose Molina	NYY	21	12	0	19	52
Gabe Kapler	Mil	8	6	0	38	52
Miguel Olivo	KC	14	3	-2	37	52
Fernando Tatis	NYM	8	-1	-2	47	52
Khalil Greene	SD	23	-2	-2	33	52
Carlos Ruiz	Phi	24	-2	2	28	52
Gary Matthews Jr.	LAA	13	-6	-2	47	52
Carlos Gonzalez	Oak	13	11	0	27	51
Jesus Flores	Was	20	1	-4	34	51
Jose Bautista	2 Tms	14	-4	-3	44	51
Craig Counsell	Mil	12	7	1	30	50
Doug Mientkiewicz	Pit	8	0	0	42	50
Emil Brown	Oak	11	0	-3	42	50
Chris Coste	Phi	18	-2	-2	36	50
Chris Davis	Tex	8	-8	0	50	50